THE OFFICIAL
PRICE GUIDE TO
Antiques
and Other
Collectibles

BY
THE HOUSE OF COLLECTIBLES, INC.

We have compiled the information contained herein through a *patented computerized process* which relies primarily on a nationwide sampling of information provided by noteworthy collectible experts, auction houses and specialized dealers. This unique retrieval system enables us to provide the reader with the most current and accurate information available.

EDITOR
THOMAS E. HUDGEONS III

SIXTH EDITION
THE HOUSE OF COLLECTIBLES, INC., ORLANDO, FLORIDA 32809

IMPORTANT NOTICE. The format of **THE OFFICIAL PRICE GUIDE SERIES,** published by **THE HOUSE OF COLLECTIBLES, INC.,** is based on the following proprietary features: **ALL FACTS AND PRICES ARE COMPILED THRU A COMPUTERIZED PROCESS** which relies on a nationwide sampling of information obtained from noteworthy experts, auction houses, and specialized dealers. **DETAILED "INDEXED" FORMAT** enables quick retrieval of information for positive identification. **ENCAPSULATED HISTORIES** precede each category to acquaint the collector with the specific traits that are peculiar to that area of collecting. **VALUABLE COLLECTING INFORMATION** is provided for both the novice as well as the seasoned collector: How to begin a collection; How to buy, sell, and trade; Care and storage techniques; Tips on restoration; Grading guidelines; Lists of periodicals, clubs, museums, auction houses, dealers, etc. **AN AVERAGE PRICE RANGE** takes geographic location and condition into consideration when reporting collector value. **A SPECIAL THIRD PRICE COLUMN** enables the collector to compare the current market values with last year's average selling price indicating which items have increased in value. **INVENTORY CHECKLIST SYSTEM** is provided for cataloging a collection. **EACH TITLE IS ANNUALLY UPDATED** to provide the most accurate information available in the rapidly changing collector's marketplace.

All of the information, including valuations, in this book has been compiled from the most reliable sources, and every effort has been made to eliminate errors and questionable data. Nevertheless the possibility of error, in a work of such immense scope, always exists. The publisher will not be held responsible for losses which may occur in the purchase, sale, or other transaction of items because of information contained herein. Readers who feel they have discovered errors are invited to **WRITE** and inform us, so they may be corrected in subsequent editions. Those seeking further information on the topics covered in this book are advised to refer to the complete line of Official Price Guides published by The House of Collectibles.

Published by: The House of Collectibles, Inc.
               Orlando Central Park
               1904 Premier Row
               Orlando, FL 32809
               Phone: (305) 857-9095

Printed in the United States of America

Library of Congress Catalog Card Number: 80-84705

ISBN: 0-87637-271-X / Paperback

TABLE OF CONTENTS

Market Review 1
An In-Depth Overview of
    The Marketplace 3
Investing 17
Building a Collection 18
Condition 20
Fakes 21
Buying Tips 22
    Buying From Dealers 22
    Buying at Auctions 24
Selling Tips 25
    Selling by Auction 26
Flea Market Directory 28
Publications 34
How to Use This Book 38
Advertising Collectibles 39
Akro Agate 44
Almanacs 50
American Indian Artifacts 52
Animal Collectibles 57
Animated Cels 60
Art Deco 63
Art Glass 67
Art Nouveau 100
Audubon Prints 104
Autographs 107
Aviation Memorabilia 112
Avon Bottles 114
Banks 116
Barbed Wire 121
Baseball Cards 123
Baskets 127
Batman 131
Battlestar Galactica 133
The Beatles 135
Beer Cans 141
Bells 148
Belt Buckles 152
Bennington Pottery 154
Bibles 158
Bicentennial 160
Bicycles 162
Black Memorabilia 164

Boehm 169
Bookplates 171
Books 172
Bottles 176
Boxes 181
Boxing 186
Brass 189
Breweriana 192
British Royalty Memorabilia .. 197
Bronze 201
Buck Rogers 202
Buttons 204
Cambridge Glass 208
Cameras 214
Canes and Walking Sticks ... 216
Carnival Glass 217
Carousel Animals 220
Cars 222
Chalkware 227
Children's Books 228
Children's Dishes 233
Christmas Decorations 237
Chrome 240
Cigar Box Labels 241
Circus Memorabilia 245
Civil War Memorabilia 248
Clocks 254
Clothing 257
Coca-Cola Collectibles 260
Coins 264
Comic Art 271
Comic Books 276
Cookbooks 284
Cookie Cutters 288
Cookie Jars 291
Copper 295
Coverlets 298
Cracker Jack Memorabilia ... 300
Crocks 302
Currency 305
Currier & Ives Prints 309
Cut Glass 313
Dairy Collectibles 317

Daum Nancy Glass 318
Decoys 322
Depression Glass 326
Disneyana 331
Dollhouses 337
Dolls 339
Doorstops 344
Duck Stamps 346
Eggs 349
Elvis Presley Memorabilia ... 351
Embroidery 358
Eyeglasses 360
Ezra Brooks Bottles 362
Fans 366
Farm Equipment 370
Fiesta Ware 372
Fire Fighting Equipment 375
Fishing Tackle 377
Flash Gordon 379
Flasks 382
Folk Art 387
Football Cards 390
Fostoria Glass 396
Frankoma Pottery 423
Fruit Crate Labels 425
Fruit Jars 436
Cookbook of Tested Recipes . 442
Furniture 571
Galle Glass 577
Games 582
Garnier Bottles 587
George Ohr Pottery 589
Ginger Beer Bottles 591
Golf Memorabilia 595
Graniteware 596
Greeting Cards 601
Grueby Pottery 606
Hall China 608
Handguns 618
Harlequin Ware 622
Harmonicas 624
Heisey Glass 627
Holiday Decorations 636
Hull Pottery 639
Hummels 643

Hutchinson Bottles 648
Icart Prints 652
Inkwells and Inkstands 656
Insulators 659
Irons 662
Ironware 663
Jewelry 667
Jim Beam Bottles 671
Jukeboxes 674
Knives 677
Lalique 681
Lamps and Lighting Fixtures . 683
Lenox 688
License Plates 691
Lightning Rod Ornaments ... 692
Lincolniana 693
Lunch Boxes 697
Luxardo Bottles 699
Magazines 701
Maps 706
Marblehead Pottery 711
Marbles 712
Maxfield Parrish Prints 714
McCormick Bottles 717
McCoy Pottery 718
Menus 725
Military Collectibles 727
Military Medals and
  Decorations 730
Mining Collectibles 733
Molds 735
Movie Costumes 740
Movie Posters 742
Music Boxes 747
Nautical Memorabilia 749
Needleworking Tools 751
Newcomb College Pottery ... 753
Newspapers 754
Niloak Pottery Company 759
Nippon 761
Occupied Japan 764
Ocean Liner Collectibles 766
Old Commonwealth 768
Old Sleepy Eye Pottery 770
Old West Memorabilia 771

Opera Memorabilia 774
Oriental Furniture 777
Oriental Paintings 782
Oriental Prints 784
Oriental Textiles 785
Ott & Brewer Pottery 791
Owls 794
Paper Collectibles 797
Paper Dolls 802
Paperweights 809
Pattern Glass 811
Pens and Pencils 815
Phonographs 817
Photographs 822
Pipes 828
Pisgah Forest Pottery 830
Plates 832
Player Pianos 835
Playing Cards 837
Police Memorabilia 840
Political Buttons 843
Political Memorabilia 845
Postcards 848
Premiums 850
Prints 853
Puppets 857
Quilts 859
Radios 866
Railroadiana 867
Razors 873
Records 875
Red Wing Pottery 876
Robots 878
Rookwood 882
Roseville Pottery 884
Royal Doulton 886
Samplers 888
Saturday Evening Girls 890
Schoenhut Dolls and Toys ... 891
Scouting 894
Scrimshaw 896
Sears Roebuck Catalogs 897
Shaker 899
Shawnee Pottery 902
Sheet Music 904

Shenandoah Valley Pottery .. 906
Ship Models 908
Shirley Temple Dolls 910
Shotguns 913
Silhouettes 915
Silver 917
Stamps 919
Stangl Pottery 923
Star Trek Collectibles 925
Star Wars Collectibles 928
Steins 930
Stereographs 932
Stock Certificates 934
Stoves 936
Superman 938
Telephones 941
Television Memorabilia 943
Theatrical Memorabilia 948
Thimbles 951
Third Reich Collectibles 952
Tiffany Glass 955
Tiffany Pottery 959
Tin 960
Tintypes 965
Tobacco Jars 967
Tools 968
Toy Cars 973
Toy Soldiers 977
Toy Trains 980
Trade Cards 983
Trade Catalogs 985
Trucks 987
TV Guides 988
Uncle Sam and Statue of
  Liberty Collectibles 991
Valentines 992
Van Briggle 995
Vanity Fair Lithographs 998
Watches 999
Waterford Crystal 1001
Weather Vanes 1003
Wicker 1006
Wood 1009

ACKNOWLEDGEMENTS

The House of Collectibles would like to express its appreciation to the following individuals and organizations for their assistance in the preparation of this publication: Phillips-Fine Art Auctioneers and Appraisers, 867 Madison Avenue, NY 10021; The Topps Chewing Gum Co., Brooklyn, NY 11232; The Fleer Corp., Philadelphia, PA 19141; Juke Box Saturday Nite, Steve Schussler, Chicago, IL 60610; Carrousel Midwest, Dale Sorenson, North Lake, WI; Clocks and Things, Cindy and Joseph Fanelli, New York, NY; Abe Kessler Appraisal Service, Queens Village, NY; Central Florida Depression Glass Club, Elizabeth Faust, Five Points Antiques, Longwood, FL; Millie Downey, Millie's Glass and China Shop, Orlando FL; Alfred J. Young, Police Academy Museum, New York, NY; Kruse Auction International Auburn, IN; Donald Z. Sokal, Airplanes, Pottstown, PA; Rita Nolth, Tacoma, WA; Michael Auclair, Lace, NYC; Selma Sternheim, Majolica, Monsey, NY; Eugene H. Brown, Lightbulbs, Dodge City, KS; George S. James Pen Fancier's Club, Washington, DC; Fridolt Johnson, Bookplates, Woodstock, NY; H.D. Lazuras, Toy Trains, Panorama City, CA; C.B. Goodman, Telegraphica, Chicago, IL.

A special thanks extended to Ted Hake of Hake's Americana & Collectibles for providing many photos for this book. Since 1967, Mr. Hake has published catalogues specializing in radio premiums, movie and television items, comic and cowboy collectibles and Disneyana. For a sample of his next catalogue send $2.00 to: Hake's Americana, POB 1444Y York, PA 17405.

PHOTOGRAPHIC RECOGNITION

Cover Photograph: Photographer — Bernie Markell, Orlando, FL 32809; *Courtesy of:* Five Points Antiques, Elizabeth Faust, proprietor, 1725 Highway 17-92, Longwood, FL 32746.

NOTE TO READERS

MARKET REVIEW

Strong prices along with increased collector interest and dealer aware-
ness account for the continued strength in most antiques and collectibles
fields across the board. If there is a problem it is that prices are constantly
rising on many rare yet always sought after collectibles. Fields that deserve
special attention this year include Americana, furniture, textiles, silver,
jewelry, Orientalia, paintings, pottery, dolls, toys and glassware.

Country and Americana collectibles are at their peak according to
experts with decoys and weathervanes among the big sellers. A rare
"Golden Plover" decoy sold recently for $50,000 while a rare Canvasback
Drake, signed by A. Elmer Crowell and dated 1915, sold for $12,000. A 19th
century molded copper and zinc trotting horse weathervane sold for $1,540
and a 19th century copper and zinc jersey Cow sold for $2,640.

Wood, tin, iron and copper kitchenware also remain popular. A wooden
cheese drainer recently sold for $900 which was twice the pre-sale esti-
mate. The ever popular graniteware is still on the rise.

Quilts, tapestries, samplers, hooked rugs and embroidery are also top
priority Americana items today. An early 20th century rug featuring a deer
sold for $330; an 18th century linsey-woolsey quilt with the wild goose
chase pattern sold for $935; and an 1870 Pennsylvania quilt, featuring the
heart and leaf pattern, sold for $2,200. A Boston needlework picture from
the mid-18th century broke all records when it sold for $63,000.

Dealers claim that young people are the big country buyers and they
seek both accessories and furniture. These buyers are discriminating: they
know what they want and are willing to pay the price. Finding good country
pieces is difficult and dealers believe that the supply is starting to dwindle.

On the whole, however, the American furniture market remains strong
and many auction records were set in recent months. Experts feel that
Federal period furniture may be the new favorite among collectors and
buyers. In recent months a Federal mahogany and painted wood bedstead
sold for $18,000; while a mahogany serving table sold for $900 and an inlaid
mahogany work table sold for $5,000. A Chippendale chest sold for
$115,500; a Boston Queen Anne desk and bookcase sold for $90,000; and a
Boston Queen Anne high chest of drawers, once belonging to John Adams,
sold for $150,000.

Arts and Crafts furnishings are on the rise in the Northeast. At recent
auctions a Gustav Stickley inlaid oak bed designed by Harvey Ellis sold for
$20,000; a Gustav Stickley oak sideboard sold for $3,300; and a three-sec-
tioned oak screen sold for $6,000. Some experts feel that Art Deco and Art
Nouveau furniture may become even more sought after as well and catch
up with Country in popularity.

Art Deco and Art Nouveau designs are certainly on the rise in the jewelry
market. This year's jewelry trends seem to be sapphires, Art Deco and
animal jewelry. A Bulgari ring set with sapphires and diamonds sold for
$6,000. An Art Deco and calibre sapphire bracelet sold above pre-sale
estimates at $16,000; a pair of Art Deco emerald and diamond ear pen-
dants, signed by Van Cleef and Arpels sold for $16,000. Animal pieces are
also sought after and a Russian emerald, diamond and pearl serpent
brooch sold for $40,000.

On a more moderate price level, fashion and costume jewelry was
singled out this year. Venetian glass woven beads from the 1920s are

worth $85 to $125; Art Deco Bakelite drop earrings from the 1930s are worth $25 to $35; and a brooch of Bohemian Crystals from the 1940s is worth $35 to $45.

A greater interest also emerged for top quality silver items. A 1720 sterling porringer by Simeon Soumain of New York City sold for $27,500; and a Paul Revere tablespoon sold for $3750. An Art Deco/Art Nouveau jewel mounted silver vitrine featuring secessionist maidens sold for $275,000. Silverplate flatware is also sought after and highly collectible, especially the Art Nouveau and Art Deco patterns.

Art Nouveau and Art Deco reached stable levels in other collectible fields as well. Art glass is doing well and particularly French cameo pieces as a Daum Nancy lamp recently sold for $26,500. A red Tiffany Tel El Amarna vase sold for $64,000. Experts expect an increase in the popularity of Lalique and less expensive art glass in the coming months.

Overall the glassware market boasts healthy prices, though some glass is faring better than others. Prices are good for Carnival glass and they remain quite high on some rare sought after pieces. Depression glass is also going strong though prices are constantly increasing and are hard to pinpoint. Now, however, is the time to buy Cut Glass as even the Brilliant Period pieces are at affordable levels.

It is currently a buyers market for some types of art pottery as well. Buy Zanesville art pottery, including Roseville, Owens and Weller, now as their current prices are one third to one half of what they were a few years ago. Other art pottery pieces are rising again after a decline of the past few years. A Dedham Pottery rabbit border plate with the Fairbanks house sold for $2,200 and a rabbit border plate featuring a coat of arms sold for $16,000.

The Oriental ceramics market continues to be very strong with a large decorated guanyao basin selling recently for $325,014. Archaic items also showed vigor when a Shang Dynasty archaic bronze cauldron sold for $187,000, and Oriental textiles showed strength too. A rare Imperial Kesi dragon robe from the Quianlong period sold for $17,600.

As far as other artistic fields are concerned, paintings had an interesting year with a continued interest in American works. Today's market is subject oriented and a mediocre painting by a lesser artist may sell at a premium price if the subject is a popular one.

There is also a revived interest in 19th Century European painters. Recent prices include $50,000 for "Le Recreation Pastorale" by William Bouguereau; $200,000 for "Autumn on the Thames," by J.J.J. Tissot; and $15,000 for "Dans Les Champs" by E.G. Bouguereau. There is also an increased interest in Chinese paintings.

The Print market is doing well and setting record prices. Both historical American and new American artists are in demand.

Of particular note this year are framed animation cels which have reached enormous heights of collector interest. Amazing records were set at a recent auction of Disney animation cels with a 1938 cel from "Brave Little Tailor" selling for $19,000 and a 1936 cel from "Through the Mirror" selling for $10,000.

Interesting happenings also occurred in the book market this year when a record setting $36,000 was paid for a cookbook. The book was published in Venice in 1475 by Bartholomaeus Sacchi. A rare third edition of the first American cookbook, Amelia Simmon's "American Cookery" sold for $20,000. A 1953 paperback, "Giant" by Edna Ferber, containing the rare signature of James Dean sold for $1263.

Items of a more historical nature also did well. One of 48 copies of an "Authorized Edition" of the 1863 Emancipation Proclamation sold for $270,000, while a George Washington letter sold for $110,000.

Such notable sales and prices extend to the fascinating world of dolls and toys as well. Wooden dolls, especially those by Schoenhut, currently rank high in collector interest as do the French bebes. An 1880 14″ Jumeau doll marked "Jumeau 5" sold for more than $5500. A Bru Jeune sold for $9350. The modern doll market is also doing well with Barbie leading the way. Perhaps the Barbie 25th anniversary sparked new collector interest.

Collectors are also hot on the trail of trains today especially those by Bing, Lionel and Ives. A Lionel No. 840 Power Station sold for $2,000 recently. Mechanical banks are also in demand and a merry-go-round bank recently sold for $12,000. The interest in clockworks and mechanicals is reflected in the $900 price paid for an 1880 clockwork dancing black couple.

Other markets also fared well this year and all indications point toward another year with fine prices and interesting happenings.

AN IN-DEPTH OVERVIEW OF THE MARKETPLACE

AMERICANA

For over a decade, there has been substantial interest paid to Americana antiques and collectibles. Each year the number of serious collectors and dealers has grown considerably. Many experts feel that there is no better time than the present to buy quality Americana items at good prices. Across the country, flea markets, auction houses, fairs and antiques shops are crowded with Americana items.

Americana antiques and collectibles span a broad range. On the one hand, there is the affordable and durable kitchen and household collectibles and primitives found in abundance at local flea markets and garage sales. Then there is the more fragile, more valuable items such as the molded copper and zinc Indian weather vane that sold for over $41,000 at a recent New York City auction or the small, Shaker-style oval box that sold for over $3000 at a recent show.

Noteworthy Americana on today's secondary market includes tramp art, old photographs, political buttons and advertising collectibles.

Tramp art is the name given to a form of nineteenth century American folk art, but it has just recently been receiving attention because of the folk art craze currently sweeping the country. Tramp art can usually be found in flea markets, out of the way junk shops and garage sales. It got its name from its unusual, transient artists (hobos or tramps). Tramp art items include elaborately carved picture frames, odd shaped boxes, lighting devices and furniture.

Old photographs can usually be found in dusty piles at local flea markets and country auctions. Truly unique photos of historical events, landmarks and people are sought by both collectors and museum curators.

Picture political buttons are considered more valuable than those with just a logo or name. Consequently, buttons featuring presidential running mates are more valuable than one candidate buttons. Particularly popular with collectors are those buttons featuring local and national candidates together.

Since the country has just held a national election, there is no better time to start a collection of political buttons while they are still readily available and affordable.

Collectors of advertising memorabilia have plenty to be pleased about this year. A museum consisting of a plethora of Nabisco Brand products and other related items recently opened in New Jersey. Items such as posters, biscuit tins and signs are displayed depicting the history of the company as well as the age of advertising in America.

In addition, an advertising art collector recently sold his accumulation spanning twenty-five years. One of the most significant items was a 1922, five-panel Coca-Cola screen priced at $22,500. Also, a 1928 General Electric calendar by Norman Rockwell sold for $400.

Americana items appeal to the casual collector as well. The casual collector is one who is searching for a few items to decorate his home or office. Especially appealing to the casual collector are baskets, fruit crate art, decoys, carousel animals, Disneyana and railroadiana. Fortunately, for the casual and serious collector, enough of these items exist to satisfy both interests.

However, earnest collectors are anxiously awaiting the big celebration in 1986. The Statue of Liberty will celebrate her centennial then and already numerous antiques and collectibles saluting her abound. Most important of all is the original terra cotta model made of her 109 years ago by F.A. Bartholdi, her creator. Through the efforts of the Statue of Liberty Commemorative Gallery in New York, permission was obtained for a mold to cast a 19½″ bronze of the model. The bronzes sell for $2500 each (10% of which goes to the restoration foundation), and will be issued in a limited edition of 4000.

Adding to the excitement, a rare, 49½″ model of the Statue of Liberty, one of only six known to exist, went on the auction block in December for over $100,000. This masterpiece, from around 1883, is considered to be the first of the six models of Liberty used in the campaign to raise funds for her construction.

This summer, another auction of Lady Liberty models and reductions to benefit the restoration foundation is planned.

Beginning collectors should not be discouraged. Practically anything dealing with America and her different eras is considered an "Americana collectible". It is not too late to search out holiday ornaments, kitchen collectibles, brass, cigar box labels, circus memorabilia, etc. Above all else, it is most important to enjoy the hunt!

BOTTLES

Auction sales results of recent months only bring good news to bottle collectors this year. The bottle market remains strong with collector/buyer enthusiasm high.

Recent sales reports indicate that bottles, flasks and inks are topping buyer priority. Inks currently are the best bet with rare ones bringing notable prices at auction. Two rare inks made by Pitkin Glass Works in Connecticut recently sold for more than $1000 each. Free blown utilitarian ink and spirit bottles also did nicely with a barrel shaped whimsey selling for $1300.

Historical flask prices at auction compare favorably with prices from previous years. An olive green coventry GI-84, Lafayette-Masonic sold for

$1000; while an aqua GII-60, Eagle-Charter Oak fetched $375; and a deep green GVIII-14 Sunburst went for $1100.

Also bringing notable prices in recent sales were food containers, pickle jars in particular. A medium green cathedral pickle jar sold for $700; while a light blue cathedral pickle bottle went for $300.

Though seriously collected for many years, milk bottles have taken an important place among bottle collectors only recently. Perhaps this is a result of last year's milk bottle centennial celebration. Many milks can be found for $5 to $10, though the rare and unusual sell for more than $100. Round pyroglazed quarts rank among the current best-sellers in this category.

The collecting of commemorative Coca Cola bottles is also becoming popular.

Commercial bottles can be found and bought in a price range from $8 to $75. Before values are decided, certain determinations must be made however. Condition is a major factor as bottles must be examined for cracks, cloudiness and excessive stains. The selling location is also a factor. Not every bottle has universal appeal: an old West Virginia bottle may bring a higher price in West Virginia than it would in Alabama. In general, the collecting of local or regional bottles is escalating with prices rising as well.

CARS

The experts are predicting another prosperous year for the collector car market. Many cars are selling at auctions, swap meets and private sales for much higher prices than have been seen for the past few years. The buyer's demand is much greater and more educated as we approach the 1990s. If this should continue, the market is apt to be increasingly strong for years to come.

The most outstanding market news took place at a recent California liquidation sale. An all-time record was set when a sporty red, 1956 300 SL Mercedes was sold for an astonishing $116,000. The bidding started at $50,000 and increased by $5,000 with every bid until it climaxed at $100,000. Thereafter, two bidders tried to outsmart each other until the final price of $116,000 was realized. At the same sale, a 1966 AC Cobra 427 was sold at the bargain price of $67,000 and a 1982 Porsche 930 Turbo in good condition went for $63,000. In total, over $1 million was raised at the one day event.

Also making headlines was the recent vintage car auction held in Las Vegas. Over 300 classic cars were put on the auction block for 8,000 prospective bidders. Prices varied from just under $10,000 to over $300,000. At this event, another record was set when $800,000 was paid for a 1936 Duesenberg Rollston convertible. A Stutz Super Bearcat sold for $120,000, a 1906 Knox tourist stopped the bidding at $15,000 and $300,000 was spent on a 1922 Mercedes Targia Florio racer.

Celebrity car auctions are also in the spotlight this year. The Batmobile, of the Batman television show, was sold for $77,000 along with celebrity vehicles belonging to Liberace and Zsa Zsa Gabor among others. In the late fall, Steve McQueen's vast collection of automobiles and motorcycles was auctioned in Nevada and was met with huge success.

Investors can expect to see high prices at the majority of important car auctions. Beginners should not be discouraged, however. There are plenty of collector cars, in various states of condition, available at reasonable prices. Corvettes, Mustangs and Thunderbirds, in particular, have seen a bit of action this past year and are experiencing an upward trend in prices and demand.

Because of the increasing sophistication among current collectors and investors, the beginner must always be aware of current trends in the market nationwide. Some cars may go for higher or lower prices depending on region, condition, color, model, etc. In order to keep abreast of the market, collectors should make it a point to visit the new museums cropping up across the country (one will be opening soon sponsored by the Classic Car Club of America), join a specialized car club (an extensive directory is provided in this guide), subscribe to the various collector publications, frequent sales as a spectator and keep this guide handy. It is a time consuming task to keep up with this hobby and its trends but; in the end, it will prove necessary and well worth the trouble.

DOLLS

Everyone wants dolls. The popularity of collectible dolls has skyrocketed along with the rest of the antique market. The future looks bright for doll collectibles. More and more doll clubs and publications are starting internationally and doll auctions and fairs are boasting record crowds and record prices. In addition, new lines of collectibles are being produced.

The busines of auctioning dolls has grown highly competitive. World records were broken at a 1983 auction when $38,000,00 was paid for 1915 antique A. Marque doll—the highest price ever paid for an antique doll. At a recent New York auction in the latter part of the year, a Bru French bisque head bebe went on the auction block for $4,000.00 while the bidding started at $3,000.00 for a Kestner German bisque head character baby, The big news is the $11,500.00 paid for an Izannah Walker doll in January, 1984.

The recent success of doll fairs and shows indicates that the market is back on the upswing. A recent Maryland show played host to record buyers and quality antique dolls. A 20″ Kestner Gibson Girl boasted a price of $3500.00 and a Simon & Halbig 18″ Oriental also was offered for $3500.00. Surprisingly, a recent London doll fair had to be closed because of the overwhelming crowds.

In keeping with the doll collectible frenzy, various companies of collectibles have introduced new dolls on the market.

House of Nisbet debuted its 18″ H.R.H. Prince William of Wales (deemed first in a Nisbet Royal Baby collection) for close to $60.00. For their new collection, Effanbee added "Judy Garland as Dorothy in the Wizard of Oz" to their exclusive Legend Series and have started a Great Moments in Music and a Great Moments in History collector series. A 15½″ Louis Armstrong and a 16½″ Winston Churchill headline these new collections respectfully. Jan Hagara's "Laurel" springs to life in the new 15″ Effanbee doll. Plus Hasbro debuted the Charmkins Family from Charmworld, a hidden place of fun and adventure. These new, whimsical characters are sure to delight collectors of all ages. In addition, the Cabbage Patch dolls are the collectibles to watch in the next few years.

As a sideline, Theiraults is expanding its list of mail-order doll books, doll calendars and doll stationery, and is setting up educational seminars, lectures and clinics on dolls.

Kewpie dolls are once again in the spotlight. The 70 year old kewpies have been a hot item since their introduction on March 14, 1913. The Kewpie doll, as we know it today, was originally the creation of Rose O'Neill and debuted in *The Ladies Home Journal* in 1909. In 1911, O'Neill commissioned sculptor Joseph Kallus to fashion the dolls out of bisque and celluloid, which were sent to Germany to be manufactured by the George Borgfeldt Company in 1913. The Kewpie doll craze continues to this day and a wide range of Kewpies appeals to collectors. The experienced Kewpie collectors seek the one of a kind Kewpies fashioned by Joseph Kallus while the new collector can easily run across the more available Kewpies made of vinyl, paper, plaster of paris, and celluloid. The Kewpie doll's original Cameo label (a company founded by Joseph Kallus) was replaced by Jesco Imports in 1983, However, Jesco will include the Cameo seal on all new lines of Kewpie dolls.

EPHEMERA

The paper collectibles market is flourishing. This market, which covers any type of item made from paper, is seeing renewed collector interest. Although the traditional paper collectibles like Thomas Jefferson autographs are still viable collectibles, recent material is enjoying heightened collector interest.

The March 29, 1976 cover of New Yorker Magazine, illustrated by Saul Steinberg, which shows New York as a large center in a very small world, fetches $40 at auction. The original newsstand price was 75¢.

A revival of Katy Keene, a popular comic book published by Archie Comics from 1942 to 1961, is occurring. Originally drawn by cartoonist Bill Woggons, the Katy Keene character was called "comic's fashion queen" because of the unusual yet fashionable clothing she wore. The clothing designs were often submitted by readers. Because of the revival, the original comic books of this series are commanding higher prices.

Recently, a monumental find was stumbled upon in a New Jersey warehouse. Forty crates of musical scores by George Gershwin, Cole Porter and Richard Rogers among others were found. Some of the works were unpublished making the pieces even more valuable.

In autograph collecting, a trend is forming toward motion picture stars' autographic material. Items like autographed photos, checks or passports from stars like Shirley Temple, Clark Gable, Rita Hayworth, Mae West and John Wayne command high prices. A Grace Kelly autographed photo from a scene in the movie *High Noon* captured $130 to $140 at auction.

Of course, traditional autographs from America's past are always highly popular among collectors. A one page letter signed by John Quincy Adams commands $700 while a signed two page letter from Benjamin Franklin dated April 9, 1773 fetches $4,500 at auction. A one page letter signed by Thomas Jefferson dated February 25, 1804 sells for $3,000 while a one page letter signed by Charles Lindbergh sells for $1,000 at auction.

One of the rarest autographed documents is the signed resignation papers of former President Richard Nixon. Although not for sale, they arevalued at $100,000. Currently, they are housed at the National Archives in Washington.

Although controversial, Third Reich paper collectibles are fetching astounding prices with Adolf Hitler items commanding the highest. A letter signed by Hitler went for $6,500 at auction recently. However, the last known letter written by him is valued at $50,000.

Postcards are another area of interest in paper collectibles. Highly popular with collectors are cards from the Columbia Exposition held in Chicago in 1893 with the World's Fair Station cancels.

Other World's Fair paper items are also popular with collectors including an 80 page color printed booklet from the 1901 Pan American Exposition which sell for $15 and stereoscope view cards from the 1876 Philadelphia Exhibition which sells for $38 for a set of seven.

Rare books are a very stable market for investing. Eighteenth and 19th century first editions are usually of more value than other more recent editions. A book of poems by John Keats published in 1894 sells for $1,000 while one of 250 signed copies of James Joyce's *Ulysses* published in 1935 commands $2,500. This book is especially valuable because it is signed by Joyce and illustrator Henri Matisse.

Paper collectibles are enjoying an upswing in the market. Because this area is broad, naturally some items will experience more movement than others. Collectors should take note of movie memorabilia, World's Fair items and rare books when perusing this collectible field.

GLASSWARE

The glassware market is growing stronger each month, reflecting the increased confidence, collectors have as the result of an improved economy. The biggest news in the art glass world this year was made during March when the United States government had the confiscated Tiffany collection of a convicted drug racketeer sold at auction. Presale estimates provided no indication of the final outcome with 66% of the lots bringing much more than their high estimates. The big surprise was that Tiffany vases, long undervalued, brought record prices. Some prices realized are as follows: red and amber favrile Tel El Marna vase, $64,900; peony lamp, $46,200; filigree poppy lamp, $23,100; laburnum lamp with gilt bronze base, $57,200; and tulip table lamp, $30,800.

Midwestern mold blown glass brought very strong prices during an April auction held in Ohio. Auctioneers refused to estimate the collection because there had been no comparable glass sold in the past years to base estimates on. Dealers could only watch as collectors drove prices into the astronomical range. Highlights of the auction include the following: amethyst Pillsbury compote, $16,100; green Ohio diamond pattern sugar bowl, $11,250; blue-gray blown molded creamer, $17,000; and green Midwest Kent bowl, $11,750. Many of the pieces had been in very prestigious collections in the past and collectors were anxious to acquire them as they seldom appear on the market.

Cut glass continues to be a buyers market. Very fine Brilliant period pieces can be obtained at reasonable prices across the country. Even fine signed pieces are very affordable and the market offers no indication of change in the near future.

The Carnival glass auction scene is a healthy one with prices continuing to be strong, especially for rarities. However, there hasn't been a great deal of change in the market for more plentiful pieces. Some of the prices realized at a recent carnival glass auction held in Missouri include: square purple Farmyard bowl, $2,200; purple Garden Patch chop plate, $900; blue opalescent Vintage bowl, $750; Millersburg green Trout and Fly bowl, $350; Millersburg amethyst nesting swan bowl, $120; Northwood green Peacock at Urn ice cream bowl, $550; Northwood purple Acorn Burrs punch set, $700; Fluffy Peacock amethyst water set, $560; Nuart green Chrysanthemum plate, $900; and a blue Elks plate, $725.

The Depression glass market is fairly stable with the exception of rarities which command very high prices. It is extremely difficult to keep up on prices for these as they increase monthly. Collectors seem to be acquiring these pieces at any price when they find them. This seems to be motivated by the fear that certain pieces are quickly becoming unobtainable.

All in all, this has been a good year for the glassware market. Look for increased activity in Lalique and less expensive quality Art glass as collectors seek an alternative to Tiffany. Cut glass and pattern glass are good investments at this time as prices are on the low side. Carnival and depression rarities continue to skyrocket and the elegant glassware of Heisey, Cambridge, Fostoria and others is attracting new collectors in record numbers.

HUMMELS

The Fiftieth Annivery of the production of M.I. Hummel Figurines will be celebrated in a big way! Goebel has announced their plans for 1985 which include fifteen new issues and the suspension of production of twenty Hummels.

Of special interest is the commemorative figurine "Jubilee" which features a singing boy and girl carrying flowers and gifts including a special envelope sealed with a heart. The boy carries a pot of flowers which has a banner marked "50" on it. This figurine will be in production only during 1985 and will have its own special backstamp.

The other totally new figurines include "Baking Day," Just Fishing, "Going Home," and "Sing With Me."

Five Hummels already in production will be introduced in new smaller sizes this year. These are "Chick Girl," "Hear Ye, Hear Ye," "For Mother," "Sensitive Hunter" and "Stormy Weather."

Production will cease for an undetermined amount of time on the following Hummels.

6/II "Sensitive Hunter"
13/II "Meditation"
33 "Joyful" — ashtray
45/0/W "Madonna With Halo" — white
45/0/6 "Madonna With Halo" — decorated
46/0/6 "Madonna Without Halo" — decorated
46/0/W "Madonna Without Halo" — white
48/II "Madonna" plaque
49/I "To Market"
50/I "Volunteers"
50/I "Village Boy"
52/I "Going To Grandma's"
60/A&B "Farm Boy" and Goose Girl" — bookends

61/A&B "Playmates" and "Chick Girl" — bookends
72 "Spring Cheer"
172/II "Festival Harmony With Mandolin"
173/II "Festival Harmony With Flute"
196/I "Telling Her Secret"
322 "Little Pharmacist" — German Issue
392 " Little Band"

Goebel has already announced that the 1985 Anniversary plate "Auf-Wiedersehen" will close the popular Anniversary Plate series which began in 1975, issuing a plate every five years.

Goebel introduced a totally new concept in 1984. It is a miniature line of plates and companion figurines beginning with a miniature "Little Fiddler" figurine 3″ tall and a miniature "Little Fiddler" plate 4″ in diameter. These are the first issues in "The Little Music Maker" series. The miniplates are being issued at $30 and the figurines at $39. The moderate price should attract buyers.

The most exciting figurine released in recent years was "Supreme Protection" (364) issued in 1984 to commemorate the seventy-fifth Anniversary of the birth of Sister Berta Hummel. This exquisite rendition of the Madonna and Child was available only during 1984 and quickly sold out. It is expected that the secondary market value will show a dramatic increase from the issue price of $150.

The biggest news in the world of Hummels is the resolution of the long, and at times, bitter conflict between Goebel and Schmid over the right to reproduce geniune Hummel art. The ramifications of this new agreement are not yet known, but obviously the potential exists for major changes in the marketing and, or, production of Hummel objects. It is a distinct possibility that the secondary market value of Hummel collectibles produced by Schmid will increase dramatically as result of this news. This is definitely a situation which bears close scrutiny in 1985.

LIMITED EDITIONS

Collector enthusiasm still remains at a peak in the field of plate collecting. In 1985, there was a significant increase in the number of plate collectors, shows, artists, distributors, dealers, manufacturers and plates. This sudden flood has caused some serious consequences.

First, sales have become sluggish because of the over saturation in the marketplace. The casual collector has become fickle letting his tastes wander from plate to plate, while the dedicated hobbyist has chosen to be selective and wait out this phase in the market.

Another result of this influx has been the production of less quality work, and more mass produced items. No true hobbyist will add these kinds of plates to a fine collection, and the market has suffered because of it. It appears that collectors are demanding quality over quantity this year.

However, plates of fine craftsmanship are still readily available today. For example, Knowles China has acquired the sponsorship of Encyclopedia Brittanica for a new series of plates featuring birds in their natural habitats. "The Cardinal" was the first release in this series. Also, Royal Orleans has begun to manufacture a series of plates commemorating the popular television show "Dynasty." The first issue, by artist Shell Fisher, is $35 and will be in production for one year only.

Plates featuring celebrities of famous characters of fiction are constantly in demand. Collectors should keep watch for the newest releases in the Knowles' "Gone With The Wind" series especially. Its value has quadrupled since the first issue in 1978. Also, Wedgwood is celebrating its 225th anniversary this year. Look for commemorative issues as well as an increase in prices throughout the year.

Some plate artists to watch for in 1986 include Sandra Kuck, Susie Morton, Rusty Money, Edna Hibel, Rosemary Calder and Donald Zolan.

The collector plate market is experiencing some growing pains right now, but it should emerge healthy and glowing in 1986!

PRINTS

The past year has been a prosperous one for the collector print market. Large audiences at exhibitions and furious bidding at auctions point to an active market for American prints and sales have rarely been stronger. In addition, there have been new releases from practically every major artist and new artists continue to rise in the field every day.

In the market today there is a mounting interest in American regionalism prints — a longing for days gone by that live in the artists imagination and this popularity is demonstrated in strong market results. Art prints from such familiar names as Norman Rockwell and Currier & Ives are consistent best-sellers. Current artists such as Americana artist Charles Wysocki and P. Buckley Moss are also highly favored.

Still influencing the collector print market is wildlife art and this was demonstrated last winter at an auction of John James Audubon's First Octavo Edition of the seven volume "Birds of America" complete with 500 handcolored plates. The exquisite collection was sold for $12,500.00 to the highest bidder. Other sales indicate that this interest will continue: the first edition of "Ross's Geese" by Edward Bierly can go as high as $2,000.00 on today's market plus "Springtime Enchantment-Wild Turkeys," an original by Owen Gromme, recently sold for $25,000.00.

The year 1984 marked the 50th anniversary of the first Federal Migratory Bird Stamp first issued in 1934. To commemorate this occasion, the 1984 issue will be a reproduction of the original stamp designed by J. N. "Ding" Darling. In addition, a limited edition color print will also be published. As the years pass, first edition prints of Federal Stamps have been known to appreciate as high as $4,000.00 on today's market.

Maynard Reece, the renowned wildlife artist and five time winner of the Federal Duck Stamp Competition, was commissioned by the sponsors of a recent wildlife art show to produce a work exclusively for auction at the show. The work, "Wetland Heritage-Canada Geese" sold for the astonishing record price of $20,000.00. The show was such an overwhelming success that the exhibiting artists were proclaiming it the best they had ever participated in. Record sales have also been reported at art exhibitions all over the country. For example, over ninety artists from across the nation showed their latest releases in a Missouri exhibition recently and the event brought more than 5,000 collectors to the two day affair. Each of the artists contributed a work for auction and over $50,000.00 was raised to aid in conservation efforts. Plus, over 550 works were submitted for an Ohio wildlife art competition this year and helped to further establish wildlife art as a pure art form and not just scientific or technical illustration.

Both wildlife and western art were represented in Minneapolis recently at a show that set both audience and exhibitor records. Featured artists at the show were Robert Abbett and Ken Riley.

Awards and honors have been plentiful this past year as well. At the conference between the U.S. Trade and Economic Council and Soviet officials, General Secretary Konstantin Chernenko of the Soviet Union was presented with an opaque watercolor of barred owls by wildlife artist John A. Ruthven. In addition, Frame House Gallery has received six awards in printing excellence from the Printing Industries of America. These prints include "The Pursuit" and "Bobcat" by Peter Skirka and Jim Harrison's "Mountain Bridge."

This is not to say that wildlife art is the only print on today's market to collect. Quite the contrary is true. The collector art print market is very competitive with a wide variety of subject matter done by experts and imaginative artists. In fact, a vast majority of collectors collect more than one artist and more than one subject. However, most aggressive investors and one theme only collectors can be found in the Federal or State Duck Stamp print market.

Art remains a profitable investment but the investor/collector must be knowledgeable before venturing into the field. For example, there is no written guarantee that any print will appreciate in value. Only the passage of time and market forces can move prices above their original retail values. If the prints consistently sell out, as this past year has indicated, and the secondary market value rises over a given period of time, then the prints and the artist should be considered a lucrative investment.

From all indications, the collector print market is stronger than ever this year and the only obstacle facing the collector at this point is the difficulty of choice.

MUSIC

Music collectors are fortunate. The music market is strong for the upcoming year especially in the areas of 18th century musical instruments and early 1900s music machines. Memorabilia of famous singers from opera to rock and roll comprises another section of highly valuable music collectibles.

Music is an interesting collectible field because of the vast array of items offered to collectors. From instruments to jukeboxes, sheet music to records, this collectible area offers any hobbyist the satisfaction of purchasing items that will usually increase in value. For example, an Edison Model A Home Phonograph made in 1901, is bringing $100 to $150 more over last year's prices. Its current selling price is between $500 and $700. An unusual musical vanity set that plays three different tunes when its lid is lifted brings about $640 to $750 on the current market.

Jukeboxes are an especially prized collector's item. Rarely found in restaurants or other public establishments, these colorful machines brighten any collection of music collectibles. Currently, jukeboxes in good condition are selling higher than last year. For example, a Wurlitzer Model 1015 jukebox made in 1947 is selling for $6,000 to $7,500, a jump of $1,000 to $1,500 over last year. This same machine owned by ex-Beatle member John Lennon can bring as much as $9,000 at auction.

Musical instruments will usually bring a premium at auctions. Although many 1800s instruments are museum pieces or for buyers with exquisite tastes, these beautiful instruments are worth memtioning. Violins are especially noteworthy. A handsome model made by Italian Francesco Ruggieri in the early 1700s usually brings between $40,000 and $45,000 at auction.

For the less extravagant collector, banjos, one of the most familiar instruments of folk music, is a good item to collect. Not only affordable, these instruments can be found crudely crafted or rather extensively decorated. Most American banjos from the late 1800s and early 1900s run from $150 to $300 depending on the wood, decoration and condition.

Other items more affordable to the average collector are memorabilia of music stars. In the rock and roll genre, The Beatlles followed by Elvis Presley are the most collectible stars. Rolls of Beatles wallpaper, now hard to find, sell for $100 to $125 at auction, four tickets to an August 23, 1966 Beatles concert at Shea Stadium sells for $200, while the Beatles gold album commemorating the sale of more than 500,000 copies of "Hey Jude," is selling for $8,000 to $10,000.

An Elvis Presley autographed photograph taken in the early 1970s currently sells for $250 on the music market, while a gray coat and velour hat owned by "the King" sells for $4,000.

Not only are Beatles and Elvis collectors growing immensely, but opera collectors are buying extensively. Although there are many big names in the opera area that are collectible, the biggest name is Enrico Caruso, Caruso autographs are one of the highest price items in this market bringing as much as $2,000 at auction.

Other opera items that beginning collectors can usually find and afford are signed paper programs, unreleased records and authorized limited edition statues or busts. Of course, the value of these items which can range from a few dollars to thousands of dollars depends on the artist.

Records, especially 78's are fetching higher prices over last year. Although still affordable, these thick black records are becoming quite collectible. For example, Gene Autry recordings take $100 to $150 at auctions while Duke Ellington 78's go for $50 to $75.

Old records is a new hobby still in its infancy. Most people bought them to add an authentic touch to their phonographs, which they did collect. This has changed. Records are becoming a viable market on its own.

Although the music collectible market is immense, areas collectors should watch include memorabilia of country and western singers, opera recordings of stars like Caruso, John McCormack and Geraldine Farrar and most Beatles memorabilia including 1960s manufactured items like dolls and lunch boxes.

ORIENTAL

The Oriental market has been confusing even to the experts this year. Auction houses report record prices for very unique pieces, such as a Tang Dynasty carved marble hare which was estimated at $20,000 to $30,000 and brought $104,500. In March, an album of 150 China trade watercolors estimated in the $25,000 to $35,000 range gaveled down an astonishing $181,500. During the same sale, a Qianlong period dragon robe was purchased for $16,000, which is the highest price ever paid for an Oriental textile.

However, during the past year many rarities failed to meet reserves or sold for disappointing prices. Rare archaic bronzes made a poor showing overall, with the exception of a few pieces which sold for astronomical prices.

Tang burial figures were also sold this year with most of the pieces realizing far less than their estimates. The exception was a piece which brought $88,000, twice as much as predicted.

The cloisonne market is equally mystifying. An 18th century ice chest brought $47,300, twice as much as its presale estimate. However, almost half of the pieces offered at the same auction failed to sell. While several pieces of jade sold higher than expected, almost half of the lots did not meet reserves and went unsold.

Growth in the value of Chinese ceramics has slowed to a halt this year. Some experts feel this is due to the increased availability of pieces that have been difficult to find in the past. However, extremely rare, fine examples continue to climb in price.

An enameled famille rose glass snuff bottle from the Qianlong period sold for $44,000 this spring reflecting the considerable popularity of this Oriental collecting area.

Although experts are baffled by the unpredictable nature of the current Orientalia market, no one seriously expects a decline. The superb quality and craftsmanship of these items will bolster oriental antiques and collectibles back to the leading edge of the market eventually. This is an excellent time to add some exceptional pieces to one's collection at much better prices than usual.

TOYS

Hang on to your hat. The collectible toy market is once again on a decidely unpredictable spin. Trends continue to rise and fall at a fast pace while the quality toys, as always, are in demand. Toy museums report planned expansions and toy fairs and shows continue to spring up all over the world to accommodate the demands of the collectors. Plus the major auction houses continue to provide a variety of quality toy collectibles resulting in, at times, record prices.

Recently, at a London auction, a record price of nearly $10,000.00 was paid for a Carette four-seater, hand painted, open phaeton car built around 1910. Also overseas, a German Marklin electric train set went for $1,250.00 and a painted wood toy farm circa 1900 realized $1,500.00 — a price far above the expected presale estimate. In addition, the highly collectible miniature figures, a Britains, Set #1177 Royal Presentation Box, in its original box, sold for $1,320.00.

In the late 1970s and beginning 1980s, all antique toys went through a slump in both market price and activity. Today some toys are experiencing a renaissance on the antique toy collectible market. For example, the tin toys of Marklin, Falk and Lehmann among others have become important and rare. This interest is evidenced at a recent sale where $5,830.00

was paid for a George Brown painted tin balancing toy of an equestrienne. In addition, the post-war Japanese tin toys are now sought heavily by collectors.

Emerging from their nearly eight year silence, cast-iron toys are hot on the secondary market. A "merry-go-round" cast-iron mechanical band in mint condition sold for $12,100.00 this year. There is also a surge of interest in clockwork and windup toys especially those made so exquisitely by Lehmann.

Mechanical banks and pull toys are still very much in demand. In the South, collectors are clamoring after toys from the 1930s and earlier. Surprisingly, miniature composition figures, largely ignored in the past, are starting to outprice their counterparts in lead and tin. Airplanes, cars and boats are emerging strongly while robots and other related toys are levelling off.

The Christmas season was a banner year for toys on the retail level. Sales were up by as much as 35% in some areas. Much can be attributed to the success of movie and television collectibles such as Star Wars, Star Trek and The A-Team as well as the new educational toys. But the teddy bear has hit an all new high in popularity and collectors should take note that great profits can be gained on the teddy bear market. Teddy bears are omnipresent not only in their familiar form but also on calendars, stationery, clothes and cartoons. This new call for bears has brought to the collector's attention the earlier bears of Steiff in particular. Early indications point to the black or white pre-1912 Steiff teddy bears as the bears to be had. Their unusual color makes them a rarity and high in demand. In addition, the modern teddy bears are fast disappearing off the store shelves and look to be the collectibles of the future.

As a side issue, Disneyana is being collected by insiders of the Hollywood movie industry and should be very much in the headlines in the future. Donald Duck has just celebrated his fiftieth birthday and new collectibles should be out soon.

Toys, like art, are a reflection of their times and the wise collector should make a careful study of this market and of this guide before venturing out.

WICKER

The prices for collectible wicker have basically leveled off over the past two years. However, very fine and rare pieces are steadily increasing in value, especially those from the Victorian era. Last year, record prices were realized at auction for a Victorian Morris chair which brought $1,100 and a fancy Victorian square table which sold for $1,300.

Generally, wicker prices are the highest in Florida, New York, and Southern California. The best area overall for fine quality collectible wicker continues to be New England. This is due to the fact that the original wicker manufacturing industry in America was basically concentrated there. Vintage wicker from the 1920s is most plentiful in Florida.

Items to look for now include children's wicker and salesmen's samples which can still be found at reasonable prices. Finding salesmen's samples can present a bit of a challenge but the results can be most gratifying. These lovely pieces were scaled down replicas or models of full-size furniture and were carried by salesmen to demonstrate new lines. Now avidly sought by collectors for their unique charm, these delightful pieces are a valuable addition to any collection. Experts feel that prices for these pieces are bound to escalate in the coming years.

Another factor which has greatly contributed to the popularity of collectible wicker is the current design trend espousing the charming Victorian and "country" look in home decoration. These styles feature a return to the romanticism and comfort of a bygone era. New Victorian-style homes are being built today and are furnished with stained glass, lace curtains and wicker furniture. It is important to remember that vintage wicker is still a good buy when one considers the expense of new furniture. Certainly there is little comparison between the two in terms of charm and quality for the money spent. In the past, Victorian, Turn of the Century and Art Deco collectibles have been regarded with disdain among the elite corps of antique collectors. This has been due to the fact that objects from this period were often machine made and the antiques world has traditionally regarded anything so produced as being inherently inferior to handcrafted pieces. (This was not the case with wicker, however, which was, for the most part handmade.) In addition, these collectibles were regarded largely as curio pieces due to their size and elaborate style, and did not have the distinction of being old enough to qualify as a genuine antique. But time passed and new generations of collectors entered the marketplace looking for distinctive pieces at affordable prices. These young collectors were unable to afford the finest old pieces and did not like the new modern styles. What they did discover was that Victorian, Art Nouveau and Art Deco furnishings had charm, verve, uniqueness and durability and could be purchased inexpensively. While price may have been the determining factor in the beginning, this new design style soon took hold as more and more people were exposed to the delightful results. Also, the craftsmanship of these styles, which has largely been ignored for fifty years, became more and more evident to the public. Vintage wicker was the very core of this new school of design. Unlike the inferior reproduction wicker which has flooded the market, old wicker is very sturdy, having been built with solid hardwood frames. It is quite heavy compared to the poor quality oriental pieces imported today.

Collectible wicker is avidly sought by the most prestigious interior designers in the country for its quality and charm. Once viewed only as informal accent pieces, this furniture is found in every possible setting today from the most affluent, elegant homes right down to log cabins — and every economic strata in between. This wide acceptance of wicker is one of the most important considerations when assessing and projecting its market performance and potential. For while wicker may have its slow periods in terms of price increases, it is most unlikely that values will ever drop. Without a doubt, the values of fine wicker of the Victorian, Turn-of-the-Century and Art Deco periods will continue to climb.

INVESTING

Investment in collectors items on a *grand scale* began overseas slightly before it began in the U.S. In Japan and Western Europe, where inflation was more drastic than in America, investors were turning to art and antiques in the early seventies. When prices for collectibles boomed abroad, as of course they did from the super-strong competition, the effect was dramatic on the U.S. market. Foreign investors by the score started buying from American dealers to take advantage of the savings. But the savings did not last long. Very shortly, U.S. prices for art, antiques and other collectibles were on a par with those of Japan and Western Europe. And the level of investor buying in all these far-flung regions of the globe was about the same — as it is today.

Today, as we approach the mid 1980's, antiques, art, coins and other "collectible investing" has been with us long enough to give us a fairly good perspective on its long-term potential, and to draw some conclusions which would have been impossible to arrive at (without a crystal ball) as recently as five years ago.

Collectible investment has proven itself more resilient than its critics believed. They were convinced that the first wave of heavy SELLING by investors — returning their purchases to the marketplace and taking their profit on them — would seriously reduce values and discourage any further investment. These collectibles would, they felt, be treated in the same manner as declining stocks.

Well, the first wave of heavy investment selling has come and gone — followed by more selling, in a rather balanced flow, since the late seventies. A VERY sizable amount of the merchandise bought by investors during the 1970's has gone back on the market, and some of it has passed through the hands of dealers and/or auctioneers half a dozen times since then. The disaster predicted by critics did not occur. Some slumps were evident in certain areas of collectibles, but these have occurred historically through the years without any influence from investors. In most cases, the slumps were not of long duration because new investors came in to snatch up bargains that resulted from falling prices.

The first requirement for successful investing is that the buyer knows what he's purchasing: what sort of investment prospects it has, and whether the particular specimen merits investment.

In other words, you cannot simply "invest in collectibles." You choose your subject, analyze the field, and buy methodically.

Even then, you are not GUARANTEED success. But your chances of turning a profit, on a well-selected collectors' item bought for investment, are unquestionably in your favor.

So many subtle considerations are involved that we cannot detail them all here. For a much more thorough exploration of investing in collectors' items — with all the pros, cons, and professional strategy — the interested reader is advised to consult the series of books on that subject published by The House of Collectibles, 1900 Premier Row, Orlando, Florida 32809. These include *The Official Investors' Guide to Gold, Silver and Diamonds; The Official Investors' Guide to Gold Coins; The Official Investors Guide to Silver Coins;* and *The Official Investors Guide to Silver Dollars.* The basic methods outlined in these works can be applied to any types of collectors' items.

The person who contemplates investing is, often, misled by the changing values of collectors' items. This is one basic "hurdle" for a new investor to clear. For example, someone has purchased a certain antique five years ago for $100. He opens a magazine today and discovers an advertisement offering the item for $200. The instinctive reaction is that he could double his money, in five years, by purchasing additional specimens for investment. There ARE some collectors' items, in fact quite a few of them, on which the investor can profit in five years or even less. But in this example, he would be ill-advised to go out and put a great deal of money into the item that rose from $100 to $200. The simple fact is that you DON'T double your money on something which rises in value that gradually. You may actually end up taking a loss on it, depending on circumstances.

Let's explore things a bit further.

When that item is selling for $200, this represents the retail market value — such as is given in the listings section of this book for thousands and thousands of collectors' items. If YOU, as a private owner, sell the item to a dealer, you will not receive $200. You may get only 50% of the retail market value, which means getting back the $100 you paid for it five years ago. But you still aren't even "breaking even." In the meantime, inflation has reduced the buying power of money. One hundred dollars isn't worth as much, today, as it was five years ago. You would need to receive CLOSE TO $200 JUST TO BREAK EVEN, in terms of the actual value of the money. So what appears on paper or in your imagination to be an excellent investment is really not one at all.

To be a worthwhile investment, an item would need to recover the cost price (when sold); PLUS compensate for the declining value of the dollar; PLUS leave you a profit when BOTH OF THESE FACTORS have been taken into consideration. To accomplish this, the investment item needs to rise in value at a fast pace. In addition, YOU the investor must watch the market and be aware of developments occurring on collectibles at that time — so you can seize the proper moment to sell.

BUILDING A COLLECTION

Virtually every type of collectors' item offers the possibility of building a collection, and adopting a hobby that can last a lifetime. All of those listed in this book, as obscure or remote as some may appear, fall into that category. And there are numerous others, hundreds in fact, which space limitations prevent us from covering. A visit to any antique shop will introduce you to many of them. So will a casual glance through the hobbyist periodicals, which are available at your public library.

Collecting need not be expensive. And it needn't be time-consuming, if you don't want it to be. This depends on you, and on what you want from your hobby. The goals and motives of collectors are diverse. Some collectors receive most of their pleasure and satisfaction from seeing their collection grow. Others enjoy the hunt and chase: tracking down hard-to-find items, following their trail wherever it leads. To them, browsing for three hours in a crowded antique shop and leaving with dust-laden hands and clothing is a prime exhilaration. And still others enjoy collecting because it leads to meeting other collectors and widening out their circle of friends and social activities.

Your selection of a collecting topic depends on finances, space, and other considerations, but mainly on your own personal tastes and inclinations. It's largely a matter of what you'll be most comfortable with. Looking through this book will provide a kaleidoscope of suggestions. While you're thinking, here are some points to ponder. Most areas of collecting can be pursued inexpensively and adapted to fit just about any budget. But this is not, unfortunately, true of EVERY type of collectible. You cannot collect Tiffany lamps or Currier & Ives lithographs without spending rather substantial amounts for each acquisition. This has nothing to do with the size or scope of the particular hobby. Competition is a factor in price, but so is availability. There are millions of coin and stamp collectors — far more than for Tiffany lamps — yet the vast majority of stamps and coins are inexpensive. These are hobbies in which great rarities exist alongside pieces that can be bought for a few pennies. Book collecting is another pursuit in which prices run the scale from zero to lofty heights. Original art, antique furniture, and porcelain are others in that category (plenty to choose from, pricewise). And there are some collecting areas in which the MOST valuable existing items are not expensive at all.

One thing you may want to consider, in thinking about your choice of a collecting hobby, is whether you'd like to collect objects that bear a DIRECT relationship to each other — such as sets. Set collecting can be done with material which was originally issued as a set (as in silverware), or carries dates or numbers that permit set assembly (such as comic books or coins). A typical example of a "set collection" is a run of Lincoln cents, beginning with the earliest one for 1909 and continuing up to the present. With this sort of collection, you always have a clear direction and you don't lose sight of your purpose. But for many people, set collecting is not creative enough. Each component in the set is, in many instances, very similar to every OTHER component. A group of 70 Lincoln cents on which all the "heads" (obverse sides) are identical except for the dates is simply boring in the view of some hobbyists. They want more variety. If you fall into that category, set collecting is definitely not for you!

Another point to consider is whether you'd like to participate in a well-established hobby that's amply supplied with reference literature, clubs and periodicals, or get in on the "ground floor" of one that's just in the process of developing. There are pros and cons on both sides of the fence, so it becomes — as usual — a matter of personal preference. With a well-established hobby, you receive the benefit of all the work already done by experts in terms of research, classification, and inquiry into fakes and counterfeits. On the other hand, items in such a group all carry an equally well-established market value, so there is less chance of finding bargains or making any discoveries on your own. In a hobby which has not yet been well developed, you could get some really excellent buys (things that might be soaring skyward in values, next year or five years from now), but they'll be somewhat harder to find and possibly trickier to authenticate. In some instances, if the hobby is really new, the dealers may not have had the chance to accumulate much knowledge and will hesitate to proclaim an item "genuine" or "fake."

But what it really boils down to is: What do you like? What do you enjoy owning, looking at, handling, thinking about? Do you like detective shows on TV? You might be at home collecting first editions of detective novels; or police memorabilia; or old "wanted" posters.

Like pets? Many collections have been made of animal-motif items, such as porcelain dogs and cats, or mechanical banks in the shape of animals.

Are you a travel enthusiast? Stamps and coins take you to faraway places. So do foreign banknotes and many other collectibles.

Into cooking? There are old and scarce and VERY curious cookbooks to be collected, as well as the implements used by our forebears in cooking and eating.

In other words, just about anything that interests you in LIFE can be turned into a hobby, even if you never thought about it from the standpoint of "collecting." For the sports fan, there are baseball and football cards, autographs, team equipment, yearbooks and plenty of other collectibles. For the car buff, there are antique components rescued from vintage autos, as well as all kinds of automotive ephemera.

And how about your job? Love it or hate it, it occupies a good deal of your attention. Are you ever curious about the way your predecessors in THAT TYPE OF JOB worked 50 or 100 years ago? The implements they used? Quite a few collectors get curious enough to become historians of their pro fession.

More doctors and dentists build collections around their profession than anyone else. In the hobbyist publications, you will encounter many ads placed by doctors and dentists, seeking to buy medical or dental memorabilia of yesteryear. These are, of course, ideal fields for collecting, because the professions are very old, have a well-documented history, and have produced a vast quantity of collectible items of every description.

Think about your job, and whether it might contain the spark for a collection.

CONDITION

The condition, or physical preservation of collectors' items, is receiving increasing attention. Collectors are becoming more demanding with regard to condition. For investors condition is of extreme importance, since it has been shown beyond a doubt that collectors' items in the best grades of condition rise sharpest in value.

Nearly ALL collectors' items in well-preserved condition have a higher rarity factor than the VERY SAME ITEMS in lesser condition. This is because the majority of existing specimens are, almost invariably, in less than outstanding condition. With some items, there may be one "mint" specimen in circulation for every ten showing signs of wear, use or abuse.

With others, the ratio could be 1-to-100 or even 1-to-1000. It varies, of course, with the type of collectible, the age, and other factors.

Condition, therefore, is a prime influence in buying or selling collectors' items. Whether the beginning collector is really concerned about condition or not, he needs to learn something about it and its effect on prices. Otherwise he is likely to see bargains where they do not exist, or accuse a seller of overpricing when a premium is being charged because of noteworthy condition. If you're bidding at auction sales, you must be even MORE alert to condition and the difference it makes in values.

No grading system fits all varieties of collectors' items. Each item has to be judged in terms of its material, age, the use for which it was intended, and other considerations. Something made as a household decoration to be hung on a wall and admired is in a far different category than a tool or cooking utensil. You would not expect a 19th century sledgehammer to be free of any nicks and scratches.

Don't expect the impossible, but don't settle for slipshod specimens of items that COULD have been preserved much better.

FAKES

Develop a critical sense, a vital quality which the bargain-hunter and casual shopper usually lack.

In nearly all cases, fakes fall into one of the following categories:

1. The outright fake. This is what most people think of as a fake, being unaware that other kinds exist. An outright fake is made wholly by the faker, "from scratch." He obtains materials and uses his own processes to create the object, and his goal is to defraud the eventual buyer.

2. The honest reproduction. These are multiplying in number. An honest reproduction is a facsimile of a collectors' item made as a decoration, souvenir, curio, or for some other legitimate purpose without the intent to defraud. They are, however, sometimes mistaken for originals.

3. The doctored item. This is a genuine collectors' item which the faker changes in some way or other to make it appear more valuable, such as a coin on which a mintmark is removed or a silver porringer to which an inscription and date are added.

4. The hybrid. These are objects made from components of two or more collectors' items. Hybrids occur most frequently in furniture. A faker will take two tables, one with good legs and the other with a good top, and marry together the well-preserved components.

Of these four categories of fakes, objects falling into the first (outright fakes) are automatically worthless, except for intrinsic value if they happen to contain a precious metal.

Honest reproductions can, and usually do, have some value, but the value is considerably less than that of the model. There are occasional exceptions to this rule. When a reproduction is made as a limited edition, in a deluxe manner using the best materials and workmanship, it can be a desirable collectors' item in itself and POSSIBLY of even greater value than the original. Some reproductions of antique firearms (for example) attain very high collector value.

Doctored items tend to be considered "spoiled" by collectors, even if they had a substantial value originally. As for the last category, hybrids, these are very commonplace on the antique market and are sold regularly. While the collector value or historical value of any hybrid is open to debate, there is definitely a good demand for them. They have the look of an antique and have a utilitarian value, if the object is a piece of furniture; and many noncollecting buyers will ask no further questions. So it is open to argument, really, whether the maker of hybrids can be called a faker.

One of your chief weapons against buying fakes (of any variety) is to buy only from the more respected sources of supply. This advice makes obvious sense. Specialist dealers who handle just one type of collectors' item are likely to be expert on that type of collectors' item. The specialist dealers, because of their reputation for knowing their subject, are very seldom offered fakes for sale. Anyone who knowingly wants to sell a fake will, nine times in ten, take it to a general antique dealer. This may mean a little lower price, but the danger of detection is lower too, and this is what counts in such situations. The less careful and less expert the dealer is, the more careful and more expert his customers must be!

BUYING TIPS

BUYING FROM DEALERS

There may be occasional problems or drawbacks in buying from dealers, but on the whole they serve a vital purpose. Most of the collecting hobbies covered in this book could not exist without the professional dealers. They do the legwork for you, in finding the material and bringing a large selection of it together for your perusal. They serve as a kind of buffer between you and the counterfeiters and forgers who manufacture bogus collectibles. Sometimes fakes do get on dealers' shelves; but without the dealers as a line of defense, things would be far worse. Dealers can be helpful to you in many ways. They have contacts within the trade which would be hard for a private hobbyist to duplicate. If they know exactly what type of item you're looking for, even if it's something very offbeat or scarce, they can usually find it for you.

There are basically two types of dealers in collectors' items. The first is the general dealer. Most antique dealers fall into that category. They offer a broad variety of collectors' items, and possibly some objects which could not be called collectors' items, but are decorative or interesting. The second type is the specialist dealer. He sells primarily — or exclusively — collectors' items of a certain kind, such as stamps, comic books, or prints. Today there are specialist dealers for nearly every type of collectible. Naturally the bigger hobbies have the most specialist dealers; thousands of dealers specialize in coins, for example, while only a handful restrict themselves to something like firefighting memorabilia. This is governed strictly by the degree of hobbyist activity and the amount of money being spent in each field. What are the basic differences in buying from a general dealer as opposed to buying from a specialist?

In the shops of general antique dealers, you will find many of the identical items offered by specialist dealers. There IS a difference, though. The prices are usually a bit lower. When you buy from a general dealer, you will usually pay a lower price for the same item than if you had acquired it from a specialist. The savings might be only 5% or 10%, but it could be as much as 50% or even more.

The general dealer does not have as large a selection of specialist items. If you collect Depression Glass, for example, the general dealer might have a dozen pieces — or perhaps he might have none at all. A specialist dealer in glassware will be displaying HUNDREDS of examples of Depression Glass. The general antique dealer does not, in most instances, profess to be an expert on everything in his stock. His wares represent a conglomeration of his purchases from many different sources, and he offers them "as they come." Not all general antique dealers fall into that category, as some deal in a higher grade of merchandise and have experts on their staff to appraise and identify incoming stock. In return for the opportunity to get a bargain, the onus falls upon you — the customer — to decide whether an item is exactly what it appears to be.

The specialist dealer goes to more trouble than the general dealer. He inspects his merchandise more carefully. He has expert knowledge of his pet subject and, usually, a reputation within the field. There is very little likelihood that fakes, counterfeits, or restorations can slip by him.

Price Variations. The question most often asked by beginners about buying in antique shops is: How firm are the prices? What will happen if I make a counter-offer? Will the dealer be offended? Do I stand much chance of getting an item for less than the named price?

The situation is generally this: the dealer has a price in mind (it may be tagged on the item, or truly "in mind") that he would LIKE to get — a price that would cover his cost and leave a favorable margin of profit. It may be double the sum he paid, or even triple: this varies depending on the item and its nature, and also his style and volume of business. A dealer will be more apt to show flexibility on a price if the item has been in stock for months or (in some cases) a year or more. When stock is relatively new, the dealer holds out, hoping that it will sell for the full price he wishes to get. As time passes and it fails to sell, it becomes evident that the price may need to be adjusted. With some dealers, the waiting period before price adjustment is very short, as they like to turn over their stock rapidly.

The term "reducing the price" is apt to be misleading. To determine whether the reduction results in a favorable buy, you would need to know if the ORIGINAL price was in line with the true market value. If a dealer prices something at $300 when the average market price is $200, he can reduce it by 20% and still be charging more than most of his competitors.

As far as the reaction you'll receive from dickering, this varies with the dealers. Some are insulted. Some pretend to be insulted, but aren't. Some welcome a no-holds-barred discussion about price, because it gets the customer talking and a talking customer is likely to end up buying. You're apt to get a more favorable reception by not drawing attention to flaws or taking a an overly casual approach. The skilled bargainer always takes a positive attitude about the item under discussion. He never asks for a discount because the item isn't EXACTLY what he really wants. Rather, he acknowledges his interest in it, and says something like, "If I could get this for $50, I wouldn't hesitate a minute," or words to that effect. If you have experience at all with antique shops and their proprietors, you can usually tell when dickering will be successful and when it won't. If you and the owner are TOO far apart in price, it's just a waste of your time to get into a bargaining session. Don't delude yourself into believing that you can work the price down to half the original sum. In most cases, a discount of 10% or 15% is the most you're going to get — because 10% off the

PRICE means at least 20% off the PROFIT in most cases. There are many possible variations on approaches to bargaining — far too numerous to enter into here. One novel method is worth mentioning. There was a collector who would browse around an antique shop until he found something he wanted — say a tin pelican priced at $30. He would pretend he hadn't seen the item, then casually ask the dealer, "Do you happen to have any tin pelicans for around $20?" This is a very effective approach, because it establishes YOUR price range before the dealer has the chance to establish HIS price range. It's a way of bargaining without appearing to be bargaining.

BUYING AT AUCTIONS

Auction buying is exciting, and offers more opportunities for bargains than in buying from dealers, but carries somewhat greater risks. As a rule, auction buying is more suitable for the experienced collector. But there is no reason why a beginner, using caution and common sense, cannot attend auctions and try his luck in the competition.

If you buy at an auction, you are apt to be involved in bidding under a broad variety of circumstances. You will sometimes be bidding on a lot for which YOUR maximum bid represents one-tenth the sum another bidder is ready, willing, and able to pay. And you will, just as frequently or perhaps more so, come prepared to give a small fortune for an item that not a single other bidder wants.The price that something brings at an auction is not, therefore, an indication of its value, but only of its value to the bidders in that particular sale. If sold again the next day, with different bidders on the floor, it could go considerably higher or lower.

If it sounds as though auction buying entails a substantial measure of uncertainty, it does indeed. But if you know the mechanics of auctions, have a relatively cool head and sound judgment about collectors' items, you can do very well in the auction arena. The important thing is to keep a rein on your emotions and not overpay unless the item is something extra-special. Also important is to know what you're bidding on: if it's authentic, if it's in good condition, and whether it truly merits the size of the bid you intend to place.

If you're going to attend the sale, don't fail to also attend the *presale exhibition.*

You could (as many bidders do) wander around the presale exhibit and see what catches your fancy. This is time-consuming, though, and a better approach is to check off — in the catalogue — lots which SEEM as though they appeal to you. Then, at the presale exhibit, you can go directly to them and spend your time giving each a thorough examination.

As you make your inspections, mark your bid limit for each item in the catalogue. This is the time to think about price, not during the heat of competition. At the presale exhibit, you're not being influenced by the prices OTHER bidders are willing to pay. You can make a much sounder judgment of how much you want it and how much it's worth to you in dollars and cents.

SELLING TIPS

Many factors enter into the price you receive (or the price you're offered) when selling collectibles. Let's take a look at some of them:

1. Dealer's stock on hand. This, of course, varies from dealer to dealer, and even among the same dealers at different times of the year. You aren't in a position to know what kind of stock the dealer has on hand, or what he has coming in, yet this does play a role in determining (a) whether he'll be interested in purchasing your antiques, and (b) the extent of investment he cares to make in them. When a dealer says he's overstocked, this is not necessarily a ploy to induce you to accept a low price. All dealers in collectors' items DO become overstocked periodically — and they become *understocked,* too. It all hinges on the pace at which material moves in and out, and that's governed largely by circumstances over which the dealer has only partial control. Sometimes he'll go for weeks without anyone offering to sell him anything. Then armies of sellers all arrive at the same time. This works fine if the volume and flow of buying is comparable to that of selling. But if the dealer has been buying more than he's been selling, he has no choice but to slow down for a while. No dealer likes to bypass the opportunity to buy worthwhile merchandise, but he can't have more cash going out than coming in.

2. The Dealer's clientele. Every dealer — whether he sells antiques, militaria, dolls, or whatever — has his own special group of customers, who are the life and blood of his business. Some of them are sure to be general collectors, but others are specialists, and the specialties of these clients can be very exclusive in some cases. An antique dealer may have a customer who wants nothing but augers (old tools uses to bore holes in wood). You could survey 99 other antique dealers and find NONE who have customers for augers, but this particular dealer has one — and an avid one to boot. The customer possibly has one of the largest collections of augers in the country. He wants to buy any specimens and ALL specimens that he can find, regardless of size, shape or color. He never says "no" to an auger. Consequently, the dealer knows he can sell any augers that come into his stock. When an auger is offered to him, he automatically buys it, and he may pay a higher proportion of the retail value than he pays for other antiques. He has a sure sale at a sure price, so his degree of risk is just about zero.

The type of items that a dealer displays in his shop may be a clue to those in which he's most interested in buying. Certainly if you find an antique shop whose stock consists mainly of glass, this would be a more likely place to sell a collection of glassware than to a "general" antique shop. But it does not always work that way. In the example given above — of augers — you would not find a single auger in the shop, even though its proprietor would rather buy them than anything else. Why? Because every one he purchases is sold immediately to his special customer, without ever going out on display in the shop. This is the situation with many kinds of merchandise in many collectors' shops. What you see "out front" displayed to the public is the general stock. Articles that have been bought for special clients aren't around any longer.

3. Geographical location. With some types of collectors' items the PLACE of sale can be a factor in their price. Values given in this book are averages for the country as a whole. If an item has definite *regional inter-*

est, it can be counted on to sell somewhat higher in that locality and, usually, a bit lower than the average elsewhere. More collectors' items have regional interest than you might imagine, though it is not usually strong enough to influence the value by more than 10% or at the most 15%.

It also happens, sometimes, that certain collecting hobbies thrive a bit stronger in some parts of the country than others, for no really explainable reason. This has been the case with knife collecting, to name one; it has been more popular in the southern states than elsewhere. In the earlier days of *rock and roll record collecting,* nearly all collecting activity was confined to New York and California (this has since changed). Comic book collecting was a big hobby in New York before it surfaced anywhere else.

4. Condition. The inescapable fact is: when an item is worn, damaged, or otherwise not in the best of condition, it is not worth the full retail value. It may still be collectible and salable to a dealer, but it represents a kind of question mark for him. Maybe if the item was in "mint" condition he would not hesitate to purchase it. In inferior condition, he will automatically wonder how long it will take to sell, and whether it will sell at all. Some dealers do not care to stock damaged or defective items. Others will do so, in certain cases, but their buying offer will be CONSIDERABLY less than their offer for a mint or near-mint specimen. It may be just 10% of the retail value of a mint specimen or even less. If that seems unfair, you should stop to consider that the dealer is in a bind when he handles merchandise of that nature. He has to offer his customers a very healthy discount on it, possibly selling it for a third as much as a mint specimen. Therefore he can put very little money into it.

If you have a collection which is mostly in good condition but contains some defective items, it may be best to REMOVE the defective items before offering it for sale. These sub-par components in a collection will always catch the dealer's eye and may give him a negative feeling toward the collection as a whole. Then, when you discuss price, the dealer is sure to point out the inferior condition of these items. Just like your garden, your collection may need weeding out before selling it. Put it in the best shape you can, and you'll stand an excellent chance of getting a satisfactory price for it.

SELLING BY AUCTION

Maybe you enjoy buying at auction. Have you considered the possibility of selling your collection in that fashion, when the time comes to sell?

Auction sales have become a much more popular method for selling all types of collectors' items. The chief attraction of selling by auction is that you have the chance — with a little luck — of realizing more than a dealer would pay for your collection. A dealer has to resell the material, so of course he takes a deduction from its retail market value in figuring up his purchase price. At auction, the sky is the limit. If two or three determined bidders lock horns on something YOU own, they could drive the price up far beyond the retail market value. Even after the auctioneer's "house commission" is deducted from the selling price, you would end up doing better than selling outright to a dealer.

Of course, it doesn't always work that way. Auctions are unpredictable. Just as you have the opportunity, at auction, of realizing more than a dealer would pay, the possibility also exists that your collection will bring LESS than a dealer would have given. Those are the breaks of the auction game.

Consider the type of collection you have for sale, its contents and value, and you may be able to judge fairly accurately which method of sale holds out the brighter prospects.

The best types of collections to sell by auction are those which are highly specialized and those containing a large proportion of investment items. But as you will see by attending auctions or just reading the reports of them, many collections are sold — thousands of them annually — which do not fall into either of these categories. Their owners chose the auction route, when they could have sold to a dealer and received quicker payment.

There are all types of auctions. They range from posh sales of art and jewels, accompanied by lavish catalogues which serve as reference books in themselves. At a sale of this type, bids totaling more than a million dollars might be recorded in less than an hour. At the other end of the scale are country auctions and estate sales, at which anything under the sun is apt to turn up and where lots can go for as low as $1 each. (But do not underestimate the country or estate sale, either — when desirable collectors' items are included, as they sometimes are, dealers and collectors flock to them and the prices can get very, very strong.)

Some auctioneers are specialists while others handle whatever comes along, so long as it falls in the nature of secondhand property. The biggest groups of specialist auctioneers are those handling coins and stamps. Material of this nature requires specialist knowledge to appraise and classify, so it is very seldom sold by the general art or antique auctioneers. If you have a specialized collection, it is advisable (when selling by auction) to seek out an auctioneer whose sales are geared to that type of merchandise. Such an auctioneer has an established mailing list of active buyers for THAT PARTICULAR KIND OF COLLECTIBLE, and you're sure to do much better pricewise than if you select a local auctioneer just because of convenience.

The procedures vary among auction houses, in terms of the arrangements made with sellers and also the actual rules and regulations of their sales. The amount of their commissions varies, too, but this usually proves to be a rather minor detail. You should not automatically choose the auctioneer who offers the lowest commission rate (i.e., the percentage he deducts from the sale price of each lot before settling with the owner). When one house is operating on a 10% commission and another on 15%, it might seem as though the 10% house is the obvious choice. This just isn't so. Usually when an auctioneer is charging slightly higher commission rates than the competition, it's because he spends a great deal more in advertising and promoting his sales, and on the preparation of his catalogues. Therefore, the prices realized at his sales are likely to be MUCH higher — so you would do better selling through him, even though his commission rate might seem discouraging. A low commission rate is, often, an indication that the house has a hard time attracting property for sale. When an auction house has an established record of successful sales and satisfied clients, it has no problem getting material to sell. So do not allow yourself to be influenced by differences in commission rates.

When you put material up for sale by auction, it is never sold immediately. It has to be lotted and catalogued and the catalogues have to be distributed. All of this takes time. It may be two to three months, between placing the merchandise in the auctioneer's hands and the actual date of sale. And, thereafter, it might be another 30 days before you receive settlement. Settlement is seldom made quickly. Each auction house works by contract. You and the auctioneer sign a sales contract at the time of placing the material in the auctioneer's care. The contract spells out all these details — the rate of commission, the sale date, and the length of waiting time between the sale date and receiving your payment.

FLEA MARKET DIRECTORY

The following flea markets are listed in alphabetical order according to state. Within each state the listings are in alphabetical order according to city or town. If you would like to have your flea market listed free of charge in the next edition of this book, please send us your information using the format found below. We provide this directory as a service to our readers and would like to expand it to include as many flea markets as possible.

One word of caution — be sure to verify flea market dates and hours of operation before driving long distances to attend.

CALIFORNIA

GARDEN GROVE
Westminster Abbey
Antique Mall — 11751
Westminster Ave.
Daily 10:00-5:00, Friday 10:00-9:00
PM — Closed Tuesday

FLORIDA

BRANDON
Joe & Jackie's Flea Market
3 miles north of Brandon between
Parsons and Kingsway on
Hwy. 574
Daily — (305) 689-6318

FT. LAUDERDALE
Oakland Park Boulevard
Flea Market
3161 W. Oakland Park Blvd.

HIALEAH *(Miami area)*
DAV Swap Meet
1000 E. 56th St. — (305) 685-1296

HIALEAH GARDENS *(Miami area)*
Palmetto Flea Market
7705 NW 103rd St.
(305) 821-8901 — 822-4478 —
825-9605

LAKELAND - AUBURNDALE
International Market World
Highway 92 East of Lakeland
Friday, Saturday and Sunday —
(813) 665-0062

MIAMI
Flea Bazaar
14501 W. Dixie Hwy.
(305) 945-3553

MIAMI
Metro Flea Markets
701 SW 27th Ave.
(305) 541-3400

MIAMI
Turnpike Drive In Theatre
Flea Market
12850 WN 27th Ave.
Wednesday, Friday, Saturday,
Sunday — (305) 681-7150

MIAMI
119th St. Flea Market
1701 NW 119th Street
(305) 687-0521

MIAMI BEACH
World's Largest Indoor
Flea Market
1901 Convention Center Dr.
(305) 673-8071

NORTH MIAMI
Seventh Avenue Flea Market Inc.
13995 NW 7th Ave.
(305) 688-3852

NORTH MIAMI
North Miami Flea Market
14135 NW 7th Ave.
(305) 685-7721

MT DORA
Florida Twin Markets, Jim
Renninger — proprietor
Highway 441 in Mt. Dora, ½ mile
north of Highway 46
Every Saturday and Sunday —
8 AM - 5 PM
(305) 886-8946

ORLANDO
Bobbie's Flea Market
5620 W. Colonial Dr.
Daily — (305) 298-0386

ORLANDO
House of Bargains
6021 E. Colonial Dr.
Thursday through Sunday — (305)
273-5555

ORLANDO
Northgate Flea Market
1725 Lee Rd.
Weekends — (305) 293-3600

ORLANDO
Orlando Flea Market
5022 S. Orange Blossom Trail
(305) 857-0048

PALMETTO *(Tampa area)*
Country Fair
U.S. Highway 301 and 41
(813) 722-5633

PLANT CITY *(Tampa area)*
Country Village Flea Market
One mile north of 1-4 Exit 13 on
St. Rd. 39
Wednesday, Saturday and Sunday
— (813) 752-4670

SANFORD *(Orlando area)*
Flea World
Hwy. 17-92 between Orlando
and Sanford
Friday, Saturday, Sunday —
8 AM - 5 PM
(305) 645-1792

SARASOTA
Trail Outdoor Flea Market
6801 Tamiami Tr N, across 41
from Sarasota airport
(813) 355-6329

TAMPA
Bargain Barn Flea Market
2400 Gehman PL.
(813) 248-1208

TAMPA
Buccaneer Flea Market Inc.
4260 Dale Mabry Highway S
(813) 831-4499

TAMPA
Oldsmar Flea Market
180 Race Track Rd.
(813) 855-5306

TAMPA
Seminole Flea Market
7407 Hillsborough Ave.
(813) 623-5662

TAMPA
Top Value Flea Market
8120 Anderson Rd. corner of
Anderson and Waters
Saturday and Sunday —
(813) 884-7810

THONOTOSSASA *(Tampa area)*
North 301 Flea World Inc.
11802 US Hwy. 301 N, one mile
north of Fowler Ave.
Thursday, Friday, Saturday,
Sunday — 8 AM - 5 PM
(813) 896-1344

VENICE
Dome Flea Market
5115 St. Rd. 775, one mile off 41
(813) 493-2446

WEST PALM BEACH
Farmer's Flea Market
1200 S. Congress Ave.
(305) 965-1500

WEST PALM BEACH
West 45th Street Flea Market
3500 45th St.
(305) 684-8444

GEORGIA

ATLANTA
A Flea Market at Moreland Ave.
1400 Moreland Ave. SE
Every Friday and Saturday from
10 AM to 7 PM
Sunday from 12 AM to 6 PM —
(404) 627-0831

ATLANTA
Arnold's Flea Market
2298 Cascade Rd. SW
Every day — (404) 752-9507

ATLANTA
Flea Market at Forest Square
4855 Jonesboro Rd. FPK. just
outside 1-285
1½ miles south
Friday and Saturday 10 AM
to 9 PM
Sunday 12 AM to 6 PM —
(404) 361-1221

ATLANTA
Flossie's Flea Market
636 Lindbergh Way NE, behind
Victoria Station at Piedmont
Monday through Saturday 11 AM
to 6 PM
(404) 237-6273

ATLANTA
Funtown Flea Market
500 Northside Dr. SW
(404) 659-9806

ATLANTA
Golden Key Flea Market
833 Cascade Rd. SW
(404) 758-8780

ATLANTA
Scavenger Hunt on Peachtree
4090 Peachtree NE
Seven days a week 10 AM - 6 PM
(404) 237-9789

ATLANTA
The Second Act Inc.
82 Peachtree St. SW, one block
from Five Points
(404) 523-9490

CHAMBLEE *(Atlanta area)*
North Perimeter Flea Market
5000 Buford Highway
(404) 451-2893

CHAMBLEE *(Atlanta area)*
Atlanta Flea Market and
Antique Center
5360 Peachtree Industrial
Blvd. Cham.
(404) 458-0456

DECATUR *(Atlanta area)*
Bailey's Flea Markets
3372 Memorial Drive
(404) 298-9726

DECATUR *(Atlanta area)*
Decatur Flea Market
724 W. College Ave.
(404) 378-4784

DECATUR *(Atlanta area)*
Kudzu Flea Market
2874 Ponce de Leon Blvd.
(404) 373-6498

DECATUR *(Atlanta area)*
Let's Make a Deal Flea Market
205 E. Ponce De Leon at Church
(404) 377-8676

DECATUR *(Atlanta area)*
Sims Flea Market
902 W. College Ave. between East
Lake Marta Station and Agnes
Scott College
Monday through Saturday 9 AM -6
PM — (404) 371-8032

ILLINOIS

AMBOY
Antique Show and Flea Market
Route 30, 4-H Fairgrounds
Third Sunday in each month
8 AM - 4 PM

BELLEVILLE
Belleville Flea Market
Route 13 and 159, just off 460,
Belleclair Exposition Center
Third weekend of every month

BELVIDERE
Boone County Flea Market
Boone County Fairgrounds
Check ahead of time; the
dates vary

BLOOMINGTON
McLean County Flea Market
McLean County Fairgrounds
Check ahead

CHICAGO
A Mart Flea Market
1839 S. Pulaski Rd.
(312) 542-6619

CHICAGO
Archer & Damen Flea Mart
3450 S. Archer
(312) 927-3556

CHICAGO
Buyers Flea Market
1126 N. Kolmar
(312) 227-1889

CHICAGO
The Christian Hope Enterprise
8357 S. Halstead
(312) 488-5025

CHICAGO
First Chicago Flea Market
4840 N. Pulaski Rd.
(312) 545-3149

CHICAGO
North Side Flea Market
5906 N. Clark
(312) 334-8982

CHICAGO
Paris Flea Market
Sheridan Drive in Theatre,
7701 South Harlem Ave.
Every weekend — (312) 233-2551

CHICAGO
Roseland Great American
Flea Market
10131 S. Michigan Ave.
(312) 995-5503

CICERO *(Chicago area)*
Flap Jaws Flea Market
1823 Cicero
Every day — (312) 656-3616

ROCKFORD
Greater Rockford Indoor-Outdoor
Antique Market
Highway 251 South, corner of
11th St. and Sandy Hollow Road
Every weekend 9 AM - 5 PM —
(815) 397-6683

ST CHARLES
Kane County Flea Market
Kane County Fairgrounds,
Route 64
Check ahead

INDIANA

CEDAR LAKE
The Barn & Field Flea Market
151 St. and Parrish, one mile east
on Route 41
Every weekend — (219) 696-7368

CENTERVILLE
Webb's Antique Mall
200 W. Union and 106 E. Main
Daily 9 AM to 6 PM

EATON
Robyn's Nest Flea Market
and Antiques
103 W. Harris St.
Monday through Saturday
9:30 AM - 5 PM

FRANKLIN
Antique Show and Flea Market
4-H Fairgrounds
Third weekend of every month —
(317) 535-5084

FT WAYNE
The Speedway Mall
across from 84 Lumber
Friday, Saturday and Sunday —
(219) 484-1239

INDIANAPOLIS
The Antique Mall
3444 N. Shadeland Ave.
Every day

INDIANAPOLIS
Traylor's Flea Market
7159 E. 46th Street
Every weekend

INDIANAPOLIS
West Washington Flea Market
6445 W. Washington St.
Every Friday, Saturday and
Sunday — (317) 244-0941

MUNCIE
Highway 28 Flea Market
State Road 28, east of Highway
3 North
Every weekend, 9 AM - 6 PM —
(317) 282-5414

NEW WHITELAND
The New Whiteland Flea Market
1-465 on U.S. 31, 10 miles south
of Indianapolis
Friday, Saturday, Sunday —
(317) 535-5907

RICHMOND
Yester Years Flea Market
The Old Melody Skating Rink
1505 S. 9th Street
Thursday 11-5 — Friday 11-7,
Sat/Sund 9-5

SOUTH BEND
Thieve's Market
2309 E. Edison at Ironwood
Every weekend

KENTUCKY
LOUISVILLE
Louisville Antique Mall
900 Goss Avenue
Daily 10 AM - 6 PM Mon-Sat;
1-5 PM Sunday
(502) 635-2852

LOUISIANA
BATON ROUGE
Deep South
5350 Florida Blvd.
Friday, Saturday, Sunday —
(504) 923-0142

LAFAYETTE
Deep South
3124 NE Evangeline Thorway
Friday, Saturday, Sunday —
(318) 237-5529

MASSACHUSETTS
NORTON
Norton Flea Market
Route 140, take exit 11 off
Route 495
Every Sunday

MICHIGAN
YPSILANTI
Giant Flea Market
214 East Michigan at Park
Every weekend — (313) 971-7676,
487-5890 (weekends)

MISSOURI
SPRINGFIELD
Olde Towne Antique Mall and
Flea Market
Every day except Thursday —
(417) 831-6665

SPRINGFIELD
Park Central Flea Market
429 Boonville
Every day — (417) 831-7516

SPRINGFIELD
Viking Flea Market
North Grant and Chase
Every day except Wednesday —
(417) 869-4237

NEVADA
LAS VEGAS
Tanner's Flea Market
Nevada Convention Center
Call (702) 382-8355 for dates

NEW YORK
BROOKLYN
Duffield Flea Market
223 Duffield Street between
Fulton and Willoughby
Monday through Saturday 11 AM
to 6 PM
(212) 625-7579

DELKALB JUNCTION
Antiques Flea Market
Route 11
Every Friday 10 AM-4 PM,
Saturday and Sunday 9 AM-5 PM
(315) 347-3393

DUANESBURG
Gordon Reid's Pine Grove Farm
Antique Flea Market
Junction of U.S. Rte. 20,
NY Route 7 and I-88
1985 Dates: May 3-4; July 5-6;
Sept. 6-7
(518) 895-2300

OHIO

AMHERST
Jamie's Flea Market
West of Route 58 on Route 113
Wednesday evenings, Saturday
and Sunday
(216) 986-4402

AURORA
Aurora Farms Flea Market
Route 43, one mile south of
Route 82
Every Wednesday and Sunday —
(216) 562-2000

CINCINNATI
Ferguson Antiques Mall and
Flea Market
3742 Kellog Ave.
Every Saturday and Sunday —
(513) 321-7341

CINCINNATI
Paris Flea Market
Ferguson Hills Drive in Theatre,
2310 Ferguson Road
Every Saturday and Sunday
(513) 223-0222 weekdays;
451-1271 weekend

CINCINNATI
Strickers Grove
Route 128, one mile south
of Ross
Every Thursday, June through
September
(513) 733-5885

DAYTON
Paris Flea Market
Dixie Drive in Theatre
6201 N. Dixie
Every Saturday and Sunday
7 AM - 4 PM
(513) 223-0222 weekdays;
890-5513 weekend

FERNALD (Cincinnati area)
Web Flea Market
1-74, Exit 7, north 5 miles to
New Haven Road
Every Saturday and Sunday —
(513) 738-2678

MONTPELIER
Fairgrounds Flea Market
Williams County Fairgrounds
Every Thursday — (419) 636-6085
L & K Promotions
Rt 1, Montpelier, OH 43543

SPRINGFIELD
Antique Show and Flea Market
Clark County Fairgrounds
Call for information:
(513) 399-7351 or 399-2261

TIFFIN
Tiffin Flea Market
Seneca County Fairgrounds
April through October
Call for information:
(419) 983-5084

WILMINGTON–WAYNESVILLE
Caesar Creek Flea Market
Intersection of 1-71 and
State Route 73
Every Saturday and Sunday —
(513) 382-1669

PENNSYLVANIA

BEAVER FALLS
The Antique Emporium
818 7th Ave.
Everyday except Monday —
(412) 847-1919

MANSFIELD
Antique Show and Flea Market
Richland County Fairgrounds
Last weekend of the month,
February through November

PUBLICATIONS

Periodicals for collectors include those of a general or specialized nature. Since magazines are prone to ownership or address changes, the information below is not guaranteed for long-term accuracy.

AMERICAN ART AND ANTIQUES
1515 Broadway, New York City, NY 10036

AMERICAN INDIAN ART
7045 Third Avenue, Scottsdale, AZ 85251

AMERICAN RIFLEMAN
National Rifle Association
1600 Rhode Island Avenue, N.W., Washington, D.C. 20036

ANTIQUE COLLECTING
P.O. Box 327, Ephrata, PA 17522

ANTIQUE COLLECTOR
Chestergate House, Vauxhall Bridge Road, London SW1V 1HF, England

ANTIQUE MONTHLY
P.O. Drawer 2, Tuscaloosa, AL 35401

ANTIQUE TOY WORLD
3941 Belle Plaine, Chicago, IL 60618

ANTIQUE TRADER
Dubuque, IA 52001

ANTIQUES (The Magazine Antiques)
551 Fifth Avenue, New York City, NY 10017

ANTIQUES AND THE ARTS WEEKLY
Newtown Beem, Newtown, CT 06470

ANTIQUES JOURNAL
P.O. Box 1046, Dubuque, IA 52001

ANTIQUES WORLD
P.O. Box 990, Farmingdale, L.I., NY 11737

ARMS GAZETTE
13222 Saticoy Street, North Hollywood, CA 91605 *(firearms)*

BANKNOTE REPORTER
Iola, WI 54945 *(paper money)*

BIE NEWSLETTER
4601 NE Third Avenue, Ft. Lauderdale, FL 33308 *(odd and error coins)*

BLUE RIDGE COIN NEWS
Banner Publishing Co., Camden, SC 29020

CLARION, THE (America's Folk Art Magazine)
49 West 53rd Street, New York City, NY 10019

CLASSICS READER
Box 1191, Station Q, Toronto, Canada M4T 2P4 *(comics)*

COINage
16001 Ventura Boulevard, Encino, CA 91316

COIN HOBBY NEWS
300 Booth Street, Anamosa, IA 52205

COIN PRICES
Iola, WI 54945

COINS MAGAZINE
Iola, WI 54945

COIN SLOT
P.O. Box 612, Wheatridge, CO 80033 *(coin-operated machines)*

COIN WHOLESALER
P.O. Box 893, Chattanooga, TN 37401

COIN WORLD
P.O. Box 150, Sydney, OH 45367

COLLECTIBLES ILLUSTRATED
Dublin, NH 03444

COLLECTIBLES MONTHLY
P.O. Box 2023, York, PA 17405

COLLECTOR'S DREAM
P.O. Box 127, Station T, Toronto, Canada M6B 3Z9

COLLECTOR EDITIONS QUARTERLY
170 Fifth Avenue, New York City, NY 10010

COLLECTOR'S PARADISE
P.O. Box 3658, Cranston, RI 02910

COLLECTOR'S SHOWCASE
P.O. Box 6929, San Diego, CA 92106

COLLECTORS UNITED
P.O. Box 1160, Chatsworth, GA 30705 *(dolls)*

COLONIAL NEWSLETTER
P.O. Box 4411, Huntsville, AL 35802 *(colonial coins)*

COMIC INFORMER
3131 West Alabama, Houston, TX 77098

COMIC TIMES
305 Broad, New York City, NY 10007

COMIXINE
10 Geneva Drive, Redcar, Cleveland T510 1JP, United Kingdom

DEPRESSION GLASS DAZE
P.O. Box 57, Otisville, MI 48463

DOLL TIMES
1675, Orchid, Aurora, IL 60505

DYNAZINE
8 Palmer Drive, Canton, MA 02021 *(comics)*

ERB-DOM
Route 2, Box 119, Clinton, LA 70722 *(Edgar Rice Burroughs)*

ERRORSCOPE
P.O. Box 695, Sidney, OH 45365 *(coin errors)*

ERROR TRENDS
P.O. Box 158, Oceanside, NY 11572 *(coin errors)*

ESSAY-PROOF JOURNAL
225 South Fischer Avenue, Jefferson, WI 53549 *(coins)*

FANTASY TRADER
34 Heworth Hall Drive, York, England *(comics)*

FANTASY UNLIMITED
47 Hesperus Crescent, Millwall, London, E.14, England *(comics)*

FUTURE GOLD
4146 Marlene Drive, Toledo, OH 43606 *(investment)*

GOBRECHT JOURNAL
5718 King Arthur Drive, Kettering, OH 45429 *(relating to life and work of Christian Gobrecht, 19th century coin designer)*

GOLDMINE
700 E. State Street, Iola, WI 54990 *(records)*

GRAPHIC TIMES
25 Cowles Street, Bridgeport, CT 06607

GUN REPORT
P.O. Box 111, Aledo, IL 61231

HOBBIES
1006 South Michigan Avenue, Chicago, IL 60605

INDIAN TRADER
P.O. Box 31235, Billings, MT 59107 *(Indian relics)*

INSIGHT ON COLLECTABLES
P.O. Box 130, Durham, Ontario NOG 1RO

JOEL SATER'S ANTIQUE NEWS
P.O. Box B, Marietta, PA 17547

JOURNAL OF NUMISMATICS AND FINE ARTS
P.O. Box 777, Encino, CA 91316 *(ancient coins and classical antiquities)*

JUKEBOX TRADER
P.O. Box 1081, Des Moines, IA 50311

LOOSE CHANGE
21176 South Alameda Street, Long Beach, CA 90810 *(coin-operated machines)*

MAIN ANTIQUES DIGEST
P.O. Box 358, Waldoboro, ME 04572

MEMORY LANE
P.O. Box 1627, Lubbock, TX 79408

NATIONAL ANTIQUES COURIER
P.O. Box 500, Warwick, MD 21912

NATIONAL VALENTINE COLLECTORS ASSOC.
Box 1404, Santa Ana, CA 92702

NEW YORK/PENNSYLVANIA COLLECTOR
Wolfe Publications, 4 South Main Street, Pittsford, NY 14534

NINETEENTH CENTURY (Forbes)
60 Fifth Avenue, New York City, NY 10011

NUMISMATIC NEWS
Iola, WI 54945

NUMISMATIST, THE
P.O. Box 2366, Colorado Springs, CO 80901

OHIO ANTIQUE REVIEW
72 North Street, Worthington, OH 43085

OLD CARS WEEKLY
Iola, WI 54990

OLD TOY SOLDIER NEWSLETTER
209 North Lombard, Oak Park, IL 60302

OWL'S NEST
P.O. Box 5491, Fresno, CA 93755 *(owl-motif items)*

PEN FANCIER
1169 Overcash, Dunedin, FL 33528 *(writing instruments)*

POLITICAL COLLECTOR
503 Madison Avenue, York, PA 17404

POSTCARD COLLECTOR
700 E. State Street, Iola, WI 54990

PRINTS
Art On Paper Inc., P.O. Box 1468, Alton, IL 62002

RECORD PROFILE MAGAZINE, INC.
24361 Greenfield, Suite 201, Southfield, MI 48075

TAMS JOURNAL
P.O. Box 127, Scandinavia, WI 54977 *(tokens and medals)*

THE DOLL AND TOY COLLECTOR
International Collectors Publications, Inc.
168 Seventh Street, Brooklyn, NY 11215

THE MILK ROUTE
4 Oxbow Road, Westport, CT 16880

THE PLATE COLLECTOR
Collector's Media, Inc.
P.O. Box 1729, San Marcos, TX 78667

THE SHAKER MESSENGER
P.O. Box 45, Holland, MI 49423

WHEELS OF TIME
American Truck Historical Society
Saunders Building, 201 Office Park Drive, Birmingham, AL 35223

WORLD COIN NEWS
Iola, WI 54945

WORLD WIDE AVON NEWS
44021 7th Street East, Lancaster, CA 93534

HOW TO USE THIS BOOK

The editors of this book have tried to include as many of the major collecting categories as possible. We have also included unusual, yet interesting collecting areas. We have not intended to cover each subject thoroughly, instead an overview of each collecting market is given. For more information on most of the categories listed, consult the complete series of *The Official Price Guides,* published by The House of Collectibles.

The sections in this book have been alphabetized for easy reference. Within each section is information describing the topic and alphabetized listings. Each listing provides relevant information about the item.

A price range is shown for each item. It represents a range of dealers average retail sums and auction results. A third price column shows last year's average value for each item. This feature measures market performance and should be helpful to investors, dealers and collectors.

ADVERTISING COLLECTIBLES

TOPIC: Advertising collectibles are considered to be any items with a company's name or logo on them.

TYPES: Advertising collectibles can be found in any form. Common items used for advertising range from ashtrays to posters to yo-yos.

PERIOD: Advertising has been around almost since humanity became literate, but advertising collectibles of interest to the modern enthusiast began around 1800. Pre-1900 items are scarce and valuable.

MATERIALS: These items are usually made of ceramics, glass, paper or tin, although the material depends on the item.

COMMENTS: Many large companies (such as Coca-Cola) put much effort into producing promotional items that are now very collectible. Because of this, a collector may focus on procuring items that pertain to a particular company. Other enthusiasts, however, collect a certain item (mirrors, for example) regardless of the company or product that is advertised.

ADDITIONAL TIPS: The listings in this section are arranged in the following order: item, company or product advertised, title, description, what it was used for, material, shape, size and date manufactured. Other information was included where relevant.

	Current Price Range		P/Y Average
☐ **Ashtray,** Armstrong Tire, clear, red decal, round, 5⅞" diameter	9.00	12.00	10.50
☐ **Ashtray,** Bacardi Rum, white china, round, 4½" diameter	3.50	7.00	5.00
☐ **Ashtray,** Budweiser, glass, round, 5" diameter	3.00	5.00	4.00
☐ **Ashtray,** Camel Cigarettes, Camel logo in center, tin, round, 3½" diameter	1.50	2.50	2.00
☐ **Ashtray,** Chivas Regal, Wade china, triangular with rounded sides, 11½"	5.00	9.00	7.00

	Current Price Range		P/Y Average
☐ **Ashtray,** Firestone Tire, 1936 Texas Central Expo	13.00	18.00	15.00
☐ **Ashtray,** Goodrich, for Silvertown Heavy Duty Cord, round, 6⅜″ diameter	6.00	12.00	9.00
☐ **Ashtray,** Goodrich, for Silvertown Cord tires, 1776 decal, round, 6¼″ diameter	10.00	16.00	13.00
☐ **Ashtray,** Labatt's Stout-Lager-Ales, cream colored porcelain, round, 6½″ diameter	3.00	7.00	5.00
☐ **Ashtray,** Michelob Beer, round, 5½″ diameter	3.00	7.00	5.00
☐ **Ashtray,** Pennsylvania, for Balloon Cord tires, round, 6⅛″ diameter	8.00	12.00	10.00
☐ **Ashtray,** Salem Cigarettes, metal, round, 3½″ diameter	.50	1.50	1.00
☐ **Ashtray,** White Horse Whiskey, white, figural horse head, 5″ x 3¾″	8.00	10.00	9.00
☐ **Ashtray,** Winston Cigarettes, tin	.03	.07	.05
☐ **Ashtray,** Winston Cigarettes, Winston logo in center, tin, round, 3½″ diameter	1.50	2.50	2.00
☐ **Bag,** Knox Knit Hosiery, picture of woman, 5″ x 7″	1.00	2.00	1.50
☐ **Bank,** Pepsi Cola, 75 Year Commemorative, red, tin can style, 1973	2.00	5.00	3.50
☐ **Bank,** R.C.A. Dog, "Nipper," ceramic, 6½″ tall	8.00	12.00	10.00
☐ **Bank,** Texaco Oil Can, one quart, 1970s	1.00	3.50	2.25
☐ **Banner,** De Soto Auto, red, gold and black fringed silk, 38″ x 66″, 1951	55.00	65.00	60.00
☐ **Bell,** Cherry Smash, porcelain, 6″ high	1.25	2.25	1.75
☐ **Bell,** Full O' Juice, porcelain, 4″ high	1.50	2.65	2.07
☐ **Bell,** Honeymoon Tobacco, porcelain, 4″ high	1.50	2.50	2.00
☐ **Bell,** Minster Beer, porcelain, 4″ high	1.25	2.50	1.87
☐ **Blotter,** Jersey Cream, picture of children, 4″ x 9″, 1920s	1.00	3.00	2.00
☐ **Blotter,** Smith Brother's Chewing Gum and Cough Drops, c. 1930	10.00	15.00	12.50
☐ **Book,** Kellogg's, "Kellogg's Funny Jungleland Moving Pictures, 6″ x 8″, 1909	35.00	42.00	39.00
☐ **Booklet,** Budweiser Beer, 20 pages, 5″ x 7″ 1965	.50	2.00	1.25
☐ **Booklet,** Camel Cigarettes, "Know Your Nerves," 3″ x 4″, 1934	12.00	16.00	14.00
☐ **Booklet,** Hire's Root Beer, "Hire's Magic Story," 1934	13.00	17.00	15.00
☐ **Booklet,** Old Dutch Cleanser, 3″ x 6″	2.00	6.00	4.00
☐ **Booklet,** Royal Baking Powder, "The Comical Cruises of Captain Cooky," 1926	14.00	18.00	16.00
☐ **Booklet,** Royal Baking Powder, making biscuits, 1927	2.50	3.50	3.00
☐ **Booklet,** Rumford Baking Powder	2.50	3.50	3.00
☐ **Bottle Carrier,** Coca-Cola, holds six miniature bottles, 2″ tall, 1953	.75	2.00	1.25
☐ **Bottle Opener,** Coca-Cola, cast iron	1.00	2.00	1.50
☐ **Bottle Opener,** Dr. Pepper, cast iron	1.00	2.00	1.50
☐ **Bottle Opener,** Falstaff, cast iron	1.00	2.00	1.50
☐ **Bottle Opener,** Pepsi Cola, cast iron	1.00	2.00	1.50

	Current Price Range		P/Y Average
☐ **Bottle Opener,** Seven-Up, cast iron	1.00	2.00	1.50
☐ **Bottle Opener,** Squirt, cast iron	1.00	2.00	1.50
☐ **Box,** Barricini Candies, resembles wood, 9″ x 7″ x 2″ with 12″ x 9″ base	8.00	12.00	10.00
☐ **Box,** Chandler's One-Day Tablets, 1″ x 5″ x 6″	.25	.50	.37
☐ **Box,** Coca-Cola, red and gold snap lid, for pencils, 1″ x 3″ x 8″, 1937	18.00	30.00	24.00
☐ **Box,** Portola Tuna, picture of Portola and tuna, cardboard, 8½ ″ x 14″ 1929	3.50	7.00	5.00
☐ **Box,** Solace Tobacco, blue with gold print, cardboard, 8½ ″ x 11″ x 5″, 1862	35.00	45.00	40.00
☐ **Calendar,** Alka Seltzer, 1942	3.50	5.75	4.25
☐ **Calendar,** Blatz Beer, girl in red, 1904	135.00	175.00	155.00
☐ **Calendar,** Camel Cigarettes, 1963	32.00	38.00	35.00
☐ **Calendar,** Coca Cola, pictures of beautiful women, six pages, 13″ x 17″, 1957	20.00	25.00	22.50
☐ **Calendar,** Dr. Mile's Remedies, picture of girl and boy, 1908	12.50	16.50	14.00
☐ **Calendar,** Dr. Pepper, 1950	22.00	27.00	24.00
☐ **Calendar,** Equitable Life Insurance, 1904 ...	20.00	28.00	24.00
☐ **Calendar,** Fairy Soap, picture of Naval officer, 1899	13.00	19.00	16.00
☐ **Cannister,** Sir Walter Raleigh Smoking Tobacco, round	18.00	22.00	20.00
☐ **Catalog,** Lionel Trains, 8″ x 11″, 1958	3.00	6.00	4.50
☐ **Catalog,** Williams Manufacturing Company, picture of the factory, for baskets, 1891	20.00	25.00	22.50
☐ **Catalog,** Wurlitzer Juke Box, 8″ x 11″, 1950s .	2.00	5.00	3.50
☐ **Chalkboard,** Hires Root Beer, for restaurants, tin, 10″ x 20″, 1940s	16.00	20.00	18.00
☐ **Clicker,** Butternut Break, tin cricket, 1¾″ diameter, c. 1930	.75	1.75	1.25
☐ **Clock,** Anheuser Busch, wood	25.00	30.00	27.50
☐ **Clock,** Bardahl Petroleum, square, electric ..	40.00	48.00	44.00
☐ **Clock,** Canada Dry Sport Cola, 13″ x 18″	25.00	30.00	27.50
☐ **Clock,** Coca-Cola, metal, round	35.00	45.00	40.00
☐ **Clock,** Falstaff Beer, illuminated	50.00	58.00	54.00
☐ **Clock,** Florsheim Shoes, wood, illuminated .	35.00	45.00	40.00
☐ **Clock,** General Electric, metal, refrigerator style	50.00	60.00	55.00
☐ **Clock,** Mr. Peanut, with alarm	25.00	30.00	27.50
☐ **Clock,** Pearl Beer, illuminated	30.00	40.00	35.00
☐ **Clock,** Seven-Up, metal, round	30.00	40.00	35.00
☐ **Clock,** St. Joseph's Aspirin for Children, 14″ diameter	55.00	65.00	60.00
☐ **Coaster,** Olympia Beer, metal, round, 3½ ″ diameter	.50	1.10	.85
☐ **Comb,** Coca-Cola, red, plastic, embossed, pocket-size, 1960s	1.00	4.00	2.50
☐ **Decal,** Bull Dog Malt Liquor, picture of a bulldog, square, 7″, 1940s	3.00	7.00	5.00
☐ **Decal,** Planters and Clark Bar, for candy machine, 4″ x 8″, 1950s	1.25	2.00	1.62
☐ **Decal,** Red Goose Shoes, 1930s	1.00	3.00	2.00
☐ **Decal,** Seven-Up, 4″ x 4″, 1931-57	1.50	3.00	2.25

	Current Price Range		P/Y Average

☐ **Decal,** Triple AAA, 5¢ Root Beer, picture of a girl, 6″ x 9″, 1940s 1.00 4.00 2.50

☐ **Doll,** Campbell Kid, early 1900s style clothing, rag 23.00 28.00 25.00

☐ **Door Handle,** Dandy Bread, picture of loaf and slices, metal, 3″ x 13″, 1940s 12.00 17.00 15.00

☐ **Fan,** 666 Liquid Medicine, picture of two children on a horse, wicker handle, c. 1935 ..... 1.50 2.50 2.00

☐ **Figurine,** R.C.A. Dog, "Nipper," ceramic, 3″ . 3.00 4.50 3.75

☐ **Folder,** Philadelphia Buckeye Wood Pumps, 6″ x 14″ 9.00 14.00 11.50

☐ **Key Chain,** Mr. Peanut, 5″ .... .50 1.50 1.00

☐ **Key Holder,** Dr. Pepper, 1″ x 2″, 1930s 1.50 3.00 2.25

☐ **License Plate,** Coca-Cola, red and white, embossed, 6″ x 12″, 1970s 2.50 5.00 3.75

☐ **License Plate Top,** Ford, reflective, metal, 3″ x 10″, 1952 .... 12.00 15.00 14.00

☐ **Lighter,** Camel Cigarettes, metal 2.50 4.50 3.50

☐ **Magazine Ad,** any automobile, 1911-1920 ... 2.50 3.50 3.50

☐ **Magazine Ad,** any automobile, 1921-1930 ... 1.50 2.00 1.75

☐ **Magazine Ad,** Coca-Cola, pre-1900 .... 14.00 18.00 16.00

☐ **Magazine Ad,** Coca-Cola, 1901-1910 .... 9.00 12.00 10.50

☐ **Magazine Ad,** Coca-Cola, 1911-1920 .... 6.00 8.00 7.00

☐ **Magazine Ad,** Coca-Cola, 1921-1930 .... 3.00 4.00 3.50

☐ **Magazine Ad,** any photograph, pre-1900 .... 4.00 5.50 4.75

☐ **Magazine Ad,** radio, 1920-1925 .... 3.00 4.00 3.50

☐ **Magazine Ad,** TV set, pre-1945 .... 2.00 3.00 2.50

☐ **Matchbook,** Hires Root Beer, miniature, 1940s .... .50 1.25 .87

☐ **Mirror,** Aunt Jemima, from Breakfast Club, round .... .75 1.25 1.00

☐ **Mirror,** Coca-Cola, pocket-size, 2″ x 3″ ...... .25 1.25 .75

☐ **Mirror,** Palmolive Soap, picture of the Dionne Quintuplets and doctor .... .50 1.50 1.00

☐ **Mug,** Anheuser-Busch, crockery, embossed with eagle, 7″ tall, 1940 .... 10.00 15.00 12.50

☐ **Pen Holders,** Falstaff Beer, for a pocket, 1960s 1.00 3.00 2.00

☐ **Pin,** Coca-Cola, bottle cap style, for a lapel, enameled, 1968 .... 3.00 5.00 4.00

☐ **Pitcher,** Ambassador Scotch, white 8.00 10.00 9.00

☐ **Pitcher,** Glenfiddich, black 8.00 10.00 9.00

☐ **Poster,** Granger Pipe Tobacco, picture of Joe Heistand Champion trap shooter, 14″ x 20″ .. 25.00 30.00 27.50

☐ **Poster,** Planters Presents Sheindele the Chazente, cardboard, 11″ x 17″ 22.00 27.00 24.00

☐ **Poster,** Shoat Sale, announcing auction of 175 pigs, 12″ x 19″, c. 1920 .... 7.00 10.00 8.50

☐ **Poster,** Yeast Foam, picture of a little girl, tin rimmed, 10″ x 14″, 1920s 18.00 22.00 20.00

☐ **Pot Holders,** Campbell Kid 8¼″ x 8½″, set of two 8.00 12.00 10.00

Mr. Peanut Peanut Butter Maker, *plastic,* **$25.00**

	Current Price Range		P/Y Average
☐ **Sign,** American Agriculturist, tin, embossed, 6½″ x 13½″, 1920s	7.00	10.00	8.50
☐ **Sign,** Arrow Trailer Rentals, picture of U.S. map, embossed, 14″ x 18″, 1940s	12.00	16.00	14.00
☐ **Sign,** Barnum's Animal Crackers, commemorative, tin 4″ diameter, 6″ tall, 1979	3.00	5.00	4.00
☐ **Sign,** Bayer Aspirin, tin, 15″ x 18″	25.00	35.00	30.00
☐ **Sign,** Beechnut Tobacco, rectangular	12.00	17.00	14.50
☐ **Sign,** Borden, glass, 12″ x 20	62.00	72.00	68.00
☐ **Sign,** Budweiser, plastic, with bottle, lighted, 5″ x 12″	12.00	18.00	15.00
☐ **Sign,** Bunny Bread, red and white, tin, embossed, 3½″ x 28″, 1930s	8.00	12.00	10.00
☐ **Sign,** Burma shave, wooden, 10″ x 3½″	1.50	2.50	2.00
☐ **Sign,** Busch Ginger Ale, picture of eagle, porcelain, 10″ x 20″, 1920s	75.00	85.00	80.00
☐ **Sign,** Camel Cigarettes, picture of blond woman, cardboard, 20″ x 11″, c. 1941	13.00	18.00	15.00
☐ **Sign,** Canadian Club, for a ceiling fan, round, 7″ diameter, 1930	2.50	5.00	3.75

AKRO AGATE

DESCRIPTION: This glass is found in a wide range of colors and types, including clear, opaque and marbleized. The patterns listed here are children's dishes.

HISTORY: The Akro Agate Company of Akron, Ohio began producing marbles and toys in 1911. For economic reasons the company moved to Clarksburg, West Virginia several years later. By the late 1920s Akro Agate was the largest marble producer in the country. However, competition soon forced the company into diversification, and in 1935 new lines were introduced which included ashtrays and children's dishes. When the Brilliant Glass Company burned in 1936, Akro Agate bought the surviving molds and materials and began producing bathroom fixtures, flower pots, planters, vases and novelty items. They also produced a full line of children's dishes in transparent, opaque and marbleized glass which were very popular in the early 1940s. However, as plastic was developed Akro Agate wares suffered a decline in popularity and finally closed down in 1951.

COLORS: Crystal; transparent amber, various shades of green, blue, brown, yellow, etc.; translucent amber; satin lemonade and oxblood; opaque white, various shades of blue, green, yellow, black amethyst, beige; marbled blue-white, brown-white, green-white, red-white, orange-white, pumpkin-white, lemonade-oxblood and shiny black opaque.

MARKS: A Flying Crow: Made in USA; Westite: Ramses (embossed); Ashtrays: 245, 246, 249, 252; Flower Pots: 297, 296, 305, 307; Bowls/Candlesticks: 320, 321, 323, 340; Six sided small urn: 764; Cornucopia Vase: 765.

CHIQUITA

Green opaque is the most common color found in this pattern made for J. Pressman.

	Current Price Range		P/Y Average
Complete Set, *16 pieces, in box*			
green opaque	48.00	60.00	51.00
cobalt	110.00	125.00	114.00
crystal	150.00	180.00	160.00
baked-on color	57.00	60.00	58.00
Complete Set, *22 pieces, in box*			
green opaque	63.00	75.00	65.00
Creamer, *1½"*			
green opaque	4.00	5.00	4.25
cobalt	9.00	10.00	9.25
crystal	13.00	15.00	13.50
baked-on color	5.50	6.50	5.75
Cup, *1½"*			
green opaque	3.50	4.50	3.75
cobalt	5.00	6.00	5.25
crystal	10.00	12.00	10.50
baked-on color	4.25	5.00	4.50
Plate, *3¾"*			
green opaque	2.00	2.50	2.15
cobalt	5.25	6.00	5.50
crystal	10.00	12.00	10.50
baked-on color	1.75	2.25	1.85
Saucer, *3⅛"*			
green opaque	1.75	2.25	1.85
cobalt	2.75	3.25	2.85
crystal	4.75	5.75	5.00
baked-on color	1.25	1.50	1.30
Sugar, *1½"*			
green opaque	3.75	4.25	3.85
cobalt	7.00	8.00	7.25
crystal	11.00	13.00	11.50
baked-on color	4.25	4.75	4.35

CONCENTRIC RIB

	Current Price Range		P/Y Average
Complete Set, *7 pieces, in box*			
green and white	23.00	27.00	24.50
other opaque colors	27.00	32.00	28.00
Creamer, *1¼"*			
green and white	3.75	4.75	4.00
other opaque colors	4.50	6.00	5.00
Cup, *1¼"*			
green and white	2.25	2.75	2.35
other opaque colors	2.75	3.75	3.00

	Current Price Range		P/Y Average
Saucer, *2¾"*			
□*green and white*	1.75	2.25	1.85
□*other opaque colors*	1.75	2.50	2.00
Sugar, *1¼"*			
□*green and white*	4.00	5.00	4.25
□*other opaque colors*	4.50	6.00	5.00

CONCENTRIC RING

Made in a large and small children's size, this pattern is similar to Concentric Rib. However, Concentric Ring is of better quality than Concentric Rib.

Complete Set, *21 pieces, large size, in box*			
□*cobalt*	335.00	385.00	345.00
□*blue marble*	430.00	470.00	440.00
Complete Set, *16 pieces, small size, in box*			
□*cobalt*	240.00	270.00	250.00
□*blue marble*	300.00	335.00	310.00
Cereal Bowl, *3⅜"*			
□*cobalt*	24.00	26.00	24.50
□*blue marble*	29.00	33.00	30.00
□*other opaque colors*	16.00	19.00	17.00
Creamer, *1⅜"*			
□*cobalt*	23.00	26.00	24.00
□*blue marble*	32.00	37.00	33.00
□*other opaque colors*	11.00	14.00	12.00
Creamer, *1¼"*			
□*cobalt*	19.00	22.00	20.00
□*blue marble*	25.00	28.00	26.00
□*other opaque colors*	9.00	11.00	9.50
Cup, *1⅜"*			
□*cobalt*	23.00	26.00	24.00
□*blue marble*	27.00	31.00	28.00
□*other opaque colors*	13.00	15.00	13.50
Cup, *1¼"*			
□*cobalt*	25.00	28.00	26.00
□*blue marble*	28.00	31.00	29.00
□*other opaque colors*	9.00	11.00	9.50
Plate, *4¼"*			
□*cobalt*	11.00	14.00	12.00
□*blue marble*	16.00	19.00	17.00
□*other opaque colors*	6.50	8.00	7.00
Plate, *3¼"*			
□*cobalt*	11.00	13.00	11.50
□*blue marble*	12.00	14.00	12.50
□*other opaque colors*	4.50	6.00	5.00

	Current Price Range		P/Y Average
Saucer, 3⅛"			
☐ cobalt	6.00	8.00	6.50
☐ blue marble	8.50	10.00	9.00
☐ other opaque colors	4.50	5.50	4.75
Saucer, 2¾"			
☐ cobalt	8.00	10.00	8.50
☐ blue marble	9.00	11.00	9.50
☐ other opaque colors	3.00	4.00	3.25
Sugar, 1⅞"			
☐ cobalt	31.00	34.00	32.00
☐ blue marble	37.00	42.00	39.00
☐ other opaque colors	17.00	20.00	18.00
Sugar, 1¼"			
☐ cobalt	19.00	22.00	20.00
☐ blue marble	25.00	27.00	25.50
☐ other opaque colors	9.00	11.00	9.50

INTERIOR PANEL

This pattern was made in a large and a small children's size.

Complete Set, 21 pieces, in box, large size			
☐ green	130.00	145.00	135.00
☐ yellow	110.00	130.00	115.00
☐ blue and white	305.00	330.00	310.00
☐ red and white	330.00	360.00	335.00
☐ green and white	245.00	275.00	250.00
☐ lemonade and oxblood	320.00	350.00	330.00
Complete Set, 8 pieces, in box, small size			
☐ pink	38.00	50.00	40.00
☐ green	38.00	50.00	40.00
☐ blue	110.00	115.00	105.00
☐ yellow	110.00	115.00	105.00
☐ green	33.00	45.00	35.00
☐ topaz	33.00	45.00	35.00
☐ blue and white	105.00	120.00	110.00
☐ red and white	90.00	100.00	93.00
☐ green and white	60.00	70.00	63.00
Complete Set, 16 pieces, in box, small size			
☐ pink	110.00	125.00	115.00
☐ green	110.00	125.00	115.00
☐ blue	215.00	240.00	220.00
☐ yellow	215.00	240.00	220.00
☐ green	80.00	95.00	85.00
☐ topaz	80.00	95.00	85.00
☐ blue and white	215.00	230.00	220.00
☐ red and white	200.00	225.00	210.00
☐ green and white	120.00	140.00	125.00

	Current Price Range		P/Y Average

Creamer, 1⅜″

☐ blue and white.........................	21.00	24.00	22.00
☐ red and white	23.00	26.00	24.00
☐ green and white	17.00	19.00	17.50
☐ lemonade and oxblood.................	23.00	27.00	24.00
☐ green	10.00	12.00	10.50
☐ topaz	9.00	11.00	9.50

Creamer, 1¼″

☐ pink...................................	21.00	23.00	21.50
☐ green	21.00	23.00	21.50
☐ blue...................................	25.00	28.00	26.00
☐ yellow	25.00	28.00	26.00
☐ green	9.00	11.00	9.50
☐ topaz.................................	9.00	11.00	9.50
☐ blue and white.........................	21.00	24.00	22.00
☐ red and white	23.00	27.00	24.00
☐ green and white	14.00	17.00	15.00

Cup, 1⅜″

☐ green	5.50	7.00	6.00
☐ topaz	4.50	6.00	5.00
☐ blue and white.........................	19.00	21.00	19.50
☐ red and white	20.00	23.00	21.00
☐ green and white	14.00	17.00	15.00
☐ lemonade and oxblood.................	19.00	22.00	20.00

Cup, 1¼″

☐ pink...................................	7.00	9.00	7.50
☐ green	7.00	9.00	7.50
☐ blue...................................	24.00	27.00	25.00
☐ yellow	24.00	27.00	25.00
☐ green	6.00	7.50	6.50
☐ topaz	6.00	7.50	6.50
☐ blue and white.........................	19.00	22.00	20.00
☐ red and white	21.00	24.00	22.00
☐ green and white	14.00	17.00	15.00

Plate, 4¼″

☐ green	4.50	6.00	5.00
☐ topaz	3.50	6.00	4.00
☐ blue and white.........................	9.00	11.00	9.50
☐ red and white	9.00	11.00	9.50
☐ green and white	7.50	10.00	8.00
☐ lemonade and oxblood.................	10.00	12.00	10.50

Plate, 3¾″

☐ pink...................................	4.00	5.00	4.25
☐ green	4.00	5.00	4.25
☐ blue...................................	4.50	6.50	5.00
☐ yellow	4.50	6.50	5.00
☐ green	3.00	4.00	3.25
☐ topaz	3.00	4.00	3.25

	Current Price Range		P/Y Average
☐ blue and white.........................	9.00	10.00	9.25
☐ red and white	6.50	8.00	7.00
☐ green and white	5.50	7.00	6.00
Saucer, 3⅛"			
☐ green	3.00	4.00	3.25
☐ topaz	2.50	3.50	3.00
☐ blue and white.........................	6.50	8.00	7.00
☐ red and white	7.50	9.00	8.00
☐ green and white	6.50	8.00	7.00
☐ lemonade and oxblood...................	6.50	8.00	7.00
Saucer, 2⅜"			
☐ pink	3.00	4.00	3.25
☐ green	3.00	4.00	3.25
☐ blue	6.00	8.00	6.50
☐ yellow	6.00	8.00	6.50
☐ green	3.25	4.00	3.50
☐ topaz	3.25	4.00	3.50
☐ blue and white	6.50	8.00	7.00
☐ red and white	6.50	8.00	7.00
☐ green and white........................	3.25	4.00	3.50
Sugar, 1⅞"			
☐ green	14.00	17.00	15.00
☐ topaz	14.00	17.00	15.00
☐ blue and white.........................	29.00	32.00	30.00
☐ red and white	30.00	33.00	31.00
☐ green and white	22.00	25.00	23.00
☐ lemonade and oxblood..................	30.00	33.00	31.00
Sugar, 1¼"			
☐ pink	21.00	24.00	22.00
☐ green	21.00	24.00	22.00
☐ blue	25.00	28.00	26.00
☐ yellow	25.00	28.00	26.00
☐ green	9.00	11.00	9.50
☐ topaz	9.00	11.00	9.50
☐ blue and white.........................	21.00	24.00	22.00
☐ red and white	23.00	26.00	24.00
☐ green and white	15.00	18.00	16.00

ALMANACS

DESCRIPTION: Almanacs are annual publications that include astrological and meterological data as well as general information of the year. Farmers use the information in almanacs to determine how weather and other variables may affect their crops.

VARIATIONS: A variety of almanacs have been published. Among the best known are the *Farmer's Almanac* and *Poor Richard's Almanack.*

PERIOD: Almanacs date to the 17th century.

COMMENTS: Collectors are primarily concerned with almanacs published before 1800. Publisher and literary content are also factors in determining price and importance.

ADDITIONAL TIPS: Almanac listings are in chronological order, and the name of the publisher is given. Prices from year to year vary greatly. For additional information refer to *The Official Price Guide to Paper Collectibles.*

	Current Price Range		P/Y Average
☐ The New-England Almanack, Lodowick, 1695	3000.00	3750.00	3400.00
☐ The Farmer's Almanack, Whittemore, 1714 ...	900.00	1200.00	1050.00
☐ An Almanack of the Coelestial Motions and Aspects, Travis, 1717	300.00	375.00	337.00
☐ The New-England Diary, Bowen, 1724	350.00	435.00	392.00
☐ The New-England Diary, Bowen, 1725	330.00	390.00	360.00
☐ The Rhode-Island Almanack, Stafford, 1738 ..	1100.00	1375.00	1237.00
☐ Poor Job's Almanack, Shepherd (James Franklin), 1753	1400.00	1900.00	1650.00
☐ An Astronomical Diary; Or, An Almanack, Ames, 1753	240.00	315.00	277.00
☐ An Astronomical Diary, Ames, 1764	75.00	95.00	85.00
☐ The New-England Almanack, West, 1775	240.00	315.00	277.00
☐ The North-American's Almanack, Stearns, 1775	90.00	120.00	110.00
☐ Bickerstaff's Boston Almanack, 1775	170.00	210.00	190.00
☐ Bickerstaff's Boston Almanack, 1778	150.00	180.00	165.00
☐ American Almanack, Russell, 1782	90.00	115.00	105.00

Almanacs, *advertising Seven Barks, 1900s,*
$8.00-$10.00

	Current Price Range		P/Y Average
☐ Webster's Connecticut Pocket Almanack, Nickerstaff, 1787	145.00	180.00	165.00
☐ An Astronomical Diary, Strong, 1788	115.00	150.00	132.00
☐ An Astronomical Diary, Sewall, 1794	115.00	150.00	132.00
☐ Strong's Almanack, 1796	115.00	150.00	132.00
☐ Farmer's Almanack, Thomas, 1799	27.00	36.00	32.00
☐ Greenleaf's New-York, Connecticut and New Jersey Almanack, 1801	90.00	115.00	105.00
☐ New England Almanack, Daboll, 1805	35.00	47.00	41.00
☐ New England Almanack, Daboll, 1808	22.00	30.00	26.00
☐ New England Almanack, Daboll, 1810	33.00	41.00	37.00
☐ Law's Boston, 1812	16.00	21.00	19.00
☐ New England Almanack, Daboll, 1813	27.00	36.00	32.00
☐ New England Almanack, Daboll, 1816	28.00	35.00	31.00
☐ National Comic Almanack, 1851	10.00	14.00	12.00
☐ True Americans Almanack, 1855	50.00	65.00	57.00
☐ Western Almanack, 1867	16.00	21.00	19.00
☐ Hagerstown Town and Country Almanack, 1869	8.00	12.00	10.00
☐ Farmer and Mechanics Almanac, Scovill, 1871	10.00	14.00	12.00
☐ Tarrytown Almanack, 1872	9.00	13.00	11.00
☐ United States Almanack, Hostetter, 1874	9.00	13.00	11.00
☐ Hagerstown Almanack, Gruber, 1880	9.00	13.00	11.00
☐ Humans and Horses, 1881	11.00	16.00	13.00
☐ Presto-Fertilizer Co., 1885	7.00	10.00	8.50
☐ Mandrahe Bitters Almanack, 1886	8.00	11.00	9.50
☐ Kendall Doctor At Home	8.00	11.00	9.50

	Current Price Range		P/Y Average
☐ Williams And Clark Fertilizers, colored cover, 1888	9.00	13.00	11.00
☐ Wright's Pictorial Family Almanack, 1888	9.00	13.00	11.00
☐ Home Almanack, 1897	5.00	7.00	6.00
☐ Barker's Guide/Cookbook, 1900	11.00	15.00	13.50
☐ Swamp Root, 1902	4.00	6.00	5.00
☐ Diamond Dye #6, 1908	11.00	15.00	13.00
☐ Ranson's, 1912	7.00	10.00	8.50
☐ Royster's, 1912	6.00	8.00	7.00
☐ Dr. Ayer's (American Health), 1915	6.00	8.00	7.00
☐ Lady's Birthday Almanack, 1917	7.00	10.00	8.50
☐ Poor Richard's Almanack, 1919	6.00	8.00	7.00
☐ Hood Farm, 1923	6.00	8.00	7.00

AMERICAN INDIAN ARTIFACTS

TOPIC: American Indian artifacts are appreciating quickly as more and more people are attracted to these unique and historical items.

TYPES: Types of artifacts range from jewelry to woven products to weapons.

PERIOD: Though some items may be prehistoric, as a rule these collectibles will date from around 1600 to 1925. More recent artifacts are usually valued according to rarity and quality of workmanship.

ORIGIN: These artifacts may originate anywhere in the United States, but the Plains and the Southwest have provided a disproportionate amount of items.

MATERIALS: The material depends on the artifact, and so, leather, stone, wood and ceramics are used extensively.

COMMENTS: Many collectors focus on specific tribes and items, such as Navajo rugs or Hopi Kachina dolls. Others do not limit themselves so strictly, and may collect all Indian artifacts from a certain period or area.

ADDITIONAL TIPS: The following listings are organized by item. The tribe name follows, and the description after that will include types, colors and decorations. The material is next, followed by the dimensions of the item and the date, if known. Other information was included where relevant.

Hopi Kachina Doll, *75 years old,* **$475.00**

	Current Price Range		P/Y Average
☐ **Armband,** Sioux, beaded, green and white, set of two	45.00	75.00	60.00
☐ **Arrow,** Yuma, cane and hardwood, 37″. c. 1890	30.00	49.00	40.00
☐ **Axe,** Creek, wraparound eye, steel head, handle 20″, head 6″, c. 1837	125.00	175.00	150.00
☐ **Bag,** Araphaho, beaded, white, black and pink, buffalo hide, 5″ x 8″, c. 1885	65.00	95.00	80.00
☐ **Bag,** Cheyenne, beaded, red, yellow and blue, 2″ diameter	15.00	25.00	20.00
☐ **Bag,** Chippewa, beaded, peco edging, 4″ wide, 6″ long	25.00	45.25	35.00
☐ **Basket,** Cherokee, red and black, tub-shaped, split oak, 5″ wide, 6″ high	45.00	57.25	51.00
☐ **Basket,** Chocataw, for berries, cane, 6″ high .	15.00	25.25	20.00
☐ **Basket,** Jicarilla, multicolored, 13″ x 18″ x 3″ .	125.00	145.25	135.00
☐ **Basket,** Maidu, tray type, redbud motif, 15″ diameter, 7″ high	115.00	140.25	127.00
☐ **Basket,** Objibwa, painted, splint and sweet grass, c. 1895	20.00	35.25	27.00
☐ **Basket,** Paiute, wedding type, 13″ wide, 4″ high	85.00	145.25	115.00
☐ **Basket,** Washo, three rod style, 14″ wide, 8″ high	165.00	275.00	220.00

	Current Price Range		P/Y Average
☐ **Belt,** Apache, children's, beaded, white, blue and red, 2″ x 27″	125.00	225.00	175.00
☐ **Belt,** Cheyenne, square conchos style	65.00	95.00	80.00
☐ **Blanket,** Navajo, red, black, brown, orange and white, nine spot pattern	1200.00	1650.00	1400.00
☐ **Blanket,** Navajo, red, blue, black, green, yellow, fourth phase nine spot pattern	1500.00	1800.00	1650.00
☐ **Blanket,** Navajo, red, white, blue and black, nine spot pattern with diamond shapes	1800.00	2100.00	1950.00
☐ **Bolo,** Navajo, turquoise stone	25.00	45.00	35.00
☐ **Boot Liners,** Eskimo, woven	35.00	45.00	40.00
☐ **Bracelet,** Navajo, silver and petrified wood, c. 1945	70.00	95.00	85.00
☐ **Bracelet,** Zuni, turquoise and coral	90.00	110.00	100.00
☐ **Broach,** Navajo, silver, turquoise, c. 1910	45.00	75.00	60.00
☐ **Brow Band,** Sioux, quilled, purple, white and red, 15″ x 4″, c. 1905	80.00	110.00	95.00
☐ **Canoe,** Chippewa, miniature, quilled, diamond and cross pattern, birch, 12″ long, 3″ high	25.00	42.00	34.00
☐ **Canteen,** Acoma, fineline, with heart-line deer, 7″ tall, c. 1975	48.00	72.00	60.00
☐ **Club,** Apache, "flop-knob" type, stone, wood and rawhide	100.00	125.00	112.00
☐ **Club,** Shoshone, stone, wood and rawhide, 22″	35.00	55.00	45.00
☐ **Club,** Sioux, stone, wood and rawhide	27.00	37.00	30.00
☐ **Coat,** Cheyenne, beaded, leather, c. 1900	250.00	395.00	322.00
☐ **Cradleboard,** Apache, beaded, rawhide and wood, c. 1900	110.00	135.00	122.00
☐ **Doll,** Hopi, Kachina type, corn cob style body, 6″ tall	23.00	42.00	31.00
☐ **Doll,** Hopi, Kachina type, 8″ tall, c. 1963	40.00	55.00	47.00
☐ **Doll,** Hopi, Kachina type, 7″ tall, c. 1915	45.00	65.00	55.00
☐ **Doll,** Hopi, Kachina type, leather clothing, 15″ tall	80.00	98.00	89.00
☐ **Doll,** Plains, beaded, rawhide, 11″ tall, c. 1915	50.00	65.00	57.00
☐ **Doll,** Plains, "scalp" type, rawhide, 1800s	185.00	225.00	205.00
☐ **Drum,** Apache, ceremonial, leather and brass, 7″ wide, 3″ wide	75.00	125.00	105.00
☐ **Drum,** Pawnee, 10″ wide, 4″ high	15.00	23.00	19.00
☐ **Drum,** Yaqui, leather and wood, 7″ wide, 24″ tall	48.00	78.00	63.00
☐ **Effigy,** Papago, 4″ wide, 6″ high	35.00	55.00	45.00
☐ **Fan,** Navajo, peyote type, goose feathers	35.00	48.00	42.00
☐ **Fob,** Kickapoo, beaded, black and white, diamond design, 2″ x 6″	28.00	48.00	38.00
☐ **Hat,** Hupa, bands, step design	135.00	175.00	155.00
☐ **Head Band,** Comanche, beaded, red, blue and white, diamond design, 1″ x 23″	23.00	33.00	30.00
☐ **Hobbles,** Navajo, rawhide, c. 1890	18.00	30.00	24.00
☐ **Jar,** Hohokam, shoulder type, painted, 6″ wide, 4″ high	175.00	280.00	225.00
☐ **Jar,** Papago, redware, 10″ tall	80.00	115.00	95.00

Zuni Grain Jar, *archaic, museum quality,* **$5,000.00 +**

	Current Price Range		P/Y Average
☐ **Jar,** Zuni, head pot, red, green and white, 10″ wide, 8″ high, c. 1922	335.00	435.00	385.00
☐ **Knife Case,** Sioux, beaded, quilled, 7½″, c. 1885	210.00	250.00	230.00
☐ **Knife Sheath,** Osage, beaded, white, green, blue and red, 8″	85.00	130.00	107.00
☐ **Leggings,** Nez Perce, men's style, beaded, fringed, c. 1915	220.00	260.00	245.00
☐ **Leggings,** Osage, men's style, blue, c. 1880	150.00	175.00	162.00
☐ **Leggings,** Plains, beaded, blue and white, rawhide, c. 1925	180.00	225.00	102.00
☐ **Moccasins,** Apache, beaded, black and white, set of two	80.00	115.00	97.00
☐ **Moccasins,** Arapaho, blue, yellow and green, set of two	60.00	110.00	75.00
☐ **Moccasins,** Sioux, children's, beaded, green, red and white, set of two	45.00	75.00	60.00
☐ **Moccasins,** Sioux, beaded, white, red and blue, set of two	138.00	178.00	158.00
☐ **Necklace,** Blackfoot, beaded, rawhide, 37″	40.00	60.00	50.00
☐ **Paddle,** Creek, mush style, 24″, 1800s	28.00	48.00	38.00
☐ **Paddles,** Haida, painted, 56″, set of two	70.00	90.00	80.00
☐ **Pillow Cover,** Plains Cree, beaded, leather, fringed, 17″ x 20″	310.00	350.00	330.00
☐ **Pin,** Zuni, Rainbird Kachina Dancer motif	75.00	90.00	82.00
☐ **Pipe,** Calumet, catlinite bowl and stem, tomahawk shape, c. 1850	400.00	450.00	425.00

	Current Price Range		P/Y Average
☐ **Plaque,** Hopi, red, green and black, coil ware, 15″ wide	80.00	129.00	105.00
☐ **Pot,** Papago, black and red, chain design, 7″ wide, 7″ tall, c. 1910	25.00	42.00	33.00
☐ **Pot,** Zia, bird type, 7½″ wide, 6″ high, c. 1980	80.00	95.00	87.50
☐ **Pouch,** Cheyenne, medicine type, beaded, blue, leather	28.00	38.00	32.00
☐ **Purse,** Comanche, red, white, and green, fret design, 3½″ wide, 5″ long	45.00	58.00	52.00
☐ **Rattle,** Hopi, white and black, gourd style, feather streamers	18.00	28.00	20.00
☐ **Ring,** Navajo, horseshoe design, silver, turquoise stone	12.00	18.00	15.00
☐ **Rug,** Navajo, blue and white, Yei figure design, 24″ x 15″, c. 1978	75.00	95.00	85.00
☐ **Rug,** Navajo, red, black and white, diamond motif, c. 1935	700.00	900.00	800.00
☐ **Saddle,** Kiowa, tacked, 18″ long, 12″ high, c. 1858	225.00	295.00	260.00
☐ **Saddlebag,** Parfleche, multicolored, fringed, 11″ x 10″	185.00	215.00	200.00
☐ **Saddle Blanket,** Plateau, elkhide, c. 1885	330.00	370.00	350.00
☐ **Serape,** Navajo, orange, blue, green, yellow and gray, 45″ x 65″, c. 1890	3000.00	3700.00	3400.00
☐ **Serape,** Navajo, blue, white and red, late terraced style, 52″ x 68″, c. 1890	4200.00	4600.00	4400.00
☐ **Serape,** Navajo, blue, white and red, 54″ x 72″	8700.00	10500.00	9600.00
☐ **Snowshoes,** Chippewa, wood and rawhide, 29″, c. 1875	150.00	175.00	162.00
☐ **Totem Pole,** Tsimshian, carved faces, painted, 12″ long	65.00	89.00	77.00
☐ **Vase,** Hopi, wedding type, 10″	165.00	195.00	180.00
☐ **Vase,** Jemez, wedding type, red and green, 12″ tall	75.00	125.00	100.00
☐ **Wrist Band,** Hopi, net woven, c. 1895	30.00	45.00	37.00
☐ **Yoke,** Mohave, beaded, 17″ wide, 9″ long ...	20.00	35.00	27.00

ANIMAL COLLECTIBLES

DESCRIPTION: Animal collectibles are highly popular among all types of collectors. The older Steiff bears, for instance, are experiencing stiff competition from the new, limited edition issues. Collectible bears and cats are extremely popular in the current market.

COMMENTS: The following list is merely a sample guide to the animal collectibles currently available on today's retail and secondary markets. All categories, bears, cats, cows, dogs, pigs, rabbits and unicorns, are listed alphabetically.

ADDITIONAL TIPS: For further information, refer to the directory located in the front of this books.

BEARS	Current Price Range		P/Y Average
☐ **Aloysius,** North American Bear Co., plaid ribbon, brown, 20″	35.00	45.00	37.00
☐ **Amelia Bearhart,** North American Bear Co., flight suit, hat and goggles, discontinued	45.00	55.00	47.00
☐ **Anniversary Bear,** Merry Thought, commemorative, has growling mechanism, off-white	100.00	150.00	105.00
☐ **Baby Bear,** Bear Haus USA, tan, jointed, #1301, 14″	12.00	15.00	13.00
☐ **Baby Bear,** Bear Haus USA, tan, jointed, #3019, 10″	10.00	15.00	11.00
☐ **Bare Bear,** North American Bear Co.	35.00	45.00	37.00
☐ **Bentley Bear,** Dakin, jointed, has growling mechanism, 21″	35.00	45.00	37.00
☐ **Bialosky Bear,** North American Bear Co., sailor middy, 13″	25.00	35.00	26.00
☐ **Bialosky Bear,** North American Bear Co., sailor middy, 18″	45.00	55.00	47.00
☐ **Bialosky Bear,** North American Bear Co., satin tuxedo, 18″	45.00	55.00	47.00

	Current Price Range		P/Y Average

☐ **Edwardian Bear,** Merry Thought, mohair, jointed, has growling mechanism, #HE18 ... `80.00` `110.00` `84.00`

☐ **Humphrey Beargurt,** North American Bear Co., trench coat and hat, 19″ .... `40.00` `50.00` `42.00`

☐ **Kareem Abdul Jabear,** North American Bear Co., black bear in basketball uniform .... `40.00` `50.00` `42.00`

☐ **Lauren Bearcall,** North American Bear Co., in fur coat and veiled hat .... `40.00` `50.00` `42.00`

☐ **Little Bear,** Bear Haus USA, tan, jointed, #1502, 12″ .... `11.00` `16.00` `12.00`

☐ **Mama Bear,** Bear Haus USA, tan, jointed, #3100, 14″ .... `15.00` `20.00` `16.00`

☐ **Margaret Strong Teddy Bear,** Steiff, mohair, voice box .... `185.00` `200.00` `195.00`

☐ **Merry Bear,** Merry Thought, mohair, green embroidered scarf, #M914 .... `50.00` `60.00` `55.00`

☐ **Mikhail Bearishnikov,** North American Bear Co., in ballet tights, 19″ .... `40.00` `50.00` `42.00`

☐ **Papa Bear,** Bear Haus USA, tan, jointed, #3008, 16″ .... `15.00` `20.00` `16.00`

☐ **Richard Steiff Bear,** copy of original Steiff Teddy, limited edition, 1983, 12″ .... `85.00` `95.00` `89.00`

☐ **Running Bear,** jogging suit with hood ...... `40.00` `50.00` `42.00`

☐ **Scarlett O'Beara,** North American Bear Co., in traditional Southern Belle Style .... `40.00` `50.00` `42.00`

☐ **Teddy Bear,** plush brown, glass eyes, red ribbon, 7¾″ .... `50.00` `60.00` `55.50`

☐ **Teddy Bear,** baby rattle, sterling silver, with teething ring .... `80.00` `100.00` `91.00`

☐ **Teddy Bear,** cookbook, 1907 .... `35.00` `55.00` `46.00`

☐ **Teddy Bear,** on wheels, riding toy, brown mohair body stuffed with straw, glass eyes, embroidered nose, growler .... `1000.00` `1500.00` `1260.00`

☐ **Teddy Bear,** tray, rectangular, c. 1906 ...... `40.00` `50.00` `46.00`

☐ **Theodore Bear,** Dakin, jointed, 12″ .... `8.00` `12.00` `9.00`

☐ **Theodore Bear,** Dakin, jointed, 15″ .... `11.00` `18.00` `12.00`

☐ **William Shakesbear,** North American Bear Co., Shakespearean costume, 19″ .... `40.00` `50.00` `42.00`

☐ **Zsa Zsa Gabear,** North American Bear Co., fancy gown, 19″ .... `40.00` `50.00` `42.00`

CATS

☐ **Black Cat Kitchen Set,** oil and vinegar bottles `15.00` `25.00` `20.00`

☐ **Black Cat Pretzel Holder,** tail serves as dowel to collect pretzels, cat in arched position, plaster of paris, USA .... `4.00` `10.00` `6.00`

☐ **Cat Ashtray,** black cat, red bow around neck, green eyes .... `12.00` `17.00` `15.50`

☐ **Cat Baby Fork,** silver plate, "Puss 'N' Boots" `12.00` `17.00` `14.50`

☐ **Cat Bank,** plaster, painted a rust hue, black whiskers, 10″ high .... `80.00` `100.00` `90.00`

☐ **Cat Bookends,** "Halloween Cat", cast iron, signed .... `40.00` `60.00` `51.00`

	Current Price Range		P/Y Average
☐ **Cat Candy Dish,** Fenton Carnival glass, features Chessie, 1970	100.00	130.00	118.00
☐ **Cat Candy Dish,** Fenton rosalene glass, features Chessie, 1977	90.00	120.00	100.00
☐ **Cat Candy Mold ,** tin, 3½ "	20.00	30.00	24.00
☐ **Cat Doorstop,** cast iron, full figure	85.00	105.00	96.00
☐ **Cat Figurine,** Mama cat, in pink bonnet, washing the face of a kitten, both in standing position	45.00	60.00	56.50
☐ **Cat Napkin Ring,** silver plate, from the Victorian era	90.00	110.00	100.00
☐ **Cat Postcards,** cats dressed up as various people, set of 18	20.00	30.00	27.50
☐ **Cat Prints,** Currier and Ives, unframed	115.00	175.00	130.00
☐ **Cat String Holder,** white cat bust, ceramic	20.00	30.00	27.00
☐ **Garfield,** Dakin, 7"	6.00	12.00	8.00
☐ **Garfield,** Dakin, 9"	10.00	15.00	11.00
☐ **Lizzy Cat,** Steiff, 1982	35.00	45.00	37.00

COWS

☐ **Cow,** fabric covered and painted, black hooves, brown spots, glass eyes, carved wooden base, 4¼ " high	20.00	30.00	24.50
☐ **Flora The Cow,** Steiff, white, beige, #3792/25, 10"	60.00	80.00	63.00

DOGS

☐ **Dog Ashtray,** Scotty dog, plastic, black and white	12.00	20.00	17.00
☐ **Bookends,** German Shepherds, bronze, manufactured by Armor Bronze, New York	120.00	140.00	132.00
☐ **Dog Bootscraper,** Scotty in standing position, c. 1920s	8.00	15.00	12.00
☐ **Dog Matchstrike,** figural bulldog	40.00	50.00	45.00
☐ **Dog Planter,** Scotty, with ashtray, china	5.00	10.00	8.00
☐ **Dog Rattle,** with teething ring, sterling	50.00	90.00	72.00

PIGS

☐ **Pig,** brown and white stuffed	35.00	45.00	40.00
☐ **Pig Ashtray,** two pigs peering at camera, pale pink bisque	70.00	90.00	80.00
☐ **Pig Figurine,** pig driving jalopy, 3¾ "	40.00	60.00	49.75
☐ **Pig Figurine,** pig peeking out of baby bassinet, 3½ "	40.00	60.00	49.75
☐ **Pig Figurine,** pig sits beside "Boston Baked Beans" pot, 2½ "	30.00	50.00	39.50
☐ **Pig Milk Pitcher,** dressed in evening finery, 4"	10.00	20.00	14.50
☐ **Pig Pillow,** quilted pattern	7.00	17.00	13.50

RABBITS

☐ **Benjamin Bunny,** Beatrix Potter	20.00	30.00	25.00
☐ **Bunnykins,** Autumn Days	10.00	20.00	16.50
☐ **Bunnykins,** Springtime	12.00	20.00	16.50

	Current Price Range		P/Y Average
☐ **Mrs. Rabbit and Bunnies,** Beatrix Potter	22.00	32.00	27.00
☐ **Punning The Rabbit,** Steiff, mohair, sitting in a crouched position, #2960/25, c. 1960s, 10″ .	65.00	79.00	69.00
☐ **Rabbit Cake Mold,** in two pieces, cast iron, 11″	30.00	50.00	42.00
☐ **Rabbit Figurine,** Peter Rabbit, Anri	60.00	80.00	70.00
☐ **Running Rabbit,** Steiff, mohair, #131400, c. 1950s, 6″	100.00	130.00	105.00

UNICORNS

☐ **Unicorn,** Steuben crystal, etched signature, 7″ high	710.00	910.00	810.00

ANIMATED CELS

DESCRIPTION: Animated cels are sheets of celluloid with painted designs used to produce color cartoons and full length animated features. Some films use part animation and part live actors as in Disney's *Song of the South* and the Beatles' *Yellow Submarine.* Cels which combine live actors and animation are equally collectible as fully animated cels.

ORIGIN: After Walt Disney Productions' release of *Snow White* in 1937, art dealers and collectors began forseeing a market for animated cels. The public acceptance of the fanciful characters in *Snow White* encouraged Disney to preserve the cels. During the 1930s and 1940s, animated cels continued to sell well fetching prices from $5 to $50. Today animated cels of that era sell for hundreds of dollars.

MAKER: Although the animated works of Walt Disney Productions and Fleischer Studios are highly collectible, animated cels preceding the 1920s are extremely desirable.

COMMENTS: Animated cels are produced by many notable cartoonists including Walter Lantz, the creator of Woody Woodpecker and Charles Jones, the originator of the Roadrunner. Disney's works are perhaps the most desirable of all since the studio often ignored production cost in order to produce detailed cels for the cartoon features.

CARE AND CONDITION: Special care should be taken with all animated cels especially those produced prior to 1951. Cels made before 1951 were made of cellulose nitrate, a flammable material which could be a serious fire hazard if stored incorrectly. After 1951, a less flammable celluloid was used. All cels, especially nitrate cels, should be stored individually in closed metal containers. Keep the containers in a cool, well ventilated area. Do not wrap the cels in paper before storing.

ADDITIONAL TIPS: A glass mount is better than a cardboard mount. If one used cardboard, it should be made of 100 percent rag stock. Always display any cell away from heat or humidity.

Original Hand Painted Cel By Chuck Jones,
©*Warner Brothers, Inc., 1980*   **$30.00-$40.00**

	Current Price Range		P/Y Average
☐ **Adventures of Ichabod Crane and Mr. Toad,** Walt Disney Productions, full figure of Mr. Toad with whip, clicking heels together, full color, 5¼ ″ x 6½ ″, 1949	275.00	280.00	277.50
☐ **Alice in Wonderland,** Walt Disney Productions, full figure of caterpillar smoking pipe, color, 5″ x 5½ ″, 1951	175.00	200.00	187.00
☐ **Alice in Wonderland,** Walt Disney Productions, two cels which combine to produce a scene of the Dodo and a pair of birds, figures are one cel and the ocean another, full color, 7½ ″ x 11″, 1951	130.00	160.00	145.00
☐ **Alice in Wonderland,** Walt Disney Productions, full figure of the White Rabbit in three piece suit carrying umbrella, full color, 4″ x 4½ ″, 1951	175.00	200.00	187.00

	Current Price Range		P/Y Average

☐ **Art of Skiing, The,** Walt Disney Productions, air brushed background showing Goofy colliding with a tree, bears WDP stamp and Courvoisier label on reverse, 8¼″ x 7½″, 1941 . . . . — 310.00 — 335.00 — 322.00

☐ **Bambi,** Walt Disney Productions, air brushed and watercolor background showing Bambi, Thumper and friends watching a butterfly, bears Courvoisier label on reverse, 7½″ x 9¼″, 1942 . . . . — 1100.00 — 1300.00 — 1200.00

☐ **Bugs Bunny,** Chuck Jones Studio, full figure of Bugs Bunny with right leg raised, full color, 2½″ x 6½″, 1970 . . . . — 60.00 — 65.00 — 62.50

☐ **Casper the Friendly Ghost,** Famous Studios, full figure of Casper, hands at side, full color, 2″ x 3½″, 1950s . . . . — 30.00 — 40.00 — 35.00

☐ **Cinderella,** Walt Disney Productions, showing the fairy waving her wand, bears WDP copyright on reverse, 6″ x 9″, 1950 . . . . — 95.00 — 110.00 — 100.00

☐ **Cinderella,** Walt Disney Productions, showing the Grand Duke in gray and blue uniform, 12½″ x 15½″, 1950 . . . . — 70.00 — 80.00 — 75.00

☐ **Dumbo,** Walt Disney Productions, showing Dumbo cradled in his mother's trunk, 7″ x 5½″, 1941 . . . . — 1250.00 — 2450.00 — 1850.00

☐ **Fantasia,** Walt Disney Productions, showing a centaurette holding a flower from the Pastoral Symphony, 10″ x 12″, 1940 . . . . — 110.00 — 135.00 — 125.00

☐ **Fantasia,** Walt Disney Productions, showing nineteen Milkwood fairies against pine tree branches and a gray background, bears Courvoisier label on reverse, 10″ x 19″, 1940 . . . . . — 610.00 — 660.00 — 635.00

☐ **Lady and the Tramp,** Walt Disney Productions, showing Lady, 8″ x 10″, 1955 . . . . — 100.00 — 135.00 — 115.00

☐ **Mary Poppins,** Walt Disney Productions, showing pair of penguins and two small birds flying overhead, full color, 5½″ x 6½″, 1964 . — 160.00 — 200.00 — 180.00

☐ **Mickey Mouse Club,** Walt Disney Productions, showing full figure of Jiminy Cricket with a yo-yo, 5½″ x 6″, 1950s . . . . — 140.00 — 150.00 — 145.00

☐ **Peter Pan,** Walt Disney Productions, showing Wendy with hands out and palms upraised, mouth open, full color, 3½″ x 4¼″, 1953 . . . . — 100.00 — 130.00 — 115.00

☐ **Peter Pan,** Walt Disney Productions, showing John holding an umbrella and wearing a silk hat, full color, 5½″ x 7″, 1953 . . . . — 90.00 — 110.00 — 100.00

☐ **Pink Panther,** Depattee-Frelang Studio, showing Pink Panther on a steel structure high above street, 10″ x 12½″, 1965 . . . . — 195.00 — 210.00 — 202.00

☐ **Pinocchio,** Walt Disney Productions, showing Jiminy Cricket on the sea floor startled by a fish, bears Courvoisier label on reverse, 5½″ x 6½″, 1940 . . . . — 430.00 — 460.00 — 445.00

☐ **Sinking of the Lusitania, The,** Winsor McCay, showing the sinking of the Lusitania, 7½″ x 9″, 1918 . . . . — 500.00 — 800.00 — 650.00

	Current Price Range		P/Y Average
☐ **Sleeping Beauty,** Walt Disney Productions, showing Prince Philip on horseback bearing a sword and shield, full color, 5¼" x 7", 1959	220.00	250.00	235.00
☐ **Snoopy.** CBS Television, showing Snoopy in tennis clothes and racket, 10¼" x 12½", 1970s	55.00	65.00	60.00
☐ **Snow White,** Walt Disney Productions, showing Dopey standing with squirrels running past him, 8½" x 8½", 1937	335.00	360.00	347.00
☐ **Snow White,** Walt Disney Productions, showing Bashful, 7" x 5", 1937	260.00	280.00	270.00
☐ **You're An Education,** Warner Brothers Studio, Hep Cat blowing a yellow trombone, 8" x 11", 1938	70.00	90.00	80.00

ART DECO

TOPIC: ART DECO See Icart; Lalique.

DESCRIPTION: Art Deco is essentially a design movement which was named for an important exhibition in Paris in 1925 called "l'Exposition Internationale des Arts Decoratifs." The show came, however, at least five years after the movement was underway.

PERIOD: Today, we call the 1920's and 1930's the period of Art Deco. Designers were inspired by Cubist art and artifacts from ancient Egypt and North and Central America. These are all characterized by strong color and abstract geometric design. There is some time overlap with the Art Nouveau period, but the major differences are characterized by the "modernist" look of Art Deho.

TYPES: The range of Art Deco collectibles is great — from plastic bracelets to custom-designed glass vases.

Furniture in sleek modernistic lines was produced and often lacquered in black or white.

COMMENTS: The sleek designs of Art Deco are currently very popular once again. California is the leading edge of this movement with the "Hollywood" style of the 1920s and 30s being particularly popular.

ADDITIONAL TIPS: Many Art Deco items can be purchased very inexpensively at second hand shops and thrift stores across the country. Look for geometric motifs, sleek styling, pastel colors, black or white enameling, chrome, and smoked glass in a wide variety of items. These include lamp bases, smoking accoutrements, vases, mirrors, vanity accessories, dishes, glassware, figurines, objets d'art and furniture. Old bedroom suites from the 1920s abound. It is quite possible to acquire a complete bedroom suite including bed, night stands, chest of drawers, dresser and vanity for under $200. Don't be put off by the old wood veneer finish. These sets can be enameled in black, white, or even pastel colors with dazzling results!

RECOMMENDED READING: For more information on Art Deco, you may refer to the following books published by The House of Collectibles:

The Official Price Guide to Glassware,
The Official Price Guide to Antique Jewelry,
The Official Price Guide to Collector Prints,
The Official Price Guide to Pottery and Porcelain,
The Official Price Guide to Wicker,
The Official Identification Guide to Glassware and
The Official Identification Guide to Pottery and Porcelain.

**Vogue magazine
promotional,**
Art Deco style,
brass, 1926,
$70.00-$90.00

	Current Price Range		P/Y Average
☐ **Andirons,** brass, pair	255.00	300.00	270.00
☐ **Ashtray,** bronze and onyx figural, onyx bowl with flower head supporting a ballerina, inscribed Lorenzl, 12¾", c. 1925	900.00	1150.00	990.00
☐ **Bar pin,** platinum, diamond, jade and onyx with white gold clasp, c. 1925	900.00	1150.00	990.00
☐ **Bedroom Suite,** Heywood Wakefield, four piece set includes dressing table with large round mirror, tabouret, four drawer dresser, and night stand, black enamel, c. 1935	2800.00	3200.00	2850.00

	Current Price Range		P/Y Average

☐ **Chair,** occasional, black vinyl upholstery, rounded back, lower arms cut out, circular seat, white apron, 33″ high by 25″ wide, c. 1925 .... 175.00 225.00 187.00

☐ **Cigar box,** Tiffany & Company, rectangular, cedar lining, c. 1925 .... 400.00 450.00 410.00

☐ **Cigarette case,** silver and blue enamel 195.00 215.00 200.00

☐ **Clock,** desk, black onyx and sterling silver, Zenith, fifteen jewel movement, three adjustments, 2 ⅜″ 285.00 340.00 305.00

☐ **Clock,** desk, jade and enamel, square form, blue enamelled hands and black Roman numerals, Cartier, 1¼″ 2500.00 3500.00 2800.00

☐ **Clock,** desk, rock crystal gold, enamel and diamonds, Cartier, c. 1935 .... 3400.00 4000.00 3600.00

☐ **Clock,** glass and chrome-plated bronze, chrome face, black glass and chrome base, 8¾″, c. 1930 .... 305.00 475.00 315.00

☐ **Comb case,** six cabochon sapphires in gold motif, sterling silver, c. 1935 .... 500.00 600.00 515.00

☐ **Compact,** black with diamond corners, black enamel link chain attached to finger ring ... 1050.00 1320.00 1150.00

☐ **Compact,** rectangular, gold enamel and diamonds, Cartier, c. 1930 .... 3400.00 4000.00 3600.00

☐ **Desk,** curved with twin pedestal, cabinet and four drawers on either side of a large central drawer, unsigned, French, 56″ long 325.00 400.00 360.00

☐ **Desk,** drop front, English, c. 1935 .... 1200.00 1800.00 1375.00

☐ **Figure,** dancer, exotic silvered figure, marble base, inscribed Fayral, c. 1925 .... 610.00 835.00 700.00

☐ **Figure,** dancer, gilt-bronze nude figure with out-stretched arms supporting a drapery, inscribed A. Kelety, 14½″, c. 1930 .... 790.00 1200.00 900.00

☐ **Figure,** dancer, swaying, inscribed CJR Colinet, 18½″, c. 1925 .... 680.00 790.00 700.00

☐ **Figure,** Pierette and Pierrot, bronze, green marble base, inscribed Lorenzl, 16¾″, c. 1925 1375.00 1870.00 1500.00

☐ **Figure,** young sailor, bronze and ivory, marked "BRONZE," plinth inscribed A. Jorel, 9″, early 20th century 390.00 500.00 425.00

☐ **Figure,** young woman, bronze and tortoise shell 830.00 1025.00 900.00

☐ **Figure,** young woman, bronze and ivory, onyx base, Bessie Callender, 17″, c. 1930 .... 1015.00 1410.00 1150.00

☐ **Figure,** young woman, silvered and gilt-bronze figure riding on elephant, onyx and marble base, French, 24″, c. 1925 .... 1650.00 2100.00 1750.00

☐ **Floor Lamp,** skyscraper style with checkerboard design, marked Warren Allen with date of January, 1929, 55½″ 275.00 335.00 290.00

☐ **Footstool,** upholstered and aluminum, designed by Deskey, c. 1931 .... 460.00 680.00 550.00

☐ **Hall Rack,** wrought iron, made in Belgium, has pivoting mirror with hooks at either side, base serves as umbrella stand, six feet by three feet 325.00 380.00 340.00

	Current Price Range		P/Y Average
☐ **Lamp,** alabaster and metal, figural, female holding torch, diamond shaped base, 22½ ″.	350.00	450.00	380.00
☐ **Lamps,** pair, chromed metal, small circular base, cylindrical standard, one-piece bowl shaped shade, French, 19″, c. 1925	1400.00	1600.00	1425.00
☐ **Lapel watch,** black onyx panel, pin has rose-cut diamonds, platinum and gold watch, Dreicer & Co.	1485.00	1870.00	1575.00
☐ **Necklace,** faceted black glass rectangles, oval faceted pastes, black metal mountings, 15″ long, Czechoslovakian, c. 1920-30	45.00	55.00	47.50
☐ **Necklace,** fancy aluminum and round black glass beads, 16½ ″ long, c. 1920-30	120.00	140.00	122.00
☐ **Necklace,** fancy green and white plastic beads, 20″ long, c. 1920-30	45.00	55.00	44.00
☐ **Necklace,** fancy pumpkin, orange and amber colored plastic beads, 16½ ″ long, c. 1920-30	35.00	45.00	35.50
☐ **Necklace,** geometric motif, beige, apple green and white plastic beads, 17″ long, c. 1920-30	35.00	45.00	35.00
☐ **Necklace,** oval and round bittersweet amber colored plastic beads, 15½ ″ long, c. 1920-30	25.00	35.00	27.50
☐ **Necklace,** round jade green ceramic beads spaced with white metal fancy links, 15½ ″ long, c. 1920-30	35.00	45.00	35.50
☐ **Necklace,** three pendants of round pastes sandwiched between two round amber glass beads, chain of small cherry red plastic tubes, 22½ ″ long, c. 1920-30	35.00	5.00	35.50
☐ **Necklace,** triple pendant, 14K gold, American, c. 1930	750.00	950.00	765.00
☐ **Picture,** reverse painting on glass by W. Fager, floral motif, enclosed in gilt wire frame, 22″	80.00	100.00	87.00
☐ **Picture Frame,** standing, bronze with black marble base, 14¼ ″ wide, 13½ ″ tall	90.00	110.00	96.00
☐ **Picture Frames,** set of four wall hanging frames, with reverse silkscreen decoration on glass, 12″ x 10″	110.00	140.00	120.00
☐ **Rack,** hall, lacquer and brass, mirror plate, brass holders, black support, French, 5′1″, c. 1930	425.00	530.00	475.00
☐ **Ring,** one round diamond approx. .50 ct., one round diamond approx. .25 ct., 16 round diamonds approx. .32 ct., 14K white gold, c. 1935	1800.00	2200.00	1875.00
☐ **Ring,** one round diamond approx. .50 ct., six baguette diamonds, 20 round diamonds, platinum, c. 1930	2000.00	2400.00	2075.00
☐ **Ring,** one round diamond approx. 1.90 cts., six baguette diamonds, round diamonds, platinum, c. 1930	7000.00	8500.00	7200.00
☐ **Ring,** oval black onyx center, two round diamonds, 14K gold, c. 1925	475.00	575.00	490.00
☐ **Ring,** platinum, cabochon sapphire and six baguette diamonds	1800.00	2300.00	2000.00
☐ **Ring,** platinum, diamond and ruby, wide band	500.00	720.00	600.00

	Current Price Range		P/Y Average
☐ **Watch,** wrist, square geometric motif, 64 round diamonds approx. 1.26 cts., 20 baguette diamonds approx. 1.06 cts., 14K white gold, maker: Hamilton, 22 jewels, c. 1930	3200.00	3400.00	3225.00
☐ **Watch,** ring, oval motif, polychrome enamels, white enamel dial, steel hands, 18K gold case, c. 1930	1700.00	1900.00	1750.00

ART GLASS

(See also Daum Nancy; Gallé; Lalique; Tiffany Glass)

DESCRIPTION: Collectible art glass refers to various types of decorative glass which was developed all over the world and hand worked in one or all stages of development from the last half of nineteenth century until the 1930s and 1940s. It includes glass from the Victorian, Art Nouveau and Art Deco periods. Victorian Art Glass consists of the Amberina, Burmese, Peach-Blow, Opal, Silverina, Agate, Crown Milano, Napoli, Satin and Royal Flemish, to name a few. With the decline of the Victorian period and the emergence of Art Nouveau, iridized glass appeared, made in America by Louis Comfort Tiffany and Steuben, in Austria by Lotz, in France by Galle, and in England by Thomas Webb and Sons.

Art Deco replaced Art Nouveau in the 1920s and the glass of Lalique of France epitomized the sleek styles of the day.

CARE: The utmost care must be exercised in cleaning art glass. Enameled or flashed pieces can be damaged by washing. It is always wise to first wipe the object with a dry, flannel cloth, buffing gently to remove accumulated dirt and dust. Then, if need be, use a damp cloth and wipe carefully. Dry the piece thoroughly. If a piece needs washing use only mild soap in lukewarm water. Do not soak. Wash and dry quickly.

REPAIRS: Repairs must be made by an expert. To find one in your area, call local galleries or museums. But remember, generally speaking, any serious damage renders art glass virtually worthless. And most damaged glass is impossible to repair.

RECOMMENDED READING: For further information refer to *The Official Price Guide to Glassware* and *The Official Identication Guide to Glassware,* published by The House of Collectibles.

	Current Price Range		P/Y Average

AGATA

☐ **Spooner,** *green opaque, very good mottling and gold band, 4½" high* . . . . — 625.00 — 725.00 — 635.00

☐ **Tumbler,** *green opaque, excellent mottling and gold band, bottom has optic rib, 3¾" high* . . . . — 575.00 — 675.00 — 585.00

☐ **Tumbler,** *green opaque, good mottling and gold band, glass is somewhat thick, 3¾" high* . . . . — 475.00 — 575.00 — 485.00

☐ **Tumbler,** *green opaque, good mottling and gold band, bottom has optic rib, 3¾" high* . . — 525.00 — 625.00 — 535.00

AMBER

☐ **Beer Stein,** *amber applied handle, green applied berry prunts, pewter base and hinged lid with thumbpiece, hold ¼ liter, 6⅞" high, 3" diameter* . . . . — 180.00 — 230.00 — 190.00

☐ **Beer Stein,** *amber applied handle, applied green berry prunts, pewter base and lid, 6¾" high, 3" diameter* . . . . — 180.00 — 230.00 — 190.00

☐ **Cologne Bottle,** *cut glass with matching stopper, 7" high, 3¾" diameter* . . . . — 150.00 — 200.00 — 155.00

☐ **Liqueur Cruet,** *pewter stopper, pewter mounted, 8" high, 3" diameter* . . . . — 100.00 — 130.00 — 105.00

☐ **Liqueur Cruet,** *swirl, amber rigaree, applied foot, pewter stopper, 8½" high, 3⅛" diameter* — 120.00 — 150.00 — 125.00

☐ **Vinegar Cruet,** *applied handle and ball stopper with enameled decorations, enameled white dabs and blue fans on cruet, bulbous shaped mouth, 6¾" high, 3½" diameter* . . . . — 130.00 — 180.00 — 135.00

☐ **Vinegar Cruet,** *inverted thumbprint style, applied handle and bubble stopper, bulbous shape, 5¼" high, 3" diameter* . . . . — 100.00 — 150.00 — 110.00

AMBERINA

☐ **Bowl,** *swirl, deep fluted, rich cranberry shades evenly to amber, amber wafer foot, decorated with gold branches, berries and leaves, 7½" x 10¾"* . . . . — 350.00 — 450.00 — 365.00

☐ **Bowl,** *swirl, fluted, rich red shades to amber, irridized finish, 4" high, 7⅝" diameter* . . . . . . — 140.00 — 190.00 — 150.00

☐ **Champagne Glass,** *hollow stem, 6" high* . . . . — 175.00 — 250.00 — 185.00

☐ **Cruet,** *Mt. Washington, Venetian Diamond, deep fuschia shading to honey amber, original stopper* . . . . — 250.00 — 350.00 — 275.00

☐ **Cruet,** *ruby shaded to amber, applied handle, 5" high* . . . . — 25.00 — 50.00 — 35.00

☐ **Fingerbowl and Underplate,** *Libbey, bowl is more red than underplate which is fuschia, 2½" high, signed LIBBEY, 1917* . . . . — 525.00 — 625.00 — 535.00

☐ **Pitcher,** *diamond quilted, applied amber handle, red shaded to amber, round mouth, shape of tankard, belltone, 7" high, 4⅛" diameter* . . . . — 350.00 — 400.00 — 375.00

	Current Price Range		P/Y Average

☐ **Ramekin,** *rich color, glass has minute ribbing, belltone, 2¼" high, 2¾" diameter ....* **230.00** **280.00** **250.00**

☐ **Salt and Pepper Shakers,** *set, inverted thumbprint, deepest fuschia color, original tops, 1880s ....* **250.00** **350.00** **265.00**

☐ **Spooner,** *Mt. Washington, diamond quilted, deep fuschia, square top ....* **275.00** **350.00** **290.00**

☐ **Tumber,** *cranberry shaded to amberina quilted design, 3" high ....* **25.00** **50.00** **35.00**

☐ **Vase,** *flower petal shaped top, fancy amber applied spiral trim, cranberry shades evenly to amber, 10" high, 5⅝" diameter ....* **140.00** **190.00** **150.00**

☐ **Vase,** *swirl, fan shaped top, rich cranberry shaded to golden amber, amber edging around top, amber applied wishbone feet, 8⅛" high, 6⅜" diameter ....* **120.00** **175.00** **130.00**

☐ **Vases,** *Jack-In-Pulpit, decorated in gold with amber edging around top, cranberry shaded to amber, decoration of flowers and leaves in heavy gold, pair, 14¾" high, 5⅜" diameter ..* **475.00** **520.00** **480.00**

☐ **Water Tumbler,** *diamond quilted, belltone, 3⅝" high, 2½" diameter ....* **100.00** **120.00** **110.00**

☐ **Whiskey Tumbler,** *diamond quilted, deep red shaded to amber, belltone, 2⅝" high, 2⅛" diameter ....* **170.00** **200.00** **185.00**

AMBERINA, REVERSE

☐ **Pitcher,** *bulbous, olive amber shades evenly to cranberry, round mouth, clear reeded applied handle, colored enameled leaves and flowers, red and green jewel decorations, 7⅞" high, 5¼" diameter ....·...............* **225.00** **325.00** **240.00**

☐ **Salt Shaker,** *inverted baby thumbprint, pewter top ....* **150.00** **220.00** **160.00**

☐ **Tumbler,** *amber shaded to cranberry at base, pink, yellow and blue enameled flowers with applied red jewels to centers, 5⅛" high, 2⅝" diameter ....* **90.00** **130.00** **95.00**

ARGY-ROUSSEAU

☐ **Bowl,** *pate-de-verre, cylinder shape tapering towards the base, red background, molded with pineapples and leaves inside medallion-like designs which encircle the shoulder in a band, in black and red, signed, 4½" diameter, c. 1925 ....* **1100.00** **1400.00** **1150.00**

☐ **Bowl,** *pate-de-verre, expanding cylinder, mottled lavender and green background, molds with roses, signed, 2¾" high, c. 1925 ....* **800.00** **1200.00** **850.00**

☐ **Box,** *covered, circular, light amber, orange, and gray, molded with leaves, strapwork, and stars with a red mask on the lid, signed, 6" diameter, c. 1925 ....* **2200.00** **2800.00** **2250.00**

BOHEMIAN

	Current Price Range		P/Y Average
☐ **Bowl,** *overlay of cobalt, cut hobstars and fans, starcut design on base, tapered sides, round shape, 3½" high, 12" diameter*	60.00	80.00	70.00
☐ **Bowl,** *overlay of cobalt, cut hobstars and fans, tapered sides, starcut design on base, tapered sides, round shape, 3½" high, 12" diameter*	60.00	80.00	70.00
☐ **Cake Plate,** *overlay of amethyst, cut wave design surrounding hobstars and diamonds, notched and scalloped rim, 11¼" diameter*	40.00	60.00	50.00
☐ **Cologne Bottle,** *ruby red with frosting around center, ruby circles and medallion have etched scene of deer, ruby cut stopper, 7⅜" high, 2½" diameter*	150.00	200.00	160.00
☐ **Compote,** *overlay of green, triangles with caning, thumbprints and sunburst design, notched and paneled shafts, starcut design on base, 6" high, 7½" diameter*	35.00	70.00	45.00
☐ **Decanter,** *cobalt with bullseye and fan cuts, paneled neck, clear stopper, 12½" high*	55.00	75.00	65.00

Bohemian Decanter, *cranberry forest design, etched, 15" high,* **$185.00-$200.00**

	Current Price Range		P/Y Average
☐ **Dish,** *overlay of green with three large cut fans, thumbprint and marquise on border, footed, round shape, 3¼" high, 8" diameter* .	45.00	65.00	50.00
☐ **Vase,** *overlay of amethyst, graduated sizes of cut panels, 10" high*	25.00	50.00	35.00
☐ **Vase,** *overlay of cobalt, trumpet shape, cut pinwheels, diamonds and fans, 12" high*	60.00	100.00	80.00
☐ **Vase,** *overlay of cobalt, trumpet shape, graduated sizes of cut panels, 7" high*	30.00	50.00	40.00
☐ **Vase,** *overlay of cranberry, cut spiked diamond and notched leaves, tapered base, cylindrical shape*	60.00	80.00	70.00
☐ **Vase,** *overlay with diamond cuts*	80.00	110.00	90.00

BRISTOL

	Current Price Range		P/Y Average
☐ **Cologne Bottle,** *finish of apple green satin, green reeded handles trimmed in gold, matching scalloped stopper, 9⅜" high, 3⅜" diameter*	130.00	190.00	140.00
☐ **Lustres,** *gold decorated blue combination of glossy and satin finish, each lustre has eight crystal cut, spear point prisms, 10¾" high, 5" diameter*	320.00	370.00	325.00

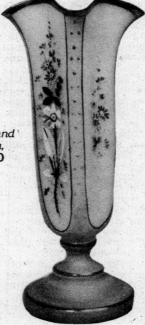

Bristol Vase, *frosted mauve and white, enamel floral decoration, 10½" high,* **$85.00-$100.00**

	Current Price Range		P/Y Average

☐ **Sweetmeat Jar,** *of pink overlay, silver plated lid, handle and rim around base, white interior, floral decoration of blue and white and enameled duck in flight, 5" high 3" diameter* — 120.00 / 160.00 / 135.00

☐ **Vase,** *decorated turquoise blue, gray, purple and yellow bird of enamel on front, flowers of pink and white with green leaves, bug decoration on back, dots of white and bands of gold adorn pedestal base, flattened oval shape, 2½" high, 4¼" diameter* . . . . — 200.00 / 240.00 / 210.00

☐ **Vase,** *of pink overlay, scalloped cut top with gold trim, decorated in blue, white and orange enameled flowers, white heron outlined in blue dot pattern, 15" high, 5" diameter* . . . . — 210.00 / 270.00 / 230.00

☐ **Vases,** *narrow necks, globular shape, 6½" high* — 25.00 / 40.00 / 30.00

BURGUN & SCHVERER

☐ **Bowl,** *half-spherical, wide mouth with sawtooth, light green streaked with red, enameled with cherry blossoms and leaves in light pink, white, green, and brown, overlaid and carved in clear, gilding, 7" diameter, c. 1895* . — 4000.00 / 6000.00 / 4100.00

☐ **Bowl,** *waisted dome body, flaring rolled lip, lobed circular foot, brownish-yellow streaked with green background, cut with wild animals and flowers within black enamel bands, background cut with spiraling garlands, enameled orange leaves around mouth, 5⅛" diameter, c. 1895* . . . . — 3000.00 / 4000.00 / 3250.00

☐ **Bowl,** *wide circular body, waisted standard, slightly flaring foot, sawtooth rim, light green with red-streaked background, enameled with poppies, grass, and leaves in light pink, white, green, and brown, overlaid clear with carving, gilding, 6", diameter, c. 1895* . . . . . . — 4000.00 / 5000.00 / 4100.00

☐ **Vase,** *bulbous body, cylinder neck slightly expanding towards sawtooth lip, pale yellow with brown streaks, enameled with flowers and leaves in blue and green, overlaid in clear, an applied scroll of foliage twining around neck, gilding, 5½" high, c. 1895* . . . . — 2000.00 / 3000.00 / 2100.00

☐ **Vase,** *bulbous body with long cylinder neck, gray shading towards base to lavender, overlaid in clear, carved with flowers and leaves of white, light yellow, and green, sawtooth neck, gilding, 5¾" high, c. 1895* . . . . . . — 2000.00 / 3000.00 / 2100.00

☐ **Vase,** *cabinet, baluster shape, sawtooth neck, yellow and beige background, overlaid in clear, carved with flowers and leaves of lavender, white, green, and brown, gilding, 5¼" high, c. 1895* . . . . — 3000.00 / 4000.00 / 3100.00

	Current Price Range		P/Y Average

☐ **Vase,** *cabinet, spherical body, short cylinder neck with flaring lip, three clear feet, frosted gray with lavender streaked background, overlaid in lavender, cut with bleeding hearts and leaves, gilding highlights, 3⅛" high, c. 1895* .. | 600.00 | 800.00 | 615.00

BURMESE

☐ **Cruet,** *Mt. Washington, acid finish, melon ribbed, undecorated, second fired yellow edge on spout, very fine color, 6½" high* .... | 900.00 | 1400.00 | 950.00

☐ **Cruet,** *Mt. Washington, acid finish, ribbed, matching ribbed stopper, yellow handle, 7" high, 3¾" diameter* .... | 775.00 | 900.00 | 785.00

☐ **Fairy Lamp,** *acid finish, superb color, deep salmon pink shades evenly to creamy yellow, rare pressed burmese base, clear inside cup, base marked Clarke, 5" high, 3⅞" diameter* .. | 375.00 | 475.00 | 385.00

☐ **Fairy Lamp,** *acid finish, superb color, rich salmon pink shades evenly to yellow, on matching ruffed reversible base, clear marked Clarke cup, 5¾" high, 7" diameter* .... | 500.00 | 700.00 | 525.00

☐ **Fairy Lamp,** *Webb, acid finish, dome on signed Clarkes candle cup* .... | 225.00 | 250.00 | 230.00

☐ **Fairy Lamp,** *Webb, acid finish, gold decorated Aladdin shape muted green Tunnecliffe pottery base, shade is decorated with red flowers and green leaves, base marked Clarke inside, 6½" high* .... | 675.00 | 750.00 | 685.00

☐ **Fairy Lamp,** *Webb, acid finish, superb color, matching unsigned fluted burmese bowl base with three yellow feet, pressed burmese insert signed Clarke, clear candle cup, large burmese dome shade, 6½" high, 4¼" diameter* .... | 685.00 | 800.00 | 700.00

☐ **Muffineer,** *Mt. Washington, acid finish, white and colored dots form delicate blossoms, attributed to Timothy Canty, 4½" high* ..... | 575.00 | 650.00 | 580.00

☐ **Rosebowl,** *miniature, Webb, acid finish, crimped top, decorated with red berries, green and brown leaves, unsigned, 2½" high, 2¾" diameter* .... | 275.00 | 350.00 | 285.00

☐ **Sugar and Creamer Set,** *Mt. Washington, acid finish, no decoration, 3¾" creamer has applied handle, open sugar is 2⅛" high* ..... | 550.00 | 650.00 | 575.00

☐ **Table Lamp,** *probably Mt. Washington, shade has satin exterior, shiny interior, fine color, base is originally Kerosene, converted to electricity, made of Brittania metal in England, has embossed florals, shade is 10" diameter, total height is 15"* .... | 1000.00 | 2000.00 | 1200.00

☐ **Toothpick Holder,** *acid finish, bulbous with square top, decorated with dainty brown leaves, white and blue enameled flowers, 3" high, 2½" diameter* .... | 230.00 | 330.00 | 245.00

	Current Price Range		P/Y Average

☐ **Toothpick Holder,** *acid finish, square top, 2⅝" high, 2½" diameter* 125.00   175.00   135.00

☐ **Vase,** *acid finish, ribbed, scalloped top, 3¾" high, 2½" diameter* 150.00   225.00   165.00

☐ **Vase,** *shiny finish, ruffled top, 3¾" high, 3" diameter* 150.00   200.00   160.00

☐ **Vase,** *acid finish, salmon pink shades evenly to yellow, enameled decoration features red buds and green leaves unsigned but attributed to Webb, 8" high, 4" diameter* 700.00   900.00   725.00

☐ **Vase,** *acid finish, undecorated, 3¾" high, 5¼" diameter at widest point* 175.00   275.00   180.00

☐ **Vase,** *Mt. Washington, beautiful coloration, enameled multicolor stylized blossoms and foliage, two applied handles, 10½" high* 1150.00   1350.00   1200.00

☐ **Vase,** *Mt. Washington, bottle, acid finish, salmon pink evenly shaded to yellow, white enameled mums and dainty green foliage, 6⅜" high, 3¼" diameter* 225.00   325.00   250.00

☐ **Vase,** *Mt. Washington, bulbous base, long slender neck, decorated with sacred ibis, oasis scene in raised gold, 12" high, 7" diameter at widest point* 2500.00   3500.00   750.00

☐ **Vase,** *Mt. Washington, egg shaped, acid finish, decorated with daisies and foliage in three shades of gold enamel, designs outlined in raised gold, 9" high, 4¾" diameter at widest point* 650.00   750.00   75.00

☐ **Vase,** *Mt. Washington, jack-in-pulpit, acid finish, very good color, flared crimped top, 12½" high, 5" diameter at top* 600.00   700.00   625.00

☐ **Vase,** *Mt. Washington, teardrop shape, elaborate blossom and foliage multicolored and gold decoration, raised gold dots, fancy scrolls, 10½" high, 5½" diameter at widest point* 1500.00   2500.00   1750.00

☐ **Vase,** *Webb, acid finish, flower petal top, salmon pink shades evenly to yellow, decorated with green leaves and red berries, 3⅜" high, 3⅛" diameter* 300.00   385.00   315.00

☐ **Vase,** *Webb, acid finish, fluted top, slightly embossed striped effect, 3½" high, 3" diameter* 175.00   270.00   185.00

☐ **Vase,** *Webb, acid finish, ruffled top and base, 4½" high, 2¾" diameter* 175.00   270.00   185.00

☐ **Vase,** *Webb, acid finish, ruffled top, salmon pink shades evenly to yellow, decorated with lavender five petal flower, green and brown leaves, unsigned, 4⅛" high, 2¾" diameter* . .   295.00   395.00   300.00

☐ **Vase,** *Webb, acid finish, ruffled top, widely flared, ball shape body, unsigned, 3⅛" high* .   175.00   275.00   180.00

☐ **Vase,** *Webb, acid finish, salmon pink shades evenly to yellow, decorated with green foliage and red buds, unusual shape, 4⅜" high, 2½" diameter* 300.00   400.00   325.00

	Current Price Range		P/Y Average

☐ **Vase,** *Webb, Queen's, acid finish, bottle, salmon pink shades evenly to yellow green ivy leaf enameled decoration, signed Thos. Webb Queens Burmese Ware, 7¾" high, 4½" diameter* 800.00 1000.00 825.00

☐ **Vase,** *Webb, Queen's, acid finish, flower petal top. salmon pink shades evenly to yellow, decorated with green and brown leaves, red berries, signed Thos. Webb Queens Burmese Ware, 2¾" high, 3¼" diameter* 375.00 475.00 400.00

☐ **Vase,** *Webb, Queen's, acid finish, flower shaped top, unusual frosted edging, salmon pink shades evenly to yellow, tan pine cone enameled decoration, signed Thos. Webb Queens Burmese Ware, 5⅝" high, 3⅛" diameter* 500.00 700.00 550.00

☐ **Whiskey Tumbler,** *Mt. Washington, acid finish, diamond quilted, reheated yellow top edge, 2¾" high, 2¼" diameter* 150.00 220.00 165.00

CAMEO

☐ **Bowl,** *English, ribbed, thin outer layer of various pink shades, white inner layer, acid cut back in fish scale motif, decorated with morning glory vine and butterfly in gold enamel, 3" base, 7½" at widest point, 6¼" top diameter, signed in enamel G.L.F., paper label Whitlow collecton* 900.00 1100.00 950.00

☐ **Perfume Bottle,** *English, round, dark blue ground, profusely decorated with deeply carved and finely detailed white blossoms, foliage and butterfly, sterling, screw-type stopper, 7¼" high, 5" diameter* 1800.00 2500.00 1900.00

☐ **Vase,** *English, four layers, white to red to clear to green, depicts raspberries and foliage, very elaborate top border, 7" high, 4½" diameter at widest point, unsigned* 2000.00 3000.00 2250.00

☐ **Vase,** *signed by Michel Paris, translucent, frosted background with brown cut to yellow, sailboat scene, three detailed acid cuttings, 8½" high, 3½" diameter* 800.00 850.00 820.00

CASED

☐ **Lustres,** *white with cranberry banding, circular medallions, hand painted flowers, ruffled rims, pedestal bases, spearpoint prisms, 12⅝" high* 70.00 160.00 110.00

☐ **Perfume Bottle,** *decorated yellow, clear ball stopper has covering of gold, sanded gold leaves and ribbon studded with applied jewels of green and red, 5½" high, 2⅛" diameter* 100.00 140.00 110.00

	Current Price Range		P/Y Average

☐ **Rose Bowl,** *amethyst, applied flower in white with transparent, applied branch and leaf, 3¾" high, 4" diameter, rare* . . . . | 150.00 | 200.00 | 175.00 |

☐ **Rose Bowl,** *pink hobnail design, eight crimp top, 3⅛" high, 3⅝" diameter* . . . . | 90.00 | 130.00 | 115.00 |

CORALENE

☐ **Pitcher,** *orange glass, amber applied handle and rigaree of amber surrounds neck, water lilies of white and green leaves in Coralene beading decoration, 6¼" high, 4" diameter* . | 210.00 | 250.00 | 215.00 |

☐ **Lamp Base,** *satin glass of decorated yellow, fern leaf sprays of pale yellow in beaded Coralene of yellow, original brass burner, 7⅝" high, 3" diameter* . . . . | 150.00 | 200.00 | 160.00 |

☐ **Vase,** *seaweed decoration on pale blue diamond quilted mother of pearl, coralene blossoms have applied jewel center, 7" high* . . . . | 450.00 | 550.00 | 475.00 |

☐ **Vase,** *seaweed, pink decoration on gold diamond quilted mother of pearl, 6¾" high* . . . . | 450.00 | 550.00 | 475.00 |

CRANBERRY

☐ **Bowl,** *applied crystal berries on top edge, berry pontil plus three crystal fans applied around top, three reeded scroll feet, 5½" high, 5½" diameter* . . . . | 280.00 | 330.00 | 290.00 |

☐ **Bowl,** *clear reeded scroll feet, six clear berry prunts around top, three crystal fan shaped applied designs on bowl, berry on base, 5⅜" high, 6⅛" diameter* . . . . | 225.00 | 300.00 | 250.00 |

☐ **Bowl,** *two rows of crystal applied shell trim, applied rigaree around center, three crystal reeded scroll feet, base has berry prunt, 4¾" high, 8" diameter* . . . . | 420.00 | 480.00 | 430.00 |

☐ **Cologne Bottle,** *frosted with gold decorations, clear ball stopper adorned in gold, 5¾" high, 3⅛" diameter* . . . . | 180.00 | 220.00 | 185.00 |

☐ **Fairy Lamp,** *frosted, shade has crimped top, signed Clarke base, 3¾" high, 2⅞" diameter* | 110.00 | 150.00 | 115.00 |

☐ **Liqueur Set on Tray,** *decorated in heavy gold, tray has square, scalloped edge, 8" diameter, bottle has applique on sides with flower basket and butterfly decoration, 9¼" high, set of six glasses, matching, 2" high* . . . . | 250.00 | 300.00 | 255.00 |

☐ **Lustres,** *clear crystal prisms, pair, 11" high* . | 110.00 | 160.00 | 130.00 |

☐ **Pitcher,** *inverted thumbprint, bulbous with square top, clear applied handles, 5⅞" high, 3½" diameter* . . . . | 85.00 | 120.00 | 90.00 |

☐ **Vase,** *clear reeded applied handles, enameled flowers of blue and white with gold foliage, 11½" high, 6¾" diameter* . . . . | 320.00 | 360.00 | 325.00 |

Cranberry Pickle Castor, *sterling holder with fork, 11¾" high,* **$225.00-$250.00**

Cranberry Thumbprint Basket, *applied crystal handle, 10" high,* **$65.00-$80.00**

	Current Price Range		P/Y Average
☐ **Vase,** *decorated with gold enamel and blue and white forget-me-nots, 11" high, 4" diameter*	120.00	160.00	130.00
☐ **Vase,** *ewer, Moser-type, enameled, clear twig handle, 11½" high*	30.00	70.00	45.00
☐ **Vase,** *fan shaped, deep cranberry color, clear applied ruffle around top edge, clear applied wishbone feet, decorated with small enameled multicolored leaves, blue and white flowers on gold panel, 10¾" high*	185.00	225.00	190.00
☐ **Vase,** *hand painted circular plaque of young child in porcelain, some fired gold foliage and bird design, pedestal base, inverted heart shape, 5" high*	30.00	60.00	45.00

	Current Price Range		P/Y Average
☐ **Vases,** *pair, decorated with gold sanded flowers and leaves outlined in white with blue centers, small white enameled flowers and branches, gold sanded top and bottom bands, 10" high, 3¾" diameter*	275.00	330.00	285.00
☐ **Vases,** *pair, deep cranberry color, lavishly decorated with gold, blue and white flowers and leaves, 11" high, 4" diameter*	300.00	400.00	325.00
☐ **Water Pitcher,** *optic effect, clear applied handle, very large, 12¾" high, 6¼" diameter* . . .	250.00	320.00	275.00
☐ **Wine Glasses,** *cranberry bowls with clear stems and feet, belltone, set of six, 5⅛, 2¼" diameter*	160.00	200.00	165.00

CROWN MILANO

	Current Price Range		P/Y Average
☐ **Ewer,** *Mt. Washington, applied handle, profuse eight-color geometric decoration, 13" high, unsigned*	1600.00	2000.00	1700.00
☐ **Ewer,** *Mt. Washington, unusual pastel lilac decoration depicts reclining shepherdess with her sheep, back decorated with birds and roses, raised gold wreaths surround both panels, small pastel lilac wreaths elsewhere, 10½" high, 8½" diameter across front*	2500.00	3500.00	2650.00

Crown Milano Biscuit Jar, *enamel decoration, silver plated lid,* **$900.00-$1000.00**

	Current Price Range		P/Y Average
☐ **Cracker Jar,** Mt. Washington, melon ribbed, cream ground, colorful nasturtuim enameled decoration, silver plated bail and lid, lid is signed J.P.C.E.P.N.S., 8" high to top of fully extended bail, 7" diameter	500.00	600.00	530.00
☐ **Decanter,** with hollow stopper, shiny finish, decorated with exquisite enamel roses and profuse gold scrolls on neck and stopper, 10" high and 6" wide at bulbous base, rare early Albertine/Crown Milano signature	1000.00	1400.00	1150.00
☐ **Jam Jar,** white body, slightest hint of pink at shoulders and base, decorated with very delicate blue and white forget-me-nots, silver plated lid and bail is signed Sant & Co., signed jar, body is 4" high, overall height to top of extended bail is 7"	350.00	450.00	375.00
☐ **Pickle Castor,** Mt. Washington-Pairpoint, pansy decoration, silver plated lid signed M.W., holder has Pairpoint mark, both resilvered, bowl is 4" high, 4½" diameter, holder is 10" tall	1000.00	1200.00	1025.00
☐ **Plate,** rose and fired gold scrolling, enameled dots on three reserves, 11" diameter	120.00	180.00	150.00
☐ **Rose Bowl,** Mt. Washington, all over decoration of roses, buds, leaves, gold trim, purple numbered pontil	350.00	425.00	365.00
☐ **Salt Shaker,** cockle shell, Mt. Washington, white satin body, dainty enamel blossoms, silver plated top shaped like seashell	385.00	485.00	390.00
☐ **Tray,** Mt. Washington, shiny finish, rolled and serrated edges, enamel thistle and foliage decoration, outlined with raised gold, 9½" long, 7" wide, signed	825.00	1000.00	40.00
☐ **Urn,** with rare crown shaped lid, raised gold blossom and foliage decoration, 16½" high, 8" wide, 5½" deep, signed	2800.00	3300.00	2900.00
☐ **Vase,** early Guba, tall and slender, shiny finish, decorated with four flying ducks over raised gold wheat field, 17" high, 4½" diameter, signed with Crown Milano/Albertine mark which features a crown within a crown	3500.00	4200.00	3650.00
☐ **Vase,** Guba, decorated with five ducks on front, three in back, two applied handles, excellent professional repair to base	2000.00	2250.00	2100.00
☐ **Vase,** Mt. Washington, bulbous, cream colored body with slender neck, gold blossoms and jewels covered with gold enamel, 12½" high, signed	825.00	1000.00	840.00
☐ **Vase,** Mt. Washington, cone shaped, enamel floral bouquet decoration, 8¾" high, signed	850.00	975.00	865.00
☐ **Vase,** square shaped, rounded corners, two delicate applied handles, decorated with pastel enamels in tiny free form geometric patterns, 8" high, unsigned	720.00	820.00	730.00

	Current Price Range		P/Y Average

☐ **Vase,** Mt. Washington, square with rounded corners, two applied scroll handles, cream ground, decoration of gold and colorful enamel oak leaves and gold acorns, original paper label, 8¼ " high 950.00 1100.00 975.00

D'ARGENTHAL

☐ **Bowl,** double-conical shape, wide with waisted neck and foot, slightly flaring rim, yellow background, overlaid in red, carved with roses, leaves, and branches, signed, 12" diameter, c. 1900 . . . . 1000.00 1400.00 1100.00

☐ **Bowl,** swollen spherical, indulated rim scalloped, yellow background, overlaid in maroon, cut with roses, signed, 6" diameter, c. 1900 . . . . 600.00 700.00 650.00

☐ **Box,** covered, shallow circular shape, dark yellow background, overlaid in brown and umber, cut with wildflowers and leaves, signed, 3¾" diameter, c. 1915 . . . . 400.00 600.00 425.00

☐ **Vase,** baluster shape, light yellow background splashed with red, overlaid in red, cut with landscape of lake, arched bridge, and trees, signed, 13¾" high, c. 1910 . . . . 2000.00 3000.00 2100.00

☐ **Vase,** baluster shape, turquoise background, overlaid in dark blue, cut with flowers and leaves, signed 7" high, c. 1900 . . . . 400.00 500.00 425.00

☐ **Vase,** cylinder shape tapering towards lip, short circular foot, orange-yellow background, overlaid in red, cut with leafy branches, trumpet blossoms, signed, 11¾" high, c. 1900 . . . . 700.00 1000.00 750.00

☐ **Vase,** cylinder, slight tapering towards base, waisted neck, flaring lip, frosted yellow background, overlaid in brown, cut with scrolling vines in bloom, signed, 13¾" high, c. 1900 . . 1000.00 1500.00 1100.00

☐ **Vase,** ovoid body, pink shading to lavender, cut with orchids and leaves, signed, 6" high, c. 1900 . . . . 400.00 600.00 425.00

DESIRE CHRISTIAN

☐ **Bowl,** bulbous shape, wide mouth, short circular foot, pale green shading to lime green and turquoise, overlaid in lime green, carved lily pads, blossoms, and flying dragonfly, signed, 6" diameter, c. 1895 . . . . 1200.00 1400.00 1250.00

☐ **Vase,** bud, compressed spherical body with long cylinder neck tapering towards flared rim, dark burnt brown with lavender tinge shading to olive green and beige, overlaid in lavender, carved with milkweeds, leaves, and grass, signed, 12⅝" high, c. 1895 . . . . 3000.00 4000.00 3100.00

	Current Price Range		P/Y Average

☐ **Vase,** *elongated cylinder expanding to swollen neck, knopped base, spreading foot, gray splashed with red background, carved with two orchids on two long stems and leaves and grass around base, signed, 14⅜" high, c. 1895* 2000.00 3000.00 2100.00

DE VEZ

☐ **Vase,** *acid finish background, dark green shaded to rose landscape scene in three acid cuttings, signed, 9⅜" high, 2⅝" diameter ....* 620.00 680.00 630.00
☐ **Vase,** *acid finish background of blue with mountain landscape scenes on three, detailed acid cuttings, signed, 11½" high, 3¾" diameter ....* 720.00 770.00 730.00
☐ **Vase,** *acid finish background of shell pink with navy blue shaded to yellow shaded to pink in three acid cuttings, mountain scene, signed, 6½" high, 2⅞" diameter ....* 630.00 690.00 640.00
☐ **Vase,** *bulbous body sloping towards long cylinder neck, light pink background, overlaid in yellow and blue, cut with scene with squirrels in trees in the foreground and mountains in the distance, signed, 13" high, c. 1900 ....* 1100.00 1400.00 1150.00
☐ **Vase,** *cylinder shape expanding toward a flaring rim, flaring circular foot, yellow background splashed with orange and green, cut with river scene, signed, 5¼" high, c. 1910 ..* 700.00 800.00 725.00
☐ **Vase,** *cylinder shape tapering toward the neck, milky, overlaid in lavender shading to pink, cut with cartouches enclosing river landscape, 9¾" high, c. 1900 ....* 800.00 1000.00 810.00
☐ **Vase,** *elongated pear shape, short cylinder neck, yellow background streaked with orange, overlaid in dark blue, cut with river scene, signed, 5½" high, c. 1910 ....* 700.00 800.00 725.00
☐ **Vase,** *pear shape body, long cylinder neck, flared rim, yellow background, overlaid in orange and blue, cut with a river scene, signed, 6" high, c. 1910 ....* 700.00 800.00 725.00
☐ **Vase,** *trumpet, acid finish background, navy blue shaded to rose in three acid cuttings, bird on branch, foliage frames scene, gold plated brass base with leaves, 18¾" high, 6⅜" diameter ....* 2000.00 2200.00 2100.00

DURAND

☐ **Plate,** *flashed ruby with white pulled feathers, hatched pontil, underside features Bridgeton Rose engraving by Charles Link, 8" diameter ....* 275.00 375.00 285.00
☐ **Vase,** *baluster shape, waisted and flaring neck, flattened circular foot, amber iridescence with opalescent trails, 8⅛" high, c. 1900-1930 ....* 300.00 400.00 350.00

	Current Price Range		P/Y Average

☐ **Vase,** *bulbous shape, iridescent blue, wide flared neck, 8½" high* .... — 175.00 — 230.00 — 210.00

☐ **Vase,** *compressed bulbous, flattened shoulders, waisted and lobed neck, flaring rim, blue iridescence, signed, 8½" diameter, c. 1905-1930* .... — 350.00 — 450.00 — 375.00

☐ **Vase,** *compressed spherical base, cylinder neck expanding into trumpet-shape, green background, undulating bands in amber iridescence, signed, 12" high, c. 1905-1930* .... — 1200.00 — 1600.00 — 1250.00

☐ **Vase,** *compressed spherical body, lobed neck, blue, 8½" high* .... — 350.00 — 450.00 — 375.00

☐ **Vase,** *compressed spherical, trumpet-like neck, short circular foot, blue iridescence, signed, 9¼" high, c. 1905-1930* .... — 300.00 — 400.00 — 350.00

☐ **Vase,** *conical, iridescent gold leaf and vine design, flared rim, 7" high* .... — 250.00 — 400.00 — 310.00

☐ **Vase,** *cylindrical, flaring rim, circular base, amber decorated with opalescent interlacing designs, 8⅛" high* .... — 700.00 — 800.00 — 725.00

☐ **Vase,** *cylindrical, iridescent platinum "King Tut" pattern, wide, narrow mouth, 8" high* ... — 250.00 — 400.00 — 310.00

☐ **Vase,** *cylindrical, scalloped rim, short circular base, opalescent glass decorated with green hearts and vines, 11" high* .... — 700.00 — 800.00 — 725.00

☐ **Vase,** *cylindrical, expanding towards the shoulders, waisted neck, flaring rim, flattened circular foot, blue iridescent, amber iridescent foot, signed, 14¼" high* .... — 300.00 — 400.00 — 375.00

☐ **Vase,** *cylindrical, swollen shoulders, everted lip, silvery-blue, signed, 6⅛" high, c. 1905-1920* .... — 300.00 — 500.00 — 375.00

☐ **Vase,** *elongated ovoid, waisted neck, flattened flaring rim, short circular foot, blue iridescent background, opalescent clinging heart vine, 10½" high, c. 1905-1930* .... — 300.00 — 500.00 — 375.00

☐ **Vase,** *ovoid shape, flaring neck, iridescent blue, signed, 10¼" high, c. 1905-1925* ...... — 400.00 — 500.00 — 425.00

☐ **Vase,** *urn shape, blue iridescent background, with white heart and trailing vine overlay, 7⅛" high, 1905-1925* .... — 400.00 — 600.00 — 425.00

LE VERRE FRANCAIS

☐ **Vase,** *cameo, ovoid-shaped, waisted neck, flaring rim, mottled pink background, cut in daisies around the shoulder, overlaid in lavender deepening to amethyst around the base, 4½" high, c. 1925* .... — 200.00 — 300.00 — 250.00

☐ **Vase,** *cameo, trumpet-shaped, mottled orange and yellow background, cut with bouquets of flowers and leaves in bright orange darkening to a deep purple, signed, 18⅛" high, c. 1925* .... — 200.00 — 300.00 — 250.00

Le Verre Français Vase,
*French Cameo glass, orange
and blue, signed, 5" high,*
$600.00-$700.00

	Current Price Range		P/Y Average
☐ **Vase,** compressed spherical tapering to trumpet-shaped neck, green background, overlaid in mottled orange, brown, and green, carved with flowers with honeycomb pattern around the base, 16¾" high, c. 1920	400.00	600.00	425.00
☐ **Vase,** cylinder body tapering towards neck, waisted neck and foot slightly flaring rim, mottled pink background, overlaid in orange shading to green and turquoise, cut with blossoms and leaves, honeycomb design on neck, 26" high, c. 1930	600.00	800.00	650.00
☐ **Vase,** spherical-shaped with thin cylinder neck, flaring rim, yellow background, cut in flowers and tendrils in blue and orange, signed, 12" high, c. 1925	250.00	400.00	275.00

LOETZ

	Current Price Range		P/Y Average
☐ **Biscuit Jar,** iridescent purple shaded to black, swing handle, silverplate lid, 9" high . .	60.00	120.00	90.00
☐ **Bowl,** bulbous body with waisted base and neck, flaring rim, magenta background, silvery-blue designs of ripples, 10" diameter, c. 1900	900.00	1100.00	950.00
☐ **Bowl,** bulbous shape, green iridescent, swirl decoration, pinched form, 5½" high	80.00	130.00	100.00
☐ **Bowl,** circular, green iridescent, fluted, 7½" diameter	70.00	100.00	85.00

	Current Price Range		P/Y Average
□ **Bowl,** deeply curved, pinched rim which curves in, clear, silvery-blue oil spots, 7" high, c. 1900	100.00	150.00	115.00
□ **Bowl,** ovoid shape, crimped lip and sides, slightly flaring rim, short circular foot, oil-spotted yellow background with blue striations, 10¼" long, c. 1900	900.00	1000.00	920.00
□ **Bowl,** ovoid-shaped, silvery amber iridescent background, amber iridescent wave pattern, ruffled neck, unsigned, c. 1900	300.00	400.00	310.00
□ **Lamp,** iridescent cylinder body with spherical shade, sits in bronze stand which encircles the cylinder body and ends in a triangular base, body in salmon with amber and silvery-blue oil spots, 19½" high, c. 1900	600.00	1000.00	700.00
□ **Lamp,** melon-shaped base, silvery-blue oil spots, helmet-shaped shade in avocado green, both with four vertical hobnail band, 11" high, c. 1900 . . . .:	1000.00	1500.00	1100.00
□ **Vase,** baluster body, expanding to swollen ovoid at upper portion, waisted neck, flaring lip, flaring circular foot, amber iridescent background, loops and trails in orange, silvery-blue, and amber iridescent, 6¼" high, c. 1900	600.00	800.00	650.00
□ **Vase,** baluster shape, flaring lip, spreading circular base, pale iridescent orange, orange straited lappets around lip, rose spotting around the foot, 8¼" high, c. 1900	200.00	300.00	220.00

Loetz Vase, *art nouveau design, metallic overlay,* 6" *high,*
$345.00-$370.00

	Current Price Range		P/Y Average

☐ **Vase,** *baluster shape, triangular mouth, orange oil spots, loops and swirls in silvery-blue and iridescent amber, 8¼" high, c. 1900* — 200.00 — 300.00 — 215.00

☐ **Vase,** *bulbous base tapering to long cylinder neck, everted rim, light orange background, lavender feathering, silvery-blue iridescent oil spots, overlaid in silver, 10½" high, c. 1900* .... — 600.00 — 1000.00 — 650.00

☐ **Vase,** *blue and green, iridescent pinched shoulder and ruffled collar, Loetz Austria etched on bottom, 7" high* .... — 320.00 — 420.00 — 375.00

MARY GREGORY

☐ **Box,** *cobalt blue, round, hinged lid, ormolu feet, white enameled decoration depicts young girl holding bird, white floral sprays, 5" high, 5⅜" diameter* .... — 350.00 — 450.00 — 365.00

☐ **Box,** *emerald green, puffy shape, lift off lid, white enameled decoration depicts young girl, 3" high, 3⅝" diameter* .... — 90.00 — 130.00 — 95.00

☐ **Box,** *lime green, hinged lid, white enameled decoration depicts young boy, hinged, 1¾" high, 2⅜" diameter* .... — 120.00 — 150.00 — 125.00

☐ **Box,** *lime green, round, hinged lid, white enameled decoration depicts young girl, floral sprays on sides, 3" high, 3¼" diameter* — 130.00 — 175.00 — 135.00

☐ **Box,** *patch, cobalt, round, hinged lid, white enameled decoration depicts little boy, white enamel dots around sides, 1⅛" high, 2" diameter* .... — 150.00 — 180.00 — 155.00

☐ **Box,** *patch, round, lime green, white enameled decoration depicts young girl, hinged, 1⅜" high, 2⅛" diameter* .... — 120.00 — 150.00 — 125.00

☐ **Box,** *sapphire blue, round, hinged lid, white enameled decoration depicts young girl, white dot trim around sides, 2⅝" high, 3¼" diameter* .... — 130.00 — 175.00 — 135.00

☐ **Plate,** *cobalt, white enameled decoration depicts girl with butterfly net, original ormolu compote stand, three round rings hang from holder, 6¼" diameter* .... — 140.00 — 170.00 — 145.00

☐ **Spa Glass,** *amber, flattened oval shape, white enameled decoration depicts little girl carrying basket, 4⅛" high, 2⅜" diameter* .... — 90.00 — 120.00 — 95.00

☐ **Tumbler,** *cranberry, white enameled decoration depicts young girl, 4¼" high, 2½" diameter* .... — 50.00 — 85.00 — 60.00

☐ **Vase,** *covered, cobalt blue, white enameled decoration depicts young girl carrying flower basket, enameled dot bands around top and lid, 14" high, 5½" diameter* .... — 275.00 — 375.00 — 285.00

☐ **Vase,** *cranberry, white enameled decoration depicts young boy wearing hat, 7¾" high* ... — 100.00 — 150.00 — 110.00

	Current Price Range		P/Y Average
☐ **Vase,** *green, with applied handles in clear, boy picking flowers decoration in white enamel, 10½" high*	130.00	180.00	145.00
☐ **Vase,** *sapphire blue, cut scalloped top, white enameled decoration depicts young boy holding goblet, fancy metal base mount of plated brass with woman's head handles on each side, 14¼" high, 3¾" diameter*	200.00	275.00	220.00
☐ **Wine Bottle,** *cranberry, white enameled decoration depicts girl holding bouquet, original clear bubble stopper, 9" high, 3⅛" diameter* .	140.00	170.00	145.00

MOSER

☐ **Box,** *decorated amethyst, three applied salamanders in amber for feet that are trimmed in gold, amber salamander trimmed in gold on lid, enameled flowers of pink and green foliage, hinged, 4⅜" high*	600.00	650.00	610.00

Moser Cup and Saucer, *lavender with gold gild decor,* **$150.00-$170.00**

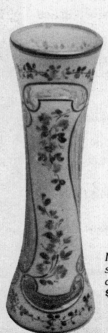

Moser Karsbad Bud Vase, *cut scroll design frames enamel floral decor,* *6" high,* **$125.00-$150.00**

	Current Price Range		P/Y Average

☐ **Juice Glass,** *cranberry, gold enamel branches, yellow, pink, turquoise and blue enamel leaves, leaves and veins outlined in raised gold, acorns, gold band at rim and base, 4" high* 150.00 225.00 175.00

☐ **Libation Jug,** *enameled decorations, strap, twig handle, signed, 9½" high* 30.00 70.00 45.00

☐ **Tumbler,** *crystal top shades to blue at base, engraved with ruffed grouse and landscape scene, acid cut decorative band at rim with gold enamel, cutting at base, 5" high, 3" diameter, signed* 350.00 400.00 360.00

☐ **Vase,** *decorated opaque pink shaded to clear, four amber reeded applied scroll feet covered in gold, gold rigaree on sides of vase, enameled eagle in relief on front, multicolored oak leaves, enameled insect decoration, applied glass acorns, 7⅞" high, 7" diameter* 1500.00 2000.00 1600.00

☐ **Vase Ewer,** *gold over crystal, enameled, multicolored flowers and green leaves, pedestal base, 5¾" high, 2¾" diameter* 150.00 200.00 160.00

☐ **Vase,** *opalescent deep pink at top shading to almost clear at base, applied crimped glass handles burnished with gold on each end of the flattened oval shape body, parrot, acorns, leaves and branches in relief and gold and multicolor enamel decoration, elaborate decoration around neck, 7½" high, 7¾" at widest point, 2½" deep, Moser signature* 850.00 950.00 875.00

☐ **Vase,** *multicolored enameled grape leaves and bee with applied yellow and red grape bunches, four applied feet of amber rosette, 5½" high, 2¼" diameter* 350.00 400.00 360.00

MOTHER-OF-PEARL

☐ **Bowl,** *blue diamond quilted, oblong, four applied feet, 8" long, 7" wide, 3" high* 250.00 350.00 275.00

☐ **Creamer,** *satin, blue raindrop, bulbous, round top, white lining, blue frosted reeded applied handle, 4½" high, 3⅛" diameter* 200.00 250.00 215.00

☐ **Fairy Lamp,** *satin glass, swirl shaded pink, white interior, clear insert cup for bulb, ruffled lampshade and base, 5" high, 5½" diameter* 420.00 480.00 435.00

☐ **Fruit Bowl,** *thin pink interior layer, air trap of interlocking diamond mother of pearl, thick exterior layer of white glass, thorn handle at one end, 10½" long, 5¾" high* 530.00 630.00 540.00

☐ **Peg Lamp,** *swirl satin glass ruffled shade and font, clear chimney, classical lady candlestick of heavy brass, 19½" high, 3½" diameter* 620.00 700.00 640.00

☐ **Perfume Bottle,** *satin glass, diamond quilted blue, white interior, silver top, 4½" high, 2⅝" diameter* 250.00 300.00 270.00

MULLER FRERES

	Current Price Range		P/Y Average

☐ **Bowl,** *inverted cone shape, waisted neck and foot, flaring rim, short circular foot, overlaid, carved, and enameled in flurogravure, harvest scene of workers in rust, orange and ochre, signed, 6¼" high, c. 1900* **2000.00 3000.00 2250.00**

☐ **Ewer,** *inverted cone shape, cylinder neck, upright spout, applied c-scroll handle, waisted short circular foot, frosted and green background, overlaid, carved, and enameled in flurogravure with blossoms and leaves, signed, 19" high, c. 1900* **2000.00 3000.00 2200.00**

☐ **Vase,** *baluster shape, frosted gray background streaked with purple and orange, enameled in black with trees, signed, 12" high, c. 1910* **800.00 1200.00 810.00**

☐ **Vase,** *baluster shape, waisted neck, spreading circular foot, frosted blue background, overlaid, carved, and enameled in flurogravure in yellow and off-white, winter scene with two dogs and hanging pheasant, signed, 9" high, c. 1900* **1800.00 2200.00 1900.00**

☐ **Vase,** *bulbous double gourd shape, background of purple acid with cameo carved decoration, narrow neck, signed, 6¼" high* **350.00 500.00 400.00**

☐ **Vase,** *bulbous shape, waisted neck, lobed lip, orange background, overlaid in black, cut with country landscape, signed, 4¼" high, c. 1910* **700.00 900.00 725.00**

☐ **Vase,** *cylinder body expanding towards shoulder, cylinder neck, applied serpentine handle, green background, enameled in flurogravure of branches of berries and leaves, in orange, brown, mustard, and gray, signed, 10¼" high, c. 1910* **1000.00 1400.00 1100.00**

OPALESCENT

☐ **Bowl,** *diamond quilted light green shaded to pink, ruffled, polished pewter frame, 17¾" high, 11¾" diameter* **210.00 250.00 215.00**

☐ **Bowl,** *flashed rainbow, fluted edge, decorated with enamel florals, 5" high* **270.00 330.00 275.00**

☐ **Ewer,** *striped white shaded to green, vaseline applied leaf and handle, appliqued flowers in pink, 8½" high, 3" diameter* **130.00 180.00 140.00**

☐ **Fairy Lamp,** *amber swirl, signed Clarke base, shaped like a pyramid, 3¾" high, 3⅛" diameter* **100.00 120.00 110.00**

☐ **Fairy Lamp,** *blue swirl satin finish, light blue glass cup and candle cup, matching square ruffled base, rare, 6½" high, 5¾" diameter* . **530.00 590.00 540.00**

☐ **Fairy Lamp,** *pink and white frosted swirl decoration, dome shape, signed Clarke candle cup, matching square ruffled vase, 5½" high, 6" diameter* **520.00 600.00 535.00**

	Current Price Range		P/Y Average

☐ **Fairy Lamp,** *pressed glass, blue embossed rib design, signed Clarke base, 3³/₄" high, 2⁷/₈" diameter* . . . . `100.00` `150.00` `110.00`

☐ **Vase,** *Jack-In-Pulpit, fluted with purple edge, 7" high, 3⁷/₈" diameter* . . . . `70.00` `100.00` `80.00`

☐ **Vase,** *white opalescent Monot Stumpf, pink shaded to off-white, pantin fan shape, belltone, interior is of lustered glass, 7" high, 6¹/₈" diameter* . . . . `220.00` `270.00` `230.00`

☐ **Vase,** *white opalescent Monot Stumpf, pink shaded to striped white, pantin ruffled fan shape, belltone, 7³/₄" high, 7¹/₂" diameter* . . . `280.00` `330.00` `290.00`

☐ **Water Tumbler,** *cranberry, ten row hobnail, 3³/₄" high, 2³/₄" diameter* . . . . `125.00` `160.00` `140.00`

☐ **Water Tumbler,** *decorated peach, white flowers have gold leaves and centers, 4" high, 2³/₄" diameter* . . . . `50.00` `100.00` `60.00`

☐ **Water Tumbler,** *lavender, light row hobnail, 3³/₄" high, 2³/₄" diameter* . . . . `125.00` `160.00` `140.00`

ORREFORS

☐ **Beaker,** *cylinder body, flaring neck, four ball feet set on flattened dome base, clear, etched jungle scene with men, women, children, palm trees, exotic birds, squirrels, and monkeys, signed, 10¹/₂" high, c. 1930* . . . . `1000.00` `1400.00` `1100.00`

☐ **Bottle,** *cylinder body, short cylinder neck, elongated dome stopper, light green, clear, decorated internally with sea grass and starfish in maroon, signed, 6¹/₄" high, c. 1938* . . . `1200.00` `1400.00` `1275.00`

☐ **Bottle,** *cylinder, thick-walled, clear, cartouche with dove and strapework, signed 6¹/₄" diameter, c. 1940* . . . . `2500.00` `3000.00` `2600.00`

☐ **Bottle,** *circular, thick-walled, stepped interior, green garlands and air bubbles embedded in walls, signed, 6¹/₂" diameter, c. 1940* . `600.00` `700.00` `620.00`

☐ **Bottle,** *cylinder with expanding neck, clear, cut with hunting scenes, signed, 8³/₄" long, c. 1927* . . . . `700.00` `800.00` `780.00`

☐ **Bottle,** *flaring, blue-tinted background, engraved scene of two maidens catching a dolphin in a net on one side, engraved dolphin on the other, stylized sunset and clouds above, scalloped border engraved around the rim, with stand, 8¹/₂" long, c. 1925* . . . . `500.00` `700.00` `550.00`

☐ **Bottle,** *octagon shape, light gray, cut with nude females and foilage, signed, 11¹/₂" long, c. 1928* . . . . `550.00` `650.00` `575.00`

OVERLAY

☐ **Bowl,** *shaded pink, fan shape with amber applied edging, hobnail effect around top, ormolu holder with tassels, 7¹/₄" high, 9³/₄" diameter* . . . . `260.00` `300.00` `265.00`

	Current Price Range		P/Y Average

□ **Fairy Lamp,** *candy striped in pink, matching candle cup, embossed, pink rib dome shade, clear applied feet, ruffled base, white interior, three parts, 5¼" high, 4⅜" diameter* . . . . — 375.00 — 420.00 — 380.00

□ **Fairy Lamp,** *dark green, shade has white interior, signed Clarke base, 4⅜" high, 3⅞" diameter* . . . . — 130.00 — 180.00 — 140.00

□ **Fairy Lamp Shade,** *dark green with white interior, signed Clarke base, 4½" high, 4" diameter* . . . . — 120.00 — 170.00 — 125.00

□ **Finger Lamp and Chimney,** *blue, shaded, clear reeded applied handle, pink and white enameled flowers and gold color foliage, 5½" high, 4¼" diameter* . . . . — 125.00 — 165.00 — 130.00

□ **Finger Lamp and Chimney,** *pink shaded, clear handle, red roses trimmed in green and dots of white, 6" high, 5" diameter* . . . . — 175.00 — 225.00 — 200.00

□ **Finger Lamp and Chimney,** *satin, lemon yellow, embossed shell and leaf, frosted reeded applied handle, 5" high, 3⅞" diameter* . . . . . . — 150.00 — 180.00 — 160.00

□ **Finger Lamp,** *blue, shaded, clear reeded, applied handle, embossed designs, 6" high, 4¼" diameter* . . . . — 135.00 — 175.00 — 140.00

□ **Goblet,** *white on crystal, dainty multicolor floral decoration, white cut to clear and outlined in gold in places, continental* . . . . — 140.00 — 160.00 — 145.00

□ **Hand Lamp and Chimney,** *shaded chartreuse green, clear reeded applied handle, scroll decoration in beige, base has panelled pattern, 5" high, 3⅝" diameter* . . . . — 130.00 — 180.00 — 140.00

□ **Rose Bowl,** *diamond quilted rose satin cut velvet, eight crimp top, white interior, 3½" high, 3¼" diameter* . . . . — 220.00 — 270.00 — 230.00

□ **Rose Bowl,** *shaded blue with embossed swirl rib design, eight crimp top, white interior, 5" high, 6" diameter* . . . . — 180.00 — 210.00 — 185.00

□ **Table Lamp,** *mushroom shape shade has pink embossed flowers and a ruffled top and clear chimney, white interior, silverplated base, 17¼" high, 6" diameter* . . . . — 330.00 — 380.00 — 340.00

□ **Vase,** *Jack-In-Pulpit, amber edged ruffled top, pink and white applied flowers with amber leaves on cream, white interior, 6⅞" high, 6⅛" diameter* . . . . — 150.00 — 200.00 — 160.00

□ **Vase,** *Jack-In-Pulpit, cranberry edged, white background, 7½" high, 6" diameter* . . . . — 130.00 — 180.00 — 140.00

□ **Vase,** *Jack-In-Pulpit, decorated blue with multicolored, enameled flowers, branches and butterfly, decorated blue interior, 5⅝" high, 4⅝" diameter* . . . . — 130.00 — 170.00 — 135.00

□ **Vase,** *Jack-In-Pulpit, green, white background, clear applied feet, 7" high, 5" diameter* . . . . — 120.00 — 150.00 — 130.00

□ **Vase,** *Jack-In-Pulpit, purple, ruffled top, white background, 7½" high, 6" diameter* . . . . — 130.00 — 180.00 — 140.00

	Current Price Range		P/Y Average

☐ **Vase,** *Jack-In-Pulpit, purple shaded to lavender, ruffled, 7¼" high, 6" diameter* 120.00   170.00   125.00

☐ **Vase,** *Jack-In-Pulpit, shaded green, clear applied feet, scalloped edges, 6⅝" high, 5½" diameter* 120.00   170.00   125.00

☐ **Vase,** *Jack-In-Pulpit, shaded maroon, white background, ruffled edging, 7" high, 6½" diameter* 140.00   175.00   150.00

☐ **Vase,** *pink, large applied crystal flower and branch, crystal around base, white interior, 8¾" high, 4⅜" diameter* 130.00   180.00   140.00

☐ **Vase,** *silver floral leaves and swag etched over green, narrow, flaring neck, pear shape, 5" high* 40.00   80.00   50.00

☐ **Vases,** *white with enameled blue flowers, clear applied edge around ruffled top, ormolu handled holder, pink interior, 12¾" high, 7" diameter* 260.00   310.00   265.00

☐ **Water Tumbler,** *overlay of decorated shaded pink, with satin blue and white flower with green leaves, gold trim, white interior, 4⅛" high, 3" diameter* 150.00   200.00   160.00

OVERSHOT

☐ **Fairy Lamp,** *amber embossed swirl, signed Clarke base, 3½" high, 2⅞" diameter* 120.00   170.00   125.00

☐ **Fairy Lamp,** *cranberry, embossed hob design, signed Clarke base, 4" high, 3" diameter* 140.00   200.00   160.00

☐ **Fairy Lamp,** *cranberry, embossed ribs, signed Clarke base, 3¾" high, 2⅞" diameter*   135.00   195.00   155.00

☐ **Fairy Lamp,** *opaque yellow, with embossed swirl pattern, signed Clarke base, 3½" high, 2⅞" diameter* 150.00   200.00   170.00

☐ **Pitcher,** *ruffled, pink and white spatter glass, bulbous three way top, clear reeded applied handle, 7⅞" high, 5¼" diameter* 150.00   200.00   160.00

PEACHBLOW

☐ **Bowl,** *New England, flared scalloped rim, 2¾" high, 5½" at widest point* 700.00   800.00   725.00

☐ **Bowl,** *porridge, New England, shiny finish, deep rich color dominates, 2¾" high, 4½" diameter* 400.00   475.00   425.00

☐ **Cruet,** *Wheeling, deepest mahogany color at top gradually shading to cream at base, clear amber faceted handle, reeded handle, 6¾" high* 1100.00   1400.00   1200.00

☐ **Pitcher,** *Wheeling, shiny finish, exquisite color, applied amber handle, 9½" high* 1000.00   1500.00   1100.00

☐ **Shade,** *gas light, New England, shiny finish, very good color, 4½" high, 6¼" diameter at top, 2¼" fitting, rare* 350.00   450.00   375.00

	Current Price Range		P/Y Average
☐ **Sugar and Creamer Set,** *Mt. Washington, pink to gray shading, egg-shell thin glass, squatty creamer is 1¾" high and 5½" across including extension of two applied handles, corset shaped pitcher is 3¾" high and 2" wide at base*	4000.00	5000.00	4300.00
☐ **Toothpick Holder,** *ruffled rim, cylindrical shape, 2¼" high*	110.00	130.00	120.00
☐ **Tumbler,** *New England, shiny finish, wild rose upper half, 3¾" high*	350.00	425.00	375.00
☐ **Vase,** *lily, New England, satin finish, beautiful wild rose color, original paper label, 8¼" high*	820.00	920.00	830.00
☐ **Vase,** *lily, New England, shiny finish, deep wild rose color covers 3" of this 9¾" high piece*	750.00	850.00	775.00
☐ **Vase,** *Morgan, Wheeling, shiny finish, exquisite candy apple red, 7¾" high*	900.00	1100.00	935.00
☐ **Vase,** *Mt. Washington, acid finish, cast in Webb Burmese shape, pink shaded to blue, flower top, very rare, 3¼" high, 3" diameter* .	800.00	1200.00	850.00
☐ **Vase,** *Mt. Washington, trumpet (lily), acid finish, pink shaded to blue, rare, 6¼" high, 2½" diameter*	900.00	1400.00	1000.00
☐ **Vase,** *New England, Wild Rose, satin finish, double gourd, deepest raspberry shading to white, 7" high, 1880s*	500.00	700.00	550.00
☐ **Vase,** *satin finish, ribbed pear design, narrow neck, 9" high*	65.00	100.00	75.00
☐ **Vase,** *Webb, glossy, dark red and pink with raised gold prunus, cream lining, 3¼" high, 2⅜" diameter*	250.00	450.00	275.00
☐ **Vase,** *Webb, glossy, rose red and pink with raised gold prunus and bird decoration, cream lining, 9" high, 4" diameter*	400.00	700.00	450.00
☐ **Vase,** *Webb, satin, rose and pink with floral and butterfly decoration in heavy gold, cream lining, 8" high, 3" diameter*	375.00	600.00	425.00
☐ **Vase,** *Webb, two applied handles, raised gold, green and silver decoration features squirrels, grapes and grape vines, 10" high*	450.00	550.00	475.00
☐ **Vases,** *rose shaded to cream, Japanese style blossoming branches, slender necks, pair, 7" high*	210.00	310.00	250.00
☐ **Water Pitcher,** *Wheeling, finest color, square top, applied amber handle, 10" high*	1000.00	1500.00	1200.00

POMONA

☐ **Juice Glass,** *first grind, delicate hobnail interior, tapered, 3¾" high, base 1½" in diameter, 2¼" in diameter at top*	60.00	80.00	65.00
☐ **Lemonade Pitcher,** *first grind, cylindrical shape, two rows of blue tinted cornflowers, 12" high, 4" diameter at base, 3" diameter at top*	950.00	1075.00	975.00

	Current Price Range		P/Y Average

☐ **Pitcher,** *New England, first grind, miniature, square top* . . . . | 90.00 | 130.00 | 100.00

☐ **Tumbler,** *New England, second grind, cornflower staining* . . . . | 60.00 | 100.00 | 70.00

☐ **Water Carafe,** *New England, second grind, cornflower staining* . . . . | 175.00 | 225.00 | 185.00

☐ **Water Set,** *pitcher and six tumblers, first grind, pitcher is 6¾" high* . . . . | 700.00 | 900.00 | 725.00

☐ **Water Tumbler,** *New England, blue cornflower pattern, second grind, 3¾" high, 2½" diameter* . . . . | 160.00 | 200.00 | 165.00

QUEZAL

☐ **Bowl,** *circular, shallow, flaring lip, mounted on circular base, iridescent, signed, 11¾" diameter, c. 1901-1925* . . . . | 300.00 | 400.00 | 320.00

☐ **Dish,** *circular shape, two ribbed handles, amber iridescence, 5½" diameter, c. 1901-1925* . . . . | 125.00 | 175.00 | 135.00

☐ **Light Shade,** *flower form, with scalloping, flared rim, iridescent yellow, signed, 5¼" high, c. 1900* . . . . | 150.00 | 200.00 | 160.00

☐ **Vase,** *elongated baluster, domed foot, light yellow background, green feather designs, highlighted with amber iridescence, 19½" high, c. 1901-1925* . . . . | 1000.00 | 1400.00 | 1100.00

☐ **Vase,** *Jack-In-The-Pulpit, flower face slightly ruffled, thin cylinder stem, flattened circular foot, opalescent, amber iridescent, striated green feathering, amber iridescence on foot, signed, 10¼" high, c. 1901-1925* . . . . | 1500.00 | 2000.00 | 1600.00

☐ **Vase,** *ovoid body with vertical lobing, wide cylinder neck, slightly flaring lip, opalescent background, green and amber iridescent draping bands, applied stringing in free form design, 6¼" high, c. 1901-1925* . . . . | 1400.00 | 1600.00 | 1480.00

☐ **Vase,** *pear shape, amber iridescent, overlaid in silver, chased with flowers and leaves, strapwork, signed, 8¾" high, c. 1905-1920* . . | 600.00 | 1000.00 | 700.00

SATIN

☐ **Bowl Vase,** *decorated yellow webb with prunus blossoms and butterfly in heavy gold, trimmed in gold, 3½" high, 4¼" diameter* . . . | 350.00 | 400.00 | 375.00

☐ **Bride's Bowl,** *overlay of decorated pink, white on bottom, maroon flowers, green, yellow and lavender leaves, frosted, ruffled edging, gold trim, 4½" high, 10½" x 9¼"* . . . . | 270.00 | 350.00 | 310.00

☐ **Ewer,** *overlay of decorated, shaded pink, applied frosted handle, small flowers of white and branches of gold, three petal top, white interior, 7¾" high, 3¼" diameter* . . . . . | 110.00 | 160.00 | 130.00

	Current Price Range		P/Y Average

☐ **Ewer,** *overlay of decorated, shaded pink, applied frosted handle, enameled flowers of white and pink, foliage of gold, white interior, 8½" high, 4¼" diameter* 140.00 190.00 165.00

☐ **Ewer,** *overlay of decorated, shaded pink, frosted, applied handle, with enameled flowers of white and pink with yellow centers, three petal top, white interior, 9¼" high, 3¾" diameter* 120.00 170.00 145.00

☐ **Fairy Lamp,** *Webb-like decoration, brown and tan leaves with cones on cream background, signed Clarke base, rare, 5⅜" high, 3⅞" diameter* 240.00 300.00 245.00

☐ **Lacemaker's Lamp,** *shade has embossed leaves, scrolls and overlapping petals with chimney, brass handled base, 18" high, 10" diameter* 520.00 570.00 530.00

☐ **Peg Lamps,** *shaded yellow, embossed completely, set in candleholders made of brass, 17" high, 6" diameter, pair* 1300.00 1500.00 1350.00

☐ **Perfume Bottle,** *decorated Webb, ivory, prunus blossoms and butterfly in heavy gold, silver, hallmarked top, 3¼" high, 2⅜" diameter* 260.00 300.00 275.00

☐ **Rose Bowl,** *embossed flowers of rose shaded to pink, white interior, eight crimp top, 3½" high, 4" diameter* 130.00 180.00 155.00

☐ **Rose Bowl,** *overlay of blue diamond quilted cut velvet, four crimp, white interior, 3¼" high, 3½" diameter* 175.00 220.00 185.00

☐ **Rose Bowl,** *overlay of decorated blue, egg shape, florals in cream with typical coralene foliage, frosted petal applied feet, eight crimp top, white interior, 6¼" high, 3½" diameter* 150.00 200.00 155.00

☐ **Rose Bowl,** *overlay of decorated blue, flowers in white and pink with Monarch butterfly decoration, petal applied feet, four crimp top, white interior, 5½" high, 4½" diameter* 150.00 200.00 155.00

☐ **Rose Bowl,** *overlay of decorated light blue, applied, frosted feet of leaf motif, enameled daisies of white and foliage of cream, center of flower has red jewel, light crimp top, white interior, 4½" high, 4½" diameter* 150.00 200.00 175.00

☐ **Rose Bowl,** *overlay of decorated rose, applied, frosted petal feet, decoration of green foliage and morning glory of tan and cream, four crimp top, 5¼" high, 4½" diameter* 155.00 200.00 170.00

☐ **Rose Bowl,** *overlay of decorated rose shaded to pink, egg shape, mauve and yellow pansies, frosted petal applied feet, four crimp top, white lining, 5½" high, 3⅜" diameter* ... 150.00 200.00 155.00

☐ **Vase,** *circular pinched form, flared rim of petal design, 8" high* 35.00 60.00 45.00

	Current Price Range		P/Y Average
☐ **Vase,** *overlay of diamond quilted, rose cut velvet, white interior, ruffled, 7¼" high, 3¼" diameter*	200.00	240.00	205.00
☐ **Vases,** *overlay of decorated rose shaded to pink, with enameled flowers of white, foliage of gold, white interior, 6⅞" high, 4½" diameter, pair*	220.00	300.00	250.00
☐ **Water Tumbler,** *decorated shaded pink overlay, enameled flowers of blue and white with green and yellow leaves, white interior, 4¼" high, 3" diameter*	150.00	200.00	160.00

SPATTER

☐ **Box,** *cased glass, egg shaped, decorated yellow, three applied feet in clear gold, branches and leaves of gold and white, floral decoration is blue bell shaped, 7½" high, 4½" diameter*	260.00	300.00	270.00
☐ **Jar,** *yellow, small forget-me-nots in blue, applied finial is clear, lid, 6¼" high, 3½" diameter*	75.00	100.00	80.00
☐ **Finger Lamp and Chimney,** *peach with white and brown spatter, clear applied handle, 6¼" high, 4¼" diameter*	130.00	180.00	150.00
☐ **Vase,** *Jack-In-Pulpit, ruffled, diamond quilted, green, white and peach, 9¼" high, 5½" diameter*	80.00	120.00	90.00
☐ **Water Tumbler,** *green and white embossed swirl, 3¾" high, 2¾" diameter*	60.00	100.00	70.00

STEUBEN

☐ **Bowl,** *circular shape, incurved neck and flaring rim, amber aurene and calcite, 5½" diameter, c. 1902-1932*	150.00	200.00	175.00
☐ **Bowl,** *lobed circular, short circular foot, clear, scrolling flowers in dark blue, dark blue band at rim, 5¼" diameter, c. 1930*	3500.00	4500.00	3700.00

Steuben Dish, *calcite finish, gold over white, 10" diameter,*
$300.00-$350.00

	Current Price Range		P/Y Average
□ **Compote,** *blue aurene and calcite, inside iridescent blue, 6" high, c. 1902-1932*	200.00	400.00	210.00
□ **Figure,** *fish rising from a breaking wave, scalloped base, 5¾" high, c. 1940*	3000.00	4000.00	3200.00
□ **Finger Bowls,** *bell shape, on pedestal base of selenium red, fluted body, 5" diameter, c. 1930*	40.00	50.00	42.00
□ **Flask,** *flattened circular body, cylindrical neck, handles, sides have irregular air trapped bubbles, blue neck to white shoulders, signed, 10" high, c. 1925*	600.00	700.00	620.00
□ **Glasses,** *wine, crystal, bell shape with fluting, long pedestal stems of selenium red, 5" high, c. 1930*	40.00	50.00	43.00
□ **Gobiets,** *crystal, inverted bell shape, fluted, long pedestal stem with circular base, stems selenium red, 8⅜" high, c. 1930*	40.00	50.00	42.00
□ **Vase,** *baluster body, short waisted neck, spreading circular foot, amber body decorated with gold peacock feathering, signed, 8½" high*	1400.00	1600.00	1480.00
□ **Vase,** *baluster shape, cylinder neck slightly flaring, knopped at bottom of base, domed and flattened circular foot, off-white background with green feathering, amber iridescent clinging hearts and vines, 10" high, c. 1905-1925*	1600.00	1800.00	1680.00
□ **Vase,** *trumpet shape on slightly domed circular foot, amber iridescent, signed, 8⅛" high, c. 1904-1930*	400.00	500.00	410.00

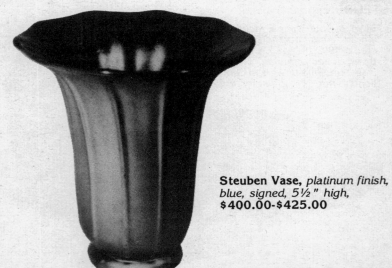

Steuben Vase, *platinum finish, blue, signed, 5½" high,* **$400.00-$425.00**

STEVENS AND WILLIAMS

	Current Price Range		P/Y Average
☐ **Fairy Lamp,** *satin finish, striped green and white, base is signed Clarke, 5¼" high, 4" diameter*	200.00	250.00	225.00
☐ **Plate,** *Pastil, blue with fleur-de-lis, signed, 7¾" diameter*	40.00	80.00	55.00
☐ **Vase,** *Arboresque, frosted cranberry with opaque white, frosted, reeded applied handles and pedestal foot, ruffled top, 6⅛" high, 3⅛" diameter*	140.00	180.00	145.00
☐ **Vase,** *cream colored ribbed tubular body on random molded amber base, caramel Northwood pull up decoration, applied glass branches and blue flower, 5½" high*	650.00	675.00	665.00
☐ **Vase,** *green rib design, pinched floral form, 6" diameter*	30.00	60.00	40.00
☐ **Vase,** *overlay amber applied edging around ruffle, off-white opaque with amber branches with multicolored flowers and leaves, pink interior, 6⅝" high, 3¼" diameter*	150.00	200.00	160.00
☐ **Vase,** *overlay, amber handle and branch on white background with amber plum, pink and amber leaf, square top in pink, amber edging, 8" high, 3½" diameter*	125.00	175.00	130.00

Stevens & Williams Vase, *cranberry, applied feet and filigree, 6¼" high,* **$245.00-$260.00**

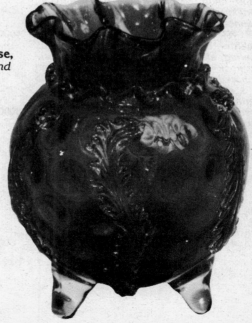

THOMAS WEBB AND SONS

	Current Price Range		P/Y Average
☐ **Berry Bowl and Underplate,** *alexandrite, crimped edge bowl is 5" in diameter, matching underplate is 6½" diameter, set is 2¼" high*	1000.00	1100.00	1050.00
☐ **Bowl,** *fruit, white opal exterior lined with thin pink glass, two tone gold decoration of bird and flowering branch, three heavy textured applied feet, 6" high, 8" diameter, signed with spider Webb mark over E*	450.00	550.00	475.00
☐ **Decanter,** *bell shape, paneled and tapered sides, signed, 11¾" high*	55.00	80.00	70.00
☐ **Bottle,** *perfume, inverted teardrop shape, cylinder neck with silver, domed lid, red background, overlaid in white, cut on one side with wildflowers and leaves, the other side with ferns, 4¼ high*	800.00	1000.00	900.00
☐ **Bottle,** *perfume, squared, cylinder neck with silver, flaring rim, flattened knop, dark green background, overlaid in white, cut with blossoms and leaves, signed, 5¼" high, c. 1901*	3000.00	4000.00	3300.00
☐ **Bottle,** *spherical body, cylinder neck of applied silver, flattened lid, turquoise background, overlaid in white, cut with shells and underwater plants, 3⅞" high, c. 1900*	1600.00	2000.00	1800.00
☐ **Bowl,** *squared, lobed at lip tapering to spherical shape, short circular foot, red background, overlaid in white, cut with roses, poppies, and bowknots, floral band around lip, 6½" diameter, c. 1895*	4000.00	5000.00	4100.00
☐ **Decanter,** *bulbous body, long cylinder neck tapering, silver domed cover with hinge, silver neck band chased with foliage and anchored with a chain hooked to lug handle on shoulder, greenish-yellow background, overlaid in pink and white, cut with apple blossoms, 9½" high, c. 1886*	6000.00	8000.00	6500.00
☐ **Plaque,** *circular shape, dark brown background, overlaid in white, carved with birds perched in blossoming branches in green, pink, blue, and rust, stylized border around rim, signed, 18¼" diameter, c. 1890*	3500.00	4500.00	3600.00
☐ **Potpourri Jar,** *ivory satin, decorated with panels of enameled pink, blue and yellow flowers, green leaves, all outlined in gold, green bands with gold trim and decoration gold washed ormulu feet, pierced top rim and lid with hinged inside cover, very ornate, 6½" high, 4¾" diameter*	500.00	700.00	550.00

Thomas Webb and Sons Vase,
Peachblow, enamel floral decor,
9½" high, **$300.00-$400.00**

	Current Price Range		P/Y Average
☐ **Rose Bowl,** *blue ground with white morning glory blossoms and foliage, reverse side has butterfly, three applied blue feet, one of which has been ground, 4" high, 6" diameter*	730.00	975.00	740.00
☐ **Rose Bowl,** *miniature, chartreuse green satin overlay ground with white cut to pink carved flowers and foliage, white lining, unsigned, 2½" high, 2¾" diameter*	900.00	1200.00	950.00
☐ **Rose Bowl,** *satin glass, peachblow, signed, 6" high*	110.00	160.00	125.00
☐ **Toothpick Holder,** *Alexandrite, rare, 2½" high*	900.00	1000.00	925.00
☐ **Vase,** *acid cut back, cream colored background, decorated with pink flowers outlined heavily in gold, gold spider in web decoration*	450.00	500.00	470.00
☐ **Vase,** *baluster shape, yellow background, overlaid in pink and white, cut with apple blossoms, leaves, and butterfly, 6½" high, c. 1895*	400.00	500.00	420.00

	Current Price Range		P/Y Average
☐ **Vase,** *bulbous body, acid red background with white floral decoration, narrow neck, bulbous shape, 5½" high*	575.00	700.00	620.00
☐ **Vase,** *bulbous body, cylinder neck, peach shading to light, overlaid in white, cut with poppies and leaves, 7½" high, c. 1895*	4000.00	6000.00	4150.00
☐ **Vase,** *bulbous body, long cylinder neck, greenish-gray background, overlaid in white and pink, cut with morning glories and leaves, stylized coils around neck, 8½" high, c. 1890*	4000.00	6000.00	4300.00

ART NOUVEAU

TOPIC: ART NOUVEAU See Daum Nancy; Galle; Lalique; Maxfield Parrish; Tiffany.

DESCRIPTION: Art Nouveau is the term applied to an international style of decorative art which flourished around the world from the 1880s to 1920s. The Art Nouveau style was a rebellion against the imitativeness of the Victorian period and the mass production of the Industrial Revolution. It came out of the Arts and Crafts movement in England and the belief of its founder, William Morris, that all decorative arts should be handmade. The Art Nouveau style is characterized by a return to nature in motifs executed by sensual, flowing lines with a heavy oriental influence.

PERIOD: The period of Art Nouveau decorative and fine arts ranges from the last fifteen years or so of the 19th century to the second decade of the 20th century. The name derives from an 1895 opening of a design shop in Paris, the name of which was a L'Art Nouveau.

TYPES: The Art Nouveau style was interpreted in jewelry, ceramics, glass, textiles, furniture, metalwork and architecture. Two of the most important aspects of Art Nouveau are asymmetry and femininity. There is a wide use of maidens with flowing hair, flowers, scrolls, tendrils, snakes and anything else with sinuous curves. Art Nouveau objects, particularly fine jewelry, are in great demand today.

COMMENTS: The works of Louis Comfort Tiffany are considered to be the finest examples of Art Nouveau artistry in America.

RECOMMENDED READING: For more in-depth information on Art Nouveau, you may refer to *The Official Price Guide to Glassware* and *The Official Price Guide to Jewelry,* published by The House of Collectibles.

Bracelet,
Art Nouveau motif in a swirl design, faceted amethyst and colored stones, gold, Tiffany & Co., early 1900s,
$5500.00-$6000.00

	Current Price Range		P/Y Average
☐ **Andirons,** pair, bronze finials, patinated metal bases, finials are molded with the face of a woman, 28″, c. 1900	1575.00	1950.00	1600.00
☐ **Basket,** silver, four flower molded feet, calla lily handles, Austrian, Maker's Mark R. O., 14″, c. 1900	550.00	650.00	580.00
☐ **Bell,** bronze, curtsying woman in gown, inscribed P. Tereszczuk, 2½″, c. 1900	255.00	340.00	290.00
☐ **Bookends,** metal, painted gold, figure of young knight and his lady, square plinth, 7¾″	55.00	65.00	50.00
☐ **Bookends,** reclining nude female figure on rocky base, inscribed S. Morani, 7½″, c. 1914	120.00	180.00	135.00
☐ **Bookends,** bronze busts, brown and green patinas, inscribed Gruber, pair, 5″, late 19th c.	560.00	670.00	595.00
☐ **Bracelet,** bangle, Art Nouveau motif in a swirl design with faceted amethyst and colored stones, gold, maker: Tiffany & Co., American, c. 1915	5500.00	6000.00	5650.00
☐ **Bracelet,** bangle, water lily motif, chased, blank initial medallions, gold, probable maker: Riker Bros., Newark, NJ, American, c. 1900	2000.00	2200.00	2050.00
☐ **Bracelet,** lady head bracelet, two Georgian chains with eight miniatures of ladies heads, heads in Art Nouveau style, c. 1890-1920	2300.00	2700.00	2350.00
☐ **Brooch,** Art Nouveau motif, 11 round diamonds approx. .90 ct., one pearl, lapel watch holder, gold, c. 1890	1800.00	1900.00	1825.00
☐ **Brooch,** dragon, diamond mouth, ruby eye, gold, c. 1880	650.00	800.00	675.00
☐ **Brooch,** fire opal, old mine diamonds, gold, c. 1890	1400.00	1500.00	1425.00
☐ **Brooch,** flower motif, translucent pink and yellow enamel flowers with seed pearls, rose diamond in silver leaves, gold, c. 1905	2500.00	2900.00	2550.00

	Current Price Range		P/Y Average
Brooch, flowers, ivory with opals, 3½ " Dia. . .	495.00	535.00	495.00
Brooch, flowing scroll motif, 11 round diamonds approx. 3.75 cts., gold and platinum, c. 1900	3400.00	3800.00	3450.00
Brooch, gold Egyptian goddess, outspread wings and serpent tail, Austrian, maker's mark M.L., 2⅛" Dia., c. 1920	420.00	510.00	445.00
Brooch, gold eagle with outstretched wings, open beak and curled talons, French, 2¼" Dia., c. 1910	450.00	535.00	475.00
Brooch, ladies heads motif, carved, gold, c. 1900	140.00	160.00	145.00
Brooch, leaf motif, translucent enamel, seed pearls, gold, c. 1900, pair	450.00	500.00	460.00
Brooch, lily-of-the-valley flower motif, seed pearls, translucent green enamel, gold, c. 1915, pair	425.00	475.00	435.00
Brooch, medallion portrait of a winged warrior with helmet, gold, 1" diameter, inscribed: V. Prouve, French, c. 1900-10	1500.00	1700.00	1550.00
Brooch, miniature of a lady, translucent pink and red enamel, emeralds in tiara, six cabochon opals in bar, engraved, gold, c. 1900	1500.00	1700.00	1550.00
Brooch, pelican, translucent pink and yellow enamel body, baroque pearl, green translucent plique-a-jour wings with rose diamonds in edges, c. 1890-1910	4500.00	5000.00	4575.00
Brooch, peridot, seed pearls, 14K gold, c. 1890	250.00	275.00	260.00
Brooch, scroll freeform motif, 14 old mine diamonds, round and rose diamonds, 18K gold, c. 1890-1900	2500.00	2900.00	2575.00
Brooch, translucent enamel portrait of a lady, diamonds in headband, two pearls, gold, c. 1890-1910	1500.00	1700.00	1575.00
Brooch, tulip motif, rubies, sapphires, diamonds, pink tourmadend, pink sapphires, old mine diamonds, natural pearls, blue green and orange translucent enamel, platinum, gold, c. 1900	16000.00	18000.00	16500.00
Centerpiece bowl, sterling silver, undulating rim, embossed floral chasing, the torso of a young girl on one end with torso of young boy on the other, footed, Gorham, 23", c. 1900 . . .	8500.00	11500.00	8750.00
Chatelaine, morning glory plaque with memo pad, pencil and glass scent bottle, white metal, c. 1895	180.00	200.00	190.00
Desk set, sterling silver, etched with flowers, leaves and children's faces, includes ruler, quill holder/sharpener, glass inkwell with hinged silver lid on stand and four corner blotter mounts, Tiffany & Company, c. 1900 .	775.00	1150.00	900.00
Clock, desk type, nude nymph, metal case . .	58.00	90.00	70.00
Dining room suite, buffet, table sideboard and five chairs, Belgian, c. 1900	3200.00	3900.00	3400.00

	Current Price Range		P/Y Average

☐ **Locket,** medallion portrait of a lady and birds, 14K gold, c. 1900 . . . . — 400.00 500.00 — 410.00

☐ **Locket,** medallion portrait of a lady, rose diamonds, slides to open, gold, maker: Diolot, c. 1890 . . . . — 2000.00 2200.00 — 2050.00

☐ **Locket,** swirl motif, one round diamond, 14K gold, American, c. 1900 . . . . — 375.00 475.00 — 385.00

☐ **Match safe,** cigar cutter base, engraved initials, sterling silver, c. 1910 . . . . — 175.00 225.00 — 185.00

☐ **Miniature,** portrait of a lady, round diamonds in border, 18K gold, signed: Gollay Fils & Stah, Geneve, c. 1890 . . . . — 2200.00 2400.00 — 2225.00

☐ **Mirror,** hand, with woman's head and flowing hair, flowers and swans, sterling silver, Unger Bros., c. 1900 . . . . — 105.00 160.00 — 125.00

☐ **Mirror,** vanity, brass, c. 1900 . . . . — 60.00 88.00 — 68.00

☐ **Necklace,** choker, Art Nouveau scroll links, lozenge-shape peridots, 54 old mine diamonds approx. 4.50 cts., forms two bracelets, maker: Harvey & Gore, English, c. late 19th . . — 6250.00 6750.00 — 6300.00

☐ **Necklace,** flower and festoon motif, seed pearls, one fresh water pearl, red glass, enamel, gold, c. 1890-1910 . . . . — 575.00 675.00 — 585.00

☐ **Necklace,** flower motif, blue and green plique a jour enamel, fresh water pearls, silver, c. 1900 . . . . — 650.00 850.00 — 675.00

☐ **Necklace,** flower motif, oval cabochon opals, demantoid garnets, c. 1900 . . . . — 4400.00 4600.00 — 4475.00

☐ **Necklace,** flower motif, pearls, one fresh water pearl, lime green to pale rose plique a jour enamel, "900" silver, French . . . . — 1000.00 1200.00 — 1050.00

☐ **Necklace,** flowers and fleur-de-lys motif, enameled, seven pearls, gold, c. 1890-1910 . . — 675.00 875.00 — 695.00

☐ **Necklace,** lady with dragonfly wing motif, green and blue plique-a-jour wings with one calibre sapphire surrounded by rose diamonds, one Holland-rose diamond set in hair of lady, 11 calibre sapphires in tail, two baroque pearls, opaque enamelled cattails, detachable pin and chain, gold, c. late 19th . — 22000.00 26000.00 — 23000.00

☐ **Necklace,** leaf and swirl motif, translucent green and yellow enamel, one oval and two round faceted peridots, one large baroque pearl suspended from center, smaller baroque pearls spaced in chain, 14K gold, American, c. 1890-1910 . . . . — 675.00 875.00 — 695.00

☐ **Necklace,** leaf motif, peridots, seed pearls, citrines, green enamel, 18K gold . . . . — 2000.00 2200.00 — 2075.00

☐ **Necklace,** openwork pendant with one small round diamond and a fresh water pearl drop attached to a double link chain spaced with seed pearls, gold, c. 1900 . . . . — 475.00 575.00 — 485.00

☐ **Pendant,** flower motif, pearls, fresh water pearls, green enamel leaves, pink enamel flower, "900" silver, c. 1900 . . . . — 275.00 375.00 — 285.00

	Current Price Range		P/Y Average
☐ **Vase,** bronze, tapered cylindrical with four dragonflies forming handles, inscribed H.E.-T., 10″ H., c. 1900	200.00	310.00	245.00
☐ **Vase,** cameo glass, cranberry and mauve, inscribed Galle, 5¼″ H., c. 1900	425.00	535.00	465.00
☐ **Vase,** enamel cameo glass, russet, mustard and dark green on brown and mustard ground, Daum Nancy, 5″ H., c. 1900	305.00	425.00	355.00
☐ **Vase,** girl with doves, German, 12″ H., c. 1900	240.00	300.00	255.00
☐ **Vase,** pottery, cherry blossoms in shades of white, iron-red, tan and brown, sea blue at base, Rookwood, 9″ H., c. 1883	680.00	1200.00	880.00
☐ **Vase,** pottery, forest scene, dolphin handles enameled in gilt, Amphora, 7¼″ H., c. 1920 . .	425.00	635.00	515.00
☐ **Vase,** pottery, iridescent with tendrils and leafage, amber, green and red glaze, French, 6½″ H., c. 1900	175.00	230.00	190.00
☐ **Wall shelf,** fruitwood frame and shelf, cameo glass half moon panel depicting idyllic landscape, signed Jacques/Gruber, 20″, c. 1900 .	1350.00	1950.00	1450.00
☐ **Watch fob,** Art Nouveau motif, two cabochon sardonyx stones in fob, gold, c. 1890	675.00	725.00	685.00

AUDUBON PRINTS

DESCRIPTION: John James Audubon is a name synonymous with bird pictures. His "Birds of America" series is recognized worldwide.

PERIOD: Between 1826 and 1842, Audubon traveled throughout the United States and Canada gathering material to paint this famous work.

COMMENTS: Today, experts believe there are less than 200 sets of "Birds of America" actually bound in volumes. The work was engraved by R. Havell and son in London. There are 435 plates in a complete set.

ADDITIONAL TIPS: This section lists many of the original prints in the set with the current market price. For a complete list of all the prints refer to *The Official Price Guide to Collector Prints* published by The House of Collectibles.

PLATE NUMBER	SUBJECT	CURRENT RETAIL PRICE	PLATE NUMBER	SUBJECT	CURRENT RETAIL PRICE
☐ 1	Turkey Cock	$30,000.00	☐ 30	Vigor's Vireo	1,430.00
☐ 2	Yellow-billed Cuckoo	2,090.00	☐ 31	White-headed Eagle	7,425.00
☐ 3	Prothonotary Warbler	990.00	☐ 32	Black-billed Cuckoo	5,775.00
☐ 4	Purple Finch	825.00	☐ 33	American Goldfinch	2,640.00
☐ 5	Bonaparte's Flycatcher ...	715.00	☐ 34	Worm-eating Warbler.....	1,430.00
☐ 6	Hen Turkey	14,300.00	☐ 35	Children's Warbler	1,045.00
☐ 7	Purple Grackle	3,960.00	☐ 36	Stanley Hawk...........	3,520.00
☐ 8	White-throated Sparrow...	1,760.00	☐ 37	Golden-winged	
☐ 9	Selby's Flycatcher	605.00		Woodpecker...........	3,520.00
☐ 10	Brown Lark	715.00	☐ 38	Kentucky Warbler	1,320.00
☐ 11	Bird of Washington	5,225.00	☐ 39	Crested Titmouse........	2,145.00
☐ 12	Baltimore Oriole	6,325.00	☐ 40	American Redstart	1,870.00
☐ 13	Snow Bird	715.00	☐ 41	Ruffed Grouse	10,175.00
☐ 14	Prairie Warbler..........	1,320.00	☐ 42	Orchard's Oriole	3,630.00
☐ 15	Blue Yellow-backed		☐ 43	Cedar Waxwing	3,520.00
	Warbler	1,760.00	☐ 44	Summer Tanager	3,850.00
☐ 16	Great Footed Hawk	3,080.00	☐ 45	Traill's Flycatcher	1,100.00
☐ 17	Carolina Pigeon	12,100.00	☐169	Mangrove Cuckoo	1,850.00
☐ 18	Bewick's Wren	1,045.00	☐170	Gray Tyrant............	935.00
☐ 19	Louisiana Water Thrush ...	825.00	☐171	Barn Owl..............	9,000.00
☐ 20	Blue-winged Yellow		☐172	Blue-headed Pigeon	2,000.00
	Warbler	2,200.00	☐173	Barn Swallow..........	2,500.00
☐ 21	Mockingbird	7,150.00	☐174	Olive Sided Flycatcher....	660.00
☐ 22	Purple Martin...........	2,640.00	☐175	Marsh Wren............	1,650.00
☐ 23	Maryland Yellow Throat ...	1,430.00	☐176	Spotted Grouse.........	6,000.00
☐ 24	Roscoe's Yellow Throat ...	825.00	☐177	White-crowned Pigeon....	7,150.00
☐ 25	Song Sparrow	715.00	☐178	Orange-crowned Warbler..	825.00
☐ 26	Carolina Parrot	17,600.00	☐179	Wood Wren............	2,650.00
☐ 27	Red-headed Woodpecker..	3,410.00	☐180	Pine Finch.............	1,350.00
☐ 28	Solitary Flycatcher	1,045.00	☐181	Golden Eagle...........	4,000.00
☐ 29	Towhe Bunting..........	1,980.00	☐182	Ground Dove...........	3,250.00

Red Breasted Merganser, *plate 401,*
$6500.00

PLATE NUMBER	SUBJECT	CURRENT RETAIL PRICE	PLATE NUMBER	SUBJECT	CURRENT RETAIL PRICE
☐183	Golden-crested Wren.....	900.00	☐317	Surf Scoter	1,540.00
☐184	Mangrove Hummingbird..	2,650.00	☐318	Avocet	3,000.00
☐185	Bachman's Warbler......	2,750.00	☐319	Lesser Tern	2,000.00
☐186	Pinnated Grouse.........	7,250.00	☐320	Little Sandpiper	1,600.00
☐187	Boat-tailed Grackle......	3,500.00	☐321	Roseate Spoonbill	28,750.00
☐188	Tree Sparrow...........	1,300.00	☐322	Red-head Duck	6,500.00
☐189	Snow Bunting...........	1,000.00	☐323	Black Skimmer	3,500.00
☐190	Yellow-bellied Woodpecker	1,600.00	☐324	Bonaparte's Gull	2,500.00
☐191	Willow Grouse..........	5,500.00	☐325	Bufflehead	5,000.00
☐192	Great American Shrike....	1,500.00	☐326	Gannet................	6,000.00
☐193	Lincoln Finch...........	2,300.00	☐327	Shoveller Duck	8,500.00
☐194	Canadian Titmouse......	1,200.00	☐328	Blackneck Stilt.........	3,000.00
☐195	Ruby-crowned Wren.....	2,000.00	☐329	Yellow Rail.............	850.00
☐196	Labrador Falcon.........	3,500.00	☐330	Plover	385.00
☐197	American Crossbill.......	2,500.00	☐331	American Merganser	6,500.00
☐198	Worm-eating Warbler.....	1,650.00	☐332	Labrador Duck	4,300.00
☐199	Little Owl..............	1,500.00	☐333	Green Heron...........	5,700.00
☐200	Shore Lark.............	700.00	☐334	Black-bellied Plover	550.00
☐201	Canada Goose..........	21,000.00	☐335	Red-bellied Sandpiper	1,100.00
☐202	Red-throated Diver.......	4,500.00	☐336	Yellow Crowned Night Heron	7,370.00
☐203	Fresh Water Marsh Wren..	2,750.00			
☐204	Salt Water Marsh Wren...	1,850.00	☐337	American Bittern	3,500.00
☐205	Virginia Rail...........	2,000.00	☐338	Bemaculated Duck	5,000.00
☐206	Summer or Wood Duck...	13,750.00	☐339	Little Auk	900.00
☐207	Booby Gannet...........	3,250.00	☐340	Stormy Petrel..........	700.00
☐208	Esquimaux Curlew.......	715.00	☐341	Great Auk.............	5,000.00
☐209	Wilson's Plover.........	385.00	☐342	Golden-eyed Duck	4,500.00
☐210	Least Bittern..........	2,500.00	☐343	Ruddy Duck	4,150.00
☐211	Great Blue Heron........	42,000.00	☐344	Long-legged Sandpiper ...	1,000.00
☐212	Common Gull...........	1,900.00	☐345	American Widgeon.......	4,300.00
☐213	Puffin................	2,475.00	☐346	Black Throated Diver	9,750.00
☐214	Razor Bill..............	935.00	☐347	American Bittern	3,500.00
☐215	Phalarope.............	660.00	☐348	Gadwall Duck...........	5,000.00
☐216	Wood Ibis.............	10,450.00	☐349	Least Water Hen	1,500.00

PLATE 203 HAVELL EDITION "Fresh Water Marsh Wren (King Rail)"

PLATE NUMBER	SUBJECT	CURRENT RETAIL PRICE	PLATE NUMBER	SUBJECT	CURRENT RETAIL PRICE
☐217	Louisiana Heron	15,400.00	☐351	Great Cinereous Owl	6,200.00
☐218	Foolish Guillemar	715.00	☐352	Black-winged Hawk	1,650.00
☐219	Black Guillemar	577.00	☐353	Titmouse, Etc.	1,700.00
☐220	Piping Plover	550.00	☐354	Louisiana Tanager	3,000.00
☐221	Mallard Duck	25,500.00	☐355	MacGillivray's Finch	1,400.00
☐222	White Ibis	9,250.00	☐356	Marsh Hawk	3,750.00
☐223	Pied Oyster Catcher	825.00	☐357	American Magpie	3,000.00
☐224	Kittiwake Gull	825.00	☐358	Pine Grosbeak	880.00
☐225	Kildeer Plover	715.00	☐359	Arkansas Flycatcher	1,210.00
☐226	Whooping Crane	14,000.00	☐360	Winter and Rock Wren	1,900.00
☐227	Pin-tailed Duck	7,250.00	☐361	Long-tailed Grouse	3,500.00
☐228	Green-wing Teal	5,500.00	☐362	Yellow-billed Magpie	2,640.00
☐229	Scaup Duck	3,850.00	☐363	Bohemian Chatterer	1,500.00
☐230	Ruddy Plover	850.00	☐364	White-winged Grossbill	2,000.00
☐231	Long-billed Curlew	20,000.00	☐365	Lapland Longspur	990.00
☐232	Hooded Merganser	4,500.00	☐366	Iceland Falcon	25,500.00
☐233	Sora or Rail	1,700.00	☐367	Band-tailed Pigeon	4,750.00
☐234	Tufted Duck	3,250.00	☐368	Rock Grouse	3,300.00
☐235	Sooty Tern	900.00	☐369	Mountain Mockingbird	1,400.00
☐236	Night Heron	10,500.00	☐370	American Water Ouzel	700.00
☐237	Great Esquimaux Curlew	2,400.00	☐371	Cock of the Plains	6,000.00
☐238	Great Marbled Codwit	2,500.00	☐372	Common Buzzard	3,000.00
☐239	American Coot	2,400.00	☐373	Evening Grosbeak	1,100.00
☐240	Roseate Tern	3,000.00	☐374	Sharp Shinned Hawk	990.00
☐311	White Pelican	30,000.00	☐375	Lesser Red Poll	850.00
☐312	Old Squaw	3,200.00	☐376	Trumpeter Swan	9,500.00
☐313	Blue-winged Teal	5,000.00	☐377	Scolopaceys Courlan	3,000.00
☐314	Laughing Gull	880.00	☐378	Hawk Owl	1,900.00
☐315	Sandpiper	1,100.00	☐379	Ruff-necked Hummingbird	2,860.00
☐350	Rocky Mountain Plover	385.00			

AUTOGRAPHS

DESCRIPTION: Original autographs of celebrities, including presidents, entertainers, writers and artists, are fairly available and always sought after.

PERIOD: Autographs that date to the middle ages exist.

COMMENTS: Autographs have established cash values though they vary greatly in price because each specimen is unique. Single signatures are generally less expensive than signatures that are part of a letter. Often values depend on buyer demand.

ADDITIONAL TIPS: A holograph letter, AL, is a letter written entirely in the person's handwriting. A letter with the body written or typed by a secretary is referred to as an L. D is for a signed document, and N is for a signed note.

Listed alphabetically by celebrity name, prices are given for ALs, Ls, signed photo, manuscript page, document and plain signatures. For further information on autographs see *The Official Price Guide to Old Books and Autographs.*

Give tea to my Third: 'tis a name I assign
To plate, pictures, or wine,
Which is yours and not mine.

Give no tea to my Whole: it will keep her awake,
And her small head will ache,
And a riot she'll make,
Till, for quietness' sake,
You supply her with cake.

Lewis Carroll.
Mar. 16. 1880.

Portion Of A Page Of Verse, *written and signed by Lewis Carroll,*
$750.00-$1000.00

AMERICAN PRESIDENTS

	ALs	Ls	Document	Signed Photo	Plain Signature
☐ Washington, George	$8000.00- 35,000.00	$1800.00- 9500.00	$1500.00- 4000.00		$450.00- 600.00
☐ Adams, John	4000.00- 7000.00	1250.00- 4000.00	1000.00- 2500.00		300.00- 400.00
☐ Jefferson, Thomas	6000.00- 30,000.00	2000.00- 8000.00	1200.00- 3000.00		400.00- 500.00
☐ Madison, James	1000.00- 3000.00	500.00- 1400.00	200.00- 800.00		100.00- 150.00
☐ Monroe, James	500.00- 1500.00	450.00- 1200.00	150.00- 300.00		75.00- 100.00
☐ Adams, John Q.	500.00- 1500.00	450.00- 1200.00	150.00- 300.00		80.00- 125.00
☐ Jackson, Andrew	1000.00- 3000.00	700.00- 2000.00	400.00- 650.00		150.00- 200.00
☐ Van Buren, Martin	400.00- 900.00	200.00- 600.00	150.00- 200.00		65.00- 85.00
☐ Harrison, William H.	700.00- 1500.00	300.00- 1000.00	350.00- 475.00		80.00- 100.00
☐ Tyler, John	500.00- 1000.00	300.00- 600.00	150.00- 200.00		60.00- 75.00
☐ Polk, James K.	500.00- 1000.00	300.00- 600.00	150.00- 200.00		60.00- 70.00
☐ Taylor, Zachary	750.00- 2000.00	350.00- 1100.00	275.00- 600.00		60.00- 100.00

	ALs	Ls	Document	Signed Photo	Plain Signature
☐ Fillmore, Millard	200.00- 400.00	150.00- 300.00	100.00- 200.00		50.00- 60.00
☐ Pierce, Franklin	200.00- 400.00	150.00- 275.00	100.00- 200.00		50.00- 60.00
☐ Buchanan, James	200.00- 400.00	150.00- 275.00	100.00- 200.00		50.00- 60.00
☐ Lincoln, Abraham	4000.00- 30,000.00	2000.00- 12,000.00	750.00- 2500.00	4000.00- 7000.00	350.00- 350.00
☐ Johnson, Andrew	800.00- 2200.00	400.00- 1000.00	150.00- 200.00	1800.00- 2500.00	50.00- 60.00
☐ Grant, U. S.	600.00- 1200.00	400.00- 750.00	85.00- 150.00	100.00- 175.00	40.00- 45.00
☐ Hayes, R. B.	250.00- 500.00	150.00 150.00	65.00- 65.00	250.00- 300.00	30.00- 38.00
☐ Garfield, James	300.00- 600.00	200.00 350.00	100.00- 90.00	350.00 700.00	38.00- 50.00
☐ Arthur, Chester A.	200.00- 300.00	120.00- 250.00	60.00- 85.00	850.00- 1200.00	30.00- 38.00
☐ Cleveland, Grover	140.00- 200.00	80.00- 120.00	50.00- 70.00	100.00- 200.00	26.00- 32.00
☐ Harrison, Benjamin	300.00- 400.00	145.00 175.00	65.00- 85.00	325.00- 450.00	28.00- 32.00
☐ McKinley, William	500.00- 750.00	190.00- 300.00	95.00- 140.00	175.00- 225.00	38.00- 42.00
☐ Roosevelt, Theodore	300.00- 350.00	100.00- 190.00	60.00- 60.00	100.00- 400.00	32.00- 38.00
☐ Taft, William H.	150.00- 190.00	90.00- 100.00	45.00- 50.00	150.00- 180.00	28.00- 35.00
☐ Wilson, Woodrow	500.00- 700.00	140.00- 190.00	60.00- 70.00	160.00- 220.00	38.00- 45.00
☐ Harding, Warren G.	700.00- 900.00	250.00- 350.00	60.00- 75.00	110.00- 140.00	28.00- 35.00
☐ Coolidge, Calvin	475.00- 700.00	140.00- 180.00	75.00- 70.00	75.00- 100.00	28.00- 35.00
☐ Hoover, Herbert	4000.00- 6000.00	150.00- 190.00	45.00- 60.00	150.00- 200.00	28.00- 35.00
☐ Roosevelt, Franklin	600.00- 1000.00	100.00- 265.00	95.00- 150.00	120.00- 180.00	33.00- 39.00
☐ Truman, Harry	1200.00- 1900.00	140.00- 350.00	80.00- 120.00	150.00- 180.00	39.00- 45.00
☐ Eisenhower, Dwight	1000.00- 1500.00	200.00- 275.00	80.00- 100.00	200.00- 300.00	28.00- 35.00
☐ Kennedy, John F.	1500.00- 4000.00	450.00- 900.00	175.00- 350.00	500.00- 1000.00	80.00- 100.00
☐ Johnson, Lyndon B	1300.00- 1800.00	300.00- 500.00	80.00- 100.00	140.00- 190.00	35.00- 48.00
☐ Nixon, Richard M	4500.00- 6500.00	450.00- 800.00	150.00- 190.00	250.00- 375.00	50.00- 75.00
☐ Ford, Gerald	700.00- 1000.00	250.00- 400.00	80.00- 110.00	140.00- 190.00	28.00- 35.00
☐ Carter, James	700.00- 1000.00	200.00- 350.00	70.00- 90.00	120.00- 150.00	25.00- 35.00
☐ Reagan, Ronald	1000.00- 1500.00	175.00- 250.00	85.00- 125.00	70.00- 100.00	25.00- 30.00

ARTISTS

	ALS		S	
☐ Barbieri, Giovanni Francesco	600.00-	800.00	150.00-	170.00
☐ Benson, Frank W.	18.00-	23.00	4.00-	6.00
☐ Cass, George N.	12.00-	15.00	2.50-	3.50
☐ Cellini, Benvenuto	3750.00-	6000.00	350.00-	450.00
☐ Cezanne, Paul	400.00-	700.00	30.00-	40.00
☐ Chagall, Marc	170.00-	200.00	22.00-	28.00
☐ Church, Frederick S.	110.00-	140.00	12.00-	15.00
☐ Corot, Camille	85.00-	100.00	17.00-	22.00
☐ Cruikshank, George	100.00-	150.00	12.00-	17.00
☐ DaVinci, Leonardo	35000.00-	60000.00	1750.00-	2250.00
☐ Degas, Edgar	375.00-	550.00	60.00-	75.00
☐ Duran, Carolus	18.00-	23.00	2.50-	3.50
☐ Eastlake, Sir Charles L.	85.00-	100.00	8.00-	10.00
☐ Fildes, Sir Luke	18.00-	23.00	3.00-	4.00
☐ Forain, Jean	12.00	15.00	3.00-	4.00
☐ Forrester, Alfred Henry	28.00-	34.00	3.00-	4.00
☐ Gauguin, Paul	650.00-	850.00	22.00-	28.00
☐ Gibson, Charles D.	50.00-	70.00	7.00-	10.00
☐ Gifford, R. Swain	8.00-	10.00	2.50-	3.50
☐ Landseer, Sir Edwin	22.00-	27.00	3.50-	4.75
☐ Lawrence, Sir Thomas	120.00-	150.00	6.00-	8.00
☐ Lear, Edward	175.00-	225.00	12.00-	15.00
☐ Leslie, C. R.	40.00-	50.00	4.00-	6.00
☐ Low, Will H.	9.00-	12.00	2.50-	3.75
☐ Matisse, Henri	140.00-	190.00	20.00-	30.00
☐ Menzel, Morlan	18.00-	25.00	2.50-	3.75
☐ Michelangelo Buonarroti	15000.00-	22000.00	1250.00-	1600.00
☐ Millais, J. E.	28.00-	34.00	4.00-	6.00
☐ Modigliani, Amedeo	700.00-	1000.00	70.00-	100.00
☐ Monet, Claude	70.00-	100.00	12.00-	15.00
☐ Morghen, Raphael	60.00-	80.00	6.00-	8.00
☐ Pissarro, Camille	140.00-	190.00	25.00-	33.00
☐ Raphael, Sanzio	35000.00-	60000.00	1750.00-	2500.00
☐ Redoute, Pierre J.	80.00-	100.00	6.00-	8.00
☐ Rembrant van Rijn	75000.00-	150000.00	4000.00-	6000.00
☐ Remington, Frederick	500.00-	900.00	30.00-	50.00
☐ Renoir, Pierre A.	350.00-	500.00	60.00-	85.00
☐ Rossetti, Dante G.	250.00-	350.00	30.00-	40.00
☐ Rouault, George S, ...	150.00-	200.00	25.00-	35.00
☐ Rubens, Peter Paul	9000.00-	12000.00	700.00-	1000.00
☐ Sargent, J. S.	110.00-	150.00	12.00-	15.00
☐ Sully, Thomas	110.00-	150.00	12.00-	15.00
☐ West, Benjamin	170.00-	200.00	12.00-	15.00
☐ Whistler, James A. M.	120.00-	160.00	17.00-	22.00
☐ Wyeth, N. C.	70.00-	100.00	7.00-	10.00

AUTHORS

AMERICAN

	ALS	MS Page
☐ Alcott, Louisa M.	$250.00-$350.00	$500.00-$700.00
☐ Aldrich, Thomas B.	100.00- 130.00	200.00- 275.00
☐ Alger, Horatio	30.00- 40.00	200.00- 275.00
☐ Bates, Arlo	12.00- 16.00	17.00- 22.00
☐ Botta, Ann Lynch	8.00- 10.00	12.00- 15.00
☐ Brooks, Fred Emerson	8.00- 10.00	12.00- 15.00
☐ Browne, Chas. F. (Artemus Ward)	22.00- 26.00	28.00- 35.00
☐ Bryant, William C.	75.00- 95.00	150.00- 190.00
☐ Burnett, Frances H.	17.00- 22.00	30.00- 35.00
☐ Burroughs, John	35.00- 50.00	75.00- 100.00
☐ Butler, Ellis P.	8.00- 10.00	14.00- 18.00
☐ Curtis, George W.	12.00- 15.00	16.00- 20.00
☐ Dana, R. H., Jr.	30.00- 35.00	100.00- 150.00
☐ Davis, Richard H.	8.00- 10.00	14.00- 18.00
☐ Dixon, Thomas	6.00- 8.00	12.00- 15.00
☐ Dodge, Mary Mapes	12.00- 15.00	22.00- 28.00
☐ Dreiser, Theodore	125.00- 160.00	250.00- 300.00
☐ Field, Eugene	80.00- 100.00	150.00- 200.00
☐ Field, Kate	6.00- 8.00	12.00- 15.00
☐ Fiske, John	8.00- 10.00	12.00- 15.00
☐ Flagg, Wilson	8.00- 10.00	12.00- 15.00
☐ Guiterman, Arthur	6.00- 8.00	12.00- 15.00
☐ Hale, Edward E.	12.00- 15.00	22.00- 28.00
☐ Harris, Joel C.	100.00- 150.00	300.00- 400.00
☐ Harte, Bret	200.00- 300.00	400.00- 500.00
☐ Hawthorne, Nathaniel	1500.00-2000.00	2000.00-3000.00
☐ Headley, Joel T.	6.00- 8.00	12.00- 15.00
☐ Hearn, Lafcadio	250.00- 400.00	400.00- 700.00
☐ Hemingway, Ernest	1500.00-3500.00	3000.00-5000.00
☐ Hubbard, Elbert	18.00- 23.00	35.00- 40.00
☐ Huneker, James	8.00- 10.00	18.00- 23.00
☐ Irving, Washington	1000.00-1500.00	3000.00-4000.00
☐ Jackson, Helen Hunt	8.00- 10.00	18.00- 23.00
☐ James, Henry	300.00- 600.00	800.00-1200.00
☐ Jewett, Sarah	12.00- 15.00	22.00- 27.00
☐ Kilmer, Joyce	175.00- 225.00	400.00- 500.00
☐ Longfellow, H. W.	150.00- 180.00	250.00- 300.00
☐ Lowell, Amy	100.00- 150.00	275.00- 325.00
☐ Lowell, James R.	45.00- 60.00	120.00- 160.00
☐ McCutcheon, George B.	8.00- 10.00	17.00- 22.00
☐ Markham, Edwin	18.00- 23.00	35.00- 40.00
☐ Melville, Herman	3750.00-6000.00	4500.00-7000.00
☐ Mencken, H. L.	75.00- 100.00	100.00- 200.00
☐ Morley, Christopher	40.00- 55.00	60.00- 80.00
☐ Nye, E. W.	55.00- 70.00	110.00- 140.00
☐ O'Neill, Eugene	800.00-2000.00	1500.00-2250.00
☐ O'Reilly, John B.	22.00- 27.00	60.00- 75.00
☐ Parsons, T. W.	8.00- 10.00	18.00- 23.00
☐ Payne, John H.	175.00- 225.00	325.00- 400.00
☐ Percival, J. G.	60.00- 80.00	120.00- 150.00
☐ Pierpont, John	30.00- 40.00	60.00- 80.00
☐ Porter, W. S. (O. Henry)	800.00-1000.00	800.00-1000.00
☐ Prescott, Mary N.	30.00- 40.00	60.00- 80.00
☐ Randall, James R.	120.00- 150.00	300.00- 375.00
☐ Sikes, William W.	12.00- 22.00	30.00- 35.00

AMERICAN	ALS		MS Page	
☐ Stockton, Frank	40.00-	50.00	85.00-	110.00
☐ Stoddard, R. H.	30.00-	40.00	60.00-	80.00
☐ Stowe, H. B.	140.00-	170.00	400.00-	550.00
☐ Tarkington, Booth	175.00-	225.00	250.00-	350.00
☐ Taylor, Bayard	40.00-	50.00	80.00-	100.00
☐ Terhune, Albert P.	17.00-	22.00	28.00-	33.00
☐ Thoreau, Henry D.	1200.00-	1500.00	1750.00-	2250.00
☐ Thorpe, Thomas B.	40.00-	50.00	80.00-	100.00
☐ Tomlinson, Everett	14.00-	18.00	30.00-	40.00
☐ Wolfe, Thomas	400.00-	700.00	1200.00-	1600.00

AVIATION MEMORABILIA

DESCRIPTION: Aviation memorabilia includes any item dealing with airplanes. From commercial airlines to the air force, hobbyists are collecting any type of aviation memorabilia available.

TYPES: Stewardess wings, pilot goggles, pins, buttons, helmets, entire airplanes or just parts of airplanes are all types of memorabilia collected by hobbyists.

COMMENTS: Finding aviation collectibles could be difficult. A good source to contact is the World Airline Hobby Club, 3381 Apple Tree Lane, Erlanger, KY 41018.

	Current Price Range		P/Y Average
☐ **Activity Book For Children,** cut-out book with seven different planes of the classic era including Lockheed Vega, Stinson, Curtiss Robin, Spirit of St. Louis, full color, 10″ x 15″, 1930, price is for an intact specimen.	40.00	55.00	44.00
☐ **Bombadeer's Panel,** with wing lights, bomb bay lights, bomb salvo switch, door on/off switch, World War II	100.00	150.00	117.50
☐ **Book,** *The Romance Of Air Fighting* by R.W. Anderson, soft cover, 31 pages, published in Great Britain, 1917	35.00	45.00	38.00
☐ **Book,** *Signal Corps Pilot's Book,* used by a cadet in 1917, hardcover, 5½″ x 6″	50.00	65.00	55.00

	Current Price Range		P/Y Average

☐ **Booklet,** Souvenir of the Harvard/Boston Aviation Meet, 1911, with photographs of Glen Curtis, Willard, Graham White and many other notables of the Wright Brothers era ... **100.00 130.00   110.00**

☐ **Button,** brass, pictures world globe and reads "U.S. Air Mail," c. 1930 .... **10.00   15.00   11.00**

☐ **Cap,** canvas with built-in earphones, bakelite phones, c. 1930-1934 .... **50.00   65.00   54.75**

☐ **Cockpit Instrument Panel (fragment),** portion of instrument panel from World War II craft, unidentified, with starter, landing lights, light prop, feathering switch, some wiring, 10″ x 12″ **100.00 150.00   117.50**

☐ **Coffee Mug,** porcelain, reads Tactical Air Command/General White, white with gold, 3″ **15.00   20.00   16.75**

☐ **Drinking Cup,** leather, Pan American Airways System, 4″, c. 1930 .... **15.00   20.00   17.00**

☐ **Game,** Flying For Fun, aviation card game based on stunt pilot maneuvers, boxed with instructions, 1928 .... **40.00   50.00   43.00**

☐ **Game, Squadron Scramble,** card game, World War II era picturing many different allied and axis aircraft, no indication of publisher **25.00   33.00   28.00**

☐ **Magazine, The Alexander Aircrafter,** September, 1927, full color cover, 22 pages, 5½″ x 8″ **30.00   35.00   31.00**

☐ **Military Pass to MacDill Air Field, Florida,** dated August 14, 1942 .... **13.00   17.00   14.25**

☐ **Notebook,** personal notes of 2nd Lieut. L.H. Thayer taken in Officer's Training Course at Kelly Field, Texas, from January to April, 1918, including nomenclature and diagrams . **75.00 100.00   82.00**

☐ **Pamphlet,** National Air Races, International Aeronautical Exposition, details of prizes with entry blank, features nonstop flight New York to Los Angeles, Orville Wright listed as Chairman, 8″ x 11″, 1928 .... **50.00   65.00   56.00**

☐ **Pilot Goggles,** bakelite with elastic band, screw off lenses, made by Wilson, c. 1930 ... **35.00   45.00   38.50**

☐ **Pilot Goggles,** fur lined, yellow tinted lenses, elastic band, c. 1920-1930 .... **30.00   40.00   32.50**

☐ **Pinback Button,** Autogiro, full color celluloid premium from Bond's Bread **7.00   10.00   7.75**

☐ **Pinback Button,** Byrd's Floyd Bennet, full color celluloid premium from Bond's Bread . **7.00   10.00   7.75**

☐ **Pinback Button,** Earhart's Friendship, full color celluloid premium from Bond's Bread . **7.00   10.00   7.75**

☐ **Pinback Button,** The Hero Of Niagara: Lincoln Beachey, black and white portrait of the famous pioneer aviator and stunt pilot, 1¾″, 1915 .... **55.00   70.00   59.00**

	Current Price Range		P/Y Average
Pocket Watch, Graf Zeppelin, silvered case has embossed view of New York City skyline, black and gold dial, reads "Trail Blazers Around The World: Magellan 1522, c. 1929-1930	275.00	325.00	290.00
Postcard, biplane over Paris, black and white, unused, c. 1910-1912	14.00	18.00	15.20
Postcard, Hanriot Monoplane in flight with Hanriot at controls, black and white, unused	19.00	24.00	21.00
Postcard, Hudson-Fulton Celebration, $10,000 prize contest to any aviator who could fly from New York City to Albany, reproduction of Biedermann painting, 1909 .	25.00	32.00	27.00
Slides, set of one hundred study slides of planes in silhouette enclosed in original box, World War II	60.00	80.00	67.00
Trade Catalogue, Bird Aircraft Corporation, seventeen page catalogue of airplanes available for sale, 1931	35.00	43.00	37.00
Watch Fob, aluminum shell, pictures dirigible, reads "U.S. Navy, Duralumin," c. 1930s .	25.00	30.00	26.00
Wreck Fragment, piece of a Douglas SBD-3 dive bomber salvaged from wreckage, yellow metal with portions of attached canvas, 5", World War II	20.00	25.00	20.25

AVON BOTTLES

DESCRIPTION: The oldest toiletry company that issues decorative bottles, Avon is the modern leader in the non-liquor bottle field.

TYPES: There are a variety of Avon bottle types, including figurals shaped as animals, people, cars, etc., cologne bottles, hand lotion bottles, among others.

PERIOD: Based on door-to-door sales, Avon began as the California Perfume Company more than 50 years ago. Since 1939 the name Avon has been used exclusively.

COMMENTS: Everything relating to Avon, including bottles, brochures and magazine ads are highly collectible. Older Avon memorabilia is usually of more value than recent products.

ADDITIONAL TIPS: The listings in this section are alphabetized by item name, followed by date of issue, description and, when possible, issue date. For more information, consult *The Official Price Guide to Bottles, Old and New,* published by The House of Collectibles.

Avon Bottle,
owl cream sachet,
1½ oz., 1972.
$5.00 - $6.50

WOMEN'S FIGURALS	Current Price Range		P/Y Average
☐ **Baby Owl,** clear glass, gold cap, 1 oz. 1975-76. Original price $2.00	2.00	4.00	2.50
☐ **Bath Urn,** white glass and cap with gold top band under the cap, 5 oz., 1971-73	4.00	6.00	4.25
☐ **Bath Treasure Snail decanter,** clear glass, gold head, 6 oz., 1973-76. Original price $6.00	6.00	8.00	6.50
☐ **Beautiful Awakening,** clear glass, painted gold in shape of an alarm clock, with clock face on front, 3 oz., 1973-74	5.00	7.00	5.50
☐ **Betsy Ross decanter,** clear glass painted white, 4 oz., 1976. Original price $10.00	8.00	12.00	8.50
☐ **Bird of Paradise cologne,** blue glass, gold cap, 1.5 oz., 1975-76. Original price $3.00	3.00	5.00	3.50
☐ **La Belle Telephone,** telephone figurine, clear glass, gold top, 1 oz., 1974-76. Original price $7.00	7.00	9.00	7.50
☐ **Lady Bug perfume decanter,** frosted glass, gold cap, ¼ oz., 1975-76. Original price $4.00	3.00	5.00	3.50
☐ **Lady Spaniel,** opal glass, plastic head, 1.5 oz., 1974-76. Original price $3.00	3.00	5.00	3.50

	Current Price Range		P/Y Average
☐ **Leisure Hours,** white milk glass in shape of clock with face of clock design on the front, gold cap, 5 oz., 1970-72. Original price $4.00 ..	4.00	6.00	4.50
☐ **Love Song decanter,** frosted glass, gold cap, 6 oz., 1973-75. Original price $6.00	5.50	7.50	5.75
☐ **Magic Pumpkin Coach,** clear glass, gold cap, 1 oz., 1976. Original price $5.00	2.50	4.50	2.75
☐ **Ming Blue Lamp,** blue glass in shape of lamp, white plastic shade, 5 oz., 1974-76. Original price $6.00	6.00	8.00	6.50
☐ **Ming Cat cologne,** tall seated cat, white glass, blue trim, neck ribbon, 6 oz., 1971	8.00	11.00	8.50
☐ **One dram perfume,** clear glass with ribbing, gold cap, 1974-76. Original price $4.25	3.00	5.00	3.50
☐ **Parisian Garden perfume,** white milk glass, in shape of pitcher with floral design on front, gold cap, 3.3 oz., 1974-75. Original price $5.00 .	5.00	7.00	5.50
☐ **Parlor Lamp,** lower portion in white milk glass, top portion in light amber glass, gold cap, 3 oz., 1971-72. Original price $7.00	8.00	11.00	8.50
☐ **Partridge cologne decanger,** white milk glass, white plastic lid, 5 oz., 1973-75. Original price $5.00	5.00	7.00	5.50
☐ **Roaring Twenties fashion figurine,** clear glass painted purple, plastic purple top, 3 oz., 1972-74	6.00	8.00	6.50
☐ **Robin Red-Breast cologne decanter,** red frosted glass, silver plastic, 2 oz., 1974-75. Original price $4.00	4.00	6.00	4.50
☐ **Royal Coach,** white milk glass, in shape of coach with gold cap on top, 5 oz., 1972-73. Original price $5.00	5.00	7.00	5.50

BANKS

TOPIC: Banks make saving coins more enjoyable. Besides providing a receptacle for the hoard of coins, they are interesting and amusing in themselves.

TYPES: Banks are either still or mechanical. Still banks are simply receptacles and do not move or react when a coin is deposited. Mechanical banks, however, respond to the coin (via a series of levers and springs) and put on a small show for the depositor.

PERIOD: Still banks were first made in the United States in the early 1790s; mechanical banks were introduced about seventy years later.

MATERIALS: Cast iron is the favorite material for banks.

COMMENTS: Banks make good collectibles because they are entertaining, attractive and often ingenious.

Bank, *tin, lithographed, Towle's Log Cabin Syrup, made in Hong Kong, 1950s,*
$13.00-$20.00

	Current Price Range		P/Y Average
☐ **Airplane,** tin, single propeller, length 8″	43.00	53.00	48.00
☐ **Alamo,** replica of Alamo, height 1⅞″	73.00	83.00	78.00
☐ **Alice In Wonderland,** English, cube with embossed designs on each side, brass, height 4¼″	53.00	103.00	78.00
☐ **Alphabet,** drum shaped, children's scenes around the outside, band with alphabet around the top, tin, height 3″	23.00	33.00	28.00
☐ **Alphabet,** multisided spherical object, each side has embossed letter, height 3¼″	78.00	128.00	103.00
☐ **Amish Lady,** carries food on a plate in her left hand, height 5½″	48.00	58.00	53.00

	Current Price Range		P/Y Average

□ **Animal Bank,** drum shaped, embossed designs of animals around the outside, height 3" 23.00 33.00 28.00
□ **Apple,** apple sits on apple leaves, height 3½ " 103.00 203.00 143.00
□ **Apple,** apple sits on embossed stand, medallion on front of apple, height 2½ " 103.00 203.00 153.00
□ **Armored Bank,** tin, length 6¼ " 23.00 33.00 28.00
□ **Atlas,** statuette of Atlas carrying the world on his shoulders, height 4¾ " 103.00 203.00 153.00
□ **Baseball On Three Bats,** three bats criscrossed to form a stand with a disproportionately large baseball between them, height 5" 78.00 128.00 103.00
□ **Baseball,** painted white with red tiger head on one side and red pegasus (Mobil gas) on the other, glass 23.00 33.00 28.00
□ **Battleship,** not authentic appearing, height 8½ " 153.00 253.00 203.00
□ **Battleship Maine,** does not appear authentic, "Maine" embossed on front, height 4½ " ... 103.00 203.00 143.00
□ **Battleship Oregon,** not authentic appearing, "Oregon" embossed on the side, height 6¼ " 103.00 203.00 153.00
□ **Blanket Chest,** rectangular shaped, two medieval window shapes on front, height 2" . 378.00 478.00 428.00
□ **Boot,** old fashioned shoe, height 3" 53.00 103.00 78.00
□ **Boy Scout,** holds flag pole to his right side, height 6" 73.00 83.00 78.00
□ **Boy With Top Hat,** German, white metal, height 4½ " 18.00 28.00 23.00
□ **Brinks Armored Truck,** Die Cast, height 4¾ " 33.00 43.00 38.00
□ **Buffalo,** authentic looking, height 3" 43.00 53.00 48.00
□ **Buffalo,** "Amherst Stoves," printed on the side, height 5" 78.00 128.00 103.00
□ **Century Of Progress,** long building with one tall tower in the center, height 6⅞ " 353.00 453.00 403.00
□ **Charlie Chaplin,** glass, candy container, height 3¾ " 63.00 73.00 68.00
□ **Chest,** embossed designs, height 2" 43.00 53.00 48.00
□ **Chest,** lid opens up, height 6" 33.00 43.00 35.00
□ **Christmas Bank,** tin, cylinder shape, design on the outside, height 3" 23.00 33.00 28.00
□ **Church,** pot metal, bell tower, height 4" 23.00 33.00 28.00
□ **Church,** cathedral style, tall bell tower on one side, height 6" 48.00 58.00 53.00
□ **Churchill,** bust, composition, height 4¾ " ... 33.00 43.00 38.00
□ **Coronation Crown,** four shell feet, beaded border over the top, height 4½ " 73.00 83.00 78.00
□ **Cottage,** two storied with small chimneys on each side, height 3⅝ " 38.00 48.00 43.00
□ **Cottage,** pot metal, single storied, height 2" . 18.00 28.00 23.00
□ **Cow,** authentic looking, height 2½ " 43.00 53.00 48.00
□ **Cow,** authentic looking, height 3½ " 43.00 53.00 48.00
□ **Coronation Crown Prince Phillip,** pot metal, height 3¾ " 13.00 23.00 18.00
□ **County Bank,** English, height 4¼ " 53.00 103.00 78.00
□ **Crystal Bank,** cylinder shade glass with domed top, three feet 18.00 28.00 23.00

	Current Price Range		P/Y Average
☐ **Cup,** tin, with lid and handle, height 2½ "	11.00	15.00	13.00
☐ **Fez,** Shriner's hat with tassel, height 1½ " ...	103.00	203.00	153.00
☐ **Fireman,** height 5½ "	78.00	128.00	103.00
☐ **Football Player,** old fashioned uniform, height 5¾ "	103.00	203.00	143.00
☐ **Football Player With Ball Overhead,** disproportionately, height 5"	103.00	153.00	123.00
☐ **Fort Dearborn,** three-storied, log building, height 6"	53.00	103.00	78.00
☐ **Fortune Ship,** small pole, one mast, "Marie" and "U.S.A." printed on the side	78.00	128.00	103.00
☐ **French Artillery Hat,** height 1¾ "	38.00	68.00	53.00
☐ **General Butler,** comical looking character, with large mustache, height 6½ "	153.00	253.00	203.00
☐ **General Sherman,** rides rearing horse, height 5½ "	128.00	228.00	178.00
☐ **German Ship,** length 7¼ "	78.00	128.00	103.00
☐ **Globe On Arc,** on pedestal stand	103.00	203.00	143.00
☐ **Globe With Eagle,** pedestal foot, small eagle on top	153.00	253.00	203.00
☐ **Globe Savings Fund,** height 7"	78.00	128.00	103.00
☐ **Goose,** authentic looking, height 4"	53.00	103.00	78.00
☐ **Goose,** "Red Goose Shoes" printed on side, height 4½ "	43.00	53.00	48.00
☐ **Goose,** height 5"	63.00	73.00	68.00
☐ **Grapette Cat,** with label, glass	5.00	10.00	6.00
☐ **Grapette Cat,** without label, glass	6.00	8.00	7.00
☐ **Grapette Clown,** glass	6.00	8.00	7.00
☐ **Grapette Elephant,** glass	6.00	8.00	7.00
☐ **Grandpa Dukes,** comical head with flat hat, height 2¼ "	23.00	33.00	28.00
☐ **Grandpa's Hat,** upside down, top hat, height 2¼ "	53.00	103.00	78.00
☐ **Guardhouse,** tin, soldier stands in archway, large striping on building, height 3½ "	33.00	43.00	38.00
☐ **Hand Grenade,** height 3¾ "	63.00	73.00	68.00
☐ **Happy Fats,** chubby figure stands on drum, candy container, height 4½ "	73.00	83.00	78.00
☐ **Hen On Nest,** height 3"	103.00	203.00	143.00
☐ **Hippo,** authentic looking, height 2½ "	103.00	203.00	153.00
☐ **Indian Family,** combination busts of Indian, squaw, and papoose, height 3¾ "	73.00	83.00	78.00
☐ **Indian Maiden,** pot metal, wears headband and one feather at the side, height 3½ "	18.00	28.00	23.00
☐ **Iron Maiden,** canister shape with head on the top, height 4¾ "	103.00	203.00	153.00
☐ **Jarmulowsky Building,** brick design, height 8"	78.00	128.00	103.00
☐ **Keene Savings Bank,** tin, replica of a bank, double doors	68.00	98.00	83.00
☐ **Key,** stands on end, height 5½ "	53.00	103.00	78.00
☐ **Koop's Mustard Barrel Bank,** glass	9.00	11.00	10.00
☐ **Kroger's Country Club Mustard Barrel Bank,** glass	9.00	11.00	10.00
☐ **Ladies Slipper,** old-fashioned style, height 2½ "	48.00	58.00	53.00

	Current Price Range		P/Y Average
☐ **Liberty Bell,** amber, iridescent, glass	11.00	15.00	13.00
☐ **Liberty Bell,** embossed lettering, height 4″ ..	53.00	103.00	78.00
☐ **Lighthouse,** keeper's house with tall tower, domed top, on rocky base	103.00	203.00	178.00
☐ **Lucky Joe Mustard,** with paper lips, glass ...	15.00	21.00	18.00
☐ **Lucky Joe Mustard,** without paper lips, glass	11.00	15.00	13.00
☐ **Mail Box,** pot metal, type that attaches or inserts into a wall, height 5¼″	13.00	23.00	18.00
☐ **Mail Box,** free standing type, four legs, "Letters" embossed on front, height 5½″	38.00	68.00	53.00
☐ **Mail Box,** small box type on pedestal stand, "Airmail U.S." embossed on front, height 6½″	53.00	103.00	78.00
☐ **Globe Savings Fund,** height 7″	78.00	128.00	103.00
☐ **Mickey Mouse With Banjo,** pot metal, sits on drum with one leg dangling over the side, height 5″	53.00	103.00	78.00
☐ **Miniature Taxi,** height 2½″	153.00	253.00	203.00
☐ **Rearing Horse On Oval Base,** "Beauty" printed on side of horse, height 4¾″	63.00	73.00	68.00
☐ **Rearing Horse On Pebbled Base,** height 7½″	78.00	128.00	103.00
☐ **Reclining Man,** pottery, fat, hands behind head, feet crossed	28.00	78.00	43.00
☐ **½ red Goose Shoes,** name printed on goose's wing, height 3¾″	78.00	128.00	103.00
☐ **Refrigerator,** height 3¾″	33.00	43.00	38.00
☐ **Reid Library,** replica, height 5½″	53.00	103.00	78.00

Mechanical Bank, *cast iron, Trick Dog, no underplate, repainted,* **$125.00-$150.00**

	Current Price Range		P/Y Average
☐ **Rocking Chair,** unusual design, openwork, height 6½ "	153.00	253.00	203.00
☐ **Roly Poly Monkey,** tin, globe shaped body with ovoid head, cone hat, height 6 "	23.00	33.00	28.00
☐ **Round Clown,** spherical with nub feet, height 2¼ "	23.00	33.00	28.00
☐ **Safe,** rectangular, free standing with four feet, height 3 "	13.00	23.00	15.00
☐ **Safe,** free standing, double doors, height 6 " .	38.00	68.00	53.00
☐ **Sailor,** saluting with one hand, holds paddle at his side with other hand, height 5¾ "	78.00	128.00	103.00
☐ **Santa,** holds a toy in each hand, height 5½ " .	153.00	253.00	203.00
☐ **Santa With Pack,** peaked hat, simplistic face	128.00	178.00	153.00

BARBED WIRE

DESCRIPTION: Barbed wire was first used by Western farmers who installed it on their land to deter cattlemen. Railroads used it in some areas to keep cattle and buffalo off the tracks.

VARIATIONS: There are various types of barbed wire including ribbon wire, double round wire with two points and single round wire with two points.

ORIGIN: The first wire fencing was patented in 1853. Between 1868 and 1900 more than 750 patents were issued for various barbed wire styles.

COMMENTS: Barbed wire is collectible because of its historical importance during the settlement of western territories.

ADDITIONAL TIPS: Prices vary from $1 to more than $400 for a stick which is an 18 inch piece of barbed wire.

The listings in this section are alphabetical according to barbed wire type. When available, the date of manufacture is given. Along with the price range, a previous year average price is included.

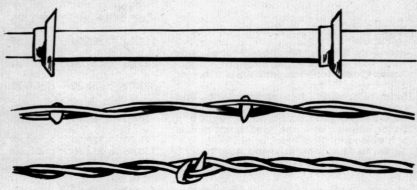

From Top to Bottom: *Brinkerhoff Ribbon wire, Daniel C. Stover two line wire and Scutt's Single Clip wire, late 1800s,* **$20.00-$30.00**

SINGLE ROUND WITH TWO POINTS

	Current Price Range		P/Y Average
☐ Bakers Single Strand, c. 1883	3.15	5.15	3.50
☐ Charles D. Rogers, c. 1888	3.15	5.15	3.50
☐ Dobbs and Booth Single Line, c. 1875	5.15	7.15	5.50
☐ Gunderson, c. 1881	5.15	7.15	5.50
☐ Half-Hitch, c. 1877	3.50	7.00	3.75
☐ H. M. Rose Wrap Barb, c. 1877	3.25	5.25	4.00
☐ L. E. Sunderland No Kink, c. 1884	3.15	5.15	4.15
☐ Mack's Alternate, c. 1875	12.50	18.50	15.50
☐ Nelson Clip, c. 1876	85.00	105.00	95.00
☐ Putnams Flat Under Barb, c. 1877	16.00	21.00	16.50
☐ R. Emerson, c. 1876	165.00	195.00	180.00
☐ Rose Kink Line, c. 1877	4.00	6.00	4.75
☐ Single Line Wide Wrap Barb, c. 1878	85.00	105.00	95.00
☐ Sunderland Hammered Barb, c. 1884	3.75	4.75	4.50
☐ "Two Point Ripple Wire"	7.50	9.50	8.50

DOUBLE ROUND WITH TWO POINTS

	Current Price Range		P/Y Average
☐ Australian Loose Wrap	4.00	6.00	3.75
☐ Baker's Half-Round Barb	2.50	3.50	2.00
☐ C. H. Salisbury, c. 1876	15.00	20.00	16.00
☐ Decker Parallel, c. 1884	7.00	9.00	6.00
☐ Figure 8 Barb, Wright, c. 1881	22.00	28.00	23.00
☐ "Forked Tongue," c. 1887	4.00	6.00	4.50
☐ Haish's Original "S," c. 1875	3.00	5.00	3.50
☐ Glidden Barb on Both Lines	4.50	7.50	5.00
☐ J. D. Curtis "Twisted Point"	2.50	3.50	2.50
☐ J. D. Nadlehoffer, c. 1878	45.00	60.00	50.00
☐ Kangaroo Wire, c. 1876	4.00	6.50	4.50
☐ L. E. Sunderland Barb on Two Line Wire, c. 1884	110.00	140.00	115.00
☐ Missouri Hump Wire Staple Barb, c. 1876	9.00	12.00	9.50
☐ Peter P. Hill Parallel, c. 1876	160.00	185.00	150.00
☐ Rose Barb on Copper Lines, c. 1877	5.50	7.50	5.50
☐ W. Edenborn	4.00	6.00	4.50
☐ W. Edenborn's Locked in Barb, c. 1885	3.00	5.00	3.50

RIBBON WIRE

	Current Price Range		P/Y Average
☐ Allis Barbless Ribbon and Single Wire, c. 1881	16.00	24.00	16.00
☐ Allis Flat Ribbon Barb, c. 1892	16.00	24.00	16.00
☐ Brinkerhoff's Ribbon Barb, c. 1881	4.50	6.50	5.00
☐ Cast Iron Buckthorn	6.50	10.00	8.00
☐ Factory Splice on Thin Barbed Ribbon, c. 1892	40.00	55.00	40.00
☐ F. D. Ford Flat Ribbon, c. 1885	4.50	6.50	5.00
☐ John Hallner's "Greenbriar," c. 1878	1.75	4.00	2.00
☐ Harbaugh's Torn Ribbon, c. 1881	6.50	10.50	7.50
☐ Kelly's Split Ribbon, c. 1868	22.00	35.00	25.00
☐ Kelmer Ornamental Fence, c. 1885	16.00	20.00	16.00
☐ "Open Face" by Brinkerhoff, c. 1881	8.00	12.00	9.00
☐ Scutt's Smooth Ribbon	14.00	24.00	14.00
☐ Scutt's Ridged Ribbon, c. 1883	55.00	70.00	55.00
☐ Three-Quarter Inch Ribbon	10.00	16.00	10.00
☐ Very Light and Narrow Ribbon, c. 1868	60.00	70.00	60.00

BASEBALL CARDS

DESCRIPTION: Baseball cards usually have the picture of a baseball player on one side and the player's baseball record on the other. Baseball cards were made in different sizes depending on the era and the company.

ORIGIN: Baseball cards were introduced in the middle 1880s. At first they were made exclusively by tobacco companies for distribution with cigarettes or other tobacco products. From 1900 to 1930, other firms also printed baseball cards, but not on a regular basis. The modern era of baseball cards began during the Depression when gum companies began packaging cards along with bubblegum. At first, the motive was to simply boost gum sales, but as the public became more interested in the cards, card issuing developed into a thriving industry.

TYPES: There are basically two types of cards — the old cards from before the 1930s and the modern cards after the 1930s.

COMPANIES: Major companies that produced baseball cards in the late 1800s and early 1900s include Goodwin and Company, Allen and Ginter, P.H. Mayo and Brothers Tobacco Company and D. Buchner.

From the early 1930s, modern card companies like Goudey Gum Company, Delong Gum Company and Frank H. Fleer were major card producers. The Topps Chewing Gum Company, which began distributing cards in the 1970s, is one which most people associate with baseball cards.

ADDITIONAL INFORMATION: For more information, consult *The Official Price Guide to Baseball Cards,* published by The House of Collectibles.

Barney McCosky,
outfielder, Philadelphia Athletics,
No. 84 in 1951
Bowman Gum card series,
$2.00-$2.25

MEAT PACKERS CARDS

Hunter's Wieners, *set of 29 cards, 2"x4¾", issued in 1955, depicts players, coaches, etc. of the St. Louis Cardinals, the cards are not numbered, this set was locally distributed in the St. Louis area, had a small printing and became very scarce within a few years of its appearance, the most valuable single card is that of Stan Musial, now selling for $85-110, the rest are bringing $70-90.*

	G-VG		FINE	
☐ Complete set	650.00	825.00	1150.00	1475.00

Hygrade Meats, *set of nine cards, 3¾"x4½", issued in 1957, depicts members of the Seattle Pacific Coast League team, the cards are not numbered, values:*

☐ **Dick Aylward**	23.00	31.00	45.00	60.00
☐ **Bob Balcena**	23.00	31.00	45.00	60.00
☐ **Jim Dyck**	23.00	31.00	45.00	60.00
☐ **Mario Fricane**	23.00	31.00	45.00	60.00
☐ **Bill Glynn**	23.00	31.00	45.00	60.00
☐ **Bill Kennedy**	23.00	31.00	45.00	60.00

	G-VG		FINE	
☐ Ray Orteig	23.00	31.00	45.00	60.00
☐ Joe Taylor	23.00	31.00	45.00	60.00
☐ Maury Wills	55.00	70.00	100.00	135.00
☐ Complete set	280.00	340.00	500.00	750.00

Koester's Bread, set of 52 cards, 3½"x2", issued in 1921, depicts members of the New York Giants and New York Yankees, and is entitled "World Series Issue" (these teams met in the World Series of 1921, the first so-called "subway series" to be played in New York), the cards are unnumbered, more valuable specimens:

☐ New York Giants - Frankie Frisch	18.00	24.00	39.00	49.00
☐ New York Giants - George Kelly	16.00	22.00	33.00	42.00
☐ New York Giants - John McGraw	19.00	25.00	40.00	50.00
☐ New York Giants - Charles D. Stengel ...	23.00	32.00	45.00	60.00
☐ New York Yankees - Waite Hoyt	15.00	20.00	30.00	39.00
☐ New York Yankees - Carl Mays	16.00	22.00	33.00	42.00
☐ New York Yankees - Babe Ruth	28.00	37.00	55.00	75.00
☐ Complete set	850.00	1075.00	1675.00	2000.00

Red Heart Dog Food, set of 33 cards, 2½"x3¾", issued in 1954, depicts players from the American and National Leagues, the cards are not numbered, this set would appear to be somewhat scarcer than the current market value indicates.

☐ Complete set	65.00	85.00	120.00	155.00

Stahl-Meyer Frankfurters, set of 12 cards, 3¼"x4½", issued in 1953, depicts players from the New York Yankees, New York Giants, and Brooklyn Dodgers, this set was distributed exclusively in the New York metropolitan area, the cards are not numbered, more valuable specimens:

☐ Roy Campanella	33.00	42.00	60.00	80.00
☐ Gil Hodges	45.00	60.00	85.00	110.00
☐ Monte Irvin	37.00	50.00	75.00	95.00
☐ Mickey Mantle	37.00	50.00	75.00	95.00
☐ Duke Snider	33.00	42.00	60.00	80.00
☐ Complete set	415.00	490.00	725.00	900.00

Sugardale Meats, set of four cards, 3¾"x5¼", issued in 1962, depicts members of the Pittsburgh Pirates, cards are lettered, values:

☐ A. Dick Groat	10.00	14.00	20.00	28.00
☐ B. Roberto Clemente	17.00	22.00	33.00	42.00
☐ C. Don Hoak	10.00	14.00	20.00	28.00
☐ D. Dick Stuart	10.00	14.00	20.00	28.00
☐ Complete set	78.00	105.00	120.00	145.00

TOBACCO CARDS

Fatima Cigarettes, set of 16 cards, 5¾"x2½", issued in 1913, depicts group portraits of all the major league teams then in existence (8 National League, 8 American League), the cards are not numbered, values:

American League

☐ Boston	24.00	33.00	45.00	60.00
☐ Chicago	16.00	22.00	31.00	40.00
☐ Cleveland	16.00	22.00	31.00	40.00
☐ Detroit	36.00	46.00	70.00	95.00

	G-VG		FINE	
☐ New York	32.00	42.00	60.00	80.00
☐ Philadelphia	17.00	22.00	33.00	42.00
☐ St. Louis	60.00	80.00	110.00	140.00
☐ Washington	17.00	22.00	33.00	42.00

National League

☐ Boston	16.00	22.00	31.00	40.00
☐ Brooklyn	16.00	22.00	31.00	40.00
☐ Chicago	16.00	22.00	31.00	40.00
☐ Cincinnati	16.00	22.00	31.00	40.00
☐ New York	16.00	22.00	31.00	40.00
☐ Philadelphia	16.00	22.00	31.00	40.00
☐ Pittsburgh	16.00	22.00	31.00	40.00
☐ St. Louis	33.00	43.00	65.00	85.00
☐ Complete set	475.00	600.00	875.00	1195.00

Fez Cigarettes, set of 126 cards (of which 100 are baseball players, the balance boxers), entitled "Prominent Baseball Players and Athletes," 5¾"x8", issued in 1911, depicts players of the National and American Leagues, the identical set was also distributed with Old Mill cigarettes; values are the same regardless of the imprint, more valuable specimens:

☐ # 5 Sam Crawford	20.00	27.00	40.00	55.00
☐ # 6 Hal Chase	17.00	22.00	33.00	43.00
☐ # 8 Fred Clarke	18.00	23.00	35.00	45.00
☐ # 9 Ty Cobb	23.00	32.00	45.00	57.00
☐ # 23 Nap Lajoie	20.00	27.00	40.00	55.00
☐ # 26 John McGraw	20.00	27.00	40.00	55.00
☐ # 27 Christy Mathewson	25.00	35.00	45.00	60.00
☐ # 35 Joe Tinker	16.00	21.00	32.00	41.00
☐ # 36 Tris Speaker	21.00	29.00	43.00	59.00
☐ # 39 Rube Waddell	24.00	38.00	47.00	62.00
☐ # 42 Cy Young	21.00	29.00	43.00	59.00
☐ # 47 Frank Chance	19.00	24.00	36.00	47.00
☐ # 80 Chief Bender	20.00	25.00	38.00	52.00
☐ # 87 Eddie Collins	21.00	27.00	40.00	55.00
☐ #125 Ed Walsh	17.25	22.25	33.00	40.00
☐ Complete set (including boxers)	no recent recorded sales, price would be over $3000.00 in FINE			

Note: Cards of boxers are ommitted from the above listing.

BASKETS

TOPIC: The art of basketry is indeed a reflection of America's cultural past. Long before this nation's first colonization, the American Indian had achieved artistic excellence as a basket weaver. Indian baskets are said to be the world's finest. Each basket was woven for a specific purpose and with the utmost care. These baskets were not only used to hold food and water and for ceremonial purposes, but some were also used for cooking. Their works are unique because they used only materials from nature — pine needles, straw, leaves, willow, porcupine quills, vines, reeds and grass. Dyes were made from bark, roots or berries. Their distinctive designs have made them sought-after by most basket enthusiasts.

TYPES: There are several types of basket construction. Wickerwork, the most common and widely used technique, is nothing more than an over and under pattern. Twining is similar except that two strands are twisted as they are woven over and under producing a finer weave. Plaiting gives a checkerboard effect and can be either a tight weave or left with some open spaces. Twillwork is much the same except that a diagonal effect is achieved by changing the number of strands over which the weaver passes. Coiling is the most desirable weave to the collector. This technique has been carefully refined since its conception around 7000 BC. Fibers are wrapped around and stitched together to form the basket's shape. Most of these pieces were either used for ceremonial purposes or for holding liquids, since the containers made in this fashion were tightly woven and leakproof.

COMMENTS: Baskets are available in a wide range of prices and types. Because of their decorative appeal they are now avidly sought by collectors. They may be collected by general category such as Indian, Appalachian, Nantucket, etc., or simply acquired in a wide variety of types and styles.

ADDITIONAL TIPS: Baskets are easy to care for but a few basic rules must be followed.
  1. Never wash an Indian basket. Dust it gently using a very soft sable artist's brush.

2. Do not subject Indian baskets to the sun as it will fade the patterns.

3. Do not wash any basket made of pine needles, straw, grass or leaves.

4. Willow, oak, hickory and rattan baskets may be washed in a mild solution of Murphy's Oil Soap and dried in a sunny location.

Basket, *Indian, coiled, 1880s,* **$200.00-$220.00**

	Current Price Range		P/Y Average
☐ **American Indian,** 10″ Dia.	180.00	220.00	155.00
☐ **Apache burden basket,** 2½″ x 2½″	25.00	35.00	22.50
☐ **Apache burden basket,** rawhide bottom, plain, 11½″ H.	300.00	375.00	300.00
☐ **Apache burden basket,** geometric pattern, tin cones hanging from leather straps, 6½″ x 5″	60.00	75.00	62.00
☐ **Apache burden basket,** negative pattern, tin cones hanging from leather straps, 12″ x 10½″	225.00	300.00	238.00
☐ **Apache coiled storage basket,** round body, dark brown with geometric motifs, 12½″ H. .	725.00	925.00	800.00
☐ **Apache coiled storage basket,** round body, flaring rim, dark brown with animals and human figures, 16¾″ H.	725.00	925.00	800.00
☐ **Apache coiled basket,** flat base, dark brown with snowflake motif, 8⅜″ Dia.	325.00	425.00	350.00
☐ **Apache grain barrel basket,** geometric design with human figures, 10″ x 11″	375.00	475.00	400.00
☐ **Apache plaque basket,** geometric design, 16″ x 5″	550.00	650.00	575.00
☐ **Apache miniature basket,** star design, 5½″ x 1″	145.00	210.00	160.00

	Current Price Range		P/Y Average
☐ **Apache tray,** 10½ " Dia., c. 1890s	110.00	160.00	125.00
☐ **Apache wedding basket,** 13" Dia., c. 1880 . . .	30.00	45.00	32.00
☐ **Bannock berry basket,** 8" x 8½ "	55.00	80.00	58.00
☐ **Buttocks basket,** tightly woven splint, 7" . . .	150.00	190.00	155.00
☐ **California,** tightly woven, light brown, diamond motif, 5¾ " Dia.	150.00	175.00	138.00
☐ **Caushatta effigy baskets,** pine cones and needles: Crawfish, 9" x 6½ "	25.00	35.00	22.50
☐ Crab, 6" x 5"	25.00	35.00	22.50
☐ Alligator, 9" x 2¾ "	25.00	35.00	22.50
☐ Turtle, 6½ " x 3"	25.00	35.00	22.50
☐ **Cheese basket,** splint	125.00	175.00	100.00
☐ **Cheese shaker,** round, 12" Dia.	250.00	275.00	225.00
☐ **Chehalis basket,** geometric and cross design, 4¼ " x 6¼ "	200.00	250.00	160.00
☐ **Chemehuevi basket,** two concentric geometric bands, 11½ " x 2"	350.00	450.00	375.00
☐ **Clothes basket,** round with two handles	75.00	95.00	62.00
☐ **Cowlitz lidded basket,** 3" x 4¼ "	80.00	130.00	100.00
☐ **Drying basket,** New England, 30" x 48", shallow rim, 1850s	325.00	500.00	330.00
☐ **Field basket,** oak splint, 1880s	100.00	175.00	110.00
☐ **Havasupi coiled basket,** triangle design, 11¾ " Dia.	175.00	200.00	150.00
☐ **Hopi coiled basket,** rectangular body in brown, orange and yellow raincloud and thunder motif, 5⅝"	110.00	160.00	125.00
☐ **Hopi corn sifter basket,** wicker with hoop around top, spiral design	80.00	110.00	82.00
☐ **Hopi coiled bowl basket,** floral design, 9¼ " Dia.	90.00	140.00	110.00
☐ **Hopi coiled plaque,** 14½ " Dia., c. 1930	110.00	160.00	125.00
☐ **Hopi tray,** mythological motif, 11" Dia.	80.00	130.00	100.00
☐ **Japanese,** tightly woven in brown and tan, circular, 7½ " Dia.	55.00	80.00	62.00
☐ **Karok basket,** oval, bottom inverted, 10" x 7"	110.00	160.00	125.00
☐ **Klamath tray,** 14" Dia., c. 1900	210.00	260.00	225.00
☐ **Laundry basket,** oak splint, 1910	50.00	70.00	55.00
☐ **Lillooet basket,** 12½ " x 16"	160.00	210.00	175.00
☐ **Maidu basket tray,** 8½ " Dia.	60.00	80.00	65.00
☐ **Makah basket,** zigzag designs, 7" Dia.	55.00	80.00	62.00
☐ **Mandan basket,** wood splint, circular	180.00	230.00	200.00
☐ **Mission basket tray,** 12" Dia.	330.00	410.00	360.00
☐ **Miwok basket,** 7" Dia., c. 1900	230.00	280.00	250.00
☐ **Modoc basketcap,** diamond design, 6" Dia. . .	120.00	140.00	125.00
☐ **Nantucket lightship basket,** 5" x 10"	400.00	465.00	415.00
☐ **Navajo wedding basket,** 10" Dia.	130.00	180.00	150.00
☐ **Nootka whaler's hat,** 10½ " x 10½ "	230.00	280.00	250.00
☐ **Paiute coiled basket,** exterior is beaded, 5" Dia.	180.00	210.00	182.00
☐ **Paiute lidded basket,** 10" H., c. 1900	90.00	125.00	100.00
☐ **Paiute water jar,** horse-hair handles, 5½ " x 7½"	80.00	110.00	82.00
☐ **Panamint basket,** reverse diamond design, 10½ " x 4"	310.00	410.00	350.00
☐ **Papago basket,** geometric design, 13" Dia. . .	80.00	110.00	82.00

	Current Price Range		P/Y Average
☐ **Papago coiled basket,** body woven in dark brown with bands of swastikas, 11⅝" Dia. ...	230.00	280.00	250.00
☐ **Papago plaque,** concentric square design, 15" Dia.	130.00	180.00	150.00
☐ **Papago waste paper basket,** men and dogs motif, 10" Dia.	100.00	130.00	110.00
☐ **Pima basket bowl,** 16" Dia.	260.00	335.00	295.00
☐ **Pima coiled basket,** flat base, flaring body, dark brown with pattern of human figures, 11¼" Dia.	260.00	360.00	300.00
☐ **Pima coiled basket,** shallow, dark brown with crosses in the field, 9¼" Dia.	110.00	160.00	125.00
☐ **Pima grain barrel,** geometric design, 11" Dia.	430.00	530.00	475.00
☐ **Pima plaque,** 11" Dia.	180.00	230.00	200.00
☐ **Pomo basket,** decorated with feathers, 12" Dia.	180.00	230.00	200.00
☐ **Sewing basket,** wicker	55.00	80.00	58.00
☐ **Skokomish berry basket,** 7" x 8"	110.00	135.00	112.50
☐ **Southwest coiled storage basket,** flat base, dark brown with arrow motifs, 27" H.	730.00	830.00	775.00
☐ **Splint collecting basket,** tightly woven, 8" x 9"	55.00	85.00	62.00
☐ **Splint cradle,** hooded, c. early 19th century, 19" x 8"	100.00	130.00	110.00
☐ **Splint hickory basket,** open handles	55.00	80.00	58.00
☐ **Splint,** oval, with wooded handles	145.00	195.00	150.00
☐ **Splint,** back pack	65.00	165.00	90.00
☐ **Split,** oak buttocks	55.00	80.00	58.00
☐ **Split,** oak buttocks, large	80.00	160.00	120.00
☐ **Tlingit basket,** geometric design, 6" Dia.	330.00	380.00	350.00
☐ **Tlingit basket,** 5" Dia., c. 1880	330.00	380.00	350.00
☐ **Tlingit lidded basket,** 4½" x 6½"	430.00	510.00	460.00
☐ **Tlingit twined spruce root basket,** cylindrical body, pale yellow bands with orange zigzag decoration, 5" Dia.	360.00	460.00	400.00
☐ **Tulare basket,** step pattern, squaw stitch, 7½" Dia.	130.00	210.00	162.00
☐ **Tulare basket,** rattlesnake design	110.00	135.00	112.50
☐ **Tulare coiled basket,** flat base, rounded sides, rattlesnake bands in black and reddish brown, 14½" Dia.	1250.00	1350.00	1150.00
☐ **Washo basket,** tightly woven, band design, 7" Dia.	85.00	115.00	80.00
☐ **Washo basket,** geometric design, 7"	65.00	95.00	75.00
☐ **Washo coiled trinket basket,** red, blue, black and green on white ground, 4¼" Dia.	110.00	160.00	125.00

BATMAN

DESCRIPTION: Batman is one of the early comic strip super heroes.

VARIATIONS: Included among Batman memorabilia are comics, toy cars and toy figures.

ORIGIN: The first Batman comic was published more than 40 years ago, and "Batman" was a popular TV show in the 1960s.

ADDITIONAL TIPS: Batman memorabilia has been listed here. For Batman comics look in the comics chapter of this book. For further information, see *The Official Price Guide to Comic Books and Collectibles.*

Batman Coloring Book,
Western Publishing Company, Inc.
$4.00-$6.00

	Current Price Range		P/Y Average
☐ **Bank,** ceramic figure of batman, 7″	30.00	45.00	37.50
☐ **Bank,** ceramic figures of Batman and Robin, c. 1966	65.00	85.00	75.00
☐ **Batbike,** toy, c. 1978	5.00	7.00	6.00
☐ **Batmobile,** toy, c. 1966	5.00	7.00	6.00
☐ **Batmobile And Batbike,** Corgi, c. 1968	10.00	15.00	12.50
☐ **Book,** *Batman and Robin,* hardcover, *From The 30s to the 70s,* 7½″ x 10½″, Bonanza, c. 1971	12.50	17.50	15.00
☐ **Book,** *Batman and Robin: From Alfred to Zowie!* by Ruthanna Thomas, Golden Press, 1966, book is die cut in shape of Batman's head	1.50	2.00	1.62
☐ **Book And Record Set,** *Gorilla City and Mystery of the Scarecrow Corpse,* Peter Pan Industries/National Periodical Publications, 1976	4.00	5.00	4.35
☐ **Bookends,** Batman and Robin, 4″ x 7″, c. 1966	25.00	50.00	35.00
☐ **Bubble Bath,** Avon, plastic Batmobile bottle which originally contained bubble bath	7.00	10.00	8.00
☐ **Button,** Batman and Robin Official Member, full color, 3½″, mid 1960s	6.00	8.00	6.65
☐ **Button,** lithographed tin, Batman in flight, TV inspired, 1966	7.00	10.00	8.10
☐ **Charm Bracelet,** with five figures (Batman, Robin, Penguin, The Riddler, The Joker), on original store card, 1966	10.00	14.00	11.00
☐ **Clock,** Bradley/National Periodical Publications, lucite desk model, c. 1966	15.00	18.00	16.00
☐ **Coloring Book,** Western Publishing Co., with the Western series number 1002, undated ...	4.00	6.00	4.45
☐ **Coloring Book,** *Batman Meets Blockbuster,* Whitman, 8″ x x 10¾″, 1956	4.00	4.75	4.20
☐ **Costume,** with mask, gray outfit, large yellow monogram with black bat on chest, blue cape, black half-mask, c. 1960	27.00	39.00	30.00
☐ **Figurine,** plastic, Wilton/National Periodical Publications, 4″	2.50	3.50	2.65
☐ **Game,** Hasbro, 1965	10.00	12.00	10.25
☐ **Game,** board game, Milton Bradley/National Periodical Publications, assorted playing pieces, box measures 9½″ x 19″	10.00	14.00	11.00
☐ **Jigsaw Puzzle,** three scenes of Batman and The Joker taken from Neal Adams' artwork in Batman Comics #251	18.00	23.00	19.00
☐ **License Plate,** 4″ x 7¼″, 1966	6.00	9.00	7.25
☐ **License Plate,** metal, 6″ x 12″, National Periodical Publications, c. 1966	6.00	9.00	7.50
☐ **Lunch Box And Thermos Set**	25.00	30.00	26.75
☐ **Model Kit,** Aurora, unopened, 1964	25.00	35.00	28.00
☐ **Mug,** white plastic with illustrations of Batman and Robin by Carmine Infantino	26.00	34.00	28.00
☐ **Music Box,** Price/National Periodical Publications, figural ceramic, 7″, late 1970s	22.00	29.00	24.00

	Current Price Range		P/Y Average
☐ **Music Box,** The Joker, Price/National Periodical Publications, figural ceramic, 7", late 1970s	22.00	29.00	24.00
☐ **Music Box,** Penguin, Price/National Periodical Publications, figural ceramic, 7", late 1970s	22.00	29.00	24.00
☐ **Music Box,** The Riddler, Price/National Periodical Publications, figural ceramic, 7", late 1970s	22.00	29.00	24.00
☐ **Paint By Numbers Set,** Hasbro, reproduction of the cover of Batman Comics #1 to be colored	5.00	10.00	7.00
☐ **Phonograph Record,** 12" LP on 20th Century Fox label, sleeve has photos of Burt Ward and Adam West with wording, "Exclusive Original Television Soundtrack Album ... Hear the Actual Television Voices of Batman and Robin, Plus Great Villains: The Penguin, Zelda, Mr. Freeze, The Riddler," etc.	20.00	25.00	21.00
☐ **Presto Paints,** undated	19.00	24.00	21.00
☐ **Token,** Batcoin #16, picturing Robin and The Riddler, TV inspired, 1966	4.00	5.00	4.30
☐ **Wallet,** 1966	11.00	15.00	12.00
☐ **Wristwatch,** Dabs, in box, c. 1977	30.00	35.00	31.00

BATTLESTAR GALACTICA

TOPIC: Battlestar Galactica was originally a science fiction movie and later a television show. It starred Lorne Greene, Richard Hatch and Dirk Benedict. The story involves a group of humans whose ancestors settled a distant part of the universe. These people are attacked and nearly annihilated by hostile "Cylons" (alien creatures who control an army of robots). The survivors flee in a small fleet of spaceships led by a battlestar (fighting spaceship) called "The Galactica." The fleet's destination is earth. The Cylons are in constant pursuit.

TYPES: Memorabilia from Battlestar Galactica may come in the form of trading cards, toys, posters or other promotional items.

PERIOD: The television show ran in 1978.

COMMENTS: Although Battlestar Galactica experienced a limited run on television, it was popular and collectors still treasure memorabilia from the show.

ADDITIONAL TIPS: For more complete listings, please refer to *The Official Price Guide to Science Fiction and Fantasy Books and Collectibles*, published by the House of Collectibles.

Battlestar Galactica Rub N' Play Magic Transfer Set, *made by Colorforms, under license from Universal City Studios, set of transfer sheets with likenesses of characters, 1978,* **$3.00-$5.00**

	Current Price Range		P/Y Average
☐ **Posters,** set of four, small	12.00	15.00	13.50
☐ **Poster,** standard size	10.00	13.00	11.50
☐ **Scripts,** group of four, "The Super Scout" and "The Night the Cyclone Landed," total of 219 pages	42.00	50.00	45.50
☐ **Trading cards,** full set of 132, Topps, 2½″ x 3½″, 1978	13.00	16.00	14.00
☐ **Trading card,** Topps, A Direct Hit, #116, 2½″ x 3½″, 1978	.10	.13	.11
☐ **Trading card,** Topps, A Planet in Peril, #101, 2½″ x 3½″, 1978	.10	.12	.11
☐ **Trading card,** Topps, A World in Flames, 11, 2½″ x 3½″, 1978	.09	.12	.10
☐ **Trading card,** Topps, Adar's Final Moments, #13, 2½″ x 3½″, 1978	.10	.12	.11
☐ **Trading card,** Topps, Annihilation of the Human Colonies, #19, 2½″ x 3½″, 1978	.10	.12	.11
☐ **Trading card,** Topps, An Ovion Warrior, #59, 2½″ x 3½″, 1978	.10	.12	.11

	Current Price Range		P/Y Average
☐ **Trading card,** Topps, Conferring with Seetol, #55, 2½″ x 3½″, 1978	.09	.13	.11
☐ **Trading card,** Topps, Escape from Fiery Death, #57, 2½″ x 3½″, 1978	.09	.12	.10
☐ **Trading card,** Topps, For the Love of Gold Cubits, #7, 2½″ x 3½″, 1978	.10	.13	.11
☐ **Trading card,** Topps, Hitting Outrageously High Notes, #70, 2½″ x 3½″, 1978	.09	.12	.10
☐ **Trading card,** Topps, Landram to the Rescue, #123, 2½″ x 3½″, 1978	.09	.13	.11
☐ **Trading card,** Topps, Night of the Metal Monsters, #90, 2½″ x 3½″, 1978	.09	.12	.11
☐ **Trading card,** Topps, Panic in Caprica Mall, #15, 2½″ x 3½″, 1978	.10	.13	.11
☐ **Trading card,** Topps, Richard Hatch is Captain Apollo, #3, 2½″ x 3½″, 1978	.09	.12	.10
☐ **Trading card,** Topps, The President's Council, #14, 2½″ x 3½″, 1978	.09	.13	.11
☐ **Trading card,** Topps, War of the Wiles, #69, 2½″ x 3½″, 1978	.09	.12	.11
☐ **Trading card,** Topps, Where the Elite Meet, #64, 2½″ x 3½″, 1978	.10	.12	.11

THE BEATLES

VARIATIONS: There is an unlimited variety of Beatles memorabilia. Records are quite collectible as well as buttons, posters and other souvenir items.

ORIGIN: The Beatles formed in Liverpool, England in the late 50s and early 60s. Band members included Paul McCartney, John Lennon, Ringo Starr and George Harrison. They took America by storm in 1964 when they appeared on the Ed Sullivan Show. Credited with starting the musical British invasion, The Beatles contributed much to rock and roll.

COMMENTS: The Beatles, along with Elvis Presley, are more collected than other recording artists. From the start of Beatlemania, anything Beatle related has become collectible. As the 20th anniversary of the Beatles arrival in the U.S. is celebrated, Beatle memorabilia should be more sought after than ever before.

ADDITIONAL TIPS: The listings in this section include memorabilia and records. The memorabilia section is listed alphabetically by item. Records are also listed alphabetically by title, followed by whether the record is an LP or a 45, the record company, issue number and other pertinent information.

For further information, refer to *The Official Price Guide to Records,* or *The Official Price Guide to Music Collectibles.*

Beatles, *still, if signed would be worth considerably more,* **$1.50-$2.00**

	Current Price Range		P/Y Average
☐ **Bandaid Dispenser,** promotional item from "Help"	2.00	5.00	2.75
☐ **Bank,** date register bank, with pictures and signatures, 1964	15.00	30.00	21.00
☐ **Belt buckle,** with "Beatles" and illustrations	60.00	80.00	67.00
☐ **Book,** *"A Cellarful of Noise" by Brian Epstein, clothbound reprint of the now-scarce 1964 first edition*	13.00	17.00	14.00
☐ **Book,** *"A Day in the Life" by Tom Schultheiss, paperback, 334 pages*	8.00	11.00	9.00
☐ **Book,** *"A Hard Day's Night" by John Burke, published by Dell, paperback*	15.00	20.00	16.00
☐ **Book,** *"A Spaniard in the Works" by John Lennon, clothbound first edition*	20.00	25.00	21.00

This price represents the average range but published offers differ considerably. When autographed by Lennon it is, of course, worth substantially more.

	Current Price Range		P/Y Average

☐ **Book,** *"The Beatles Down Under" by Glenn Baker, paperback, 128 pages* .... 13.00 17.00 — 14.00
Story of the group's Australian tour.

☐ **Book,** *"The Beatles' England" by David Bacon and Norman Maslov, paperback, 138 pages* .... 11.00 14.00 — 12.00

☐ **Book,** *"The Beatles for the Record," authorship uncredited, 96 pages, measures 12" square* .... 8.00 11.00 — 9.00

☐ **Book,** *"The Beatles Forever" by Nicholas Schaffner, clothbound, 218 pages* .... 13.00 17.00 — 14.00
An identical edition in paperback is selling at $6-8.

☐ **Book,** *"The Beatles in Their Own Words" by Miles (author who uses no last name), paperback* .... 5.00 7.00 — 6.00

☐ **Book,** *"The Beatles on Record" by J. P. Russell, paperback, 682 pages* .... 6.00 8.00 — 7.00

☐ **Book,** *"The Beatles' Record in Australia" by Bruce Hamlin, paperback, published in Australia* .... 8.00 11.00 — 9.00

☐ **Book,** *"The Beatles Reader" by Charles P. Neises, clothbound* .... 13.00 17.00 — 14.00

☐ **Book,** *"The Beatles Who's Who" by Bill Harry, paperback, 190 pages* .... 8.00 11.00 — 9.00
Biographies of everyone who played a role in the Beatles' lives.

☐ **Book,** *"The Book of Lennon" by Bill Harry, paperback, 223 pages* .... 9.00 12.00 — 10.00

☐ **Book,** *"Come Together" by Jon Wiener, paperback, 379 pages* .... 10.00 13.00 — 11.00

☐ **Book,** *"The Complete Beatles Quiz Book" by Edwin Goodgold and Dan Carlinsky, clothbound, 128 pages* .... 3.00 3.50 — 3.10

☐ **Book,** *"Dakota Days" by John Green, clothbound, 260 pages* .... 11.00 14.00 — 12.00

☐ **Book,** *"George Harrison Yesterday and Today" by Ross Michaels, paperback, 96 pages, published in Great Britain* .... 6.00 8.00 — 6.50

☐ **Book,** *"Growing Up With the Beatles" by Rom Schaumburg, paperback, 160 pages* .... 7.00 10.00 — 8.00

☐ **Book,** *"In His Own Write" by John Lennon, clothbound first edition* .... 25.00 30.00 — 26.00
Multiply that by about ten if it's personally autographed.

☐ **Book,** *"Lennon and Me" by Pete Shotton, paperback, 399 pages* .... 3.50 4.50 — 3.75

☐ **Book,** *"Lennon and McCartney" by Malcolm Doney, clothbound, 126 pages* .... 8.00 11.00 — 9.00

☐ **Book,** *"John Lennon: A Family Album" by Nishi F. Saimaru, paperback, 128 pages* ..... 32.00 40.00 — 33.00

☐ **Book,** *"John Lennon in His Own Words" by Miles (author who uses no last name), paperback* .... 5.00 7.00 — 6.00

	Current Price Range		P/Y Average
☐ **Button,** movie promo, "I've Got My Beatles Movie Tickets, Have You?", 2¼ "	.75	1.50	1.10
☐ **Car mascots,** bobbing headed Beatles, set of four	700.00	900.00	780.00
☐ **Card,** autographed wallet photo card, 2½ " x 3", 1964	.50	1.25	.75
☐ **Cards,** gum cards, set of 65, question and answer series, color, Topps, 1964	45.00	60.00	51.00
☐ **Cards,** gum cards, set of 50, Yellow Submarine, Primrose Confectionary (Britain), 1968	90.00	120.00	105.00
☐ **Card,** individual gum card, question and answer series, color, 1964	.75	1.25	1.00
☐ **Card,** individual gum card, Yellow Submarine, Primrose Confectionary (Britain), 1968	1.25	2.00	1.60
☐ **Cards,** playing cards with picture of group, 1964	3.50	6.00	4.25
☐ **Change purse,** picture of the Beatles, 1964 . .	2.00	4.50	3.00
☐ **Coasters,** set of six plastic coasters with illustrations and words, c. 1960s	25.00	35.00	29.00
☐ **Coloring book,** "Beatles Coloring Book," Saalfield Publishing Co., 1964	50.00	65.00	57.00
☐ **Comb,** John Lennon promotional	.75	1.50	1.05
☐ **Coin,** brass commemorative U.S. visit coin, 1964	6.00	14.00	9.00
☐ **Dolls,** blow up dolls, 16", 1966, set of four . . .	40.00	60.00	48.00
☐ **Doll,** John Lennon, fully dressed, base of doll is a radio, 8½ "	14.00	25.00	19.00
☐ **Game,** The Beatles Flip Your Wig Game, Milton Bradley, 1964	40.00	55.00	47.00
☐ **Hair brush,** 1964	10.00	15.00	12.00
☐ **Ink stamp,** self inking stamps, set of four, 1964	10.00	20.00	14.00
☐ **Jigsaw puzzle,** for fan club members, not sold in stores, 8½ " x 11", 1964	6.00	14.00	9.00
☐ **Key fob,** figural, promotional item for 1965 Shea Stadium Concert	.75	1.50	1.05
☐ **Key ring,** John Lennon, "Walls and Bridges" album, 1972	.75	1.50	1.05
☐ **Lunchbox,** laminated tin with color drawings of the Beatles	185.00	200.00	192.00
☐ **Magazine,** *Rolling Stone*, featuring John Lennon as "Man of the Year," 1970	30.00	45.00	37.00
☐ **Mirror,** black and white picture pocket mirror, features picture of group playing, 1964	.75	1.50	1.05
☐ **Mirror,** color picture of the Beatles, 1964	1.00	3.50	2.00
☐ **Pencil,** picture of Beatles, set of four, 1964 . .	3.00	4.00	3.30
☐ **Pencil case,** picture of Beatles, 1964	5.00	15.00	7.00
☐ **Pen,** magic picture pen, color photo	3.00	5.00	4.00
☐ **Pennant,** felt pennant with "Beatles" in block letters and illustrations of the group	40.00	60.00	48.00
☐ **Pin,** flasher pin flashes from group shot to four heads	1.50	3.00	2.10
☐ **Pin,** "I Like Beatles" flasher pin	1.00	2.00	1.40
☐ **Pin,** "I'm a Beatles Booster," 1965	.75	1.50	1.05
☐ **Pin,** John Lennon "Give Peace a Chance" . . .	.75	1.50	1.05

	Current Price Range		P/Y Average
Pin, John Lennon "Remember Love," 1¼" ..	.75	1.50	1.05
Pin, official fan pin, 2¼", 1965	.75	1.50	1.05
Pin, tin litho picture of Beatles, 1964	.75	1.50	1.05
Pin, Yellow Submarine, 1966	.75	1.50	1.05
Pocketbook, canvas, illustrated with "Beatles" and pictures	40.00	50.00	44.00
Pocket knife, John Lennon, "In Memory of a Great Beatle," 1980	1.00	3.00	2.00
Poster, Beatles at London Paladium, full color, 20" x 27", 1963, reissued in 1975	1.00	3.00	2.00
Poster, fan club souvenir poster, full color, 20" x 30", 1968	175.00	225.00	200.00
Poster, features 12 full color Beatles photos, 24" x 28", 1979	1.50	3.50	2.00
Poster, John Lennon commemorative, 1980 .	1.00	3.00	2.00
Poster, John Lennon, "Imagine There's No Lennon," 17" x 25", 1980	1.00	3.50	2.00
Poster, record shop poster advertising "A Hard Day's Night"	175.00	210.00	188.00
Press kit, Paul McCartney, Apple, 1970	60.00	80.00	66.00
Press kit, Paul McCartney and Wings, 1973 ..	80.00	110.00	93.00
Program, George Harrison, 1974 concert tour program	3.50	7.00	5.00
Record fob, metal with faces of the Beatles, 1964	.75	1.50	1.05
Ring, individual color flasher ring, set of four	.75	1.50	1.05
Ruler, 12", with signatures, photos and information, 1965	3.00	5.00	4.00
Scarf, colored with pictures and signatures, 1964	5.00	12.00	8.00
Strap, for carrying schoolbooks, features "Beatles" with musical notes	15.00	20.00	17.00
Tablecloth, printed with illustrations of the Beatles	60.00	85.00	67.00
Tickets, concert tickets	40.00	55.00	47.00
Tie tack, official fan club item, black and gold, 1964	1.50	3.00	2.25
Tie tack, raised figural face, set of four, 1964	8.00	16.00	11.00
Whistle, police style from the movie "Help," 1966	1.50	4.00	2.75
Wig, long hair Beatles wig	30.00	45.00	37.00
Wrist watch, full color picture on dial	15.00	25.00	19.00
Writing tablet, cover photo of the Beatles ...	25.00	45.00	34.00

RECORDS

Abbey Road, LP, Apple, 383, stereo	8.00	20.00	10.00
All You Need Is Love/Baby You're A Rich Man, 45, Capitol, 5964, promotional copy ...	35.00	80.00	42.00
Orange label	2.00	4.50	3.00
And I Love Her/If I Fell, 45, Capitol, 5235, orange label	2.00	4.50	3.25
Picture sleeve	11.00	25.00	13.00
The Beatles, LP, Apple, 101, stereo	13.00	30.00	19.00
The Beatles, 1962-1966, LP, Apple, 3403, stereo	6.00	13.00	8.00

	Current Price Range		P/Y Average

☐ **The Beatles, 1967-1970,** LP, Apple, 3404, stereo 6.00 13.00 8.00
☐ **The Beatles Second Album,** LP, Capitol, 2080, stereo, green label 10.00 24.00 13.00
☐   Black label 8.00 18.00 11.00
☐ **Christmas Fan Club Album,** LP, Apple, 100, stereo 33.00 75.00 40.00
☐ **Come Together/Something,** 45, Apple, 2654, Apple and Capitol markings 4.00 8.50 5.00
☐ **Do You Want To Know A Secret?/Thank You Girl,** 45, Capitol Starline, 6064 .... 8.00 20.00 11.00
☐ **Do You Want To Know A Secret?/Thank You Girl,** 45, Vee Jay, 587, label name in brackets 6.00 13.00 8.00
☐ **Do You Want To Know A Secret?/Thank You Girl,** 45, Vee Jay, 587, label name in oval with a picture sleeve 26.00 56.00 35.00
☐ **The Early Beatles,** LP, Capitol, 2309, stereo, green label 7.00 13.00 9.00
☐   Black label 7.50 15.00 9.50
☐ **Eight Days A Week/I Don't Want To Spoil The Party,** 45, Capitol, 5371, orange label 2.00 4.50 3.00
☐ **From Me To You/Please Please Me,** 45, Vee Jay, 581, picture sleeve with label name in brackets 50.00 110.00 70.00
☐ **A Hard Day's Night/I Should Have Known Better,** 45, Capitol, 5222, orange label 2.00 4.50 3.25
☐   Picture sleeve 9.00 20.00 12.00
☐ **Hey Jude/Revolution,** 45, Apple, 2276 .... 3.00 6.50 4.00
☐ **Hey Jude,** LP, Apple, 385, stereo 4.00 9.00 6.00
☐ **I Want To Hold Your Hand/I Saw Her Standing There,** 45, Apple, 5112 .... 2.50 5.50 3.50
☐ **I Want To Hold Your Hand/I Saw Her Standing There,** 45, Capitol, 5112, orange label 2.00 4.00 3.00
☐   Orange, yellow label 4.00 7.50 5.00
☐ **In The Beginning,** LP, Polydor, 24-4504, stereo 5.00 11.00 7.00
☐ **Lady Madonna/The Inner Light,** 45, Capitol, 2138, orange label 2.00 4.50 3.00
☐   Orange and yellow label 4.00 8.00 5.50
☐ **Let It Be/You Know My Name,** 45, Apple, 2764 2.50 5.50 3.50
☐ **Let It Be,** LP, Apple, 3401, stereo 4.00 9.00 6.00
☐ **The Long and Winding Road/For You Blue,** 45, Apple, 2832 .... 2.50 5.50 3.50
☐   Picture sleeve 8.50 21.00 10.00
☐ **Magical Mystery Tour,** LP, Apple, 2853, stereo 6.00 13.00 8.00
☐ **Meet The Beatles,** LP, Apple, 2047, stereo ... 4.00 9.00 6.00
☐ **Meet The Beatles,** LP, Capitol, 2047, stereo, green label 7.00 13.00 9.00
☐   Black label 8.00 23.00 10.00
☐ **My Bonnie/The Saints,** 45, Polydor, 66-833, Tony Sheridan and the Beatles, most valuable Beatles 45 .... 1400.00 3000.00 1700.00
☐ **Please Please Me/Ask Me Why,** 45, Vee Jay, 498, Beatles is misspelled, "Beattles," and it is in thick letters 130.00 275.00 150.00
☐ **Revolver,** LP, Apple, 2576, stereo 5.00 11.00 7.00
☐ **Rubber Soul,** LP, Apple, 2442, stereo 5.00 11.00 7.00

	Current Price Range		P/Y Average
☐ Sergeant Pepper's Lonely Hearts Club Band, LP, Apple, 2652, stereo	5.00	11.00	7.00
☐ Twist And Shout/There's A Place, 45, Capitol Starline, 6061	8.00	20.00	11.00
☐ Yellow Submarine, LP, Apple, 153, stereo ...	4.00	9.00	6.00
☐ Yesterday/Act Naturally, 45, Apple, 5498	2.50	5.50	3.50
☐ Yesterday/Act Naturally, 45, Capitol, 5498, orange label	2.00	4.50	3.00
☐ Orange and yellow label, picture sleeve ...	9.50	24.00	12.00
☐ Yesterday And Today, LP, Apple, 2553, stereo	13.00	30.00	19.00
☐ Yesterday And Today, LP, Capitol, 2553, stereo, butcher cover	270.00	570.00	300.00
☐ Revised cover	135.00	285.00	155.00
☐ New cover	8.00	21.00	12.00

BEER CANS

DESCRIPTION: Beer cans are highly collectible items. Beer cans were produced in different shapes, the most common include flat tops, cone tops and pull tabs.

PERIOD: Cans were first produced by breweries in 1935. The first cans were called flat tops because of the shape of the can top. Cone tops were produced shortly afterward, but they were not as popular with consumers, therefore by the 1960s they were virtually extinct. Today, cans with pull tabs are currently being produced.

ADDITIONAL TIPS: There are different ways to have a beer can collection. Some hobbyists collect full cans or empties while others collect unfinished cans called flats. See *The Official Price Guide to Beer Cans,* published by the House of Collectibles for more detailed information about this subject.

CONE TOPS

	Current Price Range		P/Y Average
☐ **Altes Lager,** Tivoli, 12 oz., silver and black -CROWNTAINER	40.00	50.00	45.00
☐ **American,** American, 12 oz., red, white, blue and gold, brand name in blue script lettering	100.00	125.00	112.00
☐ **Bavarian's Old Style,** Bavarian, 12 oz., white, gold and red, brand name in gold lettering (very ornate) with red initials	70.00	85.00	77.00
☐ **Becker's Uinta Club Mellow,** Becker, 12 oz., silver, blue and red, bucking bronco symbol . *Note: This is the correct spelling: Uinta. But it frequently appears as "unita" on trade lists.*	135.00	165.00	150.00
☐ **Ben Brew,** Franklin, 12 oz., yellow and gold, brand name in blue, red ribbon with "100% Grain Beer"	95.00	115.00	105.00
☐ **Sunshine,** Barbey, 12 oz., white and brown, brand name in white lettering against brown band, slogan "Since 1861" near top with sunburst - CROWNTAINER	500.00	600.00	550.00
☐ **Sunshine Vitamin D,** Schilitz, 12 oz., brown and white	52.00	65.00	58.50
☐ **Topaz,** Koller, 12 oz., silver, red stripes near bottom - CROWNTAINER	80.00	100.00	90.00
☐ **Topper Draught,** Standard, gallon	32.00	43.00	37.50

Cone Top, Eastside Beer, *Los Angeles Brewing Co., 12 oz.,* **$35.00-$45.00**

(photo courtesy of ©Rogalski Brothers, Gainesville, FL, 1984)

	Current Price Range		P/Y Average

☐ **Tropical Premium,** Florida, 12 oz., brown and white, slogan "Taste Tells" 480.00 575.00 527.00
☐ **Wagner's Gambrinus,** Wagner, 12 oz., gold and multi-colored 120.00 150.00 135.00
☐ **Wiedemann,** Wiedemann, 12 oz., - CROWN-TAINER 40.00 50.00 45.00

FLAT TOPS

☐ **A-1 Pilsner,** Arizona, 12 oz., white with "A-1" in block characters within gold frame 37.00 45.00 41.00
☐ **A-1 Pilsner,** Arizona, 12 oz., white and red, oval medallion with white lettering on red background 52.00 65.00 58.50
☐ **Banner Extra Dry,** Cumberland, 12 oz., white and red, "Premium Beer" in blue 15.00 20.00 17.50
☐ **Bantam,** Goebel, 8 oz. squat, white and dark green 26.00 33.00 29.50
☐ **Bantam Ale,** Goebel, 8 oz., squat, white and light green 31.00 40.00 35.50
☐ **Bartels Pure,** Lion, 12 oz., white and red, illustration of man with long beard 65.00 80.00 72.50
☐ **Bavarian Jay Vee,** Grace, 12 oz., blue and white 90.00 115.00 105.00
☐ **Becker's,** Becker, 12 oz., red, white and blue, brand name in white against red background 32.00 41.00 36.50
☐ **Becker's Best,** Becker, 12 oz., silver with black lettering 76.00 95.00 85.00
☐ **Burger,** Burger, 12 oz., white and red, letters in brand name have no black outlines and the red is a strong burgundy-red 10.00 14.00 12.00
☐ **Burgemeister Premium,** Warsaw, 12 oz., cream white, red and gold, light gold banding at top and bottom 3.00 4.00 3.50
☐ **Country Club,** Goetz, 12 oz., white, red and gold 18.00 23.00 20.50
☐ **Country Club Malt Liquor,** Goetz, 8 oz., squat, white with "Country Club" in red, gold band at bottom 21.00 29.00 26.00
☐ **Drewry's Extra Dry,** Drewry, 16 oz., blue shield, no crown, brand name in white 16.00 21.00 19.00
☐ **Drewry's Lager,** Drewry, 12 oz., silver red and black 21.00 28.00 24.50
☐ **Drewry's Malt Liquor,** Drewry, 12 oz., red, green and white, brand name in white lettering on green background, slogan "A Man's Drink" at bottom 235.00 290.00 262.00
☐ **Highlander Premium,** Missoula, 12 oz., red and white, white portion of can has slight greyish tinge (revised version) 13.00 16.50 14.75
☐ **Hillman's Export,** Best, 12 oz., brown and black, grained effect 50.00 65.00 57.50
☐ **Hillman's Superb,** Empire, 12 oz., blue and gold 62.00 78.00 69.00
☐ **Hillman's Superb,** United States Brewing, 12 oz., blue and gold 60.00 75.00 67.50

	Current Price Range		P/Y Average

☐ **Hofbrau,** Hofbrau, 12 oz., cream white and red, illustration of German village inn 16.00 21.00 19.00

☐ **Hoffman House,** Walter, 12 oz., white, brown and red 5.00 6.50 5.75

☐ **Holiday Special,** Potosi, 12 oz., white and brown with blue bands at top and bottom ... 12.00 16.00 14.00

☐ **Holihan's Light Ale,** Diamond Springs, red and cream white .... 55.00 70.00 · 62.00

☐ **Krueger,** Krueger, 12 oz., pink, dark red and silver, without traditional company symbol (pictorial letter "K") 24.00 32.00 28.00

☐ **Krueger,** Krueger, 12 oz., yellow, red and white, "Light Lager" in black 42.00 53.00 48.50

☐ **Meister Brau,** Peter Hand, 12 oz., white, gold and red, red band at top 5.00 7.00 6.00

☐ **Mile Hi,** Tivoli, 12 oz., red, white and blue, illustration of Colorado mountain 43.00 54.00 48.00

☐ **Mile Hi,** Tivoli, 12 oz., red, white and blue, illustration of Colorado mountain, reads "Light Premium Quality" in bands at bottom, mountain illustration has dark blue background 37.00 46.00 42.00

☐ **Miller Select,** Miller, 12 oz., red, white and blue, quarter-moon emblem in blue medallion 50.00 65.00 57.50

☐ **Milwaukee's Best,** Gettelman, 12 oz., blue and white, illustration of stein 16.00 21.00 19.00

☐ **Milwaukee Premium,** Waukee, 12 oz., white, red and gold 13.00 18.00 15.00

☐ **Mitchell's Premium,** Mitchell, 12 oz., red, white and blue 82.00 100.00 91.00

☐ **Old Milwaukee,** Schlitz, 12 oz., gold and red, scene within rectangular frame 25.00 33.00 29.00

☐ **Old Milwaukee,** Schlitz, 12 oz., red and white, dark printing on shield symbol 5.00 7.00 6.00

☐ **Pabst Blue Ribbon,** Pabst, 12 oz., red, white and blue 5.75 7.25 6.50

☐ **Pabst Blue Ribbon,** Pabst, 12 oz., gold, white and blue, slogan above gold band at bottom . 7.00 9.50 8.50

☐ **Pabst Blue Ribbon,** Pabst, 12 oz., gold, white and blue, slogan on gold band at bottom 7.00 9.50 8.50

☐ **Pfeiffer's,** Pfeiffer, 12 oz., gold, white and red, horizontal striping 8.00 11.00 9.50

☐ **Pickwick Ale,** Haffenreffer, 12 oz., gold, black and white 100.00 130.00 115.00

☐ **Piel's,** Piel's, 12 oz., gold, silver and black, brand name in white 10.00 13.75 11.67

PULL TABS

☐ **A-1 Light Pilsner,** National, 12 oz., cream white and brown .... .40 .60 .50

☐ **ABC Premium,** Garden State, 16 oz., dark red and white 2.50 3.25 2.87

☐ **ABC Premium,** Wagner, 12 oz., red and white, "AGED" in rectangular frame 1.75 2.50 2.12

☐ **ABC Premium Ale,** Eastern, 12 oz., dark green with "AGED" in rectangular frame .... .85 1.20 1.02

	Current Price Range		P/Y Average
☐ **Ballantine Ale,** Falstaff, 16 oz.	1.25	1.65	1.45
☐ **Ballantine Bock,** Ballantine, 12 oz., gold with ram's head in red circle	2.00	2.50	2.25
☐ **Ballantine Bock,** Falstaff, 12 oz., gold with ram's head in red circle	.85	1.15	1.00
☐ **Ballantine Draft,** Falstaff, 12 oz., white with "Draft" in large red letters, "Genuine" in red letters at top, three-ring sign in gold	.85	1.15	1.00
☐ **Black Dallas Malt Liquor,** Walter, 12 oz., blue and black, evening skyline	24.00	31.00	27.50
☐ **Black Dallas Malt Liquor,** Walter, 12 oz., blue and black, evening skyline	24.00	31.00	27.50
☐ **Black Horse Ale,** Black Horse, 12 oz., white, red and black, profile portrait of black horse .	.90	1.20	1.05
☐ **Buckhorn,** Olympia, 12 oz., yellow with illustration of antelope head in gold medallion, brand name in silver lettering	.45	.65	.55
☐ **Buckhorn,** Olympia, 12 oz., dark yellow with illustration of antelope head in dark brassy gold medallion, brand name in bluish silver .	.45	.65	.55
☐ **Budweiser,** Anheuser-Busch, 12 oz., white and red, current	.40	.60	.50
☐ **Budweiser,** Anheuser-Busch, 12 oz., red and white, "Tab Top" lettered around base	2.25	3.25	2.75
☐ **Budweiser,** Anheuser-Busch, 16 oz., "Tab Top"	4.00	5.75	4.87
☐ **Budweiser Malt Liquor,** Anheuser-Busch, 12 oz., black, brand name in red	1.75	2.35	2.05
☐ **Budweiser Malt Liquor,** Anheuser-Busch, 16 oz.	10.00	13.25	11.62
☐ **Buffalo,** Blitz Weinhard, 12 oz., light brown with illustration of buffalo	1.00	1.50	1.25
☐ **Busch Bavarian,** Anheuser-Busch, 12 oz., white and blue, snow-covered mountains, no clouds in background	1.75	2.50	2.12
☐ **Busch Bavarian,** Anheuser-Busch, 12 oz., white and blue, snow-covered mountains, no clouds in background, does not read "Tab Top," brand name encircled by thin red frame	.40	.60	.50
☐ **Carling's Black Label,** Carling, 12 oz., red and black, brand name within tilted medallion, "Carling" in red within medallion, coat-of-arms in gold, gold band at top	.50	.70	.60
☐ **Carling's Tuborg,** Carling, 12 oz., dark gold and dark red	.40	.60	.50
☐ **Cascade,** Blitz Weinhard, 12 oz., blue and white, brand name in white on blue background	1.85	2.50	2.17
☐ **Cascade,** Blitz Weinhard, 16 oz., does not state "King Size"	2.00	2.50	2.25
☐ **Cascade,** Blitz Weinhard, 16 oz., states "King Size" near top	11.00	15.00	13.00
☐ **Cee Bee,** Colonial, 12 oz., white and red	10.00	13.25	11.62
☐ **Hof-Brau,** General, 12 oz., red and white, brand name in bright blue lettering, bright blue frame around medallion	.85	1.15	1.00

	Current Price Range		P/Y Average
☐ **Hof-Brau,** Maier, 12 oz., red and white, brand name in grey-blue lettering	4.75	6.25	5.50
☐ **Kingsbury Real Draft,** Kingsbury, 12 oz., white, brown and red, lower portion of can has wood-grain finish	5.50	7.50	6.50
☐ **Kingsbury Wisconsin Pale,** Kingsbury, 12 oz., red, white and blue	4.75	6.25	5.50
☐ **Knickerbocker Natural,** Jacob Ruppert, 7 oz., white with red and blue ribbons, blue lettering	4.75	6.25	5.50
☐ **Koch's Golden Anniversary,** Koch, 12 oz., red, white and gold, "The Best in Flavor" at top of can	.40	.60	.50
☐ **Kodiak Ale,** Schmidt, 12 oz., blue and gold, illustration of mountain peaks	.90	1.20	1.05
☐ **Koehler,** Erie, 12 oz., dark blue and white, no bright orange trim around brand name	13.00	17.00	15.00
☐ **Koehler,** Erie, 12 oz., dark blue and white, bright orange trim around brand name	2.75	3.50	3.12
☐ **Koehler,** Erie, 12 oz., blue and white	1.25	1.65	1.45
☐ **Koehler,** Erie, 12 oz., blue and white, Bicentennial	.90	1.20	1.05
☐ **Koehler,** Erie, 12 oz., red and white, Bicentennial	.90	1.20	1.05
☐ **Koehler Lager,** Erie, 12 oz., red and white	1.75	2.25	2.00
☐ **Koenig Brau,** Koenig Brau, 12 oz., gold and white	6.25	8.00	7.12
☐ **Lucky Lager,** Lucky Lager, 12 oz., pale blue and gold, brand name slightly curved	4.00	6.00	5.00
☐ **Lucky Lager,** Lucky, 16 oz.	12.00	16.00	14.00
☐ **Lucky Light Draft,** General, 12 oz., white and tan, pictorial illustration and lengthy text . . .	.90	1.20	1.05
☐ **Lucky Malt Liquor,** Lucky, 16 oz.	25.00	33.00	29.00
☐ **Lucky Red Carpet,** General, 12 oz., red and white	.90	1.20	1.05
☐ **Maier Select,** Maier, 12 oz., red, white and blue, blue leaf near top	4.00	6.00	5.00
☐ **Malt Duck Grape,** National, 12 oz., purple and white	35.00	45.00	40.00
☐ **Manheim,** Reading, 12 oz., red and white	8.00	11.00	9.50
☐ **Mark Meister Premium Lager,** Eastern, 12 oz., blue and white	5.00	7.00	6.00
☐ **Mark V,** Pittsburgh, 12 oz., red, white and blue, brand name in black	1.75	2.35	2.05
☐ **Mark V,** Pittsburgh, 12 oz., red, white and blue, brand name in blue	.65	.85	.75
☐ **Miller High Life,** Miller, 12 oz., gold, white and red	.40	.60	.50
☐ **Old Crown,** Old Crown, 12 oz., white and red, without symbol (figure of man)	.90	1.20	1.05
☐ **Old Crown,** Old Crown, 12 oz., white and red, with symbol (figure of man)	2.00	2.50	2.25
☐ **Old Crown Bock,** Old Crown, 12 oz., brown and white, illustration of ram's head	1.75	2.50	2.12

	Current Price Range		P/Y Average

☐ **Schlitz,** Schlitz, 12 oz., white and brown, slogan "The Beer That Made Milwaukee Famous" is printed in dark brown scrip letters	.90	1.20	1.05
☐ **Schlitz,** Schlitz, 12 oz., white and brown, slogan "The Beer That Made Milwaukee Famous" is printed in dark brown script letters, dated 1971	.80	1.05	.92
☐ **Schlitz Malt Liquor,** Schlitz, 12 oz., white and gold, brand name blue	2.75	3.50	3.12
☐ **Schlitz Malt Liquor,** Schlitz, 12 oz., blue, black and white, illustration	.90	1.20	1.05
☐ **Schlitz Malt Liquor,** Schlitz, 16 oz., dark blue bull	1.00	1.35	1.17
☐ **Schlitz Stout Malt Liquor,** Schlitz, 12 oz., white and gold, blue lettering, "Stout" positioned above "Malt Liquor" instead of all on one line	3.00	3.75	3.37
☐ **Stag,** Stag, 12 oz., gold, white and red, small brand name	.40	.60	.50
☐ **Stag,** Carling, 16 oz., "Half Quart" in large white letters near top	4.50	6.00	5.25
☐ **Stag,** Carling, 16 oz., does not state "Half Quart"	1.75	2.25	2.00
☐ **Stallion XII,** Gold Medal, 12 oz., gold, white and red, illustration of horse	75.00	95.00	85.00
☐ **Standard Cream Ale,** Standard Rochester, 12 oz., green, white and gold	14.00	18.00	16.00
☐ **Standard Dry Ale,** Eastern, 12 oz., blue, white and gold	.85	1.15	1.00
☐ **Standard Dry Ale,** Standard Rochester, 12 oz., blue, white and gold	3.75	4.75	4.25
☐ **Stegmaier Bock,** Stegmaier, 12 oz., brown and white, slogan "Truly Brewed"	1.00	1.50	1.25
☐ **Stegmaier Gold Medal,** Stegmaier, 12 oz., gold and white	.90	1.20	1.05
☐ **Winchester Malt Liquor,** Walter, 12 oz., pale blue	4.50	5.75	5.12
☐ **Winchester Malt Liquor,** Walter, 16 oz.	12.00	16.00	14.00
☐ **Wisconsin Club Premium Pilsner,** Huber, 12 oz., white and gold, brand name in white	1.00	1.35	1.17
☐ **Wisconsin Gold Label,** Huber, 12 oz., white and gold, brand name in gold, very ornate gold designing	.90	1.20	1.05
☐ **Wisconsin Gold Label Premium,** Huber, 12 oz., gold and white	5.75	7.25	6.50
☐ **Wisconsin Holiday,** Holiday, 12 oz., white and red	1.80	2.25	2.02
☐ **Wisconsin Holiday,** Huber, 12 oz., white and red	1.00	1.30	1.15
☐ **Wisconsin Premium,** Heileman, 12 oz., white, red and blue, small map of Wisconsin	1.00	1.30	1.15
☐ **Wunderbar,** Minneapolis Brewing, 12 oz., light gold and dark gold with blue and white	9.50	12.50	11.00
☐ **Wunderbrau Malt Beverage, Near Beer,** Erie, 12 oz., blue and white, coat of arms	11.75	15.50	13.62

	Current Price Range		P/Y Average
☐ **Yorktown Extra Fine Premium,** Reading, 12 oz., red, white and black	9.00	12.00	10.50
☐ **Yuengling Premium,** Yuengling, 12 oz., silver and red, eagle symbol near top, in red	.90	1.20	1.05

BELLS

TOPIC: Bells have been used for thousands of years to signal important events such as births, weddings, enemy attacks and holidays.

TYPES: Bells can be divided into many categories, including closed and open mouth bells, figurine bells, jingle bells, chimes and gongs.

PERIODS: Bells have existed for thousands of years, although they were introduced to Europe about 1500 years ago.

MATERIALS: Brass, iron, silver, gold, bronze, wood, glass and porcelain are frequently used to make bells.

COMMENTS: Bells are very popular among collectors because of their interesting shapes and musical qualities.

☐ **Alaska bell,** colored totem handle, original	42.00	58.00	48.00
☐ **Alexander's helmet bell,** no clapper, 5½" Dia.	13.00	18.00	14.00
☐ **Bayreuther bell,** hand painted porcelain, lilies of the valley	72.00	92.00	80.00
☐ **Brass bell,** stork	34.00	50.00	38.00
☐ **Brass clapper bell**	110.00	130.00	112.50
☐ **Brass dinner bell**	8.00	12.00	7.50
☐ **Brass hotel call bell,** 4" Dia.	50.00	65.00	52.00
☐ **Brass musical chime bell**	32.00	68.00	42.00
☐ **Brass school bell,** 4⅜" Dia., c. 1910	20.00	28.00	21.00
☐ **Brass bell,** wooden handle, 4"	12.00	18.00	12.50
☐ **Brass bell,** wooden handle, 6"	18.00	22.00	20.00
☐ **Brass bell,** wooden handle, 7"	28.00	38.00	30.00
☐ **Brass bell,** wooden handle, 8"	28.00	38.00	30.00
☐ **Bronze art figurine bells,** very detailed, rare	210.00	360.00	275.00
☐ **Bronze bell,** angel holder	95.00	115.00	100.00
☐ **Cast iron bell,** mechanical	130.00	160.00	138.00
☐ **Charlie Chaplin bell,** solid brass, cane and typical pose	18.00	22.00	17.50

Call Bell, *dome shaped, round base, spring operated clapper,* **$20.00-$45.00**

	Current Price Range		P/Y Average
☐ **China bell,** cobalt, 5″	50.00	63.00	52.00
☐ **China bell,** German, painted clown	68.00	82.00	72.00
☐ **Chinese brass gong bell,** 9″	45.00	60.00	48.00
☐ **Church bell,** solid brass, single tier	110.00	135.00	112.50
☐ **Church bell,** solid brass, triple tier	180.00	220.00	195.00
☐ **Church bell,** old, 1100 pounds	575.00	675.00	600.00
☐ **Church bell,** without wheel	130.00	160.00	138.00
☐ **Coast Guard,** brass, Herculoy, mounted on walnut base, 16″, 1945	625.00	825.00	690.00
☐ **Conestoga,** graduated on strap (4), brass ...	210.00	260.00	225.00
☐ **Cow bell,** iron ring with strap attachment ...	32.00	48.00	38.00
☐ **Cow bell,** leather collar	12.00	16.00	12.50
☐ **Cow bell,** clapper	28.00	38.00	30.00
☐ **Cow bells,** hand riveted	28.00	38.00	30.00
☐ **Crystal bell,** faceted drummer boy handle, Blair-Reubel	35.00	50.00	38.00
☐ **Cutter bells,** 4 bells, 2½ ″ - 2¾ ″ Dia.	45.00	60.00	48.00
☐ **Cutter-type bell,** iron strap	80.00	110.00	82.00
☐ **Damascus bell,** bronze, inlaid gold and green leaves with red berries	55.00	75.00	60.00
☐ **Dinner bell,** crystal	55.00	75.00	60.00
☐ **Dinner bell,** enamel on metal	55.00	75.00	60.00
☐ **Dinner bell,** nickel	13.00	17.00	12.50
☐ **Dinner bell,** ornate sterling silver	65.00	90.00	72.00
☐ **Dog bells,** sculptured handles, pair, 4″	80.00	110.00	87.50
☐ **Doorbell,** Abbe's patent double strike	35.00	50.00	38.00
☐ **Doorbell,** brass	55.00	75.00	60.00
☐ **Early American thumbprint bell,** design around skirt	50.00	65.00	48.00

	Current Price Range		P/Y Average
☐ Elephant bell, brass	45.00	60.00	48.00
☐ Elephant bell, cloisonne	110.00	130.00	112.00
☐ Fire Alarm bell	48.00	58.00	48.00
☐ Fire Truck bell, eagle mounted on top of original mounting bracket, nickel plated, c. 1925 .	700.00	900.00	760.00
☐ Fire Truck bell, solid brass, brass acorn finial, polished, 10″, c. 1920	450.00	550.00	480.00
☐ Fire Truck bell, solid brass, brass finial, 10″, c. 1900	175.00	225.00	195.00
☐ French flint glass bell, cordinated handle and clapper	420.00	495.00	430.00
☐ Glass bell, amber, glass	120.00	185.00	112.00
☐ Glass bell, bristol, 11½ ″	120.00	185.00	112.00
☐ Glass bell, bristol wedding bell, 14″	130.00	160.00	138.00
☐ Glass bell, carnival	18.00	22.00	17.50
☐ Glass bell, cranberry glass, clear handle	160.00	200.00	170.00
☐ Glass bell, clear dark green	90.00	115.00	90.00
☐ Glass bell, cut glass including handle	145.00	175.00	150.00
☐ Glass bell, nailsea bell, solid glass handle, loops and swirls in color	210.00	260.00	225.00
☐ Glass Bell, venetian, ruby red, enamel decoration	90.00	110.00	90.00
☐ Glass Bell, venetian glass bell, latticino, pink, 14″	160.00	195.00	165.00
☐ Glass Bell, venetian, goose bell	22.00	32.00	25.00
☐ Hand bell, brass	110.00	135.00	112.50
☐ Hand bell, brass with decorations	80.00	110.00	82.00
☐ Hand bell, brass with wooden handle	110.00	135.00	112.50
☐ Iron bell, bronze, lion and sun motif, bas relief	90.00	110.00	90.00
☐ Iron bell, cow	18.00	22.00	17.50
☐ Iron bell, dinner	110.00	135.00	112.50
☐ Iron bell, farm	230.00	280.00	250.00
☐ Iron bell, sleigh	60.00	78.00	60.00
☐ Johannes Afine bell, (Joseph Von Ende) bronze, wreath and cherub, bas relief	95.00	120.00	105.00
☐ Lady sculptured bell, 4″	160.00	190.00	170.00
☐ Lennox-Imperial bell, off-white porcelain, 18K gold, 6″	60.00	80.00	65.00
☐ Locomotive bell, brass, New York City, brass finial, polished, 17″, c. 1920-1930	550.00	650.00	580.00
☐ Locomotive bell, steam bell by Howard, brass, from narrow guage era, 13″	800.00	1000.00	860.00
☐ Locomotive bell, with yoke and cradle, from steam locomotive, 17″	1200.00	1600.00	1375.00
☐ Majolica bell, dog	40.00	55.00	42.00
☐ Mass bell, solid brass	80.00	110.00	82.00
☐ Meissen bells, decorated, antique	110.00	135.00	112.50
☐ Meissen bells, raised decorations	210.00	260.00	225.00
☐ Meneely bell, bronze, original clapper, polished, 19″, 1858	775.00	975.00	850.00
☐ Meneely Tower bell, raised letters, large brass hexball finial, 28″, weights about 950 pounds with cradle, age undetermined	3600.00	4400.00	3775.00
☐ Mission bell, min. clapper	80.00	110.00	82.00
☐ Mission bell, Spanish	110.00	135.00	112.50

	Current Price Range		P/Y Average

☐ **Navy bell,** main deck bell from battleship, brass, large raised letters, large brass finial, 25″, c. 1920-1930 .... **3000.00 3400.00 3125.00**

☐ **Pewter sterling bell** **22.00 32.00 25.00**

☐ **Pressed glass bell,** smokey **6.00 12.00 7.50**

☐ **Quimper lady bell,** colored, 8″ **75.00 95.00 80.00**

☐ **Roeland Ghend,** bronze, sand cast, crusade handle **65.00 85.00 70.00**

☐ **Saddle chimes,** set of 3 with pinwheel on each **145.00 175.00 150.00**

☐ **School bell,** bronze, 20″ iron yoke, Jones and Hitchcock, c. 1856 .... **860.00 960.00 900.00**

☐ **School bell,** metal, wooden handles, small .. **80.00 110.00 82.00**

☐ **School bell,** metal, wooden handle, large ... **90.00 110.00 90.00**

☐ **School bell,** 5″ **50.00 65.00 52.00**

☐ **School bell,** 6½″ **72.00 92.00 80.00**

☐ **School bell,** 8¼″ **95.00 115.00 100.00**

☐ **School bell,** 9½″ **95.00 115.00 100.00**

☐ **Sculptured bell,** lady 4″ **55.00 75.00 60.00**

☐ **Sculptured bell,** little boy on a coal pile, original clapper, detailed **155.00 190.00 170.00**

☐ **Sculptured bell,** old woman on the green from "Canterbury Tales", detailed **110.00 160.00 125.00**

☐ **Sheep bell** **55.00 75.00 60.00**

☐ **Ship bell,** brass, c. 1845 .... **210.00 260.00 235.00**

☐ **Ship bell,** brass dolphin **225.00 250.00 235.00**

☐ **Ship bell,** H.M.S. Wilstar, c. 1880, 14″ diameter **475.00 575.00 510.00**

☐ **Ship bell,** nickel plated bronze, acorn finial, matching bronze mounting bracket, 10″, c. 1910 .... **275.00 325.00 290.00**

☐ **Silver-plated bell,** wooden handle, 7″ H. **40.00 50.00 45.00**

☐ **Silver-plated call bell,** foot operated, embossed trim, 36″ H. **80.00 92.00 85.00**

☐ **Sleigh bells,** leather strap of 17 bells **210.00 260.00 225.00**

☐ **Sleigh bells,** leather strap of 20 bells **260.00 285.00 262.00**

☐ **Sleigh bells,** iron string of 25 bells **280.00 330.00 300.00**

☐ **Sleigh bells,** brass string of 25 bells **230.00 280.00 250.00**

☐ **Sleigh bells,** all brass, 29 bells mounted on a jointed brass strap, old **170.00 205.00 178.00**

☐ **Soldier,** roman **55.00 75.00 60.00**

☐ **Sterling silver bell,** Reed & Barton, "Pointed Antique" **25.00 32.00 29.00**

☐ **Sterling silver bell,** twisted handle, engraved scroll design **30.00 36.00 33.00**

☐ **Sterling silver bell,** woman **120.00 150.00 132.00**

☐ **Swedish bell,** heavy brass, double throated, 2¾″ Dia. **20.00 26.00 20.50**

☐ **Swedish bell,** heavy brass, triple throated, 3″ Dia. **22.00 32.00 25.00**

☐ **Town Crier,** long with wooden handle **110.00 135.00 112.50**

☐ **Trolley car,** 8″ Dia. **80.00 110.00 82.00**

☐ **Turtle,** German mechanical **80.00 110.00 82.00**

☐ **Waterford crystal bell** **60.00 80.00 65.00**

☐ **Wedgwood,** porcelain, c. 1979 .... **30.00 40.00 30.00**

BELT BUCKLES

DESCRIPTION: Belt buckles have become a very popular collectible as the interest in vintage clothing has grown. They can be found in thrift shops and second hand clothing stores as well as in pawn shops, antique shops and flea markets. They have been made in a wide variety of styles, utilizing many different materials.

RECOMMENDED READING: For further information you may refer to *The Official Price Guide to Antique Jewelry* by Arthur Guy Kaplan, published by The House of Collectibles.

Scroll Motif Buckles, *gold, c. 1900,* **$700.00-$800.00**

		Current Price Range		P/Y Average
☐	Buckle and button set, translucent apple green enamel, silver, English, c. 1920-30 .	220.00	240.00	225.00
☐	Cameo motif, carved lava, gold plated, c. late 19th	220.00	240.00	225.00
☐	Circular motif buckle with beaded edge and slide with beaded edge, sterling silver, American, c. 1896	135.00	145.00	137.00
☐	Cluster motif pair of buckles, rhinestone, white metal, c. 1930-40	10.00	15.00	11.00
☐	Fan and scroll motif buckle, champleve opaque black and white enamel, gold, c. 1870	1200.00	1300.00	1210.00

	Current Price Range		P/Y Average
☐ Fancy shape motif pair of buckles, rhinestone, white metal, c. 1930-40	12.00	18.00	13.00
☐ Oval Etruscan granulation motif, buckle pin, gold, c. 1870	240.00	260.00	247.00
☐ Oval motif, paste, silver	400.00	500.00	410.00
☐ Oval motif pair of buckles, cut steel, c. late 19th	35.00	45.00	37.00
☐ Oval wreath motif pair of buckles, cut steel, c. late 19th	25.00	30.00	26.00
☐ Rectangular buckle and floral motif slide, floral motif belt, sterling silver, American, c. 1896	75.00	85.00	78.00
☐ Rectangular buckle and floral motif slide, floral motif belt, sterling silver, American, c. 1896	75.00	85.00	78.00
☐ Rectangular buckle with beaded rim and slide, sterling silver, American, c. 1896 . . .	85.00	110.00	88.00
☐ Rectangular flower motif pair of buckles, cut steel, marked: France, c. late 19th . . .	40.00	50.00	42.00
☐ Rectangular motif buckle, 64 emerald-cut sapphires, 114 round diamonds, platinum, gold, French, c. 1890	3200.00	3400.00	3250.00
☐ Rectangular motif pair of buckles, silver plated, c. mid 20th	12.00	18.00	13.00
☐ Rectangular motif pair of buckles, silver plated, c. mid 20th	10.00	15.00	11.00
☐ Rectangular pair of buckles, engraved, sterling silver, c. 1920	50.00	60.00	55.00
☐ Ribbon and leaf motif, gold, French, c. 1870	950.00	1100.00	955.00
☐ Scroll motif buckles, gold, c. 1900	700.00	800.00	710.00
☐ Scroll motif buckle, gold, c. 1890	500.00	600.00	520.00
☐ Scroll motif buckle and slide, sterling silver, American, c. 1896	160.00	180.00	165.00
☐ Scroll motif buckle and slide with beaded rim, sterling silver, American, c. 1896	130.00	140.00	135.00
☐ Scroll and flower motif, cloisonne and guilloche enamel, Arts and Crafts, c. late 19th	250.00	300.00	255.00
☐ Shell motif buckle, two round diamonds, six round demantoid garnets, gold, c. 1880	1300.00	1400.00	1350.00
☐ Snake motif buckle, enamelled, three round diamonds, gold, c. 19th	1600.00	1800.00	1650.00
☐ Square crescent motif pair of buckles, cut steel, c. 19th	35.00	40.00	36.00
☐ Square motif buckle, seed pearl border, cobalt blue enamel, 14K gold, c. 1920	300.00	350.00	310.00
☐ Square motif buckle with beaded edge and slide with beaded edge, sterling silver, American, c. 1896	155.00	165.00	160.00
☐ Wide rectangular motif buckle and slide, sterling silver, American, c. 1896	85.00	110.00	90.00

BENNINGTON POTTERY

TOPIC: Bennington ranks in a special class among American pottery. It was the first U.S. factory to gain an international reputation, and the first to produce truly creative artistic works. The popularity of Bennington among collectors stretches back before the beginning of the America's antique trade. By as early as 1890, the wares had become solidly established as collector's items. Since the factory's operations closed in 1858, all of its products have been ranked as antiques for many years.

HISTORY: The period of *true Bennington* was brief, extending from 1842 to 1858, but this may be deceiving since the output during those 16 years was heavy. For the actual beginnings of Bennington, we must delve into the 18th century. In 1793, John Norton established a pottery works of rather humble proportions in the town of Bennington, Vermont. Its products were red earthenware and mason's bricks. During the War of 1812, Norton installed a stoneware kiln and began making English-style wares. Brown glazed wares were also produced. The earlier Bennington wares were all sold locally apparently without any effort to invade the more lucrative market of the mid-Atlantic states. From all available information, it seems that production during these years was modest. Things took a dramatic change in the winter of 1842 to 1843, when Julius Norton (a grandson of the founder) went into partnership with Christopher Fenton. The aim of this new alliance was to diversify the Bennington line and bring it fully up to par with the imported English stonewares. With the kind of ambition that characterized few American potters of that era, Norton and Fenton set out to duplicate the much admired bold surface finished of Rockingham wares. This they accomplished and as many collectors would agree even surpassed Rockingham in their best specimens.

STYLE: The Bennington products were marvels of free-spirited designing. Among the best known are its stoneware figures with mottled, deep-brown color. The same type of unique coloration also appears on water pitchers, conventional tableware and other items. In 1849, the company filed for a patent on colored glazes, the first of its kind in the United States. The secret of the Bennington process was to take the fired wares and coat them with metallic oxides. Next they were dipped in flint enamel — the glaze was *not* brush-painted. The myth of brush-painted glaze on Bennington stoneware was probably inspired by what appear to be brush markings. These, however, were the result of natural texturing as the liquid glaze gradually solidified. If the glaze was thick on some areas of a piece, which was almost inevitable from the dipping process, it gathered into the crevices before drying. Much to the credit of Bennington, it never strove to achieve a smooth ware, free of mottling. The company was quite proud of the individuality of its product, and public response confirmed this confidence. In its time, however, the popularity of Bennington was small compared to heights reached later on the antique market.

The company underwent several name changes. From the original name of "Norton and Fenton," it became "Fenton's Works," then "Lyman, Fenton and Co." Finally, the name was changed to "United States Pottery" in 1850 which was in use at the time of the company's collapse in 1858.

In addition to the instantly recognizable wares mentioned above, Bennington also produced parianware. This was a minor phase of its operations.

MARKS: The earliest mark upon the association of Norton and Fenton in 1842, was a circle composed of the wording *NORTON & FENTON, BENNINGTON, Vt.* Block lettering was used without any symbol. When the company name was changed, after Norton left in 1847, the mark became *FENTON'S WORKS; BENNINGTON, VERMONT* enclosed in a rectangular decorative border. This distinctive mark was set in two styles of lettering with *FENTON'S WORKS* in slanting characters resembling italics. The address was set in standard vertical lettering. The next mark, that of Lyman, Fenton and Co., was contained within a plain oval frame and read *LYMAN FENTON & CO., FENTON'S ENAMEL, PATENTED 1849, BENNINGTON, Vt.* This ushered in the era of colored glazes. Within this mark, the year (1849) is very prominently displayed. When the name became United States Pottery Co., two different marks were introduced, both reading *UNITED STATES POTTERY Co., BENNINGTON, Vt.* One carries the wording within an oval frame and contains two small ornamental flourishes; the other is a modified diamond-shape composed of decorative printer's type, but without further ornamentation.

	Current Price Range		P/Y Average
☐ Baker, *10", oval, mottled brown glaze*	65.00	85.00	68.00
☐ Basin, *12", mottled brown Rockingham glaze*	70.00	80.00	72.00
☐ Bed pan, *mottled brown Rockingham glaze* .	70.00	80.00	72.00
☐ Bottle, *10½", figure of coachman wearing hat and cape without tassels, c. 1847-58*	200.00	225.00	210.00
☐ Bowl, *6", Rockingham glaze, bell-shaped* . . .	90.00	100.00	95.00
☐ Bowl, *7½", mottled brown glaze*	90.00	100.00	95.00
☐ Bowl, *9", mottled brown Rockingham glaze* .	70.00	80.00	72.00
☐ Bowl, *10" oval, mottled brown Rockingham glaze*	70.00	80.00	72.00
☐ Box, covered, *5¾" oval, all white, parian, shell-molded base and lid with shell finial* . . .	80.00	95.00	82.00
☐ Box, *5¾", square, all white parian, shell finial*	95.00	105.00	97.00

	Current Price Range		P/Y Average
□ **Box,** 4⅜″, square, parian, top with figure, Lion of Lucerne	120.00	130.00	122.00
□ **Candlesticks,** 11″, mottled brown glaze, pair	210.00	250.00	215.00
□ **Churn,** mottled brown glaze, wooden lid and dasher	230.00	270.00	235.00
□ **Compote,** on low footed base, molded design on body	120.00	130.00	122.00
□ **Creamer,** cow, mottled brown glaze	180.00	200.00	185.00
□ **Cream pot,** 1 qt., cobalt floral, covered, J. & E. Norton	145.00	160.00	147.00
□ **Crock,** 2 gal., gray, cobalt blue foliage, impressed "E. Norton & Co., Bennington, Vt.", c. 1883-94	140.00	50.00	142.00
□ **Crock,** 4 gal., yellow-brown with "4" impressed with cobalt blue	310.00	350.00	315.00
□ **Crock,** 6-gal., handled, gray, cobalt blue floral & ribbon motif, impressed "E. & L.P. Norton, Bennington, Vt." C. 1861-81	160.00	170.00	165.00
□ **Cuspidor,** 8½″, mottled brown glaze, shell pattern	130.00	150.00	135.00
□ **Dish,** 2½″, brown Rockingham glaze	60.00	70.00	62.00
□ **Dove,** 7½″, modeled in flight, molded feathers, made to hang, c. 1847-48	550.00	570.00	555.00
□ **Egg cup,** molded lily pad feet, all white, set of 6	130.00	150.00	135.00
□ **Flask,** 5½″, yellow and brown glaze	480.00	520.00	485.00
□ **Flower pot,** 6″, Rockingham glaze, eagles in relief on sides	30.00	40.00	32.00
□ **Inkwell,** 5″x2½″, mottled brown Rockingham glaze	120.00	140.00	122.00
□ **Inkwell,** 4 quill holes, usual color, design in relief	210.00	250.00	215.00
□ **Inkwell,** cylindrical, Rockingham glaze	105.00	125.00	110.00
□ **Jar,** covered, two handled, mottled brown Rockingham glaze, impressed 1849	555.00	565.00	560.00
□ **Jar,** 1 gal., gray stoneware, cobalt blue, butterfly and floral decor, impressed "E. & L. Norton, Bennington, Vt."	115.00	125.00	117.00
□ **Jar,** 2 gal, 11″, ovoid, handled, gray, cobalt blue floral motif, impressed "E. & L.P. Norton, Bennington, Vt.," c. 1861-81	200.00	220.00	210.00
□ **Jug,** 11¼″, gray, cobalt blue bird motif, impressed "J. & E. Norton, Bennington, Vt." c. 1850-59	230.00	240.00	235.00
□ **Jug,** 16″, gray, cobalt blue floral spray, impressed "Julius Norton, Bennington, Vt.," c. 1838-45	240.00	250.00	242.00
□ **Jug,** 1 gal., gray stoneware, cobalt blue tree design, marked "E. Norton, Bennington, Vt.," c. 1881-83	140.00	150.00	142.00
□ **Jug,** 1 gal., 10½″, gray, cobalt blue bird and branch motif, impressed " J. Norton & Co., Bennington, Vt."	225.00	235.00	227.00
□ **Jug,** 1½ gal., 9½″, mottled brown glaze	150.00	170.00	155.00

	Current Price Range		P/Y Average
☐ **Jug,** *2 gal, gray, brushed cobalt blue rabbit motif, impressed "Julius Norton, Bennington, Vt."*	230.00	240.00	235.00
☐ **Jug,** *gal., gray, cobalt blue floral spray, impressed "J. & E. Norton, Bennington, Vt.," c. 1850-59*	230.00	240.00	235.00
☐ **Jug,** *2 gal., gray stoneware with cobalt blue scrolling feather design, impressed "E. & L.P. Norton, Bennington, Vt."*	130.00	175.00	135.00
☐ **Jug,** *2 gal., blue and green, flint enamel*	100.00	115.00	105.00
☐ **Jug,** *2 gal, 13½", gray, cobalt blue bird motif, impressed "J. & E. Norton, Bennington, Vt.," c. 1850-59*	335.00	350.00	340.00
☐ **Jug,** *3 gal., 16", gray stoneware with cobalt blue floral decor, impressed "E. & L.P., Bennington, Vt.," 1861-81*	130.00	175.00	135.00
☐ **Jug,** *3 gal., ovoid, gray stoneware with cobalt blue floral decor, impressed "Norton & Fenton, Bennington, Vt."*	150.00	170.00	155.00
☐ **Mug,** *6", Rockingham glaze*	110.00	125.00	115.00
☐ **Ornament,** *form of a cow with tree trunk at rear, dark brown and yellow-brown glaze with some green.*	925.00	950.00	930.00
☐ **Pie plate,** *10½", mottled brown Rockingham glaze*	120.00	140.00	125.00
☐ **Pitcher,** *5½", tulip and sun flower pamotif*	55.00	65.00	60.00
☐ **Pitcher,** *7", hunting scene with dogs and hunters on horseback in relief, mottle brown Rockingham glaze*	100.00	110.00	102.00
☐ **Pitcher,** *7½", parian, relief-molded white palm trees and exotic flowers designed for syrup cover, marked "U.S.P." on base*	100.00	110.00	102.00
☐ **Pitcher,** *8¼", tulip and heart, flint enamel*	160.00	180.00	165.00
☐ **Pitcher,** *8½", parian, blue and white, molded grape cluster leaves*	120.00	130.00	122.00
☐ **Pitcher,** *8¾", Rockingham glaze, castle scene*	360.00	400.00	365.00
☐ **Pitcher,** *10", hunting scene, mottled brown Rockingham glaze*	330.00	340.00	332.00
☐ **Pitcher,** *11", hexagonal, brown birds and flowers*	280.00	330.00	285.00
☐ **Snuff jar,** *3⅞", flint enamel, flat bottom*	760.00	850.00	765.00
☐ **Teapot,** *7¾", "Rebecca at the Well"*	70.00	80.00	72.00
☐ **Teapot,** *2 qt., mottled brown glaze*	125.00	140.00	127.00
☐ **Tile,** *7", mottled olive brown glaze, impressed 1849*	530.00	540.00	532.00
☐ **Tobacco jar,** *11", mottled brown glaze, covered*	210.00	250.00	215.00
☐ **Toby creamer,** *6⅛", mottlmd brown Rockingham glaze, seated Toby*	340.00	375.00	345.00
☐ **Vase,** *basket of roses in medallion*	30.00	38.00	32.00
☐ **Vase,** *7¼", mottled brown glaze, ear of corn shape*	100.00	120.00	105.00
☐ **Vase,** *7½", all white, parian*	50.00	60.00	52.00
☐ **Vase,** *7½", flint enamel, tulip in relief*	260.00	300.00	265.00

BIBLES

DESCRIPTION: The Bible, comprised of Old and New Testaments, is the religious book used by Christians.

PERIOD: The Bible holds the distinction of being the first book ever printed. Johann Gutenberg printed it during the middle 1400s. Since then, the Bible has been reprinted more than any other book.

COMMENTS: There are several ways to collect Bibles. Some collectors buy only the rare Bibles of the 15th and 16th centuries. Others specialize in miniature Bibles or Bibles that have been translated into several languages. Another popular way to collect Bibles is specializing in first editions.

ADDITIONAL TIPS: This section is organized according to date beginning with the 1500s through the 1800s. For more information, consult *The Official Price Guide to Old Books and Autographs,* published by The House of Collectibles.

	Current Price Range		P/Y Average
☐ **English,** includes Tyndals Prologues, London, N. Hyll, 1551	650.00	900.00	775.00
☐ **English,** Breeches Bible, with the Book of Common Prayer, London, Barker, 1578	350.00	500.00	425.00
☐ **English,** London, Barker, 1583	350.00	500.00	425.00
☐ **English,** London, Barker, 1594	250.00	325.00	287.00
☐ **English,** London, Barker, 1606	85.00	120.00	102.00
☐ **English,** Breeches Bible, London, R. Barker, 1608	275.00	350.00	312.00
☐ **English,** The New Testament, London, Barker, 1612	50.00	75.00	62.00
☐ **English,** The Holy Bible, London, Barker, 1615	125.00	185.00	155.00
☐ **English,** New Testament, Cambridge, England, 1628	130.00	175.00	152.00
☐ **English,** The Holy Bible, Cambridge, England, 1630	125.00	160.00	137.00
☐ **English,** London, Barker and Bill, 1630	450.00	650.00	530.00
☐ **English,** London, H. Hill and J. Field, 1660	325.00	400.00	362.00
☐ **English,** London, 1711	100.00	135.00	117.00

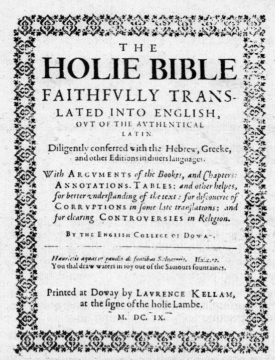

THE

HOLIE BIBLE

FAITHFVLLY TRANS-
LATED INTO ENGLISH,
OVT OF THE AVTHENTICAL
LATIN.

Diligently conferred with the Hebrew, Greeke,
and other Editions in diuers languages.

With ARGVMENTS of the Bookes, and Chapters:
ANNOTATIONS. TABLES: and other helpes,
for better vnderstanding of the text : for discouerie of
CORRVPTIONS in some late translations: and
for clearing CONTROVERSIES in Religion.

BY THE ENGLISH COLLEGE OF DOWAY.

Hauritis aquas in gaudio de fontibus Saluatoris. Isaie.12.
You shal draw waters in ioy out of the Sauiours fountaines.

Printed at Doway by LAVRENCE KELLAM,
at the signe of the holie Lambe.

M. DC. IX.

**Title Page Of The First Edition Of The Roman Catholic
Old Testament In English,** *printed in Douai, France
which was spelled "Doway."*
$200.00-$235.00

	Current Price Range		P/Y Average
☐ **English,** Baskett Bible, Oxford, 1759, two volumes	120.00	150.00	135.00
☐ **English,** Blayney's Bible, Oxford, 1769	140.00	190.00	165.00
☐ **English,** Old and New Testament, illustrated with engravings by Fittler, London, Bensley, 1795, two volumes	120.00	150.00	135.00
☐ **American,** Philadelphia, 1794, pocket size	45.00	65.00	55.00
☐ **American,** Philadelphia, 1813	300.00	400.00	350.00
☐ **American,** N.Y., 1822, pocket size	75.00	100.00	87.00
☐ **American,** Brattleboro, Vt., 1823	300.00	400.00	350.00

BICENTENNIAL

DESCRIPTION: The bicentennial, celebrated on July 4, 1976, was the 200th birthday of the United States as an independent nation. It was on July 4, 1776 that the Declaration of Independence was signed in Philadelphia, PA and the U.S. declared its freedom from England.

PERIOD: Bicentennial memorabilia was produced from the early 1970s until 1976.

COMMENTS: A variety of bicentennial commemoratives were made, from inexpensive trinkets to fine plates and silver.

ADDITIONAL TIPS: The listings are alphabetical by item. Other information includes, when possible, a description of the item, manufacturer, country of manufacture, production quantity and date. The first price listed is the issue price of the item; the second price is the current value of the item.

For more information on bicentennial memorabilia refer to *The Official Guide to Collector Plates* and *The Official Guide to American Silver and Silver Plate.*

	Current Price Range		P/Y Average
☐ **Knife,** The American Eagle Bicentennial Series, commemorative set of five knives, handcrafted, solid nickel silver bolsters, brass linings, stainless steel blades	165.00	195.00	180.00
☐ **Medal,** July 4, 1976, set of 12, sterling silver, 39 mm., Franklin Mint, U.S., production quantity 4,675, 1976 ....each	25.00	45.00	35.00
☐ ....set	245.00	325.00	275.00
☐ **Medal,** sterling silver, 64 mm., Franklin Mint, U.S., production quantity 18,849, 1975-1976 .	80.00	105.00	90.00
☐ **Medal,** sterling silver, 32 mm., Franklin Mint, U.S., production quantity 238,192, 1976	15.00	27.00	20.00
☐ **Medal,** thirteen original states, set of 13 medals, sterling silver, 39 mm., Franklin Mint, U.S., production quantity, 10,264 ......each	20.00	31.00	22.00
☐ ....set	250.00	305.00	275.00

	Current Price Range		P/Y Average

☐ **Plate,** Across the Delaware, Wedgwood, Great Britain, 1975 .... 45.00 90.00 67.00

☐ **Plate,** Boston Tea Party, silver, Gorham Collection, U.S., production quantity 750, 1973 .. 560.00 630.00 590.00

☐ **Plate,** Burning of the Gaspee, pewter, Gorham Collection, U.S., production quantity 5,000, 1971 .... 40.00 50.00 45.00

☐ **Plate,** Calm Before the Storm, Armstrong's, U.S., production quantity 250, 1971 .... 255.00 280.00 265.00

☐ **Plate,** Constellation, Kirk, U.S., production quantity 825, 1972 .... 80.00 90.00 82.00

☐ **Plate,** Crossing the Delaware, Stieff, U.S., production quantity 10,000, 1975 .... 55.00 60.00 57.00

☐ **Plate,** The Declaration, Castleton China, U.S., production quantity 7,600, 1973 .... 65.00 70.00 67.00

☐ **Plate,** The Declaration, porcelain, scalloped border, 9¾″, Haviland, France, production quantity 10,000, 1976 .... 40.00 50.00 42.00

☐ **Plate,** Declaration Signed, Wedgwood, Great Britain, 1976 .... 47.00 62.00 53.00

☐ **Plate,** E. Pluribus Unum, Bing and Grondahl, Denmark, 1976 .... 55.00 60.00 56.00

☐ **Plate,** Eagle, blue satin glass, Fenton Art Glass, U.S., 1974 .... 20.00 30.00 22.00

☐ **Plate,** Eagle, chocolate glass, Fenton Art Glass, U.S. 1975 .... 16.00 29.00 22.00

☐ **Plate,** Eagle, white satin glass, Fenton Art Glass, U.S. 1976 .... 16.00 29.00 22.00

☐ **Plate,** First in War, Ridgewood, U.S. production quantity 12,500, 1974 .... 42.00 45.00 43.00

☐ **Plate,** Gaspee Incident, Armstrong's, U.S., production quantity 175, 1972 .... 260.00 270.00 262.00

☐ **Plate,** Independence Hall, Bayel of France, France, production quantity 500, 1975 ...... 62.00 65.00 62.50

☐ **Plate,** John Hancock Signs the Declaration of Independence, sterling silver, bas-relief, 24kt gold inlaid and electro plated, 8″, Franklin Mint, U.S. production quantity 10,166, 1976 .. 180.00 215.00 195.00

☐ **Plate,** Liberty Bell, Bayel of France, France, production quantity 500, 1974 .... 55.00 60.00 57.00

☐ **Plate,** Monticello, damascene silver, Reed and Barton, U.S., production quantity 1,000, 1972 .... 80.00 90.00 82.00

☐ **Plate,** Mt. Vernon, damascene silver, Reed and Barton, U.S., 1973 .... 80.00 90.00 82.00

☐ **Plate,** A New Dawn, Castleton China, U.S., production quantity 7,600, 1972 .... 65.00 67.00 66.00

☐ **Plate,** One Nation, Castleton China, U.S., production quantity 7,600, 1974 .... 65.00 67.00 66.00

☐ **Plate,** Paul Revere, porcelain, scalloped border, 9¾″, Haviland, France, production quantity 10,000, 1975 .... 35.00 55.00 42.00

BICYCLES

ORIGIN: A steerable wooden horse on wheels, the Draisienne, is considered to be the first modern bicycle. It was built in 1818. The first pedal driven bike appeared in Scotland in 1839. Later versions include the Velocipede, the High-Wheeler and the safety bike.

MAKER: Top manufacturers of the early bicycle were the Wright Brothers of Dayton, OH, and Columbia.

COMMENTS: Bicycles built before 1900 are the most collectible. Of particular note are the 1861 Velocipede with front wheel pedals and the 1885 Rover. Tricycles and quadricycles are especially rare and collectible.

ADDITIONAL TIPS: The listings are in alphabetical order, they are followed by the year of manufacture. Prices include a current price range as well as an average price for the previous year.

	Current Price Range		P/Y Average
☐ Adult tricycle, 1885	5000.00	5800.00	5200.00
☐ Boneshaker, 1850	1750.00	2500.00	2100.00
☐ Boneshaker, 1870	1250.00	1800.00	1400.00
☐ Buggy spoked triangle pedal high wheeler, 1886	600.00	700.00	630.00
☐ Chainless, 1853	160.00	225.00	190.00
☐ Chainless safety, 1900	225.00	280.00	240.00
☐ Columbia chainless, 1856	225.00	280.00	240.00
☐ Columbia high wheeler, 1901	1350.00	2000.00	1500.00
☐ Columbia, three wheeler tandem tricycle, 1888	3350.00	4000.00	3500.00
☐ Eagle, 50 inch high wheeler, 1872	2250.00	2800.00	2500.00
☐ Eagle, high wheeler with brake, 1865	3250.00	4000.00	3500.00
☐ Fifty inch high wheeler, 1878	1350.00	1800.00	1450.00
☐ Fifty-six inch high wheeler, 1898	720.00	950.00	800.00
☐ High wheeler bicycle, 1885	1250.00	1850.00	1450.00
☐ Scooter, 1927	225.00	290.00	240.00
☐ Solid tire safety, 1890	820.00	1500.00	1000.00

Child's Bike, *Otto, iron, weighs 60 pounds, 1887,*
$250.00-$500.00

	Current Price Range		P/Y Average
☐ **Spring fork,** on sta1862	650.00	800.00	725.00
☐ **Tandem,** 1914	275.00	350.00	300.00
☐ **Tandem,** adult tricycle, 1885	6500.00	7500.00	7000.00
☐ **Tandem,** bicycle, 1895	380.00	500.00	425.00
☐ **Two wheeler,** 1896	380.00	500.00	425.00
☐ **Two wheeler,** 1914	150.00	200.00	175.00

BLACK MEMORABILIA

DESCRIPTION: A wide variety of items depicting blacks was produced from 1900 to 1960. Many were advertising promotions featuring Uncle Remus and Aunt Jemima type characters. Figural mammy kitchenware, slavery postcards, cast iron banks and doorstops, chalkware statues, dolls, figurines, etc., were very popular.

COMMENTS: Many of these items were extremely derogatory in nature and depicted blacks as slovenly and ignorant. The civil rights movement of the 1960s put an end to the production of racist depictions of blacks.

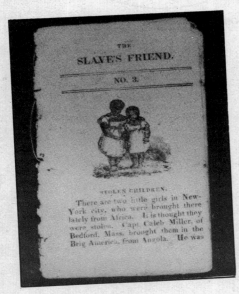

The Slave's Friend,
miniature children's magazine,
1842, **$40.00-$50.00**

	Current Price Range		P/Y Average

☐ **Advertising Poster,** Cascarets laxative, pull-man passenger and black porter, wording "Is the road clear?" lithographed on heavy cardboard, 13″ x 17″ . . . . `60.00` `80.00` `64.00`

☐ **Advertising Sign,** Coon's Ice Cream, cardboard trimmed in tin, lithographed, red, cream with black stripes, 21″ x 60″, c. 1920 . . `110.00` `135.00` `117.00`

☐ **Bank,** Aunt Jemima, new, cast iron, 8″ . . . . . . `8.00` `10.00` `9.00`

☐ **Bell,** Mammy, new, bisque, red and yellow dress with white apron, holding mixing bowl `4.00` `5.00` `4.50`

☐ **Book,** *Old Voices* by Howard Weeden, published by Doubleday, collection of black poetry, pictorial cover, 1904 . . . . `25.00` `30.00` `26.25`

☐ **Book,** *Ten Little Nigger Girls,* children's book with full color cover and colored illustrations along with rhymes, published in New York by E.P. Dutton, 9″ x 11″, c. 1900-1910 . . . . `175.00` `225.00` `190.00`

☐ **Booklet,** advertising, Excelsier Improved Varnish, 1940s, cover depicts black boy, read "Won't Turn White," eight pages long . . . . . . `1.00` `2.00` `1.50`

☐ **Broom Holder,** Mammy, cast iron . . . . `140.00` `145.00` `142.00`

☐ **Button,** advertising, new, black boy holding raccoon, Two Coons Axle Grease, color, 2¼″ `1.00` `2.00` `1.50`

☐ **Button,** advertising, new, Black Man, Georgia Cane Syrup, color, 2¼″ . . . . `1.00` `1.50` `1.25`

☐ **Button,** advertising, new, Pickaninny Girl with Watermelon, color, 2¼″ . . . . `1.00` `1.50` `1.25`

☐ **Candy Box,** Amos n' Andy . . . . `75.00` `80.00` `77.00`

☐ **Cookie Jar,** Mammy, new, bisque, very colorful, 9½″ . . . . `15.50` `18.50` `16.50`

☐ **Cookie Jar,** Mammy, new, Rockingham Pottery, lid is on belly, brown and red with white trim, 9″ . . . . `16.50` `18.50` `17.00`

☐ **Doll,** Aunt Jemima Pancake Flour, cloth, uncut . . . . `65.00` `70.00` `67.00`

Black Musicians, *Made in Japan,* **$90.00-$125.00**

	Current Price Range		P/Y Average
☐ **Doll,** baby, new, bisque, jointed arms and legs, three braided pigtails, red polka dot dress, 3½".................................	5.00	6.00	5.00
☐ **Doll,** black baby, bisque, three patches of hair with ribbon, handpainted features, made in Japan, 3", c. 1930-1940	80.00	100.00	84.00
☐ **Doll,** black girl, bisque, jointed, made in Japan, 4½", c. 1940	30.00	40.00	32.00
☐ **Doll,** Bye-Lo Baby, new, black bisque head, arms and legs, lace trimmed gown and bonnet, 11"	9.00	11.00	10.00
☐ **Doll,** girl, new, bisque, jointed arms and legs, three braided pigtails, red polka dot dress, 6"	7.00	8.00	7.50
☐ **Doll,** Mammy, new, bisque head, arms, legs, stuffed body, fully dressed in colorful outfit with apron and bandana 16"	11.00	15.00	12.00
☐ **Doll,** Mammy, rag, new, Mammy flips over to Southern Belle doll, 14"	6.50	8.50	7.50
☐ **Doll,** Uncle Mose, cloth, uncut	65.00	70.00	67.00
☐ **Figurine,** Black Boy Eating Watermelon, new, bisque, colorful, 2"	2.50	3.50	2.75
☐ **Figurine,** Black Boy on Potty, bisque, dressed in yellow nightgown and red night cap, holding a slice of watermelon	4.00	6.00	4.75
☐ **Figurines,** set of five, new, New Orleans Jazz Band, bisque, five musicians dressed in tuxedos playing banjo, clarinet, horn, saxophone and drums, 3"	17.00	20.00	18.50
☐ **Figurine,** same as set above except old, made in Japan	90.00	125.00	95.00

Figurine, *German Bisque,* **$75.00**

	Current Price Range		P/Y Average

☐ **Game,** Comic Conversation Cards, question and answer cards with black themes, lithograph of black man and woman on box lid playing the game, published by Ottmann, box measures 5¼″ x 7¼″, c. 1910 . . . . — 175.00 — 225.00 — 190.00

☐ **Jigsaw Puzzle,** Amos and Andy, Pepsodent premium (they were sponsors of the show), full color, 8″ x 10″, c. 1930-1935 . . . . — 100.00 — 130.00 — 110.00
Note: Price is for specimen in the original mailing envelope.

☐ **Kewpie,** vinyl, Rose O'Neill wings, 4½″ . . . . . — 1.50 — 2.50 — 1.75

☐ **Label,** cane syrup, Uncle Remus, 1924, stone lithograph, says "Dis' Sho' Am Good," 6¾″ x 20″ . . . . — 8.00 — 8.50 — 8.25

☐ **Medal,** anti-slavery, white metal (imitation silver), British and Foreign Antislavery Society, pictures kneeling slave with legend, "Am I Not a Man and a Brother," also reads "A Voice from Great Britain to America," 1834 . . — 90.00 — 115.00 — 97.00

☐ **Mirror,** advertising, Merrick Thread, depicts black boy hanging by thread over open mouthed alligator, saying "Fooled Dis Time Cully Dis Cotton Ain't Gwine To Break," 2″ x 3″ . . . . — 1.50 — 2.50 — 1.75

☐ **Mirror,** Aunt Jemima, round, color . . . . — 1.00 — 1.50 — 1.25

☐ **Oven Paddle,** Mammy, new, wooden, full color picture of Mammy, 15½″ . . . . — 2.50 — 4.50 — 2.75

☐ **Pail,** peanut butter, pickaninny . . . . — 20.00 — 25.00 — 22.00

☐ **Phonograph Record,** "Coon Band Contest," Columbia Wax Cylinder #531412, banjo solo, artist unbilled, c. 1890 . . . . — 40.00 — 60.00 — 45.00

☐ **Phonograph Record,** "If the Man in the Moon Were a Coon," Oxford Wax Cylinder #33083, soprano solo, artist unbilled, c. 1905 . . . . — 28.00 — 42.00 — 31.00

☐ **Photograph,** carte-de-visite of Sojourner Truth, early female activist for black equality, holds photo in her lap of Abraham Lincoln . . — 200.00 — 250.00 — 215.00

☐ **Pin Back,** Aunt Jemima, color, 2¼″ . . . . — 1.00 — 1.50 — 1.25

☐ **Postcards,** set of twelve, shows different scenes of slavery, color . . . . — 6.00 — 8.00 — 6.50

☐ **Postcards,** 1940s, set of 25 assorted, Ashville Postcard Company, full color, variety of subjects including comical, Mammy, plantation, pickaninnies, etc . . . . — 12.00 — 15.00 — 13.00

☐ **Poster,** broadside, anti-slavery, "Remarks on the Slave Trade" by Samuel Wood, 362 Pearl Street, New York City, woodcut of deck plan of slave ship showing overcrowding and atrocities to which slaves were subjected, 7¼″ x 12½″, undated, c. 1830-1840 . . . . — 600.00 — 800.00 — 640.00

	Current Price Range		P/Y Average

☐ **Print,** "Pore Lil Mose," lithographed page from book of the same name by cartoonist R.F. Outcault, full color, typical stereotyped likenesses and dialogue, 10" x 14", c. 1900-1905 .... — 40.00 — 50.00 — 43.00
Note: This value is for a single illustrated page. Complete copies of the book are rare.

☐ **Puzzle Postcard,** "Pick the Pickaninnies" by Ulman Manufacturing Company, lithographed card with five folding flaps, 3½" x 5½", 1907 .... — 65.00 — 85..00 — 72.00
Note: The flaps picture white and black children. Object of the puzzle is to fold the flaps so that only black children can be seen.

☐ **Salt and Pepper Shakers,** Aunt Jemima and Uncle Mose, new, ceramic, colorful, pair, 3¾" — 4.00 — 5.00 — 4.50

☐ **Salt and Pepper Shakers,** Mammy and Chef, new, porcelain, colorful, pair, 4½" .... — 4.00 — 5.00 — 4.50

☐ **Salt and Pepper Shakers,** Mammy, new, bisque, colorful, pair, 3" .... — 4.00 — 5.00 — 4.50

☐ **Salt and Pepper Shakers,** Mammy, new, celluloid, colorful, pair, 5" .... — 3.50 — 5.50 — 4.50

☐ **Sampler,** embroidered, pictures black boy and black girl dancing with wording "We're Free," red and black on white background, 8" x 6", 1863 .... — 250.00 — 300.00 — 260.00

☐ **Sheet Music,** "Three Little Words" from the motion picture "Check and Double Check," pictures Amos and Andy on cover, 9" x 12", 1930 .... — 20.00 — 30.00 — 23.00

☐ **Sign,** railroad station sign for rest rooms with arrow pointing in one direction for "white," another for "colored," reverse painting on glass, B. & J. Signs, 12" x 4", 1929 .... — 75.00 — 100.00 — 82.00

☐ **Sign,** Picaninny Freeze, Hendler's Ice Cream, full color cartoon of black baby eating slice of watermelon with price 5¢, 11" x 14", 1922 . — 50.00 — 65.00 — 54.00

☐ **String Holder,** Mammy, new, chalkware, wall mounted .... — 8.00 — 9.00 — 8.50

☐ **Thermometer,** composition, standing figural showing stereotyped wide-eyed black boy looking out from behind thermometer, wearing diaper, almost certainly a carnival giveaway, 5½", c. 1940-1950 .... — 40.00 — 50.00 — 43.00

☐ **Thermometer,** Mammy, new, metal picture of Mammy cooking, 7½" .... — 2.00 — 3.00 — 2.50

☐ **Thimble,** Mammy, bisque, new, figural, very colorful .... — 2.00 — 3.00 — 2.50

☐ **Token,** anti-slavery, front shows black beside tree waiting to board African slave ship, reverse reads "American Colonization Society, One Cent, Founded AD 1816," apparently dates from 1830s .... — 175.00 — 225.00 — 190.00

☐ **Toothpick Holder,** Mammy, new, bisque, colorful, 3" .... — 2.00 — 3.00 — 2.50

	Current Price Range		P/Y Average
☐ **Toy,** Alabama Coon Jigger, clockwork, lithographed tin figure of black man attached to tin base by rod, "dances" when wound up, made in Germany for Strauss of New York, M.I.B., 10″, 1912	325.00	400.00	340.00
☐ **Toy,** Amos and Andy Fresh Air Taxi by Marx, lithographed tin, clockwork motor, 8″, 1930 ..	400.00	500.00	430.00
☐ **Toy,** dancing black man, carved and painted wood, fixed to bamboo rod and paddle, jointed at arms, hips and knees, unmarked, possibly folk art, figure is 4″ tall with 26″ paddle, c. early 1900s	200.00	250.00	215.00
☐ **Toy,** dancing black man, sheet metal figure mounted on a wood frame, curved arms, painted, believed to be the work of a blacksmith, figure is 11″ tall and the frame measures 20″, mid 1800s	700.00	875.00	740.00
☐ **Toy,** Jazzbo Jim, "The Dancer on the Roof," clockwork, lithographed tin figure of black man who dances on roof of house, made by Ferdinand Strauss, 10″, c. 1920	325.00	400.00	355.00
☐ **Toy,** Mammy by Lindstrom, clockwork, lithographed tin, figure of black woman wearing apron, shakes when wound, 8″, c. 1930-1940 .	200.00	250.00	215.00
☐ **Tape Measure,** Aunt Jemima, new, retractable, colorful	1.50	2.50	1.75
☐ **Wall Plaques,** Mammy and Chef chalkware, new, with hooks for hanging pot holders, 6″ .	7.00	8.00	7.50
☐ **Wall Plaques,** set of two, black boy and girl with umbrellas, new, chalkware, 8″	9.00	10.00	9.50

BOEHM

ORIGIN: Edward Marshall Boehm founded a pottery studio in Trenton, New Jersey in 1949. Following Mr. Boehm's death, his wife Helen took over the company. In addition to the Trenton studio there are Boehm studios in England.

The information here, including the prices listed below, is secondhand material gleaned from trade journals and Boehm advertising material. Boehm figurines are beautifully made and show a great deal of time and

170 / BOEHM

attention to detail. They are owned by American presidents as well as the crowned heads of Europe and the entire world.

PRICES: Following are selected auction results for items which are no longer being made. Because they are all pre-1971 items, it is assumed they were made in Trenton.

RECOMMENDED READING: For further information refer to *The Official Price Guide to Pottery and Porcelain* published by The House of Collectibles.

	Current Price Range		P/Y Average
☐ Blue Grosbeak	900.00	1100.00	925.00
☐ Bobolink	1000.00	1200.00	1050.00
☐ Boxer, *large size*	1050.00	1200.00	1075.00
☐ Carolina Wrens	5000.00	5750.00	5100.00
☐ Catbird	1675.00	1975.00	1700.00
☐ Crested Flycatcher	2150.00	2550.00	2200.00
☐ Downy Woodpecker	1350.00	1550.00	1400.00
☐ Fledgling Blue Jay	150.00	160.00	152.00
☐ Fledgling Canada Warbler	1450.00	1650.00	1500.00
☐ Fledgling Goldfinch	190.00	220.00	192.00
☐ Fledgling Magpie	680.00	800.00	690.00
☐ Fledgling Red Poll	170.00	190.00	175.00
☐ Green Jays	4425.00	4925.00	4450.00
☐ Lazuli Bunting Paperweight	130.00	140.00	132.00
☐ Mourning Doves	4625.00	5125.00	4650.00
☐ Nuthatch	235.00	285.00	240.00
☐ Oven–Bird	1350.00	1550.00	1355.00
☐ Parula Warbler	2350.00	2850.00	2355.00
☐ Polo Player	3750.00	4300.00	3775.00
☐ Prothonotary Warblers	420.00	470.00	425.00
☐ Road Runner	4400.00	4800.00	4450.00
☐ Rufous Hummingbirds	1800.00	2100.00	1850.00
☐ Scottish Terrier	460.00	550.00	470.00
☐ Standing Poodle, *apricot-colored*	1450.00	1650.00	1475.00
☐ Thoroughbred and Exercise Boy, *decorated*	6800.00	8000.00	6900.00
☐ Towhee	1850.00	2150.00	1900.00
☐ Tufted Titmice	1075.00	1275.00	1100.00
☐ Varied Buntings	4625.00	5125.00	4650.00
☐ Whippets	3250.00	4000.00	3275.00

Note: Current items range all the way from an $18 cup and saucer to a $35,000 Prince Rudolph's Blue Bird of Paradise.

BOOKPLATES

TOPIC: Bookplates are printed paper labels which identify the owner of a book.

PERIOD: These items were produced primarily during the 1600s and 1700s.

ORIGIN: The first bookplates were printed in Germany in the 15th century.

MATERIALS: Paper was used to make bookplates.

COMMENTS: Many enthusiasts collect bookplates that have similar designs, while others do not limit themselves. In Europe, where bookplate collecting is presently very popular, it is common to buy mixed packets of bookplates, much as mixed packets of stamps are offered to stamp collectors in the United States.

ADDITIONAL TIPS: The following listings are organized by artist.

	Current Price Range		P/Y Average
☐ **Bell, Robert,** *design for Fanny Nicholson, c. 1900*	7.00	9.00	8.10
☐ **Gill, Eric,** *design for Scott Cunningham*	7.00	10.00	8.50
☐ **Kent, Rockwell,** *most designs*	6.00	9.00	7.00
☐ **Parrish, Maxfield**	9.00	16.00	12.50
☐ **American Bookplates,** *18th century, except Revere or Hurd*	6.00	8.00	6.50
☐ **Armorials,** *18th century, not done for famous people*	4.75	8.00	5.00
☐ **Mixed Packet,** *50 different, 18th century*	12.00	18.00	12.50
☐ **Mixed Packet,** *100 different, 18th century* ...	25.00	40.00	28.00
☐ **Mixed Packet,** *50 different, 19th century*	8.00	11.00	9.50
☐ **Mixed Packet,** *100 different, 19th century* ...	14.00	17.00	14.50

BOOKS

TOPIC: Books have been extremely important in man's history, for they allow him to record information and distribute it to others in unaltered form.

TYPES: Books fall into two categories, fiction and non-fiction. The non-fiction books can be further subdivided by the subjects they deal with, such as medicine or natural history.

PERIOD: Books first began to be printed around 1450, although handwritten books were in existence earlier than that.

MATERIALS: Paper was used almost exclusively in producing books.

COMMENTS: Many book collectors limit themselves to one or two favorite writers or a favorite subject, since the field of book collecting is vast. A collection is judged on quality rather than quantity, since the number of books that would be appropriate in a collection is so large.

CONDITION: It is important that the book be in good condition. Books with water damage, fire damage, broken bindings or missing pages are worth significantly less than similar books in good condition.

TIPS: For further information please refer to *The Official Price Guide to Old Books and Autographs,* published by The House of Collectibles.

	Current Price Range		P/Y Average
☐ **Bronte, Charlotte,** *Jane Eyre,* London, 1847, three vols.	1000.00	1350.00	1150.00
☐ **Bronte, Charlotte,** *Shirley,* London, 1849, three vols.	1500.00	1900.00	1700.00
☐ **Bronte, Charlotte,** *The Professor,* London, 1857, two vols.	150.00	185.00	165.00
☐ **Bronte, Emily,** *Wuthering Heights,* London, 1847, three vols. The third volume is titled *Agnes Grey.* Only 1,000 copies were printed, though this was not a "limited edition" in the true sense of the term	9000.00	12000.00	10500.00
☐ **Brooke, Rupert,** *1914 and Other Poems,* London, 1915, softbound	40.00	55.00	46.00
☐ **Brooke, Rupert,** *Lithuania,* Chicago, 1915	165.00	190.00	170.00

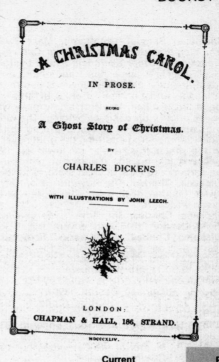

A Christmas Carol,
*title page, first edition,
by Charles Dickens*
$400.00-$500.00

	Current Price Range		P/Y Average
☐ **Brooke, Rupert,** *Letters from America,* London, 1916	40.00	55.00	47.00
☐ **Brooke, Rubert,** *The Old Vicarage,* London, 1916, softbound	90.00	115.00	100.00
☐ **Brooks, Van Wyck,** *The Confident Years,* N.p., N.Y., 1922	30.00	35.00	32.00
☐ **Brooks, Van Wyck,** *The American Caravan,* N.Y., 1927	18.00	23.00	20.00
☐ **Brooks, Van Wyck,** *Sketches in Criticism,* N.Y., 1932	28.00	34.00	31.00
☐ **Browning, Elizabeth B.,** *Two Poems,* London, 1854, softbound	40.00	55.00	46.00
☐ **Browning, Elizabeth B.,** *Aurora Leigh,* N.Y., 1857, first American edition	40.00	55.00	46.00
☐ **Browning, Elizabeth B.,** *Poems Before Congress,* London, 1860, blindstamped cloth	120.00	150.00	133.00
☐ **Browning, Elizabeth B.,** *Last Poems,* London, 1862, purple cloth	60.00	80.00	69.00
☐ **Browning, Elizabeth B.,** *Psyche Apocalypse,* London, 1876, softbound	50.00	70.00	59.00
☐ **Browning, Elizabeth B.,** *Sonnets from the Portuguese,* London, 1887, one of eight copies on vellum	450.00	575.00	500.00
☐ **Browning, Robert,** *Paracelsus,* London, 1835, boards with paper label	450.00	525.00	480.00

	Current Price Range		P/Y Average

☐ **Clemens, Samuel Langhorne,** *Mark Twain The Celebrated Jumping Frog of Calaveras County and Other Sketches,* edited by John Paul. The first issue has traditionally been identified by a page of yellow ads before the titlepage, and a normal letter "i" in "this" on page 198, last line. An effort is now under way to fix priority on basis of binding. The bindings are in assorted colors, but in some the gold-stamped frog adorning the front cover is at the center, in others at the lower left. It is believed (cautiously) the former represents an earlier or at least scarcer state, N.Y., 1867

	2175.00	2700.00	2400.00

☐ **Dickens, Charles,** *The Adventures of Oliver Twist,* London, 1846, third edition, ten parts, green wrappers 900.00 1200.00 1050.00

☐ **Dickens, Charles,** *The Adventures of Oliver Twist,* London, 1846, hard covers 250.00 300.00 265.00

☐ **Dickens, Charles,** *Nicholas Nickleby,* first issue has misspelling "vister" for "sister," page 123, line 17 of part four, London, 1838-1839, 19 parts, green wrappers 425.00 500.00 460.00

☐ **Dickinson, Emily,** *Poems,* edited by M.L. Todd and T.W. Higginson, Boston, 1890 . . . . 325.00 400.00 355.00

☐ **Eliot, T.S.,** *Charles Whibley,* London, 1931, softbound 40.00 55.00 47.00

☐ **Eliot, T.S.,** *After Strange Gods,* London, 1934 60.00 80.00 70.00

☐ **Eliot, T.S.,** *The Rock,* London, 1934 . . . . 35.00 45.00 40.00

☐ **Eliot, T.S.,** *Murder in the Cathedral,* London, 1935 . . . . 28.00 35.00 31.00

☐ **Eliot, T.S.,** *Four Quartets,* N.Y., 1943 . . . . 1250.00 1600.00 1400.00

☐ **Faulkner, William,** *Mosquitoes,* N.Y., 1927, blue cloth 1400.00 1900.00 1600.00

☐ **Faulkner, William,** *Sartoris,* N.Y., n.d., 1929 . . 600.00 800.00 700.00

☐ **Faulkner, William,** *These Thirteen,* N.Y., n.d., 1931 . . . . 50.00 65.00 56.00

☐ **Faulkner, William,** *Idyll in the Desert,* N.Y., 1931, limited signed edition 600.00 800.00 700.00

☐ **Faulkner, William,** *Sanctuary,* N.Y., n.d., 1931 1000.00 1475.00 1200.00

☐ **Faulkner, William,** *Light in August,* N.Y., n.d., 1932 . . . . 110.00 140.00 125.00

☐ **Faulkner, William,** *Miss Zilphia Gant,* N.Y., 1932 . . . . 600.00 800.00 700.00

☐ **Faulkner, William,** *Salmagundi,* Milwaukee, 1932, softbound, limited edition 500.00 700.00 600.00

☐ **Garside, Alston H.,** *Cotton Goes to Market,* N.Y., 1934, 411 pp. 25.00 30.00 27.00

☐ **Gates, Charles M.,** *Messages of the Governors of the Territory of Washington to the Legislative Assembly, 1854-1889,* Seattle, 1940, 297 pp., softbound 35.00 42.00 38.00

☐ **Hemingway, Ernest,** *The Sun Also Rises,* first state copies have misspelling "stopped" on page 181, line 26, N.Y., 1926, black cloth 600.00 800.00 700.00

	Current Price Range		P/Y Average
☐ **Hemingway, Ernest,** *Men Without Women,* N.Y., 1927, weighs 15 to 15½ ounces in the first state	225.00	300.00	260.00
☐ **Hemingway, Ernest,** *Death in the Afternoon,* N.Y., 1932, black cloth, for fine copy in dust-jacket	400.00	500.00	450.00
☐ **Hemingway, Ernest,** *Winner Take Nothing,* N.Y., 1933, black cloth	150.00	200.00	170.00
☐ **Hemingway, Ernest,** *God Rest You Merry Gentlemen,* N.Y., 1933, red cloth	350.00	425.00	380.00
☐ **Hemingway, Ernest,** *Green Hills of Africa,* N.Y., 1935, green cloth	110.00	140.00	127.00
☐ **Highbee, Elias and Thompson, R.B.,** *The Petition of the Latter-Day Saints, commonly known as Mormons,* Washington, D.C., 1840, 13 pp., softbound	220.00	270.00	240.00
☐ **Hill, Jasper S.,** *The Letters of A Young Miner, Covering the Adventures of Jasper S. Hill during the California Goldrush, 1848-1852,* San Francisco, 1964, 111 pp., limited to 475 copies, with a folding map	65.00	80.00	72.00
☐ **Smith, Samuel,** *Memoirs of the Life of Samuel Smith,* Middleborough, Mass., 1853 .	140.00	170.00	155.00
☐ **Smith, Samuel,** *History of the Province of Pennsylvania,* Philadelphia, 1913, 231 pp. . . .	15.00	20.00	17.00
☐ **Smith, Sara S.,** *The Foundrs of the Massachusetts Bay Colony,* Pittsfield, Mass., 1897, 372 pp., bound in cloth	40.00	50.00	44.00
☐ **Steinbeck, John,** *Saint Katy the Virgin,* N.p., n.d. (N.Y., 1936), limited to 199 signed copies, rare	1200.00	1500.00	1350.00
☐ **Steinbeck, John,** *Nothing So Monstrous,* N.Y., 1936, limited to 370 copies	300.00	375.00	330.00
☐ **Steinbeck, John,** *In Dubious Battle,* N.Y., n.d., 1936, orange cloth	125.00	160.00	136.00
☐ **Steinbeck, John,** *The Red Pony,* N.Y., 1937, limited to 699 signed copies, boxed	150.00	180.00	166.00
☐ **Steinbeck, John,** *Of Mice and Men,* N.Y., n.d., 1937, beige cloth	90.00	115.00	100.00
☐ **Wilder, Thornton,** *The Angel That Troubled the Waters,* N.Y., 1928, limited, signed	35.00	45.00	40.00
☐ **Wilder, Thornton,** *The Long Christmas Dinner,* N.Y., 1931	35.00	45.00	40.00
☐ **Wilder, Thornton,** *The Ides of March,* N.Y., 1948, limited to 750, signed	85.00	110.00	95.00
☐ **Williams, Tennessee,** *The Glass Menagerie,* N.Y., 1945	125.00	150.00	133.00
☐ **Williams, Tennessee,** *A Streetcar Named Desire,* N.p., n.d., (Norfolk, 1947)	125.00	150.00	133.00
☐ **Williams, Tennessee,** *The Roman Spring of Mrs. Stone,* N.p., n.d., (N.Y., 1950), limited to 500, signed	185.00	235.00	205.00
☐ **Williams, Tennessee,** *Cat on a Hot Tin Roof,* N.p., n.d., (N.Y., 1955)	40.00	50.00	45.00

BOTTLES

DESCRIPTION: With the availability of cheaper containers made of plastic, aluminum and paper, glass bottles are declining rapidly as a form of storage. With the decline of bottle production, more collectors are realizing how important old bottles are especially as they relate to history.

TYPES: There are many types of bottles found on the collectible market including ale and gin, beer, cosmetic, bitters, crocks, cure, food, ink, medicine, mineral water, poison, pontil, soda and spirits. Because of their collector appeal, flasks, fruit jars and Hutchinson bottles are listed separately.

ADDITIONAL TIPS: This section is organized alphabetically by bottle type. For additional information on bottles, consult *The Official Price Guide to Bottles Old & New* published by The House of Collectibles.

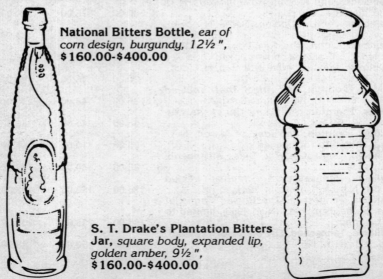

National Bitters Bottle, *ear of corn design, burgundy, 12½",* **$160.00-$400.00**

S. T. Drake's Plantation Bitters Jar, *square body, expanded lip, golden amber, 9½",* **$160.00-$400.00**

Berkshire Bitters Bottle, *pig,*
9½ ", **$160.00-$400.00**

American Life Bitters Bottle,
cabin design, amber, 9",
$160.00-$400.00

	Current Price Range		P/Y Average
☐ **Bitters,** Baker's High Life, the Great Nerve Tonic embossed on back, tapered top, machine made, pint	15.00	25.00	20.00
☐ **Bitters,** Baxter's Mandrake, Lord Bros. Prop. Burlington, Vt. on vertical panels, amethyst, 6½ "	10.00	20.00	15.00
☐ **Bitters,** Begg's Dandelion Bitters in three lines, tapered top, base to neck a plain band, amber, 7¾ "	21.00	26.00	22.50
☐ **Bitters,** Dr. Boyce's Tonic label, sample size, twelve panels, aqua, 4½ "	13.00	17.00	14.75
☐ **Bitters,** The Bitters Pharmacy on label, clear, 4½ "	4.00	6.00	5.00
☐ **Bitters,** Caroni, pint, amber	10.00	20.00	15.00

	Current Price Range		P/Y Average
□ **Bitters,** Celery & Chamomile on label, square, amber, 10″	10.00	20.00	15.00
□ **Bitters,** Dr. E. Chyder Stomach Bitters, N.O., amber, 10″	18.00	23.00	20.00
□ **Bitters,** Compound Calisaya Bitters in two lines, tapered top, square, amber, 9½″	14.00	18.00	15.75
□ **Bitters,** Fer-Kina Galeno on shoulder, beer type bottle, brown, machine made, 10⅛″	10.00	15.00	12.50
□ **Cure,** Dr. Taylor's Sure Chill Cure, on side Richardson Taylor Med. Co., ring top, aqua, 5½″	5.00	10.00	7.00
□ **Cure,** Twenty-Four Hour Cure Guaranteed, ring top, clear, 5″	8.00	12.00	9.50
□ **Cure,** Veno's Lightning Cough Cure, double ring top, aqua, 7¼″	7.00	10.00	8.25
□ **Cure,** White's Quick Healing Cure, amber, 6¼″	9.00	12.00	10.25
□ **Cure,** Wood's Great Peppermint Cure for Coughs and Colds, clear, 6½″	7.00	10.00	8.50
□ **Food,** Hires Improved Root Beer, Panel, Mfg. by The Charles Hires Co., panel, Philadelphia Pa., U.S.A., panel, Make five Gallons of a Delicious Drink, aqua, 4¾″	4.00	6.00	4.60
□ **Food,** Joslyn's Maple Syrup, eight sides, round lip, aqua, 8″	5.00	8.00	6.50
□ **Food,** Kelloggs, oval, clear	1.00	2.00	1.40
□ **Food,** Mason, Belvidere, Ill in center, Dairy in a circle, ½ pt. base M, dots on shoulder, clear	12.00	18.00	14.50
□ **Food,** My Wife's Salad Dressing, machine made, blue green, 8″	5.00	8.00	6.20
□ **Food,** Nut House, figure of house, store jar, ball shape, clear	12.00	18.00	14.50
□ **Food,** Peppermint, marble in center of neck, aqua, 7¼	9.00	12.00	9.90
□ **Food,** Planters, same in back, square, glass top with peanut nobs, clear	28.00	38.00	31.00
□ **Food,** Red Snapper Sauce Co., Memphis, Tenn., six sides, clear, 9½″	8.00	12.00	9.75
□ **Food,** Warsaw Pickle Co., aqua, 8¾″	7.00	10.00	8.20
□ **Ink,** Angus & Co., cone, aqua, 3½″	4.00	6.00	4.75
□ **Ink,** Arnold's round, clear or amethyst, 2½″ .	5.00	7.00	5.75
□ **Ink,** B&B, pottery bottle, tan, 7½″	5.00	8.00	6.50
□ **Ink,** Billing & Co., Banker's Writing Ink, aqua, 2″	10.00	15.00	12.00
□ **Medicine,** Balsam of Honey, pontil, aqua, 3¼″	25.00	35.00	29.00
□ **Medicine,** Dr. Barkman's Never Failing Liniment printed on front, light green, 6¼″	5.00	7.00	5.75
□ **Medicine,** T.B. Barton, clear or amethyst, 4½″	3.00	5.00	3.75
□ **Medicine,** Batemans Drops, vertical, cylindrical, amethyst, 5¼″	3.00	5.00	4.00
□ **Medicine,** Dr. Bell's, The E.E. Sutherland Medicine Co., Paducah, Ky., Pine Tar Honey, aqua, 5½″	3.00	5.00	3.75
□ **Medicine,** Borax, clear, 5¼″	12.00	18.00	14.50
□ **Medicine,** B & P, amber, Lyons Powder on shoulder of opposite side, 4¼″	3.00	5.00	3.75

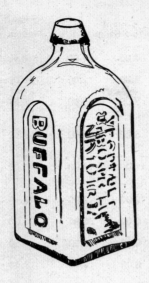  

Left to Right: *Vaughn's Vegetable Lithontriptic Mixture Medicine Bottle, blue, 8½"; Rohrer's Wild Cherry Tonic Medicine Bottle, pyramid shape, amber, 10½"; Swaim's Panacea Medicine Bottle, yellow green, 8¼".*
$45.00-$75.00

	Current Price Range		P/Y Average
☐ **Medicine,** F. Brown's, aqua, 5½ "	4.00	6.00	4.75
☐ **Medicine,** Brown Sarsaparilla, aqua, 9½ " ...	6.00	9.00	7.50
☐ **Medicine,** Brown's Instant Relief for Pain, aqua, embossed, 5¼ "	3.00	5.00	3.75
☐ **Medicine,** Burnett, clear, 6¾ "	8.00	11.00	9.25
☐ **Medicine,** California Fig Syrup Co., Califig, Sterling Products Successor on front, rectangular, clear, 6¾ "	3.00	5.00	3.60
☐ **Mineral,** San Francisco Glass works, tapered neck, blob top, green, 6⅞"	14.00	19.00	16.00
☐ **Mineral,** Saratoga Spring, honey amber, 9¾ "	30.00	40.00	34.00
☐ **Mineral,** Shasta Water Co., Mineral Water Co., amber, 10½ "	7.00	9.00	7.70
☐ **Mineral,** UTE Chief of Mineral Water, Maniton, Colo., U.T. on base, crown top, clear or purple, 8 "	5.00	8.00	6.50
☐ **Mineral,** Veronica Mineral Water printed around shoulder, square, amber, clear 10¼ "	8.00	11.00	9.50
☐ **Mineral,** Weller Bottling Works, Saratoga, N.Y., blob top, aqua	8.00	12.00	9.75
☐ **Mineral,** Adam W. Young, Canton, Ohio, graduated collar, aqua, 9¼ "	7.00	9.00	7.70
☐ **Poison,** Baltimore, MD. printed on bottom, amber, 3 "	3.00	4.00	3.25

	Current Price Range		P/Y Average
Poison, Browns Rat Killer, under it C. Wakefield Co., applied lip, aqua, 3″	7.00	11.00	8.50
Poison, DPS, skull and cross on front, cross on four sides, ring top, cobalt	8.00	12.00	10.00
Poison, Eli Lilly & Co., Poison on each panel, amber, 2″	7.00	10.00	8.50
Poison, Evans Medical Ltd., Liverpool, label, Chloroform B.A. Poison, number and U.Y.B. under bottom, ABM, amber, 6½″	5.00	8.00	6.50
Poison, F.S. & Co. on base, Poison vertically, surrounded by dots, two sides plain, ringtop, amber, 2¾″	11.00	16.00	13.00
Poison, R.C. Millings Bed Bug Poison, Charleston, S.C. shoulder strap on side, clear, 6¼″	12.00	17.00	14.00
Poison, Rat Poison printed horizontal on round bottle, clear or amethyst, 2½″	18.00	26.00	21.00
Poison, Tincture Iodine printed in three lines under skull and crossbones, square, amber .	6.00	9.00	7.50
Poison, Triloids printed on one panel of bottle, Poison on another, cobalt, 3¼″	6.00	9.00	7.50
Poison, Wyeth Poison printed vertical on back, round ring base and top, cobalt, 2¼″ .	10.00	15.00	12.00
Pontil, Allen Mrs. S.A. printed on one side, on front World's Hair Balsam, 355 Broone St printed in three lines, aqua, 6½″	19.00	27.00	22.00
Pontil, Bake's Dr. printed on front, tapered top, pale aqua, 5″	24.00	37.00	29.00
Pontil, Balsam of Honey printed on three lines, round bottle, ring top, aqua, 3″	19.00	27.00	23.00
Pontil, Brown's, F., Ess of Jamaica Ginger, Philad. printed on four lines, tapered top, oval, aqua, 5½″	10.00	15.00	12.00
Pontil, Cannington Shaw & Co., St. Helens on top of L.D. beaded decoration around shoulder	14.00	21.00	17.00
Pontil, Cooke's Carmine Ink printed on two lines, bell shaped, ring top, aqua, 1½″	15.00	21.00	17.50
Pontil, Dalby's Carminate printed on two lines, round, light ring top, 3¾″	20.00	27.00	24.00
Pontil, Harrison's Columbia Ink printed on three lines, round, ring top, cobalt, 4½″	30.00	42.00	33.00
Pontil, Hauel, J., Phila. on two lines in sunken panel, oval, light ring top, aqua, 3¾″	12.00	18.00	14.00
Pontil, Hoover, Phila. 12 panels, ring top, light green	18.00	27.00	22.00
Pontil, Snuff, label, flare top, short neck, beveled corners, olive amber, 4½″	12.00	18.00	14.50
Pontil, Taylor & Co., Varparaiso Chile printed on three lines, blob top, dark green, 7¼″	45.00	63.00	52.00
Spirits, Acker Merrall, label, A9 on bottom, amber, 11″	8.00	11.00	9.50
Spirits, Bailey's Whiskey, clear or amethyst, 9¾″	8.00	11.00	9.75
Spirits, B&B, clear or amber	4.00	6.00	4.75

	Current Price Range		P/Y Average
☐ **Spirits,** Belle of Nelson, label, whiskey, M.M. on bottom, clear, 12″	6.00	9.00	7.25
☐ **Spirits,** E.R. Betterton & Co., distillers Chattanooga, Tenn. printed on three lines in sunken panel on back, raised panel plain, flask, three ribs on each side, twenty ribs around neck, on bottom a diamond with letter Y, brown	7.00	10.00	8.75

BOXES

DESCRIPTION: Versatile and charming, boxes not only have a variety of uses but they are also quite collectible.

MATERIALS: Boxes are made using a variety of materials including straw, wood, china and glass.

COMMENTS: In the 18th and 19th centuries boxes were mostly for utilitarian use such as perishable food storage. Special boxes were made to hold such items as wedding dresses. Small boxes, for trinkets, matches or cigarettes, seem to be especially intricate and collectible.

ADDITIONAL TIPS: The listings in this section are alphabetical according to type of box, followed by descriptions and date.

☐ **Apple Box,** footed, smoked finish	260.00	310.00	275.00
☐ **Apple Box,** pine, painted, 11″ x 8½″	55.00	80.00	62.00
☐ **Ballot Box,** maple, oblong, sliding top	105.00	135.00	120.00
☐ **Band Box,** oval, painted, schoolhouse, flowers and trees on lid, 9″ x 6″	1400.00	1900.00	1600.00
☐ **Band Box,** man and woman with flowers on lid, flowers on sides	1300.00	1800.00	1500.00
☐ **Band Box,** hunter shooting deer	600.00	700.00	585.00
☐ **Bible Box,** carved oak, English, mid 1600's ..	430.00	480.00	450.00
☐ **Book-shaped Box,** inlaid, large	85.00	110.00	90.00
☐ **Book-shaped Box,** with name and dated 1861	325.00	375.00	350.00
☐ **Book-shaped Box,** Pennsylvania German, painted wood	55.00	110.00	75.00
☐ **Book-shaped Box,** inlaid colored wax hearts, stars	30.00	45.00	38.00

	Current Price Range		P/Y Average
☐ **Box,** Wilcox, quadruple plate, scrolls, pointer dogs, lock lion's paw feet, 9″ x 5″	185.00	210.00	182.00
☐ **Brass Box,** covered with leather, shape of coffin	50.00	70.00	55.00
☐ **Bride's Box,** painted flowers, dark green, c. 1817	275.00	325.00	275.00
☐ **Bride's Box,** oval, painted bride and groom with floral motif, 18″	385.00	435.00	400.00
☐ **Bride's Box,** German or Pennsylvania German, oval, 19th c.	210.00	260.00	225.00
☐ **Butter Box,** six individual containers	110.00	145.00	118.00
☐ **Candle Box,** cherry, carved, scalloped arch . .	410.00	460.00	425.00
☐ **Candle Box,** geometric design, carved and inlaid, 8″	110.00	145.00	118.00
☐ **Candle Box,** pine, sliding lid, red border, knob on lid, 14″	385.00	430.00	400.00
☐ **Candle Box,** tin, hanging, round	180.00	230.00	200.00
☐ **Cheese Box,** tree and leaf design, inlaid mahogany, 7″ Dia.	380.00	430.00	400.00
☐ **Cigar Box,** coromandel with brass fittings, mid 19th c.	180.00	230.00	200.00
☐ **Cigarette Box,** "Wavecrest," cream, blue, white, pink forget-me-nots, word "Cigarettes," 4″ H.	260.00	310.00	275.00
☐ **Cigarette Box,** cloisonne, cylindrical, unmarked	65.00	110.00	80.00

Cigarette Box, *Lenox, shape #3033, rose design,* **$50.00-$55.00**

	Current Price Range		P/Y Average
☐ **Cigarette or Chocolate Box,** brass, Princess Mary, WW1, with Mary, and names of Allies around lid	38.00	48.00	40.00
☐ **Cigarette Box,** green, Lenox wreath mark, Lenox	29.00	33.00	31.00
☐ **Cigarette Box,** pink daisy design, square with lid, 4½ ", Southern Potteries	6.00	8.00	7.00
☐ **Cigarette Box,** rounded corners, ribbing, relief apple blossom design, green with white flowers, Lenox wreath mark, Lenox	49.00	55.00	52.00
☐ **Cigarette Box,** rounded corners, ribbing, relief apple blossom design, Lenox wreath mark, Lenox	34.00	38.00	36.00
☐ **Cigarette Box,** white with Lenox Rose trim, Lenox wreath mark, Lenox	43.00	48.00	45.00
☐ **Cigarette Box,** white with Ming trim, Lenox wreath mark, Lenox	49.00	55.00	52.00
☐ **Coin Box,** oak, changer, c. 1823	260.00	310.00	275.00
☐ **Collar Box,** man's, with drawer, black with red lining	9.00	13.00	10.00
☐ **Cookie Box,** round with lid and handle, Pennsylvania Dutch design	280.00	330.00	300.00
☐ **Cutlery Box,** triple compartments, walnut, 10″ x 16″	60.00	70.00	60.00
☐ **Deed Box,** wood, carved	80.00	105.00	82.00
☐ **Desk Box,** mahogany, compartments for writing tools and ink, original hardware, 5″ x 4½ ″ x 14″	280.00	330.00	300.00
☐ **Desk Box,** painted red, slant lid, 17½ ″ W. . . .	110.00	135.00	112.00
☐ **Dome Top Box,** bird motif, 10″ W.	460.00	510.00	475.00
☐ **Dresser Box,** orange plush with molded celluloid trim, all tools intact	30.00	40.00	30.00
☐ **Glove Box,** coromandel, gilt brass with green stones inlaid	65.00	95.00	75.00
☐ **Glove Box,** covered with wallpaper	80.00	110.00	82.00
☐ **Hat Box,** covered with bird motif wallpaper . .	135.00	160.00	138.00
☐ **Hat Box,** wooden, original finish and hardware, c. 1874-90	110.00	135.00	112.00
☐ **Herb Box,** oval, original paint and lid	280.00	330.00	300.00
☐ **Jewel Box,** miniature, antique Japanese bronze d'or and black laquer, gold design, two drawers, footed, 2½ ″ x 2″, 19th century .	300.00	360.00	325.00
☐ **Jewelry Box,** plated silver (replated), cherubs playing, 8″ x 6″ x 3″	110.00	160.00	125.00
☐ **Jewel Casket,** Simpson, Hall and Miller silverplate, round on pedestal with three cupids with wings, finial, another cherub	110.00	160.00	125.00
☐ **Jewel Box,** Jenning Bros. ormolu, scenes of lovers, children in relief, pink plush lining, 2½ ″ H.	22.00	32.00	25.00
☐ **Jewel Box,** Pairpont "Wavecrest," 9″ Dia. . . .	725.00	825.00	750.00
☐ **Jewel Box,** "Wavecrest," ormolu mounts, square shape, 7″ x 7″ x 5″	425.00	475.00	425.00
☐ **Knife Box,** curly maple, dovetailed	55.00	70.00	58.00
☐ **Knife Box,** pine, scalloped, dovetailed	160.00	185.00	162.00
☐ **Knife Box,** walnut, carved handle	110.00	135.00	112.00

	Current Price Range		P/Y Average
☐ **Lacquered Box**, octagonal, yellow with Oriental designs, early 19th c.	280.00	330.00	300.00
☐ **Lap desk**, brass inlaid, walnut, 15″ W.	140.00	190.00	150.00
☐ **Leather Box**, pressed design	14.00	20.00	15.00
☐ **Lectern Box**, carved, painted, with carved book on top	17000.00	18000.00	17000.00
☐ **Lunch Box**, oval, 19th c.	45.00	55.00	45.00
☐ **Lunch Box**, tin, Art Deco design, nursery characters	45.00	55.00	45.00
☐ **Match Box**, shaped like treasure chest with acorn finial, unmarked, 3″, Willets Manufacturing Company	40.00	50.00	43.00
☐ **Match Box**, wooden, carved, 5″ H.	32.00	42.00	35.00
☐ **Miniature Box**, antique Satsuma, rectangular, children and swans on cover and interior, 3½″, 18th century	300.00	360.00	330.00
☐ **Pantry Box**, Scandinavian Bentwood	110.00	150.00	125.00
☐ **Pantry Box**, varnished, 10″	28.00	42.00	32.00
☐ **Pantry Box**, two-fingered round, small size . .	110.00	150.00	120.00
☐ **Pantry Box**, three-fingered oval, painted red (possibly Shaker)	135.00	180.00	150.00
☐ **Pantry Box**, oval, two-fingered, c. 1820	135.00	180.00	150.00
☐ **Pantry Boxes**, five graduated, round, painted	160.00	210.00	180.00
☐ **Patch Box**, Royal Bayreuth tapestry, five sheep on lid, gray mark, 2½″ x 1½″	140.00	180.00	150.00
☐ **Pencil Box**, sliding lid, dovetailed	22.00	32.00	25.00
☐ **Pipe Box**, pine, drawer, dovetailed	330.00	360.00	338.00
☐ **Pottery Box**, covered, oval, all white with shell molded base, shell finial on lid, 5¾″, Bennington	80.00	95.00	84.00
☐ **Pottery Box**, square with Lion of Lucerne figure, Bennington	120.00	130.00	124.00
☐ **Rouge Box**, round, embossed rims and ornate finial, undecorated, C.A.C. green palette mark, Lenox	40.00	50.00	44.00
☐ **Salt Box**, curved front, flat black, painted red	55.00	70.00	62.00
☐ **Salt Box**, maple and cherry, striped wood, hinged cover, hanging	110.00	135.00	112.00
☐ **Salt Box**, pine, dovetailed, open, hanging . . .	90.00	110.00	92.00
☐ **Salt Box**, walnut, dovetailed, slant lid, hanging	140.00	170.00	150.00
☐ **Salt Box**, Pennsylvania Dutch design, two compartments, open	180.00	210.00	182.00
☐ **Seed Box**, compartments, sliding lid	135.00	160.00	138.00
☐ **Shaving Box**, brush	45.00	55.00	45.00
☐ **Snuff Box**, Austrian silver gilt, musical with sectional comb, 9 cm., hallmarked Vienna, c. 1828	2300.00	2700.00	2460.00
☐ **Snuff Box**, French tortoiseshell, musical with sectional comb, 9 cm., c. 1810	1200.00	1800.00	1450.00
☐ **Snuff Box**, Mauchline ware, boxwood, 3½″ W.	55.00	80.00	62.00
☐ **Snuff Box**, horn, acorn-shaped, screw-on top, 1¾″	28.00	38.00	30.00
☐ **Snuff Box**, pewter	38.00	48.00	40.00
☐ **Snuff Box**, treenware, 2¾″ Dia.	18.00	24.00	18.00

	Current Price Range		P/Y Average

Spice Box, cherry, nine drawers, original, 13″ H.	150.00	175.00	152.00
Spice Box, curly maple, twelve drawers, brass pulls	315.00	365.00	325.00
Spice Box, oak, eight drawers, wooden pulls, hanging	80.00	110.00	82.00
Spice Box, pine, eight drawers, porcelain pulls, hanging	100.00	130.00	102.00
Spice Box, tin, eight drawers, painted black .	100.00	130.00	102.00
Spice Box, walnut, two drawers, carved back, dovetailed	280.00	330.00	300.00
Stamp Box, brass, footed, covered	45.00	55.00	45.00
Stamp Box, pewter, hinged top	65.00	85.00	70.00
Stamp Box, sterling with enameled lid, chair and finger ring	28.00	38.00	30.00
Stationery Box, walnut with brass and ivory decoration, 7″ H., late 19th c.	120.00	170.00	135.00
Tea caddy, Marguetry, English, c. 1780	550.00	650.00	562.00
Tea caddy, imitation tortoise shell, green, English, early 19th c.	230.00	280.00	250.00
Tin Box, with brass rings, hand embossed arch and bullseye, c. 1880	30.00	40.00	33.00
Tin Box, "Breethem" breath sweetener box, picture of a woman and product slogan	1.50	3.00	2.10
Tobacco Box, Pennsylvania Dutch design, 19″ H.	55.00	70.00	62.00
Tool Box, oak	28.00	32.00	30.00
Tool Box, child's, with tools, c. 1930	45.00	55.00	45.00
Tramp Art Box, footed, geometic design, hinged top, 14″ x 15″	185.00	210.00	182.00
Tramp Art Wall Boxes, small	32.00	48.00	38.00
Trinket Box, Art Deco, woman on cover, 6½″, Fulper Pottery	195.00	205.00	199.00
Trinket Box, painted, one drawer	325.00	375.00	325.00
Trinket Box, papier mache and antique sulphide, design features four women, 2¾″, 18th century	350.00	400.00	360.00
Trinket Box, rectangle, hand painted red roses with gold trim, 2″ x 4″, Lenox palette mark, Lenox	75.00	85.00	77.00
Trinket Box, round, Ming pattern, 3¾″, Lenox wreath mark, Lenox	115.00	125.00	119.00
Trinket Box, round, undecorated, 3¾″, Lenox pallette mark, Lenox	42.00	48.00	44.00
Trinket Box, wooden, carved, painted flowers, 6″ H.	325.00	375.00	325.00
Wall Box, open top, painted brown, 19th c.	160.00	210.00	175.00
Writing Box, oak, English, 13½″ W., 18th c.	135.00	185.00	150.00
Writing Box, Shaker, two drawers	135.00	185.00	150.00

BOXING

DESCRIPTION: Boxing draws many fans into its realm each year. This fascinating sport keeps collectors on their toes searching for memorabilia relating to their favorite athlete.

PERIOD: Boxing began in the late 1800s and has continued to thrive through the twentieth century.

TYPE: There are many different items boxing enthusiasts can collect including autographed photos, magazines, posters, cards and programs.

ADDITIONAL TIPS: This section is alphabetized according to item. For more information about boxing memorabilia, consult *The Official Price Guide to Sports Collectibles* published by The House of Collectibles.

Poster,
Sugar Ray Leonard vs. Thomas Hearnes for the Welterweight Championship, September 16, 1981, Caesar's Palace, Las Vegas, full color, signed "Moss," 24" x 18½",
$15.00-$25.00

	Current Price Range		P/Y Average
☐ Autograph, Muhammad Ali, *plain card ink* ...	4.00	6.00	4.75
☐ Autograph, Muhammad Ali, *plain card, pencil*	3.00	4.00	3.25
☐ Autograph, Mahammad Ali, *8" x 10", black and white photo, ink*	12.00	17.00	14.00
☐ Autograph, Muhammad Ali, *8" x 10", color photo, ink*	15.00	20.00	17.00
☐ Autograph, Cassius Clay, *plain card, ink*	50.00	70.00	59.00
☐ Autograph, Cassius Clay, *plain card, pencil* .	40.00	50.00	45.00
☐ Autograph, James Corbett, *small photo, ink* .	50.00	65.00	57.00
☐ Autograph, Jack Dempsey, *plain card, ink* ...	5.00	8.00	6.00
☐ Autograph, George Foreman, *plain card, ink* .	1.00	2.00	1.30
☐ Autograph, George Foreman, *8" x 10", black and white photo, ink*	2.00	4.00	3.00
☐ Autograph, Joe Frazier, *plain card, ink*	1.00	2.00	1.30
☐ Autograph, Joe Frazier, *8" x 10", black and white photo, ink*	2.00	4.00	3.00
☐ Autograph, Rocky Graziano, *plain card, ink* .	1.00	2.00	1.30
☐ Autograph, Rocky Graziano, *8" x 10", black and white photo, ink*	2.00	4.00	3.00
☐ Autograph, James Jeffries, *plain card, ink* ..	20.00	25.00	22.00
☐ Autograph, James Jeffries, *check, ink*	50.00	65.00	57.00
☐ Autograph, James Jeffries, *letter, ink*	60.00	80.00	70.00
☐ Autograph, Stanley Ketchel, *plain card, ink* .	23.00	29.00	26.00
☐ Autograph, Stanley Ketchel, *letter, ink*	42.00	57.00	48.00
☐ Autograph, Sugar Ray Leonard, *plain card, ink*	1.00	2.00	1.30
☐ Autograph, Sugar Ray Leonard, *8" x 10", black and white photo, ink*	2.00	4.00	3.00
☐ Autograph, Joe Louis, *plain card, ink*	15.00	20.00	17.00
☐ Autograph, Rocky Marciano, *plain card, ink* .	20.00	30.00	25.00
☐ Autograph, Rocky Marciano, *8" x 10", black and white photo, ink*	30.00	40.00	35.00
☐ Autograph, Harry Wills, *plain card, ink*	18.00	24.00	21.00
☐ Autograph, Harry Wills, *contract, ink*	300.00	400.00	345.00
☐ Boxing Card, Tommy Loughran, *Knock-Out Bubble Gum Cards, Leaf Gum Cards, 1948* ..	1.00	2.00	1.30
☐ Same as Above, Harry Greb	1.00	2.00	1.30
☐ Boxing Card, George Carpenter, *Magnoms Cigarettes, British Boxing Card, 1914, 25 cards in set*	2.00	3.00	2.40
☐ Same as Above, *complete set*	25.00	35.00	29.00

	Current Price Range		P/Y Average
☐ Boxing Card, Willy Beecher, *Mecca Cigarettes, early 1900s*	1.00	2.00	1.30
☐ Same as Above, Joe Coburn	1.00	2.00	1.30
☐ Same as Above, Pal Moore	1.00	2.00	1.30
☐ Boxing Card, Gene Tunney, *Pugilists in Action, British Cigarette Card, 1928, 50 cards in set* .	2.00	3.00	2.40
☐ Same as Above, Mickey Walker	1.00	2.00	1.30
☐ Same as Above, *complete set*	50.00	60.00	54.00
☐ Boxing Cards, Jimmy Flood, *Topps Ringside, 1950s*	1.00	2.00	1.30
☐ Same as Above, Randy Turpin	2.00	4.00	2.80
☐ Same as Above, Tony Zale	2.00	4.00	2.80
☐ Boxing Card, William Papke, *Turkey Red Cigarette Cards, early 1900s*	30.00	35.00	32.00
☐ Same as Above, Tommy Murphy	20.00	25.00	22.00
☐ Same as Above, Johnny Coulon	15.00	20.00	17.00
☐ Magazine, Boxing Illustrated, *1975, Ali vs. Frazier "Super Fight III"*	3.00	4.00	3.20
☐ Magazine, Ring Magazine, *most single issues, 1922*	28.00	35.00	31.00
☐ Magazine, World Boxing Magazine, *May, 1974*	1.00	2.00	1.30
☐ Poster, Muhammad Ali, *exhibition against unnamed opponent, May 29, 1979, Royal Albert Hall, London, paper, 16" x 23"*	9.00	19.00	13.00
☐ Poster, Joe Brown vs. Dave Charnley, *February 25, 1963, Manchester, England, paper 6½" x 8"*	4.00	8.00	6.00
☐ Poster, George Foreman vs. Joe Roman, *Heavyweight Championship, August 31, 1973, Tokyo, Japan, cardboard, 14" x 22"*	17.00	29.00	22.00
☐ Poster, Marvin Hagler vs. Fully Obel, *Middleweight Championship, January 17, 1981, Boston, 18" x 23"*	16.00	27.00	21.00
☐ Poster, Andy Kendall vs. Mike Quarry, *October 3, 1973, Orlando, Florida, cardboard, 14" x 22"*	9.00	17.00	13.00
☐ Poster, Sugar Ray Leonard vs. Pete Ranzany, *Welterweight Championship, August 12, 1979, Las Vegas, paper, 19" x 25"*	15.00	27.00	19.00
☐ Poster, Joe Louis vs. Tony Galento, *Heavyweight Championship, June 28, 1939, New York, theater film poster, 14" x 22"*	40.00	60.00	50.00
☐ Poster, Leon Spinks, *exhibition with unnamed opponents, Freeport, Bahamas, cardboard, 14" x 22"*	15.00	27.00	21.00
☐ Poster, Leon Spinks vs. Muhammad Ali, *Heavyweight Championship, September 15, 1978, 21" x 28"*	4.00	10.00	6.00
☐ Program, Max Baer vs. Tony Galento, *Heavyweight Championship, July 2, 1940, Vienna, Austria, 18 pp.*	7.00	9.00	8.00
☐ Program, Rocky Graziano vs. Charley Fusari, *Middleweight bout, September 14, 1949, Polo Grounds, New York, 24 pp.*	25.00	30.00	27.00

	Current Price Range		P/Y Average
☐ **Program, Sugar Ray Leonard vs. Bruce Finch,** *Welterweight Championship, February 15, 1982, Centennial Coliseum, Reno, Nevada, 32 pp.*	9.00	12.00	10.00
☐ **Program, Ernie Terrell vs. George Chuvalo,** *November 1, 1965, Toronto, Canada, autographed by Chuvalo*	15.00	20.00	17.00

BRASS

DESCRIPTION: Brass is an alloy of copper and zinc and has been used since antiquity. Because of its malleable nature it can be fashioned into a wide variety of utensils, tools and decorative objects.

COMMENTS: Decorative brassware has been imported from the Orient since the turn of the century. These wares feature very intricate engraving and tooling. Brass is very durable and although it tarnishes quickly it can be polished and restored to its lovely golden color very easily. Brassware can often be found in garage sales very cheaply as many people are unwilling to polish it regularly.

Ice Cream Server,
nickeled brass,
1930s, **$23.00-$30.00**

	Current Price Range		P/Y Average
☐ **Andirons,** pair, solid brass fluted column and ball finial with solid brass feet, 20½ "	110.00	120.00	112.50
☐ **Ashtray,** brass dog standing on edge, marked China, 4½ "	18.00	20.00	18.50
☐ **Ashtray,** fashioned from World War II artillery shell, very heavy, marked FSC 8/19/43, 7-V 50 cal., 4½ "	10.00	15.00	10.50
☐ **Ashtray,** ivy leaf shape, marked English Ivy by Cambron, 5¾ " x 4½ "	12.00	15.00	12.50
☐ **Ashtray,** shaped like coal scuttle, enameled with scene of men studying books around table, marked China	10.00	12.00	10.50
☐ **Ashtray,** shaped like handled bowl, enameled in floral, geometric, and scenic motifs, marked China	13.00	15.00	13.50
☐ **Ashtray,** square, cast oriental characters, 3"	4.00	5.00	4.25
☐ **Ashtray,** tooled and enameled, marked India Benares Brass, 3⅝ " x 1⅞ "	7.00	8.00	7.25
☐ **Ashtrays,** pair, slipper shape, floral engraving, marked India	5.00	6.00	5.25
☐ **Ashtrays,** set of four, nesting, scalloped, engraved flowers, marked China, 3½ " x 2¾ "	10.00	12.00	10.75
☐ **Bell,** cow shape, 3¼ "	6.00	8.00	6.50
☐ **Bell,** lady in ruffled skirt holds fan, shawl around shoulders, 3¼ "	20.00	25.00	22.50
☐ **Bell,** lady in ruffled skirt holds parasol, 4½ " .	28.00	32.00	30.00
☐ **Bowl,** sits on brass stand, marked China, 4½ "	21.00	24.00	22.00
☐ **Bowl,** tooled flowers and leaves, marked India, 6½ " x 1¾ "	9.00	11.00	9.25
☐ **Box,** oval, pierced hinged lid and sides, top handle hasp, marked India, 4" x 2½ " x7" ...	5.00	6.00	5.25
☐ **Candelabra,** five arms, marked China, 15½ " x 14"	45.00	50.00	47.50
☐ **Candelabra,** pair, each has three arms, elaborate styles, 15"	140.00	160.00	145.00
☐ **Candle Sconces,** pair, pierced 6" arm with hinge, engraved wall plate, marked China ...	28.00	33.00	29.50
☐ **Candleholders,** pair, spiral shaft, marked China, 10"	65.00	70.00	67.50
☐ **Candlestick,** heavy, teardrop and saucer turning, square footed base, 9¾ "	32.00	38.00	32.50
☐ **Candlesticks,** pair, heavy, 3"	10.00	12.00	10.50
☐ **Centerpiece,** shaped like Viking ship on stand with columns, hand hammered and footed, 17" long x 11" tall x 7" deep	34.00	40.00	35.00
☐ **Cigarette Jar with Lid,** cylindrical, dome lid, floral engraving, marked China, 3½ " x 3" ...	12.00	15.00	12.50
☐ **Cigarette Set,** three pieces, includes cigarette box, match box cover, ashtray, enameled, marked China	60.00	65.00	58.50
☐ **Coal Scuttle,** engraved, marked China, 4" x 3½ "	6.00	7.00	6.25
☐ **Coaster,** heavy, engraved flowers and leaves, marked China, 3½ "	4.00	5.00	4.25
☐ **Desk Lamp,** marble base	30.00	38.00	32.50

	Current Price Range		P/Y Average
☐ **Desk Set,** eight pieces, floral scroll design, pen tray, covered stamp safe, calenrar, letter holder, ink well with glass insert and hinged cover, rolling blotter, spring clip paper holder, Bradley and Hubbard, 1890s	285.00	315.00	290.00
☐ **Dish,** animal relief border, 4″	4.00	6.00	4.25
☐ **Dish,** footed, tooled and enameled decoration, marked Banares Brass, 2″ x 6″	9.00	11.00	9.50
☐ **Dish,** hammered, 4″	3.00	4.00	3.25
☐ **Dish,** heavy cast brass with elaborate scrolled surface, tri-footed, 4¼″	4.50	6.50	4.75
☐ **Dish,** pedestal, incised dragon, 4½″ x 3¼″	7.00	9.00	7.25
☐ **Door Knocker,** lion, 3½″ x 2½″, marked with impressed C & A	20.00	25.00	22.50
☐ **Figurine,** Art Deco style, nude dancer, domed base, very heavy, 8½″	120.00	130.00	125.00
☐ **Fireplace Tools and Stand,** small, stand is 16″ tall, tools are 11″ to 12″ tall and include hearth broom, poker, shovel, engraved heraldic crests, marked Made in England	120.00	130.00	125.00
☐ **Gong,** with stand and wooden striker, 7″	8.00	10.00	8.50
☐ **Incense Burner,** lid pierced with I Ching symbols, two tall pierced ear handles, three legs, 4½″ x 7″	22.00	28.00	23.50
☐ **Incense Burner,** pierced lid and tooled base, 2″ x 2″	2.00	4.00	2.25
☐ **Incense Burner,** pierced lid, tooled, scalloped rim, marked India, 1½″ x 2¼″	3.50	5.00	3.75
☐ **Incense Burner,** pierced lid, tooling, tri-footed, marked India, 3¼″ x 2″	4.00	6.00	4.25
☐ **Jar,** cylindrical, open, engraved trees, marked China, 1¾″	4.00	5.00	4.25
☐ **Jardiniere,** floral basket frieze around rim, ring handles, tri-footed, 9″ x 10½″	28.00	36.00	28.50
☐ **Jardiniere,** hammered texture, 2½″ band of sculptured roses in heavy relief around rim, 9¾″ x 11½″	32.00	38.00	33.50
☐ **Jelly Pot,** iron basket handle, 15″ x 5¾″	55.00	65.00	57.500
☐ **Keys,** group of seven, old	12.00	15.00	12.50
☐ **Letter Holder,** depicts jockey on horse in front of horseshoe, 6⅝″ x 4½″	32.00	38.00	35.00
☐ **Miniature Andirons,** pair, 1¾″	5.00	6.00	5.25
☐ **Miniature Bottle,** solid with screw in stopper, 1¾″	8.00	10.00	8.50
☐ **Miniature Candlestick,** solid base, 1¼″	3.00	4.00	3.25
☐ **Miniature Candlesticks,** very heavy, 1¾″	10.00	12.00	10.50
☐ **Miniature Decanter,** very heavy, 1¾″	8.00	10.00	8.50
☐ **Miniature Incense Burner,** pair, shaped like candlesticks, 2½″	4.00	5.00	4.25
☐ **Miniature Pestle,** 1¼″	3.50	4.50	3.75
☐ **Miniature Slipper,** pair, 1½″	4.00	5.00	4.25
☐ **Mint Dish,** hand tooled floral and leaf band and center, pedestal base, marked India, 5″ x 2″	8.00	10.00	8.50
☐ **Mug,** no handle, 3″ x 3″	3.00	4.00	3.25
☐ **Pig,** solid, 2½″	10.00	12.00	11.00

	Current Price Range		P/Y Average
☐ **Pig,** solid, 3″	15.00	17.00	16.00
☐ **Pig,** solid, 4¼″	24.00	28.00	25.00
☐ **Plate,** covered with tooled leaf engraving, 4¾″	4.00	5.00	4.25
☐ **Plate,** heavy cast brass with scalloped rim, features people in elaborate relief at center and around rim	6.00	8.00	6.50
☐ **Platter,** pedestal, marked China, 8″	19.00	21.00	18.50
☐ **Soap Dish,** Victorian bath tub with four curved feet, 5½″ x 2⅜″	9.00	11.00	10.00
☐ **Spittoon,** 6⅝″ x 4¾″	32.00	35.00	33.00
☐ **Table Lighter,** engraved leaves, marked India, 4½″	8.00	10.00	8.50
☐ **Table Top,** round, brass clad, covered with intricate Mid-Eastern engraving and caligraphy, 24″ diameter x 1⅝″ thick	130.00	150.00	140.00
☐ **Tongs,** claw end, hanging ring, 11″	15.00	18.00	16.50
☐ **Tray,** hammered, 5½″	4.00	5.00	4.25
☐ **Tray,** octagonal, hammered, 15″ x 10″	15.00	18.00	15.50
☐ **Tray,** two handles, engraved peacocks and flowers, marked India, 29″ x 8″	24.00	28.00	25.00
☐ **Vase,** bronze birds and flowers, marked China, 6″	28.00	32.00	28.50
☐ **Vase,** heavy, square top, two Foo dog handles, marked China, 9½″	65.00	75.00	67.50
☐ **Wall Brush Set,** includes mirror, and two bristle brushes with leaf scroll tooling, brushes hang from two hooks below mirror	45.00	48.00	46.00
☐ **Wax Seal,** bee shape	3.00	4.00	3.25
☐ **Wax Seal,** leaf shape	3.00	4.00	3.25

BREWERIANA

TOPIC: Breweriana is beer related memorabilia.

TYPES: Popular types of breweriana include serving trays, coasters, bottle and can openers and advertising signs.

PERIOD: Breweriana that dates back to 17th century England can be found, but most collectible breweriana was made after 1800. Contemporary products such as advertising mirrors are presently quite popular.

COMMENTS: Although some breweriana enthusiasts collect beer cans and beer bottles also, many limit themselves to breweriana and a specific company. Others collect certain items such as ashtrays.

ADDITIONAL TIPS: The following listings are arranged by company. For more extensive listings, refer to *The Official Price Guide to Beer Cans*, published by The House of Collectibles.

Iroquois Tray, *made by Charles Snowk, 1905, scarce, 12"*
$350.00-$400.00
(photo courtesy of ©Paul Michel, Buffalo, NY, 1984)

MISCELLANEOUS	Current Price Range		P/Y Average
☐ **Albion,** mirror, "Gold Medal Award from the 1924 Breweries Exhibition, To Albion Brewery, Championship Cup and Gold Medal Ales," 7"x 9"	130.00	170.00	150.00
☐ **American,** non-illuminated sign, glass and wood, "Brewer's Best Premium," 13" x 13"	22.00	28.00	25.00
☐ **American,** poster, "Salute to National Tavern Month," 11¼" x 14"	.40	.60	.50
☐ **Ballantine,** coaster, circular, red and black, "We Serve Ballantine Ale and Beer," probably late 1940's, 4¼"	4.00	6.00	5.00
☐ **Ballantine,** foam scraper, white and red, smile mug with logo and "Ballantine Draught Beer," dated 1964, 9"	8.50	11.50	10.00
☐ **Ballantine,** opener, copper plated, front: "Ballantine Ale and Beer" with three-ring sign, reverse: "Ballantine Ale and Beer," stamped Vaughn, 1,996,550	4.25	5.00	4.62

	Current Price Range		P/Y Average

☐ **Ballantine,** opener, front: "Drink Ballantine Ale and Beer," three-ring sign at top; reverse: blank **7.00 9.00 8.00**

☐ **Ballantine,** tray, three-ring sign with beer mug in red, yellow and black on white background . **6.50 9.50 8.00**

☐ **Ballantine's Ale and Beer,** tray, three ring sign, 11¾" **10.00 14.00 12.00**

☐ **Barbey's Sunshine,** tray, "Since 1861," gold with blue background, rounded sizes **31.00 39.00 36.00**

☐ **Bavarian,** coaster, circular, red and black, "Bavarian Type Beer, Mount Carbon Brewery, Pottsville, Pa., Union Made," 1940's, 4¼" **3.50 4.50 4.00**

☐ **Blatz,** illuminated sign, octagonal, brand name at center, mounted on pillar-type decorative bar with brass finial, gold and brown, 14" x 7" **8.00 10.00 9.00**

☐ **Blatz,** miniature bottle, 4" **13.00 17.00 15.00**

☐ **Braumeister,** coaster, oval, red, blue and yellow, "Braumeister Special Pilsner Beer, Milwaukee's Choicest, Independent Milwaukee Brewery," World War II era, 4¼" **4.00 6.00 5.00**

☐ **Black Horse Ale,** tap marker **6.50 8.50 7.50**

☐ **Brunswick Bock,** poster, "Brunswick Bock Beer," ram's head in white against green background, 1930's-40's, 23" x 34" **60.00 80.00 70.00**

☐ **Budweiser,** opener, wooden bottle with Bud label **10.00 14.00 12.00**

☐ **Budweiser,** paper hat, white with red lettering, "We Feature Budweiser Beer," c. 1950-60 .... **8.50 11.50 10.00**

☐ **Budweiser,** tip tray, Budweiser logo and "King of Beers," red with white lettering, rectangular, 3" x 7" **10.00 14.00 12.00**

☐ **Budweiser,** tray, "Duquoine State Fair, 50th Anniversary," gold and red, cream white background, 11¾" **13.00 17.00 15.00**

☐ **Budweiser,** tray, "King of Beers," eagle and trademark in red, green and yellow on white, 13¼" **9.00 12.00 10.50**

☐ **Budweiser,** tray, "Where There's Life, There's Budweiser," red, white and blue, 13¼" **11.00 15.00 13.00**

☐ **Columbia,** tray, hops and stars, multicolored with gold, 11¾" **19.00 25.00 22.00**

☐ **Columbia Five Star,** tray, Shenandoah, Pennsylvania, grain, hops and shield in multicolors and gold **22.00 28.00 26.00**

☐ **Coors,** tray, "America's Fine Light Beer," white lion, red striped background, 13¼" **8.00 10.00 9.00**

	Current Price Range		P/Y Average

☐ **Coors,** poster, reprint, "Coors Golden Brewery, Golden, Colo.," Gibson girl, 14″ x 19″ ... — 8.50 — 11.50 — 10.00

☐ **Dinkel Acker,** plastic, white with black and yellow border, logo and brand name .... — .90 — 1.20 — 1.05

☐ **Edelweiss,** non-illuminated sign, "Stop Here for Edelwiss Light Beer," thick cardboard in black, red, yellow and white, has circle marked "Special" with space for price to be written, c. 1950-60 .... — 22.00 — 28.00 — 25.00

☐ **Esslinger,** salt and pepper set, 4″ .... — 21.00 — 27.00 — 24.00

☐ **Esslinger's,** opener, "Esslinger's Premium Beer, Over the Top" .... — 8.00 — 10.00 — 9.00

☐ **Falls City,** tray, "70th Anniversary," illustration of brewery, multicolors, 11¾″ .... — 19.00 — 25.00 — 22.00

☐ **F and S Beer and Ale,** tray, multicolored drum major .... — 22.00 — 29.00 — 25.00

☐ **Genesee,** tray, "Ask for Jenny," illustration of Jenny, white, black and yellow against reddish background, 11¾″ .... — 14.00 — 18.00 — 16.00

☐ **Genesee,** tray, still life with pheasant on table, multicolored, 11¾″ .... — 15.00 — 19.00 — 17.00

☐ **Gibbons Mellow-Pure Beer and Ale,** tray, white, black and red, 11¾″ .... — 13.00 — 17.00 — 15.00

☐ **Gibbons Premium,** tray, "Gibbons is Good," white with black and red lettering, 13¼″ .... — 8.00 — 10.00 — 9.00

☐ **Grain Belt,** tray, logo with grain, hops, mug and lake in background, multicolored, 13¼″ — 12.00 — 16.00 — 14.00

☐ **Hamm's,** tray, bear with lake in woodland scene, multicolored, 11¾″ .... — 14.00 — 18.00 — 16.00

☐ **Hamm's,** tray, canoer on lake, multicolored, 13¼″ .... — 15.00 — 19.00 — 17.00

☐ **Hamm's,** tray, lion crest in gold with white lettering on red background, 13¼″ .... — 8.00 — 10.00 — 9.00

☐ **Hamm's,** tray, woodland scene with hiker and bear, multicolored, 13¼″ .... — 15.00 — 19.00 — 17.00

☐ **Hamm's Preferred Stock,** tray, view of brewery on front and reverse of tray, red and black against white background, 13¼″ .... — 24.00 — 32.00 — 28.00

☐ **Heineken,** pocket knife-opener combination, brand name on handle, "Solingen, Germany" on base of blade .... — 44.00 — 52.00 — 49.00

☐ **Heineken,** shoe, wood, "Heineken Beer," yellow with illustration of Dutch boy and windmill, 10″ .... — 22.00 — 28.00 — 25.00

☐ **Hofbrau Bavaria,** mug, ceramic .... — 4.00 — 6.00 — 5.00

☐ **Holsten,** ashtray, ceramic, circular, "Holsten Beer" in black lettering on white, made in Germany, 4″ .... — 17.00 — 23.00 — 20.00

☐ **Iroquois,** coaster, red and white, head of Indian chief, "Iroquois Indian Head Beer and Ale, Iroquois Beverage Corp., Buffalo, N.Y.," c. 1940-50, 4″ .... — 5.00 — 7.00 — 6.00

☐ **Iroquois,** tip tray, Indian chief trademark with "Iroquois Brewery, Buffalo," circular, c. 1930-40, 4½″ .... — 100.00 — 140.00 — 120.00

	Current Price Range		P/Y Average

☐ **Jacob Ruppert,** non-illuminated sign, oval, wire stand-up device on back, "Ruppert Beer and Ale, New York," reverse-painted on glass, black with silver lettering, imitation wood frame, 18″ x 12″ **50.00 70.00 60.00**

☐ **Knickerbocker,** opener, "Jacob Ruppert Brewery, New York, The Brew that Satisfies, Save this Opener, Order by the Case" **17.00 23.00 20.00**

☐ **Kuebler,** tip tray, "Kuebler Beer, Easton, Pa., 1852," black and orange, illustration of top-hatted man with mug, circular, believed to date from late 1940's, 4½″ **35.00 45.00 40.00**

☐ **Lone Star,** tray, star logo in gold and red against white background, 13¼″ **11.00 15.00 13.00**

☐ **Lowenbrau,** tray, gold heraldic lion, blue background, 13¼″ **5.00 7.00 6.00**

☐ **McSorley's Cream Stock Ale,** tray, tavern interior scene, dated 1936, 11¾″ **40.00 50.00 45.00**

☐ **Michelob,** coaster, circular, red and black, emblem on front, on back: "Have a Michelob, It's an Unexpected Pleasure," c. 1970-80, 3½″ .... **.90 1.20 1.05**

☐ **Miller Lite,** non-illuminated sign, plastic, white with blue lettering, 18″ x 14″ **4.00 5.00 4.50**

☐ **Old German,** thermometer, circular, 10″ diameter **22.00 28.00 25.00**

☐ **Old German,** tie clip, "Herman" **13.00 17.00 15.00**

☐ **Old Shay Ale,** ashtray, metallic, silver color, "Old Shay Ale, Product of Fort Pitt Brewing Co., Jeannette, Pa. Plant" in black lettering . **13.00 17.00 15.00**

☐ **Old Style,** illuminated sign, octagonal, brand name at center, mounted on pillar-type decorative bar with brass finial, gold and brown, 14″ x 7″ **8.00 10.00 9.00**

☐ **Pabst Blue Ribbon,** illuminated sign, standard logo, raised seal and lettering in a plaque-like frame, blue and white, 15″ x 20″ . **16.00 20.00 18.00**

☐ **Pabst Blue Ribbon,** illuminated sign, circular, silver and gold mug with large brand name at top of frame, logo at bottom, 15″ x 15″ **10.00 14.00 12.00**

☐ **Pabst Blue Ribbon,** tray, girl in flapper outfit, multicolored, 13¼″ **7.00 9.00 8.00**

☐ **Pabst Blue Ribbon,** tray, 1976 Bicentennial tray with view of old brewery, 13¼″ **7.00 9.00 8.00**

☐ **Piel's** tray, "Enjoy Piel's Beer," multicolored caricatures of Bert and Harry Piel, white background, 13¼″ **15.00 19.00 17.00**

☐ **Piel's Light,** tray, elf carrying tray, multicolored against gold background, 11¾″ **15.00 19.00 17.00**

☐ **Rheingold Extra Dry,** tray, Liebman, black and white on red background, 11¾″ **7.00 9.00 8.00**

☐ **Rheingold Extra Dry Lager,** tray, logo in black and red against white background, red sides, 13¼″ **8.00 10.00 9.00**

☐ **Ruppert Knickerbocker,** tray, Father Knickerbocker, multicolored, 13¼″ **10.00 14.00 12.00**

	Current Price Range		P/Y Average
☐ **Ruppert Old Knickerbocker,** tray, eagle in gold and white, gold and red on red background, 13¼ "	18.00	24.00	21.00
☐ **Schaefer,** tray, logo and grain symbol in red, white and gold, repeated on reverse, 13¼ " ...	7.00	9.00	8.00
☐ **Schaefer,** tray, red and white with mottos, 11¾ "	9.00	13.00	11.00
☐ **Schlitz,** illuminated sign, shield-shaped, "Light Beer" with word "Light" in very large lettering, decorative molding, 20″ x 18″	21.00	27.00	24.00
☐ **Schmidt's,** non-illuminated sign, "Schmidt's of Philadelphia, Beer and Ale," small sign on black wooden stand, black with silver lettering, c. 1940-50, 8″ x 6″	43.00	57.00	50.00
☐ **Whitebread,** astray, plastic, circular, blue, "Whitebread Tankard Helps me Excel," made in Great Britain, 9″	4.00	6.00	5.00
☐ **Yuengling,** coaster, circular, green and red, front: "Yuengling Premium Beer, Since 1829," reverse: "America's Oldest Breweries," 3¼ " .	1.85	2.30	2.10
☐ **Yuengling,** opener, "Drink Yuengling's Beer and Ale, D.G. Yuengling & Son, Inc., Pottsville, Pa."	8.00	10.00	9.00

BRITISH ROYALTY MEMORABILIA

VARIATIONS: A wide variety of British Royalty commemoratives have been made, from inexpensive tourist trinkets to fine pieces of porcelain.

COMMENTS: The pageantry and elegance that surrounds British royalty intrigues and attracts collectors of royalty memorabilia.

ADDITIONAL TIPS: This section is listed alphabetically according to item. Included after the item are the royal figures being honored, and when available, special events, decoration on the item, color, special features, maker, height and price,

Royal Baby Doll, *commemorating the birth of Prince William of Wales, born June 21, 1982, Heirloom series, limited edition of 2,500,* **$275.00-$325.00**

	Current Price Range		P/Y Average
☐ **Ashtray,** King Edward VIII, Edward's head and flags, Paladin china, 4½"	5.00	10.00	7.00
☐ **Box,** King George VI and Queen Elizabeth, king, queen, two princesses, tin, 5" x 4" x 3".	12.00	18.00	14.00
☐ **Box,** Prince Albert, impressed head of prince, round, brass, 2½"	20.00	30.00	24.00
☐ **Covered Jar,** Queen Elizabeth II, Coronation 1953, cream pottery with gold scrolls, portrait, coat of arms, 5"	40.00	50.00	45.00
☐ **Cover Jar,** Queen Victoria, cover shaped like Victoria's head with necklace, veil, crown, round jar has coat of arms, milkglass, 8"	55.00	65.00	60.00
☐ **Cup,** King George V and Queen Mary, Coronation 1911, king, queen, prince of Wales, enamel	50.00	60.00	53.00
☐ **Cup,** King George V and Queen Mary, Coronation 1911, portraits of royal couple, monograms, crowns, Royal Doulton	45.00	55.00	50.00
☐ **Cup,** King George V and Queen Mary, Silver Jubilee, king, queen, flags, green glass, handle	25.00	35.00	28.00

	Current Price Range		P/Y Average

☐ **Cup,** King Edward VII and Queen Alexandra, Coronation 1902, photos of royal couple, flags, enamel, 3½ " .... | 45.00 | 55.00 | 48.00

☐ **Cup,** King George VI and Queen Elizabeth, family portrait of king, queen and two princesses, roses, thistles,castles, Spode, 3½ " . | 30.00 | 40.00 | 33.00

☐ **Cup,** Queen Elizabeth II, Coronation 1953, green garland, raised heads of Elizabeth and Philip, red glaze interior, tan and white outside, double handle .... | 25.00 | 35.00 | 31.00

☐ **Cup,** Queen Victoria, scroll design with portrait of queen, palace, enamel .... | 45.00 | 55.00 | 50.00

☐ **Finger Bowl,** King Gerorge V and QueenMary, Coronation 1911, portraits of royal couple, flags, flowers .... | 45.00 | 55.00 | 50.00

☐ **Mug,** King Edward VIII, color portrait, lion, unicorn, flags, ribbon, china, 3" .... | 15.00 | 25.00 | 20.00

☐ **Mug,** King Edward VIII, Coronation 1937, Edward's head on red background in blue frame, oak leaves, 3½ " .... | 25.00 | 35.00 | 30.00

☐ **Mug,** King Edward VIII, family motto, crown, oak branches, tapered, 3½ " .... | 25.00 | 35.00 | 30.00

☐ **Mug,** King Edward VIII, picture of king on front, medallion on back blue and white, Wedgwood, 3½ " .... | 25.00 | 35.00 | 30.00

☐ **Mug,** King Edward VIII, official design, "May 1937 Coronation of King Edward VIII," around rim, bulbous handle, 4½ " .... | 30.00 | 40.00 | 37.00

☐ **Mug,** King Edward VII and Queen Alexandra, Coronation 1902, picture of royal couple, crown, coat of arms, Royal Doulton, 4" ..... | 40.00 | 50.00 | 44.00

☐ **Mug,** King George VI and Queen Elizabeth, king and queen in gold frames, flags, crown, china, " .... | 10.00 | 20.00 | 14.00

☐ **Mug,** Queen Elizabeth II, Coronation 1953, date of coronation around rim, portrait of queen surrounded by leaves and flowers, Copeland Spode, handle, 3½ " .... | 15.00 | 25.00 | 20.00

☐ **Mug,** Queen Elizabeth II, Coronation 1953, portrait of queen, lion, unicorn, flags, ribbons, handleless, flared, 3½ " .... | 25.00 | 35.00 | 28.00

☐ **Mug,** Queen Elizabeth II, gold framed picture of Elizabeth, blue ribbons, pink roses, Royal Albert bone china, handle, 4½ " .... | 30.00 | 40.00 | 33.00

☐ **Mug,** Queen Elizabeth II, official design with photo, flags, crown and flowers, Johnson Brothers, glazed pottery, 3½ " .... | 15.00 | 25.00 | 20.00

☐ **Mug,** Queen Elizabeth II, photo in frame, lion, unicorn, flags, handle, 3½ " .... | 15.00 | 25.00 | 18.00

☐ **Mug,** Queen Elizabeth II, photo of queen surrounded by roses, shamrocks, daffodils, thistles, Tuscan bone china, handle, 3½ " .... | 25.00 | 35.00 | 28.00

☐ **Mug,** Queen Elizabeth II, picture of queen on front, coat of arms on back, green, handle, 3" | 8.00 | 15.00 | 12.00

☐ **Mug,** Queen Elizabeth II, picture of queen on front, coat of arms on back, pink, handle, 3" .. | 8.00 | 15.00 | 12.00

	Current Price Range		P/Y Average
Mug, Queen Elizabeth II, raised head of queen, thistles, daffodils, roses, shamrocks, white glazed pottery, handle, 3½ "	15.00	25.00	18.00
Mug, Queen Elizabeth II, Silver Jubilee, photo of queen, handle, 3½ "	20.00	30.00	25.00
Mug, Queen Elizabeth II, Silver Jubilee, portrait, Royal Worcester fine porcelain, 3½ "	25.00	35.00	30.00
Pierced Dish, King George VI and Queen Elizabeth, figures of king and queen impressed in bowl of dish, round, 5"	25.00	35.00	30.00
Pitcher, King Edward VII and Queen Alexandra, 25th wedding anniversary, flat sided	60.00	70.00	65.00
Pitcher, King Edward VII and Queen Alexandra, young royal couple as Prince and Princess of Wales, flow blue, 7"	90.00	100.00	93.00
Pitcher, King George V and Queen Mary, portraits of king and queen, flags, flowers, china, rose and white, 5"	35.00	45.00	40.00
Pitcher, King George V and Queen Mary, royal couple in garlands of roses, saying on back, clear and frosted glass, 4"	30.00	40.00	37.00
Pitcher, Queen Victoria, 50th Anniversary, picture of queen, sayings, white, flat sided, 5"	80.00	90.00	85.00
Picture, Queen Victoria, figure and flowers in enamel, black glazed redware, 6"	90.00	100.00	95.00
Plate, King Edward VIII, Edward's head with crown, flags, square, 8½ "	15.00	25.00	20.00
Plate, King Edward VII, photograph of Edward, fleur-de-lis border, glass, 7"	20.00	30.00	24.00
Plate, King Edward VII and Queen Alexandra, portrait of Edward, scalloped border, white around rim, flow blue, 9"	35.00	45.00	40.00
Plate, King George V and Queen Mary, picture of royal couple, coat of arms, color with blue border, 6"	25.00	35.00	30.00
Plate, Queen Alexandra, photograph of Alexandra, fleur-de-lis border, glass, 7"	20.00	30.00	25.00
Plate, Queen Elizabeth II, large painted crown, bright colors on white china, 5½ "	8.00	14.00	11.00
Plate, Queen Elizabeth II, oak leaves, acorns, portrait, square	20.00	30.00	25.00
Plate, Queen Elizabeth II, official pottery makers design, square, 8"	15.00	25.00	20.00
Plate, Queen Elizabeth II, official pottery makers design, 9"	20.00	30.00	25.00
Plate, Queen Victoria, portrait of queen surrounded by emblems of Canadian provinces	25.00	35.00	30.00
Plaque, Queen Elizabeth II, Coronation 1953, round, brass, 8"	20.00	30.00	25.00
Sugar and Creamer, King Edward VIII, Edward's head, gold leaves, decorations	30.00	40.00	35.00
Sugar and Creamer, Queen Elizabeth II, photograph, flags, flowers, bone china	35.00	45.00	40.00

	Current Price Range		P/Y Average
☐ **Tea Set,** King Edward VII and Queen Alexandra, 6½", teapot, sugar and creamer, 9" cake plate, deacorated with coat of arms, figures, white glazed Foley china with gold trim, melon shaped	300.00	350.00	325.00
☐ **Tumbler,** Queen Victoria, silhouette of queen, garland, black milk glass, 5"	20.00	30.00	24.00
☐ **Tumbler,** Queen Victoria, triple rows of beading, "To Commemorate Queen Victoria's Reign of 60 Years," clear, heavy	25.00	35.00	30.00
☐ **Vase,** King George VI and Queen Elizabeth, Coronation 1937, shamrocks, thistles, roses, crystal, cut, etched, flared, 8"	40.00	50.00	45.00

BRONZE

DESCRIPTION: Sculptures and other decorative objects were cast in bronze, and usually made in limited numbers.

TYPES: Bronze statues were often made in classical styles, such as gods and goddesses, animals and warriors; also vases, urns, bookends and similar items.

PERIOD: Though bronze sculpture is of ancient origin, most of the collectible specimens on the market are Victorian to early 20th century.

CARE AND CONDITION: Clean and polish bronze with a good bronze polish, this will guard against corrosion.

☐ **Ashtray,** bronze resting on onyx base, the tray measures 6", the base 4½" x 7"	27.00	34.00	30.00
☐ **Bonheur, Rosa,** set of bookends modeled after a work by her, picturing horses in relief .	50.00	60.00	55.00
☐ **Bookends,** set with anchor motif	30.00	35.00	32.00
☐ **Book Rack,** Bradley and Hubbard, expandable, leafwork motif with screen sides	40.00	50.00	44.00
☐ **DeAngelis, Sabatino,** figure of an armored horseman, signed Sabatino DeAngelis, and Fils (son), Naples, 1908, mounted on a green marble base	300.00	400.00	340.00

	Current Price Range		P/Y Average
☐ **Diana The Huntress,** *anonymous bronze sculpture of the mythological goddess with quiver, mounted on a bronze stand, French, undated, probably late 19th century, 33½"* ..	900.00	1150.00	950.00
☐ **D'Ore, Jean B.,** *bronze sculpture of an angel, signed, 17"*	1000.00	1500.00	1200.00
☐ **Horse And Dog,** *modeled after a work by P. J. Mene, horse is shown bending over the dog, signed, 18"*	2200.00	2800.00	2500.00
☐ **Jockey And Horse,** *modeled after a work by Yves Benoist Gironiere, horse in racing motion, signed, 31" in length by 13" high*	1600.00	2000.00	1750.00
☐ **Mercury,** *modeled after a work by Jean de Bologne, large room-size mythological bronze, intended as a corner piece for large room, mounted on marble platform, 49½"*	800.00	1100.00	950.00
☐ **Milles, Carl,** *figure of man in frock coat, kneeling, signed and dated 1948 and bearing the number four along with a foundry mark, 17"* .	1200.00	1600.00	1300.00
☐ **Mongniez, J.,** *figural grouping, sculptured bronze, signed*	1200.00	1450.00	1300.00
☐ **Picault, E.,** *bronze sculpture of an unidentified nobleman, signed*	2200.00	2800.00	2450.00
☐ **Portrait Bust,** *man in ribboned hat, modeled after a work by C. Kauba, signed, marked Gershutz with the mold number 4529, 5"*	110.00	140.00	125.00
☐ **Temple Musicians,** *set of eight figurines of various musicians, all seated, wearing headdresses and elaborate costumes, playing different musical instruments, ranging in height from 3" to 3½", set*	135.00	170.00	150.00
☐ **Turtle,** *French bronze sculpture in the likeness of a turtle, unsigned, 6½"*	180.00	220.00	200.00

BUCK ROGERS

DESCRIPTION: Buck Rogers began as a futuristic comic strip conceived by Philip Nowlan in 1929. Since then, comic books, radio programs, television series and movies have been produced about this space hero.

TYPES: Because of its popularity among children, all types of items including premiums, toys, school supplies and dishes have featured Buck Rogers characters.

COMMENTS: Collectors of Buck Rogers memorabilia will find that items produced in its early years are usually more valuable then recent objects.

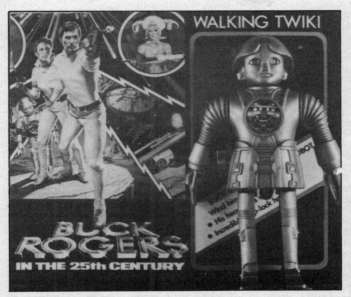

Buck Rogers Walking Twiki, *made by Mego under license from Robert C. Dille, hard molded plastic, head turns when he walks, has grip lock hands, 6½", 1979,* **$5.00-$8.00**

	Current Price Range		P/Y Average
☐ **Badge,** Buck Rogers Solar Scout badge, Cream of Wheat premium, dated 1935	35.00	45.00	40.00
☐ **Button,** Buck Rogers in the 25th Century, celluloid, multicolored	35.00	45.00	40.00
☐ **Button,** Buck Rogers Satellite Pioneer, lithographed tin in red, white and black, illustration of space vehicle with balcony encircling it, astronauts walking on balcony, words, "Rocket Rangers" in small letters	95.00	115.00	110.00
☐ **Button,** Buck Rogers Solar Scout membership button, Cream of Wheat premium, celluloid, 1935	20.00	25.00	22.50
☐ **Figure,** Buck Rogers in the 25th Century, Ardella, Mego, plastic, 1979	9.00	12.00	10.50
☐ **Figure,** Buck Rogers in the 25th Century, Draco, Mego, plastic, 1979	9.00	12.00	10.50
☐ **Figure,** Buck Rogers in the 25th Century, Killer Kane, Mego, plastic, 1979	9.00	12.00	10.50

	Current Price Range		P/Y Average

☐ **Gun,** Buck Rogers Atomic Pistol, Daisy Manufacturing Co., Plymouth, Michigan, cast pot metal with chrome plating, beaded grip . — 50.00 / 70.00 — 60.00

☐ **Gun,** Buck Rogers Copper Disintegrator Cap gun, cast iron, picture of Buck Rogers with wording "Buck Rogers in the 25th Century" . — 120.00 / 150.00 — 135.00

☐ **Gun,** Buck Rogers Pocket Pistol, Daisy Manufacturing Co., lithographed tin . . . . — 100.00 / 130.00 — 120.00

☐ **Gun,** Buck Rogers Rubber Band Gun, Onward School Supply Co., large lithographed cardboard card from which the gun and targets punch out . . . . — 35.00 / 45.00 — 40.00

☐ **Gun,** Buck Rogers Sonic Ray Gun, Norton Engineering and Manufacturing Co., Chicago, plastic, battery powered . . . . — 30.00 / 40.00 — 35.00

☐ **Holster,** Buck Rogers combat set holster, 1934 . . . . — 100.00 / 120.00 — 110.00

☐ **Kite,** Buck Rogers Strato-Kite, Aero Kite Co., 1946 . . . . — 45.00 / 55.00 — 40.00

☐ **Matchbook Cover,** Buck Rogers, carries ad for ice cream with ad for Buck Rogers radio network program . . . . — 7.00 / 10.00 — 8.50

☐ **Pencil Case,** Buck Rogers Pencil Case, cardboard, multicolored, top has picture of Buck Rogers, 1938 . . . . — 25.00 / 35.00 — 30.00

☐ **Printing Set,** Buck Rogers, set of 22 stamps used to create comic book stories . . . . — 115.00 / 135.00 — 125.00

☐ **Rocket Ships,** Buck Rogers Battlecruiser, Tootsie Toy Co., lithographed tin, blue and yellow, moves on string or wire, 1937 . . . . — 60.00 / 80.00 — 70.00

☐ **Rocket Ship,** Buck Rogers Laserscope Fighter, Mego, plastic, complex design, 1979 — 20.00 / 25.00 — 22.50

☐ **Rocket Ship,** Buck Rogers Tootsietoy Rocket Ship #1033, Attack Ship, cast metal, white and red . . . . — 130.00 / 160.00 — 145.00

BUTTONS

DESCRIPTION: Dating to the 13th century, buttons were first used for decoration. Early buttons had very elaborate and exquisite designs. Later buttons were more commonly used as fasteners. Both types are collectible.

VARIATIONS: A variety of button types have been made including, heads of famous people, animals, picture buttons, story buttons, sporting buttons, among others. "Realistics" were plastic buttons made in the 1930s and 1940s that looked like everyday items in miniature. Examples include fruit, animals and food.

MAKER: Most antique and collectible buttons on the market today are American, French or English made.

MATERIALS: Buttons have been made from materials including painted tin, metal, mother-of-pearl, pewter, brass, glass, gilt, plastic, ivory, ceramic, cloisonne and celluloid.

MARKS: Some early buttons, from the 18th and 19th centuries, had backmarks which identify the maker. Some collectors collect by backmark rather than by button design.

COMMENTS: Currently buttons from the 18th century to the present are the most available and collectible. They are a lovely and usually inexpensive collectible.

ADDITIONAL TIPS: The listings are arranged alphabetically by button material. A description follows.

For further button information, contact: The National Button Society, Box 39, Eastwood, Kentucky 40018.

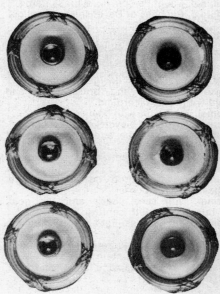

Buttons,
mother of pearl,
sapphire inset,
Tiffany & Co., 1915,
$675.00-$800.00

	Current Price Range		P/Y Average
☐ **Black Glass,** cameo head	12.50	20.00	14.00
☐ **Black Glass,** elephant under palm tree	7.50	13.00	8.50
☐ **Black Glass,** faceted ball, gold foil top	35.00	45.00	37.00
☐ **Black Glass,** mountain with house scene, beaded gilt edge	35.00	45.00	37.00
☐ **Black Glass,** shape of a slipper	10.00	15.00	12.00
☐ **Black Onyx,** with 14K gold, ball shaped, 19th century	60.00	70.00	63.00
☐ **Black Onyx,** gold filled, ball shaped, 19th century	20.00	25.00	21.00
☐ **Brass,** Aesop's Fable, frog and rabbit	21.50	30.00	24.00
☐ **Brass,** Aesop's Fable, two mice	35.00	45.00	37.00
☐ **Brass,** angry rooster	10.00	15.00	12.00
☐ **Brass,** cherubs with cornucopia and goat	4.50	8.00	6.50
☐ **Brass,** children playing game, Victorian era	21.00	30.00	24.00
☐ **Brass,** dancing gypsy girl with goat	48.00	60.00	53.00
☐ **Brass Disc,** bridge and river scene, black and white	75.00	105.00	84.00
☐ **Brass,** Indian hunter	35.00	45.00	37.00
☐ **Brass,** mother feeding child, high relief	21.50	30.00	25.00
☐ **Brass,** rooster standing on wheat shaft	16.00	25.00	18.00
☐ **Celluloid,** angel head, gold background, gilt rims	35.00	45.00	37.00
☐ **Celluloid,** Count Fersen, floral brass frame	21.00	30.00	22.00
☐ **Celluloid,** Duchess of Devonshire, pastel colors	42.00	55.00	47.00
☐ **Celluloid,** Marie Antonette	10.00	15.00	12.00
☐ **Ceramic,** bird, black and white	25.00	35.00	28.00
☐ **Ceramic,** bird with branch in beak, scalloped border	35.00	45.00	37.00
☐ **Ceramic,** cupid, scroll design on edge	45.00	55.00	47.00
☐ **Cloisonne,** birds flying, brass, black and white with red background	82.00	115.00	95.00
☐ **Enamel,** lighthouse with boat scene	47.00	58.00	50.00
☐ **Enamel,** lady riding bicycle, cut steel border	62.00	77.00	65.00
☐ **Enamel,** maiden, blue and white, diamond paste border	52.00	67.00	55.00
☐ **Enamel,** portrait of lady, black background, 18th c.	62.00	78.00	65.00
☐ **Enamel,** rose colored scene on white, embossed scroll border	200.00	245.00	220.00
☐ **Enamel,** with seed pearls and 14K gold, ladybug design, 19th century	575.00	600.00	580.00
☐ **Enamel,** shepherdess, light purple, diamond paste border	47.00	58.00	50.00
☐ **Enamel,** star shape decorated with cut steels	16.00	25.00	20.00
☐ **Enamel,** woman at fountain	55.00	75.00	60.00
☐ **Glass,** black liberty cap and flag, silver frame, 18th c.	55.00	75.00	60.00
☐ **Glass,** French Revolution motif, copper rim	70.00	88.00	74.00
☐ **Glass,** molded opaque, brown bird design	25.00	35.00	28.00
☐ **Gold,** 14K, ball shape with ribbing, 19th century	60.00	70.00	63.00
☐ **Gold,** 14K, button set with chain, 19th century	50.00	60.00	52.00
☐ **Gold,** 14K, engraved collar button, 19th century	30.00	35.00	31.00

	Current Price Range		P/Y Average
☐ **Gold,** 14K, pearl shape, 19th century	60.00	70.00	63.00
☐ **Gold,** 14K, scrolled edge design, 19th century	60.00	70.00	63.00
☐ **Gold,** woven hair under swirls, cartwheel design, 19th century	110.00	130.00	118.00
☐ **Gold,** woven hair under swirls, cartwheel design with scalloped edge, 19th century ...	130.00	150.00	138.00
☐ **Gold-filled,** ball shape with ribbing, 19th century	20.00	25.00	21.00
☐ **Gold Plated,** dragon	7.50	13.00	8.00
☐ **Ivory,** carved Royal Salamander	30.00	40.00	34.00
☐ **Ivory,** cut-out girl and bird, blue background .	150.00	180.00	155.00
☐ **Ivory,** painted cherub in chariot drawn by two horses	90.00	110.00	95.00
☐ **Ivory,** painted girl and dog chasing butterflies	90.00	110.00	95.00
☐ **Ivory,** painted lady and dog, silver rim	48.00	60.00	53.00
☐ **Ivory,** painted Oriental head	35.00	45.00	40.00
☐ **Mother-of-pearl,** 14K gold, simple button, 19th century	75.00	85.00	80.00
☐ **Oriental,** fan design, multicolored, scalloped border	30.00	40.00	33.00
☐ **Oriental,** floral motif, enameled	35.00	45.00	37.00
☐ **Pewter,** owl's head	4.50	8.00	5.50
☐ **Pierced Brass,** Little Red Riding Hood	13.00	20.00	15.00
☐ **Porcelain,** cherub catching butterflies, pink, black and white	20.00	30.00	23.00
☐ **Porcelain,** cupid, scroll design on edge	48.00	65.00	52.00
☐ **Porcelain,** flowers and butterfly, 18th c.	17.50	30.00	20.00
☐ **Porcelain,** pasture scene with children	30.00	40.00	34.00
☐ **Porcelain,** with gold, painted angels, 19th century	520.00	540.00	528.00
☐ **Silver,** Bacchus, God of Wine, etched design	25.00	35.00	27.00
☐ **Stamped Brass,** two children fighting and pulling hair	21.00	30.00	24.00
☐ **Steel,** floral design	4.50	8.00	5.50
☐ **Turquoise,** with 14K gold, button set with chain, 19th century	95.00	105.00	98.00
☐ **Victorian,** figure, black glass disc	8.50	14.00	9.00
☐ **Wedgwood,** classic figures, white relief on blue, cut steel border, 18th c.	250.00	295.00	270.00
☐ **Wedgwood,** classic figure, white on royal blue, gilt rim, 18th c.	235.00	275.00	245.00
☐ **Wedgwood,** classical figures, white relief on light blue	52.00	70.00	60.00
☐ **Wedgwood,** floral design, diamond paste border, silver frame	200.00	250.00	215.00
☐ **Wedgwood,** warrior, white relief on royal blue, copper border	225.00	275.00	230.00

CAMBRIDGE GLASS

HISTORY: The Cambridge Glass Co., located in the Ohio town of that name, was chiefly a producer of cut glass, though it sold other types as well. Its operations were very extensive and for many years, especially during the 1920s and 1930s, it maintained a near monopoly on the manufacture of cut glass tableware. Some of its designs were most creative.

COMMENTS: The glassware listed here has come to be known as "elegant" depression glass.

MARKS: Most Cambridge elegant depression glass was unmarked. A triangle with a C inside or "Near-cut" appear on some pieces of Cambridge glass.

RECOMMENDED READING: For further information refer to *The Official Price Guide to Depression Glass* published by The House of Collectibles.

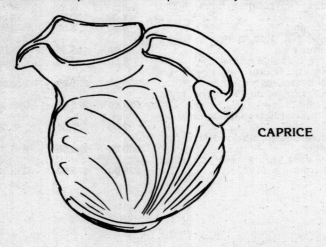

CAPRICE

CAPRICE

Caprice was first made in the 1940s. Colors are crystal, blue, amber and amethyst. Pieces in blue are the most collectible and sought after.

	Current Price Range		P/Y Average
Ashtray, *triangle shape, 4½"*			
blue	13.00	18.00	14.00
crystal	9.00	12.00	10.00
Bon Bon Dish, *square with handle, 6"*			
blue	26.00	34.00	28.00
crystal	16.00	20.00	17.00
Bread And Butter Plate, *6½"*			
blue	17.00	21.00	18.00
crystal	11.00	14.00	12.00
Cake Plate, *footed, 13"*			
blue	230.00	275.00	240.00
crystal	95.00	110.00	98.00
Candy Box, *footed, with lid, 6"*			
blue	82.00	92.00	84.00
crystal	47.00	55.00	50.00
Claret Goblet, *4½ oz.*			
blue	40.00	50.00	42.00
crystal	23.00	30.00	25.00
Coaster, *3½"*			
blue	23.00	28.00	25.00
crystal	13.00	18.00	15.00
Cocktail Goblet, *3½ oz.*			
blue	37.00	45.00	39.00
crystal	22.00	29.00	24.00
Creamer, *medium*			
blue	13.00	18.00	14.50
crystal	6.00	9.00	7.00
Decanter, *with stopper, 36 oz.*			
blue	130.00	170.00	140.00
crystal	72.00	90.00	77.00
Dinner Plate, *9½"*			
blue	87.00	110.00	90.00
crystal	35.00	45.00	37.00
Luncheon Plate, *8½"*			
blue	23.00	30.00	24.00
crystal	13.00	19.00	14.00
Pitcher, *ball shaped, 32 oz.*			
blue	170.00	185.00	175.00
crystal	87.00	100.00	90.00
Rose Bowl, *footed, 8"*			
blue	93.00	105.00	95.00
crystal	56.00	68.00	60.00
Salad Bowl, *footed, 8"*			
blue	40.00	50.00	42.00
crystal	22.00	32.00	25.00
Salad Plate, *7½"*			
blue	18.00	24.00	20.00
crystal	13.00	17.00	14.00

	Current Price Range		P/Y Average
Sherbet, *tall, 7 oz.*			
☐ blue	23.00	30.00	25.00
☐ crystal	18.00	24.00	20.00
Sugar, *medium size*			
☐ blue	13.00	18.00	15.00
☐ crystal	6.50	9.00	7.50
Tumbler, *footed, 3 oz.*			
☐ blue	21.00	26.00	22.00
☐ crystal	15.00	20.00	16.00
Tumbler, *footed, 5 oz.*			
☐ blue	21.00	26.00	22.00
☐ crystal	15.00	20.00	16.00
Tumbler, *footed, 10 oz.*			
☐ blue	30.00	37.00	32.00
☐ crystal	18.00	24.00	20.00
Tumbler, *footed, 12 oz.*			
☐ blue	33.00	40.00	35.00
☐ crystal	21.00	27.00	22.00
Vase, 5½″			
☐ blue	57.00	65.00	59.00
☐ crystal	43.00	49.00	45.00
Vase, 8½″			
☐ blue	87.00	95.00	89.00
☐ crystal	53.00	60.00	54.00
Wine Goblet, *3 oz.*			
☐ blue	43.00	52.00	45.00
☐ crystal	25.00	32.00	27.00

DECAGON

Made in the shape of a decagon, this pattern was made in the 1930s. Colors range from pastels to red and cobalt blue.

	Current Price Range		P/Y Average
Almond Bowl, 2½″			
☐ green	8.50	11.50	9.50
☐ pink	8.50	11.50	9.50
☐ light blue	8.50	11.50	9.50
☐ red	15.00	20.00	16.50
☐ cobalt	15.00	20.00	16.50
Berry Bowl, 10″			
☐ green	8.50	11.50	9.50
☐ pink	8.50	11.50	9.50
☐ light blue	8.50	11.50	9.50
☐ red	15.00	20.00	16.00
☐ cobalt	15.00	20.00	16.00
Bon Bon Bowl, *handles, 5½″*			
☐ green	8.50	11.50	9.50
☐ pink	8.50	11.50	9.50
☐ light blue	8.50	11.50	9.50
☐ red	15.00	19.00	16.00
☐ cobalt	15.00	19.00	16.00
Bread And Butter Plate, 6¼″			
☐ pink	2.00	4.00	2.50

DECAGON

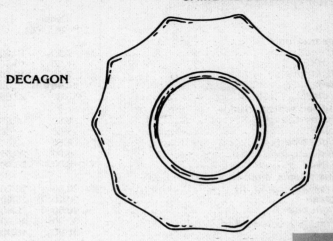

	Current Price Range		P/Y Average
green	2.00	4.00	2.50
light blue	2.00	4.00	2.50
red	4.00	6.00	4.50
cobalt	4.00	6.00	4.50
Celery Tray, *11"*			
green	8.50	11.50	9.50
pink	8.50	11.50	9.50
light blue	8.50	11.50	9.50
red	18.00	22.00	19.00
cobalt	18.00	22.00	19.00
Cereal Bowl, *bell shaped, 6"*			
green	6.00	8.00	6.50
pink	6.00	8.00	6.50
light blue	6.00	8.00	6.50
red	11.00	14.00	12.00
cobalt	11.00	14.00	12.00
Cereal Bowl, *flat rim, 6"*			
green	5.00	7.00	5.50
pink	5.00	7.00	5.50
light blue	5.00	7.00	5.50
red	9.50	12.50	10.50
cobalt	9.50	12.50	10.50
Comport, *7"*			
green	15.00	20.00	16.00
pink	15.00	20.00	16.00
light blue	15.00	20.00	16.00
red	25.00	30.00	26.00
cobalt	25.00	30.00	26.00
Cream Soup, *with liner*			
green	8.00	11.00	9.00
pink	8.00	11.00	9.00
light blue	8.00	11.00	9.00
red	13.00	17.00	14.00
cobalt	13.00	17.00	14.00

	Current Price Range		P/Y Average
Creamer, *footed*			
□ green	7.50	10.50	8.50
□ pink	7.50	10.50	8.50
□ light blue	7.50	10.50	8.50
□ red	18.00	22.00	19.00
□ cobalt	18.00	22.00	19.00
Creamer, *scalloped edge*			
□ green	6.50	9.50	7.50
□ pink	6.50	9.50	7.50
□ light blue	6.50	9.50	7.50
□ red	16.00	20.00	17.00
□ cobalt	16.00	20.00	17.00
Cruet, *handle, stopper, 6 oz.*			
□ pink	20.00	25.00	21.00
□ green	20.00	25.00	21.00
□ light blue	20.00	25.00	21.00
□ red	35.00	40.00	37.00
□ cobalt	35.00	40.00	37.00
Cup			
□ green	5.00	7.00	5.50
□ pink	5.00	7.00	5.50
□ light blue	5.00	7.00	5.50
□ red	8.50	11.50	9.50
□ cobalt	8.50	11.50	9.50
Dinner Plate, *9½"*			
□ green	8.50	11.50	9.50
□ pink	8.50	11.50	9.50
□ light blue	8.50	11.50	9.50
□ red	15.00	19.00	16.00
□ cobalt	15.00	19.00	16.00
Grill Plate, *10"*			
□ green	6.50	9.50	7.50
□ pink	6.50	9.50	7.50
□ light blue	6.50	9.50	7.50
□ red	12.00	16.00	13.00
□ cobalt	12.00	16.00	13.00
Mayonnaise Dish, *with liner and ladle*			
□ green	16.00	20.00	17.00
□ pink	16.00	20.00	17.00
□ light blue	16.00	20.00	17.00
□ red	26.00	34.00	28.00
□ cobalt	26.00	34.00	28.00
Pickle Tray, *9"*			
□ green	8.50	11.50	9.50
□ pink	8.50	11.50	9.50
□ light blue	8.50	11.50	9.50
□ red	15.00	20.00	16.00
□ cobalt	15.00	20.00	16.00
Plate, *handles, 7"*			
□ pink	8.00	11.00	8.50
□ green	8.00	11.00	8.50
□ light blue	8.00	11.00	8.50
□ red	13.00	17.00	14.00
□ cobalt	13.00	17.00	14.00

	Current Price Range		P/Y Average
Salad Plate, *8½"*			
□*green*	5.00	7.00	5.50
□*pink*	5.00	7.00	5.50
□*light blue*	5.00	7.00	5.50
□*red*	8.50	11.50	9.50
□*cobalt*	8.50	11.50	9.50
Sauce Boat, *with saucer*			
□*green*	20.00	24.00	21.00
□*pink*	20.00	24.00	21.00
□*light blue*	20.00	24.00	21.00
□*red*	36.00	44.00	38.00
□*cobalt*	36.00	44.00	38.00
Saucer			
□*green*	.75	1.75	1.00
□*pink*	.75	1.75	1.00
□*light blue*	.75	1.75	1.00
□*red*	1.50	3.50	2.00
□*cobalt*	1.50	3.50	2.00
Service Tray, *handles, 13"*			
□*green*	18.00	22.00	19.00
□*pink*	18.00	22.00	19.00
□*light blue*	18.00	22.00	19.00
□*red*	26.00	34.00	28.00
□*cobalt*	26.00	34.00	28.00
Sugar, *footed*			
□*green*	6.50	9.50	7.50
□*pink*	6.50	9.50	7.50
□*light blue*	6.50	9.50	7.50
□*red*	16.00	20.00	17.00
□*cobalt*	16.00	20.00	17.00
Sugar, *scalloped edge*			
□*green*	6.00	9.00	6.50
□*pink*	6.00	9.00	6.50
□*light blue*	6.00	9.00	6.50
□*red*	15.00	20.00	16.00
□*cobalt*	15.00	20.00	16.00
Vegetable Bowl, *oval, 9½"*			
□*green*	10.50	13.50	11.50
□*pink*	10.50	13.50	11.50
□*light blue*	10.50	13.50	11.50
□*red*	20.00	24.00	21.00
□*cobalt*	20.00	24.00	21.00

CAMERAS

DESCRIPTION: Camera collecting is a favorite hobby for thousands of people. Not only do hobbyists collect cameras, but everything associated with photography including film, postcards that picture cameras, ads selling cameras and signs from photo stores.

TYPES: Box, folding, panoramic, miniature and 35 mm cameras are all favorite types to collect.

ORIGIN: Although the photographic process was invented by Louis Jacques Mande Daguerre of Paris in 1839, it wasn't until the late 1800s that photography was accessible to the masses. An American, George Eastman, was the major influence in manufacturing cameras to sell to the public.

COMMENTS: Since Kodak was the first company to sucessfully produce cameras for the public, its cameras are very popular collector's items.

ADDITIONAL INFORMATION: For more information about camera collectibles, consult *The Official Price Guide to Collectible Cameras,* published by The House of Collectibles.

	Current Price Range		P/Y Average
☐ **Kodak,** Autographic Junior No.1, F77/100 mm lens, 1915	15.00	25.00	20.00
☐ **Kodak,** Brownie, No.2, 50th Anniversary box camera giveaway, 1930	15.00	20.00	17.50
☐ **Kodak,** Bulls-Eye No.3, uses 124 film, 1910 ..	40.00	50.00	45.00
☐ **Kodak,** Duo-620 Series II folding camera, f3.5/75 mm lens, 1940	50.00	60.00	55.00
☐ **Kodak,** Eureka No.4, uses 109 film, 1899	85.00	95.00	80.00
☐ **Kodak,** Folding Pocket No.3, uses 122 film, 1905	30.00	50.00	40.00
☐ **Kodak,** Ordinary, box, wooden, 4″ x 5″, 1890s	800.00	1200.00	1000.00
☐ **Kodak,** Premo, box camera, achromatic lens, automatic shutter, 4″ x 5″, 1910	20.00	30.00	25.00
☐ **Kodak,** Quick Focus, achromatic lens, rotary shutter, 3¼″ x 5½″, 1908	125.00	150.00	137.00
☐ **Kodak,** Vest Pocket Kodak Model B, rotary shutter, 1930s	80.00	120.00	100.00

	Current Price Range		P/Y Average
☐ **Leica,** model IIc, highest shutter speed 500, 1940s	150.00	200.00	175.00
☐ **Minolta,** Semi-Automatic, folding, Promar lens, 1937	40.00	60.00	50.00
☐ **Nikon,** Model S, later replaced by Model S2, 1951	100.00	125.00	112.00
☐ **Pentacon,** model FBM, exposure meter, 1957	55.00	80.00	67.00
☐ **Peerless,** box camera, uses glass plates	60.00	80.00	70.00
☐ **Rex Magazine Camera, Co.,** 4″ x 5″, 1899	175.00	220.00	200.00
☐ **Teddy Camera Co.,** Model A, takes direct positive prints, developing tank below camera, 1924	325.00	425.00	375.00

▣◀══▶▣◀══▶▣◀══▶▣◀══▶▣◀══▶▣◀══▶▣◀══▶▣◀══▶▣◀══▶▣◀══▶

CANES AND WALKING STICKS

TOPIC: Canes and walking sticks were popular accessories in the 17th and 18th centuries. They were both fashionable and utilitarian, because they could be used for protection if needed.

TYPES: Canes are either simple walking sticks or "gadget" canes which conceal a sword, pistol, musical instrument or other device.

PERIOD: Canes are descendents of the sticks early man used to defend himself, and as such date back into early human history. The stylish canes of Europe came into vogue in the 17th and 18th centuries, while the 19th century saw gadget canes reaching a peak of popularity.

MATERIAL: Wood is used for the shafts of almost all canes. Handles may be made out of wood, ivory, bone or metal.

COMMENTS: Canes are fascinating collectibles whether they contain concealed devices or not. The ones that do are particularly interesting because ingenious guns or other weapons may be hidden in them. It is advisable to use caution when handling old canes because a concealed weapon might be inadvertently triggered.

ADDITIONAL TIPS: When buying a cane or walking stick, examine it closely for indications of hidden compartments. Many devices are so well concealed in canes that they go undiscovered for years.

	Current Price Range		P/Y Average
☐ **Amethyst,** *cut glass handle*	180.00	220.00	190.00
☐ **Bamboo,** *curved handle*	17.00	20.00	18.00
☐ **Blown Glass,** *green*	85.00	95.00	87.00
☐ **Bottle Cane,** *glass liner holds liquor, 36"*	150.00	180.00	160.00
☐ **Clenched Hand,** *ivory*	180.00	280.00	195.00
☐ **Dog's Head,** *Fox Terrier, plainted and carved wood*	210.00	230.00	215.00
☐ **Dog's Head,** *wood with brown eyes, c. 1900* ..	40.00	60.00	45.00
☐ **Dog's Head,** *glass eyes, c. 1900*	45.00	60.00	47.00

	Current Price Range		P/Y Average
☐ **Hound's Head,** *ivory*	70.00	115.00	85.00
☐ **Monkey,** *hand carved*	95.00	120.00	105.00
☐ **Mother-Of-Pearl,** *gold*	65.00	85.00	70.00
☐ **Parade Cane,** *china clown head*	40.00	50.00	42.00
☐ **Umbrella Cane,** *wood case, 34"*	90.00	120.00	95.00
☐ **Walking Stick,** *gold head*	110.00	130.00	115.00
☐ **Walking Stick,** *sterling head*	50.00	60.00	52.00

CARNIVAL GLASS

DESCRIPTION: In 1905, Taffeta, or Carnival glass as it has come to be known, was born out of the turn of the century craze for iridescent art glass. Using mass production and new chemical techniques, Carnival glass was widely produced toward the end of the Art Nouveau period. Tastes changed, however, ushering in the streamlined Art Deco period. Even though it continued to be produced until 1930, by 1925 Carnival glass was on the way out. With a dwindling market, this glass was sold by the trainload to fairs and carnivals to be given away as prizes. Hence, it has come to be called Carnival glass.

ADDITIONAL TIPS: Intense collector interest has already driven the prices of Carnival glass into the astronomical range. An amethyst Carnival farmyard plate sold for $8,000 just this year. The tables have really been turned in this field over the years as this originally cheap imitation of Art glass now far exceeds in value the high quality glass it sought to imitate. Long regarded with disdain by serious dealers, collectors and auction houses, Carnival glass is now turning up on the most prestigious auction blocks in the country. Carnival glass auctions demonstrated one thing clearly — Carnival glass continues to command higher and higher prices with no ceiling in sight. Examples of auction results are: rare, one-of-a-kind Acan Burrs aqua-opalescent punch bowl, base and five cups, $12,500; purple Christmas compote, $1550; large green Hobstar and Feather rosebowl, $1150; amethyst Inverted Thistle pitcher, $2100; teal blue Grape and Cable plate, $1150; and amethyst Farmyard bowl, $1400.

RECOMMENDED READING: For more in-depth information on Carnival glass, you may refer to *The Official Price Guide to Carnival Glass, The Official Price Guide to Glassware* and *The Official Identification Guide to Glassware,* published by The House of Collectibles.

Bowl, *Marigold Carnival Glass, Luster Rose pattern, three footed, marked,* **$85.00-$100.00**
(photo courtesy of ©BJ Warner, Surfside Beach, SC, 1984)

	Current Price Range		P/Y Average
ACORN — Fenton			
Bowl, *diameter 7" - 8½"*			
□ *marigold*	20.00	30.00	25.00
□ *purple*	28.50	50.00	30.00
□ *green*	28.50	50.00	30.00
□ *blue*	28.50	50.00	30.00
□ *amethyst*	28.50	50.00	30.00
□ *peach opalescent*	120.00	135.00	125.00
□ *vaseline*	110.00	125.00	115.00
□ *red*	225.00	325.00	260.00
Plate, *diameter 9"*			
□ *marigold*	120.00	135.00	125.00
□ *purple*	285.00	340.00	300.00
□ *green*	285.00	340.00	300.00
□ *blue*	285.00	340.00	300.00
□ *amethyst*	285.00	340.00	300.00
APPLE BLOSSOMS — Dugan			
Bowl, *diameter 7" - 9"*			
□ *marigold*	35.00	45.00	37.50
□ *purple*	40.00	50.00	42.00
□ *green*	40.00	50.00	42.00
□ *blue*	40.00	50.00	42.00
□ *amethyst*	40.00	50.00	42.00
□ *white*	60.00	80.00	65.00
□ *ices*	60.00	80.00	65.00
Plate, *diameter 8½"*			
□ *marigold*	45.00	57.50	48.50
□ *purple*	65.00	85.00	70.00
□ *green*	65.00	85.00	70.00
□ *blue*	65.00	85.00	70.00

	Current Price Range		P/Y Average
□ amethyst	65.00	85.00	70.00
□ white	85.00	110.00	90.00
□ ice blue	85.00	110.00	90.00
□ ice green	85.00	110.00	90.00

BANDED DRAPE — *Fenton*

Tumbler

□ marigold	15.00	20.00	17.00
□ blue	28.00	32.00	29.00
□ amethyst	28.00	32.00	29.00
□ ice green	35.00	41.00	37.00
□ white	35.00	41.00	37.00

Water Pitcher

□ marigold	70.00	85.00	72.00
□ blue	185.00	200.00	190.00
□ amethyst	185.00	200.00	190.00
□ ice green	240.00	275.00	245.00
□ white	240.00	275.00	245.00

BEADED CABLE — *Northwood*

Candy Dish

□ marigold	22.50	30.00	25.00
□ purple	32.50	40.00	35.00
□ green	32.50	40.00	35.00
□ blue	32.50	40.00	35.00
□ amethyst	32.50	40.00	35.00

Rose Bowl

□ marigold	32.50	40.00	35.00
□ purple	50.00	62.50	52.00
□ green	50.00	62.50	52.00
□ blue	50.00	62.50	52.00
□ amethyst	50.00	62.50	52.00
□ aqua opalescent	175.00	225.00	180.00
□ ices	175.00	190.00	180.00

CHRYSANTHEMUM — *Fenton*

Bowl, *flat, diameter 10"*

□ marigold	33.00	37.00	35.00
□ blue	47.00	55.00	50.00
□ green	47.00	55.00	50.00
□ ice green	95.00	110.00	100.00
□ white	95.00	110.00	100.00
□ red	500.00	600.00	550.00

Bowl, *footed, diameter 10"*

□ marigold	33.00	37.00	35.00
□ blue	47.00	55.00	50.00
□ green	47.00	55.00	50.00
□ ice green	95.00	110.00	100.00
□ white	95.00	110.00	100.00
□ red	500.00	600.00	525.00

ELKS — *Fenton*	Current Price Range		P/Y Average
Bowl, *Detroit*			
☐ *purple*	325.00	375.00	330.00
☐ *green*	325.00	375.00	330.00
☐ *blue*	325.00	375.00	330.00
☐ *amethyst*	325.00	375.00	330.00
Bowl, *Parkersburg*			
☐ *purple*	350.00	425.00	360.00
☐ *green*	350.00	425.00	360.00
☐ *blue*	350.00	425.00	360.00
☐ *amethyst*	350.00	425.00	360.00

CAROUSEL ANIMALS

DESCRIPTION: The collecting of carousel animals is one of the most unusual areas of collectibles. These beautiful, hand-carved and sculptured creations are true examples of a lost art.

PERIOD: The "golden age" of carousel animals in America began shortly after the Civil War. Circuses at that time were beginning to incorporate rides into their side-shows, and larger more elaborate rides were being set up at permanent amusement parks. By 1890 the carousel or "merry-go-round" had become a standard attraction at all amusement parks and many other places of entertainment. They became so popular that a number of public parks installed them, including New York's Central Park — whose 19th century carousel is still in operation. Outstanding quality in carousel animals called for expert wood carvers. Most of those who worked in America were Italians who had learned the art of wood carving in Italy.

☐ **Armitage Hershell Jumpers,** track type, no holes through horse, c. 1890	825.00	925.00	875.00
☐ **Carmel Borrelli,** 60″ x 50″	3000.00	3500.00	3250.00
☐ **Carmel Borrelli,** 54″ x 56″	3500.00	4000.00	3750.00
☐ **Carmel Borrelli,** 49″ x 49″	2500.00	3000.00	2750.00
☐ **Carmel Borrelli,** stander	3500.00	4000.00	3750.00
☐ **Dentzel Jumping Mare,** Pittsburg, PA Carrousel	2500.00	3000.00	2750.00
☐ **Metal Illions Jumper,** off kiddie machine, 36″	200.00	220.00	210.00
☐ **Muller,** medium stander, 71″	2000.00	2500.00	2250.00

Jumping Horse, *Philadelphia Toboggan Co., carved by Frank Caretta,* **$900.00-$1500.00**

	Current Price Range		P/Y Average
☐ **Muller Dentzel,** parrots on back of saddle, 79₀	3800.00	4000.00	3900.00
☐ **Parker,** large flowers with jewel centers	1000.00	1200.00	1100.00
☐ **Parker Jumper,** super sweet horse	900.00	1000.00	950.00
☐ **Parker Style Aluminum Horse,** 52″ x 29″	400.00	500.00	450.00
☐ **Spillman,** nice flowing mane, shield, 66″	1000.00	1200.00	1100.00
☐ **Trojan Jumper,** 66″	750.00	950.00	850.00

CARS

PERIOD: While groundwork for the automobile was laid in the 18th century, it wasn't until 1896 that Henry Ford operated his first car — a twin cylinder, four-horse power quadricycle. Since then the car business and car collecting business has blossomed, and car collectors specialize in cars from that early date up to the more current cars of the 1970s. Car collecting is only about thirty years old, but it is a solid hobby.

COMMENTS: At first the collector car hobby centered around the Brass Era of the 1930s and 1940s. The pace of car collecting quickened in the 50s, and the nostalgia boom of the 1960s produced an increased interest in the Brass Era and Classic Car era. Today collectors buy a variety of cars — from the early ones to the muscle cars of the 1960s.

ADDITIONAL TIPS: The listings in this section are alphabetical according to the car maker. Following the maker is the date of manufacture, model, type of engine, type of body and price range. Prices do vary according to the condition of the car.

For further information see *The Official Price Guide to Collector Cars.*

YEAR	MODEL	ENGINE	BODY	F	G	E
B.M.W. (Deutschland, Germany, 1928-to-date)						
1932	320	1971cc	Touring	6800	14000	22000
1935	315	1.5 Litre	Cabriolet	3250	6800	12500
1953	Type 328		Drop Head			
			Coupe	2100	4400	9800
1965	2000 CS		Coupe	3800	6800	13000
1972	Sport	6 cyl.	Sedan	3600	4900	9900
BUICK (United States, 1903-to-date)						
1903	Model B	2 cyl.	Touring			
			Runabout	28500	66000	175000
1904	Model B	2 cyl.	Touring	12000	34000	83000
1905	Model C	2 cyl.	Touring	7000	10200	24200
1906	Model G	2 cyl.	Runabout	4940	11100	30700
1907	Model G	4 cyl.	Runabout	5600	11400	32000
1908	Model D	4 cyl.	Roadster	6040	12000	34000
1909	Model 10	4 cyl.	Roadster	3525	6770	15200
1910	Model 14	2 cyl.	Roadster	4500	11700	29000

YEAR	MODEL	ENGINE	BODY	F	G	E
1911	Model 33	4 cyl.	Roadster	4650	7250	12375
1912	Model 35	4 cyl.	Touring	3400	11300	26000
1913	McLaughlin	4 cyl.	Touring	2800	9450	24000
1914	Model 24	4 cyl.	Roadster	2700	9230	24000
1915	C-25	4 cyl.	Touring	6000	9550	14550
1916	D-35	6 cyl.	Touring	4500	10900	26600
1917	D-44	6 cyl.	Roadster	4300	7500	13500
1918	G-47	6 cyl.	Sedan	4000	7000	13000
1919	H-44	6 cyl.	Roadster	4000	6575	13000
1920	K-50	6 cyl.	Touring	4000	6575	13000
1921	21-46	6 cyl.	Coupe	3400	9200	14500
1922	22-44	6 cyl.	Sport Roadster	5000	11400	28500
1923	23-44	4 cyl.	Roadster	3900	10000	28000
1924	24-55	6 cyl.	Sport Touring	4700	10000	29500
1925	Standard	6 cyl.	Coach	3900	7100	22000
1926	40	6 cyl.	Touring	4800	11400	28500
1927	Master 6	6 cyl.	Roadster	5300	100000	29000
1928	28-54	6 cyl.	Sport Roadster	4500	13500	30600
1929	Big Six	6 cyl.	Cabriolet	4700	13200	30700
1930	30-46 S	6 cyl.	Sport Coupe	3200	6400	13000
1931	94	8 cyl.	Roadster	8900	23000	42000
1932	90	8 cyl.	Phaeton	6700	14000	34000
1933	90	8 cyl.	7 Passenger Sedan	3000	6000	17100
1934	40	8 cyl.	2 Door Sedan	2500	5000	13000
1935	66	8 cyl.	Sport Coupe Rumble Seat	3900	8200	15000
1936	Special	8 cyl.	Sport Coupe	4200	7200	14000
1937	Special	8 cyl.	2 Door Sedan	1500	3300	10000
1938	Roadmaster	8 cyl.	Sedan	1575	3250	10500
1939	Special	8 cyl.	Convertible Phaeton	5000	8000	16000
1940	Super	8 cyl.	Coupe	2200	4200	10200
1941	Special (44-S)	8 cyl.	Coupe	2300	6200	12900
1942	Roadmaster	8 cyl.	Sedan	2300	6200	12900
1946	Super	8 cyl.	2 Door Sedan	2300	4700	10200
1947	Super	8 cyl.	Convertible	5100	7800	14400
1948	Super	8 cyl.	Convertible	3550	6550	14200
1949	Super	8 cyl.	Sedanet	2000	4000	7550

CADILLAC (United States 1903-to-date)

YEAR	MODEL	ENGINE	BODY	F	G	E
1903	A	1 cyl.	Touring	4700	11000	25500
1904	A	1 cyl.	Roadster	4800	8050	23500
1905	B	1 cyl.	Roadster	3900	9700	26500
1906	K	1 cyl.	Runabout	3700	8800	24500
1907	K	1 cyl.	Roadster	4000	9500	26100
1908	T	1 cyl.	Runabout	4000	6000	20000
1909	30	4 cyl.	Touring	4000	6000	21000
1910	30	4 cyl.	Town	4300	11200	28600
1912	30	4 cyl.	Opera Coupe	3450	9200	15700

YEAR	MODEL	ENGINE	BODY	F	G	E
1913	30	4 cyl.	6 Passenger Touring	4400	6600	24000
1914	30	4 cyl.	Touring	4200	7000	29300
1915	51	(V) 8 cyl.	Touring	4500	11300	29300
1916	53	(V) 8 cyl.	Touring	4500	11300	29300
1917	55	(V) 8 cyl.	Touring	4200	8900	23000
1918	57	(V) 8 cyl.	7 Passenger Touring	4200	8900	23000
1919	57	(V) 8 cyl.	Touring	3700	5000	18000
1920	59	(V) 8 cyl.	7 Passenger Touring	3700	7900	22000
1921	59	(V) 8 cyl.	7 Passenger Touring	3800	8000	21500
1922	61	(V) 8 cyl.	7 Passenger Phaeton	4600	8500	25000
1923	61	(V) 8 cyl.	Sport Phaeton	4400	8200	29300
1924	V-63	(V) 8 cyl.	Phaeton	6600	11500	34500
1925	V-63	(V) 8 cyl.	Dual Cowl Phaeton	8450	20950	46000
1926	314	(V) 8 cyl.	Sedan	3650	8400	16750
1927	314	(V) 8 cyl.	Town Sedan	4700	9900	22000
1928	Fleetwood	(V) 8 cyl.	Cabriolet	8600	16800	33500
1929	341-B SM		Town Sedan	8575	13500	42500
1930	353	(V) 8 cyl.	Coupe Roadster	7000	12500	29800
1931	452	(V) 16 cyl.	Sedan	12600	22000	46000
1932	355B	(V) 8 cyl.	Club Sedan	6400	16700	26200
1933	355C	(V) 8 cyl.	Convertible Sedan	13600	37500	69000

CHEVROLET (United States, 1911-to-date)

1912	Classic Six	6 cyl.	Touring	5700	9300	32000
1913	Baby Grand	4 cyl.	Touring	3900	11400	24000
1914	Baby Grand	4 cyl.	Touring	4100	10900	26000
1915	Baby Grand	4 cyl.	Touring	3400	11400	26000
1916	Special	6 cyl.	Roadster	4700	11500	22700
1917	D	(V) 8 cyl.	Roadster	6800	13100	27000
1918	490	4 cyl.	Coupe	1900	2900	7100
1919	490	4 cyl.	Touring	3300	4500	15100
1920	490	4 cyl.	Coupe	2100	3100	8200
1921	490	4 cyl.	Touring	3300	4500	15100
1922	FB	4 cyl.	Sport Touring	4100	10600	18800
1923	FB	4 cyl.	Sedan	1800	5200	10900
1924	Superior	4 cyl.	Sedan	2700	4900	12900
1925	Superior	4 cyl.	Roadster	3100	4300	14500
1926	Superior V	4 cyl.	Coupe	2500	4900	13000
1927	AA	4 cyl.	Roadster	3400	4400	14600
1928	AB	4 cyl.	Sedan	2000	3000	7600
1929	AC	6 cyl.	Touring	4300	6600	24000

FORD (United States, 1903-to-date)

1903	A	2 cyl.	Runabout	9600	13000	25500
1904	A-AC	2 cyl.	Runabout	6900	17650	29250
1905	C	2 cyl.	Runabout	4600	9825	18850
1906	F	2 cyl.	Touring	5000	9600	20000

Ford, Model T Touring Car, *1915,* **$3000.00-$14000.00**
(photo courtesy of ©James Lemen, Summit Point, WV)

YEAR	MODEL	ENGINE	BODY	F	G	E
1907	N	4 cyl.	Runabout	5000	8600	14500
1907	K	6 cyl.	Runabout	19375	57700	115000
1908	S	4 cyl.	Runabout	2800	6500	17800
1909	T	4 cyl.	Town	4600	9725	20950
1910	T	4 cyl.	Runabout	3100	6900	14000
1911	T	4 cyl.	Tourabout	5000	8500	18850
1912	T	4 cyl.	Roadster	3100	6900	15500
1913	T	4 cyl.	Touring	4000	7200	15500
1913	T	4 cyl.	Town	3600	7225	18850
1914	T	4 cyl.	Roadster	3500	7200	14500
1915	T	4 cyl.	Coupelet	3700	7840	21950
1916	T	4 cyl.	Roadster	2500	4800	14860
1917	T	4 cyl.	Center Door Sedan	3600	5400	9000
1918	T	4 cyl.	Roadster	2300	3600	11200
1918	T	4 cyl.	Touring	2000	4000	13495
1918	T	4 cyl.	Center Door Sedan	3600	4600	9000
1919	T	4 cyl.	Roadster	2600	3600	10500
1920	T	4 cyl.	Coupe	1600	2500	6500
1921	T	4 cyl.	Roadster	1600	3500	10000
1922	T	4 cyl.	Roadster	1600	3000	11500
1922	T	4 cyl.	Touring	1600	3000	11500
1923	T	4 cyl.	Roadster	1600	3000	11500
1924	T	4 cyl.	Roadster	2095	4000	10500
1925	T	4 cyl.	Fordor	2000	3800	12235
1926	T	4 cyl.	Roadster	2000	3800	11500
1927	T	4 cyl.	Fordor	1900	3200	5800
1928	AR	4 cyl.	Touring	4600	10400	24050

YEAR	MODEL	ENGINE	BODY	F	G	E
1928	A	4 cyl.	Fordor	1900	4800	7500
1929	A	4 cyl.	Roadster	4000	9400	26000
1930	A	4 cyl.	Victoria	2800	5650	14450
1931	A	4 cyl.	Roadster	4300	7400	26500
1931	A	4 cyl.	Town Sedan	2700	6200	13600
1932	B	4 cyl.	Roadster	6500	10000	28500
1933	40	(V) 8 cyl.	Cabriolet	5600	8200	23500
1934	40	(V) 8 cyl.	Roadster	6000	9000	30500
1935	48	(V) 8 cyl.	Station Wagon	3700	6000	13100
1935	48	(V) 8 cyl.	Sedan Delivery	2800	7200	14600
1936	68	(V) 8 cyl.	Roadster	7400	11200	27100
1937	78	(V) 8 cyl.	Station Wagon	4000	6000	14500
1938	Standard	(V) 8 cyl.	Coupe	2000	3800	7500
1939	Deluxe	(V) 8 cyl.	Fordor	1750	3600	6700
1939	Deluxe	(V) 8 cyl.	Station Wagon	3100	6000	13500
1940	Standard	(V) 8 cyl.	Coupe	2600	4100	10600
1941		(V) 8 cyl.	Pickup	1300	4400	8400
1942	Special	6 cyl.	Coupe	1900	4000	7200

MERCEDES-BENZ (1926-to-date)

YEAR	MODEL	ENGINE	BODY	F	G	E
1901		4 cyl.	Phaeton	13000	26000	52000
1901		4 cyl.	Racing	19000	39000	82000
1902		4 cyl.	Tonneau	13000	26000	52000
1902		4 cyl.	Touring	15000	33000	70000
1903	'60'	4 cyl.	Racing	19000	39000	115000
1904	Simplex	4 cyl.	Tonneau	19000	39000	115000
1905		4 cyl.	Tonneau	22000	42000	88000
1906	45	4 cyl.	Limousine	13000	26000	52000
1907		6 cyl.	Landaulet	13000	26000	49000
1908		6 cyl.	Landaulet	9800	19000	39000
1909		6 cyl.	Sport	9600	19000	39000
1910	14/30	4 cyl.	Sport	6700	13000	26000
1911	16/40	4 cyl.	Phaeton	15000	32000	67000
1912	14/30	4 cyl.	Limousine	7900	14000	33000
1913	38/70	4 cyl.	Sport Phaeton	11000	26000	61000
1914	GP	4 cyl.	Racing	9100	15000	35000
1915		4 cyl.	Sport	6700	16000	41000
1916		6 cyl.	Racing	7900	23000	60000
1917		6 cyl.	Limousine	7900	14000	30000
1918		6 cyl.	Limousine	7900	14000	31000
1919		4 cyl.	Racing	9400	27000	61000
1920		6 cyl.	Coupe	5900	11000	23000
1921	6/18	4 cyl.	Sport	7900	19000	44000
1922	10/40/65	4 cyl.	Touring	11000	23000	62000
1923	24/100/140	6 cyl.	Touring	13000	26000	71000
1924	25-40	6 cyl.	Touring	10400	23000	64000
1925	SS	6 cyl.	Touring	19000	52000	120000
1926	K	6 cyl.	Touring	13000	26000	78000
1927	SS	6 cyl.	Touring	26000	94000	240000
1928		8 cyl.	Convertible	19000	39000	97000
1929	K	8 cyl.	Limousine	16000	33000	52000

CHALKWARE

DESCRIPTION: Items made from plaster of paris and painted in bright colors are called chalkware.

TYPES: Animal and bird figurines were the main items produced as chalkware.

PERIOD: Chalkware, which was produced as a cheap imitation of Staffordshire and Bennington ware, was found in middle class homes during the 1800s.

COMMENTS: Chalkware is now associated with Folk Art and can be found in antiques stores specializing in that area.

ADDITIONAL TIPS: Animals with nodding heads are especially rare. Few were produced and even fewer have survived through the years.

	Current Price Range		P/Y Average
☐ **Bank,** apple with red cheeks	28.00	32.00	27.50
☐ **Basket,** fruit filled	310.00	360.00	325.00
☐ **Bird,** nesting	260.00	310.00	280.00
☐ **Black Boy with Watermelon,** 4″	18.00	22.00	17.50
☐ **Bookends,** pirates, painted, pair	42.00	48.00	42.00
☐ **Boy,** reading books, 10½″	90.00	110.00	92.00
☐ **Cat,** 4½″	160.00	185.00	162.00
☐ **Cat,** 10½″	185.00	235.00	200.00
☐ **Charley McCarthy,** 15″	22.00	28.00	22.50
☐ **Dancing Lady,** 14″	18.00	32.00	22.00
☐ **Deer,** 9½″	435.00	485.00	450.00
☐ **Dog,** 8½″	135.00	155.00	138.00
☐ **Dove,** green with blue wings, 12″	210.00	235.00	212.00
☐ **Dove,** green and yellow wings, 6″	260.00	310.00	275.00
☐ **Duck**	140.00	165.00	142.00
☐ **Eagle,** spread, 9½″	285.00	335.00	300.00
☐ **Gnome,** German, 11″, 1930s	22.00	28.00	22.50
☐ **Horn of Plenty,** 14″	18.00	32.00	22.00
☐ **Indian,** Cigar Store, reclining, 23″	210.00	235.00	212.00
☐ **Lamb,** gray body, 8½″	260.00	310.00	275.00
☐ **Lamb,** rectangular base, 6½″	135.00	160.00	138.00
☐ **Owl,** 12″	185.00	210.00	182.00

	Current Price Range		P/Y Average
☐ **Parrot,** 10½ "	1300.00	1600.00	1400.00
☐ **Pigeon,** 10"	135.00	160.00	138.00
☐ **Poodles,** 7¾ "	185.00	235.00	200.00
☐ **Rabbit,** sitting, 8"	160.00	185.00	162.00
☐ **Rooster,** 6"	335.00	385.00	350.00
☐ **Santa Claus,** 24"	155.00	180.00	160.00
☐ **Sheep,** mother with babies, 7"	185.00	210.00	182.00
☐ **Shepherd,** German, 17½ "	85.00	105.00	85.00
☐ **Squirrel,** 10"	185.00	210.00	182.00
☐ **Stag,** rectangular base, 15"	260.00	310.00	275.00

CHILDREN'S BOOKS

DESCRIPTION: A children's book includes any title written specifically for children usually between the ages of three and thirteen.

VALUE: Condition and author play important roles in determining value. The more notable authors usually command higher prices. Lewis Carroll is a good example of an author whose children's books are extremely valuable.

COMMENTS: Children's books of the 1800s are especially collectible.

☐ **Abbott, Jacob,** *Rollo's Correspondence,* Boston, 1841	100.00	150.00	125.00
☐ **Abbott, Jacob,** *Marco Baul's Travels and Adventures: Erie Canal,* Boston, 1848, colored frontispiece and four colored plates	55.00	75.00	65.00
☐ **Abbott, Jacob,** *Rollo at School,* Boston, 1849	175.00	225.00	200.00
☐ **Adams, Hannah,** *An Abridgement of the History of New England for the Use of Young Persons,* Boston, 1807, second edition	20.00	30.00	25.00
☐ **Aikin, Lucy,** *Juvenile Correspondence, or Letters . . . for Children of Both Sexes,* Boston, 1822, calf	30.00	40.00	35.00
☐ **Alcott, Louisa M.,** *Little Women,* Boston, 1869, second issue	70.00	90.00	80.00
☐ **Alcott, Louisa M.,** *Little Men,* Boston, 1871 ..	240.00	315.00	277.00
☐ **Alcott, Louisa M.,** *Silver Pitchers,* Boston, 1876	35.00	42.00	38.00

Alphabet books, $12.00-$35.00, *Photo courtesy of Lou McCulloch, Highland Heights, OH 44143*

	Current Price Range		P/Y Average
☐ **Alcott, Louisa M.,** *Jo's Boys,* Boston, 1886 . .	35.00	42.00	38.00
☐ **Berquin, M.,** *The Blossoms of Morality; Intended for the Amusement and Instruction of Young Ladies and Gentlemen,* London, 1821, quarter roan, gilt	12.00	15.00	13.50
☐ **Berquin, M.,** *The Beauties of the Children's Friend,* Boston, 1827	35.00	45.00	40.00

	Current Price Range		P/Y Average

☐ **Bible in Miniature,** *Thumb Bible,* Troy, N.Y., 1823, measures 2″ x 1⅝″ .... — 150.00 — 200.00 — 175.00

☐ **Bible Natural History,** containing a description of Quadrupeds, Birds, Trees, Plants, Insects, etc., mentioned in the Holy Scriptures, London, 1852 .... — 6.00 — 8.00 — 7.00

☐ **Bisset, J.,** *The Orphan Boy,* A Pathetic Tale, founded on fact, Birmingham, n.d., 1799, third edition .... — 18.00 — 23.00 — 20.00

☐ **Blewitt, Mrs. Octavian,** *The Rose and the Lily,* A Fairy Tale, London, 1877 .... — 8.00 — 10.00 — 9.00

☐ **Book of Riddles,** *N.Y., 1816, 28 pp., softbound, on some copies the wrapper incorrectly reads "History of Insects,"* rare .... — 150.00 — 200.00 — 175.00

☐ **Bouton, Eliz. Gladwin,** *Grandmother's Doll,* N.Y., n.d., 1931 .... — 45.00 — 60.00 — 53.00

☐ **Brereton, Captain F. S.,** *In the Grip of the Mullah,* A Tale of Adventure in Somililand, London, 1904 .... — 8.00 — 10.00 — 9.00

☐ **Brereton, Captain F. S.,** *The Hero of Panama,* A Tale of the Great Canal, London, 1912 ..... — 8.00 — 10.00 — 9.00

☐ **Browning, Robert,** *The Pied Piper of Hamelin,* London, n.d. .... — 25.00 — 30.00 — 27.50

☐ **Burnett, Francis H.,** *Little Lord Fauntleroy,* N.Y., 1886 .... — 150.00 — 200.00 — 175.00

☐ **Burnett, Francis H.,** *Editha's Burglar,* Boston, 1888, second issue .... — 15.00 — 20.00 — 17.50

☐ **Butterworth, Hezekiah,** *Zig-Zag Journeys in Europe,* Boston, 1880, first edition .... — 40.00 — 50.00 — 45.00

☐ **Caldecott, Randolph,** *The House that Jack Built,* London, n.d., 1878 .... — 25.00 — 30.00 — 27.50

☐ **Carroll, Lewis,** *Phantasmagoria and Other Poems,* London, 1869, blue cloth .... — 100.00 — 130.00 — 115.00

☐ **Carroll, Lewis,** *Through the Looking-Glass, and What Alice Found There,* London, 1872, with 50 drawings by Tenniel, red cloth ...... — 350.00 — 425.00 — 387.00

☐ **Carroll, Lewis,** *The Hunting of the Snark,* London, 1876 .... — 175.00 — 225.00 — 200.00

☐ **Carroll, Lewis,** *Rhyme? and Reason?,* London, 1883, green cloth .... — 80.00 — 110.00 — 95.00

☐ **Carroll, Lewis,** *A Tangled Tale,* London, 1885 . — 80.00 — 110.00 — 95.00

☐ **Carroll, Lewis,** *Sylvie and Bruno,* London, 1889 .... — 120.00 — 150.00 — 135.00

☐ **Carroll, Lewis,** *Sylvie and Bruno Concluded,* London, 1893 .... — 120.00 — 150.00 — 135.00

☐ **Carter, Nicholas ("Nick Carter"),** *The Chain of Clues,* N.Y., n.d., 1907 .... — 18.00 — 23.00 — 20.00

☐ **Champney, Lizzie W.,** *Three Vassar Girls Abroad,* Boston, 1883, first edition, the binding should be red cloth, copies in brown cloth bring somewhat less .... — 120.00 — 150.00 — 135.00

☐ **Champney, Lizzie W.,** *Three Vassar Girls in England,* Boston, 1883 .... — 40.00 — 50.00 — 45.00

☐ **Child's Favorite,** *A Gift for the Young,* By a Lady, Philadelphia and N.Y., 1847, ten colored plates .... — 30.00 — 35.00 — 32.50

	Current Price Range		P/Y Average
☐ **Child's Instructor**, New Haven, 1831	12.00	15.00	13.50
☐ *Cinderella or the Little Glass Slipper*, Baltimore, n.d., c. 1850, softbound	60.00	75.00	67.00
☐ **Cock Robin**, *The Tragi-Comic History of the Burial of Cock Robin; with the Lamentation of Jenny Wren ...*, Philadelphia, 1821, softbound	100.00	150.00	125.00
☐ **Coolidge, Susan**, *What Katy Did*, Boston, 1873	70.00	90.00	80.00
☐ **Cox, Palmer**, *The Brownies, Their Book*, N.Y., n.d., 1887, second edition	120.00	150.00	135.00
☐ **Cranch, Christopher P.**, *Kobboloozo: A Sequel to the Last of the Huggermuggers*, Boston, 1857	25.00	30.00	27.50
☐ **Crowquill, Afred**, *The Pictorial Grammar*, London, n.d., c. 1840s	50.00	65.00	57.00
☐ **Cupples, Mrs. George**, *A Nice Secret and Other Stories*, London, 1876	12.00	15.00	13.50
☐ **Dame Trot And Her Comical Cat**, *The Adventures of*, Baltimore, n.d., c. 1840s, softbound, rare	120.00	150.00	135.00
☐ **Day, Thomas**, *The History of Sandford and Merton: a Work Intended for the Use of Children*, London, 1818, two vols.	50.00	65.00	57.00
☐ **Denslow, W.W.**, *Denslow's House that Jack Built*, N.Y., n.d., 1903	60.00	75.00	67.00
☐ **Denslow, W.W.**, *Denslow's Simple Simon*, N.Y., n.d., 1904	45.00	60.00	52.00
☐ **Denslow, W.W.**, *Denslow's Animal Fair*, N.Y., n.d., 1904	70.00	90.00	80.00
☐ **Disney, Walt**, *Who's Afraid of the Big Bad Wolf*, Philadelphia, 1933	120.00	150.00	135.00
☐ **Disney, Walt**, *Donald Duck and his Cat Troubles*, Whitman, Wisconsin, 1945	60.00	80.00	70.00
☐ **Dodge, Mary Mapes**, *Hans Brinker or the Silver Skates*, N.Y., 1874	50.00	65.00	57.00
☐ **Dwight, Nathaniel**, *Geography of the World by Way of Question and Answer*, Hartford, 1802	25.00	30.00	27.50
☐ **Emerson, Joseph**, *The Evangelical Primer*, Boston, 1814	18.00	23.00	20.50
☐ **Emmet, Rosina**, *Pretty Peggy and Other Ballads*, N.Y., 1880	23.00	28.00	25.50
☐ **Entick, John**, *The Child's Best Instructor in Spelling and Reading*, London, 1773, sixth edition	275.00	325.00	300.00
☐ *Marmaduke Multiply*, N.Y. and Boston, n.d., c. 1840	65.00	80.00	72.00
☐ *Mary's Little Lamb*, Dearborn, Mich., 1928 ...	25.00	32.00	28.50
☐ **May, Sophie**, *Dotty Dimple (Little Prudy Series)*, Boston, 1856	34.00	40.00	37.00
☐ *Merry's Book of Travel and Adventure*, N.Y., 1860	18.00	23.00	20.50
☐ **Milne, A.A.**, *Fourteen Songs from When We Were Very Young*, N.Y., 1925, first American edition	22.00	28.00	25.00

	Current Price Range		P/Y Average
Milne, A.A., *A Gallery of Children,* Philadelphia, n.d., 1925, first American edition	55.00	70.00	62.00
Milne, A.A., *Winnie-the-Pooh,* London, 1926	200.00	250.00	225.00
Milne, A.A., *The Ivory Door,* N.Y., 1938, first American edition	18.00	23.00	20.50
Molesworth, Mrs., *A Christmas Child,* London, 1880	19.00	24.00	21.50
Moore, Clement C., *A Visit from St. Nicholas,* in *The New York Book of Poetry,* N.Y., 1837	110.00	140.00	125.00
Murray, Lindley, *English Grammar,* Philadelphia, 1829	18.00	23.00	20.50
Newberry, Elizabeth, *A New History of the Grecian States,* designed for the use of Young Ladies and Gentlemen, London, 1795	120.00	160.00	140.00
New Doll, The, or, Grandmama's Gift, London, 1826	90.00	115.00	102.00
Newell, Peter, *The Rocket Book,* N.Y., n.d., 1912, one of the earliest books on the subject for children	150.00	190.00	170.00
New-England Primer, Massachusetts, printed for the purchaser, 1808	80.00	100.00	90.00
New-England Primer, New England, printed for the purchaser, n.d., c. 1810	225.00	275.00	250.00
New-England Primer, Boston, n.d., c. 1820	130.00	160.00	145.00
New-England Primer, Hartford, 1820	130.00	160.00	145.00
New-England Primer, Brookfield, Mass., 1822	90.00	120.00	105.00
Night Before Christmas, London, n.d., c. 1905, softbound	23.00	30.00	26.00
Old Ironside, the story of a shipwreck, Salem, 1855	18.00	23.00	20.50
Optic, Oliver, *The Prisoners of the Cave,* N.Y., n.d., 1915, softbound	8.00	10.00	9.00
Ottis, James, *Toby Tyler or Ten Weeks with a Circus,* N.Y., 1881	165.00	195.00	180.00
Otis, James, *Jenny Wren's Boarding House,* Boston, n.d., 1893, first edition	65.00	85.00	75.00
Otis, James, *The Cruise of the Comet,* Boston, 1898	40.00	55.00	47.00
Page, Thomas N., *Two Little Confederates,* N.Y., 1888	65.00	85.00	75.00
Phillips, E.O., *Birdie and Her Dog,* London, n.d., c. 1885	14.00	18.00	15.50
Pinchard, Mrs., *The Blind Child or Anecdotes of the Wyndham Family,* London, n.d., c. 1818	50.00	65.00	57.00

CHILDREN'S DISHES
(See Akro Agate)

DESCRIPTION: This chapter includes both toy dishes and children's tableware. These items were produced extensively throughout America, Europe and the Orient from the 1880s through the 1950s. They are found in every material full size dishes and tablewares are made of. Indeed, they were intended to be miniatures of "Mother's" dishes and many are accurate down to the smallest detail.

ADDITIONAL TIPS: This area is gaining rapidly in popularity and prices are going up accordingly.

RECOMMENDED READING: For further information on Children's glass dishes refer to *The Official Price Guide to Depression Glass* published by The House of Collectibles.

Roy Rogers Plate And Bowl, *set,* **$10.00-$15.00**
(photo courtesy of ©Hake's Americana, York, PA, 1984)

	Current Price Range		P/Y Average
☐ **Bowl,** Blue Marble, England, oval, 4½″	28.00	33.00	30.00
☐ **Bowl,** Blue Willow, Made in Japan, 3½″	10.00	15.00	12.00
☐ **Bowl,** glass, Hopalong Cassidy, white milk glass with black enameled pictures of Hopalong Cassidy, 5″	10.00	15.00	12.00
☐ **Bowl,** glass, Shirley Temple, blue, 6½″	50.00	65.00	55.00
☐ **Butter Dish,** pattern glass, Bead and Scroll, clear, with dome lid, 4″	135.00	155.00	140.00
☐ **Casserole,** Blue Willow, Made in Japan, 4¾″	15.00	20.00	17.50
☐ **Casserole,** Blue Willow, Made in Japan, 5″	15.00	20.00	17.50
☐ **Casserole,** Blue Willow, Occupied Japan	15.00	20.00	17.50
☐ **Casserole,** graniteware, blue and white, with lid, 2⅞″	42.00	50.00	43.00
☐ **Casserole,** Noritake, Bluebird, 6″	30.00	40.00	35.00
☐ **Casserole,** Pagodas, England, with lid, 5½″	40.00	50.00	42.00
☐ **Coffee Pot,** aluminum, tapered with full length wooded handle, hinged lid is embossed with advertising slogan "Drink Thomson Malted Milk," lid has wooden knob, 5″, 1930s	15.00	20.00	17.50
☐ **Coffee Pot,** tin, hinged top with wooden knob, tapered sides, long spout, curved full length handle, engraved decoration, 5½″, 1890	25.00	35.00	30.00
☐ **Creamer,** Blue Willow, Made in Japan, 1½″	6.00	8.00	7.00
☐ **Creamer,** Blue Willow, Made in Japan, 2″	6.00	8.00	7.00
☐ **Creamer,** Blue Willow, Occupied Japan	5.00	10.00	7.50
☐ **Creamer,** depression glass, Cherry Blossom, pink, 2¾″	25.00	30.00	27.50
☐ **Creamer,** depression glass, Doric and Pansy, pink, 2¾″	25.00	30.00	27.00
☐ **Creamer,** glass, Akro Agate, Chiquita, green opaque, 1½″	3.50	4.50	4.00
☐ **Creamer,** Noritake, Bluebird, 1⅞″	10.00	15.00	12.00
☐ **Creamer,** pattern glass, Acorn, clear, 3½″	70.00	80.00	72.00
☐ **Creamer,** Sunset, Made in Japan, 1⅞″	3.00	5.00	3.25
☐ **Creamer,** Water Hen, England, 3⅛″	20.00	25.00	21.00
☐ **Crock,** lid, brown and gray, 4″, 1920s	9.00	15.00	12.50
☐ **Cup And Saucer,** Blue Willow, Made in Japan, 1⅛″ cup, 3⅜″ diameter saucer	6.00	8.00	6.50
☐ **Cup And Saucer,** Blue Willow, Made in Japan, 3½″ cup, 3¾″ diameter saucer	6.50	10.00	7.50
☐ **Cup And Saucer,** Blue Willow, Occupied Japan	10.00	12.00	11.00
☐ **Cup And Saucer,** depression glass, Cherry Blossom, pink, 1½″ cup, diameter of saucer is 4½″	25.00	28.00	26.00
☐ **Cup And Saucer,** depression glass, Doric and Pansy, ultramarine, 1½″ cup, diameter of saucer is 4½″	25.00	30.00	22.00
☐ **Cup And Saucer,** Noritake, Bluebird	7.00	12.00	10.00
☐ **Cup And Saucer,** Noritake, Silhouette, pale lavender with black silhouette of little girl pushing a doll buggy, 1¼″ cup, 3¾″ saucer	9.00	12.00	10.00
☐ **Cup And Saucer,** Silhouette, Made in Japan, 1½″ cup, diameter of saucer is 3¾″	6.00	8.00	6.50
☐ **Cup And Saucer,** Sunset, Made in Japan, 1¼″ cup, diameter of saucer is 3⅜″	6.00	8.00	6.50

	Current Price Range		P/Y Average

☐ **Cup And Saucer,** Water Hen, England, 2″ cup, 4½″ diameter saucer ... — 15.00 — 18.00 — 16.50

☐ **Dishpan,** aluminum, flat sides, rolled edge, loop handles, 4″ ... — 4.00 — 8.00 — 5.00

☐ **Frying Pan,** graniteware, blue and white, 4½″ — 28.00 — 35.00 — 30.00

☐ **Grater,** graniteware, blue and white, 4″ ... — 50.00 — 55.00 — 52.00

☐ **Gravy Boat,** Blue Marble, England, 1½″ ... — 28.00 — 33.00 — 30.00

☐ **Gravy Boat,** Blue Willow, Made in Japan ... — 15.00 — 20.00 — 17.50

☐ **Grill Plate,** Blue Willow, Made in Japan, 5″ ... — 15.00 — 20.00 — 17.50

☐ **Mold,** graniteware, blue and white, fluted, 2¾″ ... — 30.00 — 35.00 — 32.00

☐ **Mug,** glass, Hopalong Cassidy, white milk glass with black enameled picture of Hopalong Cassidy, 3″ ... — 5.00 — 7.00 — 5.50

☐ **Penny Candy Tray,** with spoon, pressed tin, shaped like cream skimmer, originally sold in 1920s filled with candy, 3″ x 1″ x ⅛″ ... — 5.00 — 10.00 — 7.50

☐ **Pitcher And Wash Bowl,** ironstone, white background with pastel green shading, 24 Kt gold bands, roses, scalloped edges, scroll handle, 4″, 1890 ... — 25.00 — 30.00 — 27.50

☐ **Pitcher And Wash Bowl,** porcelain, very fancy, pitcher is 4″ tall, bowl has 5″ diameter, white with pale green and gold trim, decorated with roses, marked with gold crown, the letter L and the number 5725 ... — 60.00 — 70.00 — 65.00

☐ **Pitcher,** graniteware, blue and white, 2½″ ... — 40.00 — 48.00 — 42.00

☐ **Plate,** Blue Marble, England, 4″ ... — 9.00 — 12.00 — 10.00

☐ **Plate,** Blue Willow, Made in Japan, 3¾″ ... — 2.00 — 4.00 — 2.50

☐ **Plate,** Blue Willow, Made in Japan, 5″ ... — 13.00 — 15.00 — 14.00

☐ **Plate,** Blue Willow, Occupied Japan ... — 3.50 — 5.00 — 4.00

☐ **Plate,** depression glass, Cherry Blossom, pink, 5⅞″ ... — 7.00 — 9.00 — 8.00

☐ **Plate,** depression glass, Doric and Pansy, pink, 5⅞″ ... — 6.00 — 8.00 — 7.00

☐ **Plate,** glass, Akro Agate, Concentric Rib, green opaque, 3¼″ ... — 1.50 — 2.50 — 1.75

☐ **Plate,** glass, Hopalong Cassidy, white milk glass with black enameled picture of Hopalong Cassidy and his horse, 7″ ... — 14.00 — 18.00 — 15.00

☐ **Plate,** Noritake, Bluebird, 4¼″ ... — 3.50 — 5.00 — 4.00

☐ **Plate,** Pagodas, England, 4½″ ... — 10.00 — 12.00 — 10.00

☐ **Plate,** Sunset, Made in Japan, 4¼″ ... — 1.00 — 2.00 — 1.25

☐ **Platter,** Blue Marble, England, 4½″ ... — 25.00 — 30.00 — 27.00

☐ **Platter,** Blue Willow, Made in Japan, 4⅝″ ... — 7.00 — 10.00 — 7.50

☐ **Platter,** Blue Willow, Made in Japan, 6″ ... — 7.00 — 10.00 — 7.50

☐ **Platter,** Blue Willow, Occupied Japan ... — 10.00 — 15.00 — 12.00

☐ **Platter,** Noritake, Bluebird, 7⅛″ ... — 10.00 — 15.00 — 12.00

☐ **Platter,** Pagodas, England, 7⅛″ ... — 25.00 — 32.00 — 27.00

☐ **Presentation Cup,** porcelain, "To My Sister," pink roses, 24 Kt scrolling, closed loop handle, 2⅜″, 1890 ... — 15.00 — 20.00 — 17.50

☐ **Sugar Bowl,** Blue Willow, Made in Japan, with lid, 2″ ... — 7.00 — 10.00 — 8.50

☐ **Sugar Bowl,** Blue Willow, Made in Japan, with lid, 2¾″ ... — 5.00 — 10.00 — 6.00

	Current Price Range		P/Y Average
Sugar Bowl, Blue Willow, Occupied Japan, with lid	10.00	15.00	12.00
Sugar Bowl, depression glass, Cherry Blossom, pink, 2⅝"	20.00	25.00	22.00
Sugar Bowl, depression glass, Doric and Pansy, pink, 2½"	20.00	24.00	21.00
Sugar Bowl, Noritake, Bluebird, with lid, 2¾"	14.00	20.00	15.00
Sugar Bowl, pattern glass, Block, blue, with lid, 4½"	90.00	105.00	95.00
Sugar Bowl, Sunset, Made in Japan, with lid, 3⅛"	3.00	5.00	3.50
Sugar Bowl, Water Hen, England, with lid, 4½"	25.00	30.00	26.50
Table Utensils, tin, ten pieces, five knives with two piece riveted bone handles, five forks, 3½", 1910	25.00	35.00	30.00
Teapot, Blue Willow, Made in Japan, with lid, 2⅝"	35.00	45.00	32.00
Teapot, Blue Willow, Made in Japan, with lid, 3¾"	30.00	40.00	32.00
Teapot, Blue Willow, Occupied Japan, with lid	20.00	25.00	17.50
Teapot, glass, Akro Agate, J.P., Transparent green, with lid, 1½"	25.00	30.00	26.50
Teapot, Noritake, Bluebird, with lid, 3½"	30.00	40.00	35.00
Teapot, Noritake, Silhouette, pale lavender with black silhouette of little girl pushing a doll buggy, 3½"	30.00	40.00	32.00
Teapot, Silhouette, Made in Japan, with lid, 4"	6.00	8.00	6.50
Teapot, Sunset, Made in Japan, with lid, 3¾"	5.00	7.00	5.50
Teapot, Water Hen, England, with lid, 5¼"	35.00	40.00	36.50
Tea Set, china, nine pieces, covered teapot, creamer, covered sugar, two cups, two saucers, white with blue shading, 24 Kt gold decoration, scalloped edges, tallest piece is 5½", German, 1910	75.00	100.00	85.00
Tea Set, depression glass, Homespun, fourteen pieces, pink, original box	190.00	220.00	195.00
Tea Set, glass, Akro Agate, Chiquita, twenty-two pieces, green opaque, original box	55.00	75.00	60.00
Tea Set, glass, Akro Agate, Concentric Ring, twenty-one pieces, marbleized blue, original box	400.00	475.00	420.00
Tea Set, glass, Akro Agate, Interior Panel, eight pieces, transparent topaz, original box	25.00	42.00	30.00
Tea Set, Palissy china, twenty-three pieces, covered teapot, creamer, covered sugar, six cups, six saucers, six plates, white with brown flower berry and leaf decoration, gold trim, very elaborate shape, teapot is 4½" high, perfect condition, Palissy blue mark, early 1800s	150.00	250.00	175.00
Tea Set, porcelain, eight pieces, covered teapot, creamer, covered sugar, two cups, two saucers, teddy bear decoration	8.00	10.00	8.50

	Current Price Range		P/Y Average
□ **Tea Set,** porcelain, seven pieces, covered teapot, sugar, creamer, two cups, two saucers, Dolly Dingle decoration	6.00	10.00	7.50
□ **Tea Set,** porcelain, seven pieces, covered teapot, sugar, creamer, two cups, two saucers, Peter Rabbit decoration	6.00	10.00	7.50
□ **Toleware,** tin, set of three pieces, pitcher, cup, saucer, pitcher is 2″, cup is 1⅝″, painted blue and cream with still life scenes, 1920 . . .	9.00	15.00	12.00
□ **Tureen,** Blue Willow, Made in Japan, with lid, 4″	15.00	20.00	17.00
□ **Tureen,** Blue Willow, Occupied Japan, with lid	20.00	25.00	22.00
□ **Tureen,** ironstone, lid, moss rose decoration, rococo styling, 24 Kt trim on handles, 1890 . .	25.00	35.00	30.00
□ **Tureen,** semi-porcelain, Johnson Brothers, lid, white with gold trim and sprays of tiny roses, 7″ x 4½″, 1800s	50.00	60.00	55.00
□ **Turkey Roasting Pan,** aluminum, oval, lid, riveted iron handles on ends of pan and top of lid, 5½″ x 3½″ x 1½″, 1920s	5.00	10.00	7.50

CHRISTMAS DECORATIONS

DESCRIPTION: Christmas tree ornaments were first manufactured and sold to consumers in the 1870s. Replacing homemade decorations, most of these early ones were simple shapes made in small German villages. Dresden ornaments are the rarest and most valuable. Being made of embossed cardboard and covered with metallic paper, these intricate handcrafted specimens were soon superceded by easily produced blown glass items. It is estimated that by the 1920s, over 5,000 different designs were used for ornaments.

COMMENTS: Age, rarity and, therefore, value are determined by the ornament's construction, design, patina and the material of which it is made. The best place to find old ornaments at a reasonable price is most likely in great-grandma's attic. Since they are in great demand at the moment, dealer prices are high, even for specimens in average condition.

ADDITIONAL TIPS: Also quite collectible are Christmas tree lights dating from the 1920s and 1930s, even if they no longer work. The most collectible of these are the blown glass ones made in molds in Occupied Japan. A variety of shapes and sizes are available.

Ornament, Gorham,
silver plated,
$13.00-$17.00

	Current Price Range		P/Y Average
☐ **Light,** Andy Gump, milk glass	15.00	17.00	16.00
☐ **Light,** bear with guitar, milk glass	15.00	17.00	16.00
☐ **Light,** blue bird, milk glass	15.00	17.00	16.00
☐ **Light,** clock	15.00	17.00	16.00
☐ **Light,** clown, milk glass	20.00	24.00	22.00
☐ **Light,** elephant, milk glass	7.00	9.00	8.00
☐ **Light,** fish, milk glass	13.00	15.00	14.00
☐ **Light,** gingerbread man	13.00	15.00	14.00
☐ **Light,** grapes, milk glass	8.00	10.00	9.00
☐ **Light,** house, milk glass	13.00	15.00	14.00
☐ **Light,** Humpty Dumpty, milk glass	15.00	17.00	16.00
☐ **Light,** lantern	13.00	15.00	14.00
☐ **Light,** parrot, milk glass	7.00	9.00	8.00
☐ **Light,** Pinocchio	20.00	22.00	21.00
☐ **Light,** Puss N' Boots, milk glass	20.00	22.00	21.00
☐ **Light,** Santa, painted	20.00	22.00	21.00
☐ **Light,** snowman, milk glass	13.00	15.00	14.00
☐ **Light,** zeppelin with flag	20.00	22.00	21.00
☐ **Ornament,** angel's face, blown glass, 2½ " ..	22.00	28.00	24.00
☐ **Ornament,** baby in bunting, blown glass, embossed script lettering, 4 "	65.00	85.00	73.00

	Current Price Range		P/Y Average
Ornament, ball, amber	23.00	25.00	24.00
Ornament, ball, canary, blown glass	20.00	22.00	21.00
Ornament, basket, fruit filled, blown glass	23.00	25.00	24.00
Ornament, bear with muff, blown glass	48.00	50.00	49.00
Ornament, camel, Dresden	30.00	32.00	31.00
Ornament, carrot, blown glass, embossed detail, pre-1920, 4″	40.00	50.00	43.00
Ornament, child, milk glass	10.00	12.00	11.00
Ornament, church, blown glass	30.00	32.00	31.00
Ornament, clown head, blown glass	53.00	55.00	54.00
Ornament, cuckoo clock, blown glass, white/orange/green, embossed and painted	22.00	28.00	23.50
Ornament, doll's head, blown glass, silver and flesh color with blown glass eyes, 3″	50.00	70.00	55.00
Ornament, elephant, mercury glass with blown milk glass tusks, label reads "Made in Germany," 4″	30.00	40.00	33.00
Ornament, fence, wood	23.00	25.00	24.00
Ornament, fish, blown glass	53.00	55.00	54.00
Ornament, football player, milk glass	20.00	22.00	21.00
Ornament, Foxy Grandpa, blown glass with applied legs, 4½″	150.00	175.00	160.00
Note: High value because this was an early comic strip character.			
Ornament, girl, blown glass	34.00	36.00	35.00
Ornament, girl's head, blown glass with blown glass eyes, 2½″	25.00	30.00	26.75
Ornament, Happy Hooligan, blown glass with applied legs, 4½″	200.00	250.00	215.00
Note: Happy Hooligan, a comic strip character of the early 1900s, was created by Frederick Burr Opper.			
Ornament, heart, blown glass, large	35.00	37.00	36.00
Ornament, icicle, glass	20.00	24.00	22.00
Ornament, lamp	55.00	57.00	56.00
Ornament, lion, Dresden	20.00	22.00	21.00
Ornament, man in the moon, blown glass, green, 3″	36.00	44.00	39.00
Ornament, monkey holding stick, blown glass, 2½″	50.00	65.00	56.00
Ornament, musical instrument	20.00	22.00	21.00
Ornament, peacock, blown glass, brush tail	20.00	22.00	21.00
Ornament, penguin, blown glass, blue, silver, red, embossed feet, 1¾″	37.00	45.00	40.00
Ornament, pinecone, blown glass	7.00	9.00	8.00
Ornament, pipe, blown glass	23.00	25.00	24.00
Ornament, pocket watch, blown glass with paper watch face, pre-1920, 2″	40.00	50.00	43.00
Ornament, purse, blown glass	33.00	35.00	34.00
Ornament, Santa, celluloid	33.00	35.00	34.00
Ornament, Santa carrying bag of toys, blown glass, 2½″	18.00	23.00	20.00
Ornament, Santa, with plaster face	23.00	25.00	24.00
Ornament, Scottie dog, blown glass, yellow and blue, size unavailable	50.00	65.00	55.00

	Current Price Range		P/Y Average
☐ **Ornament,** smiling snowman with broom, blown glass, pre-1920, 3½ ″	35.00	45.00	36.75
☐ **Ornament,** stag, blown glass, blue with gold antlers, label reads "Made in Germany," 3″ .	30.00	40.00	33.00
☐ **Ornament,** star, Dresden	20.00	22.00	21.00
☐ **Ornament,** swan, blown glass	23.00	25.00	24.00
☐ **Ornament,** teapot	23.00	25.00	24.00
☐ **Ornament,** turkey, blown glass with tinsel wings and tail, 5″	10.00	15.00	12.00
☐ **Ornament,** umbrella, tinsel	23.00	25.00	24.00

CHROME

DESCRIPTION: Glossy metal used in various types of manufacturing, such as decorative trimmings on autos and trucks, sailboats, etc.

TYPES: Chrome collectibles include not only auto items, which are perhaps the most familiar to the general public, but a wide variety of decorative household objects and novelties.

PERIOD: Chrome came into extensive use in the 1920s and has remained popular thereafter. It was one of the more important substances of the Art Deco era.

CARE AND CONDITION: Clean with any metal cleaning polish recommended for use on chrome. Do not use an abrasive tool, nor even steel wool, as this will result in fine scratches that mar the surface. As chrome is very durable, it presents no problem in storage or display.

☐ Bud Vase, chased, 4½ ″ cylinder resting on a 3½ ″ base	16.00	20.00	18.00
☐ **Cocktail Set,** shaker with six matching flared goblets, height of goblets 7″, set	30.00	35.00	32.00
☐ **Cocktail Shaker,** footed, etched banding with grape leaf cluster motif, red plastic handle, 11¾ ″	10.00	14.00	12.00
☐ **Cocktail Shaker,** grape etching, with cap and lid	9.00	12.00	10.25

	Current Price Range		P/Y Average
☐ **Cordial Dispenser,** clear glass and chrome, plunger type with six jiggers, the glass decorated with horizontal ribbing, jiggers have plastic belts, set	22.00	28.00	24.00
☐ **Cordial Dispenser,** keg resting on pedestal with six small mugs, price for full set	14.00	18.00	16.00
☐ **Farber Cocktail Shaker And Six Glasses,** hammered texture, shaker with plastic handle (black), height of glasses 6¼″, set	27.00	34.00	30.00
☐ **Lazy Susan,** 2-tier bar, green plastic central handle, top has six small jiggers with green and yellow striping, bottle has twelve jiggers, set	32.00	40.00	35.00
☐ **Liquer Dispenser,** decorative sphere with six shot glasses, set	20.00	25.00	22.00
☐ **Tray,** large, ceramic with chrome trim and chrome handles, the ceramic painted with purple grapes, 13¾″ diameter	21.00	28.00	23.00

CIGAR BOX LABELS

TOPIC: Cigar box labels are brightly colored, artistically decorated labels that adorn cigar boxes.

TYPES: The major types of cigar box labels are inside lids (which are placed on the inside lid of the box), box end labels (which are placed on the ends of the box) and box sealers (which seal the lid to the sides).

PERIOD: These labels came into use in the middle of the 19th century.

MAKERS: Witsch & Schmitt of New York created many artistic labels.

COMMENTS: Labels which were damaged while being removed from their boxes are automatically worth less. In the early 1900s printers often sold unused bands directly to collectors.

ADDITIONAL TIPS: Most labels in the ten to fifteen dollar price range are multicolored stone lithographs dating from around 1900. Prices decrease as age decreases.

Labels, *cigar box, 1900s, each,* **$10.00-$20.00**

	Current Price Range		P/Y Average
☐ **Acropolis,** inside lid, 6″ x 9″, c. 1920	3.00	5.50	4.25
☐ **A Dream,** small boy riding bicycle, full colors, 4″ x 5½″	20.00	25.00	21.25
☐ **Africora,** box end label, 4″ x 4″	.50	1.50	1.00
☐ **Alcazar,** inside lid, 6″ x 9″, c. 1920	1.00	3.00	2.00
☐ **American Twins,** pictures twin girls, full colors, 6″ x 9″, c. 1880-1890	40.00	50.00	43.00
Note: This brand of cigar was sold by the pair.			
☐ **Barrister,** inside lid, 6″ x 9″, c. 1895	8.00	11.00	9.50
☐ **Barrister,** inside lid, 6″ x 9″, c. 1895	8.00	11.00	9.50
☐ **Big Five,** inside lid, 6″ x 9″, c. 1935	.20	.30	.25
☐ **Big Wolf,** box sealer, 2″ x 3″	.50	1.50	1.00

	Current Price Range		P/Y Average
☐ **Blue Bird**, inside lid, 6″ x 9″, c. 1930	1.00	3.00	2.00
☐ **Blue Goose**, box end label, 4″ x 4″	.20	.30	.25
☐ **Blue Goose**, inside lid, 6″ x 9″, c. 1935	.50	1.50	1.00
☐ **Brick House**, box end label, 2″ x 5″	.25	.75	.50
☐ **Calender**, inside lid, 6″ x 9″, c. 1905	13.00	18.00	15.50
☐ **Castellanos**, inside lid, 6″ x 9″, c. 1930	1.00	3.00	2.00
☐ **Castle Hall**, inside lid, 6″ x 9″, c. 1940	.25	.75	.50
☐ **Christy Girl**, box end label, 4″ x 4″	.50	1.50	1.00
☐ **Christy Girl**, inside lid, 6″ x 9″, c. 1932	2.00	3.00	2.50
☐ **Clipper**, box end label, 4″ x 4″	1.00	3.00	2.00
☐ **Clubhouse**, box end label, 2″ x 5″	.20	.30	.25
☐ **College Inn**, box sealer, 2″ x 3″	.25	.75	.50
☐ **College Inn**, inside lid, 6″ x 9″, c. 1910	8.00	12.00	10.00
☐ **Custom House**, inside lid, 6″ x 9″, c. 1930	3.00	5.00	4.00
☐ **Damasco**, inside lid, 6″ x 9″, c. 1900	13.00	17.00	15.00
☐ **Diamond Crown**, box end label, 2″ x 5″	.20	.30	.25
☐ **Diamond Crown**, inside lid, 6″ x 9″, c. 1940 . . .	.50	1.50	1.00
☐ **Don Alfonso**, inside lid, 6″ x 9″, c. 1905	14.00	16.00	15.00
☐ **Don Nieto**, box end label, 2″ x 5″	.20	.30	.25
☐ **Don Nieto**, inside lid, 6″ x 9″, c. 1940	.20	.30	.25
☐ **Duo Art**, box end label, 4″ x 4″	.25	.75	.50
☐ **Duo Art**, inside lid, 6″ x 9″, c. 1930	.25	.75	.50
☐ **Edmund Halley**, inside lid, 6″ x 9″, c. 1900	8.00	12.00	10.00
☐ **El Escudero**, box end label, 4″ x 4″	.20	.30	.25
☐ **El Escudero**, inside lid, 6″ x 9″, c. 1940	.20	.30	.25
☐ **El Guardo**, inside lid, 6″ x 9″, c. 1910	4.00	7.00	5.50
☐ **Elsie**, box end label, 4″ x 4″	.50	1.50	1.00
☐ **Farragut**, inside lid, 6″ x 9″, c. 1905	8.00	13.00	10.50
☐ **Fidelity**, box end label, 4″ x 4″	.25	.75	.50
☐ **Fidelity**, inside lid, 6″ x 9″, c. 1945	.25	.75	.50
☐ **First Blush**, box end label, 4″ x 4″	4.00	6.50	5.25
☐ **Flor de Franklin**, Benjamin Franklin flying a kite, full color, 3″ x 5″	30.00	35.00	31.50
☐ **For Cash Only**, illustration of man buying cigar at counter with female clerk behind counter, full color, 6″ x 6″, believed to date from 1880s	40.00	50.00	43.00
Note: In the late 1800s many restaurants kept open boxes of cigars at the cashier's desk and patrons were welcome to take one for free. Better grade cigars were available for purchase, and this brand — For Cash Only — wanted to make certain it wasn't mistaken for a freebie.			
☐ **Fragancia**, box end label, 4″ x 4″	.50	1.50	1.00
☐ **Gallatin**, box end label, 2″ x 5″	.25	.75	.50
☐ **Garcia Y Garcia**, inside lid, 6″ x 9″, c. 1937 . . .	.50	1.25	.80
☐ **Garcia Y Hermanos**, box end label, 4″ x 4″ . .	4.00	6.00	5.00
☐ **Garcia Y Hermanos**, inside lid, 6″ x 9″, c. 1920	3.50	5.50	4.50
☐ **Golden Horn**, pictures Arabian female, full colors, size unavailable, c. 1880-1890	25.00	30.00	26.00
☐ **Golden Sun**, box end label, 4″ x 4″	.25	.75	.50
☐ **Grand Council**, box end label, 4″ x 4″	1.00	3.00	2.00
☐ **Group of 40**, colored and gilded, includes Prudential, Airdale, Montebello, Lyra, Red Tips, others	17.00	25.00	20.50

	Current Price Range		P/Y Average
☐ **Longfellow,** box end label, 2″ x 5″	.50	1.50	1.00
☐ **Lopez-Alvaraz,** box end label, 4″ x 4″	.20	.30	.25
☐ **Lord Puffer,** portrait of elegantly dressed man seated by fire with cigar and whisky nearby, 5½″ x 8½″	25.00	30.00	26.75
☐ **Lord Vernon,** inside lid, 6″ x 9″, c. 1930	2.00	4.50	3.25
☐ **Lucky Bill,** box end label, 2″ x 5″	.20	.30	.25
☐ **Madrigal,** inside lid, 6″ x 9″, c. 1930	.25	.75	.50
☐ **Malta,** box end label, 4″ x 4″	.20	.30	.25
☐ **Manila Blunts,** inside lid, 6″ x 9″, c. 1942	.20	.30	.25
☐ **Memorata,** box end label, 4″ x 4″	4.00	6.00	5.00
☐ **Miss Pluck,** pictures woman and corset, full colors, 6″ x 9″, c. 1880-1890	35.00	45.00	37.00
☐ **Mission,** box end label, 4″ x 4″	.50	1.50	1.00
☐ **Moosariana,** box end label, 4″ x 4″	1.00	3.00	2.00
☐ **Moro Light,** inside lid, 6″ x 9″, c. 1938	.50	1.50	1.00
☐ **Navy Ribbon,** box end label, 2″ x 5″	.25	.75	.50
☐ **Newport Club,** men in top hats ride stage coach past hotel, full color, 4¼″ x 5¼″	20.00	25.00	21.75
☐ **Nutura,** box end label, 4″ x 4″	.20	.30	.25
☐ **Old Abe,** portrait of Abraham Lincoln in gray and white with embossed gold, 7″ x 9″	20.00	25.00	21.50
☐ **Old Hickory,** box end label, 4″ x 4″	.25	.75	.50
☐ **Old Hickory,** inside lid, 6″ x 9″, c. 1930	.50	1.50	1.00
☐ **Old Hickory,** portrait of Andrew Jackson, full color, 7″ x 8″	20.00	25.00	26.00
☐ **Our Bird,** pictures the Lindbergh aircraft Spirit of St. Louis, red/white/blue, 7″ x 9″ ...	25.00	30.00	26.25
Note: As the historic Lindbergh flight was made in 1927 this label probably dates to the years immediately thereafter.			
☐ **Our Fire Laddies,** pictures uniformed firemen and engine, full colors, c. 1880	30.00	40.00	33.00
☐ **Our Kitties,** box sealer, 2″ x 3″	.25	.75	.50
☐ **Peace Time,** box end label, 4″ x 4″	.25	.75	.50
☐ **Peace Time,** inside lid, 6″ x 9″, c. 1927	.25	.75	.50
☐ **Pearl,** inside lid, 6″ x 9″, c. 1925	3.00	6.00	4.50
☐ **Pony Post,** box end label, 4″ x 4″	4.00	6.00	5.00
☐ **Prima Rosa,** inside lid, 6″ x 9″, c. 1930	2.00	3.50	2.75
☐ **Prize Beauty,** picture of a young girl, 1880s ..	4.00	6.50	5.75
☐ **Pug,** inside lid, 6″ x 9″, c. 1903	7.00	12.00	9.50
☐ **Quaker Quality,** box end label, 4″ x 4″	.50	1.50	1.00
☐ **Quaker Quality,** inside lid, 6″ x 9″, c. 1934 ...	.50	1.50	1.00
☐ **Red Ball,** couple on ice skates pushing huge red ball, full color, 4¼″ x 5¼″	30.00	35.00	31.50
☐ **Red Cloud,** pictures Indian chief on horse, full colors, 6″ x 10″, undetermined age	25.00	30.00	26.25
☐ **Red Dandies,** inside lid, 6″ x 9″, c. 1900	14.00	16.50	15.25
☐ **Red Tips,** box end label, 2″ x 5″	.20	.30	.25
☐ **Regal X Ten,** inside lid, 6″ x 9″, c. 1920″	3.00	6.00	4.50
☐ **Reina Bella,** box end label, 4″ x 4″	.25	.75	.50
☐ **Rigoletto,** inside lid, 6″ x 9″, c. 1929″	1.00	3.00	2.00
☐ **Rolamo,** inside lid, 6″ x 9″, c. 1945	.20	.30	.25
☐ **Rosa Moro,** inside lid, 6″ x 9″, c. 1940	.25	.75	.50
☐ **Rosa Y O,** box sealer, 2″ x 3″	.25	.75	.50
☐ **Round-Up,** box end label, 2″ x 5″	.25	.75	.50

CIRCUS MEMORABILIA

VARIATIONS: All circus-related items are considered collectible, including posters, photographs, ticket stubs, programs as well as large items such as cages and tents.

ORIGIN: The first American circus opened in 1793 in Philadelphia. The show was modeled after already established English circuses. The show traveled from town to town in order to entertain rural communities. About 30 years after the first American circus, tents and big tops were introduced. In 1919 the top three competing circuses, P. T. Barnum, James A. Bailey and Ringling Brothers combined their shows.

COMMENTS: The year 1984 marks the centennial for Ringling Brothers. This special celebration may add to the already high interest in circus memorabilia.

ADDITIONAL TIPS: The following listings are alphabetical according to title. A description and price range follows.

	Current Price Range		P/Y Average
☐ **Band Wagon,** horse drawn	400.00	450.00	405.00
☐ **Book,** *Barnum's Wonders, An Illustrated History of the Hindoo Hairy Family and other Prodigious and Exclusive Features of "The Greatest Show on Earth,"* 16 pp., c. 1890	60.00	75.00	65.00
☐ **Book,** *Buffalo Bill's Wild West,* programmed and descriptive booklet, c. 1885	125.00	175.00	136.00
☐ **Book,** *Burdett Twins,* Fanny and Major, age, 22 years, height 38", New York, c. 1890	55.00	75.00	60.00
☐ **Book,** *The Curious and Amusing Exhibition of The Educated Fleas,* by L. Bertolotto, 5th edition, 245 pp., New York, c. 1876	85.00	115.00	100.00
☐ **Book,** *Dr. Doolittle's Circus,* by Hugh Loftring, New York, c. 1924	90.00	120.00	95.00
☐ **Book,** *The Genial Showman,* depicts the life of Artemus Ward, New York, c. 1870	50.00	65.00	53.00
☐ **Book,** *The Man of the Mountain,* by Frederic Farnsworth, Boston, c. 1818	150.00	180.00	160.00

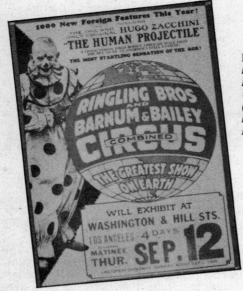

Booklet,
*Ringling Bros. Barnum &
Bailey, 1929,*
$25.00-$35.00
*(photo courtesy of ©Lou
McCulloch, Highland,
Heights, OH)*

	Current Price Range		P/Y Average
☐ **Book,** *Tom Thumb,* life of Charles S. Stratton, 28″ high and 15 pounds, 24 pp. booklet, published by Barnum, New York, c. 1847	200.00	280.00	224.00
☐ **Booklet,** *Barnum and Bailey Circus,* color cover, features biographies, pictures and descriptions of the circus, c. 1910	65.00	85.00	70.00
☐ **Booklet,** *Forepaugh and Sells Circus,* color cover, features biographies, pictures and descriptions of the circus, c. 1910	55.00	75.00	60.00
☐ **Booklet,** *Walter L. Main Circus,* 8 pp., color, wraps	16.00	25.00	18.00
☐ **Broadside,** Bailey Bros. Circus, red, white, blue, 14″ x 41″	20.00	30.00	24.50
☐ **Broadside Handbills,** illustrated, 10″ x 28″, c. 1920s	20.00	30.00	23.00
☐ **Button,** "Souvenir Ringling Bros. — World's Greatest Shows," black and white, 1½″, c. 1900s	75.00	100.00	87.50
☐ **Courier,** *Illustrated News,* by P. T. Barnum, 16 pp., c. 1897	42.00	58.00	44.00
☐ **Cabinet Photo,** "Che — Mah, The Chinese Dwarf" from Barnum and Bailey, c. 1900	25.00	35.00	29.50
☐ **Elephant,** tin lithograph, Unique Art Mfg. Co., "Flying Circus" marked on base, c. 1930s . . .	100.00	125.00	115.00
☐ **Folder,** Barnum and Bailey, full color, 14 pp., c. 1910	30.00	50.00	40.00
☐ **Lithograph,** *The Tigers Are Ferocious and They Bite,* by Adam Forepaugh, c. 1880	135.00	175.00	160.00

	Current Price Range		P/Y Average
☐ **Lithograph,** *The Circus Kings of All Time,* window card, 14″ x 22″, mid 1830s	32.50	40.00	35.00
☐ **Herald Or Handbill,** *Sparks Circus,* c. 1921 ..	16.00	25.00	18.00
☐ **Magazine,** *Barnum and Bailey Circus,* bright color cover, c. 1918	55.00	75.00	60.00
☐ **Magazine,** *Magazine of Wonders and Daily Review,* by Ringling Brothers, color, c. 1914 ..	60.00	80.00	70.00
☐ **Photograph,** Downie Brothers Circus, groups of photos features various artists, 5″ x 7″, c. 1930	35.00	50.00	40.00
☐ **Photograph,** Russell Brothers Circus, groups of photos features various artists, 5″ x 7″, c. 1930	15.00	25.00	18.00
☐ **Poster,** Adam Forepaugh Circus and Roman Hippodrome, 7 part composite, 30½″ x 40″, c. 1885	185.00	215.00	195.00
☐ **Poster,** Adam Forepaugh's "Queen of The Ring," 30″ x 40½″c. 1885	135.00	175.00	145.00
☐ **Poster,** Adam Forepaugh and Sells circus, pictures Aurora Zoaves	52.00	70.00	58.00
☐ **Poster,** Barnum and Bailey Circus, color, depicts naval battle against Spanish fleet, 25″ x 36″, c. 1898	180.00	220.00	195.00
☐ **Poster,** Clyde Beatty Circus, action scene, 21″ x 28″, c. 1930	75.00	100.00	80.00
☐ **Poster,** Clyde Beatty, training lions and tigers, c. 1930	80.00	100.00	89.00
☐ **Poster,** Dale's animal three-ring circus	15.50	25.00	18.00
☐ **Poster,** "Lady Viola, The Most Beautiful Tattoed Woman in The World," painted in oils over large photo, 40″ x 40″, New York, c. 1925	450.00	495.00	460.00
☐ **Poster,** "Lilla," high-wire act, 34″ x 45″, c. 1895	230.00	250.00	237.00
☐ **Poster,** "Princess Topaze, Star of The Casino de Paris," female midget, 35″ x 48″	300.00	340.00	310.00
☐ **Poster,** P. T. Barnum and Co., Lake Front, Chicago, Monday, July 19th	20.00	28.00	23.00
☐ **Poster,** "Terrell Jacobs The Liong King," 28″ x 40″, c. 1935	60.00	70.00	63.00
☐ **Poster,** Terrell Jacobs in Big Top, surrounded by lions, 28″ x 40″, c. 1934	75.00	85.00	77.00
☐ **Program,** Ringling Brothers, Barnum and Bailey, c. 1948	15.00	23.00	17.00
☐ **Program,** Hagenbeck-Wallas	20.00	28.00	23.00
☐ **Sheet Music,** Children At The Circus, c. 1909 .	25.00	35.00	28.00
☐ **Sheet Music,** Whe It's Circus Day Back Home, c. 1917	25.00	35.00	27.00
☐ **Song Book,** Barnum and London Musical Album, large size	25.00	35.00	27.00
☐ **Stationery,** Sparton Brothers, ornate, unused	4.50	8.00	6.00
☐ **Tickets,** Barnum's Circus, c. 1890	15.00	24.00	17.00
☐ **Tickets,** Hunts Brothers, illustrated with clown, 100 large, c. 1940s	10.00	15.00	12.00
☐ **Ticket,** P. T. Barnum Circus, c. 1890	15.00	25.00	17.00

	Current Price Range		P/Y Average
☐ **Toy,** Barnum and Bailey circus cage, elephant drawn, painted, stained and lithographed wood, c. 1930	180.00	280.00	220.00
☐ **Toy,** circus cage, decorative wagon, c. 1928 ..	150.00	200.00	175.00
☐ **Toy,** circus train, tin, eight pieces, c. 1950s ..	112.00	140.00	117.00
☐ **Toy,,** clown, Rolly-Poly, Shoenhut, 9″	25.00	35.00	27.00
☐ **Toy,** clown, wooden, hinged	75.00	100.00	80.00
☐ **Toy,** elephant pulling animals in cage, mechanical, c. 1935	170.00	210.00	180.00
☐ **Toy,** lion cage, driver and lions	130.00	190.00	143.00
☐ **Toy,** tin clown holding balloon, long gown with feet protruding, 6⅞″, c. 1930	100.00	140.00	110.00
☐ **Toy Wagon,** wood and tin with scene of circus on wagon, 17½″ L.	115.00	160.00	130.00

CIVIL WAR MEMORABILIA

DESCRIPTION: The Civil War produced some of the most collectible antiques in today's marketplace. Items are available all over the world. Collecting Civil War memorabilia can be a most gratifying hobby for the collector as he delves into the history of each item and discovers the principles upon which this country has grown.

COMMENTS: The most sought-after collectible in this category is that of firearms. This period in time marked a technological transition from a single shot gun to one that would shoot several times, including the first machine gun. Other collectible areas include uniforms, buttons, belt buckles, canteens, knapsacks, insignias and personal effects, such as diaries, letters, and photographs.

ADDITIONAL TIPS: Auctions are a great place to pick up such items as well as dealer shops. Prices are as varied as the items so even the novice can afford to begin this type of collection.

RECOMMENDED READING: For more in-depth information and listings, you may refer to *The Official Price Guide to Military Collectibles* by Colonel Robert H. Rankin, published by The House of Collectibles.

AUTOGRAPHS (ALs stands for autographed letters)

	ALs		Document		Plain Signature	
☐ Ammen, Rear Admiral Daniel .	$35.00-	$42.00	$18.00-	$23.00	$4.00-	$6.00
☐ Andrew, John A.	18.00-	23.00	8.00-	10.00	3.00-	4.00
☐ Anderson, James P.	36.00-	43.00	18.00-	23.00	5.00-	6.00
☐ Anderson, Brig. Gen. Robert .	60.00-	75.00	25.00-	33.00	7.00-	11.00
☐ Augur, Christopher C.	14.00-	16.00	4.00-	7.00	1.00-	1.50
☐ Badeau, Adam	14.00-	16.00	4.00-	7.00	1.00-	1.50
☐ Banks, Nathaniel P.	50.00-	65.00	18.00-	23.00	8.00-	11.00
☐ Barnard, John G.	18.00-	22.00	8.00-	10.00	3.00-	5.00
☐ Beauregard, G. T.	275.00-	350.00	90.00-	110.00	14.00-	19.00
☐ Benton, James G.	10.00-	12.00	8.00-	9.00	2.00-	3.00
☐ Berdan, Hiram	43.00-	50.00	14.00-	18.00	4.00-	6.00
☐ Bocock, Thomas S.	20.00-	26.00	8.00-	10.00	2.00-	3.00
☐ Bonham, M. L.	14.00-	18.00	8.00-	10.00	2.00-	3.00
☐ Bragg, Braxton	42.00-	50.00	18.00-	23.00	8.00-	11.00
☐ Buchanan, Thomas McKean .	125.00-	175.00	38.00-	50.00	20.00-	27.00
☐ Burnside, A. E.	90.00-	120.00	33.00-	45.00	12.00-	18.00
☐ Butterfield, Daniel	20.00-	28.00	10.00-	15.00	4.00-	7.00
☐ Cleburne, Patrick R.	240.00-	300.00	100.00-	140.00	35.00-	55.00
☐ Corse, Brig. Gen. John M.	14.00-	20.00	8.00-	11.00	3.00-	5.00
☐ Cosby, George B.	20.00-	28.00	10.00-	15.00	4.50-	7.00
☐ Crittenden, Thomas	20.00-	28.00	10.00-	15.00	4.50-	7.00
☐ Custer, George A.	850.00-	875.00	250.00-	330.00	60.00-	90.00
☐ Dahlgren, Rear Admiral John .	33.00-	40.00	20.00-	28.00	4.50-	7.00
☐ Davis, Jefferson	1100.00-	2000.00	325.00-	475.00	50.00-	80.00
☐ Dix, Gen. John A.	45.00-	60.00	20.00-	28.00	4.50-	7.00
☐ Early, Jubal A.	90.00-	130.00	50.00-	70.00	8.00-	13.00
☐ Farragut, Admiral David G. ...	275.00-	350.00	125.00-	200.00	15.00-	22.00
☐ Floyd, John B.	20.00-	29.00	8.00-	13.00	3.00-	5.00
☐ Forney, Maj. Gen. John H. ...	20.00-	29.00	8.00-	13.00	3.00-	5.00
☐ Foster, John G.	17.00-	23.00	8.00-	12.00	3.00-	5.00
☐ Fremont, Gen. J. C.	35.00-	43.00	10.00-	15.00	6.00-	9.00
☐ French, Samuel G.	40.00-	56.00	10.00-	15.00	6.00-	9.00
☐ Gardner, Franklin	25.00-	35.00	8.00-	13.00	3.00-	5.00
☐ Garnett, Robert S.	32.00-	43.00	11.00-	18.00	3.00-	5.00
☐ Gilmore, Gen. Quincy A.	25.00-	34.00	8.00-	11.00	3.00-	5.00
☐ Gladden, Adley H.	70.00-	95.00	21.00-	30.00	10.00-	15.00
☐ Gordon, John B.	32.00-	42.00	10.00-	14.00	3.00-	5.00
☐ Gorgas, Josiah	32.00-	42.00	10.00-	14.00	3.00-	5.00
☐ Halleck, H. W.	45.00-	60.00	22.00-	29.00	5.00-	8.00
☐ Hancock, W. S.	35.00-	43.00	15.00-	20.00	3.00-	5.00
☐ Heintzelman, S. P.	22.00-	28.00	10.00-	14.00	3.00-	5.00
☐ Hooker, Gen. Joseph	34.00-	42.00	12.00-	19.00	5.00-	8.00
☐ Humphries, A. A.	34.00-	42.00	12.00-	19.00	5.00-	8.00
☐ Ingraham, Duncan N.	40.00-	58.00	15.00-	20.00	5.00-	8.00
☐ Iverson, Alfred	35.00-	45.00	15.00-	20.00	3.00-	5.00
☐ Jackson, "Stonewall"	2800.00-	4500.00	700.00-	1200.00	150.00-	200.00
☐ Jackson, W. H.	36.00-	47.00	15.00-	20.00	6.00-	9.00
☐ Johnston, Joseph E.	45.00-	60.00	20.00-	32.00	6.00-	9.00
☐ Jones, David R.	95.00-	130.00	45.00-	70.00	15.00-	22.00
☐ Kearny, Philip	200.00-	275.00	70.00-	95.00	20.00-	28.00
☐ Lee, FitzHugh	32.00-	45.00	15.00-	20.00	3.00-	5.00
☐ Lee, Robert E.	500.00-	900.00	200.00-	325.00	80.00-	110.00
☐ Logan, Maj. Gen. John A.	26.00-	35.00	15.00-	10.00	4.00-	7.00
☐ Longstreet, James	26.00-	35.00	10.00-	15.00	4.00-	7.00

	ALs		Document		Plain Signature	
☐ Luce, Admiral Stephen	33.00-	40.00	10.00-	15.00	4.00-	7.00
☐ Lyon, Gen. Nathaniel	110.00-	150.00	45.00-	70.00	20.00-	28.00
☐ Mahone, William	33.00-	40.00	10.00-	15.00	4.00-	7.00
☐ McArthur, John	40.00-	50.00	15.00-	22.00	4.00-	7.00
☐ McClellan, Geo. B.	58.00-	75.00	22.00-	32.00	6.00-	9.00
☐ Mason, James M.	275.00-	350.00	80.00-	120.00	20.00-	29.00
☐ Meade, George G.	45.00-	58.00	18.00-	26.00	6.00-	10.00
☐ Meagher, Thomas F.	26.00-	36.00	10.00-	15.00	4.00-	7.00
☐ Mosby, John S.	26.00-	36.00	10.00-	15.00	4.00-	7.00
☐ Pickett, George E.	300.00-	415.00	115.00-	170.00	18.00-	25.00
☐ Porter, Admiral David D.	110.00-	170.00	50.00-	75.00	8.00-	12.00
☐ Porter, FitzJohn	45.00-	65.00	15.00-	23.00	5.00-	8.00
☐ Porter, Horace	33.00-	42.00	15.00-	23.00	3.00-	5.00
☐ Price, Sterling	40.00-	60.00	20.00-	29.00	5.00-	8.00
☐ Pryor, Roger A.	47.00-	75.00	20.00-	29.00	5.00-	8.00
☐ Ransom, Robert, Jr.	60.00-	100.00	22.00-	30.00	5.00-	8.00
☐ Reagan, John H.	33.00-	47.00	15.00-	22.00	4.00-	7.00
☐ Richardson, J. B.	33.00-	47.00	15.00-	22.00	4.00-	7.00
☐ Ripley, R. S.	38.00-	50.00	15.00-	22.00	4.00-	7.00
☐ Rosecrans, W. S.	80.00-	110.00	22.00-	28.00	8.00-	12.00
☐ Scott, Winfield	200.00-	300.00	80.00-	130.00	15.00-	20.00
☐ Seddon, James A.	110.00-	150.00	35.00-	50.00	7.00-	12.00
☐ Seward, William H.	150.00-	210.00	47.00-	65.00	10.00-	15.00
☐ Sherman, William T.	220.00-	300.00	70.00-	100.00	15.00-	22.00
☐ Sigel, Franz	37.00-	50.00	15.00-	22.00	4.00-	7.00
☐ Sneed, John L. T.	40.00-	62.00	22.00-	28.00	5.00-	8.00
☐ Stanton, Edwin M.	130.00-	220.00	45.00-	85.00	10.00-	15.00
☐ Stephens, Alexander H.	80.00-	110.00	23.00-	32.00	5.00-	8.00
☐ Sumner, Charles	80.00-	110.00	23.00-	32.00	5.00-	8.00
☐ Taylor, Richard	100.00-	140.00	35.00-	50.00	8.00-	11.00
☐ Thomas, Maj. Gen. George H.	150.00-	200.00	47.00-	62.00	11.00-	15.00
☐ Thompson, M. J.	110.00-	140.00	35.00-	50.00	8.00-	11.00
☐ Toombs, Robert	90.00-	110.00	22.00-	28.00	5.00-	9.00
☐ Twiggs, David E.	40.00-	65.00	15.00-	22.00	4.00-	7.00
☐ Waterhouse, Richard	50.00-	75.00	15.00-	22.00	5.00-	8.00
☐ Welles, Gideon	75.00-	110.00	22.00-	28.00	5.00-	8.00
☐ Wheeler, Gen. Joseph	50.00-	75.00	22.00-	28.00	5.00-	8.00
☐ Winslow, Admiral John A.	75.00-	110.00	30.00-	39.00	5.00-	8.00
☐ Wool, John E.	50.00-	75.00	22.00-	28.00	3.00-	5.00

MISCELLANEOUS

	Current Price Range		P/Y Average
☐ Bayonet Scrabbard Tip, excavated	2.00	3.00	2.40
☐ Belt, Union, infantry, oval belt plate marked SNY, issued by the state of New York early in the war, black bridle leather belt	325.00	350.00	337.50
☐ Belt, Union, infantry, standard issue leather belt with U.S. oval buckle	75.00	80.00	77.50
☐ Belt Plate, rectangular with eagle motif, M1851, used from the 1850s into the early days of the Civil War	100.00	125.00	110.00
☐ Blanket, Union, Regular Army issue, medium brown, very fine condition	300.00	325.00	312.50

	Current Price Range		P/Y Average

☐ **Bond,** Confederate States of America, $500 coupon bond, issued under Act of February 17, 1864, vignette of sailing vessel, printed by Evans and Cogswell of Columbia, South Carolina **1100.00 1500.00 1275.00**

☐ **Bond,** Confederate States of America, $1,000 coupon bond, issued under Act of August 19, 1861, pictures C.G. Memminger, printed by B. Duncan of Columbia, South Carolina **60.00 80.00 67.00**

☐ **Bond,** State of Louisiana $500 coupon bond, issued under Act of January 13, 1862, typeset, signed by governor and other state officials, state seal vignette at upper center **185.00 230.00 205.00**

☐ **Book,** *The Story of the Fourth Regiment, Ohio Volunteer Cavalry,* 216 pages, published 1912 **5.00 7.00 5.60**

☐ **Books,** *Millers Photographic History,* set of ten volumes, contains original photographs on nearly every page, 8″ x 11″, each is around 350 pages, published in 1911, the classic Civil War reference work **330.00 350.00 340.00**

☐ **Buckle,** Confederate, forked tongue, found buried near Fredericksburg, Virginia, 3⅝″ x 2¼″ **190.00 200.00 195.00**

☐ **Bugle,** cavalry, solid brass, 8½″ **365.00 385.00 375.00**

☐ **Bugle,** infantry, 17¾″ **320.00 330.00 325.00**

☐ **Bullet,** .44 cal. Colt Dragoon .... **.60 1.00 .80**

☐ **As Above,** .44 cal. Colt Army .... **.80 1.35 1.05**

☐ **Bullet,** .52 cal. Sharps carbine .... **.60 1.00 .80**

☐ **Bullet,** .58 cal. Gardner, Confederate States of America .... **.75 1.25 1.00**

☐ **Bullet,** .58 cal. U.S. standard "minie ball" ... **.50 1.00 .75**

☐ **Candleholder,** camp, spike on bottom and side, cast iron, 4½″ **45.00 50.00 47.50**

☐ **Canteen,** smooth body pattern, tin spout, thought to be Confederate. It is very difficult to distinguish Union from Confederate canteens **50.00 65.00 54.00**

☐ **Cap Pouch,** black leather, stamped "Ohio" .. **70.00 100.00 82.00**

☐ **Card Game,** "The Commander of Our Forces," in multi colored box picturing Zouaves and ironclad ships, price is for specimen in box and with original instruction sheet **45.00 60.00 51.00**

☐ **Cartridge And Bullet,** .56 cal. Spencer carbine **2.00 3.00 2.40**

☐ **Cartridge Box,** black leather, brass U.S. box plate, tin inserts, average condition **35.00 45.00 38.00**

☐ **Cavalry Boots,** leather, very tall above-knee type, soft tops to conform with leg contour, square toes, high heels, spurs missing, 31″ high, pair **400.00 500.00 430.00**

☐ **Cavalry Bugle,** solid brass, dark patina, cord rings on inside of loops, 8½″ in length, diameter across bell 3⅝″ **300.00 400.00 335.00**

	Current Price Range		P/Y Average

□ **Drummers Plate,** solid brass, worn on drum sling, iron wire hooks, stamped in back is C.L. Carrington/AP/4th, excellent condition, 3¼ " wide by 3½ " high **225.00** **250.00** **237.50**

□ **Drumsticks,** rosewood, pair **90.00** **100.00** **95.00**

□ **Envelope,** at left a portrait of Liberty seated with sixth corp's badge, gold link, by Magnuss **20.00** **25.00** **21.75**
Note: Value is for specimen bearing a common or damaged postage stamp. A stamp of premium value would of course add value to the item as a whole.

□ **Flag,** Confederate, regimental battle flag of the Confederate Army of Northern Virginia, infantry size, 4' x 4', superb condition, very rare .... **9500.00** — —

□ **Flag,** Confederate, small version used to show patriotism during parades and rallies, polished cotton on wooden stick, 6" x 8", excellent condition, 1863 .... **65.00** **75.00** **70.00**

□ **Flag,** Confederate, small type used in local parades and celebrations, 8" x 11", with original carrying stick **50.00** **65.00** **54.00**

□ **Flask,** whiskey, Confederate, glass body with pewter top and cup which slides over lower half of flask, engraved, 7", marked on bottom by hand Richmond/1863/B.A./1st VA. REG. ... **175.00** **195.00** **185.00**

□ **Grape Shot,** solid iron, approximately 4½ " diameter **40.00** **55.00** **44.00**
Note: These come in various sizes, all the way up to huge ones that can hardly be lifted. One word of caution: not all are solid. Some are powder loaded and set with a percussion fuse. Even after 120 years they can still explode.

□ **Gun Wrench,** Springfield type, excavated ... **2.00** **3.00** **2.40**

□ **Holster,** Confederate, full flap holster for dragoon sized revolver, brass stud closure, single wide belt loop on back, typical reddish brown Richmond leather, excellent condition **475.00** **500.00** **487.50**

□ **Hook,** brass, for knapsack, excavated ...... **.50** **.75** **.62**

□ **Infantry Bugle,** brass, engraved, chain guard for mouthpiece, 17¾ " in length, 6" diameter across bell **225.00** **300.00** **260.00**

□ **Jacket,** Union, artillery shell, regulation issue, dark blue with red piping, twenty eagle buttons, fully lined, small to medium, excellent condition **475.00** **500.00** **487.50**

□ **Kit,** boot care, black japanned tin hinged case lid, contains three compartments which hold cake of saddle soap, chamois, and four brushes, marked Tiffany & Co. in gold letters on lid **185.00** **205.00** **195.00**

	Current Price Range		P/Y Average

☐ **Knapsack,** Confederate, box style, black oil cloth over wood frame with leather reinforced corners, white buff straps, imported from England, marked "S.Isaacs Campbell/London." . . . . — 150.00 · 170.00 · 160.00

☐ **Knapsack,** Union, so-called "softpack" without wooden frame, made of tar-covered fabric, leather straps and shoulder sling, sling has inspection stamp . . . . — 35.00 · 45.00 · 38.00

☐ **Lantern,** camp and signal, tin, japanned finish, scalloped peaked roof, cylindrical body with large glass lens on door, oil burner, wire loop handles, wire belt hook, 6½ ", excellent condition . . . . — 65.00 · 85.00 · 75.00

☐ **Letter,** Confederate, written by General John Bell Hood, commander of the Texas Cavalry, 8″ x 10″, dated March 2, 1864, framed . . . . . . — 175.00 · 185.00 · 180.00

☐ **Letter,** soldier's letter by Union Lieutenant writing to wife of a Colonel in his unit who was taken ill, reporting on his condition, has had fever averaging 103 for twenty days, 7¾ " x 12¼ ", August 16, 1863 . . . . — 16.00 · 20.00 · 17.00

Note: We list this specimen as an example only. Civil War soldiers' letters vary considerably in price depending on content.

☐ **Lincoln Portrait Bust,** stamped on copper sheet with very detailed relief, coated with frosted silver plate, applied to velvetized tin background and mounted in a circular frame of gilded plaster over wood, bust is 7″ high, frame is 16″ in diameter, done at the end of the Civil War, signed and dated, J. Powell, Patented 1865 . . . . — 250.00 · 270.00 · 260.00

☐ **Map,** Confederate, pocket map of Virginia published by West & Johnston in Richmond, 1862 . . . . — 325.00 · 350.00 · 337.50

☐ **Mirror,** cased, recovered from battlefield of Chicamauga . . . . — 35.00 · 45.00 · 38.00

☐ **Musket,** Confederate, 3 band rifled, marked Potts & Hunt, London, good condition . . . . . . — 775.00 · 825.00 · 800.00

☐ **Musket Hammer,** escavated . . . . — 3.00 · 4.00 · 3.50

Note: Whenever a Civil War relic is identified by a dealer as "excavated," this means it was in the ground for a century or more and is rusty, twisted, etc.

☐ **Naval Cutlass,** model 1860, brass hilt, half-basket guard, leather grip, blade dated 1862 and hallmarked U.S.N. . . . . — 210.00 · 265.00 · 230.00

☐ **Officers Frock Coat,** Union, field grade officers model, regulation army, finest quality materials and workmanship, double breasted with eighteen buttons bearing the Rhode Island state seal, excellent condition . . . . — 600.00 · 650.00 · 625.00

	Current Price Range		P/Y Average
☐ **Stereopticon Photo,** view of contraband camp at Harper's Ferry, Virginia, #369 from the John Soule series of Civil War views, 1865	26.00	34.00	28.75
☐ **Stereopticon Photo,** view of the headquarters of General Meade at the battle of Gettysburg, #557 from the W.H. Tipton series of Gettysburg views, undated	25.00	30.00	26.75
☐ **Stereopticon Photo,** view of the interior of Fort Sumpter looking toward Morris Island, #343 from the John Soule series of Civil War views, 1865	25.00	30.00	26.00
☐ **Sword,** Foot Officer's, double sided engraved blade, American eagle and floral patterns on one side of blade, Union inscription, leather grip, leather scabbard	280.00	335.00	300.00
☐ **Sword Belt,** Confederate, consists of two piece sword belt plate on original belt, plate marked CS	975.00	1000.00	987.50
☐ **Sword,** officers, staff and field, rayskin grips, Horstmann blade, etched eagle, scabbard is brass mounted steel	650.00	660.00	655.00
☐ **Trousers,** red wool for Zouaves or other units wearing red tousers, part machine and part hand sewn, pewter buttons, believed to be made in France	600.00	800.00	675.00

CLOCKS

TOPIC: Clocks, of course, are devices that measure time in hours, minutes and sometimes seconds. Usually they have circular faces with arabic or roman numerals. Two or three hands on the face is standard.

TYPES: There are numerous types of clocks, including alarm clocks, atmospheric clocks, dresser clocks, gingerbread clocks, tall case (Grandfather) clocks, mantel clocks, regulator clocks, travel clocks and wall clocks.

PERIOD: Most collectors focus on 18th and 19th century clocks. Domestic clocks originated around the 1500s.

ORIGIN: Clocks developed in Europe.

MATERIALS: Clock cases may be of wood, glass, plastic, metal or porcelain. The workings are porcelain. The workings are metal.

MAKERS: Seth Thomas is one of the most famous clockmakers from New England. Well known clock companies include: Ansonia, W.L. Gilbert, E. Ingraham, Jerome, New Haven and Waterbury.

COMMENTS: Clocks cover a great range of sizes, varieties and designs. The collector can focus on a specific type of clock, such as a wall clock, and further specialize in banjo style specimens.

ADDITIONAL TIPS: The listings are arranged in the following order: type of clock, manufacturer, style, material, description, dimensions and date. For further information, please refer to *The Official Price Guide to Antique Clocks.*

Ingraham 8 Day Clock, *strikes half hour and hour,* **$90.00-$125.00**

	Current Price Range		P/Y Average
☐ **Alarm Clock,** Victorian, cherrywood	35.00	56.00	45.50
☐ **Atmospheric Clock,** Lecoultre, brass and glass, 9½ " H.	225.00	300.00	262.00
☐ **Carriage Clock,** French, hourly bell, one piece case, 6½ " H., c. 1845	950.00	1050.00	1000.00
☐ **Carriage Clock,** French, porcelain, 6¼ " H., c. 1880	2100.00	2500.00	2300.00
☐ **Carriage Clock,** French, by Margaine, gilded brass, 7" H.	1000.00	1250.00	1125.00
☐ **Carriage Clock,** Japan, tin, music box alarm, 6" H., 5¼ " W.	55.00	75.00	65.00
☐ **Carriage Clock,** tin, music box alarm, 6" x 5½ "	40.00	60.00	50.00
☐ **Carriage Clock,** Waterbury, gilded metal, 6" H.	180.00	235.00	207.00

	Current Price Range		P/Y Average
☐ **Dresser Clock,** New Haven, Art Noveau, 7¼″ H.	40.00	55.00	48.00
☐ **Dresser Clock,** Gilbert, wood, key wind, 8″ x 5″	15.00	25.00	20.00
☐ **Dresser Clock,** Western Clock Company, brass, 5″ H.	25.00	40.00	32.00
☐ **Gingerbread Clock,** elaborate decoration	110.00	135.00	122.00
☐ **Gingerbread Clock,** Gilbert, grape design	110.00	130.00	120.00
☐ **Gingerbread Clock,** Victorian, oak, eglomise painting, 21″ x 14″	70.00	100.00	85.00
☐ **Mantel Clock,** American, onyx, c. 1880	175.00	250.00	212.00
☐ **Mantel Clock,** American Bisque, wedgwood style, c. 1865	175.00	245.00	210.00
☐ **Mantel Clock,** Ansonia, ceramic	175.00	225.00	200.00
☐ **Mantel Clock,** Ansonia, slate, gilded, 15″ x 10″ x 6″	245.00	295.00	270.00
☐ **Mantel Clock,** French, Art Deco, brass and marble, c. 1900	350.00	450.00	400.00
☐ **Mantel Clock,** Empire, 14″ H., 9½″ W.	40.00	60.00	50.00
☐ **Mantel Clock,** French, bronze and beveled glass, key wind, 10½″ H.	265.00	345.00	305.00
☐ **Mantel Clock,** French, by Chardon, bronze, on rhinoceros base, 18″ H., 13½″ L.	1750.00	2300.00	1900.00
☐ **Mantel Clock,** French, d'ore bronze, porcelain plaques, 14″ H., 14″ W.	1200.00	1550.00	1325.00
☐ **Mantel Clock,** French, Empire, bronze, 18¼″ H., c. 1815	850.00	950.00	900.00
☐ **Mantel Clock,** French, Empire, gilt metal, 18½″ H.	70.00	100.00	85.00
☐ **Mantel Clock,** French, marble and d'ore bronze, pillars, 24″ H.	550.00	650.00	600.00
☐ **Mantel Clock,** German, mahogany, scrolled, 21½″ L.	80.00	120.00	100.00
☐ **Mantel Clock,** Ingraham, banjo shape, 40″	320.00	400.00	360.00
☐ **Mantel Clock,** Ingraham, wood, black, gilt	125.00	200.00	162.00
☐ **Mantel Clock,** Italian, baroque, brass 15″ H.	200.00	280.00	240.00
☐ **Mantel Clock,** marble and onyx, columns, 10¾″ H., 1800s	55.00	85.00	70.00
☐ **Mantel Clock,** Parisien, bronze, pendulum, 24″ H.	3600.00	4100.00	3850.00
☐ **Mantel Clock,** rococo, porcelain, painted, 11½″ H., c. 1900	225.00	265.00	245.00
☐ **Mantel Clock,** Sessions	40.00	55.00	48.00
☐ **Mantel Clock,** Seth Thomas, key wind, domed case	30.00	50.00	40.00
☐ **Mantel Clock,** Seth Thomas, marbleized, lions	60.00	85.00	72.00
☐ **Mantel Clock,** Seth Thomas, pillars and scrolls, 32″ H., 16½″ W., 1800s	175.00	250.00	200.00
☐ **Mantel Clock,** Victorian, rococo, gilt metal, 11½″ H.	120.00	150.00	135.00
☐ **Mantel Clock,** Victorian, walnut, pendulum, 19½″ x 12″	225.00	325.00	275.00
☐ **Mantel Clock,** Waterbury, pillars and ornaments	40.00	60.00	50.00

	Current Price Range		P/Y Average
☐ **Regulator Clock,** Waterbury, mahogany, pendulum, 22″	180.00	230.00	205.00
☐ **Tall Case Clock,** Chippendale, Boston, mahogany, calendar, seconds dial, 94½″ H., 17½″ W., 8½″ Dp., c. 1800	7500.00	8000.00	7750.00
☐ **Tall Case Clock,** Colonial Manufacturing Company, German works, 73¼″ H.	800.00	1100.00	950.00
☐ **Tall Case Clock,** Federal, Massachusetts, maple, 85″ H., 17½″ W., 10½″ Dp., c. 1800 .	2700.00	3200.00	2950.00
☐ **Tall Case Clock,** Jacobean, Colonial Manufacturing Company, oak, German works, strikes on the quarter hour, half hour and hour, 86″ H., 20¼″ W.	1300.00	1750.00	1525.00
☐ **Travel Clock,** Swiss, silver, 3½″ x 3″	50.00	85.00	67.00
☐ **Wall Clock,** Gilbert, calendar, for a school, octagonal, 24½″ H.	80.00	130.00	105.00
☐ **Wall Clock,** Dutch, friese, painted, 41¾″ H., c. 1865	190.00	400.00	295.00
☐ **Wall Clock,** Dutch, Stoeltjes, wood and lead, gilded, pendulum, c. 1860	200.00	300.00	250.00
☐ **Wall Clock,** French, brass, round, strikes on hour, pendulum	325.00	475.00	400.00
☐ **Wall Clock,** German, walnut, 38″ H.	190.00	290.00	240.00
☐ **Wall Clock,** New Haven, banjo shape, 30″ H. .	100.00	140.00	120.00
☐ **Wall Clock,** New Haven, banjo shape, 33″ H. .	110.00	160.00	135.00
☐ **Wall Clock,** Sessions, banjo shape, 28″ H. . . .	130.00	150.00	140.00
☐ **Wall Clock,** Tiffany, New York, bronze, banjo shape, 38″ H., 1800s	5000.00	5700.00	5350.00
☐ **Wall Clock,** Victorian, painted, gilded, 11″ diameter	40.00	60.00	50.00

CLOTHING

DESCRIPTION: Vintage clothing is collected by those who wish to add it to their wardrobes as well as by collectors who wish only to display it.

VARIATIONS: Clothes of all ages are collectible. Currently, the most sought after are Victorian era clothes as well as clothes from the 1920s, 1930s and 1940s.

MATERIALS: Among the popular material types collected are silk, taffeta, silk velvet, chiffon, crepe de chine and beadwork. Current fashions rarely are made of such fine fabrics so such clothes are especially collectible.

COMMENTS: As with any collectible, clothing becomes less valuable when damaged. Alterations and construction details are factors in determining price, while skilled workmanship or handmade trims often increase value. Clothing with beadwork is also a good investment.

CARE AND CONDITION: Vintage clothing requires careful handling. Textiles are perishable: light, humidity, dust and body oil are potentially harmful. The acids in wood, cardboard and tissue paper can also hurt clothing. When storing pieces, it is best to wrap items in white sheets and use mothballs. Hang lightweight clothing on padded hangers, and store heavy clothing flat.

ADDITIONAL TIPS: The listings are alphabetical according to clothing item. Also included is a description and, when available, date. For further information on vintage clothing, contact The Costume Society of America, c/o The Costume Institute, The Metropolitan Museum of Art, NY, NY 10028.

Vintage Jacket, *black bouclé with ecru cotton lace insert,* $40.00-$50.00

	Current Price Range		P/Y Average
☐ **Apron,** embroidered, Hungarian, c. 1930	32.00	45.00	38.00
☐ **Baby Shoes,** hand stitched satin shoes with mocassin style lowers and double ribbon drawstring through uppers	10.00	20.00	13.00
☐ **Baby Shoes,** kidskin leather button shoes, three buttons on uppers, c. 1880	35.00	65.00	45.00
☐ **Baby Shoes,** velvet top button shoes, leather lowers, five buttons on uppers, c. 1880	50.00	75.00	60.00

	Current Price Range		P/Y Average
☐ **Baby Slippers,** white kid Mary Janes, strap, fastened with mother-of-pearl button, soft leather sole	30.00	50.00	40.00
☐ **Bonnet,** for Christening, lace with white silk tie ribbons	25.00	45.00	35.00
☐ **Coin Purse,** nickel plated metal with mother-of-pearl panels, compartments in red leatherette	12.00	20.00	14.00
☐ **Dress,** black faille damask, cap sleeves, tie belt, c. 1940	50.00	90.00	60.00
☐ **Dress,** floor length, horizontal stripes and metallic thread, tiered	60.00	100.00	80.00
☐ **Dress,** for child, tucked bib, lace trim, embroidered	30.00	60.00	40.00
☐ **Dress,** handmade traveling dress, c. 1890s ..	200.00	240.00	210.00
☐ **Dress,** for infant, lace, long sleeves	20.00	50.00	35.00
☐ **Dress,** for infant, scalloped collar, embroidered	25.00	50.00	37.00
☐ **Dress and Jacket,** blue lace over rose, velvet ribbon straps, short jacket	40.00	75.00	55.00
☐ **Evening Bag,** Victorian, crochet flowers, metal beads	115.00	130.00	120.00
☐ **Evening Bag,** Victorian, petit point flowers on silk	115.00	130.00	122.00
☐ **Gloves,** cotton crochet, c. 1890	14.50	22.00	16.00
☐ **Gloves,** long, brown suede	8.00	16.00	11.00
☐ **Gloves,** short, white kid	8.00	16.00	13.00
☐ **Gloves,** white cotton	8.00	16.00	13.00
☐ **Hat,** fox fur	15.00	30.00	18.00
☐ **Hat,** man's beaver top hat	45.00	65.00	55.00
☐ **Mantilla,** Blonde de Caen lace, cream colored, c. 1820	120.00	160.00	130.00
☐ **Mantilla,** black lace	45.00	60.00	53.00
☐ **Purse,** clear crystal beads, white cloth liner, drawstring, beaded decoration, c. 1920s	20.00	40.00	30.00
☐ **Robe,** embroidered silk, Japanese, c. 1890 ..	282.00	350.00	300.00
☐ **Shawl,** peach silk, bright silk embroidered flowers, c. 1920s	165.00	225.00	180.00
☐ **Skirt,** crocheted, floor length, fringed bottom	30.00	50.00	40.00
☐ **Wedding Gown,** lace, satin, pearls and white beaded flowers, high neck, cap sleeves, train, c. 1960s	75.00	150.00	100.00

COCA-COLA COLLECTIBLES

DESCRIPTION: Coca-Cola collectibles are any items made by or for the largest soft drink company in the world, the Coca-Cola Company. Although this company produces several types of cola, its most popular soft drink is Coke.

ORIGIN: The Coca-Cola Company produced its first Coke in Atlanta, GA in 1886. It was created by John Pemberton, an Atlanta pharmacist. The familiar Coca-Cola logo was created by Pemberton's bookkeeper, Frank Robinson.

COMMENTS: Although the company produced thousands of different items promoting its soft drinks, because of the large number of Coca-Cola collectors, many items are valued higher than similar objects for other soft drink company's advertising memorabilia.

	Current Price Range		P/Y Average
☐ **Ashtray,** aluminum, c. 1955	3.00	6.00	3.00
☐ **Ashtray And Match Holder,** c. 1940	180.00	200.00	177.00
☐ **Ashtray,** metal, c. 1963	18.00	22.00	17.50
☐ **Ashtray,** Mexican, painted aluminum	3.00	4.00	2.50
☐ **Ashtray,** picture of Atlanta plant	18.00	22.00	20.00
☐ **Ashtray,** set of card suites, c. 1940	55.00	60.00	52.00
☐ **Badge,** Coca-Cola Vendor's License, brass 1¾"	1.00	4.00	3.00
☐ **Bank,** Coca-Cola, metal cap	1.00	2.00	1.50
☐ **Bank,** pop bottle machine, tin	28.00	38.00	30.00
☐ **Bingo Game**	55.00	65.00	55.00
☐ **Blackboard,** c. 1939	38.00	48.00	40.00
☐ **Blotter,** "Delicious and Refreshing," c. 1904	11.00	14.00	10.50
☐ **Blotter,** "Duster Girl" in auto, c. 1904	11.00	14.00	10.50
☐ **Blotter,** "Icy Style COLD Refreshment," c. 1939	7.00	9.00	7.00
☐ **Blotter,** "Restores Energy and Strengthens Nerves," c. 1906	9.00	11.00	9.00
☐ **Blotter,** Santa Claus with children, c. 1938	7.00	9.00	8.00

Radio, *speaker behind Coca-Cola logo, 1930s,* **$325.00-$350.00**

	Current Price Range		P/Y Average
☐ **Blotter,** Sprite with bottle-top hat, c. 1953 . . .	3.25	4.25	3.50
☐ **Blotter,** Sprite with bottle-top hat, c. 1956 . . .	2.25	3.25	2.50
☐ **Book Cover,** c. 1939	6.50	8.50	7.00
☐ **Book Cover,** c. 1951	6.00	8.00	6.00
☐ **Bookmark,** Coke can, c. 1960	9.00	12.00	9.00
☐ **Bookmark,** Hilda Clark, c. 1899	140.00	160.00	142.00
☐ **Bookmark,** Hilda Clark, c. 1900	135.00	155.00	138.00
☐ **Bookmark,** little girl with bird house, c. 1904 .	160.00	180.00	160.00
☐ **Bookmark,** Lillian Russel, c. 1904	80.00	90.00	80.00
☐ **Bookmark,** owl on perch, c. 1906	105.00	115.00	100.00
☐ **Bookmark,** Valentine, c. 1899	110.00	130.00	110.00
☐ **Bookmark,** Victorian Lady	175.00	190.00	172.00
☐ **Bottle Holder Protector,** paper envelope, c. 1932	6.00	8.00	6.00
☐ **Bottle Holder Protector,** six bottle type, c. 1933	38.00	45.00	37.50
☐ **Bottle,** "Best by a Dam Site," c. 1936	38.00	45.00	37.50
☐ **Bottle,** light green, c. 1905	12.00	16.00	11.00
☐ **Bottle,** applied paper label, c. 1915	38.00	42.00	37.50
☐ **Bottle,** display 20″ H., red or clear, c. 1923 . . .	125.00	235.00	120.00
☐ **Bottle,** Donald Duck, 7 oz., painted	5.00	10.00	6.00

	Current Price Range		P/Y Average
□ **Cigarette Lighter,** aluminum, c. 1963	8.00	12.00	8.50
□ **Cigarette Lighter,** Coke bottle shape, c. 1940	9.00	14.00	10.00
□ **Cigarette Lighter,** Coke can, c. 1950	28.00	32.00	27.50
□ **Cigarette Lighter,** music box plays "Dixie" . .	20.00	28.00	22.00
□ **Cigarette Lighter,** musical, c. 1960	30.00	38.00	32.00
□ **Clock,** brass mantle type, c. 1954	95.00	125.00	190.00
□ **Clock,** dome style, c. 1950	185.00	200.00	192.00
□ **Clock,** electric brass wall model, c. 1915	260.00	310.00	270.00
□ **Clock,** leather boudoir, c. 1919	220.00	260.00	230.00
□ **Clock,** re-issue of Betty, c. 1974	55.00	75.00	65.00
□ **Clock,** small boudoir style, c. 1915	250.00	270.00	250.00
□ **Clock,** spring operated wall style, brass pendulum	310.00	360.00	325.00
□ **Clock,** walnut wall model, c. 1960	225.00	250.00	225.00
□ **Cooler,** c. 1930	310.00	385.00	340.00
□ **Cuff Links,** bottle cap, c. 1954	8.00	12.00	9.00
□ **Cuff Links,** blue pearl	75.00	90.00	78.00
□ **Cuff Links,** gold burnish links and tie clip, c. 1952	14.00	18.00	14.00
□ **Cuff Links,** salesman's sterling silver links and tie tack, c. 1930	55.00	65.00	55.00
□ **Cuff Links,** sterling silver, c. 1923	50.00	60.00	48.00
□ **Cutouts,** uncut, c. 1930	85.00	115.00	92.00
□ **Cutouts,** uncut, c. 1932	55.00	80.00	62.00
□ **Dice,** white and red imprint, pair	1.00	2.00	1.50
□ **Door Pull,** bottle shape	48.00	58.00	50.00
□ **Flashlight,** bottle shaped plastic	6.00	8.00	6.00
□ **Fountain Dispenser**	85.00	120.00	85.00
□ **Glass,** 5¢ with arrow, c. 1905	130.00	155.00	132.00
□ **Glass,** flair type, c. 1900	185.00	195.00	180.00
□ **Glass,** flair lip, c. 1923	35.00	45.00	35.00
□ **Glass,** fountain type with syrup line, c. 1900 .	52.00	62.00	55.00
□ **Glass,** fountain type, no syrup line	8.00	12.00	8.50
□ **Glass,** home promotion type, red and white .	4.00	6.00	4.00
□ **Glass,** pewter, c. 1930	72.00	82.00	75.00
□ **Ice Pick And Opener,** c. 1940	8.00	12.00	8.50
□ **Key Chain,** amber replica bottle with brass chain, c. 1964	6.00	8.00	6.00
□ **Key Chain,** car key style, c. 1950	28.00	32.00	27.50
□ **Key Chain,** red with gold bottle, c. 1955	18.00	28.00	20.00
□ **Key Chain,** 50th Anniversary Celebration, c. 1936	12.00	18.00	12.50
□ **Knife,** pocket, "Enjoy Coca-Cola"	80.00	110.00	82.00
□ **Knife,** pocket, two blades	12.00	18.00	12.50
□ **Menu Board,** tin, c. 1940	42.00	62.00	50.00
□ **Milk Glass,** light shade, c. 1920	385.00	410.00	382.00
□ **Mirror,** pocket-size, "Bathing Beauty," c. 1918	285.00	300.00	282.00
□ **Mirror,** pocket-size, "Betty," c. 1914	110.00	130.00	110.00
□ **Mirror,** pocket-size, "Coca-Cola Girl," c. 1909	130.00	150.00	135.00
□ **Mirror,** pocket-size, "Coca-Cola Girl," c. 1911	130.00	150.00	130.00
□ **Mirror,** pocket-size, "Drink Coca-Cola 5¢," c. 1914	260.00	285.00	262.00
□ **Mirror,** pocket-size, "Elaine," c. 1917	155.00	165.00	155.00
□ **Mirror,** pocket-size, "Enjoy Thirst," c. 1930 . .	80.00	95.00	82.00
□ **Mirror,** pocket-size, "Garden Girl," c. 1920 . . .	260.00	285.00	262.00
□ **Mirror,** pocket-size, "Juanita," oval, c. 1905 . .	195.00	210.00	292.00

	Current Price Range		P/Y Average
Mirror, pocket-size, "Lillian Russel," round, c. 1904	72.00	82.00	75.00
Mirror, pocket-size, oval, c. 1903	140.00	160.00	140.00
Mirror, pocket-size, "Relieves Fatigue," c. 1906	160.00	190.00	170.00
Mirror, pocket-size, "St. Louis Exposition," c. 1904	110.00	120.00	105.00
Mirror, pocket-size, "St. Louis Fair," c. 1904	135.00	150.00	138.00
Music Box, cooler, c. 1951	55.00	80.00	62.00
Note Book, brown leather, embossed, c. 1903	280.00	360.00	372.00
Note Pad, celluloid covered, c. 1902	80.00	100.00	85.00
Opener, bone handle knife, c. 1908	140.00	160.00	140.00
Opener, Nashville Anniversary, c. 1952	55.00	70.00	58.00
Opener, skate key style, c. 1935	38.00	48.00	40.00
Opener, "Starr X," c. 1925	3.00	5.00	3.00
Opener, stationary wall model, c. 1900	22.00	28.00	22.00
Paperweight, Coca-Cola gum, c. 1916	80.00	90.00	80.00
Paperweight, "Coke is Coca-Cola," c. 1948	75.00	95.00	80.00
Paperweight, hollow glass, tin bottom, c. 1909	260.00	285.00	262.00
Pen, ball point with telephone dialer	6.00	8.00	6.00
Pen, baseball bat, c. 1940	22.00	33.00	25.00
Pencil Box, c. 1930	40.00	55.00	42.00
Pencil Holder, celluloid, c. 1910	130.00	140.00	130.00
Pencil Holder, miniature ceramic, c. 1960	70.00	80.00	70.00
Pencil Holder, tin, c. 1925	4.50	7.00	5.00
Pencil Sharpener, plastic, c. 1960	6.00	12.00	7.50
Pencil Sharpener, red metal, c. 1933	14.00	18.00	13.50
Playing Cards, Airplane Spatter, (deck), c. 1942	12.00	18.00	11.00
Playing Cards, Coca Cola Girls, (deck), c. 1909	52.00	62.00	55.00
Plate, glass and Coke bottle, c. 1920	70.00	85.00	72.00
Pocket Knife, Chicago World's Fair, 3½"	1.00	3.00	2.00
Pocket Knife, Coca Cola in bottles, 3½"	1.00	3.00	2.00
Pocket Knife, picture of Coke bottle, 3½"	1.00	3.00	2.00
Pocket Secretary, leather bound, c. 1920	32.00	42.00	35.00
Postcard, "All Over the World," c. 1913	115.00	125.00	112.00
Postcard, "Duster Girl" driving car, c. 1906	95.00	105.00	95.00
Postcard, girl with picture hat, c. 1909	28.00	38.00	30.00
Postcard, horse and delivery wagon, c. 1900	130.00	150.00	130.00
Postcard, men in speedboat, c. 1913	105.00	120.00	105.00
Postcard, picture of bottling plant, c. 1905	120.00	140.00	120.00
Postcard, school teacher at blackboard, c. 1913	88.00	98.00	90.00
Postcard, truck carrying cases of Coke, c. 1913	135.00	155.00	135.00
Postcard Set, Dick Tracy series, c. 1942	140.00	160.00	145.00
Poster, "Bathing Beauty," c. 1918	410.00	435.00	412.00
Poster, "Betty," c. 1914	260.00	280.00	260.00
Poster, "Early Display with Young Lovers," c. 1891	460.00	490.00	465.00
Poster, "Flapper Girl," c. 1929	160.00	180.00	160.00
Poster, "Florine McKinney," c. 1936	40.00	50.00	40.00
Poster, "Girl in Hammock," c. 1900	435.00	460.00	438.00
Poster, "Hilda Clark Cuban," c. 1901	310.00	335.00	312.00

	Current Price Range		P/Y Average
☐ **Tray,** "Hilda Clark," c. 1904	260.00	285.00	262.00
☐ **Tray,** "Johnny Weismuller and Maureen O'Sullivan," c. 1934	185.00	210.00	188.00
☐ **Tray,** "Juanita," round, c. 1905	150.00	175.00	158.00
☐ **Tray,** "Olympic Games," 15″ x 11″, c. 1976 ...	12.00	18.00	12.50
☐ **Tray** (serving), plastic, c. 1971	50.00	60.00	52.00
☐ **Tray,** replica of "Duster Girl," c. 1972	28.00	42.00	32.00
☐ **Tray,** "Sailor Girl," c. 1940	28.00	42.00	32.00
☐ **Tray,** "Saint Louis Fair," oval, c. 1904	160.00	190.00	170.00
☐ **Tray,** "Santa Claus," 15″ x 11″, c. 1973	22.00	32.00	25.00
☐ **Tray,** "Soda Fountain Clerk," c. 1927	80.00	110.00	82.00
☐ **Tray,** "Springboard Girl," c. 1939	45.00	60.00	46.00
☐ **Tray,** "Summer Girl," c. 1921	185.00	235.00	200.00
☐ **Tray,** T.V., candle design, c. 1972	20.00	28.00	21.00
☐ **Tray,** T.V., picnic basket	28.00	38.00	30.00
☐ **Tray,** T.V., Thanksgiving motif, c. 1961	20.00	28.00	21.00
☐ **Tray,** "Topless," c. 1908	510.00	710.00	600.00
☐ **Tray,** "Two Girls at Car," c. 1942	32.00	42.00	35.00
☐ **Tray,** "Vienna Art Nude," c. 1905	210.00	285.00	238.00
☐ **Tray,** "Western Bottling Co.," c. 1905	110.00	160.00	125.00
☐ **Vendor's Umbrella,** "Pause that Refreshes" .	135.00	160.00	138.00
☐ **Wallet,** Coke bottle emblem, c. 1915	75.00	85.00	75.00
☐ **Wallet,** Coca-Cola script, c. 1922	88.00	98.00	90.00
☐ **Wallet,** embossed coin purse, c. 1906	150.00	165.00	148.00
☐ **Watch Fob,** bulldog, c. 1925	55.00	85.00	65.00
☐ **Watch Fob,** "Drink Coca-Cola in Bottles" ...	60.00	80.00	65.00

COINS

DESCRIPTION: Coins are metallic objects, usually circular, designed as a medium of exchange. The earlier series of U.S. coins comprised base metal for the lowest denominations; silver for the medium to high denominations; and gold for very high denominations, up to $20. Today, all U.S. coins, regardless of denomination, are made of base metal; neither silver nor gold is used. For present-day U.S. coins of 10¢ and higher denominations, a nickel exterior coating is bonded to a copper interior. The front of a coin, which on U.S. issues carries a portrait, is called the "obverse." The back is the "reverse."

PERIOD: U.S. coins were first struck in 1793, though earlier coins issued by the colonial governments had preceded them. They have been struck continually since then, though with various changes in denominations and of course in designs. The U.S. has had coins with face values of 2¢, 3¢, 20¢ and other odd amounts.

MATERIALS: When precious metal was used in U.S. coins, it was usually a .900 grade. That is, silver coins were 90% silver vs. 10% copper; gold coins were 90% gold vs. 10% copper. The very earliest U.S. coins did not precisely conform to these standards, but all later ones did. Thus the term "coin silver" means .900 silver.

MARKS: While there are numerous types of marks that could potentially be found on coins (double strikes, small letters, etc.), the most frequent are the "Mint marks," which are placed intentionally. These are small letters indicating the Mint from which that particular coin has originated, such as S for San francisco and D for Denver. Traditionally the Mint did not place any mark on its Philadelphia coins, but this practice has been changed in recent years.

ADDITIONAL TIPS: Do not attempt to clean or polish coins; the surfaces are much more delicate than you may imagine and can be easily injured. Though coin collecting is a hobby and pastime, coin *buying* is more akin to a science. Coin fakes are very numerous, often of high quality and undetectable except by a trained expert. It is therefore important to buy, as much as possible, from the recognized coin dealers rather than from flea markets or other questionable sources.

The following values were compiled with silver selling in the range of $8 to $10 per ounce. In the following listings, ABP means Average Buying Price.

For a complete explanation of coins, see *The Official Blackbook Price Guide to U.S. Coins,* published by The House of Collectibles.

SMALL CENTS — INDIAN HEAD, 1859-1887

DATE	MINTAGE	ABP	G-4 Good	F-12 Fine	EF-40 Ex. Fine	MS-60 Unc.	PRF-65 Proof
☐ 1859 Copper-Nickel	36,400,000	3.50	5.00	9.50	62.00	300.00	4375.00
☐ 1860 Copper-Nickel	20,566,000	2.00	4.00	7.50	23.00	135.00	2750.00
☐ 1861 Copper-Nickel	10,100,000	4.50	8.50	17.00	42.00	215.00	2750.00
☐ 1862 Copper-Nickel	28,075,000	1.50	3.00	6.00	20.00	110.00	2750.00
☐ 1863 Copper-Nickel	49,840,000	1.50	2.75	5.00	18.00	110.00	2750.00
☐ 1864 Copper-Nickel	13,740,000	4.00	7.50	13.00	34.00	145.00	2750.00
☐ 1864 Bronze	39,233,714	1.50	3.00	8.00	28.00	100.00	2500.00
☐ 1864 L on Ribbon		16.00	37.00	60.00	140.00	360.00	15000.00
☐ 1865	35,429,286	1.25	2.75	7.00	26.00	78.00	1300.00
☐ 1866	9,826,500	11.00	22.00	35.00	95.00	275.00	1300.00
☐ 1867	9,821,000	11.00	22.00	35.00	95.00	275.00	1300.00
☐ 1868	10,266,500	11.00	22.00	35.00	95.00	275.00	1300.00
☐ 1869	6,420,000	15.00	32.00	72.00	170.00	400.00	1400.00
☐ 1869 over 8		42.00	80.00	220.00	500.00	1300.00	
☐ 1870	5,275,000	10.00	24.00	52.00	115.00	285.00	1425.00
☐ 1871	3,929,500	17.00	33.00	70.00	125.00	330.00	1425.00
☐ 1872	4,042,000	23.00	40.00	80.00	170.00	410.00	1425.00
☐ 1873	11,676,500	3.50	8.50	17.00	45.00	155.00	1200.00
☐ 1873 Doubled Liberty						EXTREMELY RARE	
☐ 1874	14,187,500	3.50	7.00	16.00	57.00	155.00	1200.00
☐ 1875	13,528,000	3.50	7.00	16.00	62.00	155.00	1200.00

Nickel, *Liberty Head, issued 1883-1912,* **$20.00-$1500.00**

DATE	MINTAGE	ABP	G-4 Good	F-12 Fine	EF-40 Ex. Fine	MS-60 Unc.	PRF-65 Proof
☐1876	7,944,000	4.50	11.00	23.00	52.00	185.00	1200.00
☐1877	852,500	130.00	250.00	450.00	825.00	1675.00	3750.00
☐1878	5,799,850	4.50	11.00	26.00	58.00	200.00	1200.00
☐1879	16,231,200	1.10	2.15	6.50	20.00	85.00	975.00
☐1880	38,964,955	.50	1.35	5.00	15.00	77.00	975.00
☐1881	39,211,575	.50	1.35	3.75	15.00	77.00	975.00
☐1882	38,581,100	.50	1.35	3.75	15.00	77.00	975.00
☐1883	45,598,109	.50	1.35	3.75	17.00	77.00	975.00
☐1884	23,261,742	.75	1.90	7.00	33.00	82.00	975.00
☐1885	11,765,384	1.25	3.50	9.00	38.00	95.00	975.00
☐1886	17,654,290	1.00	2.25	7.00	25.00	85.00	975.00
☐1887	45,226,483	.50	1.00	2.50	10.50	72.00	975.00

SMALL CENTS — LINCOLN HEAD, 1909-1920

(1909-1942 COMPOSITION-95 TIN AND ZINC)

DATE	MINTAGE	ABP	G-4 Good	F-12 Fine	EF-40 Ex. Fine	MS-60 Unc.	PRF-65 Proof
☐1909	72,702,618	.22	.45	.70	1.00	2.00	16.00	900.00
☐1909 V.D.B.	27,995,000	1.15	2.00	2.75	3.10	3.75	15.00	3000.00
☐1909S	1,825,000	20.00	42.00	55.00	70.00	90.00	210.00	
☐1909S V.D.B.	484,000	105.00	210.00	300.00	375.00	400.00	575.00	
☐1910	146,801,218	.08	.15	.35	.50	2.00	15.00	1500.00
☐1910S	6,045,000	2.50	5.00	9.00	12.00	20.00	85.00	
☐1911	101,177,787	.08	.20	.40	1.40	3.00	20.00	800.00
☐1911D	12,672,000	1.50	3.00	6.00	11.00	24.00	90.00	
☐1911S	4,026,000	6.00	10.00	15.00	19.00	30.00	140.00	
☐1912	68,153,060	.18	.30	1.50	3.50	6.00	37.00	700.00
☐1912D	10,411,000	1.65	3.75	7.00	12.00	27.00	150.00	
☐1912S	4,431,000	4.50	9.00	14.00	17.50	26.00	110.00	
☐1913	76,532,352	.15	.30	1.25	2.75	5.00	30.00	800.00

DATE	MINTAGE	ABP	G-4 Good	F-12 Fine	EF-40 Ex. Fine	MS-60 Unc.	PRF-65 Proof
☐1913D	15,804,000	1.00	2.00	4.00	6.00	18.00	75.00	
☐1913S	6,101,000	2.50	5.00	8.50	12.00	19.00	100.00	
☐1914	75,238,432	.20	.40	1.00	3.00	6.75	58.00	900.00
☐1914D	1,193,000	28.00	45.00	100.00	180.00	380.00	1000.00	
☐1914S	4,137,000	4.00	7.00	13.00	18.00	29.00	165.00	
☐1915	29,092,120	.35	.80	3.50	7.00	26.00	115.00	1350.00
☐1915D	22,050,000	.30	.70	1.25	3.75	10.00	45.00	
☐1915S	4,833,677	3.25	6.00	10.00	11.50	21.00	100.00	
☐1916	131,838,677	.07	.20	.25	.75	2.50	12.00	1575.00
☐1916D	35,956,000	.09	.17	1.15	1.75	6.00	50.00	
☐1916S	22,510,000	.35	.70	1.50	2.50	6.50	60.00	
☐1917	196,429,785	.07	.20	.30	.60	2.00	13.00	
☐1917D	55,120,000	.10	.23	.65	1.75	5.00	60.00	
☐1917S	32,620,000	.18	.37	.70	2.00	5.00	65.00	
☐1918	288,104,634	.07	.12	.40	.70	2.00	12.00	
☐1918D	47,830,000	.11	.20	.75	2.00	6.00	58.00	
☐1918S	34,680,000	.11	.20	.55	1.75	5.25	65.00	
☐1919	392,021,000	.06	.12	.25	.45	1.50	11.00	
☐1919D	57,154,000	.10	.20	.55	2.00	4.00	42.00	
☐1919S	139,760,000	.06	.12	.30	.65	2.50	45.00	
☐1920	310,165,000	.05	.09	.25	.45	1.50	11.50	
☐1920D	49,280,000	.07	.13	.50	1.50	3.50	55.00	
☐1920S	46,220,000	.07	.13	.35	1.50	3.25	67.00	

NICKELS — LIBERTY HEAD, 1883-1909

DATE	MINTAGE	ABP	G-4 Good	F-12 Fine	EF-40 Ex. Fine	MS-60 Unc.	PRF-65 Proof
☐1883 no cents	5,479,519	1.00	2.20	5.00	12.00	55.00	1850.00
☐1883 w/cents	16,032,983	4.00	7.00	15.00	40.00	310.00	1050.00
☐1884	11,273,942	4.25	8.00	18.00	47.00	320.00	1050.00
☐1885	1,476,490	165.00	320.00	575.00	1075.00	1400.00	2475.00
☐1886	3,330,290	24.00	55.00	139.00	300.00	600.00	1700.00
☐1887	15,263,652	3.50	7.00	22.00	42.00	310.00	1050.00
☐1888	10,720,483	4.00	9.00	21.00	50.00	310.00	1050.00
☐1889	15,881,361	2.25	5.00	20.00	40.00	310.00	1050.00
☐1890	16,259,272	2.25	5.00	18.00	40.00	310.00	1050.00
☐1891	16,834,350	2.00	4.50	17.00	40.00	310.00	1050.00
☐1892	11,699,642	2.25	4.75	20.00	40.00	310.00	1050.00
☐1893	13,370,195	2.25	4.50	19.00	40.00	310.00	1050.00
☐1894	5,413,132	3.00	6.00	25.00	80.00	330.00	1050.00
☐1895	9,979,884	2.00	4.00	23.00	45.00	315.00	1050.00
☐1896	8,842,920	2.25	4.50	24.00	45.00	320.00	1050.00
☐1897	20,428,735	.50	1.10	4.50	27.00	180.00	1050.00
☐1898	12,532,087	.50	1.15	4.50	25.00	260.00	1050.00
☐1899	26,029,031	.40	.80	3.25	25.00	118.00	1050.00
☐1900	27,255,995	.40	.80	3.25	25.00	118.00	1050.00
☐1901	26,480,213	.40	.80	3.25	25.00	118.00	1050.00
☐1902	31,480,579	.40	.80	3.25	25.00	118.00	1050.00
☐1903	28,006,725	.40	.80	3.25	25.00	118.00	1050.00
☐1904	21,404,984	.40	.80	3.25	25.00	118.00	1050.00
☐1905	29,827,276	.40	.80	3.25	25.00	118.00	1050.00
☐1906	38,613,725	.40	.80	3.25	25.00	118.00	1050.00
☐1907	39,214,800	.40	.80	3.25	25.00	118.00	1050.00
☐1908	22,686,177	.40	.80	3.25	25.00	118.00	1050.00
☐1909	11,590,526	.50	1.00	3.25	25.00	118.00	1050.00

DIMES — MERCURY DIMES, 1916-1927

DATE	MINTAGE	ABP	G-4 Good	F-12 Fine	EF-40 Ex. Fine	MS-60 Unc.	PRF-65 Proof
☐1916	22,180,000	.60	3.50	4.50	6.00	9.50	35.00
☐1916D	264,000	200.00	400.00	825.00	1150.00	1575.00	2325.00
☐1916S	10,450,000	.60	3.00	6.00	8.00	14.00	47.00
☐1917	55,230,000	.60	1.75	2.50	5.00	7.00	28.00
☐1917D	9,402,000	.60	3.00	7.00	12.00	30.00	100.00
☐1917S	27,330,000	.60	2.00	2.75	6.00	8.00	55.00
☐1918	26,680,000	.60	2.25	4.00	10.00	22.00	65.00
☐1918D	22,674,800	.60	2.25	3.75	8.00	18.00	80.00
☐1918S	19,300,000	.60	2.00	2.75	6.00	12.00	50.00
☐1919	35,740,000	.60	1.50	2.75	5.00	8.00	39.00
☐1919D	9,939,000	.60	3.50	5.50	13.75	32.00	120.00
☐1919S	8,850,000	.60	3.25	5.00	12.75	27.00	120.00
☐1920	59,030,000	.60	1.35	2.00	4.50	7.00	30.00
☐1920D	19,171,000	.60	2.20	4.00	6.50	14.00	65.00
☐1920S	13,820,000	.60	2.20	4.00	6.50	13.00	65.00
☐1921	1,230,000	11.00	20.00	63.00	115.00	330.00	775.00
☐1921D	1,080,000	15.00	32.00	85.00	160.00	350.00	775.00
☐1923*	50,130,000	.60	2.00	3.50	4.00	7.00	19.00
☐1923S	6,440,000	.60	2.20	4.00	7.00	18.00	75.00
☐1924	24,010,000	.60	2.00	3.50	4.50	7.00	50.00
☐1924D	6,810,000	.60	2.20	4.00	7.00	17.50	90.00
☐1924S	7,120,000	.60	2.15	4.00	6.00	16.00	85.00
☐1925	25,610,000	.60	2.15	3.50	4.00	7.00	40.00
☐1925D	5,117,000	2.00	5.00	8.00	20.00	65.00	235.00
☐1925S	5,850,000	.60	1.25	3.50	6.50	17.00	110.00
☐1926	32,160,000	.60	1.25	2.00	3.75	6.00	18.00
☐1926D	6,828,000	.60	1.25	4.00	6.00	14.00	65.00
☐1926S	1,520,000	4.00	8.00	15.00	30.00	75.00	365.00
☐1927	28,080,000	.60	1.00	1.50	4.00	5.50	18.00
☐1927D	4,812,000	.60	2.50	6.00	13.00	30.00	160.00

*All dimes with 23D date are counterfeit.

QUARTERS — WASHINGTON, 1932-1943

DATE	MINTAGE	ABP	G-4 Good	F-12 Fine	EF-40 Ex. Fine	MS-60 Unc.	PRF-65 Proof
☐1932	5,404,000	1.50	3.00	5.00	10.00	25.00	
☐1932D	436,800	22.00	42.00	75.00	185.00	550.00	
☐1932S	408,000	22.00	40.00	55.00	110.00	275.00	
☐1934	31,912,052	1.50	3.00	4.00	7.00	28.00	
☐1934 Double Die			35.00	45.00	100.00	250.00	
☐1934D	3,527,200	1.50	3.00	9.50	20.00	95.00	
☐1935	32,484,000	1.50		4.00	7.00	25.00	
☐1935D	5,780,000	1.50		8.00	18.00	90.00	
☐1935S	5,550,000	1.50		6.00	12.00	80.00	
☐1936	41,303,837	1.50		5.00	8.00	30.00	1150.00
☐1936D	5,374,000	1.50		10.00	30.00	200.00	
☐1936S	3,828,000	1.50		6.00	11.50	100.00	
☐1937	19,701,542	1.50		5.00	8.00	30.00	300.00
☐1937D	7,189,600	1.50		4.00	12.00	40.00	
☐1937S	1,652,000	1.50		8.00	20.00	125.00	
☐1938	9,480,045	1.50		5.00	15.00	65.00	275.00
☐1938S	2,832,000	1.50		6.00	11.00	55.00	
☐1939	33,548,795	1.50		3.50	7.00	16.00	180.00
☐1939D	7,092,000	1.50		4.00	9.00	35.00	
☐1939S	2,628,000	1.50		6.00	12.00	55.00	

DATE	MINTAGE	ABP	G-4 Good	F-12 Fine	EF-40 Ex. Fine	MS-60 Unc.	PRF-65 Proof
☐1940	35,715,246	1.50		4.00	6.00	15.00	120.00
☐1940D	2,797,600	1.50		7.00	16.00	80.00	
☐1940S	8,244,000	1.50		3.00	7.00	17.00	
☐1941	79,047,287	1.50		2.75	6.00	8.00	115.00
☐1941D	16,714,800	1.50		2.75	3.50	25.00	
☐1941S	16,080,000	1.50		2.75	3.50	25.00	
☐1942	102,117,123	1.50		2.75	3.50	7.00	115.00
☐1942D	17,487,200	1.50		2.75	3.50	15.00	
☐1942S	19,384,000	1.50		2.75	3.50	50.00	
☐1943	99,700,000	1.50		2.75	3.50	8.00	
☐1943D	16,095,600	1.50		2.75	3.50	16.00	

HALF DOLLARS — LIBERTY WALKING, 1916-1936

DATE	MINTAGE	ABP	G-4 Good	F-12 Fine	EF-40 Ex. Fine	MS-60 Unc.	PRF-65 Proof
☐1916	608,000	8.00	17.00	52.00	190.00	425.00	
☐1916D on obverse	1,014,400	4.00	9.00	30.00	130.00	380.00	
☐1916S on obverse	508,000	15.00	30.00	105.00	350.00	800.00	2400.00
☐1917	12,292,000	2.00	4.00	10.00	32.00	160.00	
☐1917D on obverse	765,400	3.00	8.00	25.00	160.00	500.00	
☐1917D on reverse	1,940,000	3.00	6.00	20.00	125.00	550.00	
☐1917S on obverse	952,000	7.00	11.00	30.00	350.00	1000.00	2400.00
☐1917S on reverse	6,554,000	2.00	4.00	15.00	45.00	265.00	
☐1918	6,634,000	2.00	4.00	8.75	115.00	360.00	
☐1918D	3,853,040	2.00	4.50	8.75	130.00	725.00	
☐1918S	10,282,000	2.00	4.00	8.50	42.00	275.00	
☐1919	962,000	3.00	9.50	31.00	350.00	1050.00	
☐1919D	1,165,000	3.00	9.00	30.00	400.00	2050.00	
☐1919S	1,552,000	3.00	7.00	20.00	350.00	1925.00	
☐1920	6,372,000	2.75	5.00	9.00	50.00	250.00	
☐1920D	1,551,000	2.75	5.00	25.00	250.00	1000.00	
☐1920S	4,624,000	2.75	5.00	6.00	105.00	850.00	
☐1921	246,000	35.00	65.00	200.00	1000.00	2150.00	
☐1921D	208,000	55.00	115.00	260.00	1100.00	2375.00	
☐1921S	548,000	7.00	13.00	35.00	1100.00	6750.00	
☐1923S	2,178,000	2.75	4.50	8.75	140.00	900.00	
☐1927S	2,393,000	2.75	4.50	8.75	75.00	800.00	
☐1928S	1,940,000	2.75	4.50	8.75	95.00	850.00	
☐1929D	1,001,200	2.75	4.50	8.75	70.00	360.00	
☐1929S	1,902,000	2.75	4.50	8.75	70.00	360.00	
☐1933S	1,786,000	2.75	4.50	8.75	55.00	360.00	
☐1934	6,964,000	2.75	4.00	5.75	12.00	90.00	
☐1934D	2,361,400	2.75	4.00	5.75	30.00	180.00	
☐1934S	3,652,000	2.75	4.00	5.75	22.00	350.00	
☐1935	9,162,000	2.75	4.00	5.75	15.00	75.00	
☐1935D	3,003,800	2.75	4.00	5.75	30.00	185.00	
☐1935S	2,854,000	2.75	4.00	5.75	22.00	230.00	
☐1936	12,617,901	2.75	4.00	5.75	11.00	65.00	2000.00

SILVER DOLLARS — LIBERTY HEAD or "MORGAN,"1878-1892

DATE	MINTAGE	ABP	G-4 Good	F-12 Fine	EF-40 Ex. Fine	MS-60 Unc.	PRF-65 Proof
☐1878 7 Tail Feathers	416,000		9.25	18.00	25.00	65.00	8350.00
☐1878 8 Tail Feathers	750,000		9.25	20.00	30.00	75.00	5775.00
☐1878 7 over 8 Tail Feathers			9.25	22.00	40.00	85.00	
☐1878CC	2,212,000		9.25	28.00	47.00	135.00	
☐1878S	9,774,000		9.25	18.00	20.00	65.00	
☐1879	14,807,100		9.25	16.00	20.00	55.00	6000.00
☐1879CC	756,000		35.00	65.00	260.00	890.00	

DATE	MINTAGE	ABP	G-4 Good	F-12 Fine	EF-40 Ex. Fine	MS-60 Unc.	PRF-65 Proof
☐1879O	2,887,000		9.25	15.50	19.00	60.00	
☐1879S	9,110,000		9.25	15.50	19.00	56.00	
☐1880	12,601,355		9.25	15.50	19.00	54.00	5500.00
☐1880CC	591,000		25.00	50.00	90.00	210.00	
☐1880 over 79CC			25.00	54.00	90.00	215.00	
☐1880O	5,305,000		9.25	15.50	19.00	85.00	
☐1880S	8,900,000		9.25	15.50	19.00	65.00	
☐1881	9,163,975		9.25	15.50	19.00	60.00	5500.00
☐1881CC	206,000		50.00	80.00	110.00	220.00	
☐1881O	5,708,000		9.25	16.00	20.00	55.00	
☐1881S	12,760,000		9.25	16.00	20.00	60.00	
☐1882	11,101,000		9.25	16.00	20.00	60.00	5500.00
☐1882CC	1,133,000		17.00	30.00	50.00	110.00	
☐1882O	6,090,000		9.25	16.00	20.00	55.00	
☐1882O, O over S			14.00	17.00	20.00	55.00	5500.00
☐1882S	9,250,000		9.25	16.00	20.00	60.00	
☐1883	12,191,039		9.25	16.00	20.00	55.00	5500.00
☐1883CC	1,204,000		15.00	28.00	45.00	112.00	
☐1883O	8,725,000		9.25	16.00	20.00	55.00	
☐1883S	6,250,000		9.25	19.00	30.00	575.00	
☐1884	14,070,875		9.25	16.00	21.00	60.00	5500.00
☐1884CC	1,136,000		20.00	33.00	50.00	112.00	
☐1884O	9,730,000		9.25	16.50	20.00	50.00	
☐1884S	3,200,000		9.25	18.00	35.00	1075.00	
☐1885	17,787,767		9.25	16.00	20.00	50.00	5500.00
☐1885CC	228,000		80.00	138.00	170.00	240.00	
☐1885O	9,185,000		9.25	15.50	20.00	50.00	
☐1885S	1,497,000		9.25	15.50	28.00	130.00	
☐1886	19,963,886		9.25	15.50	20.00	50.00	5500.00
☐1886O	10,710,000		9.25	15.50	20.00	380.00	
☐1886S	750,000		9.25	28.00	40.00	130.00	
☐1887	20,290,710		9.25	15.50	20.00	50.00	5500.00
☐1887O	11,550,000		9.25	15.50	20.00	57.00	
☐1887S	1,771,000		9.25	18.00	23.00	75.00	
☐1888	19,183,833		9.25	15.50	20.00	50.00	5500.00
☐1888O	12,150,000		9.25	15.50	20.00	50.00	
☐1888S	657,000		16.00	25.00	45.00	130.00	
☐1889	21,726,811		9.25	15.50	20.00	50.00	5500.00
☐1889CC	350,000		145.00	275.00	700.00	4825.00	
☐1889O	11,875,000		9.25	16.00	21.00	100.00	
☐1889S	700,000		9.25	34.00	45.00	75.00	
☐1890	16,802,590		9.25	16.00	21.00	60.00	5500.00
☐1890CC	2,309,041		16.00	29.00	48.00	250.00	
☐1890O	10,701,000		9.25	16.00	21.00	65.00	
☐1890S	8,230,373		9.25	18.00	21.00	65.00	
☐1891	8,694,206		9.25	18.00	23.00	95.00	5500.00
☐1891CC	1,618,000		16.00	29.00	48.00	215.00	
☐1891O	7,954,529		9.25	16.00	23.00	95.00	
☐1891S	5,296,000		9.25	16.00	22.00	65.00	
☐1892	1,037,245		9.25	18.00	24.00	170.00	5500.00
☐1892CC	1,352,000		23.00	43.00	87.00	375.00	
☐1892O	2,744,000		9.25	17.00	24.00	150.00	
☐1892S	1,200,000		21.00	40.00	175.00	4425.00	

COMIC ART

TOPIC: Original comic art is the drawings and paintings from which final printed reproductions are made.

TYPES: Comic art can be from comic strips that ran in a newspaper or from comic books. Original artwork for magazine cartoons also falls into this category but is considered a specialized field by collectors. The art may be a "penciled rough" (which is sketched very lightly in pencil), or a finished drawing (which has been enhanced by drawing ink).

PERIOD: With rare exceptions, comic art in America will have been produced during the 1900s.

MAKERS: Famous comic artists include Walt Kelly, Alex Raymond, Jack Kirby and Arthur Suydam.

COMMENTS: Original art is unique and has more visual impact than the printed reproduction. Most of it is priced within the range of the average collector, although some art by famous artists is quite valuable.

ADDITIONAL TIPS: With original comic art, prices do not reflect scarcity. They are determined by the number of admirers a certain artist has, and how much these admirers are willing to pay for the work. For more information and more extensive listings, please refer to *The Official Price Guide to Comic Books and Collectibles,* published by The House of Collectibles. The following listings are organized by artist.

ADAMS, NEAL

	Current Price Range		P/Y Average
☐ **Amazing Adventures #18,** *War of the Worlds, page 8, pencil layout on translucent paper, signed*	30.00	40.00	34.00
☐ **Batman #236,** *cover, scene from story Wail of the Ghost Bride*	275.00	325.00	290.00
☐ **Ben Casey,** *daily strip for March 19, 1966*	26.00	34.00	29.00
☐ **Ben Casey,** *Sunday page for February 13, 1966*	110.00	140.00	120.00
☐ *Black and white illustrations for 1976 D.C. calendar, depicting Superman; inking by Giordano, 15" x 14"*	250.00	300.00	265.00

	Current Price Range		P/Y Average

☐ **Brave And The Bold #83,** *page 16 (featuring Batman and the Ten Titans)* 30.00 40.00 33.00
☐ **Brave And The Bold #83,** *page 24* 40.00 50.00 44.00
☐ **Creepy #15,** *large splash of Ty Rex* 140.00 180.00 152.00
☐ **The Flash #226,** *page one (Green Lantern story)* 135.00 165.00 145.00
☐ **The Flash #226,** *page one of second story (splash page) featuring The Green Lantern* .. 130.00 170.00 145.00
☐ **The Flash #226,** *page 5* 110.00 140.00 122.00
☐ **The Flash #226,** *page 7* 110.00 140.00 122.00
☐ **The Green Lantern #78,** *page 20, featuring The Black Canary* 70.00 90.00 77.00
☐ **Justice League of America #79,** *cover* 110.00 140.00 123.00
☐ **Justice League of America #139,** *cover without logo* 110.00 140.00 122.00
☐ **Superboy #158,** *cover* 90.00 110.00 97.00
☐ **Teen Titans #22,** *page 5, featuring Wonder Girl and Kid Flash, inking by Cardy* 60.00 80.00 66.00
☐ **Tomahawk #128,** *cover* 130.00 170.00 143.00

BUSCEMA, JOHN

☐ **Avengers #82,** *page 14* 35.00 45.00 37.75
☐ **Captain America #115,** *page 10, featuring The Red Skull* 45.00 55.00 47.00
☐ **KaZar #7,** *cover* 45.00 55.00 47.00
☐ **Marvel Preview #27,** *page 19, featuring The Phoenix* 28.00 36.00 30.25
☐ **Marvel Two In One #8,** *page 17* 4.00 6.00 4.20
☐ **Peter Parker #38,** *page 27* 22.00 28.00 23.50
☐ **Savage Sword Of Conan #10,** *page 57* 26.00 34.00 27.80
☐ **Savage Sword Of Conan #10,** *page 63* 26.00 34.00 27.80
☐ **Savage Sword Of Conan #10,** *page 64* 26.00 34.00 27.80
☐ **Thor #226,** *page 26, featuring Glactus and Hercules* 17.00 23.00 18.35
☐ **Thor #241,** *page 26* 16.00 20.00 17.00

CHAN, ERNIE

☐ **Batman Family Giant #9,** *cover* 13.00 17.00 14.20
☐ **Conan The Barbarian,** *daily strip for December 21, 1978, featuring Red Sonja* 30.00 40.00 32.20
☐ **Conan The Barbarian,** *daily strip for January 20, 1979, featuring The Great White Worm* ... 30.00 40.00 32.20
☐ **Conan The Barbarian,** *daily strip for January 22, 1979, featuring The Great White Worm* ... 30.00 40.00 32.20
☐ **Conan The Barbarian,** *daily strip for January 24, 1979, featuring The Great White Worm* ... 30.00 40.00 32.20
☐ **Conan The Barbarian,** *daily strip for February 23, 1979, featuring The Shadow Bats* 30.00 40.00 32.20

	Current Price Range		P/Y Average

FRAZETTA, FRANK

	Current Price Range		P/Y Average
☐ **Danger Is Our Business #1,** *page 5, signed* ..	1000.00	1200.00	1050.00
☐ *Sketch of nude figure, described only as "small"*	350.00	450.00	365.00
☐ **Yours, Mine And Ours,** *watercolor for movie poster (Lucille Ball/Henry Fonda movie, 11" x 15"*	1600.00	2000.00	1715.00

FREAS, KELLY

☐ *Ace paperback cover of a spaceship and a city, from unidentified novel, 1967*	26.00	34.00	29.00
☐ *Double page spread for a Marvel black and white horror magazine (specific title and issue not known)*	110.00	140.00	122.50
☐ *Preliminary sketch (in ink) for title page of The Art of Science Fiction, 3" x 18"*	22.00	28.00	24.15

FREEMAN, GEORGE

☐ *Framed painting of Red Sonja battling cavemen; she has two swords and they have spears. No information on whether published or not, 13" x 18"*	300.00	350.00	310.00

FRENZ, RON

☐ **KaZar #16,** *page 9*	8.50	11.50	9.35
☐ **KaZar #16,** *page 22*	8.50	11.50	9.35
☐ **KaZar #17,** *page 4*	17.00	23.00	18.15
☐ **KaZar #17,** *page 14*	22.00	28.00	23.60
☐ **Peter Parker #80,** *page 10*	6.50	8.50	6.80
☐ **Peter Parker #80,** *page 15*	6.50	8.50	6.80

FULLER, VING

☐ **Doc Syke,** *Sunday page from 1946*	42.00	58.00	47.00

GAMMILL, KERRY

☐ **Marvel Team-Up #127,** *page 2*	14.00	18.00	14.20
☐ **Marvel Team-Up #127,** *page 3*	11.00	15.00	11.75
☐ **Marvel Team-Up #127,** *page 5*	14.00	18.00	14.20
☐ **Marvel Team-Up #127,** *page 8*	11.00	15.00	11.75
☐ **Marvel Team-Up #127,** *page 9*	14.00	18.00	14.20
☐ **Marvel Team-Up #127,** *page 10*	11.00	15.00	11.75
☐ **Marvel Team-Up #127,** *page 12*	14.00	18.00	14.20
☐ **Marvel Team-Up #127,** *page 13*	14.00	18.00	14.20

KIRBY, JACK AND NEAL ADAMS

☐ **Jimmy Olson #148,** *cover*	90.00	110.00	91.15

KIRBY, JACK AND MICKY DEMEO

☐ **Tales To Astonish #74,** *page 3 (Hulk)*	65.00	85.00	67.00
☐ **Tales To Astonish #74,** *page 4 (Hulk)* ...	65.00	85.00	67.00
☐ **Tales To Astonish #74,** *page 5 (Hulk)*	60.00	70.00	61.15
☐ **Tales To Astonish #74,** *page 6 (Hulk)*	40.00	50.00	42.20

	Current Price Range		P/Y Average

MAYERICK, VAL

☐ **Micronauts #35,** *page 1 (splash page)*	40.00	50.00	42.25
☐ **Micronauts #35,** *page 8*	22.00	28.00	23.15
☐ **Micronauts #35,** *page 9*	22.00	28.00	23.15
☐ **Micronauts #35,** *page 11*	17.00	23.00	17.70
☐ **Micronauts #35,** *page 15*	13.00	17.00	13.45
☐ **Micronauts #35,** *page 16*	22.00	28.00	23.15
☐ **Micronauts #35,** *page 35*	22.00	28.00	23.15

MAXON, REX

☐ **Tarzan,** *set of six daily strips from 1940, matted into an area 25" x 36"*	175.00	215.00	187.50

McCAY, WINSOR

☐ **Drawing Of Christ,** *surrounded by followers, signed twice, believed to date from about 1900, 27" x 11"*	700.00	900.00	785.00
☐ **Little Nemo,** *Sunday pages, 1906*	5500.00	6200.00	5700.00
☐ **Dream Of The Rarebit Friend,** *1905*	1000.00	1200.00	1050.00

McDONELL, LUKE

☐ **Iron Man #166,** *page 18*	26.00	34.00	26.75
☐ **Iron Man #166,** *page 22*	35.00	45.00	36.00
☐ **Iron Man #166,** *page 31*	30.00	40.00	31.15
☐ **Iron Man #167,** *page 19*	40.00	50.00	41.20
☐ **Micronauts #46,** *page 5*	22.00	28.00	22.90
☐ **Micronauts #46,** *page 7*	26.00	34.00	26.75
☐ **Micronauts #46,** *page 10*	26.00	34.00	26.75
☐ **Micronauts #46,** *page 12*	22.00	28.00	22.90

MYERS, RUSS

☐ **Broomhilda,** *daily strip from 1970*	60.00	85.00	70.00
☐ **Broomhilda,** *Sunday page from 1972*	140.00	165.00	150.00

NINO, ALEX

☐ **The Burial Of Death,** *oil painting, 42" x 60"* ..	900.00	1200.00	1025.00

ROMITA, JOHN

☐ **Amazing Spiderman #107,** *page 20*	26.00	34.00	27.10
☐ **Amazing Spiderman #39,** *page 7*	60.00	70.00	61.75
☐ **Amazing Spiderman #39,** *page 9*	60.00	70.00	61.75
☐ **Amazing Spiderman #39,** *page 11*	60.00	70.00	61.75
☐ **Amazing Spiderman #39,** *page 19*	60.00	70.00	61.75
☐ **Amazing Spiderman #41,** *page 1*	65.00	85.00	67.90
☐ **Amazing Spiderman #41,** *page 12*	50.00	60.00	52.00
☐ **Amazing Spiderman #41,** *page 14*	50.00	60.00	52.00
☐ **Amazing Spiderman #41,** *page 16*	50.00	60.00	52.00
☐ **Amazing Spiderman #41,** *page 17*	50.00	60.00	52.00
☐ **Amazing Spiderman #43,** *page 1 (splash page)*	65.00	85.00	67.90
☐ **Amazing Spiderman #43,** *page 8*	52.00	68.00	53.85
☐ **Amazing Spiderman #43,** *page 9*	52.00	68.00	53.85
☐ **Amazing Spiderman #43,** *page 12*	52.00	68.00	53.85
☐ **Amazing Spiderman #43,** *page 13*	52.00	68.00	53.85

	Current Price Range		P/Y Average

	Current Price Range		P/Y Average
☐ Amazing Spiderman #43, *page 16*	52.00	68.00	53.85
☐ Amazing Spiderman #43, *page 17*	52.00	68.00	53.85
☐ Amazing Spiderman #43, *page 19*	52.00	68.00	53.85
☐ Amazing Spiderman #210, *page 6*	8.50	11.50	9.10
☐ Amazing Spiderman #210, *page 13*	8.50	11.50	9.10
☐ Daredevil #14, *page 11, featuring Foggy and Karen*	22.00	28.00	22.50
☐ Dr. Strange #7, *page 32, featuring Clea and demons*	20.00	25.00	21.10
☐ Incredible Hulk #196, *cover*	65.00	85.00	67.25

ROMITA, JOHN JR.

☐ Amazing Spiderman #244, *cover*	50.00	70.00	51.75
☐ Amazing Spiderman #245, *cover*	50.00	70.00	51.75

ROMITA, JOHN JR. AND LAYTON

☐ Iron Man #123, *page 26*	22.00	28.00	22.50

ROSENBERGER, JOHN

☐ The Fly #11, *page 1*	26.00	34.00	26.90
☐ The Fly #11, *page 3*	26.00	34.00	26.90
☐ The Fly #11, *page 6*	26.00	34.00	26.90
☐ The Fly #11, *page 7*	26.00	34.00	26.90
☐ The Fly #11, *page 9*	26.00	34.00	26.90
☐ The Fly #11, *page 11*	26.00	34.00	26.90

ROTH, WERNER

☐ X-Men #20, *page 1 (splash page)*	80.00	100.00	84.15
☐ X-Men #21, *page 1 (splash page), without logo*	55.00	75.00	57.75
☐ X-Men #33, *page 1 (splash page)*	80.00	100.00	84.15

SUYDAM, ARTHUR

☐ Epic #1, *page 3 of the story Heads*	350.00	450.00	345.00
☐ Epic #1, *page 4 of the story Heads*	350.00	450.00	345.00
☐ Epic #1, *page 5 of the story Heads*	350.00	450.00	345.00
☐ Heavy Metal *for January, 1980, page 1 of the story Food For My Children (splash page)* ...	350.00	450.00	345.00
☐ Heavy Metal *for January, 1980, page 2 of the story Food For My Children*	325.00	375.00	305.00
☐ Heavy Metal *for January, 1980, page 3 of the story Food For My Children*	325.00	375.00	305.00
☐ Heavy Metal *for January, 1980, page 4 of the story Food For My Children*	325.00	375.00	305.00

SWAN, CURT

☐ Action #383, *page 1 (splash page from The Killer Costume)*	22.00	28.00	23.70
☐ Action #489, *page 1*	22.00	28.00	23.70
☐ Action #495, *page 1*	22.00	28.00	23.70
☐ Action #515, *page 13*	11.00	14.00	11.45
☐ Action #515, *page 14*	11.00	14.00	11.45
☐ Action #515, *page 16*	11.00	14.00	11.45
☐ Action #515, *page 18 (featuring Superman)* ..	16.00	20.00	16.90

	Current Price Range		P/Y Average
☐ **Action #515,** *page 20 (featuring Superman)* ..	16.00	20.00	16.90
☐ **Action #527,** *page 12*	16.00	20.00	16.90
☐ **Action #527,** *page 13*	16.00	20.00	16.90
☐ **Action #527,** *page 14*	16.00	20.00	16.90
☐ **Action #527,** *page 15*	16.00	20.00	16.90
☐ **Adventure #377,** *pencil for cover (unpublished)*	110.00	140.00	117.00
☐ **D.C. Presents #6,** *page 15*	11.00	14.00	11.45
☐ **Jimmy Olson #75,** *page 5*	45.00	55.00	46.40
☐ **Jimmy Olson #122,** *cover*	22.00	28.00	23.10
☐ **Superboy #62,** *page 1*	60.00	80.00	62.75
☐ **Superman #233,** *page 2, inking by Murphy Anderson*	25.00	32.00	26.20
☐ **Superman #233,** *page 10, inking by Murphy Anderson*	28.00	38.00	29.40
☐ **Superman #242,** *page 6, inking by Anderson* .	22.00	28.00	23.30
☐ **Superman #261,** *a page featuring Star Sapphire*	22.00	28.00	23.30

YOUNG, CHIC

☐ **Blondie,** *Sunday page from May 31, 1931, 17" x 16"*	350.00	425.00	375.00

COMIC BOOKS

TOPIC: Comic books are collections of sequential cartoons that tell a story. Each illustrated frame progresses the story line.

TYPES: Comic books are categorized by publisher; for instance, D-C/National Periodical, Fawcett and Marvel.

PERIOD: Most collectible comic books were published from 1940 to the early 1970s.

COMMENTS: Comic books make wonderful collectibles because they are both historic and artistic.

ADDITIONAL TIPS: The following listings are organized by publisher. The order of the remaining information is: name and date of the series, name of the issue, issue number, main characters and descriptive information. For more information and extensive listings, please refer to *The Official Price Guide to Comic Books and Collectibles,* published by The House of Collectibles.

Left to Right: *#9, Four Favorites,* ©*Ace Magazines,* **$33.00-$41.00;** *#1, Lightning,* ©*Ace Magazines,* **$125.00-$150.00**

D-C/NATIONAL PERIODICAL PUBLICATIONS

ACTION COMICS, 1938	Current Price Range		P/Y Average
☐ **7, Superman,** *(Pep Morgan, Scoop Scanlon), Adventures of Marco Polo, Superman on cover*	1500.00	1775.00	1615.00
☐ **14, Superman vs. Ultra,** *(Pep Morgan, Chuck Dawson, Clip Carson), Adventures of Marco Polo, (Zatara) on cover*	425.00	485.00	440.00
☐ **17, Superman vs. Ultra,** *last installment of Adventures of Marco Polo, Superman on cover*	360.00	410.00	375.00
☐ **18, Three Aces,** *begins*	375.00	425.00	390.00
☐ **19, Superman vs. Ultra,** *(Chuck Dawson, Clip Carson, Three Aces), Superman on cover* . . .	335.00	375.00	345.00
☐ **20, Superman vs. Ultra**	335.00	375.00	345.00
☐ **22, Last Chuck Dawson,** *(had appeared continuously from #1)*	265.00	315.00	275.00

	Current Price Range		P/Y Average

☐ **23, Superman vs. Luthor,** *Luthor shown with red hair initially, first appearance of (The Black Pirate), created by Sheldon Moldoff, this short-lived series ran for only nineteen issues and was never regarded as a major feature but it was superbly illustrated* 385.00   450.00   405.00

☐ **33, Mr. America,** *origin of Mr. America, created by artist Bernard Bailey* 275.00   330.00   290.00

☐ **37, Superman Charged With Violation Of Law,** *first appearance of Congo Bill, created by Whitney Ellsworth, first appeared as a minor feature in D-C's More Fun Comics for eleven issues, then was dropped. But one month later, Action Comics introduced a new series of Congo Bill in which he suddenly became a movie star. The movie serial turned out to be one of the better ones of the 1940's* 230.00   285.00   245.00

☐ **42, Origin Of The Vigilante,** *last (Black Pirate, Mr. America) uses his cape as a flying carpet for the first time, Vigilante soon became one of D-C's star attractions and he headlined their new entry, Leading Comics, which began as a quarterly publication in January 1942* 275.00   330.00   290.00

☐ **43, The Vigilante vs. The Shade,** *(Billy Gunn)* .   220.00   270.00   235.00

☐ **45, The Vigilante,** *first appearance of (Stuff, the Chinatown Kid)* 215.00   260.00   225.00

☐ **46, The Vigilante vs. Rainbow Man** 215.00   260.00   225.00

☐ **51, Superman vs. The Prankster,** *first appearance of (The Prankster)* 220.00   270.00   235.00

☐ **52, Origin Of Americommando,** *cover features montage with Superman, Zatara, Congo Bill and The Vigilante* 175.00   230.00   180.00

☐ **56, Americommando vs. Dr. Ito** 130.00   160.00   140.00

☐ **60, Lois Lane, Superwoman** 175.00   230.00   185.00

☐ **64, Superman vs. The Toyman,** *first appearance of (The Toyman)* 160.00   200.00   170.00

☐ **68, Lois Lane's,** *(niece Susie is introduced)* . .   130.00   160.00   145.00

BATMAN (1940)

☐ **2, The Crime Master,** *(Adam Lamb), The Case of the Missing Link (Hackett and Snead, Professor Drake)* 1150.00   1375.00   1230.00

☐ **3, The Ugliest Man In The World,** *(Carlson, Ugly Horde, Detective McGonicle), The Crime School for Boys (Big Boy Daniels), Batman vs. the Cat Woman, first appearance of Cat Woman in costume, cover: Batman and Robin running toward reader with capes flying* 700.00   875.00   760.00

☐ **4, More Whirlwind Adventures Of Batman And Robin,** *Blackbeard's Crew and the Yacht Society (Thatch), cover: Batman climbing rope ladder* 575.00   700.00   615.00

☐ **5, The Case Of The Honest Crook,** *(Smiley Sikes), The Riddle of the Missing Card (Queenie, Diamond Jack Deegan, Clumbsy),*

	Current Price Range		P/Y Average

cover: Batman weighing fugitives on balance scale, "scales of justice." Last issue to be published quarterly. Switches to semi-monthly (six issues per year) with #6 .... **500.00 625.00 545.00**

☐ **6, Suicide Beat,** (Jimmy Kelly, Fancy Dan, Alderman Skigg) **350.00 450.00 385.00**

☐ **7, The Trouble Trap,** (Linda Page, Commissioner Gordon), The People vs. the Batman (Horatio Delmar, Weasel Venner, Freddie Hill) **350.00 450.00 385.00**

☐ **8, The Strange Case Of Professor Radium,** (Professor Rose), Stone Walls Do Not Prison A Make, The Superstition Murders (Johnny Glim), The Cross-Country Crimes (Namtab I/Batman; Nabtab is Batman spelled backwards) **375.00 450.00 400.00**

☐ **9, The Case Of The Lucky Law Breakers,** The White Whale (Capt. Burly), (Bob Crachit, Timmy Cratchit) **325.00 400.00 350.00**

☐ **10, Sheriff Of Ghost Town,** (Five Aces Frogel), Report Card Blues (Tommy Trent) **300.00 375.00 330.00**

☐ **11, Four Birds Of A Feather,** (Buzzard Benny, Joe Crow, Canary, The Penguin), Payment in Full (Joe Dolan) **275.00 330.00 290.00**

☐ **12, The Wizard Of Words,** (The Jocker), They Thrill to Conquer (Joe Kirk) **300.00 375.00 330.00**

☐ **13, The Story Of The 17 Stones,** (Rocky Grimes), Comedy of Tears (The Joker) **275.00 335.00 295.00**

☐ **14, Prescription For Happiness,** (Pills Mattson), Swastika over the White House (Count Felix, Fritz Hoffner), The Case Batman Failed to Solve **275.00 335.00 295.00**

☐ **15, Your Face Is Your Fortune,** (Elva Barr), The Loneliest Man in the World (Dirk Dagner, Tom Wick), The Boy who Wanted to be Robin (Knuckles Conger, Bobby Deen) **260.00 320.00 287.50**

☐ **16, Grade-A Crimes,** (Winthrop, character without first name), Here Comes Alfred (Alfred the Butler), Adventures of the Branded Tree (Squidge, character without first name), The Joker Reforms (Joe Kerswag) **295.00 340.00 310.00**

☐ **17, Adventure Of The Vitamin Vandals,** (Archie Gibbons), The Penguin Goes a-Hunting, Rogues' Pageant (Alfred the Butler) **140.00 170.00 152.75**

☐ **18, The Secret Of The Hunter's Inn,** (Alfred the Butler, Tweed Cousins), first appearance of Police Stories **140.00 170.00 152.75**

☐ **19, Collector Of Millionaires,** (Ali, Ali's Health Resort), The Case of the Timid Lion (The Joker), Atlantis Goes to War (Emperor Taro, Empress Lanya) **140.00 170.00 152.75**

☐ **20, The Centuries Of Crime,** (Ecla Tate, Swami Meera Kell, The Joker), Bruce Wayne Loses the Guardianship of Dick Grayson (Alfred the Butler, Fatso Foley), The Trial of Titus Keyes (Slick Fingers/George Collins) **145.00 175.00 155.00**

	Current Price Range		P/Y Average

☐ **21, Batman And Robin Whoop It Up In Four Whirlwind Action Stories**, *The Streamlined Rustlers (Brule, character without first name), His Lordship's Double (Lord Hurley Burleighm C.L.J. Carruthers), The Three Eccentrics (The Penguin), Blitzkreig Bandats (Chopper Gant, Hannibal B. Brown)* **140.00 170.00   148.00**

☐ **47, Special! The Peril-Packed Inside Story Of The Origin Of Batman!**, *(retold), The Chain Gang Crimes (Warden Beltt, Whiskers Mob), cover: Batman (as a boy) reading Gotham Gazette with headline Socialite Thomas Wayne Slain By Mystery Killer! Thomas Wayne was Batman's father. The Gotham Gazette neglected to mention that Batman's mother was killed at the same time, although it is not celar whether she was also slain by the gunman or suffered a fatal heart attack as an onlooker* **235.00 285.00   247.00**

☐ **48, the Thousand Secrets Of The Batcave**, *(Wolf Brando), Fowls of Fate (The Penguin), Crime from Tomorrow (Morton, character without first name)* **60.00   80.00   65.00**

☐ **49, Scoop Of The Century**, *(Jervis Tetch, Vicki Vale), Batman's Arabian Nights (The Crier, Professor Carter Nichols, The Joker)* **65.00   85.00   72.75**

☐ **50, The Second Boy Wonder**, *(Waxey Wilson), Lights — Camera — Crime (Vicki Vale, Stilts Tyler, Tom Macon)* **60.00   80.00   64.85**

☐ **51, The Stars Of Yesterday**, *(Rufus Lane), Pee-Wee the Talking Penguin, The Wonderful Mr. Wimble (Warts)* **55.00   75.00   60.00**

☐ **52, Batman And The Vikings**, *(Olaf Erickson, Professor Carter Nichols), The Man with the Automatic Brain (Alfred the Butler), The Happy Victims (The Joker, Mrs. Carlin)* **60.00   80.00   64.50**
Note: Batman and the Vikings is another Prof. Nichols time travel story. This one is about the Viking exploration of North America in the 10th century A.D.

☐ **57, The Walking Mummy**, *(Andrews, character without a first name — he was a museum curator), The Funny Man Crimes (The Joker)* . **45.00   60.00   49.00**

☐ **58, The Brand Of A Hero**, *(Joaquin Murieta), The State Bird Crimes (The Penguin), The Black Diamond (Bulls-Eye Kendall, Barracuda Brothers, Nitro Nelson) Joaquin Murieta was a real-life desperado of the Old West, here worked into a time-travel piece* **45.00   60.00   49.00**

☐ **59, Batman In The Future**, *(Erkham, character without first name), The Man who Replaced Batman (Deadshot/Floyd Lawton, Commissioner Gordon), The Forbidden Celler (Professor Vincent)* **40.00   55.00   44.75**

☐ **60, The Auto Circus Mystery**, *(Lucky Hooton)* **35.00   45.00   38.00**

	Current Price Range		P/Y Average
☐ **61, The Birth Of Batplane II,** *(Boley Brothers), Wheelchair Crimefighter (Vicki Vale), Mystery of the Winged People (The Penguin)*	37.00	48.00	40.00

SUPERMAN (1939)

	Current Price Range		P/Y Average
☐ **2, Superman vs. Luthor,** *first appearance of Luthor*	2300.00	3000.00	2350.00
☐ **4, Superman vs. Luthor**	1275.00	1500.00	1270.00
☐ **10, Superman vs. Luthor**	400.00	500.00	395.00
☐ **12, Superman vs. Luthor**	400.00	500.00	395.00
☐ **19, Superman Movie Cartoons,** *redone into book format*	320.00	375.00	310.00
☐ **20, Cover Taken From Hardcovered Superman Book,** *(by this time Superman products of all kinds were one the market)*	320.00	375.00	310.00
☐ **30, Superman vs. Mr. Mxyztplk,** *first appearance of Mr. Mxyztplk; in later issues the name was spelled Mxyzptlk*	235.00	285.00	215.00
☐ **45, Lois Lane,** *Superwoman (Hocus, Pocus)* .	210.00	260.00	190.00
☐ **53, Anniversary Issue,** *origin retold*	245.00	310.00	215.00
☐ **54, Superman vs. The Wrecker,** *first appearance of the Wrecker*	100.00	130.00	95.00
☐ **61, Superman Returns To Krypton,** *first Kryptonite story*	150.00	200.00	145.00
☐ **76, Guest Appearances By Batman And Robin**	275.00	340.00	245.00
☐ **78, Lois Lane's Meeting With Lana Lang**	90.00	115.00	80.00
☐ **81, Superman's Secret Workshop,** *discovered by arch-foe Luthor*	65.00	90.00	60.00
☐ **100, Origin Retold,** *for the second time*	75.00	100.00	72.75
☐ **113, The Superman Of The Past,** *part I*	28.00	37.00	26.75
☐ **114, The Superman Of The Past,** *part II*	28.00	37.00	26.75
☐ **115, The Superman Of The Past,** *part III*	28.00	37.00	26.75
☐ **123, Girl Of Steel**	22.00	30.00	19.50
☐ **125, Clark Kent In College**	26.00	33.00	21.75
☐ **127, Return Of Titano**	25.00	32.00	22.00
☐ **128, Kryptonite Story**	27.00	37.00	23.50
☐ **130, Krypto Grows Up**	26.00	33.00	23.00
☐ **133, How Parry White Hired Clark Kent**	20.00	25.00	17.25
☐ **135, Lori Lemaris**	19.00	24.00	16.75
☐ **138, Lori Lemaris**	19.00	24.00	16.75
☐ **139, Story Of Red Kryptonite**	23.00	31.00	19.00
☐ **140, Superman And The Son Of Bizarro**	19.00	24.00	18.00
☐ **141, Superman Returns To Krypton And Meets Lyla Lerrol**	20.00	25.00	18.50
☐ **142, Guest Appearances By Batman And Robin**	50.00	70.00	42.75
☐ **143, Return Of Bizarro**	22.00	30.00	17.75
☐ **144, Superboy's First Public Appearance**	28.00	37.00	23.50
☐ **145, Great Boo-Boo**	16.00	21.00	14.75
☐ **146, Superman's Life Story**	65.00	85.00	60.00
☐ **147, Superman vs. The Legion Of Super Villains,** *first appearance of The Legion of Super Villains*	45.00	60.00	41.50
☐ **148, Guest Appearance By Aquaman**	45.00	60.00	39.75

	Current Price Range		P/Y Average
☐ 149, **Death Of Superman,** *(fantasy)*	50.00	70.00	43.50
☐ 156, **Last Days Of Superman,** *with appearances by Batman and Robin*	65.00	85.00	57.75
☐ 158, **Nightwing And Flamebird**	16.00	21.00	13.25

FAWCETT

CAPTAIN MARVEL (1941)

☐ 19, **Cover:** *Santa Claus riding on Captain Marvel's back, with Mary Marvel alongside, wording (at upper right), "On sale every third Friday"*	150.00	180.00	160.00
☐ 26, **Cover:** *Captain Marvel soaring skyward against huge American flag, wording "War Stamps for Victory"*	65.00	80.00	69.75
☐ 27, **Captain Marvel Joins The Navy,** *cover: Captain Marvel rearing back to hurl bomb as if it were a football. Wording: "This is the insignia recently adopted by a naval air squadron." (Referring to the lightning bolt on Captain Marvel's shirt-front)*	60.00	75.00	63.25
☐ 28, **Cover:** *Captain Marvel standing at attention with hands at sides, receiving medal being pinned on him by Unclm Sam while column of soldiers watch*	55.00	70.00	58.15
☐ 31, **Captain Marvel In Buffalo, City Saved From Doom; Captain Marvel Fights His Own Conscience,** *cover: Captain Marvel in close-up with an angel on one shoulder and a devil on the other (relating to the story, Captain Marvel fights his own conscience)*	55.00	70.00	58.00
☐ 42, **Cover:** *close-up portrait of Captain Marvel in Christmas wreath, wording "Season's Greetings"*	40.00	55.00	44.50
☐ 47, **Cover:** *Captain Marvel stands facing old man with long beard who holds scroll. On wall are names Solomon, Hercules, Atlas, Zeus, Achilles, Mercury. Also on cover, "Seventh War Loan, buy stamps and bonds"*	40.00	55.00	44.50
☐ 60, **Captain Marvel Battles The Dread Atomic War,** *cover: Captain Marvel in nuclear-devastated city, poised to catch falling atomic bomb in his arms*	75.00	100.00	82.75
☐ 70, **Captain Marvel And The Horror In The Box,** *cover: Captain Marvel, with astonished expression on face, peering into box that has a question mark on the lid*	37.00	45.00	40.00
☐ 73, **Cover:** *Captain Marvel speeds past skyscraper (Woolworth Building in New York)* ...	32.00	38.00	34.50
☐ 97, **Captain Marvel Is Wiped Out!,** *cover: Captain Marvel standing full-length, while a hand with an eraser is "wiping out" the drawing. He exclaims, "Holy moley! What goes on?"* .	21.00	27.00	23.00

	Current Price Range		P/Y Average

☐ **104, Mr. Tawny's Masquerade,** *cover: Mr. Tawny (with cape) delivering knockout punch, while Captain Marvel exclaims, "Attaboy, Mr. Tawny"* . . . . | 18.00 | 24.00 | 20.00

☐ **112, Captain Marvel And The Strange Worrybird,** *cover: Worrybird pacing ground with dark cloud of gloom over its head, as Captain Marvel stands by mystified* . . . . | 18.00 | 24.00 | 20.00

MARVEL COMICS GROUP

AMAZING SPIDERMAN (1963)

☐ **1, Origin Retold,** *Spiderman vs. Chameleon, (John Jameson, Fabulous Four), Ditko artwork, Lee stories, Dee lettering, inking unknown* . . . . | 1100.00 | 1350.00 | 1175.00

☐ **2, Duel To The Death With The Vulture,** *Uncanny Threat of the Terrible Tinkerer, Ditko artwork, Lee stories, Duffy lettering, inking unknown* . . | 420.00 | 500.00 | 460.00

☐ **3, Spiderman vs. Dr. Octopus,** *(Human Torch), Ditko artwork, Lee stories, Duffy lettering, inking unknown* . . . . | 220.00 | 260.00 | 237.00

☐ **4, Nothing Can Stop The Sandman,** *(Betty Brant), Ditko artwork, Lee stories* . . . . | 170.00 | 200.00 | 182.00

☐ **5, Marked For Destruction By Dr. Doom,** *(Fabulous Four), Ditko artwork, Lee stories, Rosen lettering* . . . . | 105.00 | 125.00 | 112.00

☐ **6, Face To Face With The Lizard,** *Ditko artwork, Lee stories, Simek lettering* . . . . | 105.00 | 125.00 | 112.00

☐ **7, Return Of The Vulture,** *Ditko artwork, Lee stories, Simek lettering* . . . . | 80.00 | 100.00 | 87.00

☐ **8, Living Brain,** *Spiderman Tackles the Human Torch, (Fabulous Four), Kirby and Ditko artwork, Lee stories, Simek lettering, Ditko inking* . . . . | 80.00 | 100.00 | 87.00

☐ **9, Man Called Electro,** *Ditko artwork, Lee stories, Simek lettering* . . . . | 80.00 | 100.00 | 87.00

☐ **10, Enforcers,** *(Fredrick Foswell, The Ox, Montana, Fancy Dan), Ditko artwork, Lee stories, Rosen lettering* . . . . | 80.00 | 100.00 | 87.00

☐ **11, Turning Point,** *(Spiderman Tracer, Dr. Octopus), Ditko artwork, Lee stories, Rosen lettering* . . . . | 45.00 | 60.00 | 52.00

☐ **12, Unmasked By Dr. Octopus,** *Ditko artwork, Lee stories, Simek lettering* . . . . | 45.00 | 60.00 | 52.00

☐ **13, Menace Of Mysterio,** *Ditko artwork, Lee stories, Simek lettering* . . . . | 45.00 | 60.00 | 52.00

☐ **14, Green Goblin,** *(Hulk, Enforcers, Ox, Montana, Fancy Dan), Ditko artwork, Lee stories, Simek lettering, (premium value because of Hulk appearance)* . . . . | 80.00 | 100.00 | 87.00

☐ **15, Kraven The Hunter,** *(Chameleon), Ditko artwork, Lee stories, Simek lettering* . . . . | 45.00 | 60.00 | 52.00

COOKBOOKS

PERIOD: Cookbooks have been published for close to 500 years.

ORIGIN: European in origin, the earliest cookbooks usually featured recipes for medicine.

COMMENTS: Rare first edition cookbooks, and those published before 1850, can be very expensive. However, most collectible cookbooks are reasonably priced. Many cookbooks from the early 20th century were given away as advertising premiums.

CONDITION: Cookbooks were usually used heavily so they are not expected to be in mint condition. Notations in margins are common.

ADDITIONAL TIPS: The following listings are alphabetical according to the author's name. For further information, refer to *The Official Guide to Kitchen Collectibles,* or *The Official Guide to Old Books and Autographs.*

	Current Price Range		P/Y Average
☐ **Acton, Eliza,** *The English Bread-Book for Domestic Use,* practical receipts for many varieties of bread, etc. London, 1857, cloth-bound	40.00	53.00	45.00
☐ *Adventures In Good Cooking And The Art of Carving In The Home,* Duncan Hines, Inc., 1947	`3.00	7.00	4.50
☐ **Allen, Elaine,** *Watkins Salad Book,* J.R. Watkins Co., 1946	6.00	10.00	8.50
☐ **Allen, H. Warner,** *Sherry,* London, 1934, cloth-bound	12.00	17.00	14.00
☐ **Allen, Mrs. Ida Cogswell Bailey,** *Golden Rule Cook Book,* Golden Rule House, 1918	10.00	30.00	17.50
☐ **Ames, Richard,** *The Bacchanalian Sessions; or, The Contenion of Liquors: With a Farewell to Wine,* by the author of *The Search After Claret,* London, for E. Hawkins, 1693	250.00	325.00	265.00
☐ **Ames, Richard,** *Fatal Friendship, or, The Drunkard's Misery,* being a satry against hard drinking, London, for Randal Taylor, 1693, bound in calf. "Satry" meant, of course, "satire"	230.00	275.00	245.00

Advertising Cookbooks,
1920s, each, **5.00-$8.00**

	Current Price Range		P/Y Average
☐ *Archdeacon's Kitchen Cabinet,* Chicago, 1876	30.00	45.00	40.00
☐ **Armstrong, John,** *The Young Women's Guide to Virtue, Economy and Happiness With a Complete and Elegant System of Domestic Cookery,* Newcastle (England), n.d. (c. 1819), with engraved frontis and ten engraved plates, calfbound, mainly a handbook for young ladies who intended going into domestic service	100.00	130.00	120.00
☐ *Cornerstones — A Cookbook by Assistance League,* Marshalltown, Iowa, spiral bound, 441 pp., 1976	4.00	8.00	5.50
☐ *Could I Have Your Recipe?* An international Cookbook published by The United Nations Nursery School, Geneva, Switzerland, spiral bound, 287 pp., 1957	4.00	8.00	5.50
☐ **Croly, Mrs. J.C.,** *Jennie June's American Cookery Book,* N.Y., 1870	40.00	53.00	48.00

	Current Price Range		P/Y Average

☐ *Dainty Dishes for Slender Incomes,* New York, 1900 . . . . 20.00 28.00 23.00

☐ **Darby, Charles,** *Bacchanalia, or, A Desscription of a Drunken Club,* London, for Robert Boulter, 1680, folio, 16 pp., calfbound 300.00 400.00 320.00

☐ **Decker, John W.,** *Cheese Making,* Wisconsin, 1909 . . . . 25.00 33.00 26.00

☐ **Degraf, Mrs. Belle,** *Asparagus For Delicacy And Variety,* Canners League of California, c. 1920s 4.00 14.00 7.00

☐ **De Loup, Maximillan,** *The American Salad Book,* McClure, Phillips & Co., New York, 1901 29.00 45.00 37.00

☐ *Dining And Its Amenities,* by *A Lover of Good Cheer,* New York, 1907 . . . . 25.00 33.00 28.00

☐ **Escoffier, A.,** *A Guide to Modern Cookery,* McClure, Phillips & Co., New York, 1907 . . . . . . 50.00 70.00 59.00

☐ *Experienced American Housekeeper,* Hartford, 1836, with four engraved plates, one of which is a folding plate, price given is for a sound copy 130.00 170.00 140.00

☐ **Farley, John,** *The London Art of Cookery and Housekeeper's Complete Assistant,* eighth edition, London, John Fielding, J. Scatcherd and J. Whitacker, 1796, with portrait and 12 engraved plates, showing menus for every month of the year 190.00 235.00 190.00

☐ **Farmer, Fannie M.,** *Food And Cooking For The Sick And Convalescent,* Little, Brown & Co., Boston, 1911 . . . . 25.00 35.00 30.00

☐ *Fifty Good Ways of Serving Woodcock Macaroni,* New York, 1919 . . . . 6.00 10.00 8.00

☐ **Frederick, Mrs. Christine,** *Meals That Cook Themselves,* Sentinel Mfg. Co., New Haven, 1915 . . . . 10.00 15.00 13.00

☐ **Gillette, Mrs. F. L.,** *White House Cook Book,* Chicago, 1889 . . . . 75.00 95.00 80.00

☐ **Lemery, Louis,** *A Treatise of all Sorts of Foods, both Animal and Vegetable: also of Drinkables,* giving an account how to choose the best sort of all kinds, London, 1745, calfbound 250.00 325.00 275.00

☐ **Leslie, Miss,** *75 Receipts for Pastry, Cakes and Sweetmeats, by a Lady of Philadelphia,* Boston, n.d. (1828) 150.00 200.00 175.00

☐ **Leslie, Miss,** *Directions for Cookery,* Philadelphia, 1863, 59th edition 20.00 27.00 23.00

☐ *Lessons of Thrift Published for General Benefit,* by a member of the Save-All Club, London, 1820, with 12 colored aquatints by Cruikshank, bound in gilt morocco. Though largely a satirical work, the illustrations give a fairly accurate view of (for example) proceedings in a no-frills chophouse of the era. Theft of tableware was such a problem that knives, forks, etc., were chained to the table . 200.00 260.00 230.00

	Current Price Range		P/Y Average
☐ Lincoln, Mary, *The Peerless Cook Book,* Boston, 1901, softbound	14.00	19.00	16.00
☐ Lincoln, Mrs., *Boston Cook Book, What To Do and What Not To Do in Cooking,* Boston, 1884	475.00	575.00	550.00
☐ Lincoln, Mrs., *Carving and Serving,* Boston, 1915	17.00	23.00	20.00
☐ Lincoln, Mrs. D.A., *Boston School Kitchen Textbook,* Boston, 1887	25.00	33.00	28.00
☐ Lippman, B.F., *Aunt Betty's Cook Book,* Cincinnati, 1918	15.00	21.00	17.00
☐ Llanover, Lady Augusta, *The First Principles of Good Cookery,* London, 1867, illustrated, clothbound	70.00	90.00	80.00
☐ Lockhart, Marion, *Standard Cook Book for All Occasions,* New York, 1925	12.00	17.00	15.00
☐ McCann, Alfred W., *Thirty Cent Bread,* New York, 1917, bound in boards. Alfred W. McCann hosted the first food-and cooking radio show	14.00	19.00	17.00
☐ MacDougall, A.F., *Coffee and Waffles,* New York, 1927	11.00	16.00	12.00
☐ MacKenzie, Colin, *MacKenzie's Five Thousand Receipts,* Philadelphia, 1825	150.00	190.00	175.00
☐ Maddocks, Mildred, *The Pure Food Cook Book,* New York, 1914	17.00	24.00	20.00
☐ Manchester, Herbert, *The Evolution of Cooking and Heating,* published by Fuller and Warren, 1917	55.00	70.00	60.00
☐ Nelson, Harriet S., *Fruits and Their Cookery,* New York, 1921	14.00	19.00	17.00
☐ *New Family Receipt-Book,* containing 800 truly valuable receipts in various branches of domestic economy, selected from the works of British and foreign writers, London, 1811, half calf	80.00	100.00	90.00
☐ *New Family Receipt-Book,* containing 800 truly valuable receipts in various branches of domestic economy, selected from the works of British and foreign writers, London, 1837 edition, half calf	70.00	90.00	75.00
☐ Nichol, Mary E., *366 Dinners, by "M.E.N."* New York, 1892	20.00	27.00	23.00
☐ Nicholson, Elizabeth, *What I Know; or, Hints on The Daily Duties of a Housekeeper,* Philadelphia, 1856	130.00	165.00	150.00
☐ Norton, Caroline T., *The Rocky Mountain Cook Book,* Denver, 1903	30.00	39.00	32.00
☐ Nutt, Frederick, *The Complete Confectioner, or, The Whole Art of Confectionary Made Easy,* with receipts for liqueurs, home-made wines, etc., new edition, with additions, London, 1809, with ten plates, half calf	150.00	190.00	170.00
☐ Owen, Catherine, *Culture and Cooking,* New York, 1881	30.00	39.00	32.00
☐ Owen, Catherine, *Choice Cookery,* New York, 1889	30.00	39.00	32.00

	Current Price Range		P/Y Average
☐ **Owens, Mrs. F.,** *Cook Book and Useful House-hold Hints,* Chicago, 1883	20.00	27.00	23.00
☐ **Panchard, E.,** *Meats, Poultry and Game,* New York, 1919	14.00	19.00	16.00
☐ **Parloa, Maria,** *The Appledore Cook Book,* Boston, 1878	25.00	33.00	28.00
☐ **Parloa, Maria,** *Choice Receipts,* Dorchester (Mass.), 1895, softbound	12.00	17.00	14.00
☐ **Paul, Mrs. Sara T.,** *Cookery from Experience,* Philadelphia, 1875	25.00	33.00	28.00
☐ **Parker, T.N.,** *Remarks on The Malt Tax,* with reference to the debate in the House of Commons on the 10th March, 1835, Shrewsbury (England), 1835, 34 pp.	25.00	33.00	28.00
☐ **Pereira, J.,** *A Treatise on Food and Diet,* New York, 1843	45.00	60.00	52.00
☐ **Poindexter, Charlotte M.,** *Jane Hamilton's Recipes,* Chicago, 1909	17.00	23.00	20.00
☐ **Poole, H.M.,** *Fruits and How to Use Them,* New York, 1890	20.00	27.00	23.00

COOKIE CUTTERS

TOPIC: Cookie cutters are outlines or molds that shape cookie dough into a specific design.

TYPES: Cookie cutters are generally divided into the hand-crafted variety versus the manufactured variety. They can also be categorized according to shape or design.

PERIOD: Cookie cutters have been widely used since at least the 16th century. There is evidence that they have existed in some form for thousands of years.

ORIGIN: Cookie cutters are thought to have originated in Europe.

MATERIAL: The oldest cookie cutters are made of wood. These are seldom seen on the market today. Aluminum became popular around 1920, and plastic usurped aluminum around 1940. Other metals, especially tin, occur frequently also.

COMMENTS: Backplates can sometimes be used to approximate the date of manufacture of a cookie cutter. In the late 1800s, these backings were trimmed to echo the shape of the cutter design. After the turn of the century, backplates were usually rectangular.

ADDITIONAL TIPS: Scarcity and age are not good indicators of cutter prices. In general, the price depends on the quality of the piece and the interest the individual collector has in it. Cutters with names on them are often more valuable than similar nameless ones. The following listings are organized by design.

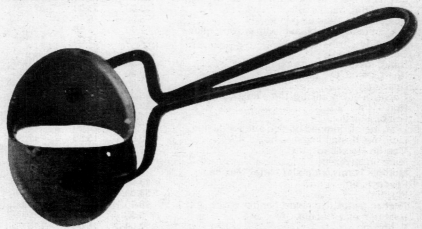

Cookie Cutter, *aluminum, late 19th c.,* **$6.50-$10.00**

	Current Price Range		P/Y Average
☐ **Acorn,** metal, European	4.00	7.00	6.00
☐ **Animals,** tin	8.00	15.00	8.50
☐ **Bear,** metal, oval backplate, holes form a star	12.00	18.00	15.00
☐ **Bear,** metal, trimmed backplate, two holes, 6¼ "	75.00	100.00	83.00
☐ **Bear,** tin, 4" high	15.00	25.00	16.00
☐ **Bird,** aluminum, 4¾ "	1.00	2.50	1.75
☐ **Bird,** metal, flying, handle, 2¾ " x 5¼ "	20.00	29.00	24.50
☐ **Bird,** metal, flying, two holes, 4¾ "	100.00	125.00	112.50
☐ **Bird,** metal, standing, one hole, 3¾ "	20.00	30.00	25.00
☐ **Bird,** tin, 3" long	20.00	35.00	19.00
☐ **Butterfly,** tin	15.00	26.00	19.00
☐ **Cat,** metal, sitting, curling tail, one hole, handle, 5"	110.00	125.00	117.00
☐ **Cat,** metal, sitting, French	20.00	30.00	25.00
☐ **Chick,** metal, holes form a star, 4"	17.00	25.00	21.00
☐ **Chick,** tin	10.00	20.00	10.50
☐ **Christmas Tree,** metal, thick trunk, handle, 4⅝"	80.00	95.00	87.50
☐ **Christmas Tree,** tin, 4¾ "	4.00	6.50	5.25
☐ **Circle,** aluminum, open handle, late 1800s ...	7.00	10.00	8.50
☐ **Circle,** metal, crimped, handle, 4"	5.00	8.00	6.50
☐ **Circle,** tin, handle, 3" diameter	2.00	4.00	3.00

	Current Price Range		P/Y Average
☐ **Club (of cards),** tin, 3½ " long, 1¾ " high	1.00	3.00	2.00
☐ **Deer,** tin, jumping	30.00	42.00	31.00
☐ **Diamond,** metal, painted wood handle	.50	1.50	1.00
☐ **Dog,** metal, Husky, one hole, 3⅜ " x 4⅜ "	35.00	50.00	42.50
☐ **Donkey,** tin, lying down	16.00	26.00	19.00
☐ **Duck,** metal, 4 "	5.00	8.00	7.00
☐ **Duck,** metal, embossed, "Davis Baking Powder"	4.00	8.00	6.00
☐ **Elephant,** metal, one hole, 4½ "	100.00	115.00	107.50
☐ **Fish,** metal, handle, 6 "	20.00	35.00	27.50
☐ **Gingerbread Man,** aluminum, 6 "	3.50	6.50	5.00
☐ **Gingerbread Man,** plastic, with crown, yellow .	1.00	3.50	2.25
☐ **Goose,** tin, flying	32.00	47.00	37.00
☐ **Guitar,** tin	20.00	30.00	21.00
☐ **Heart,** metal, painted wood handle	.50	1.50	1.00
☐ **Heart,** metal, two holes, handle, 4½ "	40.00	65.00	47.50
☐ **Heart,** tin	4.00	10.00	5.50
☐ **Horse,** metal, prancing, three holes, 5¼ "	135.00	160.00	148.00
☐ **Horse,** tin	12.00	24.00	13.00
☐ **Lamb,** aluminum, 4 "	1.00	3.50	2.25
☐ **Leaf,** metal, crimped border, interior design . .	12.00	20.00	16.00
☐ **Lion,** metal, standing, two holes, 4½ "	10.00	15.00	12.50
☐ **Man on Horseback,** tin	15.00	21.00	17.00
☐ **Man,** tin, stylized	20.00	30.00	21.00
☐ **Multiple Forms (animals),** metal, Mexican	3.00	7.00	5.00
☐ **Peacock,** tin	18.00	30.00	21.00
☐ **Pig,** tin	33.00	46.00	37.00
☐ **Pitcher,** metal, two holes, handle, 5¼ "	90.00	110.00	100.00
☐ **Rabbit,** metal, handle, 3 "	5.00	15.00	10.00
☐ **Rabbit,** tin	10.00	25.00	13.00
☐ **Santa Claus,** tin	11.00	18.00	13.00
☐ **Set,** tin, "Junior Card Party Cake Cutters," a heart, spade, diamond and club, 2 "	10.00	15.00	12.50
☐ **Spade,** tin, handle, 3½ "	2.00	4.00	3.00
☐ **Star in Crescent Moon,** metal, 2¾ "	15.00	28.00	21.50
☐ **Star,** tin, six points	22.00	37.00	27.00
☐ **Swan,** metal, standing, two holes, 3¼ "	25.00	40.00	32.50
☐ **Tulip,** metal, crimped border, contemporary . .	10.00	20.00	15.00
☐ **Whale,** metal, multiple holes, 3¾ "	20.00	35.00	27.50
☐ **Woman,** aluminum, 5¼ "	2.50	4.00	3.25
☐ **Woman,** metal, stylized, 3 "	10.00	20.00	15.00

COOKIE JARS

MAKER: A variety of pottery and glassware companies have made cookie jars. It is sometimes difficult to identify the maker because different companies often used similar molds.

COMMENTS: Cookie jars are collected by those interested in pottery as well as those interested in kitchen items. Prices on cookie jars, unless very rare or very old, are usually moderate.

ADDITIONAL TIPS: The listings are alphabetical according to cookie jar shape. When available, a description, color, height and company are listed.

RECOMMENDED READING: For more information, see *The Official Price Guide to Pottery and Porcelain.*

	Current Price Range		P/Y Average
☐ **Alice in Wonderland**	26.00	38.00	30.00
☐ **Animals,** *"Cookies," in relief*	19.00	36.00	24.00
☐ **Antique Wall Phone,** *Cardinal pottery*	15.00	25.00	28.00
☐ **Apple,** *yellow, red, green, with lid*	10.00	15.00	12.00
☐ **Autumn Leaf,** *Hall China Company, c. 1936, 1939*	75.00	80.00	77.00
☐ **Bananas,** *McCoy pottery*	16.00	24.00	18.00
☐ **Bear,** *cookies in pocket, McCoy pottery*	22.00	26.00	23.00
☐ **Bear,** *manufactured by Royhlmare*	25.00	35.00	30.00
☐ **Bear,** *McCoy pottery*	20.00	26.00	22.00
☐ **Bear,** *with open eyes, manufactured by A.B. Co.*	20.00	30.00	24.50
☐ **Bears,** *manufactured by Turnabout*	12.00	17.00	14.50
☐ **Bell,** *"Ring Fo Cookies," with lid*	15.00	24.00	28.00
☐ **Bird Feed Sack,** *manufactured by McCoy Pottery*	10.00	20.00	16.00
☐ **Bird,** *flying, 9" diameter*	341.00	380.00	350.00
☐ **Brown,** *with red flowers*	14.00	20.00	16.00
☐ **Butter Churn,** *flowers*	19.00	25.00	22.00
☐ **Cat,** *fluffy*	23.00	33.00	26.00
☐ **Cat,** *in basket*	17.00	30.00	21.00
☐ **Cat,** *leaves and flowers, with lid*	15.00	23.00	18.00
☐ **Cat,** *on beehive*	17.00	26.00	20.00
☐ **Cat,** *seated, yellow, black, pink, white*	18.00	37.00	22.00

McCoy Cookie Jar, $10.00-$13.00

	Current Price Range		P/Y Average
☐ **Chef,** *manufactured by McCoy Pottery*	35.00	45.00	40.00
☐ **Chick,** *on chicken*	19.00	39.00	25.00
☐ **Chick,** *wearing a beret, manufactured by A.B. Co.*	25.00	35.00	27.00
☐ **Chick,** *wearing a blue jacket*	13.50	18.00	15.00
☐ **Clown,** *head only, with black boater hat, lid is formed by hat, McCoy pottery*	18.00	23.00	20.00
☐ **Clown,** *in barrel, tan and white, McCoy pottery*	16.00	24.00	18.00
☐ **Clown,** *on stage, manufactured by A.B. Co.* .	25.00	37.00	29.00
☐ **Coffee Grinder,** *with lid, McCoy pottery*	18.00	25.00	20.00
☐ **Coffee Pot,** *imprinted cookies and cup, white*	14.00	20.00	16.00
☐ **Collegiate Owl,** *manufactured by A.B. Co.*	20.00	30.00	25.00
☐ **Cookie Boy,** *manufactured by McCoy Pottery*	25.00	35.00	29.00
☐ **Cookie Garage**	16.00	22.00	18.00
☐ **Cookie Truck,** *manufactured by A.B. Co.*	45.00	60.00	53.50
☐ **Coors USA**	25.00	35.00	30.00
☐ **Covered Wagon,** *with lid, McCoy pottery*	25.00	35.00	30.00
☐ **Cow,** *manufactured by A.B. Co.*	20.00	25.00	22.50
☐ **Cow,** *manufactured by Brush*	60.00	80.00	74.00
☐ **Daffodil,** *gold trim, Hall China Company*	27.00	33.00	30.00
☐ **Dog,** *in basket*	11.00	22.00	14.00
☐ **Donald Duck,** *with nephews, Disney*	32.00	40.00	35.00
☐ **Dutch Boy,** *American Bisque*	14.00	28.00	17.00
☐ **Dutch Boy,** *manufactured by Shawnee*	40.00	50.00	46.00

	Current Price Range		P/Y Average
☐ **Dutch Girl,** *brown, manufactured by Red Wing*	35.00	45.00	39.50
☐ **Dutch Girl,** *stoneware, manufactured by McCoy Pottery*	20.00	30.00	24.50
☐ **Dutch Girl,** *tulips on skirt*	19.00	40.00	24.00
☐ **Dutch Windmill**	16.00	34.00	20.00
☐ **Ear of Corn,** *manufactured by McCoy Pottery*	55.00	65.00	59.50
☐ **Elephant,** *grinning, blond, in blue bonnet and jacket, ice cream cone in trunk, with lid*	16.00	24.00	18.00
☐ **Elephant,** *honking, crossed legs*	21.00	28.00	23.00
☐ **Elf's Head**	23.00	30.00	25.00
☐ **Farmer Pig,** *manufactured by Shawnee*	40.00	50.00	46.00
☐ **Fat Man**	16.00	28.00	20.00
☐ **Fat Policeman,** *manufactured by R.R.P. Co.*	25.00	35.00	29.50
☐ **Flowers,** *stoneware, manufactured by McCoy Pottery*	10.00	20.00	16.00
☐ **Flower Forms,** *gold, pink, lilac, blue, raised gold stems, 2 handles*	100.00	120.00	105.00
☐ **French Chef,** *manufactured by Red Wing*	40.00	45.00	42.50
☐ **Frog,** *manufactured by Holiday*	20.00	30.00	25.00
☐ **Frontier Scene,** *manufactured by McCoy Pottery*	25.00	35.00	29.50
☐ **Gingerbread Man and Baker,** *"Cookies," hexagonal*	16.00	24.00	18.00
☐ **Gingerbread Man,** *candy cane handle*	32.00	60.00	36.00
☐ **Grandma,** *manufactured by A.B. Co.*	35.00	45.00	39.50
☐ **Grandma,** *red skirt, glasses, hair bun forms lid*	27.00	32.00	29.00
☐ **Hobby Horse,** *manufactured by McCoy Pottery*	35.00	45.00	40.00
☐ **Honey Bear,** *manufactured by McCoy Pottery*	20.00	30.00	27.50
☐ **Honeycomb,** *manufactured by McCoy Pottery*	15.00	25.00	19.50
☐ **Humpty Dunpty,** *in cowboy attire, manufactured by Brugh*	30.00	40.00	34.50
☐ **Humpty Dumpty,** *yellow, with lid*	12.00	16.00	14.00
☐ **Jack-In-The-Box,** *manufactured by A.B. Co.*	30.00	40.00	37.00
☐ **Kitchen Jar,** *pink, manufactured by Hull*	7.00	15.00	9.50
☐ **Kitten,** *in basket, McCoy Pottery*	22.00	26.00	24.00
☐ **Kitten,** *on barrel, manufactured by Hull*	20.00	30.00	25.00
☐ **Kitten,** *on basketweave, manufactured by McCoy Pottery*	30.00	40.00	34.50
☐ **Kitten,** *on beehive, manufactured by A.B. Co.*	25.00	35.00	29.50
☐ **Lady Pig,** *manufactured by A.B. Co.*	25.00	35.00	29.50
☐ **Lamb,** *manufactured by A.B. Co.*	20.00	25.00	22.00
☐ **Lion,** *wears cowboy hat, manufactured by Balmont*	30.00	40.00	34.50
☐ **Log Cabin,** *manufactured by McCoy Pottery*	30.00	40.00	34.50
☐ **Ma And Pa Owls,** *manufactured by McCoy Pottery*	25.00	35.00	29.50
☐ **Mammy,** *manufactured by McCoy Pottery*	50.00	100.00	75.00
☐ **Mammy,** *red kerchief, "Mammy," Pearl china*	18.00	25.00	20.00
☐ **Mickey And Minnie,** *manufactured by Turnabout*	25.00	35.00	30.00
☐ **Milk Can,** *blue, white and gray, 9"*	20.00	30.00	25.00
☐ **Monk,** *"Thou Shalt Not Steal"*	26.00	50.00	35.00

	Current Price Range		P/Y Average
☐ **Mother Goose,** *manufactured by McCoy Pottery*	50.00	60.00	54.50
☐ **Owl,** *glossy brown, McCoy Pottery*	15.00	25.00	18.00
☐ **Owl,** *white and brown, one eye closed, Shawnee Pottery Company*	11.00	15.00	13.00
☐ **Pair of Boots,** *manufactured by A.B. Co.*	40.00	50.00	44.50
☐ **Penguins,** *kissing, McCoy pottery*	24.00	28.00	26.00
☐ **Picnic Basket,** *McCoy pottery*	30.00	35.00	32.00
☐ **Pig,** *dressed as farmer, white, Shawnee Pottery Company*	32.00	36.00	34.00
☐ **Pig,** *manufactured by Brush*	60.00	80.00	74.00
☐ **Pig,** *Smiley, red bandana, flowers, Shawnee Pottery Company, with lid*	30.00	40.00	35.00
☐ **Pineapple,** *McCoy Pottery*	22.00	25.00	23.00
☐ **Polar Bear,** *manufactured by McCoy Pottery*	22.00	32.00	27.00
☐ **Pot Belly Stove,** *black, McCoy Pottery*	10.00	16.00	12.00
☐ **Puppy,** *holding sign, manufactured by McCoy Pottery*	20.00	30.00	26.00
☐ **Puppy,** *in blue pot, manufactured by A.B. Co.*	20.00	30.00	24.50
☐ **Rabbit In Hat,** *manufactured by A.B. Co.*	30.00	45.00	39.00
☐ **Raggedy Ann,** *manufactured by McCoy Pottery*	35.00	45.00	39.50
☐ **Red And White,** *with lid, 10" diameter*	26.00	50.00	35.00
☐ **Red Riding Hood,** *with lid, Hull Pottery*	30.00	40.00	33.00
☐ **Rooster,** *tail is handle, with lid, pale green, Red Wing pottery*	26.00	32.00	28.00
☐ **Rooster,** *yellow, manufactured by McCoy Pottery*	20.00	30.00	24.50
☐ **Sailor Boy,** *manufactured by Shawnee*	45.00	55.00	49.50
☐ **School Girl's Face,** *glasses and pigtails, "Cooky," Abingdon Pottery*	15.00	25.00	20.00
☐ **Schoolhouse Bell,** *manufactured by A.B. Co.*	20.00	30.00	24.50
☐ **Sheriff Pig,** *manufactured by R.R.P. Co.*	30.00	40.00	24.00
☐ **Strawberry,** *manufactured by Sears*	12.00	17.00	14.50
☐ **Strawberry,** *McCoy Pottery*	22.00	28.00	24.00
☐ **Sunset Scene,** *house and church in background, jeweling on three legs and finial, 7½"*	160.00	180.00	168.00
☐ **Teapot,** *copper and bronze, McCoy Pottery*	22.00	28.00	24.00
☐ **Toy Soldier,** *manufactured by A.B. Co.*	7.00	15.00	11.00
☐ **Train,** *manufactured by A.B. Co.*	25.00	35.00	29.50
☐ **Truck,** *with perched bird, yellow*	14.00	20.00	16.00
☐ **Tug Boat,** *manufactured by A.B. Co.*	55.00	65.00	59.50
☐ **Windmill,** *blue, manufactured by McCoy Pottery*	25.00	35.00	29.50
☐ **Wishing Well,** *McCoy Pottery*	16.00	24.00	18.00
☐ **Wise Bird,** *manufactured by R.R.P. Co.*	30.00	40.00	37.00
☐ **Woodsey Owl,** *manufactured by McCoy Pottery*	30.00	40.00	34.50

COPPER

DESCRIPTION: This versatile metal has been used extensively by mankind in every conceivable way. Copper is an excellent conductor of heat and electricity and is also very malleable. It has been made into wire, cooking utensils, coins, decorative objects and countless other useful items.

RECOMMENDED READING: For more in-depth information on copper you may refer to *From Hearth to Cookstove* by Linda Campbell Franklin and *The Official Price Guide to Kitchen Collectibles*, published by The House of Collectibles.

Copper Boiler, $75.00-$100.00

	Current Price Range		P/Y Average
☐ Cream Skimmer	35.00	45.00	36.00
☐ Cup	35.00	45.00	38.00
☐ Dipper, *19th century*	55.00	72.00	63.00
☐ Egg Poacher, *long iron handle, holds nine eggs*	35.00	65.00	40.00
☐ Egg Poacher, *two brass handles, holds 16 eggs, large*	35.00	65.00	40.00
☐ Dipper, *many types*	25.00	50.00	35.00
☐ Evaporating Pan, *iron bail handle, swinging, with ring handles*	85.00	95.00	84.00
☐ Funnel, *23" high*	155.00	210.00	156.00
☐ Funnel, *8" diameter*	35.00	45.00	32.00
☐ Funnel, *tube shaped, with screen attachment, 8" diameter*	35.00	45.00	32.00
☐ Hot Water Bottle, *12"*	40.00	45.00	36.00
☐ Hot Water Bottle, *egg shaped, with brass cap, unmarked*	35.00	40.00	32.00
☐ Hot Water Bottle, *circular, with brass cap, unmarked*	35.00	40.00	33.00
☐ Hot Water Bottle, *bail handle, brass lid, late 19th century*	50.00	55.00	49.00
☐ Hot Water Urn	250.00	300.00	255.00
☐ Hot Water Urn, *early 19th century*	300.00	500.00	425.00
☐ Kettle, *for apple butter, mid-1800's, dove-tail bottom, 25" diameter*	450.00	500.00	459.00
☐ Kettle, *apple butter, c. 1880-1900*	75.00	125.00	82.00
☐ Kettle, *copper with brass, wood handle, one gallon, Portugal*	14.00	18.00	15.00
☐ Kettle, *bail handle, iron, swinging, molded lip, iron stand*	460.00	475.00	462.00
☐ Kettle, *early 20th century*	50.00	60.00	51.00
☐ Kettle, *early 19th century*	115.00	125.00	112.00
☐ Kettle, *iron bail handle, jelly kettle*	60.00	75.00	62.00
☐ Kettle, *apple butter, used outdoors, 25" diameter*	110.00	130.00	115.00
☐ Kettle, *apple butter, used outdoors, 28" diameter*	130.00	150.00	128.00
☐ Kettle, *19th century, kitchen, brass knop, 15" high*	90.00	110.00	92.00
☐ Kettle, *mid 19th century, 9"*	260.00	300.00	257.00
☐ Kettle, *early American, 10" in diameter, 15" high*	130.00	175.00	132.00
☐ Lid, *set, 19th century, 6" diameter*	215.00	250.00	213.00
☐ Measure, *pint*	46.00	52.00	47.00
☐ Measure, *quart*	46.00	52.00	47.00
☐ Measure, *set, one pint to 2½ quarts*	170.00	190.00	172.00
☐ Measure, *flared spout, soldered handle, narrowing sides, early 19th century, 11"*	80.00	110.00	83.00
☐ Measure, *set, 19th century, harvest measures*	600.00	750.00	625.00
☐ Measuring Cups, *set, wide based, marked, seven in all, pure copper*	1400.00	2000.00	1600.00
☐ Measure, *1 quart, handle, brass knob*	50.00	60.00	55.00
☐ Measure, *pours, sloping edges, holds one pint*	25.00	30.00	26.00
☐ Measure, *pours, sloping edges, holds one quart*	30.00	35.00	32.00

	Current Price Range		P/Y Average
☐ **Measures,** *a trio of measures for rum, large to small, 19th century*	600.00	750.00	615.00
☐ **Milk Bucket,** *iron bail, handle, late 19th century*	100.00	125.00	105.00
☐ **Milk Churn,** *19th century, European, molded brass ring handles, 32" high*	850.00	1200.00	848.00
☐ **Milk Jug**	80.00	95.00	82.00
☐ **Milk Pail**	110.00	108.00	105.00
☐ **Mixing Bowl,** *circular base, one handle, 15" diameter, 8" deep*	45.00	65.00	48.00
☐ **Mixing Bowl,** *15" diameter, 8" deep*	50.00	80.00	55.00
☐ **Miniatures,** *pan, 5" diameter, 8" deep*	10.00	16.00	14.00
☐ **Miniatures,** *pan for frying, 5" diameter, handle of heavy brass*	12.00	22.00	16.00
☐ **Miniatures,** *wash tub, brass trim, and handles, 3" diameter*	10.00	14.00	12.00
☐ **Miniatures,** *kettle, pours, iron bail handle, swinging, 3" diameter*	9.00	14.00	12.00
☐ **Miniatures,** *tea kettle, 2" high, pure brass, European*	7.00	12.00	8.00
☐ **Mold,** *bird*	30.00	45.00	32.00
☐ **Mold,** *bundt*	95.00	110.00	95.00
☐ **Mold,** *Easter egg, rabbit*	55.00	65.00	55.00
☐ **Mold,** *jelly or pudding*	50.00	70.00	53.00
☐ **Mold,** *quart size*	30.00	45.00	32.00
☐ **Mold,** *pint size*	25.00	40.00	29.00
☐ **Mold,** *circular base with fruit or floral motif, quart size*	30.00	40.00	31.00
☐ **Mold,** *circular base, with fruit or floral motif, pint size*	15.00	26.00	15.00
☐ **Mold,** *fluted with scroll design along edge, 8"*	3.00	6.00	4.50
☐ **Mold,** *twelve tube, c. 1860*	130.00	150.00	129.00
☐ **Mold,** *pan*	140.00	155.00	138.00
☐ **Mold,** *pan, iron, handle, hanging eye*	150.00	165.00	149.00
☐ **Mold,** *dull finish, copper handles, 6" x 20" diameter*	150.00	165.00	149.00
☐ **Mold,** *iron handle, 13" diameter*	70.00	75.00	68.00
☐ **Pitcher**	40.00	55.00	41.00
☐ **Plate,** *9"*	10.00	20.00	12.00
☐ **Pot,** *crafted by hand, handled, early 19th century, 15" diameter*	95.00	110.00	98.00
☐ **Pots,** *hollow iron handles, tin interiors, with lids, set of three, 6", 7" and 8" diameter*	30.00	40.00	36.00
☐ **Reservoir,** *from kitchen stove, 19" x 8¾" x 11½"*	15.00	25.00	19.00
☐ **Salt Box**	50.00	65.00	52.00
☐ **Saucepan,** *covered, one long brass handle, lined with tin, one quart*	50.00	65.00	52.00
☐ **Saucepan,** *covered, one long handle, lined with tin, two quart*	50.00	67.00	52.00
☐ **Saucepan,** *covered, one long brass handle, lined with tin, three quart*	55.00	84.00	53.25
☐ **Saucepan,** *covered, one long brass handle, lined with tin, four quart*	60.00	93.00	65.00
☐ **Saucepan,** *double boiler, one quart*	35.00	43.00	39.00

COVERLETS

DESCRIPTION: Coverlets are bedspreads that have been woven on a loom.

VARIATIONS: The many types of designs produced by weavers fall into two categories: geometrics and Jacquards. The geometrics are the earliest coverlets made and they have small simple designs such as the star, diamond or snowball. The Jacquards, produced using a loom device made by Frenchman Joseph Jacquard, have curving, ornate designs such as flowers, birds and trees.

PERIOD: Coverlets were made from the 18th to the 20th century in the East, South and Midwest. Some are made today in isolated areas.

MAKER: The early geometric coverlets were woven at home usually by women. The Jacquards were more often made by professional male weavers. The Jacquard device enabled the weaver to put his name on his work, the simple loom didn't.

MATERIALS: Two threads are used in weaving. The warp threads, which are vertical are usually cotton, and the weft threads are horizontal and usually wool. All-cotton or all-wool coverlets are fairly rare. Red and blue dye was primarily used until the middle of the 19th century when synthetic dyes brought a greater color variety.

COMMENTS: The Jacquards are more popular with collectors than the geometrics. Most coverlets, especially the geometrics, are reasonably priced. The Jacquards go for the highest prices. Prices are also higher for the more rare all-cotton or all-wool coverlets. The development of the power loom brought an end to most manual loom weaving.

ADDITIONAL TIPS: The listings are identified as geometric or Jacquard. Following the identification are color, description and dates, when available.

RECOMMENDED READING: For further information contact the Colonial Coverlet Guild of America, 7931 Birchdale Ave., Elmwood Park, IL 60635.

	Current Price Range		P/Y Average
☐ **Geometric,** blue and white, double woven	175.00	210.00	185.00
☐ **Geometric,** blue and white, c. 1840	270.00	375.00	300.00
☐ **Geometric,** blue and white, design, c. 1830 ...	350.00	400.00	375.00
☐ **Geometric,** indigo and cream, double woven .	300.00	400.00	320.00
☐ **Geometric,** log cabin design	300.00	375.00	315.00
☐ **Geometric,** red, white, blue, center seam	275.00	325.00	290.00
☐ **Jacquard,** black and white, birds and flowers .	375.00	440.00	390.00
☐ **Jacquard,** blue and white, crossed rose sprays and stars center, potted rose plant border with eagle corners, double woven, c. 1850	750.00	800.00	760.00
☐ **Jacquard,** blue and white, floral and geometric motifs, house, horse and tree border, double woven, center seam, c. 1835	460.00	520.00	475.00
☐ **Jacquard,** blue and white, floral medallions and florals with American eagles and star border, double woven, c. 1830	575.00	650.00	600.00
☐ **Jacquard,** blue and white garlands and flowers, spread winged American Eagle, double woven, center seam, c. 1855	575.00	625.00	585.00
☐ **Jacquard,** blue and white, patriotic motif, signed, c. 1860	1050.00	1500.00	1200.00
☐ **Jacquard,** blue and white, rosettes, leaves, snowflakes, double woven	500.00	580.00	520.00
☐ **Jacquard,** red and white, floral motif	350.00	450.00	365.00
☐ **Jacquard,** red and white, lilies and floral sprays, signed	375.00	425.00	385.00
☐ **Jacquard,** red, blue, green, white, double house border, single weave, center seam	750.00	800.00	765.00
☐ **Jacquard,** red, eagle motif, signed	400.00	450.00	410.00
☐ **Jacquard,** red, eagle motif, unsigned	400.00	480.00	415.00
☐ **Jacquard,** red, green, white, oak leaf and flower design	400.00	450.00	415.00
☐ **Jacquard,** red, gold, blue, stars and leaves with grapes on border, center seam, c. 1850 ..	700.00	800.00	730.00
☐ **Jacquard,** red, tan, ivory, eagle motif, "Independence, Virtue, Liberty"	850.00	950.00	875.00
☐ **Jacquard,** red, white, blue, exotic birds	750.00	900.00	800.00
☐ **Jacquard,** red, white, blue, star and flower motif	350.00	450.00	365.00
☐ **Jacquard,** red, white, gold, bird medallions, double weave	340.00	420.00	360.00
☐ **Jacquard,** red, white, gold, green, central medallions and floral borders, double woven .	350.00	450.00	365.00
☐ **Jacquard,** red, white, green, flowers, stars, spread winged American eagle	400.00	500.00	420.00
☐ **Jacquard,** tree of life, signed, c. 1948	525.00	550.00	600.00

CRACKER JACK MEMORABILIA

ORIGIN: This famous mixture of popcorn, peanuts, and molasses was developed in 1893 and sold at the Columbian Exposition in Chicago where it was an overnight sensation. In 1896 it was named Cracker Jack and in 1910 the prizes were introduced. At first coupons were used which the customer could trade for various prizes. The company began putting the actual prize in each box in 1912.

MATERIAL: Cracker Jack prizes have been made of lead, paper, porcelain, plastic, tin and wood.

	Current Price Range		P/Y Average
☐ Clicker, Whistle, metal, embossed CJ, 2"....	15.00	25.00	20.00
☐ Corkscrew, Angelus, metal, 3¾" wide	25.00	50.00	37.50
☐ Flip Book, Charlie Chaplin, pre-1922	50.00	75.00	62.50
☐ Fortune Teller, 2" H.	25.00	50.00	37.50
☐ Game #1, red, white and blue, 2½"	20.00	50.00	35.00
☐ Horse And Wagon, metal, 2" long	50.00	100.00	75.00
☐ Hummer Band, metal, embossed, 1" diameter	15.00	25.00	20.00
☐ Air Corps Wings, metal, embossed	25.00	50.00	37.50
☐ Badge, junior detective, metal, embossed, 1¼"	5.00	25.00	15.00
☐ Baseball Card, #124, Earl Moore, Buffalo Federals, red, white and black	25.00	75.00	50.00
☐ Baseball Card, #150, W.R. Johnston, Cleveland Americans, red, white, blue and black ..	25.00	75.00	50.00
☐ Card, #95, Victoria Cross Heroes series, 3" x 2½", made by Lowney	5.00	25.00	15.00
☐ Charm For Bracelet, blue celluloid, comical head of man fully shaped with chain attached to top of head	20.00	25.00	21.00
☐ Clicker, metal, black and silver, instructions on front, 2⅛" H	5.00	25.00	15.00
☐ Iron-Ons, paper, set of four attached on a folded sheet, c. 1940-1950	5.00	10.00	7.00

	Current Price Range		P/Y Average

☐ **Jumper,** tin, frog, green and silver, 1⅞″, c. 1935 .... 25.00 35.00 28.00

Note: Jumpers were among the most numerous of Cracker Jacks premiums. These little novelties, always made of lightweight lithographed sheet tin, had a spring device on the underside. The end of the spring was pressed into a small wad of tar and the jumper placed on the ground. After a few seconds (or longer, depending on how hard you pressed) the spring worked itself free and the jumper sprang up into the air. Larger versions were commercially sold.

☐ **Magazine Advertisement,** *Saturday Evening Post,* June, 1919, red, white and blue 5.00 15.00 10.00

☐ **Magic Puzzle,** donkey, paper and plastic, 1½″ 5.00 15.00 10.00

☐ **Magic Puzzle,** fish 5.00 15.00 10.00

☐ **Magic Puzzle,** man with cigar, marked CJ Co. on reverse 5.00 15.00 10.00

☐ **Paper Booklet,** #12, Bess and Bill, 2½″ 15.00 50.00 32.50

☐ **Paper Frog,** outside is green black and white, opens to red and tan inside 15.00 25.00 20.00

☐ **Paper Golf Top,** red, white and blue, rules back, intact 15.00 50.00 32.50

☐ **Paper Prize,** Jack at the blackboard, turn dial and Jack writes and erases his name from blackboard, black, white, red, blue, and brown, 2″ square 25.00 75.00 50.00

☐ **Pin,** Lady 15.00 25.00 20.00

☐ **Pin,** Lady, celluloid, paper insert in back for "CJ 5 Cents" 15.00 25.00 20.00

☐ **Pocket Watch,** tin, gold, black, and white, 1½″ diameter 15.00 25.00 20.00

☐ **Postcard,** bears, #13 .... 5.00 25.00 15.00

☐ **Postcard,** bears, #15 .... 5.00 25.00 15.00

☐ **Puzzle Book,** #1, 4″, copyright 1917 .... 15.00 50.00 32.50

☐ **Puzzles,** #1-15, complete set 100.00 200.00 150.00

☐ **Rainbow Spinner,** blue and white on one side, other side is red, blue and yellow, 2½″ long, 1940s 15.00 25.00 20.00

☐ **Sign,** cardboard, string at top for hanging, red, white and blue box on blue background, 11″ x 15″ 200.00 500.00 350.00

☐ **Spinner,** tin, red/white/blue with illustration of Cracker Jacks package, 1½″ 10.00 15.00 12.00

Note: This was something like a top (very popular in the 1930s) but you spun it by hand without a string.

☐ **Tin,** Coconut Corn Crisp, full color round tin, 8½″ tall 45.00 60.00 49.00

☐ **Tin Stand-Up,** Harold Teen 25.00 50.00 37.50

☐ **Tin Stand-Up,** Orphan Annie 5.00 50.00 37.50

☐ **Tin Stand-Up,** Perry 25.00 50.00 37.50

☐ **Tin Top** 5.00 25.00 15.00

☐ **Tin Top,** fortune teller 25.00 50.00 37.50

	Current Price Range		P/Y Average
☐ **Truck,** plastic, embossed on all four sides, gold, 1⅝" long, late 1940s	5.00	15.00	10.00
☐ **Truck,** tin, red, white and black, one side says Cracker Jack, the other says Angelus, 1⅝" long	15.00	25.00	20.00
☐ **Whistle,** metal, embossed CJ	15.00	50.00	32.50
☐ **Whistle,** paper, red and white, reverse marked CJ Whistle, 2" H	15.00	25.00	20.00
☐ **Whistle,** paper, 2⅜", rare	15.00	50.00	30.00
☐ **Whistle,** plastic, red and white, embossed, 1½", 1950s	5.00	15.00	10.00
☐ **Whistle,** tin, silver and blue, 2½", no later than 1940s	15.00	25.00	18.00

CROCKS

DESCRIPTION: A crock is a container made of thick earthenware. Early crocks were intended as storage containers for food.

PERIOD: Crocks were made in the U.S. as early as 1641. Most household crocks were made in the 19th century however, and those with an interior glaze were made after 1900.

COMMENTS: The automatic glassblowing machine, introduced in 1903, made glass bottle making easier and the use of pottery crocks declined. Today they are popular collectibles.

RECOMMENDED READING: For further information on crocks please refer to *The Official Price Guide to Bottles Old and New.*

☐ **Jug Style,** *floral pattern, 2¾" diameter*	35.00	45.00	37.00
☐ **P. H. Alders, Compliments of The Eagle Saloon,** *St. Joseph, MO, cream and brown, 3"*	35.00	45.00	37.00
☐ **Ale,** *label, tan, 8½"*	15.00	25.00	17.00
☐ **American Stone Ware,** *in two lines, blue letters also near top a large six, gray, 13½"*	32.00	42.00	35.00
☐ **F.A. Ames & Co.,** *Owensboro KY in back, flat, tan and brown, 3½"*	38.00	48.00	43.00
☐ **Anderson's Weiss Beers,** *7¼"*	10.00	16.00	12.00

Western Stoneware Jar, *impressed Monmouth, Ill, 2,*
$45.00-$65.00

	Current Price Range		P/Y Average
☐ **Armour & Company,** *Chicago, jug, pouring spout, white, 7¼"*	24.00	30.00	26.00
☐ **B. & J. Arnold,** *London, England, Master Ink, dark brown, 9"*	15.00	25.00	18.00
☐ **B & H,** *cream, 3"*	30.00	40.00	33.00
☐ **Bass & Co.,** *NY, cream, 9½"*	18.00	27.00	21.00
☐ **Bean Pot,** *label, light blue, 4¼"*	5.00	8.00	6.00
☐ **L. Beard,** *on shoulder, cream and blue, blob top, 8½"*	20.00	26.00	22.00
☐ **Bellarmine Jug,** *superb mask, two horseshoe decorations below mask, 13"*	26.00	36.00	30.00
☐ **Biscuit Slip Glaze Stone Porter,** *blob top with small impressed ring for string, firmly impressed towards base, J, Heginbotham, Kings Arms, Stayley Bridge, reserve has other letters impressed below shoulder which cannot be clearly deciphered: UBL?T ??? ?EA TODY, towards base are a further possible 14 characters which cannot be deciphered, MINT STATE and EARLY 1800's, 9½"*	50.00	70.00	56.00
☐ **Compliments of Beniss & Thompson,** *Shelbyville, KY, tan and brown, 3¾"*	30.00	42.00	35.00
☐ **Jas. Benjamin, Stoneware Depot,** *Cincinnati, OH, blue stencil lettering, mottled tan, 9"*	38.00	48.00	42.00
☐ **Jas. Benjamin, Stoneware Depot,** *Cincinnati, OH, blue stencil lettering, tan, 13½"*	38.00	48.00	42.00

	Current Price Range		P/Y Average

☐ **Black's Family Liquor Stone,** *H.P. Black, 2042-43 Fresno in blue glaze letters, 1 gal. jug, ivory and dark brown* 30.00 40.00 33.00
☐ **Bitter,** *label, olive, brown trim, 10¼"* 35.00 50.00 40.00
☐ **B.B. Bitter Mineral Water,** *Bowling Green, MO, white, five gallon, 15"* 35.00 50.00 38.00
☐ **Black Family Liquor Store,** *stamped in blue glaze, brown and tan, gallon* 20.00 28.00 23.00
☐ **Blanchflower & Sons,** *homemade, four price medals, GT, Yarmouth, Norfolk, cream with black, six sided lid* 20.00 28.00 22.00
☐ **Blue Picture Print Ginger Jar,** *picture extends entire circumference of jar, building and junk in sail, 3½"* 25.00 35.00 27.00
☐ **Blue Print Ointment Pot Beach & Barnicott,** *successors to Dr. Roberts Bridgeport, poor man's friend, crisp print* 12.00 18.00 14.00
☐ **Blue Top And Print Cream Pot,** *Golden Pastures, thick rich cream, chard, picture of maid milking cow* 14.00 21.00 16.00
☐ **Brownings Pale Ale,** *Lewes, sparkled biscuit glazed finish, string rim at neck, cork closure, impressed, 8¾"* 18.00 24.00 20.00
☐ **Brownings Pale Ale,** *Lewes, potters mark: Stephen Green's Lambeth* 18.00 24.00 20.00
☐ **Boston Baked Beans,** *HHH on back, brick color. 1½"* 6.00 10.00 7.00
☐ **Boston Baked Beans,** *OK on back, brick color, 1½"* 6.00 10.00 7.00
☐ **Bowers Three Thistles Snuff,** *cream color with blue lettering, two to three gallon* 40.00 55.00 45.00
☐ **Burgess, John & Son,** *anchovy paste, warehouse 107 stand, black print on white, 3½", curved shoulder type, print 2" x 2¾"* 30.00 40.00 33.00
☐ **Bryant & Woodruff,** *Pittsfield, ME, handled jug, blue gray, 7"* 26.00 37.00 29.00
☐ **Bynol Malt & Oil,** *Allen & Hanbury's, black on white, print 2¾" x 3¾", height, lots of writing on this pot, 4⅕"* 20.00 27.00 22.00
☐ **Butter,** *no label, handle, blue-gray decoration, 4"* 26.00 37.00 28.00
☐ **Butter,** *no label, blue-gray decoration, 5¼"* . . 20.00 30.00 24.00
☐ **California Pop,** *pat. Dec. 29, 1872, blob top, tan, 10½"* 60.00 80.00 65.00
☐ **California Cough Balm,** *dose teaspoon full, children ½, 10-brown, crock jug with handle, 3¼"* 95.00 125.00 103.00
☐ **Cambridge Springs Mineral Water,** *in two lines, 2½", brown and tan* 20.00 30.00 23.00
☐ **Canning,** *inscribed Hold Fast That Which is Good, dark brown, 6½"* 25.00 36.00 28.00
☐ **Canning,** *wax sealer, 6"* 22.00 30.00 24.00
☐ **Canning,** *wax sealer, reddish brown, 8"* 22.00 30.00 24.00
☐ **Canning,** *blue with a gray decorative design, 8½"* 22.00 30.00 24.00
☐ **Canning,** *mustard color, 7"* 18.00 24.00 20.00

	Current Price Range		P/Y Average
☐ **Canning**, *maple leaf design in lid, caramel color, 6"*	12.00	18.00	14.00
☐ **Canning**, *brown, 5"*	16.00	22.00	17.50
☐ **Canning**, *wax channel, brown, 8½"*	17.00	24.00	18.00
☐ **Canning**, *reddish brown, green on the inside, 6¾"*	18.00	24.00	19.00
☐ **Canning**, *crude, brown, 4"*	12.00	18.00	13.00
☐ **Canning**, *wax sealer, dark brown, 5½"*	16.00	24.00	18.00
☐ **Canning**, *wax sealer, tan, 5½"*	16.00	24.00	18.00
☐ **Canning**, *wax sealer, dark brown, 5½"*	12.00	17.00	14.00
☐ **Canning**, *wax sealer, dark brown, 6½"*	11.00	16.00	13.00
☐ **Canning**, *wax sealer, mottled gray, 5"*	10.00	15.00	12.00
☐ **Canning**, *wax sealer, brown, 5½"*	13.00	18.00	14.50
☐ **Canning**, *barrel, dark brown, 5½"*	13.00	18.00	14.50
☐ **Canning**, *lid, star design, dark brown, 8¾"* ..	18.00	25.00	20.00
☐ **Canning**, *dark brown, 7½"*	16.00	22.00	17.00
☐ **Canning**, *tan, 9"*	18.00	25.00	20.00
☐ **Canning**, *wax channel, brown, 7½"*	18.00	25.00	20.00

CURRENCY

DESCRIPTION: Currency notes issued by the federal government, as a medium of exchange ("legal tender").

MAKER: Today all U.S. paper money is produced by the U.S. Department of Printing and Engraving at Washington, D.C. Early specimens were contracted for with private firms. From its origin to the present day, all U.S. paper money has been *engraved.* This is considered the most difficult process to counterfeit.

MATERIALS: A special paper is used for U.S. paper money, of high quality and with tiny blue and red threads running through it. This paper is not available to the public.

MARKS: Various standard markings appear on U.S. paper money, including the Treasury Seal, district number, district name, control number, and the serial number. The serial number is green and appears twice on each note, at the lower left and upper right. When the numbers on a note are not alike, or missing, or wrongly positioned, it is regarded as a freak note and commands a premium price.

COMMENTS: Traditionally, collectors were interested only in the early types or "large size" currency. (In 1929 the government reduced the physical size of notes to their present proportions.) Today, all paper money is collectible, though common specimens must be in strictly uncirculated condition to be regarded as such.

ADDITIONAL TIPS: Paper money deteriorates in circulation very rapidly. When a note is said to be uncirculated it has no creases, wrinkles, fading, or signs of fatigue; the paper is crisp and the printing fresh and bright. Notes in very deteriorated condition, with holes or corners missing, etc., are not deemed collectible unless the type is very rare.

Early U.S. paper money is often found with tiny pinholes, even when the condition is otherwise excellent. This is due to the common practice among old-time storekeepers of impaling notes on nails, before the use of cash registers. Since this defect is so commonplace, it does not cause a great reduction in value, unless the hole occurs on the portrait.

Twenty Dollar Note, *Federal reserve bank note, 1929, portrait of President Jackson, small size,* **$20.00-$100.00**

ONE DOLLAR NOTES (1969) FEDERAL RESERVE NOTES
(Small Size)   NOTE NO. 18A

SERIES OF 1969—ELSTON-KENNEDY, GREEN SEAL

Boston 2.70	Cleveland 2.70	Chicago 2.70	Kansas City 2.70
New York 2.70	Richmond 2.70	St. Louis 2.70	Dallas 2.70
Philadelphia 2.70	Atlanta 2.70	Minneapolis 2.70	San Francisco . . . 2.70

SERIES OF 1969A—KABIS-KENNEDY, GREEN SEAL

Boston 2.70	Cleveland 2.70	Chicago 2.70	Kansas City 2.70
New York 2.70	Richmond 2.70	St. Louis 2.70	Dallas 2.70
Philadelphia 2.70	Atlanta 2.70	Minneapolis 2.70	San Francisco . . . 2.70

SERIES OF 1969B—KABIS-CONNALLY, GREEN SEAL

Boston 2.70	Cleveland 2.70	Chicago 2.70	Kansas City 2.70
New York 2.70	Richmond 2.70	St. Louis 2.70	Dallas 2.70
Philadelphia 2.70	Atlanta 2.70	Minneapolis 2.70	San Francisco . . . 2.70

SERIES OF 1969C—BANUELOS-CONNALLY, GREEN SEAL

Boston 2.15	Cleveland 2.15	Chicago 2.15	Kansas City 2.15
New York 2.15	Richmond 2.15	St. Louis 2.15	Dallas 2.15
Philadelphia 2.15	Atlanta 2.15	Minneapolis 2.15	San Francisco . . . 2.15

SERIES OF 1969D—BANUELOS-CONNALLY, GREEN SEAL

Boston 2.15	Cleveland 2.15	Chicago 2.15	Kansas City 2.15
New York 2.15	Richmond 2.15	St. Louis 2.15	Dallas.........2.15
Philadelphia 2.15	Atlanta 2.15	Minneapolis 2.15	San Francisco...2.15

SERIES OF 1974—NEFF-SIMON, GREEN SEAL

Boston 2.15	Cleveland 2.15	Chicago 2.15	Kansas City 2.15
New York 2.15	Richmond 2.15	St. Louis 2.15	Dallas.........2.15
Philadelphia ...2.15	Atlanta 2.15	Minneapolis 2.15	San Francisco...2.15

SERIES OF 1977—MORTON-BLUMENTHAL, GREEN SEAL

Boston 2.10	Cleveland 2.10	Chicago 2.10	Kansas City 2.10
New York 2.10	Richmond 2.10	St. Louis 2.10	Dallas.........2.10
Philadelphia 2.10	Atlanta 2.10	Minneapolis 2.10	San Francisco...2.10

SERIES OF 1977A—MORTON-MILLER, GREEN SEAL

Boston 2.10	Cleveland 2.10	Chicago 2.10	Kansas City 2.10
New York 2.10	Richmond 2.10	St. Louis 2.10	Dallas.........2.10
Philadelphia ...2.10	Atlanta 2.10	Minneapolis 2.10	San Francisco...2.10

SERIES OF 1981—TORTEGA-REGAN, GREEN SEAL

Issued for all Federal Reserve Banks....................................CURRENT

FIVE DOLLAR NOTES (1950-1963) FEDERAL RESERVE NOTES
(Small Size)   NOTE NO. 57

SERIES OF 1950 — SIGNATURES OF CLARK-SNYDER, GREEN SEAL

BANK & CITY	A.B.P.	V.FINE	UNC.	BANK & CITY	A.B.P.	V.FINE	UNC.
☐Boston	5.15	7.00	15.75	☐Chicago	5.15	7.00	16.00
☐New York	5.15	7.00	13.75	☐St. Louis	5.15	7.00	17.00
☐Philadelphia	5.15	7.00	15.00	☐Minneapolis	5.15	7.00	17.50
☐Cleveland	5.15	7.00	15.00	☐Kansas City	5.15	7.00	17.00
☐Richmond	5.15	7.00	14.75	☐Dallas.........	5.15	7.00	17.00
☐Atlanta	5.15	7.00	15.00	☐San Francisco ..	5.15	7.00	16.00

SERIES OF 1950A — PRIEST-HUMPHREY, GREEN SEAL

Boston 14.25	Cleveland....14.25	Chicago 14.25	Kansas City ...14.25
New York.....14.25	Richmond 14.25	St. Louis 14.75	Dallas 14.25
Philadelphia ..14.25	Atlanta.......14.25	Minneapolis ...14.75	San Francisco .14.25

SERIES OF 1950B — PRIEST-ANDERSON, GREEN SEAL

Boston 13.60	Cleveland....13.00	Chicago 12.00	Kansas City ...14.25
New York.....13.00	Richmond 13.00	St. Louis 14.50	Dallas 13.80
Philadelphia ...13.00	Atlanta.......13.00	Minneapolis ...15.00	San Francisco .14.35

SERIES OF 1950C — SMITH-DILLON, GREEN SEAL

Boston 12.50	Cleveland.....12.85	Chicago 13.75	Kansas City ...13.65
New York.....12.25	Richmond 12.85	St. Louis 12.85	Dallas 15.75
Philadelphia ..12.85	Atlanta.......12.85	Minneapolis ...13.75	San Francisco .14.25

SERIES OF 1950D — GRANAHAN-DILLON, GREEN SEAL

Boston 12.30	Cleveland.....12.30	Chicago 12.30	Kansas City ...12.75
New York.....12.30	Richmond 12.30	St. Louis 12.30	Dallas 12.75
Philadelphia ..12.30	Atlanta.......12.30	Minneapolis ...12.75	San Francisco .12.30

SERIES OF 1950E — GRANAHAN-FOWLER, GREEN SEAL

New York.....16.25	Chicago 17.00	San Francisco .16.50

This Note was issued by only three banks.

TEN DOLLAR NOTES (1934) FEDERAL RESERVE NOTES
(Small Size)   **NOTE NO. 83B**

SERIES OF 1934A—SIGNATURES OF JULIAN-MORGENTHAU, GREEN SEAL

BANK & CITY	A.B.P.	V.FINE	UNC.	BANK & CITY	A.B.P.	V.FINE	UNC.
☐Boston	10.50	13.75	26.00	☐Chicago	10.50	13.75	25.00
☐New York	10.50	13.75	26.00	☐St. Louis	10.50	13.75	31.00
☐Philadelphia	10.50	13.75	26.00	☐Minneapolis	10.50	13.75	31.00
☐Cleveland	10.50	13.75	28.00	☐Kansas City	10.50	13.75	25.00
☐Richmond	10.50	13.75	29.00	☐Dallas	10.50	13.75	25.00
☐Atlanta	10.50	13.75	29.00	☐San Francisco* .	14.00	25.00	250.00

*San Francisco - 1934A with brown seal and overprinted HAWAII on face and back. Special issue for use in combat areas during World War II. Value in V. Fine $45.00, Value in Unc. $220.00.

SERIES OF 1934B — SIGNATURES OF JULIAN-VINSON, GREEN SEAL

BANK & CITY	A.B.P.	V.FINE	UNC.	BANK & CITY	A.B.P.	V.FINE	UNC.
☐Boston	10.75	15.00	29.00	☐Chicago	10.75	15.00	29.00
☐New York	10.75	15.00	29.00	☐St. Louis	10.75	15.00	29.00
☐Philadelphia	10.75	15.00	29.00	☐Minneapolis	10.75	15.00	29.00
☐Cleveland	10.75	15.00	31.00	☐Kansas City	10.75	16.00	31.00
☐Richmond	10.75	15.00	29.00	☐Dallas	10.75	15.00	31.00
☐Atlanta	10.75	15.00	29.00	☐San Francisco ..	10.75	15.00	29.00

SERIES OF 1934C — SIGNATURES OF JULIAN-SNYDER, GREEN SEAL

BANK & CITY	A.B.P.	V.FINE	UNC.	BANK & CITY	A.B.P.	V.FINE	UNC.
☐Boston	10.25	12.75	21.75	☐Chicago	10.25	12.75	21.00
☐New York	10.25	12.75	21.00	☐St. Louis	10.25	12.75	21.00
☐Philadelphia	10.25	12.75	21.00	☐Minneapolis	10.25	12.75	22.00
☐Cleveland	10.25	13.00	23.00	☐Kansas City	10.25	12.75	22.00
☐Richmond	10.25	12.75	21.00	☐Dallas	10.25	12.75	22.00
☐Atlanta	10.25	12.75	21.00	☐San Francisco ..	10.25	12.75	21.00

SERIES OF 1934D — SIGNATURES OF CLARK-SNYDER, GREEN SEAL

BANK & CITY	A.B.P.	V.FINE	UNC.	BANK & CITY	A.B.P.	V.FINE	UNC.
☐Boston	10.25	12.75	21.50	☐Chicago	10.25	12.75	21.50
☐New York	10.25	12.75	21.50	☐St. Louis	10.25	12.75	21.50
☐Philadelphia	10.25	12.75	21.50	☐Minneapolis	10.25	12.75	23.00
☐Cleveland	10.25	12.75	22.00	☐Kansas City	10.25	12.75	23.50
☐Richmond	10.25	12.75	21.50	☐Dallas	10.25	12.75	22.00
☐Atlanta	10.25	12.75	21.50	☐San Francisco ..	10.25	12.75	21.50

TWENTY DOLLAR NOTES (1928) FEDERAL RESERVE NOTES
(Small Size)   **NOTE NO. 99**

SERIES OF 1928 — SIGNATURES OF TATE-MELLON, GREEN SEAL

BANK	A.B.P.	V.FINE	UNC.	BANK	A.B.P.	V.FINE	UNC.
☐Boston	22.00	28.00	65.00	☐Chicago	22.00	28.00	53.00
☐New York	22.00	28.00	57.00	☐St. Louis	22.00	32.00	70.00
☐Philadelphia	22.00	28.00	60.00	☐Minneapolis	22.00	35.00	80.00
☐Cleveland	22.00	28.00	60.00	☐Kansas City	22.00	32.00	80.00
☐Richmond	22.00	35.00	70.00	☐Dallas	22.00	32.00	80.00
☐Atlanta	22.00	32.00	65.00	☐San Francisco ..	22.00	30.00	70.00

SERIES OF 1928A — SIGNATURES OF WOODS-MELLON, GREEN SEAL

CITY	A.B.P.	V.FINE	UNC.	CITY	A.B.P.	V.FINE	UNC.
☐Boston	22.75	40.00	60.00	☐Chicago	22.75	37.00	70.00
☐New York	22.75	37.00	70.00	☐St. Louis	22.75	40.00	65.00
☐Philadelphia	22.75	37.00	60.00	☐Minneapolis		NOT ISSUED	
☐Cleveland	22.75	37.00	65.00	☐Kansas City	22.75	45.00	85.00
☐Richmond	22.75	40.00	70.00	☐Dallas	22.75	35.00	75.00
☐Atlanta	22.75	40.00	65.00	☐San Francisco ..		NOT ISSUED	

TWENTY DOLLAR NOTES (1928) FEDERAL RESERVE NOTES
(Small Size) NOTE NO. 100

SERIES OF 1928B — SIGNATURES OF WOODS-MELLON, GREEN SEAL FACE AND BACK DESIGN SIMILAR TO PREVIOUS NOTE. NUMERAL IN FEDERAL RESERVE SEAL IS NOW CHANGED TO A LETTER.

BANK	A.B.P.	V.FINE	UNC.	BANK	A.B.P.	V.FINE	UNC.
☐Boston	21.85	31.50	53.00	☐Chicago	21.85	31.50	53.00
☐New York	21.85	31.50	53.00	☐St. Louis	21.85	31.50	55.00
☐Philadelphia	21.85	31.50	53.00	☐Minneapolis	21.85	31.50	55.00
☐Cleveland	21.85	31.50	53.00	☐Kansas City	21.85	31.50	55.00
☐Richmond	21.85	31.50	53.00	☐Dallas	21.85	31.50	60.00
☐Atlanta	21.85	31.50	55.00	☐San Francisco	21.85	31.50	55.00

SERIES OF 1928C — SIGNATURES OF WOODS-MILLS, GREEN SEAL ONLY TWO BANKS ISSUED THIS NOTE.

☐Chicago	28.00	55.00	225.00	☐San Francisco	28.00	55.00	225.00

TWENTY DOLLAR NOTES (1934) FEDERAL RESERVE NOTES
(Small Size) NOTE NO. 100A

FACE AND BACK DESIGN SIMILAR TO PREVIOUS NOTE. "REDEEMABLE IN GOLD" REMOVED FROM OBLIGATION OVER FEDERAL RESERVE SEAL. SIGNATURES OF JULIAN-MORGENTHAU, GREEN SEAL.

BANK	GOOD	V.FINE	UNC.	BANK	GOOD	V.FINE	UNC.
☐Boston	——	29.00	50.00	☐St. Louis	——	30.00	47.00
☐New York	——	29.00	47.00	☐Minneapolis	——	30.00	55.00
☐Philadelphia	——	29.00	47.00	☐Kansas City	——	30.00	47.00
☐Cleveland	——	29.00	47.00	☐Dallas	——	30.00	47.00
☐Richmond	——	29.00	47.00	☐San Francisco	——	30.00	47.00
☐Atlanta	——	29.00	47.00	☐*San Francisco			
☐Chicago	——	29.00	47.00	(HAWAII)	50.00	150.00	925.00

CURRIER & IVES PRINTS

ORIGIN: Nathaniel Currier began his career in lithography in 1828. At that time, he was apprenticed at the age of 15, to Pendleton of Boston, one of the earliest American lithographic firms known. After five years, he left and engaged in various business ventures, one of which was with Stodart in New York. It was at this time in 1834 that the print *"Dartmouth College"* was published by Currier.

The venture with Stodart was short-lived; and, in 1835, Currier started his own firm at 1 Wall Street in New York. James Ives joined the firm in 1852 as a bookkeeper, after being recommended to Nathaniel Currier by his brother Charles, who also worked in the business. (Ives was married to Charles' sister-in-law.) The firm was located in New York City during its entire existence but occupied several locations over the years.

DESCRIPTION: The firm was unique in its ability to combine artistic talent, skilled craftsmanship, appropriate technology, and merchandising acumen into a successful business enterprise. Well-known artists of the day including Maurer, Palmer, Tait, and Worth were a few who were employed at various times. Appropriate attention to detail is manifest in the work as examination of a clipper ship print or a country scene will attest. Only the finest materials were used: stones from Bavaria (where lithography was invented), lithographic crayons from France, and colors from Austria. The firm contributed to technology by inventing a lithographic crayon, reputed to be superior to any others available anywhere. It also produced a lithographic ink, which contained beef suet, goose grease, white wax, castile soap, gum mastic, shellac, and gas black. Innovative merchandising techniques were used. Mass distribution and low cost were the keys to success. Cost was important. Uncolored prints sold for as little as six cents each and even large-colored folios sold for no more than three dollars. Anyone could afford a print at these prices. Prints were sold door-to-door by peddlers, in the streets by pushcart vendors, in geographically remote places through distributors, and even overseas through agents. Although an estimated ten million prints were sold, only a small percentage are in existence today.

The prints were published in various sizes but are commonly grouped into folio sizes shown below:

Very Small	Up to approximately 7″ x 9″
Small	Approximately 8.8″ x 12.8″
Medium	Approximately 9″ x 14″ to 14″ x 20″
Large	Anything over 14″ x 20″

The sizes pertain to the picture only, not to the margin around the picture. Often, print owners trimmed the margins of the pictures. Therefore, an uncut print is more valuable than a pared one.

Most of the prints were made in black and white and then hand-colored. Although occasionally sold uncolored, usually a group of workers colored the prints by working from a professional artist's rendition. Because of this method, different colorings of the same print were found. Folio sizes very small, small and medium were completed in this manner. However, the large folios were sometimes partially printed in color and then finished by hand usually by only one artist.

Currier and Ives were successful men who worked well together. Currier retired in 1880 and died in 1888. Ives continued to run the business until his death in 1895. Although the sons of both men ran the business from 1895, it soon dissolved in 1907.

COMMENTS: Currier and Ives' prints are not only attractive and historically informative, but they represent a sound investment value. Studies indicate these prints have increased in value by 300 to 500 percent in the past twenty years. For example, the large folio "The Life of a Hunter-A Tight Fix" sold in 1928 for $3,000. Recently it sold at an auction for $7,500.

Currier and Ives prints are found in public and private collections. A large collection exists at the New York City Museum which holds over 2,885 of their prints. However, no known collection contains all of the prints because previously unknown titles are uncovered occasionally.

RECOMMENDED READING: For further information you may refer to *The Official Price Guide to Collector Prints,* published by The House of Collectibles.

AMERICAN HOMESTEAD WINTER.

American Homestead Winter *by Currier and Ives,* **$460.00-$635.00**

THE BEST FIFTY (small folio)

	Current Price Range		P/Y Average
☐ 1. The Express Train - 1790*	750.00	1000.00	770.00
☐ 2. American Railroad Scene - Snowbound -187*	900.00	1200.00	920.00
☐ 3. Beach Snipe Shooting - 445	900.00	1100.00	920.00
☐ 4. Ice-boat Race on the Hudson - 3021	1000.00	1800.00	1100.00
☐ 5. Central Park in Winter - 953	900.00	1200.00	920.00
☐ 6. The Star of the Road - 5701	250.00	500.00	270.00
☐ 7. The High Bridge at Harlem, N. Y. - 2810*	250.00	400.00	270.00
☐ 8. Maple Sugaring, Early Spring in the Northern Woods - 3975	400.00	600.00	410.00
☐ 9. Shakers Near Lebanon - 5475	600.00	900.00	620.00
☐10. Winter Sports - Pickerel fishing - 6747	750.00	900.00	780.00
☐11. The American Clipper Ship Witch of the Wave - 115	600.00	800.00	620.00
☐12. Gold Mining in California - 2412	700.00	900.00	720.00
☐13. The Great International Boat Race - 2623	800.00	1000.00	820.00
☐14. Wild Turkey Shooting - 6677	400.00	600.00	420.00
☐15. Perry's Victory on Lake Erie - 4754	400.00	550.00	420.00
☐16. Washington at Mount Vernon, 1797 - 6515	250.00	350.00	270.00
☐17. The Whale Fishery. ''Laying On'' - 6626	900.00	1200.00	920.00
☐18. Chatham Square, New York - 1020	450.00	600.00	470.00
☐19. Water Rail Shooting - 6567*	500.00	650.00	520.00
☐20. The Sleigh Race - 5554*	500.00	800.00	520.00
☐21. Franklin's Experiment - 2128*	300.00	500.00	320.00

	Current Price Range		P/Y Average
☐22. Washington Crossing the Delaware - 6523*	250.00	350.00	270.00
☐23. American Homestead Winter - 172	400.00	600.00	420.00
☐24. Washington Taking Leave of the Officers of His Army - 6547	250.00	350.00	270.00
☐25. Steamboat Knickerbocker - 5727	250.00	350.00	270.00
☐26. Kiss Me Quick! - 3349*	200.00	250.00	220.00
☐27. On the Mississippi Loading Cotton - 4607	250.00	350.00	270.00
☐28. Bound Down the River - 627	350.00	500.00	370.00
☐29. American Whalers Crushed in the Ice - 205	800.00	1000.00	820.00
☐30. Dartmouth College - 1446*	1000.00	1300.00	1100.00
☐31. Terrific Combat Between the Monitor, 2 Guns, and the Merrimac, 10 Guns - 5996*	350.00	500.00	370.00
☐32. General Francis Marion - 2250	200.00	300.00	220.00
☐33. Art of Making Money Plenty - 275	200.00	300.00	220.00
☐34. Hon. Abraham Lincoln - 2895*	150.00	250.00	170.00
☐35. Gen. George Washington (with cape) - 2261*	150.00	250.00	170.00
☐36. Black Bass Spearing - 543	1100.00	1300.00	1200.00
☐37. Early Winter - 1652	1500.00	2000.00	1600.00
☐38. Woodcock Shooting - 6773*	450.00	600.00	470.00
☐39. ''Dutchman'' and ''Hiram Woodruff'' - 1640	600.00	700.00	620.00
☐40. Great Conflagration at Pittsburg, Pa. - 2581	500.00	600.00	520.00
☐41. Bear Hunting, Close Quarters - 446*	1500.00	2000.00	1600.00
☐42. The Destruction of Tea at Boston Harbor - 1571	600.00	800.00	620.00
☐43. Cornwallis is Taken - 1258	250.00	400.00	270.00
☐44. Landing of the Pilgrims at Plymouth, 11th Dec., 1620-3435*	200.00	300.00	220.00
☐45. The Great Fight for the Championship - 2613	300.00	500.00	320.00
☐46. Benjamin Franklin - 499*	150.00	300.00	170.00
☐47. Noah's Ark - 4494*	150.00	200.00	170.00
☐48. Black Eyed Susan - 551*	125.00	150.00	140.00
☐49. The Bloomer Costume - 574*	150.00	175.00	160.00
☐50. The Clipper Yacht ''America'' - 1173*	700.00	1000.00	720.00

THE BEST FIFTY (large folio)

	Current Price Range		P/Y Average
☐ 1. Husking - 3008	4000.00	8500.00	4500.00
☐ 2. American Forest Scene-Maple Sugaring - 157	3000.00	4500.00	3200.00
☐ 3. Central Park Winter-The Skating Pond - 954	3000.00	5000.00	3200.00
☐ 4. Home to Thanksgiving - 2882	7000.00	8000.00	7200.00
☐ 5. Life of a Hunter-A Tight Fix - 3522	12000.00	15000.00	12500.00
☐ 6. Life on the Prairie-The Buffalo Hunt - 3527	5500.00	6000.00	5600.00
☐ 7. The Lightning Express Trains Leaving the Junction - 3535* .	5000.00	6500.00	5200.00
☐ 8. Peytona and Fashion - 4763	7000.00	8000.00	7200.00
☐ 9. The Rocky Mountains-Emigrants Crossing the Plains - 5196	7500.00	10000.00	7800.00
☐10. Trolling for Blue Fish - 6158	3000.00	4000.00	3200.00
☐11. Whale Fishery-The Sperm Whale in a Flurry - 6628*	7000.00	8000.00	7200.00
☐12. Winter in the Country-The Old Grist Mill - 6738	5500.00	7000.00	5700.00
☐13. American Farm Scenes No. 4 (Winter) - 136	2000.00	4000.00	2200.00
☐14. American National Game of Baseball - 180	8000.00	10000.00	8200.00
☐15. American Winter Sports-Trout Fishing on Chateaugay Lake -210*	3000.00	4500.00	3200.00
☐16. Mink Trapping-Prime - 4139	7500.00	8000.00	7600.00
☐17. Preparing for Market - 4870*	1500.00	3000.00	1750.00
☐18. Winter in the Country-Getting Ice - 6737	5000.00	7500.00	5500.00
☐19. Across the Continent-Westward the Course of Empire Takes its Way - 33	7500.00	8000.00	7600.00
☐20. Life on the Prairie-The Trappers Defense - 3528	5500.00	6000.00	5700.00
☐21. The Midnight Race on the Mississippi - 4116*	2000.00	3500.00	2200.00
☐22. The Road-Winter - 5171	6000.00	8000.00	6200.00
☐23. Summer Scenes in New York Harbor - 5876	2000.00	3000.00	2200.00
☐24. Trotting Cracks at the Forge - 6169	2000.00	3500.00	2200.00
☐**25. View of San Francisco - 6409**	4000.00	6000.00	4200.00
☐26. Wreck of the Steamship ''San Francisco'' - 5492	3500.00	4500.00	3700.00
☐27. Taking the Back Track ''A Dangerous Neighborhood'' - 5961	5000.00	5500.00	5200.00
☐28. American Field Sports-Flush'd - 149	1500.00	3000.00	1600.00
☐29. American Hunting Scenes-A Good Chance - 174	1500.00	3000.00	1600.00

	Current Price Range		P/Y Average
☐30. American Winter Scenes-Morning - 208	4000.00	6000.00	4200.00
☐31. Autumn in New England-Cider Making - 322	2500.00	3500.00	2600.00
☐32. Catching a Trout-"We Hab You Now, Sar" - 845	800.00	1000.00	850.00
☐33. Clipper Ship "Nightingale" - 1159	5500.00	7000.00	5700.00
☐34. The Life of a Fireman-The Race - 3519	2000.00	4000.00	2200.00
☐35. Mac and Zachary Taylor-Horse Race - 3848	1000.00	2000.00	1100.00
☐36. New England Winter Scene - 4420	3500.00	5000.00	3600.00
☐37. Rail Shooting on the Delaware - 5054	3500.00	5000.00	3600.00
☐38. Snowed Up-Ruffed Gouse-Winter - 5581	3000.00	4000.00	3200.00
☐39. Surrender of General Burgoyne at Saratoga - 5907	3000.00	3500.00	3200.00
☐40. Surrender of Cornwallis at Yorktown - 5906	3000.00	3500.00	3200.00
☐41. Clipper Ship "Red Jacket" - 1165*	4000.00	5000.00	4200.00
☐42. American Winter Sports-Deer Shooting on the Shattagee -209	3000.00	5000.00	3200.00
☐43. The Bark "Theoxana" - 371	1500.00	2500.00	1700.00
☐44. The Cares of a Family - 814*	2000.00	2500.00	2100.00
☐45. The Celebrated Horse Lexington - 887*	1600.00	1800.00	1700.00
☐46. Grand Drive-Central Park - 2481	2000.00	3000.00	2100.00
☐47. The Great Fire at Chicago - 2615	2000.00	3000.00	2100.00
☐48. Landscape, Fruit and Flowers - 3440	1500.00	2500.00	1600.00
☐49. The Life of a Fireman-The Metropolitan System - 3516	2000.00	4000.00	2100.00
☐50. The Splendid Naval Triumph on the Mississippi - 5659	750.00	1000.00	780.00

Note: Those titles followed by an asterisk are known to appear on more than one composition.

CUT GLASS

DESCRIPTION: Cut glass features deep prismatic cutting in elaborate, often geometrical designs. The edges are very sharp, thus allowing light to be refracted easily. Its high lead content makes it heavier than most blown glass. It also has a distinct bell tone when struck.

ORIGIN: It developed during the 16th century in Bohemia and was very popular until the invention of molded pressed glass in America about 1825 which was an inexpensive imitation of cut glass. It enjoyed a revival during the Brilliant period of cut glass in America which dated from 1876-1916.

PROCESS: The making of cut glass was a time consuming process requiring the patience and talent of master craftsmen. The glass was handblown of the finest 35-45% lead crystal and poured into molds to produce the shaped piece, called a blank. These blanks were anywhere from ¼" - ½" thick in order to achieve the deep cutting which distinguished this glass from later periods. The resulting finished product was, therefore exceedingly heavy.

The cutting and polishing was accomplished in four steps. The first step involved making the desired pattern on the blank with crayons or paint. Next the deepest cuts were made by rough cutting. This was accomplished by pressing the blank on an abrasive cutting wheel of metal or stone which was lubricated by a small stream of water and sand. In the third step, the rough cuts were smoothed with a finer stone wheel and water only. Finally, polishing or "coloring" was done on a wooden wheel with putty powder or pumice, in order to produce the gleaming brilliant finish.

RECOMMENDED READING: For more in-depth information on cut glass, you may refer to *The Official Price Guide to Glassware,* and *The Official Identification Guide to Glassware,* published by The House of Collectibles.

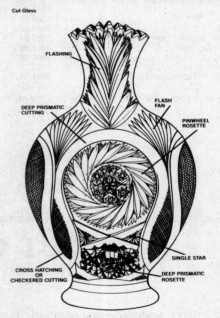

PATTERN MOTIFS

	Current Price Range		P/Y Average
☐ **Ashtray,** rectangular	55.00	80.00	62.00
☐ **Ashtray,** richly cut, signed	80.00	110.00	88.00
☐ **Basket,** floral design, handle, 10″	210.00	260.00	225.00
☐ **Basket,** scalloped edge, handle, 6″	160.00	210.00	175.00
☐ **Basket,** floral and miter cut, twisted handle, 8″	170.00	195.00	172.00
☐ **Bell,** diamond and fan	110.00	135.00	112.00
☐ **Bell,** star design	135.00	160.00	138.00
☐ **Bonbon,** diamond shape, 6″	70.00	95.00	78.00
☐ **Bonbon,** heart shape, 6″	80.00	110.00	88.00
☐ **Bonbon,** oval, 5¼″	28.00	38.00	30.00
☐ **Bonbon,** pedestal, pair	460.00	510.00	475.00

	Current Price Range		P/Y Average
☐ **Candy Dish,** American, Clarke	90.00	140.00	110.00
☐ **Candy Dish,** sterling and crystal, Hawkes . . .	160.00	210.00	175.00
☐ **Carafe,** block and fan	32.00	42.00	35.00
☐ **Carafe,** diamond and strawberry	185.00	210.00	188.00
☐ **Carafe,** hobstar and clover	55.00	80.00	62.00
☐ **Carafe,** prism and fan	80.00	110.00	88.00
☐ **Carafe,** Russian, starred buttons	235.00	335.00	275.00
☐ **Carafe,** water, Harvard, prism stem	110.00	135.00	112.00
☐ **Carafe,** water, hobstar and notched prism . .	80.00	110.00	88.00
☐ **Carafe,** water, pinwheel, crosscut diamond and flasked fan	90.00	120.00	98.00
☐ **Carafe,** water, pinwheel cut flowers	80.00	110.00	88.00
☐ **Carafe,** wine, hobstar and fan, sterling collar	135.00	160.00	138.00
☐ **Celery,** Harvard, Libbey	260.00	310.00	275.00
☐ **Celery,** hobstar and fan, signed Hawkes	135.00	160.00	138.00
☐ **Celery,** strawberry, diamond and fan, Hawkes	185.00	210.00	188.00
☐ **Champagne,** Russian, rayed star base	80.00	110.00	88.00
☐ **Compote,** Harvard, hobstar base, intaglio cut, 9″	310.00	360.00	325.00
☐ **Compote,** hobstar, strawberry, diamond and fan, 8″	360.00	410.00	375.00
☐ **Compote,** pinwheel, hobstar, prism cut, 7½″	135.00	160.00	138.00
☐ **Compote,** square, signed Hoare	510.00	585.00	538.00
☐ **Cordial,** crystal and silver, pair	760.00	835.00	780.00
☐ **Cordial,** Russian	80.00	110.00	88.00
☐ **Cordial,** sterling, blown glass	135.00	185.00	150.00
☐ **Creamer,** hobstar	80.00	95.00	82.00
☐ **Creamer,** pinwheel	55.00	70.00	58.00
☐ **Creamer,** Waterford, c. 1930's	45.00	65.00	50.00
☐ **Cruet,** Harvard, signed Hoare	160.00	185.00	162.00
☐ **Cruet,** Middlesex	75.00	95.00	80.00
☐ **Cruet,** prism, signed Libbey	155.00	175.00	155.00
☐ **Cruet,** pyramid shape, 7½″	55.00	80.00	62.00
☐ **Decanter,** Art Deco, pressed pattern of Chrysler Building	110.00	160.00	125.00
☐ **Decanter,** Harvard, 8″	95.00	140.00	110.00
☐ **Decanter,** hobstar, diamond and fan, cut stopper	160.00	185.00	162.00
☐ **Decanter,** original stopper, numbered	185.00	210.00	188.00
☐ **Decanter,** pineapple cut	110.00	135.00	112.00
☐ **Decanter,** pineapple fan, brilliant cut	80.00	130.00	100.00
☐ **Decanter,** pinwheel	185.00	210.00	188.00
☐ **Dish,** cheese and cracker, signed Hoare	310.00	410.00	350.00
☐ **Dish,** cheese and cracker, hobstar, strawberry and diamond	100.00	125.00	105.00
☐ **Dish,** cheese, pinwheel	285.00	335.00	300.00
☐ **Dish,** cheese, diamond and fan, covered	385.00	460.00	412.00
☐ **Dish,** ice cream, hobstar	385.00	435.00	400.00
☐ **Dish,** lemon, signed Hawkes	40.00	55.00	42.00
☐ **Dish,** nut, signed Libbey, pair	285.00	335.00	300.00
☐ **Dish,** olive, hobstar and comet	40.00	55.00	42.00
☐ **Dish,** shell, signed Hoare	110.00	135.00	112.00
☐ **Dish,** signed Omega	50.00	65.00	52.00
☐ **Dish,** square, Imperial, signed Libbey	185.00	235.00	200.00
☐ **Dish,** four sections, strawberry, and diamond point	160.00	210.00	175.00

	Current Price Range		P/Y Average
☐ **Dish,** condiment, heavily cut, c. 1900's	135.00	185.00	150.00
☐ **Dish,** pedestal	285.00	335.00	300.00
☐ **Glass,** etched, signed Libbey, pair	110.00	160.00	125.00
☐ **Glass,** magnifying, Art Nouveau, sterling . . .	135.00	185.00	150.00
☐ **Glass,** magnifying, ivory handles	1250.00	1450.00	1300.00
☐ **Glass,** magnifying, mother-of-pearl	135.00	185.00	150.00
☐ **Goblet,** panel, prism cut	55.00	80.00	62.00
☐ **Goblet,** prism cut, signed Hawkes	60.00	85.00	68.00
☐ **Goblet,** Russian	110.00	135.00	112.00
☐ **Goblet,** spiral pinwheel	40.00	55.00	42.00
☐ **Goblet,** Vintage	55.00	80.00	62.00
☐ **Inkwell,** crystal	235.00	310.00	262.00
☐ **Inkwell,** silver and crystal	535.00	610.00	562.00
☐ **Inkwell,** sterling lid, 2″	40.00	55.00	42.00
☐ **Jar,** Art Nouveau, sterling lid	45.00	65.00	50.00
☐ **Jar,** candy, Hawkes, 11″	210.00	260.00	225.00
☐ **Jar,** mustard, signed Webb	55.00	80.00	62.00
☐ **Jar,** powder, Art Nouveau, hobstar and fan . .	110.00	135.00	112.00
☐ **Jar,** powder, Reine Des Fleurs	80.00	110.00	88.00
☐ **Jar,** powder, sterling lid, 3″ x 3″	80.00	110.00	88.00
☐ **Jar,** tobacco, sterling top, 7″	135.00	160.00	138.00
☐ **Jug,** whiskey, Clarke	285.00	335.00	300.00
☐ **Knife Rest,** c. 1920's	22.00	32.00	25.00
☐ **Knife Rest,** ball ends, diamond cut	28.00	38.00	30.00
☐ **Knife Rest,** signed Hawkes	45.00	65.00	50.00
☐ **Lamp,** diamond cut, 17″	385.00	485.00	425.00
☐ **Lamp,** table, mushroom shade, 18″	485.00	585.00	525.00
☐ **Matchstrikes,** antique, pair	210.00	260.00	225.00
☐ **Muffineer,** sterling, cone shaped	80.00	130.00	100.00
☐ **Nappy,** hobstar and fan, signed Clarke	65.00	80.00	68.00
☐ **Nappy,** pinwheel	50.00	65.00	52.00
☐ **Nappy,** strawberry and diamond	45.00	60.00	48.00
☐ **Pitcher,** cider, prism and bull's eye, hobstar base, 8″	160.00	185.00	162.00
☐ **Pitcher,** claret, Encore by Strauss, 12″	260.00	310.00	275.00
☐ **Pitcher,** Harvard, signed Libbey, 8″	160.00	210.00	175.00
☐ **Pitcher,** hobstar and fan, 8″	160.00	210.00	175.00
☐ **Pitcher,** milk, Russian, starred buttons, 5″ . .	360.00	435.00	380.00
☐ **Pitcher,** milk, deep cutting, twelve point star base, signed Hawkes, 5½″	185.00	235.00	200.00
☐ **Pitcher,** pinwheel, strawberry and diamond, 9″	135.00	160.00	138.00
☐ **Platter,** ice cream, oval, Russian	310.00	370.00	330.00
☐ **Punch Bowl,** two pieces, flower with star, box pattern	1250.00	1450.00	1300.00
☐ **Punch Bowl,** two pieces, signed Tuthill, 10½″	660.00	760.00	700.00
☐ **Relish Dish,** Harvard	95.00	125.00	100.00
☐ **Relish Dish,** hobstar, strawberry and diamond, 11½″	185.00	235.00	200.00
☐ **Relish Dish,** Royal, 7″	95.00	125.00	100.00
☐ **Rose Bowl,** Harvard, signed Libbey	310.00	360.00	325.00
☐ **Rose Bowl,** hobstar and fan, footed, 4″	185.00	235.00	200.00
☐ **Rose Bowl,** hobstar, diamond and fan	210.00	260.00	225.00
☐ **Salt and Pepper Shakers,** 6″	25.00	35.00	30.00
☐ **Stickpin,** antique cameo	160.00	185.00	162.00
☐ **Stickpin,** cameo	145.00	185.00	155.00

DAIRY COLLECTIBLES

DESCRIPTION: All items pertaining to the American dairy industry.

TYPES: Dairy collectibles include articles used on dairy farms such as pails, milking devices and churns, containers to transport and retail milk and other dairy products; and advertising items, brochures, signs generated by the dairy industry.

PERIOD: Though dairy farming in America dates to the early colonial era, collectibles available on the market date from the 1700s. Most of them are of the period from about 1850 to the early 1900s. This era ushered in large scale factory production of such items as milk cans and store bottles.

COMMENTS: This is another of various fields of collecting in which charm and historical appeal take precedence over immaculate condition.

	Current Price Range		P/Y Average
☐ **Bottle Filler,** three wooden legs, glass window at front, brass spigot, 36″ tall	27.00	34.00	30.00
☐ **Butter Churn,** Dazy Churn and Manufacturing Co., glass, model No. 40, made in St. Louis, square, four quart capacity, wood paddles . .	43.00	57.00	48.00
☐ **Centrifugal Butter Fat Tester,** Vermont Farm Machinery Co., Bellows Falls, Vermont, 100 revolutions per minute, embossed cover, brass gears and brass bottle holders, galvanized rack and tank, 8½″ x 6″ x 7″	90.00	115.00	98.00
☐ **Metal Sign,** Turner Centre Ice Cream, reads "It's Frozen Health," embossed black letters on yellow background, nailhole at top, 1928 .	90.00	105.00	95.00
☐ **Milk Bottle,** B & S Pasteurizing Co., Tamaque, Pennsylvania, glass, quart, round, slug plate	6.00	8.00	7.00
☐ **Milk Bottle,** Bloomingdale Dairy Co., Inc., 136 to 40 Hunterdon St., Newark, New Jersey, glass, quart, round	7.00	10.00	8.20
☐ **Milk Bottle,** Chestnut Farm Chevy Chase Dairy, Washington, D.C., reads "Milk for Babies," glass, quart, round	6.00	8.00	7.00

	Current Price Range		P/Y Average
☐ **Milk Bottle,** D.A. Delano, Norway, Maine, "Tel. 6-24," glass, quart, round, slug plate ...	7.00	10.00	8.50
☐ **Milk Bottle,** Edward Carlson, East Walpole, glass, quart, round	6.00	8.00	7.00
☐ **Milk Bottle,** Granite Farm Pure Milk and Cream, Brunswick, Maine, glass, quart, round, slug plate	7.00	10.00	8.50
☐ **Milk Bottle,** Laudholm Farms, Wells, Maine, glass, quart, round	7.00	10.00	8.50
☐ **Milk Bottle,** The Lawson Milk Co., Akron, Ohio, glass, quart, round, slug plate	6.00	8.00	7.00
☐ **Milk Bottle,** Petersburg Creamery, Petersburg, Ohio, reads "Safe Milk Every Morning," glass, quart, round	9.00	12.00	10.20
☐ **Milk Bottle,** R.O. Stockman, Portland, Maine, glass, quart, round	6.00	8.00	7.00
☐ **Milk Bottle,** Wonder Brook Farm, A.F. Smith, Kennebunk, Maine, glass, quart, round stubby style	9.00	12.00	10.25
☐ **Milk Bottle Cap,** Parson's Jersey Dairy, plug type, 56 mm.	.10	.15	.12
☐ **Milk Bottle Cover,** National Milk Co., Boston, aluminum with pouring lip.	9.00	12.00	10.20
☐ **Milk Strainer,** filter type, homemade filter holder	4.00	6.00	5.00
☐ **Porch Box,** Blais Dairy, Lewiston, Maine, stenciled name, double box, holds eight milk bottles	22.00	28.00	24.00
☐ **Porch Box,** Needham Dairy Inc., embossed double box, holds six milk bottles	20.00	26.00	22.00

DAUM NANCY GLASS

DESCRIPTION: August and Jean Daum of Nancy, France produced exquisite cameo glass although they had never received their just due until recent years. Their work is similar to that of Gallé but the background colors differ; Daum-Nancy cameo glass often has orange and yellow grounds as contrasted to the cream ground so often used by Gallé. This glass was produced from 1900 through the 1920s.

RECOMMENDED READING: For more in-depth information on Daum Nancy glass you may refer to *The Official Price Guide to Glassware* and *The Official Identification Guide to Glassware,* published by The House of Collectibles.

Vase, Daum Nancy, *French Cameo glass, sterling base and feet, thistle motif, 5",* **$550.00-$650.00**

	Current Price Range		P/Y Average
☐ **Beaker,** *flaring cylinder, gray shading to light pink and green, enameled black winter landscape, signed, 6" high, c. 1910*	600.00	800.00	610.00
☐ **Bottle,** *compressed spherical body, inverted bell shaped lid, mottled gray shading to lavender, overlaid and enameled in lavender and green, gilding, cut with violets and leaves, strapwork on base, signed, 4" high, c. 1910* . . .	700.00	800.00	710.00
☐ **Bottle,** *perfume, stopper, ovoid shape flattened on two sides, tapering to cylinder neck, concave disc-shaped stopper, mottled blue background, overlaid, cut and enameled with yellow iris and green leaves, signed, 5½" high, c. 1910*	600.00	700.00	620.00
☐ **Bottle,** *perfume, stopper, ovoid shape, short cylinder neck, fan-shaped stopper, gray background shading to darkish-yellow and pink, cut and enameled with wildflowers in blue, red, and gray, gilding, 3½" high, c. 1910*	550.00	650.00	565.00
☐ **Bowl,** *elongated diamond shape, waisted shoulder, dipped rim, mottled pink and blue background, overlaid and enameled with flowers and leaves in blue, green, dark brown, signed, 12" high, c. 1910*	800.00	1000.00	850.00

	Current Price Range		P/Y Average

☐ **Bowl,** *enameled, short ovoid body, background of yellow sea and orange and grey sunset, overlaid with greyish-brown sailboats, signed, 5¼" high, c. 1900* .... | 400.00 | 600.00 | 420.00 |

☐ **Bowl,** *enameled, frosted and yellow background, cut with trailing violets and leaves enameled in light green and lavender, 4⅜" high, c. 1900* .... | 300.00 | 350.00 | 320.00 |

☐ **Bowl,** *fish bowl shape, shading from green at neck to pale green at base, cut and enameled into bowl is river scene, signed, 5½" high, c. 1900* .... | 350.00 | 450.00 | 375.00 |

☐ **Box,** *covered, bulging circular, domed lid with knop finial, mottled brown and green with gilt foil inclusions, signed, 6" diameter, c. 1925* .. | 400.00 | 500.00 | 420.00 |

☐ **Box,** *covered, circular, domed lid, mottled gray background, overlaid in pink, green, red, cut with blossoms and leaves, signed,3½" diameter, c. 1915* .... | 300.00 | 500.00 | 325.00 |

☐ **Box,** *covered, flattened circular lid, enameled gray winter scene, bowl enameled with river scene, opalescent background, signed, 6" diameter, c. 1910* .... | 800.00 | 1000.00 | 825.00 |

☐ **Box,** *covered, waisted spherical shape, domed lid, mottled aquamarine and gray shading to dark blue, overlaid in green and blue, cut with peacock feathers, signed, 6" diameter, c. 1910* | 900.00 | 1100.00 | 935.00 |

☐ **Creamer,** *ovoid shape, applied silver handle with foliage, silver flattened lid chased with lilies of the valley and leaves, opalescent, enameled scene with windmills and sailboats in charcoal, signed, 4¼" high, c. 1910* ...... | 600.00 | 800.00 | 625.00 |

☐ **Dish,** *clover shape, mottled ochre, etched and enameled with columbines and leaves in rust and green, signed, 5¾" diameter, c. 1915* | 400.00 | 600.00 | 450.00 |

☐ **Ewer,** *elongated teardrop, applied loop handle, short circular foot, mottled yellow and orange, overlaid and enameled in red and green poppies and leaves, band of flowers around base, 9½" high, c. 1910* .... | 800.00 | 1200.00 | 850.00 |

☐ **Figure,** *woman in classical dress, standing on rectangular base, hand raised over head, glass shading progressively downward from light purple to green and dark purple, signed, 10" high, c. 1915* .... | 3500.00 | 4500.00 | 3600.00 |

☐ **Goblet,** *domed, cylinder stem with lobe, domed circular foot, cut with croix de Lorraine and hatched scrolls, enameled in red, gray, black, and white croix de Lorraine, heraldic crests, and thistles, gilding, signed, 4¼" high, c. 1890* .... | 800.00 | 1000.00 | 830.00 |

☐ **Lamp,** *domed shade with upper section lobed, on three-arm support of wrought-iron, baluster shape stand with knopped neck and*

	Current Price Range		P/Y Average

circular spreading foot, deep blue shading to light blue with gold foil inclusions, signed, 18½" high, c. 1920 . . . . **1500.00 2000.00 1600.00**

☐ **Lamp,** helmet shape shade with large domed finial, supported by angular wrought-iron arms, baluster standard, knopping above the spreading circular foot, signed, 15" high, c. 1910 . . . . **3500.00 4500.00 3600.00**

☐ **Lamp,** lobed domed shade supported by wrought-iron angular arms, baluster standard, knopped above the slightly domed foot, mottled yellow-brown background overlaid in lavender, cut with lake scene, signed, 14¾" high, c. 1910 . . . . **6000.00 7000.00 6100.00**

☐ **Lamp,** lobed domed shade with uneven edge, supported by angular wrought-iron arms, baluster standard with spiraling grooves and knopped above slightly domed foot, mottled blue shading to green, standard mottled in green shading to blue-green and lavender, signed, 21½" high, c. 1915 . . . . **700.00 800.00 720.00**

☐ **Pitcher,** ovoid shape, slightly flaring rim with small spout, scrolling handle, mottled blue shading to green, cut and enameled with wildflowers and leaves, signed, 3½" high, c. 1910 . . . . **700.00 800.00 720.00**

☐ **Pitcher,** slender cylindrical body, flat shoulder, straight cylindrical neck, elongated spout, streaked burgundy sides overlaid in purple shading to blue, cut around neck and shoulder with scrolling strapwork against a tooled ground, sides tooled with lily blossoms and leaves, signed, 16½" high, c. 1900 **800.00 900.00 850.00**

☐ **Salt,** circular bowl shape with two notched portions of the rim extending as handles, gray background, enameled Dutch scene of the seashore in gray, signed, 1¾" high, c. 1910 . . . . **300.00 400.00 320.00**

☐ **Tumbler,** cylinder shape, expanding towards the rim, gray streaked with ochre, burgundy, and yellow, overlaid in ochre, green, yellow, blue, burgundy, and rust, cut with leafy branches with raspberries, signed, 5" high, c. 1915 . . . . **600.00 800.00 610.00**

☐ **Vase,** baluster shape tapering towards the neck, waisted neck and base, knopped base with spreading foot, mottled gray streaked with green and mustard background, etched and enameled with wildflowers, leaves, and grass in pink, green, and brown, signed, 16¾" high, c. 1915 . . . . **600.00 700.00 615.00**

DECOYS

TOPIC: A decoy is a representation of some animal used to lure others of that species within shooting range.

TYPES: Decoys most often represent waterfowl, but frog, fish, owl and crow decoys are not uncommon. Decoys can be solid, hollow or slat-bodied. They can be either of the floating variety or the "stick-up" variety, which is driven into the ground.

PERIOD: Decoys produced after the mid-nineteenth century are most popular among collectors.

ORIGIN: American Indians have made and used decoys since 1000 A.D.

MAKERS: Famous decoy carvers include Ira Hudson, Charles Wheeler, Albert Laing and Mark Whipple.

MATERIALS: Decoys are usually carved out of wood, although metal and other materials are found.

COMMENTS: Enthusiasts usually collect decoys by carver, species or flyway (the path of migration). Decoys made for actual use are more favored by collectors than those intended only for show.

TIPS: The condition of the paint on a decoy is a good indicator of age. Many cracked layers of paint mean that the decoy is probably old. Original paint is favored by collectors.

	Current Price Range		P/Y Average
☐ **B.W. Teal**, P. Wilcoxen	80.00	130.00	105.00
☐ **B.W. Teal**, glass eyes, pre-1900	1300.00	1700.00	1500.00
☐ **B.W. Teal**, preening, Ohio	75.00	100.00	87.50
☐ **Beach Duck**, papier-mache, paper label, Mackey	170.00	220.00	195.00
☐ **Beach Duck**, cork body, Thomas H. Gelston	125.00	175.00	150.00
☐ **Black Duck**, August mock drake, c. 1900	200.00	250.00	225.00
☐ **Black Duck**, Cobb Island, carved wing tips	175.00	225.00	200.00
☐ **Black Duck**, Dan English	525.00	575.00	550.00
☐ **Black Duck**, handcarved, c. 1900	90.00	110.00	100.00
☐ **Black Duck**, hollow, carved, Ken Anger	350.00	400.00	375.00
☐ **Black Duck**, hollow, carved, Stanley Grant	150.00	200.00	175.00

	Current Price Range		P/Y Average
☐ **Black Duck,** hollow, carved, John Heisler	375.00	425.00	400.00
☐ **Black Duck,** hollow, carved, K. Peck	275.00	325.00	300.00
☐ **Black Duck,** hollow, carved, Harry V. Shourds .	150.00	190.00	170.00
☐ **Black Duck,** bird standing with wings spread, Ira Hudson	1500.00	1700.00	1600.00
☐ **Black Duck,** sleeping, set of five, original paint	850.00	1050.00	950.00
☐ **Black Duck,** swimming, Down East Decoy Co.	160.00	190.00	175.00
☐ **Blue Jay,** signed, A. Elmer Crowell	1400.00	1600.00	1500.00
☐ **Brant,** carved cedar	300.00	500.00	400.00
☐ **Brant,** Cobb Island, carved wings	175.00	225.00	200.00
☐ **Brant,** hollow, Harry Shourds	200.00	300.00	250.00
☐ **Brant,** hollow, carved, New Jersey, carved wings	300.00	350.00	325.00
☐ **Brant,** Long Island, cork body	175.00	225.00	200.00
☐ **Brant,** Mason's	190.00	230.00	210.00
☐ **Brant,** swimming, carved wings	200.00	240.00	220.00
☐ **Broadbill,** Chauncey Wheeler	300.00	360.00	330.00
☐ **Bufflehead,** drake, Doug Jester	115.00	145.00	130.00
☐ **Bufflehead,** drake, Ira Hudson	300.00	425.00	362.50
☐ **Bufflehead,** drake, California	75.00	125.00	100.00
☐ **Bufflehead,** glass eyes	600.00	900.00	750.00
☐ **Bufflehead,** drake, hollow, carved, Charles Parker	300.00	360.00	330.00
☐ **Bufflehead,** drake, primitive, Oscar Ayers	115.00	145.00	130.00
☐ **Canada Goose,** Nathan Cobb	450.00	500.00	475.00
☐ **Canada Goose,** Hurley Conklin	650.00	750.00	700.00
☐ **Canada Goose,** John Furlow	275.00	325.00	300.00
☐ **Canada Goose,** solid, Madison Mitchell	160.00	200.00	180.00
☐ **Canada Goose,** L. Parker	275.00	325.00	300.00
☐ **Canada Goose,** Harvey V. Shourds	380.00	420.00	400.00
☐ **Canada Goose,** swimming, signed, c. 1880 . . .	1900.00	2100.00	2000.00
☐ **Canvasback,** drake, balsa wood, Harry Megargy	90.00	120.00	105.00
☐ **Canvasback,** drake, feeding, A. Elmer Crowell	415.00	475.00	430.00
☐ **Canvasback,** drake, Lohrman	130.00	180.00	155.00
☐ **Canvasback,** drake, Madison Mitchell	100.00	170.00	135.00
☐ **Canvasback,** drake, Michigan bobtail	190.00	220.00	205.00
☐ **Canvasback,** drake, Samuel Denny	245.00	285.00	260.00
☐ **Canvasback,** hen, Mason's	90.00	120.00	205.00
☐ **Canvasback,** hen, Frank Schmidt	270.00	330.00	300.00
☐ **Canvasback,** Michael Pavolich	150.00	200.00	175.00
☐ **Coot,** J.W. Johnson, 1960	60.00	100.00	80.00
☐ **Coot,** Mason's	300.00	330.00	315.00
☐ **Coot,** Benjamin J. Schmidt	170.00	200.00	185.00
☐ **Crow,** hollow, late 1800s	325.00	425.00	375.00
☐ **Crow,** hollow, carved, Charles H. Perdew Co. .	325.00	375.00	350.00
☐ **Crow,** wooden, glass eyes, c. 1900	475.00	525.00	500.00
☐ **Curlew,** Barnegat	615.00	645.00	630.00
☐ **Curlew,** Cobb Island, running	760.00	790.00	775.00
☐ **Curlew,** Eskimo, carved wings, signed	740.00	780.00	760.00
☐ **Curlew,** Mason's	2800.00	3000.00	2900.00
☐ **Curlew,** sickle-billed, Harry Shourds, contemporary	225.00	325.00	275.00
☐ **Dowitcher,** Long Island	275.00	325.00	300.00
☐ **Duck,** J. H. Whitney	90.00	120.00	105.00
☐ **Duck,** Labrador	770.00	790.00	780.00

	Current Price Range		P/Y Average
☐ **Duck,** Pacific Northwest	45.00	75.00	60.00
☐ **Duck,** papier-mache	35.00	55.00	45.00
☐ **Eider duck,** primitive	160.00	180.00	170.00
☐ **Fish,** carved and painted, pair, 19th c.	340.00	360.00	350.00
☐ **Gadwell,** hen, Ken Anger	270.00	290.00	280.00
☐ **Golden Eye,** drake, Doug Jester	125.00	200.00	161.50
☐ **Golden Eye,** drake, Mason's	290.00	320.00	305.00
☐ **Golden Eye,** drake, Steven's Decoy Factory .	400.00	440.00	420.00
☐ **Golden Eye,** hen, Harry Shourds	160.00	180.00	170.00
☐ **Golden Eye,** hen, Bob White	325.00	375.00	350.00
☐ **Golden Plover**	75.00	90.00	82.50
☐ **Goose,** standing, aggressive stance, hollow, Prince Edward Island	400.00	550.00	475.00
☐ **Great Blue Heron,** sheet metal, painted	375.00	425.00	400.00
☐ **Gull,** with iron weight, J. W. Carter	2500.00	2700.00	2600.00
☐ **Heron,** primitive	650.00	750.00	700.00
☐ **Lesser Yellowlegs,** Bay Head	250.00	280.00	265.00
☐ **Lesser Yellowlegs,** Mason's	650.00	700.00	675.00
☐ **Lesser Yellowlegs,** William Matthews	315.00	335.00	325.00
☐ **Lesser Yellowlegs,** c. 1896	300.00	320.00	210.00
☐ **Mallard,** drake, J. N. Dodge Decory Factory .	75.00	95.00	85.00
☐ **Mallard,** drake, Elliston	2400.00	2800.00	2600.00
☐ **Mallard,** drake, Old Illinois River	360.00	380.00	370.00
☐ **Mallard,** drake, Charles H. Perdew Co.	550.00	580.00	565.00
☐ **Mallard,** hen, Mason's	80.00	100.00	90.00
☐ **Mallard,** hen, Ward Brothers, c. 1920	220.00	250.00	235.00
☐ **Mallard,** papier-mache	25.00	30.00	27.50
☐ **Mallard,** drake, cork body	28.00	32.00	30.00
☐ **Merganser,** drake, red-breasted, Hurley Conklin	170.00	190.00	180.00
☐ **Mallard,** crude, Kansas	30.00	45.00	37.50
☐ **Merganser,** hen, Doug Jester	500.00	540.00	520.00
☐ **Merganser,** Long Island	370.00	400.00	385.00
☐ **Merganser,** Harold Haertel	2900.00	3000.00	2950.00
☐ **Merganser,** primitive, American	150.00	200.00	175.00
☐ **Merganser,** red-breasted, drake	125.00	225.00	175.00
☐ **Merganser,** tack eyes	700.00	1000.00	850.00
☐ **Old-Squaw,** drake, Mark English	850.00	890.00	870.00
☐ **Owl,** balsa wood, glass eyes	480.00	500.00	490.00
☐ **Owl,** 19th c.	225.00	275.00	250.00
☐ **Pigeon,** English wood, Austin Johnson	275.00	350.00	311.50
☐ **Pigeon,** Lou Schifferell	275.00	295.00	285.00
☐ **Pintail,** drake, carved cedar	280.00	300.00	290.00
☐ **Pintail,** drake, carved wings and feathers ...	275.00	325.00	300.00
☐ **Pintail,** drake, A. Elmer Crowell	230.00	300.00	265.00
☐ **Pintail,** drake, Ira Hudson	850.00	890.00	870.00
☐ **Pintail Duck,** green beak	60.00	80.00	70.00
☐ **Pintail,** hen, Mason's	170.00	200.00	185.00
☐ **Pintail,** hen, Lem and Steve Ward	1500.00	2000.00	1750.00
☐ **Pintail,** hen and drake, L. T. Ward, pair	3000.00	3500.00	3250.00
☐ **Plover,** black-bellied, Cobb Island	390.00	410.00	400.00
☐ **Plover,** black-bellied, A. Elmer Crowell	1500.00	1700.00	1600.00
☐ **Plover,** black-bellied, William Matthews	340.00	380.00	360.00
☐ **Plover,** black-bellied, Charles E. Wheeler	1700.00	2100.00	1900.00
☐ **Redhead,** drake, Ben Schmidt	600.00	750.00	675.00
☐ **Redhead,** hen, Frank Schmidt	160.00	200.00	180.00

	Current Price Range		P/Y Average
☐ **Redhead,** drake, Lloyd Parker	200.00	325.00	262.50
☐ **Redhead,** Michael Pavolich	150.00	200.00	175.00
☐ **Redhead,** drake, turned head, solid body	700.00	1100.00	900.00
☐ **Redhead,** cork body	180.00	200.00	190.00
☐ **Redhead,** drake, Thomas Gelston	140.00	160.00	150.00
☐ **Redhead,** drake, hollow, carved, signed	1400.00	1500.00	1450.00
☐ **Redhead,** drake, sleeping, Mason's	340.00	370.00	355.00
☐ **Redhead,** hen, Nate Quillen	530.00	590.00	560.00
☐ **Ruddy Duck,** hen, L. T. Ward	150.00	170.00	160.00
☐ **Sanderling,** A. Elmer Crowell	830.00	860.00	845.00
☐ **Sanderling,** Taylor Johnson	280.00	300.00	290.00
☐ **Sandpiper,** Cobb Island	260.00	280.00	270.00
☐ **Sandpiper,** primitive	70.00	90.00	80.00
☐ **Scaup,** drake, Elliston	230.00	280.00	255.00
☐ **Scaup,** hen, F. Bach	250.00	300.00	275.00
☐ **Scaup,** drake, glass eyes	300.00	500.00	400.00
☐ **Scaup,** drake, Bart Clayton	170.00	190.00	180.00
☐ **Scaup,** drake, Henry Grant	600.00	640.00	620.00
☐ **Scaup,** drake, hollow, carved feathers	1800.00	2000.00	1900.00
☐ **Scaup,** drake, Roland Horner	440.00	460.00	450.00
☐ **Scaup,** drake, Joe King, hollow, carved	80.00	100.00	90.00
☐ **Scaup,** hen, Mason's	500.00	600.00	550.00
☐ **Scaup,** hen, Chauncey Wheeler	250.00	300.00	275.00
☐ **Shorebird,** carved head, glass eyes	380.00	400.00	390.00
☐ **Shorebird,** Dodge Decoy Factory	100.00	130.00	115.00
☐ **Snipe,** robin, Cobb Island	220.00	240.00	230.00
☐ **Snipe,** robin, Dodge Decoy Factory	220.00	230.00	225.00
☐ **Snipe,** robin, Joe King	270.00	290.00	280.00
☐ **Snipe,** robin, primitive	120.00	130.00	125.00
☐ **Swan,** hollow, carved	900.00	950.00	925.00
☐ **Swan,** c. 1900	450.00	500.00	475.00
☐ **Widgeon,** A. Elmer Crowell	110.00	150.00	130.00
☐ **Widgeon,** c. 1880	170.00	190.00	180.00
☐ **Willet,** carved wings	400.00	500.00	450.00

DEPRESSION GLASS

DESCRIPTION: Colored glassware was machine made during the Depression years of the late 1920s and early 1930s. The glass was available in ten cent stores, given away at filling stations, theatres, and used for promotional purposes. There are approximately 150,000 collectors and the popularity is steadily increasing each year. There are over 80 Depression Glass clubs which sponsor shows with attendance in the thousands.

COMMENTS: Of the approximately 100 different patterns and colors produced, rose pink remains the favorite color. Luncheon sets of 16 pieces sold new for as low as $1.29. Today a dinner service, depending on the scarcity of the pattern, may cost from $100.00 to $1000.00.

RECOMMENDED READING: For more in-depth information on Depression Glass you may refer to *The Official Price Guide to Depression Glassware, The Official Price Guide to Glassware* and *The Official Identification Guide to Glassware,* published by The House of Collectibles.

	Current Price Range		P/Y Average
BOWKNOT (Green)			
☐ **Berry Bowl,** *diameter 4½"*	6.50	9.50	7.25
☐ **Cereal Bowl,** *5½"*	9.00	12.00	10.00
☐ **Cup**	3.50	5.50	4.00
☐ **Salad Plate,** *diameter 7"*	5.00	8.00	6.00
☐ **Sherbet**	6.50	9.50	7.50
☐ **Tumbler,** *10 oz.*	8.50	11.50	9.00
☐ **Tumbler,** *footed, 10 oz.*	8.50	11.50	9.00
CIRCLE (Green — *Hocking Glass Co.*)			
☐ **Bowl,** *diameter 4½"*	2.00	4.00	2.50
☐ **Bowl,** *diameter 8"*	4.50	7.50	5.25
☐ **Creamer**	3.50	5.50	4.00
☐ **Cup**	1.50	3.50	2.00
☐ **Decanter,** *handled*	14.00	18.00	15.00
☐ **Dinner Plate,** *diameter 9½"*	4.50	7.50	5.25
☐ **Juice Tumbler,** *4 oz.*	2.50	4.50	3.00
☐ **Pitcher,** *80 oz.*	15.00	19.00	16.00
☐ **Saucer**	.50	1.75	.75
☐ **Sherbet,** *diameter 3⅛"*	2.50	4.50	3.00

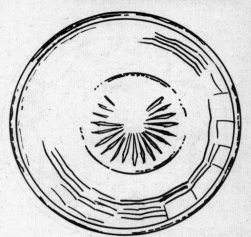

CIRCLE

Circle (Green-Hocking Glass Co.)

	Current Price Range		P/Y Average
☐ **Sherbet,** *diameter 4¾"*	3.50	5.50	4.00
☐ **Sherbet Plate,** *diameter 6"*	1.00	3.00	1.50
☐ **Sugar Bowl**	3.50	5.50	4.00
☐ **Vase,** *hat shape*	16.00	19.00	17.00
☐ **Water Goblet,** *8 oz.*	5.00	8.00	6.00
☐ **Water Tumbler,** *8 oz.*	3.50	5.50	4.00
☐ **Wine Goblet,** *height 4½"*	3.00	5.00	3.50

FOREST GREEN (Green — *Anchor Hocking Glass Co.*)

☐ **Ashtray**	1.50	3.50	2.50
☐ **Creamer,** *flat*	3.00	5.00	4.00
☐ **Cup**	1.50	3.00	1.75
☐ **Lunch Plate,** *diameter 8"*	3.00	5.00	3.50
☐ **Pitcher,** *circular, 3 qt.*	18.00	21.00	19.00
☐ **Platter,** *rectangular*	8.50	10.50	9.50
☐ **Salad Bowl,** *diameter 7"*	5.00	7.00	6.00
☐ **Salad Plate,** *diameter 6½"*	1.25	2.25	1.75
☐ **Saucer**	.75	1.50	1.00
☐ **Soup Bowl,** *diameter 6"*	5.00	7.00	6.00
☐ **Tumbler,** *5 oz.*	1.25	2.25	1.75
☐ **Vase,** *height 6"*	3.00	5.00	3.25

GEORGIAN (Green — *Federal Glass Co.*)

☐ **Berry Bowl,** *diameter 4"*	4.25	5.25	4.75
☐ **Berry Bowl,** *diameter 7½"*	37.00	40.00	38.50
☐ **Bowl,** *steep sided, diameter 6½"*	42.00	46.00	44.00
☐ **Butter Dish,** *with cover*	60.00	70.00	65.00
☐ **Cereal Bowl,** *diameter 5¼"*	12.00	14.00	13.00
☐ **Creamer,** *pedestal foot, diameter 3"*	7.00	9.00	8.00
☐ **Creamer,** *pedestal foot, diameter 4"*	8.00	10.00	9.00
☐ **Cup**	6.00	8.00	7.00
☐ **Dinner Plate,** *diameter 9¼"*	15.00	17.00	16.00
☐ **Lunch Plate,** *diameter 8"*	5.25	6.25	5.75

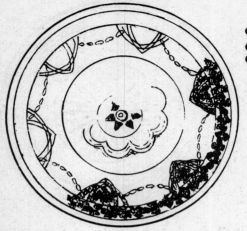

GEORGIAN

Georgian (Green-Federal Glass Co.)

	Current Price Range		P/Y Average
□ **Plate,** *central medallion and band on rim, diameter 9¼"*	14.25	15.25	14.75
□ **Platter,** *tab handle, diameter 11¼"*	42.00	46.00	44.00
□ **Saucer**	1.75	2.75	2.25
□ **Sherbet Dish,** *stemmed*	7.00	9.00	8.00
□ **Sherbet Plate,** *diameter 6"*	2.25	3.25	2.75
□ **Sugar Bowl,** *pedestal foot, height 3"*	7.00	9.00	8.00
□ **Sugar Bowl,** *pedestal foot, diameter 4"*	8.25	9.25	8.75
□ **Sugar Lid**	21.00	23.00	22.00
□ **Tumbler,** *height 4"*	33.00	36.00	34.50
□ **Tumbler,** *height 5¼"*	56.00	62.00	59.00
□ **Vegetable Bowl,** *length 9"*	42.00	46.00	44.00

HOLIDAY (Pink — Jeannette Glass Co.)

	Current Price Range		P/Y Average
□ **Berry Bowl**	6.25	7.25	6.75
□ **Butter Dish**	32.00	36.00	34.00
□ **Candlesticks,** *pair*	47.00	51.00	49.00
□ **Creamer**	5.25	6.25	5.75
□ **Cup And Saucer**	7.25	8.25	7.75
□ **Plate,** *diameter 9"*	8.75	9.75	9.25
□ **Pitcher,** *diameter 7"*	23.00	26.00	24.50
□ **Sherbet,** *footed*	2.25	3.25	2.75
□ **Sugar And Creamer**	10.00	13.00	11.50
□ **Tumbler,** *footed, diameter 4"*	23.00	26.00	24.50

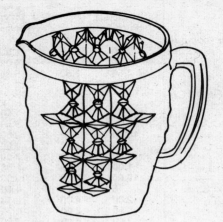

Holiday (Pink-Jeannette Glass Co.)

Moonstone (Opalescent Crystal-Anchor Hocking Glass Co.)

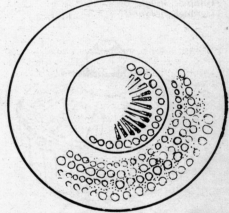

MOONSTONE (Opalescent Crystal — *Anchor Hocking Glass Co.)*

	Current Price Range		P/Y Average
☐ **Berry Bowl,** *diameter 5"*	5.50	8.50	6.50
☐ **Bon Bon,** *heart shape*	5.50	8.50	6.25
☐ **Bowl,** *flat, diameter 7½"*	6.50	9.50	7.25
☐ **Bowl,** *fluted edge, diameter 9"*	11.00	14.00	12.00
☐ **Bowl,** *fluted rim, with handle*	5.50	8.50	6.25
☐ **Bud Vase,** *height 5"*	7.00	10.00	8.00
☐ **Candlesticks,** *pair*	13.00	17.00	14.00
☐ **Candy Jar,** *with lid, diameter 5"*	16.00	18.50	16.75
☐ **Cigarette Bowl,** *with lid*	13.00	16.00	13.75
☐ **Creamer**	4.50	7.50	5.25
☐ **Cup**	4.50	7.50	5.25
☐ **Dessert Bowl,** *fluted rim, diameter 5"*	4.50	7.50	5.25
☐ **Goblet,** *height 5½"*	13.00	16.00	14.00
☐ **Lunch Plate,** *diameter 8"*	7.00	9.50	8.00
☐ **Puff Box,** *with lid, diameter 4½"*	13.00	17.00	14.00
☐ **Relish Bowl,** *two compartments, diameter 7"*	6.00	9.00	7.00

	Current Price Range		P/Y Average
☐ Relish Dish, *clover shapes, three compartments*	7.00	10.00	8.00
☐ Sandwich Plate, *diameter 10"*	13.00	17.00	14.00
☐ Sherbet Dish, *pedestal foot*	4.50	7.50	5.25

RIBBON (Green — *Hazel Atlas Glass Co.*)

☐ Berry Bowl, *diameter 4"*	1.00	3.00	1.50
☐ Berry Bowl, *diameter 8"*	5.00	7.00	5.50
☐ Candy Dish, *with cover*	18.00	22.00	19.00
☐ Creamer, *pedestal foot*	2.50	4.50	3.00
☐ Cup	1.50	3.50	2.00
☐ Lunch Plate, *diameter 8"*	1.00	3.00	1.50
☐ Salt And Pepper	13.00	17.00	14.00
☐ Saucer	.75	2.25	1.00
☐ Sherbet Dish, *pedestal foot*	2.00	4.00	2.50
☐ Sherbet Plate, *diameter 6"*	.50	2.00	.75
☐ Sugar Bowl, *pedestal foot*	2.00	4.00	2.50
☐ Tumbler, *height 6"*	4.00	7.00	5.00
☐ Tumbler, *height 7"*	5.00	8.00	6.00

Ribbon (Green-Hazel Atlas Glass Co.)

ROSE CAMEO
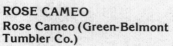
Rose Cameo (Green-Belmont Tumbler Co.)

ROSE CAMEO (Green — Belmont Tumbler Co.)	Current Price Range		P/Y Average
☐ Berry Bowl, *diameter 5"*	2.75	4.00	2.85
☐ Cereal Bowl, *diameter 5"*	5.00	7.00	5.25
☐ Salad Plate, *diameter 7"*	3.50	5.50	4.00
☐ Sherbet Dish	3.50	5.50	4.00
☐ Tumbler, *diameter 5"*	9.00	10.00	9.25

DISNEYANA

DESCRIPTION: Disneyana refers to all items made by or for Walt Disney Productions, the company that gave Americans Mickey Mouse, Donald Duck, Snow White and a host of other cartoon characters.

TYPE: There are many different types of Disney collectibles. Disney characters have been reproduced on every item from animated cels to dishes.

COMMENTS: Some hobbyists collect Disneyana by character or item, while others collect anything which features a Disney character. Older Mickey Mouse items are especially valuable, since this was the first character produced by the company.

ADDITIONAL TIPS: For more information, consult *The Official Price Guide to Collectible Toys,* published by The House of Collectibles.

☐ **Aristocats, The,** Schmid, Walt Disney Prod., set of five figural music boxes, all play different tunes, height 6"	110.00	135.00	112.50
☐ **Baloo,** Walt Disney Prod., ceramic figurine of the "Jungle Book" bear, height 5½", c. 1965	21.00	25.00	18.00
☐ **Bambi,** Anri, wooden music box, figures of Bambi and Thumper revolve on this Italian Disney item, c. 1971	85.00	110.00	95.00
☐ **Bambi And Thumper,** Schmid, pair of two pewter figurines, recent	30.00	40.00	30.00
☐ **Cinderella,** drinking glass, #8, red, yellow and blue, shows her being fitted for shoe, height 4⅝", c. 1950	9.00	12.00	6.00
☐ **Cinderella,** planter, ceramic	20.00	25.00	22.00
☐ **Clarabelle Cow,** drinking glass, full figure in red, seated in front of mirror primping, height 4¾", c. 1930	25.00	30.00	22.50

	Current Price Range		P/Y Average
☐ **Clarabelle Cow,** drinking glass, full figure in red, walking to the right, height 4¾", c. 1930 .	23.00	25.00	20.00
☐ **Clarabelle Cow,** drinking glass, full figure in red, height 4⅜"	23.00	25.00	20.00
☐ **Dalmatians,** Schmid, ceramic figural "Playmates" music box, mother, father dog watching pups play, plays "Whistle A Happy Tune," first limited edition, height 6½", c. 1982	35.00	45.00	35.00
☐ **Dalmatians,** Schmid, ceramic "Playmate" figurine, mother and father with pups, first edition "Mother's Day 1981," height 4½", c. 1981	21.00	25.00	18.00
☐ **Dalmatians,** pin back button, promoting Disney, re-release of movie, diameter 3½", c. 1979	12.00	19.00	6.00
☐ **Disney,** Ben Rickert, Inc., Snow White, Goofy, Mickey Mouse and Donald Duck, c. 1980	15.00	19.00	12.00
☐ **Disney,** Fort Productions, pewter collectible shovel spoon set, figures of Mickey, Minnie Donald and Goofy on handles, length 4¼" . . .	25.00	35.00	25.00
☐ **Disney,** Fort Productions, silver plate collectible spoon set, four different with their name: Mickey, Minnie, Donald and Goofy on the handles, length 4"	28.00	32.00	25.00
☐ **Disney,** party baskets, plastic, features colorful figures of Mickey, Donald and Minnie, set of approximately 29 figures in original box, made by Best Toy Novelties, 7½" x 11" x 4" .	125.00	150.00	120.00
☐ **Donald Duck and Nephews,** colorful rug, 21" x 38"	100.00	130.00	95.00
☐ **Donald Duck,** badge, "Happy Birthday Donald Duck 1934-1984," enamel on metal, issued by the Disney channel, 1983	25.00	50.00	27.50
☐ **Donald Duck,** doll, Lenci, felt	350.00	400.00	375.50
☐ **Donald Duck,** night light, ceramic, Walt Disney Productions	32.00	52.00	42.00
☐ **Donald Duck,** night light, figure on black base, 9½"	55.00	65.00	53.00
☐ **Donald Duck,** paint box, c. 1930s	15.00	25.00	20.50
☐ **Donald Duck,** watering can, tin, Walt Disney Enterprises, c. 1930s	35.00	45.00	41.00
☐ **Donald Duck,** United China, Co., bisque and painted figurine, he's sitting in pool of water next to golf club, with ball on his head, height 3"	13.00	17.00	20.00
☐ **Donald Duck,** United China, Co., bisque hand painted figurine, in his bathing suit, ready to jump off diving board, height 4"	13.00	17.00	10.00
☐ **Donald Duck,** bisque hand painted figurine, standing on surf board riding a wave, height 4"	13.00	17.00	10.00
☐ **Donald Duck,** Morris Plastics, "The Bubble Duck," mouth clacks, blows bubbles, in original box, c. 1955	16.00	22.00	14.00
☐ **Donald Duck,** California Originals, ceramic cannister cookie jar, Donald's Cookie Express, height 10", c. 1970	18.00	22.00	15.00

Mickey Mouse Top, *8" diameter,* **$10.00-$20.00**

Mickey Mouse Handcar Set, *windup, metal handcar with tracks,* **$550.00-$650.00**

	Current Price Range		P/Y Average

□ **Donald Duck,** ceramic figural cowboy bank, height 6½ ", c. 1940 . . . . — 47.00 — 52.00 — 44.50
□ **Donald Duck,** ceramic figural milk pitcher, height 6½ ", c. 1940 . . . . — 29.00 — 35.00 — 27.50
□ **Dopey,** figurine, plaster, 14" high, c. 1930s . . — 70.00 — 90.00 — 78.00
□ **Dumbo,** California Originals, ceramic figural cookie jar, says "Dumbo's Greatest Cookies On Earth," height 12" . . . . — 25.00 — 43.00 — 24.00
□ **Dumbo,** ceramic figural toothbrush holder, height 4", c. 1940 . . . . — 27.00 — 35.00 — 26.50
□ **Dumbo,** ceramic planter, height 3¾ ", c. 1940 — 21.00 — 25.00 — 18.00
□ **Dumbo,** Cameo Doll Co., composition figure, swiveling trunk and "Googlie Eyes," height 9", c. 1941 . . . . — 110.00 — 160.00 — 125.00
□ **Dumbo,** Gare Mold Co., glazed figurine, height 9" . . . . — 35.00 — 40.00 — 32.50
□ **Dumbo,** Schmid, pewter figurine . . . . — 28.00 — 32.00 — 25.00
□ **Dumbo,** American Pottery, seated version of "Baby" Dumbo with Bonnet, #41 on bottom, height 5½ ", c. 1940 . . . . — 55.00 — 65.00 — 55.00
□ **Dumbo And Timothy,** Gare Mold Co., pair of figurines, height 9" . . . . — 35.00 — 42.00 — 33.50
□ **Fantasia,** "Lionel Train" box car, depicts scenes from this Disney classic, from 1970s . — 20.00 — 24.00 — 17.00
□ **Goofy,** Schmid, pewter figurine, c. 1980 . . . . . — 25.00 — 32.00 — 23.50
□ **Goofy,** die cast and plastic auto, "Politoy," in pictorial box, marked #W5, c. 1965 . . . . — 13.00 — 15.50 — 9.50
□ **Goofy And Morty,** Schmid, ceramic Christmas ornament, height 3½ ", c. 1981 . . . . — 15.00 — 19.00 — 12.00
□ **Goofy, Morty And Huey,** Schmid, Christmas ceramic figural, sleigh ride music box, plays "We Wish You A Merry Xmas," first limited edition, height 7¼ ", c. 1980 . . . . — 32.00 — 35.00 — 28.50
□ **Goofy And Wilbur,** Disney All Star Parade drinking glass, height 4⅜", c. 1939 . . . . — 15.00 — 19.00 — 12.00
□ **Grandma Duck,** die cast and plastic auto, "Politoy," Donald's grandma in 1/43rd scale, Italian, c. 1970 . . . . — 15.00 — 19.00 — 12.00
□ **Greedy Pig And Colt,** Disney All Star Parade drinking glass, red and black, height 4⅜", c. 1937 . . . . — 12.00 — 16.00 — 9.25
□ **Grumpy,** Christmas light bulb, c. 1940 . . . . . . — 9.00 — 11.00 — 5.00
□ **Horace Horsecollar,** drinking glass, full figure in red, bending over for coin, height 4¾ ", c. 1930 . . . . — 25.00 — 30.00 — 22.50
□ **Horace Horsecollar,** juice glass, full figure in black, bending over for coin, height 3½ ", c. 1930 . . . . — 19.00 — 23.00 — 16.00
□ **Huey, Dewey, And Louie,** frosted glass figurine, Donald's three nephews, Italian, height 3½ ", c. 1970 . . . . — 18.00 — 22.00 — 15.00
□ **Jiminy Cricket,** Christmas light bulb, c. 1950 . — 12.00 — 13.00 — 7.50
□ **Jiminy Cricket,** drinking glass, in green with poem on back, height 4⅜" . . . . — 21.00 — 25.00 — 18.00
□ **Jiminy Cricket,** drinking glass, with poem on reverse side, height 4¾ ", c. 1940 . . . . — 22.00 — 28.00 — 20.00

	Current Price Range		P/Y Average

☐ **Jiminy Cricket,** frosted glass figurine, Italian, first series, height 4⅝″, c. 1970 . . . . 15.00 20.00 12.50

☐ **Jiminy Cricket,** Gare Mold, glazed Hi-gloss figurine, height 9″ 33.00 41.00 32.00

☐ **Jiminy Cricket,** Gund, vinyl and cloth hand puppet, in original box, c. 1960 . . . . 12.00 17.00 9.50

☐ **Jiminy Cricket,** oval "cameonyx" jewelry box, showing him in poses raised on cover, white on blue, height 6″, c. 1980 . . . . 41.00 48.00 40.00

☐ **Lady And Tramp,** double bisque figurine, having spaghetti dinner over candlelight, height 7″, c. 1970 . . . . 30.00 35.00 27.50

☐ **Lady And The Tramp,** Grolier bisque Christmas figurine in original box, c. 1980 . . . . 43.00 47.00 40.00

☐ **Mickey Mouse,** Page Productions, 50th birthday paint set in tin lithoed box, 45 large colors, length 9½″ 13.00 17.00 10.00

☐ **Mickey Mouse,** 50th birthday pin back button, marked "Disneyland," diameter 3½″, c. 1978 11.00 15.00 8.00

☐ **Mickey Mouse,** Page of England, paint set, lithoed tin box, Mickey Mouse, Minnie, Morty, Ferdy, Goofy doing yard work, length 9¾″ . . 10.00 12.00 6.00

☐ **Mickey Mouse,** pie-eyed Santa full figure . . . 9.00 11.00 10.00

☐ **Mickey Mouse,** pie-eyed Santa face 9.00 11.00 10.00

☐ **Mickey Mouse,** pie-eyed "Telephone" 10.00 12.00 11.00

☐ **Mickey Mouse and Minnie,** pie-eyed on roller skates 13.00 16.00 14.50

☐ **Mickey Mouse,** pin back button, "Globe Trotters' Member," diameter 1¼″, c. 1930 . . . . . . 43.00 52.00 47.00

☐ **Mickey Mouse,** plastic figural head drinking cup, the bandleader in red, height 4″, c. 1930 12.00 15.00 13.50

☐ **Mickey Mouse,** "Politoy," die cast plastic automobile, Italian, marked #W600, c. 1960 . . 12.00 16.00 14.00

☐ **Mickey Mouse,** Royal Orleans, bisque figurine, dressed as Santa going down chimney, height 4″, c. 1980 . . . . 14.00 18.00 16.00

☐ **Mickey Mouse,** recipe scrap book, premium by "Peter Pan Bread," height 6¼″, c. 1930 . . 37.00 48.00 42.50

☐ **Mickey Mouse,** Colorforms, seed packets, c. 1977 . . . . 5.00 8.00 4.50

☐ **Mickey Mouse,** Bransford, silverplate spoon, has pie-eyed full figure of Mickey on handle, his name down the stem, length 5½″, c. 1930 15.00 22.00 15.00

☐ **Mickey Mouse,** set of three different Christmas pin back buttons, diameter 1¾″ 6.00 8.00 7.00

☐ **Mickey Mouse,** Schmid, 50th birthday ceramic figural music box, Mickey in formal attire lighting candle on cake 45.00 53.00 47.00

☐ **Mickey Mouse,** Viletta, 50th birthday ceramic plate 85.00 95.00 85.00

☐ **Mickey Mouse,** Studios Giveaways, 50th birthday commemorative match box, box of 50, c. 1978 . . . . 45.00 90.00 55.00

	Current Price Range		P/Y Average

□ **Mickey Mouse,** Schmid, 50th birthday globe ornament, in box	15.00	22.00	14.50
□ **Mickey Mouse and Donald Duck,** J. Chein and Co., tin sand pail, also shows Daisy and nephews at the zoo, height 4½″, c. 1940	29.00	37.00	28.00
□ **Mickey Mouse, Donald Duck And Goofy,** Masterwork, Bicentennial belt buckle, item laminated with colorful scene of the three of them marching and carrying flag as "Minutemen," c. 1976	8.00	12.00	8.00
□ **Mickey Mouse, Donald Duck And Goofy,** Schmid, ceramic Christmas ornament, height 3½″	18.00	22.00	15.00
□ **Mickey Mouse, Donald Duck And Goofy,** "Triple Bisque" Bicentennial figurine, depicting the three of them dressed as "Minutemen," marching and playing instruments, c. 1976 . .	310.00	430.00	390.00
□ **Mickey Mouse, Donald Duck And Goofy,** Mattel, "Skediddlers" toys, set of three in original boxes, c. 1960	45.00	53.00	47.00
□ **Mickey Mouse, Donald Duck And Pluto,** "Patriot China" cup, shows them in a tug of war scene, c. 1930	10.00	13.00	11.00
□ **Mickey Mouse And Goofy,** Schmid, Christmas ceramic figural "Happy Holidays" music box, Mickey and Goofy are holding wreaths around their necks, plays "Rudolph The Red Nosed Reindeer," height 7″, c. 1981	35.00	43.00	34.00
□ **Mickey Mouse And Minnie Mouse,** Royal Orleans, bisque figurine with stocking caps, she's holding Christmas sock with Christmas package in it, he's holding a big Christmas package, c. 1980	25.00	30.00	27.00
□ **Mickey Mouse And Minnie Mouse,** bisque toothbrush holder, they're standing arm-in-arm, height 4½″, c. 1930	90.00	100.00	85.00
□ **Mickey Mouse And Minnie Mouse,** Schmid, "Caroling" pewter figurines, they're holding book marked "Noel"	30.00	36.00	33.00
□ **Mickey Mouse And Minnie Mouse,** Dan Brechner, ceramic salt and pepper shakers, seated on a wooden park bench, height 4½″, c. 1950	35.00	45.00	40.00
□ **Mickey Mouse And Minnie Mouse,** drinking glass, full figures in black on pink, height 5⅞″, c. 1950	13.00	15.00	14.00
□ **Mickey Mouse And Minnie Mouse,** "Nifty Nineties" double bisque figurine, Mickey's sporting striped coat, straw hat, bow-tie and cane, Minnie in polka dot dress with bow in hair	32.00	37.00	34.00
□ **Pluto,** Walt Disney Productions, composition figural bank, sitting down with tongue hanging out, height 6½″	13.00	17.00	15.00
□ **Pluto And Goofy,** Radnor, set of two bone china thimbles, in box, c. 1970	18.00	22.00	20.00

DOLLHOUSES

PERIOD: Dollhouses have been manufactured by toy companies since the Industrial Revolution. The most elaborate American dollhouses date from the Victorian period which is considered to be the "golden age" of toys.

COMMENTS: Many of the loveliest examples are handmade. Traditionally fathers and grandfathers have made dollhouses for their little girls, often a miniature version of their actual house.

ADDITIONAL TIPS: Because of the tremendous popularity of all types of miniature collectibles the demand for vintage dollhouses is at its greatest peak ever.

	Current Price Range		P/Y Average
☐ **Dollhouse,** Bliss, 13″	155.00	175.00	165.00
☐ **Dollhouse,** fireplaces in all rooms, simulated carved shingles, stucco exterior, late 1920's .	730.00	830.00	780.00
☐ **Dollhouse,** lithographed, c. 1930	80.00	100.00	90.00
☐ **Dollhouse,** lithographed, wood, 2 wooden figures, 13″ L.	275.00	325.00	300.00
☐ **Dollhouse,** wood, faced with paper, painted, brick styled chimney, 17½″ L.	90.00	110.00	100.00
☐ **Dutch Colonial,** wood, accessories, c. 1925 . .	475.00	575.00	520.00
☐ **English,** four rooms with staircase, two fireplaces, original, late 1800	850.00	950.00	900.00
☐ **French chateau-style,** windows on three sides, working door, c. 1890	650.00	750.00	700.00
☐ **German,** curtained windows, attic, steps leading to front door, c. 1890	1475.00	1575.00	1525.00
☐ **German castle,** ½″ to 1′ scale, molded after a late Gothic castle, c. 1875	2200.00	3200.00	2250.00
☐ **German,** small, embossed paper railing on second floor, unfurnished, c. 1900	310.00	360.00	335.00
☐ **Nineteenth century style,** roof shingled, clapboard sides, four rooms with hallways and staircase, two fireplaces, Victorian furnishings	3000.00	4000.00	3500.00
☐ **Swiss chalet style,** oak base on wheels, stenciled design on exterior, five rooms, Victorian furnishings, fourteen figures	2600.00	3600.00	3100.00

	Current Price Range		P/Y Average
□ **Tootsietoy**	35.00	45.00	40.00
□ **Tudor style,** Schoenhut	300.00	340.00	320.00
□ **Twentieth century style,** four rooms with hall-ways and staircase, conventional furnishings	270.00	370.00	325.00
□ **Walt Disney,** six-room, metal	60.00	90.00	75.00

DOLLHOUSE FURNITURE

□ **Bathtub,** tin, paint worn, 2½", late 19th c.	25.00	35.00	30.00
□ **Bedroom suite,** four pieces: chairs, bureau	40.00	50.00	45.00
□ **Bedroom suite,** three pieces, painted, c. 1920	50.00	80.00	65.00
□ **Bowfront chest,** Tynietoy, scale	55.00	65.00	60.00
□ **Broom holder,** tin, with brooms and dust pan	50.00	60.00	55.00
□ **Dining table,** golden oak, scale 1" to 1'	70.00	90.00	80.00
□ **Drum table,** rosewood, top tilts, edge lines in velvet, 3" Dia.	45.00	50.00	47.50
□ **Fireplace,** open hearth, pine mantel	25.00	35.00	30.00
□ **Hepplewhite sofa,** Tynietoy, scale	70.00	90.00	80.00
□ **Ice cream parlor set,** 2 chairs with wire mesh seats, table 3½"	50.00	55.00	52.50
□ **Rope bed,** ticking mattress and pillow, 15½" x 10½"	30.00	40.00	35.00
□ **Rug,** needlepoint, 3½" Dia.	12.00	16.00	14.00
□ **Shaving mirror,** mahogany frame and stand, mirror beveled glass, 4"	35.00	45.00	40.00
□ **Stove,** cast iron	70.00	90.00	80.00
□ **Stove,** tin kitchen, with utensils 11" H.	115.00	125.00	120.00
□ **Teakettle,** brass with trivet	55.00	75.00	65.00
□ **Victrola,** four-legs, painted wood, 4½"	55.00	75.00	65.00

FINE MINIATURE FURNITURE

□ **Chest of drawers,** George III, mahogany, late 18th c., 14" H.	365.00	465.00	420.00
□ **Chest of drawers,** George III style, mahogany, 10" H.	110.00	120.00	115.00
□ **Tea caddy,** George III, 4½" H., 18th c.	110.00	150.00	130.00
□ **Victorian dining room set,** walnut table and sideboard with marble tops, upholstered chairs	240.00	290.00	265.00
□ **Wing chair,** Federal, upholstered in brocade, 8¼" H.	265.00	285.00	275.00

DOLLS

COMMENTS: Doll collecting has grown phenomenally in the last 25 years to become one of the top hobbies in the United States. Individual appeal seems to be the magic ingredient in the world of doll collecting. Some dolls made of common materials show exquisite workmanship and detailing, while others made of fine porcelain bisque are crudely fashioned.

ADDITIONAL TIPS: The prices of dolls cover such a wide range that any collector can find specimens to fit his budget. While the French and German fashion dolls are out of the financial reach of many collectors, most of the more recent composition dolls are relatively plentiful and inexpensive. Interesting and varied collections may be assembled by specializing in dolls of a certain era, a certain construction material, those dressed in similar nationalistic costumes, or all the various dolls made by a single manufacturer. Prices given are for dolls in excellent to mint original condition. Deductions must be made for any missing parts, worn-out or faded clothes, and broken or cracked heads.

RECOMMENDED READING: For more extensive information, see *The Official Price Guide to Dolls,* published by The House of Collectibles.

ALEXANDER

	Current Price Range		P/Y Average
☐ **Alexanderkin,** hard plastic, wears bathing suit, sandals, robe, square sunglasses, carries beach bag, 8″	65.00	85.00	80.00
☐ **Amy,** plastic sleep eyes, blonde looped curls, 14″	90.00	105.00	103.00
☐ **Cissy,** hard plastic, jointed at knees and elbows, long flowing yellow cape-style coat, sleep eyes, high heel open dress shoes, 21″	85.00	110.00	102.50
☐ **Laurie,** vinyl head, sleep eyes, sad, long eyelashes, black hair, wears double-breasted jacket, plaid trousers, 12″	10.00	17.00	18.50
☐ **Scarlett O'Hara,** vinyl, sleep eyes, long black glossy hair, satin gown with trimming, satin bonnet, wears cameo on a chain at the neck, marked Alexander 1961, 21″	105.00	135.00	125.00

Georgene Averill Doll, *Bonnie Babe, marked Copr. by Georgene Averill Germany, 16", ***$850.00-$950.00**

	Current Price Range		P/Y Average
☐ **Sleeping Beauty,** Disney special edition, 1959, 9"	195.00	495.00	350.00
☐ **M.I.B.**	445.00	595.00	475.00
☐ **Wendy,** hard plastic, sleep eyes, dressed as tennis player with racquet, skirt, opentoe shoes, 8"	85.00	110.00	102.00
☐ **Wendy Ann,** hard plastic, sleep eyes, puffy cheeks, blond hair, wears jacket and skirt of matching style, two buttons on jacket, 8"	65.00	85.00	80.00

ARMAND MARSEILLE

☐ **Bisque,** socket head set on toddler body, fully jointed construction, open mouth showing two teeth, fixed eyes, marked Armand Marseille/Germany 996/A. 3 M., 16"	130.00	180.00	155.00
☐ **Bisque,** socket head, sleep eyes, open mouth with two teeth, five-piece body, marked G.B. 327/A. 12 M. Germany, 21"	335.00	385.00	360.50
☐ **Bisque,** five-piece composition body, set eyes, open mouth showing four teeth and traces of others, marked A.M. 560a/DRGM R 232/1, 14"	280.00	330.00	305.00
☐ **Bisque,** socket head, five-piece composition body, sleep eyes, open mouth with two teeth, marked Germany/971/A.4.M., 15"	90.00	140.00	115.00

	Current Price Range		P/Y Average

ARRANBEE

☐ **Army Boy,** composition head and limbs, body stuffed with excelsior, molded hair, painted eyes, wears U.S. soldier's uniform of post-World War I era, featuring reproductions (in reduced size) of Lincoln cents for jacket buttons, 15″ **75.00 95.00 70.00**

☐ **Baby Marie,** vinyl head, vinyl arms and legs, plastic body, sleep eyes, molded hair, partially open mouth, shaped for insertion of nursing bottle, wears diaper, quilt jacket, 8¼ ″ **5.00 7.00 5.00**

☐ **Scarlet,** composition head, composition arms, legs and body, sleep eyes (green), long eyelashes, closed mouth, wears long ball gown of U.S. Civil War era and large bonnet, gown is trimmed with silk ribbons, marked R & B, 15″ . **50.00 65.00 48.00**

☐ **Sonja Heinie,** composition head and body, brunette wig attached by adhesive, sleep eyes (brown), marked R & B, made in 1945, 21¼ ″ .. **49.00 58.00 47.00**

☐ **Taffy,** plastic, sleep eyes (green), marked R & B, made in 1954, 16½ ″ **55.00 67.00 52.00**

FISHER PRICE

☐ **Audrey,** vinyl head, cloth body, rooted hair, painted eyes, blouse with small heart pattern, marked 168240, 1973, Fisher Price Toys, 14″ .. **11.00 15.00 10.00**

☐ **Baby Ann,** vinyl head, cloth body, rooted blond hair, painted eyes, floral print dress with large sash ribbon, marked 60, 188460, 1973, Fisher Price Toys, 13½ ″ **10.00 14.00 9.00**

☐ **Elizabeth,** black, vinyl head, cloth body, rooted hair, closed mouth in semi-smile, painted eyes, marked 18, 168630, 1973, Fisher Price Toys, 13½ ″ **11.00 15.00 10.00**

☐ **Mary,** vinyl head, cloth body, rooted hair, upturned eyes (painted), angelic facial expression, wears print dress and white apron, marked 168420, 1973, Fisher Price Toys, 14″ .. **10.00 14.00 9.00**

☐ **Natalie,** vinyl head, cloth body, rooted hair, upturned eyes (painted), grinning smile, marked 168320, 1973, Fisher Price Toys, 13½ ″ **11.00 15.00 10.00**

HASBRO

☐ **Baby Ruth,** vinyl head, stuffed body, vinyl hands, molded and painted features, blonde hair, rooted, sold originally with a tag reading Baby Ruth 1971, used as a premium by the Curtis Candy Co., 10″ **5.00 7.00 5.00**

☐ **Flying Nun,** vinyl, brunette hair, rooted, molded and painted features, marked 1967 Hasbro, Hong Kong, 5″ **10.00 13.00 9.00**

☐ **G.I. Joe,** Action Marine, plastic, molded hair, brown, brown eyes, painted, marked 7700, G.I. Joe TM Copyright by Hasbro Patent Pending, made in U.S.A., made in 1964, 11½ ″ **35.00 43.00 31.00**

	Current Price Range		P/Y Average

IDEAL

☐ **Baby, Baby,** vinyl, rooted hair (blonde), fixed eyes (blue), nursing mouth, marked 115 Ideal, made in Hong Kong in 1974, 7″ . . . . — 7.00 — 10.00 — 8.00

☐ **Baby Belly Button,** black, vinyl, black hair (rooted), painted features, brown eyes, smiling closed mouth, in the likeness of an infant, Baby Belly Button has a knob at its stomach which, when turned, makes the arms, legs and head move, dressed in a diaper and white lace-edged smock, marked Ideal Toy Corp., E9-2-H-165, made in Hong Kong in 1970, 9″ . . . — 5.50 — 7.00 — 5.00

☐ **Baby Big Eyes,** vinyl, blonde hair (rooted), sleep eyes (blue), closed mouth, marked Ideal Doll, made in 1954, 21″ . . . . — 45.00 — 56.00 — 42.00

☐ **Snow White,** composition head, arms and legs, cloth body, molded and painted hair, molded and painted features, open mouth, eyes turned to side, marked Ideal, made c. 1939, 17½″ . . . . — 70.00 — 85.00 — 65.00

☐ **Tressy,** plastic/vinyl, black hair (rooted), sleep eyes (blue), pug nose, closed mouth, hair has "grow" feature (portion of wig is fitted inside head; when hair is pulled gently, it gives the appearance of "growing" out of the scalp), marked 1969, Ideal Toy Corp., GH-18, also marked (on hip) with Patent No. 3162976, made in Hong Kong . . . . — 8.00 — 10.00 — 7.00

JUMEAU

☐ **Bebe Parle,** talker, bisque, sleep eyes (round-ish), painted lashes on upper and lower lids, long arching brows, partially open mouth, narrow nose, joined at the elbows, talking mechanism operated by pullcord, says two words ("mama" — "papa"), date of manufacture unknown, probably c. 1895, 32″ . . . . — 950.00 — 1150.00 — 950.00

☐ **Cody,** bisque, fixed eyes (medium size, dark), lightly painted lashes on upper and lower lids, naturalistic brows (slightly arched), closed mouth, thin pale lips, narrow nose with well-defined nostrils, long thin face, found dressed as a child or adult, marked 13, date of manufacture unknown, c. 1887, one of the most famous and sought-after of the Jumeau dolls, 26″ — 4000.00 — 4500.00 — 3800.00

☐ **Bisque,** fixed eyes (large, prominent, dark), painted lashes on the upper and lower lids, arching brows (rather bushy), partially open mouth (the lower lip much smaller than the upper), narrow nose, squarish jaw, conventional ears, representing a girl about 5 or 6 years of age, marked Depose E-3J, date of manufacture unknown, 10½″ . . . . — 1000.00 — 1200.00 — 1000.00

	Current Price Range		P/Y Average

☐ **G.I. Joe,** Action Marine, plastic, molded hair, brown, brown eyes, painted, marked 7500, G.I. Joe, Copyright 1964 by Hasbro, Pat. No. 3,277,602, made in U.S.A., no problem distinguishing this 1967 version from the previous: the patent is no longer pending, a patent number is shown, 11½ " 21.00 25.00 19.00

HEINRICH HANDWERCK

☐ **Bisque,** head with bisque shoulder plate, fixed eyes, large, almond shaped, short painted lashes on top of eye socket, much longer painted lashes beneath, open mouth showing teeth, wide nose, thick prominent eyebrows, roundish jaw, prominent ears, marked with the letters HcH and the mold number 5/0, additionally marked with a device which resembles an airplane propeller or a flower with two petals, date of manufacture unknown, but the absence of the word "Germany" from the marking would suggest a dating of pre-1892, 17 " 230.00 280.00 210.00

☐ **Bisque,** head with bisque shoulder plate, fixed eyes, medium large, partially open mouth showing teeth, long face with prominent cheeks and jaw, moderately arched eyebrows, representing a girl of 4 or 5 years of age, marked with a four-petaled flower and the letters HcH, and also with the mold number 9/0, date of manufacture unknown, but the absence of the word "Germany" from the marking would suggest a dating of pre-1892, 14¾ " 160.00 190.00 150.00

HORSMAN

☐ **Athlete,** mechanical, plastic/vinyl, molded and painted hair, molded and painted features, stands on platform, operates by spring-driven motor, marked Horsman 1967, 5½ " 5.00 7.00 5.00

☐ **Babs,** composition, sleep eyes, blue, molded and painted hair, made in 1931, 10 " 63.00 75.00 55.00

☐ **Baby Chubby,** composition head, cloth body, composition arms and legs, molded and painted hair, reddish blonde, sleep eyes, blue, marked A-Horsman, made in 1940, 23 " 27.00 36.00 25.00

☐ **Bootsie,** black, plastic/vinyl, rooted hair, black, sleep eyes, brown, marked 1125-4-Horsman, made in 1969, 12 " 26.00 34.00 23.00

☐ **Campbell Kid,** composition body and head, molded and painted hair, painted shoes and socks, 1948, 12 " 90.00 110.00 85.00

☐ **Campbell Soup Kids,** plastic, boy in chef hat, girl with ribbon 25.00 32.00 22.00

MATTEL
BARBIE AND BARBIE-RELATED

	Current Price Range		P/Y Average
☐ **Barbie,** plastic, molded and painted features, bubble hairdo, wears red swimsuit (one piece), marked 850, made in 1962, 11½ "	330.00	430.00	380.00
☐ **Barbie's Friend Christie,** black, plastic, molded and painted features, talker, brown hair (parted), wears knitted green shirt and red shorts, marked 1126, sold in 1968, 11½ "	120.00	150.00	100.00
☐ **Bendable Ken,** plastic, molded and painted features, bendable legs, wears blue jacket and red trunks, marked 1020, sold in 1965, 12 "	14.00	18.00	12.00
☐ **Busy Barbie,** plastic, molded and painted features, wears checked skirt and denim sunsuit, marked 3311, sold in 1972, 11½ "	7.00	10.00	6.00
☐ **Chef Boy-Ar-Dee Barbie,** plastic, molded and painted features, painted lashes, wears green and red suit (one piece), marked 1190, sold in 1971, 11½ "	8.00	11.00	7.00

DOORSTOPS

DESCRIPTION: Doorstops are small, heavy figures, usually made of iron, that are used to hold open doors.

ORIGIN: While things such as stones have always been used to prop open doors, the use of decorative figures for such a purpose dates to late 18th century England.

MATERIALS: Doorstops are usually made of cast iron that has been painted or bronzed. Some are made of other metals, and those made of brass tend to be the most valuable.

COMMENTS: Doorstops made prior to 1920 are the most collectible. Age, rarity and condition affect the price.

ADDITIONAL TIPS: The listings are alphabetical according to the figure. Measurements and descriptions follow as available. Unless otherwise noted, the doorstops are made of cast iron.

	Current Price Range		P/Y Average
☐ Airedale	35.00	45.00	37.00
☐ American Eagle	50.00	65.00	53.00
☐ Aunt Jemima	65.00	75.00	67.00
☐ Basket of Flowers, height 6¼"	17.00	26.00	19.00
☐ Basket of Red Poppies, height 8", Hubley	25.00	35.00	28.00
☐ Basket of Fruit, height 10", aluminum	20.00	28.00	22.50
☐ Black Bear	40.00	50.00	43.00
☐ Boxer	30.00	42.00	33.00
☐ Bull	35.00	45.00	37.00
☐ Bulldog	37.50	47.00	40.00
☐ Campbell Kid, with teddy bear	170.00	210.00	185.00
☐ Cat, black	28.00	35.00	30.00
☐ Cat, black, green eyes	40.00	50.00	43.00
☐ Cat, height 7", seated, black body with green eyes, red mouth and yellow whiskers	80.00	100.00	87.00
☐ Cat, white, blue eyes, bell at throat, Hubley	80.00	100.00	87.00
☐ Cockatoo, height 7½", red, yellow and green paint, B. Noyes & Co.	55.00	75.00	62.00
☐ Cockatoo	28.00	34.00	29.00
☐ Colonial Lady, height 11½", black dress, holding yellow hat	40.00	55.00	42.00
☐ Conestoga Wagon, height 10"	60.00	80.00	67.00
☐ Court Jester, with animal	50.00	60.00	53.00
☐ Dog, Boston Terrier, height 8½", length 7"	40.00	58.00	45.00
☐ Dog, Boston Terrier, height 9½", length 8", facing left	65.00	80.00	70.00
☐ Dog, Cocker Spaniel	40.00	50.00	43.00
☐ Dog, German Shepherd	35.00	50.00	40.00
☐ Dog, Russian Wolf Hound, height 9½", length 15½"	130.00	155.00	138.00
☐ Dog, Scotty, length 10¼"	70.00	85.00	75.00
☐ Doll, with toy	40.00	50.00	43.00
☐ Drum Major	115.00	140.00	125.00
☐ Elephant	30.00	40.00	32.00
☐ Fiddler, with violin	33.00	40.00	34.00
☐ Flowers, in basket, solid brass	60.00	75.00	63.00
☐ Fox, brass	70.00	80.00	72.00
☐ Frog, solid bronze	92.00	115.00	95.00
☐ Fruit, in bowl	28.00	35.00	30.00
☐ General Robert E. Lee, height 7¼"	70.00	95.00	75.00
☐ Girl, height 11⅜", standing, bonnet on head, holding skirt by hem, white and blue paint, B&H	100.00	120.00	105.00
☐ Boy and Girl, Dutch, Hubley	80.00	97.00	85.00
☐ Golfer, in knickers	140.00	165.00	150.00
☐ Horses	45.00	55.00	47.00
☐ Indian, riding horse	78.00	90.00	80.00
☐ Jenny Lind, height 4½"	60.00	75.00	65.00
☐ Kitten	38.00	45.00	40.00
☐ Lamb, black	48.00	55.00	50.00
☐ Lighthouse	68.00	80.00	70.00
☐ Lion	45.00	55.00	47.00
☐ Little Red Riding Hood and The Wolf, pair	68.00	80.00	70.00
☐ Mail Coach	50.00	60.00	52.00
☐ Mammy, height 9"	110.00	135.00	115.00
☐ Monkey	40.00	50.00	42.00

	Current Price Range		P/Y Average
☐ Parrot	28.00	35.00	29.00
☐ Peacock	78.00	95.00	85.00
☐ Penguin, height 10½", black and white paint	73.00	90.00	79.00
☐ Peter Rabbit, height 11¾"	58.00	73.00	65.00
☐ Popeye	50.00	60.00	53.00
☐ Punch, with dog	92.00	115.00	95.00
☐ Rabbit	35.00	45.00	37.00
☐ Red Riding Hood and Wolf	68.00	85.00	75.00
☐ Rooster	50.00	60.00	52.00
☐ Spanish Dancer	45.00	53.00	47.00
☐ Squirrel	37.00	45.00	39.00
☐ Stagecoach	45.00	55.00	47.00
☐ Tiger Lilies	43.00	55.00	46.00
☐ Windmill	40.00	50.00	42.00
☐ Wolf	35.00	45.00	37.00
☐ Woodpecker	78.00	98.00	85.00

DUCK STAMPS

TOPIC: Duck Stamps are similar to hunting licenses in that the proceeds are used to procure and maintain refuges for waterfowl, and every waterfowl hunter over sixteen years of age must buy one from the government. The Duck Stamps themselves are not as collectible as the Duck Stamp prints, which the artist markets independently. Duck Stamps and the corresponding prints feature new pictures of waterfowl each year.

TYPES: Duck Stamps may be issued by either the state or the federal government. The listings given here are for federal Duck Stamp prints. Please refer to *The Official Price Guide to Collector Prints,* published by The House of Collectibles, for additional information and listings.

PERIOD: The first Duck Stamps and prints were issued by the federal government in 1934. The first state-issued stamps were released in 1971.

ORIGIN: The Duck Stamp program was begun as a response to a serious decline in the waterfowl population, resulting from loss of habitat.

COMMENTS: Many collectors frame both the print and its corresponding stamp. The second winning design is scarce; only 100 were issued. Because of this, no more than 100 complete sets of federal Duck Stamp prints can exist.

YEAR	PRINT DESIGN	ARTIST	MEDIUM	EDITION	CURRENT RETAIL PRICE
☐1934	MALLARDS	Ding Darling	Etching	300	4,400.00
☐1935	CANVASBACKS	Frank W. Benson	Etching	100	6,800.00
☐1936	CANADA GEESE	Richard E. Bishop	Etching	unlimited	1,000.00
☐1937	GREATER SCAUP	J. D. Knap	Gravure	260	3,000.00
☐1938	PINTAILS	Roland Clark	Etching	300	3,700.00
☐1939	GREEN WING TEAL	Lynn Bogue Hunt	Stone Litho	1st ed. 100	6,200.00
				2nd ed. 100	5,700.00
☐1940	BLACK DUCKS	Francis L. Jacques	Stone litho	1st ed. 30	7,000.00
				2nd ed. 30	6,000.00
				3rd ed. 200	3,500.00
☐1941	RUDDY DUCKS	E. R. Kalmback	Gravure (rev.)	100-110	3,600.00
			(reg.)	unknown	1,300.00
☐1942	WIGEON	A. Lassell Ripley (signed by Mrs. Ripley)	Etching	unlimited	1,200.00
					600.00
☐1943	WOOD DUCKS	Walter E. Bohl	Etching	unlimited	1,000.00
				2nd ed.	500.00
☐1944	WHITE FRONT GEESE	Walter A. Weber	Stone litho (rev.)	100	4,500.00
				2nd ed. 200	2,500.00
				3rd ed. 90	850.00
☐1945	SHOVELERS	Owen J. Gromme	Gravure	250	6,200.00
☐1946	REDHEADS	Robert W. Hines	Stone litho	1st ed. 300	2,000.00
				2nd ed. 380	150.00
☐1947	SNOW GEESE	Jack Murray	Gravure	300	2,400.00
☐1948	BUFFLEHEADS	Maynard Reece	Stone litho	200	1,200.00
				150	1,000.00
				400	600.00
☐1949	GOLDEN EYES	Roger E. Preuss	Stone litho	250	3,200.00
☐1950	TRUMPETERS	Walter A. Weber	Gravure	1st ed. 250*	1,500.00
				2nd ed. 300	400.00
☐1951	GADWALL	Maynard Reece	Stone litho	1st ed. 250	1,100.00
				2nd ed. 400	750.00
☐1952	HARLEQUINS	John H. Dick	Stone litho	250*	1,100.00
☐1953	BLUE WING TEAL	Clayton B. Seagears	Stone litho	250*	1,100.00
☐1954	RING NECKS	Harvey D. Sandstrom	Stone litho	275	1,100.00
☐1955	BLUE GEESE	Stanley Stears	Etching	1st ed. 1st pr. 250	1,100.00
				1st ed. 2nd pr. 53	1,100.00
				2nd ed. 100	600.00
☐1956	MERGANSERS	Edward J. Bierly	Etching	1st ed. 325	1,000.00
				2nd pr. 125	800.00
☐1957	EIDERS	Jackson Miles Abbott	Stone litho	1st ed. 253	1,100.00
				500	300.00
☐1958	CANADA GEESE	Leslie C. Kouba	Stone litho	1st ed. 250	1,100.00
				2nd ed. 250	1,000.00
☐1959	LABRADOR DOG	Maynard Reece	Stone litho	1st ed. 400	2,700.00
				2nd ed. 300	1,600.00
				3rd ed. 400	900.00
☐1960	REDHEADS	John A. Ruthven	Litho	1st ed. 400	1,000.00
				2nd ed. 400	600.00
☐1961	MALLARDS	Edward A. Morris	Etching	275	1,100.00
☐1962	PINTAILS	Edward A. Morris	Etching	275	1,100.00
☐1963	BRANT	Edward J. Bierly	Etching	1st ed. 550	1,000.00
				2nd pr. 125	800.00
☐1964	NENE GEESE	Stanley Stearns	Stone litho	1st ed. 300	1,100.00
				2nd ed. 300	700.00
☐1965	CANVASBACKS	Ron Jenkins	Stone litho	1st ed. 700	850.00
				2nd ed. 100	600.00
				3rd ed. 250	200.00
☐1966	WHISTLING SWANS	Stanley Stearns	Stone litho	1st ed. 300	1,100.00
				2nd ed. 300	500.00
☐1967	OLD SQUAWS	Leslie C. Kouba	Etching	275	900.00
☐1968	MERGANSERS	Claremont G. Pritchard	Stone litho	750	1,100.00
☐1969	SCOTERS	Maynard Reece	Stone litho	750	1,000.00

YEAR	PRINT DESIGN	ARTIST	MEDIUM	EDITION	CURRENT RETAIL PRICE
☐1970	ROSS GEESE	Edward J. Bierly	Photo litho-rem.	1,000	**3,200.00**
			-reg.	total	**2,500.00**
				2nd ed. 2,150	**150.00**
☐1971	CINNAMON TEAL	Maynard Reece	Stone litho	950	**5,000.00**
☐1972	EMPEROR GEESE	Arthur M. Cook	Photo litho-rem.	950	**4,000.00**
			-reg.	total	**2,800.00**
☐1973	STELLER'S EIDERS	Lee LeBlanc	Photo litho-rem.	1,000	**2,300.00**
			-reg.	total	**2,000.00**
☐1974	WOOD DUCKS	David A. Maass	Photo litho	unknown	**1,300.00**
☐1975	CANVASBACK DECOY	James Fisher	Photo litho-rem.	3,150	**1,300.00**
			-reg.	total	**1,100.00**
☐1976	CANADA GEESE	Alderson Magee	Photo litho with companion pc.	1,000	**2,100.00**
			without companion pc.	3,600	**900.00**
☐1977	ROSS' GEESE	Martin Murk	Photo litho-rem.	5,800	**750.00**
			-reg.	total	**600.00**
☐1978	HOODED MERGANSER	Albert Earl Gilbert	Photo litho-rem.	5,800	**1,100.00**
			-reg.	total	**550.00**
☐1979	GREEN WING TEAL	Ken Michaelson	Photo litho with companion pc.		**600.00**
			-reg.		**450.00**
☐1980	MALLARDS	Richard Plasschaert	Photo litho	N/A	**500.00**
☐1981	RUDDY DUCKS	John Wilson	Photo litho	N/A	**250.00**
☐1982	CANVAS BACK	David Maass	Photo litho	N/A	**200.00**
☐1983	PINTAILS	Phil Scholer	Photo w/medallion-		
			-rem.		**250.00**
			-reg.		**135.00**

EGGS

DESCRIPTION: Eggs are considered very beautiful art objects and are quite collectible.

VARIATIONS: Eggs are made for various purposes, from simple wooden darning eggs to jeweled egg boxes.

COMMENTS: The most famous eggs, prized for their beauty and rarity, are the Russian eggs created by Peter Carl Faberge. Today the decorated Easter is the egg most sought after by collectors. Prices tend to be reasonable.

ADDITIONAL TIPS: The listings are alphabetical according to type of egg, followed by description, manufacturer, year and price range.

For further information on eggs, contact The Egg Art Guild, 1174 Glenwood Dale, Cape St. Claire, MD 21408.

	Current Price Range		P/Y Average
☐ **Art Glass Egg,** iridescent, large, Vanderbelt ..	35.00	45.00	37.00
☐ **Art Glass Egg,** pink, gold flowers	138.00	165.00	145.00
☐ **Box,** china, painted with flowers and birds, hinged lid, brass fittings, 9½ "	140.00	180.00	145.00
☐ **Easter Candy Container,** papier-mache, egg being drawn by rabbit, 4"	12.50	20.00	14.00
☐ **Easter Egg,** baby chick, Goebel, c. 1978	17.50	25.00	19.00
☐ **Easter Egg,** dove on cover, Wedgwood, c. 1977	60.00	75.00	63.00
☐ **Easter Egg,** glass, raised lettering	40.00	50.00	44.00
☐ **Easter Egg,** glass, undecorated, large, set of four	40.00	50.00	44.00
☐ **Easter Egg,** porcelain, Royal Bayreuth, c. 1979	25.00	35.00	28.00
☐ **Easter Egg,** porcelain, floral decoration, Furstenberg, c. 1974	20.00	30.00	23.00
☐ **Easter Egg,** silver and enamel, lilies and forget-me-nots, Faberge, by Ruckert, c. 1900	11750.00	14000.00	12000.00
☐ **Jewel case,** mother-of-pearl, gilded metal, egg "wheelbarrow"	68.00	85.00	72.00

Minton Emperor's Garden,
of the egg series,
1982, **$95.00-$110.00**

	Current Price Range		P/Y Average
☐ **Mary Gregory Glass Egg,** raised lettering and design	25.00	35.00	27.00
☐ **Milk Glass Egg,** raised lettering and design .	30.00	40.00	32.00
☐ **Minton Emperor's Garden,** Royal Doulton, edition size 3500, 1982	100.00	115.00	103.00
☐ **Minton 19th Century,** Royal Doulton, edition size 3500, 1979	80.00	100.00	85.00
☐ **Rouge Flambe,** Royal Doulton, edition size 3500, 1980	110.00	120.00	112.00
☐ **Vinaigrette,** ivory, screw lid with grill inside, English	175.00	250.00	185.00
☐ **Vinaigrette,** silver and enamel, figure of a woman, French	700.00	800.00	720.00
☐ **Vinaigrette,** silver and enamel, purple, gold, white, French	950.00	1300.00	1050.00
☐ **Wooden Egg,** pine, hen, painted	7.50	12.00	8.00

ELVIS PRESLEY MEMORABILIA

DESCRIPTION: Elvis Presley, a rock and roll legend, was one of the greatest influences on music. His twenty year career spanned from 1956 until his untimely death in 1977. Because of the millions of Elvis Presley fans throughout the world, any items belonging to the "King of Rock and Roll" are valuable among collectors.

TYPES: There are all kinds of Elvis memorabilia from clothes, cars and contracts to autographed photos and school items. One of the largest collecting areas is his records.

COMMENTS: Some Elvis fans collect only his records while others collect all types of his memorabilia.

ADDITIONAL TIPS: For more information, consult *The Official Price Guide to Music Collectibles,* and *The Official Price Guide to Records* published by The House of Collectibles.

MEMORABILIA	Current Price Range		P/Y Average
☐ **Book,** *The Army Years by Nick Corvino, 93 pages, clothbound, 5½" x 8½".* Fictionalized story of the years spent by Elvis in the army.	5.00	7.00	5.50
☐ **Book,** *The Complete Elvis by Martin Torgoff, paperback, 256 pages.*	9.00	12.00	9.50
☐ **Book,** *Elvis by Dave Marsh, clothbound, 246 pages.*	30.00	40.00	31.00
☐ **Book,** *Elvis by Albert Goldman, clothbound.*	13.00	17.00	14.00
☐ **Book,** *Elvis: The Final Years by Jerry Hopkins, clothbound, 258 pages.*	11.00	15.00	12.00
☐ **Book,** *Elvis: The Illustrated Discography by Martin Hawkins and Colin Escott, paperback.*	5.00	7.00	6.00
☐ **Book,** *Elvis: The Illustrated Record by Roy Carr and Mick Farren, 12" square format.*	11.00	15.00	12.00
☐ **Book,** *Elvis in His Own Words by Mick Farren and Pearce Marchbank, paperback, 128 pages.*	5.00	7.00	6.00

	Current Price Range		P/Y Average
☐ **Book,** *Elvis: The Legend and the Music by John Tobler and Richard Wooten, clothbound, 192 pages.*	10.00	13.00	11.00
☐ **Book,** *Elvis Presley: A Complete Reference by Wendy Sauers, clothbound, 194 pages.*	16.00	20.00	17.00
☐ **Book,** *Elvis Presley Reference Guide and Discography by John Whisler, clothbound, 250 pages.*	13.00	17.00	14.00
☐ **Book,** *Elvis Presley: A Study in Music by Robert Matthew-Walker, paperback, 154 pages.*	5.00	7.00	6.00
☐ **Book,** *Elvis Presley News Diary by Bill Johnson, 230 pages, spiral binding, 9½" x 12", 1981.*	8.00	10.00	8.50
☐ **Book,** *The Illustrated Elvis by W. A. Harbinson, 160 pages, softbound, 8" x 10½".*	2.00	3.00	2.50
☐ **Book,** *Jailhouse Rock by Lee Cotten and Howard A. DeWitt, clothbound, 368 pages.* . . .	16.00	20.00	16.50
☐ **Book,** *Private Elvis, author uncredited, 199 pages, softbound, 8½" x 11", 1978.*	10.00	13.00	10.50
☐ **Book,** *Up and Down With Elvis Presley by Marge Crumbaker and Gabe Tucker, clothbound, 254 pages.*	11.00	15.00	11.50
☐ **Book,** *When Elvis Died by Neal Gregory and Janice Gregory, clothbound, 290 pages.*	12.00	16.00	12.50
☐ *Elvis Presley child's guitar, plastic.*	28.00	38.00	29.00
☐ *Elvis Presley school bag.*	35.00	50.00	36.00
☐ *8x10 photo with guitar, signed and inscribed, 1957.*	350.00	450.00	355.00
☐ *Printed postcard photo, facsimile signature.* . .	5.00	8.00	6.00
☐ *Lifesize cardboard figure of Elvis, c. 1961, used for theater promotion, full color.*	375.00	475.00	380.00
☐ *8x10 color photo, signed.*	400.00	600.00	405.00
☐ *Signature on label of 45rpm record - add $225-$300 to value of record as listed above.*			
☐ *Signature on label of 33⅓rpm long-play record - add $275-$375 to value of album as listed above.*			
☐ *Signature on cover of 33⅓rpm long-play album - add $300-$400 to value of album if record is present. If record is not present, cover alone is worth $300-$400.*			
☐ *Elvis Presley drinking mug, ceramic, picture on side.*	23.00	32.00	24.00
☐ *Handkerchief, colored silk, illustrated.*	20.00	27.00	21.00
☐ *Typewritten note by Col. Tom Parker (his manager), signed.*	9.00	12.00	10.00
☐ *8x10 photo, unsigned, black and white.*	2.00	4.00	3.00
☐ *8x10 motion picture still, unsigned, black and white.*	1.50	3.00	1.75
☐ *8x10 color photo, unsigned (**not** clipped from magazine or book).*	6.00	10.00	6.50
☐ *8x10 motion picture still, unsigned, color.* . . .	5.00	8.00	5.50
☐ *8x10 motion picture still, black and white, signed.*	250.00	375.00	255.00
☐ *8x10 motion picture still, color, signed.*	300.00	450.00	305.00

Elvis Presley, *still,*
if signed would be worth
considerably more,
$1.50-$2.00

	Current Price Range		P/Y Average
☐ *Typewritten letter, signed, ½ page*	150.00	225.00	155.00
☐ *Typewritten letter, signed, 1 page*	180.00	250.00	185.00
☐ *Typewritten letter, signed, 2 pages*	275.00	375.00	280.00
☐ *Handwritten letter, signed, ½ page*	275.00	375.00	280.00
☐ *Handwritten letter, signed, 1 page*	450.00	600.00	455.00
☐ *Handwritten letter, signed, 2 pages*	600.00	800.00	610.00
☐ *Handwritten letter, signed, 3 pages*	750.00	1100.00	755.00
☐ *Note in his handwriting, one line.*	150.00	200.00	160.00
☐ *Signature on an otherwise blank sheet of paper or card.*	80.00	100.00	85.00
☐ *Typewritten letter **to him** from record company executive.*	40.00	50.00	45.00
☐ *Typewritten letter **to him** from motion picture executive.*	35.00	49.00	40.00
☐ *Typewritten letter **to him** from TV producer.* .	31.00	42.00	32.00
☐ *Typewritten letter **to him** from music agent.* .	29.00	39.00	30.00
☐ *Typewritten letter **to him** from U.S. Armed Forces.*	235.00	310.00	240.00
☐ *Typewritten letter **to him** from author seeking an interview.*	9.00	14.00	10.00
☐ *Typewritten letter **to him** from Ed Sullivan.* ...	140.00	200.00	145.00
☐ *Draft card issued to him by Selective Service.*	1750.00	3000.00	1800.00
☐ *Magazine cover with full color photo.*	.50	1.00	.75
☐ *News cuttings (most).*	.50	2.00	.75

ELVIS PRESLEY — 45 SINGLES

☐ **Sun 209** *That's All Right/Blue Moon of Kentucky.*	195.00	350.00	198.00
☐ **210** *Good Rockin' Tonight/I Don't Care If the Sun Don't Shine.*	175.00	275.00	180.00

	Current Price Range		P/Y Average

☐ **215** *Milkcow Blues Boogie/You're a Heartbreaker.*	250.00	375.00	255.00
☐ **217** *Baby Let's Play House/I'm Left, Your Right, She's Gone.*	140.00	240.00	145.00
☐ **223** *Mystery Train/I Forgot to Remember to Forget.*	130.00	240.00	135.00
☐ **RCA6357** *Mystery Train/I Forgot to Remember to Forget.*	15.00	24.00	16.00
☐ **6380** *That's All Right/Blue Moon of Kentucky.*	15.00	24.00	16.00
☐ **6381** *Good Rockin' Tonight/I Don't Care If the Sun Don't Shine.*	15.00	24.00	16.00
☐ **6382** *Milkcow Blues Boogie/You're a Heartbreaker.*	15.00	24.00	16.00
☐ **6383** *Baby Let's Play House/I'm Left, You're Right, She's Gone.*	15.00	24.00	16.00
☐ **6420** *Heartbreak Hotel/I Was the One.*	5.00	9.00	5.50
☐ **6540** *I Want You, I Need You, I Love You/My Baby Left Me.*	5.00	9.00	5.50
☐ **6604** *Don't Be Cruel/Hound Dog.*	5.00	9.00	5.50
☐ **6636** *Blue Suede Shoes/Tutti Fruitti.*	15.00	24.00	16.00
☐ **6637** *I Got a Woman/I'm Countin' on You.*	15.00	24.00	16.00
☐ **6638** *I'm Gonna Sit Right Down and Cry Over You/I'll Never Let You Go.*	15.00	24.00	16.00
☐ **6639** *Tryin' to Get to You/I Love You Because.*	15.00	24.00	16.00
☐ **6640** *Blue Moon/Just Because.*	15.00	24.00	16.00
☐ **6641** *Money Honey/One-Sided Love Affair.*	15.00	24.00	16.00
☐ **6642** *Shake, Rattle and Roll/Lawdy Miss Clawdy.*	15.00	24.00	16.00
☐ **6643** *Love Me Tender/Anyway You Want Me.*	4.50	8.00	16.00
☐ **6800** *Too Much Playing For Keeps.*	4.50	8.00	5.00
☐ **6870** *All Shook Up/That's When Your Heartaches Begin.*	4.50	8.00	5.00
☐ **7000** *Teddy Bear/Loving You.*	4.50	8.00	5.00
☐ **7035** *Jailhouse Rock/Treat Me Nice.*	4.50	8.00	5.00
☐ **7150** *Don't/I Beg of You.*	4.50	8.00	5.00
☐ **7240** *Wear My Ring Around Your Neck/Doncha Think It's Time.*	4.50	8.00	5.00
☐ **7280** *Hard Headed Woman/Don't Ask Me Why.*	4.50	8.00	5.00
☐ **7410** *One Night/I Got Stung.*	4.50	8.00	5.00
☐ **7506** *A Fool Such As I/I Need Your Love Tonight.*	3.75	6.00	4.00
☐ **7600** *A Big Hunk O' Love/My Wish Came True.*	3.75	6.00	4.00
☐ **7740** *Stuck on You/Fame and Fortune.*	3.25	5.50	3.50
☐ **7740** *Stuck on You/Fame and Fortune (stereo single).*	70.00	125.00	72.00
☐ **7777** *It's Now or Never/A Mess of Blues.*	3.25	5.50	3.50
☐ **7777** *It's Now or Never/A Mess of Blues (stereo single).*	70.00	125.00	72.00
☐ **7810** *Are You Lonesome Tonight?/I Gotta Know.*	3.25	5.50	4.00
☐ **7810** *Are You Lonesome Tonight?/I Gotta Know (stereo single).*	70.00	125.00	72.00
☐ **7850** *Surrender/Lonely Man.*	3.25	5.50	3.50
☐ **7850** *Surrender/Lonely Man (stereo single).*	95.00	165.00	97.00
☐ **7880** *I Feel So Bad/Wild in the Country.*	3.25	5.50	3.50

	Current Price Range		P/Y Average
☐ **7880** *I Feel So Bad/Wild in the Country (stereo single).*	95.00	165.00	97.00
☐ **098** *His Latest Flame/Little Sister.*	3.00	5.00	3.50
☐ **7968** *Can't Help Falling in Love/Rock-A-Hula-Baby.*	3.00	5.00	3.50
☐ **7992** *Good Luck Charm/Anything That's a Part of You.*	3.00	5.00	3.50
☐ **8041** *She's Not You/Just Tell Her Jim Said Hello.*	3.00	5.00	3.50
☐ **8100** *Return to Sender/Where Do You Come From?*	3.00	5.00	3.50
☐ **8134** *One Broken Heart For Sale/They Remind Me Too Much of You.*	3.00	5.00	3.50
☐ **8188** *Devil in Disguise/Please Don't Drag That Sting Around.*	3.00	5.00	3.50
☐ **8234** *Kissin' Cousins/It Hurts Me.*	3.00	5.00	3.50
☐ **8360** *What's I Say/Viva Las Vegas.*	3.00	5.00	3.50
☐ **8400** *Such a Night/Never Ending.*	3.00	5.00	3.50
☐ **8440** *Ask Me/Ain't That Loving You Baby.*	3.00	5.00	3.50
☐ **8500** *Do the Clam/You'll Be Gone.*	3.00	5.00	3.50
☐ **8585** *(Such An) Easy Question/It Feels So Right.*	3.00	5.00	3.50
☐ **8740** *Tell Me Why/Blue Rider.*	3.00	5.00	3.50
☐ **8780** *Frankie and Johnny/Please Don't Stop Loving Me.*	3.00	5.00	3.50
☐ **8870** *Love Letters/Come What May.*	3.00	5.00	3.50
☐ **8941** *If Every Day Was Like Christmas/How Would You Like To Be.*	4.50	8.00	4.75
☐ **9056** *Indescribably Blue/Fools Fall in Love.*	3.00	5.00	3.50
☐ **9115** *Long Legged Girl/That's Someone You Never Forget.*	3.00	5.00	3.50
☐ **9287** *There's Always Me/Judy.*	3.00	5.00	3.50
☐ **9341** *Big Boss Man/You Don't Know Me.*	3.00	5.00	3.50
☐ **94258** *Guitar Man/High Heeled Sneakers.*	3.00	5.00	3.50
☐ **9465** *U.S. Male/Stay Away Joe.*	3.00	5.00	3.50
☐ **9547** *Let Yourself Go/Your Time Hasn't Come Yet Baby.*	3.00	5.00	3.50
☐ **9600** *You'll Never Walk Alone/We Call on Him.*	3.00	5.00	3.50
☐ **9610** *A Little Less Conversation/Almost in Love.*	3.00	5.00	3.50
☐ **9670** *If I Can Dream/Edge of Reality.*	2.75	4.50	3.00
☐ **9731** *Memories/Charro.*	2.75	4.50	3.00
☐ **9741** *In the Ghetto/Any Day Now.*	2.75	4.50	3.00
☐ **9747** *Clean Up Your Own Back Yard/The Fair is Moving On.*	2.75	4.50	3.00
☐ **9764** *Suspicious Minds/You'll Think of Me.*	2.75	4.50	3.00
☐ **9768** *Don't Cry Daddy/Rubberneckin'.*	2.75	4.50	3.00
☐ **9791** *Kentucky Rain/My Little Friend.*	2.75	4.50	3.00
☐ **9835** *The Wonder of You/Mama Liked the Roses.*	2.75	4.50	3.00
☐ **9873** *I've Lost You/The Next Step is Love.*	2.75	4.50	3.00
☐ **9916** *You Don't Have to Say You Love Me/Patch It Up.*	2.75	4.50	3.00
☐ **9960** *I Really Don't Want To Know/There Goes My Everything.*	2.75	4.50	3.00

	Current Price Range		P/Y Average
☐ **9980** *Where Did They Go, Lord?/Rags to Riches.*	2.75	4.50	3.00
☐ **9985** *Life/Only Believe.*	2.75	4.50	3.00
☐ **9998** *I'm Leavin'/Heart of Rome.*	2.75	4.50	3.00
☐ **1017** *It's Only Love/The Sound of Your Cry.*	2.75	4.50	3.00
☐ **0619** *Until It's Time for You to Go/We Can Make the Morning.*	2.75	4.50	3.00
☐ **0672** *An American Trilogy/The First Time I Ever Saw Your Face.*	2.75	4.50	3.00
☐ **0769** *Burning Love/It's a Matter of Time.*	2.50	4.00	2.75
☐ **0815** *Separate Ways/Always on My Mind.*	2.50	4.00	2.75
☐ **0910** *Steamroller Blues/Fool.*	2.50	4.00	2.75
☐ **0088** *Raised on Rock/For Ol' Time Sake.*	2.50	4.00	2.75
☐ **0196** *I've Got a Thing About You Baby/Take Good Care of Her.*	2.50	4.00	2.75
☐ **0280** *If You Talk in Your Sleep/Help Me.*	2.50	4.00	2.75
☐ **10074** *Promised Land/It's Midnight.*	2.50	4.00	2.75
☐ **10191** *My Boy/Thinking About You.*	2.50	4.00	2.75
☐ **10278** *T-R-O-U-B-L-E/Mr. Songman.*	2.50	4.00	2.75
☐ **10401** *Bringing It Back/Pieces of My Life.*	2.50	4.00	2.75
☐ **10601** *Hurt/For the Heart.*	2.50	4.00	2.75
☐ **18057** *Moody Blue/She Thinks I Still Care.*	2.50	4.00	2.75

EXTENDED PLAY (EP)

	Current Price Range		P/Y Average
☐ **RCA 1254** *Elvis Presley (double-pocket).*	90.00	165.00	95.00
☐ **747** *Elvis Presley.*	12.00	25.00	13.00
☐ **821** *Heartbreak HoteL.*	14.00	27.00	15.00
☐ **830** *Elvis Presley.*	14.00	27.00	15.00
☐ **940** *The Real Elvis.*	14.00	27.00	15.00
☐ **965** *Anyway You Want Me.*	14.00	27.00	15.00
☐ **4006** *Love Me Tender.*	12.00	25.00	15.00
☐ **992** *Elvis, Vol. I.*	12.00	25.00	15.00
☐ **993** *Elvis, Vol. II.*	14.00	27.00	15.00
☐ **994** *Strictly Elvis.*	14.00	27.00	15.00
☐ **1-1515** *Loving You, Vol. I.*	14.00	27.00	15.00
☐ **2-1515** *Loving You, Vol. II.*	14.00	27.00	15.00
☐ **4041** *Just for You.*	14.00	27.00	15.00
☐ **4054** *Peace in the Valley.*	12.00	25.00	15.00
☐ **4108** *Elvis Sings Christmas Songs.*	14.00	27.00	15.00
☐ **4114** *Jailhouse Rock.*	14.00	27.00	15.00
☐ **4319** *King Creole, Vol. I.*	14.00	27.00	15.00
☐ **4321** *King Creole, Vol. II.*	14.00	27.00	15.00
☐ **4325** *Elvis Sails.*	27.00	48.00	29.00
☐ **4340** *Christmas with Elvis.*	14.00	27.00	16.00
☐ **4368** *Follow That Dream.*	8.25	14.00	8.50
☐ **4371** *Kid Galahad.*	8.25	14.00	8.50
☐ **4382** *Easy Come, Easy Go.*	9.50	18.00	10.00
☐ **4383** *Tickle Me.*	9.50	18.00	10.00
☐ **5088** *A Touch of Gold, Vol. I (maroon label).*	35.00	56.00	38.00
☐ **5088** *A Touch of Gold, Vol. I (black label).*	12.00	25.00	14.00
☐ **5120** *The Real Elvis (reissue) (maroon label).*	35.00	54.00	38.00
☐ **5120** *The Real Elvis (reissue) (black label).*	9.50	15.00	10.00
☐ **5121** *Peace in the Valley (reissue) (maroon label).*	35.00	54.00	38.00

	Current Price Range		P/Y Average

☐ 5151 *Peace in the Valley (reissue) (black label).*	9.50	15.00	10.00
☐ 5122 *King Creole, Vol. I (reissue) (maroon label).*	35.00	54.00	38.00
☐ 5122 *King Creole, Vol. I (reissue) (black label).*	9.50	15.00	10.00
☐ 5101 *A Touch of Gold, Vol. II (maroon label).*	35.00	54.00	38.00
☐ 5101 *A Touch of Gold, Vol. II (black label).*	12.00	25.00	14.00
☐ 5141 *A Touch of Gold, Vol. II (maroon label).*	35.00	54.00	38.00
☐ 5141 *A Touch of Gold, Vol. III (black label).*	12.00	25.00	13.00
☐ 5157 *Elvis Sails (reissue) (maroon label).*	40.00	70.00	45.00
☐ 5157 *Elvis Sails (reissue) (maroon label).*	12.00	25.00	15.00

COMPACT 33's

☐ RCA 37-7850 *Surrender/Lonely Man.*	48.00	115.00	52.00
☐ 37-7880 *I Feel So Bad/Wild in the Country.*	75.00	175.00	80.00
☐ 37-7908 *His Latest Flame/Little Sister.*	75.00	175.00	80.00
☐ 37-7968 *Can't Help Falling in Love/Rock-A-Hula Baby.*	75.00	175.00	80.00
☐ 37-7992 *Good Luck Charm/Anything That's Part of You.*	75.00	175.00	80.00
☐ 37-8041 *She's Not You/Just Tell Her Jim Said Hello.*	90.00	250.00	95.00
☐ 37-8100 *Return to Sender/Where Do You Come From?*	90.00	250.00	95.00

LP'S

THE ALBUMS BELOW WERE FIRST ISSUED ONLY IN MONO

☐ RCA 1254 (M) *Elvis Presley.*	25.00	56.00	30.00
☐ 1382 (M) *Elvis.*	25.00	56.00	30.00
☐ 1515 (M) *Loving You.*	17.00	39.00	20.00
☐ 1035 (M) *Elvis' Christmas Album (double-pocket).*	75.00	190.00	80.00
☐ 1707 (M) *Elvis' Golden Records.*	17.00	39.00	20.00
☐ 1884 (M) *King Creole.*	17.00	39.00	20.00
☐ 1951 (M) *Elvis' Christmas Album (reissue) (photo on back).*	17.00	39.00	20.00
☐ 1990 (M) *For LP Fans Only.*	24.00	56.00	30.00
☐ 2011 (M) *A Date with Elvis (double pocket).*	34.00	84.00	38.00
☐ 2011 (M) *A Date with Elvis (single pocket).*	17.00	39.00	20.00
☐ 2075 *Elvis' Golden Records, Vol. II.*	17.00	39.00	20.00

THE ALBUMS BELOW HAVE EQUIVALENT VALUE IN MONO AND STEREO

☐ 2231 (M) *Elvis is Back.*	17.00	39.00	20.00
☐ 2256 (M) *G.I. Blues.*	17.00	39.00	20.00
☐ 2328 (M) *His Hand in Mine.*	12.00	29.00	15.00
☐ 2370 (M) *Something for Everybody.*	17.00	39.00	18.00
☐ 2436 (M) *Blue Hawaii.*	17.00	39.00	18.00
☐ 2523 (M) *Pot Luck.*	17.00	39.00	18.00
☐ 2621 (M) *Girls! Girls! Girls!*	17.00	39.00	18.00
☐ 2697 (M) *It Happened at the World's Fair.*	17.00	39.00	18.00
☐ 2697 (M) *Fun in Acapulco.*	15.00	35.00	16.00
☐ 2765 (M) *Elvis' Golden Records, Vol. III.*	15.00	35.00	16.00
☐ 2894 (M) *Kissin' Cousins.*	15.00	35.00	16.00
☐ 2999 (M) *Roustabout.*	15.00	35.00	16.00

	Current Price Range		P/Y Average
☐ 3338 **(M)** *Girl Happy.*	15.00	35.00	16.00
☐ 3450 **(M)** *Elvis for Everyone.*	15.00	35.00	16.00
☐ 3468 **(M)** *Harum Scarum (with photo enclosed).*	20.00	35.00	22.00
☐ 3553 **(M)** *Frankie and Johnny.*	17.00	39.00	18.00
☐ 3643 **(M)** *Paradise, Hawaiian Style.*	15.00	35.00	16.00
☐ 3702 **(M)** *Spinout.*	17.00	39.00	18.00
☐ 3758 **(M)** *How Great Thou Art.*	15.00	35.00	16.00
☐ 3787 **(M)** *Double Trouble.*	15.00	35.00	16.00
THE ALBUMS BELOW HAVE A HIGHER VALUE IN MONO			
☐ 3893 **(M)** *Clambake.*	40.00	100.00	45.00
☐ 3893 **(S)** *Clambake.*	17.00	39.00	20.00
☐ 3921 **(M)** *Elvis' Golden Records, Vol. IV.*	90.00	240.00	95.00
☐ 3921 **(S)** *Elvis' Golden Records, Vol. IV.*	17.00	39.00	18.00
☐ 3989 **(M)** *Speedway.*	320.00	800.00	325.00
☐ 3989 **(S)** *Speedway.*	17.00	39.00	18.00

EMBROIDERY

DESCRIPTION: Embroidery is decorative needlework using diverse threads such as silk, gold, wool or cotton stitched into any type of fabric including cloth or leather.

PERIOD: The most valuable and rarest embroidery work is from the 1700s. Embroidery pieces from the 1800s and 1900s are more readily available.

VALUE: The condition, workmanship, materials, design and age of a piece are equally important in determing value.

COMMENTS: Many hobbyists collect all types of embroidery while others collect by motif, stitch or country.

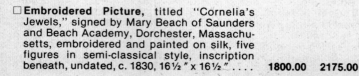

☐ **Embroidered Picture,** titled "Cornelia's Jewels," signed by Mary Beach of Saunders and Beach Academy, Dorchester, Massachusetts, embroidered and painted on silk, five figures in semi-classical style, inscription beneath, undated, c. 1830, 16½″ x 16½″	1800.00	2175.00	1975.00

Tea Cloth, *royal blue with white embroidery and crocheted trim, 1930s,* **$10.00-$15.00**

	Current Price Range		P/Y Average
☐ **Embroidered Picture,** titled "Spring," anonymous, showing two women and a man in a field, one of the women seated, an overhanging tree nearby, place of origin not known, probably late 18th century or early 19th century, 16½" x 18"	625.00	750.00	670.00
☐ **Embroidered Picture on Silk,** titled "Timoclea," signed by Harriet Valentine, a classical scene from the legend of Timoclea with numerous figures clad in robes, the embroidery done in chenille and silk thread, undated, c. 1840, 26" x 36"	850.00	1075.00	920.00
☐ **Embroidered Picture on Silk,** untitled, an American eagle with spread wings near the top, in the central portion a vignette of a World War I naval gunnery ship surrounded by flags, also cannon and anchor devices, probably made in the Orient for sale on the U.S. market at the time of World War I, c. 1918, 42" x 25½"	450.00	575.00	500.00
☐ **Needlework Map of Maryland,** also showing portions of New Jersey and Pennsylvania, signed by Harriet Beall, done in a variety of stitches and colors, undated, probably very early 19th century, 13" x 17½"	800.00	1000.00	875.00

	Current Price Range		P/Y Average
☐ **Silk and Chenille Embroidered Floral Picture,** signed with initials "G.M.," worked in various colors of chenille thread against solid beige silk background, picturing a basket filled with an assortment of flowers, place of origin unknown, c. 1820, 22″ x 19″	375.00	450.00	410.00
☐ **Tent-Stitched Picture,** titled "Fishing Lady," shows lady at pond hooking fish while man stands by with hat in hand, various colors of wool thread woven into a canvas backing, Connecticut origin, mid 1700s, 16″ x 20″	4475.00	5600.00	4800.00
☐ **Yarn-sewn Wall Picture,** untitled, signed by Christine Wuerpel, showing a male and female rider in a sleigh being drawn across a snow-covered field by a light and dark horse, undated, c. 1880, 22″ x 33″	325.00	425.00	365.00

EYEGLASSES

TOPIC: Eyeglasses are devices that enhance eyesight. They consist of one or two glass or plastic lenses, and a frame to help the user keep the lenses in front of his eyes.

TYPES: Common types of eyeglasses that collectors are interested in include the quizzing glass, scissors-glasses, temple spectacles and the lorgnette. The quizzing glass was an early version of the monocle. Scissors-glasses consisted of two eyepieces connected by a hinged handle that was held under the nose. Temple spectacles employ two bars that press against the temples; these are modern eyeglasses. The lorgnette is a pair of eyepieces with a handle on one side.

PERIOD: Although eyeglasses have been available since the 1200s, they did not come into general use until the 1780s.

COMMENTS: Wild styles of eyeglasses from the 1960s are currently in demand among collectors. Prices for these and other types of eyeglasses are still reasonable.

ADDITIONAL TIPS: Old eyeglasses can be found through Lions and Rotary Clubs, which collect eyeglasses for the needy. Optometrist offices are another good source for collectible specimens.

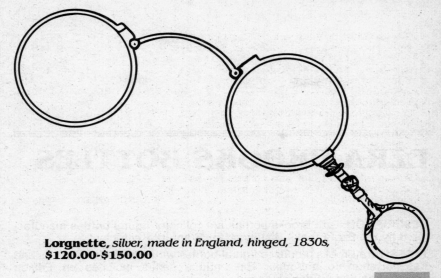

Lorgnette, *silver, made in England, hinged, 1830s,*
$120.00-$150.00

	Current Price Range		P/Y Average
☐ **Harold Lloyd,** bone frame, c. 1920	60.00	78.00	69.00
☐ **Lorgnette,** English, gilded, c. 1840	130.00	150.00	140.00
☐ **Lorgnette,** mother-of-pearl, c. 1800	70.00	90.00	80.00
☐ **Lorgnette,** sterling silver, c. 1840	160.00	190.00	175.00
☐ **Lorgnette,** tortoiseshell, c. 1800	130.00	150.00	140.00
☐ **Magnifying,** plain silver frame, c. 1910	30.00	40.00	35.00
☐ **Monocle,** gold frame, silk cord, c. 1800	50.00	80.00	65.00
☐ **Quizzing,** monocle, gold and silver, c. 1800 . .	80.00	100.00	90.00
☐ **Scissor,** gold plated, ornate, c. 1880	85.00	95.00	90.00
☐ **Spectacles,** pinch, Art Deco, wire frame, c. 1930	60.00	80.00	70.00
☐ **Spectacles,** pinch, Edwardian, 16k gold	100.00	130.00	115.00
☐ **Spectacles,** pinch, hard rubber, c. 1860	65.00	85.00	75.00
☐ **Spectacles,** pinch, sterling silver, c. 1920 . . .	85.00	105.00	95.00
☐ **Spectacles,** pinch, wire frame, c. 1920	63.00	83.00	73.00
☐ **Spectacles,** steel framed with ties, c. 1800 . .	110.00	120.00	115.00
☐ **Spectacles,** steel framed, wire temples, c. 1800	100.00	130.00	115.00

CASES

☐ **Engraved Silver,** oval, clasp works, c. 1900 . . .	140.00	160.00	150.00
☐ **Papier-mache,** with mother-of-pearl inlay, c. 1850-1860	145.00	175.00	160.00

EZRA BROOKS BOTTLES

DESCRIPTION: Ezra Brooks bottles are collector figural bottles manufactured by the Ezra Brooks Distilling Co., Franfurt, Kentucky.

TYPES: Ezra Brooks produces figural bottles with themes from sports and transportation to antiques. The antique series includes an Edison phonograph and a Spanish cannon.

COMMENTS: Ezra Brooks rivals Jim Beam as one of the chief whiskey companies manufacturing figural bottles.

ADDITIONAL TIPS: For more information, consult *The Official Price Guide to Bottles, Old and New,* published by The House of Collectibles.

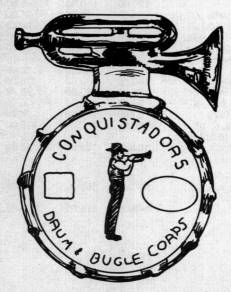

Ezra Brooks Drum and Bugle Conquistador, *(1971),* $10.00-$15.00

	Current Price Range		P/Y Average
☐ **Alabama Bicentennial,** (1976)	10.00	15.00	12.50
☐ **American Legion,** (1971), distinguished embossed star emblem born out of WWI struggle. Combination blue and gold. On blue base	25.00	34.00	29.00
☐ **American Legion,** (1972), Ezra Brooks salutes the American Legion, its Illinois Department, and Land of Lincoln and the city of Chicago, host of the Legion's 54th National Convention	60.00	70.00	65.00
☐ **American Legion,** (1973), Hawaii, our fiftieth state, hosted the American Legion's 1973 annual Convention. It was the largest airlift of a mass group ever to hit the islands. Over 15,000 Legionnaires visited the beautiful city of Honolulu to celebrate the Legion's fifty-fourth anniversary	10.00	15.00	12.50
☐ **American Legion,** (1977) Denver	20.00	30.00	25.00
☐ **American Legion,** (1973) Miami Beach	8.00	12.00	10.00
☐ **Amvets,** (1974) Dolphin	16.00	20.00	18.00
☐ **Amvet,** (1973) Polish Legion	16.00	22.00	19.00
☐ **Antique Cannon,** (1969)	5.00	8.00	6.50
☐ **Antique Phonograph,** (1970), Edison's early contribution to home entertainment. White, black, "Morning Glory" horn, red. Richly detailed in 24k gold	8.00	12.00	10.00
☐ **Arizona,** (1969), man with burro in search of "Lost Dutchman Mine", golden brown mesa, green cactus, with 22k gold base, "ARIZONA" imprinted	5.00	8.00	6.50
☐ **Auburn 1932,** (1978) Classic Car	30.00	40.00	35.00
☐ **Badger No. 1,** (1973) Boxer	14.00	20.00	17.00
☐ **Badger No. 2,** (1974) Football	16.00	24.00	20.00
☐ **Badger No. 3,** (1974) Hockey	16.00	24.00	20.00
☐ **Baltimore Oriole Wild Life,** (1979)	35.00	45.00	40.00
☐ **Bare Knuckle Fighter,** (1971)	6.00	10.00	8.00
☐ **Baseball Hall of Fame,** (1973), baseball fans everywhere will enjoy this genuine Heritage China ceramic of a familiar slugger of years gone by	16.00	21.00	19.00
☐ **Basketball Player,** (1974)	8.00	12.00	10.00
☐ **Bear,** (1968)	5.00	8.00	6.50
☐ **Bengal Tiger Wild Life,** (1979)	32.00	40.00	36.00
☐ **Betsy Ross,** (1975)	12.00	18.00	15.00
☐ **Big Bertha,** Nugget Casino's very-own elephant with a raised trunk, gray, red, white and black, yellow & gold trim. "Blanket" and stand	8.00	12.00	10.00
☐ **Big Daddy Lounge,** (1969), salute to South Florida's "STATE" liquor chain, and "Big Daddy's" lounges. White, green, red	5.00	10.00	7.50
☐ **Bighorn Ram,** (1973)	8.00	11.00	9.50
☐ **Bird Dog,** (1971)	10.00	18.00	14.00
☐ **Bordertown,** Borderline Club where California and Nevada meet for a drink. Brown, red, white. Club Building with Vulture on roof stopper, and outhouse	5.00	10.00	7.50

	Current Price Range		P/Y Average
☐ **Bowler,** (1973)	5.00	10.00	7.50
☐ **Brahma Bull,** (1972)	12.00	18.00	15.00
☐ **Clown,** (1978), Imperial Shrine	20.00	28.00	24.00
☐ **Club Bottle,** (1973), the third commemorative Ezra Brooks Collector Club bottle is created in the shape of America, each gold star on the new club bottle represents the location of an Ezra Brooks Collectors Club	21.00	28.00	24.00
☐ **Clydesdale Horse,** (1973), in the early days of distilling, Clydesdales carted the bottles of whiskey from the distillery to towns all across America	10.00	16.00	13.00
☐ **Colt Peacemaker,** (1969), flask	4.00	8.00	6.00
☐ **Conquistadors,** tribute to a great drum & bugle corps, silver colored trumpet attached to drum	6.00	12.00	8.00
☐ **Conquistador's Drum & Bugle,** (1972)	10.00	18.00	14.00
☐ **Corvette Indy Pace Car,** (1978)	40.00	50.00	45.00
☐ **Maine Lobster,**(1970), bottle in Lobster shape, complete with claws, pinkish-red color, bottle is sold only in Maine	20.00	28.00	24.00
☐ **Maine Lighthouse,** (1971)	16.00	20.00	18.00
☐ **Man-O-War,** (1969), "Big Red" captured just about every major horse-racing prize in turf-dom, replica of famous horse in brown and green, 22k gold base, embossed, "MAN-O-WAR"	10.00	16.00	13.00
☐ **M & M Brown Jug,** (1975)	18.00	24.00	21.00
☐ **Map,** (1972), U.S.A. Club Bottle	8.00	14.00	11.00
☐ **Masonic Fez,** (1976)	10.00	18.00	14.00
☐ **Max,** (1976), the hat, Zimmerman	25.00	30.00	27.50
☐ **Military Tank,** (1971)	15.00	22.00	19.50
☐ **Minnesota Hockey Player,** *(1975)*	18.00	22.00	20.00
☐ **Minuteman,** (1975)	12.00	18.00	14.00
☐ **Missouri Mule,** (1972), brown	12.00	15.00	13.50
☐ **Moose,** (1973)	22.00	30.00	26.00
☐ **Mr. Maine Potato,** (1973), from early begin-nings the people of Maine have built the small potato into a giant industry, today potatoes are the number one agricultural crop in the state, over thirty-six billion pounds are grown every year	6.00	10.00	8.00
☐ **Mr. Foremost,** (1969), an authentic reproduc-tion of the famous bottle-shaped symbol of Foremost Liquor stores, "Mr. Foremost" known for good wines and spirits, red, white and black	9.00	12.00	10.50
☐ **Mr. Merchant,** (1970), JUMPING MAN, Whim-sical, checkered-vest caricature of amiable shopkeeper, leaping into the air, arms out-stretched, yellow, black	8.00	12.00	10.00
☐ **Motorcycle,** motorcycle rider and machine, rider dressed in blue pants, red jacket, with stars 'n stripes helmet, motorcycle black with red tank on silver base	8.00	12.00	10.00

	Current Price Range		P/Y Average
☐ **Mountaineer,** (1971), figure dressed in buckskin, holding rifle, "MOUNTAINEERS ARE ALWAYS FREE" embossed on base, bottle is hand-trimmed in platinum, one of the most valuable Ezra Brooks figural bottles	40.00	60.00	50.00
☐ **Mustang Indy Pace Car,** (1979)	12.00	18.00	15.00
☐ **New Hampshire State House,** (1970), 150-year old State House, embossed doors, windows, steps, eagle topped stopper, gray building with gold	10.00	14.00	12.00
☐ **Nebraska—Go Big Red!** (1972), genuine Heritage China reproduction of a game ball and fan, trimmed in genuine 24k gold	10.00	14.00	12.00
☐ **North Carolina Bicentennial,** (1975)	10.00	14.00	12.00
☐ **Nugget Classic,** replica of golf pin presented to golf tournament participants, finished in 22k gold	8.00	10.00	9.00
☐ **Oil Gusher,** bottle in shape of oil drilling rig, all silver, jet black stopper in shape of gushing oil	5.00	8.00	6.50
☐ **Old Capital,** (1971), bottle in shape of Iowa's seat of government when the corn state was still frontier territory, embossed windows, doors, pillars, "OLD CAPITAL/IOWA 1840-1857" on base, reddish color with gold dome stopper	15.00	22.00	19.00
☐ **Old Ez,** (1977), No. 1, barn owl	45.00	55.00	50.00
☐ **Old Ez,** (1978), No. 2, eagle owl	62.00	66.00	64.00
☐ **Old Ez,** (1979), No. 3, snow owl	40.00	45.00	42.50
☐ **Panda—Giant,** (1972), Giant Panda ceramic bottle	14.00	18.00	16.00
☐ **Penguin,** (1972), Ezra Brooks salutes the penguin with a genuine Heritage China ceramic figural bottle	8.00	12.00	10.00
☐ **Reno Arch,** (1968), honoring the "biggest little city in the world", Reno, Nevada, arch shape with "RENO" embossed on yellow, front of bottle multi-color decal of: dice, rabbits foot, roulette wheel, slot machine, etc., white and yellow, purple stopper	5.00	10.00	7.50
☐ **San Francisco Cable Car,** (1968)	10.00	16.00	13.00
☐ **Sailfish,** (1971), leaping deep water Sailfish with a sword-like nose and large spread fin, blue-green luminous tones on green "waves" base	8.00	12.00	10.00
☐ **Salmon,** (1971), Washington King	12.00	18.00	15.00
☐ **San Francisco Cable Car,** (1968)	10.00	16.00	13.00
☐ **Sea Captain,** (1971), salty old seadog, white hair and beard, in blue "captains" jacket with gold buttons and sleeve stripes, white cap, gold band, holding pipe, on "wooden" stanchion base	10.00	14.00	12.00

	Current Price Range		P/Y Average
□ **Senator,** (1971), cigar-chomping, whistle-stopping State Senator, stumping on a platform of pure nostalgia, black "western" hat and swallow-tail coat, red vest, string tie, gold, black red, white	12.00	16.00	14.00
□ **Senators of the U.S.,** (1972), Ezra Brooks honors the Senators of the United States of America with this genuine Heritage Ceramic "Old Time" courtly Senator	12.00	16.00	14.00
□ **Setter,** (1974)	12.00	18.00	15.00
□ **Shrine King Tut Guard,** (1979) . . . .·. . . .	30.00	38.00	34.00
□ **Silver Saddle,** (1973)	24.00	30.00	27.00
□ **Silver Spur Boot,** (1971), cowboy-boot shaped bottle with silver spur buckled on, "SILVER SPUR—CARSON CITY NEVADA" embossed on side of boot, brown boot with platinum trim	8.00	14.00	11.00
□ **1804 Silver Dollar,** (1970), commemorates the famous and very valuable "1804 Silver Dollar," embossed replica of the Liberty Head dollar, platinum covered round dollar shaped bottle on black or white base	5.00	8.00	6.50

FANS

ORIGIN: Folding fans were popular and fashionable accessories for women of means during the 18th, 19th and even into the early 20th centuries. Aside from the obvious function of being used to cool oneself, fans were used to show not only one's social position and wealth, but also for coquetry or flirting.

The Oriental version — like all Oriental artifacts — was a symbolic and functional device, essential to the proper code of daily living. Men as well as women utilized them, from the scented fans of the elderly, to the black and red implements of the military. A popular export item (particularly the delicate ivory fans, carved under water and much sought after as wedding gifts), fans served many functions in Oriental society. They were used for cooling of course, but also as an essential fashion accessory, for fanning flames, to direct military troops, as message carriers, in dances, stories, games and wrestling matches.

CONSTRUCTION: Folding fans were constructed in one of two ways. The more common method was the insertion of sticks into a pleated piece of material called a "leaf." Leaves were made of silk lace, paper, or even vellum (very thin goatskin). The other type of folding fan was called a "brise." The brise fan was made up of wide, overlapping sticks and joined by a ribbon. Nearly all fans of both types have scenes or designs painted on them.

Another type, considered quite stylish from the 1870s until about 1910, was the feather fan. Usually made of ostrich feathers, this type was quite perishable and is now relatively rare.

Beautifully drawn, painted, or inscribed, Oriental fans fell into two main structural categories. Women's fans were usually non-folding, consisting of a roundish piece of paper glued to a flat bamboo handle. Folding fans, used more extensively in ritual ceremonies, or by high born citizens, were made of paper or silk, with wooden, bamboo, ivory, or mother-of-pearl ribs.

ADDITIONAL TIPS: Because fans are not durable collectibles, their numbers tend to be rather low and prices accordingly high. Once a beautiful fan is acquired, the methods of display and preservation are vital factors. Special attention should be paid to store the item in an airtight container that screens out damaging ultraviolet rays. Most specimens do well when placed in a protective frame.

RECOMMENDED READING: For more in-depth information on fans you may refer to *The Official Price Guide to Oriental Collectibles,* published by The House of Collectibles.

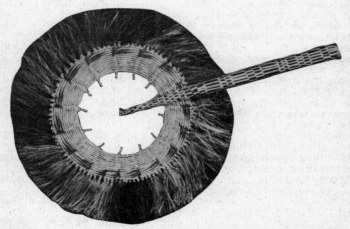

Fan, *woven straw with tortoiseshell, 1920s,* **$8.00-$10.00**

	Current Price Range		P/Y Average
□ **Advertising,** Hire's Root Beer, 6½″, c. 1930 . .	10.00	15.00	12.50
□ **Advertising,** Homer's 5 Cigar, 7″, c. 1910	10.00	15.00	12.50
□ **Advertising,** lithographed, late 19th c.	10.00	15.00	12.50
□ **Black net,** with sequins	20.00	30.00	25.00
□ **Bride's,** lace, hand painted	20.00	30.00	25.00
□ **Bride's,** lace, sequins, ivory sticks	35.00	45.00	37.50
□ **Brise,** child's, painted, ribbon and floral design	65.00	75.00	70.00
□ **Brise,** gilded, painted with three vignettes, loop	130.00	160.00	145.00
□ **Brise,** Regency, painted floral design, amber guards	120.00	130.00	125.00
□ **Brise,** Regency, painted vase of flowers	40.00	60.00	50.00
□ **Celluloid,** carved flower	40.00	60.00	50.00
□ **Celluloid,** miniature	40.00	60.00	50.00
□ **Celluloid,** Oriental design	20.00	30.00	25.00
□ **Celluloid,** sequins, chiffon	45.00	50.00	47.50
□ **Cockade,** silver and cut steel pique, middle quizzing glass	275.00	300.00	237.50
□ **Feather,** celluloid sticks	45.00	55.00	50.00
□ **Feather,** ivory sticks	100.00	140.00	120.00
□ **Feather,** painted, c. 1870	100.00	110.00	105.00
□ **Feather,** tortoiseshell sticks	100.00	110.00	105.00
□ **Feather,** small, late 19th c.	120.00	130.00	125.00
□ **Feather,** signed Duvelleroy, 19th c.	500.00	600.00	550.00
□ **French,** painted, ivory sticks	175.00	185.00	170.00
□ **French,** painted, tortoise sticks, sequins	175.00	185.00	170.00
□ **French,** painted, signed Jolivet, 19th c.	500.00	700.00	600.00
□ **French,** painted, carved, signed	75.00	85.00	80.00
□ **Garrett Snuff,** advertising, paper, c. 1928	15.00	20.00	17.50
□ **George Washington and Cherry Smash,** lithographed	20.00	30.00	25.00
□ **Gold edge,** pink silk, ebony ribs	30.00	35.00	32.50
□ **Hand painted,** floral design, wood	20.00	30.00	25.00
□ **Horn,** carved, painted pansies, blue ribbon . .	100.00	130.00	115.00
□ **Lacquered,** black, silver flower	75.00	85.00	80.00
□ **Lacquered,** white, silver handle	55.00	65.00	60.00
□ **Marabou feathers,** satin, hand painted, 20″ .	125.00	145.00	135.00
□ **Oriental,** bamboo, 7″ x 20″, 1900s, signed Liang Zhuang-cheng	450.00	650.00	550.00
□ **Oriental,** bamboo and birds, 8″ x 23″, c. 1820-1875, signed by Hezhong	450.00	650.00	550.00
□ **Oriental,** bamboo, rock and trees, 6″ x 18″, c. 1910-1930, by Wu Hafan	8000.00	12000.00	1000.00
□ **Oriental,** bird and fruit blossoms, 6″ x 18″, c. 1620-1665, by Ren Yi	2050.00	3100.00	2500.00
□ **Oriental,** birds and bamboo, 6″ x 18″, c. 1830-1845, by Ren Yi	10000.00	12000.00	11000.00
□ **Oriental,** birds, flowers, rocks, bamboo, 6″ x 19″, c. 1820-1865, by Ren Yi	850.00	1250.00	1050.00
□ **Oriental,** blossom, 7″ x 21″, c. 1820-1875, by Hu Gongshou	450.00	650.00	550.00
□ **Oriental,** blossoms, 8″ x 21″, c. 1820-1875, by Hu Gongshou	550.00	750.00	650.00
□ **Oriental,** calligraphy, 7″ x 20″, c. 1820-1895, by Liu Rongsi	450.00	650.00	550.00

	Current Price Range		P/Y Average
□ **Oriental,** calligraphy, 6″ x 21″, c. 1620-1665, by Yilin	1050.00	1250.00	1150.00
□ **Oriental,** city scene, 7″ x 20″, c. 1820-1875, by Wang Kun	450.00	650.00	550.00
□ **Oriental,** cricket and mulberries, 8″, x 21″, c. 1890-1910, by Wang Kun	15000.00	20000.00	17500.00
□ **Oriental,** egrets, 8″ x 21″, c. 1850-1895, by Wang Kun	6000.00	8000.00	7000.00
□ **Oriental,** female, 7″ x 21″, c. 1820-1875, figure preparing to mount horse, by Gu Luo	555.00	750.00	650.00
□ **Oriental,** flowers and wood, 6″ x 17″, c. 1505-1575	850.00	1050.00	950.00
□ **Oriental,** fruit and blosssoms, 7″ x 21″, c. 1820-1875, by Deng Qichang	650.00	850.00	750.00
□ **Oriental,** immortal and goose, 6″ x 18″, c. 1930-1950, by Ren Yi	12000.00	15000.00	13500.00
□ **Oriental,** landscape and calligraphy, 7″ x 21″, c. 1890-1910, by PuRu	6000.00	8000.00	7000.00
□ **Oriental,** landscape, 7″ x 22″, c. 1720-1795, by Fang Shishu	1250.00	1550.00	1400.00
□ **Oriental,** landscape, 7″ x 20″, c. 1820-1890, by Dai Jian	350.00	550.00	450.00
□ **Oriental,** landscape, 7″ x 21″, c. 1820-1875, by Yongbo	550.00	750.00	650.00
□ **Oriental,** landscape, 7″ x 20″,1620-1665, artist unknown	1550.00	2050.00	1800.00
□ **Oriental,** landscape, 7″ x 20″, c. 1720-1795, by Huang Yi	1050.00	1250.00	1175.00
□ **Oriental,** lohan, 7″ x 20″, c. 1820-1875, by Ren Xun	4000.00	6000.00	5000.00
□ **Oriental,** lohans, 6″ x 18″, c.1820-1875, signed Fanglan	650.00	850.00	750.00
□ **Oriental,** lotus flower, 7″ x 20″, c.1930-1950, by Zhang Daqian	25000.00	30000.00	27500.00
□ **Oriental,** magnolia, 6″ x 18″, c.1910-1930, by Shao'ang	3000.00	3500.00	3250.00
□ **Oriental,** man and youth, 7″ x 20″, c.1820-1875, by Fena Ning	450.00	650.00	550.00
□ **Oriental,** man at tablem 7″ x 20″, c.1820-1875, by Ren Xun	1250.00	1550.00	1375.00
□ **Oriental,** mountain scene, 8″ x 22″, by Juru Bao	450.00	650.00	550.00
□ **Oriental,** pavilions, 8″ x 21″, c.1820-1875, artist unknown	2100.00	2550.00	2325.00
□ **Oriental,** poem in character, 7″ x 20″, c.1620-1665, by Jiang Jie	710.00	920.00	815.00
□ **Oriental,** poem, 7″ x22″, c.1620-1665, by Shu Youzhang	550.00	650.00	600.00
□ **Oriental,** poem, 8″ x 21″, c.1820-1870, artist unknown	450.00	650.00	550.00
□ **Oriental,** riverscape, 6″ x 20″, by Shu Youzhang	550.00	950.00	850.00
□ **Oriental,** rocks and bamboo, 7″ x 21″, c. 1890-1910, artist unknown	350.00	500.00	425.00
□ **Oriental,** sailboats, 6″ x 20″, 1505-1575, artist unknown	850.00	1250.00	925.00

	Current Price Range		P/Y Average
□ **Oriental,** scholar in a landscape scene, 6″ x 18″, c. 1890-1910, by PuRu	6000.00	8000.00	7000.00
□ **Oriental,** the court, 75 x 2″, c. 1620-1675, artist unknown	250.00	350.00	300.00
□ **Oriental,** tiger and priest, 8″ x 21″, c. 1820-1875, by Cao Hua	450.00	650.00	550.00
□ **Oriental,** wiseman on the water, 7″ x 215, c. 1720-1795, by Bi Han	650.00	850.00	750.00
□ **Oriental,** straw, lacquered handle	15.00	20.00	17.50
□ **Oriental,** silk, Geisha figure	10.00	15.00	12.50
□ **Ostrich plume,** tortoise shell sticks	50.00	60.00	55.00
□ **Pearl sticks,** sequin design, 8″	35.00	45.00	40.00
□ **Puzzle,** four scenes, two-way opening	150.00	170.00	160.00
□ **Satin flower center,** carved, ivory sticks	150.00	170.00	160.00
□ **Silk,** embroidered, ivory sticks	75.00	85.00	80.00
□ **Silk,** hand painted animal figure and books . .	25.00	35.00	30.00
□ **Silk,** hand painted figures and floral designs, original storage container	65.00	75.00	70.00
□ **Silk,** Oriental design, ivory and bamboo	45.00	55.00	50.00
□ **Souvenir Centennial,** historical buildings, 12″	100.00	110.00	105.00
□ **Wedding,** ivory sticks, lace	65.00	75.00	70.00

FARM EQUIPMENT

DESCRIPTION: Farm equipment includes any implement used for agriculture.

TYPES: Farm equipment includes tractors, potatoe diggers, pitchforks, plows and cultivators.

PERIOD: Americans began using farm machinery during the early 1800s. Although farm equipment from the early years was often impractical inventions that did not survive, those which did are highly collectible.

MAKER: In the 1800s and early 1900s, there were many manufacturers who later went out of business. The obscure company's equipment is usually more valuable due to rarity than an existing company's equipment. Rock Island Plow Company, the Minneapolis Threshing Machine Company and the Avery Manufacturing Company are examples of relatively obscure companies, while John Deere and International Harvester are companies which have existed since the 1800s.

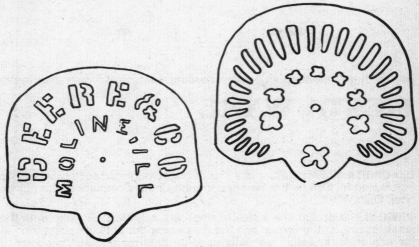

Left to Right: *tractor seat, iron, Deere & Co., Moline, ILL imprinted in seat, $20.00-$40.00; tractor seat, J.I. Case, Racine, WI, 1800s, $100.00-$120.00*

	Current Price Range		P/Y Average
☐ **Avery steam engine,** 40 hp. with full extension wheels, 1912	1650.00	1850.00	1700.00
☐ **Baker steam engine,** 20 hp. single cylinder side mount, 1920	3250.00	3550.00	3350.00
☐ **Case Tractor,** model "C," 4 cylinder, rubber wheels, restored, good condition, c. 1927	800.00	1050.00	900.00
☐ **Case Tractor,** VAC model, rubber wheels, restored, good condition, c. 1931	360.00	510.00	420.00
☐ **Chilled Plow,** Richland Farm Implements, iron and oak, for two or three horses	150.00	250.00	200.00
☐ **International Harvester Tractor,** model "H," rubber wheels, restored, good condition, c. 1937	800.00	1050.00	900.00
☐ **John Deere Tractor,** model "B," rubber wheels, restored, good condition, c. 1935	420.00	620.00	500.00
☐ **Russell Traction Steam Machine,** 8 hp., restored	3550.00	4050.00	3750.00
☐ **Sattley's Timber Saw,** kerosene engine	1250.00	1450.00	1300.00

FIESTA WARE

DESCRIPTION: Fiesta Ware is a line of brightly colored pottery tableware introduced in 1935 by the Homer Laughlin China Company of East Liverpool, Ohio.

DESIGN: The design is a series of rings which graduate in size, with the smallest ring at the center and the greatest width between rings also at the center. This design is mostly used on the rims and at the center of items such as plates, bowls, etc. It is also used on pieces with small pedestal bases and on lids.

COLOR: The colors used for these wares are Fiesta red, rose, dark green, medium green, light green, chartreuse, yellow, old ivory, gray, turquoise and dark blue. Red is the most valuable.

COMMENTS: Fiesta began to be actively collected in the 1960s and a big surge of popularity followed in the next decade. Prices on the secondhand market zoomed from an average of 25¢ to 35¢ to the $5 to $10 range. This seemed unbelievable, because everyone knew Fiesta ware was very common — it had been one of the most widely manufactured tablewares of the 20th century. Nevertheless, buyer demand was strong, and with this kind of demand anything can happen to retail prices.

MARKS: Each piece, except a very few, is marked with the Fiesta trademark, either in the mold or an ink handstamped mark.

RECOMMENDED READING: For more in-depth information on Fiesta Ware you may refer to *The Official Price Guide to Pottery and Porcelain* and *The Official Identification Guide to Pottery and Porcelain*, published by The House of Collectibles.

	Current Price Range		P/Y Average
Blue			
☐ **Bowl,** *dessert, 6", 1959*	9.00	11.00	9.50
☐ **Bowl,** *salad, 10", footed*	65.00	75.00	68.00
☐ **Candleholders,** *pair, spherical body on square base, 1936*	62.00	72.00	64.00

	Current Price Range		P/Y Average
□ **Carafe**	28.00	32.00	29.00
□ **Plate,** *13"*	15.00	20.00	16.00
□ **Tumbler,** *footed*	18.00	22.00	19.00
Gray			
□ **Bowl,** *dessert, 4½"*	8.00	12.00	9.00
□ **Bowl,** *fruit, 5½"*	8.00	12.00	9.00
□ **Plate,** *9½"*	7.00	9.00	8.00
Ivory			
□ **Carafe,** *three pint, cork seal top, 1940s*	29.00	34.00	30.00
□ **Creamer**	4.00	6.00	5.00
□ **Gravy Boat**	16.00	22.00	17.00
□ **Plate,** *6"*	3.00	5.00	4.00
□ **Plate,** *9½"*	6.50	8.00	7.00
□ **Plate,** *10½"*	18.00	22.00	19.00
□ **Plate,** *13"*	9.00	15.00	10.00
□ **Relish,** *three compartments*	40.00	50.00	42.00
□ **Soup Plate,** *scalloped rim*	9.00	12.00	10.00
□ **Tray,** *relish, 1939*	37.00	42.00	38.00
Light Green			
□ **Bowl,** *fruit, 5½"*	6.00	8.00	7.00
□ **Coffeepot,** *lidded*	25.00	30.00	26.00
□ **Creamer,** *ring handle, small pedestal base* ..	6.00	8.00	7.00
□ **Cup And Saucer**	10.00	15.00	11.00
□ **Plate,** *11"*	8.00	10.00	9.00
□ **Platter,** *12"*	9.00	12.00	10.00
□ **Salt and Pepper Shakers**	9.00	12.00	10.00
□ **Sauceboat,** *handled, on small pedestal base, 1939*	11.00	14.00	12.00
Medium Green			
□ **Bowl,** *dessert, 1959*	22.00	27.00	23.00
□ **Bowl,** *fruit, 4¾", flared rim*	22.00	27.00	24.00
□ **Cup And Saucer**	20.00	30.00	21.00
□ **Tray,** *utility, extended rim*	11.00	14.00	12.00
Red			
□ **Ashtray**	18.00	25.00	19.00
□ **Coffeepot,** *notched lid and handle, 1930s* ...	52.00	62.00	53.00
□ **Cup and Saucer**..........................	13.00	16.00	14.00
□ **Pitcher,** *juice*	20.00	30.00	22.00
□ **Plate,** *6"*	4.00	6.00	4.50
□ **Plate,** *11"*	10.00	15.00	11.00
□ **Sugar And Creamer,** *1940s*	13.00	17.00	14.00
□ **Teapot,** *large, holds eight cups, ring handle, 1930s*	27.00	35.00	28.00
□ **Teapot,** *small, lidded*	50.00	60.00	52.00
□ **Tumbler,** *footed*	15.00	17.00	16.00
Turquoise			
□ **Bowl,** *4½"*	7.50	9.50	8.00
□ **Carafe**	32.00	38.00	33.00
□ **Creamer**	52.00	67.00	54.00
□ **Mug**	22.00	27.00	24.00

Pitcher,
water, Fiesta pattern,
$20.00-$30.00

	Current Price Range		P/Y Average
☐ Plate, *10½", three compartments, flared rim,* 1940s	8.00	11.00	9.00
☐ Platter, *12", oval, with extended rim, 1939*	8.00	11.00	9.00
☐ Relish, *three compartments*	45.00	55.00	46.00
☐ Soup Plate, *scalloped rim*	9.00	12.00	10.00
☐ Sugar Bowl, *lidded*	10.00	14.00	11.00
☐ Tray	52.00	62.00	53.00
☐ Tumbler, *footed*	11.00	14.00	12.00
☐ Tumbler, *5 ounces, cylindrical*	11.00	14.00	12.00
Yellow			
☐ Ashtray, *floral design*	20.00	30.00	21.00
☐ Ashtray, *three impressions, 1930s*	17.00	22.00	18.00
☐ Bowl, *salad, 9½", pronounced rim*	27.00	32.00	29.00
☐ Candleholders, *pair, tripod*	32.00	34.00	33.00
☐ Casserole, *French Baker*	60.00	70.00	62.00
☐ Casserole, *notched lid and plug handle*	66.00	82.00	67.00
☐ Coffeepot, *lidded*	40.00	80.00	42.00
☐ Creamer	5.00	7.00	6.00
☐ Creamer, *experimental, ring handle*	22.00	27.00	23.00
☐ Creamer, *yellow, on small pedestal base*	9.00	12.00	10.00
☐ Cup And Saucer	10.00	15.00	11.00
☐ Mug	22.00	27.00	23.00
☐ Pitcher, *juice, disk shape, handled*	9.00	11.00	10.00
☐ Pitcher, *water*	20.00	30.00	21.00
☐ Plate, *6"*	4.00	6.00	5.00
☐ Plate, *9½"*	6.00	8.00	7.00
☐ Plate, *13"*	12.00	16.00	13.00

	Current Price Range		P/Y Average
☐ **Plate,** *chop, 6"*	6.00	8.00	7.00
☐ **Plate,** *dessert, 6"*	6.00	8.00	7.00
☐ **Platter,** *12", oval*	11.00	14.00	12.00
☐ **Soup Plate,** *scalloped rim*	9.00	12.00	10.00
☐ **Sugar Bowl,** *lidded*	9.00	12.00	10.00
☐ **Teapot,** *lidded*	35.00	45.00	36.00
☐ **Tray**	52.00	62.00	53.00
☐ **Tray,** *utility, 1940s*	8.00	11.00	9.00
☐ **Tumbler,** *5 ounces*	11.00	14.00	12.00

FIRE FIGHTING EQUIPMENT

VARIATIONS: All types of fire fighting equipment is collected, from fire engines to fire marks, axes and buckets.

PERIOD: Organized fire fighting began in the late 1650s in the United States when citizens were asked to keep leather buckets in their homes to put fires out with.

COMMENTS: Much equipment used by firemen received heavy use so today many early items are scarce. This accounts for price variations and the high price often placed on small items.

ADDITIONAL TIPS: The listings are in alphabetical order according to item. Following the item are descriptions, dates and price ranges.

Fireman's Ax,
hardwood handle,
nickel plated head,
curved pick, used in parades,
mid-1800s,
$300.00-$350.00

	Current Price Range		P/Y Average
☐ **Axe,** nickel-plated head, c. 1850, ...	212.00	275.00	225.00
☐ **Banner,** for parades, with lantern, axe and trumpet	115.00	130.00	120.00
☐ **Bell,** brass, hand crank	275.00	350.00	300.00
☐ **Belt,** parade belt, leather	65.00	100.00	75.00
☐ **Belt,** parade belt, leather with black, white and red trim, shiled on buckle	35.00	50.00	38.00
☐ **Belt Buckle,** brass with fire engine engraved, c. 1970	68.00	85.00	72.00
☐ **Book,** *Our Fireman,* by A.E. Costello, history of New York fire departments, c. 1887	215.00	240.00	222.00
☐ **Bucket,** leather, decorated with helmet and hatchet	212.00	240.00	220.00
☐ **Bucket,** leather, painted	185.00	230.00	195.00
☐ **Bucket,** leather with red design	330.00	360.00	340.00
☐ **Bucket,** tin	30.00	40.00	32.00
☐ **Bucket,** with owner's name inscribed, 19th century	920.00	1500.00	970.00
☐ **Bucket,** wooden with iron bandings and leather strap handle, height 13″	20.00	30.00	23.00
☐ **Cap,** fireman's dress cap with badge	75.00	90.00	80.00
☐ **Extinguisher,** glass	52.00	70.00	57.00
☐ **Extinguisher,** brass	30.00	45.00	33.00
☐ **Extinguisher,** bulb shape	12.50	20.00	13.50
☐ **Extinguisher,** tin	13.00	23.00	14.00
☐ **Fire Bell,** nickel plated bronze, outside mechanism, mounted on board	180.00	220.00	195.00
☐ **Fire Engine,** American LaFrance, Auburn V-12 engine with ladders, siren, bell, c. 1944	1100.00	1400.00	1200.00
☐ **Fire Engine,** American LaFrance, 6 cyl., pumper, c. 1948	1350.00	1650.00	1400.00
☐ **Fire Engine,** American LaFrance, 6 cyl., type 40 pumper, c. 1917	15000.00	18000.00	16500.00
☐ **Fire Engine,** American LaFrance, 6 cyl., type 75 pumper, c. 1924	2200.00	2600.00	2300.00
☐ **Fire Engine,** Chevrolet, 4 cyl., one ton, restored, excellent condition, c. 1927	4100.00	4500.00	4250.00
☐ **Fire Engine,** Ford, 8 cyl., restored, c. 1941 ...	1750.00	2500.00	2000.00
☐ **Fire Engine,** Ford, F-6, V-8, equipped, c. 1948 .	1900.00	2500.00	2100.00
☐ **Fire Engine,** Ford, unrestored, c. 1947	1100.00	1400.00	1200.00
☐ **Fire Engine,** Seagrave, Model "A," 4 cyl., restored, c. 1928	16500.00	19500.00	17500.00
☐ **Fire Mark,** cast iron, c. 1860	240.00	280.00	250.00
☐ **Fire Mark,** hands clasped, Germantown National Fire, c. 1843	138.00	170.00	145.00
☐ **Fire Mark,** hydrant, F.A., brass plaque, c. 1817	200.00	240.00	210.00
☐ **Fire Mark,** hydrant, F.A., brass plaque, c. 1843	92.00	120.00	100.00
☐ **Fire Mark,** Insurance Co. of Florida, c. 1841 ..	250.00	295.00	263.00
☐ **Fire Mark,** Mutual Assurance Co., iron plaque	125.00	175.00	140.00
☐ **Fire Mark,** Twentieth Century	38.00	60.00	45.00
☐ **Helmet,** aluminium with eagle finial	58.00	75.00	65.00
☐ **Helmet,** brass with eagle finial	225.00	275.00	240.00
☐ **Helmet,** hand painted shield, c. 19th century .	525.00	575.00	540.00
☐ **Helmet,** leather, black embossed with brass eagle, c. 1889	88.00	120.00	95.00

	Current Price Range		P/Y Average
☐ **Helmet,** leather, ornamental parade helmet, 18th century	675.00	750.00	700.00
☐ **Helmet,** leather, 6-seam, front shield	60.00	80.00	65.00
☐ **Helmet,** leather, white with eagle, 19th century	112.00	140.00	120.00
☐ **Helmet,** leather with trumpet finial	127.00	160.00	135.00
☐ **Helmet,** spike top, used for parades	135.00	170.00	142.00
☐ **Helmet,** three cornered, 19th century	1350.00	1650.00	1430.00
☐ **Honor Roll,** watercolor	312.00	350.00	320.00
☐ **Hose Nozzle,** brass, 12″	60.00	85.00	65.00
☐ **Hose Nozzle,** brass, 15″	78.00	108.00	85.00
☐ **Hose Nozzle,** copper, 25″	82.00	115.00	95.00
☐ **Horn,** brass	262.00	325.00	275.00
☐ **Lantern,** brass	100.00	175.00	120.00
☐ **Lantern,** nickel plated	80.00	95.00	83.00
☐ **Lantern,** wagon style with brass font	170.00	200.00	178.00
☐ **Spotlight,** nickel plated brass	160.00	180.00	165.00
☐ **Tickets,** fireman's benefit, 19th century	6.25	10.00	7.50
☐ **Trumpet,** brass, engraved	350.00	395.00	360.00
☐ **Trumpet,** nickel plated	138.00	170.00	148.00
☐ **Trumpet,** silver plated with red tassel	285.00	325.00	300.00
☐ **Trumpet,** sterling silver	438.00	500.00	450.00
☐ **Watch Fob,** copper	25.00	40.00	30.00
☐ **Watercolor Drawing,** pumpers, crowd, 19th century	385.00	440.00	400.00

FISHING TACKLE

DESCRIPTION: Rods, reels, flies and lures comprise the majority of collectible fishing tackle. The manufacture of fishing tackle did not begin in the United States until around 1810. Prior to that time, all fishing supplies were imported from Europe.

MAKERS: Reels made by J. F. and B. F. Meeks, B. Milam and Pfleuger are favored, as are rods made by Hiram Leonard. Flies, fake bait made by tying feathers, fur or other materials around the shaft of a hook, are also popular. There are over 5,000 patterns and sizes of flies, each with its own name. The manufacturer, or tier, of individual flies is very difficult to discern, unless the fly is in its original marked container.

Artificial Lure, *tin,* "*Arbogast,*" **$5.00-$8.00**

	Current Price Range		P/Y Average
☐ **Casting rod,** Heddon, split bamboo, 6', c. 1920	85.00	100.00	115.00
☐ **Casting rod,** split bamboo, straight handle, 5', c. 1800	45.00	55.00	50.00
☐ **Casting rod,** Tonkin. cane, 5½', c. 1900	55.00	65.00	60.00
☐ **Casting rod,** Union Hardware, 5', c. 1920	20.00	30.00	25.00
☐ **Casting rod,** Winchester, split bamboo, c. 1925	20.00	30.00	25.00
☐ **Creel fishing basket,** splint weave, pine lid, c. 1900	85.00	125.00	105.00
☐ **Creel fishing basket,** wicker with leather straps, c. 1880	115.00	165.00	140.00
☐ **Fishhooks,** set of 50, c. 1910	20.00	24.00	22.00
☐ **Flies,** English, set of 12, c. 1880	420.00	440.00	430.00
☐ **Fly box,** metal, round, c. 1910	25.00	35.00	30.00
☐ **Fly box,** wooden, 6" x 10", c. 1900	55.00	65.00	60.00
☐ **Fly rod,** Heddon, split bamboo, 9½', c. 1922	65.00	75.00	70.00
☐ **Fly rod,** H. L. Leonard, 8½', c. 1890	165.00	185.00	175.00
☐ **Fly rod,** H. L. Leonard, 7', c. 1885	320.00	340.00	330.00
☐ **Lure,** Heddon, wooden plug, Dowagiac Minnow	10.00	15.00	12.00
☐ **Lure,** Heddon, wooden plug, Heddon's Minnow, #100 series	10.00	12.00	11.00
☐ **Lure,** Heddon, wooden plug, Meadow Mouse, #4000 series	8.00	10.00	9.00
☐ **Lure,** Shakespeare, wooden plug, Darting Shrimp, #135 series	13.00	15.00	14.00
☐ **Reel,** Billinghurst, fly, nickel plated, c. 1869	190.00	250.00	220.00
☐ **Reel,** Coxe, casting, aluminum, c. 1940	120.00	140.00	130.00
☐ **Reel,** English fly, silver, c. 1850	520.00	620.00	570.00
☐ **Reel,** Heddon, casting, silver, c. 1925	55.00	85.00	70.00
☐ **Reel,** Hendryx, fly, brass, c. 1890	25.00	35.00	30.00
☐ **Reel,** Leonard, fly, bronze, silver trim, c. 1878	470.00	570.00	520.00
☐ **Reel,** Leonard, fly, silver, c. 1925	270.00	300.00	285.00
☐ **Reel,** Meek, casting, brass, c. 1855	520.00	620.00	570.00
☐ **Reel,** Meek, casting, silver, c. 1930	145.00	185.00	165.00
☐ **Reel,** Meisselbach, casting, c. 1920	55.00	75.00	65.00
☐ **Reel,** Meisselbach, fly, nickel plated, c. 1895	50.00	70.00	60.00
☐ **Reel,** Meisselbach, trolling, wood, c. 1910	25.00	35.00	30.00
☐ **Reel,** Milam, casting, brass, c. 1865	420.00	520.00	470.00
☐ **Reel,** Milam, casting, silver, c. 1898	170.00	230.00	200.00
☐ **Reel,** Mills, fly, nickel, c. 1895	120.00	170.00	145.00
☐ **Reel,** Orvis, fly, nickel plated, c. 1874	120.00	170.00	145.00
☐ **Reel,** Orvis, fly, solid silver, c. 1874	620.00	720.00	670.00
☐ **Reel,** Pennell, casting, nickel plated, c. 1920	40.00	60.00	50.00
☐ **Reel,** Pfleuger, casting, brass, c. 1910	25.00	35.00	30.00

	Current Price Range		P/Y Average
☐ **Reel,** Pfleuger, casting, silver, c. 1925	60.00	110.00	85.00
☐ **Reel,** Pfleuger, fly, rubber, c. 1905	120.00	170.00	145.00
☐ **Reel,** Pfleuger, trolling, brass, c. 1915	30.00	40.00	35.00
☐ **Reel,** Pfleuger, trolling, silver, c. 1890	40.00	60.00	50.00
☐ **Reel,** Sage, fly, solid silver, c. 1848	770.00	870.00	820.00
☐ **Reel,** Shakespeare, casting, plastic, c. 1940 .	50.00	70.00	60.00
☐ **Reel,** Shakespeare, casting, level wind, c. 1922	40.00	60.00	50.00
☐ **Reel,** Shakespeare, universal, take down, c. 1922	40.00	60.00	50.00
☐ **Reel,** Shipley, casting, brass, c. 1885	190.00	270.00	230.00
☐ **Reel,** Snyder, casting, brass, c. 1820	520.00	670.00	595.00
☐ **Reel,** South Bend, fly, aluminum, c. 1940	45.00	65.00	55.00
☐ **Reel,** Talbot, casting, silver, c. 1920	95.00	145.00	120.00
☐ **Reel,** Union Hardware, fly, nickel plated, c. 1920	35.00	55.00	45.00
☐ **Reel,** Vom Hofe, fly, nickel, small, c. 1890 . . .	145.00	195.00	165.00
☐ **Reel,** Vom Hofe, trolling, rubber, c. 1918	170.00	240.00	195.00
☐ **Reel,** Yawman and Erbe, fly, aluminum, c. 1889	120.00	170.00	145.00
☐ **Reel,** Zwarg, trolling, rubber, c. 1950	195.00	275.00	235.00
☐ **Rod case,** wood, brass trim, 5′, c. 1880	100.00	120.00	110.00
☐ **Steel casting rod,** Wards, telescopic, 9″, c. 1922	35.00	45.00	40.00
☐ **Steel casting rod,** Wards, with case, agate guides, 5½′, c. 1922	35.00	45.00	40.00
☐ **Tackle box,** wooden and brass trim, 14″, c. 1910	55.00	65.00	60.00
☐ **Tackle box,** metal and brass trim, 16″, c. 1925	55.00	65.00	60.00

FLASH GORDON

DESCRIPTION: Flash Gordon is a fantasy futuristic comic strip featuring Flash Gordon as the heroic figure conquering space.

ORIGIN: Alex Raymond produced Flash Gordon for King Features Syndicate. The strip first appeared in Sunday newspapers on January 7, 1934.

TYPES: Flash Gordon has appeared in many types of media from newspaper comic strips and comic books to movies. Items relating to any facet of the comic strip are collectible.

RECOMMENDED READING: For further information refer to *The Official Price Guide to Comic Books and Collectibles* and *The Official Price Guide to Science Fiction and Fantasy Collectibles,* published by The House of Collectibles.

Flash Gordon Signal Pistol, *The Screaming Signal Gun,*
$200.00-$400.00
Photo courtesy of Hake's Americana, York, PA.

	Current Price Range		P/Y Average
☐ **Button,** Flash Gordon Dueling Ming, copyright by King Features Syndicate, signed by Alex Raymond	6.00	10.00	8.00
☐ **Christmas Card,** portrait of Flash Gordon surrounded by holly wreath, interior shows rocket ship, 1951	9.00	10.00	10.50
☐ **Christmas Light Covers,** made by Textolite under license from King Features Syndicate, set of eight, hard plastic with decal illustrations, contained in a stiff paper box with lithographed illustration, all artwork by Alex Raymond (creator of Flash Gordon), undated, almost certainly 1930's	70.00	90.00	77.00
☐ **individually**	6.00	8.00	6.80
☐ **Compass, Flash Gordon Space Compass,** flexible plastic band, white with red artwork, portrait in red, white and blue	20.00	25.00	22.50

	Current Price Range		P/Y Average

☐ **Decals, Flash Gordon Easter Egg Decals,** also features The Phantom and other characters, dated 1940 . . . . — 25.00 — 35.00 — 27.50

☐ **Figure, Flash Gordon,** standing at attention, wood, 5"tall . . . . — 80.00 — 100.00 — 85.00

☐ **Figures, Flash Gordon Solar Commando,** made by Premier, a lithographed card with three plastic figures, each 3" tall, dated 1952, the card measures 6¾" x 9¾"and the price is for the intact card (the loose figures would sell for much less). . . . . — 40.00 — 53.00 — 46.00

☐ **Gun Flash Gordon Arresting Ray Gun,** copyright by King Features Syndicate, maker unidentified, lithographed tin, red/yellow/blue with profile of Flash Gordon on butt, name in large letter on barrel . . . . — 80.00 — 90.00 — 83.00

☐ **Gun, Flash Gordon Radio Repeater,** lithographed tin, red, black and silver, illustrations of Flash Gordon along with planet and star. Bears a King Features copyright notice as licensee to Marx Toy Co., 4½" x 10" . . . . — 175.00 — 220.00 — 187.00

☐ **Guns,** set of two ray guns made by Louis Marx, 1935, rare . . . . — 1500.00 — 2000.00 — 1625.00

☐ **Record, Flash Gordon In The City Of Caves,** 78 r.p.m. Record Guild of America record, pictures disc on which both sides of the record comprise large pictures, dated 1948 . . . . — 60.00 — 80.00 — 63.00

☐ **Premium,** Kelloggs Pep Cereal, lithographed tin button, multicolored, 1940s . . . . — 7.00 — 10.00 — 8.50

☐ **Premium,** Kelloggs Pep Cereal, lithographed tin button, portrait facing full front, based on drawing by Alex Raymond, 1946 . . . . — 25.00 — 30.00 — 27.50

☐ **Rocket Ship, Flash Gordon Rocket Fighter,** copyright by King Features Syndicate, manufacturer unidentified, clockwork, lithographed tin, red/yellow/black/white, 1937, 12½" . . . . . . — 225.00 — 250.00 — 230.00

☐ **Rocket Ship,** Marx, lithographed tin, Flash Gordon seated in open cockpit with gun, wears crash helmet, 13" . . . . — 110.00 — 140.00 — 122.00

☐ **T-Shirt,** Flash Gordon iron on . . . . — 6.00 — 8.00 — 7.00

FLASKS

DESCRIPTION: Flasks are containers which have a broad body and narrow neck often fitted with a closure. Usually they were used to hold alcoholic beverages.

TYPES: There were many variations of flask bottles produced including figural and portrait flasks.

PERIOD: Usually collectors search for flasks from the early 1800s through the early 1900s. Before 1810, few glass containers were manufactured.

COMMENTS: Flasks with portraits of Presidents or others politicians are highly sought after by collectors.

ADDITIONAL TIPS: For more information, consult *The Official Price Guide to Bottles, Old and New,* published by The House of Collectibles.

Poison Flask, *diamond motif, 4",* **$55.00-$75.00**

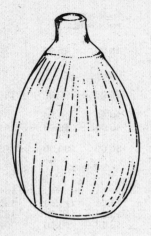

Pitkin Flask, *vertical ribbing, amber, 7",* **$55.00-$75.00**

Keene Marlboro Street Glassworks, *sunburst design, green,* **$310.00-$390.00**

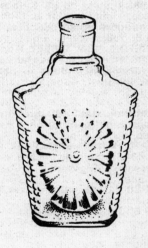

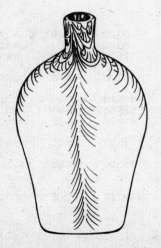

Nailsea Flask, *blue with white loopings, 6⅞",* **$200.00-$250.00**

	Current Price Range		P/Y Average

□ **A.G.W.L.** Under bottom, saddle flask, amber, ½ pint **15.00** **25.00** **20.00**

□ **ALL SEEING EYE,** Star and large eye in center, under it A.D., in back, six-pointed star with arms, Masonic emblem, under it G.R.J.A., pontil, sheared top, amber, pint . . . **230.00** **300.00** **265.00**

□ **ANCHOR FLASK,** double ring, amber or clear, ½ pint, quart **30.00** **40.00** **35.00**

□ **AQUAMARINE,** pint **40.00** **50.00** **45.00**

□ **BALTIMORE GLASS WORKS,** Aqua, very thin glass, pontil, on back a stack of wheat **150.00** **200.00** **175.00**

□ **BALTIMORE MONUMENT,** And under it Balto. door with step railing, in back sloop with pennant flying, sailing to right above it Fells below point, ½ pt. 3 ribbed on side, plain top, pontil, aqua, qt. (c. 1840) **125.00** **175.00** **150.00**

□ Same as above, except plain bottom, ... **115.00** **145.00** **130.00**

□ **B.P. & B.,** Yellow green, ½ pint **45.00** **60.00** **52.00**

□ **BRIDGETON, NEW JERSEY,** Around a man facing to left, in back a man facing to the left with Washington around it, ribbed sides, sheared top, pontil, aqua, pint **80.00** **100.00** **90.00**

□ **CALABASH,** Hunter and fisherman, aqua, quart **45.00** **60.00** **52.00**

□ **CHAPMAN P., BALT., MD,** Soldier with a gun on front, a girl dancing on a bar in back, sheared top, aqua, pint **160.00** **200.00** **180.00**

□ **CLASPED HANDS - Eagle Flask,** (c. 1860-75) Union 13 stars, clasped hands, eagle above banner mark, "E", Wormer & Co., Pittsburg, aqua, quart **100.00** **130.00** **115.00**

□ **CLASPED HANDS — Eagle Flask,** (c. 1860-75) Deep golden amber, ½ pint **110.00** **150.00** **130.00**

□ **CLASPED HANDS — Flask,** (c. 1860-75) One with eagle and banner, above oval marked Pittsburgh, Pa., other cannon to left, flag and cannonballs, aqua, pint **80.00** **100.00** **90.00**

□ **Delicate powder blue,** ½ pint **40.00** **50.00** **45.00**

□ **18 diamond quilted flask,** green, 6¼ " **115.00** **135.00** **125.00**

□ **DOG,** in center, in back man in uniform on a horse, pontil, sheared top, aqua, quart **120.00** **155.00** **137.00**

□ **DOUBLE EAGLE,** (eagles lengthwise), open pontil, olive green **110.00** **150.00** **130.00**

□ **DOUBLE EAGLE,** aqua, pint **135.00** **175.00** **155.00**

□ **DOUBLE EAGLE,** light green, pint **110.00** **135.00** **122.00**

□ **DOUBLE EAGLE,** beneath unembossed oval, sheared top, pontil, amber, 6¼ " **35.00** **45.00** **40.00**

□ **DOUBLE EAGLE, STODDARD, N.H.,** olive or amber, pint **110.00** **135.00** **122.00**

□ **DUCK FLASK,** picture of a duck in water, under duck SWIM, above duck WILL YOU HAVE A DRINK, aqua, pint **140.00** **160.00** **150.00**

	Current Price Range		P/Y Average

☐ **EAGLE,** on oval panels, 25 sun rays in ¼ circle around eagle head, 8 vertical bars on shield. End of olive branch & arrows under claws in oval frame with 23 small pearls around. T.W.D., in back full sailing to right. U.S. flag at reas., waves beneath frigate and in semi-circle beneath Franklin pt. 3 vertically ribbed on side, sheared top, pontil, aqua, (c. 1830) 125.00 175.00 150.00
☐ **EAGLE,** and Stag, aqua, ½ pint 175.00 225.00 200.00
☐ **EAGLE,** and Tree, aqua, pint 90.00 110.00 100.00
☐ **FLORA TEMPLE,** Aqua, pint 200.00 250.00 225.00
☐ **FLORA TEMPLE,** Handle, puce or amber, pint 200.00 250.00 225.00
☐ **FLORIDA UNIVERSAL STORE BOTTLE,** Clear, pint 6.00 10.00 8.00
☐ **H. FRANK, PAT'D. AUG. 6th 1879,** Under bottom, two circles in center, reverse plain, ring top, ribs on sides 40.00 50.00 45.00
☐ **H. FRANK, PAT. AUG. 6, 1872,** All on bottom, circular shaped flask, two circles in center on front, reverse side plain, wide rib on sides, ring neck, aqua, pint 45.00 60.00 52.00
☐ **FRANKLIN & FRANKLIN,** Aqua, quart 130.00 170.00 150.00
☐ **GEN. MACARTHUR and GOD BLESS AMERICA,** Purple or green, ½ pint 12.00 18.00 15.00
☐ **G.H.A.,** Concord, N.Y. 1865, aqua, ½ pint . . . 20.00 28.00 24.00
☐ **GIRL FOR JOE,** Girl on bicycle, aqua, pint . . . 70.00 90.00 80.00
☐ **GRANITE GLASS CO.,** In three lines, reverse Stoddard, N.H.; sheared top, olive, pint 150.00 200.00 175.00
☐ **GUARANTEED FLASK,** Clear or amethyst, 6¼" 6.00 10.00 8.00
☐ **GUARANTEED FULL,** Clear, 6½" 8.00 12.00 10.00
☐ **HISTORY FLASK,** Label, aqua, side panels, 7¼" 15.00 22.00 18.00
☐ **IRON,** Pontil, double collared, pint 40.00 50.00 45.00
☐ **ISABELLA G.W.,** Sheaf of wheat, pint 75.00 95.00 85.00
☐ **JENNY LIND,** With wreath, reverse picture of glass works, above is FISLERVILLE GLASS WORKS, wavy line on neck, pontil, tapered top, aqua, quart 110.00 150.00 130.00
☐ Same as above, except S. HUFFSY 60.00 80.00 70.00
☐ **JENNY LIND LYRE,** Aqua, pint 110.00 150.00 130.00
☐ **L.C. & R. CO.,** On bottom, Eagle in a circle, reverse plain, clear, ½ pint 40.00 50.00 45.00
☐ **LEGENDARY GRANDFATHER,** Broken swirl pattern, reddish amber 110.00 150.00 130.00
☐ **PIKE'S PEAK** Man with pack and cane walking to left, reverse eagle with ribbon in beak in oval panel, aqua, pint 100.00 150.00 125.00
☐ Same as above, except several colors 75.00 95.00 85.00
☐ **FOR PIKE'S PEAK** Reverse side, man shooting a gun at a deer, aqua, 9½" 35.00 45.00 40.00
☐ **FOR PIKE'S PEAK** Old rye, aqua, pint 35.00 45.00 40.00
☐ **PITTSBURGH** Double eagle, aqua, pint 30.00 40.00 35.00

	Current Price Range		P/Y Average

□ **PITTSBURGH, PA.** In raised oval circle at base, with an eagle on front, back same except plain for label, aqua, applied ring at top, pint, 7½ ″ **40.00 50.00 45.00**

□ PITKIN type, light green, pint **55.00 75.00 65.00**

□ POTTERY FLASK, figure of a man and horse, same on reverse side, pint **275.00 350.00 312.00**

□ **RAILROAD — Eagle Flask** (c. 1830-48) Amber, pint **160.00 200.00 180.00**

□ **RAILROAD FLASK** (c. 1860) On oval panels, horse drawing long cart on rail to right. Cart filled with barrels and boxes, under it Lowell and above it Railroad in back eagle facing left. Shield with 7 vertical & 2 horizontal bars on breast, 3 arrows in eagles left claw, olive branch in right, 13 large stars surround edge, ½ pt. 3 ver. ribbed on side, sheared top, pontil, O. amber **110.00 150.00 130.00**

□ **RAILROAD FLASK** Designs on oval panels, crude locomotive to left on rail, embossed success to the Railroad, reading around locomotive-back but the line connecting the tender with rear wheel shows a slight break and E in success carries a conbex dot attached to the upper bar pt. 3 vertically ribbed on side, sheared top O. amber, (c. 1830) **120.00 175.00 147.00**

□ **RAVENNA GLASS WORKS — Star Flask** (c. 1857-60) Ohio, aqua, pint **150.00 190.00 170.00**

□ **RAVENNA GLASS WORKS** In three lines, ring top, yellow green, pint **130.00 175.00 152.00**

□ **RAVENNA** In center, anchor with rope, under it GLASS COMPANY, ring top, aqua, pint ... **140.00 175.00 157.00**

□ **RAVENNA TRAVELERS COMPANION** Pontil, amber, quart **250.00 350.00 300.00**

□ **REHM BROS** Bush & Buchanan Sts & O'Farrel & Mason Sts, in a sunken circle, ribbed bottom, two rings near shoulder, coffin type, metal and cork cap, clear or amethyst, ½ pint **100.00 145.00 122.00**

□ **SPRINGFIELD G.W. and CABIN** aqua, ½ pint **65.00 85.00 75.00**

□ **SPRING GARDEN** in center, anchor, under it GLASS WORKS, reverse side, log cabin with a tree to the right, ring top, aqua, ½ pint **130.00 160.00 145.00**

□ STAG and TREE, aqua, pint **65.00 85.00 75.00**

□ **STAR — Cornucopia Flask,** STAR with a circle around it on shoulder, light amber, saddle flask, ½ pint **12.00 18.00 15.00**

□ **STODDARD** double eagle, *GRANITE GLASS CO., STODDARD, N.H.*Pontil, golden amber, pint **100.00 130.00 115.00**

	Current Price Range		P/Y Average
☐ **WILLINGTON — Eagle Flask** (c, 1860- 72) brite green, pint	100.00	130.00	115.00
☐ Same as above, except olive amber, ½ pint ...	100.00	130.00	115.00
☐ **WILLINGTON GLASS CO., WEST WILLINGTON, CONN.** on four lines, reverse eagle and shield, under it a wreath, on shoulder LIBERTY, amber, pint	100.00	130.00	115.00
☐ **WILL YOU TAKE A DRINK? WILL A DUCK SWIM?** aqua, pint	150.00	175.00	162.00
☐ WINTER and SUMMER FLASK, tree with leaves and a bird on right side, above it SUMMER, reverse side tree without leaves and bird, above it WINTER, tapered top aqua, quart and pint ..	110.00	150.00	130.00
☐ Same as above, but with Summer on front and Winter on back	100.00	130.00	115.00
☐ **ZANESVILLE CITY GLASS WORKS** In oval panel, reverse plain, ring top, amber	100.00	130.00	110.00
☐ Same as above, except aqua	65.00	85.00	70.00

FOLK ART

DESCRIPTION: Originally the term used to describe painting and sculpture done by untrained artists, today the term is given to all hand-crafted items.

TYPES: Various types of folk art sculpture include dolls, toys, animals, jewelry and bottlecap sculpture. Four types of folk art painting include: paintings done by stencil called theorems; drawings that display unique penmanship skills called calligraphic; frakturs which were ornately designed certificates of birth, baptism or marriage; and mourning pictures to commemorate the death of a loved one.

PERIOD: Folk art has no specific period; it is still made today.

ORIGIN: The original popularity of folk art dates to the 1920s and the first Folk Art exhibits at the Whitney Studio Club (later the Whitney Museum of American Art) and the Museum of Modern Art.

COMMENTS: Until the 1920s the value of folk art was largely ignored because its distortion of size and scale was not considered artistic. Today such Americana collectibles are quite sought after. Reasonably priced pieces can be found, especially those from the 19th and 20th centuries.

	Current Price Range		P/Y Average
☐ **Banjo,** *snake skin head, three string, 31"*	60.00	80.00	63.00
☐ **Barber's Pole,** *with hitching post*	152.00	178.00	155.00
☐ **Bird,** *cloth, Victorian*	48.00	75.00	52.00
☐ **Bird In Hoop,** *green and yellow painted wood parrot perched in a wrought-iron hoop, 19th c., 14"*	675.00	725.00	720.00
☐ **Blanket Chest,** *Chippendale, front is painted with a comport filled with red and yellow flowers and bordered with yellow floral vines on a painted red and black background, signed Miss H. Taylor in pencil inside lid, 19th c., 8" x 19" x 7¼"*	1000.00	1500.00	1200.00
☐ **Boat,** *model, wood, c. 1900*	48.00	75.00	52.00
☐ **Boot Jack,** *wooden, unpainted*	17.00	27.00	21.00
☐ **Bottlecap Sculpture,** *snake*	162.00	190.00	165.00
☐ **Bottlecap Sculpture,** *carved heads of a man and woman, c. 1930*	82.00	115.00	85.00
☐ **Box,** *hinged lid has three overlapping hearts carved, edge is painted black, green sponge decoration on bottom, 14" x 9" x 5"*	75.00	95.00	84.50
☐ **Bride's Box,** *painted bentwood, late 18th c., 6½" x 18¼"*	395.00	495.00	445.00
☐ **Butcher's Shop Sign,** *carved pig painted pink-orange, inscribed MEAT in black letters, wrought-iron tail, iron suspension rings, c. 1930, 12" x 26"*	1400.00	1500.00	1435.00
☐ **Candle Box,** *pine planked construction, painted red, 14"*	300.00	350.00	335.00
☐ **Carving,** *bird, wood, painted, 6"*	40.00	60.00	45.00
☐ **Cigar Store Indian,** *Princess, c. 1880, 61"*	4500.00	5500.00	5000.00
☐ **Coffee Pot,** *Toleware, decorated with painted red flowers on green stems with yellow leaves, dark brown background, convex hinged lid, conical shape, 19th c., 8¼"*	900.00	950.00	936.00
☐ **Cow,** *felt, painted face, 9"*	30.00	40.00	32.00
☐ **Cradle,** *doll, pine, original paint, 18th c.*	225.00	275.00	240.00
☐ **Crock,** *marked White's-Utica 3, decorated with a dark blue flower, stem and leaves, open top* .	160.00	185.00	174.00
☐ **Decoy,** *swan, original paint, hollow construction, cedar*	950.00	1075.00	1050.00
☐ **Decoy,** *wooden bluebill, glass eyes, weighted bottom, some bullet marks*	35.00	55.00	48.00
☐ **Decoy,** *wooden bluebill, painted eyes, original paint*	45.00	55.00	50.00
☐ **Decoy,** *wooden, Canadian Goose in gray, white, black and brown, 27"*	40.00	50.00	46.00
☐ **Doll,** *dancer, jointed wood, hand operated, 14½", 19th c.*	200.00	240.00	210.00
☐ **Doll,** *reversible face, dress and color, 14"*	275.00	320.00	285.00
☐ **Face Mask,** *carved, man's face*	125.00	145.00	130.00

	Current Price Range		P/Y Average

☐ **Figure,** *black preacher, carved and painted wood, initials DC carved on chest, 10"* **3000.00** **3120.00** **3085.00**

☐ **Figure,** *cast-iron form of a woman holding two trays in her hands, painted polychrome, 12⅝" x 11"* **1000.00** **1100.00** **1050.00**

☐ **Flute,** *pine, 15"* **60.00** **80.00** **65.00**

☐ **Footstool,** *wooden, pumpkin top with two ends black and red underneath, 12" x 8" x 7"* .   **55.00** **75.00** **67.50**

☐ **Footstool,** *wooden with turned legs, square nailed construction, 10" x 9" x 6"* **40.00** **50.00** **46.00**

☐ **Fraktur,** *part printed, part hand-colored, Victorian frame* **50.00** **70.00** **55.00**

☐ **Game,** *checkered game board, splined, signed, 19" x 29"* **82.00** **115.00** **85.00**

☐ **Game,** *ring toss, 5 rings, c. 1900* **52.00** **80.00** **60.00**

☐ **Game,** *skittles, ornate steeple in center, 19th c.* **200.00** **250.00** **220.00**

☐ **Gate Post Finial,** *carved Statue of Liberty finial made of pine, wrought-iron crown spokes, traces of black and yellow polychrome, c. 1900, 19¾"* **2500.00** **3500.00** **3000.00**

☐ **Hooked Rugs,** *picture of dog in the middle encircled in dark blue with purple border, set of two, c. 1910, 45" x 26"* **300.00** **400.00** **350.00**

☐ **Hooked Rug,** *two black and two white horses on vertical striped background, 49" x 26"* . . .   **150.00** **250.00** **190.00**

☐ **Miniature,** *bookcase on chest, accessories, 11¾" x 9½"* **160.00** **200.00** **170.00**

☐ **Miniature,** *furniture, set of 3 chairs, painted* .   **60.00** **80.00** **65.00**

☐ **Miniature,** *windmill, wood, tin blades, 21"* . . .   **75.00** **100.00** **80.00**

☐ **Mourning Picture,** *embroidery on silk, 16" x 20"* **338.00** **365.00** **345.00**

☐ **Oil On Board,** *little girl in hooded cape, 7" x 9", c. 1820* **125.00** **175.00** **130.00**

☐ **Oil On Board,** *rat terrier with rat, 19th c.* **275.00** **325.00** **290.00**

☐ **Oil On Canvas,** *apples and book, 8" x 10"* . . .   **390.00** **425.00** **400.00**

☐ **Oil On Canvas,** *boy, girl, lamb, mid-19th c.* . . .   **138.00** **170.00** **145.00**

☐ **Oil On Canvas,** *fruit and bird, unframed, 24" x 18", c. 1835* **550.00** **650.00** **570.00**

☐ **Oil On Canvas,** *Irish Setter, 16" x 19", framed* .   **325.00** **380.00** **340.00**

☐ **Picture,** *cut paper, white cut into a design against a red background, c. 1850* **425.00** **500.00** **450.00**

☐ **Portraits,** *man and woman (pair), unsigned, 19th c.* **350.00** **395.00** **360.00**

☐ **Portrait,** *miniature, on ivory, bust of man in coat, gold frame with leaves and flowers, 19th c.* **1900.00** **2400.00** **2100.00**

☐ **Portraits,** *pair, signed, G.H. Blackburn, 30" x 28" framed, c.1886* **325.00** **375.00** **335.00**

☐ **Rag Doll,** *Amish, embroidered face* **90.00** **100.00** **95.00**

☐ **Rag Doll,** *Amish, faceless, Amish outfit* **65.00** **75.00** **70.00**

☐ **Rag Doll,** *handmade of floss eyes, nose, mouth and hair, blue and white dress, 11"* . . .   **25.00** **50.00** **37.50**

☐ **Rag Doll,** *made from a printed pattern, c. 1930s* **40.00** **50.00** **46.00**

	Current Price Range		P/Y Average
☐ **Rocking Horse,** wooden shoo-fly, with seat between sides of horse	100.00	200.00	145.00
☐ **Sewing Stand,** to hang on wall, set of three spool holders on top shelf, hand carved diamond design around top border, carved heart and three initials on second shelf, natural pine darkened with time	55.00	75.00	64.00
☐ **Shelves,** two shelves, stripped down with blue, red and gray showing, checkerboard showing on the bark, 10" x 14" x 4"	45.00	55.00	49.50
☐ **Spreaders,** wooden, original mustard colored paint, set of two, 29"	20.00	30.00	24.00
☐ **Storks,** carved and painted, c. 1910, 20", pair	380.00	420.00	410.00
☐ **Toy,** baby rattle, hand carved, 9"	82.00	115.00	85.00
☐ **Toy,** climbing clown, flat, made of cardboard in red and blue polka dots	17.00	25.00	21.50
☐ **Toy,** "Froggie" of the Andy Devine Show, green, red, white and black rubber, 5"	10.00	20.00	14.50
☐ **Toy,** monkey on pole, hand carved	72.00	100.00	75.00
☐ **Toy,** pecking chicken, hand carved	62.00	85.00	65.00
☐ **Toy,** rocking horse, handmade	62.00	85.00	65.00
☐ **Toy,** sheep on wheels, hand carved	138.00	170.00	145.00
☐ **Toy,** train, hand carved, painted, 23", 19th c. .	112.00	135.00	115.00
☐ **Whirligig,** black man made of wood wearing a yellow hat and jacket, red pants and black boots, paddle baffles on the arms, round base, Maine, early 20th c.	3900.00	4400.00	4190.00
☐ **Whirligig,** cast iron, painted, man turning grindstone	475.00	545.00	490.00
☐ **Whirligig,** wooden duck, glass eyes, mounted on a wood fence post	60.00	75.00	66.00
☐ **Whirligig,** wooden Indian, carved and painted, 11½"	1700.00	1800.00	1750.00

FOOTBALL CARDS

DESCRIPTION: Football cards usually have the picture of a football player on one side and his statistics or biography on the other.

ORIGIN: The first football cards we produced by Goudey Gum in 1933.

MAKER: There are several companies who have produced football cards including Topps, Fleer, O-Pee-Chee and Bowman.

COMMENTS: Although the popularity of collecting football cards lags behind the well established baseball card hobby, football's tremendous popularity assures the growth of football card collecting.

ADDITIONAL TIPS: The most valuable cards to watch for are old sets, famous player cards and rookie cards. For more information, consult *The Official Price Guide to Football Cards,* published by The House of Collectibles. **VG** — very good; **PYM** — prior year mint.

BOWMAN — 1950 (2¹⁄₁₆″ x 2½ ″, Numbered 1-144, Color)

			MINT	VG	PYM
☐		Complete Set	375.00	225.00	227.00
☐	1	Doak Walker, Detroit Lions back	5.20	4.20	4.70
☐	5	Y.A. Tittle, Baltimore Colts, quarterback	11.00	7.00	7.48
☐	6	Lou Groza, Cleveland Browns, tackle	1].00	6.00	5.35
☐	16	Glenn Davis, Los Angeles Rams, back	5.10	4.10	4.60
☐	27	Sid Luckman, Chicago Bears, quarterback	10.75	6.75	5.53
☐	45	Otto Graham, Cleveland Browns, quarterback	12.00	8.00	11.98
☐	78	Dante Lavelli, Cleveland Browns, end	4.40	3.40	3.90
☐	100	Sammy Baugh, Washington Redskins, quarterback	14.00	9.50	11.75
☐	132	Chuck Bednarik, Philadelphia Eagles, center	5.00	3.00	4.95

BOWMAN — 1951 (2¹⁄₁₆″ x 3⅛″, Numbered 1-144, Color)

☐		Complete Set	425.00	275.00	235.00
☐	2	Otto Graham, Cleveland Browns, quarterback	10.50	6.50	10.65
☐	4	Norm VanBrocklin, Los Angeles Rams, quarterback	7.00	4.50	6.60
☐	12	Chuck Bednarik, Philadelphia Eagles, center	6.50	4.00	5.05
☐	20	Tom Landry, New York Giants, back	12.50	8.80	10.65
☐	34	Sammy Baugh, Washington Redskins, quarterback	16.00	10.00	10.65
☐	75	Lou Groza, Cleveland Browns, tackle	8.00	5.00	8.18
☐	76	Elroy Hirsch, Los Angeles Rams, back	7.00	4.00	5.05
☐	102	Bobby Layne, Detroit Lions, quarterback	10.20	7.70	8.95
☐	105	Joe Perry, San Francisco 49ers, back	3.50	2.00	5.10

BOWMAN — 1952 (2¹⁄₁₆″ x 3⅛″, Numbered 1-144, Color)

☐		Complete Set	375.00	225.00	337.00
☐	1	Norman Van Brocklin, Los Angeles Rams, quarterback	11.50	8.45	9.98
☐	2	Otto Graham, Cleveland Browns, quarterback	14.25	12.35	110.45
☐	16	Frank Gifford, New York Giants, back	22.00	14.00	11.85
☐	30	Sammy Baugh, Washington Redskins, quarterback	17.50	10.00	11.85

			MINT	VG	PYM
☐	78	**Bobby Layne**, Detroit Lions, quarterback	12.75	9.00	11.00
☐	127	**Ollie Matson**, Chicago Cardinals, back	4.50	2.75	5.68
☐	137	**Bob Waterfield**, Los Angeles Rams, quarterback	6.50	4.00	9.25
☐	142	**Tom Landry**, New York Giants, back ...	15.00	9.00	9.88

BOWMAN — 1953 (2½" x 3¾", Numbered 1-96, Color)

			MINT	VG	PYM
☐		Complete Set	280.00	175.00	206.00
☐	9	**Marion Motley**, Cleveland Browns, back	4.25	3.25	3.75
☐	11	**Norm Van Brocklin**, Los Angeles Rams, quarterback	8.50	5.00	6.73
☐	21	**Bobby Layne**, Detroit Lions, quarterback	10.20	7.80	9.00
☐	26	**Otto Graham**, Cleveland Browns, quarterback	12.50	8.80	10.65
☐	32	**Hugh McElhenny**, San Francisco 49ers, back	34.00	2.50	5.13
☐	43	**Frank Gifford**, New York Giants, back .	15.00	9.00	10.60
☐	53	**Emlen Tunnel**, New York Giants, back	3.00	1.75	3.75
☐	88	**Leo Nomellini**, San Francisco 49ers, tackle	4.00	2.50	3.75
☐	95	**Lou Groza**, Cleveland Browns, tackle ..	7.00	4.50	5.13

BOWMAN — 1954 (2½" x 3¾", Numbered 1-128, Color)

			MINT	VG	PYM
☐		Complete Set	225.00	150.00	117.00
☐	6	**Joe Perry**, San Francisco 49ers, back ..	4.00	2.50	2.83
☐	7	**Kyle Rote**, New York Giants, end	3.55	2.60	3.08
☐	8	**Norm Van Brocklin**, Los Angeles Rams, quarterback	5.20	4.20	4.70
☐	23	**George Blanda**, Chicago Bears, quarterback	7.40	5.50	6.45
☐	40	**Otto Graham**, Cleveland Browns, quarterback	5.00	5.50	8.35
☐	42	**Y.A. Tittle**, San Francisco 49ers, quarterback	7.00	4.50	4.95
☐	53	**Bobby Layne**, Detroit Lions, quarterback	7.40	5.50	6.45
☐	55	**Frank Gifford**, New York Giants, back .	12.00	8.00	8.35
☐	56	**Leon McLaughlin**, Los Angeles Rams, center	1.00	.60	.63

BOWMAN — 1955 (2½" x 3¾", Numbered 1-160, Color)

			MINT	VG	PYM
☐		Complete Set	165.00	115.00	110.00
☐	7	**Frank Gifford**, New York Giants, back .	12.00	8.00	7.98
☐	16	**Charley Conerly**, New York Giants, quarterback	2.75	1.75	1.75
☐	32	**Norm Van Brocklin**, Los Angeles Rams, quarterback	5.50	4.40	4.95
☐	37	**Lou Groza**, Cleveland Browns, tackle, kicker	5.10	4.10	4.60
☐	44	**Joe Perry**, San Francisco 49ers, back ..	2.95	2.15	2.55
☐	52	**Pat Summerall**, Chicago Cardinals, end	3.00	1.75	2.80
☐	62	**George Blanda**, Chicago Bears, quarterback	6.85	4.90	5.88
☐	71	**Bobby Layne**, Detroit Lions, end	8.00	4.75	8.15

FLEER — 1960 (2½ ″ x 3½ ″, Numbered 1-132, Color)

		MINT	VG	PYM
☐	Complete Set	75.00	50.00	56.50
☐	7 **Sid Gillman,** Los Angeles Chargers (AFL), coach	1.00	.60	.74
☐	20 **Sammy Baugh,** New York Titans (AFL), coach	5.00	4.00	4.55
☐	58 **George Blanda,** Houston Oilers (AFL), quarterback/kicker	4.00	3.00	3.53
☐	66 **Billy Cannon,** Houston Oilers (AFL), back/end	1.50	.90	1.90
☐	73 **Abner Haynes,** Dallas Texans (AFL), back	1.50	.90	1.90
☐	76 **Paul Lowe,** Los Angeles Chargers (AFL), back	1.25	1.00	1.13
☐	116 **Hank Stram,** Los Angeles Chargers (AFL), back	2.20	1.60	1.90
☐	118 **Ron Mix,** Los Angeles Chargers (AFL), tackle	2.20	1.60	1.90
☐	124 **John Kemp,** Los Angeles Chargers (AFL), quarterback	7.75	5.00	4.55

FLEER — 1961 (2½ ″ x 3½ ″, Numbered 1-220, Color)

		MINT	VG	PYM
☐	Complete Set	135.00	80.00	113.00
☐	11 **Jim Brown,** Cleveland Browns, back	19.00	12.00	17.13
☐	30 **John Unitas,** Baltimore Colts, quarterback	6.60	4.80	5.70
☐	41 **Don Meredith,** Dallas Cowboys, quarterback	7.50	5.00	6.25
☐	69 **Kyle Rote,** New York Giants, end	2.20	1.60	1.90
☐	88 **Bart Starr,** Green Bay Packers, quarterback	5.50	5.00	4.40
☐	90 **Paul Horning,** Green Bay Packers, back	4.50	3.00	3.08
☐	117 **Bobby Layne,** Pittsburg Steelers, quarterback	4.00	2.50	4.25
☐	155 **John Kemp,** San Diego Chargers (AFL), quarterback	8.00	5.00	6.23
☐	166 **George Blanda,** Houston Oilers (AFL), quarterback/kicker	5.50	4.40	4.95

TOPPS — 1956 (2⅝ ″ x 3⅝ ″, Numbered 1-120, Color)

		MINT	VG	PYM
☐	Complete Set	175.00	100.00	135.00
☐	6 **Norm Van Brocklin,** Los Angeles Rams, quarterback	5.25	3.00	4.25
☐	28 **Chuch Bednarik,** Philadelphia Eagles, center	2.50	1.50	2.83
☐	29 **Kyle Rote,** New York Giants, end	4.00	2.50	3.08
☐	36 **Art Donvan,** Baltimore Colts, tackle	1.50	.90	1.90
☐	53 **Frank Gifford,** New York Giants, back	14.00	8.00	7.30
☐	60 **Lenny Moore,** Baltimore Colts, back	2.75	1.75	2.83
☐	78 **Elroy Hirsch,** Los Angeles Rams, end/back	3.50	2.00	2.83
☐	87 **Ernie Stautner,** Pittsburgh Steelers, tackle	2.75	1.75	1.63

		MINT	VG	PYM
☐	**101 Roosevelt Grier,** New York Giants, tackle	1.75	1.00	1.90
☐	**110 Joe Perry,** San Francisco 49ers, back ..	1.75	1.00	2.83

TOPPS — 1957 (2½″ x 3½″, Numbered 1-154, Color)

		MINT	VG	PYM
☐	Complete Set	215.00	125.00	155.00
☐	**11 Roosevelt Brown,** New York Giants, tackle	1.50	.90	1.50
☐	**22 Norman Van Brocklin,** Los Angeles Rams, quarterback	6.50	3.50	4.20
☐	**28 Lou Groza,** Cleveland Browns, tackle, kicker	3.50	2.00	2.70
☐	**30 Y.A. Tittle,** San Francisco 49ers, quarterback	6.00	3.25	5.00
☐	**31 George Blanda,** Chicago Bears, quarterback/kicker	8.50	4.50	7.20
☐	**32 Bobby Layne,** Detroit Lions, quarterback	7.00	4.00	7.45
☐	**88 Frank Gifford,** New York Giants, back .	12.00	7.00	7.98
☐	**119 Barr Starr,** Green Bay Packers, quarterback	23.00	14.00	11.75
☐	**151 Paul Horning,** Green Bay Packers, back	17.00	10.00	11.80

TOPPS — 1958 (2½″ x 3½″, Numbered 1-132, Color)

		MINT	VG	PYM
☐	Complete Set	165.00	95.00	135.00
☐	**2 Bobby Layne,** Detroit Lions, quarterback	5.00	3.25	5.05
☐	**22 John Unitas,** Baltimore Colts, quarterback	7.50	4.50	6.75
☐	**62 Jim Brown,** Cleveland Browns, back ...	40.00	25.00	42.50
☐	**66 Bart Starr,** Green Bay Packers, quarterback	6.75	4.00	5.05
☐	**73 Frank Gifford,** New York Giants, back .	13.00	8.00	6.75
☐	**86 Y.A. Tittle,** San Francisco 49ers, quarterback	5.50	3.75	5.05
☐	**90 Sonny Jurgensen,** Philadelphia Eagles, quarterback	15.00	9.00	6.75
☐	**122 Hugh McElhenny,** San Francisco 49ers, back	2.50	1.50	2.55
☐	**129 George Blanda,** Chicago Bears, quarterback/kicker	6.50	4.25	5.05

TOPPS — 1959 (2½″ x 3½″, Numbered 1-176, Color)

		MINT	VG	PYM
☐	Complete Set	145.00	80.00	118.00
☐	**1 Johnny Unitas,** Baltimore Colts, quarterback	8.00	5.00	6.38
☐	**5 Hugh McElhenny,** San Francisco 49ers, back	2.00	1.25	2.25
☐	**7 Kyle Rote,** New York Giants, end	3.00	1.75	2.25
☐	**10 Jim Brown,** Cleveland Browns, back ...	18.00	11.00	18.00
☐	**20 Frank Gifford,** New York Giants, back .	11.00	7.00	6.00
☐	**23 Bart Starr,** Green Bay Packers, quarterback	7.00	4.00	4.68
☐	**40 Bobby Layne,** Pittsburg Steelers, quarterback	5.00	3.00	5.03

			MINT	VG	PYM
☐	82	**Paul Horning,** Green Bay Packers, back	5.25	3.00	3.95
☐	130	**Y.A. Tittle,** San Francisco 49ers, quarterback	4.75	3.00	3.83

TOPPS — 1960 (2½″ x 3½″, Numbered 1-132, Color)

			MINT	VG	PYM
☐		Complete Set	120.00	75.00	83.60
☐	1	**John Unitas,** Baltimore Colts, quarterback	7.00	4.00	5.53
☐	23	**Jim Brown,** Cleveland Browns, back ...	18.00	11.00	16.25
☐	51	**Bart Starr,** Green Bay Packers, quarterback	6.00	3.75	4.96
☐	74	**Frank Gifford,** New York Giants, back .	10.00	6.00	5.53
☐	87	**Chuck Bednarik,** Philadelphia Eagles, center	1.75	1.00	2.20
☐	93	**Bobby Layne,** Pittsburgh Steelers, quarterback	4.75	3.00	4.45
☐	113	**Y.A. Tittle,** San Francisco 49ers, quarterback	5.00	3.00	3.25
☐	114	**Joe Perry,** San Francisco 49ers, back ..	1.75	1.00	2.20
☐	116	**Hugh McElhenny,** San Francisco 49ers, back	2.00	1.25	2.20

TOPPS — 1961 (2½″ x 3½″, Numbered 1-198, Color)

			MINT	VG	PYM
☐		Complete Set	139.00	80.00	103.50
☐	1	**John Unitas,** Baltimore Colts, quarterback	7.50	4.50	5.60
☐	39	**Bart Starr,** Green Bay Packers, quarterback	6.00	4.00	4.85
☐	58	**Y.A. Tittle,** San Francisco 49ers, quarterback	5.00	3.00	3.38
☐	59	**John Brodie,** San Francixco 49ers, quarterback	3.00	1.75	2.75
☐	71	**Jim Brown,** Cleveland Browns, back ...	20.00	13.00	18.50
☐	77	**Cleveland Browns Action Card,** Jimmy Brown	10.00	6.00	7.33

FOSTORIA GLASS

ORIGIN: Founded in Fostoria, Ohio in 1887, Fostoria continues in production at their Moundsville, West Virginia factory today. Many of their lovely glassware lines are considered to be "elegant" depression era glass and these patterns are avidly sought by collectors today.

RECOMMENDED READING: For further information refer to *The Official Price Guide to Depression Glassware,* published by The House of Collectibles.

AMERICAN

This classic cube style design has become a favorite glass of collectors. Prices should escalate as a result of Fostoria's announcement that its manufacturing process will no longer include handwork. American was mostly made in crystal, some green, amber, blue and yellow was also made. Some pieces of American are still being produced.

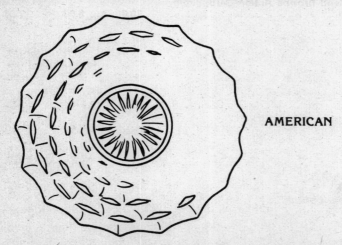

AMERICAN

	Current Price Range		P/Y Average
Appetizer, *individual, 3¼"*			
☐ *crystal*...............................	15.00	40.00	20.00
Ashtray, *square, 5"*			
☐ *crystal*...............................	17.00	25.00	19.00
Baby Set, *tumbler and bowl*			
☐ *crystal*...............................	40.00	50.00	42.00
Banana Split Bowl, *9"*			
☐ *crystal*...............................	28.00	42.00	32.00
Bell			
☐ *crystal*...............................	17.00	27.00	19.00
Bon Bon Dish, *3 toes, 6"*			
☐ *crystal*...............................	8.00	13.00	9.50
Bowl, *rolled edge, 11½"*			
☐ *crystal*...............................	30.00	45.00	33.00
Bread And Butter Plate, *6"*			
☐ *crystal*...............................	5.00	7.50	6.00
Bud Vase, *footed, flared, 6"*			
☐ *crystal*...............................	13.00	17.00	14.00
Bud Vase, *footed, flared, 8½"*			
☐ *crystal*...............................	20.00	26.00	21.00
Butter Dish, *with lid, round*			
☐ *crystal*...............................	95.00	108.00	98.00
Butter Dish, *oblong, ¼ lb.*			
☐ *crystal*...............................	30.00	40.00	32.00
Cake Plate, *footed, 12"*			
☐ *crystal*...............................	37.00	46.00	39.00
Candlesticks, *pair, 3"*			
☐ *crystal*...............................	22.00	35.00	25.00
Candlesticks, *pair, 6"*			
☐ *crystal*...............................	50.00	70.00	57.00
Centerpiece Bowl, *3 corners, 11"*			
☐ *crystal*...............................	30.00	45.00	34.00
Coaster, *3¾"*			
☐ *crystal*...............................	4.00	8.00	5.00
Cocktail Goblet, *footed, 3 oz., 2⅞"*			
☐ *crystal*...............................	11.00	14.00	12.00
Cologne Bottle, *8 oz., 7½"*			
☐ *crystal*...............................	43.00	60.00	46.00
Comport, *flat, 8½"*			
☐ *crystal*...............................	40.00	50.00	42.00
Comport, *flat, 9½"*			
☐ *crystal*...............................	40.00	50.00	42.00
Condiment Tray, *4 sections*			
☐ *crystal*...............................	30.00	40.00	32.00
Cream Soup			
☐ *crystal*...............................	20.00	30.00	22.50

	Current Price Range		P/Y Average
Creamer, *9½ oz., 4¼"*			
☐ crystal...............................	9.00	14.00	11.00
Creamer, *tea*			
☐ crystal...............................	6.00	9.00	7.00
Cup, *footed, 7 oz.*			
☐ crystal...............................	6.00	10.00	7.00
Decanter, *with stopper, 24 oz., 9¼"*			
☐ crystal...............................	68.00	85.00	72.00
Dinner Plate, *9½"*			
☐ crystal...............................	18.00	24.00	20.00
Finger Bowl, *4½"*			
☐ crystal...............................	17.00	24.00	18.00
Finger Bowl Plate, *6½"*			
☐ crystal...............................	8.00	12.00	9.00
Fruit Bowl, *footed, 12"*			
☐ crystal...............................	85.00	110.00	90.00
Fruit Bowl, *footed, 16"*			
☐ crystal...............................	60.00	90.00	68.00
Fruit Nappy, *flared, 4¾"*			
☐ crystal...............................	8.00	12.00	9.00
Goblet, *footed, 10 oz., 6⅞"*			
☐ crystal...............................	14.00	19.00	15.00
Goblet, *low, 9 oz., 5½"*			
☐ crystal...............................	9.00	13.00	10.00
Handkerchief Box, *with cover, 5½" x 4½" x 2"*			
☐ crystal...............................	110.00	140.00	115.00
Hurricane Lamp, *12"*			
☐ crystal...............................	70.00	80.00	72.00
Ice Bucket			
☐ crystal...............................	40.00	50.00	42.00
Iced Tea Tumbler, *footed, flared, 12 oz., 5¾"*			
☐ crystal...............................	13.00	17.00	14.00
Jam Pot, *with cover, 4½"*			
☐ crystal...............................	40.00	50.00	42.00
Jelly Comport, *regular, 4¼"*			
☐ crystal...............................	12.00	18.00	13.00
Juice Tumbler, *footed, 5 oz., 4¾"*			
☐ crystal...............................	10.00	14.00	11.00
Lemon Dish, *with cover, 5½"*			
☐ crystal...............................	26.00	34.00	28.00
Mayonnaise Dish, *with liner*			
☐ crystal...............................	24.00	32.00	25.00
Mayonnaise Ladle			
☐ crystal...............................	10.50	14.50	11.50
Muffin Tray, *handled*			
☐ crystal...............................	21.00	29.00	22.50

	Current Price Range		P/Y Average
Mustard Dish, *with cover and spoon, 3¾"*			
☐ *crystal*	28.00	35.00	30.00
Napkin Ring			
☐ *crystal*	5.00	8.00	6.00
Nappy, *flared, 7"*			
☐ *crystal*	30.00	40.00	32.00
Nappy, *flared, 9"*			
☐ *crystal*	30.00	45.00	33.00
Nappy, *shallow, 7"*			
☐ *crystal*	27.00	35.00	28.00
Nappy, *3 corners, handle, 5"*			
☐ *crystal*	8.00	12.00	9.00
Oil Cruet, *7 oz., 6¾"*			
☐ *crystal*	35.00	45.00	37.00
Old Fashioned Tumbler, *flat, 6 oz., 3⅜"*			
☐ *crystal*	9.00	13.00	10.00
Oyster Cocktail, *4½ oz., 3½"*			
☐ *crystal*	11.00	14.00	12.00
Pickle Jar, *with cover, 6"*			
☐ *crystal*	135.00	165.00	142.00
Pitcher, *with lip, 3 pints, 6½"*			
☐ *crystal*	45.00	55.00	47.00
Pitcher, *with lip, ½ gallon, 8¼"*			
☐ *crystal*	70.00	80.00	72.00
Platter, *oval, 12"*			
☐ *crystal*	60.00	70.00	62.00
Preserve Bowl, *with cover and handle, 5½"*			
☐ *crystal*	30.00	45.00	33.00
Puff Box, *with cover, 3" x 3" x 2⅞"*			
☐ *crystal*	68.00	85.00	72.00
Punch Bowl, *with base, 3¾ gallons, 18"*			
☐ *crystal*	230.00	260.00	240.00
Punch Cup, *flared, 6 oz.*			
☐ *crystal*	6.00	9.00	7.00
Relish Tray, *for olives, oval, 6"*			
☐ *crystal*	8.00	12.00	9.00
Relish Tray, *for pickles, oval, 8"*			
☐ *crystal*	11.00	15.00	12.00
Relish Tray, *oval, 3 sections, 11"*			
☐ *crystal*	28.00	35.00	30.00
Rose Bowl, *3½"*			
☐ *crystal*	13.00	22.00	15.00
Rose Bowl, *5"*			
☐ *crystal*	18.00	25.00	19.00
Salad Plate, *8½"*			
☐ *crystal*	13.00	17.00	14.00

	Current Price Range		P/Y Average
Salt And Pepper, *round bottom, 3½"*			
☐ crystal	13.00	17.00	14.00
Salt Dish, *individual*			
☐ crystal	3.00	7.00	4.00
Sandwich Plate, *11½"*			
☐ crystal	20.00	30.00	22.00
Saucer			
☐ crystal	2.50	4.50	3.00
Serving Bowl, *with handle, 9"*			
☐ crystal	20.00	30.00	22.00
Sherbet, *low, flared, 5 oz., 3¼"*			
☐ crystal	7.50	11.50	8.50
Sherbet, *with handle, 4½ oz., 3½"*			
☐ crystal	13.00	17.00	14.00
Sugar, *tea*			
☐ crystal	5.50	8.50	6.00
Sugar, *with cover and handle, 5¼"*			
☐ crystal	19.00	25.00	21.00
Sugar Shaker, *4¾"*			
☐ crystal	110.00	140.00	120.00
Sundae, *6 oz., 3⅛"*			
☐ crystal	8.00	11.50	9.00
Sweet Pea Vase, *4½"*			
☐ crystal	88.00	105.00	92.00
Toothpick, *2¼"*			
☐ crystal	16.00	23.00	17.00
Urn, *square, 7½"*			
☐ crystal	30.00	40.00	32.00
Utility Tray, *handled, round, 9"*			
☐ crystal	21.00	29.00	22.00
Vase, *8"*			
☐ crystal	32.00	45.00	34.00
Vase, *10"*			
☐ crystal	42.00	55.00	44.00
Vegetable Bowl, *oval, 2 sections, 10"*			
☐ crystal	27.00	37.00	30.00
Water Bottle, *44 oz., 9¼"*			
☐ crystal	130.00	160.00	138.00
Water Tumbler, *footed, 9 oz., 4⅜"*			
☐ crystal	9.00	15.00	10.00
Wedding Bowl, *pedestal, 6½"*			
☐ crystal	28.00	37.00	30.00
Whiskey Tumbler, *flat, 2 oz., 2½"*			
☐ crystal	7.00	11.00	8.00
Wine Goblet, *footed, 2½ oz., 4¾"*			
☐ crystal	12.00	17.00	13.00

BAROQUE

Made in crystal, blue and yellow, this elegant pattern features ornamental scrolls and designs on simple, delicately scalloped pieces.

BAROQUE

	Current Price Range		P/Y Average
Ashtray, *oval*			
☐ *blue*	13.00	17.00	14.00
☐ *yellow*	11.00	14.00	12.00
☐ *crystal*	7.00	10.00	8.00
Bowl, *flared, 12"*			
☐ *blue*	26.00	34.00	28.00
☐ *yellow*	21.00	29.00	22.00
☐ *crystal*	15.00	20.00	16.00
Bowl, *handles, 10½"*			
☐ *blue*	31.00	39.00	32.00
☐ *yellow*	26.00	34.00	28.00
☐ *crystal*	17.00	23.00	18.00
Bowl, *oval, 6½"*			
☐ *blue*	13.00	20.00	14.00
☐ *yellow*	11.00	16.00	12.00
☐ *crystal*	8.00	12.00	9.00
Bread And Butter Plate, *6"*			
☐ *blue*	5.00	7.00	5.50
☐ *yellow*	3.50	5.50	4.00
☐ *crystal*	2.00	4.00	2.50
Cake Plate, *handles, 10"*			
☐ *blue*	20.00	25.00	21.00
☐ *yellow*	15.00	20.00	16.00
☐ *crystal*	11.00	14.00	12.00
Candelabra, *3 lights, 9¼"*			
☐ *blue*	68.00	82.00	71.00
☐ *yellow*	54.00	66.00	56.00
☐ *crystal*	40.00	50.00	42.00

	Current Price Range		P/Y Average
Candlesticks, *4"*			
☐ blue	22.00	29.00	23.00
☐ yellow	18.00	22.00	19.00
☐ crystal	13.00	17.00	14.00
Candlesticks, *5½"*			
☐ blue	26.00	34.00	28.00
☐ yellow	22.00	28.00	23.00
☐ crystal	18.00	22.00	19.00
Celery Dish, *oval, 11"*			
☐ blue	22.00	29.00	23.00
☐ yellow	14.00	19.00	15.00
☐ crystal	11.00	14.00	12.00
Cereal Bowl, *6"*			
☐ blue	26.00	34.00	28.00
☐ yellow	20.00	25.00	21.00
☐ crystal	14.00	20.00	15.00
Cocktail Tumbler, *footed, 3¾ oz., 3"*			
☐ blue	15.00	20.00	16.00
☐ yellow	12.00	16.00	13.00
☐ crystal	8.00	12.00	9.00
Compote, *6½"*			
☐ blue	18.00	22.00	19.00
☐ yellow	14.00	18.00	15.00
☐ crystal	8.00	11.00	10.00
Cream Soup			
☐ blue	26.00	34.00	28.00
☐ yellow	20.00	25.00	21.00
☐ crystal	14.00	19.00	15.00
Creamer, *footed, 3¾"*			
☐ blue	14.00	18.00	15.00
☐ yellow	11.00	14.00	12.00
☐ crystal	6.00	10.00	7.00
Cruet, *with stopper, 3½ oz., 5½"*			
☐ blue	230.00	270.00	240.00
☐ yellow	230.00	270.00	240.00
☐ crystal	23.00	29.00	24.00
Dinner Plate, *9"*			
☐ blue	26.00	34.00	28.00
☐ yellow	20.00	25.00	21.00
☐ crystal	13.00	17.00	14.00
Floating Garden Bowl, *10"*			
☐ blue	35.00	45.00	37.00
☐ yellow	31.00	39.00	32.00
☐ crystal	21.00	29.00	22.00
Ice Bucket, *metal handle*			
☐ blue	78.00	97.00	82.00
☐ yellow	55.00	65.00	57.00
☐ crystal	31.00	39.00	32.00

	Current Price Range		P/Y Average

Iced Tea Tumbler, *14 oz., 5¾"*

☐ *blue*	31.00	39.00	32.00
☐ *yellow*	25.00	30.00	26.00
☐ *crystal*	15.00	20.00	16.00

Juice Tumbler, *5 oz., 3¾"*

☐ *blue*	20.00	25.00	21.00
☐ *yellow*	18.00	22.00	19.00
☐ *crystal*	11.00	14.00	12.00

Luncheon Plate, *8"*

☐ *blue*	9.00	13.00	10.00
☐ *yellow*	7.00	11.00	8.00
☐ *crystal*	5.00	9.00	6.00

Mayonnaise, *5½"*

☐ *blue*	24.00	31.00	26.00
☐ *yellow*	20.00	24.00	21.00
☐ *crystal*	17.00	21.00	18.00

Nappy, *5"*

☐ *blue*	14.00	20.00	15.00
☐ *yellow*	11.00	15.00	12.00
☐ *crystal*	8.00	12.00	9.00

Old Fashioned Tumbler, *6¾ oz., 3½"*

☐ *blue*	21.00	29.00	22.00
☐ *yellow*	18.00	22.00	19.00
☐ *crystal*	11.00	14.00	12.00

Pickle Dish, *8¼"*

☐ *blue*	14.00	19.00	15.50
☐ *yellow*	11.00	16.00	12.00
☐ *crystal*	7.50	11.50	8.50

Pitcher, *44 oz.*

☐ *blue*	625.00	675.00	635.00
☐ *yellow*	525.00	575.00	535.00
☐ *crystal*	135.00	165.00	145.00

Punch Cup, *6 oz.*

☐ *blue*	18.00	22.00	19.00
☐ *crystal*	6.00	9.00	7.00

Relish Tray, *3 sections, handled*

☐ *blue*	24.00	31.00	26.00
☐ *yellow*	20.00	25.00	21.00
☐ *crystal*	11.00	14.00	12.00

Rose Bowl, *3¾"*

☐ *blue*	26.00	34.00	28.00
☐ *yellow*	19.00	26.00	21.00
☐ *crystal*	13.00	17.00	14.00

Rose Bowl, *8¾"*

☐ *yellow*	26.00	34.00	28.00

	Current Price Range		P/Y Average
Salad Plate, *7"*			
☐ *blue*	7.00	11.00	8.00
☐ *yellow*	6.00	10.00	7.00
☐ *crystal*	4.00	7.00	5.00
Salt And Pepper Shakers			
☐ *blue*	100.00	130.00	110.00
☐ *yellow*	87.00	103.00	90.00
☐ *crystal*	30.00	40.00	32.00
Saucer			
☐ *blue*	4.50	6.50	5.00
☐ *yellow*	3.00	5.00	3.50
☐ *crystal*	1.00	3.00	1.50
Serving Plate, *center handle, 11"*			
☐ *crystal*	14.00	19.00	15.00
Sherbet, *5 oz.*			
☐ *blue*	16.00	21.00	17.00
☐ *yellow*	12.00	16.00	13.00
☐ *crystal*	7.00	10.00	8.00
Sugar, *footed, 3½"*			
☐ *blue*	12.00	15.00	13.00
☐ *yellow*	9.00	13.00	10.00
☐ *crystal*	6.00	9.00	6.50
Tray, *oval, 11¼"*			
☐ *blue*	20.00	25.00	21.00
☐ *yellow*	15.00	20.00	16.00
☐ *crystal*	11.00	14.00	12.00
Vase, *8¼"*			
☐ *blue*	26.00	34.00	28.00
☐ *yellow*	21.00	28.00	22.00
☐ *crystal*	16.00	20.00	17.00

COLONY

Colony was made from the 1920s to the 1970s. This pattern was mostly made in crystal, though other colors include green, blue and yellow.

	Current Price Range		P/Y Average
Almond Bowl, *footed*			
☐ *crystal*	3.00	5.00	3.50
Bowl, *low foot, 9"*			
☐ *crystal*	13.00	17.00	14.00
Candlestick, *9¾"*			
☐ *crystal*	11.00	14.00	12.00
Candy Dish, *with lid, 6½"*			
☐ *crystal*	18.00	22.00	19.00
Celery Bowl, *11½"*			
☐ *crystal*	10.50	13.50	11.50
Cocktail Goblet, *3½ oz., 4"*			
☐ *crystal*	7.50	10.50	8.50

	Current Price Range		P/Y Average
Creamer			
□ crystal	6.50	9.50	7.50
Finger Bowl, *4³⁄₄"*			
□ crystal	5.00	8.00	6.00
Goblet, *9 oz., 5¹⁄₄"*			
□ crystal	10.50	13.50	11.50
Oyster Cocktail, *4 oz., 3³⁄₈"*			
□ crystal	7.00	10.00	8.00
Pickle Bowl, *9¹⁄₂"*			
□ crystal	8.50	11.50	9.50
Plate, *6"*			
□ crystal	1.50	3.50	2.00
Plate, *7"*			
□ crystal	2.00	4.00	2.50
Plate, *8"*			
□ crystal	2.50	4.50	3.00
Plate, *9"*			
□ crystal	3.50	5.50	4.00
Plate, *10"*			
□ crystal	6.00	9.00	7.00
Sherbet, *5 oz., 3⁵⁄₈"*			
□ crystal	7.50	11.50	8.50
Sugar			
□ crystal	4.00	6.00	4.50
Tumbler, *5 oz.*			
□ crystal	6.50	9.50	7.50
Tumbler, *9 oz.*			
□ crystal	8.50	11.50	9.50

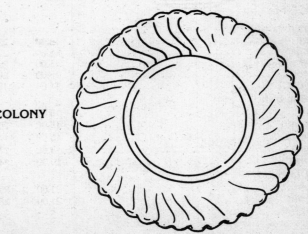

COLONY

	Current Price Range		P/Y Average
Tumbler, *footed, 5 oz., 4½"*			
□ *crystal*	8.00	11.00	9.00
Tumbler, *footed, 12 oz., 5¾"*			
□ *crystal*	10.00	13.00	11.00
Tumbler, *12 oz.*			
□ *crystal*	10.50	13.50	11.50
Vase, *8"*			
□ *crystal*	15.00	20.00	16.50
Wine Goblet, *3¼ oz., 4¼"*			
□ *crystal*	8.50	11.50	9.50

FAIRFAX

This plain simple pattern was made from the 1920s to the 1940s. Other patterns were created using Fairfax and adding a design.

FAIRFAX

Ashtray			
□ *blue*	18.00	22.00	19.00
□ *orchid*	18.00	22.00	19.00
□ *pink*	16.00	20.00	17.00
□ *green*	16.00	20.00	17.00
□ *amber*	11.00	15.00	12.00
Bon Bon Dish			
□ *blue*	15.00	20.00	16.00
□ *orchid*	15.00	20.00	16.00
□ *pink*	13.00	17.00	14.00
□ *green*	13.00	17.00	14.00
□ *amber*	10.00	14.00	11.00
Bowl, *footed, 11¾"*			
□ *blue*	21.00	25.00	22.00
□ *orchid*	21.00	25.00	22.00

	Current Price Range		P/Y Average
☐ *pink*	17.00	21.00	18.00
☐ *green*	17.00	21.00	18.00
☐ *amber*	13.00	17.00	14.00
Bowl, *oval, 10½"*			
☐ *blue*	25.00	30.00	26.00
☐ *orchid*	25.00	30.00	26.00
☐ *pink*	22.00	28.00	23.00
☐ *green*	22.00	28.00	23.00
☐ *amber*	15.00	20.00	16.00
Bread And Buttler Plate, *6"*			
☐ *blue*	3.50	5.50	4.00
☐ *orchid*	3.50	5.50	4.00
☐ *pink*	3.00	5.00	3.50
☐ *green*	3.00	5.00	3.50
☐ *amber*	2.00	4.00	2.50
Cake Plate, *handles, 10"*			
☐ *blue*	15.00	20.00	16.00
☐ *orchid*	15.00	20.00	16.00
☐ *pink*	13.00	17.00	14.00
☐ *green*	13.00	17.00	14.00
☐ *amber*	11.00	14.00	12.00
Candy Dish, *with lid, 3 sections*			
☐ *blue*	42.00	52.00	44.00
☐ *orchid*	42.00	52.00	44.00
☐ *pink*	33.00	41.00	34.00
☐ *green*	33.00	41.00	34.00
☐ *amber*	29.00	35.00	31.00
Cereal Bowl, *6"*			
☐ *blue*	13.00	17.00	14.00
☐ *orchid*	13.00	17.00	14.00
☐ *pink*	11.00	14.00	12.00
☐ *green*	11.00	14.00	12.00
☐ *amber*	8.50	11.50	9.50
Cigarette Box			
☐ *blue*	31.00	39.00	33.00
☐ *orchid*	31.00	39.00	33.00
☐ *pink*	23.00	33.00	25.00
☐ *green*	23.00	33.00	25.00
☐ *amber*	20.00	25.00	21.00
Claret Goblet, *4 oz.*			
☐ *blue*	23.00	28.00	24.00
☐ *orchid*	23.00	28.00	24.00
☐ *pink*	20.00	25.00	21.00
☐ *green*	20.00	25.00	21.00
☐ *amber*	17.00	21.00	18.00

	Current Price Range		P/Y Average
Coaster, *3½"*			
blue	5.00	7.00	5.50
orchid	5.00	7.00	5.50
pink	3.00	5.00	3.50
green	3.00	5.00	3.50
amber	2.00	4.00	2.50
Cocktail Goblet, *3 oz.*			
blue	20.00	25.00	21.00
orchid	20.00	25.00	21.00
pink	18.00	22.00	19.00
green	18.00	22.00	19.00
amber	15.00	20.00	16.00
Compote, *7"*			
blue	20.00	25.00	21.00
orchid	20.00	25.00	21.00
pink	18.00	22.00	19.00
green	18.00	22.00	19.00
amber	14.00	18.00	15.00
Cordial Goblet, *¾ oz.*			
blue	26.00	34.00	28.00
orchid	26.00	34.00	28.00
pink	25.00	30.00	26.00
green	25.00	30.00	26.00
amber	21.00	26.00	23.00
Cream Soup			
blue	12.00	15.00	13.00
orchid	12.00	15.00	13.00
pink	10.50	13.50	11.50
green	10.50	13.50	11.50
amber	8.50	11.50	9.50
Creamer, *footed*			
blue	8.50	11.50	9.50
orchid	8.50	11.50	9.50
pink	6.50	9.50	7.50
green	6.50	9.50	7.50
amber	5.00	7.00	5.50
Cruet, *footed, with handle*			
blue	112.00	140.00	117.00
orchid	112.00	140.00	117.00
pink	98.00	122.00	104.00
green	98.00	122.00	104.00
amber	82.00	98.00	85.00
Cup, *footed*			
blue	7.00	10.00	8.00
orchid	7.00	10.00	8.00
pink	4.50	7.50	5.50
green	4.50	7.50	5.50
amber	4.00	6.00	4.50

	Current Price Range		P/Y Average
Dinner Plate, *10¼"*			
☐*blue*......................................	25.00	30.00	26.00
☐*orchid*...................................	25.00	30.00	26.00
☐*pink*.....................................	22.00	28.00	23.00
☐*green*....................................	22.00	28.00	23.00
☐*amber*...................................	18.00	22.00	19.00
Finger Bowl, *4⅝" x 2"*			
☐*blue*.....................................	13.00	17.00	14.00
☐*orchid*...................................	13.00	17.00	14.00
☐*pink*.....................................	11.00	15.00	12.00
☐*green*....................................	11.00	15.00	12.00
☐*amber*...................................	8.50	11.50	9.50
Fruit Bowl, *5"*			
☐*blue*.....................................	7.50	11.50	8.50
☐*orchid*...................................	7.50	11.50	8.50
☐*pink*.....................................	5.00	8.00	6.00
☐*green*....................................	5.00	8.00	6.00
☐*amber*...................................	5.00	7.00	5.50
Grill Plate, *10¼"*			
☐*blue*.....................................	15.00	20.00	16.00
☐*orchid*...................................	15.00	20.00	16.00
☐*pink*.....................................	11.00	14.00	12.00
☐*green*....................................	11.00	14.00	12.00
☐*amber*...................................	8.50	11.50	9.50
Ice Bucket, *with metal handle*			
☐*blue*.....................................	36.00	44.00	38.00
☐*orchid*...................................	36.00	44.00	38.00
☐*pink*.....................................	31.00	39.00	33.00
☐*green*....................................	31.00	39.00	33.00
☐*amber*...................................	25.00	30.00	26.00
Luncheon Plate, *9½"*			
☐*blue*.....................................	7.50	10.50	8.50
☐*orchid*...................................	7.50	10.50	8.50
☐*pink*.....................................	6.50	9.50	7.50
☐*green*....................................	6.50	9.50	7.50
☐*amber*...................................	6.00	8.00	6.50
Mayonnaise Dish			
☐*blue*.....................................	13.00	17.00	14.00
☐*orchid*...................................	13.00	17.00	14.00
☐*pink*.....................................	9.50	12.50	10.50
☐*green*....................................	9.50	12.50	10.50
☐*amber*...................................	7.50	10.50	8.50
Mayonnaise Ladle			
☐*blue*.....................................	18.00	22.00	19.00
☐*orchid*...................................	18.00	22.00	19.00
☐*pink*.....................................	13.00	17.00	14.00
☐*green*....................................	13.00	17.00	14.00
☐*amber*...................................	13.00	17.00	14.00

	Current Price Range		P/Y Average
Oyster Cocktail, *footed, 5½ oz.*			
□ *blue*	14.50	18.50	15.50
□ *orchid*	14.50	18.50	15.50
□ *pink*	12.00	16.00	13.00
□ *green*	12.00	16.00	13.00
□ *amber*	8.50	11.50	9.50
Parfait, *footed, 6½ oz.*			
□ *blue*	15.00	20.00	16.00
□ *orchid*	15.00	20.00	16.00
□ *pink*	12.00	16.00	13.00
□ *green*	12.00	16.00	13.00
□ *amber*	11.00	14.00	12.00
Pitcher, *footed, 48 oz.*			
□ *blue*	175.00	220.00	180.00
□ *orchid*	175.00	220.00	180.00
□ *pink*	150.00	190.00	160.00
□ *green*	150.00	190.00	160.00
□ *amber*	120.00	150.00	127.00
Platter, *oval, 15"*			
□ *blue*	42.00	52.00	45.00
□ *orchid*	42.00	52.00	45.00
□ *pink*	38.00	46.00	40.00
□ *green*	38.00	46.00	40.00
□ *amber*	32.00	39.00	33.00
Relish Tray, *2 sections, 8½"*			
□ *blue*	13.00	16.00	14.00
□ *orchid*	13.00	16.00	14.00
□ *pink*	11.00	14.00	12.00
□ *green*	11.00	14.00	12.00
□ *amber*	8.50	11.50	9.00
Relish Tray, *3 sections, 11½"*			
□ *blue*	20.00	25.00	21.00
□ *orchid*	20.00	25.00	21.00
□ *pink*	15.00	20.00	16.00
□ *green*	15.00	20.00	16.00
□ *amber*	11.00	14.00	12.00
Relish Tray, *3 sections, round*			
□ *blue*	15.00	20.00	16.00
□ *orchid*	15.00	20.00	16.00
□ *pink*	12.00	15.00	13.00
□ *green*	12.00	15.00	13.00
□ *amber*	8.50	11.50	9.50
Sauce Boat			
□ *blue*	31.00	39.00	33.00
□ *orchid*	31.00	39.00	33.00
□ *pink*	26.00	34.00	28.00
□ *green*	26.00	34.00	28.00
□ *amber*	23.00	28.00	24.00

	Current Price Range		P/Y Average

Saucer
☐ blue	2.50	4.50	3.00
☐ orchid	2.50	4.50	3.00
☐ pink	1.50	3.50	2.00
☐ green	1.50	3.50	2.00
☐ amber	1.50	3.50	2.00

Sherbet, *low, 6 oz.*
☐ blue	14.00	17.00	15.00
☐ orchid	14.00	17.00	15.00
☐ pink	12.00	15.00	13.00
☐ green	12.00	15.00	13.00
☐ amber	11.00	14.00	12.00

Sherbet, *tall, 6 oz.*
☐ blue	15.00	20.00	16.00
☐ orchid	15.00	20.00	16.00
☐ pink	12.00	16.00	13.00
☐ green	12.00	16.00	13.00
☐ amber	12.00	16.00	13.00

Soup Bowl
☐ blue	15.00	20.00	16.00
☐ orchid	15.00	20.00	16.00
☐ pink	13.00	17.00	14.00
☐ green	13.00	17.00	14.00
☐ amber	11.00	14.00	12.00

Sugar, *footed*
☐ blue	7.50	10.50	8.50
☐ orchid	7.50	10.50	8.50
☐ pink	6.00	8.00	6.50
☐ green	6.00	8.00	6.50
☐ amber	4.00	6.00	4.50

Tray, *handle, 11"*
☐ blue	25.00	30.00	26.00
☐ orchid	25.00	30.00	26.00
☐ pink	20.00	25.00	21.00
☐ green	20.00	25.00	21.00
☐ amber	15.00	20.00	16.00

Tumbler, *footed, 12 oz.*
☐ blue	18.00	22.00	19.00
☐ orchid	18.00	22.00	19.00
☐ pink	16.00	20.00	17.00
☐ green	16.00	20.00	17.00
☐ amber	14.00	18.00	15.00

Tumbler, *footed, 9 oz.*
☐ blue	15.00	20.00	16.00
☐ orchid	15.00	20.00	16.00
☐ pink	12.00	16.00	13.00
☐ green	12.00	16.00	13.00
☐ amber	10.50	13.50	12.50

	Current Price Range		P/Y Average
Tumbler, *footed, 5 oz.*			
☐ *blue*	12.00	16.00	13.00
☐ *orchid*	12.00	16.00	13.00
☐ *pink*	9.50	12.50	10.50
☐ *green*	9.50	12.50	10.50
☐ *amber*	7.50	10.50	8.50
Tumbler, *footed, 2½ oz.*			
☐ *blue*	12.50	15.50	13.50
☐ *orchid*	12.50	15.50	13.50
☐ *pink*	9.50	12.50	10.50
☐ *green*	9.50	12.50	10.50
☐ *amber*	7.50	10.50	8.50
Water Goblet, *10 oz.*			
☐ *blue*	20.00	25.00	21.00
☐ *orchid*	20.00	25.00	21.00
☐ *pink*	16.00	20.00	17.00
☐ *green*	16.00	20.00	17.00
☐ *amber*	15.00	18.00	16.00

JUNE

This understated, lacy pattern is built around a series of wide, bowknot motifs, separated one from the other by a trailing garland about the rim. It was issued in crystal, blue, topaz and rose.

	Current Price Range		P/Y Average
Ashtray			
☐ *yellow*	27.00	34.00	32.00
☐ *pink*	27.00	34.00	32.00
☐ *blue*	27.00	34.00	32.00
☐ *crystal*	20.00	25.00	22.00
Baking Dish, egg shape, length 9″			
☐ *yellow*	70.00	80.00	72.50
☐ *pink*	40.00	45.00	42.00
☐ *blue*	50.00	60.00	55.00
☐ *crystal*	30.00	35.00	32.00
Bon Bon, stemmed			
☐ *yellow*	20.00	25.00	22.00
☐ *pink*	15.00	20.00	17.00
☐ *blue*	18.00	22.00	19.00
☐ *crystal*	10.00	14.00	11.00
Bouillon Bowl, pedestal foot with under-plate			
☐ *pink*	20.00	25.00	22.00
☐ *yellow*	20.00	25.00	24.00
☐ *crystal*	10.00	14.00	11.00
☐ *blue*	33.00	36.00	34.00
Bowl, diameter 10″			
☐ *yellow*	33.00	38.00	34.00
☐ *pink*	38.00	43.00	39.00
☐ *blue*	48.00	53.00	49.00
☐ *crystal*	22.00	28.00	24.00

	Current Price Range		P/Y Average
Bread And Butter Plate, diameter 6″			
yellow	5.00	7.00	6.00
pink	5.00	7.00	6.00
blue	6.00	8.00	7.00
crystal	4.00	6.00	5.00
Cake Plate, handled, diameter 10″			
yellow	33.00	38.00	34.00
pink	35.00	40.00	37.00
blue	43.00	48.00	46.00
crystal	23.00	28.00	24.00
Canape Plate			
yellow	12.00	15.00	13.00
pink	12.00	15.00	13.00
blue	14.00	15.00	16.00
crystal	8.00	10.00	9.00
Candlesticks, pair, height 2 ″			
yellow	33.00	38.00	34.00
pink	35.00	40.00	37.00
blue	40.00	45.00	42.00
crystal	28.00	33.00	29.00
Candlesticks, pair, height 3″			
yellow	35.00	40.00	37.00
pink	38.00	43.00	39.00
blue	45.00	50.00	46.00
crystal	30.00	35.00	32.00
Candlesticks, pair, height 5″			
yellow	40.00	45.00	42.00
pink	45.00	50.00	47.00
blue	55.00	60.00	56.50
Candy Jar, with lid, capacity two cups			
yellow	95.00	110.00	97.00
pink	105.00	115.00	107.50
blue	145.00	155.00	147.00
crystal	63.00	68.99	64.00
Candy Jar, with lid, capacity six cups			
yellow	70.00	90.00	75.00
pink	145.00	155.00	147.00
blue	145.00	155.00	147.00
crystal	40.00	50.00	45.00
Celery Dish, length 11″			
yellow	33.00	37.00	34.00
pink	33.00	38.00	34.00
blue	38.00	43.00	40.00
crystal	20.00	25.00	22.00
Centerpiece Bowl, oval, length 11″			
yellow	30.00	50.00	32.00
pink	40.00	50.00	42.00
blue	40.00	50.00	42.00
crystal	20.00	25.00	22.00
Cereal Bowl, diameter 6″			
yellow	25.00	30.00	27.00
pink	20.00	25.00	22.00
blue	23.00	27.00	24.50
crystal	14.00	16.00	15.00

	Current Price Range		P/Y Average
Cheese And Cracker Set			
☐ *yellow*	30.00	35.00	32.00
☐ *pink*	40.00	44.00	42.00
☐ *blue*	40.00	44.00	42.00
☐ *crystal*	20.00	25.00	22.00
Chop Plate, diameter 12″			
☐ *yellow*	35.00	40.00	37.00
☐ *pink*	35.00	40.00	37.00
☐ *blue*	40.00	45.00	42.00
☐ *crystal*	20.00	25.00	22.00
Condiment Bottle, footed, with stopper			
☐ *yellow*	240.00	260.00	245.00
☐ *pink*	290.00	310.00	295.00
☐ *blue*	370.00	380.00	372.00
☐ *crystal*	145.00	155.00	148.00
Comport, diameter 5″			
☐ *yellow*	22.00	38.00	23.00
☐ *pink*	30.00	34.00	30.00
☐ *blue*	30.00	34.00	30.00
☐ *crtstal*	28.00	34.00	29.50
Comport, diameter 6″			
☐ *yellow*	50.00	60.00	53.00
☐ *pink*	55.00	65.00	58.00
☐ *blue*	65.00	75.00	68.00
☐ *crystal*	38.00	43.00	39.50
Comport, diameter 7″			
☐ *yllow*	55.00	65.00	58.00
☐ *pink*	60.00	70.00	63.00
☐ *blue*	80.00	90.00	83.50
☐ *crystal*	43.00	48.00	44.00
Comport, diameter 8″			
☐ *yellow*	65.00	75.00	67.50
☐ *pink*	70.00	80.00	73.50
☐ *blue*	90.00	100.00	94.50
☐ *crystal*	57.00	63.00	58.50
Cordial Cup			
☐ *yellow*	30.00	35.00	32.00
☐ *pink*	38.00	43.00	39.50
☐ *blue*	45.00	55.00	48.50
☐ *crystal*	20.00	25.00	22.00
Cordial Cup Saucer			
☐ *yellow*	8.00	10.00	8.50
☐ *pink*	9.00	11.00	9.50
☐ *blue*	11.00	14.00	12.00
☐ *crystal*	6.00	8.00	7.00
Cordial Glass, stemmed			
☐ *yellow*	62.00	68.00	63.00
☐ *pink*	55.00	65.00	58.00
☐ *blue*	68.00	73.00	69.00
☐ *crystal*	30.00	40.00	35.00

	Current Price Range		P/Y Average
Creamer, collar base			
☐ *yellow*	23.00	28.00	24.00
☐ *pink*	28.00	33.00	29.50
☐ *blue*	33.00	38.00	34.00
☐ *crystal*	20.00	25.00	22.00
Creamer, pedestal foot			
☐ *yellow*	16.00	18.00	17.00
☐ *pink*	16.00	18.00	17.00
☐ *blue*	20.00	22.00	21.00
☐ *crystal*	16.00	18.00	16.50
Cup, pedestal foot			
☐ *yellow*	20.00	22.00	21.00
☐ *pink*	20.00	25.00	22.00
☐ *blue*	25.00	30.00	26.00
☐ *crystal*	14.00	16.00	14.50
Decanter, with glass stopper			
☐ *yellow*	390.00	410.00	395.00
☐ *pink*	440.00	460.00	445.00
☐ *blue*	490.00	510.00	495.00
☐ *crystal*	290.00	310.00	295.00
Dessert Bowl, handled, diameter 8″			
☐ *yellow*	45.00	55.00	48.00
☐ *pink*	55.00	65.00	59.00
☐ *blue*	60.00	70.00	64.00
☐ *crystal*	38.00	43.00	39.00
Dinner Plate, diameter 9″			
☐ *yellow*	20.00	25.00	22.00
☐ *pink*	14.00	16.00	15.00
☐ *blue*	16.00	18.00	17.00
☐ *crystal*	11.00	14.00	11.50
Dinner Plate, diameter 10¼″			
☐ *yellow*	33.00	38.00	34.00
☐ *pink*	35.00	40.00	37.00
☐ *blue*	40.00	50.00	43.00
☐ *crystal*	23.00	28.00	24.00
Fan Vase, pedestal foot			
☐ *yellow*	90.00	100.00	94.00
☐ *pink*	95.00	105.00	98.00
☐ *blue*	120.00	130.00	124.00
☐ *crystal*	70.00	80.00	74.00
Finger Bowl			
☐ *yellow*	23.00	28.00	24.00
☐ *pink*	23.00	28.00	24.00
☐ *blue*	30.00	38.00	32.50
☐ *crystal*	15.00	20.00	17.00
Fruit Bowl, diameter 5″			
☐ *yellow*	17.00	20.00	18.00
☐ *pink*	15.00	20.00	16.00
☐ *blue*	20.00	25.00	22.00
☐ *crystal*	11.00	13.00	11.50

	Current Price Range		P/Y Average
Mayonnaise Compote			
☐ yellow	30.00	35.00	32.50
☐ pink	35.00	40.00	37.00
☐ blue	45.00	50.00	47.00
☐ crystal	25.00	35.00	28.00
Mint Dish			
☐ yellow	20.00	25.00	22.00
☐ pink	23.00	28.00	24.00
☐ blue	27.00	33.00	28.00
☐ crystal	14.00	18.00	15.00
Nappy, flat, diameter 7″			
☐ yellow	15.00	20.00	16.00
☐ pink	15.00	20.00	16.00
☐ blue	18.00	20.00	19.00
☐ crystal	10.00	14.00	11.00
Nappy, pedestal foot, diameter 6¼″			
☐ yellow	315.00	20.00	16.00
☐ pink	15.00	20.00	16.00
☐ blue	18.00	20.00	19.00
☐ crystal	10.00	14.00	11.00
Oil Cruet, pedestal foot			
☐ yellow	280.00	320.00	290.00
☐ pink	340.00	360.00	345.00
☐ blue	420.00	430.00	425.00
☐ crystal	140.00	160.00	150.00
Oyster Plate			
☐ yellow	20.00	24.00	22.00
☐ pink	20.00	24.00	22.00
☐ blue	28.00	32.00	30.00
☐ crystal	20.00	26.00	22.00
Parfait Glass			
☐ yellow	40.00	45.00	42.00
☐ pink	24.00	28.00	25.00
☐ blue	30.00	35.00	32.00
☐ crystal	18.00	20.00	19.00
Pitcher			
☐ yellow	340.00	360.00	345.00
☐ pink	340.00	360.00	345.00
☐ blue	465.00	485.00	470.00
Platter, diameter 11″			
☐ yellow	40.00	45.00	42.00
☐ pink	43.00	48.00	44.00
☐ blue	45.00	55.00	48.00
☐ crystal	30.00	40.00	34.00
Platter, diameter 15″			
☐ yellow	85.00	95.00	87.00
☐ pink	95.00	105.00	97.00
☐ blue	115.00	135.00	120.00
☐ crystal	55.00	65.00	58.00
Relish Dish, two compartments, length 8¼″			
☐ yellow	20.00	24.00	21.50
☐ pink	25.00	30.00	26.00
☐ blue	25.00	30.00	26.00
☐ crystal	14.00	16.00	15.00

	Current Price Range		P/Y Average
Sugar Bowl, small with lid			
☐ *yellow*	20.00	25.00	22.00
☐ *pink*	25.00	30.00	27.00
☐ *blue*	33.00	38.00	34.00
☐ *crystal*	20.00	25.00	22.00
Tray, loop handle, diameter 11″			
☐ *yellow*	33.00	38.00	34.00
☐ *pink*	38.00	43.00	39.50
☐ *blue*	45.00	55.00	49.50
☐ *crystal*	25.00	30.00	27.50
Tumbler, height 3½″			
☐ *yellow*	30.00	35.00	32.00
☐ *pink*	30.00	35.00	32.00
☐ *blue*	35.00	40.00	36.00
☐ *crystal*	20.00	30.00	22.00
Tumbler, height 5″			
☐ *yellow*	20.00	30.00	22.00
☐ *pink*	20.00	30.00	22.00
☐ *blue*	25.00	30.00	26.00
☐ *crystal*	14.00	16.00	15.00
Vase, height 7½″			
☐ *yellow*	95.00	100.00	97.50
☐ *pink*	95.00	100.00	97.50
☐ *blue*	185.00	205.00	187.50
☐ *crystal*	30.00	40.00	35.00
Water Glass, stemmed			
☐ *yellow*	20.00	30.00	22.50
☐ *pink*	30.00	35.00	32.00
☐ *blue*	28.00	33.00	29.50
☐ *crystal*	18.00	22.00	19.50
Whipped Cream Bowl, large			
☐ *yellow*	110.00	120.00	112.00
☐ *pink*	123.00	128.00	124.00
☐ *blue*	140.00	160.00	145.00
☐ *crystal*	65.00	85.00	70.00
Whipped Cream Bowl, small			
☐ *yellow*	18.00	22.00	19.00
☐ *pink*	20.00	25.00	22.00
☐ *blue*	23.00	28.00	24.00
☐ *crystal*	15.00	20.00	17.00
Whiskey Tumbler, shot, 2½ oz			
☐ *yellow*	30.00	35.00	32.00
☐ *blue*	30.00	35.00	32.00
☐ *pink*	40.00	45.00	41.50
☐ *crystal*	20.00	25.00	22.00
Wine Glass, stemmed			
☐ *yellow*	40.00	45.00	42.00
☐ *pink*	35.00	40.00	37.00
☐ *blue*	45.00	50.00	47.00
☐ *crystal*	19.00	23.00	20.00

TROJAN

This is an interesting symmetrical pattern made up of spade-like motifs created by framing ridgework with a curly scroll, trapping a floral design that is reminiscent of a fleur-de-lis. These shapes alternate around the outer rim with draped scrollwork delicately drawn in low relief. The rest of the glass is plain, with no center medallions or base designs.

	Current Price Range		P/Y Average
Ashtray, *large*			
□ pink	25.00	35.00	25.50
□ yellow	25.00	35.00	25.50
Bon bon Bowl			
□ pink	10.00	20.00	12.00
□ yellow	10.00	20.00	12.00
Bouillon Bowl, *footed*			
□ pink	14.00	25.00	15.00
□ yellow	14.00	25.00	15.00
Cereal Bowl, *diameter 6"*			
□ pink	16.00	26.00	17.50
□ yellow	16.00	26.00	17.50
Compote, *height 6"*			
□ pink	20.00	30.00	22.00
□ yellow	20.00	30.00	22.00
Creamer, *footed*			
□ pink	15.00	25.00	16.50
□ yellow	15.00	25.00	16.50
Dinner Plate, *diameter 10¼"*			
□ pink	25.00	35.00	26.50
□ yellow	25.00	35.00	26.50
Finger Bowl, *with liner*			
□ pink	20.00	30.00	22.00
□ yellow	20.00	30.00	22.00
Grill Plate, *diameter 10"*			
□ pink	25.00	35.00	26.50
□ yellow	25.00	35.00	26.50
Luncheon Plate, *diameter 8¾"*			
□ pink	10.00	20.00	12.00
□ yellow	10.00	20.00	12.00
Mayonnaise Bowl, *with liner*			
□ pink	25.00	35.00	26.50
□ yellow	25.00	35.00	26.50
Parfait			
□ pink	24.00	34.00	25.00
□ yellow	24.00	34.00	25.00
Pitcher			
□ pink	225.00	300.00	235.00
□ yellow	225.00	300.00	235.00
Platter, *diameter 12"*			
□ pink	28.00	38.00	30.00
□ yellow	28.00	38.00	30.00
Platter, *diameter 15"*			
□ pink	40.00	50.00	42.00
□ yellow	40.00	50.00	42.00

	Current Price Range		P/Y Average
Relish Dish, *diameter 8½"*			
□ *pink*	10.00	20.00	12.00
□ *yellow*	10.00	20.00	12.00
Relish Dish, *three compartments*			
□ *pink*	20.00	30.00	22.00
□ *yellow*	20.00	30.00	22.00
Saucer			
□ *pink*	4.00	10.00	6.00
□ *yellow*	4.00	10.00	6.00
Sherbet, *height 4¼"*			
□ *pink*	14.00	20.00	16.00
□ *yellow*	14.00	20.00	16.00
Sugar Bowl, *footed*			
□ *pink*	15.00	25.00	17.00
□ *yellow*	15.00	25.00	17.00
Tray, *diameter 11", center handle*			
□ *pink*	25.00	35.00	26.50
□ *yellow*	25.00	35.00	26.50
Tumbler, *height 4½"*			
□ *pink*	18.00	28.00	20.00
□ *yellow*	18.00	28.00	20.00
Tumbler, *height 5¼"*			
□ *pink*	14.00	24.00	15.00
□ *yellow*	14.00	24.00	15.00
Tumbler, *height 6"*			
□ *pink*	18.00	28.00	20.00
□ *yellow*	18.00	28.00	20.00
Vase, *height 8"*			
□ *pink*	55.00	65.00	57.50
□ *yellow*	55.00	65.00	57.50
Whipped Cream Tub			
□ *pink*	65.00	80.00	70.00
□ *yellow*	65.00	80.00	70.00

VERSAILLES

This pattern was Fostoria's pride and joy during the time of the depression and was expensive given the economic conditions of the time. Now collectors have made it a favorite and the prices reflect it. It is a scrolled pattern, consisting of sprays of ornate curves around a stylized fern-like center. The variety of shapes is enormous with many interesting handles and lids. The glass is delicate, the moldwork excellent, the design well conceived.

	Current Price Range		P/Y Average
Ashtray			
□ *blue*	28.00	38.00	30.00
□ *green*	22.00	32.00	23.00
□ *pink*	22.00	32.00	22.00
□ *yellow*	25.00	35.00	26.50

	Current Price Range		P/Y Average
Bonbon Bowl			
blue	12.00	22.00	14.00
green	10.00	20.00	12.00
pink	10.00	20.00	12.00
yellow	10.00	20.00	12.00
Bouillon Bowl			
blue	20.00	30.00	21.50
green	15.00	25.00	17.00
pink	15.00	25.00	17.00
yellow	16.00	26.00	17.50
Bread and Butter Plate, *diameter 6"*			
blue	4.00	10.00	5.00
green	3.00	9.00	4.00
pink	3.00	9.00	4.00
yellow	3.00	9.00	4.00
Cereal Bowl, *diameter 6"*			
blue	25.00	35.00	27.00
green	18.00	28.00	20.00
pink	18.00	28.00	20.00
yellow	20.00	30.00	22.00
Chop Plate, *diameter 13"*			
blue	33.00	43.00	35.00
green	28.00	38.00	30.00
pink	28.00	38.00	30.00
yellow	30.00	40.00	32.00
Compote, *height 6"*			
blue	28.00	38.00	30.00
green	20.00	30.00	22.00
pink	20.00	30.00	22.00
yellow	25.00	35.00	26.00
Compote, *height 7"*			
blue	33.00	43.00	34.00
green	23.00	33.00	24.00
pink	23.00	33.00	24.00
yellow	28.00	38.00	30.00
Creamer, *footed*			
blue	18.00	28.00	20.00
green	13.00	23.00	15.00
pink	13.00	23.00	15.00
yellow	13.00	23.00	15.00
Demitasse Cup and Saucer			
blue	45.00	55.00	47.00
green	20.00	30.00	22.00
pink	20.00	30.00	22.00
yellow	30.00	40.00	32.00
Decanter			
blue	175.00	250.00	185.00
green	125.00	200.00	135.00
pink	125.00	200.00	135.00
yellow	140.00	180.00	145.00

	Current Price Range		P/Y Average

Finger Bowl, *with liner*
☐ blue	25.00	35.00	26.50
☐ green	18.00	28.00	18.50
☐ pink	18.00	28.00	18.50
☐ yellow	23.00	33.00	24.50

Fruit Bowl, *diameter 5"*
☐ blue	15.00	25.00	16.50
☐ green	12.00	22.00	14.00
☐ pink	12.00	22.00	14.00
☐ yellow	13.00	23.00	14.00

Ice Bucket
☐ blue	77.00	87.00	80.00
☐ green	60.00	70.00	62.00
☐ pink	60.00	70.00	62.00
☐ yellow	73.00	84.00	74.50

Lemon Bowl
☐ blue	12.00	22.00	14.00
☐ green	8.00	18.00	10.00
☐ pink	8.00	18.00	10.00
☐ yellow	10.00	20.00	12.00

Luncheon Plate, *diameter 8¾"*
☐ blue	8.00	18.00	10.00
☐ green	6.00	16.00	7.50
☐ pink	6.00	16.00	7.50
☐ yellow	8.00	18.00	10.00

Mayonnaise Bowl, *with liner*
☐ blue	45.00	55.00	47.00
☐ green	33.00	43.00	35.00
☐ pink	33.00	43.00	35.00
☐ yellow	38.00	48.00	40.00

Parfait
☐ blue	28.00	38.00	30.00
☐ green	24.00	34.00	25.00
☐ pink	24.00	34.00	25.00
☐ yellow	25.00	35.00	26.50

Pitcher
☐ blue	380.00	440.00	400.00
☐ green	240.00	280.00	245.00
☐ pink	240.00	280.00	245.00
☐ yellow	280.00	330.00	295.00

Platter, *diameter 12"*
☐ blue	38.00	48.00	40.00
☐ green	28.00	38.00	30.00
☐ pink	28.00	38.00	30.00
☐ yellow	33.00	43.00	34.50

Platter, *diameter 15"*
☐ blue	58.00	68.00	59.50
☐ green	43.00	53.00	44.00
☐ pink	43.oO	53.00	44.00
☐ yellow	45.00	55.00	46.50

	Current Price Range		P/Y Average
Relish, *diameter 8½"*			
☐ blue	38.00	48.00	39.50
☐ green	28.00	38.00	32.00
☐ pink	28.00	38.00	32.00
☐ yellow	33.00	43.00	34.50
Sauce Boat and Underplate			
☐ blue	57.00	67.00	58.00
☐ green	43.00	53.00	44.00
☐ pink	43.00	53.00	44.00
☐ yellow	38.00	48.00	40.00
Saucer			
☐ blue	4.00	10.00	5.00
☐ green	3.00	9.00	4.00
☐ pink	3.00	9.00	4.00
☐ yellow	3.00	8.00	3.50
Soup Bowl, *diameter 7"*			
☐ blue	28.00	38.00	30.00
☐ green	23.00	33.00	24.50
☐ pink	23.00	33.00	24.50
☐ yellow	25.00	35.00	26.50
Sugar, *footed*			
☐ blue	18.00	28.00	20.00
☐ green	13.00	23.00	15.00
☐ pink	13.00	23.00	15.00
☐ yellow	13.00	23.00	15.00
Tray, *diameter 11", with center handle*			
☐ blue	28.00	38.00	30.00
☐ green	18.00	28.00	20.00
☐ pink	18.00	28.00	20.00
☐ yellow	23.00	33.00	24.50
Tumbler, *height 4½", 5 oz.*			
☐ blue	22.00	32.00	23.50
☐ green	18.00	28.00	21.50
☐ pink	18.00	28.00	21.50
☐ yellow	20.00	30.00	22.50
Tumbler, *height 5¼", 9 oz.*			
☐ blue	23.00	33.00	24.50
☐ green	18.00	28.00	19.50
☐ pink	18.00	28.00	19.50
☐ yellow	19.50	29.50	20.00
Tumbler, *height 6", 12 oz.*			
☐ blue	25.00	35.00	26.50
☐ green	20.00	30.00	22.00
☐ pink	20.00	30.00	22.00
☐ yellow	23.00	33.00	24.50
Vase, *height 8"*			
☐ blue	120.00	150.00	127.50
☐ green	70.00	90.00	72.50
☐ pink	70.00	90.00	72.50
☐ yellow	90.00	125.00	97.50

FRANKOMA POTTERY

DESCRIPTION: Founded in 1933 by John Frank, the Frankoma Pottery continues to produce earthenwares made from Oklahoma clays to the present day. Located in Sapula, Oklahoma, the wares of this company are known for their color and durablility.

TYPES: Many types of objects have been produced by Frankoma including jewelry, limited edition plates, miniatures, trivets, Christmas cards, sculpture, novelties and of course dinnerware.

RECOMMENDED READING: For more in-depth information you may refer to *The Official Price Guide to Pottery and Porcelain* and *The Official Identificaion Guide to Pottery and Porcelain,* published by The House of Collectibles.

Mug, *1969, Nixon-Agnew Presidential,* **$75.00-$85.00**

	Current Price Range		P/Y Average
☐ **Bowl, divided,** 11″, item #49d, peach glow, ..	6.00	8.00	7.00
☐ **Bowl,** 14 ounces	3.50	5.00	4.25
☐ **Creamer And Sugar,** 8 ounces, item #4a, peach glow...........................	8.00	10.00	9.00
☐ **Cup,** item #4c, clay blue	4.00	5.50	4.75
☐ **Dish, butter,** item #4k, peach glow, lidded ...	7.00	10.00	8.50
☐ **Juice,** 6 ounces	3.00	4.00	3.50
☐ **Lazy Suzette,** 5 sections, on ball bearing base, made from 1957-1982	22.00	24.00	23.00
☐ **Pitcher,** item #4d, two quart, clay blue	9.00	12.00	10.50
☐ **Platter, serving,** 12⅞″, item #4p, clay blue ...	11.00	14.00	12.50
☐ **Plate, dinner,** 10″, item #4f, peach glow	5.00	6.00	5.50
☐ **Pot,** 3 quart, lid, handled	16.00	18.00	17.00
☐ **Saucer,** 5¼″, item #4e, clay blue	1.75	2.00	1.85
☐ **Soup Cup,** 11 ounces, ...	4.00	6.00	5.00
☐ **Spoon Holder,** 6″	3.00	5.00	4.00
☐ **Tumbler,** 12 ounces	4.00	6.00	5.00
☐ **Vegetable,** 24 ounces	5.00	7.00	6.00
☐ **Bowl, salad,** 20 ounces, item #7x1, woodland moss	6.00	8.00	7.00
☐ **Bowl, sugar,** item #7b, prairie green, unlidded .	9.00	12.00	10.50
☐ **Bowl, vegetable,** one quart, item #7n, woodland moss	7.00	9.00	8.00
☐ **Creamer and sugar,** items #7a, 7b, woodland mossand, C-shape handles, the sugar bowl's lid with a plug-type handle, the creamer featuring a vaulted pouring spout.	13.00	16.00	14.50
☐ **Cup,** item #7c, woodland moss, sculptured handle.	4.00	5.00	4.50
☐ **Dish, fruit,** 8 ounces, item #7xo, woodland moss	4.00	5.50	4.75
☐ **Dish, sauce,** 10 ounces, item #7s, desert gold, lidded	2.50	3.25	2.75
☐ **Mug,** item #7cl, woodland moss, modified loop handle.	3.00	4.00	3.50
☐ **Pitcher,** item #7d, woodland moss, pot form with tall loop handle.	10.00	14.00	12.00
☐ **Plate,** 7″	3.00	4.00	3.50
☐ **Plate, dinner,** 9″, item #7f, woodland moss ..	4.00	5.50	4.75
☐ **Plate,** 10″	6.00	8.00	7.00
☐ **Plater,** 13″, shallow	7.00	10.00	8.50
☐ **Plate,** 15″	16.00	18.00	17.00
☐ **Platter,** 11″	5.00	6.00	5.50
☐ **Saucer,** 5″, item #7e, woodland moss	2.75	3.75	3.25
☐ **Shakers,** salt and pepper	5.00	6.00	5.50
☐ **Teapot,** 2 cup	7.00	9.00	8.00
☐ **Teapot,** 6 cup, tall, short lip spout	10.00	12.00	11.00
☐ **Tray,** 9″	5.00	7.00	6.00

FRUIT CRATE LABELS

DESCRIPTION: The decorative labels that adorned the sides of wooden fruit crates have become popular collectibles.

PERIOD: The oldest and most rare fruit crate labels date to the 1880s.

ORIGIN: Fruit crate labels were originally designed to attract potential fruit buyers. In the 1950s collecting such art work began when the use of decorated wooden crates declined.

COMMENTS: Rarity and design are the important variables with fruit crate labels. California labels are usually worth more than Florida labels, and orange labels usually have more ornate designs. Label designs changed over the years, and some collectors focus on labels that have undergone design changes.

ADDITIONAL TIPS: The listings are alphabetical according to fruit company name. Following names are descriptions of the label art, type of fruit and price range. Size of label and states are listed when available.

	Current Price Range		P/Y Average
☐ **Ahtanum, WA.** *Pear, three pears, mountains, stock label #947, pictorial*	3.00	5.00	4.00
☐ **Airline, CA.** *Citrus, globe with wings, stars in red, white and blue, 10" x 11"*	.75	1.75	1.00
☐ **Airship, CA.** *Citrus, pictures commercial airplane, royal blue, 10" x 11"*	6.00	10.00	8.00
☐ **Ak-Sar-Ben, CA.** *Citrus, picture of oranges on a blue background, 10" x 11"*	.75	1.75	1.00
☐ **All American, WA.** *Apple, flag type shield, patriotic appearance, blue background, pictorial*	4.00	6.00	5.00
☐ **Altissimo, CA.** *Citrus, pictures mountains in pink and blue on a blue sky background, dated 1918, 10" x 11"*	.75	1.75	1.00
☐ **All Year, CA.** *Citrus, black border frames landscape scene, 12½" x 8¾"*	.50	1.50	1.00
☐ **Alpine Orchards, WA.** *Pear, three pears, yellow, red, black background, pictorial.*	2.00	4.00	3.00

	Current Price Range		P/Y Average

☐ **Blue Mountain, WA.** *Apple, silhouette of trees and mountains, one red and one golden apple in right corner, orange background, blue border* **9.00** **11.00** **10.00**

☐ **Blue Streak, WA.** *Large red ribbon seal with two red apples, brown border* **3.00** **5.00** **4.00**

☐ **Blue Tip, CA.** *Citrus, picture of a large feather, 9" x 9"* .... **.50** **1.00** **.74**

☐ **Blue Winner, WA.** *Apple, cowboy on horse-back picking up an apple in a rodeo, blue and white background* **3.00** **5.00** **4.00**

☐ **Boa Vista Ranch, CA.** *Apple, mountains, orchard and farm house, one red and one golden apple, blue border* **1.50** **3.50** **2.50**

☐ **Bolero, CA.** *Apple, Spanish dancer with two guitarists, black background* **4.50** **6.50** **5.50**

☐ **Bounty, CA.** *Pear, bright yellow background, blue and red lettering, blue border* **1.00** **3.00** **2.00**

☐ **Boy Blue, WA.** *Apple, boy with horn, white lettering* **3.50** **5.50** **4.50**

☐ **Boy Blue, WA.** *Pear, boy about to blow an old horn, blue background, white letters* **2.50** **4.50** **3.50**

☐ **Briant, WA.** *Apple, Washington State map, white and blue lettering, blue background* ... **1.00** **3.00** **2.00**

☐ **Briskey, WA.** *Apple, snowy scene from Naches Pass, mountains and two red apples, black background, blue border* **2.00** **4.00** **3.00**

☐ **Broadway, CA.** *Pear, red and black lettering (old) graphic type, gold leaf, blue background, blue-green border* **2.00** **4.00** **3.00**

☐ **Bronco, CA.** *Citrus, old stone litho of fully dressed cowboy riding a wild horse, very colorful* **3.00** **5.00** **4.00**

☐ **Brownie's, CA.** *Citrus, pictures Brownies preparing orange juice against a yellow sun and blue background, 10" x 11"* **1.00** **3.00** **2.00**

☐ **Buckaroo, WA.** *Apple, cowboy breaking a bucking horse, mountains and desert, yellow sky* **5.50** **7.50** **6.50**

☐ **Buddy.** *Michigan broker label, smiling baby, blue background, green border, 1920* **3.50** **5.50** **4.50**

☐ **Buffalo, CA.** *Apple, angry looking buffalo, red lettering, blue background, green border* **3.50** **5.50** **4.50**

☐ **Bunting, WA.** *Apple, one red apple, ribbon sash through the center, red lettering, blue background* **3.00** **5.00** **4.00**

☐ **Butler's Pride, WA.** *Apple, branch with large red apple, white lettering, graphic, blue background* .... **.75** **2.75** **1.50**

☐ **Caledonia, CA.** *Citrus, picture of Scotch thistles on plaid background, 10" x 11"* ..... **.50** **1.00** **.74**

☐ **Cal-Flavor, CA.** *Citrus, oranges, blossoms and leaves against a woodgrained and black background, 10" x 11"* **1.00** **3.00** **2.00**

	Current Price Range		P/Y Average

□ **Cambria, CA.** *Citrus, brown border frames a brown eagle and two torches against a blue background, 10" x 11"* **1.00** **3.00** **2.00**

□ **Carefree, CA.** *Citrus, pictures a girl with blonde hair laughing against a blue background, 10" x 11"* **1.00** **3.00** **2.00**

□ **Carro Amano Aranci, CA.** *Citrus, pictures Italian fruit peddler with a cart full of oranges, 10" x 11"* **1.00** **3.00** **2.00**

□ **Chere Best, WA.** *Apple, aqua inset with block lettering, blue background* .... **.75** **2.75** **1.50**

□ **Chief Joseph, WA.** *Apple, large white arrow head with Chief Joseph's image in front of it, dressed in full headdress and beads, historic, red lettering, blue background* **7.00** **9.00** **8.00**

□ **Cho Paka, WA.** *Apple, trees, mountains, distant orchard scene, blue background* **8.00** **10.00** **9.00**

□ **Circle A&F, WA.** *Apple, yellow and black lettering, circle in center with A&F in white letters, black background* **3.00** **5.00** **4.00**

□ **Clasen, WA.** *Apple, old litho of orchard homes and Mt. Adams in the background, two red apples on a limb, red lettering, 40 Lbs. (old)* **2.50** **4.50** **3.50**

□ **Cliff, WA.** *Apple, rock cliffs with raging waterfall, span bridge over water with old sedan driving over it, orchard hills, blue sky and red lettering, brown border* **3.00** **5.00** **4.00**

□ **Clipper, FL.** *Citrus, three-masted schooner, 7" x 7"* .... **.75** **1.75** **1.00**

□ **Clipper Ship, WA.** *Apple, large sailing ship on the ocean, blue background* **17.50** **19.50** **18.50**

□ **Coed, CA.** *Citrus, pictures smiling girl in graduate cap and gown against a purple background, 10" x 11"* **1.00** **3.00** **2.00**

□ **Color Guard, WA.** *Apple, blue bottom, yellow lettering, graphic, black background* **2.00** **4.00** **3.00**

□ **Columbia, WA.** *Apple, mountains, cliffs, Columbia River gorge, farm, houses, orchards, ghostly Statue of Liberty with torch in background (the torch is emitting a light on two large apples), blue background, beautiful, rare* **45.00** **47.00** **46.00**

□ **Columbia Bell, WA.** *Apple, patriotic dressed lady with crown and holding a drawn sword, one red apple, blue and white background* .. **3.00** **5.00** **4.00**

□ **Congdon Refrigerated, WA.** *Apple, first edition label, one red apple frozen in a block of ice, art deco lettering, black background* **15.00** **17.00** **16.00**

□ **Congdon Refrigerated, WA.** *Pear, pear frozen in a block of ice* **4.00** **6.00** **5.00**

□ **Corona Lily, CA.** *Citrus, white and gold speckled lily against a black background, 10" x 11"* **1.00** **3.00** **2.00**

	Current Price Range		P/Y Average

□ **Desert Bloom, CA.** *Citrus, white, blooming yucca with desert greenery and mountains against a blue sky background, 10" x 11"* .... | 1.00 | 3.00 | 2.00

□ **Dewy Fresh, WA.** *Apple, modern green leaf, fairy in leafy skirt holding a wand, believed to be one of the last label printed, white and red background, 1956* .... | 1.50 | 3.50 | 2.50

□ **Diamond, OR.** *Apple, red diamonds in center with white letters saying Hood River Apples (cartoon of apple head man), green background* .... | 6.00 | 8.00 | 7.00

□ **Diamond, OR.** *Pear, Mt. Hood scene, red diamond shipper is Apple growers service* ..... | 2.00 | 4.00 | 3.00

□ **Diamond S, CA.** *Pear, two horse heads, blue diamond, black-tan background* .... | 6.00 | 8.00 | 7.00

□ **Di Giorgio, CA.** *Pear, two gold pears, white letters, dark blue background, light blue border* .... | 1.50 | 3.50 | 2.50

□ **Dinner Gong, WA.** *Apple, one red apple with leaves and stem, black bottom, blue background* .... | 1.00 | 3.00 | 2.00

□ **Diving Girl, CA.** *Apple, 1920s girl in swimming suit diving into the lake* .... | 6.50 | 8.50 | 7.50

□ **Dixie Boy, FL.** *Citrus, picture of a black boy, 9" x 9"* .... | 2.00 | 4.00 | 3.00

□ **Don Juan, CA.** *Pear, orchard scene in upper left corner, blue/black/red background* ..... | 1.50 | 3.50 | 2.50

□ **Donnater, TX.** *Citrus, pink grapefruit against a black background, 9" x 9"* .... | .25 | .75 | .50

□ **Don't Worry, WA.** *Apple, blond boy holding apple with bite out of it, written white letters, shiny black background* .... | 4.00 | 6.00 | 5.00

□ **Double A, CA.** *Citrus, train supported by two capital letter As on a trestle, 10" x 11"* ...... | .75 | 1.75 | 1.00

□ **Duckwall, OR.** *Apple, stone wall with a very colorful duck in front, red background* ...... | 15.00 | 17.00 | 16.00

□ **Dunbar, OR.** *Pear, cartoon pear skiing down snowy hill, yellow letter, blue sky* .... | 2.50 | 4.50 | 3.50

□ **Eagle, CA.** *Pear, eagle and two pears, red lettering, blue background, yellow border* ..... | 3.50 | 5.50 | 4.50

□ **Eatmor, WA.** *Pear, 1920s boy in plaid knickers, holding a pear, red lettering, green background, rare* .... | 20.00 | 22.00 | 21.00

□ **Eat One, CA.** *Citrus, pictures arrow pointing to an orange, aqua background, 10" x 11"* ... | 1.00 | 3.00 | 2.00

□ **Eatum, WA.** *Apple, one red and one golden apple, yellow letters, graphic type label, blue and black background* .... | 1.00 | 3.00 | 2.00

□ **El Mejor, CA.** *Citrus, pictures Sunkist orange, 10" x 11"* .... | .75 | 1.75 | 1.00

□ **Emerald Beauty, WA.** *Pear, Spanish lady playing a guitar, rare* .... | 17.50 | 19.50 | 18.50

□ **Emerald Green, WA.** *Apple, suit of armor head with shield with a large emerald on it, green background* .... | 3.00 | 5.00 | 4.00

	Current Price Range		P/Y Average

Empire, WA. Apple, evaporated apples, old litho of mountains, orchards and trees 3.00 5.00 4.00

Empire Builder, WA. Apple, mountains, large warehouse, trucks, train orchards, large apple covered wagon and four oxen 1.50 3.50 2.50

Endurance, CA. Citrus, night scene pictures walking camels against a purple and black background, 10" x 11" 5.00 7.00 6.00

Esperanza, CA. Citrus, pictures a Senorita with a carnation in her hair, wearing a lace mantilla and holding a lace fan against a blue background, 10" x 11" .... .75 1.75 1.00

Exeter, CA. Citrus, Tulare Co. map against a multicolored background, 10" x 11" .... .75 1.75 1.00

Fido, CA. Citrus, white puppy with black spot against a black background, 12½" x 8¾" ... 9.00 11.00 10.00

Fiesta, TX. Citrus, girl dressed in gown against a black background, 10" x 11" ...... .25 .75 .50

Fillmore Crest, CA. Citrus, blue border frames three oranges and green leaves against a turquoise background, 10" x 11" .. .75 1.75 1.00

First Blue, WA. Apple, photo of three apples, light blue and orange letters, on a yellow sash, blue background 1.50 3.50 2.50

Flavor Crest. Treasure chest full of red and golden apples (apple label from New York), blue background 5.00 7.00 6.00

Florida Cowboy, FL. Citrus, cowboy astride bucking bronco with diamond K brand palm trees in background, 9" x 9" 3.00 7.00 5.00

Florita, CA. Citrus, dancing senorita and two guitarists against a black background, 10" x 11" 3.00 5.00 4.00

Flying V, WA. Apple, photo of red apple, yellow written letters and A V with wings on it, blue background 3.50 7.50 5.50

Foothills, OR. Pear, old stone litho of orchard, mountain, river and two pears 4.50 6.50 5.50

For The Kids Of Austin, WA. Apple, stock label, two red apples and a leafy limb, Kiwanis International insignia, tufted yellow, blue background 3.00 5.00 4.00

Full O' Juice, CA. Citrus, pictures half peeled orange and a glass of orange juice, lavender background, 10" x 11" 1.00 3.00 2.00

Galleon, CA. Citrus, galleon sailing on the open sea, sky background, 12½" x 8¾" 1.00 3.00 2.00

Gladiola, CA. Citrus, two gladiola sprays on a gold and tan background, 10" x 11" 1.00 3.00 2.00

Globes O' Gold, CA. Citrus, pictures three oranges, blossoms, leaves, 10" x 11" .... .75 1.75 1.00

Gold Buckle, CA. Citrus, outline of a belt with a gold buckle frames an orchard scene against a blue background, 10" x 11" 1.00 3.00 2.00

Gold Circle, CA. Pear, gold circle, yellow circle, two pears, graphic, blue background ... 2.00 4.00 3.00

	Current Price Range		P/Y Average

☐ **Kentucky Cardinal, KY.** *Apple, three apples and a red cardinal on a blossoming apple limb, 1918 stone litho* 17.50 19.50 **18.50**

☐ **King David, CA.** *Citrus, king with white beard in royal robes and crown, 10" x 11"* 1.00 3.00 **2.00**

☐ **Kings Park, CA.** *Citrus, pictures a waterfall and mountain stream, 10" x 11"* 1.00 3.00 **2.00**

☐ **Lakecove, CA.** *Pear, barefoot boy with straw hat on, leaning on a tree, lake and mountain* . 5.00 7.00 **6.00**

☐ **Lake View, WA.** *Apple, two goldens with a red apple between them, scene of the Pajaro Valley, old, blue background, green border* .. 5.00 7.00 **6.00**

☐ **Lamb, WA.** *Apple, Lamb's first printing, lamb standing on a hillside with orchard mountain background, two red apples hanging over its head, blue/black border, 1920s artwork, beautiful* 55.00 57.00 **56.00**

☐ **La Reina, CA.** *Citrus, hacienda scene with Spanish senorita holding a black fan against a blue background, 10" x 11"* .... .50 1.50 **1.00**

☐ **Lauree, CA.** *Citrus, pictures oranges, berries, laurel leaves, blue background, 10" x 11"* .... .50 1.50 **1.00**

☐ **Laurie, CA.** *Apple, little girl with an apple in each hand, she has a pink dress on, blue background, 1930s label, rare* 10.00 12.00 **11.00**

☐ **Leavenworth, WA.** *Pear, two green pears with white letters, blue background* 1.50 3.50 **2.50**

☐ **Legal Tender, CA.** *Citrus, pictures U.S. currency in a $250 bundle against a blue and black background, 10" x 11"* 1.00 3.00 **2.00**

☐ **Lemonade, CA.** *Citrus, three lemons in foreground, orchard scene in background, 12½" x 8¾"* .... .25 .75 **.50**

☐ **Lily, CA.** *Citrus, two white calla lilies, green leaves on a black background, 10" x 11"* 1.00 3.00 **2.00**

☐ **Lincoln, CA.** *Citrus, portrait of Lincoln with oranges and leaves, 10" x 11"* 1.00 3.00 **2.00**

☐ **Loch Lomond, CA.** *Citrus, Scottish scene on blue and green plaid background, 10" x 11"* .. .50 1.50 **1.00**

☐ **Loop Loop, WA.** *Apple, Indian chief on a palomino horse, he is picking an apple from the horse's back* 10.00 12.00 **11.00**

☐ **Loot Of Ventura County, CA.** *Citrus, multicolored, 10" x 11"* 1.00 3.00 **2.00**

☐ **Lucky Lad, WA.** *Apple, large red apple with image of the 1920s farm boy in front of it, gold letters, black background, green border* 50.00 52.00 **51.00**

☐ **Lure, WA.** *Apple, image of a big, largemouth bass hooked on a fish plug, bright red letters, blue border* 25.00 27.00 **26.00**

☐ **Luxor, WA.** *Apple, big red maltese cross with the name Luxor in white on it, blue background* 10.00 12.00 **11.00**

☐ **M Brand, WA.** *Apple, big blue M with some kind of gold lance behind it, red background, rare* 7.00 9.00 **8.00**

	Current Price Range		P/Y Average

☐ **Nimble, CA.** *Citrus, pictures an orange and blossoms against an orchard landscape, aqua background, 10" x 11"* .... .50 1.50 1.00

☐ **Nob Hill, CA.** *Pear, Metropolitan skyscrapers, autos and street cars* 5.00 7.00 6.00

☐ **Nuchief, WA.** *Apple, little cartoon Indian chief with an apple in his right hand and a tomahawk in his left, says Apples from Washington State, blue background* 4.00 6.00 5.00

☐ **Orchard King, CA.** *Citrus, orange, with crown, royal blue background, 10" x 11"* .... .50 1.50 1.00

☐ **Orchard, OR.** *Pear, old stone litho, Model T truck on a road, orchard and mountains, white background* 5.00 7.00 6.00

☐ **Oriole, CA.** *Citrus, oriole perched on a branch with nearby orange, blossoms and leaves, black background, 10" x 11"* 3.00 5.00 4.00

☐ **Orland, CA.** *Citrus, pictures old dam scene, 10" x 11"* 4.00 6.00 5.00

☐ **Our Pride WA.** *Apple, parrot sitting on a twig, one red apple, black background, blue border, copy 1923, 40 lbs.* 5.00 7.00 6.00

☐ **Outboard, WA.** *Apple, modern race boat zooming across a lake; houses, orchards and mountains in the background, red lettering* .. 17.50 19.50 18.50

☐ **Ox Team, WA.** *Apple, covered wagon pulled by a team, driver with whip in hand, desert in the background, red and green border, 1937 label* 10.00 12.00 11.00

Pacific Fruit & Produce Co., WA, *peaches,* **$3.00-$6.00**

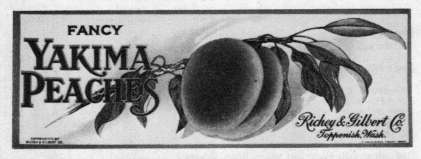

Top: Richey & Gilbert Co., WA, *peaches*, $3.00-$6.00; Bottom: Pacific Fruit & Produce Co., WA, *cantaloupes*, $3.00-$6.00

	Current Price Range		P/Y Average
☐ **Princess, CA.** *Citrus, princess in royal robes and crown jewels, with grapefruits, leaves on a blue background, dated 1911*	1.50	2.50	2.00
☐ **Pure Gold, CA.** *Citrus, pictures prospector and his mule, blue background, 10" x 11"* . . .	.75	1.75	1.00
☐ **Pyramid, Canada.** *Apple, three pyramids with river, palm trees, camel and rider, blue background*	10.00	12.00	11.00
☐ **Queen Esther, CA.** *Citrus, elegant queen dressed in turquoise gown, golden crown, 10" x 11"*	2.00	4.00	3.00
☐ **Queen Fruits, WA.** *Pear, two pears, old queen in full dress, blue background*	10.00	12.00	11.00
☐ **Quercus Ranch, CA.** *Pear, orchard, sky, lake, mountains and two pears*	3.00	5.00	4.00
☐ **Rancheria, CA.** *Pear, Indian Chief on horse by a maiden, teepees, black background*	2.50	4.50	3.50
☐ **Red Bird, CA.** *Citrus, large red eagle, black background, 10" x 11"*	.50	1.50	1.00
☐ **Red Label, WA.** *Apple, valley scene with town, roads, river and mountains, two large red apples in the sky, red border*	15.00	17.00	16.00
☐ **Redlands Best, CA.** *Citrus, four blue arrows pointing to big orange in center, 10" x 11"* . . .	2.00	4.00	3.00

	Current Price Range		P/Y Average

☐ **Redman, WA.** *Apple, Indian brave, behind him are cave drawings, two apples - one red and one golden, blue background* 4.00 6.00 5.00

☐ **Red Peak, CA.** *Citrus, landscape scene, 10" x 11"* .... .50 1.50 1.00

☐ **Red Seal, WA.** *Apple, red ribbon with old time red wax seal, two red apples, white letters, green background* 2.00 4.00 3.00

☐ **Red Star, CA.** *Apple, big red star in the center, red and white letters, black background, red border* 4.00 6.00 5.00

☐ **Red Streak, WA.** *Apple, two drawn apples, one red and one golden, red lightning streak shooting through the label, black background, red border* 15.00 17.00 16.00

☐ **Red Wagon, WA.** *Apple, cartoon boy pulling a red wagon full of red and golden apples, black background, yellow border* 8.00 10.00 9.00

☐ **Red Winner, WA.** *Apple, picture inset of Indian maiden in leather and beads, on a white horse, grassy plains, desert and mountains, red and yellow letters, red and white background* 4.00 6.00 5.00

☐ **Reindeer, CA.** *Citrus, reindeer and grove scene against a yellow background, 10" x 11"* 2.00 4.00 3.00

☐ **Repetition, WA.** *Apple, three identical boys in front of three identical boxes of apples with the same label on them, black background* .. 10.00 12.00 11.00

☐ **Rider, FL.** *Citrus, jockey in white and green silks astride a brown race horse, 9" x 9"* .... .50 1.50 1.00

☐ **Rocky Hill, CA.** *Citrus, Indian chief on horse standing on cliff against a blue background, 10" x 11"* .... .50 1.50 1.00

☐ **Rose, WA.** *Apple, two large red roses with thorns and leaves, white letters, blue background* 3.50 5.50 4.50

☐ **Round Robin, OR.** *Pear, big red robin standing on a hill, old, blue background* 8.00 10.00 9.00

☐ **Royal Feast, CA.** *Citrus, pictures orange, blossoms, dark blue leaves with two lions in black framed by a black checkered border, 10" x 11"* .... .50 1.50 1.00

☐ **Royal Knight, CA.** *Citrus, knight on horseback against a yellow background, 10" x 11"* .50 1.50 1.00

☐ **Rubaiyat, CA.** *Citrus, pictures desert scene under a full moon, 10" x 11"* .... .50 1.50 1.00

☐ **Safe Hit, TX.** *Vegetables, 1920s baseball player hitting a ball, grandstand in the background, 7" x 9"* 2.00 4.00 3.00

☐ **Sails, WA.** *Apple, large sailing ship in a rough choppy sea, yellow and red letters, blue background, red penline border, 40 lbs.* 5.00 7.00 6.00

☐ **Sam Birch, OR.** *Apple, one red apple, yellow strip through the label with blue letters on it, blue background* 8.00 10.00 9.00

	Current Price Range		P/Y Average
Sunshine Ranch, WA. *Apple, large warehouse with Mt. Adams in the background at sunrise, letters in the orange sky say EAT GOOD APPLES FOR VITAMINS/EAT APPLES FOR HEALTH, blue border*	10.00	12.00	11.00
Sun Smile, CA. *Pear, smiling face of the sun, blue letters, also a blue anchor, sunburst background*	3.00	5.00	4.00
Sun Sugared, OR. *Pear, photo of an orange pear, black background*	1.00	3.00	2.00
Super Crisp, WA. *Apple, two-and-a-half apples, one red and one golden, orchard, house, hill, writing in the sky, blue border, c. 1948*	1.50	3.50	2.50
Super-Pak, WA. *Apple, blue ribbon in a triangle with the lettering on it, black background*	1.00	3.00	2.00
Sure Mark, CA. *Pear, red stripes, blue background*	3.00	5.00	4.00
Surety, WA. *Apple, stone litho of a steamship in a cove with pine trees, orchards, mountains, red sky with blue letters in the sky, in the corner it says "FROM TREE TO TRADE," a busy red lace type border*	5.00	7.00	6.00
Swan, WA. *Apple, big white swan on the water, orange letters, black background*	6.00	8.00	7.00
Sweet Sue, WA. *Apple, three red apples in the center of the label with an inset in front of them with 1920s lady's face, white letters, brown and green border*	9.00	11.00	10.00
Talisman, CA. *Citrus, three talisman roses against a blue and black background, 10" x 11"*	1.00	3.00	2.00
Tasty Treet, WA. *Apple, three apples, two reds with one golden in the center, blue stripe with white lettering on it, on the tail of the last "t" it says YOUR TASTY TREAT TO HEALTH, black background*	1.50	3.50	2.50

Swan Apples, *black background, white swan,* **$7.00-$10.00**

Hi-Tone Pears, *red background, yellow pears, colorful orchard in center,* **$3.00-$5.00**

Tulip Apples, *black background, blue, orange and yellow tulips,* **$4.00-$6.00**

	Current Price Range		P/Y Average
☐ **The Dalls Cherries.** *Photo of cherries background with the printing on it, small lug label*	.75	2.75	1.75
☐ **Tom Cat, CA.** *Citrus, black and white cat reclining on a pillow, 12½" x 8¾" ....*	20.00	30.00	25.00
☐ **Topaz, WA.** *Apple, there is a big topaz in the word topaz where the o should be, blue background ....*	2.50	4.50	3.50
☐ **Triton, WA.** *Apple, King Neptune sitting on a rock by the ocean holding a spear and an apple, he is wearing a gold crown, the sky is orange and pink, blue and light blue border ..*	5.00	7.00	6.00
☐ **Trojan, WA.** *Apple, Roman Gladiator with sword and shield in front of a man size red apple, he is standing on a globe of the world, with horse mounted gladiators on each side of him, black back round, blue border with a red penline border, rare ....*	15.00	17.00	16.00
☐ **Trout, WA.** *Apple, white arrowhead with Indian brave's head in front of it, large Rainbow trout jumping in the center of the label, white lettering, blue background ....*	2.50	4.50	3.50

	Current Price Range		P/Y Average
☐ **Tulip, WA.** *Apple, three tulips, one red, one yellow and one blue, orange letters, black background*	4.00	6.00	5.00
☐ **Uncle Sam, WA.** *Apple, has a repetition design of one apple, one American shield border and letters of white, also a stone litho of Uncle Sam with tophat in hand, green background*	5.00	7.00	6.00
☐ **Valencia, CA.** *Apple, orchards, farms, hills, mountains, purple sky with lettering*	3.00	5.00	4.00
☐ **Valley Queen Cantaloupes, WA.** *Half a cantaloupe on an Early American dinnerware plate, vase of flowers, farm valley and a plateau range*	1.00	3.00	2.00
☐ **Vandalia, CA.** *Citrus, male peacock against a blue background, 10″ x 11″*	.50	1.50	1.00
☐ **Velvet, CA.** *Citrus, Sunkist orange against draped blue velvet, dated 1929, 10″ x 11″*	.50	1.50	1.00
☐ **Victoria, CA.** *Citrus, portrait of Queen Victoria, 10″ x 11″*	1.00	3.00	2.00

FRUIT JARS

DESCRIPTION: Fruit jars are glass containers which were sold empty and were intended for use in the home preservation of food.

TYPES: There were several types of fruit jars produced including those with either the manufacturer's name or a decorative motif printed on the jar.

MAKER: One of the most familiar names in fruit jars is the Mason jar produced by John Landis Mason in the early 1800s. One of Mason's innovations was a zinc lid which provided greater air tightness.

COMMENTS: Fruit jars of the 1800s are highly collectible. Before 1810, few glass containers were manufactured.

ADDITIONAL TIPS: For more information, consult *The Official Price Guide to Bottles, Old and New,* published by The House of Collectibles.

Ball Fruit Jar,
Perfect Mason,
Aqua, c. 1960,
$3.00 - $5.00

	Current Price Range		P/Y Average
☐ **Anchor Mason's,** *patent in 3 lines, sheared top, Mason seal, qt., clear*	35.00	45.00	40.00
☐ **Atlas EZ Seal,** *in 3 lines all in a circle, sheared top, lightning seal, qt., aqua, lt. blue*	13.00	18.00	15.00
☐ **Atlas E.Z,** *seal all in 3 lines, under bottom Atlas E-Z seal, aqua pt. jar, clear or aqua*	1.50	2.50	2.00
☐ **Atlas Improved Mason** *(c. 1890's), glass lid, metal screw band, aqua or green*	8.00	10.00	9.00
☐ **Atlas Mason's Patent** *(c. 1900), zinc lid, olive green, quart*	18.00	20.00	19.00
☐ **Atlas Mason's Patent Nov. 30, 1858,** *zinc lid, olive green, ½ gallon*	20.00	28.00	24.00
☐ **Atlas Mason's Patent Nov. 30th, 1858,** *screw top, olive green, quart*	20.00	28.00	24.00
☐ **Atlas Mason's Patent,** *screw top, green, quart*	4.00	6.00	5.00
☐ **Atlas Special** *(c. 1910), screw top, clear or blue*	6.00	8.00	7.00
☐ **B & Co. Ld,** *under bottom, stopper finish (neck) per glass stopper, cork jacket (English) 2 Sizes lt. green*	8.00	10.00	9.00
☐ **Baker Bros.** *(c. 1865), wax sealer, groove ring, green or aqua, pint*	30.00	35.00	32.50
☐ **Ball,** *vaseline glass, screw top, pint, quart* . . .	6.00	8.00	7.00
☐ **Ball** *(c. 1890), screw top, green, three sizes* . .	7.00	10.00	8.50
☐ **The Ball** *(c. 1890), screw top, green, quart* . . .	7.00	10.00	8.50
☐ **Ball** *in script,* **Ideal,** *wire top clamp, clear, 3" or 4¾"*	6.00	8.00	6.00

	Current Price Range		P/Y Average
☐ **Ball** *in script,* **Ideal,** *in back, Pat. July 14, 1908, wire top clamp, green or clear, three sizes*	5.00	7.00	6.00
☐ **Ball Ideal Patd July 14 1988,** *(error in date), blue green, pint*	18.00	24.00	21.50
☐ **Boyd Mason** *(c. 1910), zinc lid, olive green, pint, quart*	40.00	50.00	45.00
☐ **Boyd Perfect Mason,** *zinc lid, green, ½ pint, pint, quart*	5.00	7.00	6.00
☐ **Boyds Genuine,** *Mason under bottom inside of diamond IG Co. sheared top, Mason seal, qt., aqua*	3.00	5.00	4.00
☐ **Braun Safetee Mason,** *zinc lid, aqua*	5.00	7.00	6.00
☐ **Brayton & Co. A.P.,** *In half moon, under it San Francisco, Cal. Pressed on laid on ring, Iron closure, William Haller, Patd. Aug. 7, 1860, aqua, quart*	420.00	510.00	465.00
☐ **Brelle Jar,** *glass lid and wire clamp, wide mouth, clear, quart*	15.00	20.00	17.50
☐ **Brighton** *(c. 1890), glass lid, metal wire clamp, clear, amber or amethyst, quart*	50.00	60.00	55.00
☐ **Geo. D. Brown & Co.** *(c. 1875), glass lid and heavy metal clamp, green, quart*	60.00	70.00	65.00
☐ **The Burlington** *(c. 1880), zinc band, clear or aqua, quart*	40.00	60.00	50.00
☐ **Decker's Iowana,** *glass lid and wire bail, clear, quart*	3.00	5.00	4.00
☐ **Dexter** *(c. 1865), zinc band with glass insert, aqua, quart*	30.00	60.00	45.00
☐ **Diamond Fruit Jar,** *glass lid and full wire bail, clear, quart*	3.00	5.00	4.00
☐ **Dictator D.D.I. Holcomb Patented Dec. 14th, 1869,** *wax seal, blue, quart*	75.00	100.00	87.00
☐ **Dillon** *(c. 1890), wax seal, round, aqua, quart .*	10.00	12.00	11.00
☐ **Dominion** *(c. 1886), zinc band and glass insert, round, clear, quart*	75.00	100.00	87.00
☐ **Dominion Widemouth Special,** *zinc lid, round, clear, quart*	2.00	3.00	2.50
☐ **Doolittle, The Self Sealer,** *glass lid, wide mouth, clear, quart*	50.00	75.00	62.00
☐ **Drey Ever Seal,** *glass lid and full wire bail, clear or amethyst, quart*	2.00	3.00	2.50
☐ **Economy,** *metal lid and spring wire clamp, amethyst, pint, quart, ½ gallon*	2.50	4.50	3.50
☐ **Economy, Trade Mark,** *clear or amethyst, quart*	2.50	4.50	3.50
☐ **Economy, Trade Mark, Pat. June 9, 1903,** *clear or amethyst, quart*	2.50	4.50	3.50
☐ **E.G.Co.** *(monogram)* **Imperial,** *clear, quart*	9.00	12.00	10.50
☐ **Electric,** *glass lid and wire bail, round, aqua, quart*	10.00	12.00	10.50
☐ **Electric Fruit Jar** *(c. 1900-15), glass lid and metal clamp, round, aqua, quart*	60.00	70.00	65.00
☐ **Electroglas N.W.,** *clear, quart*	3.00	4.50	3.75
☐ **Empire,** *in maltese cross, clear, quart*	8.00	11.00	9.50

	Current Price Range		P/Y Average

☐ **Empire** *(c. 1860), glass stopper, deep blue, quart* 55.00 75.00 65.00

☐ **The Empire** *(c. 1866), glass lid with iron lugs to fasten it, aqua, quart* 65.00 75.00 70.00

☐ **Erie Fruit Jar** *(c. 1890), screw top, clear, quart* 75.00 100.00 87.00

☐ **Erie Lightning,** *clear, quart* 20.00 25.00 22.50

☐ **Eureka** *(c. 1864), wax dipped cork or other, extending neck, aqua, pint* 35.00 45.00 40.00

☐ **Eureka, Pat. Feb 9th, 1864, Eureka Jar Co. Dunbar, W. VA.** *(c. 1870), aqua, quart* 14.00 20.00 17.00

☐ **Everlasting Improved Jar** *(c. 1904), in oval, quart* 15.00 20.00 17.50

☐ **Everlasting Jar** *(c. 1904), glass lid and double wire hook fastener, round, green, pint, quart, ½ gallon* 15.00 20.00 17.50

☐ **Excelsior** *(c. 1880-90), zinc screw band and glass insert, aqua, quart* 48.00 55.00 51.00

☐ **Gilberds Improved Jar** *(c. 1885), glass lid and wire bail, aqua, quart* 40.00 55.00 47.00

☐ **Gilberds Jar** *(c. 1884), glass lid and screw band, aqua, quart* 55.00 75.00 65.00

☐ **Gilchrist** *(c. 1895), zinc lid and dome shaped opal liner, wide mouth, aqua green, quart* . . . 7.00 10.00 8.50

☐ **Glassboro** *(c. 1880-1900), trademark, zinc band and glass insert, light to dark green, three sizes* 15.00 20.00 17.50

☐ **Glassboro Improved** *(c.1880), wide zinc screw band and glass insert, aqua or pale green, quart* 15.00 20.00 17.50

☐ **Glenshaw G. Mason,** *(G in square), clear, quart* 3.00 5.00 4.00

☐ **Globe,** *glass lid, metal neck band, top wire bail and bail clamp, amber, green or clear, quart* 12.00 18.00 15.00

☐ **Glocker, Pat. 1911 Other Pending Sanitary,** *aqua, quart* 12.00 15.00 13.50

☐ **Haines** *(c. 1882), glass lid and iron clamp, green, quart* 40.00 55.00 47.00

☐ **Haines Improved** *(c. 1870), glass lid and top wire bail, aqua green, quart* 175.00 200.00 187.00

☐ **Hamilton Glass Works,** *green, quart* 14.00 20.00 17.00

☐ **Hansee's Place Home Jar,** *pat. Dec. 19 1899 under bottom, aqua, 7"* 40.00 50.00 45.00

☐ **Harris** *(c. 1860), metal lid, ground top, deep green, quart* 125.00 150.00 137.00

☐ **Harris Improved** *(c. 1875-1880), glass lid and iron clamp, green, quart* 45.00 60.00 52.00

☐ **Haserot Company** *(c. 1915-1925), zinc lid, green, quart* 12.00 15.00 13.50

☐ **The Haserot Company, Cleveland Mason Patent,** *screw top, ground top, green, quart* . . 15.00 18.00 16.50

☐ **E.C. Hazard & Co., Shrewsbury, N.J.,** *wire clamp, aqua, quart* 10.00 12.00 11.00

☐ **Hazel,** *glass lid and wire bail, aqua, quart* . . . 12.00 15.00 13.50

☐ **Hazel-Atlas Lightning Seal,** *full wire bail and glass lid, green, quart* 6.00 10.00 8.00

	Current Price Range		P/Y Average
☐ H. & D. *(c. 1915), glass top, metal band*	5.00	7.00	6.00
☐ Helme's Railroad Mills, *amber, 7¾"*	12.00	15.00	13.50
☐ Helmes Railroad Mills, *amber, quart*	12.00	16.00	14.00
☐ The Improved Hero, *glass top, metal band, green, base, Patd Nov. 26, 1867*	15.00	20.00	17.50
☐ Hero, *with cross and lightning at top, green, quart*	25.00	30.00	27.50
☐ The Heroine, *wide zinc screw band and glass insert, light green, quart*	25.00	30.00	27.50
☐ The High Grade, *zinc screw-on top, clear*	20.00	25.00	22.50
☐ Kerr Economy Trade Mark, *Chicago on base, metal lid and narrow clip band, clear or amethyst, pint, quart*	2.00	4.00	3.00
☐ Kerr Economy *in script, under it* TRADE MARK, *under bottom Kerr Glass Mfg. Co., Sand Spring, Okla., clear, 3¾"*	2.00	4.00	3.00
☐ Same as above, except Chicago Pat. under bottom	2.00	4.00	3.00
☐ Kerr Wide Mouth Mason, *clear, ½ pint*	15.00	22.00	18.00
☐ KG, *in oval, wire clamp, clear, quart*	1.50	3.00	2.25
☐ The Kilner Jar, *zinc screw band and glass insert, clear, quart*	2.00	4.00	3.00
☐ King, *full wire bail and glass lid, clear or amethyst, quart*	10.00	12.00	11.00
☐ Kinsella True Mason *(c. 1874), zinc lid, clear, quart*	6.00	8.00	7.00
☐ Kline Pat. Oct. 27, 1863, *a on glass stopper, aqua, quart with jar*	100.00	150.00	125.00
☐ Kline A. *(c. 1863), glass fitting lid and clamp, aqua, quart*	25.00	30.00	27.50
☐ Leotric, *in oval, glass lid, ground top, medium green, quart*	8.50	10.00	9.25
☐ Lightning Trade Mark Registered U.S. Patent Office, *Putnam 4 on bottom, lid with dates, aqua, pint*	2.00	4.25	3.12
☐ Lightning Trade Mark, *Putnam 199 on bottom, aqua, ½ gallon*	6.00	8.00	7.00
☐ Same as above, except wire and lid, pint	6.00	8.00	7.00
☐ Lightning Trademark, *glass top, round, aqua, 6"*	7.00	10.00	8.50
☐ Same as above, except Putnam on base, aqua, quart, ½ gallon	8.00	11.00	9.50
☐ Same as above, except amber, pint, quart, ½ gallon	15.00	20.00	17.50
☐ Lightning, *Putnam 824 under bottom, sheared top, aqua*	9.00	12.00	10.50
☐ Lindell Glass Co. *(c. 1870), wax sealer, amber, quart*	70.00	100.00	85.00
☐ Lockport Mason, *zinc top, aqua, ½ gallon* . . .	4.50	8.00	6.25
☐ Lockport Mason, Improved, *zinc screw band, glass insert, aqua, quart*	4.00	6.00	5.00
☐ Lorillard & Co, *on base, glass top, metal clamp, amber, pint*	12.00	15.00	13.50
☐ P. Lorillard & Co., *sheared top, amber, 6¼"* .	10.00	12.00	11.00
☐ Lustre R.E. Tongue & Bros. Co. Inc. Phila., *in circle or shield, wire clamp, quart*	6.00	8.00	7.00

	Current Price Range		P/Y Average
☐ **Mason's**, *swirled milk glass, 7¼"*	75.00	90.00	82.00
☐ **Mason's CG, Patent Nov. 30, 1858,** *zinc lid, green, quart*	5.00	8.00	6.50
☐ **Mason's-C-Patent Nov. 30th 1858,** *green, 7"* .	10.00	12.00	11.00
☐ **Mason's Improved Butter Jar,** *sheared top, aqua, ½ gallon*	10.00	14.00	12.00
☐ **Mason's Improved,** *ground top with zinc lid, quart, blue*	7.00	14.00	10.00
☐ **Mason's Improved,** *Hero F J Co. in cross above, zinc band and glass lid covered with many patent dates, earliest Feb. 12, '56, aqua*	10.00	14.00	12.00
☐ **Mason's Improved,** *zinc screw band and glass insert, aqua or green, pint*	10.00	14.00	12.00
☐ **Mason's Keystone** *(c. 1869), zinc screw band and glass insert, aqua, quart*	15.00	20.00	17.50
☐ **Mason's "M" Patent Nov. 30th 1858,** *green, 7"*	5.00	8.00	6.50
☐ **Mason's,** *under it* **"M" Patent Nov. 30th 1898,** *screw top, aqua, quart*	11.00	15.00	13.00
☐ **Mason's Patent 1858,** *zinc lid, amber or green, pint*	15.00	20.00	17.50
☐ **Peerless,** *wax dipped cork, green, quart*	55.00	75.00	65.00
☐ **The Penn,** *metal cap and wax seal, green, quart*	30.00	35.00	32.50
☐ **Peoria Pottery,** *metal top and wax seal, glazed brown stoneware, quart*	15.00	18.00	16.50
☐ **Perfection,** *double wire bail and glass top, clear, quart*	35.00	40.00	37.50
☐ **The New Perfection,** *clear or amethyst, ½ gallon*	19.00	26.00	22.00
☐ **Perfect Seal,** *full wire bail and glass top, clear, quart*	4.00	6.00	5.00
☐ **Perfect Seal** *in shield,* **Made In Canada,** *clear, quart*	1.50	2.50	2.00
☐ **Pet,** *glass stopper, green, quart*	45.00	60.00	52.00
☐ **Pet,** *glass stopper and wire bail, aqua, quart* .	30.00	35.00	32.50
☐ **H.W. Pettit, Wesville N.H.,** *under bottom, ground top, aqua, quart*	8.00	12.00	10.00
☐ **The Goragas Pierie Co., Phila., Royal Peanutene,** *sheared top, clear, quart*	9.00	12.00	10.50
☐ **Pine Deluxe Jar,** *full wire bail and glass top, clear, quart*	4.00	6.00	5.00
☐ **Pine** *(P in square)* **Mason,** *zinc top, clear, quart*	4.00	5.00	4.50
☐ **Porcelain Lined,** *zinc top, aqua, quart*	15.00	20.00	17.50
☐ *Same as above, except green, 2 gallon*	12.00	17.00	14.50
☐ **Potter & Bodine Philadelphia,** *in script, glass top and clamp, aqua, quart*	85.00	95.00	90.00
☐ **Premium Coffeyville Kas.,** *wire ring and glass top, clear or amethyst, quart*	14.00	18.00	16.00
☐ **Premium Improved,** *glass top and side wire clips, clear, quart*	15.00	20.00	17.50
☐ **Presto,** *screw-on top, clear*	2.50	3.25	2.82
☐ **Presto Fruit Jar,** *screw-on top, clear*	2.50	3.25	2.82

COOK-BOOK
OF
TESTED RECIPES

Collecting involves so much more than the mere acquisition of objects. One of the most enjoyable and interesting aspects of collecting is research. Today's collector is more informed than ever before and pursues knowledge by every method available. For example, one very popular field is kitchen collectibles. Indeed, many collectors have charming kitchens filled with old graniteware, baskets, cast iron, tin, treen and stoneware. Many take great pleasure in using their kitchen collectibles to cook and serve authentic old recipes gleaned from vintage cookbooks. These old cookbooks are highly prized by collectors who enjoy them not only for their quaint phrasing but also for the insight they provide into the kitchens of bygone eras. The enjoyment of collecting kitchen items is enhanced by the knowledge gained from reading these old cookbooks.

Therefore, for both the pleasure and education of our readers, we have reprinted a charming turn of the century cookbook entitled Cook-Book of Tested Recipes in its entirety. This book was originally published in 1896 as a fund raiser by "the ladies of the Presbyterian Church, corner of High Street and Second Avenue, Union City, Pennsylvania." Since 1896, fund raising cookbooks have grown in popularity and are published by church groups, women's clubs, and garden clubs. In fact, just about every non-profit organization in the country produces one. We thought you would enjoy reading this early version of what has become an American phenomenon; the privately printed fund-raiser cookbook.

This delightful cookbook not only contains delicious recipes, it also includes wonderful old advertisements. These ads provide us with an opportunity to travel back in time to life in America at the turn of the century.

Many collectors enjoy preparing authentic old recipes and the Cook-Book of Tested Recipes provides hundreds which are easily made in today's kitchens. It was common during the turn of the century to measure ingredients by weight such as "1 lb. flour," etc. The ladies of the Presbyterian Church of Union City, Pennsylvania have provided us with a conversion chart which translates weight into measure. It is found on page 448 at the beginning of the cake chapter.

We hope you enjoy this new addition to The Official Price Guide to Antiques and Other Collectibles. Bon Appetit!

Cook=Book

OF

Tested Recipes,

Prepared by the Ladies

OF THE

Presbyterian Church,

Union City, Pa.

1896.

THE TIMES PRINT, UNION CITY, PA.
1896.

To those that never learned the culinary art,
Buy this book and you will act well your part ;
It is for laborer, statesman or king,
It has the right directions for cooking everything.

"We may live without poetry, music or art,
We may live without conscience, and live without heart ;
We may live without friends ; we may live without books ;
But civilized man cannot live without cooks.
He may live without books,—what is knowledge but grieving?
He may live without hope,—what is hope but deceiving?
He may live without love,—what is passion but pining?
But where is the *man* that can live without dining."

My bread and cake are baked with speed,
And I have time to stop and read ;
Because the dough I need not knead,
With Royal Baking Powder.

"Forsake not the assembling of yourselves together."

Presbyterian Church,

Of Union City, Pa.

Corner of High Street and Second Avenue.

A. J. HERRIES, Pastor,

Schedule of Regular Meetings.

SABBATH.—Preaching Service at 11 A. M. and 7.30 P. M.

SABBATH.—Bible School at 12.15 P. M.

SABBATH.—Y. P. S. C. E. Prayer Meeting at 6.30 P. M.

THURSDAY.—Prayer Meeting, 7.30 P. M.

LAST TUESDAY OF MONTH.—Women's Missionary Meeting, 3 P. M.

SEATS FREE.   STRANGERS INVITED.

Table of Contents.

BREAD AND BISCUITS... 34
CAKE.. 6
COOKIES.. 44
CONFECTIONERY 50
CROQUETTES.. 54
DOUGHNUTS... 56
DRINKS... 60
ICES.. 70
JELLIES... 70
MEATS.. 74
MISCELLANEOUS... 131
OYSTERS AND FISH... 82
OMELETS... 88
POULTRY... 90
PUDDINGS AND SAUCES.. 92
PASTRY... 109
PICKLES.. 113
PRESERVES AND SWEET PICKLES........................... 116
SALADS... 118
SCALLOPS.. 122
SOUPS... 123
SUNDRIES.. 125
TIME TABLE FOR COOKING VEGETABLES 127
VEGETABLES.. 127

L. S. CLOUGH,

WHOLESALE DEALER IN

Hardwood Lumber.....

Office and Yard, Warren, Pa.
Mills and Yard at McCray's, Pa.

WE SOLICIT STOCK LISTS OF ALL KINDS OF SHIPPING
DRY HARDWOOD LUMBER.

When Prices and Quantity are an Inducement, will inspect at your Mill.

WE PAY CASH.

Cake.

Measures and Weights.

One quart sifted flour (heaped) weighs 1 lb.
Three coffeecups sifted flour (level) weigh 1 lb.
Four teacups sifted flour (level) weigh 1 lb.
One quart sifted corn meal weighs 1 lb 1 oz.
One pint soft butter (packed) weighs 1 lb.
Two teacups soft butter (packed) weigh 1 lb.
One and one-third pints powdered sugar weigh 1 lb.
Two coffeecups powdered sugar (level) weigh 1 lb.
One and one-half coffeecups granulated sugar (level) weigh
1 lb.
Two teacups granulated sugar (level) weigh 1 lb.
One and three-quarter coffeecups coffee A sugar (level) weigh
1 lb.
Two teacups coffee A sugar (heaped) weigh 1 lb.
One and three-quarter coffeecups best brown sugar (level)
weigh 1 lb.
Two and one half teacups best brown sugar (level) weigh 1 lb.
Three and one half teacups corn meal (level) equal 1 qt.
One tablespoon (heaped) granulated sugar weighs 1 oz.
Two tablespoons (rounded) powdered sugar, or flour,
weigh 1 oz.
One tablespoon (rounded) soft butter weighs 1 oz.
Seven tablespoons granulated sugar (heaped) equal 1
teacup.
Six tablespoons sifted flour, or meal, (heaped) equal 1
teacup.
Four tablespoons soft butter (heaped) equal 1 teacup.
Two teaspoons (heaped) flour, sugar, or meal, equal 1
heaping tablespoon.

Atkins Cake.

Mrs. H. C. Cheney.

One cup of sugar, one-third cup of butter, one and one-half
cups of flour, two teaspoons baking powder, one-half cup of milk,
two eggs. Beat the whites and yokes separately, then beat together; flavor.

6

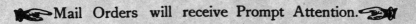

Snow Drift Cake.

Mrs. J. R. Mulkie.

Three cups of flour, two of sugar, one half of butter, one of sweet milk, two heaping teaspoons Royal baking powder, the whites of five eggs, beaten to a stiff froth, cream, butter and sugar, add milk and flour, lastly the eggs, put in the flour and baking powder and stir the cake well before the eggs are added. Do all the mixing with the hands.

Sponge Cake.

Mrs. J. R. Mulkie.

Two eggs, one cup of sugar, one and one-half cups of flour, one and one-half teaspoons Royal baking powder, one-half cup of boiling water; put on the last thing. Bake slowly.

I am partial to Royal baking powder.

Sponge Cake.

Mrs. George Read.

One and one-half cups fine granulated sugar, four eggs, beaten twenty minutes with sugar; pour two-thirds cup boiling water over this; add two cups flour, two teaspoons baking powder. Flavor with orange or vanilla; little salt.

Princess Cake.

Mrs. James Woods.

One cup butter, three cups sugar (pulverized), one cup sweet milk, four and one-half flour, ten eggs, whites only; one tablespoon baking powder, one teaspoon lemon, one-fourth citron, sliced.

Pond Lily Cake.

Mrs. E. P. Clarke.

Whites of four eggs, one-half cup butter, two-thirds cup milk, two and one-half cups Pond Lily flour, one and one-half cups sugar, three level teaspoons baking powder.

Pound Cake.

Mrs. A. G. Sweet.

Two cups sugar, one cup butter, one cup sweet milk, two cups flour, ten eggs; season with nutmeg.

8

Ocean Cake.

Mrs. Arthur Young.

Two cups sugar, one cup butter creamed, yolks of three eggs, one small cup sweet milk, three cups flour, two teaspoons baking powder, whites of three eggs beaten stiff and added last; flavor to taste.

Angels' Food.

Mrs. S. G. Shepard.

Whites of eleven eggs beaten stiff, one and one-half tumblers granulated sugar, one tumbler flour, one teaspoon cream of tartar, one of vanilla. Beat whites of eggs stiff, add sugar gently to eggs, then the flour and cream of tartar, lastly vanilla; bake in moderate oven forty-five minutes. Sift flour and sugar seven times each, and measure before sifting.

Angel Cake.

Mrs. C. B. Geer.

Whites of nine large or ten smaller eggs, one and one quarter cups sifted granulated sugar, one cup sifted flour, one-half teaspoon cream tartar, a pinch of salt added to eggs before beating; after sifting flour four or five times, measure and set aside one cup; then sift and measure one and one-quarter cups granulated sugar, beat white of eggs about half, add cream tartar, and beat until very, very stiff; stir in sugar thoroughly and flour very lightly; flavor to taste. Bake in a moderate oven from forty to sixty minutes. Do not open oven door for twenty minutes at least.

Angels' Food.

Mrs. Arthur Treat.

Sift one tumbler flour four times, measure after sifting; sift one and one-half tumblers granulated sugar twice, measure after sifting and return to seive; now beat the whites of eleven eggs to a stiff froth, add one teaspoon vanilla. Put them on a large platter and sift the sugar over them, add one teaspoon cream tartar to the flour, mix thoroughly and sift on top of eggs and sugar. Stir all together very gently, not stirring any more than is necessary to mix evenly. This should be put together quickly and turned immediately in the pan (not greased), and baked in a moderate oven forty minutes. Do not open oven door for first twenty minutes.

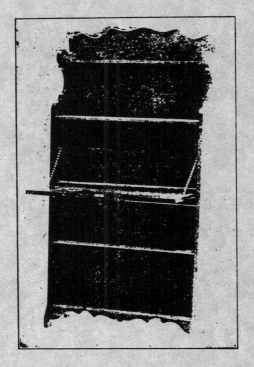

HANSEN discovered the North Pole, but the people have long since discovered that we make the best, prettiest and cheapest

Oak Book Case and Desk,

in all that territory lying between the North Pole and the South Pole. We have'nt sold to all the people yet, but they are coming our way pretty rapidly. How is it with you?

Price, only $4.00.

Size, 60 ins. high ; 30 ins. wide ; 10 ins. deep.
¼-inch brass rod for curtain.

NOVELTY WOOD WORKS,
Union City, Pa.

11

White Cake.

Mrs. D. A. W.

Two cups granulated sugar, one-half cup butter, two-thirds cup sweet milk, three cups flour, three teaspoons baking powder, whites of six eggs beaten stiff, and added the last thing; flavor to taste.

White Cake.

Mrs. W. E. Jackson.

Whites of four eggs well whipped, one and one-half cups granulated sugar, one-half cup butter, one cup sweet milk, two teaspoons baking powder, two cups sifted flour, one teaspoon vanilla.

White Cake.

Mrs. Addie C. Burnham.

One and one half cups sugar, two-thirds of butter, one-half of milk, whites of eight eggs, two and a half cups flour, two teaspoons baking powder.

Bride's Cake.

Mrs. V. D.

Whites of twelve eggs, three cups sugar, cup of butter, one of milk, four small cups flour, one-half cup corn starch, two teaspoons cream of tartar in flour, and one of soda in half the milk; or you can use two teaspoons Royal baking powder, half teaspoon each Royce's lemon and vanilla.

White Mountain Cake.

Mrs. H. N. Neal.

Two cups pulverized sugar, one-half cup butter creamed, one-half cup sweet milk, two and one-half cups flour, three teaspoons baking powder, whites of eight eggs.

Snow Cake.

Mrs. James S. Thompson.

One-half cup butter, one cup sugar, one and one-half cups flour, one-half cup sweet milk, whites of four eggs, one teaspoon baking powder; flavor with lemon.

The Brownies' Favorite.

Abner Royce.

Sift, measure, and set aside two-thirds cup flour, one cup granulated sugar; beat yolks of five eggs thoroughly, wash beater; beat whites of seven eggs about half, add a third of a teaspoon of

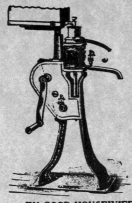

13

cream tartar, and beat very stiff, one-half teaspoon of Royce's Violet vanilla, stir in sugar lightly, then yolks thoroughly, then flour. Bake in tube pan from thirty to fifty minutes.

Sunshine Cake.

Mrs. H. C. Cheney.

Two cups of sugar, three cups of flour, one cup of milk, two teaspoonsful Royal baking powder, three-fourths cup butter, yolks of eleven eggs; flavor with Royce's vanilla.
I always use Royal baking powder.

Delicate Cake.

Mrs. C. B. Geer.

Whites of four eggs, two cups sugar, one cup of milk, two-thirds cup of butter, three cups flour, two teaspoons baking powder; flavoring.

Lemon Cream Cake.

Mrs. C. B. Geer.

One cup sugar, one-half cup butter, two eggs, one-half cup milk, two and one-half cups flour, two teaspoonsful baking powder.
Jelly—The juice and grated rind of one lemon, two tablespoonsful cornstarch, one cup boiling water, one egg, three-fourths cup sugar, a little butter.

Delicate Cake.

Mrs. C. B. Geer.

Two cups of sugar, one cup butter, one cup milk, one cup of cornstarch, two and one-half cups flour, whites of six eggs, two teaspoons baking powder; flavoring.

Layer Cake.

Mrs. D. A. W.

Two cups sugar, butter size of an egg, one cup sweet milk, two and one-half cups flour, three eggs, two teaspoons baking powder.

Madge's One-Egg Cake.

One even cup of sugar, one heaping teaspoon of butter, one egg, mixed to a cream with the hands; add one cup cold water, two even cups flour, two teaspoons baking powder, sifted with flour.

14

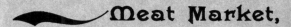
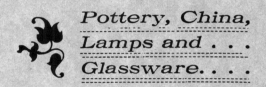
15

Fig Cake.

Mrs. Herries.

Two cups sugar, one-half cup butter creamed, half cup sweet milk, two and a half cups flour, sifted twice, two and a half teaspoons baking powder sifted in flour, whites of eight eggs. Bake in layers and put together with boiled frosting.

Frosting.

Boil together two cups sugar, a little water until it threads, pour slowly over the well-beaten whites of two eggs, beat till cool; spread a thin layer of frosting over cake, then a layer of figs cut in pieces, then frosting.

Ice Cream Cake.

Mrs. M. W. Shreve.

Two cups sugar, one cup butter, one cup sweet milk, three cups flour, three teaspoons baking powder, whites of five eggs. Bake in two layers; put together with boiled frosting.

Ice Cream Cake.

Mrs. J. R. Mulkie.

One and one-half cups of sugar, one-half cup butter. stir to a cream, add the whites of four eggs, one at a time without previously beating; one-half cup of sweet milk. two and one-half cups flour, two teaspoons Royal baking powder. Bake in layers.

Ice Cream—Two cups white sugar, boil to a soft wax, whites of two eggs, tartartic acid, size of a pea, dissolved in water.

Lemon Jelly Cake.

Mrs. F. E. McLean.

One and one-half cups of sugar, one-half of butter, one-half of sweet milk, two and one-half of flour, three eggs, whites and yolks beaten separately, and two teaspoons baking powder.

Jelly—One cup of sugar, one egg, grate the rind and use the juice of one lemon, one tablespoon of water, one teaspoon flour; put your dish in a kettle of boiling water, and let it come to a boil; have your cake ready and put your jelly between the layers.

Peach Cake.

Mrs. L. D. Rockwell.

Three eggs, one cup sugar, one-half cup thin sweet cream, one and one-half cups flour, one teaspoon baking powder, a little salt and flavoring. Bake in one tin, split it, and spread with canned peaches. Then pour over whipped cream; also put cream on the top layer.

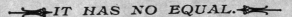

17

Orange Cream Cake.
Miss Daisy Bissell.

Three-fourths cup butter, one of sugar, one cup sweet milk, two and one-half flour, two teaspoons baking powder, whites of three eggs. Bake in layers.

Cream Filling—One cup sugar, one half cup cream, one teaspoon cornstarch; boil till thick, and add orange flavoring.

Orange Cake.
Mrs. P. H. T.

Two cups of sugar, one-half cup of butter, one-half cup of cold water, three cups of flour, yolks of three eggs, and whites of four beaten well, three teaspoonsful baking powder, juice and grated rind of one orange. Whites of two eggs well beaten, add sugar until almost too thick to stir, then add juice and grated rind of one orange, and spread between the layers.

Orange Cake.
Mrs. George Burnham.

Two cups of sugar, yolks of five eggs, whites of four, two cups flour, two teaspoons baking powder, one-half cup cold water, pinch of salt, grated rind and juice of one large or two small oranges; saving a little juice for filling.

Cream—Two-thirds cup sugar, same of water, one heaping teaspoon cornstarch, one egg; flavor with orange juice. Cook till thick. Spread between layers; frost top.

Marsh-Mallow Cake.
Mrs. Bissell.

Two cups granulated sugar, three cups flour, one cup sweet milk, one-half butter, whites of five eggs, beaten stiff, two teaspoons baking powder.

Filling—Usual boiled frosting, melt five marsh-mallows, and stir into icing; beat until cool.

Sponge Cake With Filling.
Mrs. H. S. Thompson.

Three eggs well beaten, one and a half cups of sugar, one cup flour, well beaten together; one-half cup cold water, a pinch of salt, one cup more of flour, one heaping teaspoon baking powder; flavor with vanilla. Bake in a large, square tin. When done cut the cake open, as two layers would be, and put the prepared filling between and frost.

Filling—Two eggs well beaten, one and one-fourth cups of sugar, one-half cup flour, well stirred, one cup sweet milk; stir this in one cup of boiling milk. Cook until thick and flavor.

Date Cake.
Mrs. W. J. Sloan.

One cup sugar, one-half cup sweet milk, one half cup butter, two cups flour, two eggs, two teaspoons baking powder; bake in layers.

Filling—One cup dates, one cup raisins, chopped fine, one-half cup water, one cup sugar; boil until thick and spread between layers. Use boiled frosting for top layer.

Caramel Cake.
Mrs. Bissell.

Three cups flour, two cups granulated sugar, one cup sweet milk, one-half cup butter, whites of five eggs, beaten stiff, two teaspoons baking powder.

Caramel—Two cups sugar, one cup milk, one half cup chocolate, yolk of one egg, piece of butter size of walnut; flavor with vanilla.

Caramel Cake.
Mrs. Coleman.

One cup of sugar, one-half cup of sweet milk, one-half cup butter, two cups of flour, two eggs, two teaspoonsful Royal baking powder.

Filling and Frosting—Two cups sugar, two-thirds cup of sweet milk, butter size of an egg, boil fifteen minutes, beat until cold, and flavor with vanilla.

Devil Cake (Elegant).
Mrs. Caflisch.

Dark Part, No. 1—One cup brown sugar, one cup grated chocolate, half cup sweet milk; boil this until dissolved. Spices are nice in this part.

No. 2—One cup of brown sugar, half cup butter, yolks of three eggs, half cup sweet milk, two heaping cups of flour, one teaspoon of soda; when cool put No. 1 in No. 2. Flavor. Bake slowly and carefully.

Devil's Food Cake.
Miss Madge McLean.

Part 1—One cup of brown sugar, two and a half cups flour, one-half cup butter, three-fourths cup sweet milk, yolks of three eggs, one teaspoon soda sifted into flour.

Part 2—One cup grated chocolate, one-half cup sweet milk, one cup brown sugar. Set part 2 on stove until it melts, but do not let it boil. When cold stir into part 1. Bake in layers and put together with chocolate or white frosting.

Henry L. Stem, M. D.,

Homeopathic Physician and Surgeon.

Office and Residence,
Over Van Dusen & Seigfried's Clothing Store,
Yealey Block,

UNION CITY, PA.

Office Hours, 10 to 12 a. m , 1 to 4 p. m., and evenings.

Dr. W. J. HUMPHREY,

Office on Main Street,

UNION CITY, PA.

A. C. Sherwood, M. D.,

PHYSICIAN AND SURGEON.

Office at Residence,
Corner First Avenue and High Street,

UNION CITY, PA.

Office Hours, 10 to 12 a. m , 2 to 5 and 7 to 9 p. m.

L. D. ROCKWELL, M. D.,

Office and Residence,

South Main Street.   Union City, Pa.

21

Chocolate Cake.

Mrs. D. B. Honeywell.

Two cups of brown sugar, three-quarter cups butter, one cup sour milk, one-third cup grated chocolate, three cups flour, three eggs, one teaspoonful cloves, one teaspoonful cinnamon, one teaspoonful soda. Bake in a loaf. Very fine, indeed.

Black Chocolate Cake (Fine).

Mrs. James Woods.

Two cups sugar, one-half butter, two and a half flour, one-half boiling water, one-fourth cake chocolate, two eggs, two teaspoonsful baking powder.

Chocolate Layer Cake.

Mrs. James Woods.

Three eggs (reserve the white of one for frosting), two-thirds cup grated chocolate, one-half cup of sweet milk. Boil chocolate, eggs and milk until thick, stirring all the time. Then add one cup of sugar, one-half cup milk or water, one tablespoon vanilla, one and one-half cups flour. Bake in three layers; put together with boiled frosting.

Chocolate Cake.

Mrs. H. M. Rogers.

One-third cup Baker's chocolate, one-half cup milk, one cup sugar ; cook all over boiling water until it thickens, then let cool. Cake : One cup sugar, one-half cup butter, three-fourths cup milk, two and one half cups flour, two eggs, three teaspoons baking powder, and mix in the part previously cooked and bake.

Frosting—Four cups sugar, whites of four eggs, one-half pint water. Boil water and sugar; add eggs.

Almond Cake.

Mrs. Bissell.

Three-fourths cup butter, two cups granulated sugar, three cups flour, sifted three times. Add to creamed sugar and butter two cups of the flour, a small amount at a time ; sift the remaining cup of flour, with two teaspoons of baking powder, and whip lightly into the batter, adding quickly the whites of twelve eggs, well beaten. Bake in four layers in deep cake tins.

Filling—Beat one half cup of thick sour cream until light, add yolks of six eggs, well beaten; one-half cup powdered sugar, one-half teaspoon extract of almonds, one pound blanched almonds, chopped fine. Cover top with soft icing. Decorate with cream almonds.

JOHNSON & HUNTER.

THE LEADING HOUSE IN EVERY
RESPECT FOR

DRY GOODS,

Foreign and Domestic

Fancy Goods,
Notions,
Dress Goods,
Silks, Hosiery,
Gloves, Underwear,
Waists, Skirts,
Lace Curtains,
Cloaks and Capes.

JOHNSON & HUNTER,

——— UP-TO-DATE ———

Men's,
Boys'
and
Youth's,

Women's,
Misses',
Children's
and
Infants'

→❈ SHOES. ❈←

UNION CITY, - - PENNA.

We cater to your trade and it is our aim to thoroughly
please our customers.

☞ IT WILL PAY YOU TO COME AND SEE US. ☜

23

French Cream Cake.

Mrs. P. H. Thompson.

Four eggs, one and a half cups sugar, beat well together ; two tablespoons cold water, a little salt, one and two-thirds cups flour, two even teaspoons Royal baking powder.

Cream—One-half pint milk, let boil; then add two small tablespoons cornstarch, and two eggs well beaten ; stir in while boiling. When cool add butter size of an egg. Sweeten and flavor to taste.

Nut Filling for Cake.

Mrs. J. C. McLean.

One cup of cream, sweet or sour, one cup hickorynut meat, chopped, one cup sugar. Cook till thick.

Cream Frosting.

Add to white of one egg, equal measure of cold water, stir into this confectioner's sugar until the right consistency to spread ; flavor. This will remain soft and creamy, and cut without breaking.

Milk Frosting.

One cup white sugar, five tablespoons sweet milk, one-half teaspoon butter. Boil about five minutes, stir until cool and spread on cold cake.

Frosting.

Mrs. A. G. Sweet.

Whites of two eggs, five tablespoons granulated sugar. Beat a little and put over a tea kettle and steam fifteen or twenty minutes. Stir until cold. Flavor to taste.

Angel Cakelets.

Mrs. M. Green.

Sift together four times one-half cup of fine granulated sugar, one half cup of flour, one-half level teaspoon of cream tartar. Beat the whites of four eggs until stiff and dry. Then gradually mix in sugar and flour ; flavor with one-half teaspoon almond, rose or vanilla extract. Drop with a teaspoon on buttered paper an inch or two apart, sprinkle with sugar ; bake in a moderate oven fifteen minutes. This quantity makes two dozen.

Cream Puffs.

Mrs. A. G. Sweet.

One cup boiling water, one cup flour, one-half cup butter, four eggs. Place a small tin on the stove containing water and

TO ONE SPOONFUL

Of common sense, add a little money, together with a pleasant walk, and the result? Why, don't you see? You have purchased some beautiful articles at

N. B.—This recipe should be tried often, for the old saying is "practice makes perfect."

Goodnough's Jewelry Store.

KING & KEIM,

At No. 34 South Centre St., CORRY,

Are giving great bargains in

Furniture.

LATE STYLES, LOW PRICES, FAIR DEALING.

**Call and see them before you buy.
They can and will save you money.**

WE ARE PRACTICAL UNDERTAKERS AND EMBALMERS.

Our prices in this line are as low as good work can be done for.   .   .   .   .

Respectfully, KING & KEIM.

butter, let come to a boil, beat in flour at once, beat until the whole cleaves from the tin; remove from stove and beat in the eggs, one at a time. Drop on a buttered tin, and bake in an even oven twenty minutes. When done let cool, open and fill with whipped cream flavored.

Cream Puffs.
Mrs. J. R. Mulkie.

One cup hot water, one-half cup butter. Boil together, and while boiling stir in one cup dry flour. Remove from fire and stir to a smooth paste. After this cools stir in three unbeaten eggs, stirring five minutes. Drop teaspoonful on a buttered tin and bake in a quick oven thirty minutes, being careful not to open the door oftener than is absolutely necessary. Do not let them touch each other in the pan. This makes twelve puffs.

Cream—One and one-half cups milk, three-fourths cup sugar, one egg, two tablespoons cornstarch; flavor with vanilla. When both this and the puffs are cool open a little way with a knife and fill with cream.

Queen's, or Hickory Nut Cake.
Mrs. E. G. Stranahan.

One and one-half cups granulated sugar, two thirds cup butter, one cup sweet milk, three whole eggs, or six whites. three cups flour, two cups hickorynut meats broken, one and a half cups seeded raisins; dredge the fruit in flour, add salt and vanilla, three teaspoons baking powder. Makes one large, or two small cakes.

Jam Cake.
Mrs. Belle Everson.

One cup sugar, three eggs, three-fourths cup butter, one cup blackberry jam, one half nutmeg, one tablespoon cinnamon, one teaspoon cloves, one teaspoon soda, three tablespoons sour milk, two cups flour.

Spiced Cake.
Mrs. E. C. Richards.

Two cups of brown sugar, two eggs, one-half cup butter, one cup of sour milk, one cup chopped raisins, two and three-fourths cups of flour, one teaspoon soda, one tablespoon cinnamon, one teaspoon cloves.

Cocoa Spice Cake.
Mrs. Belle Everson.

One and a half cups light brown sugar, one-half cup of molasses, one-half sour milk, one-half butter, one-third of cocoa,

27

three eggs beaten separately, one-half teaspoon cloves, one teaspoon of cinnamon, one-fourth of nutmeg, one teaspoon vanilla, one of soda, three cups flour.

Spice Layer Cake.

Mrs. Will Fuller.

One cup brown sugar, one cup molasses, one-half cup butter, one cup sour milk, three and one half cups flour, two eggs beaten separately, one teaspoon cinnamon, one-half teaspoon cloves, one teaspoon soda, one cup chopped raisins or currants rolled in flour, and added last.

Spanish Buns.

Mrs. J. S. Bissell.

One and a half coffeecups granulated sugar, three fourths of butter, one of sweet milk, five eggs, leaving whites of three for icing; two and three-fourths cups flour, one and a half teaspoons soda, three of cream tartar, one of cloves,.one of allspice, one heaping teaspoon cinnamon, one-half teaspoon nutmeg.

Icing—One and one-half cups granulated sugar, one-half boiling water; boil until it threads. Whites of three eggs beaten.

Spice Cake.

Mrs. A. J. Bartholme.

One egg, one-half cup brown sugar, one cup molasses, one cup sour milk, one-half cup shortening, three cups flour. onefourth teaspoon cinnamon, same of cloves, one teaspoon soda.

Coffee Cake,

Mrs. Belle Everson.

One cup of brown sugar, one cup of molasses, one cup of butter, one cup strong coffee, two eggs, one teaspoon soda, one teaspoon cloves, one tablespoon cinnamon, one pound raisins, onehalf pound currants, four and one-half cups of flour.

Coffee Cake.

Mrs. Will Clark.

Three eggs, two cups brown sugar, one-half of molasses, one of butter, one of cold coffee, four of flour, four teaspoons baking powder, one tablespoon cinnamon, one of cloves, one nutmeg grated, one pound raisins chopped. one pound English currants, one-fourth pound citron cut fine. Bake slowly an hour or more.

ROYAL

BAKING
POWDER
Absolutely Pure.

Sour Cream Fruit Cake.

Mrs. D. A. Wright.

One cup sour cream, one cup butter, four cups flour, two cups brown sugar, two and a half cups raisins chopped, one teaspoon each soda, cloves, cinnamon. Bake slowly.

Black Fruit Cake.

Mrs. F. E. Donnelly.

One lb. flour, two pounds raisins, two of currants, one pound brown sugar, one of butter, one-half pound citron, one-fourth pound each candied lemon and orange peel, ten eggs, one-half cup molasses, two nutmegs, one teaspoon cloves, two of cinnamon, one of lemon, and one of vanilla, one-half cup flour, with fruit added last. One large teaspoon soda in molasses. Will keep for years.

Fig Cake.

Mrs. Bole.

Two cups sugar, one cup sweet milk, three cups flour, whites of six eggs, two teaspoons baking powder, one small cup butter.

Fig Dressing—One pound figs, one cup of brown sugar, chop figs, add a little sugar and boiling water to moisten; a little orange extract.

Fig Layer Cake.

Mrs. O. Glezen.

One cup of sugar, three even tablespoonsful of butter, one egg and the yolks of two, two-thirds of a cup of milk, two cups of flour, one teaspoonful of soda, two of cream tartar; bake in three layers.

Fig Paste—One cup of sugar, one-fourth cup of water, boil till thick; test by dropping a little in cold water, like candy; beat the white of one egg to a stiff froth, chop eight figs very fine, take the sugar from the stove, cool five minutes, add the white of an egg, beat five minutes and add the figs. Spread on the cake.

Dried Apple Cake.

Mrs. H. M. Rogers.

Soak three cups dried apples over night, in morning chop fine and simmer two hours in two cups molasses, when near cold add the cake, made as follows: One cup sugar, one-half cup butter, one cup sour milk, four cups flour, two eggs, one teaspoon soda; spices to taste.

The Essentials

of good cooking comprise nothing that is of more importance than good shortening. Your food will be deliciously light and free from the greasiness and richness that make lard so objectionable if shortened with or fried in pure, clean, sweet

Cottolene

Bath Ginger Bread.

Mrs. D. A. Wright.

Put a scant two-thirds cup of butter and two cups of molasses in a saucepan; when it begins to boil add three teaspoons soda and tablespoon ginger. Take from fire and add one cup sour milk and one beaten egg; three cups flour before sifting; bake in large pan in hot oven twenty minutes. Cut in pan or it will break.

Soft Ginger Bread.

Mrs. Herries.

One cup brown sugar, one cup butter, one cup molasses, one cup sweet milk, one tablespoon vinegar put in the milk; one large teaspoon soda, dissolved in warm water; two eggs, three and a half cups of flour, one tablespoon ginger mixed in the flour. This can be made and only part of it baked. The remainder will keep for ten days.

Molasses Cake.

Mrs. H. S. Thompson.

One-half cup molasses, one-half cup sugar, one egg, butter size of an egg, one-half cup sour milk, one teaspoon soda, one cup raisins; spice to taste. Flour to make rather stiff batter.

Fairy Gingerbread.

Mrs. O. Glezen.

One cupful of butter, two of sugar, one of milk, four of flour, three-fourths of a teaspoonful of soda, one tablespoon of ginger. Beat the batter to a cream. Add the sugar gradually, and when very light, the ginger, the milk in which the soda has been dissolved, and finally the flour. Turn baking pans upside down and wipe the bottoms very clean. Butter them and spread the cake mixture very thin on them. Bake in a moderate oven until brown, While still hot cut into squares with a case-knife and slip from the pan. Keep in a tin box. This is delicious. With the quantities given, a large dish of gingerbread can be made. It must be spread on the bottom of the pan as thin as a wafer, and cut the moment it comes from the oven.

SMILEY BROS'. STORE

——— IS THE ———

Leading Dry Goods
——— AND ———
Boot and Shoe House

Of Union City, Penna.

WE AIM always to have the best and most desirable goods
as soon as they are placed upon the market.

Located in the Old Brick Store.   **Union City, Pa.**

HANIEL CLARK & CO.,
The Union City Mills.

Manufacture Highest Grades

Winter and Spring Wheat Flours

Pond Lily, Fancy Winter Wheat Patent,
Northern Queen, Spring Patent, Blue Jay,
Moss Rose,   White Clover,   Diamond.
Reliance.

Best Bread Flours.   All Warranted.

TO BE FOUND AT ALL GROCERS.

TRY THE "NORTHERN QUEEN."

33

Bread.

Lightening Yeast.

Mrs. Tillotson.

One quart mashed potatoes, one quart potato water; take a three gallon jar, put in one teacup granulated sugar, one cup flour; scald with potato water, add potatoes, and beat thoroughly. When milk warm add yeast; always keep a starter of this. Stir down three or four times, then set in a cool place. You can use yeast cakes to start with, but it is better to use a starter.

Potato Yeast.

Scald one-half cup flour into two cups mashed potatoes, thin with cold water. When luke warm add half cup any soft yeast; let rise, stir down two or three times, then add one tablespoon salt, one of ginger, two of sugar; cover tight in a jar, and set in a cool place.

Lightening Yeast Bread.

Mrs. Tillotson.

For three loaves, take one quart water, one pint yeast, one teaspoon salt, little lard; pour about two tablespoons boiling water on lard, add wetting, make a batter, and add yeast; mix in hard loaf. Let rise very light, then mould into tins, letting it rise only twice. Can be baked in four hours, no matter how much yeast you use. If using whole wheat flour do not knead quite so stiff.

Graham Bread.

Mrs. C. F. Blair.

When making white bread take one quart of sponge, one quart warm water, one-half cup brown sugar, one-half teaspoon soda, one small cup wheat flour, and graham flour to make a little thicker than loaf cake. Fill quart tomato cans half full. When light bake one hour; in half an hour turn over on side.

White Bread.

Mrs. O. Glezen.

Three medium-sized potatoes boiled and mashed very fine, one tablespoon lard, one of sugar, one of salt, one-half cake compressed

Brooklyn • Clothing • House.

WE ARE AT IT AGAIN.

If you just look through our line,
You will surely say, it is all very fine ;
    It cannot be beat !
    And then, how very cheap.
You had better come to us, or write,
For samples we send with great delight ;
    And we are sure you will find
    Stylish goods of every kind.
All our lines are now full and complete,
And we are ready and willing to compete.

Ready-Made Clothing and Outfitters.

FINE————
MERCHANT TAILORING
A SPECIALTY.

Van Dusen & Siegfried,

UNION CITY, PENNA.

yeast, and warm water for two loaves bread ; mix stiff and knead twenty minutes. Mix at night, let stand in a warm room until morning, then mould into loaves. Do not get it too light. Bake in a moderate oven half an hour.

Salt Rising Bread.

Mrs. Will King.

Two teaspoons corn meal, wet with enough boiling milk to scald ; set this the day before you wish to use it. Let rise, it will take ten or twelve hours.

Bread—In the morning put in a bowl enough warm water for rising, stir quite thick and add railroad yeast ; let it rise. Put flour in a pan, make a hole in center and pour in a pint of boiling water, then cool with either milk or water, then knead into loaves. The secret of good salt rising bread is to keep it warm.

Graham Bread.

Mrs. Belle Everson.

One-half cup molasses, one-half brown sugar, one teaspoon salt, two teaspoons soda, three teacups butter milk, five cups graham flour. Bake in slow oven one hour. This makes two loaves.

Brown Bread.

Four cups sour milk, four of cornmeal, one of molasses, two of flour, two teaspoons soda, salt. Steam in a two-quart basin two hours, and bake twenty minutes.

Brown Bread.

Mrs. M. M.

Two cups sour milk, two cups cornmeal, two cups graham flour, one cup N. O. molasses, one teaspoon soda and salt. Steam three hours and brown in oven.

Graham Bread.

Mrs. Hazelton.

Four cups sweet milk. two cups molasses, two teaspoons soda, little salt, nine cups graham flour, five teaspoons baking powder. Bake slowly.

Graham Bread.

Mrs. C. F. Blair.

Two cups buttermilk, two handsful cornmeal, one tablespoon salt, four of sugar ; add Schumacher's graham flour till a little thicker than loaf cake. This makes two loaves.

37

Steamed Indian Bread.
S. L. Honeywell.

Two cups sour milk, one cup molasses, two cups cornmeal, two cups flour, two tablespoons melted butter, one teaspoon soda, salt. Steam two hours, then brown in oven.

Corn Bread.
Mrs. V. D.

Two cups sour milk, three-fourths cup N. O. molasses, two even cups corn meal, two of white flour, two teaspoons soda sifted in flour, teaspoon salt. Steam three hours, bake one-half hour.

Brown Bread.
Mrs. L. E.

Two and one-half cups sour milk, one-half cup molasses; add one heaping teaspoon soda, two scant cups cornmeal, one and one-half graham flour, one teaspoon salt. Steam three hours.

Sweet Brown Bread.
Mrs. R. E. Ashley.

One cup baking molasses, one-half cup brown sugar, one heaping teaspoon soda, two cups sweet milk, one-half cup drawn butter, one egg well beaten, one teaspoon ground cloves; dissolve soda in one cup milk. Wheat flour to make stiff batter, about three cups. Steam three hours.

Spider Corn Cake.
Mrs. A. G. Sweet.

Two and one-third cups Indian meal, one-third cup flour, one teaspoon salt, one-fourth cup sugar, three teaspoons baking powder, sift together. Beat two eggs very light, add one and one-half cups sweet milk, two eggs, and add to the dry mixture; beat well. Put one tablespoon butter in spider, and when very hot pour in and place on top of stove until it bubbles, then pour over it one cup sweet milk without stirring. Bake half an hour.

Old-Fashioned Johnny Cake.
Mrs. George Alden.

One cup flour, one cup yellow corn meal, one-fourth cup sugar, one and a half teaspoons salt, two-teaspoons baking powder, one egg well beaten, one cup milk, one tablespoon butter, softened. Mix in order given; beat well. Bake in a moderate oven from twenty to twenty-five minutes.

39

Splendid Johnny Cake.
Mrs. C. F. Blair.

One egg beaten light, two cups sour milk or buttermilk, two teaspoons soda, one-half cup brown sugar, one teaspoon salt, one large handful graham flour, add cornmeal to make a thin batter ; last add one tablespoon lard, smoking hot. Have tins very hot, and bake in quick oven.

Rolls.
S. L. Honeywell.

Three pints flour, two teaspoons salt, four tablespoons brewers' yeast, or six of home-made yeast, one pint luke warm water, knead ten minutes. Then divide into small rolls and knead each separately. Let rise till light.

Breakfast Gems.
Mrs. H. C. Cheney.

One and one-half cups flour, two teaspoons baking powder (Royal), two teaspoons melted Cottolene, one teaspoonful sugar, one egg ; milk to make moderate thick batter. Stir the baking powder into the flour, add the milk, Cottolene, sugar and eggs, well beaten, then beat all thoroughly. Heat the gem pans hot on the top of the stove. Bake in a very hot oven.

Light Biscuit.
Mrs. C. F. Blair.

Put in a crock one-half cup butter, three tablespoons white sugar. Boil one quart sweet milk, and pour over butter and sugar, when cool add flour for thick sponge, and one-half cup yeast. Let rise over night. In morning knead, let rise, then make into biscuits.

Graham Gems.
Mrs. O. Glezen.

One-half cup sugar, one tablespoon melted butter, one egg, one large cup sweet milk, one cup graham flour (sifted), one-half teaspoon salt, two teaspoons baking powder, wheat flour to thicken to consistency of thick batter.

Waffles.
Mrs. Stevens.

Yolks of three eggs beaten, one quart buttermilk or sour milk, three teaspoons salt, three tablespoons melted butter, flour to make like pancakes, one heaping teaspoon soda, the whites of the eggs beaten and added last.

41

Baking Powder Biscuits.

Three pints flour, one teaspoon salt, three teaspoons baking powder sifted twice with flour, two tablespoons lard or butter rubbed in flour ; sweet milk for soft dough. Hot oven.

Cream Biscuits.

Three large cups flour, two teaspoons baking powder, little salt ; sift together. As much sweet cream as will make a soft dough. Bake in a quick oven.

Bread Pancakes.

Take stale bread, what will be enough, and soak over night in sour milk or buttermilk ; rub through a colander, add sour milk, as much as needed, salt, soda, one egg, flour to make batter a little thicker than wheat pancakes.

Wheat Muffins.

Mrs. O. Glezen.

One pint of new milk, two eggs, one tablespoonful yeast, one of butter, teaspoonful of salt. If wanted for breakfast, stir at night and they will be light in the morning—if for tea, stir in the morning.

Corn Muffins.

One quart of Indian meal, sifted, heaping spoonful of butter, one quart of milk, saltspoon of salt, two tablespoonsful distillery yeast, one of molasses. Let it rise four or five hours. Bake in muffin rings, or shallow pans.

Cream Muffins.

Mrs. H. C. Cheney.

Two teaspoonsful baking powder (Royal), one-half teaspoon salt, one pint sifted flour, two eggs, one-half cup milk, one-third cup Cottolene. Mix the baking powder and salt with the flour. Beat the yolks of eggs lightly, add to them the milk and stir quickly into the flour. Then stir in the Cottolene, soften, and lastly the eggs, whites, well beaten. Fill greased muffin pans two-thirds full, and bake about fifteen minutes in a very hot oven.

F. M. McClintock,

Attorney and Counsellor at Law

—— Main Street, ——

Union City, Penna.

M. W. SHREVE,

Attorney-at-Law,

Main Street,

UNION CITY, PA.

WM. C. JACKSON,

NOTARY PUBLIC,

Justice of the Peace and Conveyancer.

UNION CITY, ERIE CO., PA.

Deeds, Bonds, Mortgages, Pension Vouchers, &c., executed with legal accuracy.

J. W. Sproul.   W. O. Morrow.

Sproul & Morrow,

ATTORNEYS-AT-LAW,

UNION CITY, - - - - - PENNA.

Cookies.

Ginger Snaps.

Mrs. Mulkie.

Tea cup molasses heated, stir one egg, one cup sugar, large tablespoon vinegar, heaping teaspoon ginger, same of soda together; pour molasses over when cool. Thicken and bake soon as possible.

Ginger Cookies.

Mrs. W. L. Fuller.

One cup brown sugar, one cup dark molasses, one cup butter or lard, one cup hot coffee, one teaspoon ginger, one of cinnamon, and one of soda. Flour enough to drop from spoon; not too stiff.

Ginger Cookies.

S. K. Thompson.

One cup butter and lard mixed, one cup sugar, one cup molasses, one-half cup cold coffee, one teaspoon ginger, one of cloves, one of cinnamon, one teaspoon soda dissolved in hot water, flour for quite a stiff dough. Sift sugar over top before baking.

Molasses Cookies.

Mrs. G. J. Warden.

One cup black molasses, one cup shortening, one cup cold water, one cup sugar, one teaspoon soda, one teaspoon ginger, one teaspoon cinnamon, one-half teaspoon cloves; mix soft.

Ginger Cookies.

Mrs. Herries.

One cup brown sugar, one cup N. O. molasses, two-thirds cup lard, one egg, one tablespoon ginger, one tablespoon vinegar, one tablespoon soda (just level), six tablespoons boiling water. Do not make too stiff.

Ginger Cookies.

Mrs. V. D.

One cup N. O. molasses, one cup granulated sugar, one cup shortening, two eggs, one-half cup sour milk, one tablespoon ginger, one level tablespoon soda, one tablespoon vinegar, one tablespoon cinnamon; mix soft as can be handled. Salt.

UNION CITY CHAIR COMPANY,

Manufacturers of CHAIRS.

Correct Styles,   Right Prices,   Prompt Deliveries.

Office and Factory, Crooked Street.　　　　**UNION CITY, PA.**

Ginger Cookies.

Mrs. W. Bush.

One cup molasses, one cup sugar, one cup lard, one cup sweet milk, one teaspoon salt, one tablespoon ginger, three teaspoons soda. Mix as stiff with flour as can be made with a spoon, let it stand over night in a cool place ; roll quite thin and bake in a hot oven.

Cinnamon Drops.

Mrs. James Woods.

One-half pint N. O. molasses, one-half pound brown sugar, one-half pound butter, one-half pint sour milk, two teaspoons soda, two of cinnamon, four eggs. Beat the whites to a stiff froth, add last, then flour to make a stiff batter, and drop in places with a spoon. Bake in a quick oven.

Ginger Cookies.

Mrs. J. W. Middleton.

One cup molasses, one cup butter, one cup sugar, one tablespoon ginger, one of cinnamon, two teaspoons soda, dissolved in three tablespoons boiling water.

Fruit Snaps.

Mrs. J. S. Bissell.

One and one-half cups sugar, one-half cup molasses, one cup butter, one cup chopped raisins, two cups currants, three eggs, one teaspoon of soda, one of ginger, one of cinnamon, one of allspice, one of cloves, one teaspoon nutmeg ; mix soft as can be rolled.

Hermits.

Gertrude Boyd.

Two eggs, two cups sugar, two-thirds cup butter, one tablespoon water, one-half teaspoon soda, one cup chopped and seeded raisins, two tablespoons cinnamon ; flour. Mix soft and bake a nice brown.

Sugar Cookies.

Mrs. D. A. W.

One and one-half cups sugar, one cup butter, one-half cup cold water, one-half teaspoon soda dissolved in water, one egg ; flour to make a stiff dough. Sprinkle with sugar before putting in oven.

Eggless Sugar Cookies.
Mrs. V. D.

One cup sugar, one-half cup butter, one-half cup sweet milk, one-half teaspoon soda; season with nutmeg.

Sugar Cookies.
Mrs. W. E. Jackson.

Two cups sugar, one cup butter, one cup sour cream, two eggs, one teaspoon soda; flavor with vanilla. Flour to roll. Bake in a hot oven.

Mother's White Cookies.
Mrs. W. L. Fuller.

One and one-half cups sugar, one of butter, scant teaspoon soda dissolved in one-half cup sweet milk, two eggs, one teaspoon lemon extract; add flour to roll nicely.

Sour Cream Cookies.
Mrs. Rulof Fuller.

Two cups coffee A sugar, three eggs, one cup sour cream, one cup butter, one teaspoon soda, one teaspoon lemon extract; flour to make a soft dough. Very nice.

White Cookies.
Mrs. A. Clayton.

One cup butter, two cups sugar, three eggs, one cup sweet milk, three teaspoons baking powder; flavor to taste.

Soft Cookies.
Mrs. W. C. Siegfried.

One heaping cup butter, one and a half (scant) cups sugar, two eggs, whites and yolks beaten separately, three tablespoons sour milk, one small teaspoon soda, and cinnamon; flour just enough to roll. Sprinkle with sugar and nutmeg before cutting. Bake light brown.

Rock Biscuits.
Mrs. C. H. Smith.

Two even cups flour, one and a half cups sugar, three-fourths cup butter, one cup seeded and chopped raisins, one pound nut meat chopped, but not too fine; one-half cup currants, three eggs, four tablespoons sweet milk, one small teaspoon baking powder, one-half teaspoon cinnamon, a little nutmeg. Put about a teaspoonful in each biscuit, and bake same as cookies. These are a great fad, and are served on all occasions.

Camp Milling Co.,

MERCHANT MILLERS,

And Dealers in Flour, Feed and Grain.

UNION CITY, PENNA.

Our old reliable brands are guaranteed to be always up to our high standard, our motto being "highest quality" rather than "lowest price."

None but the highest grade of choicest varieties of hard winter wheat used in the manufacture of our flours, making them superior in color and strength to any in the market. A sack of any of our brands is guaranteed to make one more baking of bread than any other winter wheat flour sold in Erie County.

Test a sack of

Magnolia, Chautauqua, Camp's Best, Belle of Ohio, Red Ball, Red Cross, Anchor, Target, Columbia, Surprise, The Latest, or Up-to-Date.

We will make good our Claim as above. Prices as Low as Any for Same Quality of Flour or Feed.

CAMP MILLING CO.

Confectionery.

Hints on Candy Making.

Gertrude Boyd.

Porcelain-lined pan is best, because it does not burn so readily. Put into it one pound best loaf sugar, small teacup cold water; stir it to mix it, but cease as soon as it begins to boil. Boil ten minutes, then dip a fork into it, hold high; when a silky hair forms drop a small quantity into cold water. When it can be taken up in a soft ball it is done. Pour into a dish, put in a cool, dry place. Be careful not to shake or stir it; as soon as cool enough to dip the fingers into it, beat it briskly, until it begins to thicken, and turn white like cream. Then put the hand in and knead as dough. Unless worked quickly it will grain or turn rough.

Butter Scotch.

Mrs. Inez Thompson.

Twenty tablespoons sugar, two tablespoons vinegar, one-fourth cup butter; flavor with vanilla. Add a very little water, boil slowly; be sure and dissolve well before cooking. Pour on buttered plates, and when cool enough cut in squares. Nuts may be added.

French Candy.

Mrs. James Lydell.

Six cups fine granulated sugar, hot water to dissolve, a large fourth teaspoon cream tartar; cook until it threads or ropes. Pour in dish, and stand until cool, so the top will wrinkle; flavor with vanilla. Beat with spoon until cold and white, then mould in shapes with your hand, and place nuts on top. Use fruit coloring for pink; cocoanut rolled in for cocoanut balls. Make up the different kinds as other French candy. Excellent.

Butter Cups.

Irene Warden.

One-half cup sugar, one-half cup butter, one-half cup molasses. Boil until it hardens in water, pour out in buttered tins, crease in squares and set away to cool.

50

French Creams.

Break the white of one egg into a glass and add an equal quantity of water or milk, then stir into this enough XXXX confectioner's sugar to make stiff enough to roll into shape—about a pound and a half will be needed. Use different flavorings to make variety. Put nuts on top of some of the creams, or chop fine and add to the mixture. Cocoanut, figs and dates may be used if desired.

Chocolate Caramels.

One cup chocolate, one cup brown sugar, one cup molasses, one-half cup sweet milk. When nearly done add a piece of butter the size of an egg and stir constantly to keep from burning. When nearly cold mark in squares.

Chocolate Creams.

Break the white of an egg into a glass and add the same quantity of water or milk; then add XXXX confectioner's sugar until stiff enough to roll into balls. Have ready some grated chocolate and place over boiling water until soft, then roll cream in the melted chocolate and drop on buttered paper to dry. Flavor with vanilla. Will need about one and one-half pounds sugar.

Burnt Almond Caramels.

Blanch almonds, then shred them and place them in the oven to take a dark brown color. Have the irons arranged on the marble; spread the burned almonds evenly on the marble; pour on them a boiling made same as for vanilla caramels. Arrange the bars to give a sheet a little under half an inch in thickness. When cold enough mark and cut up same as for ordinary caramels. If you prefer to put the almonds in the boiling, do so just before removing it from the fire.

Crystalized Pop Corn.

Ida D. Sproul.

Put into an iron kettle one tablespoon of butter, three table spoons of water and one teacup of white sugar, boil until ready to candy, then throw in three quarts of corn nicely popped, stir briskly until the candy is evenly distributed over the corn. Care should be taken not to have too hot a fire, lest you scorch the corn when crystalizing. Nuts of any kind may be treated in the same way.

Pure Spices, ✳ Extracts, &c.

Will assist you in meeting with success in your cooking. If you want the best, call on R. FULLER.

Instead of Selling on Credit,

and asking the same old prices for groceries, and buying them likewise, he does the reverse. That is, buys for cash—gets cash discounts and discounts for large orders—and sells for cash at lowest prices ever asked.

R. FULLER.

Croquettes.

Oyster Croquettes.

Wrs. Alice Herries.

Take the hard end of the oyster, leaving the other end in nice shape for stew. Scald them, then chop fine and add an equal weight of potatoes mashed fine. To one pound of this add four ounces of butter, one teaspoon of salt, one-half tablespoon pepper, and a little cream or milk; make in small rolls, dip in eggs and grated crackers and fry in deep lard.

Egg Croquettes.

Mrs. W. J. Sloan.

Stir four minced hard boiled eggs in one-half pint boiled sauce by adding two teaspoons flour to one tablespoon butter, stirred in one cup boiling cream; season with salt and pepper and few drops of onion juice; turn out to cool. When cold form in cylinder shape, roll in fine cracker crumbs, then dip in egg, roll in cracker crumbs again. Put aside for an hour, then drop in boiling hot lard until brown. Serve with peas and cream dressing.

Ham Croquettes.

Mrs. E. C. Richards.

One cup chopped ham, one cup chopped potatoes, one cup bread crumbs, one tablespoon of butter, one egg. Make in balls, roll in bread crumbs, fry in hot lard; cook ham and potatoes first.

Chicken Croquettes.

Mrs. D. Smiley.

Two pounds of boiled chicken, one cup mashed potatoes, made soft with milk, two eggs, half cup butter, salt and pepper. Chop the chicken very fine, beat in the egg, then the potatoes and butter, salt and pepper; make into croquettes, roll in cracker crumbs and fry in hot fat.

A. G. SWEET,

Fire & Life Insurance.

One of the Oldest Agencies in the State.

UNION CITY, PA.

MURPHY'S JEWELRY STORE,

DEALER IN

Diamonds, Watches & Fine Jewelry

Cut Glass Lamps, Etc.

ORDERS FILLED BY MAIL.

918 State Street,   ERIE, PENNA.

Salmon Croquettes.

Mrs. A. L. Main.

Mix bread crumbs and salmon together in proportion of two cups of bread crumbs to one of salmon, season and mould into balls with the hands, roll in beaten eggs, then in dry crumbs; drop in boiling lard.

Chicken Croquettes.

Mrs. Mulkie.

Take one quart of chopped, cooked and seasoned chicken, one cup milk, boil and thicken with one tablespoon flour, add pinch of salt and large piece of butter, add to meat and then stir well. To form croquettes take one tablespoon of mixture, cover with egg, and roll in bread crumbs, and cook in boiling hot lard five minutes, or until nicely browned; place on brown paper to absorb fat.

Doughnuts and Fritters.

Doughnuts.

Mrs. P. H. Thompson.

Two cups sugar, two eggs, two cups sour milk, eight tablespoons melted shortening, two level teaspoons soda, nutmeg or cinnamon, flour to make medium soft; add teaspoon baking powder to flour.

Doughnuts.

Mrs. Laura Clark.

Two eggs, one heaping cup sugar, one and one-half cups sour milk, three and one-half tablespoons butter, one teaspoon soda, and two of baking powder; about five cups flour.

Doughnuts.

Mrs. J. O. Loomis.

One and one-half cups sugar, one cup sweet milk, two eggs, four tablespoons butter, two teaspoons baking powder, one of salt.

Doughnuts.

Mrs. M. E. Jackson.

One and one-half cups sugar, two cups sweet milk, three tablespoons butter, four of melted lard, two eggs, three teaspoons baking powder, half teaspoon salt; flour to roll.

57

Doughnuts.

Mrs. A. Clayton.

One-half cup sugar, one teaspoon melted butter, one egg, one cup sweet milk, two teaspoons baking powder; season with nutmeg.

Doughnuts.

Kate Cook.

Two eggs, one cup sugar, three and one-half tablespoons lard or fried meat fat, one cup cold water, one teaspoon salt, three teaspoons baking powder; flavor with what you choose. Always melt shortening before measuring. Beat whites and yolks of eggs separate. Mix soft.

Fritters.

Mrs. A. G. Sweet.

One egg, one teaspoon baking powder, one-half cup sweet cream, one-half cup of milk, two and a half cups flour; fry in hot lard. Eat with maple syrup.

Banana Fritters.

Mrs. James Woods.

Eight bananas cut in halves, put one cup flour in a dish, beat the yolks of two eggs and stir in, two-thirds cup of water, add to flour, beat smooth, a pinch of salt. Put in tablespoon melted butter, whites of eggs, one teaspoon baking powder. Dip the bananas in batter; fry hot in lard. Fine.

Fritters.

Mrs. W. L. Fuller.

One cup sour milk, one egg, one-half teaspoon soda, one-half teaspoon salt; stir thick with flour. Fry in hot lard.

Fritters.

Mrs. Martha Main.

One cup milk, one cup flour, three eggs, a little salt, scant teaspoon baking powder.

Fritters.

Mrs. Martha Main.

Two eggs, one cup milk, a little salt, flour to make a stiff batter; a little baking powder.

59

Cream Fritters.

Mrs. Martha Main.

Three eggs, three cups flour, one teaspoon baking powder, one spoonful melted lard, milk enough for thick batter; add whites of eggs, beaten stiff, last.

Potato Fritters.

Mrs. H. C. Cheney.

Grate six cold potatoes, add to them a pint of cold milk, and flour enough to make as stiff as other fritters, yolks of three eggs, then the beaten whites; a little salt Fry in hot lard.

Green Corn Fritters.

Mrs. P. H. T.

One pint grated corn, one teacup flour, one teaspoon butter, two eggs, salt and pepper; fry on griddle, like pancakes.

Apple Fritters.

Mrs. J. R. Mulkie.

Stir into the yolks of two well-beaten eggs one cup quite warm milk; add two cups flour, with one teaspoon baking powder, two tablespoons sugar, pinch salt; last the whites of eggs, beaten stiff. Have some nice tart apples pared and sliced, lay a slice on a spoon partly filled with batter, cover with batter and drop into hot lard. To be eaten with maple syrup, or sugar and cream.

Crullers.

Mrs. P. G. Stranahan.

Three eggs, three tablespoons lard, three tablespoons sugar, pinch of soda, little salt; nutmeg or lemon.

Drinks.

Coffee.

Mrs. E. J. W.

Allow one tablespoon coffee to each person. Mix coffee with white of egg and little cold water, put in coffee pot and pour on boiling water sufficient for steeping. Do not boil, let simmer. In making for six persons allow from one to two tablespoons extra. When simmered sufficiently pour on hot water, allowing one-half pint water to person. Lastly pour in few drops cold water.

61

Coffee.

Mrs. M. W. Shreve.

Using one tablespoon for each person, and "one for the pot," stir moist with egg, put in pot, and add as much cold water as you desire to serve, let it heat gradually until it comes to a boil, boil up three times, then set on back of stove and simmer until ready to serve.

Cocoa.

H. E. W.

Dissolve six tablespoons of cocoa and mix to a smooth paste with a little hot water, have ready about a quart of hot milk, turn mixed cocoa into milk and add about as much hot water; sweeten to taste. Whipped cream is very nice to place about a tablespoon on top of each cup of cocoa.

Tea.

Mrs. Mulkie.

One teaspoon tea to one cup of water is a good rule for making tea. Scald teapot. If it is green tea do not boil, but let it simmer five minutes. Black tea should be boiled at least five minutes. Pour water on tea boiling hot, and serve very hot.

Unfermented Wine for Communion.

Mrs. Wulkie,

Weigh the grapes, pick from stems, put in a porcelain kettle, add very little water, and cook till seeds and pulp separate. Strain through a thick cloth, return juice to kettle and add three pounds of sugar to every ten pounds of grapes; heat to simmering. Bottle hot and seal. This makes one gallon.

Raspberry Shrub.

Mrs. D. A. Wright.

Pour one pint of vinegar over three quarts ripe raspberries, let stand twenty-four hours, then strain through jelly bag. Take one-half pound sugar to one pint juice, and boil twenty minutes, skimming well; bottle when cold. A pleasant and refreshing drink.

Raspberry Fluff.

Mrs. H. C. Cheney.

One cup raspberries (crush with a spoon), add one cup of sugar, and white of one egg, beat together to a stiff froth (will

63

take half an hour), and set on ice until ready to use. Currants and apples can be used in same way. Will make three goblets, if properly beaten.

Raspberry Vinegar.

Mrs. D. A. W.

Procure the first berries of the season, any amount; put in stone jar and cover with vinegar. Allow them to stand from two to four hours,then strain off all the juice, add one-half pound of white sugar to one quart of juice, then boil five minutes. Cork tight when nearly cool. For drinking allow two tablespoons to glass of water.

Raspberry Acid.

Mrs. F. E. McLean.

Dissolve five ounces tartaric acid in two quarts water, turn it upon twelve pounds red raspberries in a large bowl, let stand twenty-four hours; strain it without pressing. To a pint of this juice add one and a half pounds of white sugar, stir until dissolved; bottle but do not cork for several days. When ready for use put two or three tablespoons in a glass of ice water. Makes a delicious beverage.

Strawberry Sherbet.

Mrs. Alice Herries.

One and one-half quarts of berries, one large lemon, three pints of water, the juice of one orange, three-fourths pound sugar. Crush the berries in a bowl, squeeze in the lemon and orange juice; pour the water over this and let stand several hours. Strain, add the sugar and cool on ice before serving.

Orange Sherbet.

Mrs. J. H. S.

One tablespoon of gelatine, one-half cup cold water, one-half cup boiling water, one cup of sugar, one more cold water, six oranges, or one pint of orange juice; freeze.

Milk Sherbet.

Mrs. H. C. Cheney.

Remove the juice from four lemons, strain and add one teaspoonful of Royce's lemon extract, add sufficient white sugar to make it the consistency of batter; pack the freezer with ice and salt. Pour one quart of milk into the can, add the lemon batter, cover and freeze. Turn slowly and steadily until frozen.

Kimberly Hotel,

Seventh and Peach Sts.

Opposite City Hall, One Square from Post Office.

RATES, $1.50 TO $2.00 PER DAY.

Erie, Pa.

FOR FIRST-CLASS WORK, CALL ON

W. E. JACKSON,

Contractor and Builder,

Union City, Pa.

GARY SMITH,

THE LARGEST AND BEST STOCK OF

Groceries ∴ and ∴ Crockery

IN UNION CITY.

UNION CITY, PA.

Cream Soda Water.

Five and one-half ounces tartaric acid, four and one-half pounds loaf sugar dissolved in one gallon boiling water. While hot clarify with beaten whites of five eggs. Bottle when cool and add whatever flavorings will suit the taste. When you wish to use fill the glass to the depth of about one inch, then two-thirds full with cold water (ice water), last add one-fourth teaspoon of soda, stirring it well. It effervesces as well as soda water from fountains, and is said to be more healthful.

Lemonade by the Quantity.

J. A. W.

One dozen lemons, two pounds sugar, five quarts of water, quarter lemons and squeeze into large earthen jar, let rinds drop into jar as you squeeze, adding sugar little by little at same time. Allow this to stand a few hours, then add the water. Stir with a wooden spoon until all the sugar is dissolved, and it is ready for use. A piece of ice put in with juice, rinds and sugar will improve it

Pine Apple Lemonade.

Mrs. H. C. C.

Boil one and one-half cups full sugar and one pint of water for ten minutes, add one grated pine apple, and juice of four lemons; cool just before serving. Add one quart ice water.

Ginger Lemonade.

Mrs. R. Fuller.

Take half cup vinegar, one cup of sugar, two teaspoons ginger, stir well together, put in a quart pitcher, and fill with ice water. If it is wanted sweeter or sourer than these quantities will make it, more of the needed ingredients may be put in. It is a cooling drink, almost as good as lemonade.

Gus Holloway.

Mrs. O. Glezen.

A capital ginger beer is easily made as follows: Put one pint of molasses and two teaspoonsful of pure powdered ginger into a pail half full of boiling spring water, when well stirred together fill the pail with cold water, leaving room for one pint of yeast, which must not be put in until lukewarm. Place it on a warm hearth for the night, and bottle it in the morning.

Koumiss, or Milk Beer.

Mrs. Alice Herries.

One quart new milk, three or four lumps white sugar, one gill of fresh buttermilk; mix until the sugar is dissolved. Let stand in warm place ten hours, when it will have thickened, then pour from one vessel to another until it is smooth and thick. Bottle and keep in a warm place twenty-four hours, in winter it may take thirty-six hours. Cork the bottle tight, then tie down. Shake well before using. This drink is recommended for a delicate stomach, as it aids in the assimilation of food; it is also healthy for young children.

Splendid Ginger Beer.

Mrs. F. E. M.

Five gallons of water, one-half pound ginger root boiled, four pounds sugar, one-eighth pound cream tartar, one bottle essence of lemon, one ounce of tartaric acid, one quart yeast.

Harvest Drink.

Kate Cook.

One quart water, one tablespoon sifted ginger, five tablespoons sugar, one-half pint vinegar. Mix thoroughly and put in a jug in a cool place.

Cream of Tartar Drink.

Mrs. R. Fuller.

Two teaspoonsful of cream of tartar, the grated rind of a lemon, half a cup of loaf sugar, and one pint of boiling water. This is a good summer drink for invalids, and is cleansing to the blood.

Ices and Jellies.

Ices.

The best ices are prepared by first cooking the sugar into syrup, and then adding the fruit juice and freezing. To clarify sugar for water ices or sherbets, to each quart of water allow two pounds of granulated sugar and a teaspoonful of whipped white of an egg. Boil about ten minutes, remove all scum, and set aside to cool before adding fruit juices.

Lemon Ice.

M. L. B.

The juice of four lemons and one orange, one pint of sugar, one quart of water; mix juice and water together and strain, then the sugar; put in freezer and freeze. Very simple, but nice.

Ice Cream.

Mrs. J. W. Swalley.

Two quarts of thick cream, one and a half cups granulated sugar, two teaspoonsful vanilla; put into freezer and freeze slowly.

Ice Cream.

S. M. S.

For one quart cream, whipped, add the whites of six eggs whipped, put together; flavor same as other creams, sweeten to taste, and freeze.

Coffee Ice Cream.

Mrs. A. G. Sweet.

One generous pint of milk, two cups of sugar, two eggs, two heaping tablespoons flour, one quart of cream, one cup very strong coffee. Beat the eggs and one cup sugar together, put the milk on stove, and when nearly boiling add the sugar, eggs, and flour, (which has been made smooth in a little water), stir constantly for twenty minutes; remove when cold, add second cup of sugar, coffee and cream and freeze.

Saw Mill.   Planing Mill.   Feed Mill.

GAFLISCH BROTHERS,

Manufacturers of and Dealers in

All Kinds Rough and Dressed

LUMBER.

LATH, SHINGLES, Etc., Etc.

**Sidewalk Plank Cut to Order, in Pine or Hemlock.   Also all kinds
Planing Mill Supplies, Doors, Windows, Glass, Sash
Screen Doors, Porch Columns, &c.**

Also do General Planing Mill Work.

Inside and Outside Finishing Lumber for Houses Furnished Complete

---

**High Grade of MILL FEED Constantly on Hand. Custom Grinding
a Specialty. Also have one of the best Buckwheat
Runs in the State.**

Mills and Office, cor. Bridge and Willow Sts., UNION CITY, PENNA.

OUR PRICES ARE RIGHT.   CALL AND SEE US.

Frozen Bisque.

Mamie L. Bole.

Two eggs, one pint of milk, cook in double boiler; remove from stove and chill, add one quart rich cream, one and one-half cups sugar, two dozen macaroons, rolled very fine; season with vanilla.

Jellied Oranges.

Mrs. W. E. Caldwell.

Eight oranges, one large lemon, one-half box of gelatine, two-thirds cup cold water, one cup boiling water, one and one-half cups granulated sugar. Cut oranges in two, remove juice from oranges and lemon, soak gelatine in cold water and dissolve with boiling water, add sugar, and when cold the pieces, strain and set until it begins to thicken, then fill orange shells, and when firm serve with whipped cream; sweeten and flavor to taste.

Lemon Jelly.

Helen Hecker.

Two cups of sugar, one cup lemon juice, one quart boiling water, one cup cold water, one box gelatine. Soak the gelatine in the cold water two hours, pour the boiling water on it, add sugar and lemon juice, strain through a napkin, mould and harden.

Lemon Jelly.

Mrs. A. G. Sweet.

One-half box gelatine, one scant cup cold water, one pint boiling water, one cup sugar, juice of one lemon. Soak the gelatine in the cold water until soft, then add the boiling water, when dissolved add sugar, lemon juice, and strain. Decorate with nuts.

Coffee Jelly.

Mrs. A. W. Hecker.

One pint of sugar, one of strong coffee, one pint and a half of boiling water, one half pint cold water, a box of gelatine. Soak gelatine two hours in the cold water, pour the boiling water on it, add the sugar and coffee, strain and turn into moulds; set away to harden. Serve with sugar and cream.

72

Buy Underwear and Hosiery

DIRECT FROM THE MILLS,

THROUGH

WILLIAM P. MEEHAN, ERIE, PA.

Calls at this place Every Spring and Fall.

LARGE ASSORTMENT.   ALWAYS UP TO DATE.

→❊McDONNELL & HICKEY,❊←

702 State Street, ERIE, PA.

HATTERS,

OUTFITTERS TO MEN,

AND

CUSTOM SHIRT MAKERS.

73

Meats.

General Rules for Cooking Meats.

Mrs. F. E. McLean.

All salt meat should be put on in cold water, that the salt may be extracted while cooking. Fresh meat, which is boiled to serve with sauces at the table, should be put to cook in boiling water, when the outer fibres contract the inner juices are preserved. Remove the scum when it first begins to boil. The more gently meat boils the more tender it will become. Allow twenty minutes for boiling each pound of fresh meat. Roast meats require a brisk fire; baste often. Twenty minutes is required for roasting each pound of fresh meat.

Roast Beef with Yorkshire Pudding.

Mrs. F. E. McLean.

Set a piece of beef to roast upon a grating, or several sticks laid across a dripping pan, if there is much fat in the dripping pan, before the pudding is ready to put in drain it off, leaving just enough to prevent the batter from sticking to the bottom.

Yorkshire Pudding.

Mrs. F. E. McLean.

One pint of milk, four eggs, whites and yolks beaten separately, two cups flour, one teaspoon salt; be careful in mixing not to get the batter too stiff. Bake in small patty pans, and use as a garnish for roast beef.

Roast Beef.

Mrs. F. E. McLean.

Prepare for the oven by washing and wiping dry, then sprinkle with flour, salt and pepper; have oven hot when first putting in roast, gradually letting it cool off, basting often. Turn once while roasting.

75

Yorkshire Pudding.

Mrs. F. E. McLean.

Three tablespoons flour mixed with one pint of milk, three eggs and a little salt; pour into gem tins and bake. To be used as a garnish with roast beef.

Boiled Ham.

Mrs. D. A. W.

Take a twelve-pound ham, washing and rinsing well, put in a boiler with cold water and let simmer an hour, then boil slowly three or four hours; when done place in an oven for a few minutes to absorb as much of the fat as possible.

Boiled and Baked Ham.

Mrs. F. E. McLean.

Boil ham until tender, cover it with the white of a raw egg, and sprinkle sugar or bread crumbs over it, put it in oven and brown. It is delicious also covered with a regular cake icing and browned.

Nice Way to Use Poor Meats.

Mrs. O. Glezen.

Boil it until it can be picked from bones, then shred it fine with knife and fork, the fat and lean together. Season with little butter, salt, pepper and sage if desired, add one egg, and about a quarter as many bread or cracker crumbs as meat, moisten with some of the stock it was cooked in (not too soft), mix well; press in a long bar and slice cold for tea, or fry for breakfast.

Some Cold Meat Dishes.

Mrs. F. E. McLean.

Take one pint of cold meat (beef, chicken or veal), season with one small teaspoonful salt, quarter teaspoonful pepper, soften a tablespoonful of gelatine, with a little cold stock or soup; melt a tablespoonful of butter in a saucepan, add a tablespoonful of flour, stir them over the fire until they bubble. Heat a scant cupful of stock, add the softened gelatine, then add to butter and flour, stirring until it boils; when smooth and thick, add meat and few drops of lemon, and when the mixture has become hot without boiling, spread on a dish to get cold.

"Erie" Cast Aluminum Ware.

THE FINEST EVER MANUFACTURED.

**Every Article Cast Solid in One Piece. No Seams or Joints to Leak.
Highly Polished Inside and Outside as Fine as Silver.**

The "Erie" Cast Aluminum Coffee Pot

Just out in three sizes, 2, 3 and 4 quarts.
The spout and strainer are cast on the pot
in one piece. Polished inside and out like
silver. No enamel to flake off.   No poison-
ous metal to endanger life.   They are
strictly PURE and boil coffee quicker than
any pot without overheating it. A beauty
to any table. Don't be without one.

The "Erie" Cast Aluminum Tea Kettle.

Made in four sizes and two styles, flat
or pit bottom. We have had this Tea
Kettle on the market nearly two years
and the trade have indorsed it the finest
ever made. Cast all in one piece with
no seams to leak. No plating or enamel to wear off.   Light, and with a
polish like silver. It deserves its name
as the "KING OF THE KETTLES." No kitchen perfect without
one.

———ALSO———

Kettles, Sauce Pans, Skillets, Griddles, Tea Pots, Pitchers, Chafing Dishes, 5 o'clock Tea Kettles, Etc., Etc.

Write for Catalogue and Prices to the Manufacturers.

GRISWOLD MFG. CO.,   ERIE, PENNA.

77

Croquettes.

The mixture can be made out in cork shapes, and rolled in beaten egg and cracker crumbs, and dropped in boiling fat (very hot), then drain on coarse paper.

Fritters.

Make thick batter, make the meat mixture into balls, and roll in batter, then turn carefully in the boiling fat; or still another way, make a nice crust, and roll very thin, cut into squares 4x3 inches, make out the meat mixture into small rolls, and lay on the square of paste, moisten edges, and overlap, close the ends, brush over with white of egg or milk, and bake a pale brown.

Roast Lamb.
Mrs. D. A. Wright.

Take a hind quarter of lamb, rub well with salt, pepper and flour; cut away all extra fat, have incision made, or bone removed by butcher, fill in with stuffing of bread crumbs, butter, pepper and salt, adding sage or thyme; sew firmly together to keep dressing in place. A roast of seven pounds will roast in about two hours.

Stewed Breast of Lamb.
Ellen F. Cheney.

Cut the breast into pieces and season with salt and pepper, put these in a stew pan, pour sufficient water or soup stock to cover them, stew very gently until tender, or about an hour and a half. Just before serving thicken the sauce with a little flour and butter, let it come to a boil, and pour it over the meat, which has been removed to a platter.

Green peas or finely chopped mint may be strewed over it. The breast may be cooked whole, which will require about three hours, then put into the oven and brown.

Veal Cutlets (Fried).
Mrs. Ellen P. Cheney.

Remove the bones and trim the same as beefsteak, pound thoroughly. Beat two eggs light, add a pinch of salt, one tablespoon of cold water; dip the veal steak into the crumbs, beaten eggs and crumbs again; fry in smoking hot fat. When nicely browned, turn and cook the other side in the same way, but cook each side sufficiently before turning, as one turn is sufficient. If

78

you have not allowed the butter in the frying pan to burn, pour a cup of hot water into pan, thicken with a tablespoonful of flour, let it boil up, pour over the veal, or serve in a gravy boat.

Roast Leg of Lamb.

Mrs. Ellen P. Cheney.

Cut off the shank bone, wash if necessary, and wipe dry, season with salt and pepper, put into a baking pan, add hot water, and bake in a hot oven ; basting frequently. Allow at least twenty minutes to the pound for roasting, as lamb and mutton are better if thoroughly cooked. When done remove to a hot platter, drain the drippings from the baking pan, add a little hot water, season with pepper and salt, thicken with flour; send to table in a gravy boat.

Broiled Beefsteak With Onions.

Peel and wash four medium-sized onions, slice and put in a spider with hot water enough to cover, boil until tender, pour off the water, add a little butter, and fry to a nice brown ; draw the spider to the side of the stove to keep it hot. Broil a large and tender stake, salt and pepper, cover with the onions and serve. To make a tough steak tender, pour two tablespoonfuls each of good olive oil and vinegar on a plate, and lay the steak in this mixture for several hours, until ready to broil it over a very hot fire, or fry it in a hot pan without any fat in it. The oil which has kept it moist while the vinegar was making tender the tough fibres, will not taste after it is cooked.

Smothered Steak (Pork or Beef).

Mrs. W. C. Siegfried.

After steak is fried on one side turn, mince a small onion very fine, sprinkle over, then add dressing, prepared as follows : One quart dry bread, cut in small pieces, salt, pepper and sage to taste, put in basin, then in steamer, and steam until thoroughly moistened ; take out, add piece of butter, one egg, well beaten, and very little water, if not moist enough to suit ; spread over steak, press lightly, cover a short time. Very good.

Oysters and Fish.

Oysters on Toast (Without Milk).

Strain the oyster liquor, rinse the bits of shell from the oysters, pour the liquor on them again, put into a stew pan and set them where they will boil up. Salt, pepper and butter to your taste. Have ready nicely browned toast, previously moistened in boiling water, and well buttered. Arrange this in a deep platter, and pour over it the oysters. Serve hot.

Creamed Oysters.

Mrs. H. C. Cheney.

Wash one pint of oysters, and parboil until plump, skim carefully, drain, and add to the sauce.

Sauce.

One pint of cream or milk, one tablespoonful butter, one tablespoonful flour, one-half of salt, one-half of pepper; cook butter and flour together, add cold cream slowly, then season.

Pigs in Blankets.

Season large oysters with salt and pepper, cut very thin slices of bacon, and fasten with wooden toothpick. Put in a hot spider, and cook just long enough to crisp the bacon.

Fried Oysters.

Mrs. H. C. Cheney.

Choose large oysters, drain them thoroughly, dip in rolled cracker, then in well-beaten egg, then in crackers again, fry with butter on pancake griddle, season with pepper and salt; three eggs are necessary for a quart of oysters; butter may be added as needed to griddle. Serve on hot platter.

Fried Oysters.

Mrs. Gilbert.

Choose large oysters, drain in a colander, sprinkle pepper and salt, and mix well, roll separately each oyster in sifted Indian

meal, fry in very hot lard, and have enough to cover oysters. Will brown beautifully without turning.

Oyster Pie.

Mrs. Alice Herries.

Line a deep dish with a nice paste, dredge the crust with a little flour, and put in one pint of oysters, season well with butter, salt and pepper, and sprinkle some flour over them; pour on a little of the oyster liquor, cover with a crust, open a little for steam to escape. Two hard-boiled eggs chopped coarsely, and mixed with the oysters will be found good, and instead of flour you may use cracker crumbs.

Codfish Balls.

Mrs. H. C. Cheney.

Pick fish fine and freshen, boil potatoes, mash them; mix fish and potatoes while hot, taking two-thirds potatoes and one-third fish. Put in plenty of butter and one egg, make into balls, and fry with butter on pancake griddle.

Creamed Codfish.

Mrs. W. T. Boyd.

Pick up fish, put in cold water, let come to boiling heat, drain, cover with milk or cream, piece of butter size of walnut, little pepper; let get hot, but not boil. Serve on a hot platter.

Fish.

Mrs. Alice Herries.

To remove scales from fish easily they should be dipped in boiling water, and taken out quickly.

To boil fish sew them in a cloth, put into cold water, with plenty of salt, and cook them thirty minutes.

Baked Fish.

Mrs. Alice Herries.

Prepare a stuffing of fine bread crumbs, a little salt pork, chopped very fine, season with sage, parsely, pepper and salt; fill the fish with the stuffing, sew it up, and sprinkle the outside with salt, pepper, and bits of butter; dredge with flour. Put enough water to keep the fish from sticking; baste often. Serve with hard-boiled eggs, and garnish the platter with sprigs of parsely.

FULLER & EVERSON,

PLUMBERS,

And Dealers in Hardware and Builders' Supplies.

If you think of putting in a Bath Room or doing anything in the Plumbing line, remember, we keep a complete line of Plumbing Goods, and do first-class work.

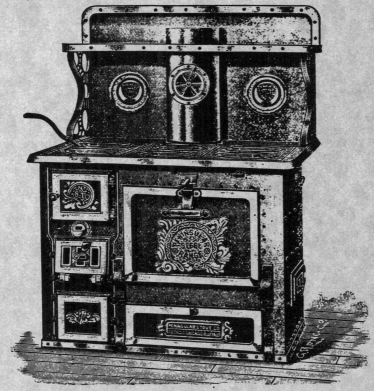

FURNACE, STOVES *AND* RANGES.

We do all kinds of Furnace work and keep a large assortment of Ranges and Coal Heaters. You will have better success with many of the within recipes, if baked in a Peninsular Range. We also keep all kinds of Kitchen Utensils.

FULLER & EVERSON, Union City, Pa.

Fish Chowder.

Mrs. Cheney.

Three or four pounds of fresh haddock or cod, carefully cleaned, and cut in pieces three inches square. Place in bottom of kettle five or six slices salt pork, fry brown, then add three onions sliced thin, fry them brown. Remove from the fire, and place on the pork and onions a layer of fish, sprinkle with salt and pepper, then a layer of peeled, sliced potatoes, then fish and potatoes till the fish is used up. Cover with water and let boil for half an hour, break up six crackers, put in with the fish, and lastly add a pint or more of milk. Let it get thoroughly heated and serve.

To Fry Fish.

Mrs. H. C. Cheney.

Clean the fish, wipe dry, rub a little salt inside, and sprinkle with a little pepper. The fat should be smoking hot when the fish is put on, and kept at the same temperature throughout the cooking. Fish may be fried in lard or clarified drippings, or what is better, the fat obtained by frying thin slices of salt pork. The quantity required depending upon the size or number of fish, but a generous quantity is desired. If a piece of bread dropped into the fat will instantly brown, it will be hot enough to put the fish in. All small fish are better fried.

Salmon Timbales with Caper Sauce.

Mrs. H. C. Cheney.

One can of salmon, one-half cup of soft bread crumbs, one tablespoon melted butter, one tablespoon lemon juice, one-half tablespoon salt, one-half saltspoon cayenne, four eggs. Remove the bones and skin, chop the salmon fine, mix with the crumbs, butter and seasoning, and moisten with beaten egg. Pack closely in buttered cups, set them in a pan of hot water, and cook in the oven one half hour. Turn out on a platter, pour sauce around them, and garnish with sprigs of parsely.

Caper Sauce.

Mrs. H. C. Cheney.

Two tablespoons flour, one-half cup butter. one pint of boiling water, pepper and salt, three tablespoons capers, one tablespoon lemon juice, cream, butter and flour together, pour in the boiling water, set mixture over the fire and stir constantly until it has reached the boiling point; season with pepper, add lemon juice and capers.

Omelets.

Veal Omelet.
Mrs. Bole.

Two pounds of chopped veal, two eggs, one-half cup butter, one cup rolled crackers, sage if desired, salt and pepper to taste; mix in two small rolls, or one large. Bake two hours in dripper, basting as for roast.

Beef Omelet.
Mrs. Beebe.

One pound and a half of beef, chopped very fine, one cup of cracker crumbs, two eggs, one large tablespoon of butter, one level tablespoon salt, one small teaspoon pepper, mix together, and put water in to make a nice loaf. Bake with a little water in the pan.

Beef, or Veal Loaf.
Mrs. A. O. Gillett.

Two pounds meat, chopped fine, two cups bread crumbs, two eggs, salt, pepper and sage to taste, a little butter, and the juice of a lemon; bake one hour and let cool. Slice very thin.

Beef Omelet.
Mrs. Loomis.

Three pounds of beef, chopped very fine, three eggs, beaten together, six soda crackers, rolled fine, one tablespoon salt, one teaspoon pepper, two tablespoons melted butter, sage to taste; mix well, make into a loaf, put a little water in pan, and small pieces of butter over it. Bake one hour and a half.

French Omelet.
Mrs. Arthur Treat,

Three eggs, one-half tablespoon corn starch, one-half cup sweet milk; add yolks and beat together. Dissolve the corn starch in a little milk, now add a little salt and the milk, beat the whites to a stiff froth, mix all together, put in frying pan butter size of an egg, let get hot, pour in the omelet and cook.

Egg Omelet.
Mrs. L. Evarts.

Soak one teacup of bread crumbs in one cup of sweet milk till soft, beat the yolks of three eggs, and mix with the bread crumbs already in the milk, then beat the whites to a stiff froth, beat all together, with a little salt, fry brown. This is sufficient for six persons, and is very nice.

The Union City Times,

McLEAN BROS., Proprietors.

PRINTERS OF

Wedding Invitations,
Party Invitations,
Plain and Fancy Programs.
Business Stationery, Etc.

ORDERS TAKEN FOR

Engraved Invitations,
Engraved Calling Cards,
Embossed Stationery,
Cuts of All Kinds, Etc.

YOUR PAPER

Shows your taste and betrays character. Don't use shabby, fuzzy note paper, when you can get something good, with your name and address neatly printed on it, at about the same price. Call and see samples.

Poultry.

Roast Turkey.

Mrs. W. C. Siegfried.

When turkey is dressed rub salt outside and in, fill with dressing, then place in roaster or dripping pan, set this in wash boiler, or other dish large enough, with some water, and a couple of nails or sticks to keep from bottom, cover boiler, steam (for a twelve-pound fowl) about three hours, occasionally sprinkle salt, then remove roaster, put in oven about an hour and a half to brown ; basting often.

Filling for Roast Fowl.

Two quarts dry bread, cut in small pieces, salt, pepper and sage to suit the taste, well mixed through it ; put in basin, then in steamer, steam until thoroughly moistened, take out and add butter size of an egg, and one egg well beaten, stir lightly with a fork. When filling the fowl shake, but not pack with a spoon.

Chicken Suffla.

Mrs. A. O. Gillett.

One cup of finely minced chicken, fish or veal, one tablespoon butter, and one tablespoon flour, melted together; then add one cup of milk, boil until like gravy, add fish or chicken, mix well, then add yolk of one egg, well beaten, then put into a well-buttered dish, have the white of one egg well beaten, and stir lightly into the top of the rest, then cover lightly with cracker crumbs, and bake twenty minutes in a very hot oven.

Pressed Chicken.

Mrs. A. O. Gillett.

Boil a chicken until tender, take out all the bones, chop very fine, season with salt, pepper and plenty of butter; add to the liquor the chicken was boiled in one cup bread crumbs, made soft with warm water, add to this the chopped chicken, when heated take out and press in a dish ; serve cold.

Deviled Chicken.

Mrs. D. G. Smiley.

Clean, split down the back, and boil until done, then lay in a dripping pan, and rub all over with a sauce made by whipping a teaspoonful of vinegar, a teaspoon of prepared mustard, and a pinch of pepper, sift fine bread crumbs over it, and set on upper grate to brown.

The Cooper House.

**REFITTED AND REFURNISHED
THROUGHOUT,**

AND IS TO-DAY ONE OF THE FINEST EQUIPPED
HOTELS IN WESTERN PENNA.

Located on Main St., Union City, Pa.

MIDWAY BETWEEN THE ERIE R. R. AND THE P. & E. R. R.

 **House Heat throughout
with Hot Air. Rooms well
ventilated. Bath Rooms,
Etc.**

SPECIAL ATTENTION GIVEN TO OUR GUESTS AT ALL
TIMES.

FINE NEW LIVERY IN CONNECTION.

M. J. WAGER, PROPRIETOR.

Puddings and Sauces.

Suet Pudding.

Mrs. Herries.

One cup chopped beef suet, one cup molasses, one cup sweet milk, three cups flour, one egg, one tablespoonful salt, three-fourths teaspoon soda, one cup raisins, one cup currants, mix well, and steam two hours; serve with liquid sauce.

Fruit Pudding.

Mrs. J. S. Bissell.

One cup of sugar, one cup fruit, one cup chopped apples, one cup bread crumbs, one cup chopped suet, six eggs, two even teaspoons of soda; steam three hours.

Favorite Fruit Pudding.

Mrs. W. T. Boyd.

One cup of sugar, one cup milk, one egg, two cups flour, one and a half teaspoons baking powder; flavor with nutmeg. Put in a pudding dish two cups sliced apples, peaches pealed and halved, cherries, or any fruit desired, pour over the mixture and bake, when done turn out on serving dish, fruit side up. Serve with liquid sauce, or sugar and cream.

Ginger Pudding.

Mrs. W. T. Boyd.

One egg, one cup molasses, half cup butter, half cup hot water, half cup seeded raisins, one teaspoon soda, one tablespoonful ginger, flour to make stiff like cake, and steam one hour.

Sauce for Ginger Pudding.

One egg, one cup sugar, one-third cup butter, one tablespoon flour, one and one-half tablespoons lemon; pour boiling water on to make like thin starch.

Poor Man's Pudding.

Mrs. V. D.

One quart milk, one-half cup rice, salt to taste, one teacup sugar, butter size of walnut, small cup raisins, put in oven cold, stir occasionally while swelling; bake slowly two hours.

93

Graham Pudding.

Mrs. A. G. Sweet.

One cup molasses, one cup raisins, one cup sour milk, one teaspoon soda, a little nutmeg and cinnamon, two cups graham flour; steam three hours.

Sauce.

One cup sugar, one-third cup butter, one egg, one-half pint boiling hot milk, one teaspoon vanilla.

Graham Pudding.

Mrs. J. Chapman.

One cup molasses, one and a half cups graham flour, one of milk, one cup each raisins and currants, one tablespoon butter, one-half a nutmeg, one-half teaspoon cinnamon, one teaspoon soda, one egg, beat all together; steam three hours.

Sauce.

Two cups sugar, two tablespoons butter, four tablespoons vinegar, four of boiling water, two eggs, beaten thoroughly.

Corn Starch Pudding.

Mrs. F. W. Minniss.

One quart milk, three tablespoons corn starch, whites of three eggs, beaten light; cook until thick.

Sauce.

One pint milk, one cup sugar, scant tablespoon corn starch, yolks of three eggs; flavor with vanilla. Cook over hot water.

Apple Tapioca Pudding.

Mrs. J. C. M.

To one-half cup tapioca add one and one half pints cold water, let it cook until cooked clear, remove, sweeten and flavor with nutmeg and lemon; put into a deep dish, in which have been placed six or eight pared and cored apples, bake until apples are done. Serve cold, with whipped cream.

Delicious Lemon Pudding.

Mrs. C. B. Fulton.

Juice and grated rind of one lemon, one cup sugar, yolks of two eggs, three heaping tablespoons flour, pinch of salt, pint rich milk, mix flour and part of milk to a smooth paste, add juice and

95

rind of lemon, sugar, yolks of eggs, well beaten, and rest of milk. Line a dish with puff paste, one-fourth inch thick, pour in custard, bake in a quick oven till done. Beat whites to a stiff froth, add two tablespoons sugar, spread over top, return to oven and brown; serve with very cold, or whipped cream.

Raisin Puffs.

Mrs. E. Decker.

Two eggs, one-half cup butter, two tablespoons sugar, two cups flour, three teaspoons baking powder, one cup milk, one cup seeded and chopped raisins; steam one-half hour in small buttered cups.

Vinegar Sauce for Puffs.

One cup brown sugar, one cup water, one teaspoon butter, one teaspoon vinegar, pinch of salt, one tablespoon flour, beat well together, then pour on the water boiling hot; let it come to a good boil.

Frosted Fruit.

Mrs. F. E. M.

Take peaches, berries, currants, or any summer fruit, and stir well through it frosting prepared as for cake, of whites of eggs and powdered sugar, spread on a platter, and set on ice till needed.

Cake Cream.

Mrs. F. E. M.

Slice stale cake, and put in a pudding dish in layers, with preserves or stoned raisins, pour over this half a cup sweet cream, well sugared, cover the top with a layer of cake, and spread on this a frosting as for cake, brown slightly in oven; serve cold.

Orange Charlotte.

Mrs. Belle L. Page.

One-fourth box gelatine, one-third cup cold water, one-third boiling water, one cup sugar, juice one lemon, one cup orange juice and pulp, three eggs (whites); line mould with sections of oranges, soak gelatine till soft, pour on boiling water, add sugar and lemon juice, strain, add juice and pulp, cool in pan of ice water. Beat whites of eggs, and add when jelly begins to harden, and beat together till stiff enough to drop; pour into moulds or orange baskets.

The Leading Dry Goods House of this section.

A. M. FULLER & CO.,

MEADVILLE, PA.

DRESS FABRICS.

Special values in Dress Goods at 25c., 50c. and upwards. Fine Crepon Suitings. Special fabrics for bridal outfits.

FINE DRESS TRIMMINGS.

Colored Lace Gimps, Jet Laces, Embroidered Chiffon, White and Ecru Band Trimmings. Jet Collars, $1.50 upwards. Fine Buttons, Narrow Jet Trimmings, Velvets in all shades.

BARGAIN COUNTERS.

Of interest—Zephyr Ginghams, 7c. yard. All Linen Twilled Crash, 8c. yard, worth 10c. Children's Spliced Knee, Fast Black Stockings, 15c. pair, worth 20c.

JACKETS, CAPES, READY-MADE SKIRTS.

We offer the largest assortment of garments in this city.

Cloth Capes, $2.50 upwards; Silk Capes, $5.00 upwards; Velvet Capes, $5.00 upwards; Ready-made Skirts, in Serge and Mohair, Brocaded Mohair and Brocaded Silks, $5.00 to $16.00. We offer a make of Skirts correct in style, well made and low in price. Ladies' Silk Waists, $4.50 upwards; Cambric Waists, 50c. upwards; Ladies' Calico, Sateen, Lawn and Dimity Wrappers, 75c., $1.00 and upwards.

Orange Baskets.

Mrs. H. S. Thompson.

One pine apple, picked in pieces, three bananas, sliced, three oranges, cut fine, mix well together. Make a syrup by boiling one cup sugar, one-fourth cup of water, add this to fruit, when a thick syrup. Fill baskets made of oranges and serve ice cold. To be eaten with cake.

Floating Island.

Mrs. A. G. Sweet.

Dissolve one heaping tablespoon cornstarch and three of sugar, in one-fourth cup of milk, add beaten yolks of four eggs, one teaspoon vanilla, stir into one quart boiling milk, cook five minutes, pour out in a deep dish, beat the whites, drop two inches apart one tablespoon of the beaten whites ; serve cold.

Snow Balls.

Mrs. Belle L. Page.

One cup sugar, yolks of three eggs beaten very light, three tablespoons water, one lemon rind grated, whites of eggs beaten to stiff froth, two tablespoons lemon juice, one cup flour, one and a half teaspoons baking powder ; pour into buttered cups and steam half an hour. When done turn out, and sift powdered sugar on top. Serve with sauce.

Sauce for Snow Balls.

Cream one-fourth cup butter, and one-half cup powdered sugar slowly (sift the sugar), add three tablespoons cream, one teaspoon vanilla, or lemon ; beat well, place over hot water, and stir until hot.

A Delicious Desert.

Miss Nellie Gillett.

Take one cracker for each person, dip in hot water, put in any pretty glass sauce dish, put on each a generous lump of jelly ; take one pint cream, sweeten to taste, flavor with vanilla, and pour over crackers.

Quick Puff Pudding.

Mrs. V. D.

Stir one pint flour, two teaspoons baking powder, and a little salt together, wet with milk till soft, place in steamer well-greased cups, put in each a teaspoonful of batter, then one of fruit, berries, apples or any sauce convenient, cover with another spoonful of batter, steam twenty minutes ; eat with sauce or sweetened cream.

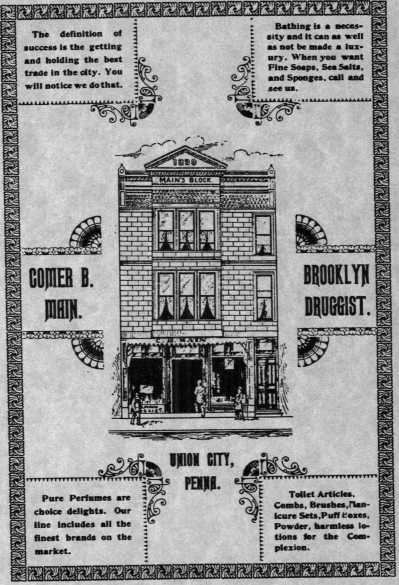

The definition of success is the getting and holding the best trade in the city. You will notice we do that.

Bathing is a necessity and it can as well as not be made a luxury. When you want Fine Soaps, Sea Salts, and Sponges, call and see us.

COMER B. MAIN.

BROOKLYN DRUGGIST.

1896

MAIN'S BLOCK.

UNION CITY, PENNA.

Pure Perfumes are choice delights. Our line includes all the finest brands on the market.

Toilet Articles, Combs, Brushes, Manicure Sets, Puff Boxes, Powder, harmless lotions for the Complexion.

Sauce.

Beat one egg and one-half cup sugar till light, stir in well one tablespoon flour, and one and one-half tablespoons lemon juice, pour over one pint boiling water.

Cranberry Cake.

Mrs. F. E. M.

Put in layers, first cranberry jelly, strained and smooth, then slices of stale white cake, then custard made of yolks of eggs, then cake, then cranberry, then cake, then a frosting made of the whites of eggs; serve cold with cream.

Cherry Pudding.

Mrs. F. M. McClintock.

One pint of flour, two teaspoons baking powder, pinch of salt, butter size of a walnut, stir together with sufficient water to make a stiff batter, into this stir one pint canned red cherries, after draining off juice ; steam one and a half hours.

Sauce.

Take cherry juice, one tablespoon flour, one-half cup sugar, beaten white of one egg ; boil together.

Orange Desert.

Mrs. E. J. W.

Mix nearly one quart water, with juice and pulp of two lemons. two cups sugar, boil sufficiently to dissolve sugar, then strain, bring again to a boil, stirring in two spoons dissolved cornstarch, stir and boil slowly ten minutes, when cool pour over one-half dozen sliced oranges ; serve with whipped cream.

Splendid Steamed Pudding.

Mrs. W. L. Fuller.

One cup sweet milk, one egg, small piece butter, two table-spoons sugar, one and one-half cups flour, two teaspoons baking powder, one teaspoon vanilla, one cup seeded raisins; steam one hour.

Sauce.

One tablespoon of butter, three of sugar, two of flour, one teaspoon vanilla, stir all together ; add boiling water to the consistency of cream.

Tapioca Cocoanut Pudding.

Mrs. V. D.

Four tablespoons tapico, soaked over night in water to cover, one quart of milk, yolks of two eggs, one-half cup sugar, let it cook ten minutes, then add two tablespoons cocoanut. Make frosting of whites of eggs, with one teaspoon cocoanut added, brown slightly in oven; eat cold.

Prune Pudding.

Mrs. J. S. Bissell.

Whites of five eggs beaten stiff, one-half cup sugar, one-fourth teaspoon salt, one-fourth cream tartar, one-fourth pound prunes cooked and chopped fine. Bake in buttered dish, in boiling water, twenty-two minutes.

Custard for Prune Pudding.

Yolks of the eggs, one large cup sweet milk, one heaping tea-spoon cornstarch, one-fourth cup sugar; flavor with vanilla. Pour around pudding after it settles and turn out.

Queen of Puddings.

N. C.

One pint bread crumbs, one quart sweet milk, oue cup sugar, yolks four eggs, butter size of an egg. After it is baked spread over the top a layer of jelly, and a frosting made of the whites of the eggs, and one cup white sugar; set in oven a few minutes to brown.

Fruit Salad.

Mrs. J. C. McLean.

One-half box gelatine, soaked in one-half cup cold water, one-half cup boiling water, one cup lemon juice, one of orange juice, one of sugar; let it stand until it begins to thicken, then beat, and and lastly add whites of five eggs, well beaten. Pack in mould with fruit.

Lemon Jelly.

One box Plymouth Rock gelatine, one pint cold water, soak half an hour, pour on one quart boiling water, squeeze out and strain juice of two lemons, stir gelatine until dissolved, then add lemon juice; sweeten to taste. Put in moulds.

103

Fruit Salad.

Use the above recipe, when cool enough to begin to jelly, pour one layer in dish you wish to serve it in, then a layer of any kind of fruit, alternate with jelly, serve with whipped cream. With light fruit, use red gelatine ; with dark fruit, use white gelatine.

Fruit Jelly.

Mrs. H. S. Thompson.

Soak one-half box gelatine in cold water to cover it well one hour, pour into this one pint boiling water, and strain through a bag into a dish containing the juice of four oranges, one-half a lemon, and one cup sugar, well dissolved, then pour the whole into a mould lined with candied cherries, and set in a cool place until firm.

Apple Snow Pudding.

Mrs. F. M. McClintock.

Bake a large tin of sour apples, when cold take a large cup of the apple, free from core and skin, one cup of granulated sugar, white of one egg, beat about fifteen minutes with egg beater, till light and foamy.

Dressing.

One and one-half pints milk, two eggs, one-third cup sugar, two level teaspoons cornstarch, one teaspoon vanilla ; serve in dishes, pouring dressing over.

Orange Pudding.

Mrs. M. Green.

One cup stale bread, soak in one-half cup of milk, beat to a pulp, mix with the grated rind of one orange and the juice of two oranges ; yolks of two eggs, beaten well with one-half cup sugar. Butter six earthen cups and set them in a pan of hot water, then beat the whites of the eggs stiff and mix lightly with the other ingredients, fill the cups two-thirds full and bake twenty minutes, when done turn out and serve with golden sauce.

Golden Sauce.

Mrs. H. C. C.

One cup powdered sugar, one-third cup of milk, one-third cup of butter, yolks of two eggs, juice of one orange ; beat the butter to a cream, then add the sugar gradually, then the eggs, without beating, next the flavoring, then the milk, a little at a time, set in a dish of hot water until ready to serve.

Orange Cream.

Mrs. D. B. Honeywell.

Cover a fourth of a box of gelatine with four tablespoons water, and soak one-half hour, add one-half cup sugar, place over tea kettle till melted, then add half pint orange juice and strain, turn in a dish, and put in a cool place, watch carefully, and stir often. Whip one-half pint cream to a stiff froth, when mixture begins to congeal, stir in cream; turn all in a mould, and put in a cold place till ready to use.

Steamed Pudding.

Mrs. L. E.

One cup brown sugar, one of seeded raisins, one third cup of butter, one quart sour milk, two eggs, one teaspoon soda, a little salt, mix to a soft batter, put in buttered basin, and tie a cloth over to prevent steam escaping; steam two hours.

Apricot Whip.

Mrs. H. C. C.

Soak one-half pound apricots over night in one-half cup of water, in the morning add one-half cup of sugar, cook until soft and thick; sift. When cold add whites of two eggs, beaten stiff, beat thoroughly. Pour around it a custard made of one pint of milk, yolks of two eggs, two tablespoons of sugar; flavor with lemon.

Apple Pudding.

A very nice pudding is made from stale cake and stewed apples, either fresh or dried, crumble the cake and put a thick layer in a buttered pudding dish, add a layer of stewed apples and add another of cake crumbs. For a quart dish of this mixture beat the yolks of two eggs, and white of one, with a pint of milk and three tablespoons sugar, pour over the cake and apples, and bake thirty minutes. Draw to the oven door and cover with a meringue, made from the whites of eggs and beaten with sugar.

Apple Snow.

Mrs. H. C. Cheney.

Peel and grate one large, sour apple, sprinkle over it a small cupful of powdered sugar as you grate it, to keep it from turning dark break into this the whites of two eggs, and beat it all constantly for half an hour; take care to have it in a large bowl, as it beats up very stiff and light, heap this in a glass dish and pour a fine, smooth custard around it and serve. A very delicate desert.

SNOW FLAKE.

GENUINE.

We make the above-named brand of Flour. It is made from choice Winter Wheat. For family use no better flour can be made. It answers every purpose. It makes excellent bread, and is equally as well adapted to pastry work. You need but the one grade. Use it for everything, Bread, Pies, Cake, etc. We guarantee every sack to please. Return, if not satisfactory.

CROUCH BROS. CO.,

ERIE, PENNA.

Almond Custard.

Mrs. O. Glezen.

Take four ounces of sweet almonds, two and a half ounces of sugar, one pint of cream, one teaspoonful rose water, the yolks of four eggs. Blanch the almonds and beat them to a smooth paste with a tablespoonful of water, using a few drops occasionally, add the rose water to the cream, the beaten yolks, almonds, and sugar, place it over boiling water, and stir until it thickens; serve in cups.

Spanish Cream.

Mrs. L. D. Rockwell.

Soak one-third box gelatine in three-fourths quart of milk for one hour, set in a dish of hot water, when boiling stir in the yolks of three eggs, beaten with three fourths cup of sugar, when well cooked remove from fire and stir in the beaten whites of three eggs; flavor and pour into moulds.

Cold Cabinet Pudding.

Mrs. E. B. Landsrath.

Soak one fourth box gelatine in one-fourth cup cold water until soft, beat yolks of three eggs, add one-fourth cup sugar, one teaspoon salt, pour on one pint boiling milk, cook like soft custard, then add the softened gelatine, strain, add one teaspoon vanilla. Decorate the bottom of mould with candied fruit, put on a layer of custard, when hard but in a layer of lady fingers soaked in custard, then a layer of macaroons, and so on; serve with whipped cream

Pudding.

Anon.

One pint scalded milk, one pint cake crumbs, scant cup cocoanut, yolks of three eggs, all beaten together, beat whites together, and last stir all together; bake half an hour. Eat with whipped cream, or cream and sugar.

Pastry

Pastry.

Mrs. J. S. Thompson.

To one pint sifted flour add one even teaspoon baking powder, and sweet cream enough to wet the flour, leaving crust a little stiff. This is enough for two pies.

Good, Common Paste.

One coffeecup lard, three of sifted flour, and a little salt. In winter soften the lard a little, but not in summer. Cut it well into the flour with a knife, then mix with cold water quickly into a moderately stiff dough, handling as little as possible. This makes four common-sized pies. After rolling spread with a teaspoon, butter, fold and roll again, using trimming, etc., for undercrust.

Chocolate Pies.

Mrs. A. G. Sweet.

One cup sugar, four eggs, whites of two for frosting, beat the yolks to a cream, one and one-half cups of sweet milk, two tablespoons Baker's chocolate, dissolve in a little hot milk, flavor with vanilla, add altogether and bake as a custard pie, then add the beaten whites, a little sugar, and brown.

Lemon Pie.

Two crusts, one lemon cut fine, one and one–half cups sugar, one cup water, heaping tablespoon cornstarch.

Lemon Pie.

Sadie Honeywell.

The juice and grated rind of one lemon, one cup hot water, one of sugar, one egg, one tablespoon cornstarch, butter size of an egg, have the water boiling, wet cornstarch and stir till it thickens, add sugar, butter and lemon, when this is cold add egg; bake with two crusts. Very fine; try it.

Lemon Pie, with Milk.

Mrs. J. Chapman.

Two eggs, one cup sugar, two tablespoonsful melted butter, one tablespoon cornstarch, one grated lemon rind and juice, beat the eggs and sugar until light, then mix in the lemon and starch one cup new milk; bake thirty minutes.

Sour Milk Pie.

Mrs. H. C. Cheney.

One cup sugar, one cup sour milk, one cup chopped and seeded raisins, two eggs, all kinds of spices; baked between two crusts.

Lemon Pie.

Mrs. M. Moore.

One grated lemon, one cup sugar, one cup water, yolk of an egg, two tablespoons cornstarch; bake the crust. Boil the custard until it thickens, pour into crust, add the whites of two well-beaten eggs, and bake a light brown.

Pie Plant Pie.

Mrs. Cheney.

One pound pie plant, one and one-half cups seeded raisins, two cups sugar, two eggs, chop pie plant and raisins together, then add the other ingredients. Makes two pies.

Mock Mince Pie.

Mrs. Moore.

One cup chopped crackers, one cup seeded raisins, two cups water, one cup sugar, one half cup molasses, one-half cup vinegar, two tablespoons butter, spice to taste; heat it hot.

Lemon Pie.

Mrs. Herries.

Two tablespoons of flour, with one of butter, mixed to a smooth paste, then add one cup of granulated sugar, one cup of milk, yolks of three eggs, rind and juice of one lemon, beat the whites of three eggs, add three tablespoons sugar, put on pie and set in oven to brown.

Cream Pie.

Mrs. D. A. Wright.

One tablespoon of cornstarch, one tablespoon of flour, one pint of milk, the yolks of two eggs, beaten in one-half cup sugar. Bake the crust first, and cook the custard, and put in the baked crust, beat the whites of two eggs to a stiff froth, and add a little sugar, put in the oven and brown slightly.

110

Mince Meat.

Mrs. P. H. Thompson.

Four pounds meat, eight pounds apples, two pounds sugar, one quart molasses, one pound raisins, one pound currants, one teacup boiled cider, four tablespoons cinnamon, two of cloves, two of allspice, three of black pepper, two of salt, one nutmeg.

Sweet Potato Pie.

Mrs. Boyd.

Steam potatoes until tender, pare and put through colander, to one pint of potatoes add one pint of milk, three eggs, from one to two cups sugar, to suit taste, flavor with ginger; one crust.

Ripe Currant Pie.

Mrs. Sweet.

One coffeecup crushed currants, small cup sugar, one tablespoon flour beaten with the yolks of two eggs, bake with one crust, then take beaten whites of two eggs, add two tablespoons sugar, put on top, and return to oven.

Peach Pie.

Mrs. J. Thompson.

Line a pie tin with puff paste, fill with pared peaches cut in halves, well covered with sugar, bake until done, remove from oven, and cover with whites of two eggs beaten to a stiff froth, with two tablespoons powdered sugar, return to oven and brown slightly.

Orange Pie.

Mrs. J. S. Thompson.

Grated rind and juice of two oranges, four eggs, four tablespoons sugar, and one of butter; cream the butter and sugar, add the beaten eggs, then the rind and juice of the oranges, and lastly the whites beaten to a froth and mixed in lightly. Bake with an undercrust.

Orange Pie.

Mrs. M. Geeen.

Juice, grated rind and pulp of one orange, one cup sugar, one cup water, one heaping tablespoon cornstarch, yolks of three eggs, bake the crust, boil the custard until it thickens, pour into crust, add the whites of eggs, well beaten, and bake a light brown.

Cocoanut Pie.

Mrs. E. C. Richards.

One cup white sugar, one half cup butter, four eggs, one cup cocoanut, one quart milk, put cocoanut with butter and sugar, add milk and beaten eggs. This makes two pies.

Pumpkin Pie.

Sadie Honeywell.

Boil the pumpkin until soft, drain perfectly dry, then beat and mash smooth and fine, add a piece of butter, and sugar to taste, while hot a little salt and pepper, nutmeg and ginger to taste; allow two eggs for each pie. Lastly add milk enough to make a pretty thick custard.

Pie Plant Cream Pie.

Line a pie tin with a rich crust, cover the bottom with pie plant, beat together one cup sugar, yolk of one egg, one tablespoon flour, one cup thin cream, and pour over pie plant. After baking beat the whites of eggs stiff, add a little sugar, put over top of pie, and brown in the oven.

Mock Mince Pie.

Mrs. Sadie Humphrey.

One cup seeded raisins, one-half cup currants, one cup cold water, one-half cup sugar, one-half cup molasses, one cup vinegar, one-half cup grated bread crumbs, one egg, big piece butter, all kinds spices and little salt and pepper. Put it in a crock on the stove and let it come to a boil. Will make two large pies. Let the mince meat get cold before using. They are immense.

Cranberry Pie.

Mrs. H. C. Cheney.

Take two cups chopped cranberries, add to them one cup of seeded and chopped raisins, one-half cup sugar, one-half cup of water, two tablespoons of flour, one egg; line pie plate with rich crust, fill with mixture, cover with an upper crust, and bake in slow oven.

Pickles.

Pickle Brine.

Mrs. F. E. McLean.

One and one-half gallons good cider vinegar, one-half gallon water, one and a half pints of salt, one-half pound alum. Dissolve alum in the water, put whole in large jar, and place pickles in as you pick them, cover with heavy weight. When you want to use them wash clean, bring them to a boiling heat in water, then put in sweet pickle while hot.

Cucumber Pickles.

Mrs. Margaret Bole.

One hundred green cumbers, rather small, soak twenty-four hours in weak salt brine, scald in very weak vinegar, with a piece of alum size of hickory nut. Place in cans, have pure cider vinegar boiling hot, reduce vinegar if too strong, sugar to taste. Put mixed spices on top of every can; also small pieces of fresh horse radish. Seal tight.

Cucumber Pickles.

C. K. Wilson.

Wash small cucumbers, pack tight in glass jars, spice to taste, with whole black pepper, white and black mustard seed, celery seed if you like, a piece of horse radish and a small red pepper to a quart can. To one gallon of good cider vinegar add one cup each of salt and sugar ("A" sugar is best), have the vinegar boiling hot, pour over the pickles, and seal at once.

Cucumber Pickles.

Mrs. Harley Thompson.

Soak cucumbers in salt and water over night, pack pickles in cans solid, put in each can pulverized alum size of a pea, then pour over scalding hot vinegar and seal. These are excellent sour pickles.

Cucumber Pickles.

Mrs. Alden.

Wash the pickles and let them stand in weak brine over night, in the morning scald in the brine and prepare a sweet, spiced vinegar, and pour over them in glass can; seal tight.

Cucumber Pickles.

Mrs. H. C. Cheney.

Three dozen large cucumbers, eighteen small onions, chop quite fine, sprinkle salt over them, and put in a colander to drain over night, then put one teacup of white mustard seed and a tablespoon of ground pepper, and cover with good, cold cider vinegar; then can.

Pickled Cucumbers.

Mrs. Arthur Young.

Wash cucumbers and place in jar, make a brine of one cup of salt to six quarts of water, when scalding hot turn over the cucumbers, repeat this two mornings, on the third morning take one gallon of vinegar, put in small piece of alum, when hot put in cucumbers, let scald, do not boil, skim out, put in jars, take one gallon vinegar, three cups sugar, one-half ounce mustard seed, three red peppers, boil fifteen minutes, pour over cucumbers. Good.

Pickled Cabbage.

Lizzie Brunstetter.

Three solid heads of cabbage sliced fine, place in a jar with a good handful of salt between the layers, put a weight upon it and let stand over night, the next day drain out the brine, and put the cabbage in a large wooden bowl, and put in one cup or more of white sugar, three green peppers chopped fine, one ounce of whole yellow mustard, mixed together, then put in a jar and cover with good cider vinegar. This will keep a long time.

Pickled Cabbage.

Mrs. James Woods.

Three heads cabbage cut fine, five sweet and three red peppers, one-half pound mustard seed, two cups sugar, two quarts vinegar. Let the cabbage stand over night, with a handful of salt sprinkled over it. In the morning squeeze it out with the hands, mix mustard seed and sugar with it, also pepper, and cover with vinegar; ready for use the next day. Will keep for months in a cool place.

Tomato Chowder.

Mrs. Hipple.

One peck green tomatoes, six large onions, chopped fine, add cup of salt, let stand over night, drain, and boil in two quarts vinegar and one quart water, boil fifteen minutes, let drain in colander, add two pounds of brown sugar, one-half pound white mustard, three quarts of vinegar, and boil twenty minutes, then add one tablespoon ground mustard, one tablespoon allspice, one tablespoon pepper, one tablespoon ginger, one tablespoon cloves, one tablespoon cinnamon.

Mustard Pickles.

Mrs. H. C. Cheney.

One pint small cucumbers. one pint green tomatoes, one pint small onions, one pint cauliflower, one quart cabbage, one-half cup flour. one half teacup mustard, one-half teacup sugar, one-half ounce timerick powder, two quarts vinegar; cut up vegetables all fine, put in salt and water over night, drain, put in vinegar, and cook until tender, take mustard, sugar, tumerick powder and stir in a little cold vinegar, then add to the above, let come to a boil; can while hot

Tag End of the Garden.

Mrs. W. C. Siegfried.

One head of cauliflower, small pieces, one quart of lima beans, two quarts cabbage, chopped fine, one and one-half quarts of green tomatoes, chopped fine, two large cucumbers, cut in short pieces, seventy five small cucumbers, one to two inches in length, six carrots, cut in small pieces, one quart small onions, one dozen ears of corn, cut from cob, two bunches of celery, cut in small pieces, a few string beans, one chopped red pepper, seeds removed, one pound brown sugar, one gallon of vinegar, one-half pound mustard. Boil the ingredients in salt and water until tender, place in colander and drain, stir the lumps out of the mustard with a little vinegar, then pour into the vinegar and let come to a boil, pour the boiling liquid over the ingredient and stir; seal in cans.

Tomato Catsup.

Sadie L. Honeywell.

One gallon strained tomatoes, four tablespoons of salt, two tablespoons black pepper, one-half tablespoon red pepper, two tablespoons white mustard seed, one tablespoon allspice, one-half tablespoon cloves, one-half tablespoon cinnamon, one pint vinegar, one cup brown sugar; boil together three hours.

Raw Tomato Catsup.

Mrs. I. L. Clifford.

One-half peck ripe tomatoes pared and chopped fine, one root of horse radish, one-half cup salt, one cup sugar, one teaspoon black pepper, one teaspoon ground cloves, two teaspoons allspice, two or three peppers, with seeds, cut fine, one quart vinegar, cork in air tight bottles; add celery if desired.

Celery Sauce.

Mrs. Glenn.

Twenty-four green tomatoes chopped fine, and let stand over night in salt and water, one small head cabbage, two small onions, one bunch celery, chopped fine ; put all in kettle and cover well with vinegar, boil one-half hour, add one-half cup mustard, five cents worth celery seed, five cents worth white mustard seed, three cents worth tumerick, one pound brown sugar.

Preserves and Sweet Pickles.

To Preserve a Husband.

Be careful in your selection, do not choose one too young, and take only such varieties as have been raised in a good moral atmosphere. When once decided upon and selected let that part remain forever settled, and give your entire time and thought to domestic use. Some insist on keeping them .in a pickle, while others are constantly keeping them in hot water. But even poor varieties may be made sweet, tender and good by garnishing with patience, well sweetened with smiles, and flavored with kisses to taste; then wrap them well in the mantle of charity, keep warm with a steady flow of domestic devotion, and serve with peaches and cream When thus prepared they will keep for years.

Quince Honey.

Mrs. Bole.

Five pounds granulated sugar, one quart of water, boil to syrup, pare, core and grate five quinces, add syrup and boil twenty minutes.

Quince Honey.

Pare and grate three large quinces, add three pounds white sugar and one quart cold water, and boil twenty minutes; seal while hot.

To Preserve Citron.

Mrs. W. E. Caldwell.

Pare citron, take out the middle, cut into slices, soak in cold water four hours to freshen, syrup, one pint of water to each pound of sugar, boil to a syrup and skim, put in citron and simmer slowly until tender enough to cut with a straw, slice in two lemons when partly done.

116

Currants Put Up Without Cooking.

Mrs. Mulkie.

Mash a few at a time, taking care that every currant is mashed, or it will not keep. Allow one quart of granulated sugar to every quart of fruit, after being mashed mix well, after sugar is dissolved, fill cans to overflowing. shake down each time you add currants, so there will be no cavity, then screw cover on tight as possible. Currants canned in this way are delicious, and the seeds are more tender.

Canned Pine Apple.

Slice pine apple thin, weigh, place in earthen or granite dish, with a very little water, stew gently until tender, drain, put one pound of sugar for each pound of fruit, add sugar to liquor turned off, boil and skim, then add fruit, boil up once, then can and seal.

Peach Butter.

Mrs. W. O. Black.

Prepare and cook your peaches, and put them through a colander, use half as much sugar as fruit, a little cinnamon, and some boiled cider if you have it, cook up and can. This does not need to be cooked, as you would apple butter.

Pickled Peaches.

Mrs. Rulof Fuller.

Five pounds peaches, three pounds of coffee A sugar, one quart of cider vinegar, wipe peaches with white flannel cloth, boil until done in the vinegar and sugar, take out, put in the vinegar and sugar, one-half ounce of cloves, and one half ounce cinnamon, boil well and pour over.

Spiced Pears.

Mrs. J. A. Humphrey.

One peck pears, three pounds white sugar, one pint vinegar, one ounce cinnamon, half ounce cloves, bring the sugar and vinegar, with the spices, in a bag, to a boil, put in the pears a few at a time, testing with a fork, to see when tender, when done place the fruit in a jar, pour the hot vinegar over and cover tight.

Green Tomato Sweet Pickles.

Mrs. C. B. Geer.

Take green tomatoes. slice and scald them in salt and water, add a little alum and boil until tender, skim them out and drain, to every quart of vinegar, add one pound of sugar, and spices to suit taste, pour over them while hot.

117

Salads.

Potato Salad.

Mrs. G. W. H. Reed.

Boil six large potatoes, when cool cut in small dice, add one onion, chopped fine, four hard boiled eggs, three stalks of celery cut small; salt and pepper.

Dressing.

Four tablespoons vinegar, yolks of two eggs, beaten, a little salt and pepper, two teaspoons sugar, one teaspoon prepared mustard, one tablespoon butter, cook until thick, when cold add half cup sweet cream, and mix with potatoes.

Cabbage Salad.

Mrs. Beebe.

One medium-sized head of cabbage, chopped fine, pepper and salt to taste.

Dressing.

Take butter size of an egg, one-half cup sour cream, one-half cup vinegar, two tablespoons sugar, let boil, add yolks of four eggs, beaten; cool before turning on cabbage.

Salad.

Mrs. H. C. Cheney.

Three cold, boiled sweet potatoes, cut into half–inch squares, cut in very small pieces two small stalks of celery, with salt and pepper, and pour over a French dressing made as follows: Three tablespoons onion juice, one saltspoon each salt and pepper, stand in cool place two hours; garnish with olives.

Stuffed Tomato Salad.

Mrs. Hecker.

Remove centers from tomatoes, place on ice, mix equal parts chicken and celery, cut in dice, with two tablespoons chopped pickles, and enough mayonaise dressing to moisten; stuff tomatoes, and serve on lettuce leaves.

English Walnut Salad.

Helen Hecker.

Take equal parts of English walnuts and celery, chopped fine, mix these well together, with an oil mayonaise dressing; serve on lettuce leaves.

Egg Salad.

Mrs. H. N. Cheney.

Boil eight eggs fifteen minutes, chop, salt and pepper them, take one teaspoon of flour, one of sugar, one of butter, one of prepared mustard and one—half cup vinegar, cook, when cold pour over eggs; garnish with parsley.

Egg Salad.

Margaret L. Bole.

Ten hard-boiled eggs, two-thirds as much shreded lettuce as eggs, remove the yolks and mash fine, with two large spoons melted butter, one of sugar, four of vinegar, a sprinkle of cayenne, mustard if desired, little salt and pepper, chop the whites in large dice, mix lightly. One-half cup sweet cream improves this salad very much.

Veal Salad.

Belle L. Page.

Cut cold veal into dice, and white, crisp celery in similar pieces, in proportion of two measures of veal to one of celery.

Dressing.

Three eggs, well beaten, one tablespoon melted butter, nine of vinegar, mix three teaspoons sugar with one scant teaspoon of mustard, one of salt, one-half of pepper together, put on stove and cook till smooth and creamy, stirring all the time.

Veal Salad.

Mrs. J. C. McLean.

Stew veal until tender, season with salt and pepper, cut into small dice, and mix with an equal amount of lettuce, pour over any preferred dressing with whipped cream.

Beef Salad.

Mrs. M. W. Shreve.

Proportions for five persons: Two pounds cold, boiled chopped beef, four hard-boiled eggs. sliced, one large onion, chopped fine, one-half spoon chopped parsely, a little salt, pepper, and melted butter.

Dressing.

One cup weak vinegar, one-half cup sugar, two tablespoons butter, one tablespoon flour, a little salt and pepper, yolks of three eggs, cook; when cold add one half cup sour cream.

Cream Dressing for Cold Slaw.

Two tablespoonsful of whipped cream, four of vinegar, two of sugar. Beat and pour over cabbage cut very fine, and seasoned with salt.

Chicken Salad.

Margaret C. Kirk.

Boil chicken till tender, season well, when cold pick from bones into small shreds, take three times the amount of celery you have of chicken, shred fine and throw into ice water. Boil four eggs hard, and slice.

Dressing.

One boiled potato, mashed fine, with the yolks of two hard-boiled eggs, add three tablespoons melted butter, or salad oil, one teaspoon prepared mustard, little salt and pepper, one-half cup weak vinegar, mix all smoothly; pour this over the chicken, mixing well, then add celery and eggs.

Salmon Salad.

Margaret Bole.

One can salmon, three cups cabbage, chopped very fine, cayenne pepper and salt to taste.

Dressing.

One small cup vinegar, two tablespoons butter, sugar to taste, two eggs, put together as cooked mayonaise dressing.

Sweet Bread Salad.

Mrs. C. B. Fulton.

Two pairs of sweet breads soaked in salt water one hour, wash with cold water, and boil twenty minutes, when cold chop fine, add one-half as much celery, chopped fine, sprinkle with salt and pepper; mix with mayonaise dressing.

Dressing.

Two tablespoons butter, one of flour, one cup sweet cream or milk, one cup vinegar, one teaspoon mustard, one-half teaspoon salt, two of sugar, one-fourth of pepper, three eggs, put butter in sauce pan, when hot stir in flour and cream, when cooked draw to one side, and stir in eggs, have the rest mixed and stir in briskly; when cold, with silver fork, toss lightly till thoroughly mixed.

Dressing for Salads.

Mrs. A. C. Sherwood.

Yolks of eight eggs, or four whole eggs, one-half cup sugar, one tablespoon each salt, mustard, black pepper and flour, a very little cayenne, mix thoroughly; add one and one-half pints of vinegar, one cup butter; let the mixture come to a boil. This will keep for weeks in hottest weather. When cold take a pint of this and add to it one cup sweet cream, beat well and pour over potatoes prepared in the proportion of six good-sized potatoes, one onion, grated or sliced fine, one good-sized cucumber, cut in small cubes; season to taste.

Salad Dressing.

Mrs. W. J. Sloan

Beaten yolks of two eggs, pinch of salt and pepper, slowly drop in oil, one drop at a time, until one-half pint of olive oil is used; occasionally cutting oil with one-half spoon lemon juice.

French Dressing.

M. H.

One tablespoon vinegar, three of olive oil, one-half teaspoon salt, one-fourth of black pepper, put the salt and pepper in a bowl. add gradually the oil; rub and mix until the salt is thoroughly dissolved, then add by degrees the vinegar, stir continually one minute, and it is ready for use.

Salad Dressing.

Mrs. W. E. Bush.

One cup cream, sweet or sour, put on stove to heat, then beat one egg with one teaspoon cornstarch, add to the cream, beat till it thickens; put in a cup one teaspoon mustard, one of sugar, a scant one of salt, adding vinegar enough to dissolve them, and put them into the mixture on the stove.

Salad Butter.

Mrs. H. C. Cheney.

One-half pound of butter, three tablespoonsful of salad oil, one tablespoon mixed mustard, salt, pepper, yolk of one egg, cream the butter, add the other things, beat well, set away to cool.

Scallops.

Potato Scalloped.

L. C. M.

Pare the potatoes very thin. In a baking dish put a layer of potatoes, sprinkle with salt, pepper and bits of butter, sift a little flour over, then another layer of potatoes until the dish is full, then cover with sweet milk and bake an hour.

Tomato Scalloped.

Mrs. Arthur Young.

Butter an earthen dish, put in a layer of fresh tomatoes, peeled and sliced, and a few slices of onion, cover with layer of bread crumbs, with small pieces of butter, sprinkle a little salt and pepper; repeat this process until dish is full; bake one-half hour; remove the cover and brown.

Onions Scalloped.

Gertrude L. Boyd.

Boil until tender, six large onions. If the onions are strong, change water once while boiling, and afterwards separate them with a large spoon, place a layer of onions and a layer of fine bread crumbs, alternately, in a pudding dish, season with pepper, salt and butter to taste, pour over enough milk to thoroughly moisten, then put into oven until nicely browned.

Oysters Scalloped.

Mrs. W. T. Boyd.

Roll oyster crackers, put in pan a layer of oysters, cover with cracker, not too thickley, season with plenty of butter, pepper and salt, more oysters, more crackers, more seasoning; have crackers for top layer; just before putting in oven pour over your oyster juice, and good tea-cup milk. Bake in hot oven until cooked entirely through and browned on top, about three-quarters of an hour.

Eggs Scalloped.

Mrs. R. Fuller.

Put small pieces of butter in bottom of pan, put in six eggs or more, put over the eggs small pieces of butter, season with salt and pepper, sprinkle thickly over the top very fine bread crumbs, pour over half cup milk, put in oven fifteen minutes.

Turkey Scalloped.

Mrs. R. Fuller.

Pick the meat from the bones of cold turkey and chop it fine, put a layer of bread crumbs on the bottom of a buttered dish, moisten them with a little milk, then put in a layer of turkey with some of the filling, and cut small pieces of butter over the top, sprinkle with pepper and salt, then another layer of bread crumbs and so on until the dish is nearly full; add a little hot water to the gravy left from the turkey and pour over it, then take two eggs, two tablespoons milk, one of melted butter, a little salt, and cracker crumbs as much as will make it thick enough to spread over the top; bake three-quarters of an hour.

Soups.

Tomato Soup.

Mrs. J. R. Mulkie.

One half can concentrated tomatoes, boil twenty minutes, with piece of butter size of walnut, a little grated onion, salt and pepper; heat two cups milk, add two teaspoons cornstarch, and beat all together slowly, adding at the very last a pinch of soda. Enough for five or six persons.

Tomato Bisque.

Mrs. C. C. Van Dusen.

One quart can tomatoes, one quart of milk, with a bit of soda stirred in; one even teaspoon cornstarch, one heaping teaspoon sugar. Stew tomatoes half an hour, with salt, pepper and sugar. Rub through a fine colander back into same pan, and heat to boiling. Scald milk in another dish, add cornstarch and heaping tablespoon butter; stir until thickened, mix with tomatoes, and bring to a quick boil and serve.

Potato Soup.

Mrs. J. C. McLean.

To one gallon water add six potatoes sliced, lump of butter size of an egg, salt and pepper. Just before taking from fire, add cup of cream or milk, and a little rolled cracker crumbs.

Beef Soup.

Take bones and trimmings from a sirloin steak, put over fire after breakfast in three quarts water; simmer slowly. An hour before dinner add two onions, one carrot, three small potatoes (slice all), some parsley cut fine, salt and pepper to taste.

Swiss Soup.

Mrs. V. D.

Four quarts water, two onions, one carrot, three potatoes, one small turnip. Slice potatoes and onions fine, chop carrot and turnip; cook till tender; season with salt and pepper and plenty of butter.

Oyster Soup.

Mrs. Boyd.

One pint oysters, one and a half pints boiling water, skim and add one teacup butter. Let them come to a boil.

Oyster Soup.

Mrs. H. C. Cheney.

One quart of oysters, three pints warm water, well seasoned with salt and pepper. Let them come to a boil. When ready to serve, add one pint of boiling milk, and butter size of an egg.

Bean Soup.

Mrs. J. C. M.

Put over beans and parboil, the same as for cooking. Drain and put on water (and a piece of pork if you wish) and cook until tender. You can then take out a part and put in oven to bake if you wish. The remainder put through a colander back into kettle, add more water, season with salt and pepper (and if no meat is used) butter and part of a cup of cream, and boil up.

Bean Soup.

Mrs. C. B. Geer.

Soak one quart of beans over night. In the morning drain, add two quarts of water; when it comes to the boiling point, pour off and add two quarts of fresh boiling water, also a quarter of a teaspoonful of soda. Boil until the beans are soft, then press through a seive, and return to the kettle; add salt and pepper to taste, and a cup of sweet cream or milk, and some butter. Crackers buttered and browned in the oven are nice to serve with this soup.

Chicken Soup.

Mrs. E. B. Landsrath.

One chicken, eight quarts cold water, one teaspoon of salt, six pepper corns, one tablespoon chopped onion, two tablespoons celery, one pint milk, one tablespoon butter, one of flour, one teaspoon salt, little pepper, one egg. When chicken is tender, should be taken from bones and bones put to boil again. Add vegetables and simmer until reduced one-fourth. Strain the stock and remove fat. Boil stock, add butter and flour cooked together and the seasoning. Pour over the egg, stirring as you pour, or it will curdle. Add cream. If not smooth, strain.

Sundries.

Stuffed Eggs.

Mrs. H. C. Cheney.

Take six hard boiled eggs, shell and split them in half lengthwise. Remove the yolks, rub them to a paste in melted butter, add four teaspoonfuls of minced ham, tongue or chicken. Season with salt, pepper, vinegar and mixed mustard. Fit the halves together and arrange them on a dish in the form of a pyramid. Garnish with sprigs of parsley or lettuce leaves.

Egg Baskets.

Mrs. C. H. Smith.

Make for lunch or supper, the day after you have had chicken. Hard boil six eggs, cut in half and remove the yolks, chop them, with a couple of pieces of cold chicken, season with salt and pepper, and moisten with a spoonful of the gravy. Cut off a slice from bottom of egg so they will stand; fill with the paste and set in shallow dish. About twenty minutes before serving, put dish in pan of hot water on back of stove, so they will warm through, and just before serving pour the heated chicken gravy over them.

Ham Sandwiches.

Mrs. F. E. McLean.

Take some boiled ham and chop it very fine, mix it with a dressing of one dessertspoon of mustard, two of oil, one raw egg beaten very light, a little salt and pepper; cut and spread the bread very thin.

Chicken Sandwiches.

Mrs. D. G. Smiley.

Mince cold chicken, freed from skin and fat, quite fine; rub in a little butter, season to your liking, and spread between thin slices of bread, pressing the pieces gently but firmly on the mixture.

Mixed Sandwiches.

Mrs. Kate Cook.

Chop fine cold ham, tongue or chicken; mix with one pint of meat, half cup of melted butter, one tablespoon mustard, a little pepper, yolk of a beaten egg; Spread on bread cut thin and buttered.

Welsh Rarebit.

Maud Humphrey.

Teacup of cheese, one cup bread crumbs, one-third cup of milk, three eggs. Put cheese in pan with two tablespoons of milk, stirring slowly; when dissolved, add bread crumbs that have been soaked in milk; beat up the eggs, stir constantly (not beat) and slowly until thoroughly cooked.

Cheese Straws.

Aunt Kate Munra.

Six ounces grated cheese, six ounces bread crumbs, six ounces flour, four of butter, pinch of salt and cayenne pepper.

Salted Almonds.

Inez Thompson.

Blanch one cup of almonds (put in hot water to remove the skins); melt one-half cup of butter, put the almonds in the butter and sprinkle well with salt; let stand one-half hour, then brown in the oven, stirring often and drain on paper. Peanuts may be salted the same way.

Curry Powder.

One ounce of mustard, one of pepper, three of coriander seed, one of ginger, three of tumerick, one-half ounce cardamon, quarter ounce cummint seed, some cayenne; pound all fine, sift and cork. One teaspoon is sufficient to season anything, nice for meats, stews and soups.

Time Table for Cooking Vegetables.

Potatoes, Boiled	30	minutes
Potatoes, Baked	60	"
Sweet Potatoes, Boiled	40	"
Sweet Potatoes, Baked	60	"
Squash, Steamed	30	"
Squash, Baked	45	"
Green Peas, Boiled	25	"
Shell Beans, "	1	hour
String " "	2	hours
Green Corn, "	25	minutes
Asparagus, "	30	"
Spinach, "	1	hour
Tomatoes, "	1	"
Cabbage, "	2	"
Turnips, "	2	"
Cauliflower, "	1	"
Dandelions, "	2	"
Beet Greens, "	1½	"
Onions, "	1½	"
Beets, "	2	"
Parsnips, "	1	"
Carrots, "	1	"
Rice, "	20	minutes

Vegetables.

Potato Puffs.

Mrs. Herries.

One cup cold mashed potatoes, stir into it one tablespoon melted butter, and beat to a white cream, then stir in one egg, well beaten, must be very light, then one teacup of milk or cream, salting to taste ; beat all together until very light, put into a baking dish and bake until nicely browned. Nice for breaefast.

Saratoga Potatoes.

Mrs. Geo. Alden.

Peel and slice thin into cold water, drain, and dry in a towel, fry a few at a time in boiling *cottolene*; salt as you take them out, and lay them on coarse brown paper for a short time.

Quirled Potatoes.

Mrs. O. Glezen.

Boil potatoes, mash fine and season well, press through a colander into the dish you wish to serve them in, set them in the oven and let them brown.

Potato Sticks.

Mrs. H. C. Cheney.

Pare and cut five or six raw potatoes, lengthwise, into strips the size of a lead pencil and length of potato. Throw them, a few at a time, into boiling lard, turning till golden brown. Drain, sprinkle with salt and pepper, and serve wrapped in a napkin.

Beets and Potatoes.

Mrs. V. D.

Boil young beets and new potatoes, and slice while hot into a warm vegetable dish, about equal parts, season with salt, pepper, butter and a little vinegar.

Scalloped Squash.

Beat two eggs, add tablespoon butter, half cup milk, and two cups squash; put through colander, beat light, put into a buttered bake dish, sift bread crumbs over, cover, bake half hour, then brown.

Cooking Turnips.

Mrs. W. C. Siegfried.

One large or two small turnips, cut in small pieces and slice very thin; cook in salt water until tender, drain, add two cups of beef stock, and half a cup sweet cream, salt and pepper and add a few fine bread or cracker crumbs.

Parsnip Balls.

Mrs. S. K. Thompson.

Boil in salted water till very tender, mash, season with salt, pepper and butter, add a little flour and two well beaten eggs; form into small balls and fry in hot fat.

Scalloped Cabbage.

Mrs. J. O. Loomis.

Take cabbage and slice, not very fine, put layer in bottom of bake dish, sprinkle over salt, pepper and bits of butter, then layer of cabbage, till dish is full, having seasoning for last layer, pour over milk, cover tightly, bake one hour.

128

FURNITURE

(See Art Deco, Art Nouveau, Oriental Furniture, Shaker, and Wicker)

COMMENTS: Interest in antique and collectible furniture is growing, according to auction houses and dealers around the country. Record prices were realized for American Federal and Victorian period pieces this year. European furniture is also very strong. Experts feel that the current design trends featuring "Country" and Victorian styles have had a major impact on this upward movement in the popularity of antique furniture. Also, prices for fine old pieces compare very favorably to the cost of new furniture.

RECOMMENDED READING: For more in-depth information on furniture you may refer to *The Official Identification Guide to Early American Furniture, The Official Identification Guide to Victorian Furniture, The Official Price Guide to Wicker, The Official Price Guide to Oriental Collectibles, The Official Guide to Buying and Selling Antiques and Collectibles* and *The Official Encyclopedia of Antiques and Collectibles,* published by The House of Collectibles.

	Current Price Range		P/Y Average
☐ **Adams Style,** English, armchairs, pair, walnut, squared back, open lyre splat, arms with beaded molding and bowfront, tapering reeded legs, 32" high, 1900.	2900.00	3100.00	400.00
☐ **Art Deco,** American, bedroom suite, five pieces, red and black laquer and chrome.	800.00	1100.00	950.00
☐ **Art Deco,** desk, burl walnut, diamond parquetry veneer on sides and top, front and rear worked in design of three concentric veneer bands, 27" high x 56" long x 29" wide.	1800.00	2200.00	2000.00
☐ **Art Deco,** French, table, mahogany, rectangular sloped base inset with six copper dividers supporting two three-drawer units united by six copper supports bearing glass top, glass ball knobs, 33" high x 50" long x 16" wide, 1920	750.00	950.00	850.00
☐ **Art Nouveau,** English, sideboard, mahogany, floral carved top section	600.00	700.00	650.00

Victorian Eastlake Renaissance Revival Bed, *walnut,*
1875, **$750.00-$1000.00**
Photo courtesy of Wood's Auction, New Carlisle, OH.

	Current Price Range		P/Y Average
☐ **Belter,** American Rococo, bedstead, carved rosewood, 1860	4000.00	8000.00	6000.00
☐ **Belter,** American Rococo, bureau with mirror, rosewood, very elaborate, 1860	10000.00	17000.00	7000.00
☐ **Biedermeier,** credenza, inlaid walnut, rectangular top above three frieze drawers over three cupboard doors, raised on tapering square legs, 39″ high x 54½″ long x 17¾″ deep	800.00	1200.00	1000.00
☐ **Brass,** canopy bed, knob and tube style, twin size, 81″ long x 43″ wide x 84″ high	800.00	1200.00	1000.00
☐ **Chippendale,** American, architectural corner cupboard, upper molded applied arch, double glazed doors each with twelve panes, 103¼″ high x 63″ wide x 25″ deep, Maryland, 1760-1790	9000.00	11000.00	4000.00
☐ **Chippendale,** American, desk, slant-front, walnut, thumb molded slant lid opening, elaborately fitted interior, six serpentine front drawers over four thumb molded graduated drawers, 42½″ high x 41″ wide x 22″ deep, Pennsylvania, 1765-1795	9000.00	11000.00	5500.00
☐ **Chippendale,** American, gaming table, serpentine shaped top, square corners, five ball and claw feet, New York, 28″ high x 32″ wide x 16¾″ deep, 1765-1785	27000.00	37000.00	32000.00

	Current Price Range		P/Y Average

☐ **Chippendale Style,** chest of drawers, mahogany, serpentine, four drawers, 1830 . . . **1000.00 1600.00 1300.00**

☐ **Chippendale Style,** china cabinet, curved glass, pierced cornice above floral frieze, astragal doors, 1850s **1750.00 2750.00 2250.00**

☐ **Directoire,** dining table, mahogany, oval top, square tapering legs, Egyptian female busts, stamped Chapius, 70″ wide, 1790 . . . . **4000.00 5000.00 4500.00**

☐ **Duncan Phyfe Style,** dining table, mahogany, reeded edge top, three reeded legs, brass paws and casters, two leaves, English, 28½″ high x 46″ wide x 51″ diameter, early 20th century **2800.00 3200.00 3000.00**

☐ **Dutch,** curio shelf, hanging, three shelves above a two door cupboard base section, the doors with inlaid floral decoration, 34½″ x 22½″ x 6″, 1800 . . . . **225.00 275.00 250.00**

☐ **Eastlake,** bureau and matching bedstead, incised mahogany and walnut, bureau has gray marble top over three long drawers, mirror has stylized floral crest, bedstead is 5′2″ high x 4′9½″ wide **400.00 500.00 450.00**

☐ **Empire,** late, side chairs, set of six, tablet crest rail centering a panel flanked by scrolls and carved leafage, molded stiles over a trapezoidal slip seat on sabre legs, 32½″ high x 19″ wide x 21½″ deep **6000.00 8000.00 3000.00**

☐ **English,** provincial, chairs, set of six, oak, ladderback, last quarter 18th century **2800.00 3200.00 3000.00**

☐ **Federal,** chest of drawers, mahogany and birch veneer, 39″ high x 40″ wide, Massachusetts, 1790-1810 . . . . **3000.00 4000.00 3500.00**

☐ **Federal,** Pembroke table, inlaid mahogany, square tapered legs with bell flower motifs, Baltimore, 28½″ high x 29¾″ wide x 19″ deep **5500.00 7500.00 650.00**

☐ **Federal,** settee, bird's eye maple, tablet crest rail above three raking stiles connected by a horizontal rail, rush seat, turned legs, 33¼″ high x 60″ wide, New England, 1810-1830 . . . . **4000.00 5500.00 1000.00**

☐ **Federal,** settee, stenciled and ochre painted, rectangular crest rail decorated with cornucopia above spindle splats, plank seat raised on cylindrical legs joined by stretchers, 6′ long, 1840 . . . . **650.00 850.00 750.00**

☐ **Federal,** side chair, painted, oval shaped back centering a pierced Prince of Wales splat, bowed seat square tapering legs, surface painted white with polychrome flowers, stems, feathers, bows and plumes, 35⅝″ x 21¼″ wide, Philadelphia, 1795-1800 . . . . **10000.00 18000.00 14000.00**

☐ **Federal,** side chairs, set of six, mahogany, heart shaped back, fan shaped reticulated splat, reeded legs, spade feet, New York, 1790-1800 . . . . **6500.00 8500.00 3000.00**

	Current Price Range		P/Y Average
Federal Style, bed, post, cherry, broken arch crest, 85″ high x 60″ wide	1100.00	1500.00	700.00
French Provincial, cupboard, walnut, hand carved, two double doors at top, two lower doors, scrolled legs, 56½″ x 91″ high, 18th century	3250.00	4250.00	3750.00
French Provincial, dresser, oak, two sections, upper section with carved crest above three open shelves, lower section with molded top above molded floral frieze, 78″ high x 80″ wide x 18″ deep	1000.00	3000.00	2000.00
George I, bureau bookcase, red lacquer chinoiserie, 87″ high x 44″ wide, 1730	5000.00	5800.00	5400.00
George III, chairs, dining, set of fourteen, mahogany, arched crest rail above a pierced interlaced splat, flared serpentine seat raised on molded square legs joined by stretchers	4500.00	5500.00	5000.00
George III Style, desk, partners, mahogany, gold embossed leather top above one long and two short drawers set upon two pedestals with three drawers each, 31″ high x 59″ wide x 41″ deep, last quarter 19th century	1200.00	4100.00	1600.00
Georgian, armchair, open, mahogany, carved in the French manner, shaped upholstered back, serpentine front seat, cabriole legs, scrolled feet, 1770	1800.00	2200.00	700.00
Georgian, English, library stand, burled walnut, adjustable tilting top, 49½″ high x 18″ wide x 14″diameter, 18th or early 19th century	2400.00	2800.00	2600.00
Hepplewhite Style, English, dining suite, eleven pieces, mahogany, table with two leaves, buffet, china cabinet, eight chairs	7000.00	8000.00	7500.00
Irish, cabinet, pine, raised panels, double doors, 1820	850.00	950.00	900.00
Louis XIV Style, armchairs, pair, oak, rectangular upholstered back, scroll arms, ball feet, 46″ high, late 19th century	1000.00	1400.00	500.00
Louis XV, bergere, walnut, molded frame enclosing leather back and seat, decorated at back with cane work, raised on cabriole legs	2000.00	2800.00	600.00
Louis XV Provincial, armoire, fruitwood, molded cornice above two grilled doors, raised on scrolled feet, 6′3″ high x 4′3″ long x 15″ deep	1000.00	2000.00	1500.00
Louis XV Provincial, table, bedside, cherry, oblong top above a conforming frieze with full drawer and scalloped apron raised on cabriole legs, 28½″ high x 19½″ wide x 13½″ deep	3000.00	3600.00	700.00
Louis XV Style, parlor set, settee, armchair and sidechair, giltwood, early 20th century	1200.00	2300.00	1200.00
Louis XVI Style, bedroom suite, eleven pieces, painted off-white, caned head and foot boards, swag decoration	1100.00	1500.00	1300.00

	Current Price Range		P/Y Average

□ **Louis XVI Style,** mirror, easel type, silvered bronze, cartouche shaped frame cast with floral garlands and ribbon pendants, raised on scrolled feet, 19½ ″ high x 15½ ″ wide ... **700.00 800.00 750.00**

□ **Louis XVI Style,** parlor set, square back, beribboned crest bowfront seat, cream gessoed woodwork, brocade upholstery **800.00 1200.00 1000.00**

□ **Oak,** golden, armchair, pressed carving in back splat, upholstered seat, 38″ high x 27″ wide ... **125.00 200.00 170.00**

□ **Oak,** golden, china cabinet, curved front, mirrored back, three glass shelves, 87″ high x 44″ wide ... **600.00 800.00 700.00**

□ **Oak,** golden, dentistry cabinet, 54″ high x 36″ wide x 13″ deep ... **800.00 1000.00 900.00**

□ **Oak,** golden, dining table, round with center pedestal and four carved feet, 1 leaf, 30″ high x 42″ diameter, 1880 ... **600.00 800.00 700.00**

□ **Oak,** golden, ice box, zinc lined, two doors, some chestnut, 42″ high x 35″ wide x 18″ deep ... **350.00 450.00 400.00**

□ **Oak,** golden, Morris Chair, 38″ high x 27″ wide x 28″ deep, 1880s ... **300.00 400.00 350.00**

□ **Oak,** golden, rocker, pressed carving ... **200.00 400.00 300.00**

□ **Oak,** golden, sideboard, mirrored, elaborate carvings, plain, quarter, and tiger stripe wood, 82″ high x 60″ wide ... **800.00 3000.00 1400.00**

□ **Queen Anne Style,** English, tea table, walnut, flip top, adjustable, brass pulls, two drawers, 22″ x 15″ x 30″ high ... **300.00 500.00 400.00**

□ **Queen Anne Style,** side chairs, set of four, spoon back, 1860 ... **2100.00 2700.00 2400.00**

□ **Regency Credenza,** calamander, brass mounted parcel gilt, 36″ high x 6′ long x 15″ deep ... **3250.00 3750.00 1750.00**

□ **Regency,** English, dining chairs, set of ten, mahogany, rectangular molded crest rail, latticework slat, reeded back supports, tapering legs, spade foot, 34″ high x 20½ ″ wide x 18″ diameter ... **5300.00 5900.00 5600.00**

□ **Regency,** games table, elm, inlaid, 44½ ″ wide, 1810 ... **4000.00 5000.00 4500.00**

□ **Regency Style,** dining chairs, set of ten, black lacquer and parcel gilt, faux bamboo turnings ... **2875.00 3575.00 3225.00**

□ **Sheraton Style,** bed, mahogany, queen size, four posters, carved and fluted columns, swan neck headboard ... **850.00 950.00 900.00**

□ **Sheraton Style,** dining chairs set of twelve, painted, rounded back, open splat, painted serpentine front, 37½ ″ high, early 20th century ... **2200.00 2700.00 1000.00**

□ **Sheraton Style,** fern stand, pair, mahogany, square tops with notched corners, turned standards, raised on tripod bases, 36″ high . **325.00 375.00 350.00**

	Current Price Range		P/Y Average

☐ **Sheraton Style,** sideboard, cornucopia inlay, single recessed cupboard below bowfronted central section, fluted malborough legs, 1840 — 2850.00 / 3250.00 / 3050.00

☐ **Sheraton Style,** table stand, mahogany, three tier, the top tier features galleried sides, fitted with an under drawer, 12″ x 18″ x 28″ high — 275.00 / 375.00 / 325.00

☐ **Stickley, Gustav,** bookcase, oak, double doors, 56″ high x 62″ wide x 12¼″ deep, 1907 — 2600.00 / 3100.00 / 2850.00

☐ **Stickley, Gustav,** desk, slant front, oak, opens to fitted interior, 40″ high x 29″ wide x 17″ deep, 1915 . . . . — 425.00 / 475.00 / 450.00

☐ **Stickley, Gustav,** table, dropleaf, oak, two hinged flaps, three drawers, 28″ high x 16¼″ deep, top is 43″ long when extended, 1910 . . — 600.00 / 700.00 / 650.00

☐ **Thonet,** chaise lounge, bentwood, elaborate, caned frame, adjustable back, unsigned, 43½″ x 21″, 1898 . . . . — 3000.00 / 3500.00 / 1200.00

☐ **Victorian,** corner cabinet, rosewood, marquetry inlaid, top has beveled glass display cabinet, 79″ high x 32″ wide x 19″ deep, late 19th century . . . . — 1000.00 / 1800.00 / 1400.00

☐ **Victorian,** hall tree, walnut and burl walnut, arched and thumb molded cornice above a central mirrored panel flanked by pilasters and brass lion head knobs, plinth base with single drawer flanked by wells, 9′8″ high x 4′11″ wide x 19½″ deep, late 19th century . . . — 750.00 / 950.00 / 850.00

☐ **Victorian,** parlor suite, six pieces, mahogany and burl walnut, includes settee, gentleman's armchair, lady's chair and three side chairs, settee is 6′8″ long, late 19th century . . . . — 1000.00 / 1900.00 / 1450.00

☐ **Victorian,** pedestal table, oak round top, pedestal base with carved lion's mask, paw feet, 30″ high x 62″ diameter . . . . — 1900.00 / 2100.00 / 500.00

☐ **Victorian,** Renaissance Revival, American, bedroom suite, two pieces, dresser and bed, black walnut, dresser has white beveled marble top, ebony finish wood drawer pulls, elaborate mirror, both bed and dresser have carved bust of Columbia at top, raised panels in burl walnut, headboard is 93½″ high x 61¼″ wide, dresser is 102″ high x 51½″ wide x 21½″ deep, made by Berkey and Gay, Grand Rapids, Michigan, 1870-1876 . . . . — 3500.00 / 5000.00 / 4250.00

☐ **Victorian,** stool, walnut, covered in needlepoint . . . . — 450.00 / 550.00 / 500.00

☐ **Victorian,** writing table, Carlton House, marquetry satinwood, 48″ wide, 19th century . . . — 5500.00 / 6500.00 / 6000.00

☐ **Welsh,** dresser, pine, upper section with wide valanced cornice over three narrow shelves, lower section with three short drawers, 78″ high x 58″ wide x 15¼″ deep, late 18th-early 19th century . . . . — 1200.00 / 1900.00 / 1550.00

	Current Price Range		P/Y Average

☐ **William and Mary,** desk, maple and pine, slant lid enclosing valanced compartments, drawers, and hidden compartment, block and turned legs, scalloped skirt, some restoration, New England, 39″ high x 22½″ wide x 15″ deep, 1740 .... **3600.00** **4300.00** **4000.00**

GALLÉ GLASS

DESCRIPTION: The greatest of all the French art glass makers was Emile Gallé who directed the acclaimed Nancy School of Art in Nancy, France. This academy was formed to promote the great Art Nouveau movement in France. Nancy developed into a colony for the artisans of this movement.

Early in his career Gallé produced enamelled and gilded transparent amber, green, or white pieces using historical themes. In the mid 1880s, he began to make pieces decorated with realistic motifs drawn from the world of nature. Flora, fauna, and even insects appeared on transparent glass objects. Gallé is probably most famous for his exquisite cameo glass which he introduced in the 1890s. With improved mass production techniques, Gallé used acid to etch designs on cased glass and remove layers of glass, leaving bas-relief designs which were then further carved by hand. Emile Gallé died in 1904 and the quality of the work produced by his factory declined dramatically. He signed his glass "Gallé", after his death the mark "Gallé*" appeared.

RECOMMENDED READING: For more in-depth information on Galle glass you may refer to *The Official Price Guide to Glassware* and *The Official Identification Guide to Glassware,* published by The House of Collectibles.

☐ **Beaker,** cylinder shape, protruding horizontal rib around lower portion, sits on a gilt-bronze foot with scalloped design, pale blue background, overlaid in red, orange, and maroon, cut with an orchid and leaves, signed, 5¼″ high, c. 1900 .... **3500.00** **4500.00** **3550.00**

Vase,
frosted,
floral design,
signed Gallé, 4½",
$250.00-$300.00

	Current Price Range		P/Y Average
☐ **Beaker,** cylinder shape tapering towards base and rim, Islamic-like designs enameled in red, white, blue, mauve, and gray, on front side cut with cartouche enclosing a woman and birds, reverse side with oval panel enclosing a king, figures yellow, signed, 4¼" high, c. 1890	800.00	900.00	815.00
☐ **Bottle,** pilgrim, flattened ovoid shape, waisted neck, canoe-shaped lip, yellow background, overlaid	2000.00	3000.00	2100.00
☐ **Bowl,** circular with cylinder ridged foot, yellow background, overlaid in maroon, and beige, carved with a lakeside scene with sailboats in the background and trees, in the foreground, 9¼" diameter, c. 1900	3500.00	4500.00	3600.00
☐ **Bowl,** cylinder shape, beige background, overlaid in amber and brown, cut with fruit-laden and leafy branches in the foreground and trees and clouds in the background, signed, 9¼" diameter, c. 1900	1800.00	2500.00	1900.00
☐ **Bowl,** deep bulbous shape with ruffled flaring rim, deep yellow, enameled with a cross of Lorraine encircled by a garland of thistles in pale orange, ivory and gilt, signed, 9" high, c. 1885	800.00	900.00	815.00
☐ **Bowl,** elongated ovoid, straight neck, gray background, carved iris blossoms and leaves in avocado, signed, 6½" long, c. 1900	300.00	500.00	320.00

	Current Price Range		P/Y Average

☐ **Bowl,** half-spherical shape with spreading cylinder foot, yellow background, cartouche in center, flowers and leaves in ivory, rose, green, and brown, gilt, decorative band around the rim, floral repousse around the bottom edge of the foot, signed, 9½″ diameter, c. 1895 .... **3000.00 3500.00 3100.00**

☐ **Bowl,** half-spherical with lobed lip, light gray background, frosted inside, overlaid in orange, cut with hanging grapes, signed, 4¾″ long, c. 1900 .... **450.00 550.00 475.00**

☐ **Bowl,** shallow with wide mouth, mottled amber shading pale to dark, green lower body, fire polished, signed, 5¼″ diameter, c. 1890 .... **600.00 800.00 625.00**

☐ **Bowl,** triangular shape, straight-sided, red background, overlaid in burgundy, cut with orange blossoms and leaves, signed, 4″ high, c. 1900 .... **300.00 500.00 310.00**

☐ **Box,** covered, circular, domed lid flat on top, yellow background, overlaid in red, cut flowers and vines, signed, 4⅛″ diameter, c. 1900 . **600.00 700.00 610.00**

☐ **Box,** covered, circular shallow shape, flattened lid, light orange background, overlaid in blue, cut with morning glories, leaves and trailings, signed, 3″ diameter, c. 1900 ...... **700.00 800.00 720.00**

☐ **Box,** covered, hexagonal, mottled gray, yellow, and pink background, overlaid in various shades of brown, cut with butterflies on lid, river scene with blossoming trees on box, signed, 6¾″ diameter, c. 1900 .... **550.00 800.00 550.00**

☐ **Box,** covered, cylinder body which tapers, yellow background with reddish brown overlay, carved branches with flowers and leaves, matching cover with three butterflies, box and cover signed, 2⅞″ diameter, c. 1900 .... **300.00 500.00 315.00**

☐ **Cordial Set,** decanter and six cups, decanter swollen ovoid body, short cylinder neck with spout, large applied handle, cups cylinder shape expanding towards the rims, mottled gray and yellow background, overlaid in bright red, cut with hanging grape vines with berries and leaves, signed, decanter 8½″ high, cups 2½″ high, c. 1900 .... **1700.00 1800.00 1750.00**

☐ **Decanter,** bell shape body with waisted shoulder, baluster neck, trumpet-shaped stopper with flaring, scalloped rim, short circular foot, spiral ribbing, upper knop above shoulder and lower portion of body carved with wildflowers, green background, signed, c. 1895 .... **1800.00 2200.00 1850.00**

	Current Price Range		P/Y Average

☐ **Decanter,** tear drop shape, slightly domed foot, knopped neck, knopped flattened stopper, light amber background, enameled with lion on one side and fleur-de-lys on the other in white, black, and gray, applied bosses on sides, signed, 10½ ″ high, c. 1895 .... **1500.00 2000.00 1600.00**

☐ **Dish,** leaf shape, scalloped rim which is rolled at two sides, light blue, enameled with dragonflies and lacy ribbons in red, pink, blue-gray, and black, gilding, signed, 12″ long, c. 1895 .... **800.00 1200.00 840.00**

☐ **Ewer,** cylinder shape with tapering towards the base and the neck, uneven rim with rising spout, short circular foot, twining applied handle, amber background, enameled in dark rose and bright red with a cross of Lorraine and a blooming thistle with leaves, gilding, signed, 10½ ″ high, c. 1900 .... **1200.00 1300.00 1250.00**

☐ **Ewer,** ovoid body, cylinder neck, applied handle, short circular foot, red and yellow, foil inclusions, carved with orchids and leaves, signed, 6¾ ″ high, c. 1900 .... **3000.00 4000.00 3050.00**

☐ **Ewer,** ovoid shape, cylinder neck with spout, short circular foot, applied handle, pale yellow, transparent, enameled in pink, citron, green, and brown, gilt with wildflowers, signed, 7½ ″ high, c. 1900 .... **800.00 900.00 810.00**

☐ **Ewer,** small, pear shape with slanted rim, spiral ribbing, small C-scroll handle, light amber background, enameled with berries and leaves in red and green, gilding around rim and handle, signed, 3½ ″ high, c. 1900 ... **700.00 1000.00 750.00**

☐ **Flacon,** compressed spherical body, waisted bulbous neck tapering into cylinder below acorn-shaped stopper, pale blue background, overlaid in red, maroon, and deep rose, carved with hanging orchids and leaves, signed, 7¼ ″ high, c. 1900 .... **6000.00 7000.00 6050.00**

☐ **Flacon,** spherical base, waisted and bulbous neck, applied handle, green background, enameled with landscape, signed, 3¼ ″ high, c. 1900 .... **600.00 700.00 620.00**

☐ **Flacon,** pear shape, lobed, rectangular sections, flattened circular stopper, dark yellow background, enameled in off-white and black undulating bands, insects and geometric shapes, gilding, signed, 5½ ″ high, c. 1890 .. **600.00 1000.00 630.00**

☐ **Flacon,** wide cylinder, flattened shoulders, slightly ribbed, short cylinder neck, flower-shaped stopper, green etched background, cut with flowers and leaves, touches of white enameling, cut in intaglio of ferns, signed, 4½ ″ high, c. 1900 .... **800.00 1200.00 825.00**

	Current Price Range		P/Y Average

☐ **Lamp,** swollen conical shade, lower border lobed, standard in baluster shape, spreading foot, shade supported by three arms of bronze, pink and gray background, overlaid in violet shading to green, cut with primroses and leaves, signed, 22¼ " high, c. 1904-1914 . **4500.00 5500.00 4600.00**

☐ **Lamp base,** baluster shape, waisted neck, flaring foot, yellow background, overlaid in red, carved roses and leaves, signed, 16½ "high, c. 1900 . . . . **600.00 800.00 610.00**

☐ **Sconces,** ovoid shape with flat top and lower section coming to a point, gilt-bronze lines the sides ending in a scrolling design at the rim and a small paneled design at the bottom, pale pink background, overlaid in purple, cut with scrolling morning glories, signed, 11" high, c. 1900 . . . . **1200.00 1300.00 1250.00**

☐ **Shade,** ceiling, half-spherical, flared rim, pale yellow background, overlaid in bright red, cut with cactus blossoms and leaves, signed, 21¼ " high, c. 1900 . . . . **1000.00 2000.00 1075.00**

☐ **Shade,** ceiling, half-spherical, flaring rim, pale yellow background, overlaid in orange, red, yellow, and maroon, cut with branches with acorns, leaves and a squirrel, signed, 20" diameter, c. 1910 . . . . **19000.00 21000.00 19100.00**

☐ **Tumbler,** cylinder shape, tapering towards neck and base, light amber background, enameled with two dragonflies in red, pink, blue, green and white, carved pinwheels, signed, 4½ " high, c. 1900 . . . . **600.00 900.00 630.00**

☐ **Vase,** baluster shape, swollen shoulders, slightly flaring foot, gray with orange streaked background, overlaid in orange, cut with chrysanthemums and leaves, signed, 7⅞" high, c. 1900 . . . . **800.00 1200.00 840.00**

☐ **Vase,** baluster shape, trumpet base, mottled amber background, overlaid in purple, carved with delphiniums, signed, 17⅛" high, c. 1900 **700.00 1000.00 715.00**

☐ **Vase,** baluster shape, waisted neck and foot, rolled foot, gray shading to turquoise background, overlaid in rose and avocado, cut with poppy blossoms, buds and leaves, signed, 11½ " high, c. 1904 . . . . **700.00 1000.00 725.00**

☐ **Vase,** baluster shape, waisted neck, flaring foot, yellow background, overlaid in red, cut with poppies and leaves, signed, 8¾ " high, c. 1900 . . . . : **600.00 1000.00 650.00**

☐ **Vase,** baluster shape, waisted neck, flaring rim, domed foot, off-white blackground, overlaid in red, cut with leafy branches and fuchias hanging, signed, 8" high, c. 1900 . . . . **1500.00 2000.00 1575.00**

	Current Price Range		P/Y Average

☐ **Vase,** baluster shape, waisted neck with slightly flaring rim, spreading foot with knob, mottled amber shading to lavender, overlaid in dark amber shading to lavender, carved with iris blossoms and leaves, signed, 13¾" high, c. 1900 .... 1500.00 2000.00 1600.00

☐ **Vase,** baluster shape with paneled sides, thick-walled, milky gray background, enameled with shells and plants, gilt, signed, 8½" high, c. 1900 .... 1100.00 1400.00 1150.00

☐ **Vase,** baluster shape with slightly everted rim, short rolled foot, gray opalescent background, overlaid in pink, rose, deep red, cut with wild roses and leaves, signed, 11¾" high, c. 1900 .... 2000.00 2200.00 2050.00

☐ **Vase,** baluster shape, yellow and gray background, overlaid in red and burgundy, cut with primroses and leaves, signed, 14¼" high, c. 1900 .... 800.00 1200.00 850.00

☐ **Vase,** bud, compressed spherical body, thin cylinder neck, gray and lavender background, overlaid in lavender, cut with blossoms and leaves, polished, signed, 8½" high, c. 1900 .. 250.00 350.00 275.00

GAMES

TOPIC: Games are amusing activities that people participate in. The games that collectors are primarily interested in are board games, which are played on the decorated surface of a board or platform.

PERIOD: The first American board game was produced 1843 by W. and S.B. Ives Company. Monopoly, the most famous of all American games, was invented around 1934.

COMMENTS: From 1850 to 1920, games were using lithography. Some parts were hand painted. The most collectible board games were made by Ives Company or the McLoughlin Brothers.

ADDITIONAL TIPS: American board games do not have a high survival rate. When selecting a collectible game, look for one in good condition and with all its pieces intact. For further information, please refer to *The Official Price Guide to Collectible Toys,* published by The House of Collectibles.

Monopoly Game by Parker Bros., *Library Edition, 1961,* **$5.00-$7.00**

	Current Price Range		P/Y Average
☐ **Across the Continent:** The United States Game, Parker Brother, board game, lid shows various modes of transportation including motorcycle and auto, game board when open measures 17″ x 32½″, 1922	130.00	160.00	140.00
Note: Apparently this game was in production a very long time. This is a 1922 version but the board has a 1901 copyright date.			
☐ **Age Cards,** Germany, seven cards, 2″ x 2″ . . .	2.00	5.00	2.50
☐ **Air Mail,** Milton Bradley, c. early 1930's, roll marble across board with obstacles	30.00	40.00	32.00
☐ **Ally Sloper,** Milton Bradley, #4110 subtitled "A Splendid Game For Many Players," instuctions in English and Spanish, colorful box, 6½″ x 13″, 1907	55.00	70.00	61.00
Note: Balls were thrown into a clown's mouth, in the style of amusement park games.			
☐ **Alphabet Game,** c.1950's, "PInkey Lee's"	7.00	14.00	6.00

	Current Price Range		P/Y Average

☐ **Action Letters,** Parker Brothers, includes play money and cards, box lid has full color illustration of rabbits attending an auction, 5½″ x 7½″, 1900 . . . . **130.00** **160.00** **142.00**

☐ **Bear Game,** lithographed paper under glass, put knife and fork in bear's hands by shaking . **20.00** **30.00** **23.00**

☐ **Ben Casey, M.D.,** Bing Crosby Productions, based on TV program, pictures Vincent Edwards on cover, box measures 9″ x 17½″, 1961 . . . . **25.00** **30.00** **26.50**

☐ **Bing Crosby's Call Me Lucky,** Parker Brothers, board game picturing Bing Crosby on cover, box measures 10″ x 20″, c. 1953 . . . . **25.00** **30.00** **26.50**

☐ **Bingo Game,** Germany, c.1920's, twelve cards, wood numbers **3.00** **6.00** **3.50**

☐ **Blackout,** World War II ear, covered with glass, tin sides, shows planes about to bomb town, object: to cover windows with rolling windows **30.00** **40.00** **33.00**

☐ **Blondie Card Game,** King Features Syndicate, deck of thirty six cards with playing instructions, in a box measuring 5″ x 6″, 1941 . . . . . . **60.00** **75.00** **65.00**

☐ **Chalk and Checkers,** The Ohio Art Company, #523, c.1960's, metal, slate, plastic, eraser, chalk **7.00** **12.00** **8.00**

☐ **Checker Board,** advertising giveaway for Preferred Accident Insurance Company, c.1930's **8.00** **12.00** **9.00**

☐ **Checkers,** empress, Japan, wood **2.00** **5.00** **2.50**

☐ **Checkers,** The Ohio Art Company, #97, c.1950's, tin, multicolored, Chinese, and regular checkers, diameter 13″ **8.00** **12.00** **9.00**

☐ **Chinese Checkers,** The Ohio Art Company, #535, 1960's, metal, marbles, multicolored . . . **8.00** **12.00** **9.00**

☐ **Chinese Checkers and Checkers,** The Ohio Art Company, #538, c.1960's, metal board, glass marbles, plastic checker **12.00** **18.00** **15.00**

☐ **Cinderella Game,** Bavaria, nine cards, 3″ x 3″ . **2.00** **5.00** **2.50**

☐ **Collage football,** Milton Bradley, board game with moving pieces and instructions, lid has colored sketch of game action, 8″ x 16″, undated but uniforms worn by players in the lid picture suggest a dating of c. 1930 . . . . **45.00** **60.00** **52.00**

☐ **Dad's Puzzler,** J. W. Hayward, c.1926, wood block puzzle game **15.00** **20.00** **16.00**

☐ **Deluxe Chinese Checkers and Checkers,** The Ohio Art Company, #539, c.1960's, metal board, glass marbles, plastic checkers, storage drawer, diameter 18″ **20.00** **25.00** **21.00**

☐ **Eddie Cantor Tell it To The Judge,** Parker Brothers **20.00** **25.00** **21.00**

☐ **Education Board,** Brill Monfort Company, New York, multiply and divide, 12″ x13″ **6.00** **12.00** **7.00**

☐ **Finance and Fortune,** Parker Brothers, board game inspired by Monopoly, box measures 10″ x 19″, c. 1936 . . . . **25.00** **30.00** **26.00**

	Current Price Range		P/Y Average

	Current Price Range		P/Y Average
☐ **Game of Chance,** c.1940's, wooden box, disc that spins causes dice to tumble	75.00	95.00	82.00
☐ **Game of Venetian Fortune Telling,** Parker Brothers	5.00	10.00	7.00
☐ **Gee-Whiz Horse Race,** Wolverine, flywheel game, tin with steel wheel, horses race to flag	50.00	60.00	53.00
☐ **Goose Game,** dice, pegs, multicolored pictures, 15″ x 11″	10.00	15.00	11.00
☐ **Heads Down,** puzzle game, under glass with tin sides, object: put trucks standing on heads, 3″ x 4″	20.00	30.00	23.00
☐ **Hold the Fort,** Parker Brother, c.1895, Civil War cover	35.00	45.00	40.00
☐ **Horsehoe Set,** The Ohio Art Company, #531, c.1950's, metal, vinyl, black, red	7.00	12.00	8.00
☐ **Howdy Doody's Own Game,** Parker Brothers, lithographed box lid pictures characters from the TV program, box measures 7″ x 15″, c. 1950-1955	60.00	80.00	68.00
☐ **Jolly Darkie Target Game,** McLoughlin, late 19th century, cardboard with colored lithographed covering, game in which the target is a likeness of a black man wide open mouth, 11½″	140.00	170.00	150.00
☐ **Jolly Old Maid,** Parker Brothers	5.00	10.00	7.00
☐ **Kick Back,** pinball game, spring action, board 15″ x 24″	20.00	30.00	23.00
☐ **Koo Koo Choo Choo,** The Ohio Art Company, #647, c.1960's, metal plastic, exploding train game, mechanical	12.00	22.00	15.00
☐ **Let 'Em Have It,** World War II era, lithographed cover and game board with battle scenes	30.00	40.00	32.00
☐ **Lightning Express,** Miltion Bradley, game board part of box	22.00	28.00	24.00
☐ **Man From U.N.C.L.E.,** Ideal Toy Co., based on TV program, Robert Vaughn and David McCallum on cover, hard plastic figures, box measures 10″ x 19½″, c.	30.00	40.00	33.00
☐ **Mickey Mouse Club Magic Adder,** battery operated, red light turns on correct answer is given	18.00	22.00	18.00
☐ **Money Box,** The Ohio Art Company, #121, c.1950's, in, multicolored, rectangular, play coins, bills	8.00	12.00	9.00
☐ **Mother Goose, E.L. Horsman,** contains fourteen cartoon pictures that must be assembled in playing the game, in box measuring 7″ x 9″, c. 1880-1890	200.00	300.00	230.00
☐ **Old Maid,** Bavaria, nine cards, 2″ x 2″	2.00	5.00	2.50
☐ **Perry Mason: Case Of Missing Suspect,** Transogram, based on TV program, pictures Raymond Burr on cover, box measures 10″ x 19½″, 1959	25.00	30.00	26.25

	Current Price Range		P/Y Average

☐ **Peter Coddles Visit to New York,** c. early 1900's, word game, lithographed cover, 5″ x 6″ **12.00 18.00 14.00**

☐ **Picture Puzzle,** McLoughlin Brothers, New York, wood backed **35.00 45.00 38.00**

☐ **Pike's Peak or Bust,** Parker Brother, c.1895 .. **15.00 20.00 17.00**

☐ **Pollyana,** Parker Brothers, c.1915, game board and cards, lithographed **30.00 40.00 33.00**

☐ **Oueen of the Prom,** Barbie Doll Game, box measures 9″ x 22″, 1960 .... **25.00 30.00 26.50**

☐ **Presidential Puzzle,** wooden playing pieces, race to White House by Herbert Hoover and Franklin D. Roosevelt, no indication of manufacturer, must have been retailed during the campaign of 1932 .... **50.00 65.00 56.00**

☐ **Ralph Edwards' This Is Your Life,** Lowell Toy Manufacturing Corporation, board game, based on TV program, box measures 13½″ x 18″, c. 1958 .... **45.00 60.00 49.00**

☐ **Ring Toss,** c.1940's, wood, rope, post length 6″ **7.00 12.00 8.00**

☐ **Roulette,** Reliable Toys, England, c.1930's, roulette wheel, metal ball **35.00 45.00 39.00**

☐ **Rubber Ball Shooting Gallery,** Schoenhut, c.1910-1915, wood and cardboard covered in lithographed paper, bell rung by clown when shooter makes a direct hit, three aditional targets, 16″ **360.00 420.00 380.00**

☐ **Schley,** card game by Chaffee of New York, fifty two cards plus instructions in a cardboard box, based on the Spanish-American War adventures of Admiral Schley, box measures 5″ x 7″, 1899 .... **100.00 130.00 112.00**

☐ **Shoot-A-Loop-Marble Game,** Wolverine **18.00 22.00 20.00**

☐ **Spinner,** lithographed box, 7″ x 7″ **12.00 18.00 14.00**

☐ **Spudsie,** The Ohio Art Company, #514, c.1960's, plastic, hotpotato game, length 7″ . **5.00 10.00 6.00**

☐ **Steeple Chase,** Bavaria, dice, marker, grand national, 15″ x 15″ **12.00 20.00 13.00**

☐ **Table Golf,** The Ohio Art Company, #549, c.1960's, metal, plastic, flet, putting green, hazards, golfers **15.00 25.00 16.00**

☐ **The Spider and The Fly,** Waverly Toy Works, c.1869, wood, glass cover, picture of spider and web, four felts, 4″ x 4″ **12.00 18.00 14.00**

☐ **Through The Locks To The Golden Gate,** Milton Bradley, comes with spinners and wooden playing pieces, label pictures Panama Canal and 1915 Expo building **8.00 12.00 9.00**

☐ **Tic Tac Toe,** Tahe Ohio Art Company, #528, c.1960's, plastic, marbles **5.00 10.00 6.00**

☐ **Tiddly Winks,** Milton Bradley, box 4″ x 5½″ . **12.00 18.00 14.00**

☐ **Touring,** Parker Brothers **8.00 12.00 10.00**

	Current Price Range		P/Y Average
□**Toy Soldiers And Battle game,** parker Brothers, lithographed paper on box, none standup paper soldiers, five wooden shells, and a wooden cannon	40.00	50.00	43.00
□**U.S. Map Puzzle,** Parker Brothers, c.1907, wood backed, diecut, 12″ x 20″	45.00	55.00	47.00
□**What's The Time,** Parker Brothers, c.1898, lithographed cover, teaches hot to tell time .	18.00	22.00	19.00
□**When My Ship Comes in,** Parker Brothers, c.1888	12.00	18.00	14.00

GARNIER BOTTLES

DESCRIPTION: Garnier bottles are collector figural and decorative liquor bottles produced by the Garnier Company.

ORIGIN: The Garnier Company began producing figural bottles in 1899.

COMMENTS: Garnier bottles produced prior to World War II are scarce. Some of the better known include the Cat, 1930; Clown, 1910; Country Jug, 1937; and Greyhound, 1930.

ADDITIONAL TIPS: For more information, consult *The Official Price Guide to Bottles, Old and New,* published by The House of Collectibles.

□**ALADDIN'S LAMP** (c. 1963), Silver. 6½ ″	38.00	48.00	42.00
□**ALFA ROMEO 1913** (c. 1970), Red body, yellow seats, black trim, 4″ x 10½ ″	15.00	25.00	20.00
□**ALFA ROMEO 1929** (c. 1969), Pale blue body, red seat, black trim, 4″ x 10½ ″	15.00	25.00	20.00
□**ALFA ROMEO RACER** (c. 1969), Maroon body, black tires and trim, 4″ x 10″	15.00	25.00	20.00
□**ANTIQUE COACH** (c. 1970), Multicolor pastel tones, 8″ x 12″	15.00	25.00	20.00
□**APOLLO** (c. 1969), Yellow quarter-moon, blue clouds, silver Apollo Spaceship, 13½ ″	12.00	17.00	15.00
□**AZTEC VASE** (c. 1965), "Stone" tan, multicolor aztec design, 11¾ ″	8.00	14.00	11.00
□**BABY FOOT-SOCCER SHOE** (c. 1963), Black with white trim, 3¾ ″ x 8½ ″	10.00	20.00	15.00
1962 soccer shoe—large	8.00	11.00	9.50

Garnier Strawberries, (1982),
decanter basket of ceramic
strawberries, contained
Strawberry liqueur.
$18.00-$26.00

	Current Price Range		P/Y Average
☐ **BABY TRIO** (c. 1963), Clear glass, gold base, 6¼ "	7.00	10.00	8.50
☐ **BACCUS—FIGURAL** (c. 1967), Purple, brown, flesh tones, 13"	12.00	16.00	14.00
☐ **BAHAMAS,** Black policeman, white jacket, and hat, black pants, red stripe, gold details .	16.00	26.00	21.00
☐ **BALTIMORE ORIOLE** (c. 1970), Multicolor, green, yellow, blue, approx. 11"	10.00	16.00	13.00
☐ **BANDIT—FIGURAL** (c. 1958), Pin ball shape, multicolor, 11½ "	10.00	14.00	12.00
☐ **BEDROOM CANDLESTICK** (c. 1967), White with hand painted flowers, 11½ "	32.00	42.00	37.00
☐ **BELLOWS** (c. 1969), Gold and red, 4" x 14½ "	14.00	21.00	17.50
☐ **CANADA,** "Mountie" in red jacket, black jodphur, brown boots	11.00	14.00	12.50
☐ **CANDLESTICK** (c. 1955), Yellow candle, brown holder with gold ring, 10¾ "	11.00	15.00	13.50
☐ **CANDLESTICK GLASS** (c. 1965), Ornate leaves and fluting, 10"	16.00	23.00	20.00

GEORGE OHR POTTERY

Description: The George Ohr pottery holds a unique position among all American pottery wares. Ohr, of Biloxi, Mississippi designed and manufactured all his products himself. He was totally unconcerned about what would appeal to the public. Rather than letting the public dictate taste to him, he dictated to the public — something which even the giant potteries would not dare to do. He took a totally casual attitude about whether or not anyone wanted to buy it. If there were no customers for one line of his products, he did not stop producing it. Instead, he made more and more, stockpiling it away, feeling certain that someday its real worth would be recognized. It is said he planned to sell his warehouse filled with pottery to the Smithsonian Institute in Washington D.C., so it could have the greatest collection of pottery in existence.

Type: The Ohr pottery is almost totally free hand work, like doodles done in clay, but some striking results were achieved. Ohr's boundless confidence in himself shows through in every piece. No matter how offbeat the idea or design, each item was created with masterful skill.

Period: Ohr ran away from home when he was a young boy and worked as a ship chandler's assistant, among various odd jobs. He entered the pottery business in the early 1880's and continued producing items until 1906. Then he simply retired, without passing on any of his trade secrets.

Comments: Today, among collectors, the Ohr pottery is loved by some and detested by others. This is the same response it received when it was being produced the only difference is that today the prices are higher. Some collectors are prejudiced against these products, believing that a potter of Ohr's background and character could not possibly have produced respectable work. The foolishness of this line of thinking can easily be seen, after examining other lives and personalities of the world's artists.

Marks: Just like the wares themselves, George Ohr's markings followed no special pattern. He seems to have experimented with marks just as much as with designs and working procedures. Most pieces are marked *G.E. OHR, BILOXI* but this can be a small or large mark, in block or script lettering, by itself or in conjunction with numbers and legends of various kinds. Some of Ohr's pieces are dated — not only with the year, but the month and day on which the mold was ready for casting or on which the piece was fired. Ohr sometimes numbered his works like limited editions. But he had no real plan in that direction, either, and would begin numbering after many pieces had already left the kiln.

	Current Price Range		P/Y Average
Bowl, 3½", beige, of squat form with cylindrical sides flaring out into a wide base, crimped along the lip and decorated with small ornaments along the base rim. Marked G.E. OHR, BILOXI, MISS. Believed to date from the late 19th or early 20th centuries.	130.00	145.00	132.00
Bowl, 2½", brown, of free form design giving the appearance of an ashtray with shaped rim, marked G.E. OHR, BILOXI, MISS. Believed to date from the late 19th or early 20th centuries.	230.00	270.00	235.00
Bowl, 2½", brown-green, of free form design giving the appearance of an ashtray, caved-in sides, high-gloss glaze. Marked G.E. OHR, BILOXI. Believed to date from the late 19th or early 20th centuries.	620.00	750.00	625.00
Bowl, 4", green and mud-brown flecked with very dark brown, circular. Marked G.E. OHR, BILOXI. Believed to date from the late 19th or early 20th centuries.	310.00	375.00	315.00
Bowl, 3¼", green and mud-brown, of squat free form design, Marked G.E. OHR, BILOXI, MISS. Believed to date from the late 19th or early 20th centuries.	240.00	290.00	245.00
Bowl, 7", various shades of brown, V-form with severely crimped sides. Marked GEO. E. OHR, BILOXI, MISS. Believed to date from the late 19th or early 20th centuries.	320.00	380.00	325.00
Ink stand, 6¼", green streaked-glaze, in the form of a semi-rectangular artist's palette with thumb-hole and molded brush, the ink-well resting to one corner. The entire palette encircled by small beadwork at the rim. Marked G.E. OHR, BILOXI. Believed to date from the late 19th or early 20th centuries. . . .	330.00	370.00	335.00
Pitcher, 5", brown with green mottling, of free form design resembling a fish in which the tail is pierced and serves as the handle. Marked G.E. OHR. Believed to date from the late 19th or early 20th centuries.	620.00	730.00	625.00
Teapot, 3⅞", brown and green splatter glaze, ovoid bulbous form with thumbprint designing, braided handle, disc-type lid. Marked GEO. E. OHR, BILOXI, MISS. Believed to date from the late 19th or early 20th centuries.	720.00	850.00	725.00
Vase, 7", blue, of modified cylindrical form with a bulging shoulder and tall neck, molded designwork along the lip. Marked G.E. OHR. Believed to date from the late 19th or early 20th centuries.	620.00	750.00	625.00

	Current Price Range		P/Y Average
☐ **Vase,** *10", blue, of basically cylindrical form widening out slightly at the bottom, very glossy glaze. Marked G.E. OHR BILOXI, MISS. Believed to date from the late 19th or early 20th centuries.*	500.00	570.00	525.00
☐ **Vase,** *3¼", brown, bulbous shaped form with pinched and dented sides. Marked G.E. OHR, BILOXI, MISS. Believed to date from the late 19th or early 20th centuries.*	215.00	240.00	220.00
☐ **Vase,** *3½", brown smear glaze, of bulbous form with crimped neck. Marked G.E. OHR. Believed to date from the late 19th or early 20th centuries.*	430.00	520.00	435.00
☐ **Vase,** *5¼", burnt orange and green glaze, in cologne-bottle form with dome-shaped bowl, pinched neck and funnel-type neck and mouth. Marked GEO. E. OHR, BILOXI. Believed to date from the late 19th or early 20th centuries.*	200.00	235.00	210.00
☐ **Vase,** *5¼", burnt orange and olive glaze with rust brown, of hurricane lamp form with a bulbous body and inverted dome neck, wide mouth. Decorated with the applied likeness of a caterpillar. Marked G.E. OHR. Believed to date from the late 19th or early 20th centuries.*	520.00	615.00	525.00

GINGER BEER BOTTLES

ORIGIN: Though Ginger Beer originated in the early 1800s in Great Britain, this section features only American Ginger Beer bottles. The heyday for Ginger Beer was from 1890 to the 1920s when the new production of grain beer won many fans. Some non alcoholic Ginger Beer is still made today, however. Unless otherwise noted in the description, the ginger beer bottles listed are made of stoneware.

COMMENTS: The bottles and prices in this section were furnished by Sven Stau of Buffalo, NY. For further information on Ginger Beer bottles, please refer to The Illustrated Stone Ginger Beer, by Sven Stau, P.O. Box 1135, Buffalo, NY 14211.

RECOMMENDED READING: For further information refer to *The Official Price Guide to Bottles Old and New,* published by The House of Collectibles.

	Current Price Range		P/Y Average
□ **AKRON GINGER BEER CO.**			
Akron, OH, English Brewed Ginger Beer	13.00	18.00	14.00
□ **ALBANY BOTTLING COMPANY**			
Albany, NY	13.00	18.00	14.00
□ **G. ASTE AND CO., INC.**			
New York, NY, Josiah Russell's Olde Fashioned Stone Ginger Beer, paper label	13.00	18.00	14.00
□ **ATLANTIC BOTTLING WORKS**			
Buffalo, New York, Ginger Beer, green glass .	3.00	7.00	3.50
□ **ATLANTIC BOTTLING WORKS**			
Buffalo, NY, pottery	95.00	110.00	96.00
□ **BARNUM'S**			
Niagara Falls, NY, Brewed Ginger Beer	20.00	30.00	21.00
□ **WILLIAM BATT**			
Tonawanda, NY, Brewed Ginger Beer	20.00	30.00	21.00
□ **C. BAUMGARTNER**			
McKeesport, PA, Ginger Beer	18.00	24.00	19.00
□ **C. H. BELL**			
Albany, NY, incised	48.00	52.00	49.00
□ **BRADFORD GINGER BEER**			
Bradford, PA, BGB	12.00	18.00	13.00
□ **HENRY BROWN CO.**			
Glendale, CA, Sierra Club Ginger Beer	22.00	26.00	23.00
□ **J. C. BUFFUM**			
Pittsburg, PA, Ginger Beer	38.00	48.00	39.00
□ **A. CARPENTER AND CO.**			
Eastman Springs, MI/Chicago, IL, U.S.A., Stone Ginger Beer	22.00	27.00	23.00
□ **CHELMSFORD SPRING CO.**			
Chelmsford, MA, Old English Ginger Beer ...	33.00	38.00	34.00
□ **CLEVERLY'S**			
Syracuse, NY, English Brewed Ginger Beer ..	16.00	23.00	17.00
□ **COBURN, LANG AND CO.**			
Boston, MA, incised quart	62.00	78.00	63.00
□ **CRESCENT BOTTLING CO.**			
Alleghany, PA, The Original Brewed Ginger Beer, 2233 Wayne St.	18.00	24.00	19.00
□ **CROWN GINGER BEER CO.**			
Cleveland, OH, English Brewed Ginger Beer .	10.00	15.00	11.00
□ **DR. BROWN'S**			
New York, NY, Ginger Pop, incised	27.00	34.00	28.00
□ **THE DOUBLE EAGLE BOTTLING CO.**			
Cleveland, OH, Ginger Beer, with picture of double eagles	18.00	24.00	19.00
□ **THE DOUBLE EAGLE BOTTLING CO.**			
Cleveland, OH, with picture of double eagles, painted label, brown glass	3.00	7.00	4.00
□ **ADRIAN FEYH**			
New York City, New York, incised	11.00	15.00	12.00
□ **FLANIGAN AND MURPHY**			
Syracuse, NY, Brewed Ginger Beer	18.00	24.00	19.00

	Current Price Range		P/Y Average
FRIEDLER'S			
Rochester, NY, High Grade English Brewed Ginger Beer	18.00	24.00	19.00
FRIER'S			
Niagara Falls, NY, Ginger Beer Bottled by A. C. Freir	20.00	30.00	21.00
GARDNER'S			
Elmira, NY, Gardner's Old English Style Ginger Beer	18.00	24.00	19.00
A. GOLDSTEIN			
Rochester, NY, Celebrated Ginger Beer	25.00	35.00	26.00
JOHN J. HALLORAN CO.			
Syracuse, NY, Imperial Brewed Ginger Beer .	13.00	18.00	14.00
HEYWORTH			
New Bedford, PA, Brewed Ginger Beer	22.00	28.00	23.00
HARRY HICKS			
New Castle, PA, English Brewed Ginger Beer	22.00	28.00	23.00
HUGHES & POTICHER			
Johnston, PA, English Brewed Ginger Beer ..	22.00	30.00	23.00
IMPERIAL BOTTLING CO.			
Buffalo, NY, English Brewed Ginger Beer ...	16.00	22.00	17.00
INTERNATIONAL DRUG CO.			
Calais, ME, Old Homestead Ginger Beer, height 6¾"	13.00	18.00	14.00
JUMBO BOTTLING WORKS			
Cincinnati, OH, Ginger Beer, with picture of elephant	48.00	56.00	49.00
KOENIG BREWERY			
Auburn, NY, Ginger Beer	33.00	38.00	34.00
LATTER AND CO.			
Seattle, WA, Home Brewed Ginger Beer	18.00	30.00	19.00
MAURICE LEWIS			
Rochester, NY, High Grade English Style Ginger Beer, brown glass	8.00	12.00	9.00
MAURICE LEWIS			
Rochester, NY, High Grade English Brewed Ginger Beer	50.00	65.00	51.00
LOUIS BRASS			
Lancaster, NY, Brewed Ginger Beer	18.00	24.00	19.00
LUCAS BROS.			
Auburn, NY, English Brewed Ginger Beer ...	11.00	15.00	12.00
McCOY AND BUSHNELL			
Watertown, NY	13.00	18.00	14.00
NEW YORK BOTTLING WORKS			
Syracuse, NY, R.D. High Grade European Style Ginger Beer	9.00	14.00	10.00
NIAGARA BOTTLING CO.			
Buffalo, NY, Brewed F&M Ginger Beer	20.00	25.00	21.00
A. NOE AND SON			
Sharpesburg, PA, Improved Ginger Beer	13.00	18.00	14.00
OHIO GINGER BEER CO.			
Toledo, OH, O. Ginger Beer, Brewed by English Process	16.00	22.00	17.00
J. OLIVER			
Savannah, GA, Ginger Pop, incised	28.00	35.00	29.00

	Current Price Range		P/Y Average

☐ J. PABST
Baltimore, MD .... 13.00 | 18.00 | 14.00

☐ PAINESVILLE MINERAL SPRINGS CO.
Painesville, OH .... 10.00 | 16.00 | 11.00

☐ PINE AND CO.
Seattle, WA, Home Brewed Ginger Beer .... 28.00 | 40.00 | 29.00

☐ RAMROTH
Troy, NY, Ginger Beer, green glass .... 3.00 | 7.00 | 4.00

☐ REX WATER CO.
New York, NY, Sir Arthur's Original Ginger Beer English Brew, Non-Alcoholic .... 22.00 | 29.00 | 23.00

☐ ROCHESTER SODA AND MINERAL WATER CO. *Rochester, NY, English Brewed Ginger Beer* .... 18.00 | 25.00 | 19.00

☐ RYCROFT ARTIC SODA CO., LTD.
Honolulu, Hawaii, Rycroft's Old Fashioned Ginger Beer, 9 fluid ounces .... 150.00 | 300.00 | 152.00

☐ THE M. SHOULER BOTTLING WORKS
Akron, OH, English Brewed Ginger Beer, Keep Cool .... 13.00 | 19.00 | 14.00

☐ SMITH AND CLODY
Buffalo, NY, Brewed Ginger Beer, Monogram Brand .... 10.00 | 15.00 | 11.00

☐ SOUTHERN ENGLISH GINGER BEER CO.
Jacksonville, FL, John's English Brew Ginger Beer, with man holding mug, height 5½" ..... 20.00 | 30.00 | 21.00

☐ SPRING BOTTLING WORKS
Utica, NY, T&C Ginger Beer .... 18.00 | 24.00 | 19.00

☐ STANDARD WATER CO.
Buffalo, NY, Ginger Beer .... 45.00 | 55.00 | 46.00

☐ STONE JUG BEVERAGE CO.
Buffalo, NY, All American Gingerbru, painted label, brown glass .... 3.00 | 7.00 | 4.00

☐ DR. SWETT'S ROOT BEER
Boston, MA, Original Root Beer, Registered ... 13.00 | 18.00 | 14.00

☐ TULLEY BOTTLING CO.
Syracuse, NY, Gay's English Brewed Ginger Beer .... 22.00 | 30.00 | 23.00

☐ VARTRAY
Buffalo, NY, Brewed Ginger Beer, Keep Cold .. 10.00 | 15.00 | 11.00

☐ VIMO CO.
Cleveland, OH, English Brewed Ginger Beer, Non-Alcoholic, Improves With Age .... 13.00 | 18.00 | 14.00

☐ WASHINGTON BOTTLING CO.
Baltimore, MD, Genuine Brewed Ginger Beer English Process .... 13.00 | 18.00 | 14.00

☐ WASHINGTON BOTTLING CO.
Baltimore, MD, Weiss Beer .... 13.00 | 18.00 | 14.00

☐ WASHINGTON BOTTLING CO.
Washington, D.C., Genuine Brewed Ginger Beer English Process .... 13.00 | 18.00 | 14.00

☐ WESTERN BOTTLING CO.
Buffalo, NY, WB .... 13.00 | 18.00 | 14.00

GOLF MEMORABILIA

TYPES: All types of golf memorabilia are collectible, from gloves to bags, balls, clubs and autographs.

COMMENTS: Golf memorabilia collectors are not as large as group as collectors of baseball and football memorabilia. Most collectors seek golf clubs, and as will most collectibles age and rarity account for high prices.

ADDITIONAL TIPS: The listings are alphabetical according to item. For further information, contact the *Golf Collectors' Society,* 638 Wagner Road, Lafayette Hill, PA 19444.

	Current Price Range		P/Y Average
☐ **Driver,** wooden shaft, c.1910	142.00	180.00	160.00
☐ **George Low Wizard 600 Putter,** flanged	490.00	720.00	610.00
☐ **Golf bag,** leather, c.1930	220.00	265.00	240.00
☐ **Golf glove,** c.1910	34.00	42.00	38.00
☐ **MacGregor R. Armour Set,** wood and irons, c.1950	1070.00	1450.00	1200.00
☐ **Marathon Wards set,** wood and irons, c.1922	238.00	312.00	275.00
☐ **Power build driver,** c.1950	120.00	150.00	135.00
☐ **Putter,** wooden shaft, c.1930	61.00	75.00	68.00
☐ **Putter,** two-way blade with wooden shaft, c.1920	71.00	85.00	78.00
☐ **Reuter Bull's Eye putter**	100.00	150.00	125.00
☐ **Score card,** Master's Tournament	59.00	97.00	78.00
☐ **Golfer's Manual by H.B. Farnie,** c.1857	625.00	725.00	675.00
☐ **Tommy Armour wedge,** c.1959	168.00	212.00	190.00
☐ **Wedge,** Walter Hagen, c.1930	112.00	137.00	125.00
☐ **Wilson,** Sam Snead set, woods and irons, c.1940	458.00	542.00	500.00
☐ **Wilson,** R-20 wedge, c.1930	168.00	212.00	190.00

GRANITEWARE

DESCRIPTION: Metal ware with an enamel coating, Graniteware often has a mottled or marbleized appearance. Most Graniteware is made for use in the kitchen.

PERIOD: 1870s to the present.

ORIGIN: First featured in 1876 at the Centennial Exposition in Philadelphia, Graniteware became popular immediately.

COMMENTS: Graniteware was made in large quantities and it's still produced today. There is a fairly consistent demand for the ware, and prices are reasonably stable.

ADDITIONAL TIPS: The listings are in alphabetical order according to item. For futher information on Graniteware, refer to *The Official Price Guide to Kitchen Collectibles.*

	Current Price Range		P/Y Average
☐ **Baby Cup,** *gray with tin lid, enamel tray*	45.00	55.00	47.00
☐ **Basin,** *salesman's sample, gray, marked Royal Granite Steelware, 6" diameter*	100.00	125.00	110.00
☐ **Basin,** *emerald and white*	40.00	60.00	42.00
☐ **Basin,** *toy, gray*	10.00	20.00	15.00
☐ **Basting Spoon,** *blue and white swirl*	10.00	22.00	11.00
☐ **Basting Spoon,** *gray, good condition, 11¾" long*	8.00	15.00	9.50
☐ **Bucket,** *turquoise swirl, three gallon, bail handle*	55.00	75.00	60.00
☐ **Bucket,** *water, blue and white swirl*	50.00	65.00	52.00
☐ **Bucket,** *water, cobalt and white swirl*	49.00	70.00	50.00
☐ **Cake Mold,** *twelve sided, tube mold*	22.00	36.00	24.00
☐ **Candleholder,** *green*	30.00	50.00	33.00
☐ **Candleholder,** *saucer, scalloped edge, curled handle*	17.00	30.00	19.00
☐ **Candlestick,** *gray, beehive*	90.00	110.00	94.00
☐ **Candlestick,** *gray swirl, black hanger, handle leveling mechanism in working order, rough on one side of base*	45.00	65.00	48.00

Flask, *ceramic cork, 9" high,*
$85.00-$125.00

	Current Price Range		P/Y Average
□ **Canner,** *gray, enamel lid, wire rack, seven quart*	25.00	40.00	28.00
□ **Canning Kettle,** *six quart size, gray*	35.00	38.00	45.00
□ **Casserole,** *gray mottled, dome lid, two quart*	24.00	34.00	36.00
□ **Chamber Pot,** *blue and white streaked, cover*	30.00	55.00	34.00
□ **Chamber Pot,** *gray speckled*	10.00	25.00	12.00
□ **Chamberstick,** *white*	60.00	75.00	62.00
□ **Cheese Grater,** *white*	37.00	50.00	40.00
□ **Coffee Boiler,** *blue and white marbleized, enameled steel, dome lid, eleven quart*	40.00	52.00	42.00
□ **Coffee Boiler,** *blue and white mottled*	37.00	47.00	38.00
□ **Coffee Boiler,** *blue and white mottled, unusual lid, small*	40.00	55.00	42.00
□ **Coffee Boiler,** *blue and white swirl*	65.00	75.00	65.00
□ **Coffee Boiler,** *brown and white marbleized, dome lid, six quart*	58.00	70.00	62.00
□ **Coffee Pot,** *gray, trimmed in pewter, ornate handle, spout, lid, tapered sides, copper bottom*	200.00	250.00	215.00
□ **Coffee Pot,** *red, six cup*	26.00	36.00	27.00
□ **Coffee Pot,** *teal mottled, 9½"*	18.00	35.00	19.50
□ **Coffee Pot,** *turquoise and white, medium*	60.00	80.00	63.00
□ **Coffee Pot,** *turquoise swirl, tin lid, hollow knob, two gallon*	45.00	65.00	50.00
□ **Coffee Pot,** *white, black handle and trim, excellent outside condition, inside repair, can be used for display only*	10.00	18.00	12.00

	Current Price Range		P/Y Average
☐ **Coffee Pot,** *white with green trim, six cup* ...	20.00	45.00	22.00
☐ **Coffee Urn,** *gray, five gallon, brass spigot, cloth strainer, enamel lid*	75.00	85.00	78.00
☐ **Colander,** *blue, 11"*	20.00	35.00	22.00
☐ **Colander,** *diffused, brown and white swirl* ...	33.00	50.00	34.00
☐ **Colander,** *gray mottled, bowl-shaped, stand, hole for hanging, some chips*	12.00	20.00	13.50
☐ **Colander,** *gray mottled, dipped wire handles, nice old seams, some chips*	8.00	16.00	9.50
☐ **Colander,** *gray mottled, rounded, some chips*	10.00	20.00	12.00
☐ **Colander,** *gray, shallow, handles, unusual*	20.00	35.00	25.00
☐ **Colander,** *white, hole for hanging, excellent usable condition, 11½" diameter*	15.00	25.00	17.00
☐ **Colander,** *white with black rim, side handles, footed*	17.00	27.00	19.00
☐ **Cream Can,** *dark gray, ribbed effect, flat lid and bail handle, two quart*	32.00	41.00	34.00
☐ **Cream Pitcher,** *gray, one pint, small spout and side handle*	35.00	50.00	38.00
☐ **Fish Poacher,** *gray, enamel lid and rack, enamel label, small*	55.00	75.00	60.00
☐ **Flask,** *gray*	40.00	60.00	43.00
☐ **Flask,** *gray, pint, flat sides, round bottom, cork stopper, small loops on top for hanging, marked H & C.A-G 1916*	65.00	85.00	70.00
☐ **Flask,** *gray ribbed*	62.00	69.00	64.00
☐ **Flask,** *screw cap*	37.00	44.00	38.00
☐ **Foot Tub,** *blue and white swirls, round*	46.00	56.00	49.00
☐ **Frying Pan,** *marbleized green and white, 9" diameter*	65.00	67.00	75.00
☐ **Funnel,** *blue and white swirls*	17.00	30.00	19.00
☐ **Kerosene Stove,** *table top, gray, very fancy, ornate nickel coated trim, includes one quart nickel plated brass teakettle with ornate gooseneck spout and lid, bell shaped bottom, wood and bail handle, tray with raised rim, made by George Haller, 11" diameter*	350.00	425.00	375.00
☐ **Kettle,** *beer, gray, five gallon, straight sides, enamel lid, pull down spigot*	75.00	95.00	80.00
☐ **Kettle,** *Berlin, blue and white mottled*	37.00	50.00	38.00
☐ **Kettle,** *Berlin, blue and white swirl*	37.00	47.00	38.00
☐ **Kettle,** *Berlin, blue swirl, with lid*	55.00	75.00	57.00
☐ **Kettle,** *Berlin, wooden finial on lid, bail handle, one quart*	11.00	17.00	13.00
☐ **Kettle,** *blue, two-tone, lid, bail handle*	30.00	50.00	35.00
☐ **Kettle,** *camp, gray, coffee boiler, bail handle, enamel lid, large*	30.00	40.00	35.00
☐ **Kettle,** *gray, strainer lip*	24.00	38.00	25.00
☐ **Kettle,** *preserve, gray, bail handle, 15½"*	25.00	45.00	27.00
☐ **Kettle,** *preserving, gray, marked L & G, 22" diameter*	35.00	50.00	37.00
☐ **Kettle,** *preserving and canning, flared pouring lip, blue and white*	17.00	30.00	18.00
☐ **Kettle,** *turquoise and white speckled, large* ..	30.00	45.00	33.00
☐ **Kitchen Sink Backplate,** *gray, brass faucets* .	110.00	130.00	115.00

	Current Price Range		P/Y Average
☐ **Milk Cream Can,** *gray mottled, side handle, seamless, tin lid, mint condition*	65.00	85.00	67.50
☐ **Milk Cream Can,** *white, dark blue trim, lid, wire bail with wood handle, two bad chips, 11" high*	12.00	18.00	13.00
☐ **Milk Pan,** *turquoise, small swirl, 10" diameter*	25.00	35.00	27.00
☐ **Miniature,** *pie plate, gray and white mottled* .	25.00	35.00	26.00
☐ **Miniature,** *platter, blue and white mottled*	20.00	34.00	22.00
☐ **Miniature,** *skillet, granite, gray*	44.00	55.00	46.00
☐ **Miniature,** *strainer, triangular*	22.00	38.00	25.00
☐ **Mixing Bowl,** *yellow and white swirl, large* . .	40.00	55.00	42.00
☐ **Mixing Bowl,** *yellow and white swirl, medium*	30.00	45.00	33.00
☐ **Mold,** *cake, tube, gray, twelve-sided, marked Agate-Seconds, chipped, 9" diameter*	35.00	45.00	38.00
☐ **Mold,** *corn, gray*	68.00	85.00	70.00
☐ **Mold,** *melon, gray, tin bottom, enamel label* .	45.00	60.00	50.00
☐ **Mold,** *octagonal, gray, cone center*	30.00	40.00	32.00
☐ **Mold,** *pudding, gray*	60.00	75.00	63.00
☐ **Mold,** *scalloped, gray*	18.00	30.00	19.00
☐ **Mold,** *scalloped, gray, no tube, small*	20.00	30.00	21.00
☐ **Mold,** *strawberry and grapes*	32.00	38.00	32.00
☐ **Mold,** *tube*	16.00	22.00	15.00
☐ **Mold,** *tube, solid cobalt, white inside, swirl design, large*	65.00	85.00	70.00
☐ **Mold,** *turban, gray swirl, tube in center, excellent overall condition* . . . . :	45.00	65.00	50.00
☐ **Mold,** *Turk's head, cobalt outside, cobalt and white inside*	45.00	65.00	48.00
☐ **Mold,** *Turk's head, gray*	25.00	45.00	30.00
☐ **Muffin Pan,** *blue and white, eight cup*	15.00	22.00	15.00
☐ **Muffin Pan,** *gray, eight swirl cups, excellent mottling*	190.00	120.00	100.00
☐ **Muffin Pan,** *gray mottled, ribbed, twelve cups*	75.00	95.00	80.00
☐ **Muffin Pan,** *gray, six cup*	28.00	40.00	29.00
☐ **Muffin Pan,** *gray, six cup, hole in top for hanging, rough corners, some chips, nice display piece*	20.00	30.00	22.50
☐ **Muffin Pan,** *gray swirl, nine cup*	70.00	90.00	80.00
☐ **Muffin Pan,** *gray, twelve cups*	25.00	45.00	26.00
☐ **Pan,** *cake, tube, gray, 11" diameter*	30.00	45.00	35.00
☐ **Pan,** *fudge, gray, one inch rim, 9" square*	20.00	30.00	22.00
☐ **Pan,** *gray mottled, handle*	17.00	25.00	18.00
☐ **Pan,** *jelly roll, blue and white swirl, 12" diameter*	16.00	26.00	18.00
☐ **Pan,** *loaf, gray and white*	12.00	18.00	14.00
☐ **Pan,** *maroon spatter, round*	7.00	18.00	8.00
☐ **Pan,** *milk, blue and white marbleized, white liner, 12"*	23.00	39.00	26.00
☐ **Pan,** *milk, gray mottled, inconspicuous chips, excellent overall condition, 12½" diameter* . . .	15.00	25.00	17.50
☐ **Pan,** *milk, gray mottled, mint condition, 12½" diameter*	15.00	25.00	17.50
☐ **Pan,** *pie, blue and white mottled*	12.00	25.00	13.50
☐ **Pan,** *pie, blue and white speckled*	15.00	25.00	17.00
☐ **Pan,** *pie, blue and white swirl*	15.00	28.00	17.00
☐ **Pan,** *pie, blue, two-tone*	12.00	25.00	13.50

	Current Price Range		P/Y Average
☐ **Pan**, *pie, blue, two-tone*	18.00	28.00	19.00
☐ **Pan**, *pie, crystolite and white swirl*	13.00	23.00	14.00
☐ **Pan**, *pie, gray and black mottled*	15.00	25.00	16.50
☐ **Pan**, *pie, gray mottled, inconspicuous chips, 9½" diameter, 1½" deep*	15.00	25.00	17.50
☐ **Pan**, *pie, gray mottled, some chips, good overall condition, 10" diameter*	5.00	10.00	6.00
☐ **Pan**, *pie, gray and white*	12.00	20.00	14.00
☐ **Roaster**, *with drip pan, gray, medium, embossed L & G Mfg. Co.*	40.00	50.00	42.00
☐ **Salt Box**, *blue and white swirl, hinged lid*	46.00	55.00	49.00
☐ **Salt Box**, *white, mint condition*	68.00	78.00	69.00
☐ **Salt Box**, *white, wall type*	39.00	49.00	39.50
☐ **Salt Box**, *wooden lid, flared*	46.00	59.00	49.00
☐ **Saucepan**, *aqua and white swirl, handle*	25.00	40.00	26.00
☐ **Saucepan**, *blue and white marbleized, two quarts*	35.00	55.00	40.00
☐ **Saucepan**, *blue and white mottled, tubular handle, large*	35.00	45.00	36.00
☐ **Saucepan**, *blue and white swirl, large*	38.00	48.00	39.00
☐ **Saucepan**, *cobalt and white*	50.00	65.00	52.00
☐ **Saucepan**, *gray*	20.00	34.00	25.00
☐ **Saucepan**, *gray, handled, 4½" diameter, small*	25.00	40.00	27.00
☐ **Saucepan**, *gray, with lid which has long curved handle, round sides, large*	20.00	30.00	25.00
☐ **Saucepan**, *one quart size, flared lip*	12.00	20.00	14.00
☐ **Saucepan**, *red and white swirl*	40.00	60.00	43.00
☐ **Spittoon**, *turquoise swirl, two piece, straight sides, flat bottom, paper label*	60.00	80.00	64.00
☐ **Spoon**, *blue and white swirl*	15.00	22.00	16.00
☐ **Spoon**, *child's, medium blue speckled with white, excellent front, conspicuous chips on back*	5.00	10.00	6.00
☐ **Spoon**, *cobalt swirl, white bowl, long handle*	15.00	25.00	18.00
☐ **Steamer**, *blue and white mottled, with lid* ...	20.00	35.00	22.00
☐ **Steamer**, *insert, gray, 12"*	52.00	68.00	55.00
☐ **Stew Pan**, *blue and white marbleized, bail handle, wood grip, dome lid*	34.00	44.00	37.00
☐ **Stew Pan**, *blue and white swirl, handle, small*	20.00	30.00	21.00
☐ **Stew Pot**, *blue, two-tone, with lid and bail handle*	25.00	50.00	27.50
☐ **Stoves**, *electric burner*	42.00	48.00	44.00
☐ **Stoves**, *kerosene*	195.00	245.00	210.00
☐ **Strainer**, *blue and white swirl, long handle* ..	12.00	22.00	14.00
☐ **Strainer**, *blue and white swirl, round*	33.00	45.00	34.00
☐ **Strainer**, *brown-gray*	20.00	33.00	21.00
☐ **Strainer**, *sink, gray, rounded, footed*	10.00	20.00	11.00
☐ **Strainer**, *turquoise and white swirl*	35.00	50.00	38.50
☐ **Sugar Bowl**, *gray mottled, black trim, dome lid*	184.00	235.00	195.00
☐ **Sugar Bowl**, *gray, no lid*	90.00	110.00	94.00
☐ **Syrup Pitcher**, *aqua and white swirl, rare*	70.00	85.00	72.00
☐ **Table**, *children's, white with blue trim, child's scene in center of top*	60.00	80.00	65.00

	Current Price Range		P/Y Average
☐ Tea Cup, *gray mottled, matching saucer, 4"* diameter	14.00	18.00	15.00
☐ Tea Kettle, *cobalt swirl, cast iron, tin lid,* gallon size	70.00	90.00	72.00
☐ Tea Kettle, *"S" curved spout, wood handle,* ten quart	30.00	40.00	32.00
☐ Tea Kettle, *whistler*	28.00	46.00	32.00
☐ Teapot, *blue*	78.00	135.00	85.00

GREETING CARDS

TYPES, All types greeting card, Christmas card, was produced in 1843. However the tradition of greeting cards didn't take hold until 1860 and the introduction of small visiting greeting cards.

MAKERS: Popular publishers of cards in Marcus Ward & Co., DeLaRue & Co., Raphael Tuck & Co. and L. Prang and Co.

COMMENTS: Greeting cards from the 19th century are the most beautiful and the most sought after. Greeting cards are easy to find and most are reasonably priced.

ADDITIONAL TIPS: The listings are alphabetical accodding to type of greeting. Also see the section in this book on Valentines.

☐ Christmas, "A Merry Christmas and Happy New Year," children playing under Christmas tree, c. 1870's	3.75	6.50	4.50
☐ Christmas, "A Merry Christmas to you All," family strolling through snow-blanketed woodland, c. 1880	5.00	8.00	6.00
☐ Christmas, blue fringed, golding, birds and flowers, c.1880	25.00	50.00	30.00
☐ Christmas, child in 19th century, bonnet	3.00	7.00	4.50
☐ Christmas, children and farm scene	3.00	6.00	4.50
☐ Christmas, flowers and birds, Merry Christmas and Happy New Year, 4 pages	9.00	20.00	13.00
☐ Christmas, Fold out Christmas card, Santa Claus	11.00	16.00	13.00

Greeting Card, *Christmas ad for Raphael Tuck & Sons,* **$28.00-$30.00**
Photo courtesy of Lou McCulloch, Highland Heights, OH 44143.

	Current Price Range		P/Y Average
☐ **Christmas,** Fold out Christmas card, Nativity scene, c. 1820	7.00	12.00	8.00
☐ **Christmas,** "Hail, Day of Joy," card by L. Prang and Co., angel kneeling with dove on finger, c. 1870's	14.00	19.00	15.00
☐ **Christmas,** "Here Comes the New Year with Lots of Good Cheer," child with Christmas tree and toys, c. 1870	10.00	16.00	12.00
☐ **Christmas,** "Here, Open the Door," card by Kate Greenaway, young messenger boy knocking on door, c. 1880	40.00	55.00	43.00
☐ **Christmas,** ice pond, boy putting skates on a girl, fringed and embroidered, German	8.00	12.00	10.00

	Current Price Range		P/Y Average
☐ **Christmas,** "Merry Christmas and Happy New Year," children romping in snow, church in background, c. 1860	3.75	6.00	4.50
☐ **Christmas,** "Merry Christmas to You All," card by L. Prang and Co., brown suited Santa in chimney, square, c. 1880's	21.00	30.00	23.00
☐ **Christmas,** "My Lips May Give a Message," card by Kate Greenaway, young girl holding letter, c. 1880	40.00	55.00	43.00
☐ **Christmas,** Pop up Christmas card, ice skating scene, England, c. 1890	22.00	30.00	25.00
☐ **Christmas,** Prang's American Third Prize Christmas Card, designed by C. C. Coleman, oriental scene	17.00	25.00	20.00
☐ **Christmas,** Victorian Christmas card, paper lace border surrounds season's greeting, c. 1800's	9.00	15.00	12.00
☐ **Christmas,** "Wishing You a Happy New Year," card by L. Prang and Co., folded, young girl on front, old man on back, fringed, tied with tasseled cord, c. 1884	24.00	34.00	27.00
☐ **Christmas,** "Wishing You a Merry Christmas," card by L. Prang and Co., fireplace scene, cat and kittens looking up chimney, square, c. 1880's	21.00	29.00	24.00
☐ **Christmas,** "With Best Christmas Wishes," card by Raphael Tuck and Sons, young girl holding spray of flowers, c. late 1800's	12.00	18.00	15.00
☐ **Christmas,** "With the Season's Greetings," card by W. S. Coleman, girl on swing (back view), c. 1890	7.00	12.00	9.00
☐ **Easter,** angels on front, by Whitney, New York, 19th century	4.00	6.00	5.00
☐ **Easter,** Bible verses, birds, late 19th century .	3.00	6.00	4.50
☐ **Easter,** booklet, poem, cross with flowers, German	2.00	5.00	3.00
☐ **Easter,** child coming out of egg, gold fringed	6.00	10.00	8.00
☐ **Easter,** cross on reef in sea, by Carter and Karrick, 19th century	4.00	8.00	6.00
☐ **Easter,** floral cross on front, German, 19th century	4.50	6.50	5.50
☐ **Easter,** girl climbing out of an egg shelf, fringed German, 19th century	8.50	15.00	12.00
☐ **Easter,** religious, floral, Tuck	10.00	18.00	14.00
☐ **Greetings,** cupid with ribbon holding flowers, 19th century	7.00	15.00	10.00
☐ **Greetings,** heads of children in flower pot, 19th century	1.00	4.00	2.00
☐ **Greetings,** Shakespears, "Heaven Give You Many Merry Days," 19th century	3.00	6.00	4.00
☐ **Happy Birthday,** blue fringed, floral design, c.1880	15.00	25.00	18.00
☐ **Happy Birthday,** booklet, flowers, 19th century	3.00	6.00	4.00
☐ **Happy Birthday,** children, 19th century	2.00	4.00	3.00

	Current Price Range		P/Y Average
Happy Birthday, maroon floral, fringed, 19th century	14.00	20.00	16.00
Happy Birthday, maroon fringed, flowers	8.00	12.00	10.00
New Year, girl holding bird under palm tree, 19th century	3.00	6.00	4.00
Religious, blue fringed, 19th century	3.00	6.00	4.00
Religious, eggs and feathers, c.1880	7.00	12.00	9.00
Religious, embossed card, "I Go to Prepare A Place for You"	1.00	2.00	1.50
Religious, Welcome to Happy Morn, 19th century	4.50	6.50	5.50
Season's Greetings, card shaped like fan	2.50	5.00	3.50
Season's Greetings, mechanical, boy with flowers, 19th century	15.00	25.00	20.00
Season's Greetings, river and small boat, 19th century	4.00	8.00	5.50
Valentine, American, heart shaped, lace, c. 1905.	9.00	16.00	9.50
Valentine, American, honeycomb, "Cupid's Temple of Love," c. 1928.	8.00	16.00	8.50
Valentine, American, Maggie and Jiggs, c. 1940.	4.00	12.00	4.25
Valentine, American, Popeye, c. 1940.	4.00	10.00	4.25
Valentine, Art Nouveau, heart shaped folder.	4.50	6.50	4.75
Valentine, Carrington, folder, lace, c. 1937.	1.50	4.50	1.75
Valentine, Comic Valentine, the "Hat Trimmer," Elton and Co., New York, illustration of glum-looking woman sewing hat, with verse, c. 1860.	22.00	30.00	22.50
Valentine, "Dainty Dimples" series, per card.	3.00	8.00	3.25
Valentine, Easel Valentine, fold back, free standing, c. early 1900s.	34.00	44.00	35.00
Valentine, German, five layer, pulldown, religious sentiment, flowers.	45.00	65.00	46.00
Valentine, German, large ship, mechanical pulldown.	55.00	85.00	56.00
Valentine, German, pulldown, children, c. 1915.	4.50	10.00	4.15
Valentine, German, pulldown, gold.	10.00	20.00	11.00
Valentine, German, pullout and stand up cottage, c. 1910.	7.00	15.00	7.50
Valentine, German, pullout and stand up steam boiler, c. 1910.	12.00	18.00	12.50
Valentine, German, stand up, little girl holding opening parasol.	15.00	25.00	15.50
Valentine, German, three layers, pulldown, lavender, pink, gold, green, c. 1920.	6.50	15.00	7.00
Valentine, Gibson Art, paper doll mechanical stand up, little girl holding doll, German.	20.00	35.00	21.00
Valentine, "Hearts Are Ripe," children picking heart shaped apples from tree.	3.00	7.00	4.00
Valentine, H. Dobbs and Co., "Pillar Post," illustration of mailbox, c. 1800.	22.00	27.00	23.00
Valentine, "It Must Be Fine, To Have a Valentine," from "Valentine Wishes" series.	7.00	12.00	7.50

	Current Price Range		P/Y Average
□ **Valentine,** "Lady Killer," comic valentine by A. J. Fisher, NY, c. 1850.	29.00	39.00	30.00
□ **Valentine,** McLoughlin, folder, no lace, c. 1905.	5.00	12.00	5.50
□ **Valentine,** McLoughlin, three layer, silver, white, lace, c. 1880.	5.00	12.00	5.50
□ **Valentine,** McLoughlin, three layer, white, gold, lace, c. 1880.	5.00	12.00	5.50
□ **Valentine,** Mansell, lace, handwritten verse, c. 1946.	75.00	100.00	78.00
□ **Valentine,** Mansell, lace paper, lovers in a park, heavily ornamented, white with silver, c. 1855.	44.00	54.00	45.00
□ **Valentine,** Mansell, cameo embossing, two lovers walking along woodland path, c. 1845.	39.00	49.00	40.00
□ **Valentine,** Mechanical, set of fifteen, c. 1920.	34.00	44.00	35.00
□ **Valentine,** Mechanical, "Such is Married Life," c. 1950.	39.00	49.00	40.00
□ **Valentine,** Mechanical, various animals, c. 1930.	10.00	15.00	11.00
□ **Valentine,** Mechanical, Walt Disney character, c. 1930.	17.00	24.00	18.00
□ **Valentine,** Meek & Son, Gibson Girl (from photo), surrounded by lace in various ornamental patterns, cherub heads, c. 1890.	54.00	65.00	55.00
□ **Valentine,** Meek, layered folder, lace, c. 1870.	8.00	15.00	9.00
□ **Valentine,** "Temple of Love'," from Raphael Tuck's "Betsy Beauties" series, young girl chasing butterfly.	5.00	9.00	6.00
□ **Valentine,** "To My Valentine," from Raphael Tuck's "Innocence Abroad" series, two young children, brief verse.	5.00	8.00	6.00
□ **Valentine,** "To My Wife," embossed woman, hearts and flowers, cutout flowers tied with satin ribbon, real lace surrounds cutout heart, c. 1936.	11.00	16.00	12.00
□ **Valentine,** Tuck, folder, heart shaped, little girl on front.	4.00	10.00	5.00
□ **Valentine,** Victorian, fold out, paper lace. . . .	20.00	25.00	21.00

GRUEBY POTTERY

DESCRIPTION: This very prestigeous art pottery manufacturer was in business rather briefly, a total of 16 years. In that time, it rose to the top of its market, was considered one of the foremost trend-setters, and established an enviable reputation for creativity and quality. Its years of operation (from 1891 to 1907) coincided with the glory years of art pottery when it not only made a resounding public splash but influenced other crafts and arts. The Grueby ware was expensive and was intended for a limited audience. Grueby did so well that, in a sense, it put itself out of business. The Tiffany Co. of New York, which had been selling fine jewelry and decorative glassware for many years, decided to add art pottery to its inventory. Rather than selling the products of another manufacturer, Tiffany would consider nothing less than manufacturing its own pottery. Since Grueby had the outstanding reputation in the industry, Tiffany approached the company with purchase offers. The purchase plan was completed in 1907 and thereafter all Grueby pottery was manufactured and sold under the name of Tiffany.

TYPE: Grueby had as diverse a line as any art pottery manufacturer. Its products included vases, ornamental wares of various kinds including statuettes, and decorative tiles.

MARKS: The majority of Grueby ware carries not only a factory stamp but an artist's marking as well. There are several variations of the company mark, which fall into two basic categories: straight-line and circular. The straight-line mark will sometimes read *GRUEBY POTTERY* and, directly beneath this in lettering of a slightly smaller size *BOSTON, U.S.A.* A.

RECOMMENDED READING: For more in-depth information you may refer to *The Official Price Guide to Pottery and Porcelain and The Official Indentification Guide to Pottery and Porcelain,* published by The House of Collectibles.

	Current Price Range		P/Y Average

☐ **Bowl,** 4½ ", greenish brown glaze (mottled), pressed bulbous form, bearing an impressed factory mark. . . . . 170.00 · 200.00 · 185.00

☐ **Bowl,** 6½ "x5", matte blue, thick glaze . . . . . 325.00 · 335.00 · 330.00

☐ **Inkwell,** 3¾ ", floral sterling silver overlay, hinged silver cover, bulbous body, marked sterling . . . . 500.00 · 550.00 · 525.00

☐ **Paperweight,** 4", matte green glaze, c. 1904 . 140.00 · 150.00 · 145.00

☐ **Tile,** 4", windmill design . . . . 120.00 · 130.00 · 125.00

☐ **Tiles,** 4", set of 4, plain, solid color . . . . 55.00 · 65.00 · 60.00

☐ **Tile,** 6", grape motif . . . . 55.00 · 65.00 · 60.00

☐ **Tile,** 6¼ " square, blue, decorated with a painting of green flowers, bearing an impressed factory mark and an artist's initials. Probably early 1900's. . . . . 310.00 · 385.00 · 347.00

Note: It should be mentioned that when such items occur for sale in groups, such as half a dozen of the same design, the price per tile is higher than for a single specimen. This is because their decorative uses are greater when one has a number of them.

☐ **Tile, Horse,** 6¼ " square, pastel blue, decorated with a painting of a white horse, bearing an impressed factory mark and an artist's initials. Probably early 1900's. . . . . 285.00 · 345.00 · 315.00

☐ **Tile, landscape,** 4" square, chiefly green and beige, bearing an impressed factory mark and hand-inked artist's initials P.S. Late 19th to early 20th centuries. . . . . 130.00 · 155.00 · 142.00

Note: While Rookwood was selling its huge tile murals (more than a yard square), Grueby was doing a good business with these small individual tiles. Naturally, each pattern was turned out in the thousands, since it would take hundreds just to cover a single wall. Nevertheless, they aren't common — because when the houses they decorated came down, they went with them.

☐ *Vase,* bulbous base, purple glaze . . . . 280.00 · 310.00 · 295.00

☐ **Vase,** 3¼ ", green, flared neck, rounded lip, thick glaze . . . . 140.00 · 150.00 · 145.00

☐ **Vase,** 4¼ ", green, molded loaf design, bulbous body, signed with initials . . . . 300.00 · 350.00 · 325.00

☐ **Vase,** 5¾ ", brown glaze (speckled), of flattened spherical form with short neck, bearing an impressed factory mark. c. 1900 . . . . 310.00 · 385.00 · 347.50

☐ **Vase,** 6¼ ", green glaze, bulbous bowl with a tall squared cylindrical neck, bearing an impressed factory mark and artist's initials. Late 19th century to early 20th century. . . . . . . 435.00 · 535.00 · 485.00

☐ **Vase,** 6¼ ", light blue matte glaze, c.1900 . . . 160.00 · 170.00 · 165.00

☐ **Vase,** 7", blue glaze . . . . 315.00 · 335.00 · 325.00

☐ **Vase,** 7", green, of modified ovoid form with molded panels encircling the body, bearing an impressed factory mark and artist's initials. Late 19th century to early 20th century. 480.00 · 570.00 · 525.00

	Current Price Range		P/Y Average
☐ **Vase,** 7½″, green, ovoid flask-style form with pinched neck, decorated by Lillian Newman, bearing an impressed factory mark. c. 1898/1901.	540.00	620.00	580.00
☐ **Vase,** 8″, matte green glaze, molded with buds on stems above leaves, artist-signed, c.1900	260.00	280.00	270.00
☐ **Vase,** 8½″, bulbous body, 3-handled, matte green glaze, leaf design	850.00	1000.00	925.00
☐ **Vase,** 10″, green, decorated by Ruth Erickson, impressed factory mark, artist's initials, c.1900	1250.00	1650.00	1450.00
☐ **Vase,** 11″, green, molded with leaves	290.00	310.00	300.00
☐ **Vase,** 11″, matte green glaze, molded with bud and leaf motif, artist-signed	530.00	580.00	555.00
☐ **Vase,** 12½″, green, cylindrical shape, leaf and bud motif, stamped and numbered 161 .	750.00	850.00	800.00

HALL CHINA

DESCRIPTION: Hall's best known dinnerwares were in white or cream usually with a gilt border and decorated with soft pastel flowers. This was the standard line which found new customers in each succeeding generation. In addition, it manufactured numerous other styles in creative patterns, including solid-color wares with richly painted decoration.

INNOVATIONS: This giant of the dinnerware industry was noteworthy not only for the volume of its sales and variety of its patterns, but because it produced the first leadless glaze in the trade. This resulted in strong hardpaste wares with non-porous surfaces which required only a single trip through the firing kiln. Not only were labor costs reduced, but the sales impact was enormous. Hall could authentically claim it was manufacturing chinaware by the same process used in China centuries earlier. The ancient Oriental potters fired their wares only once.

MARKS: There are numerous marks and variations of them, sometimes accompanied by trade names applying to the different lines. The earlier markings were very simple compared to those of later eras, usually consisting of nothing more than the words *HALL'S CHINA* arranged in a plain circular frame, containing a mold or pattern number at the center. This was sometimes accompanied by *MADE IN U.S.A.* directly beneath the stamp. Later, the name Hall was placed in a rectangular frame with wider border, with a small R in a circle beneath it (signifying registration as a trademark). A more eleborate marking reads *HALL'S SUPERIOR QUALITY KITCHENWARE* in a rectangular frame with bars above and beneath. There are also many retailers' marks to be encountered on the Hall products.

RECOMMENDED READING: For more in-depth information on Hall China you may refer to *The Official Price Guide to Pottery and Porcelain* and *The Official Identification Guide to Pottery and Porcelain,* published by The House of Collectibles.

Autumn Leaf salt and pepper range shakers, *made by Hall for Jewel Tea, pair,* $13.00-$15.00

AUTUMN LEAF *(Introduced 1933)*

Hall produced this pattern for the Jewel Tea company.

	Current Price Range		P/Y Average
☐ **Baker,** *9½"*	14.00	16.00	15.00
☐ **Bowl,** *3½"*	4.00	6.00	5.00
☐ **Bowl,** *5"*	5.00	8.00	6.50
☐ **Bowl Set,** *6", 7½" 9¼", mixing*	30.00	34.00	32.00
☐ **Bowl,** *6½"*	8.00	10.00	9.00
☐ **Bowl,** *8"*	10.00	12.00	11.00
☐ **Casserole,** *covered, round*	24.00	27.00	25.50
☐ **Casserole Set,** *covered, three pieces*	55.00	60.00	57.50
☐ **Coffeepot,** *covered, metal insert*	37.00	40.00	38.50
☐ **Cookie Jar,** *covered, c. 1936-39*	70.00	75.00	72.50
☐ **Creamer,** *ruffled*	10.00	12.00	11.00

	Current Price Range		P/Y Average
□ Creamer And Sugar, covered sugar, pair	22.00	26.00	24.00
□ Cup And Saucer pair	6.00	8.00	7.00
□ Custard Cups, set of six	30.00	34.00	32.00
□ Dish, 7½", swirl design	6.00	8.00	7.00
□ Dish, covered	95.00	105.00	00.00
□ Dish, gravy	10.00	12.00	11.00
□ Dish, pickle	12.00	15.00	13.50
□ Dish, with lid	24.00	28.00	26.00
□ Jar, cover and underplate, three piece set ...	50.00	58.00	54.00
□ Pitcher, 6"	15.00	20.00	17.50
□ Pitcher, ice lip	27.00	33.00	30.00
□ Plate, 6"	3.00	6.00	4.50
□ Plate, 7"	5.00	7.00	6.00
□ Plate, 8"	6.00	8.00	7.00
□ Plate, 9"	7.00	9.00	8.00
□ Plate, 9½"	6.00	8.00	7.00
□ Plate, 10"	10.00	12.00	11.00
□ Plate, 13", oval	13.00	16.00	14.50
□ Salad Bowl, c. 1937	12.00	15.00	13.50
□ Saucer	2.00	4.00	3.00
□ Sauce, 5½"	5.00	6.00	5.50
□ Shakers, salt and pepper, pair, c.1933	32.00	35.00	33.50
□ Stove Set, 4 pieces	28.00	32.00	30.00
□ Sugar	4.00	6.00	5.00
□ Teapot, covered	50.00	58.00	54.00
□ Vegetable Dish, covered	30.00	35.00	32.50
□ Vegetable Dish, 10½", oval, open	13.00	16.00	14.50

BLUE BOUQUET (Introduced early 1950s)

Hall produced this pattern for the Standard Coffee Company, discontinuing production in the mid 1960s.

□ Baker	12.00	15.00	12.50
□ Ball Jug #3	18.00	28.00	18.50
□ Bread and Butter Plate, 6"	1.50	3.00	2.00
□ Cake Stand	10.00	13.00	11.00
□ Casserole, covered	22.00	32.00	22.50
□ Cereal Bowl, 6"	4.00	6.00	4.50
□ Coffeepot	40.00	50.00	42.00
□ Creamer	5.00	8.00	6.00
□ Cup	3.50	5.00	3.75
□ Custard Cup	5.00	8.00	5.50
□ Dinner Plate, 9"	4.00	6.00	4.25
□ Fruit Bowl, 5½"	3.00	4.25	3.25
□ Gravy Boat	15.00	20.00	15.50
□ Luncheon Plate, 8¼"	3.00	4.25	3.25
□ Mixing Bowl, 6"	5.00	9.00	5.50
□ Mixing Bowl, 7½"	12.00	18.00	12.50
□ Mixing Bowl, 8½"	12.00	18.00	12.50
□ Pitcher	12.00	15.00	12.50
□ Platter, 11"	12.00	18.00	15.50
□ Platter, 13"	15.00	20.00	15.50
□ Salad Bowl, 9"	11.00	15.00	11.50
□ Salt and Pepper Shakers, pair	15.00	20.00	15.50
□ Saucer	1.00	2.50	1.50

	Current Price Range		P/Y Average
☐ Soup Bowl, *8½"*	9.00	13.00	9.50
☐ Soup Tureen	50.00	70.00	55.00
☐ Sugar Bowl, *with lid*	9.00	13.00	9.50
☐ Teapot, *Aladdin shape*	38.00	42.00	39.00
☐ Vegetable Bowl, *9¼"*	18.00	24.00	18.50

CAMEO ROSE (Introduced 1950s)

Hall produced this pattern for the Jewel Tea Company.

☐ Bread and Butter Plate, *6½"*	1.25	2.25	1.50
☐ Butter Dish, *covered*	25.00	35.00	26.00
☐ Casserole, *covered, two tab handles*	20.00	30.00	21.00
☐ Cereal Bowl, *6"*	2.75	3.75	3.00
☐ Creamer	5.00	6.50	5.50
☐ Cup	4.25	5.25	4.75
☐ Dessert Plate, *8"*	2.00	2.75	2.10
☐ Dinner Plate, *10"*	3.75	5.75	3.80
☐ Fruit Bowl, *5¼"*	1.75	2.75	1.90
☐ Gravy Boat	10.00	15.00	11.00
☐ Luncheon Plate, *9¼"*	2.75	3.75	3.00
☐ Platter, *11"*	8.00	11.00	9.00
☐ Platter, *13"*	10.00	13.00	11.00
☐ Relish Dish, *9"*	7.00	9.00	8.00
☐ Salt and Pepper Shakers, *pair*	10.00	15.00	11.00
☐ Saucer	.75	1.25	1.00
☐ Soup Bowl	5.00	7.00	5.50
☐ Sugar Bowl, *covered*	8.00	13.00	8.50
☐ Teapot	28.00	38.00	29.00
☐ Vegetable Bowl, *oval*	8.00	11.00	8.50
☐ Vegetable Bowl, *round, 9"*	8.00	11.00	8.50

CROCUS (Introduced 1930s)

☐ Baker	14.00	19.00	14.50
☐ Ball Jug #3	25.00	30.00	25.50
☐ Bean Pot, *with lid*	45.00	52.00	45.50
☐ Bread and Butter Plate, *6"*	1.50	3.00	1.75
☐ Butter Dish, *covered, large, rare*	325.00	385.00	300.30
☐ Cereal Bowl, *6"*	3.00	5.00	3.25
☐ Creamer	6.00	8.00	6.50
☐ Cup	3.50	5.50	3.75
☐ Custard Cup	2.50	3.75	2.75
☐ Dinner Plate, *9"*	3.00	6.00	3.50
☐ Drip Jar	20.00	24.00	21.00
☐ Dripolator, *china*	90.00	100.00	91.00
☐ Fruit Bowl, *5½"*	2.25	3.25	2.50
☐ Gravy Boat	15.00	19.00	15.50
☐ Luncheon Plate, *8¼"*	3.00	4.50	3.25
☐ Mixing Bowl, *6"*	7.00	9.00	7.25
☐ Mixing Bowl, *7½"*	9.00	11.00	9.50
☐ Mixing Bowl, *9"*	12.00	15.00	12.50
☐ Mug	20.00	30.00	21.00
☐ Pie Plate	10.00	13.00	11.00
☐ Platter, *11¼"*	10.00	13.00	11.00
☐ Platter, *13¼"*	11.00	14.00	12.00
☐ Refrigerator Jar, *rectangular*	20.00	26.00	21.00

	Current Price Range		P/Y Average
☐ Refrigerator Jar, *square*	20.00	25.00	21.00
☐ Salad Bowl, *9"*	10.00	13.00	11.00
☐ Saucer	1.00	2.00	1.25
☐ Soup Bowl, *8½"*	8.00	11.00	9.00
☐ Sugar Bowl, *covered*	8.00	13.00	9.00
☐ Teapot	20.00	30.00	21.00
☐ Tidbit Server, *3 tier*	28.00	33.00	29.00
☐ Tureen, *covered*	60.00	80.00	61.00
☐ Vegetable Bowl, *oval*	10.00	13.00	11.00

MORNING GLORY *(Introduced 1940s)*

Hall produced this kitchenware line for the Jewel Tea Company.

☐ Bowl, *6"*	5.00	9.00	5.50
☐ Bowl, *7½"*	8.00	13.00	8.50
☐ Bowl, *9"*	12.00	17.00	12.50
☐ Coffeepot, *drip, china*	55.00	70.00	56.00
☐ Custard Cup	3.00	6.00	3.50
☐ Teapot, *Aladdin shape*	35.00	47.00	36.00

MUMS

☐ Bread and Butter Plate, *6"*	.50	1.25	.75
☐ Casserole	28.00	33.00	29.00
☐ Cereal Bowl, *6"*	4.00	5.75	4.25
☐ Creamer	5.00	6.50	5.25
☐ Cup	3.50	4.75	3.75
☐ Custard Cup	2.50	3.50	2.75
☐ Dinner Plate	4.50	5.75	4.60
☐ Fruit Bowl, *5½"*	3.00	4.25	3.25
☐ Luncheon Plate, *8¼"*	2.50	3.25	2.75
☐ Platter, *11"*	11.00	13.00	11.50
☐ Platter, *13"*	13.00	15.00	13.50
☐ Salad Bowl, *9"*	9.00	13.00	9.50
☐ Salt and Pepper Shakers, *pair*	10.00	12.00	10.50
☐ Saucer	.50	1.25	.75
☐ Soup Bowl, *8½"*	6.00	7.50	6.25
☐ Sugar Bowl, *covered*	9.00	11.00	9.25
☐ Teapot	50.00	58.00	52.00

ORANGE POPPY *(Introduced 1933)*

Hall produced this dinnerware line for the Great American Tea Company.

☐ Baker	10.00	14.00	11.00
☐ Ball Jug #3	14.00	16.00	15.00
☐ Bean Pot, *covered, one handle*	35.00	40.00	36.00
☐ Bowl, *6"*	5.00	8.00	6.00
☐ Bowl, *7½"*	8.00	10.00	9.00
☐ Bowl, *9"*	12.00	15.00	12.50
☐ Bowl, *10"*	15.00	21.00	15.50
☐ Bread and Butter Plate, *7"*	2.00	5.00	2.50
☐ Bread Box, *metal*	40.00	48.00	41.00
☐ Cake Plate	10.00	13.00	10.50
☐ Canisters, *set of four, metal*	30.00	38.00	31.00
☐ Casserole, *covered, oval, 8"*	18.00	25.00	18.50

	Current Price Range		P/Y Average
☐ Casserole, *11", covered, oval*	55.00	70.00	56.00
☐ Casserole, *covered, two handles, round*	15.00	21.00	15.50
☐ Coffeepot	30.00	42.00	31.00
☐ Creamer	6.00	7.50	6.25
☐ Cup	3.00	5.00	3.50
☐ Custard Cup	13.00	15.00	13.50
☐ Drip Jar	13.00	15.00	13.50
☐ Dessert Plate, *7¾"*	4.00	6.00	4.25
☐ Dinner Plate, *9"*	5.00	6.50	5.25
☐ Fruit Bowl	2.75	3.75	3.00
☐ Platter, *11¼"*	11.00	15.00	11.50
☐ Platter, *13¼"*	15.00	19.00	15.50
☐ Pretzel Jar, *covered*	45.00	52.00	46.00
☐ Refrigerator Jar, *oval, one loop handle on top*	20.00	28.00	21.00
☐ Salad Bowl, *9"*	9.00	11.00	9.50
☐ Salt and Pepper Shakers, *pair*	5.00	10.00	5.50
☐ Saucer	1.00	2.25	1.10
☐ Sifter, *metal*	15.00	19.00	15.50
☐ Soup Bowl, *8½"*	8.00	11.00	8.50
☐ Spoon	30.00	38.00	31.00
☐ Sugar Bowl, *covered*	10.00	15.00	10.50
☐ Teapot, *Bellvue shape*	80.00	90.00	81.00
☐ Teapot, *Boston shape*	30.00	35.00	31.00
☐ Teapot, *Doughnut shape*	80.00	95.00	81.00
☐ Teapot, *Melody shape*	80.00	90.00	81.00
☐ Teapot, *Streamline shape*	40.00	48.00	41.00
☐ Teapot, *Windshield shape*	60.00	70.00	61.00
☐ Vegetable Bowl, *9¼"*	18.00	24.00	19.00

PASTEL MORNING GLORY *(Introduced 1930s)*

☐ Ball Jug #3	20.00	24.00	21.00
☐ Bean Pot, *covered, one handle*	40.00	50.00	41.00
☐ Bowl, *oval*	13.00	15.00	14.00
☐ Bread and Butter Plate, *6"*	2.00	4.00	2.50
☐ Casserole, *covered, closed tab handles*	25.00	30.00	26.00
☐ Cereal Bowl, *6"*	5.00	6.00	5.50
☐ Creamer	6.00	8.00	6.50
☐ Cup	4.00	5.50	4.25
☐ Dinner Plate, *9"*	6.00	8.00	6.25
☐ Drip Jar	14.00	16.00	14.50
☐ Fruit Bowl, *5½"*	3.50	5.00	3.75
☐ Gravy Boat	18.00	24.00	18.50
☐ Luncheon Plate, *8¼"*	3.00	5.00	3.25
☐ Platter, *11"*	12.00	15.00	12.50
☐ Platter, *13"*	15.00	19.00	15.50
☐ Salad Bowl, *9"*	10.00	13.00	10.50
☐ Salt and Pepper Shakers, *pair*	15.00	20.00	15.50
☐ Saucer	1.00	1.75	1.25
☐ Soup Bowl, *8½"*	9.00	11.00	9.50
☐ Sugar Bowl, *covered*	10.00	15.00	11.00

RED POPPY *(Introduced early 1950s)*

Hall produced this dinnerware line for Grand Union Tea Company.

☐ Ball Jug #3	20.00	28.00	21.00

	Current Price Range		P/Y Average
☐ Baker	13.00	15.00	14.00
☐ Bowl, 6″	8.00	10.00	9.00
☐ Bowl, 7½″	10.00	15.00	11.00
☐ Bowl, 9″	14.00	19.00	15.00
☐ Bread and Butter Plate, 6″	1.00	2.25	1.10
☐ Cake Plate	10.00	14.00	11.00
☐ Cereal Bowl, 6″	3.50	5.50	3.75
☐ Coffeepot	15.00	18.00	16.00
☐ Creamer	6.00	7.50	6.25
☐ Cup	4.50	5.50	4.75
☐ Custard Cup	2.50	3.50	2.75
☐ Dessert Plate, 7″	2.50	3.50	2.75
☐ Dinner Plate, 10″	6.50	7.50	6.75
☐ Fruit Bowl, 5½″	3.00	4.00	3.25
☐ Gravy Boat	18.00	24.00	18.50
☐ Luncheon Plate, 9¼″	4.50	5.50	4.75
☐ Platter, 11″	12.00	14.00	12.50
☐ Platter, 13″	15.00	17.00	15.50
☐ Salad Bowl, 9″	9.00	11.00	9.50
☐ Salt and Pepper Shakers, set	6.00	9.00	6.50
☐ Saucer	.75	1.75	1.00
☐ Soup Bowl	9.00	11.00	9.25
☐ Sugar Bowl, covered	9.00	11.00	9.25
☐ Teapot, Aladdin shape	30.00	38.00	31.00
☐ Teapot, New York shape	30.00	38.00	31.00
☐ Vegetable Bowl, oval 10″,	15.00	19.00	16.00

ROSE PARADE (Introduced 1940s)

☐ Baker	10.00	15.00	11.00
☐ Bean Pot, covered, tab handles	30.00	38.00	31.00
☐ Bowl, 6″	8.00	10.00	9.00
☐ Bowl, 7½″	10.00	15.00	11.00
☐ Bowl, 9″	12.00	16.00	12.50
☐ Casserole, covered, tab handles	15.00	19.00	15.50
☐ Creamer	5.00	9.00	5.50
☐ Custard Cup	3.75	5.25	4.00
☐ Drip Jar	14.00	19.00	15.00
☐ Pitcher, 5″	10.00	16.00	11.00
☐ Pitcher, 6½″	15.00	19.00	16.00
☐ Pitcher, 7½″	20.00	26.00	21.00
☐ Salad Bowl, 9″	10.00	13.00	10.50
☐ Salt and Pepper Shakers, pair	10.00	15.00	10.50
☐ Sugar Bowl, covered	5.50	8.50	5.75
☐ Teapot, four cup	15.00	22.00	16.00
☐ Teapot, six cup	18.00	25.00	18.50

ROSE WHITE (Introduced 1940s)

☐ Baker	8.00	13.00	8.50
☐ Bean Pot, covered, tab handles	25.00	34.00	25.50
☐ Casserole, covered, tab handles	18.00	24.00	18.50
☐ Creamer	5.00	7.00	5.25
☐ Custard Cup	3.50	5.25	3.75
☐ Drip Jar, covered, tab handles	10.00	14.00	10.50
☐ Pitcher, 5″	10.00	15.00	10.50
☐ Pitcher, 6½″	12.00	17.00	12.50

	Current Price Range		P/Y Average
☐ Pitcher, 7½"	14.00	21.00	14.50
☐ Salad Bowl, 9"	8.00	11.00	8.50
☐ Salt and Pepper Shakers, *pair*	10.00	12.00	10.50
☐ Sugar Bowl, *covered*	4.00	6.00	4.50
☐ Teapot, *four cup*	14.00	19.00	14.50
☐ Teapot, *six cup*	17.00	24.00	17.50

ROYAL ROSE (Introduced 1940s)

☐ Ball Jug #3	20.00	28.00	22.00
☐ Casserole, *covered*	18.00	23.00	19.00
☐ Drip Jar, *covered*	14.00	19.00	14.50
☐ Mixing Bowl, 6"	7.00	10.00	7.50
☐ Mixing Bowl, 7½"	10.00	14.00	11.00
☐ Mixing Bowl, 8½"	12.00	15.00	12.50
☐ Salt and Pepper Shakers, *pair*	12.00	18.00	12.50
☐ Teapot	25.00	33.00	25.50

SERENADE (Introduced 1930s)

Hall produced this dinnerware pattern for the Eureka Tea Company.

☐ Bowl, 6"	5.00	7.00	5.25
☐ Bowl, 7¼"	8.00	10.00	8.25
☐ Bowl, 9"	11.00	15.00	11.25
☐ Bread and Butter Plate, 6"	1.00	2.00	1.25
☐ Casserole, *covered*	20.00	26.00	21.00
☐ Cereal Bowl, 6"	4.00	5.00	4.25
☐ Coffeepot	15.00	19.00	16.00
☐ Cup	3.00	4.00	3.50
☐ Dinner Plate, 9"	3.00	6.00	3.50
☐ Fruit Bowl, 5½"	2.50	3.75	2.75
☐ Gravy Boat	15.00	19.00	15.50
☐ Luncheon Plate, 8¼"	2.75	3.75	2.85
☐ Platter, 11"	11.00	15.00	11.50
☐ Platter, 13"	13.00	15.00	13.50
☐ Pretzel Jar, *covered, tab handles*	40.00	48.00	41.00
☐ Salad Bowl, 9"	8.00	10.00	8.50
☐ Salt and Pepper Shakers, *pair*	15.00	20.00	15.50
☐ Saucer	1.00	2.25	1.25
☐ Soup Bowl, 8½"	8.00	10.00	8.50

SILHOUETTE (Introduced 1930s)

☐ Baker	10.00	13.00	10.50
☐ Ball Jug #3	25.00	32.00	25.50
☐ Bread and Butter Plate, 6"	5.50	6.50	5.75
☐ Casserole Dish, *covered*	20.00	25.00	21.00
☐ Cereal Bowl, 6"	5.00	6.50	5.50
☐ Coffeepot, *drip, china*	100.00	120.00	1.01
☐ Cup	4.00	6.50	
☐ Dinner Plate, 9¼"	5.50	6.50	5.75
☐ Drip Jar, *covered*	10.00	15.00	10.50
☐ Fruit Bowl, 5½"	3.00	4.00	3.25
☐ Luncheon Plate, 8¼"	3.50	4.50	3.75
☐ Mug	20.00	30.00	21.00
☐ Pitcher	15.00	25.00	15.50

	Current Price Range		P/Y Average
☐ Platter, *11"*	10.00	13.00	10.50
☐ Platter, *13"*	15.00	19.00	15.00
☐ Pretzel Jar, *covered, closed tab handles*	40.00	50.00	41.00
☐ Refrigerator Jar, *covered, rectangular*	15.00	18.00	15.50
☐ Refrigerator Jar, *covered, square*	20.00	28.00	21.00
☐ Salt and Pepper Shakers, *pair*	5.00	15.00	5.50
☐ Salad Bowl, *9"*	8.00	10.00	8.50
☐ Saucer	1.00	1.75	1.10
☐ Soup Bowl, *8½"*	9.00	11.00	9.50
☐ Sugar Bowl, *covered*	10.00	13.00	10.50
☐ Teapot, *New York shape*	45.00	55.00	45.50

SPRINGTIME

☐ Ball Jug #3	20.00	28.00	21.00
☐ Bread and Butter Plate, *6"*	1.00	1.75	1.25
☐ Casserole, *covered, two tab handles, thick* ..	20.00	26.00	21.00
☐ Cereal Bowl, *6"*	70.00	80.00	71.00
☐ Coffeepot, *drip, china*	4.00	6.00	4.25
☐ Creamer	4.00	475.00	3.25
☐ Cup	5.00	6.00	5.25
☐ Dinner Plate, *9¼"*	10.00	13.00	11.00
☐ Drip Jar, *thick*	10.00	13.00	11.00
☐ Fruite Bowl, *5½"*	3.00	3.75	3.25
☐ Gravy Boat, ...	15.00	19.00	15.00
☐ Luncheon Plate, *8¼"*	3.00	3.75	3.25
☐ Pie Plate	10.00	15.00	11.00
☐ Platter, *11"*	11.00	13.00	11.25
☐ Platter, *13"*	13.00	15.00	13.50
☐ Salad Bowl, *9"*	9.00	11.00	9.50
☐ Salt and Pepper Shakers, *pair*	15.00	20.00	15.50
☐ Saucer	.75	1.75	.85
☐ Soup Bowl, *8½"*	7.00	8.50	7.75
☐ Sugar Bowl, *covered*	9.00	13.00	9.25

TULIP

Hall produced this dinnerware line for the Cook Coffee Company.

☐ Baker................................	10.00	15.00	10.50
☐ Bread and Butter Plate, *6"*	1.00	2.00	1.25
☐ Cereal Bowl, *6"*	4.00	5.00	4.25
☐ Coffeepot, *drip, china*	65.00	75.00	65.50
☐ Creamer	4.00	7.00	4.25
☐ Cup	3.00	4.50	3.25
☐ Custard Cup	3.00	5.50	3.25
☐ Dessert Plate, *7"*	2.00	3.00	2.25
☐ Dinner Plate, *10"*	5.00	7.00	5.50
☐ Drip Jar	13.00	15.00	13.50
☐ Fruit Bowl, *5½"*	2.50	3.75	2.75
☐ Gravy Boat............................	14.00	19.00	14.50
☐ Luncheon Plate, *9"*	3.00	5.00	3.25
☐ Mixing Bowls, *nesting set of three, thick*....	30.00	40.00	31.00
☐ Platter, *11"*	12.00	14.00	12.50
☐ Platter, *13"*	13.00	17.00	13.50
☐ Salad Bowl, *9"*	8.00	10.00	8.25
☐ Salt and Pepper Shakers, *pair*	8.00	12.00	8.25

	Current Price Range		P/Y Average
☐ Saucer	.50	1.25	.60
☐ Soup Bowl, 8½″	8.00	10.00	8.25
☐ Sugar Bowl, covered	10.00	15.00	11.00

WILDFIRE (Introduced 1950s)

Hall produced this dinnerware line for the Great American Tea Company.

☐ Baker	8.00	11.00	8.25
☐ Bread and Butter Plate, 6″	1.75	2.75	1.85
☐ Casserole, covered, tab handles	20.00	30.00	21.00
☐ Cereal Bowl, 6″	4.50	5.75	4.75
☐ Coffeepot	20.00	28.00	21.00
☐ Creamer	5.00	7.00	5.50
☐ Cup	3.50	4.50	3.75
☐ Custard Cup	3.50	4.75	3.75
☐ Dessert Plate, 7″	3.00	4.25	3.10
☐ Dinner Plate, 10″	4.50	5.50	4.65
☐ Drip Jar	10.00	15.00	10.25
☐ Egg Cup	20.00	28.00	21.00
☐ Fruit Bowl, 5½″	2.50	3.25	2.75
☐ Gravy Boat	10.00	15.00	11.00
☐ Mixing Bowl, large	18.00	24.00	18.50
☐ Mixing Bowl, medium	8.00	11.00	8.50
☐ Mixing Bowl, small	6.00	8.00	6.25
☐ Pie Plate	8.00	11.00	8.50
☐ Platter, 11″	8.00	11.00	8.50
☐ Platter, 13″	10.00	13.00	10.50
☐ Salad Bowl, 9″	8.00	11.00	8.50
☐ Salt and Pepper Shaker, pair	15.00	20.00	15.50
☐ Saucer.................................	1.75	2.75	2.00
☐ Soup Bowl, 8½″	8.00	11.00	8.25
☐ Sugar Bowl, covered	8.00	11.00	8.25
☐ Teapot, Aladdin shape	30.00	35.00	31.50
☐ Tidbit Tray, 3-tier.......................	20.00	28.00	21.00

WILD POPPY (Introduced 1930s)

☐ Baker	13.00	15.00	13.50
☐ Bean Pot, covered, one loop handle	50.00	58.00	51.00
☐ Canister	55.00	65.00	56.00
☐ Casserole, oval.........................	20.00	25.00	21.00
☐ Creamer	6.00	8.00	6.50
☐ Custard Cup	3.00	4.50	3.25
☐ Mixing Bowls, set of three	20.00	28.00	21.00
☐ Salt and Pepper Shakers, pair	20.00	28.00	21.00
☐ Sugar Bowl, covered	8.00	12.00	8.50
☐ Teapot, four cup	40.00	48.00	41.00
☐ Teapot, six cup	40.00	48.00	41.00

YELLOW ROSE

☐ Baker..................................	9.00	13.00	9.50
☐ Bread and Butter Plate, 6″	1.00	2.00	1.25
☐ Casserole, covered......................	15.00	19.00	15.50
☐ Cereal Bowl, 6″	3.75	4.75	3.85
☐ Coffeepot, drip, Norse shape.	35.00	42.00	36.00

	Current Price Range		P/Y Average
☐ Creamer	4.00	7.00	4.25
☐ Cup	3.00	4.50	3.25
☐ Custard Cup	2.00	3.50	2.25
☐ Dinner Plate, *9"*	3.75	4.75	3.85
☐ Fruit Bowl, *5½"*	2.50	3.75	2.65
☐ Gravy Boat	10.00	18.00	10.50
☐ Luncheon Plate, *8¼"*	3.25	4.25	3.50
☐ Platter, *11"*	8.00	11.00	8.25
☐ Platter, *13"*	10.00	13.00	10.50
☐ Salad Bowl, *9"*	8.00	11.00	8.50
☐ Salt and Pepper Shakers, *pair*	15.00	20.00	15.50
☐ Saucer	1.00	2.00	1.25
☐ Soup Bowl, *8½"*	7.50	8.50	7.75
☐ Sugar Bowl, *covered*	8.00	11.00	8.25
☐ Teapot, *New York shape*	25.00	34.00	25.50

HANDGUNS

TOPIC: A handgun is a firearm designed to be held and fired with one hand.

TYPES: There are several common varieties of handguns. Flintlocks are muzzleloaded. They utilize a hammer holding a flint that strikes a spring-loaded frizzen/pan cover to produce ignition. A revolver is a handgun with a revolving cylinder containing multiple chambers. A semi-automatic ejects the spent case and cycles a new round into the chamber using the energy of the fired round. It only fires one shot with each pull of the trigger. A singleshot has no magazine, and thus can fire only one shot.

PERIOD: Firearms made before 1898 are considered antiques.

COMMENTS: Collecting handguns is an expensive hobby which nevertheless attracts many enthusiasts. New guns as well as antiques compose many collections, since antiques may be out of the price range of many people.

ADDITIONAL TIPS: For more information and extensive listings, please refer to *The Official Price Guide to Antique and Modern Firearms, and The Official Price Guide to Collector Handguns,* written by David Byron and published by The House of Collectibles. The following listings are for revolvers only.

COLT

Patterson, NJ 1836-1841; Whitneyville, CT 1847-1848; Hartford, CT 1848-present.

	VG	EXC.	Prior Year EXC. Value
☐ **".357 Magnum"**, *357 magnum, 6 shot, various barrel lengths, adjustable sights, target hammer, target grips, modern*	285.00	440.00	425.00
☐ **".357 Magnum"**, *.357 magnum, 6 shot, various barrel lengths, adjustable sights, modern*	250.00	285.00	375.00
☐ **125 Anniversary**, *.45 colt, single action army, commemorative, blue with gold plating, cased, curio*	450.00	700.00	700.00
☐ **Agent**, *.38 special, 6 shot, parkerized, 2" barrel, light weight, modern*	115.00	150.00	150.00
☐ **Agent**, *.38 special, 6 shot, blue, 2" barrel, lightweight, modern* . . . . !	145.00	200.00	200.00
☐ **Agent**, *.38 special, 6 shot, nickel plated, 2" barrel, lightweight, modern*	155.00	220.00	220.00
☐ **Carolina Charter Tercentennial**, *.22 L.R.R.F., and .45 Colt set, Frontier Scout & S.A.A.,commemorative, blue with gold plating, 4³/₄" barrel, cased, curio*	700.00	1050.00	1000.00
☐ **Chamizal Treaty**, *.22 L.R.R.F., Frontier Scout S.A., commemorative, blue with gold plating, 4³/₄" barrel, cased, curio*	220.00	310.00	300.00
☐ **Chamizal Treaty**, *.22 L.R.R.F., and .45 Colt set, Frontier Scout and S.A.A., commemorative, blue with gold plating, cased, curio*	1300.00	1995.00	1950.00
☐ **Chamizal Treaty**, *.45 Colt, single action army, commemorative, blue with gold plating, 5¹/₂" barrel, cased, curio*	825.00	1200.00	1150.00

REMINGTON ARMS CO.

Eliphalet Remington, Herkimer County, NY 1816-1831; Ilion, NY 1831 to date; E. Remington & Sons, 1856; Remingtion Arms Co., 1888; Remington Arms U.M.C. Co., 1910; Remington Arms Co., 1925 to date; Ilion, NY.

	VG	EXC.	Prior Year EXC. Value
☐ **Iroquois**, *.22 L.R.R.F., 7 shot, solid frame, spur trigger, single action, unfluted cylinder, antique*	280.00	420.00	395.00
☐ **Model 1875**, *.44-40 WCF, single action, Western style, solid frame, antique*	570.00	1075.00	950.00
☐ **Model 1875**, *.45 Colt, single action, Western style, solid frame, antique*	525.00	1000.00	900.00
☐ **Model 1890**, *.44-40 WCF, single action, Western style, solid frame, antique*	875.00	1700.00	1650.00
☐ **Smoot #1**, *.30 short R.F., 5 shot, solid frame, spur trigger, single action, antique*	160.00	245.00	235.00
☐ **Smoot #2**, *.32 short R.F., 5 shot, solid frame, spur trigger, single action, antique*	140.00	220.00	200.00
☐ **Smoot #3**, *.38 long R.F., 5 shot, solid frame, spur trigger, single action, birdhead grip, antique*	175.00	300.00	280.00
☐ **Smoot #3**, *.38 long R.F., 5 shot, solid frame, spur trigger, single action, saw handle grip, antique*	180.00	335.00	320.00
☐ **Smoot #4**, *.38 S & W, 5 shot, solid frame, spur trigger, single action, no ejector housing, antique*	140.00	220.00	200.00
☐ **Iroquois**, *.22 L.R.R.F., 7 shot, solid frame, spur trigger, single action, fluted cylinder, antique*	200.00	320.00	295.00

RUGER

Sturm, Ruger & Co., Southport, CT.

	VG	EXC.	Prior Year EXC. Value
☐ **.22 L.R.R.F.**, *Western style, single action, blue, lightweight, early model, modern*	240.00	335.00	300.00
☐ **"Magna-port IV"**, *.44 magnum, Western style, single action, commemorative, modern*	950.00	1450.00	1400.00
☐ **"Magna-port V"**, *.44 magnum, Western style, single action, commemorative, modern*	995.00	1750.00	1700.00
☐ **Bearcat**, *.22 L.R.R.F., Western style, single action, blue, brass grip frame, modern*	160.00	235.00	225.00
☐ **Bearcat**, *.22 L.R.R.F., Western style, single action, blue, aluminum grip frame, early model, modern*	185.00	280.00	265.00
☐ **Blackhawk**, *.30 Carbine, Western style, single action, blue, new model, modern*	140.00	170.00	160.00
☐ **Blackhawk**, *.30 Carbine, Western style, single action, blue, modern*	155.00	220.00	200.00
☐ **Blackhawk**, *.357 magnum, Western style, single action, blue, new model, modern*	135.00	165.00	160.00
☐ **Blackhawk**, *.357 magnum, Western style, single action, blue, modern*	155.00	220.00	200.00

	VG	EXC.	Prior Year EXC. Value
☐ **Blackhawk,** .357 magnum, Western style, single action, blue, flat-top frame, early model, modern	320.00	435.00	400.00
☐ **Blackhawk,** .357 magnum, Western style, single action, blue, 10" barrel, ...	475.00	675.00	650.00
☐ **Super Single Six,** .22LR/.22 WMR Combo, Western style, single action, blue, new model, modern	95.00	140.00	135.00
☐ **Super Single Six,** .22L/.22 WMR Combo, Western style, single action, blue, new model, 9½" barrel, modern	95.00	140.00	140.00
☐ **Super Single Six,** .22R/.22 WMR Combo, Western style, single action, blue, modern ..	135.00	175.00	165.00
☐ **Super Single Six,** .22LR/.22 WMR Combo, Western style, single action, blue, 9½" barrel, modern	145.00	185.00	175.00
☐ **Super Single Six,** .22LR/.22 WMR Combo, Western style, single action, stainless steel, new model, modern	135.00	165.00	160.00
☐ **Redhawk,** .44 magnum, double action, stainless, interchangeable sights, swingout cylinder, modern	180.00	275.00	275.00

SMITH & WESSON

Started in Norwich, CT in 1855 as Volcanic Repeating Arms Co., reorganized at Springfield, MA as Smith & Wesson in 1857 (Volcanic Repeating Arms moved to New Haven, CT in 1856 and was purchased in 1857 by Winchester Repeating Arms Co.).Smith & Wesson at Springfield, MA to date.

	VG	EXC.	Prior Year EXC. Value
☐ **.32 Double Action,** .32 S & W, 1st model, top break, 5 shot, straight-cut sideplate, rocker cylinder stop, antique	825.00	1400.00	1350.00
☐ **.32 Double Action,** .32 S & W, 2nd model, top break, 5 shot, irregularly-cut sideplate, rocker cylinder stop, antique	125.00	200.00	190.00
☐ **.32 Double Action,** .32 S & W, 3rd model, top break, 5 shot, irregularly-cut sideplate, antique	120.00	180.00	175.00
☐ **.32 Double Action,** .32 S & W, 4th model, round-back trigger guard, top break, 5 shot, irregularly-cut sideplate, modern	110.00	170.00	160.00
☐ **.32 Double Action,** .32 S & W, 5th model, round-back trigger guard, top break, 5 shot, irregularly-cut sideplate, front sight forged on barrel, modern	110.00	170.00	165.00
☐ **Hand Ejector,** .32 S & W long, 1st model, solid frame, swing-out cylinder hammer, actuated cylinder stop, target sights, double action, modern	325.00	485.00	475.00

HARLEQUIN WARE

ORIGIN: Harlequin tableware was introduced by the Homer Laughlin Pottery Company in 1938 and continued to be produced until 1964.

DESCRIPTION: The Harlequin wares are similar to Fiesta, having bright colors and simple shapes. They have an Art Deco flair with the same series of rings, but they are not on the rim. Instead, they appear farther into the center after a thin band with no design.

COLORS: The colors used on Harlequin are tangerine, salmon, forest green, medium green, light green, chartreuse, Harlequin yellow, gray, turquoise, mauve blue, maroon and spruce green.

MARKS: Harlequin was not marked.

RECOMMENDED READING: For more in-depth information on Harlequin tableware you may refer to *The Official Price Guide to Pottery and Porcelain* and *The Official Identification Guide to Pottery and Porcelain,* published by The House of Collectibles.

Harlequin Dinnerware By Homer Laughlin Company, *1978 reissue in commemoration of the 100th anniversary of Woolworth and Co.,* **$30.00 - $40.00**

	Current Price Range		P/Y Average

Blue

□ Bowl, *salad, 7", shallow, no rings*	5.00	7.00	5.50
□ Bowl, *fruit, 5½", flared rim*	3.00	5.00	3.50
□ Creamer, *inverted dome shape, with pointed handles*	4.00	6.00	4.25
□ Cup, *coffee, with pointed handle*	6.00	10.00	6.25
□ Plate, *6", recessed center*	1.25	2.50	1.50
□ Plate, *7", recessed center*	1.50	2.75	1.75
□ Platter, *13", oval, recessed center*	4.50	8.00	4.75
□ Sugar Bowl, *inverted dome shape, with lid* ..	5.00	8.00	5.25

Chartreuse

□ Bowl, *5", flared rim*	3.00	5.00	3.25
□ Cup, *cream, soup, with two pointed handles* .	3.00	5.00	3.25
□ Saucer, *with recessed ring for cup*	1.00	2.00	1.25

Gray

□ Bowl, *salad, 7", shallow, no rings*	6.00	8.00	6.25
□ Casserole, *with lid*	20.00	26.00	21.00
□ Creamer, *inverted dome shape, with pointed handles*	4.00	6.00	4.25
□ Cup, *cream, soup, with two pointed handles* .	5.00	9.00	5.25
□ Plate, *6", recessed center*	1.25	2.50	1.50
□ Plate, *7", recessed center*	1.25	2.50	1.50
□ Plate, *9", recessed center*	3.00	4.00	3.25
□ Plate, *10", recessed center*	4.00	6.00	4.25
□ Sauceboat, *oblong, squared, with handle* ...	6.00	8.00	6.25

Harlequin Yellow

□ Ashtray, *basketweave*	17.00	22.00	17.50
□ Baker, *9", oval, with lid and pointed handles* .	5.00	8.00	5.50
□ Bowl, *salad, 7", shallow, no rings*	6.00	10.00	6.25
□ Casserole, *with lid*	18.00	24.00	18.50
□ Creamer, *inverted dome shape, with printed handles*	2.00	5.00	2.25
□ Dish, *nut, 3", basketweave design*	5.00	8.00	5.25
□ Eggcup, *on pedestal base*	5.00	11.00	5.25
□ Jug, *water, with handle*	11.00	14.00	11.25
□ Plate, *6", recessed center*	1.25	2.50	1.50
□ Plate, *7", recessed center*	1.50	2.75	1.75
□ Plate, *9", recessed center*	3.00	4.00	3.25
□ Plate, *10", recessed center*	4.00	6.00	4.25
□ Salt And Pepper Shakers, *inverted dome shape, on small pedestal base*	3.00	8.00	3.25
□ Sugar Bowl, *with lid*	3.00	8.00	3.25
□ Teacup, *inverted dome shape, with pointed handles*	4.00	6.00	4.25
□ Teapot, *inverted dome shape, with pointed handles*	16.00	21.00	16.50

Maroon

□ Ashtray, *with three impressions*	17.00	22.00	17.50
□ Bowl, *fruit, 5½", flared rim*	3.00	5.00	3.25
□ Casserole, *with lid*	24.00	40.00	25.00
□ Dish, *nut, 3", basketweave design*	4.00	7.00	4.25
□ Jug, *22 ounce, cylindrical with pointed handle*	7.00	12.00	7.50
□ Plate, *6", recessed center*	1.25	2.50	1.50

	Current Price Range		P/Y Average
☐ Platter, *11", oval, recessed center*	5.00	8.00	5.50
☐ Sugar Bowl, *with lid*	5.00	8.00	5.50
☐ Teapot, *with handles*	13.00	17.00	13.50
Mauve Blue			
☐ Bowl, *salad, 7", shallow, no rings*	6.00	10.00	6.50
☐ Bowl, *fruit, 5½", flared rim*	3.00	5.00	3.25
☐ Baker, *oval, with lid and pointed handles* ...	5.00	8.00	5.25
Medium Green			
☐ Creamer, *inverted dome shape, with pointed handles*	4.00	6.00	4.25
☐ Plate, *10", recessed center*	3.00	6.00	3.25
Red			
☐ Ashtray, *basketweave, with three impressions*	17.00	22.00	17.50
☐ Bowl, *fruit, 5½", flared rim*	3.00	5.00	3.25
☐ Butter Dish, *with cover*	22.00	27.00	22.50

HARMONICAS

DESCRIPTION: A harmonica is a rectangular instrument with air slots. Musical tones are produced by blowing air into the slots.

PERIOD: Harmonicas were first produced in the 1800s.

COMMENTS: Material, maker and rarity play important roles in determining the value of a harmonica.

Harmonica, *Germany, 4½", 1800s,* **$35.00-$45.00**
(photo courtesy of ©The Metropolitan Museum of Art, The Crosby Brown Collection of Musical Instruments, 1889)

	Current Price Range		P/Y Average

□ **Angel's Clarion,** made by Weiss, 28 holes, brass reed plates, c. 1900 . . . . 35.00 / 50.00 / 42.00

□ **"Baseball Club Band Mouth Organ,"** 32 bell metal reeds, two sound horns, 1920s . . . . 10.00 / 15.00 / 12.50

□ **Bell Harmonica (Richter),** 10 single holes, brass reed plates, German silver covers, extended ends, one bell . . . . 30.00 / 40.00 / 35.00

□ **As Above,** with two bells . . . . 35.00 / 45.00 / 40.00

□ **Bohm's Professional Harmonica,** 10 single holes, 20 brass reeds, 1890s . . . . 25.00 / 35.00 / 30.00

□ **Bohm's Jubilee Harmonica,** 10 single holes, 20 brass reeds, brass reed plates, c. 1900 . . . 20.00 / 25.00 / 22.50

□ **Bohm's Sovereign,** 5½″ x 1½″, 16 double holes, 32 steel reeds, nickel covers . . . . 20.00 / 25.00 / 22.50

□ **The Brass Band Clarion,** by Weiss, 10 single holes, 20 reeds, c. 1900 . . . . 25.00 / 35.00 / 30.00

□ **Columbian Exhibition Harmonica,** 10 single holes, nickel reed plates and covers, bronzed wood . . . . 60.00 / 80.00 / 70.00

□ **Concert Harmonica,** two bells, 10 double holes with 40 reeds, brass reed plates, engraved German silver covers . . . . 45.00 / 60.00 / 52.00

□ **Doerfel's International,** made of celluloid, 10 double holes, 40 reeds, brass reed plates . . . 50.00 / 65.00 / 57.00

□ **Doerfel's New Best-Quality Harmonika,** 48 steel and bronze reeds, brass reed plates, in original box . . . . 11.00 / 15.00 / 13.00

□ **Doerfel's Patent Universal Harp,** made of celluloid, 10 single holes, 20 reeds, brass reed plates, one of the earliest celluloid harmonicas, 1890s . . . . 40.00 / 50.00 / 45.00

□ **Duss Band Harmonica,** 14 double holes, 28 metal reeds set on brass plates, nickel covers, 4¾″, 1920s . . . . 15.00 / 20.00 / 17.50

□ **Duss Band Tremelo,** three-in-one harmonica, each tuned to a different key, 32 double holes, 96 reeds, brass reed plates, nickel covers, 8¾″, post-World War I . . . . 20.00 / 25.00 / 22.50

□ **Duss Full Concert Harmonica,** 10 single holes, 40 reeds on brass plates, nickel covers, 4½″ . . . . 10.00 / 15.00 / 12.50

□ **Carl Essbach's French Harp #44,** 10 single holes, 20 German silver reeds, brass reed plates, nickel covers . . . . 14.00 / 20.00 / 17.00

□ **European Brass Band Harmonica,** 10 double holes, 40 reeds, brass reed plates . . . . 40.00 / 50.00 / 45.00

□ **European,** 10 single holes, white metal reed plates with steel reeds, 1890s . . . . 20.00 / 25.00 / 22.50

□ **High Art,** 16 double holes, 32 reeds, brass plates, curved mouthpiece, nickel covers, 4″ 10.00 / 15.00 / 12.50

□ **Hohner Auto Harmonica,** shaped like auto, 14 double holes, 28 reeds, metal cover . . . . 25.00 / 35.00 / 30.00

□ **Hohner Concert Harmonica,** marked "Ulm 1871-Philadelphia 1873," 20 double holes, 80 reeds, brass reed plates, nickel covers, 1890s 20.00 / 300.00 / 250.00

	Current Price Range		P/Y Average
☐ **Hohner Double Side Harmonica,** 64 reeds, brass plates, steel covers, nickel-plated, 1920s	25.00	35.00	30.00
☐ **Hohner "Grand Auditorium,"** 16 double holes, 32 reeds, brass reed plates, nickel covers . . .	130.00	200.00	165.00
☐ **M. Hohner Harmonica,** 10 single holes, brass reed plates, c. 1900	20.00	30.00	25.00
☐ **Hohner Harmonica,** 20 double holes, 80 reeds, brass reed plates, nickel covers, c. 1900	70.00	90.00	80.00
☐ **Hohner,** harp shaped, 14 double holes, 28 tremolo reeds, brass plates, nickel-plated covers, 4⅝ "	20.00	30.00	25.00
☐ **M. Hohner's Newest And Best Full Concert Harmonica,** 10 double holes, 40 reeds, brass reed plates, nickel covers	45.00	60.00	52.00
☐ **Hohner,** 10 double holes, 40 reeds, brass reed plates, nickel covers	70.00	90.00	80.00
☐ **"The Improved Emmet,"** 10 single holes, brass reed plates, nickel-plated covers, 1890s	35.00	45.00	40.00
☐ **Ludwig Harmonica,** double sided with 10 holes and 20 reeds on each side, 1890s	55.00	75.00	65.00
☐ **Ludwig Harmonica,** Richter Pattern, 10 single holes, 20 reeds, 1890s	30.00	40.00	35.00
☐ **Ludwig Harmonica,** 20 double holes, 40 brass reeds, heavy brass reed plates and nickel covers, c. 1900	65.00	85.00	75.00
☐ **Gebruder Ludwig's "Professional Concert Mouth Organ,"** 10 double holes, 40 reeds, brass reed plates, German silver covers	60.00	80.00	70.00
☐ **"The New Troubador,"** 20 single holes, ten on each side, c. 1897	25.00	35.00	30.00
☐ **"The Prairie Queen,"** 10 single holes, steel and bronze reeds, nickel-plated reed plates and covers	40.00	60.00	50.00
☐ **"The Quadruple Reed Mouth Organ,"** 160 reeds, insscribed "House Music, Best Harp for Artists from Ocean to Ocean," 7¼ "	15.00	20.00	17.50
☐ **"Radio Band" Harmonica,** two sets of reeds, pitched in different keys, in the original box, 1920s	10.00	15.00	12.50
☐ **"Radio Band Jazz Mouth Organ,"** novelty harmonica in shape of flashlight with horn at end, sold in U.S. 11″, 1929	15.00	20.00	17.50
☐ **"Reveille Mouth Organ,"** nickel-plated covers, c. 1925	6.00	8.00	7.00
☐ **Richter "C,"** 10 single holes, brass reed plates, nickel covers	14.00	20.00	17.00
☐ **"The Silver-Tongued Richter,"** 10 double holes, brass reed plates, nickel covers	42.00	60.00	51.00
☐ **Sousa's Band Harmonica,** 10 single holes, 20 brass reeds, 4″, c. 1900	25.00	35.00	30.00
☐ **Sousa Band Harmonica,** 20 holes, 40 brass reeds, 4¾ ″, c. 1900	35.00	50.00	42.00
☐ **"World's Fame,"** 10 single holes, 20 reeds, brass plates, nickel covers, 4″	5.00	10.00	7.50

HEISEY GLASS

ORIGIN: The A.H. Heisey Glass Co. was established in 1860's at Newark Ohio, by a partnership which included George Duncan and Daniel C. Ripley. It manufactured cut and pressed wares.

DESCRIPTION: Heisey Glass is of a high quality and many patterns are called "elegant depression glass"

COMMENTS: The Heisey Collectors of America Inc. publishes The Heisey News, a newsletter with information on patterns history of Heisey and advertisements. Address: Box 27, Newark O H 43055.

RECOMMENDED READING: For further information refer to *The Official Price Guide to Depression Glass* published by House of Collectibles.

CRYSTOLITE

This pattern was produced on blank #1503 in crystal, blue, green, yellow and amber.

CRYSTOLITE

	Current Price Range		P/Y Average
Ashtray, *square, 3½"*			
☐crystal...............................	2.00	4.00	2.50
Bon Bon Dish, *shell shaped, 7"*			
☐crystal...............................	15.00	19.00	16.00
Candlestick, *footed, 1 lite*			
☐crystal...............................	10.50	13.50	11.50
Candy Dish, *swan shape, 6½"*			
☐crystal...............................	31.00	39.00	32.00
Cigarette Box, *with cover, 4½"*			
☐crystal...............................	15.00	19.00	16.00
Claret Goblet, *wide blown, 3½ oz.*			
☐crystal...............................	22.00	28.00	24.00
Cocktail Goblet, *wide optic, blown, 3½ oz.*			
☐crystal...............................	18.00	22.00	19.00
Cordial Goblet, *wide optic, blown, 10 oz.*			
☐crystal...............................	55.00	65.00	57.00
Creamer			
☐crystal...............................	8.50	11.50	9.50
Flower Urn, *7"*			
☐crystal...............................	13.00	17.00	14.00
Iced Tea Tumbler, *wide optic, blown, 10 oz.*			
☐crystal...............................	18.00	22.00	19.00
Juice Tumbler, *footed, wide optic, blown, 5 oz.*			
☐crystal...............................	13.00	17.00	14.00
Mayonnaise Ladle			
☐crystal...............................	6.00	9.00	6.50
Mustard Dish, *with lid*			
☐crystal...............................	26.00	34.00	28.00
Nut Bowl, *handle, 3"*			
☐crystal...............................	13.00	17.00	14.00
Pitcher, *swan shape, ice lip, 2 quart*			
☐crystal...............................	625.00	675.00	635.00
Puff Box, *with lid, 4¾"*			
☐crystal...............................	42.00	49.00	43.50
Punch Bowl, *7½ quart*			
☐crystal...............................	70.00	80.00	72.00
Punch Cup			
☐crystal...............................	8.50	11.50	9.50
Relish Tray, *3 sections, 12"*			
☐crystal...............................	18.00	22.00	19.00
Salad Bowl, *round, 10"*			
☐crystal...............................	20.00	24.00	21.00
Salad Plate, *7"*			
☐crystal...............................	5.50	8.50	6.50
Salad Plate, *8½"*			
☐crystal...............................	13.00	17.00	14.00
Salt And Pepper			
☐crystal...............................	21.00	29.00	23.00
Sandwich Plate, *12"*			
☐crystal...............................	18.00	22.00	19.00

	Current Price Range		P/Y Average
Saucer			
☐ *crystal*	4.00	6.00	4.50
Sherbet, *6 oz.*			
☐ *crystal*	8.50	11.50	9.50
Sugar			
☐ *crystal*	8.50	11.50	9.50
Syrup Bottle, *drip and cut top*			
☐ *crystal*	45.00	55.00	47.00
Vase, *footed, 6"*			
☐ *crystal*	13.00	17.00	14.00

EMPRESS

Colors made in this pattern include crystal, green, yellow, pink, blue, alexandrite and orange.

	Current Price Range		P/Y Average
Ashtray			
☐ *crystal*	22.00	28.00	23.00
☐ *pink*	36.00	44.00	38.00
☐ *yellow*	45.00	55.00	47.00
☐ *green*	55.00	66.00	57.00
☐ *cobalt*	112.00	140.00	117.00
☐ *alexandrite*	175.00	225.00	190.00
Candlestick, *dolphin footed, 6"*			
☐ *crystal*	26.00	34.00	28.00
☐ *pink*	50.00	60.00	53.00
☐ *yellow*	55.00	65.00	57.00
☐ *green*	63.00	87.00	70.00
☐ *cobalt*	150.00	200.00	165.00
Celery Tray, *10"*			
☐ *crystal*	10.00	14.00	11.00
☐ *pink*	14.00	18.00	15.00

EMPRESS

	Current Price Range		P/Y Average
☐ yellow	20.00	24.00	21.00
☐ green	22.00	29.00	23.00
Comport, *footed, 6"*			
☐ crystal	22.00	28.00	23.00
☐ pink	36.00	44.00	38.00
☐ yellow	50.00	60.00	53.00
☐ green	60.00	70.00	63.00
Comport, *square, 6"*			
☐ crystal	31.00	39.00	33.00
☐ pink	60.00	70.00	63.00
☐ yellow	63.00	77.00	67.00
☐ green	69.00	82.00	63.00
Cream Soup			
☐ crystal	8.00	12.00	9.00
☐ pink	13.00	17.00	14.00
☐ yellow	16.00	20.00	17.00
☐ green	20.00	24.00	21.00
Creamer, *dolphin footed*			
☐ crystal	13.00	17.00	14.00
☐ pink	22.00	28.00	23.00
☐ yellow	31.00	39.00	33.00
☐ green	34.00	42.00	35.00
☐ alexandrite	175.00	225.00	190.00
Cup			
☐ crystal	6.50	9.50	7.50
☐ pink	22.00	28.00	23.00
☐ yellow	26.00	34.00	28.00
☐ green	31.00	39.00	33.00
☐ alexandrite	82.00	98.00	85.00
Floral Bowl, *rolled edge, 9"*			
☐ crystal	20.00	24.00	21.00
☐ pink	26.00	34.00	28.00
☐ yellow	31.00	39.00	33.00
☐ green	34.00	41.00	36.00
Ice Bucket, *metal handles*			
☐ crystal	31.00	39.00	33.00
☐ pink	78.00	92.00	81.00
☐ yellow	87.00	104.00	90.00
☐ green	98.00	121.00	102.00
Iced Tea, *flat bottom, 12 oz.*			
☐ crystal	13.00	17.00	14.00
☐ pink	18.00	22.00	19.00
☐ yellow	23.00	30.00	25.00
☐ green	26.00	34.00	28.00
Marmalade Dish, *with lid, dolphin footed*			
☐ crystal	26.00	34.00	28.00
☐ pink	40.00	50.00	42.00
☐ yellow	55.00	65.00	57.00
☐ green	64.00	76.00	68.00
Mayonnaise Dish, *footed, 5½"*			
☐ crystal	18.00	22.00	19.00
☐ pink	31.00	39.00	33.00
☐ yellow	41.00	49.00	43.00

	Current Price Range		P/Y Average
☐ green	45.00	55.00	47.00
☐ alexandrite	130.00	170.00	140.00
Mint Bowl, *dolphin, footed, 6"*			
☐ crystal	10.50	13.50	11.50
☐ pink	15.00	19.00	16.00
☐ yellow	20.00	24.00	21.00
☐ green	25.00	30.00	26.00
☐ alexandrite	80.00	90.00	82.00
Mustard Dish, *with lid*			
☐ crystal	18.00	22.00	19.00
☐ pink	31.00	39.00	33.00
☐ yellow	41.00	49.00	43.00
☐ green	45.00	55.00	47.00
Nappy, *4½"*			
☐ crystal	3.50	6.50	4.50
☐ pink	6.50	9.50	7.50
☐ yellow	8.00	12.00	9.00
☐ green	10.50	13.50	11.50
Nappy, *8"*			
☐ crystal	20.00	24.00	21.00
☐ pink	26.00	34.00	28.00
☐ yellow	31.00	39.00	33.00
☐ green	34.00	42.00	36.00
Oyster Cocktail			
☐ crystal	13.00	17.00	14.00
☐ pink	18.00	22.00	19.00
☐ yellow	22.00	28.00	23.00
☐ green	26.00	34.00	28.00
Pickle/ Olive Bowl, *2 sections, 13"*			
☐ crystal	8.50	11.50	9.50
☐ pink	13.00	17.00	14.00
☐ yellow	16.00	20.00	17.00
☐ green	20.00	24.00	21.00
Plate, *4½"*			
☐ crystal	1.00	3.00	1.50
☐ pink	4.00	6.00	4.50
☐ yellow	5.00	7.00	5.50
☐ green	6.00	8.00	6.50
Plate, *round or square, 6"*			
☐ crystal	4.00	6.00	4.50
☐ pink	8.50	11.50	9.50
☐ yellow	11.00	15.00	12.00
☐ green	13.00	17.00	14.00
☐ alexandrite	31.00	39.00	33.00
Plate, *round or square, 7"*			
☐ crystal	5.50	8.50	6.50
☐ pink	10.50	13.50	11.50
☐ yellow	13.00	17.00	14.00
☐ green	15.00	19.00	16.00
☐ alexandrite	40.00	50.00	42.00
Plate, *8"*			
☐ crystal	7.50	10.50	8.50
☐ pink	14.00	18.00	15.00

	Current Price Range		P/Y Average
☐ *yellow*	18.00	22.00	19.00
☐ *green*	22.00	26.00	23.00
Plate, *9"*			
☐ *crystal*	10.50	13.50	11.50
☐ *pink*	22.00	28.00	23.00
☐ *yellow*	32.00	38.00	33.00
☐ *green*	36.00	44.00	37.00
Plate, *10½"*			
☐ *crystal*	18.00	22.00	19.00
☐ *pink*	36.00	44.00	38.00
☐ *yellow*	45.00	55.00	47.00
☐ *green*	50.00	60.00	53.00
Plate, *12"*			
☐ *crystal*	22.00	27.00	23.00
☐ *pink*	41.00	49.00	43.00
☐ *yellow*	50.00	60.00	52.00
☐ *green*	55.00	65.00	57.00
Platter, *14"*			
☐ *crystal*	20.00	24.00	21.00
☐ *pink*	26.00	34.00	28.00
☐ *yellow*	31.00	39.00	32.00
☐ *green*	36.00	44.00	38.00
Punch Cup, *4 oz.*			
☐ *crystal*	8.50	11.50	9.50
☐ *pink*	22.00	28.00	23.00
☐ *yellow*	25.00	31.00	26.00
☐ *green*	26.00	34.00	28.00
Relish Bowl, *3 sections, handle, 7"*			
☐ *crystal*	13.00	17.00	14.00
☐ *pink*	19.00	23.00	20.00
☐ *yellow*	22.00	28.00	23.00
☐ *green*	25.00	31.00	26.50
Relish Tray, *3 sections, 10"*			
☐ *crystal*	16.00	20.00	17.00
☐ *pink*	22.00	28.00	23.00
☐ *yellow*	26.00	34.00	28.00
☐ *green*	31.00	39.00	33.00
Salad Bowl, *square, handles, 10"*			
☐ *crystal*	25.00	30.00	26.00
☐ *pink*	31.00	39.00	33.00
☐ *yellow*	40.00	50.00	43.00
☐ *green*	50.00	60.00	53.00
Salt And Pepper			
☐ *crystal*	36.00	44.00	38.00
☐ *pink*	60.00	70.00	62.00
☐ *yellow*	78.00	92.00	81.00
☐ *green*	88.00	102.00	92.00
Sandwich Tray, *handle, 12"*			
☐ *crystal*	26.00	34.00	28.00
☐ *pink*	44.00	54.00	46.00
☐ *yellow*	52.00	63.00	55.00
☐ *green*	60.00	70.00	62.00

	Current Price Range		P/Y Average
Saucer			
crystal	2.00	4.00	2.50
pink	6.50	9.50	7.50
yellow	12.00	16.00	13.00
green	14.00	18.00	15.00
Sherbet, *4 oz.*			
crystal	13.00	17.00	14.00
pink	18.00	22.00	19.00
yellow	22.00	28.00	23.00
green	26.00	34.00	27.00
Sugar			
crystal	13.00	17.00	14.00
pink	22.00	28.00	23.00
yellow	31.00	39.00	33.00
green	34.00	42.00	36.00
Tumbler, *dolphin, footed, 8 oz.*			
crystal	55.00	65.00	57.00
pink	78.00	97.00	82.00
yellow	108.00	133.00	115.00
green	105.00	140.00	117.00
Tumbler, *flat bottom, 8 oz.*			
crystal	10.50	13.50	11.50
pink	15.00	19.00	16.00
yellow	22.00	26.00	23.00
green	23.00	29.00	24.00
Vase, *flared, 8"*			
crystal	41.00	49.00	43.00
pink	60.00	70.00	62.00
yellow	69.00	82.00	63.00
green	78.00	93.00	82.00
Vase, *footed, 9"*			
crystal	45.00	55.00	47.00
pink	78.00	92.00	83.00
yellow	82.00	98.00	85.00
green	110.00	145.00	117.00
Vegetable Bowl, *oval, 10"*			
crystal	25.00	30.00	26.00
pink	31.00	39.00	33.00
yellow	40.00	50.00	42.00
green	50.00	60.00	52.00
Wine Goblet, *3 oz.*			
blue	25.00	30.00	26.00
orchid	25.00	30.00	26.00
pink	21.00	25.00	22.00
green	21.00	25.00	22.00
amber	18.00	22.00	19.00

GREEK KEY

Greek Key was mostly made in crystal, though some pink was also made.

GREEK KEY

	Current Price Range		P/Y Average
Almond Bowl, *footed, 5"*			
☐ *crystal*	26.00	34.00	28.00
Banana Split Dish, *flat, 9"*			
☐ *crystal*	15.00	19.00	16.00
Bowl, *low footed, shallow, 10"*			
☐ *crystal*	39.00	46.00	41.00
Bowl, *low footed, straight sides, 7"*			
☐ *crystal*	26.00	34.00	28.00
Bowl, *low footed, straight sides, 9"*			
☐ *crystal*	36.00	44.00	38.00
Burgundy Goblet, *3½ oz.*			
☐ *crystal*	78.00	93.00	80.00
Candy Jar, *with lid, ½ lb.*			
☐ *crystal*	88.00	103.00	92.00
Celery Tray, *oval, 9"*			
☐ *crystal*	13.00	17.00	14.00
Cheese and Cracker Set, *10"*			
☐ *crystal*	45.00	55.00	47.00
Claret Goblet, *4½ oz.*			
☐ *crystal*	73.00	87.00	75.00
Cocktail, *3 oz.*			
☐ *crystal*	15.00	19.00	16.00
Compote, *5"*			
☐ *crystal*	45.00	55.00	47.00
Cordial Goblet, *¾ oz.*			
☐ *crystal*	120.00	150.00	130.00

	Current Price Range		P/Y Average
Creamer			
☐ *crystal*	22.00	28.00	23.00
Egg Cup, *5 oz.*			
☐ *crystal*	41.00	49.00	43.00
Finger Bowl			
☐ *crystal*	12.00	16.00	13.00
Goblet, *7 oz.*			
☐ *crystal*	45.00	55.00	47.00
Goblet, *9 oz.*			
☐ *crystal*	53.00	67.00	56.00
Hair Receiver			
☐ *crystal*	47.00	56.00	49.00
Horseradish Jar, *with lid, large*			
☐ *crystal*	60.00	70.00	62.00
Ice Bucket, *tab handles, large*			
☐ *crystal*	55.00	65.00	58.00
Jelly Bowl, *handle, 5"*			
☐ *crystal*	26.00	34.00	28.00
Nappy, *4"*			
☐ *crystal*	6.50	9.50	7.50
Nappy, *scalloped, 8"*			
☐ *crystal*	34.00	43.00	36.00
Nappy, *shallow, 6"*			
☐ *crystal*	20.00	25.00	21.00
Nappy, *shallow, 11"*			
☐ *crystal*	39.00	46.00	41.00
Pickle Jar, *with lid*			
☐ *crystal*	72.00	87.00	75.00
Pitcher, *1 pint*			
☐ *crystal*	45.00	55.00	47.00
Pitcher, *3 pints*			
☐ *crystal*	62.00	77.00	65.00
Plate, *4½"*			
☐ *crystal*	8.50	11.50	9.50
Plate, *5½"*			
☐ *crystal*	9.50	12.50	10.50
Plate, *6½"*			
☐ *crystal*	10.00	14.00	11.00
Plate, *7"*			
☐ *crystal*	11.00	15.00	12.00
Plate, *8"*			
☐ *crystal*	13.00	17.00	14.00
Plate, *9"*			
☐ *crystal*	18.00	22.00	19.00
Plate, *10"*			
☐ *crystal*	40.00	50.00	42.00
Punch Bowl, *footed, 12"*			
☐ *crystal*	130.00	170.00	140.00
☐ *pink*	620.00	680.00	635.00
Punch Bowl, *footed, 15"*			
☐ *crystal*	90.00	125.00	97.00

	Current Price Range		P/Y Average
Punch Cup, *4½ oz.*			
☐ *crystal*	16.00	20.00	17.00
☐ *pink*	26.00	34.00	28.00
Salt and Pepper			
☐ *crystal*	45.00	55.00	47.00
Sherbet, *footed, flared rim, 4½ oz.*			
☐ *crystal*	8.50	11.50	9.50
Sherbet, *footed, straight rim, 4½ oz.*			
☐ *crystal*	8.50	11.50	9.50
Sherbet, *low footed, 6 oz.*			
☐ *crystal*	9.50	12.50	10.50
Sherry Goblet			
☐ *crystal*	100.00	130.00	110.00
Sugar			
☐ *crystal*	22.00	28.00	23.00
Tankard, *1 pint*			
☐ *crystal*	45.00	55.00	47.00
Tumbler, *flared or straight side, 5 oz.*			
☐ *crystal*	13.00	17.00	14.00
Tumbler, *flared or straight side, 7 oz.*			
☐ *crystal*	19.00	23.00	20.00
Tumbler, *flared or straight side, 10 oz.*			
☐ *crystal*	25.00	30.00	26.00
Tumbler, *flared or straight side, 12 oz.*			
☐ *crystal*	26.00	31.00	27.00
Tumbler, *flared or straight side, 13 oz.*			
☐ *crystal*	26.00	34.00	28.00
Water Tumbler, *5½ oz.*			
☐ *crystal*	14.00	18.00	15.00
Wine Goblet, *2 oz.*			
☐ *crystal*	105.00	140.00	110.00

HOLIDAY DECORATIONS

DESCRIPTION: The category of holiday decorations encompasses all holidays and all manner of decorations. The most popular collectibles are, of course, the delightful ornamentations of Christmas.

BACKGROUND: Christmas ornaments became popular in the 1870s. Previously, Christmas trees were decorated with homemade ornaments. Today collectors especially prize early figures of Santa and figural light bulbs.

COMMENTS: The following is merely a sampling of the more unusual holiday items available on the market today. All are listed alphabetically according to their respective holidays.

TIPS: For further information, refer to the directory located in the front of this book.

CHRISTMAS

	Current Price Range		P/Y Average
☐ **Angel,** cardboard, Dresden-type	200.00	250.00	230.00
☐ **Angel,** from the Danbury mint, 4″	15.00	45.00	31.00
☐ **Angel,** paper, die-cut, trimmed with tinsel . . .	7.00	15.00	12.50
☐ **Angel,** wax, wings are made of spun glass . .	45.00	70.00	59.00
☐ **Button,** "Merry Christmas," Santa with pack in household Christmas scene, lithographed tin	25.00	50.00	32.50
☐ **Button,** "Santa Claus Gave This To Me," 1½″	25.00	50.00	32.50
☐ **Button,** shows Santa reading a book titled "Good Boys - Good Girls," 1¼″	25.00	50.00	32.50
☐ **Cards,** comic characters, in original box, c. 1940s	30.00	35.00	32.00
☐ **Creche,** papier mache, stable made of wood, set of seventeen figures, c. 1930s	90.00	100.00	96.00
☐ **Decoration,** folding, life size Santa Claus, c. 1920s	100.00	150.00	125.00
☐ **Decoration,** Santa Claus doll, has pack, holds tree, composition, 1910	90.00	100.00	95.00
☐ **Figural Light Bulb,** Santa Claus holds tree, drum, doll and horn, c. 1920s, 5″	105.00	125.00	115.00
☐ **Lights,** bells on a string	7.00	15.00	11.00
☐ **Ornament,** baby in basket, cardboard, Dresden-type	40.00	65.00	57.00
☐ **Ornament,** ball, blown glass, decorated with wire tinsel, 3″	3.00	10.00	7.25
☐ **Ornament,** basket of flowers	8.00	10.00	9.00
☐ **Ornament,** boat, blown glass	25.00	30.00	27.50
☐ **Ornament,** bugle, blown glass	15.00	20.00	17.75
☐ **Ornament,** camel, cardboard, Dresden-type .	25.00	40.00	33.50
☐ **Ornament,** candy cane	12.00	15.00	13.50
☐ **Ornament,** church, blown glass	17.00	27.00	21.00
☐ **Ornament,** clown, blown glass, inscribed "My Darling," pale pink costume with silver collar, 4″	15.00	25.00	18.50
☐ **Ornament,** coiled like a snake, blown glass, metallic silver and blue	15.00	25.00	18.50
☐ **Ornament,** cornucopia, gauze, on front a die-cut Santa, loop made of tinsel	12.00	19.00	15.25
☐ **Ornament,** Dutch girl	25.00	30.00	27.00
☐ **Ornament,** ear of corn	45.00	55.00	50.00
☐ **Ornament,** elf, blown glass	20.00	32.00	26.75
☐ **Ornament,** elf sitting on a mushroom	25.00	30.00	26.50
☐ **Ornament,** enamel daisy on heart	25.00	30.00	26.50
☐ **Ornament,** gold and white ball with woodpecker	25.00	30.00	26.50

	Current Price Range		P/Y Average
☐ **Ornament,** icicle with cotton batting	20.00	30.00	27.00
☐ **Ornament,** reindeer with cotton batting	70.00	100.00	82.50
☐ **Ornament,** Santa Claus, celluloid, white and red	7.00	12.00	9.00
☐ **Ornament,** snowman, with cotton batting . . .	70.00	95.00	84.50
☐ **Ornament,** star, tin	15.00	25.00	21.00
☐ **Ornament,** Teddy Bear	20.00	25.00	22.00
☐ **Ornament,** Victorian Christmas stocking . . .	65.00	70.00	66.50
☐ **Ornaments,** pine cones, blown glass, set of three	15.00	25.00	18.50
☐ **Plate,** child's ABC's, features children and snowman	55.00	62.00	57.00
☐ **Print,** Father Christmas, chromo lithograph, die punched, c. 1890s	15.00	25.00	20.00
☐ **Santa,** blow glass, three dimensional, Santa holds a pine tree, 4½ "	25.00	50.00	37.50
☐ **Santa Claus Costume,** c. 1920s	30.00	40.00	36.00
☐ **Seals,** full sheets, 1934-38	5.00	10.00	7.00
☐ **Snowflake,** Gorham, 1972 and 1973 issues . .	25.00	45.00	35.00
☐ **Three Light,** Santa Claus has bag over one shoulder, handpainted, 4½ "	95.00	105.00	100.00

EASTER

☐ **Easter Egg Candy Containers,** red, gold and white	20.00	30.00	24.00
☐ **Easter Eggs,** blown glass	4.00	12.00	9.00

HALLOWEEN

☐ **Hat,** decorated, orange and black crepe paper	6.00	10.00	7.50
☐ **Jack-O-Lantern,** tin	75.00	126.00	95.00
☐ **Mask,** black cat, paper, round eyes, 11" x 8" .	12.00	20.00	17.00
☐ **Mask,** clown, paper, red, black and yellow, 8½ " x 9"	5.50	16.00	12.00
☐ **Mask,** devil, horns and pointed ears, 11" x 8"	12.00	20.00	16.50
☐ **Mask,** Grandma, paper, glasses and bonnet, black, white, yellow, pink and blue, 11" x 8" .	12.00	20.00	16.50
☐ **Mask,** pirate, paper, eyepatch and earrings, red, black and yellow, 9" x 8"	5.50	16.00	12.50
☐ **Mask,** pumpkin, paper, dark eyes and eyebrows, 11 " x 8"	12.00	20.00	16.50
☐ **Mask,** witch, paper, red, black and yellow, 9" x 8"	5.50	16.00	13.00
☐ **Mask,** Wizard of Oz, made by Par-T-Mask, excellent condition	205.00	305.00	250.00
☐ **Noisemaker,** with face, lithographed tin, c. 1920s, 10" x 4"	55.00	75.00	65.00

THANKSGIVING

☐ **Candlesticks,** cornucopia shape, ceramic, pair, 3½ "	5.00	10.00	7.00
☐ **Candlesticks,** pilgrims, ceramic, 2½ ", pair . .	6.00	10.00	8.00
☐ **Centerpiece,** turkey, Hallmark, c. 1940s	7.00	12.00	9.00
☐ **Cornucopia,** papier mache, c. 1910-20	7.00	17.00	10.00
☐ **Cornucopia,** made of wicker	5.00	10.00	7.00

VALENTINES DAY	Current Price Range		P/Y Average
☐ **Candlesticks,** cupids, ceramic	9.00	15.00	11.00

HULL POTTERY

DESCRIPTION: Since 1903 the Hull Pottery Co. has produced a diverse range of products. Though the firm did not work exclusively in artware, its production of art pottery rivaled that of its leading competitors. Its jugs, pitchers and vases, sometimes of heroic proportions, are typical examples of the flamboyant art pottery era. Prices for these are high. However, many Hull creations can be purchased modestly in fields other than art pottery, such as the containers it made for after-shave lotion in the 1930's. Something in the neighborhood of 11,000,000 of these were produced and retailed across the country for the Shulton Company. The diligent hobbyist will learn to inspect every item for a Hull marking, because the firm made wares of every conceivable description. Destroyed by fire in 1950, the factory was reopened in 1952 and is still active.

MARKS: The marking practices of this manufacturer were rather confusing. Most of the artware is stamped with numbers, which, suggest edition sizes: 100, 200, 300 and so on. Actually, it has nothing to do with the quantity manufactured, but relates to a coding system in which each color was referred to by an assigned number. Some Hull pottery has a paper label. The usual marking is *HULL ART U.S.*, sometimes *HULL U.S.A.* When the name is spelled without the first letter capitalized, this points to a manufacturing date of 1952 or later. This practice was not instituted after the fire and reorganization.

RECOMMENDED READING: For more in-depth information on Hull, you may refer to *The Official Price Guide to Pottery and Porcelain* and *The Official Identification Guide to Pottery and Porcelain,* published by The House of Collectibles.

CAMELIA

☐ **Basket,** shape # 107, 8″	65.00	70.00	72.50
☐ **Pitcher,** shape # 102, 8½″	30.00	40.00	35.00
☐ **Pitcher,** shape # 105, 7″	50.00	60.00	55.00
☐ **Pitcher,** shape # 128, 4¼″	25.00	30.00	27.50
☐ **Planter,** shape # 113, 7″	35.00	38.00	36.50
☐ **Swan,** shape # 102, 8½″	40.00	45.00	42.50

Basket, *Ebb Tide pattern, fish shape handle,*
$30.00-$35.00

	Current Price Range		P/Y Average
☐ **Vase,** shape # 122, 6¼″	25.00	28.00	26.50
☐ **Vase,** shape # 123, 6½″, flattened	35.00	40.00	37.50
☐ **Vase,** shape # 126, 8″, hand shape, matte white	50.00	60.00	57.50
☐ **Vase,** shape # 127, 4½″	20.00	25.00	22.50
☐ **Vase,** shape # 136, 6¼″	30.00	35.00	32.50
☐ **Vase,** shape # 138, 6¼″	30.00	35.00	32.50

CONTINENTAL

	Current Price Range		P/Y Average
☐ **Basket,** shape # USA 55, orange, c. 1959	20.00	30.00	25.00
☐ **Candleholder,** shaped # USA 61, 3½″, blue, c. 1959	20.00	30.00	25.00
☐ **Console Bowl,** shape # USA 51, 8″, persimmon, c. 1959	25.00	30.00	27.50
☐ **Planter,** shape # USA 68, 6″, green, c. 1959 ..	20.00	30.00	25.00
☐ **Vase,** shape # USA 57, 14″, gourd shape, green, c. 1959	20.00	30.00	25.00
☐ **Vase,** shape # USA 58, 13¾″, persimmon, c. 1959	20.00	30.00	25.00
☐ **Vase,** shape # USA 59, 15″, green, c. 1959 ...	25.00	30.00	27.50
☐ **Vase,** shape # USA 60, 15″, blue, c. 1959	30.00	40.00	35.00
☐ **Vase,** shape # 66, 6″, bud, persimmon, c. 1959	35.00	40.00	37.50

	Current Price Range		P/Y Average

HOUSE AND GARDEN

☐ **Beer Mug,** 3½ ", brown	3.00	5.00	4.00
☐ **Creamer,** marked Hull oven proof, brown	9.00	12.00	10.50
☐ **Creamer,** shape # 518, brown	3.50	5.50	4.50
☐ **Creamer,** shape # 518, green	9.00	11.00	10.00
☐ **Coffee Mug,** 3½ ", brown	3.00	6.00	4.50
☐ **Milk Pitcher,** 6¾ ", brown	8.00	12.00	10.00
☐ **Mug,** 3½ ", brown and orange	2.00	4.00	3.00
☐ **Pitcher,** 9½ ", brown	12.00	15.00	13.50
☐ **Shaker,** 3½ ", matte finish, brown	2.50	4.00	3.25
☐ **Saucer,** 6", brown	1.00	3.00	2.00
☐ **Sugar,** marked Hull oven proof, with cover, brown	8.00	11.00	10.50
☐ **Sugar,** shape # 519, green	9.00	12.00	10.50

OPEN ROSE

☐ **Basket,** shape # 501, 7½ ", pink and blue, c. 1949	65.00	70.00	67.50
☐ **Cornucopia,** shape # 511, 11½ ", blue and peach, c. 1949	65.00	70.00	67.50
☐ **Cornucopia,** shape # 522, 4½ ", peach, c. 1949	20.00	25.00	22.50
☐ **Cornucopia,** shape # 522, 4½ ", pink, c. 1949 .	20.00	25.00	22.50
☐ **Creamer,** shape # 111, 5", white, c. 1949	25.00	30.00	27.50
☐ **Pitcher,** shape # 128, 4¾ ", matte, white, c. 1949	12.00	14.00	13.00
☐ **Pitcher,** shape # 505, 6½ ", peach and blue, c. 1949	35.00	40.00	37.50
☐ **Planter,** shape # 514, 4", peach, c. 1949	20.00	30.00	25.00
☐ **Planter,** shape # 521, 7", peach and blue, c. 1949	35.00	40.00	37.50
☐ **Vase,** shape # 127, 4", pink and blue, c. 1949 .	20.00	25.00	22.50
☐ **Vase,** shape # 143, 8½ ", pink and blue, c. 1949	28.00	32.00	30.00
☐ **Vase,** shape # 502, 6½ ", suspended, blue and pink, c. 1949	35.00	40.00	37.50
☐ **Vase,** shape # 502, 6½ ", suspended, pink, c. 1949	35.00	40.00	37.50
☐ **Vase,** shape # 509, 6½ ", blue and cream, c. 1949	25.00	30.00	27.50
☐ **Vase,** shape # 513, 6½ ", pink, c. 1949	35.00	70.00	50.00
☐ **Vase,** shape # 515, 8½ ", pink and blue, c. 1949	40.00	45.00	42.50
☐ **Watering Can,** shape # 50T, 6½ ", with cover, beige, c. 1949	22.00	30.00	26.00

POPPY

☐ **Vase,** shape # 404, 4¾ ", peach, c. 1944	22.00	25.00	23.50
☐ **Vase,** shape # 602, 6½ ", c. 1944	35.00	40.00	37.50
☐ **Vase,** shape # 606, 6½ ", c. 1944	30.00	40.00	35.00
☐ **Vase,** shape # 606, 6½ ", pink and blue, c. 1944	45.00	50.00	47.50
☐ **Vase,** shape # 607, 8½ ", pink base, blue top, c. 1944	65.00	70.00	67.50
☐ **Vase,** shape # 607, 8½ ", blue base, pink top, c. 1944	65.00	70.00	67.50

	Current Price Range		P/Y Average

☐ **Vase,** shape # 607, 4¾", pink and blue, c. 1944 . . . . 25.00 30.00 27.50
☐ **Vase,** shape # 608, 4¾", c. 1944 . . . . 25.00 30.00 27.50
☐ **Vase,** shape # 611, 6¼", c. 1944 . . . . 30.00 40.00 35.00
☐ **Vase,** shape # 611, 6½", pink and blue, c. 1944 . . . . 45.00 50.00 47.50
☐ **Vase,** shape # 612, 6½", c. 1944 . . . . 30.00 40.00 35.00
☐ **Wall Pocket,** shape # 609, 9", pink and blue, c. 1944 . . . . 45.00 50.00 47.50

RED RIDING HOOD

☐ **Bank,** 6¾", shaped like red, c. 1938 . . . . 275.00 300.00 287.50
☐ **Butter Dish,** 7" x 5½", with cover, c. 1939 . . . 250.00 300.00 275.00
☐ **Cannister,** c. 1937 . . . . 200.00 300.00 250.00
☐ **Cookie Jar,** c. 1937 . . . . 80.00 90.00 85.00
☐ **Creamer,** 5", c. 1945 . . . . 45.00 50.00 47.50
☐ **Jam Jar,** c. 1940 . . . . 35.00 45.00 40.00
☐ **Pitcher,** 8", c. 1937 . . . . 75.00 85.00 80.00
☐ **Salt And Pepper,** 3", shaped like red, c. 1940 . 18.00 22.00 20.00
☐ **Salt And Peppers,** 5½", shaped like red, c. 1941 . . . . 30.00 40.00 35.00

SERENADE

☐ **Ashtray,** shape # S23, 13", blue, c. 1957 . . . . 20.00 22.00 21.00
☐ **Ashtray,** shape # S23, 14", blue, c. 1957 . . . . 15.00 18.00 16.50
☐ **Basket,** shape # S4, hat shape, yellow, c. 1957 . . . . 25.00 30.00 27.50
☐ **Basket,** shape # 85, 6", yellow, c. 1957 . . . . . 20.00 30.00 25.00
☐ **Basket,** shape # S14, blue, c. 1957 . . . . 65.00 70.00 67.50
☐ **Candy Dish,** shape # S3, with cover, turquoise, c. 1957 . . . . 24.00 28.00 26.00
☐ **Console Bowl,** shape # S9, 6"₀, blue, c. 1957 28.00 32.00 30.00
☐ **Creamer,** shaped S18, pink, c. 1957 . . . . 20.00 30.00 25.00
☐ **Dish,** shape # S3, on pedestal, yellow, c. 1957 15.00 17.00 16.00
☐ **Hat Vase,** shape # S4, yellow, c. 1957 . . . . . . 12.00 15.00 13.50
☐ **Pitcher,** shape # S2, 6½", pink, c. 1957 . . . . . 10.00 14.00 11.50
☐ **Pitcher,** shape # S21, pink, c. 1957 . . . . 40.00 45.00 42.50
☐ **Pitcher,** shape # 67, 10½", blue, c. 1957 . . . . 20.00 25.00 22.50
☐ **Pitcher,** shape # 67, 10½", pink, c. 1957 . . . . 22.00 24.00 23.00
☐ **Vase,** shape # S1, 6", yellow, c. 1957 . . . . 18.00 22.00 20.00
☐ **Vase,** shape # S1, 6½", yellow, c. 1957 . . . . . 11.00 15.00 13.00
☐ **Vase,** shape # S11, rectangular, blue with gold, c. 1957 . . . . 50.00 55.00 52.50

THISTLE

☐ **Vase,** shape # USA51, 6½", blue, c. 1940 . . . 35.00 36.00 35.50
☐ **Vase,** shape # USA52, 6½", pink, c. 1940 . . . 35.00 38.00 36.50
☐ **Vase,** shape # USA52, 6½", yellow, c. 1940 . 30.00 34.00 32.00
☐ **Vase,** shape # USA53, 6½", blue, c. 1940 . . . 35.00 38.00 36.50
☐ **Vase,** shape # USA 53, 6½", pink, c. 1940 . . . 35.00 40.00 37.50
☐ **Vase,** shape # USA52, 6½", blue, c. 1940 . . . 35.00 40.00 37.50
☐ **Vase,** shape # USA54, 6½", blue, c. 1940 . . . 30.00 35.00 32.50

HUMMELS

DESCRIPTION: Hummels are ceramic statuettes usually of children engaged in some activity.

ORIGIN: Berta Hummel, an artist and nun, is the creater of Hummels. In 1935 with the help of the Franz Goebel factory, the first figurine was produced.

MARKS: Although there are variations, all marks fall into one of six basic groups which include Crown Mark (CM), 1935-1949; Full Bee, 1950-1958; Stylized Bee; 1956-1963; 3-line mark, 1963-1972; Goebel/V (V-G), 1972-1979; and Goebel, 1979-present.

ADDITIONAL TIPS: Fore more information, consult *The Official Price Guide to Hummel Figurines and Plates,* published by The House of Collectibles.

	Current Price Range		P/Y Average
ACCORDION BOY			
☐ 185, Full Bee trademark, 5-6″	100.00	110.00	105.00
☐ 185, Stylized Bee, trademark 5-6″	100.00	110.00	105.00
☐ 185, 3-line mark, trademark 5-6″	83.00	90.00	87.00
ANGEL DUET			
☐ 261, 3-line mark, trademark 5″	325.00	355.00	340.00
☐ 261, Goebel/V, trademark 5″	95.00	105.00	100.00
☐ 261, Goebel, trademark 5″	88.00	98.00	93.00
APPLE TREE BOY			
☐ 142/3/0, Stylized Bee Trademark, 4-4¼″	100.00	110.00	105.00
☐ 142/3/0, Goebel trademark, 4-4¼″	65.00	70.00	68.00
☐ 142/2/1, Goebel trademark, 6-6¾″	105.00	115.00	110.00
THE ARTIST			
☐ 304, 3-line trademark, 5½″	325.00	355.00	340.00
☐ 304, Goebel/V, trademark, 5½″	110.00	120.00	115.00
☐ 304, Goebel trademark, 5½″	94.00	104.00	99.00

Baker, 128, *Full Bee Trademark,*
4¾"-5", $200.00-$220.00

BAKER

	Current Price Range		P/Y Average
☐ **128,** CM trademark, 4¾-5″	350.00	385.00	235.00
☐ **128,** Stylized Bee trademark, 4¾-5″	110.00	120.00	100.00
☐ **128,** Goebel/V trademark, 4¾-5″	82.00	90.00	62.00

BE PATIENT

☐ **197/2/0,** Goebel/V trademark, 4¼-4½ ″	95.00	105.00	100.00
☐ **197/1,** Full Bee trademark, 6-6¼ ″	250.00	275.00	262.00
☐ **197/1,** Goebel/V trademark, 6-6¼	115.00	125.00	120.00

BIRD WATCHER

☐ **300,** Goebel/V trademark	130.00	145.00	137.00
☐ **300,** Goebel trademark, 5″	100.00	110.00	105.00

BOOTS

☐ **140/0,** Goebel/V trademark, 5-5½ ″	82.00	90.00	86.00
☐ **143/1,** Goebel/V trademark, 6½-6¾ ″	150.00	165.00	157.00
☐ **143,** Stylized Bee trademark, 6¾ ″	300.00	330.00	315.00

	Current Price Range		P/Y Average

BOY WITH HORSE

☐ 117, CM trademark, 3½″	125.00	135.00	130.00
☐ 117, 3-line trademark, 3½″	30.00	35.00	32.00
☐ 117, Goebel trademark, 3½″	26.00	30.00	28.00

BUSY STUDENT

☐ 367, Stylized Bee trademark, 4¼″	260.00	285.00	272.00
☐ 367, 3-line trademark, 4¼″	110.00	120.00	115.00
☐ 367, Goebel trademark, 4¼″	72.00	80.00	76.00

CELESTIAL MUSICIAN

☐ 188, CM trademark, 7″	750.00	800.00	775.00
☐ 188, Stylized Bee trademark, 7″	200.00	220.00	210.00
☐ 188, Goebel/V trademark, 7″	130.00	140.00	135.00

CHICK GIRL

☐ 57/0, Stylized Bee trademark, 7″	125.00	135.00	130.00
☐ 57/0, Goebel/V trademark, 3½″	75.00	85.00	80.00
☐ 57/1, 3line trademark, 4¼″	150.00	160.00	155.00

CINDERELLA

☐ 337, Geobel/V trademark, 4¼″	120.00	130.00	125.00
☐ 337, Goebel trademark, 4½″	115.00	120.00	117.00

CLOSE HARMONY

☐ 336, 3-line trademark, 5¼-5½″	350.00	370.00	360.00
☐ 336, Goebel/V trademark, 5¼-5½″	140.00	150.00	130.00
☐ 336, Goebel trademark, 5¼-5½″	125.00	135.00	130.00

CONFIDENTIALLY

☐ 314, 3-line trademark, 5¾″	600.00	630.00	615.00
☐ 314, Goebel/V trademark, 5¾″	0	115.00	110.00
☐ 314, Goebel trademark, 5¾″	94.00	105.00	100.00

FEATHERED FRIENDS

☐ 344, 3-line trademark, 4¾″	250.00	260.00	255.00
☐ 344, Goebel/V trademark, 4¾″	120.00	130.00	125.00
☐ 344, Goebel trademark, 4¾″	110.00	125.00	117.00

FEEDING TIME

☐ 199/0, Goebel, trademark, 4¼-4½″	88.00	98.00	93.00
☐ 199/1, Goebel/V trabemark, 5½-5¾″	105.00	115.00	110.00
☐ 199, trademark, 5¾″	480.00	530.00	505.00

FLOWER VENDOR

☐ 381, 3-line trademark, 5¼″	350.00	370.00	360.00
☐ 381, Goebel/V trademark, 5¼″	110.00	120.00	115.00
☐ 381, Goebel trademark, 5¼″	100.00	120.00	110.00

	Current Price Range		P/Y Average

GOOD FRIENDS

☐ 183, Full Bee trademark, 4-4¼ "	250.00	275.00	262.00
☐ 182, 3-line trademark, 4-4¼ "	120.00	125.00	122.00
☐ 182, Goebel trademark, 4-4¼ "	83.00	90.00	86.00

GOOD HUNTING

☐ 307, Stylized Bee trademark,5 "	250.00	270.00	260.00
☐ 307, 3-line trademark, 5 "	175.00	185.00	180.00
☐ 307, Goebel trademark, 5 "	94.00	105.00	99.00

HAPPINESS

☐ 86, CM trademark, 4½-5 "	250.00	270.00	260.00
☐ 86, Stylized Bee trademark, 4½-5 "	100.00	120.00	110.00
☐ 86, Goebel/V trademark, 4½-5 "	65.00	75.00	70.00

HELLO

☐ 124/0, Stylized Bee trademark, 5¾-6¼ "	150.00	170.00	160.00
☐ 124/0, Goebel/V trademark, 5¾-6¼ "	85.00	95.00	90.00
☐ 124/1, Goebel/V trademark, 6¾-7 "	100.00	115.00	110.00

IN TUNE

☐ 414, Goebel trademark, 3¼ "	120.00	140.00	130.00

JOYFUL

☐ 53, trademark, 3½-4¼ "	300.00	325.00	312.00
☐ 53, Stylized Bee trademark, 3½-4¼ "	80.00	90.00	85.00
☐ 53, Goebel/V trademark, 3½-4¼ "	55.00	65.00	60.00

KNITTING LESSON

☐ 256, 3-line trademark, 7½ "	275.00	295.00	285.00
☐ 256, Goebel/V trademark, 7½ "	240.00	260.00	250.00
☐ 265, Goebel trademark, 7½ "	220.00	240.00	230.00

LET'S SING

☐ 110/0, Stylized Bee trademark, 3-3¼ "	90.00	110.00	100.00
☐ 110/0, Goebel trademark, 3-3¼ "	55.00	65.00	60.00
☐ 110/1, Stylized Bee trademark, 3½-4 "	125.00	135.00	130.00

LOST SHEEP

☐ 68/2/0, Stylized Bee trademark,4¼-4½ "	110.00	120.00	115.00
☐ 68/2/0, Goebel/V trademark,4¼-4½ "	65.00	75.00	70.00
☐ 68/0, 3-line trademark, 5½ "	110.00	120.00	115.00

MADONNA WITHOUT HALO

☐ 46/0, 3-lines trademark, 10¼-10½ "	75.00	85.00	80.00
☐ 46/1, 3-line trademark, 11¼-12 "	100.00	110.00	105.00
☐ 46/111, 3-lined trademark, 16¼-16¾ "	200.00	220.00	210.00

MISCHIEF MAKER

☐ 342, 3-lined trademark, 5 "	350.00	375.00	362.00

	Current Price Range		P/Y Average
☐ **342**, Goebel/V trademark, 5″	120.00	140.00	130.00
☐ **342**, Goebel trademark, 5″	110.00	130.00	120.00

THE PHOTOGRAPHER

☐ **178**, CM trademark, 4¾-5¼″	500.00	550.00	525.00
☐ **178**, Stylized Bee trademark,4¾-5¼″	200.00	225.00	212.00
☐ **178**, Goebel/V trademark, 4¾-5¾″	115.00	125.00	120.00

PUPPY LOVE

☐ **1**, CM trademark, 5-5¼″	350.00	380.00	365.00
☐ **1**, Stylized Bee trademark,5-5¼″	150.00	170.00	160.00
☐ **1**, Goebel/V trademark, 5-5¼″	85.00	95.00	90.00

RING AROUND THE ROSIE

☐ **348**, Line trademark, 6¾″	1750.00	1950.00	1850.00
☐ **348**, Goebel/V trademark, 6¾″	1500.00	1700.00	1600.00
☐ **348**, Goebel trademark, 6¾″	1310.00	1500.00	1400.00

STREET SINGER

☐ **131**, CM trademark, 5-5½″	300.00	330.00	315.00
☐ **131**, Stylized Bee trademark, 5-5½″	120.00	130.00	125.00
☐ **131**, Goebel/V trademark, 5-5½″	75.00	85.00	80.00

SURPRISE

☐ **94/3/0**, Stylized Bee trademark,4-4½″	90.00	100.00	95.00
☐ **94/3/0**, Goebel/V trademark,4-4½″	75.00	85.00	80.00
☐ **94/1**, Stylized Bee trademark, 5¼-5½″	175.00	195.00	185.00

TO MARKET

☐ **49/3/0**, Stylized Bee trademark,4″	150.00	170.00	160.00
☐ **49/3/0**, Goebel/V trademark, 4″	85.00	95.00	90.00
☐ **49/0**, Goebel/V trademark, 5-5½″	130.00	150.00	140.00

WATCHFUL ANGEL

☐ **194**, Full Bee trademark, 6¼-6¾″	350.00	380.00	365.00
☐ **194**, 3-lines trademark, 6¼-6¾″	175.00	195.00	185.00
☐ **194**, Goebel trademark, 6¼-6¾″	136.00	155.00	146.00

WEARY WANDERER

☐ **204**, CM trademark, 5½-6″	500.00	550.00	525.00
☐ **204**, Stylized Bee trademark, 5½-6″	200.00	220.00	210.00
☐ **204**, Goebel/V trademark, 5½-6″	100.00	110.00	105.00

HUTCHINSON BOTTLES

DESCRIPTION: Hutchinson bottles are containers with a unique stopper which consists of a rubber disc held between two metallic plates attached to a spring stem.

ORGIN: The Hutchinson bottle was produced by Charles A. Hutchinson, Chicago, in the late 1870s.

COMMENTS: Hutchinson bottles are not decorative. They were last manufactured in 1912.

ADDITIONAL TIPS; Prices on Hutchinson bottles vary more sharply by geographic locale than prices for other types of collectible bottles. For more information, consult *The Official Price Guide to Bottles, Old and New,* published by The House of Collectibles.

	Current Price Range		P/Y Average
☐ **Anchor, The Bottling Works, Cincinnati, Ohio,** all in a circle, in center of it an anchor, in back registered bottle never sold in 2 lines, on base D, panels base 6¾ " aqua	17.00	24.00	21.00
☐ **Anchor, The Bottling Works, Cincinnati, Ohio,** all in a circle, in center, anchor, aqua, 7 "	15.00	20.00	17.50
☐ **Anchor Steam Bottling Works, Shawnee, Oklahoma,** all in a circle, in center an anchor, anchor on base,6¾ "	15.00	20.00	17.50
☐ **A. Anchor Steam Bottling Works, Shawnee, Ohlahoma,** ty all in a circle, aqua, 6¾ "	45.00	65.00	55.00
☐ **Andrae, G. Port Huron, Michigan,** all in a circle, 6¾ "	25.00	35.00	30.00
☐ **Anniston, Alabama,** Coca-cola in block letters, aqua, 7¾ "	100.00	130.00	115.00
☐ **City Bottling Works, Braddock, Pennsylvania,** all in a circle, aqua, 6½ "	12.00	17.00	14.50
☐ **City Brewing Co., Wapakonet, Ohio,** in moon letter, aqua, 7 "	12.00	17.00	14.50

Delta Mfg. Co. Trade Mark, Delta *(in triangle), Greenville, Miss., rounded shoulders, short neck stopper, aqua, 7½",* **$12.00-$17.00**

Capital S.W. Co., *Columbus, Ohio, rounded shoulders, shortneck, stopper, aqua, 7¼",* **$12.00-$17.00**

Elephant Steam Bottling Works, *Birmingham, Ala., all on front under line drawing of elephant, aqua, 6½",* **$14.00-$19.00**

	Current Price Range		P/Y Average

☐ **CityIce,** in center, & Bottling Works, GEORGETOWN, under Texas, all in a circle, aqua, 6½ " 12.00 17.00 14.50

☐ **Decker Bottling, Dayton, Ohio,** on 3 panels bottle, aqua, 7" 19.00 25.00 22.00

☐ **Deis & Tibbals, Lima, Ohio,** all in a circle, aqua, 7" 12.00 17.00 15.00

☐ **Delaney & Co. Bottlers, Plattsburg, New York,** all in a circle, aqua, 7" 12.00 17.00 15.00

☐ **Delaney & Young, Eureka, California,** all in a circle, pale blue, 6½ " 15.00 20.00 17.50

☐ **Erts, J.M., Poughkeepsie, New York,** all in a circle, Reg. on base E. under bottom, clear, 7" 12.00 17.00 15.00

☐ **Esposito G., Phiade,** all in a circle, aqua, 6¾ " 12.00 17.00 14.00

☐ **Eureka California Soda Water Co., San Francisco,** in center of it, a bird, light green, 6¾ " 16.00 23.00 20.00

☐ **Evenchick Bros. Bottling Works, Cleveland, Ohio,** in center an Eagle, all in a circle, aqua, 7" 15.00 20.00 17.50

☐ **Ewa Bottling Work,** in a horse shoe letters, under it H.T., Panels base, clear, 7½ " 75.00 95.00 85.00

☐ **As Above,** also aqua 85.00 110.00 97.00

☐ **Excelsior Bottling Co., Bloomington, Illinois,** all in a circle, under bottom E.B. Co., aqua, 7" 14.00 20.00 17.00

☐ **Excelsior Bottling Co., Clarksburg, West Virginia,** all in a circle, aqua, 6¾ " 12.00 17.00 14.50

☐ **Excelsior Bottling Works, Houston, Texas,** all in a circle, aqua, 7¼ " 15.00 20.00 17.50

☐ **F.A.B.,** in a large horse shoe, in center, Galveston, TX near base, aqua, 7½ " 12.00 17.00 14.50

☐ **Fargo, The Mineral Springs, Co.,** in a horse shoe in center of it Pure & Clean, Warren O., clear, 6⅝ " 12.00 17.00 14.50

☐ **Felbrath, H. Peoria, Illinois,** all in a circle at base S.B. & Co., aqua, 7" 12.00 17.00 14.50

☐ **Fidelity Bottling Works,** Reg. Monroe, La. all in a circle, panels base, under bottom, Fidelity, aqua 7" 15.00 20.00 17.50

☐ **5th Ward Bottling Works, Houston, Texas,** , in center 5th Ward, aqua, 7¾ " 15.00 20.00 17.50

☐ **Finley And Son,** in ½ moon letters in center 1893, under it Bottlers, 1806 D St. N.W. Washington, D.C. in back, T.B.N.T.B.S., under bottom F, aqua, 6½ " 15.00 20.00 17.50

☐ **Fischer And Co., Santa Fe, New Mexico,** all in a circle, aqua, 6¼ " 15.00 20.00 17.50

	Current Price Range		P/Y Average
☐ **Lauterback, John,** letters in a horse shoe , under it Springfield, Ill., on base N.B.B.G. Co., 46, aqua, 7⅛ "	12.00	17.00	14.50
☐ **Lavin, M.F., Ashlley, Pennsylvania,** letters in a horse shoe, under it Reg., light blue, 6¾ "	12.00	17.00	14.50
☐ **Lawrence, Louis, Manaimo, B.C.,** all in a circle, aqua, 7½ "	16.00	23.00	20.00
☐ **Mahaska Bottling Works,** all in a circle, clear, 7"	12.00	17.00	14.50
☐ **Mahaska Bottling Works,** all in a circle, aqua, 6¾ "	12.00	17.00	14.50
☐ **Manfield Bottle Works, Manfield, Arkansas,** all in a circle, "M" etc. under bottom, light green, 6½ "	15.00	20.00	17.00
☐ **Manhattan, The — Bottling Co., Chicago, Illinois,** center, trade mark horse head, Registered under bottom Trademark Registered in center head, aqua, 6¾ "	16.00	23.00	20.00
☐ **Manhattan, The, Bottling Co.,** trademark registered Chicago, Ill. all in a circle, central horse head, aqua, 6½ "	12.00	17.00	14.50
☐ **Marietta Bottling Works, Marietta, Georgia,** all in a circle, clear, 7"	12.00	17.00	14.50
☐ **Marietta Bottling Works, Marietta, Oklahoma,** all in a circle, panels base, aqua, 7¼ "	75.00	100.00	87.00
☐ **Marion Bottling & Ice Cream Co.,** made from Mo-Cola, original Coca-Cola Formula not an imitation, Ocala, Fla. all in a circle, aqua, 6¾ "	12.00	17.00	14.50
☐ **Marion Bottling & Ice Cream Co.,** made from Mo-Cola original, Coca-Cola Formula, not an imitation, all in a circle, clear, 6¼ "	55.00	75.00	65.00
☐ **Marion Bottling Works, Fairmont, West Virginia,** all in a circle, aqua, 6¾ "	12.00	17.00	14.50
☐ **Markowitz, L., Brunswick, Georgia,** in 3 lines in back T.B.T.B.R., aqua, 7⅝ "	16.00	23.00	20.00
☐ **Marsh, J.I., Portmouth, O.,** all in a circle, aqua, green, 6¼ "	12.00	17.00	14.50
☐ **Omaha Bottling Co.,** in 2½ moon lines under it Omaha Nebr. "O" under bottom, light aqua, 6½ "	16.00	23.00	20.00
☐ **Ottenville, E. "MC",** in 2 lines, under bottom "25", cobalt, 6"	70.00	90.00	80.00
☐ **Ottenville, Nashville, Tennessee,** all in a circle, blue	33.00	42.00	38.00
☐ **Ottenville, E.,** "McC" on base, "25" under bottom, cobalt, 6"	70.00	90.00	80.00
☐ **Ottenville, Nashville, Tennesse,** blue, 6½ "	70.00	90.00	80.00
☐ **Pablo & Co.,** man in a canoe and dog, T.B.N.S., etc. N.O., aqua, 7"	33.00	42.00	38.00
☐ **Pablo & Co. J.,** In center, man in canoe with dog, Trade Mark, on base T.B.N.S. Seltzer & Mineral Mfg. Nos.-475-477 & 479 St. Claude, St. N.D.	17.00	23.00	20.00

ICART PRINTS

MAKER: Louis Icart was born in the small southern French city of Toulouse. This city was the home of many famous French artists, the most famous being Henri de Toulouse-Lautrec. In this atmosphere Icart became aware of the fine arts. He began his sketching at the early age of six and by the age of fifteen was sketching designs for costumes. As a fashion artist he was quite successful.

With the outbreak of World War I, Icart went to the front as a soldier. Not completely abandoning his desire as an artist, he would sketch and etch on any available material. At the end of the war, with encouragement from friends, Icart began to make prints of the etchings he had made during this period. When they were published they became an immediate international success.

TECHNIQUE: Icart's works demonstrate a mastery of dry point, line etching, aquatint, and their variations. Icart produced up to 500 prints each of over one thousand subjects. However, his works are scarce, because many have been lost or destroyed.

MARKS: Most Icart prints are easily identified. Most bear his hallmark which is usually located near the edge of the print. The following picture is his hallmark in actual size.

His signature is also easily identifiable, although subject to forgery and sometimes found on lithographic reproductions of his prints.

Earlier works will have his signature but may not bear the hallmark. Most will, however, bear the stamp of his gallery, an oval shape with the letters EM for l'estampe moderne. It is possible to have an original Icart with no hallmark at all, but this is rare.

The prints are usually numbered in the traditional manner of a first number representing the number of the print then a slash mark followed by a second number. This second number represents the number of prints in the edition (excluding artist's proofs and hors commerce prints if they exist). For example 75/120 means the print is number seventy-five of an edition of one hundred and twenty prints.

Icart pulled two editions frequently, one for Europe and one for American distribution. Sometimes the number is preceded by the letter "A" for an American edition; as in the example a 75/120. All prints were not numbered.

RECOMMENDED READING: For further information, refer to *The Official Price Guide to Collector Prints* published by The House of Collectibles.

The following is a listing of prints with current prices compiled from dealer's price lists across the country. These prices are for mint prints (perfect or near perfect), and of course, prices vary from one area of the country to another.

Coursing II *by Louis Icart*

TITLE	PRICE RANGE	
☐ After The Raid	1,550.00	2,000.00
☐ Above the Wings	1,850.00	2,250.00
☐ Amazonia	4,500.00	5,000.00
☐ Angry Buddha	800.00	
☐ Apache Dancer	750.00	
☐ Arabian Nite (1926)(Masked nude rear)	850.00	
☐ Attic Room	1,100.00	
☐ Arrival (Woman entering doorway)	700.00	
☐ Autumn Leaves	750.00	
☐ Backstage	750.00	
☐ Ballerina with roses	750.00	
☐ Bathing beauties	1,500.00	2,000.00
☐ Before the Raid	2,500.00	3,000.00
☐ Bird of Prey (Woman with eagle)	1,400.00	1,800.00
☐ Bird Seller	750.00	
☐ Black Fan	750.00	
☐ Birth of Venus	2,000.00	
☐ Blue Book	750.00	
☐ Blue Buddha	750.00	
☐ Blue Broken Jug	750.00	
☐ Blue Parasol	750.00	
☐ Bo Peep	750.00	
☐ Bubbles	1,500.00	1,800.00
☐ Butterfly Falls	1,200.00	
☐ Carmen	750.00	
☐ Cassanova	850.00	
☐ Champs (Girls in buggy)	750.00	
☐ Charm of Montmarte	750.00	
☐ Chestnut Vendor	750.00	
☐ Clipped Wings	750.00	

Fumee - Smoke *by Louis Icart*

TITLE		PRICE RANGE
☐ Cinderella	850.00	
☐ Coach, The	750.00	
☐ Conchita	1,500.00	
☐ Courage France	2,000.00	2,500.00
☐ Coursing II	850.00	1,250.00
☐ Coursing III	850.00	1,250.00
☐ Cat with paw in fishbowl	750.00	
☐ Dame Rose	750.00	
☐ Dancer (Finale)	750.00	
☐ D'Artagnan	850.00	
☐ Date Tree	750.00	
☐ Dear Friends	1,100.00	
☐ December	850.00	
☐ Defense of the Homeland	1,950.00	2,250.00
☐ Descending Coach	700.00	
☐ Dollar	500.00	
☐ Don Juan	950.00	
☐ Dream Waltz	1,200.00	
☐ Ecstacy	1,500.00	2,000.00
☐ Embrace	750.00	
☐ Eve (Nude) (Large Oval)	1,400.00	1,500.00
☐ Fair Dancer	750.00	
☐ Faust	900.00	1,000.00
☐ Favorites The	950.00	
☐ Fashion Early	700.00	
☐ Feeding Time	750.00	
☐ Finlandia	850.00	1,000.00
☐ Flower Vendor	750.00	
☐ Follies	3,000.00	4,000.00
☐ Forbidden Fruit	750.00	
☐ Fountain, The	1,000.00	1,500.00
☐ Four Dears	950.00	
☐ From From	850.00	
☐ France de Foyer	1,800.00	2,000.00
☐ French Bus	1,200.00	1,500.00

TITLE		PRICE RANGE
☐ French Doll	750.00	
☐ Gatsby 1920's	750.00	
☐ Gay Senorita	850.00	
☐ Gay Trio	1,850.00	2,000.00
☐ German Eagle	1,850.00	2,000.00
☐ Girl in Crinoline	800.00	
☐ Golden Veil	1,500.00	
☐ Goosed	700.00	
☐ Grande Eve	7,000.00	7,500.00
☐ Green Broken Jug	750.00	
☐ Guardian	900.00	
☐ Gust of Wind	1,250.00	
☐ Happy Birthday	1,200.00	1,500.00
☐ Recollections(Woman atdesk)	750.00	
☐ Red Alcove	750.00	
☐ Red Riding Hood	850.00	
☐ Reflections Pool	1,500.00	1,800.00
☐ Repose	4,000.00	4,250.00
☐ Ritz, The	1,500.00	2,000.00
☐ Salome	750.00	
☐ Sappho	750.00	
☐ Scherazade	800.00	
☐ Seashell (Nude woman on shell)	1,500.00	2,000.00
☐ Secrets or Blue Book	750.00	
☐ Singing Lesson	850.00	
☐ Sleeping Beauty	950.00	1,250.00
☐ Smoke	1,350.00	1,500.00
☐ Speed (Woman and greyhound)	850.00	1,250.00
☐ Sofa	7,500.00	
☐ Spanish Dancer	850.00	
☐ Spilled Apples	750.00	
☐ Sprintime	1,000.00	
☐ Summer Music	600.00	
☐ Swans	1,500.00	2,000.00
☐ Sweet Mystery	950.00	
☐ Symphony in Blue	850.00	
☐ Symphony in White	1,200.00	1,500.00
☐ Tennis	900.00	1,000.00
☐ Three of Four Seasons	800.00	
☐ The Coach (There are several versions)	750.00	
☐ Tosca	850.00	950.00
☐ Thoroughbreds (Woman with horse, Rare)	3,500.00	4,000.00
☐ Treasure Chest	600.00	
☐ Trenches	1,850.00	2,250.00
☐ Two Beauties	5,000.00	
☐ Unmasked	900.00	
☐ Venetian Nights	900.00	
☐ Venus (Companion to Eve)	1,500.00	
☐ Victory in the Skies	1,950.00	2,250.00
☐ Victory Wreath (Soldier holding woman holding wreath up in air, WWI)	1,850.00	2,250.00
☐ View of Montmarte	750.00	

INKWELLS AND INKSTANDS

TOPIC: Inkwells are containers for holding ink. They were used in the days before pens had their own ink supply. An inkstand is composed of two or more inkwells and a tray. Other accessories are often included.

PERIOD: Most of the collectible inkwells and inkstands will date from the 1800s and early 1900s.

ORIGIN: These items have been in use for over 4,500 years.

MATERIAL: Glass is the most common material for collectible inkwells and inkstands. Other popular materials include stone, metal, wood, pottery and porcelain.

COMMENTS: Many collectors focus on glass inkwells and inkstands. The variety and beauty of these pieces make them wonderful collectibles.

ADDITIONAL TIP: It is rare to find an inkwell with an intact separate glass cover. These pieces are valuable. Inkstands with numerous accessories in good condition are worth the most.

INKWELLS	Current Price Range		P/Y Average
☐ **Brass,** Art Deco, glass insert	45.00	55.00	50.00
☐ **Brass,** crab, glass insert, hinged lid	85.00	105.00	95.00
☐ **Brass,** cups on brass, tray, 6″ x 9″, c. 1900s .	225.00	275.00	250.00
☐ **Brass,** devil, German, c. 1900	80.00	98.00	89.00
☐ **Brass,** horse, two milk glass inserts, 5½″ x 9½″ .	115.00	135.00	125.00
☐ **Brass,** scrollwork, porcelain insert, square .	80.00	98.00	89.00
☐ **Brass,** shape of kettle, Japanese, 2½″, 1800s	230.00	260.00	245.00
☐ **Brass,** Victorian, two glass inserts	80.00	100.00	90.00
☐ **Bronze,** Art Deco, glass insert, silver inlay . .	80.00	100.00	90.00
☐ **Bronze,** Art Nouveau, ornate sailing vessel .	140.00	160.00	150.00
☐ **Bronze,** Art Nouveau, woman's head with flowing hair for lid	130.00	170.00	150.00

Inkwell, *ceramic, made in France, marked Imperial,*
$55.00-$75.00

	Current Price Range		P/Y Average
☐ **Bronze,** clay pot of natural flowers	140.00	170.00	155.00
☐ **Cast iron,** car, two glass inserts, 5½ " x 10 " .	150.00	180.00	165.00
☐ **Cast iron,** cat's head, 4", c. 1800s	225.00	275.00	250.00
☐ **Cast iron,** globe, Columbian Exposition	60.00	80.00	70.00
☐ **Cloisonne,** stone wall and tray, 7", c. 1900s .	110.00	130.00	120.00
☐ **Delft,** lion, Germany, 7½ " x 9 "	170.00	190.00	180.00
☐ **Delft,** windmill, Germany, 3" x 3½ ", c. 1800s	100.00	130.00	115.00
☐ **Glass, Cut,** eagle finial on brass lid, c. 1800s	160.00	210.00	185.00
☐ **Glass, Cut,** hinged crystal lid	100.00	126.00	113.00
☐ **Glass, Cut,** sterling silver lid, 2"	100.00	130.00	115.00
☐ **Glass, Pressed,** chair with cat on cushion, 4", c. 1800s	150.00	190.00	170.00
☐ **Glass,** blue, hinged brass lid, 2½ "	160.00	180.00	170.00
☐ **Glass,** sterling silver overlay	100.00	120.00	110.00
☐ **Glass,** umbrella shape, c. 1800s	225.00	275.00	250.00
☐ **Glass And Bronze,** Tiffany Favrile, mosaic, height 3", c. 1910	1300.00	1500.00	1400.00
☐ **Glass And Bronze,** Tiffany Favrile, mosaic, iridescent cover, height 4", c. 1910	1100.00	1400.00	1250.00
☐ **Marble,** blue and gray, cherubs, French, 4"	150.00	190.00	170.00
☐ **Metal,** enameled, camel, glass insert, c. 1900s	180.00	240.00	210.00
☐ **Metal,** enameled, camel, glass, insert, c. 1900s	180.00	240.00	210.00
☐ **Metal,** enameled, floral motif, Chinese, c. 1800s	120.00	150.00	135.00

	Current Price Range		P/Y Average
☐ **Metal,** enameled, gold and brass trim, glass inset	60.00	80.00	70.00
☐ **Milk glass,** cat on iron base, 5″	140.00	160.00	150.00
☐ **Milk glass,** dogs on iron base, 4″	120.00	140.00	130.00
☐ **Papier Mache,** Japanned, gold figures, black lacquer, length 8½″, c. 1800s	80.00	100.00	90.00
☐ **Pewter,** blue pottery insert, 9″, c. 1820	160.00	180.00	170.00
☐ **Pewter,** dome rolltop, 5″	80.00	110.00	95.00
☐ **Pewter,** pear with bees on tray, Kayserzinn	225.00	255.00	240.00
☐ **Pewter,** round, 6½″	100.00	130.00	115.00
☐ **Porcelain,** Limoges, gilded, floral motif, hinged top	70.00	85.00	77.50
☐ **Porcelain,** boy wearing hat, French, 12″, c. 1880s	150.00	170.00	160.00
☐ **Porcelain,** hinged lid, painted flowers	70.00	100.00	85.00
☐ **Porcelain,** Victorian woman, 4″	60.00	78.00	69.00
☐ **Silver-Plated,** figural, dog's head, hat is inkwell cover	55.00	65.00	60.00
☐ **Silver-Plated,** Tiffany Studios, pine needle design on white glass, 5½″	90.00	100.00	95.00
☐ **Soapstone,** carved dog on stand, Italian, 8″, 1700s	120.00	140.00	130.00
☐ **Stoneware,** dark red glaze, roped edge, four pen holes, signed, 5″	135.00	155.00	145.00
☐ **Stoneware,** round, chiseled edge	50.00	68.00	59.00
☐ **Wood,** carved, Black Forest deer	135.00	155.00	145.00
☐ **Wood,** glass insert, four pen holes, 4″	60.00	80.00	70.00
☐ **Wood,** porcelain insert, 3″	50.00	68.00	59.00

INKSTANDS

	Current Price Range		P/Y Average
☐ **Brass,** with two milk glass ink bottles, hinged lid, height 2½″	85.00	95.00	90.00
☐ **Bronze,** crab and shell, Tiffany Studios, 7″, c. 1910	2000.00	2500.00	2250.00
☐ **Bronze,** French, gilded, shell boat pulled by swan, oval stand, length 11¼″, c. 1800s	400.00	500.00	450.00
☐ **Iron,** horse, brass cap, 5″	45.00	65.00	55.00
☐ **Silver,** Austrian, oval, pierced, panel feet, beaded rim, length 11⅜″, c. 1795	900.00	1100.00	1000.00
☐ **Silver,** engraved, Paul de Lamerie	5250.00	6250.00	5750.00
☐ **Silver, George III,** rectangular, panel feet, cut-glass receptacles, length 11″, c. 1800	1200.00	1500.00	1350.00
☐ **Silver, George IV,** flowers, oblong, paw feet, c. 1822	4500.00	4800.00	4650.00
☐ **Silver,** Georgian	900.00	1300.00	1100.00
☐ **Wood,** J. R. Chappell, 3¾″	60.00	80.00	70.00

INSULATORS

DESCRIPTION: Insulators are the nonconducting glass figures used to attach electrical wires to poles.

ORIGIN: The first insulator was invented in 1844 for a telegraph line.

COMMENTS: Insulators became collectible after World War II. Old electrical lines with insulators were taken down during the early post war stages of urban development.

Color, age and design determine value. Threadless insulators are older, more rare and usually more valuable than threaded ones.

Clear glass is most common. Colors, including green, milk white, amber, amethyst and cobalt blue are more valuable.

ADDITIONAL TIP: The listings are alphabetical according to manufacturer. Other information including color and size is also included.

	Current Price Range		P/Y Average
☐ **A.G.M.**, amber, 3¾″ x 2¾″	12.00	24.00	18.00
☐ **A.T.& T. Co.**, aqua, single skirt, 2⅛″ x 3¾″, c. 1900	7.00	12.00	9.00
☐ **A.T.& T. Co.**, aqua, 3⅜″	7.00	12.00	9.00
☐ **A.T.& T. Co.**, aqua, two-piece, 2¾″ x 3⅝″	5.00	8.00	6.50
☐ **A.T.& T. Co.**, green, single skirt, 2½″ x 3¾″ .	5.00	12.00	7.50
☐ **Agee**, clear amethyst, 3⅝″ x 2¾″	12.00	16.00	14.00
☐ **American Insulator Co.**, aqua, double petticoat, 4⅛″ x 3⅛″	10.00	14.00	12.00
☐ **Armstrong**, amber 4″ x 3¼″	10.00	14.00	12.00
☐ **Armstrong**, No. 5, clear, double petticoat, 3⅛″ x 3¾″	5.00	8.00	6.50
☐ **A.U. Patent**, green, 4⅜″ x 2¾″	29.00	39.00	33.00
☐ **B. & O.**, aqua, 3⅞″ x 3¼″	29.00	39.00	34.00
☐ **B.F.G. Co.**, aqua, 4″ x 3½″	39.00	49.00	44.00
☐ **B.G.M. Co.**, clear amethyst, 3⅜″ x 2¼″	17.00	25.00	21.00
☐ **Barclay**, aqua, double petticoat, 3″ x 2¼″ . . .	17.00	25.00	21.00
☐ **Boston Bottle Works**, aqua, 4⅛″ x 3″	44.00	54.00	48.00
☐ **Brookes, Homer**, aqua, 3¾″ x 2¾″	21.00	31.00	26.00
☐ **Brookfield**, No. 36, aqua, green, 3⅞″ x 3⅛″ . . .	12.00	18.00	15.00
☐ **Brookfield**, No. 45, aqua, green, 4⅛″ x 3⅛″ . . .	7.00	12.00	9.50
☐ **Brookfield**, No. 55, aqua, green, 4″ x 2½″ . . .	12.00	18.00	14.00
☐ **Brookfield**, No. 83, aqua, green, 4″ x 3⅛″	17.00	25.00	21.00

	Current Price Range		P/Y Average
☐ **Brookfield,** dark olive green, double petticoat, 3¾" x 4"	7.00	12.00	8.50
☐ **Brookfield,** green, double petticoat, 3³⁄₁₆" x 3⅝", c. 1865	7.00	12.00	8.50
☐ **B.T. Co. of Canada,** clear, amethyst, 3½" x 2⅛"	15.00	25.00	20.00
☐ **B.T. Co. of Canada,** aqua, green, 3¼" x 2⅜"	12.00	16.00	14.00
☐ **C. & P. Tel Col.,** aqua, green, 3½" x 2⅜"	10.00	14.00	12.00
☐ **C.E.L.,** amethyst, 4⅛" x 2¾"	12.00	16.00	14.00
☐ **C.E.N.,** amethyst, 3¼" x 2½"	34.00	44.00	39.00
☐ **C.G.I.,** clear, amethyst, 3½" x 2⅛"	21.00	27.00	24.00
☐ **Cable,** aqua, green, 4½" x 3¼"	23.00	30.00	26.00
☐ **California,** aqua, green, 3½" x 2⅛"	23.00	30.00	26.00
☐ **California,** clear, amethyst, 4⅜" x 3½"	32.00	40.00	37.00
☐ **California,** clear, amethyst, 4⅛" x 3¼"	5.00	10.00	7.50
☐ **California,** CK-162, purple, double petticoat, 3¾" x 4"	7.00	12.00	9.50
☐ **Canadian Pacific,** blue, green, aqua, 3⅝" x 2¾"	44.00	54.00	49.00
☐ **Canadian Pacific,** clear, amethyst, 3½" x 2¾"	15.00	20.00	17.00
☐ **Castle,** aqua, 3⅞" x 2½"	44.00	54.00	49.00
☐ **Chester,** aqua, 4" x 2⅜"	48.00	58.00	53.00
☐ **Columbia,** aqua, green, 3¾" x 4"	38.00	48.00	33.00
☐ **Derflinger, T.N.I.,** aqua, green, 4" x 3½"	17.00	25.00	21.00
☐ **Dominion** No. 9, amber, aqua and clear, 3¾" x 2½"	3.00	6.00	4.50
☐ **Duquesne,** aqua, green, 3⅜" x 2⅜"	30.00	40.00	35.00
☐ **Dwight,** aqua, 4" x 3"	30.00	40.00	35.00
☐ **E.C. & M. Co.,** green, 4" x 2½"	23.00	30.00	26.50
☐ **Electrical Supply Co.,** aqua, green, 3⅝" x 2⅝"	30.00	40.00	35.00
☐ **Folembray,** No. 221, olive green, 2⅝" x 3⅜"	38.00	48.00	43.00
☐ **Gayner,** 36-190, aqua, 3¾" x 3¼"	10.00	14.00	12.00
☐ **Gayner,** green, double petticoat, 3³⁄₁₆" x 3⅞"	23.00	30.00	27.00
☐ **H.G. Co.,** amber, double petticoat, 3¼" x 3¾"	12.00	16.00	14.00
☐ **H.G. Co. Petticoat,** aqua, green, 3¾" x 3¾"	5.00	8.00	6.50
☐ **H.G. Co. Petticoat,** clear, 4⅛" x 3¼"	10.00	14.00	12.00
☐ **Hawley,** aqua, 3¼" x 2¼"	15.00	20.00	17.50
☐ **Hemingray,** No. 2 Cable, aqua, green, 4" x 3⅝"	22.00	30.00	26.50
☐ **Hemingray,** No. 7, aqua, green, 3½" x 2½"	3.00	6.00	4.50
☐ **Hemingray,** No. 8, aqua, green, 3⅜" x 2⅜"	14.00	18.00	16.00
☐ **Hemingray,** No. 9, aqua, single skirt, 2¼" x 3½"	17.00	23.00	20.00
☐ **Hemingray,** No. 10, clear, single skirt, 2⅝" x 3½"	12.00	16.00	14.00
☐ **Hemingray,** No. 16, green, single skirt, 2⅞" x 4"	3.00	6.00	4.50
☐ **Hemingray,** No. 19, aqua, double petticoat, 3¼" x 3"	28.00	38.00	33.00
☐ **Hemingray,** No. 25, aqua, green, 4" x 3¼"	14.00	20.00	17.00
☐ **Hemingray,** No. 95, aqua, green, 3⅝" x 2⅞"	34.00	40.00	37.00
☐ **Hemingray Beehive,** green, double petticoat, 3⅛" x 4⅜"	17.00	23.00	20.00
☐ **Hemingray Petticoat,** cobalt blue, 4" x 3¼"	30.00	40.00	35.00

	Current Price Range		P/Y Average
☐ **Hemingray Transportation,** green, 4½ " x 3¼ "	23.00	30.00	26.00
☐ **Isorex,** clear, black, green, blue, 5½ " x 3½ "	5.00	8.00	6.50
☐ **Jeffery Mfg. Co.,** aqua, 3⅝ " x 2¾ "	30.00	40.00	35.00
☐ **Jumbo,** aqua, 7¼ " x 5¼ "	21.00	27.00	25.00
☐ **Knowles Cable,** aqua, green, 4 " x 3⅝ "	32.00	40.00	36.00
☐ **Fred M. Locke,** No. 14, aqua, 4⅜ " x 3⅛ "	21.00	27.00	24.00
☐ **Fred M. Locke,** No. 21, aqua, green, 4 " x 4 "	5.00	8.00	6.50
☐ **Lynchburg,** No. 10, aqua, green, 3⅜ " x 2¼ "	7.00	14.00	10.50
☐ **Lynchburg,** No. 31, aqua, green, 3½ " x 2⅜ "	7.00	12.00	9.50
☐ **Lynchburg,** No. 44, aqua, single skirt, 2¼ " x 3⅝ "	10.00	14.00	12.00
☐ **Lynchburg,** No. 44, 4 " x 3⅝ "	5.00	8.00	6.50
☐ **Maydwell** No. 9, clear, aqua, 3⅝ " x 2⅛ "	5.00	8.00	6.50
☐ **Maydwell,** No. 9, clear, single skirt, 2⅛ " x 3½ "	5.00	8.00	6.50
☐ **Maydwell,** No. 16, amber, 3⅞ " x 2¾ "	5.00	8.00	6.50
☐ **Maydwell,** No. 20, white milk glass, 3⅝ " x 3⅛ "	21.00	27.00	24.00
☐ **McLaughlin,** No. 9, green, single skirt, 2¼ " x 3⅝ "	12.00	16.00	14.00
☐ **McLaughlin,** No. 16, amber, aqua, green, 3⅝ " x 2⅝ "	5.00	10.00	7.50
☐ **McLaughlin,** No. 19, aqua, 3¾ " x 3¼ "	3.00	6.00	4.50
☐ **McLaughlin,** No. 42, aqua, 4 " x 3⅝ "	5.00	10.00	7.50
☐ **McLaughlin,** No. 62, aqua, 3⅝ " x 3⅝ "	7.00	11.00	9.00
☐ **Mershon,** aqua, 5 " x 5½ "	31.00	38.00	34.50
☐ **Monogram H.I. Co.,** aqua, 4½ " x 3⅛ "	21.00	27.00	24.00
☐ **Mulford & Biddle,** aqua, 3¼ " x 2⅝ "	34.00	40.00	37.00
☐ **N.E.G.M. Co.,** aqua, green, 3½ " x 2⅛ "	14.00	18.00	16.00
☐ **N.E.G.M. Co.,** aqua, 3½ " x 3¼ "	17.00	23.00	20.00
☐ **N.E.T. & T. Co.,** aqua, green, 3⅝ " x 2⅜ "	5.00	8.00	6.50
☐ **N.E.T. & T. Co.,** blue, 3½ " x 3 "	12.00	16.00	14.00
☐ **Noleak,** aqua, green, 4 " x 4 "	31.00	36.00	33.00
☐ **O.V.G. Co.,** aqua, 3½ " x 2¼ "	7.00	12.00	10.00
☐ **O.V.G. Co.,** aqua, green, 3½ " x 2¼ "	12.00	16.00	14.00
☐ **Pettingel Anderson Co.,** aqua, 4 " x 2¾ "	17.00	23.00	20.00
☐ **Pony,** blue, 3⅛ " x 2⅜ "	21.00	27.00	24.00
☐ **Postal,** aqua, green, 4⅛ " x 3½ "	15.00	18.00	16.50
☐ **Pyrex,** carnival glass, 3⅛ " x 3¾ "	17.00	23.00	20.00
☐ **Pyrex,** carnival glass, 3 " x 3¾ "	12.00	16.00	14.00
☐ **Pyrex,** double threads, carnival glass, 2⅝ " x 4¼ "	14.00	18.00	16.00
☐ **S.B.T. & T. Co.,** aqua, green, 3½ " x 2¼ "	14.00	18.00	16.00
☐ **Santa Ana,** aqua, green, 4¼ " x 4¾ "	28.00	35.00	31.50
☐ **Standard,** clear, amethyst, 3⅝ " x 2¾ "	12.00	16.00	14.00
☐ **Star,** aqua, single skirt, pony, 2⅜ " x 3½ "	7.00	10.00	8.50
☐ **Sterling,** aqua, 3¼ " x 2¼ "	14.00	18.00	16.00
☐ **T.C.R.,** aqua, 4 " x 3¾ "	12.00	16.00	14.00
☐ **T.H.E. Co.,** aqua, 4 " x 3⅛ "	29.00	35.00	32.00
☐ **Thomas,** brown pottery, 2½ " x 1⅛ "	5.00	10.00	7.50
☐ **Transportation,** No. 2, aqua, 4¼ " x 2⅞ "	21.00	27.00	24.00
☐ **U.S. Tel. Co.,** aqua, 3¾ " x 2⅜ "	14.00	18.00	16.00
☐ **V.M.R. Napoli,** aqua, green, 4 " x 2¾ "	12.00	16.00	14.00
☐ **W.F.G. Co.,** clear, amethyst, 3½ " x 2⅛ "	14.00	18.00	16.00
☐ **W.G.M. Co.,** clear, amethyst, 3½ " x 2¼ "	23.00	30.00	26.00

	Current Price Range		P/Y Average
☐ **W.G.M. Co.,** clear, amethyst, 3⅞″ x 3⅛″	17.00	23.00	20.00
☐ **W.V.,** No. 5, aqua, 4¼″ x 2¾″	17.00	23.00	20.00
☐ **Westinghouse,** aqua, green, 3⅛″ x 2⅜″	27.00	33.00	30.00
☐ **Whitall Tatum,** amber, 3⅞″ x 3¼″	12.00	16.00	14.00
☐ **Whitall Tatum,** 512-A, amber, red, 3½″ x 3⅝″	5.00	10.00	7.50

IRONS

TYPES: Various types of collectible irons include: the charcoal iron; the box iron which featured a heated metal slug placed inside the hollow iron; and the sadiron, a solid iron that was heated on the hearth or stove. In 1871 Mary Potts invented a detachable handle for the sadiron. The Potts iron led to self-heating irons fueled with gasoline or cooking gas. These were dangerous and unsatisfactory. The electric iron was patented in 1882.

ORIGIN: Irons were used in Asia for centuries before their 17th century Western introduction.

COMMENTS: Collectible irons are still reasonably priced. Collectors should seek odd shaped irons.

ADDITIONAL TIP: The listings are alphabetical according to type of iron.

☐ **Alcohol Iron,** wooden handle, c. 1880	65.00	80.00	70.00
☐ **Box Iron,** heated slug, c. 1890	45.00	65.00	53.00
☐ **Box Iron,** English, heated slugs, c. 1800	82.00	125.00	90.00
☐ **Box Iron,** solid brass, punch decoration on top surface, height 5″ x 4½″	105.00	117.00	110.00
☐ **Charcoal Iron,** brass fittings, chimney vent ..	70.00	90.00	75.00
☐ **Charcoal Iron,** twisted handle, chimney vent	75.00	90.00	78.00
☐ **Charcoal Iron,** wooden handle	42.00	50.00	45.00
☐ **Charcoal Iron,** wooden handle, c. 1890	45.00	60.00	48.00
☐ **Charcoal Iron,** wooden iron, with trivet	65.00	80.00	69.00
☐ **Flat Iron,** all iron	6.00	7.50	6.50
☐ **Flat Iron,** bail handle	8.00	12.00	10.00
☐ **Flat Iron,** charcoal, chimney vent, c. 1860 ...	29.00	40.00	33.00
☐ **Flat Iron,** hollow handle	29.00	40.00	33.00
☐ **Flat Iron,** metal handle, c. 1860	29.00	40.00	35.00
☐ **Flat Iron,** no handle, asbestos	4.00	6.00	5.00

	Current Price Range		P/Y Average
☐ **Flat Iron,** no handle, Blass and Drake, Newark, New Jersey, height 6″	4.00	6.00	5.00
☐ **Flat Iron,** red, small, c. 1877	45.00	50.00	47.00
☐ **Flat Iron,** removable handle, c. 1870	29.00	38.00	32.00
☐ **Flat Iron,** rope handle	28.00	35.00	30.00
☐ **Flat Iron,** stone body, metal handle, c. 1850 .	45.00	60.00	50.00
☐ **Flat Iron,** wooden handle, child's, c. 1860 . . .	29.00	40.00	33.00
☐ **Flat Iron,** wooden handle, large	34.00	45.00	36.00
☐ **Fluting Iron,** brass rollers, with black enamel and red and gold stripes, two slugs, height 9″	85.00	95.00	89.00
☐ **Fluting Iron,** double, with holder	65.00	80.00	68.00
☐ **Fluting Iron,** Geneva, c. 1870s	50.00	65.00	57.00
☐ **Gasoline Iron,** Coleman	28.00	38.00	30.00
☐ **Gasoline Iron,** wooden handle, c. 1910	55.00	70.00	58.00
☐ **G.E. Electric Iron,** c. 1905	39.00	50.00	42.00
☐ **G.E. Electric Iron,** c. 1920	34.00	45.00	37.00
☐ **Iron,** for a child, glass base, wooden handle .	4.75	6.25	5.50
☐ **Laundry Stove,** cast iron, double burner	170.00	220.00	190.00
☐ **Laundry Stove,** cast iron, single burner	120.00	180.00	135.00
☐ **Laundry Stove,** fancy cast iron, c. 1895	500.00	600.00	520.00
☐ **Nickel Plated Iron**	24.00	37.00	27.00
☐ **Polishing Iron,** oval shaped, c. 1845	48.00	58.00	52.00
☐ **Sadiron,** alcohol iron, nickel plated, black wooden handle, Foote Manufacturing Co., Dayton, Ohio	47.00	55.00	50.00
☐ **Sadiron,** for child, removable wooden handle, 2″ x 4″	40.00	52.00	45.00
☐ **Sadiron,** waffle pattern on bottom, "Genoa"	30.00	37.00	33.00
☐ **Tailor's Iron**	34.00	45.00	37.00
☐ **Travel Iron,** asbestos	29.00	40.00	33.00

IRONWARE

DESCRIPTION: Nineteenth century kitchenware and other household items were often made of iron because of its durability.

COMMENTS: Ironware usually can be found for fairly low pieces. Marked pieces are of greater value and importance. Dates on ironware do not always stand for the year made, some dates stand for the year the patent was issued.

Oiling or polishing old ironware decreases its value.

ADDITIONAL TIPS: The listings are alphabetical according to item.
For further information, refer to *The Official Price Guide to Kitchen Collectibles,* published by The House of Collectibles.

Trivet, *nickel plated iron, c. 1900,*
$15.00-$20.00
Photo courtesy of Lou McCulloch,
Highland Heights, OH, 44133

IRONWARE	Current Price Range		P/Y Average
□ **Anvil,** regulation type, antique	1400.00	1800.00	1650.00
□ **Apple Parer,** with clamp, cast iron, Simplex Company	25.00	40.00	30.00
□ **Apple Parer,** Double Quick model	25.00	40.00	30.00
□ **Apple Parer,** Sinclair & Scott Company	25.00	40.00	30.00
□ **Apple Parer,** cast iron, c. 1870	25.00	40.00	30.00
□ **Apple Parer,** cast iron, c. 1900	25.00	40.00	30.00
□ **Apple Parer,** cast iron, Apple Parer Company, c. 1880	18.00	60.00	54.00
□ **Apple Parer,** pares, cores, and slices	18.00	25.00	21.00
□ **Apple Parer,** Hudson Parer Company	25.00	30.00	26.00
□ **Apple Parer,** cast iron, F.A. Walker, c. 1870s .	18.00	55.00	47.00
□ **Apple Parer,** Rocking Table Company	18.00	50.00	42.00
□ **Apple Parer,** White Mountain Company	18.00	48.00	39.00
□ **Apple Peeler**	39.00	47.00	41.00
□ **Apple Segmenter,** bolt type, cast iron, patented 1869	23.00	35.00	27.00
□ **Asparagus Buncher,** cast iron, on walnut board	140.00	175.00	156.00
□ **Balance Scales,** forged, hook on top, 13″ . . .	20.00	40.00	30.00
□ **Basket Spit,** spun iron basket with andiron hooks to hold meat	80.00	125.00	105.00
□ **Basket,** fireplace grate, cast iron, c. 1900, 11″ long	120.00	180.00	126.00
□ **Bathtub,** hammered tin alloy, c. 1820	500.00	625.00	575.00

Item	Current Price Range		P/Y Average
☐ **Bedwarmer,** with wooden handle, 36″	60.00	80.00	64.00
☐ **Bird Spit,** wrought iron, legged with hooks and drip pan	90.00	130.00	110.00
☐ **Bookends,** bronzed, profile of Abraham Lincoln, 4¾″	12.00	16.00	14.50
☐ **Bowl,** cast iron, diameter 9″, depth 3″	50.00	60.00	53.00
☐ **Bowl,** cast iron, flared sides, flat bottom, round spove, early 19th century, top 12″, height 3½″	160.00	185.00	167.00
☐ **Broiler,** "Reliable", cast iron, c. 1893	40.00	60.00	42.00
☐ **Broiler,** wrought iron, for fireplace, legged, round, 14″ diameter	58.00	75.00	68.00
☐ **Broiler,** wrought iron, rectangular	40.00	55.00	49.00
☐ **Butcher Flesh Fork,** wrought iron, length 15″	35.50	41.00	36.50
☐ **Butcher Set,** strainer and ladle, wrought iron, length 20″	60.00	70.00	63.00
☐ **Butter Tester,** iron pin, 17½″ long	9.00	18.00	12.00
☐ **Cabbage Cutter,** cast iron and wood, sided	45.00	55.00	48.00
☐ **Cabbage Cutter,** cast iron blades on wooden board, 33″ long	30.00	45.00	37.00
☐ **Candle Dip,** early 19th century	200.00	250.00	210.00
☐ **Candleholder,** cast iron, 7″ high	70.00	95.00	78.00
☐ **Candleholder,** cast iron, c. 1800, 7¾″ high	90.00	115.00	99.00
☐ **Candleholder,** forged iron, English, c. 1800, 11″ high	250.00	400.00	315.00
☐ **Candleholder,** forged iron, wall type, c. 1600	90.00	115.00	101.00
☐ **Candleholder,** forged iron, c. 1700	70.00	85.00	78.00
☐ **Candleholder,** forged iron with spike, wall type, c. 1600	175.00	225.00	199.00
☐ **Meat Chopper,** cast iron, tin, painted wood, c. 1865	16.00	15.00	20.00
☐ **Meat Chopper,** cast iron, with crank handle, clamps, c. 1900	10.00	15.00	13.00
☐ **Meat Chopper,** cast iron, with crank handle, clamp, Universal Company, c. 1900	13.00	16.00	15.00
☐ **Meat Chopper,** twin blades, Enterprise Company, c. 1900	12.00	16.00	15.00
☐ **Meat Hook,** tinned iron, c. 1890	12.00	16.00	13.50
☐ **Meat Slicer,** crank handle, clamp-on table type, circular blade	8.00	12.00	10.50
☐ **Meat Tenderizer,** cast iron, c. 1892	10.00	25.00	13.00
☐ **Pan,** iron and tin alloy, rolled sheet for soap-making, 10″ diameter	50.00	60.00	53.00
☐ **Paring Knife,** steel blade, wood handle, Dunlap Company	2.50	5.00	3.00
☐ **Pastry Blender,** wood nickeled iron, 1915 to 1940	8.00	15.00	8.50
☐ **Pastry Jigger,** cast iron, octagonal shape, 5½″ diameter, c. 1700	40.00	45.00	42.00
☐ **Pastry Marker,** late 19th century	8.00	15.00	10.50
☐ **Pea Huller**	37.50	37.50	20.00
☐ **Pea Sheller,** clamp on type	16.00	26.00	17.00
☐ **Peel,** cast iron, hook end, shovel head, open handle, hand cast, antique	45.00	60.00	53.00
☐ **Peel,** wrought iron, hook end, shovel head for use in fireplace	50.00	65.00	58.00

	Current Price Range		P/Y Average

Peel, wrought iron, knob end, shovel head, open handle grip 60.00 75.00 68.00

Pot Hook, wrought iron hook with wood handle 10.00 24.00 13.00

Raisin Seeder, cast iron 16.00 30.00 17.00

Raisin and Grape Seeder, clamp on, Enterprise Company 20.00 35.00 26.00

Raisin and Grape Seeder, c. 1890 .... 28.00 38.00 29.00

Raisin and Grape Seeder, inscribed "Wet your Raisins", c. 1895 .... 28.00 38.00 29.00

Rug Beater, wire pattern with wood handles, c. 1920 .... 10.00 24.00 13.00

Rug Beater, wire, including handle, spade shape, c. 1850 .... 12.00 26.00 15.00

Rushlight, iron, 10" high, c. 1850 .... 120.00 175.00 131.00

Rushlight, iron, 12" high, c. 1750 .... 540.00 750.00 580.00

Rushlight, iron, 8½" high 90.00 125.00 105.00

Rushlight, iron, snake head, 11" long, c. 1750 275.00 400.00 315.00

Rushlight, oak pedestal, 10" high, c. 1750 ... 275.00 400.00 315.00

Rushlight, yew pedestal, 8½" high, c. 1850 .. 275.00 400.00 315.00

Sausage Stuffer, cast and sheet iron, gears . 30.00 45.00 37.00

Sausage Stuffer 38.00 50.00 42.00

Saratoga Potato Chipper, clamp on type, crank handle 16.00 22.00 19.00

Sugar Cutter, nippers, shears, for snipping pointed or square shaped, solid mounds of sugar 78.00 100.00 79.00

Sugar Devil, iron, for use with brown sugar, cut off hardened lumps 75.00 95.00 84.00

Sugar Nips, late 19th century 19.00 30.00 21.00

Tailors Iron, European origin, mid 19th century, 9" long 14.00 25.00 16.00

Tallow Dipper, wrought, 18th century, 25" long 380.00 412.00 388.00

Tea Kettle, ironstone, English, c. 1870 ...... 42.00 53.00 47.00

Tenderer Steak, iron, wood, c. 1870 .... 8.00 12.00 8.50

Toaster 155.00 180.00 161.00

Toaster, two slices, supported by three legs, comes with handle, 17" long 135.00 150.00 139.00

Trivet, lacy cast iron, six pointed and circular motif, mid 19th century 78.00 95.00 79.99

Trivet, leaf and scroll 95.00 115.00 99.00

Trivet, letters 20.00 30.00 21.00

Trivet, lyre 35.00 43.00 37.00

Trivet, Maltese emblem 32.00 40.00 35.00

Trivet, Masonic emblem 42.00 55.00 47.00

Trivet, moose 12.00 18.00 15.00

JEWELRY

PERIOD: Some of the major style periods for jewelry include 18th century Georgian, 19th century Victorian, Art Nouveau and Art Deco.

COMMENTS: Usually the value of a piece of jewelry depends on the quality of material used. Designer status also accounts for some high prices. To judge material quality, the collector should use a loupe, an eyepiece magnifier. A 10-power loupe is recommended. A touchstone should be used to assess gold content in jewelry.

ADDITIONAL TIPS: The following listings are alphabetical according to item of jewelry.

For further information, refer to *The Official Price Guide to Antique Jewelry.*

Bracelet, *bangle, tiger heads, beast, flower and bird motifs, Jaipur champleve enamel in translucent red, green, blue, yellow and opaque white, rose diamonds, gold, Indian, c. 19th,* **$4600.00-$5200.00**

BRACELETS, FLEXIBLE

	Current Price Range		P/Y Average

☐ **Animal Gold Silhouettes on Green Glass,** Indian Pitch, engraved floral reverse, 22K gold, Indian, c. 19th **1300.00 1600.00 1400.00**

☐ **Button Motif,** repousse links, three round diamonds, gold, c. 1920 .... **850.00 950.00 875.00**

☐ **Coral,** three branch coral chains, seed pearls, surrounding glass locket with woven hair clasp, gold, c. 1870 .... **275.00 400.00 325.00**

☐ **Flower Motif,** robin's egg blue and white champleve enamel, gold, c. 1830 .... **625.00 675.00 650.00**

☐ **Geometric Motif Flat Links,** one round emerald, one round ruby, one round sapphire, two round diamonds, 14K gold, c. 1930 **1050.00 1300.00 1100.00**

☐ **Heart Lock Motif,** curb links, 9K gold, English, c. 20th **135.00 165.00 145.00**

☐ **Jade Carved Circular Motif,** seed pearls, gold, c. 20th **650.00 750.00 700.00**

☐ **Mesh Woven,** Greek key motif on oval slide, black enamel, gold, c. 1860 .... **840.00 940.00 865.00**

☐ **Oval Link Motif,** three round peridots and two cushion-cut peridots alternating with chain links, gold, American, c. 1900 .... **520.00 570.00 535.00**

☐ **Ribbon and Flower Motif,** center panel on wide band, 17 rose diamonds in flowers, gold, maker G. Ehnl, c. 1871 .... **3100.00 3300.00 3200.00**

☐ **Scroll Motif Links,** alternating with light green cabochon emeralds, gold **2700.00 3200.00 2850.00**

☐ **Snake,** woven flexible band, engraved head, gemstone eyes, gold, c. 1840 .... **1300.00 1450.00 1350.00**

☐ **Turquoise Pave Set,** in three clusters, old mine diamond centers, snake link bracelet, gold, c. 1840 .... **3300.00 3700.00 3450.00**

BROOCHES, ANIMAL AND BUG

☐ **Bird,** pave diamonds, center emerald-cut, emerald in closed back mounting, silver, c. 1800-10 .... **750.00 1000.00 825.00**

☐ **Cat,** pave rose diamond body, ruby eyes, pearl ball, white gold, French, c. 1935 ...... **1000.00 1250.00 1100.00**

☐ **Dragonfly,** colored stones, silver, c. mid 19th **225.00 275.00 240.00**

☐ **Fly,** cabochon ruby eyes and body, old mine diamond body and wings, pearl, gold, c. 1860 **1850.00 2050.00 1900.00**

☐ **Rams' Head,** Etruscan granulation, rope motif, gold, c. 1860 .... **1250.00 1450.00 1300.00**

☐ **Snake,** one cabochon turquoise, gold, English, c. early 20th **260.00 280.00 270.00**

☐ **Turtle,** six rose diamonds, 36 demantoid garnets, gold, c. early 20th **475.00 675.00 525.00**

	Current Price Range		P/Y Average

BROOCHES, CAMEO

☐ **Coral,** Cameo of a Lady, engraved frame, gold, c. late 19th	525.00	625.00	550.00
☐ **Hardstone Cameo,** three gentlemen and a ram, gold, c. 19th	1000.00	1200.00	1050.00
☐ **Mother-Of-Pearl,** scenic cameo with oriental figures, gold, c. 19th	435.00	485.00	445.00
☐ **Opal,** matrix cameo of the Sphinx, gold, c. 1920	2750.00	3150.00	2850.00
☐ **Sardonyx,** cameo of a lady, four round diamonds, eight seed pearls, gold, c. 1880 . .	1150.00	1300.00	1200.00
☐ **Wedgwood,** cameo of a Muse, c. 1840, blue enameled 10K gold frame, c. 1900	465.00	575.00	480.00

BROOCHES, SILVER

☐ **Angel Motif,** sterling, American, c. 1896	140.00	160.00	145.00
☐ **Flower Motif,** enameled, sterling silver, American, c. 1935	70.00	90.00	75.00
☐ **Heart Motif,** sterling, American, c. 1896	45.00	60.00	50.00
☐ **Madonna and Child Motif,** bas-relief panel, blue enamel, four half-pearls, silver, c. 1905 .	190.00	210.00	195.00
☐ **Swirl and Dangle Motif,** engraved, maker: Ellis & Son, Exeter, England, silver, c. 1869 .	130.00	165.00	140.00
☐ **Wreath Motif,** enamel, sterling, American, c. 1896	75.00	105.00	85.00

EARRINGS, GEMSTONE

☐ **Black Onyx Ball and Bar Motif,** seed pearls, gold, c. 1860-80	525.00	600.00	535.00
☐ **Circle Dangle Motif,** marcasites, sterling silver, c. 1920-30	80.00	100.00	87.00
☐ **Hoop Motif,** sead pearls, gold, c. 1860-80 . . .	425.00	475.00	435.00
☐ **Lava Cameos,** openwork frames, silver gilt, c. 1870-80	400.00	500.00	420.00
☐ **Mosaic Butterfly Dangle Motif,** gold, c. 1860	1675.00	1775.00	1700.00
☐ **Snake Motif,** pear-shape diamond in head, gold, c. 19th	1100.00	1300.00	1150.00
☐ **Teardrop Motif,** lapis lazuli, seed pearls, gold, c. 1890	425.00	475.00	450.00

	Current Price Range		P/Y Average

PENDANTS

	Current Price Range		P/Y Average
☐ **Bell Motif,** round diamond, seed pearls, 14K gold, American, c. 1920	110.00	160.00	120.00
☐ **Cameo,** mythological figure, carved snake frame, gold, c. 19th	2600.00	2750.00	2650.00
☐ **Crescent and Star Motif,** one turquoise, six seed pearls, 12 in. chain, 14K gold, American, c. 1894-95	145.00	175.00	150.00
☐ **Cutout Swirl Motif,** marcasites, sterling silver, American, c. 1920	40.00	50.00	42.00
☐ **Fire Opal,** cabochon, rose diamonds, silver, gold, c. mid 19th	1700.00	1900.00	1750.00
☐ **Flower Motif,** translucent colored enamel, one round diamond, 12 in. chain, 14K gold, American, c. 1894-95	240.00	275.00	250.00
☐ **Hardstone,** cameo of a lady, half seed pearl border, gold, pendant or brooch, c. 1880	1350.00	1700.00	1400.00
☐ **Heart Motif,** heart-shaped moonstone, rose diamonds, silver topped gold, c. 1870	500.00	550.00	520.00

WATCHES, GENTLEMEN'S POCKET

	Current Price Range		P/Y Average
☐ **Bicycle with Rider Motif,** engraved, HC, 14K gold, American, c. 1896	650.00	850.00	700.00
☐ **Initial Shield Motif,** with deep wavy engraving, 21 jewel, model 993, white porcelain dial, HC, 14K gold, 16 size, maker: Hamilton, c. 1900	875.00	1150.00	925.00
☐ **Miniature Enamel,** of an angel and a putti, pink base taille enamel background, engraved case, HC, 18K gold, Swiss, c. 19th ..../....	1300.00	1550.00	1400.00
☐ **Repeater,** quarter hour, Jaquemar, standard better grade movement, gold hands, OF, gold, maker, Vacheron, Swiss, c. 1900	3800.00	4400.00	4000.00
☐ **Sead Pearls Pave,** high grade lever movement, fusee, jeweled, OF, gold, English, c. 1830-60	14500.00	17000.00	15500.00
☐ **Train and Flower Engraved Motif,** HC, 14K gold, American, c. 1896	850.00	1150.00	950.00

JIM BEAM BOTTLES

DESCRIPTION: Jim Beam Bottles refer to the figural liquor containers first issued in the 1950s by the James B. Beam Distilling Company, Kentucky.

ORIGIN: The company was founded in 1778 by Jacob Beam. The firm now bears the name of Jacob Beam's grandson, Colonel James B. Beam.

TYPES: The company produces a variety of themes including The Executive Series, Regal China Series, and Political Figures Series.

COMMENTS: Early Beam Bottles made before the figural series are also collectible. In 1953, the company produced its first figural decanter. When the decanters sold well, Beam began producing decorative bottles on a large scale.

ADDITIONAL TIPS: For more information, consult *The Official Price Guide to Bottles, Old and New,* published by The House of Collectibles.

"Boxer," *Jim Beam 1964 Presidential Decanter,* **$27.00-$30.00**

	Current Price Range		P/Y Average

☐ **The Big Apple,** 1979, apple shaped bottle with embossed Statue of Liberty on the front with New York City in the background and the lettering "The Big Apple" over the top **10.00** **15.00** **12.50**

☐ **Bing Crosby 36th,** 1976, same as the Floro de Oro except for the medallion below the neck. Urn-shaped bottle with pastel wide band and flowers around the middle. Remainder of bottle is shiny gold with fluting and designs **28.00** **36.00** **32.00**

☐ **Ernie's Flower Cart,** 1976, replica of an old-fashioned flower cart used in San Francisco. Wooden cart with movable wheels. In honor of Ernie's Wines and Liquors of Northern California **22.00** **30.00** **25.50**

☐ **Falstaff,** 1979, replica of Sir John Falstaff with blue and yellow outfit holding a gold goblet. Second in the Austrailian Opera Series. Music box which plays "Va, vecchio, John." Limited edition of 1000 bottles **250.00** **350.00** **300.00**

☐ **Fantasia Bottle,** c. 1971, this tall, delicately handcrafted Regal China decanter is embellished with 22 karat gold and comes packaged in a handsome midnight blue and gold presentation case lined with red velvet. 16¼"   **12.00** **18.00** **15.00**

☐ **Fiesta Bowl,** c. 1973, the second bottle created for the Fiesta Bowl. This bottle is made of genuine Regal China, featuring a football player on the front side. 13¼" **10.00** **16.00** **13.00**

☐ **Figaro,** c. 1977, figurine of the character Figaro from the opera "Barber of Seville." Spanish costume in beige, rose, and yellow. Holds a brown guitar on the ground in front of him. Music box plays an aria from the opera **300.00** **350.00** **325.00**

☐ **Hawaiian Open,** c. 1973, the second bottle created in honor of the United Hawaiian Open Golf Classic. Of genuine Regal China designed in the shape of a golf ball featuring a pineapple and airplane on front, 11" **6.00** **10.00** **8.00**

☐ **Hawaiian Open,** c. 1974, genuine Regal China bottle commemorating the famous 1974 Hawaiian Open Golf Classic, 15" **6.00** **10.00** **8.00**

☐ **Hawaii Paradise,** 1978, commemorates the 200th Anniversary of the landing of Captain Cook. Embossed scene of a Hawaiian resort framed by a pink garland of flowers. Black stopper, 8¾" **20.00** **28.00** **24.00**

☐ **Hemisfair,** c. 1968, the Lone Star of Texas crowns the tall gray and blue "TOWER OF THE AMERICAS." "THE LONE STAR STATE" is lettered in gold over a rustic Texas scene. The half map of Texas has "HEMISFAIR 68 — SAN ANTONIO." Regal China, 13" **6.00** **10.00** **8.00**

	Current Price Range		P/Y Average

☐ **Hoffman,** c. 1969, the bottle is in the shape of "HARRY HOFFMAN LIQUOR STORE" with the Rocky Mountains in the background. Beam bottles, and "SKI COUNTRY — USA" are in the windows. Reverse: embossed mountain & ski slopes with skier. Regal China, 9″ **4.00 8.00 6.00**

☐ **Short Timer,** 1975, brown army shoes with army helmet sitting on top. Produced for all who have served in the armed forces, 8″ **28.00 34.00 31.00**

☐ **Shriners,** 1975, embossed camel on front of bottle in blue, green, and brown with bright red blanket flowing from the camel's saddle. A gold scimitar and star centered with a fake ruby is on the back, 10½ ″ **15.00 20.00 17.50**

☐ **Shriners' Pyramid,** 1975, white and brown pyramid with embossed emblems on the sides, 5″ **12.00 16.00 14.00**

☐ **Tall Dancing Scot,** c. 1964, a small Scotsman encased in a glass bubble in the base dances to the music of the base. A tall pylon shaped glass bottle with a tall stopper. No dates on these bottles. Glass, 17″ **12.00 18.00 15.00**

☐ **Tavern Scene,** c. 1959, two "beer stein" tavern scenes are embossed on sides, framed in wide gold band on this round decanter. Regal China, 11½ ″ **65.00 75.00 70.00**

☐ **Telephone,** 1975, replica of a 1907 phone of the Magneto Wallset type which was used from 1890 until the 1930's, 9½ ″ **55.00 65.00 60.00**

☐ **Ten-Pin,** 1980, designed as a bowling pin with two red bands around the shoulder and the neck. Remainder of the pin is white, screw lid, 12″ **4.00 8.00 6.00**

☐ **Thailand,** c. 1969, embossed elephant in the jungle and "THAILAND — A NATION OF WONDERS" on the front. Reverse: A map of Thailand and a dancer. Regal China, 12½ ″ .. **4.00 8.00 6.00**

☐ **Thomas Flayer 1907,** 1976, replica of the 1907 Thomas Flyer, 6-70 Model K "Flyabout," which was a luxury car of its day. Comes in blue or white. Plastic rear trunk covers the lid to the bottle **50.00 60.00 55.00**

☐ **Volkswagen Commemorative Bottle,** two colors, c. 1977, Commemorating the Volkswagen Beetle ... the largest selling single production model vehicle in automotive history. Handcrafted of genuine Regal China, this unique and exciting bottle will long remain a memento for bottle collectors the world over, 14½ ″ **30.00 36.00 33.00**

☐ **Washington State Bicentennial,** 1976, patriot dressed in black and orange holding drum. Liberty bell and plaque in front of drummer, 10″ **12.00 20.00 15.00**

	Current Price Range		P/Y Average
☐ **Waterman,** 1980, in pewter or glazed. Boatman at helm of his boat wearing rain gear. Glazed version in yellow and brown, 13½ ″ ..	150.00	200.00	175.00

JUKEBOXES

DESCRIPTION: A coin operated phonograph that automatically plays records is a jukebox.

PERIOD: The most collectible jukeboxes were manufactured from 1938 to 1948.

MAKER: The most popular machines were manufactured by Wurlitzer. They were prized for their imaginative cabinetry and see through mechanisms. Favored models are the 850, 950 and 1015.

ADDITIONAL TIPS: For more information, consult *The Official Price Guide to Music Collectibles,* published by The House of Collectibles.

☐ **AMI Model A,** 40 tune selections, called "Mother of Plastic," lights up, "jewels" on front of case, c. 1948	1250.00	2500.00	2000.00
☐ **AMI Model FR,** 20 tune selections, simple wood case in an Art Deco style, top glass panel is record mechanism and tune cards, c. 1932	320.00	520.00	400.00
☐ **AMI "Singing Tower,** 10 tunes, looks like an Art Deco skyscraper, 6′ H., c. 1941	2500.00	3000.00	2750.00
☐ **AMI "Top Flight,"** 20 tune selections, straight rectangular case, metal trim, rounded speaker opening, lights up, c. 1936	400.00	750.00	500.00
☐ **Capehart Jukebox,** early example, simple rectangular oak case, glass panels to view mechanism, decorative grill, 1930s	500.00	750.00	620.00
☐ **Filben "Maestro,"** 30 tune selections, very space age design, plastic top section, 1940s	1000.00	1500.00	1250.00

	Current Price Range		P/Y Average

☐ **Gabel's Charme,** 18 tune selections, all wood rectangular case, selection dial, some case decoration, tune cards inside clear glass window 275.00   500.00   400.00

☐ **Mills "Empress" Model 910,** 20 tune selections, rounded wood case, large plastic panels, small window to view tune cards, lights up 1250.00   1750.00   1500.00

☐ **Mills Jukebox,** 12 tune selections (78rpm), arranged in a "Ferris Wheel" effect, wood case, some decoration, dial tune selector, volume control, doors open on front top of case, speaker grill in bottom, 1930s 500.00   1250.00   750.00

☐ **Mills "Throne of Music,"** 20 tune selections, plastic panels, very similar in appearance to "Empress" 1000.00   1500.00   1250.00

☐ **Packard Pla-Mor (Capehart),** 24 tune selections, plastic and wood, large viewing window in top front, decorative grill in base, tune selection cards on wheel, coin mechanism in top center 750.00   1500.00   1000.00

☐ **Rock-Ola "Luxury Light-Up,"** 20 tune selections, large rounded corners case, orange and green plastic panels, push button tune selector in center, tune cards under plastic panel, decorative grill panel and trim 2000.00   2500.00   2250.00

☐ **Rock-Ola "Multi-Selector,"** 12 tune selections, clear glass, top front panel to view mechanism, push button tune selection, simple walnut case and front grill, c. 1935 . . . . . . 400.00   750.00   600.00

Rock-Ola, *style 1422, "Magic Glo," 1940s,* **$1250.00-$2000.00**

	Current Price Range		P/Y Average

☐ **Rock-Ola "Rocket" Model 1434,** 50 tune selections, push button, simple grill, colored panels, dome, top covers record mechanism, colored corner panels, 1950s . . . . — 500.00 | 1250.00 | 750.00

☐ **Rock-Ola "Rhythm King,"** 12 tune selections, wood base, plain case, viewing window to see mechanism, c. 1938 . . . . — 720.00 | 1250.00 | 1000.00

☐ **Rock-Ola Style 1426,** 20 tune, "Classic" style, push buttons, revolving lights, plastic, viewing window, c. 1947 . . . . — 1700.00 | 2250.00 | 2050.00

☐ **Seeburg Audiophone,** 8 disc records, plain rectangular case, oval glass opening on top front, "Ferris Wheel" type mechanism with 8 turntables, speaker on door in front, c. 1928 . — 400.00 | 750.00 | 600.00

☐ **Seeburg "Commander,"** 20 tune selections, "Space Age" 1930s look, plastic front, sides, top, decorative trim mouldings, button next to each tune card, c. 1940 . . . . — 750.00 | 1500.00 | 1000.00

☐ **Seeburg P147 (P148),** 20 tune selections, "washing machine" case style, plastic panels, c. 1947 . . . . — 750.00 | 1200.00 | 1000.00

☐ **Seeburg "Symphonola,"** 12 tune selections, rectangular plain case style, window to view mechanism, selector dial, c. 1936 . . . . — 500.00 | 1250.00 | 750.00

☐ **Seeburg "Symphonola Classic,"** 20 tune selections, push button, mainly wood and red plastic panels in front and top corners, decorative trim, lights up, c. 1938 . . . . — 500.00 | 1000.00 | 620.00

☐ **Seeburg "Symphonola Regal,"** 20 tune selections, plastic panels, tune cards in top section (no viewing of mechanism), c. 1940 . . . . . — 1000.00 | 1500.00 | 1250.00

☐ **Wurlitzer Model P 10,** 10 tune selections, rectangular wooden case, simple lines, glass window, tune selector dial, simple front grill on bottom, early version of "Simplex," c. 1934 . . . . — 250.00 | 500.00 | 400.00

☐ **Wurlitzer Model 35,** 12 tune selections, more elaborate walnut case, art deco style, clear glass front window to view mechanism, 1930s . . . . — 350.00 | 500.00 | 400.00

☐ **Wurlitzer Counter Model 61,** 12 tune selection, wood base and sides, some plastic (comes with floor stand), c. 1938-39 . . . . — 1000.00 | 2000.00 | 1500.00

☐ **Wurlitzer Counter Model 81,** 12 tune selections, wood base and sides, curving plastic panels, graceful front grill, small viewing window with tune selection cards, push buttons, 1940s . . . . — 1000.00 | 2000.00 | 1500.00

☐ **Wurlitzer Model 416,** 16 tune selections, simple wood case, tune selector dial, rounded front corner columns, decorative front grill over speaker, 1930s . . . . — 350.00 | 450.00 | 350.00

	Current Price Range		P/Y Average
☐ **Wurlitzer Model 616 Simplex,** 16 tune selections, wood case, rounded rectangular style, simple lines, clear glass top front viewing panel, tune selector dial, decorative grill, 1930s	750.00	1725.00	1000.00
☐ **Wurlitzer Model 700,** 24 tune selections, wood case, plastic panels on front corners and top, push button tune selections, decorative metalgrill, c. 1940	1000.00	2500.00	1750.00
☐ **Wurlitzer Model 750,** 24 tune selections, "Classic" style, plastic panels, viewing window, push buttons, c. 1937-40	2000.00	3250.00	2500.00
☐ **Wurlitzer Model 800,** 24 tune selections, wood trim and base, large orange and red plastic corner side and top panels, decorative grill, clear glass panel to view mechanism and tune selections, lights up, c. 1940 . .	1500.00	3000.00	2250.00
☐ **Wurlitzer "Victory,"** 24 tune selections, distinctive design, wood case, multicolored glass panels along front with musical instruments, harlequins, etc., small half circle viewing window, push buttons, decorative grill with colored panels behind, c. 1942-43	2000.00	3750.00	2500.00
☐ **Wurlitzer Model 1015,** 24 tune selections, "Classic" style, revolving lights in plastic bubble tubes, viewing window, c. 1946-47 . . .	3500.00	6500.00	4500.00

KNIVES

MAKER: Well known knife manufacturers include Russell, Case, Winchester and Remington.

COMMENTS: Most collectors of American knives are interested in specific types, including seaman's knives, military knives, knives adapted for hand-to-hand combat and bowie knives.

ADDITIONAL TIPS: Two prices are given for the knife section. The manufacturers, listed in alphabetical order, make a variety of knives so the prices indicate the range for each manufacturer.

For more complete information, refer to *The Official Price Guide to Collectors Knives,* published by The House of Collectibles.

Parker, *One Arm Pillbuster, genuine stag, 3⅞",* **$30.00-$40.00**

	Current Price Range		P/Y Average
☐ **A-1 Novelty Cutlery** Canton, OH	20.00	130.00	60.00
☐ **Ack Cutlery Co.** Freemont, OH	40.00	100.00	40.00
☐ **Adams & Bros.**	55.00	130.00	55.00
☐ **Adams & Sons**	40.00	100.00	55.00
☐ **Adolph Blaich,** San Francisco, CA	20.00	175.00	80.00
☐ **Adolphuis Cutlery Co.,** Sheffield, England ...	10.00	70.00	30.00
☐ **Aerial Mfg. Co.,** Marionette, WI	10.00	115.00	50.00
☐ **Akron Cutlery Co.,** Akron, OH	30.00	70.00	40.00
☐ **Alamo,** Japan	3.00	7.00	4.00
☐ **American Cutlery Co.,** U.S.A.	17.00	38.00	22.00
☐ **American Cutlery Co.,** Germany	9.00	22.00	13.00
☐ **Armstrong Cutlery Co.,** Germany	7.00	14.00	8.00
☐ **Arnex (stainless),** Solingen, Germany	5.00	11.00	7.00
☐ **Atenback,** Swanswork, Germany	12.00	60.00	28.00
☐ **Atlantic Cutlery Co.,** Germany	13.00	30.00	16.00
☐ **Autopoint,** Chicago, IL	4.00	10.00	5.00
☐ **Banner Cutlery Co.,** Germany	14.00	30.00	17.00
☐ **Banner Knife Co.**	14.00	30.00	17.00
☐ **A. F. Bannister & Co.,** New Jersey	4.00	50.00	23.00
☐ **Barhep,** Solingen, Germany	7.00	12.00	8.00
☐ **Barlett Tool Co.,** Newark, NY	18.00	70.00	35.00
☐ **Barrett & Sons**	7.00	70.00	30.00
☐ **Barton Bros.,** Sheffield, England	19.00	100.00	50.00
☐ **Bassett,** Derby, CT	10.00	30.00	15.00
☐ **Bastian Bros. Co.,** Rochester, NY	30.00	75.00	40.00
☐ **R. Bunting & Sons** Sheffield	80.00	550.00	280.00
☐ **Burkinshaw Knife Co.** Pepperell, MA	40.00	320.00	100.00
☐ **Frank Buster Cutlery Co.**	12.00	1200.00	460.00
☐ **Butler Bros.** Chicago, IL	18.00	95.00	45.00
☐ **Camden Cutlery Co.,** Germany	30.00	115.00	60.00
☐ **Camillus Cutlery Co.** Camillus, NY	10.00	115.00	50.00
☐ **Camillus,** New York, NY	7.00	30.00	15.00
☐ **Camp Buddy,** USA	10.00	30.00	16.00
☐ **Camp King**	10.00	30.00	16.00
☐ **Continental Cutlery Co.** Kansas City, MO. ...	30.00	70.00	45.00
☐ **Cook Bros.**	80.00	135.00	100.00
☐ **Copper Bros.**	10.00	20.00	13.00
☐ **Delux**	7.00	18.00	10.00
☐ **Depend-on-me-Cutlery Co.,** New York	8.00	40.00	20.00
☐ **E.A.A.** Solingen, Germany	6.00	12.00	7.00
☐ **E. F. & Co.**	70.00	100.00	75.00

	Current Price Range		P/Y Average
☐ Eagle	25.00	40.00	26.00
☐ Eagle Cutlery Co.	70.00	340.00	180.00
☐ Eagle Knife Co., U.S.A.	35.00	330.00	160.00
☐ Eagle Pencil Co.	6.00	17.00	10.00
☐ Eagleton Knife Co.	22.00	130.00	70.00
☐ Emmon Hawkins Hardware	17.00	110.00	55.00
☐ Empire Knife Co. Winsted, CT	32.00	315.00	160.00
☐ Empire, Winsted, CT	32.00	315.00	160.00
☐ Emrod Co., Germany	5.00	17.00	9.00
☐ Wm. Enders Mfg. Co., U.S.A.	17.00	130.00	68.00
☐ Faulkhiner & Co. Germany	12.00	25.00	14.00
☐ Favorite Knife Co. Germany	5.00	27.00	14.00
☐ Hibbard, Spencer, & Bartlett Chicago, IL	14.00	370.00	170.00
☐ Hickory	5.00	220.00	100.00
☐ Highcarbon Steel, U.S.A.	12.00	170.00	90.00
☐ Higler & Sons	17.00	80.00	45.00
☐ Hike Cutlery Co. Solingen, Germany	12.00	40.00	22.00
☐ Hill Bros.	22.00	65.00	40.00
☐ Honk Falls Napanoch, NY	40.00	930.00	450.00
☐ Imperial Knife Co. Providence, RI	3.00	80.00	38.00
☐ Imperial, Mexico	1.50	3.50	2.00
☐ Imperial, Germany	7.00	28.00	15.00
☐ Joseph Allen & Sons	12.00	260.00	120.00
☐ K.I.E.,Sweden	4.00	17.00	10.00
☐ Ka-Bar, U.S.A.	12.00	630.00	300.00
☐ Kabar, U.S.A.	12.00	315.00	150.00
☐ Kamp Cutlery Co. Germany	6.00	17.00	9.00
☐ Kamp Huaser Plumacher, Germany	17.00	64.00	37.00
☐ Murcott, Germany	6.00	27.00	16.00
☐ R. Murphy, Boston, MD	17.00	27.00	21.00
☐ New Port Cutlery Company Germany	13.00	20.00	15.00
☐ Newton Premier Sheffield	11.00	27.00	16.00
☐ New York Knife Company Walden, NY	30.00	1050.00	500.00
☐ Norsharp	12.00	36.00	24.00
☐ N. American, Wichita, KS	12.00	57.00	32.00
☐ Olcut, Olean, NY	45.00	320.00	145.00
☐ Old Cutlery Olean, NY	17.00	130.00	65.00
☐ Old American Knife, U.S.A.	12.00	38.00	19.00
☐ Old Hickory (Ontario Knife Company)	5.00	14.00	8.00
☐ Parker-Frost	12.00	220.00	100.00
☐ Wm. & J. Parker	110.00	420.00	200.00
☐ Petters Cutlery Company Chicago, IL	30.00	90.00	45.00
☐ Phoenix Knife Co. Phoenix, NY	12.00	140.00	70.00
☐ Pic, Germany	3.50	9.00	6.00
☐ PIC, Japan	2.50	5.75	4.10
☐ Pine Knot, U.S.A.	37.00	320.00	150.00
☐ Pine Knot James W. Price	47.00	440.00	200.00
☐ C. Platts & Sons Andover, NY	43.00	830.00	400.00
☐ Platts Bros. Andover, NY	42.00	850.00	400.00
☐ Platts Bros., Union, NY	77.00	850.00	390.00
☐ Poor Boy	6.00	110.00	50.00
☐ Pop Cutlery Co. Camillus, NY	6.00	22.00	10.00
☐ Quick Point (Winchester stamped on back of tang)	53.00	78.00	63.00
☐ R. J. Richter, Germany	5.00	17.00	8.00
☐ Ring Cutlery, Japan	1.50	5.75	3.50

	Current Price Range		P/Y Average
☐ Rivington Works	17.00	69.00	37.00
☐ Rizzaro Estilato, Milan, Italy	37.00	80.00	57.00
☐ Roberts & Johnson & Rand St. Louis, MO ...	17.00	77.00	40.00
☐ Robertson Bros. & Co. Louisville, KY	17.00	315.00	150.00
☐ Robeson, Germany	27.00	80.00	40.00
☐ Robeson, Rochester, NY	17.00	420.00	210.00
☐ Robeson, Suredge	12.00	130.00	60.00
☐ Sizeker Manstealed, Germany	12.00	17.00	14.00
☐ Sliberstein Laporte & Co.	38.00	69.00	45.00
☐ Simmons Hardware Co. Germany	22.00	320.00	150.00
☐ Simmons Hardware St. Louis, MO	27.00	315.00	150.00
☐ Simmons Warden White Co. Dayton, OH	17.00	80.00	50.00
☐ Spartts, England	37.00	95.00	60.00
☐ Spear Cutlery Co., Germany	12.00	27.00	16.00
☐ Spring Cutlery Co. Sheffield	17.00	130.00	50.00
☐ Springer, Japan	5.00	16.00	8.00
☐ Standard Cutlery Co. Germany	5.50	26.00	15.00
☐ Thomas Turner & Co. Sheffield, England	17.00	180.00	100.00
☐ United, Germany	4.00	12.00	8.00
☐ Universal Knife Co. New Britain, CT	17.00	38.00	25.00
☐ Utica Co., Czechoslovakia	13.00	38.00	24.00
☐ Utica Cutlery Co. Utica, NY	12.00	160.00	90.00
☐ Utica Knife Co., U.S.A.	12.00	160.00	90.00
☐ V. K. Cutlery Co., Germany	6.00	16.00	9.00
☐ Valley Falls Cutlery Co.	17.00	79.00	45.00
☐ Valley Forge Cutlery Co.	21.00	100.00	50.00
☐ Valor, Germany	3.50	16.00	8.00
☐ Valor, Japan	3.50	16.00	8.00
☐ Van Camp, U.S.A.	4.00	110.00	51.00
☐ Van Camp H & I Co., U.S.A.	17.00	310.00	150.00
☐ Van Camp Indianapolis, IN	17.00	310.00	150.00
☐ Van Camp, Germany	12.00	35.00	19.00
☐ Vanco, Indianapolis, IN	6.00	37.00	19.00
☐ Vernider, St. Paul, MN	6.00	37.00	19.00
☐ John Watts, Sheffield	16.00	33.00	24.00
☐ Webster, Sycamore Works U.S.A.	12.00	36.00	22.00
☐ Webster Cutlery Co., Germany	6.00	17.00	9.00
☐ Weck, N.Y.	17.00	68.00	35.00
☐ Wedgeway Cutlery Co.	15.00	39.00	27.00
☐ Weed & Co., Buffalo	36.00	77.00	52.00
☐ G. Weiland, New York	6.00	27.00	18.00
☐ Marshall Wells Hardware Co.	39.00	130.00	155.00
☐ H. C. Wentworth & Son Germany	6.00	37.00	20.00
☐ Weske Cutlery Co. Sandusky, OH	16.00	38.00	19.00
☐ Westaco, Boulder, CO	32.00	64.00	45.00
☐ Wester, B. C.	6.00	37.00	25.00
☐ Wester Bros., Germany	36.00	260.00	100.00
☐ Wester Stone, Inc., U.S.A.	16.00	118.00	50.00
☐ Western, Boulder, CO	52.00	520.00	240.00

LALIQUE

DESCRIPTION: Rene Lalique first achieved fame as a maker of Art Nouveau jewelry in the 1890s. He experimented with glass and incorporated it into his jewelry designs. His fame as a glassmaker, however, came as a result of his commission by Coty Parfums to produce decorative bottles for their fragrances. His most famous work was produced during the Art Deco period and included illuminated, frosted glass sculpture, vases and even car hood ornaments.

ADDITIONAL TIPS: The current resurgence of interest in the Art Deco period has caused the exquisite jewelry and glassware of Lalique to skyrocket in price.

RECOMMENDED READING: For more in-depth information on Lalique, you may refer to *The Official Price Guide to Glassware, The Official Price Guide to Antique Jewelry* and *The Official Identification Guide to Glassware,* published by The House of Collectibles.

	Current Price Range		P/Y Average
□ **Ashtray,** circular form, wide flat rim, amber, molded in high relief with scarabs with leaves, signed, 5¼″ high, c. 1925	300.00	500.00	350.00
□ **Ashtray,** square, stepped corners, frosted, molded with interweaving bands — one plain, the other of daisies, signed, 10″ long, c. 1925	400.00	600.00	425.00
□ **Bottle,** compressed spherical, short cylinder neck, ovoid stopper, green, molded with protruding ruffled fan designs, signed, 2½″ high, c. 1925	400.00	600.00	425.00
□ **Brooch,** sculptured lady with bat wings, translucent blue enamel, gold, maker: Lalique, French, c. 1900	5700.00	6700.00	6200.00
□ **Buckle,** rectangular shape with rounded corners, amber, molded and pierced with two twining cobras with open mouths, signed, 1¾″ long, c. 1925	800.00	1000.00	810.00

	Current Price Range		P/Y Average

☐ **Centerpiece,** round bowl with large looped-shaped handles with pierced scrolls, frosted handles molded with leaping gazelles, signed, 18½" long, c. 1925 . . . . **800.00   1200.00   825.00**

☐ **Chandelier,** domed shape, clear, molded with three bands of grape clusters and vines, pierced, signed, 13¾" diameter, c. 1925 . . . . **800.00   1000.00   850.00**

☐ **Chandelier,** domed shade, pierced and supporting four hooks, molded in high relief with peaches and leaves, 15" diameter, c. 1930 . . **1000.00   1400.00   1000.00**

☐ **Chandelier,** domed shape shade, frosted, molding on exterior of bouquets of primroses, brown wash, signed, 12" diameter, c. 1925 . . . . **600.00   800.00   615.00**

☐ **Clock,** flat panel with arched crest, molded with two females in classical dress holding garland circling etched circular clock face, on rectangular base silver painted, on four ball feet, 15¼" high, c. 1925 . . . . **8000.00   10000.00   8500.00**

☐ **Clock,** flattened rectangular frame, expands into rectangular base, clear, molded in low relief with birds perched in cherry branches, signed, 6" high, c. 1930 . . . . **800.00   1000.00   815.00**

☐ **Clock,** flattened rectangular, stepped rectangular base, clear, background of molded flowers, molded swallows flying in black enamel, signed, 6" high, c. 1925 . . . . **600.00   800.00   610.00**

☐ **Clock,** flattened square, clear and frosted, molded with nude females swimming, signed, 4½" high, c. 1925 . . . . **400.00   600.00   425.00**

☐ **Clock,** rectangular shape, frosted, pierced, molded with sparrows perched on leafy branches, signed, 6" high, c. 1925 . . . . **800.00   1000.00   800.00**

☐ **Decanter,** bell shape, short neck, clear, slightly domed stopper with molded branches of berries and leaves, signed, 8½" high, c. 1930 . . . . **600.00   800.00   650.00**

☐ **Decanter,** double-cone shape, flaring neck, teardrop on stem stopper, clear, molded with leaves radiating in bands, black ring around neck, signed, 11¼" high, c. 1925 . . . . **150.00   200.00   160.00**

☐ **Decanter,** ovoid shape, molded in pattern of blossoms on one side, the other flattened side has a large molded blossom, stopper in shape of disc with blossom design, signed, 8" high, c. 1925 . . . . **300.00   500.00   325.00**

☐ **Necklace,** priestess motif, green and blue enamel, bar link chain, gold, 3¾" long, Art Nouveau, maker: Rene Lalique, French, c. late 19th **35000.00   40000.00   37500.00**

☐ **Pendant,** flattened triangular shape with rounded corners, mold on one side with scrolling branches with berries, pierced for stringing, signed, 2" long, c. 1925 . . . . **800.00   1200.00   810.00**

	Current Price Range		P/Y Average
☐ **Pendant,** medallion motif, obverse: warrior with griffin, reverse: a lady, gold, Art Nouveau, maker: Rene Lalique, c. 1900	1000.00	1200.00	1100.00
☐ **Tray,** perfume, rectangular shape with five apertures, blossom-shaped stoppers, clear, molded with pattern of thistle branches, 8¾″ long, c. 1930	600.00	800.00	600.00
☐ **Vase,** molded, opalescent, urn shape, molded with pattern of thistles and leaves, 8½″ high, c. 1925	500.00	600.00	550.00
☐ **Vase,** opalescent, cylinder shape, flaring rim, molded with eucalyptus leaves and berries, 6½″ high, c. 1925	300.00	500.00	325.00
☐ **Vase,** opalescent, trumpet shape, frosted background, molded with bands of overlapping leaves, signed, 5⅛″ high, c. 1925	300.00	500.00	325.00
☐ **Vase,** ovoid body, rimmed neck, frosted, molded in high relief with grasshoppers and blades of grass, green and blue wash, signed, c. 1925	1000.00	1400.00	1100.00
☐ **Vase,** ovoid body, short cylinder neck, amber, molded in relief with archers hunting flying birds, signed, 10¾″ high, c. 1930	2000.00	3000.00	2200.00
☐ **Vase,** ovoid body, short cylinder neck, dark amber, molded frieze of nude men with bows and arrows hunting birds in flight, signed, 10½″ high, c. 1925	2000.00	3000.00	2200.00

LAMPS AND LIGHTING FIXTURES

TYPES: There are many different types of lighting fixtures, from grease burning to kerosene to electric. Styles of lamps and other fixtures may be named for the designer who innovated them or a distinctive feature of the lamp itself. For instance, the "Emeralite" light is a green glass shaded office lamp.

PERIOD: Lamps and lighting fixtures have been popular since the early 1700s. Collectors focus on the periods that saw significant developments in the field, such as the Art Nouveau period.

ORIGIN: Clay oil lamps have existed for at least 2000 years.

MAKERS: The most prominent makers of lamps and lighting fixtures are Tiffany, Quezal, Handel and Pairpoint. These companies produced some of the finest and most artistic lamps in existence.

COMMENTS: Although few individuals collect lamps and lighting fixtures as a hobby, these items are eagerly sought as accent pieces. Many lamps, especially the most expensive ones, are works of art as much as functional pieces.

ADDITIONAL TIPS: These listings are arranged according to the type of lighting fixture. Lamps by such distinctive makers such as Tiffany and Handel are grouped together.

LAMPS AND LIGHTING DEVICES

	Current Price Range		P/Y Average
☐ **Angle Lamp,** brass, double lacquered	190.00	280.00	235.00
☐ **Argand Lamp,** American Empire, bronze, cut glass shade	200.00	300.00	250.00
☐ **Art Nouveau Figural Lamp,** white paint, metal	170.00	210.00	190.00
☐ **Astral Lamp,** English, classical column, floral motif frosted shade, square base, 17⅜″ H., c. 1838	1100.00	1400.00	1250.00
☐ **Betty Lamp,** tin, with hanger	85.00	105.00	95.00
☐ **Boudoir Lamp,** Art Deco, Austrian porcelain, figural, fabric shade	60.00	90.00	75.00
☐ **Boudoir Lamp,** Blanc de Chine, figural base, 11½″ H. base	35.00	60.00	47.50
☐ **Bradley and Hubbard,** caramel shade, signed base, 24″ H.	550.00	700.00	625.00
☐ **Candleabrum,** Art Nouveau, bronze, figural, two lights, pate de verre shades, 20½″ H.	1200.00	1400.00	1300.00
☐ **Carriage Lamps,** brass, clear glass and red reflector lenses	275.00	325.00	300.00
☐ **Ceiling Light Fixture,** Art Deco, bronze and onyx, inverted pyramid, bronze mounts, 35″ H., c. 1933.	500.00	650.00	575.00
☐ **Ceiling Light Fixture,** pressed glass, hobnail	60.00	100.00	80.00
☐ **Chandelier,** brass and pressed glass, three lights, crystal bulbs, 24″ diameter	100.00	160.00	130.00
☐ **Chandelier,** bronze, six arms, French, 21″ diameter	60.00	100.00	80.00
☐ **Chandelier,** crystal and brass, prisms and swags, 18″ diameter	55.00	75.00	65.00
☐ **Chandelier,** Dresden, porcelain, nine arms, 24″ diameter	2400.00	3200.00	2800.00
☐ **Chandelier,** Florent, gilt metal, five lights, 17″ diameter	170.00	230.00	200.00
☐ **Chandelier,** Louis XV style, cut glass shade .	1000.00	1200.00	1100.00
☐ **Chandelier,** milk glass and cranberry overlay, prisms, five arms, 20″ diameter	120.00	200.00	160.00
☐ **Chandelier,** porcelain and d'ore bronze, six arms, blue, white and gold, 27″ diameter	180.00	260.00	220.00

	Current Price Range		P/Y Average
☐ **Chandelier,** tin circle, fifteen candle sockets, 21″ diameter, 1800s	350.00	450.00	300.00
☐ **Chandelier,** Victorian, kerosene lamp with hurricane shade, 42″ H.	270.00	350.00	310.00
☐ **Chinese Lamp,** bronze, urn form, low-relief dragon, 30″ H.	170.00	250.00	210.00
☐ **Courting Lamp,** pewter, clear and frosted front, 4″ H.	90.00	120.00	105.00
☐ **Desk Lamp,** goose neck, quezel art glass shade in trumpet form, iridescent, 15″ H., late 1800s	150.00	200.00	175.00
☐ **Emeralite Lamp,** brass, green glass globe, square brass base, 13″ H., c. 1920	110.00	150.00	130.00
☐ **Floor Lamp,** French, bronze, reeded shaft, Dresden flowers	80.00	120.00	100.00
☐ **Floor Lamp,** oak, carved diamond shaft, crossbar base	45.00	75.00	60.00
☐ **Gas Sconces,** pair, handwrought, French	300.00	360.00	330.00
☐ **"Gone With the Wind" Lamp,** umbrella shade with cupids and foliage, brass foot, 20″ H	280.00	320.00	300.00
☐ **"Gone With the Wind" Lamp,** grape pattern with green leaves, 22″ H	500.00	600.00	550.00
☐ **"Gone With the Wind" Lamp,** magnolia blossoms handpainted, 24″ H	575.00	675.00	625.00
☐ **"Gone With the Wind" Lamp,** red glass with red bull's eye, 28½″ H	650.00	750.00	700.00
☐ **Handel Desk Lamp,** square trunk base, swing porcelain shade, 15″ H.	320.00	400.00	360.00
☐ **Handel Table Lamp,** glass and metal, reverse painted, 24½″ H.	2100.00	2300.00	2200.00
☐ **Handel Table Lamp,** art glass shade, cylindrical base with handles, 24½″ H.	700.00	800.00	750.00
☐ **Handel Table Lamp,** Persian bordered glass shade, 22″ H.	1450.00	1650.00	1550.00
☐ **Hanging Lamp,** brass with chocolate glass panels, 14″ H.	65.00	85.00	75.00
☐ **Hanging Lamp,** cranberry with prisms	700.00	800.00	750.00
☐ **Hanging Lamp,** striped with canopy, 13″ H.	175.00	225.00	200.00
☐ **Hanging Lamp,** light fixture, brass and crystal, three lights, crystal bulbs, 19½″ H.	40.00	80.00	60.00
☐ **Hurricane Lamp,** pair 11″ H.	40.00	50.00	45.00
☐ **Kerosene Lamp,** Bohemian crystal, brass shaft, white marble base, cut flowers, red, 22″ H.	55.00	95.00	75.00
☐ **Kerosene Lamp,** cabbage case pattern	60.00	80.00	70.00
☐ **Kerosene Lamp,** country store fixture, brass front	140.00	160.00	150.00
☐ **Kerosene Lamp,** green pattern, milk glass base	80.00	100.00	90.00
☐ **Kerosene Lamp,** hanging fixture, cranberry glass with brass frame	180.00	220.00	200.00
☐ **Kerosene Lamp,** hobnail pattern	35.00	45.00	40.00
☐ **Kerosene Lamp,** table, Lincoln Drape pattern, amber	110.00	150.00	130.00
☐ **Kerosene Lamp,** table, overlay glass, 13″ H.	675.00	775.00	725.00

	Current Price Range		P/Y Average
Miner's Safety Lamp, brass and iron, red lens, #1000	110.00	150.00	130.00
Oil Lamp, dogtooth	30.00	40.00	35.00
Oil Lamp, Hall & Son, brass, tiered square base, frosted vintage globe, 26" H.	270.00	370.00	320.00
Oil Lamp, green depression glass	40.00	50.00	45.00
Oil Lamp, Victorian, aqua milk glass square pedestal base, hurricane chimney, 23" H., late 1800s	30.00	50.00	40.00
Oriental Lamp, elephant, bronze, wood base, 19¾" H.	400.00	580.00	490.00
Pairpoint, butterflies and roses, signed base and shade, 10" Dia.	1100.00	1300.00	1200.00
Peg Lamp, brass burner, 6" H.	70.00	90.00	80.00
Peg Lamp, ribbed glass with brass candlesticks, pair	150.00	200.00	175.00
Railroad Switch Lamp, four lenses, red and green, type 1880	40.00	80.00	60.00
Railroad Switch Lamp, Handlan, St. Louis, four lenses	50.00	80.00	65.00
Student Lamp, double brass, green glass shade with original chimney	500.00	570.00	535.00
Student Lamp, hanging double, burnished, green shade	675.00	775.00	725.00
Student Lamp, single brass front, milk glass shade	320.00	370.00	345.00
Table Lamp, American Empire, brass, glass prisms, cut frosted shade	700.00	800.00	750.00
Table Lamp, "Arrow Root," leaded glass shade with bronze base, 25½" H	8500.00	10500.00	9500.00

LANTERNS

Auto Lantern, brass, oil burning, 14½" H.	100.00	136.00	118.00
Barn Lantern, Peter Gray, Boston	100.00	150.00	125.00
Buggy Dashboard Lantern, kerosene	23.00	31.00	27.00
Candle Lantern, sheet metal painted black, 16¼" H.	65.00	85.00	75.00
Carriage Lantern, brass trim, pair	340.00	400.00	370.00
Chien Lung Period Lantern, porcelain, gourd form, pierced pedestal base, teak stand, hexagonal, 18" H., late 1700s	320.00	400.00	360.00
Chinese Junk Lantern, brass, oil	50.00	66.00	56.00
Coach Lantern, pierced, 17½" H.	170.00	210.00	190.00
Continental Lantern, brass and tin, finials, 9½" H., c. 1800s	400.00	600.00	500.00
Dietz Driving Lantern, red glass in rear, 7½" H.	125.00	165.00	145.00
Kerosene Lantern, brass base and top engraved "Joseph Gavett, Roxbury," 17" H.	250.00	300.00	275.00
Kerosene Lantern, Dietz red reflector	28.00	38.00	33.00
Miner's Lantern, tin and brass, 5½" H., Jan. 10, 1882	25.00	40.00	32.50
Paul Revere Lantern, tin with swirled punched holes	160.00	190.00	175.00

ACL Railroad Lantern, *clear globe,* $35.00-$55.00

	Current Price Range		P/Y Average
□ **Railroad Lantern,** Nazi, marked with Swastika	20.00	40.00	30.00
□ **Railroad Lantern,** New York City, red or clear globe	15.00	30.00	22.50
□ **Railroad Lantern,** San Francisco, clear globe	25.00	55.00	40.00
□ **Skater's Lantern,** brass with glass globe	75.00	100.00	87.50
□ **Ship's Lantern,** copper, pair, 16″ H.	270.00	320.00	295.00
□ **Wagon Lantern,** clamp-on type with rear red reflector	25.00	35.00	30.00
□ **Wood Lantern,** rare second material	160.00	190.00	175.00

MINIATURE LIGHTING DEVICES

□ **Acorn Burner,** brass, 6″ H.	65.00	85.00	75.00
□ **Acorn Burner,** milk glass, white, embossed with iris, clear glass chimney	180.00	220.00	200.00
□ **Acorn Burner,** opaline glass base and chimney, house scene	190.00	240.00	115.00
□ **Acorn Burner,** tin	18.00	28.00	23.00
□ **Artichoke,** red satin	50.00	70.00	60.00
□ **Aventurine,** green, glass base	40.00	60.00	50.00
□ **Banquet Lamp,** blue, glass, jeweled base, 10″ H.	270.00	350.00	310.00
□ **Bristol,** blue enamel flowers, 6½″ H.	80.00	110.00	95.00
□ **Bristol Type,** hexagonal base, figures on sides	120.00	170.00	145.00
□ **Bullseye Lamp,** by U.S. Glass Co.	45.00	55.00	50.00
□ **Christmas Tree Lamp,** clear glass	85.00	95.00	90.00
□ **Coreopsis,** green band base	45.00	55.00	50.00

	Current Price Range		P/Y Average
☐ **Cosmos,** clear glass, painted base	20.00	30.00	25.00
☐ **Cosmos,** floral motif, 8″ H.	280.00	440.00	360.00
☐ **Cosmos,** pink band base	40.00	50.00	45.00
☐ **Daisy,** by U.S. Glass	80.00	90.00	85.00
☐ **Fleur de Lis,** milk glass, by Eagle Glass Co. .	280.00	320.00	300.00
☐ **Greek Key,** clear glass	42.00	52.00	47.00
☐ **Kerosene Lamp,** pressed glass, daisy motif .	35.00	45.00	40.00
☐ **Lincoln Drape Lamp**	70.00	80.00	75.00
☐ **Melon Lamp,** yellow cased glass	60.00	70.00	65.00
☐ **Milk Glass,** chimney top with fluted stem, footed base, 5½″ H.	180.00	230.00	205.00
☐ **Night Lamp,** ribbed base	55.00	75.00	65.00
☐ **Nutmeg Burner,** brass saucer, 2″ H.	70.00	100.00	85.00
☐ **Nutmeg Burner,** clear glass base and chimney	45.00	55.00	50.00
☐ **Oil Lamp,** Greek Key	30.00	40.00	35.00
☐ **Oil Lamp,** swirl base and chimney, metal handle, 6″ H., c. 1940s	12.00	18.00	15.00
☐ **Star Lamp,** painted	40.00	60.00	50.00
☐ **Night Lamp,** swirl, narrow	40.00	50.00	45.00
☐ **Skating Lamp,** brass, link chain, 8″ H.	65.00	85.00	75.00
☐ **Table Lamp,** beehive, Pairpoint, 14½″ H. ...	450.00	600.00	525.00

LENOX

DESCRIPTION: Lenox China was founded on May 18, 1889 by Jonathan Coxon, Sr. and Walter Scott Lenox, who had met when both were employed by Ott & Brewer. The original name of the new company was the Ceramic Art Company, and Coxon was its president with Lenox as secretary/treasurer and art director. Company activities in the early years included production of both decorated and undecorated wares. By the end of the C.A.C. period, they were producing around 600 different shapes decorated both in standard and original fashion. The emphasis was on giftware instead of dinnerware, and many of the more interesting Lenox collectibles date from this time. With the formation of Lenox, Inc., in 1906, dinnerware production was greatly expanded. Hand-painting, although it would continue for another half-century, became less important than transfer decoration. By the time of World War II, the company had produced more than 3,000 different shapes decorated with thousands of different designs. Since World War II, the company has added crystal bone china, and oven-proof ware to their list. The china is now made in Pomona, NJ, and new corporate headquarters were recently opened in Lawrenceville, NJ. The Lenox corporate umbrella now covers a diversified group of companies making everything from school rings to candles.

MARKS: Lenox marks are extremely complicated. For a complete discussion refer to *The Official Price Guide to Pottery and Porcelain* and *The Official Identification Guide to Pottery and Porcelain,* published by The House of Collectibles.

	Current Price Range		P/Y Average
☐ **Ashtray,** shape #2997, coral and white apple blossom design, Lenox wreath mark	19.00	23.50	21.00
☐ **Bouillon cup and saucer,** shape #175, scalloped rim and fancy handles, hand-painted tiny roses, C.A.C. lavender palette mark	68.00	78.00	73.00
☐ **Bowl,** shape #823, 4″ x 10″, scattered hand-painted tiny flowers inside and out, gold trim, artist's initials, Lenox palette mark	90.00	100.00	95.00
☐ **Butter pat,** item #176, 3″, hand-painted little pink roses with gold trim, Lenox wreath mark	35.00	38.00	36.00
☐ **Candlesticks,** shape #147, 10½″, high, brushed gold trim, Lenox wreath mark, pair . .	115.00	125.00	120.00
☐ **Chocolate pot,** shape #107, 8″ high, beautifully done floral design on shaded background, gold trim, signed W. H. Morley, transition mark	420.00	470.00	445.00
☐ **Cigar jar,** shape #346, 3½″, x 3½″, gold trim and monogram, Lenox palette mark	35.00	38.00	36.00
☐ **Cigarette box,** shape #2424, plain green, Lenox wreath mark	29.00	33.00	30.00
☐ **Cigarette holder,** shape #2656, 2¼″, high, shape with fluting on base, plain white, Lenox wreath mark	15.00	18.00	17.00
☐ **Cigarette jar,** shape #347, 2½″ x 2½″, undecorated, Lenox wreath	20.00	23.50	21.00
☐ **Coffeepot,** shape #108, 8″ high, hand-painted scattered wild flowers, nicely done gold trim, artist signed and dated, C.A.C. lavender palette mark	135.00	150.00	140.00
☐ **Comport,** shape #441, 9¾″, open ornate handles, tall base, hand-painted roses, yellow on one side, pink on other, gold trim on rims and handles, artist signed and dated, C.A.C. lavender palette mark	130.00	145.00	140.00
☐ **Box,** shape #819, 5½″ x 3″, finial, round, medium pink with gold trim, gold finial, Lenox wreath mark	50.00	55.00	52.50
☐ **Cup and saucer,** shape #2, 2¼″, ribbed design, fancy handle, eggshell thin, beige matte finish with gold trim, C.A.C. red palette mark	70.00	78.00	75.00

	Current Price Range		P/Y Average

□ **Desk Set, Three-pieces,** unmarked rolling blotters, two-compartment standing letter holder (6″ x 8″), and covered inkwell with 5″ underplate, monochromatic blue Delft type scene with houses, children, etc., artist's initials, transition mark and Tiffany & Company mark **650.00   720.00   675.00**

□ **Ewer,** shape #444, 12″ high, hand-painted peacock on shaded background, artist signed, C.A.C. palette mark **200.00   235.00   215.00**

□ **Horn of plenty,** shape #2754, 7″ high, Lenox Rose pattern, Lenox wreath mark **110.00   120.00   115.00**

□ **Jug,** shape #534, 4″ tall, hand-painted grapes and leaves on shaded background, gold inside spout, signed G. Morley, transition mark **310.00   360.00   320.00**

□ **Ladle rest/sugar bowl,** shape #72½, 4½″ diameter, tiny pink flowers beneath rim, gold trim, artist signed and dated, C.A.C. green palette mark **58.00   63.00   62.00**

□ **Loving cup,** shape #258, three-handled, decorated with fruit on a shaded background, gold handles and rims, C.A.C. lavender palette mark **85.00   95.00   90.00**

□ **Match holder,** shape #2425, undecorated, Lenox wreath mark **42.00   47.50   44.00**

□ **Match jar,** shape #348, 1¾″ x 1¾″, undecorated, Lenox wreath mark **17.00   20.00   18.00**

□ **Muffineer,** shape number unknown, hand-painted flowers, Lenox wreath mark **70.00   75.00   72.50**

□ **Mug,** shape #251, 4⅞″ high, gold trim on handle and rims, gold monogram on front, Lenox palette mark **42.00   47.50   45.00**

□ **Pitcher,** shape #24, 5″ high, gold trim on handle and brushed gold near rims, C.A.C. wreath mark, eggshell thin **20.00   23.50   21.00**

□ **Salt shaker,** shape #882, 5″ high, hand-painted with Art Deco type design in raised enamel effect, Lenox palette mark, pair **25.00   28.00   27.00**

□ **Shaving mug,** shape #201, 4″ tall, hand-painted violets on shaded background, C.A.C. palette mark **170.00   195.00   180.00**

□ **Sugar and creamer,** shape #38, creamer 4″, sugar 4½″ diameter, raised gold paste trim, C.A.C. lavender palette mark **170.00   195.00   180.00**

□ **Teapot,** shape #946, 3¾″, hand-painted roses, pink on one side, red on the other, gold trim, artist signed, Lenox palette mark **62.00   70.00   65.00**

□ **Tea strainer,** shape #339, hand-painted roses and gold trim, transition mark **270.00   320.00   300.00**

□ **Tobacco jar,** shape #328, 7½″ high, hand-painted Indian smoking peace pipe, Lenox palette mark **180.00   220.00   200.00**

□ **Tray,** shape #983, 11⅜″ x 7⅛″, rounded-off corners, gold trim, Lenox palette mark **70.00   78.00   73.00**

Pitcher, *shape #352, transition mark,* **$340.00-$395.00**

	Current Price Range		P/Y Average
☐ **Shot glass,** shape #269, tiny ears or corn hand-painted on front, gold trim, Lenox palette mark	30.00	32.50	31.00
☐ **Vase,** item #27, 7½" high, bulbous bottom, white top with coral bottom, Lenox wreath mark, see photo	35.00	38.00	36.00
☐ **Vase,** item #27, 7½" high, bulbous, bottom, beige matte finish with raised gold paste work, lavender palette C.A.C. mark	110.00	120.00	115.00

LICENSE PLATES

MATERIAL: Pre-1910 license plates were made of various materials including leather. Since then, plates have been made of metal.

COMMENTS: License plates are the first auto collectible to attract widespread interest. Some collectors focus on plates from the same state, while others collect plates in chronological order. Older plates show changes in design, size and color. Because of materials used, most plates are not in mint condition.

ADDITIONAL TIPS: The following sampling of license plates is listed alphabetically by state. The year follows.

	Current Price Range		P/Y Average
☐ **Arkansas,** 1932	17.50	26.00	18.50
☐ **California,** 1930	17.50	26.00	18.50
☐ **Connecticut,** 1915	80.00	90.00	85.00
☐ **Iowa,** 1932	22.50	38.00	27.00
☐ **Maine,** 1920	7.50	14.00	9.00
☐ **Kansas,** 1933	13.50	20.00	15.00
☐ **Massachusetts,** 1915	22.50	38.00	27.00
☐ **Rhode Island,** 1926	12.50	18.00	14.00
☐ **Wisconsin,** 1925	12.50	18.00	14.00
☐ **Michigan,** good condition, 1916	50.00	60.00	52.00
☐ **Ohio,** good condition, 1922	60.00	70.00	62.00
☐ **Pennsylvania,** 1908	55.00	65.00	60.00

LIGHTNING ROD ORNAMENTS

TOPIC: A lightning rod ornament is a glass ball that has a hole through its middle. This allows it to be placed on a lightning rod for decoration. These ornaments resemble very large Christmas ornaments except for the hole going all the way through the ball. Other decorations for lightning rods, such as ornamental tips to surmount the rod, are also collected, though much more rarely.

TYPES: Lightning rod ornaments can be classified by type of glass or shape. Spheres are the most common shape, although the teardrop and the doorknob forms are not unusual.

PERIOD: Most of the collectible balls were produced between 1880 and 1910. Lightning rod ornaments were just coming into vogue in the mid-1800s.

MATERIALS: These items were almost exclusively made of glass. Porcelain is seen very rarely.

COMMENTS: Lightning rod ornaments can be exquisitely beautiful and they are well suited to display. Since few individuals are aware of them and collect them, prices are relatively low for most items.

ADDITIONAL TIP: These specimens can be cleaned with a mild solution of soapsuds. After cleaning, they may be rubbed with olive oil on a rag to make them sparkle.

	Current Price Range		P/Y Average
□ **Diddie Blitzer,** mercury glass ball	80.00	100.00	90.00
□ **Electra ball,** amber/brown	40.00	48.00	44.00
□ **Hawkeye,** brick red	120.00	150.00	135.00
□ **Mercury glass,** gold-toned, 4½″ Dia.	30.00	36.00	33.00
□ **Milk glass,** doorknob ball, orange	250.00	280.00	265.00
□ **Moon and star ball,** red	60.00	70.00	65.00

LINCOLNIANA

DESCRIPTION: Lincolniana is memorabilia dealing with Abraham Lincoln, America's 16th President.

TYPES: There are all types of Lincoln Memorabilia from photographs to campaign ribbons.

PERIOD: Lincoln served as president from 1861 to 1865. He was assassinated by actor John Wilkes Booth on April 14, 1865 at Ford's Theater in Washington. Most of Lincoln's collectibles are items dealing with his political life.

□ **Advertising Poster,** carte-de-visite photograph of Lincoln mounted as the centerpiece of an advertising poster, advertises a Providence, R.I. salvage dealer's business seeking to buy "papers, rags and junk metals."	45.00	60.00	51.00
□ **Banner,** cotton, bust portrait with no wording in white and black, marked Joseph Rhein, Detroit, undated, probably post-assassination, 36″ x 48″	400.00	500.00	430.00

	Current Price Range		P/Y Average

☐ **Cabinet Card,** with applied albumen photo print, card consists of lengthy eulogilistic text, marked Bancroft, Philadelphia, photo is 2½ " x 3½ ", card overall is 9" x 14", 1865 .... **170.00 200.00 180.00**

☐ **Ferrotype,** bearded Lincoln pictured, brass frame **140.00 160.00 150.00**

☐ **Locket,** with albumin portrait photograph, tortoiseshell, oval, Lincoln bearded, probably from the 1860 campaign, 1¼ " x 1¾ " **160.00 190.00 172.00**
Note: The presence or absence of a beard is one certain method of placing at least an approximate date on Lincoln portraits. He began growing the beard in late 1860.

☐ **Medal,** copper, profile bust with wording, "Repub Cand for Pres/Prot(ector) to Amer Industry, Free Homes for Free Men," from the 1860 campaign **40.00 55.00 47.00**

☐ **Medal For Funeral,** white metal (imitation silver), pictures willow tree and urn with wording, "Died by the Hands of a Rebel Assassin," black silk ribbon at top **40.00 55.00 46.00**

☐ **Medal,** North Western Sanitary Fair, bronze, profile bust facing right, official U.S. Mint issue struck in early 1865 before his assassination **250.00 350.00 280.00**
Note: The "sanitary fairs," held in various cities during the Civil War, were glorified carnivals whose proceeds went to buy medicine and clothing for Union troops.

☐ **Medal,** white metal (imitation silver), profile bust with wording, "A Foe to Traitors, No Compromise With Armed Rebels," probably from first year of Civil War **60.00 80.00 68.00**

☐ **Merchant's Token,** brass, Stoner and Shroyer Dry Goods, Adamsville, Ohio, protrait bust facing right **230.00 280.00 250.00**
Note: Merchant tokens, given to customers in place of pennies when change was scarce, where issued profusely during the Civil War in all eastern and midwest cities. This is one of the rarer examples and has a much higher value than most.

☐ **Paperweight,** Zanesville tile **35.00 45.00 39.00**

☐ **Photograph,** carte-de-visite by Matthew Brady, half length seated portrait with hands resting on arms of ornate armchair, marked "Brady's National Photographic Portrait Galleries, 352 Pennsylvania Avenue, Washington, D.C.," dated January 8, 1864 .... **500.00 600.00 540.00**

☐ **Photograph,** John Wilkes Booth, rare **125.00 135.00 130.00**

☐ **Photograph,** Lincoln and family, taken by Joseph Hoover, 1866 .... **85.00 100.00 92.00**

☐ **Photograph,** Lincoln's Tomb, three soldiers stand guard at front, taken by F.W. Ingmire . **50.00 60.00 55.00**

☐ **Picture,** Lincoln and wife Mary Todd, small .. **40.00 50.00 45.00**

Envelope, *Civil War design, Lincoln and overall bicolored motif,*
$75.00-$100.00
(photo courtesy of ©Lou McCulloch, Highland Heights, OH)

	Current Price Range		P/Y Average

☐ **Print,** portrait within oval by Kellogg, dove of peace with wording "Justice, Liberty, Equality," 12″ x 16″ **90.00 115.00 103.00**

☐ **Ribbon,** silk, made in Switzerland, multicolor, beardless Lincoln pictured, "A. Lincoln, President", written underneath picture, 1861 .... **650.00 700.00 675.00**

☐ **Ribbon,** silk, made in Switzerland, "With Charity to all, with malice for none," written above portrait of Lincoln, weeping Columbia with face buried in U.S. flag below portrait .. **250.00 300.00 275.00**

☐ **Stereo Card,** image #1312 in the "Photographic War History" series published by Taylor & Huntington after the Civil War in 1880s, from an original stereo plate done by Mathew Brady in 1864 .... **250.00 275.00 262.00**

☐ **Stereo Photograph,** box at Ford's Theater occupied by Lincoln at the time of his assassination, from the Anthony series with number 3403, made from a Matthew Brady negative **75.00 95.00 83.00**

☐ **Stereo Photograph,** chair in which Lincoln was seated at time of assassination, from the Anthony series with number 3406, made from a Brady negative **75.00 95.00 82.00**

☐ **Stereo Photograph,** funeral procession of Abraham Lincoln passing through Philadelphia (Broad Street), unmarked, housed in a flat yellow mat **160.00 190.00 172.00**

☐ **Stereo Photograph,** funeral procession of Abraham Lincoln passing through New York (lower Broadway), from the Anthony series with number 2954 .... **160.00 190.00 172.00**

☐ **Statue,** glass, Gillinder and Sons for the 1876 Centennial Exposition, portrait bust of Lincoln, 6″ **320.00 365.00 335.00**

☐ **Stereo Photograph,** half length portrait from the Anthony Prominent Portraits series, numbered 2968, housed in a mount **700.00 900.00 765.00**

☐ **Tintype,** bearded Lincoln, 2¼″ x 3⅞″, rare ... **450.00 500.00 475.00**

☐ **Tintype,** taken by Mathew Brady, 1860, 3¾″ x 2½″ **750.00 800.00 775.00**

LUNCH BOXES

DESCRIPTION: The colorful lunch boxes used by school children are avidly sought by collectors. Usually these boxes feature comic and science fiction characters. Lunch boxes from the 1950s-1980s are particularly interesting.

ADDITIONAL TIPS: Condition is extremely important and rust, scratches or dents will lower value dramatically.

RECOMMENDED READING: For further information refer to *The Official Price Guide to Science Fiction and Fantasy Collectibles* and *The Official Price Guide to Comic Books and Collectibles* published by The House of Collectibles.

	Current Price Range		P/Y Average
☐ **Battlestar Galactica,** *made by Aladdin, 7"x 7¾"*	9.00	12.00	10.50
☐ **Bionic Woman**	4.00	6.00	5.00
☐ **Captain Astro**	10.00	12.00	11.00
☐ **Enterprise,** *on the side with scenes from the television show Aladdin-Hump Backed, 1978*	50.00	70.00	60.00
☐ **Flying Nun,** *Screengems made by Aladdin, lithographed tin, illustration of Sally Field, 1968*	10.00	15.00	11.00
☐ **Green Hornet**	9.00	11.00	10.00
☐ **Jungle Book,** *Walt Disney Productions, lithographed tin, illustration of Mowgli, the Jungle Boy and other characters*	7.00	10.00	8.25
☐ **King Kong,** *Dino deLaurentis, lithographed tin, 1977*	9.00	12.00	9.75
☐ **Kirk,** *on one side, King-Seely Thermos Co., from the motion picture, Spock and McCoy on the other side, thermos captioned "Star Trek," 1979*	10.00	15.00	12.50
☐ **Marvel Comics Super Heroes,** *Marvel Comics Group, Aladdin, illustrations of The Fantastic Four, Thor, Spiderman and Captain Marvel, with vinyl thermos, 1976*	12.00	16.00	13.00
☐ **Return Of The Jedi,** *1983*	6.00	8.00	7.00
☐ **Space 1999,** *metal*	5.00	7.00	6.00

	Current Price Range		P/Y Average

Superman, *Adco-Liberty Manufacturing Co./Superman Corp./National Periodical Publications, lithographed tin, artwork shows Superman battling robot with planes circling around, 6" x 9", c. 1940-50* 120.00 150.00 **130.00**
Note: Artwork could be Wayne Boring; hard to tell for certain as a number of the Superman artists used very similar styles.
The Empire Strikes Back, *1980* 8.00 10.00 **9.00**
U.F.O., *Century 21 Merchandising Company, lithographed tin, 1973* 12.00 17.00 **13.45**

LUNCH BOX AND THERMOS SETS

Batman	25.00	27.00	**26.00**
Battlestar Galactica	8.00	10.00	**9.00**
Green Hornet	20.00	22.00	**21.00**
Land Of The Giants	12.00	15.00	**13.50**
Lost In Space, *metal*	30.00	35.00	**32.00**
Monsters	8.00	10.00	**9.00**
Planet Of The Apes, *metal*	10.00	12.00	**11.00**
Space Capsule, *1960*	8.00	10.00	**9.00**
Space 1999	10.00	12.00	**11.00**
Star Trek, *1968*	50.00	60.00	**55.00**
Superman, *1967*	12.00	15.00	**13.50**
UFO, *metal*	8.00	10.00	**9.00**

THERMOS

Astronauts, *plastic*	4.00	6.00	**5.00**
Batman	10.00	12.00	**11.00**
Munsters	10.00	12.00	**11.00**
Planet Of The Apes	4.00	6.00	**5.00**

Tom Corbett Space Cadet, *Aladdin, bearing the copyright notice of Rockhill Radio, imprinted with a brightly colored illustration, 6½", 1952* 20.00 25.00 **21.00**

Star Trek, *Paramount Pictures,* **$50.00-$60.00**

LUXARDO BOTTLES

DESCRIPTION: Luxardo bottles are figural decanters produced by the Luxardo Company of Torreglia, Italy. They were first imported to America in 1930.

TYPES: Luxardo produces both glass and majolica figural bottles. Classical and natural history themes dominate the decorative bottles.

COMMENTS: Luxardo bottles are often blends of a variety of colors. This careful blending of colors attracts collectors.

ADDITIONAL TIPS: For more information, consult *The Official Price Guide to Bottles, Old and New,* published by The House of Collectibles.

	Current Price Range		P/Y Average
☐ **Alabaster Fish,** figural, c. 1960-67-68	19.00	26.00	22.00
☐ **Alabaster Goose,** figural, c. 1960-67-68, green and white, wings, etc.	19.00	26.00	22.00
☐ **Apple Figural,** c. 1960, yellow apple, green leaves	10.00	15.00	13.50
☐ **Assyrian Ashtray Decanter,** c. 1961, gray, tan and black	16.00	22.00	19.00
☐ **Autumn Wine Pitcher,** c. 1958, hand painted country scene, handled pitcher	30.00	40.00	35.00
☐ **Babylon Decanter,** c. 1960, dark green and gold	16.00	23.00	19.50
☐ **Baby Amphoras,** c. 1956, six hand painted miniature bottles, set vari-colored	16.00	23.00	19.50
☐ **Florentine Majolica,** c. 1956, round handled decanter, painted pitcher, yellow, dragon, blue wings	21.00	27.00	24.50
☐ **Gambia,** c. 1961, black princess, kneeling holding tray, gold trim, 10¾ "	14.00	19.00	16.50
☐ **Golden Fakir,** seated snake charmer, with flute and snakes, gold	26.00	37.00	32.00
☐ **1961, Fakir 1960,** black and gray	26.00	37.00	32.00
☐ **Gondola,** c. 1959, highly glazed "abstract" gondola and gondolier in black, orange and yellow, stopper on upper prow, 12¾ "	21.00	27.00	24.50
☐ **Same as above,** miniature , 4½ "	11.00	16.00	14.50

Luxardo Calypso Girl, *figural, (c. 1962), black, West Indian girl, flower headdress in bright color,* **$14.00-$19.00**

	Current Price Range		P/Y Average
☐ **Gondola,** c. 1960, same as 1959, stopper moved from prow to stern	14.00	19.00	16.50
☐ **Same as above,** miniature	11.00	15.00	13.00
☐ **Grapes,** pear figural	24.00	34.00	29.00
☐ **Opal Majolica,** c. 1957, two gold handles, translucent opal top, pink base, also used as lamp base, 10″	14.00	19.00	16.50
☐ **Penguin,** Murano glass figural, c. 1968, black and white penguin, crystal base	26.00	37.00	32.00
☐ **Pheasant,** red and gold figural, c. 1960, red and gold glass bird on crystal base	23.00	35.00	28.00
☐ **Pheasant,** Murano glass figural, c. 1960, red and clear glass on a crystal base	26.00	37.00	32.00
☐ **Primavera Amphora,** c. 1958, two handled vase shape, with floral design in yellow, green and blue, 9¾″	14.00	19.00	17.00
☐ **Puppy,** Cucciolo glass figural, c. 1961, amber and green glass	26.00	37.00	32.00
☐ **Puppy,** Murano glass figural, c. 1960, amber glass, crystal base	26.00	37.00	32.00
☐ **Silver Blue Decanter,** c. 1952-55, hand painted silver flowers and leaves	22.00	28.00	25.00

	Current Price Range		P/Y Average
☐ **Silver Brown Decanter,** c. 1952-55, hand-painted silver flowers and leaves	26.00	37.00	32.00
☐ **Sir Lancelot,** c. 1962, figure of English knight in full armor with embossed shield, tan-gray with gold, 12″	14.00	19.00	16.50
☐ **Spring-Box Amphora,** c. 1952, vase with handle, leaping African deer with floral and lattice background, black, brown, 9¾″	14.00	19.00	16.50
☐ **Squirrel,** glass figural, c. 1968, amethyst colored squirrel on crystal base	30.00	40.00	35.00
☐ **Sudan,** c. 1960, two handle classic vase, incised figures, African motif in browns, blue, yellow and gray, 13½″	14.00	19.00	16.50
☐ **Tower OF Fruit,** majolicas, Torre Bianca, c. 1962, white and gray tower of fruit, 10¼″ ...	16.00	24.00	20.00
☐ **Torre Rosa,** c. 1962, rose tinted tower of fruit, 10¼″	16.00	24.00	20.00
☐ **Torre Tinta,** c. 1962, multicolor tower of fruit, natural shades	16.00	24.00	20.00
☐ **Tower Of Fruit,** c. 1968, various fruits in natural colors, 22¼″	16.00	24.00	20.00

MAGAZINES

DESCRIPTION: Magazines are periodicals usually containing articles and illustrations.

TYPES: There are many types of magazines including nature, sports, home, garden and news.

COMMENTS: Hobbyists enjoy magazine collecting because periodicals capture a part of history. Magazines detail world events which make interesting reading decades later.

ADDITIONAL TIPS: Many hobbyists collect the issues of only one magazine such as Life, National Geographic or Playboy. Others collect magazines topically buying periodicals with photographs and articles about their favorite Hobbywood stars, presidents or sports heroes. Another way to collect magazines is by subject.

RECOMMENDED READING: For extensive information on a wide variety of magazines refer to *The Official Price Guide to Paperbacks and Magazines,* published by The House of Collectibles.

House Beautiful, *September, 1926,* **$4.00-$6.00**

NATIONAL GEOGRAPHIC	Current Price Range		P/Y Average
☐ January, 1899	25.00	33.00	28.00
☐ February, 1899	25.00	33.00	28.00
☐ March, 1899	45.00	60.00	51.00
☐ April, 1899	50.00	65.00	57.00
☐ May, 1899	47.00	62.00	52.00
☐ June, 1899	35.00	45.00	39.00
☐ July, 1899	50.00	65.00	57.00
☐ August, 1899	25.00	33.00	28.00
☐ September, 1899	25.00	33.00	28.00
☐ October, 1899	29.00	36.00	32.00
☐ November, 1899	25.00	33.00	28.00
☐ December, 1899	29.00	36.00	32.00
☐ January, 1900	25.00	33.00	28.00
☐ February, 1900	22.00	28.00	24.50
☐ March, 1900	22.00	28.00	24.50
☐ April, 1900	22.00	28.00	24.50
☐ May, 1900	22.00	28.00	24.50
☐ June, 1900	30.00	38.00	33.00
☐ July, 1900	30.00	38.00	33.00
☐ August, 1900	22.00	28.00	24.50
☐ September, 1900	30.00	38.00	33.00
☐ October, 1900	22.00	28.00	24.50
☐ November, 1900	22.00	28.00	24.50
☐ December, 1900	22.00	28.00	24.50
☐ January, 1901	24.00	31.00	27.00

	Current Price Range		P/Y Average
☐ February, 1901	30.00	38.00	33.00
☐ March, April, May, June, July, August, September, 1901	22.00	28.00	24.50
☐ January, 1902	35.00	45.00	39.00
☐ February, March, April, May, June, 1902	22.00	28.00	24.50
☐ July, 1902	23.00	29.00	25.00
☐ August, 1902	28.00	35.00	31.00
☐ September, October, November, December, 1902	22.00	28.00	24.50
☐ January, 1903	24.00	31.00	27.00
☐ February, 1903	35.00	45.00	39.00
☐ March, April, 1903	22.00	28.00	24.50
☐ June, July, 1903	24.00	31.00	27.00
☐ August, 1903	22.00	28.00	24.50
☐ September, 1903	24.00	31.00	27.00
☐ October, 1903	22.00	28.00	24.50
☐ November, 1903	28.00	35.00	31.00
☐ December, 1903	30.00	38.00	33.00
☐ January, February, March, 1904	35.00	45.00	39.00
☐ April, 1904	24.00	31.00	27.00
☐ May, 1904	35.00	45.00	39.00
☐ June, July, August, September, 1904	24.00	31.00	27.00
☐ November, 1904	32.00	41.00	36.00
☐ December, 1904	24.00	31.00	27.00
☐ January, February, March, 1905	40.00	53.00	45.00
☐ April, 1905	17.00	22.00	19.50
☐ May, 1905	16.00	21.00	18.00
☐ June, 1905	11.00	15.00	12.50
☐ July, August, Seeptember, October, November, December, 1905	9.00	12.00	10.50
☐ January, 1906	10.00	13.00	11.50
☐ February, 1906	9.00	12.00	10.50
☐ March, 1906	10.00	13.00	11.50
☐ June, 1906 (San Francisco earthquake)	11.00	15.00	13.00
☐ July, 1906	9.00	12.00	10.50
☐ August, 1906	10.00	13.00	11.50
☐ September, 1906	9.00	12.00	10.50
☐ October, 1906	10.00	13.00	11.50
☐ November, December, 1906	9.00	12.00	10.50
☐ January, 1907	10.00	13.00	11.50
☐ February, March, 1907	9.00	12.00	10.50
☐ April, May, June, 1907	8.00	11.00	9.50
☐ July, 1907	9.00	12.00	10.50
☐ August, September, 1907	8.00	11.00	9.50
☐ October, 1907	9.00	12.00	10.50
☐ November, December, 1907	8.00	11.00	9.50
☐ January, 1908	14.00	19.00	16.00
☐ February, 1908	10.00	13.00	11.50
☐ March, 1908	9.00	12.00	10.50
☐ April, 1908	14.00	19.00	16.50
☐ May, June, July, August, 1908	9.00	12.00	10.50
☐ December, 1908	8.00	11.00	9.50
☐ January, 1909	18.00	25.00	21.00
☐ February, 1909	10.00	13.00	11.50
☐ March, 1909	9.00	12.00	10.50
☐ April, 1909	7.50	10.00	8.50

	Current Price Range		P/Y Average
☐ May, 1909	8.00	11.00	9.50
☐ June, 1909	7.50	10.00	8.50
☐ July, 1909	9.00	12.00	10.50
☐ August, 1909	7.50	10.00	8.50
☐ October, 1909	10.00	13.00	11.50
☐ January, 1910	7.50	10.00	8.50
☐ February, March, 1910	8.00	11.00	9.50
☐ July, August, September, October, November, December, 1910	7.50	10.00	8.50
☐ January, February, March, April, 1911	7.00	9.50	8.00
☐ May, 1911	7.50	10.00	8.50
☐ December, 1911	7.00	9.50	8.00
☐ January, February, 1912	7.00	9.50	8.00
☐ May, June, July, August, 1912	6.00	8.00	7.00
☐ September, 1912 (Head Hunters)	7.00	9.50	8.00
☐ December, 1912	6.00	8.00	7.00
☐ January, 1913	7.00	9.50	8.00
☐ February, 1913	6.00	8.00	7.00
☐ May, June, July, August, 1913	5.50	7.50	6.50
☐ September, 1913 (Egyptian relics)	8.00	11.00	9.50
☐ January, 1914 (North Africa)	5.00	7.00	6.00
☐ February, March, April, 1914	4.25	5.75	5.00
☐ May, 1914 (Birds)	5.00	7.00	6.00
☐ June, 1914	4.25	5.75	5.00
☐ August, 1914 (Grand Canyon)	5.00	7.00	6.00
☐ September, 1914	4.25	5.75	5.00
☐ January, February, March, April, 1915	4.00	5.50	4.75

PLAYBOY

☐ October, 1955	30.00	40.00	23.50
☐ November, 1955	30.00	40.00	23.50
☐ December, 1955	35.00	45.00	29.50
☐ January, 1956	23.00	30.00	25.00
☐ February, 1956	18.00	23.00	20.00
☐ March, 1956	18.00	23.00	20.00
☐ April, 1956	18.00	23.00	20.00
☐ May, 1956	18.00	23.00	20.00
☐ June, 1956	18.00	23.00	20.00
☐ July, 1956	18.00	23.00	20.00
☐ August, 1956	18.00	23.00	20.00
☐ September, 1956	18.00	23.00	20.00
☐ October, 1956	18.00	23.00	20.00
☐ November, 1956	18.00	23.00	20.00
☐ December, 1956	23.00	30.00	25.00
☐ January, 1957	10.00	15.00	12.00
☐ February, 1957	8.00	11.00	9.00
☐ March, 1957	8.00	11.00	9.00
☐ April, 1957	8.00	11.00	9.00
☐ May, 1957	8.00	11.00	9.00
☐ June, 1957	8.00	11.00	9.00
☐ August, 1957	8.00	11.00	9.00
☐ September, 1957	8.00	11.00	9.00
☐ October, 1957	8.00	11.00	9.00
☐ November, 1957	8.00	11.00	9.00
☐ December, 1957	10.00	15.00	12.00

	Current Price Range		P/Y Average
☐ *January, 1958*	10.00	15.00	12.00
☐ *February, 1958*	7.00	10.00	8.00
☐ *March, 1959*	7.00	10.00	8.00
☐ *July, 1958*	7.00	10.00	8.00
☐ *August, 1958*	7.00	10.00	8.00
☐ *October, 1958*	7.00	10.00	8.00
☐ *November, 1958*	7.00	10.00	8.00
☐ *December, 1958*	10.00	15.00	12.00
☐ *January, 1959*	9.00	13.00	10.00
☐ *February, 1959*	7.00	10.00	8.00
☐ *March, 1959*	7.00	10.00	8.00
☐ *August, 1959*	7.00	10.00	8.00
☐ *September, 1959*	7.00	10.00	8.00
☐ *November, 1959*	7.00	10.00	8.00
☐ *December, 1959*	9.00	13.00	10.00
☐ *January, 1960*	16.00	21.00	17.00
☐ *April, 1960*	7.00	10.00	8.00
☐ *May, 1960*	7.00	10.00	8.00
☐ *June, 1960*	7.00	10.00	8.00
☐ *July, 1960*	7.00	10.00	8.00
☐ *August, 1960*	7.00	10.00	8.00
☐ *September, 1960*	7.00	10.00	8.00
☐ *December, 1960 (five favorite "Christmas Playmates")*	16.00	21.00	17.00
☐ *February, 1961 ("Girls of New York")*	8.00	11.00	9.00
☐ *March, 1961*	7.00	10.00	8.00
☐ *April, 1961*	7.00	10.00	8.00
☐ *May, 1961 ("Girls of Sweden")*	8.00	11.00	9.00
☐ *June, 1961*	7.00	10.00	8.00
☐ *July, 1961*	7.00	10.00	8.00
☐ *August, 1961*	7.00	10.00	8.00
☐ *September, 1961*	7.00	10.00	8.00
☐ *October, 1961*	7.00	10.00	8.00
☐ *November, 1961*	7.00	10.00	8.00
☐ *December, 1961*	10.00	15.00	12.00
☐ *January, 1962*	13.00	17.00	14.00
☐ *February, 1962*	7.00	10.00	8.00
☐ *April, 1962*	7.00	10.00	8.00
☐ *June, 1962*	7.00	10.00	8.00
☐ *July, 1962 (playmate: Janet Pilgrim)*	8.00	11.00	9.00
☐ *August, 1962*	7.00	10.00	8.00
☐ *October, 1962*	7.00	10.00	8.00
☐ *November, 1962*	7.00	10.00	8.00
☐ *December, 1962*	13.00	17.00	14.00
☐ *January, 1963 (Elizabeth Taylor in "Cleopatra")*	18.00	23.00	17.00
☐ *February, 1963 (interview: Frank Sinatra)*	11.00	15.00	12.00
☐ *April, 1963 ("Girls of Africa")*	8.00	11.00	9.00
☐ *May, 1963*	5.00	8.00	6.00
☐ *June, 1963*	9.00	12.00	10.00
☐ *July, 1963*	5.00	8.00	6.00
☐ *August, 1956*	5.00	8.00	6.00
☐ *September, (Romy Schneider, Sarah Miles, Claudia Cardinale)*	13.00	17.00	14.00
☐ *October, 1963 (Elsa Martinelli)*	10.00	15.00	11.00
☐ *December, 1963 (10th anniversary special with Heffner's "Ten Favorite Playmates")*	18.00	23.00	19.00

	Current Price Range		P/Y Average
☐ January, 1964 (Marilyn Monroe)	23.00	30.00	25.00
☐ February, 1964 (Mamie Van Doren and flash-back on playmates of 1954)	9.00	12.00	10.00
☐ March, 1964 ("Girls of Russia")	7.00	10.00	8.00
☐ April, 1964	7.00	10.00	8.00
☐ May, 1964 (playmate: Donna Michelle)	10.00	15.00	11.00
☐ July, 1964 (Brigitte Bardot)	10.00	15.00	11.00
☐ August, 1964	5.00	8.00	6.00
☐ September, 1964 (Elke Sommer)	7.00	10.00	8.00
☐ October, 1964	7.00	10.00	8.00
☐ November, 1964 ("Girls of Germany")	7.00	10.00	8.00
☐ December, 1964	15.00	20.00	16.00

MAPS

TOPIC: Printed maps showing the layout of the land were printed as early as the mid-1400s. Later maps featured landmarks, altitudes, territorial boundaries and even more specialized information such as mineral deposits. Of course, the most common map found today is the road map.

TYPES: Maps can be traditional or "bird's eye" perspective of a town or other small area. "Bird's eye" maps feature the town as seen from one point in space, while traditional maps are not done in perspective.

PERIOD: Artistically and historically, maps from the 1600s are the most desirable. For the purposes of the average collector, however, most specimens date from the 1800s.

COMMENTS: Maps are collected both for their beauty and their historical importance. Often maps reflect the misconception people had about distances and relationships between land forms.

ADDITIONAL TIPS: Since maps with margins are worth more than those which have been trimmed down, examine the margin area carefully to determine its condition. Also look for creases caused by careless handling, since these lessen the value of the map. Condition is very important in the map collecting field. For more information, please refer to *The Official Price Guide to Paper Collectibles,* published by The House of Collectibles.

Atlas, *North America, J. Olney's Atlas, engraved by D. Robinson, 1829,* **$40.00-$45.00**
Photo courtesy of Lou McCulloch, Highland Heights, OH 44143.

	Current Price Range		P/Y Average

☐ A Map of the Most Inhabited Part of New England, containing the Provinces of Massachusetts Bay and New Hampshire with the Colonies of Connecticut and Rhode Island, colored outlines, two section, each measuring 21″ x 39½″, Paris, after the original by M. Le Rouge, 1777 . . . . **460.00 510.00 485.00**

☐ A Map of New England and New York, shows southwest to Chesapeake Bay, sold by Thomas Basset and Richard Chiswell, uncolored, 16½″ x 21½″, London, 1676 . . . . **460.00 560.00 510.00**

☐ A Map of Virginia and Maryland, sold by Thomas Basset and Richard Chiswell, Uncolored, 17″ x 22¼″, London, 1676 . . . . **460.00 560.00 510.00**

☐ America, engraved, 11″ x 14″, Frankfurt, Merian, second quarter of the seventeenth century **300.00 350.00 315.00**

☐ America, engraved, based on Mercator's maps, 14¾″ x 19″, Amsterdam, Hondius, 1631 . . . . **725.00 925.00 760.00**

☐ America, engraved, based on Mercator's maps, illustrations of sailing vessels and sea monsters, inset of "Terra Incognita," 15″ x 20″, Amsterdam, Jansson, second quarter of the seventeenth century **800.00 1100.00 900.00**

☐ America, engraved, bordered with likeness of native costumes and dignitaries (one identified as "King of Florida"), shows and names Martha's Vineyard, portrays California as a island, Atlantic Ocean is identified as "The North Sea," Pacific Ocean is "The South Sea," 15½″ x 20″, London, Speed, 1626 . . . . . **2000.00 3000.00 2275.00**

☐ America, engraved, has California as an island, 19″ x 23½″, Amsterdam, Allard, c. 1690-1710 . . . . **750.00 1000.00 825.00**

☐ America, engraved, shows California as an island, 19″ x 22″, London, Senex, c. 1720 . . . . **600.00 800.00 650.00**

☐ America, engraved, shows routes of Cortez, Drake and Mendana, illustrations of native birds and manners of the Indians, 19½″ x 22″, Augsburg, Seutter, c. 1735 . . . . **700.00 900.00 750.00**

☐ America, engraved, uncolored, 18″ x 21″, Nuremburg, Hasius, 1746 . . . . **700.00 1000.00 790.00**

☐ British And French Dominions In North America, engraved, a large wall map consisting of eight separate sheets, each sheet 26″ x 19″, price is for full set, London, Jefferys and Faden, c. 1765 . . . . **8000.00 10000.00 8275.00**

☐ California, engraved, shows it as an island in the Pacific crudely shaped, illustrations of wildlife, 18″ x 26″, Paris, DeFer, 1720 . . . . **1500.00 2000.00 1575.00**

☐ Caroline Meridionale et Partie de la Georgia, Par le Chevr. Bull . . . Chevr. Bryan, et de Brahn . . . colored outlines, two sheets, each measuring 29″ x 42″, A Paris, chez Le Rouge, 1777 . . . . **460.00 510.00 485.00**

	Current Price Range		P/Y Average

☐ **Carte de la Flaoride Occidentale et Louisiana,** shows coast of Louisiana to westward of New Orleans, the coasts of Mississippi and Alabama, all but the southern tip of Florida, and the Bahamas, mainly uncolored, 21″ x 54¾″, Paris, Le Rouge, 1777 . . . . **210.00 270.00 240.00**

☐ **Carte des Troubles de l'Amerique Levee,** Par Ordre du Chevalier Tryon, Capitaine General et Gouverneur de la Province de New-York Ensemble la Province de New-Jersey, Par Sauthier et Ratzer, traduit de l'Anglois, from Montreal south to Delaware Bay and Cape Henlopen and from Salem and Marbehead (northeast of Boston) westward to part of Lake Ontario, colored outlines, 29″ x 21″, Paris, Le Rouge, 1778 . . . . **275.00 325.00 300.00**

☐ **Chicago,** lithographed, very detailed street plan, most streets renamed since then but still recognizable, 22½″ x 37½″, New York, Talcott, 1836 . . . . **1500.00 1900.00 1625.00**

☐ **Chignecto Bay,** engraved, 14″ x 22½″, London, Jefferys, 1755 . . . . **450.00 600.00 510.00**

☐ **English Colonies And Canada,** engraved, 18½″ x 23½″, Amsterdam, Visscher, c. 1680 **1200.00 1600.00 1350.00**

☐ **Les Cotes aux Environs de la Riviere de Misisipi Descouvertes par Mr. de la Salle en 1683 et reconnues par M. le Chevallier d'Iberville en 1698 et 1699,** par N. de Fer, Geographe de Monseigneur le Dauphine, shows the present Gulf states, the Bahamas, Cuba and part of Mexico, colored, 9″ x 13″, Paris, 1705 . . . . **275.00 325.00 300.00**

☐ **Map of Louisiana, Mississippi and Alabama,** colored, 18¾″ x 25″, Philadelphia, A. Finley, 1827 . . . . **85.00 115.00 100.00**

☐ **Map of Maine, New Hampshire and Vermont,** colored, 18¾″ x 25″, Philadelphia, A. Finley, 1826 . . . . **125.00 175.00 150.00**

☐ **Map of Massachusetts, Connecticut and Rhode Island,** colored, 18¾″ x 24¾″, Philadelphia, A. Finley, 1826 . . . . **85.00 115.00 100.00**

☐ **Map of North and South Carolina and Georgia,** colored, 18¾″ x 24¾″, Philadelphia, A. Finley, 1827 . . . . **85.00 115.00 100.00**

☐ **Map of Pennsylvania, New Jersey and Delaware,** colored, 18¾″ x 24¾″, Philadelphia, A. Finley, 1826 . . . . **85.00 115.00 100.00**

☐ **Map of Reconnaissance Exhibiting the Country between Washington and New Orleans,** The Routes examined in reference to a contemplated National Road between those two cities, mostly uncolored, 21¾″ x 28″, N.p., 1826 . . . . **85.00 115.00 100.00**

☐ **Map of the State of Missouri and Territory of Arkansas,** colored, 18¾″ x 25″, Philadelphia, A. Finley, 1826 . . . . **100.00 140.00 120.00**

	Current Price Range		P/Y Average
☐ **Map of Virginia and Maryland,** colored, 18¾″ x 25″, Philadelphia, A. Finley, 1827	85.00	115.00	100.00
☐ **Nouvelle Carte des Cotes des Carolines (North and South)** . . . **du Cap Fear a Sud Edisto,** Levees et Sondees par N. Pocock en 1770, traduites de l'Anglois, uncolored, 21″ x 29¼″, A Paris, chez Le Rouge, 1777	230.00	300.00	265.00
☐ **Philadelphia,** engraved, includes detailed street plan as well as surrounding villages (Germantown, Derby, Frankfort), Quaker meeting houses, 18″ x 23½″, Augusburg, Scull and Heap, 1777	900.00	1150.00	985.00
☐ **Russian America,** (Alaska and surrounding territory), engraved, grossly inaccurate in many respects, 18″ x 25″, Paris, Delisle, c. 1780	800.00	1000.00	875.00
☐ **Russian America,** (Alaska and surrounding territory), engraved, 19″ x 25″, St. Petersburg (now Leningrad), Von Staehlin, 1784	400.00	550.00	470.00
Note: This was a refutation of the Delisle map of Russian America published earlier in Paris, which was so inaccurate that it caused embarrassment to the Russians.			
☐ **United States of America,** colored, 17¼″ x 22¼″, engraved by B. Tanner, Philadelphia, 1827	75.00	125.00	100.00
☐ **United States,** engraved, colored, titled "National Map of the American Republic," 24″ x 34″, Philadelphia, Mitchell, 1843	350.00	450.00	380.00
☐ **United States,** engraved, ornamental border with vignettes of major cities, 69″ x 85″, New York, Calvin Smith, 1853	1000.00	1250.00	1100.00
☐ **United States,** engraved, 16″ x 21″, Paris, Bouchon, 1825	150.00	200.00	165.00
☐ **United States,** engraved, 48″ x 56″, London, Arrowsmith, 1795	1350.00	1625.00	1475.00
☐ **Virginia, Maryland** . . . par Fry et Jefferson . . . augmente a Paris, chez Le Rouge, 1777, partly colored outlines, 29″ x 40½″	400.00	520.00	460.00
☐ **Virginiae Partis Australis, et Floridae Partis Orientalis,** shows from Chesapeake Bay to a small part of present northeastern Florida, cartouche of Indians and ships at sea, colored outlines, 18½″ x 23″, Amsterdam, Blaeu, c. 1640	325.00	375.00	350.00
☐ **World,** engraved, insets of Arctic and Antarctic, Niger River shown in Africa (its existence was only speculation at that time), 19″ x 22″, Paris, Delisle, 1700	800.00	1000.00	835.00
☐ **World,** engraved, titled "A New and Accurate Map of the World," two large hemispheres surrounded by illustrations of the elements, solar and lunar eclipse, portraits of Drake, Cavendish, Magellan and Noort (first four explorers to circle the globe), 15½″ x 20½″, London, Speed, 1651	2000.00	2500.00	2200.00

	Current Price Range		P/Y Average
World, engraved, typical world map of that era with Europe and Eastern Asia fairly accurate and distortions in North and South America, 20″ x 26″, Holland, Vander Leyden, c. 1720	800.00	1000.00	885.00
World, woodcut, figures of the Twelve Winds, 11″ x 13½″, Basle, Sebastian Munster, 1540 .	600.00	775.00	650.00
World, woodcut, titled "Charta Cosmographica," shows the world opened out and laid flat in one continuous section, illustrations off sailing vessels and allegorical subjects, South America recognizable but North America blundered, 8″ x 12″, Antwerp, Gemma Frisius, 1584	700.00	900.00	775.00

MARBLEHEAD POTTERY

ORIGIN: Marblehead Pottery was organized by Dr. Herbert J. Hall of Marblehead, Massachusetts. Doing much experimentation, Marblehead pottery started as a therapeutic resource for invalids until size forced it to branch out on its own. In 1916, it was bought by artist Arthur Baggs.

DESCRIPTIONS: The ware produced was heavy and dark using colors like gray, brown, blue and yellow. Later, a cream colored ware with multicolored decoration was introduced and included a new line of children's pieces. The company ceased production in 1936.

MARKS: Backstamps include a sailing ship with a M and P on opposite sides and a monogram of Arthur E. Baggs.

Bowl, 6″, dark blue glaze	35.00	45.00	37.00
Candlestick, 3″, blue glaze, pair	75.00	90.00	77.00
Pitcher, 4¾″, dark blue glaze	50.00	65.00	52.00
Planter, turquoise glaze, artist signed, 1934 .	225.00	250.00	230.00
Tile, 6½″ x 6½″, brown and yellow glaze, floral motif, rare	150.00	170.00	155.00
Vase, 3½″, bulbous shape, gray matt with blue flecks	70.00	80.00	75.00
Vase, 6″, black glaze	400.00	450.00	410.00
Vase, 6½″, green glaze	40.00	50.00	42.00

	Current Price Range		P/Y Average
☐ **Vase,** 7″, cylinder shape, tree motif, gray and green glaze, artist signed	275.00	325.00	280.00
☐ **Vase,** 7″, dark blue glaze	50.00	60.00	55.00
☐ **Wall Pocket,** blue glaze	50.00	60.00	55.00

MARBLES

TYPES: Most common are glass marbles. Antique marbles were made of steel, porcelain, clay, agate, onyx, rose quartz and carnelian. Marble was rarely used. Most marbles measure from ½″ to 1½″ in diameter. Larger ones were used for other types of games.

PERIOD: The most collectible marbles were handmade in Germany before World War I, though some were also made in America during that time. Since World War I most marbles have been machine made and hold little interest for the collector.

COMMENTS: Marble value is not based on age. Material, beauty, design and rarity are the variables. Most common are marbles made of crockery, stone or clay. Limestone marbles are more rare. Agate marbles are valuable, as are one-of-a-kind end of day marbles which were made of leftover glass scraps.

ADDITIONAL TIPS: The listings are alphabetical according to type of marble. For more marble information, refer to *The Official Price Guide to Collectible Toys,* published by The House of Collectibles.

☐ **Carpet Bowl,** black on white, diameter 3¼″ .	48.00	56.00	50.00
☐ **Double Ribbon,** one with red, yellow and white, one blue and white, wide ribbons, yellow and white outer strands, diameter 1¾″ .	62.00	72.00	64.00
☐ **Granite,** large dark brown and gray paint beauty, diameter 3″	77.00	87.00	78.00
☐ **Ivory,** ivory sphere, diameter 2″	8.50	12.50	10.50
☐ **Latticinio Swirl,** white core with four outer bands, two red and white, two green and yellow, diameter 1⅜″	34.00	44.00	36.00
☐ **Latticinio Swirl,** white core with six very bright outer bands, three green and white, three red and yellow, diameter 1⅜″	62.00	72.00	65.00

	Current Price Range		P/Y Average

☐ **Latticinio Swirl,** yellow core with many outer bands, each having red, white, blue and yellow, diameter 1½ " . . . . — **64.00 72.00 66.00**

☐ **Latticinio Swirl,** white core with four multicolored outer bands, diameter 1½ " . . . . — **62.00 72.00 64.00**

☐ **Latticinio Swirl,** yellow core, six outer bands, three red and blue, three red and green, diameter 1⅝" . . . . — **62.00 72.00 64.00**

☐ **Latticinio Swirl,** yellow core with four wide outer bands of blue, white and yellow, diameter 1⅝" . . . . — **47.00 57.00 48.00**

☐ **Latticinio Swirl,** white core with six outer bands, three blue and white, three red and white, diameter 1⅝ " . . . . — **57.00 68.00 59.00**

☐ **Latticinio Swirl,** yellow core with six wide outer bands, three white, one blue, one green, one red, diameter 1¾ " . . . . — **77.00 87.00 79.00**

☐ **Latticinio Swirl,** yellow core with wide red, blue and green outer bands, diameter 1¾ " . . — **53.00 65.00 55.00**

☐ **Latticinio Swirl,** white core with eight outer bands, four red, two blue and white, two green and white, diameter 1⅞" . . . . — **86.00 97.00 90.00**

☐ **Latticinio Swirl,** white core with four wide outer bands one with yellow and blue, one with red and yellow, diameter 1⅞ " . . . . — **87.00 96.00 89.00**

☐ **Latticinio Swirl,** white core with blue bands, narrow yellow alternate bands, diameter 1⅞" — **93.00 112.00 96.00**

☐ **Open Core,** wide bands, two red and white, one blue and white, one green and white, yellow outer strands, diameter 1¾ " . . . . — **80.00 97.00 83.00**

☐ **Open Core,** four very wide bands, yellow and red, yellow and green, blue and white, red and white with four sets of three outer strands, two white and two yellow, core fills the marble, diameter 1¾ " . . . . — **88.00 100.00 90.00**

☐ **Open Core,** four multicolored center bands, four sets of three yellow outer strands, diameter 1⅞ " . . . . — **88.00 100.00 90.00**

☐ **Open Core,** two red and two blue center bands, four sets of three white outer strands, gray glass, diameter 1⅞ " . . . . — **63.00 74.00 64.00**

☐ **Open Core,** three wide center bands, three sets of four yellow outer strands, diameter 2" — **93.00 114.00 95.00**

☐ **Open Core,** four wide multicolored central bands, yellow and white outer strands, diameter 2 " . . . . — **87.00 99.00 89.00**

☐ **Pottery,** modern, handpainted, glazed, diameter 1½ " . . . . — **14.00 20.00 15.00**

☐ **Pottery,** modern, handpainted, glazed, diameter 2" . . . . — **20.00 26.00 22.00**

☐ **Ribbon Swirl,** single very wide ribbon core with two wide sets of yellow outer strands, diameter 2½ " . . . . — **72.00 82.00 74.00**

☐ **Solid Core,** triple layer, center core white with narrow red, blue and green overlay stripes, narrow yellow outer strands, diameter 1½ " . — **53.00 63.00 55.00**

	Current Price Range		P/Y Average
☐ **Solid Core,** double twist, diameter 1⅝″	67.00	77.00	69.00
☐ **Solid Core,** double twist with red, white, blue and green core, yellow outer strands, diameter 1¾″	72.00	82.00	74.00

MAXFIELD PARRISH PRINTS

DESCRIPTION: Maxfield Parrish was a successful American illustrator and artist during the early 1900s.

TYPES: Parrish did ads for various national companies, magazines covers and many limited edition prints. A popular collector's item is Parrish's *Collier Magazine* covers.

PERIOD: Parrish's popularity reached extraordinary heights until the 1940s. His work regained popularity in the 1960s.

ADDITIONAL TIPS: This section only lists Parrish's prints. For additional information, consult *The Official Price Guide to Collector Prints,* published by The House of Collectibles.

	Current Retail Price
☐ **Above The Balcony,** knaves and maidens in garden	35.00
☐ **Air Castles,** nude in bubbles	125.00
☐ **Aladdin In Cave Of 40 Thieves,** 12″ x 16¼″, on quality paper	85.00
☐ **Aladdin And The Lamp,** 10″ x 12″	85.00
☐ **Ancient Trees,** large oak tree by lake	95.00
☐ **Argonauts, In Quest of the Golden Fleece, The**	40.00
☐ **Atlas,** giant holding up sky	90.00
☐ **Arizona,** landscape of mountain-rich blues 11″ x 13″	40.00
☐ **Aucassin Seeks Nicolette,** knight on horse, Bookplate SM	18.00
☐ **Autumn,** maiden standing on hilltop	30.00
☐ **Below the Balcony,** knaves and maidens in garden	35.00
☐ **Bookplate,** John Cox-His Book	20.00
☐ **Brazen, The Boatman,** 10″ x 12″	40.00
☐ **Brown And Bigelow Landscape,** the village church, 24″ x 27″	175.00

	Current Retail Price
☐ **Cadmus Showing the Dragons Teeth,** 10″ x 12″	40.00
☐ **Canyon,** maiden in canyon, 14″ x 17″	125.00
☐ **Circles Palace,** maiden standing on porch	40.00
☐ **Cleopatra,** rare, large	500.00
☐ **Community Plate,** 11″ x 13″, 1918	25.00
☐ **Contentment,** large Edison Mazda Calendar	375.00
☐ **Dawn,** maiden sitting on rock, Mazda print	42.00
☐ **Daybreak,** nude and maiden on porch, small size	65.00
☐ **Daybreak,** large size	225.00
☐ **Dinkey Bird,** nude on swing, 13½″ x 18″, 1904	125.00
☐ **Djer-Kiss Ad,** Maiden on swing in forest, 10½″ x 14″	40.00
☐ **Dreaming,** nude sitting under oak, medium size	150.00
☐ **Dreaming,** large size	450.00
☐ **Dream Castle in the Sky,** 9″ x 12″	35.00
☐ **Duchess at Prayer,** illustration for L'Allegro, 10″ x 15″, 1901	20.00
☐ **Ecstasy,** maiden standing on rock, small size	125.00
☐ **Ecstasy,** large Edison Mazda Calendar	500.00
☐ **Enchantment,** maiden standing on stars at night, 9½″ x 20½″, large	400.00
☐ **Errant Pan, The,** Pan sitting by stream, 6″ x 8″, small	25.00
☐ **Evening,** nude sitting on rock in lake	100.00
☐ **Evening,** nude sitting in lake, 13″ x 17″	90.00
☐ **Fisherman And The Geni, The,** 10″ x 12″	40.00
☐ **Florentine Fete,** maidens in garden, 10″ x 16″	30.00
☐ **Garden of Allah,** 3 maidens sitting in garden, medium size	95.00
☐ **Garden of Allah,** Large Edison Mazda Calendar	190.00
☐ **Garden Of Opportunity, The,** prince and princess	50.00
☐ **Garden of Opportunity Triptyk,** 10″ x 13″	50.00
☐ **Golden Hours,** maidens in forest, Large Edison Mazda Calendar	350.00
☐ **Hilltop,** youths sitting on mountain, medium size House of Art	200.00
☐ **Hilltop,** large size, House of Art	450.00
☐ **Hilltop,** small size	75.00

Garden of Allah *by Maxfield Parrish,* **$95.00-$190.00**

Current
Retail Price

☐ **His Christmas Dinner,** tramp having dinner 50.00
☐ **Interlude,** maidens sitting in garden playing lutes 85.00
☐ **Isola Bella Scene,** 9″ x 10″ 16.00
☐ **Jason and His Teacher Chiron The Centeur,** 1910 .... 35.00
☐ **King of the Black Isles,** king on throne, 10″ x 12″, on quality paper 85.00
☐ **Kings Son, The,** Arab in garden by fountain 40.00
☐ **Knaves and Maidens,** conversing in garden 50.00
☐ **Lamplighters, The,** Mazda Calendar, 9″ x 13″, 1924 .... 90.00
☐ **Lampseller of Bagdad, The,** maiden on steps, Mazda Calendar ... 350.00
☐ **Land of Make-Believe, The,** maiden to garden 20.00
☐ **Little Princess, The,** princess sitting by fountain 18.00
☐ **Lute Players,** small size, House of Art 70.00
☐ **Lute Players,** large size, House of Art 375.00
☐ **Milkmaid, The,** maiden walking in Mountain 20.00
☐ **Morning,** maiden sitting on rock, 13″ x 16″ 100.00
☐ **Night Call,** bare breasted girl in surf, 6″ x 8″ 25.00
☐ **October - 1900,** woman in long gown holding fruit draped in her
   gown, large orange moon behind her head, 18″ x 23″ 25.00
☐ **Old Romance,** nude sitting in pool, 6″ x 8″ 25.00
☐ **Old King Cole** 125.00
☐ **Pandora's Box,** maiden sitting by large box 50.00
☐ **Pierrot,** clown with lute and gorgeous golds in water, sky glittering,
   1912 .... 50.00
☐ **Pool of the Vista D'Este,** nude boy lying down besides luminous
   pool, 7¼″ x 10¾″ 18.00
☐ **Pipe Night,** comical men with pipes and coffee urns sitting facing
   each other at table, 9″ x 12½″ 25.00
☐ **Post standing,** by river in forest 25.00
☐ **Potpourri,** nude in garden picking flowers 20.00
☐ **Primitive Man,** unique salesman's sample, 4¾″ x 7½″ 45.00
☐ **Prince Goodad,** pirates on boat 60.00
☐ **Prince, The,** from Knave of Hearts, 10″ x 12½″, very rare 100.00
☐ **Prosperina,** maiden in the sea, 10″ x 12″ 45.00
☐ **Providing It By The Book,** 2 gents at table 18.00
☐ **Queen Gulnare,** maiden on porch, 10″ x 12″ 45.00
☐ **Reveries,** two maidens sitting by fountain 35.00
☐ **Reveries,** Large Edison Mazda Calendar 350.00
☐ **Sandman, The,** sandman with full moon, 6″ x 7½″ 30.00
☐ **Scribners One Of The Wise Men,** 10″ x 11½″ 18.00
☐ **Search For The Singing Tree** 35.00
☐ **Sea Nymphs,** 12″ x 14″, 1914 .... 45.00
☐ **Seven Green Polls At Cintra,** 6″ x 8″ 25.00
☐ **Shepherd With Sheep,** 8½″ x 13½″ 18.00
☐ **Ship In Ocean,** 11″ x 13½″ 35.00
☐ **Sinbad And The Cyclops,** 10″ x 12″ 35.00
☐ **Sing A Song Of Sixpence,** 9″ x 12″ 30.00
☐ **Singing Tree, The,** 10″ x 12″ 40.00
☐ **Stars,** House of Art, medium size, nude sitting on Rock 350.00
☐ **Stars,** House of Art, large size, nude sitting on Rock 475.00
☐ **Story From Phoebus,** 8″ x 10″, 1901 .... 16.00
☐ **Sunlit Valley,** scenic of river and mountains 125.00
☐ **Sunrise,** Edison Mazda Calendar Top 125.00
☐ **Sunrise,** Edison Mazda Calendar, rare, large 500.00
☐ **Swifts Ham Ad,** Jack Sprat and wife 40.00
☐ **Turquoise Cup, The,** Gent sitting in Villa 18.00
☐ **Twilight Had Fallen,** two figures on beach 25.00

	Current Retail Price
☐ **Valley of Diamonds,** Arab in Valley	35.00
☐ **Venetian Lamplighter,** Edison Mazda Calendar, 1924	85.00
☐ **Villa D'Este,** nude sitting by pool	30.00
☐ **Walls of Jasper,** youth and castle, 12″ x 14″	85.00
☐ **Waterfall,** small Edison Mazda Calendar	125.00
☐ **Waterfall,** large Edison Mazda Calendar	550.00
☐ **White Birch,** farmer under large birch	35.00
☐ **Wild Geese,** girl on Rock, 13″ x 16″	95.00
☐ **Knave Of Hearts Book,** mint	600.00
☐ **Dreamlight,** maiden sitting on swing in forest, large Edison Mazda Calendar, 9½″ x 20½″, 1925, large	475.00

McCORMICK BOTTLES

DESCRIPTION: McCormick bottles are figural decanters produced for retailing McCormick Irish Whiskey.

TYPES: There are four different series including Cars, Famous Americans, Frontiersman and Gunfighters. The lengthiest series is the Famous Americans. It encompasses celebrities from colonial times to the twentieth century.

ADDITIONAL TIPS: Released in limited numbers, the prices on the McCormick bottles are generally higher than other figurals. For more information, consult *The Official Price Guide to Bottles, Old and New,* published by The House of Collectibles.

	Current Price Range		P/Y Average
☐ **Airplane,** Spirit of St. Louis, 1969	80.00	90.00	85.00
☐ **American Bald Eagle,** 1982	30.00	40.00	35.00
☐ **Buffalo Bill,** 1979	45.00	55.00	50.00
☐ **Car,** Packard 1937, 1980, black or cream, first in a series of classic cars, rolling wheels and vinyl seats	65.00	75.00	70.00
☐ **Ciao Baby** 1978	25.00	35.00	30.00
☐ **Clock,** Cuckoo, 1971	25.00	35.00	30.00
☐ **Clock,** Queen Anne, 1970	25.00	35.00	30.00
☐ **De Witt Clinton Engine,** 1970	40.00	50.00	45.00
☐ **French Telephone,** 1969	28.00	34.00	31.00

	Current Price Range		P/Y Average
Jimmy Durante, 1981, with music box, plays "Inka Dinka Do."	35.00	45.00	40.00
J.R. Ewing, 1980, with music box, plays theme song from "Dallas."	35.00	45.00	40.00
Joplin Miner, 1972	20.00	28.00	24.00
Julia Bulette, 1974	150.00	180.00	167.00
Large Mouth Bass, 1982	20.00	28.00	24.00
Lobsterman, 1979	45.00	55.00	50.00
McCormick Centennial, 1956	125.00	150.00	137.00
Mikado, 1980	185.00	220.00	200.00
MO. Sesquicentennial China, 1970	8.00	12.00	10.00
MO. Sesquicentennial Glass, 1971	6.00	10.00	8.00
Muhammad Ali, 1981	20.00	28.00	24.00
U.S. Marshal, 1979	35.00	45.00	40.00
Ozark Ike, 1979	45.00	55.00	50.00
Paul Bunyan, 1979	45.00	55.00	50.00
Pony Express, 1978	40.00	50.00	45.00
Pioneer Theatre, 1972	8.00	12.00	10.00
Renault Racer, 1969	40.00	50.00	45.00
Thelma Lu, 1982	15.00	20.00	17.50
Yacht Americana, 1971	30.00	38.00	34.00
Mark Twain, 1977	25.00	35.00	30.00
Will Roger, 1977	28.00	38.00	33.00
Henry Ford, 1977	28.00	38.00	33.00
Stephen F. Austin, 1977	25.00	35.00	30.00
Sam Houston, 1977	25.00	35.00	30.00

McCOY POTTERY

DESCRIPTION: This 20th century company is noted both for its artware and general lines of tableware, as well as decorative pieces and utilitarian pottery of many kinds. The majority of its fine artware, now so avidly sought, was produced in its earlier years of operation prior to 1930. As was the case with a number of other firms, a cutback on artware production became necessary during the Depression of the 1930s, because only essential merchandise was sought by the public. Brush-McCoy's lines of popular-priced wares fared extremely well in stores throughout the nation. They were continued and expanded in the 1940s and 1950s with many sales registered by mail order via the major catalogue houses.

Today the available variety of Brush-McCoy wares for the collector is overwhelming, offering something for just about all tastes and budgets. There are even many pieces of very recent vintage, going back to the 1960s.

HISTORY: The Brush-McCoy Pottery was first established as the J.W. McCoy Pottery Company, located in Roseville, Ohio — the heart of Ohio "clay country." From all available evidence, it seems that the company got off to an ambitious start when it was incorporated in 1899. J.W. McCoy reportedly had $15,000 capital at the outset, then two years later had multiplied this investment to $100,000.

In 1909, George Brush joined the organization after a pottery works he had been operating was ruined by fire. However, It was not until two years later the name became Brush-McCoy. J.W. McCoy was not an office holder in the newly reorganized Brush-McCoy Pottery Co. Two reasons could be attributed to his lack of interest. In 1910, McCoy and son Nelson founded The Nelson McCoy Sanitary Stoneware Co., also in Roseville, Ohio. There is also speculation that McCoy's health was failing since he died three years later. After McCoy death in 1914, Nelson McCoy served on the Brush-McCoy Board of Directors until 1918. The name McCoy was dropped from the company name in 1925.

MARKS: Many different marks were used by this company for its various lines. In its earlier days and up to the Depression, it rarely marked any of its art pottery, and therefore identifiction must be made on the basis of style. Later, its artware was customarily marked. The more commonly found mark (used on later wares) is the name *BRUSH* in block capitals with flourishing serifs on the first and last letters. This is above the initials *USA*. There are several varieties of this mark. The variations are not of great help in dating as they were often used simultaneously. Several of the marks of this organization, both early and late, made a play on the word "Brush," picturing artists' brushes. These would sometimes be accompanied by an inkwell or a palette. Beginning in the late 1930's, it was customary for the object's mold number to appear in the mark. The collector of Brush-McCoy is certain to learn far more from studying the works themselves, than from studying the marks.

	Current Price Range		P/Y Average
☐ **Ashtray,** *frogs, 6½", mud brown, green and marble-white, a pair of frogs, seated at either side of a shallow bowl tray, their heads turned upward and moutns open (the open mouths designed as rests for cigars or cigarettes), the frogs have alternate stripes of brown and pale green on their legs*	6.00	8.00	6.50
☐ **Ashtray,** *turtle, 5", ivory-white and various reddish hues mixed with brown, the form of a standing turtle*	4.00	6.00	4.25
☐ **Bank,** *Emigrant, Golden Eagle*	12.00	13.00	12.50
☐ **Bank,** *frog, 3½", forest green and yellow, a bullfrog seated on a circular platform with ribbed edge, both are green, with yellow highlights*	22.00	26.00	22.50

	Current Price Range		P/Y Average

☐ **Bank,** *7¼", Williamsburg, gray with original pen holder* .... 11.00 13.00 — 11.50

☐ **Basket,** *9" x 7", green and brown, marked 1/29/3C* .... 10.00 12.00 — 10.50

☐ **Bean Pot,** *high gloss brown, marked 1/21/3A* . 6.00 7.00 — 6.25

☐ **Bean Pot,** *with lid, 2 quart, brown, marked H59/1* .... 20.00 22.00 — 21.00

☐ **Birdbath Ornament,** *frog, 8", beige and slate purple with gray, a frog seated on a tree stump, slate purple with hints of gray, his chest a pale cream-beige, the tree stump is a somewhat deeper beige with slate purple streaking to suggest wood texture* .... 25.00 30.00 — 26.00

☐ **Birdbath Ornament,** *frog, 7½", marble-white, a pair of frogs, one standing with legs crossed, the other seated with hand on knee* 24.00 28.00 — 26.00

☐ **Bookends,** *pair of birds, marked 161/2/3* .... 17.50 18.50 — 18.00

☐ **Bookends,** *"Wise Bird," 7", burnt orange, lavender and yellow, an owl wearing spectacles, holding an open book and reading, he perches upon a stump and faces a lectern which forms the support of each bookend, pair* .... 70.00 85.00 — 71.00

☐ **Same as above,** *but single bookend* .... 28.00 33.00 — 29.00

Note: Since single specimens could easily be mistaken for figurines, the value is somewhat higher than for most single bookends.

☐ **Bowl,** *8", bright canary yellow, modified pot form with molded banding, giving the appearance of graduated sections joined together, small handles* .... 7.00 10.00 — 7.50

☐ **Bowl,** *2½", shape #133, cream white, pink and rose red, inverted dome form, decorated with narrow ribbing vertically encircling the body* .... 5.00 7.00 — 5.50

☐ **Bowl,** *2½", yellow and brown, footed, marked 1/65/4A* .... 3.00 4.00 — 3.25

☐ **Bowl,** *4¾", big red roses, gold trim, side handled, four footed, scalloped rim* .... 7.00 8.00 — 7.25

☐ **Bowl,** *5" x 2¼", maroon with one handle* .... 4.00 5.00 — 4.25

☐ **Bowl,** *5¾", high gloss black* .... 2.00 3.00 — 2.25

☐ **Bowl,** *5¾", high gloss maroon* .... 2.00 3.00 — 2.10

☐ **Bowl,** *5¾" x 2", yellow* .... 2.00 3.00 — 2.10

☐ **Bowl,** *5⅝", turquoise, vertical lines and chevrons* .... 2.50 3.50 — 2.60

☐ **Bowl,** *10", pink and gray with flecking* ...... 7.00 8.00 — 7.25

☐ **Bowl,** *shape #195, ivory white streaked with jade green, to appear like carved ivory, inverted cap form, with molded decoration beneath the rim* .... 6.00 8.00 — 6.25

☐ **Bowl,** *10" wide, slate white, inverted dome form, with flared lip, decorated with a wide central black band, blocked at either side by a similar but narrower band* .... 7.00 10.00 — 7.25

	Current Price Range		P/Y Average

☐ **Box, hanging salt,** *4½", cream white with a wooden hinged lid, cylindrical form flattened at the back (to fit flush with a wall), decorated with vertical molded fluting, at the front a cartouche with the word "SALT"* **23.00**   **27.00**   **24.00**

☐ **Box, hanging salt,** *4½", marble-white and blue, with a wooden hinged lid, half-cylindrical form (flattened at the back to fit flush against a wall), with pierced hanger, decorated with a triple horizontal blue band, with the word "SALT" printed in black script characters* **43.00**   **49.00**   **44.00**

☐ **Box, hanging salt,** *6¼" x 4¼", marble-white and blue, with a wooden hinged lid, rectangular shape with pierced hanger, also set with feet for optionally standing, decorated with stenciled motifs in the upper left and lower right corners of the front panel, in blue, with the word "SALT" printed in black script characters* **38.00**   **44.00**   **39.00**

☐ **Box, hanging salt,** *6½" x 4¼", marble-white and blue, with a wooden hinged lid, rectangular shape with pierced hanger, also set with feet for optionally standing, decorated with a modified Greek key emblem at top and bottom of front panel in blue, with the word "SALT" printed in black script characters* . . .   **41.00**   **47.00**   **42.00**

☐ **Centerpiece,** *9¾" x 6" x 2", green, rectangular shape, ribbing scoring, center crosstrip with leaf relief and hole for candle* **7.00**   **8.00**   **7.25**

☐ **Console Bowl,** *6½", splotchy maroon and chartreuse, marked H127/4B* **7.00**   **8.00**   **7.25**

☐ **Cookie Jar,** *antique auto, steel gray, bone white and yellow, form of a touring car of World War I vintage, with convertible top, the body is steel gray and the top white, wheel spokes are yellow, the lid is formed by the convertible top* **18.00**   **23.00**   **19.00**

☐ **Cookie Jar,** *antique stove, white* **10.00**   **12.00**   **11.00**

☐ **Cookie Jar,** *apple* **10.00**   **12.00**   **11.00**

☐ **Cookie Jar,** *"Balloon Boy," cream white with yellow, green and other colors, representing a boy dressed like a child of the 1920's holding two balloons in his left hand. He wears a moss-green jacket, blue knickers, yellow shoes and a yellow boater hat. The balloons are magenta and pastel blue. The jar's lid is formed by his head and upper shoulders, including the balloons* **14.00**   **17.00**   **15.00**

☐ **Cookie Jar,** *bananas* **18.00**   **20.00**   **19.00**

☐ **Cookie Jar,** *bear* **22.00**   **25.00**   **23.00**

☐ **Cookie Jar,** *bear, marked 95/1/1* **25.00**   **30.00**   **26.00**

☐ **Cookie Jar,** *bear with cookies in pocket* **20.00**   **22.00**   **21.00**

	Current Price Range		P/Y Average

Planter, Turtle, *shape #205, pale lavender and beige, a standing turtle, wearing a long-sleeve sweater with ribbed collar and knitted cap, the planter is formed by the turtle's shell, World War II era* .... 3.00 / 5.00 / 3.25

Planter, Turtle, *#740, 8" x 4½", glossy green and bronze* .... 10.00 / 12.00 / 10.50

Planter, *twin shells, 8½" x 3" x 3½", glossy yellow, marked H 199/1A* .... 6.00 / 7.00 / 6.25

Planter, "Twin Swans," *bone white with black and pink, a pair of swans, face to face, their heads touching in such a manner that their necks create a heart-shaped outline, back of each hollowed out as a planter, manufactured in early 1940s* .... 7.00 / 9.00 / 7.20

Planter, *white, marked C2/23/6* .... 8.00 / 9.00 / 8.50

Planter, *window box, 4" x 8", maroon* .... 5.00 / 6.00 / 5.50

Planter, *window box, 6½" x 3¼", glossy dark green, basketweave pattern* .... 5.00 / 6.00 / 5.50

Planter, *window box, 6½" x 3¼", glossy turquoise with leaf relief* .... 4.00 / 5.00 / 4.25

Planter, *window box, 7" x 4½", pedestal base, glossy dark green, marked H 213/3C* .. 3.50 / 4.50 / 3.75

Planter, *window box, 8" x 4½", glossy dark green with swirls, footed, marked H 215/7C* .. 6.00 / 7.00 / 6.25

Planter, *window box, 9" x 3½" x 3", pale blue over turquoise with scallops and vertical ribbing* .... 5.00 / 6.00 / 5.50

Planter, *wishing well* .... 8.00 / 9.00 / 8.25

Planter, *wishing well, green and gray, rare* .. 14.00 / 15.00 / 14.50

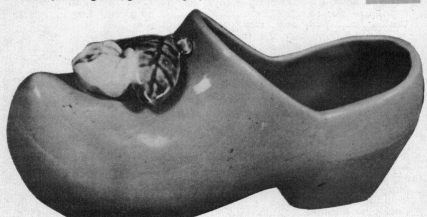

Planter, *shoe, blue with white flower,* **$6.00-$7.00**

	Current Price Range		P/Y Average

☐ **Planter,** *wood grain, 6¼", green and gold, marked C2/34/1D* 4.00   5.00   4.25

☐ **Planter,** *3½" x 4½", gold ribbed panels* 2.00   3.00   2.50

☐ **Planter,** *4½", white with vertical ribbing and horizontal ripples* 2.00   3.00   2.50

☐ **Planter,** *6½" x 3", black, footed* 3.00   4.00   3.50

☐ **Planter,** *7" x 2", high gloss green with diagonal ridges and sculptured scrolls* 3.00   4.00   3.25

☐ **Planter,** *7" x 2", ivory with curlicue relief* 3.00   4.00   3.25

☐ **Planter,** *7" x 4½" x 3", green zig-zag rim with mosaic sides* 4.00   5.00   4.25

☐ **Planter,** *8⅜" x 4" x 4", glossy turquoise with swirled ribbing, footed* 5.00   6.00   5.15

☐ **Planter,** *8½" x 3½" x 2¾", cream with rose decal, footed* 4.00   5.00   4.25

☐ **Planter,** *10", white, oval shaped* 3.00   4.00   3.25

☐ **Planter,** *#66, Chinese, 5½", black with hand painted decoration, marked C1/37* 6.50   7.50   6.75

☐ **Planter,** *#711, double flower pot, 10" x 5", two-tone green with applied yellow swallow, attached saucer, marked 1/79/711* 7.00   8.00   7.10

☐ **Planter,** *#1302, oval, 10" x 9" 3", glossy dark green, three footed* 4.50   5.50   4.65

☐ **Radio Receiver,** *9½" x 3", a ceramic bug (a beetle) which contained a radio receiver, contained a crystal receiver, value as stated is for a specimen without the receiver* 95.00 112.00   97.00

☐ **Rolling pin,** *marble-white and black, with turned wooden holders, cylindrical form with foliage designs stenciled at either end* 130.00 150.00 134.00

☐ **Vase, "Wise Bird,"** *8", deep mahogany brown with yellow and touches of green, an owl perched on a stump next to a hollow tree trunk (which forms the vase), the owl is dark brown with some black coloring to highlight the texturing of its feathers, both the stump and the lower part of the tree trunk are yellow with tones of pale and deep green* 23.00   27.00   24.00

☐ **Vase,** *5½", yellow with side handles, footed*   3.50   4.50   3.75

☐ **Vase,** *6", glossy green with side handles and vertical ribbing, footed* 5.00   6.00   5.25

☐ **Vase,** *6", lavender, swirled* 5.00   6.00   5.25

☐ **Vase,** *6", white, marked H 62/2/1* 8.00   9.00   8.25

☐ **Vase,** *6" x 5" x 3", glossy green with brown flecks, marked H 221/5B* 5.00   6.00   5.25

☐ **Vase,** *6" x 5½" x 6½", yellow flowers on pink, footed, marked H 185/3B* 6.00   7.00   6.25

☐ **Vase,** *7", orchid swirled and footed, marked C1/81/4A* 5.00   6.00   5.25

☐ **Vase,** *7¼", pink, four ribs, footed* 5.00   6.00   5.25

☐ **Vase,** *8", green and blue with ribbing and diamond medallions* 7.00   8.00   7.25

☐ **Vase,** *8", green with ribbing and side handles*   6.00   7.00   6.25

☐ **Vase,** *8", pink with ribbing and side handles* .   6.00   7.00   6.25

☐ **Vase,** *8", pink with side handles* 3.00   4.00   3.25

☐ **Vase,** *8", white with side handles* 3.00   4.00   3.25

	Current Price Range		P/Y Average
Vase, 8" x 7", yellow flowers, marked H 155/2B	9.00	10.00	9.50
Vase, 8½", maroon with stylized leaves and side handles, footed	7.00	8.00	7.25
Vase, 8¾", pink with bird in relief, handled, footed	6.50	7.50	6.75
Vase, 9", cream, marked H/191/2B	7.00	8.00	7.10
Vase, 9", flared yellow with handles, footed .	6.00	7.00	6.10
Vase, 9", glossy green with ribbing, handled and footed, marked H 197/3C	7.00	8.00	7.25
Vase, 9", glossy pink, square footed	7.00	8.00	7.25
Vase, 9", glossy turquoise, square footed ...	7.00	8.00	7.25
Vase, 9", green with square pedestal base ..	6.00	7.00	6.25
Vase, 9¼", glossy green with ribbing, handles, footed, marked C1/11/2A	6.00	7.00	6.25
Vase, 9¼", green and brown with grapes, marked C1/43/4B	13.00	14.00	13.25
Vase, 9¼", turquoise, side handles	6.00	7.00	6.25
Vase, 10", green, decorated with long leaves, side handles, marked H 199/5/2	10.00	11.00	10.50
Wall Ornament, 8", white, cream-white and brown, in the form of a cone, at the front of which is a figure of a perched owl, the cone is brown and has molded leaves at the sides, intended to give the appearance of a tree trunk, the owl is chiefly white with touches of brown and yellow	24.00	29.00	25.00
Wall Ornament, yellow, pale blue and rust brown, vertical rectangular plaque with a sculptured mermaid, tail upturned, holding a shell which serves as a rest for jewelry	13.00	16.00	14.00
Wall Ornament, boxer dog, caramel brown with violet-brown, touches of yellowish beige, extremely realistic modeling of a standing boxer dog, set against a textured background, with storage compartment	14.00	17.00	15.00

MENUS

DESCRIPTION: Collectible menu types include board menus, printed wall menus, novelty, decorated or autographed menus, White House menus and those that commemorate special events.

COMMENTS: Though fun and fairly easy to collect, the value of menus depends on their age, rarity and decoration. Board menus, written and hung on wooden boards, date to the 18th and 19th century and are quite valuable. White House menus, especially those from inaugural ball dinners, are sought after. Special menus, made to commemorate a special event, were often painted or hand lettered on special material. Menus from famous restaurants of New York, Hollywood, New Orleans and Paris are favorites of collectors.

ADDITIONAL TIPS: Menu prices vary greatly in price. The following price sampling is alphabetized according to type of menu.

	Current Price Range		P/Y Average
☐ **Board Menu,** California, 1850-1880	1800.00	2800.00	2300.00
☐ **Board Menu,** California, 1880-1910	550.00	850.00	700.00
☐ **Board Menu,** Midwestern U.S., 1860-1890 ...	800.00	1200.00	1000.00
☐ **Board Menu,** Midwestern U.S., 1890-1910 ...	270.00	420.00	330.00
☐ **Board Menu,** New England, pre-1800	1000.00	1400.00	1200.00
☐ **Board Menu,** New England, 1800-1859	800.00	1200.00	1000.00
☐ **Board Menu,** New York City, pre-1800	1400.00	1900.00	1600.00
☐ **Board Menu,** New York City, 1800-1850	900.00	1400.00	1100.00
☐ **Board Menu,** Southern states, 1800-1850	3000.00	4000.00	3200.00
☐ **Board Menu,** Southwestern, U.S., 1890-1910 .	460.00	710.00	520.00
☐ **Famous Restaurants,** menus from the heyday of noted restaurants in New York, Hollywood, New Orleans, Paris	5.50	15.00	8.00
☐ **Hand-painted Bill Of Fare,** unnamed tavern, believed to be Midwest. Flat-cut wooden board with decorative top (spindles at either side), the board painted cream color, lettering in black ink applied with a thin brush, more than 100 items listed, overall size 22″ x 31″, c. 1875	1800.00	2500.00	2000.00

Menus, *color artwork, 1890s,* **$12.00-$35.00**

	Current Price Range		P/Y Average
☐ **Leheigh Valley Railroad,** dinner menu, picture of Lehigh Valley Railroad tugboat on front cover, c. 1950-1960	4.00	5.00	4.40
☐ **Lond Boar's Head Coffee House,** paper wall menu, c. 1820	220.00	260.00	240.00
☐ **New York Central,** dinner menu advertising the Grand Central Art Galleries, various examples of this menu exist with different works of art on the cover	3.00	4.00	3.50
☐ **New York Central,** dinner menu from "The James Whitcomb Riley," color cover picturing steam loco pulling the train	6.00	8.00	6.80
☐ **New York Central,** World War II "Victory" menu with large V for Victory	5.00	7.00	5.90
☐ **Norddeutscher Lloyd Bremen,** ocean liner dinner menu, c. 1900-1910	2.50	3.50	3.00

Note: This was the forerunner of the steamship company now known as North German Lloyd.

☐ **Silver Star Cafe,** (location unknown, thought to be southwestern U.S.), hand-lettered bill of fare on wooden board. The board shellacked and painted over in various colors with decorations, artistic lettering, etc. Few dishes listed, along with house rules. 18½" x 33⅔", c. 1910	600.00	800.00	700.00
☐ **Steamship Menus,** from major steamship lines	2.00	8.00	5.00
☐ **Washington Inn,** (probably New Hampshire or Vermont), hand-lettered bill of fare on thick wooden board. The board is whitewashed, with list of dishes and prices lettered in dark brown paint. Corners worn down, some of the painted surface cracked, 13" x 18½" x 1½", c. 1835	550.00	700.00	625.00

MILITARY COLLECTIBLES

DESCRIPTION: Military memorabilia encompasses items pertaining to all branches of the military.

COMMENTS: Some hobbyist collect military memorabilia by type of item, for example badges or swords, while others collect by military branch like the Navy, Army or Air Force.

ADDITIONAL TIPS: For more information, consult *The Official Price Guide to Military Collectibles,* published by The House of Collectibles.

Whistle, *England, World War I,* **$15.00-$20.00**

BADGES AND OTHER INSIGNIA

	Current Price Range		P/Y Average
☐ **Aerial Gunner badge,** World War II	40.00	45.00	42.00
☐ **Airship Pilot badge,** c. 1921. Authorized in 1921, a dirigible took the place of the balloon in this badge	175.00	200.00	185.00
☐ **Bombardier badge,** World War II	40.00	45.00	42.00
☐ **Combat (Aircraft) Observer badge,** World War II	50.00	55.00	52.00
☐ **Command Pilot badge,** World War II	55.00	60.00	57.00
☐ **Flight Surgeon's badge,** c. 1943	60.00	65.00	62.00

SWORDS

☐ **Army Foot Artillery sword,** model 1833. Brass scaled grip cast in one piece with a short cross guard with plain disk finials. Blade marked with the American Eagle and "N.P. AMES SPRINGFIELD." An American Eagle appears on the pommel. Hilt attached to the tang of the blade by three iron traverse rivets	169.00	185.00	173.00

	Current Price Range		P/Y Average

☐ **Army Officer's sword,** model 1850. Based on French army model, half basket hilt in gilt with gilt wire wrapped leather covered grips. Phrygian helmet pattern pommel, blade single edge and slightly curved, polished black leather scabbard with gilt/brass fittings **210.00 230.00 220.00**

☐ **Army Officer's sword,** model 1902. Generally similar to the above except that the grips are notched on the inside for the fingers. Full back strap, simple rounded semicap pommel with small caspan top, "D" shape knuckle guard divides into three parts as it becomes the guard. Turned down tear shape finial, nickled scabbard **141.00 175.00 153.00**

UNIFORMS

☐ **Army Air Force Officer's Blouse.** U.S. buttons and cuff braid. Officer's U.S. and winged propellor collar insignia. Pilot's silver wings **55.00 60.00 55.00**

☐ **Army Enlisted Man's Field Jack,** World War II. So-called "Eisenhower jacket of stout OD material. Two pleated pockets. Concealed button front. Embroidered 1st Division patch on left shoulder........................ **25.00 29.00 25.00**

☐ **Army Enlisted Man's Issue Blouse.** World War I 89th Division patch on upper left sleeve. Bronze U.S. enlisted device on right collar and Signal Corps device on left side. Single overseas chevron **50.00 55.00 51.00**

☐ **Marine Corps Enlisted Man's Coat,** World War II period. Green coat with four bronze Marine Corps buttons down the front and on each of four pockets. Marine Second Division patch on upper left shoulder. Corporal's stripes and one enlistment stripe on each sleeve. Red "Ruptured Duck" discharge device on green backing on right breast **25.00 27.00 25.00**

☐ **Marine Sergeant OD Wool Blouse,** World War I period. Four pockets closed with bronze Marine Corps buttons as are pockets. Blouse has high collar with rare collar ornaments consisting of disk bearing Marine Corps emblem. Sergeant's chevrons **90.00 98.00 92.00**

MILITARY MEDALS AND DECORATIONS

TOPIC: Decorations are individual awards for specific acts of gallantry, valor or exceptional meritorious service. On the other hand, medals are given in quantity to many individuals for participation in battles or war. However, at least one decoration, the U.S. Medal of Honor, while strictly a decoration, has the word "medal" in its title.

TYPES: There are numerous different awards given for outstanding service. The highest award the United States gives is the Medal of Honor.

MATERIALS: Bronze is extremely common, although many other valuable metals are used.

COMMENTS: In connection with the collecting of decorations and medals given by the United States, it should be noted that Federal law prohibits the sale of such awards but does permit them to be offered on a trade basis. In buying such items, it is required that an article or articles of trade, such as stamps, be exchanged.

ADDITIONAL TIPS: For further information, please refer to *The Official Price Guide to Military Collectibles,* published by The House of Collectibles.

CANADA

	Current Price Range		P/Y Average
☐ **Efficiency Medal,** George VI	50.00	70.00	60.00
☐ **Forces Decoration,** Elizabeth II	60.00	80.00	70.00
☐ **Forces Decoration,** George VI	120.00	140.00	130.00
☐ **General Service Medal,** 1866-1870	375.00	400.00	387.50
☐ **General Service Medal,** 1870, Red River	1000.00	1300.00	1150.00
☐ **Korean War Medal,** 1951	40.00	60.00	50.00
☐ **Medal of Bravery,** instituted 1972, circular medallion with maple leaf	160.00	190.00	175.00
☐ **Memorial Cross,** Elizabeth II	45.00	65.00	55.00
☐ **Military Cross,** Korea	120.00	160.00	140.00

Purple Heart,
United States, with ribbon,
$26.00-$31.00

	Current Price Range		P/Y Average
GERMANY (Imperial)			
☐ **Baden Leopold Medal.** (for service in the Franco-Prussian War) With 1870-1871 bar ...	75.00	95.00	85.00
☐ **Baden World War I Honor Medal.** Medal inscribed "For Baden's Honor," dated 1914-1918	35.00	55.00	45.00
☐ **Bavarian 1870 Cross for Volunteer Nurses** ..	220.00	300.00	260.00
☐ **Bavarian Order of Military Merit,** 4th Class, with swords	135.00	155.00	145.00
☐ **Bavarian 10 Year Service Medal**	18.00	22.00	20.00
☐ **Brunswick Order of Henry the Lion,** 3rd Class	400.00	440.00	420.00
☐ **Grand Cross to the Iron Cross,** 1914	1000.00	1200.00	1100.00
☐ **Hesse Order of Philip the Good,** 4th Class ...	200.00	240.00	220.00
☐ **Iron Cross,** 1st Class, 1870	410.00	460.00	435.00
☐ **Iron Cross,** 1st Class, World War I, pin back .	60.00	80.00	70.00
☐ **Iron Cross,** 2nd Class, World War I, with ribbon	30.00	50.00	40.00
☐ **Iron Cross,** 2nd Class, 1870 (Franco Prussian War), with 25 year oak leaf	130.00	150.00	140.00
☐ **Saxon Order of Albert,** 4th Class, with swords, ribbon	140.00	170.00	155.00
☐ **Wilhelm I Commemoration Medal**	18.00	28.00	23.00
☐ **Wurttemberg Medal for Veterans,** wars of 1793-1815	80.00	100.00	90.00
☐ **Wurttemberg Silver Medal for Bravery,** World War I. This offering was for the medal together with the award certificate	90.00	110.00	100.00
GREAT BRITAIN			
☐ **Air Force Medal,** World War I	375.00	475.00	425.00

	Current Price Range		P/Y Average
☐ Air Force Medal, World War II	300.00	350.00	325.00
☐ Albert Medal, heroic actions on land or sea, oval bronze medallion surmounted by crown, classified according to monarch who made presentation:			
☐ Edward VI	1700.00	1800.00	1750.00
☐ Elizabeth II	1600.00	1700.00	1650.00
☐ George V	1600.00	1700.00	1650.00
☐ George VI	1600.00	1700.00	1650.00
☐ Victoria	1700.00	1900.00	1800.00
☐ Allied Victory Medal, Air	25.00	35.00	30.00
☐ Allied Victory Medal, awarded to all members of combat battalions in World War I, C.E.F	25.00	35.00	30.00
☐ Allied Victory Medal, Naval	25.00	35.00	30.00
☐ Anglo-Boer War Medal	70.00	90.00	80.00
☐ Arctic Medal, 1857	250.00	300.00	275.00
☐ Baltic Medal, 1854-1855	90.00	100.00	95.00
☐ Colonial Auxiliary Forces Officers Decoration, G.R.V. (George V)	80.00	90.00	85.00
☐ Colonial Auxiliary Forces Officers Decoration, V.R.I. (Victoria)	95.00	115.00	100.00
☐ Conspicuous Gallantry Medal, World War II	2600.00	2700.00	2650.00
☐ Crimea Medal, one bar "SEBASTOPOL"	85.00	95.00	90.00
☐ Defense Medal, 1939-1945	4.00	7.00	5.50
☐ Distinguished Conduct Medal, Korea	700.00	725.00	712.00

UNITED STATES

☐ Air Force Commendation Medal	25.00	35.00	30.00
☐ Airman's Medal	25.00	35.00	30.00
☐ American Campaign Medal	20.00	30.00	25.00
☐ American Defense Service Medal	20.00	30.00	25.00
☐ American Defense Medal, 1939-1946	8.00	14.00	11.00
☐ Armed Forces Reserve Medal	15.00	21.00	18.00
☐ Army Commendation Medal	16.00	22.00	19.00
☐ Bronze Medal, California, Spanish-American War, #1758	90.00	120.00	105.00
☐ Bronze Star, "Boys Remember The Maine"	15.00	25.00	20.00
☐ Dewey Relic Medal, bronze, 1899	50.00	70.00	60.00
☐ Distinguish Military Service, New Jersey, silver	20.00	30.00	25.00
☐ Gettysburg Veteran Model, 1893, bronze	25.00	35.00	30.00
☐ Good Conduct Medal, Navy, 1920	40.00	60.00	50.00
☐ Join Services Commendation Medal	35.00	45.00	40.00
☐ Korean Service Medal	14.00	20.00	17.00
☐ Legion of Merit, Commander Degree, complete with neck ribbon and lapel pin	190.00	230.00	210.00
☐ Legion of Merit, Legionnaire Degree	40.00	50.00	45.00
☐ Marine Corps Expeditionary Medal	28.00	38.00	33.00
☐ Marine Corps Good Conduct Medal	25.00	35.00	30.00
☐ Marine Corps Reserve Medal	20.00	30.00	25.00
☐ Marine Corps Yangtze Service Medal	40.00	48.00	44.00
☐ Medal For Humane Action (Berlin Air Lift)	25.00	35.00	30.00
☐ Medal Of Honor (Air Force), cased, recent issue	580.00	680.00	630.00
☐ Medal Of Honor, Civil War, bronze	1500.00	1800.00	1650.00

	Current Price Range		P/Y Average
☐ **Mexican Service Medal,** Navy and Marine Corps, 1911-1917	60.00	70.00	65.00
☐ **Navy Good Conduct Medal**	30.00	38.00	34.00
☐ **Navy Reserve Medal**	19.00	29.00	24.00
☐ **New Jersey Volunteer Medal,** Spanish-American War, 1898	70.00	90.00	80.00
☐ **Purple Heart,** with ribbon bar	29.00	39.00	34.00
☐ **Sampson Medal** (Navy)	70.00	80.00	75.00
☐ **Second Nicaraguan Campaign,** Marine Corps, 1926-1930	170.00	200.00	185.00
☐ **Service Medal,** World War I, Connecticut	15.00	20.00	18.00
☐ **Service Medal,** World War I, New York, silver	40.00	50.00	45.00
☐ **Silver Star**	60.00	80.00	70.00
☐ **Spanish War Service Medal,** # 18367	40.00	50.00	45.00
☐ **Veteran Soldier Medal,** bronze, 1861-1865 ...	10.00	20.00	15.00
☐ **Victory Medal,** World War II	5.00	10.00	7.50
☐ **Vietnam Service Medal**	14.00	18.00	16.00
☐ **World War I Victory Medal.** (Battle and sector clasps increase value)	25.00	35.00	30.00
☐ **World War II Victory Medal**	19.00	29.00	24.00

MINING COLLECTIBLES

DESCRIPTION: All memorabilia pertaining to mining operations in the U.S., such as deeds, bills of sale, stock certificates, sales brochures, posters, etc.; books on the history of mining; and actual objects used in connection with mining, such as tools, dynamite detonators, helmets, lanterns and the like.

MAKER: As the items involved are so diverse, so too are their origins and the persons responsible for them. Mining gear and equipment was usually commercially manufactured, and by the 1890s could even be ordered from mail order catalogues. It was sold by the trading posts in mining towns.

ADDITIONAL TIPS: Some items have premium value because of the specific mine or locality to which they relate; others because they happen to be more elaborate than others, such as a mining stock certificate which carries a large steel engraving.

	Current Price Range		P/Y Average

☐ **Arizona,** report on Silver Glance Claim, Silver District, Yuma County, Arizona, 1879, three handwritten pages on letterhead of the Castle Dome Mining and Smelting Co., New York — 35.00 / 45.00 / 38.00

☐ **California,** Assay Report, San Francisco Assaying and Refining Works, report to Mineral Hill Mining Co., one page, 1871 — 11.00 / 14.00 / 12.00

☐ **California,** Mining Stock Certificate, American River Water and Mining Co., Dotan's Bar, vignette of Greek figure, 1855 — 135.00 / 170.00 / 145.00

☐ **California,** Mining Stock Certificate, Gold Valley Main Tunnel and Mining Co., Poverty Hill, printed in black on white paper, dated 1867 — 22.00 / 30.00 / 25.00

☐ **Colorado,** mining lease from Free Coinage Gold Mining Co. to Christopher Peacock, three pagel legal document, undated — 18.00 / 23.00 / 20.00

☐ **Colorado,** Mining Stock Certificate, Unadilla Mining Co. of Colorado, vignette of eagle, green and black with lettering in gold, 1880 — 18.00 / 23.00 / 20.00

☐ **Memorandum Of Bullion Deposit,** California Assayer G.A. Berton, single sheet giving weights, finenesses and values of bullion, 1880, 5½ " x 11" — 22.00 / 30.00 / 25.00

☐ **Montana,** Mining Stock Certificate, Moulton Mining Co., Butte City, Montana, two vignettes of mining operations, printed by The American Bank Note Co., green on white, 1881 — 55.00 / 70.00 / 62.00

☐ **Nevada,** broadside poster of The Assay Office of the Eberhardt and Aurora Mining Co., Eberhardt City, Nevada, 1878, listing ore samples with weights and values, 8½ " x 14" — 18.00 / 23.00 / 20.00

☐ **Nevada,** Gould and Curry Mine, Virginia City, Nevada, report of mining operations, including names of employees and work done during the week, dated 1888, single sheet, 9" x 15" — 9.00 / 12.00 / 10.20

☐ **Nevada,** Mining Stock Certificate, Queen Mining Co., Flowery Mining District, Story County, Nevada, vignette of Queen Victoria, printed in black on white paper, issued at San Francisco, 1876 — 75.00 / 95.00 / 82.00

☐ **Nevada,** Mining Stock Certificate, Ruby Hill Tunnel and Mining Co., Eureka, Nevada, vignette of Columbia, issued 1882 — 17.00 / 22.00 / 19.00

☐ **Nevada,** Mining Stock Certificate, Senator Silver Mining Co., Story County, Nevada, vignette of founder, printed in black on white paper, issued at San Francisco, 1875 — 75.00 / 95.00 / 82.00

☐ **Nevada,** Mining Stock Certificate, Silver Central Consolidated Mining Co., Devil's Gate District, Lyon County, Nevada, vignette of the mine, printed in black with gold border on white paper, issued at San Francisco, 1876 — 90.00 / 110.00 / 96.00

	Current Price Range		P/Y Average
Pamphlet, Old Tuolumne 1849-1893, published by Spaulding of San Francisco, 16 pages, lists some of the prominent mines, soft covered, undated	90.00	115.00	99.00
Price List, Hydraulic Mining Equipment, Joshua Hendy Machine Works, San Francisco, California, illustrated, four pages, 1882, 8″ x 11″	32.00	40.00	35.00

MOLDS

DESCRIPTION: Molds are used to hold certain foods while they harden or gel. The food item retains the mold form or design.

VARIATIONS: There are many kinds of molds including butter, chocolate and sugar. Molds are made of wood, copper, tin, iron and graniteware.

COMMENTS: Popular collectibles, molds are often sought after by kitchen collectors. Prices of molds vary greatly, depending on rarity, condition and material.

ADDITIONAL TIPS: The listings are alphabetized according to type of mold or type of material. Descriptions and price ranges follow.

Buttermold, apple, wooden	336.00	350.00	343.00
Buttermold, eagle with branch, 3″ diameter, wooden	236.00	250.00	243.00
Buttermold, eagle, maple, round, wooden ...	215.00	260.00	230.00
Buttermold, eagle, wingtip to wingtip, c. 1800s, wooden	131.00	175.00	145.00
Buttermold, eight, number, wooden	79.00	90.00	83.00
Buttermold, encircled cross and lily, wooden	79.00	90.00	83.00
Buttermold, partridge in a pear tree, wooden	436.00	460.00	443.00
Buttermold, parrot on perch, wooden	210.00	230.00	215.00
Buttermold, c. 1890, wooden	63.00	75.00	67.00
Buttermold, hen, wooden	179.00	195.00	185.00
Buttermold, peaches, wooden	146.00	160.00	150.00
Buttermold, peony, wooden	452.00	460.00	455.00
Buttermold, pigeon, wooden	79.00	99.00	85.00

Buttermold, *pineapple motif,* **$50.00-$60.00**

	Current Price Range		P/Y Average
☐ **Buttermold,** pineapple, seratted edge, 3¾", diameter, wooden	52.00	72.00	60.00
☐ **Buttermold,** pine cone and leaf, wooden	83.00	90.00	87.00
☐ **Buttermold,** pine cones in basket, wooden	32.00	40.00	35.00
☐ **Buttermold,** pine twig stamp, wooden	32.00	40.00	35.00
☐ **Buttermold,** pine twigs, wooden	42.00	50.00	45.00
☐ **Buttermold,** plum, wooden	252.00	320.00	265.00
☐ **Buttermold,** potted tree, wooden	89.00	100.00	93.00
☐ **Buttermold,** primitive, wooden	73.00	90.00	80.00
☐ **Buttermold,** caveman, wooden	105.00	115.00	110.00
☐ **Buttermold,** name, wooden	226.00	255.00	230.00
☐ **Buttermold,** ram and floral design, 4" diameter, wooden	387.00	400.00	390.00
☐ **Buttermold,** wooden	189.00	200.00	193.00
☐ **Buttermold,** Uncle Remus, wooden	179.00	210.00	181.00
☐ **Buttermold,** rooster, wooden	138.00	150.00	140.00
☐ **Buttermold,** rose and bud, factory made, 3" diameter, wooden	37.00	50.00	40.00
☐ **Buttermold,** rosebuds, c. 1880s, 2" diameter, wooden	84.00	110.00	90.00
☐ **Buttermold,** rose, with leaves, factory made, wooden	37.00	50.00	40.00
☐ **Buttermold,** round, four pattern repeat, wooden	37.00	50.00	40.00
☐ **Buttermold,** initials, wooden	188.00	200.00	193.00
☐ **Buttermold,** name, wooden	176.00	200.00	185.00
☐ **Buttermold,** sea shell, wooden	189.00	200.00	193.00

	Current Price Range		P/Y Average
☐ **Buttermold,** sheaf stamp, wooden	42.00	55.00	47.00
☐ **Buttermold,** sheaf of wheat, hand carved, 3″ diameter, wooden	47.00	70.00	50.00
☐ **Buttermold,** sheep, with handle, wooden	141.00	160.00	145.00
☐ **Buttermold,** shell, ring border, c. 1800s, 3″ diameter, wooden	121.00	135.00	126.00
☐ **Buttermold,** fern, factory made, 2″ diameter, wooden	32.00	65.00	40.00
☐ **Buttermold,** flower, wooden	47.00	75.00	50.00
☐ **Buttermold,** flower and leaf, jagged edge, wooden	268.00	350.00	280.00
☐ **Buttermold,** ship, wooden	341.00	370.00	350.00
☐ **Buttermold,** single fish, wooden	263.00	300.00	270.00
☐ **Buttermold,** single pine, wooden	31.00	45.00	33.00
☐ **Buttermold,** single pine twig, wooden	31.00	45.00	33.00
☐ **Buttermold,** single strawberry, wooden	37.00	50.00	40.00
☐ **Buttermold,** six-leaf flower, c. 1830s, 3½″ diameter, wooden	52.00	80.00	60.00
☐ **Buttermold,** six motif, wooden	131.00	140.00	135.00
☐ **Buttermold,** six-pointed star, carven, carven .	99.00	115.00	105.00
☐ **Buttermold,** six-sided lyre, wooden	131.00	145.00	135.00
☐ **Buttermold,** snowflake, wooden	42.00	52.00	45.00
☐ **Buttermold,** star, wooden	57.00	65.00	60.00
☐ **Buttermold,** sunburst, wooden	73.00	90.00	75.00
☐ **Buttermold,** sunflower, wooden	131.00	160.00	136.00
☐ **Buttermold,** sunflower with leaves, c. 1800s, wooden	68.00	80.00	72.00
☐ **Buttermold,** swirls and flowers, wooden	436.00	535.00	450.00
☐ **Buttermold,** three feathers, wooden	105.00	115.00	107.00
☐ **Buttermold,** three leaf fern, maple, 5″ diameter, wooden	55.00	65.00	60.00
☐ **Buttermold,** three twigs, factory made, 3″ diameter, wooden	37.00	50.00	40.00
☐ **Buttermold,** thistle, wooden	47.00	60.00	50.00
☐ **Buttermold,** tobacco foliage, wooden	94.00	100.00	94.00
☐ **Buttermold,** Tree of Life, 3″ diameter, wooden	126.00	180.00	135.00
☐ **Chocolate,** turkey, tin	20.00	25.00	15.00
☐ **Chocolate,** hen, tin, German	20.00	30.00	25.00
☐ **Copper,** bird	32.00	48.00	35.00
☐ **Copper,** bundt	95.00	115.00	98.00
☐ **Copper,** Easter egg, rabbit	55.00	70.00	60.00
☐ **Copper,** jelly or pudding	53.00	75.00	58.00
☐ **Copper,** quart size	32.00	47.00	35.00
☐ **Copper,** pint size	29.00	42.00	32.00
☐ **Copper,** circular base with fruit or floral motif, quart size	31.00	45.00	33.00
☐ **Copper,** circular base, with fruit or floral motif, pint size	15.00	28.00	17.00
☐ **Copper,** twelve tube, c. 1860	129.00	155.00	135.00
☐ **Copper,** pan	138.00	160.00	142.00
☐ **Copper,** pan, iron, handle, hanging eye	149.00	170.00	153.00
☐ **Copper,** dull finish, copper handles, 6″ x 20″ diameter	149.00	170.00	152.00
☐ **Copper,** iron handle, 13″, diameter	68.00	80.00	70.00
☐ **Graniteware,** barley sheaf	27.00	36.00	29.00

	Current Price Range		P/Y Average
☐ **Graniteware,** corn	24.00	32.00	26.00
☐ **Graniteware,** food, grey, 9″, circular	25.00	36.00	28.00
☐ **Graniteware,** gelatin, pineapple	15.00	25.00	18.00
☐ **Graniteware,** pudding, blue and white swirl, ring	37.00	60.00	40.00
☐ **Graniteware,** strawberry and grapes	32.00	40.00	36.00
☐ **Graniteware,** tube	15.00	25.00	18.00
☐ **Ice Cream,** Ace of Clubs, pewter	25.00	35.00	30.00
☐ **Ice Cream,** Ace of Spades, pewter	25.00	35.00	30.00
☐ **Ice Cream,** airplane, pewter	25.00	45.00	38.00
☐ **Ice Cream,** American flag, pewter	30.00	42.00	36.00
☐ **Ice Cream,** apple, pewter	25.00	35.00	30.00
☐ **Ice Cream,** aster, pewter	25.00	38.00	32.00
☐ **Ice Cream,** ball, pewter	15.00	25.00	20.00
☐ **Ice Cream,** banana, pewter	25.00	36.00	31.00
☐ **Ice Cream,** battleship, pewter	42.00	52.00	46.00
☐ **Ice Cream,** bell, pewter	25.00	35.00	30.00
☐ **Ice Cream,** grapes, pewter	25.00	35.00	30.00
☐ **Ice Cream,** Calla Lily, pewter	25.00	35.00	28.00
☐ **Ice Cream,** carnation, pewter	30.00	40.00	35.00
☐ **Ice Cream,** cat, pewter	28.00	38.00	32.00
☐ **Ice Cream,** chicken, pewter	30.00	42.00	36.00
☐ **Ice Cream,** crysanthemum, pewter	28.00	36.00	32.00
☐ **Ice Cream,** cupid, pewter	35.00	45.00	40.00
☐ **Ice Cream,** daisy, pewter	25.00	35.00	30.00
☐ **Ice Cream,** doves, pewter	28.00	38.00	32.00
☐ **Ice Cream,** Easter Lily, pewter	25.00	35.00	30.00
☐ **Ice Cream,** egg, pewter	20.00	32.00	26.00
☐ **Ice Cream,** engagement ring, pewter	25.00	35.00	29.00
☐ **Ice Cream,** football, pewter	25.00	35.00	30.00
☐ **Ice Cream,** George Washington, pewter	45.00	55.00	50.00
☐ **Ice Cream,** harp, pewter	35.00	45.00	38.00
☐ **Ice Cream,** heart, pewter	25.00	35.00	30.00
☐ **Ice Cream,** heart with cupid, pewter	25.00	35.00	30.00
☐ **Ice Cream,** hyacinth, pewter	25.00	35.00	30.00
☐ **Ice Cream,** Liberty Bell, pewter	35.00	45.00	30.00
☐ **Ice Cream,** mutton chop, pewter	27.00	37.00	32.00
☐ **Ice Cream,** ocean liner, pewter	35.00	45.00	40.00
☐ **Ice Cream,** orange, pewter	25.00	35.00	28.00
☐ **Ice Cream,** peach, pewter	25.00	35.00	28.00
☐ **Ice Cream,** pear, pewter	25.00	35.00	28.00
☐ **Ice Cream,** petunia, pewter	25.00	35.00	30.00
☐ **Ice Cream,** potato, pewter	25.00	35.00	30.00
☐ **Ice Cream,** pumpkin, pewter	25.00	35.00	28.00
☐ **Ice Cream,** rose, pewter	25.00	35.00	30.00
☐ **Ice Cream,** rosebud, pewter	30.00	40.00	34.00
☐ **Ice Cream,** Santa Claus, pewter	35.00	45.00	40.00
☐ **Ice Cream,** smoking pipe, pewter	30.00	40.00	34.00
☐ **Ice Cream,** stork with baby, pewter	30.00	40.00	35.00
☐ **Ice Cream,** turkey, pewter	28.00	38.00	31.00
☐ **Ice Cream,** wedding bell, pewter	30.00	40.00	35.00
☐ **Ice Cream,** wedding ring, pewter	25.00	35.00	28.00
☐ **Iron Mold,** ice cream, apple	20.00	30.00	22.00
☐ **Iron Mold,** ice cream, automobile	58.00	68.00	60.00
☐ **Iron Mold,** Albany Troy Foundry, c. 1750	108.00	185.00	115.00
☐ **Iron Mold,** cheese, porcelain and metal	58.00	70.00	60.00

	Current Price Range		P/Y Average
☐ **Iron Mold,** Dariel, cast iron, c. 1870s	26.00	55.00	30.00
☐ **Iron Mold,** for ice cream, heart and cupid pattern	40.00	50.00	42.00
☐ **Iron Mold,** for ice cream, locomotive	68.00	80.00	72.00
☐ **Iron Mold,** for ice cream, pumpkin	38.00	50.00	40.00
☐ **Iron Mold,** for ice cream, rabbit, two part hinged	46.00	60.00	48.00
☐ **Iron Mold,** cast iron, two piece, 11″ long	99.00	120.00	103.00
☐ **Iron Mold,** rabbit, cast iron, two piece, mirror image	37.00	50.00	39.00
☐ **Maple Sugar,** bird	6.00	12.00	8.00
☐ **Maple Sugar,** cookie boy	5.00	9.00	7.00
☐ **Maple Sugar,** cookie girl	6.00	12.00	8.00
☐ **Maple Sugar,** cow	6.00	10.00	8.00
☐ **Maple Sugar,** crouching rabbit	6.00	12.00	8.00
☐ **Maple Sugar,** duck	5.50	10.50	7.50
☐ **Maple Sugar,** elephant	6.00	12.00	8.00
☐ **Maple Sugar,** horse	6.00	12.00	8.00
☐ **Maple Sugar,** horse and bear	12.00	18.00	14.50
☐ **Maple Sugar,** horse and pig	12.00	18.00	14.50
☐ **Maple Sugar,** lion	6.00	12.00	8.00
☐ **Maple Sugar,** pig	5.00	7.50	10.00
☐ **Maple Sugar,** rooster	6.00	12.00	8.00
☐ **Maple Sugar,** rooster and duck, two imprints	12.00	18.00	14.50
☐ **Maple Sugar,** rooster and turkey, two imprints	12.00	18.00	14.50
☐ **Maple Sugar,** sheep, two imprints	5.00	7.50	10.00
☐ **Maple Sugar,** sheep and pig, two imprints ...	12.00	18.00	14.50
☐ **Maple Sugar,** squirrel	6.00	12.00	8.00
☐ **Maple Sugar,** turkey and duck, two imprints .	10.00	18.00	14.50
☐ **Tin Mold,** bread or pudding, 11″ long	37.00	48.00	39.00
☐ **Tin Mold,** fluted edge handle, 3″ long	15.00	25.00	18.00
☐ **Tin Mold,** ice cream, c. 1880	26.00	53.00	29.00
☐ **Tin Mold,** jelly, c. 1890	26.00	53.00	29.00
☐ **Tin Mold,** lion, with base, 6″ long	23.00	35.00	28.00
☐ **Tin Mold,** embossed design gives relief on cheese, grape pattern, 6″ long	30.00	50.00	35.00
☐ **Tin Mold,** pierced tin, heart shaped, for cheese, 19th century	16.00	25.00	18.00
☐ **Tin Mold,** tubed, c. 1890	11.00	16.00	12.00

MOVIE COSTUMES

DESCRIPTION: Costumes worn by movie actors and actresses are sought after collectibles.

COMMENTS: Costumes are difficult to find and acquire. Most are one of a kind creations which makes them quite valuable.

The best way to locate costumes is through auction houses and private dealers. A studio label is usually sewn in the garment, and often the star's name or the designer's name will be on a label.

ADDITIONAL TIPS: The listings are in alphabetical order according to item. For further information on movie memorabilia, refer to *The Official Price Guide to Radio, Movie and TV Collectibles.*

	Current Price Range		P/Y Average
☐ **Coat,** men's, from MGM wardrobe, gray wool, ¾ length, lined, c. 1950s	65.00	85.00	75.00
☐ **Coat,** men's, from MGM wardrobe, MGM label, green with beige ruffles at end of sleeves, satin lined, c. 1950s	65.00	85.00	75.00
☐ **Coat,** worn by Gene Kelly in "The Black Hand," brown, 1950	180.00	225.00	190.00
☐ **Coat,** worn by Lana Turner in "The Bad And The Beautiful," fur, knee length, hood, lined .	150.00	250.00	200.00
☐ **Court Gown,** worn by Linda Darnell in "Forever Amber," heavy cut green velvet with lace trim, 1954	350.00	450.00	375.00
☐ **Dress,** worn by Susan Hayward, in "I'll Cry Tomorrow," designed by Helen Rose, black crepe dress, flares at waist, 'v' neck in back, 1956	300.00	600.00	450.00
☐ **Gown,** from MGM wardrobe, designer Ben Reig, black chiffon, bustle sewed in, lace, sequins and rhinestones trimmed on bustle, c. 1950s	150.00	250.00	200.00
☐ **Gown,** from MGM wardrobe, no label, orange satin, large satin bow, c. 1950s	125.00	250.00	187.00
☐ **Gown,** from MGM wardrobe, polyester, satin lined, sequined jacket, blue, c 1950s	50.00	75.00	87.00

	Current Price Range		P/Y Average
☐ **Gown,** worn by Anne Baxter in "My Wife's Best Friend," silver and white in the style of a Joan of Arc costume, 1952	18.00	23.00	20.00
☐ **Gown,** worn by Ava Gardner in "Lone Star," satin bodice, pink tulle ball gown, 1952	130.00	170.00	145.00
☐ **Gown,** worn by Betty Grable in "The Farmer Takes A Wife," designed by William Travilla, pink, chiffon, ribbon trim, sequins attached .	300.00	500.00	400.00
☐ **Gown,** worn by Deborah Kerr in "An Affair To Remember", designed by Charles LeMaire, strapless, chiffon, black sequins, full length slip of satin, corset sewn into garment	300.00	400.00	350.00
☐ **Gown,** worn by Debra Paget in "Prince Valiant", designed by Charles LeMaire, double layer blue over lavender chiffon	200.00	275.00	237.00
☐ **Gown,** worn by Greer Garson in "Price and Prejudice," polka dot, 1940	160.00	180.00	165.00
☐ **Gown,** worn by Jayne Mansfield in "The Girl Can't Help It," designed by Charles LeMaire, blue rayon crepe, beaded, 1956	500.00	600.00	550.00
☐ **Gown,** worn by Loretta Young in "Mother Is A Freshman," designed by Kay Nelson, green silk chiffon over pale yellow half-slip, ribbon accents, 1949	175.00	225.00	200.00
☐ **Gown,** worn by Marilyn Monroe, designed by William Travilla, white wool, flared from knee, metallic threaded piping throughout pattern, lined	400.00	600.00	500.00
☐ **Gown,** worn by Marilyn Monroe in "Don't Bother To Knock," designed by William Travilla, orange silk chiffon, 1952	350.00	450.00	400.00
☐ **Gown,** worn by Susan Hayward in "I'll Cry Tomorrow," rose chiffon, sequined, designed by Helen Rose, 1955	1000.00	1200.00	950.00
☐ **Gown,** worn by Susan Hayward in "Untamed," lime green, 1955	130.00	170.00	115.00
☐ **Gown,** worn by Mary Pickford in "The Taming of the Shrew," green silk with gold and silver edging, 1929	500.00	700.00	575.00
☐ **Jacket,** bolero style, men's, from MGM wardrobe, MGM label, brown with tan labels and sleeves, satin lined, c. 1950s	40.00	60.00	50.00
☐ **Jacket,** waist style, men's, from MGM wardrobe, MGM label, gray wool, satin lined, c. 1950s	40.00	50.00	45.00
☐ **Leotard And Skirt,** worn by Betty Grable in "When My Baby Smiles at Me," 1948	60.00	80.00	65.00
☐ **Military Coat And Pants,** worn by Rock Hudson in "Ice Station Zebra," 1968	160.00	200.00	170.00
☐ **Military Shirt,** worn by William Holden in "The Bridge on the River Kwai," 1957	100.00	125.00	90.00
☐ **Military Shirt,** worn by Cliff Robertson in "P. T. 109," 1963	38.00	48.00	42.00
☐ **Navy Shirt,** worn by Henry Fonda in "Mr. Roberts," 1955	150.00	175.00	145.00

	Current Price Range		P/Y Average
☐ **Pants,** riding, women's, from MGM wardrobe, beige wool, gold braid design on front and back, c. 1950s	40.00	50.00	45.00
☐ **Pants,** riding, women's, from MGM wardrobe, no label, beige wool, pant legs trimmed, c. 1950s	25.00	45.00	35.00
☐ **Pants,** women's, from MGM wardrobe, MGM label, black with white trim and red rhinestones, c. 1950s	50.00	75.00	63.00
☐ **Pants,** women's, from MGM wardrobe, MGM label, black wool, braided work on lower half, c. 1950s	45.00	55.00	50.00
☐ **Pants,** women's, from MGM wardrobe, MGM label, black wool with purple, pink, orange and yellow tassels attached, c. 1950s	45.00	55.00	50.00
☐ **Robe,** worn by June Allyson in "A Woman's World," pink cotton, 1954	25.00	35.00	29.00
☐ **Space Suit,** worn by Keir Dullea in "2001: A Space Odyssey," 1968	1600.00	2000.00	1500.00
☐ **Suite Dress,** worn by Greer Garson in "Scandal at Scourie," blue, 1953	20.00	25.00	22.00
☐ **Surgical Gown,** worn by Chad Everette in "Medical Center"	80.00	100.00	80.00
☐ **Toga,** worn by Esther Williams in "Jupiter's Darling," white with gold trim, 1955	180.00	220.00	185.00
☐ **Tuxedo,** worn by Elvis Presley in "Double Trouble," MGM label, three pieces including jacket, vest and pants, black wool	600.00	800.00	700.00

MOVIE POSTERS

DESCRIPTION: Movie posters are pictures of various sizes which advertise a motion picture.

TYPES: In 1909, the Motion Picture Patents Company standardized the size and purpose of posters. Currently, there are seven poster sizes including lobby card, 11″ x 14″; window card, 14″ x 22″; display card, 22″ x 28″; insert, 14″ x 36″; one sheet poster, 27″ x 41″, two sheet poster, 30″ x 40″ and three sheet poster, 41″ x 81″.

ORIGIN: The Lumiere Brothers of France produced the first movie posters in 1895. The posters featured scenes from the movie as well as pictures of the audience viewing the movie.

COMMENTS: Today, fine poster art is becoming very collectible. Factors that determine a poster's value include the death of a great performer, a new version of an old movie and rarity.

ADDITIONAL TIPS: Classic movies like *Phantom of the Opera* or *Gone With the Wind* will always command high prices. Currently, the market is showing an increased interest in western posters, especially those picturing John Wayne, and horror film posters.

For more information, consult *The Official Price Guide to Radio, TV and Movie Memorabilia,* published by The House of Collectibles.

Grand Hotel, *1932,* © *Metro-Goldwyn-Mayer, Greta Garbo, John Barrymore,* **$1200.00-$1300.00**
Photo courtesy of Poster City, Orangeburg, NY

	Current Price Range		P/Y Average
☐ **Lobby Card,** Abbott and Costello Meet the Invisible Man, 1951, Universal Pictures, Bud Abbott, Lou Costello, scene card	15.00	25.00	20.00
☐ **Lobby Card,** Andy Hardy Comes Home, 1958, Metro-Goldwyn-Mayer, Mickey Rooney, scene card	7.50	13.00	10.50
☐ **Lobby Card,** Bronco Buster, 1952, Universal Pictures, John Lund, Scott Brady, Joyce Holden, Chill Wills, title card	5.00	10.00	7.50
☐ **Lobby Card,** Caine Mutiny, The, 1954, Columbia Pictures, Humphrey Bogart, scene card . .	15.00	25.00	20.00
☐ **Lobby Card,** California Gold Rush, 1946, Republic Pictures, Wild Bill Elliott, scene card	5.00	10.00	7.50

	Current Price Range		P/Y Average
☐ **Lobby Card,** Deadline U.S.A., 1952, Twentieth Century-Fox, Humphrey Bogart, scene card ..	12.00	18.00	15.00
☐ **Lobby Card,** Great Gatsby, The, 1949, Paramount Pictures, Alan Ladd, Betty Field, Macdonald Carey, Ruth Hussey, Barry Sullivan, Howard De Silva, scene card	15.00	27.00	19.00
☐ **Lobby Card,** Gun Smoke, 1945, Monogram Pictures, Johnny Mack Brown, scene card	12.00	18.00	15.00
☐ **Lobby Card,** Invasion of the Body Snatchers, 1956, Allied Artists, Kevin McCarthy, Dana Wynter, scene card	25.00	40.00	32.00
☐ **Lobby Card,** Julius Caesar, 1953, Metro-Goldwyn-Mayer, Marlon Brando, James Mason, John Gielgud, Louis Calhern, Edmond O'Brien, Deborah Kerr, scene card	4.00	9.00	6.00
☐ **Lobby Card,** One Sunday Afternoon, 1933, Paramount Pictures, Gary Cooper, Fay Wray, scene card	65.00	85.00	75.00
☐ **Lobby Card,** Oregon Trail, 1945, Republic Pictures, Sunset Carson, title card	7.00	15.00	11.00
☐ **Lobby Card,** Outlaw of the Plains, 1946, Producers Releasing Corp., Buster Crabbe, scene card	7.00	15.00	11.00
☐ **Lobby Card,** Singing Cowboy, 1936, Republic Pictures, Gene Autry, Lon Chaney, Jr., scene card	35.00	50.00	42.00

The Misleading Lady,
1932, ©Paramount Pictures,
Claudette Colbert, Edmund Lowe,
$350.00-$400.00

	Current Price Range		P/Y Average
☐ **Lobby Card,** Sky's the Limit, The, 1943, RKO Radio Pictures, Fred Astaire, Joan Leslie, title card	27.50	43.00	34.00
☐ **Lobby Card,** Young Frankenstein, 1974, Twentieth Century-Fox, Gene Wilder, Madeline Kahn, Peter Boyle, scene card	2.00	3.50	2.75
☐ **Insert,** Hunchback of Notre Dame, The, 1957, Allied Artists, Gina Lollobrigida, Anthony Quinn	10.00	15.00	12.50
☐ **Insert,** Lady From Louisiana, 1942, Republic Pictures, John Wayne, Ona Munson	60.00	68.00	64.00
☐ **Insert,** Legend of the Lost, 1957, United Artists, John Wayne, Sophia Loren	25.00	35.00	30.00
☐ **Insert,** Man Who Knew Too Much, The, 1956, Paramount Pictures, James Stewart, Doris Day	60.00	80.00	70.00
☐ **Insert,** Reveille With Beverly, 1943, Columbia Pictures, Ann Miller, Bob Crosby and His Band, Freddie Slack and His Band, Count Basie and His Band, The Radio Rogues, Frank Sinatra, Mills Brothers	27.50	35.00	30.50
☐ **One-Sheet,** A*P*E, 1976, Worldwide Entertainment Corp., Rod Arrants, Joanna De Varona ..	3.00	7.50	5.50
☐ **One-Sheet,** Air Patrol, 1962, Twentieth Century-Fox, Willard Parker, Merry Anders, Richard Dix	3.00	8.00	5.00
☐ **One-Sheet,** Back From Eternity, 1956, RKO Radio Pictures, Robert Ryan, Anita Ekberg, Rod Steiger	3.50	7.00	5.50

It Happened One Night,
1934, ©Columbia Pictures,
Clark Gable, Claudette Colbert,
$500.00-$600.00

	Current Price Range		P/Y Average

☐ **One-Sheet,** Barbarella, 1968, Paramount Pictures, Jane Fonda . . . . — 12.50 — 16.00 — 14.50

☐ **One-Sheet,** Blood of Dracula's Castle, 1969, Crown International, John Carradine . . . . — 5.00 — 8.00 — 6.50

☐ **One-Sheet,** Bluebeard, 1972, Cinerama Releasing Corp., Richard Burton, Joey Heatherton, Raquel Welch, Virna Lisi . . . . — 2.00 — 6.00 — 4.00

☐ **One-Sheet,** Carnal Knowledge, 1971, Embassy Pictures, Jack Nicholson, Candice Bergen, Ann-Margret . . . . — 3.00 — 6.00 — 4.50

☐ **One-Sheet,** Castle on the Hudson, 1940, Warner Brothers, John Garfield, Ann Sheridan, Pat O'Brien, Burgess Meredith . . . . — 40.00 — 55.00 — 47.00

☐ **One-Sheet,** Creation of the Humanoids, The, 1962, Emerson Film Enterprises, Don Megowan, Erica Elliot . . . . — 15.00 — 25.00 — 20.00

☐ **One-Sheet,** Cross and the Switchblade, The, 1970, Dick Ross and Assoc., Pat Boone . . . . . . — 1.00 — 3.50 — 2.25

☐ **One-Sheet,** Dr. Kildare's Wedding Day, 1941, Metro-Goldwyn-Mayer, Lew Ayres, Lionel Barrymore, Laraine Day, Red Skelton . . . . — 20.00 — 30.00 — 25.00

☐ **One-Sheet,** Dr. Tarr's Torture Dungeon, 1976, Group One, Claude Brook, Ellen Sherman . . . . — 2.00 — 5.00 — 3.50

☐ **Window Card,** Alligator People, The, 1959, Twentieth Century-Fox, Beverly Garland, Bruce Bennett, Lon Chaney . . . . — 15.00 — 25.00 — 20.00

☐ **Window Card,** Big Jim McLain, 1952, Warner Brothers, John Wayne . . . . — 35.00 — 45.00 — 40.00

☐ **Window Card,** Creature Walks Among Us, The, 1956, Universal Pictures, Jeff Morrow, Rex Reason, Leigh Snowden . . . . — 75.00 — 100.00 — 87.00

☐ **Window Card,** Cyclops, The, 1957, RKO Radio Pictures, James Craig, Lon Chaney . . . . — 15.00 — 25.00 — 20.00

☐ **Window Card,** David and Goliath, 1969, Allied Artists, Orson Wells . . . . — 8.00 — 12.00 — 10.00

☐ **Window Card,** Day the World Ended, 1956, American Releasing Corp., Richard Denning, Lori Nelson, Adele Jergens, Mike Connors . . . — 25.00 — 35.00 — 30.00

☐ **Window Card,** Hot Spell, 1958, Paramount Pictures, Shirley Booth, Shirley MacLaine, Anthony Quinn, Earl Holliman . . . . — 10.00 — 20.00 — 15.00

☐ **Window Card,** Hound of the Baskervilles, The, 1959, United Artists, Peter Cushing, Christopher Lee . . . . — 65.00 — 85.00 — 75.00

☐ **Window Card,** House That Dripped Blood, The, 1971, Cinerama Releasing Corp., Christopher Lee, Peter Cushing . . . . — 5.00 — 10.00 — 7.50

===

MUSIC BOXES

DESCRIPTION: This section deals with cylinder music boxes. The cylinder has an arrangement of tiny metal pins that pluck the teeth of a tuned metal comb as the cylinder revolves. This causes the tune to play.

PERIOD: Cylinder music boxes were popular from the mid-1800s to 1890.

ORIGIN: The cylinder music box originated in 18th century Switzerland.

COMMENTS: With the advent of the disc music box and other forms of home entertainment, cylinder music boxes lost some of their popularity. Today such music boxes are quite collectible.

ADDITIONAL TIPS: Listings are alphabetical according to music box maker. Descriptions of the boxes are included.

For more complete music box listings refer to *The Official Price Guide to Music Collectibles.*

	Current Price Range		P/Y Average
☐ **A.B.H. Abrahams,** 6 tune 6¼ ″ cyl, 3 bells with butterfly strikers, grained case with transfer decoration on lid, colored tune sheet.	450.00	800.00	600.00
☐ 10 tune 6½″ cyl, 3 bells with butterfly strikers, walnut veneered case with marquetry and transfer decoration, tune sheet, 18″ wide.	300.00	650.00	350.00
☐ 12 tune 13″ cyl, drum, 5 bells with butterfly strikers, castanets, zither attachment, walnut veneer case, transfer decoration on lid, tune sheet, coin operated.	800.00	1300.00	900.00
☐ **Alexandra,** 4 tune 6″ cyl, interchangeable cyls (6), sleeve type, rosewood inlaid case, 4 bells, insect strikers, storage inside case to left of mechanism for extra cylinders, inner glass lid.	1400.00	1700.00	1500.00
☐ 6 tune 6″ cyl, interchangeable cyls (6), c. 1890, hollow cylinders that fit over brass mandrel, single comb, inner lid of glass, two compartments on either side of mechanism with pegs for extra cylinders.	1650.00	3000.00	1700.00

Regina Disc Music Box,
*style #50, table model,
serpentine case,
mahogany,* **$2800.00-$3750.00**

	Current Price Range		P/Y Average
□ **D. Allard—J. Sandoz,** 8 tune 13″ cyl, interchangeable cyls (3), some case decoration, wide base moulding hides storage drawer for extra cylinders.	2500.00	4000.00	3000.00
□ **(Geo.) Baker & Co. (Switzerland),** 6 tune 11″ cyl., sublime harmonie combs, tune sheet, tune indicator and tempo control, double spring barrel, stop/start and change levers, maple case, simple case decoration, inner glass lid.	1450.00	2500.00	1550.00
□ **Baker-Troll,** 6 tune, Sublime-Harmonie Piccolo, walnut case with mother-of-pearl decoration, inner glass lid.	1300.00	1850.00	1500.00
□ 6 tune 17″ cyl, interchangeable cyls, 6 bells, bee strikers, walnut case with brass inlay decoration, matching storage table, three part comb.	2200.00	3300.00	2500.00
□ 6 tune 19½″ cyl, interchangeable cyls (7), ornately inlaid case with brass, pewter and copper decorations, matching cabinet (wide, floor standing) for extra cylinders, decorative moldings, one large comb for cylinder and one for 10 bells, double spring drive, start/stop.	5000.00	7500.00	6000.00

	Current Price Range		P/Y Average
☐ **Bremond,** 4 tune 7″ cyl, simple case, tune card (92 teeth comb), case 15″ long.	400.00	800.00	450.00
☐ 6 tune 3½″ cyl, inlaid rosewood veneer case, inner glass lid, stop/start and change levers, single comb (42 teeth).	275.00	550.00	325.00
☐ 6 tune 8″ cyl, lever wind, simple fruitwood case, tune sheet, case 15″ wide.	550.00	800.00	600.00
☐ 6 tune 10¾″ cyl, hidden drum and bells, inner glass lid (½ size), simple case lines with inlaid decoration on lid and front panel, tune sheet.	1300.00	1800.00	1350.00
☐ **Nicole Freres,** 2 tune SNUFF BOX, tortoise shell case, c. 1825.	1050.00	1550.00	1100.00
☐ 3 tune 9¼″ cyl, ideal sublime harmonie, tune sheet, tune indicator, crank wind, oak case, zither attachment, c. 1895.	1050.00	1800.00	1200.00
☐ 4 tune 6″ cyl, double spring, inlaid case, tune card.	900.00	1300.00	1100.00
☐ 4 tune 8″ cyl, keywind, 15″ case with inlay and banding decoration, tune card.	1300.00	1550.00	1400.00
☐ 4 tune 11″ cyl, simple rosewood case with some decoration, single comb, trills.	1050.00	2050.00	1100.00

NAUTICAL MEMORABILIA

DESCRIPTION: Nautical memorabilia refers to any items about sailing including figureheads, anchors, windlasses, deadeyes and navigational and weather instruments.

TYPES: The types of objects included in this area are varied and include not only items salvaged from ships, but paper items such as ship lists, posters, and ship logs; articles created by sailors; and paintings of ships.

PERIOD: Collectors will usually find items dating from the 1800s. Items before that time are rare and usually housed in museums.

COMMENTS: Nautical memorabilia has only recently become popular collectible items. Now it is so universally popular that the finer items are very valuable on the collectible market. Yet, the determined hobbyist will still succeed in finding items. Ship salvage yards are an excellent place to search for nautical gear.

Telescope, *American, brass, rosewood, early 1800s, 17",*
$200.00-$300.00

	Current Price Range		P/Y Average
☐ **Bill of Lading,** partially printed, Liverpool to Boston, on the ship John and Phiebe, 1799, 5" x 9½"	13.00	17.00	15.00
☐ **Book,** *Sailing Craft* by Edwin Schpettle, published in New York in 1928, cloth bound, 786 pages	90.00	115.00	100.00
☐ **Deadeye,** wood braced with iron, c. 1860	70.00	90.00	80.00
☐ **Diver's Helmet,** brass with glass viewing shield, some iron and nickel components, complete with partial shoulder plate, late 1800s	300.00	375.00	335.00
☐ **Document,** British Brig Geffrared enters the Port of San Francisco, large document headed Inward Foreign Entry, 1854	35.00	45.00	40.00
☐ **Document,** Entry of Merchandise from Valpariso to San Francisco on the ship Bark Orient, partially printed, 1853, 14" x 17"	35.00	45.00	40.00
☐ **Lithograph,** Coleman's Line Clipper Ship, in the form of a huge card, undated, 9" x 12"	450.00	550.00	500.00
☐ **Oil Painting,** Clipper Ship by Antonio Jacobsen, oil on board, dated 1915, 16" x 12"	1600.00	2000.00	1800.00
☐ **Oil Painting,** Sailing in Philadelphia Harbor by James E. Buttersworth, oil on panel, 5¾" x 9¼"	4000.00	5500.00	4600.00
☐ **Print,** two ships at sea, marked Seamen's Bank for Savings, New York, 1962, 15½" x 22"	20.00	25.00	22.00
☐ **Sailor's Foot Locker,** made of rough pine joined with copper braces at the sides and back, decorated with simple incised carving of port scenes and several crude representations of sailing ships, 39" wide x 19" deep x 18" high, undated, c. 1875	350.00	450.00	400.00
☐ **Ship's Compass,** in cherrywood box with lid, brass fittings, made in England, undated, c. 1820	400.00	500.00	450.00
☐ **Ship's Log,** Nantucket whaler, 168 pages, some sketches of whales and harpooning in margins, binding loose, stained, dated 1884	500.00	650.00	570.00
☐ **Ship's Wheel,** mahogany, well preserved condition, mid to late 1800s, overall diameter including grips 39"	550.00	675.00	610.00
☐ **Ship's Wheel,** rosewood and brass, mid 1800s, overall diameter including grips 44½"	700.00	900.00	800.00

	Current Price Range		P/Y Average
☐ **Trade Sign Figure,** The Little Navigator, carved and painted wood, figure of a man in stovepipe hat holding navigational instrument, c. 1860, 27½ "	600.00	750.00	660.00

NEEDLEWORKING TOOLS

DESCRIPTION: The often exquisite sewing utensils used by past generations are sought after collectibles today.

COMMENTS: While most needleworking tools are collectible, and fairly easy to find, thimbles are the most popular. They vary in prices and were made in silver, porcelain and plastic with advertising slogans, but cut glass thimbles are the most valuable and the most rare. Scissors are also sought after, as are workboxes and small cases.

ADDITIONAL TIPS: The listings are alphabetical according to sewing item. Prices follow.

☐ **Basket,** wicker, 12″ H.	22.50	29.00	23.00
☐ **Darner,** foot-form, patented, wood, double ended	2.50	4.50	3.75
☐ **Darner,** glass, red	31.00	40.00	32.00
☐ **Darner,** glove, sterling silver	44.00	54.00	46.00
☐ **Darner,** wood, spring clip	1.50	3.50	2.75
☐ **Darner,** sock, brown	31.50	39.00	33.00
☐ **Needlebook,** embossed lithograph decoration on cover	10.00	16.00	12.00
☐ **Needle Case,** brass	16.00	22.00	18.00
☐ **Needle Case,** carved ivory	36.00	44.00	38.00
☐ **Needle Case,** sterling silver	27.00	34.00	28.00
☐ **Needle Case,** tortoise shell	85.00	110.00	92.00
☐ **Pincushion,** ball shaped, black alternating with red and white check, hangs on a ribbon, 19th century	35.00	50.00	39.00
☐ **Pincushion,** ivory, pedestal base	48.00	60.00	52.00
☐ **Pincushion,** patchwork, 8″	16.50	22.00	18.00
☐ **Pincushion,** sterling silver	120.00	160.00	130.00
☐ **Pincushion,** tomato shape in red satin with green felt leaves, 5½ " diameter, 9″ high	50.00	65.00	53.00

	Current Price Range		P/Y Average
☐ **Scissors,** *embroidery, stork, silver plate, 3″ L.*	31.50	39.00	33.00
☐ **Sewing Bird,** *brass*	49.00	60.00	52.00
☐ **Sewing Bird,** *brass, clamp-on, large with cushion*	165.00	215.00	275.00
☐ **Sewing Bird,** *iron, 6″ L.*	35.00	45.00	37.00
☐ **Sewing Bird,** *sterling silver, 6″ L.*	46.50	60.00	48.00
☐ **Sewing Machine,** *Singer, heavy duty*	260.00	340.00	300.00
☐ **Sewing Machine,** *White, Cleveland, Ohio, early 1900's*	150.00	190.00	170.00
☐ **Spinning Wheel,** *Norwegian, paint decorated, small*	205.00	255.00	220.00
☐ **Spool Cabinet,** *Eureka, walnut, 22 drawers, 16 with glass*	1250.00	1800.00	1350.00
☐ **Spool Cabinet,** *Brooks, four-drawer*	312.00	375.00	320.00
☐ **Stencil,** *copper, Old English alphabet, used to make needlework design*	8.00	16.00	10.00
☐ **Tape Measure,** *clock*	75.00	100.00	83.00
☐ **Tape Measure,** *duck and hen*	40.00	52.00	42.00
☐ **Tape Measure,** *figural turtle, sterling, brass enamel*	57.00	77.00	67.00
☐ **Tape Measure,** *owl*	26.00	34.00	28.00
☐ **Tape Measure,** *papoose, original box*	14.50	20.00	15.50
☐ **Tape Measure,** *rabbit*	36.00	45.00	38.00
☐ **Tape Measure,** *vault*	26.00	35.00	28.00
☐ **Tatting Shuttle,** *tortoise shell*	15.00	23.00	16.00
☐ **Thimble,** *brass*	18.50	26.00	20.00
☐ **Thimble,** *celluloid*	8.50	13.00	9.50
☐ **Thimble,** *engraved bird, large size, 14k gold* .	82.00	110.00	85.00
☐ **Thimble,** *gold with leather case*	95.00	125.00	105.00
☐ **Thimble,** *sterling silver marked with star trademark, in leather box*	45.00	60.00	48.00
☐ **Thimble,** *sterling silver*	47.50	62.00	50.00
☐ **Thimble,** *tortoise shell and sterling silver* ...	107.00	135.00	115.00
☐ **Thimble Holder,** *wooden acorn with hinged leaf top*	55.00	80.00	62.00
☐ **Thimble Holder,** *celluloid, with thread holder*	16.50	25.00	18.00

NEWCOMB COLLEGE POTTERY

DESCRIPTION: Pottery making and decorating became the chief specialty at the art department of Newcomb College in New Orleans. Its efforts in the field were launched in 1896. As all the work was performed under expert guidance and at a pace much slower and more conducive to artistic achievement than that of a commercial factory, some very noteworthy results were obtained. Most of the Newcomb pottery is brilliant. Its level of quality is consistently high and the decorating reflects imagination and spirit. Since its works were never produced in large quantities, they ranked as collectors' items almost from the beginning. Lovers of fine art pottery have been seeking out Newcomb products for at least 80 years.

COMMENTS: The Newcomb Pottery operations were headed by Dr. Ellsworth Woodward and Mary G. Sheerer. Newcomb wares carry underglaze designs, picturing subjects from nature. Local subject-matter predominates, as the objective was to have students paint "from life" rather than from pictures in books (which was usually the case in commercial potteries). Thus the designs present an intriguing panorama of the flowers, leaf types, birds, etc. of Louisiana.

MARKS: There are normally *five marks* on any given piece. First is the general mark of Newcomb, which will appear either as a white-on-black vase with the initials *N.C.,* or consist merely of those initials without symbolization (the N resting within the C). Another variety of the mark has *NEWCOMB COLLEGE* spelled out. Additionally, the piece will (or should) carry a potter's mark, an artist's or decorator's mark, a recipe mark, and finally a registration mark. The purpose of using potters' marks was to identify which works were produced by the students. The artists' marks were more elaborate than those of the potters, consisting usually of boldly drawn initial letters within geometrical frames. Obviously, the students took some inspiration in signing their names from the practices of artists at commercial art pottery factories. The *recipe mark* is a single capital letter, which relates to a book of clay mixtures used by the class.

RECOMMENDED READING: For further information, you may refer to *The Official Price Guide to Pottery and Porcelain,* published by The House of Collectibles.

	Current Price Range		P/Y Average
☐ **Bowl,** *painted flowers, applied roses and leaves*	105.00	115.00	110.00
☐ **Candlesticks,** *7¼", pair, trumpet shape, matte lavender glaze with green and rose, c. 1925*	350.00	375.00	360.00
☐ **Trivet,** *floral motif, signed Sadie Irvine*	200.00	220.00	205.00
☐ **Vase,** *4", green, lavender and rose, high gloss finish*	235.00	245.00	240.00
☐ **Vase,** *5", white and yellow flowers, green leaves around rim and sides, blue background, signed Sadie Irvine*	555.00	575.00	260.00
☐ **Vase,** *5", floral motif, dark blue band on neck continuing to light blue on bulbous body, matte glaze, signed Sadie Irvine, c. early 20th century*	390.00	410.00	395.00
☐ **Vase,** *5", ovoid, narcissi and leaf motif, pale cream matte glaze on blue matte background, artist signed, c. 1910*	610.00	630.00	615.00
☐ **Vase,** *6", moon shining through trees motif, blue background, signed Henrietta Bailey* ...	1450.00	1475.00	1455.00
☐ **Vase,** *6", white floral motif, blue background, signed Henrietta Bailey*	720.00	750.00	725.00
☐ **Vase,** *8", floral motif, signed Henrietta Bailey*	500.00	525.00	505.00
☐ **Vase,** *8", pale gray and beige glaze on purple, background, blossoming dogwood branches motif, signed Sarah Irvine, c. 1910*	720.00	740.00	725.00

NEWSPAPERS

DESCRIPTION: Newspapers are daily or weekly papers which contain news events, features and advertising.

TYPES: The types of newspapers that are valuable are those with major events headlining its pages. One of the most valuable twentieth century newspapers are those carrying the premature "Dewey defeats Truman" headlines.

ADDITIONAL TIPS: Prices are for whole issues, not just front pages. Front pages alone are worth less than the prices shown. For more information, consult *The Official Price Guide to Paper Collectibles,* published by The House of Collectibles.

Newspaper, *facsimile signature of George Washington, 1789,* **$35.00-$50.00**
Photo courtesy of Lou McCulloch, Highland Heights, OH 44143.

ASSASSINATIONS

	Current Price Range		P/Y Average
☐ Archduke Francis Ferdinand	7.75	11.50	9.67
☐ James Garfield Shot (still alive)	11.50	16.50	13.50
☐ James Garfield dies of wound	5.75	6.75	6.25
☐ Mahatma Gandhi	4.00	5.75	4.87
☐ Mrs. Indira Gandhi, Denver Post, news of attack without definite word on her condition	1.00	1.50	1.50
☐ John F. Kennedy	11.50	13.50	12.50
☐ Robert Kennedy Shot (still alive)	5.75	6.75	6.25
☐ Robert Kennedy dies of wound	4.00	5.75	4.87
☐ Martin Luther King, Jr.	4.00	5.75	4.87
☐ Abraham Lincoln	115.00	170.00	142.00
☐ Huey Long	6.75	7.75	7.25
☐ Huey Long — New Orleans paper	10.00	13.50	11.75
☐ William McKinley Shot (still alive)	11.50	16.50	13.50
☐ William McKinley dies of wound	6.75	7.75	7.25
☐ Benito Mussolini	25.00	35.00	29.00
☐ Anwar Sadat	.75	1.00	.87
☐ Leon Trotsky, (early report, stating he had been shot)	9.00	12.00	10.00

	Current Price Range		P/Y Average
☐ **Leon Trotsky,** (corrected report, stating he was bludgeoned with hammer)	7.00	10.00	7.50

ATTEMPTED ASSASSINATIONS

	Current Price Range		P/Y Average
☐ **Charles DeGaule**	1.35	2.00	1.67
☐ **Gerald Ford**	.65	.95	.80
☐ **Hitler,** attempt by concealed bomb fails, London Daily Telegraph	8.00	11.00	9.25
☐ **Franklin D. Roosevelt**	4.00	5.50	4.75
☐ **Harry S. Truman**	2.75	4.00	3.38
☐ **Gov. George Wallace**	2.00	3.25	2.62
☐ **Pope John-Paul II**	.75	1.00	.87

RESULTS OF PRESIDENTIAL ELECTIONS

	Current Price Range		P/Y Average
☐ **1860,** Lincoln/Douglas	33.75	47.25	40.50
☐ **1864,** Lincoln/McClellan	27.50	40.00	33.75
☐ **1868,** Grant/Seymour	8.00	13.50	10.50
☐ **1872,** Grant/Greeley	8.00	13.50	10.50
☐ **1876,** Hayes/Tilden	6.75	10.75	8.75
☐ **1880,** Garfield/Hancock	6.75	10.75	8.75
☐ **1884,** Cleveland/Blaine	6.75	10.75	8.75
☐ **1888,** Harrison/Cleveland	6.75	10.75	8.75
☐ **1892,** Cleveland/Harrison	6.75	10.75	8.75
☐ **1896,** McKinley/Bryan	8.00	12.25	10.00
☐ **1900,** McKinley/Bryan	8.00	12.25	10.00
☐ **1904,** Roosevelt/Parker	6.75	10.75	8.75
☐ **1908,** Taft/Bryan	5.50	9.50	7.50
☐ **1912,** Wilson/Roosevelt/Taft	8.00	12.25	10.00
☐ **1916,** Wilson/Hughes	5.50	9.50	7.50
☐ **1920,** Harding/Cox	4.00	6.75	5.37
☐ **1924,** Coolidge/Davis	2.75	4.75	3.75
☐ **1928,** Hoover/Smith	2.75	4.75	3.75
☐ **1932,** Roosevelt/Hoover	5.50	9.50	7.50
☐ **1936,** Roosevelt/Landon	4.00	6.75	5.37
☐ **1940,** Roosevelt/Wilkie	4.00	6.75	5.37
☐ **1944,** Roosevelt/Dewey	4.00	6.75	5.37
☐ **1948,** Truman/Dewey	4.00	6.75	5.37

Note: Papers carrying premature "Dewey Defeats Truman" headlines are worth as much as $200. The New York Times was not one of them.

	Current Price Range		P/Y Average
☐ **1952,** Eisenhower/Stevenson	2.75	4.75	3.75
☐ **1956,** Eisenhower/Stevenson	2.00	3.50	2.75
☐ **1960,** Kennedy/Nixon	8.00	12.25	10.00
☐ **1964,** Johnson/Goldwater	2.00	3.50	2.75
☐ **1968,** Nixon/Humphrey	2.00	3.50	2.75
☐ **1972,** Nixon/McGovern	2.00	3.50	2.75
☐ **1976,** Carter/Ford	1.35	2.75	2.05
☐ **1980,** Reagan/Carter	1.00	1.50	1.25
☐ **1984,** Reagan/Mondale	.75	1.00	—

DEATHS OF CELEBRATED PERSONS (WHOLE PAPER)

	Current Price Range		P/Y Average
☐ Jack Benny	1.35	2.75	2.05
☐ Charlie Chaplin	2.75	4.75	3.75
☐ Winston Churchill	4.00	6.75	5.37
☐ Calvin Coolidge	2.75	4.50	3.62
☐ Charles DeGalle	2.00	3.00	2.50
☐ Edward VII	2.75	4.50	3.62
☐ Adolph Eichmann (Executed)	5.50	9.50	7.50
☐ Dwight D. Eisenhower	2.00	3.50	2.75
☐ Judy Garland	13.50	20.00	16.50
☐ Warren Harding	2.75	4.75	3.75
☐ Adolph Hitler (unconfirmed)	20.00	27.00	24.00
☐ Herbert Hoover	2.00	3.50	2.75
☐ Lyndon Johnson	1.35	2.75	2.05
☐ Nikita Khrushchev	2.00	3.50	2.75
☐ John Lennon	1.00	1.50	1.25
☐ Ethel Merman, New York Times	1.00	1.50	1.50
☐ Marilyn Monroe	16.00	23.50	20.00
☐ Elvis Presley	12.00	16.00	14.00
☐ Queen Victoria	13.50	20.00	16.50
☐ Franklin D. Roosevelt	13.50	20.00	16.50
☐ Theodore Roosevelt	5.50	9.50	7.50
☐ William H. Taft	2.75	4.00	3.37
☐ Harry Truman	2.00	3.50	2.75
☐ John Wayne	.65	1.00	.82
☐ Woodrow Wilson	4.00	6.75	5.37

NEWS EVENTS

	Current Price Range		P/Y Average
☐ Aaron Burr Slays Alexander Hamilton In Pistol Duel	100.00	130.00	112.00
☐ Alan Ameche Scores TD In Overtime As Colts Defeat Giants For NFL Championship, Baltimore Sun	4.00	6.00	5.00
☐ Astronauts Killed in Fire	4.00	6.50	5.25
☐ Atomic Bomb Dropped on Nagasaki	33.75	45.50	39.57
☐ Battle of Little Big Horn	130.00	190.00	160.00
☐ Billy The Kid Slain By Pat Garrett	60.00	80.00	67.00
Note: This was not treated as "front page" news by most newspapers; it received just a paragraph in some. The lengthier and more prominent the coverage, the more valuable.			
☐ Body Of Bobby Greenlease Found, kidnap victim, Kansas City Times	4.00	6.00	5.00
☐ Brooklyn Dodgers Play First Night Game And Are Victims Of No-Hit Pitching By John VanderMeer, New York Daily Mirror	5.00	7.00	5.75
☐ Burning Of Morro Castle	10.00	15.00	11.75
☐ Coolidge Sworn In As President Following Death of Harding	22.00	30.00	25.00
☐ Disaster Of Excursion Boat "General Slocum" With 1,000 Killed	50.00	70.00	60.00
☐ Jack Johnson Knocks Out James J. Jeffries To Retain Heavyweight Title, New York Times, lengthy report with byline of John L. Sullivan (former heavyweight champion)	50.00	65.00	56.75
☐ Bonnie and Clyde Shot	40.00	45.00	42.50

	Current Price Range		P/Y Average
☐ John Wilkes Booth Slain	37.50	50.00	43.50
☐ Caryl Chessman Executed	2.60	4.50	3.50
☐ Chicago Fire	100.00	125.00	112.50
☐ Chicago Fire — Chicago newspaper	450.00	650.00	550.00
☐ Coronation of Elizabeth II	4.00	6.50	5.25
☐ D-Day	20.00	26.00	23.00
☐ John Dillinger Shot	33.00	40.00	36.00
☐ Germany Surrenders (World War II)	20.00	26.00	23.00
☐ John Glenn Orbits Earth	6.50	10.50	8.50
☐ Bruno Hauptmann Executed	52.00	65.00	58.00
☐ Hindenberg Explodes	52.00	65.00	58.00
☐ Jesse James Killed	70.00	100.00	85.00
☐ Japan Surrenders	26.00	32.00	29.00
☐ John F. Kennedy Inaugurated	6.50	10.50	8.50
☐ Lee Harvey Oswald Slain By Jack Ruby	10.00	15.00	11.25
☐ Charles Lindbergh Baby Kidnapped	45.00	60.00	52.00
☐ Charles Lindbergh Crosses Atlantic	100.00	160.00	130.00
☐ Marilyn Monroe Marries Joe DiMaggio	15.00	20.00	17.00
☐ Moon Landing (first, 1969)	20.00	26.00	23.00
☐ Mount St. Helens Erupts, 1981, Seattle Post-Intelligencer	3.00	4.00	3.25
☐ Police Storm Hideout Of Simbionese Liberation Army, Slay Donald DeFreese, Los Angeles Times	2.00	3.00	2.20
☐ Power Failure Blacks Out East Coast of U.S., Newark Star Ledger	3.00	4.00	3.50
☐ Richard Nixon Resigns	7.25	10.50	9.05
☐ Pearl Harbor Attacked	26.00	40.00	33.00
☐ Prince Charles/Princess Diana's Marriage	1.00	1.50	1.25
☐ Russian Sputnik Launched	15.00	22.00	19.00
☐ 1929 Stock Market Crash	52.00	65.00	58.50
☐ Titanic Sinks	78.00	105.00	91.00
☐ Triangle Shirtwaist Factory Fire	13.00	20.00	17.00
☐ Truman Relieves General MacArthur of Korean Command	10.00	15.00	12.00

NILOAK POTTERY COMPANY

DESCRIPTION: The products of this 20th century art pottery are highly creative. Prior to closing in 1946, Niloak sold decorative wares with very simple shapes, whose textures resembled marble. All the shapes and styles were inspired by so-called primitive work, by the ancient Greeks and Romans and especially by the American Indians. The Niloak pottery is essentially old classic redware, the same type you find in museums, but with the drastic difference of a marbelized texture. To achieve an even more natural, striking appearance, the company decided to stop using exterior glazes. Thus, most of the Niloak pottery has a glaze on the inside only. This interior glaze was considered necessary from a utilitarian point of view, in the event any owner wanted to keep liquids in them. It is highly doubtful, though, if anyone did more with Niloak creations than to display them as decorative objects of art. They were dazzlers, especially in a setting with subdued lighting.

Today, Niloak has become a favorite art pottery with collectors. It never fails to intrigue the general public, too, though there are many who instinctively believe it to have an Indian origin.

HISTORY: Niloak products were developed in an old family pottery business in 1909 in Benton, Arkansas, when the company was being run by Charles D. Hyten. Charles was the son of J.H. Hyten, who had come to Arkansas from Iowa many years earlier to establish a pottery works. Niloak was nothing more than an experiment at the factory when it was initially produced. The word "niloak" is kaolin spelled backwards, kaolin being the special clay which serves as chief ingredient in porcelain. Since Niloak pottery was about as opposite to porcelain as any ware could be, the use of this name was appropriate. Clays of various colors taken from the neighborhood around Benton went into Niloak. They were blended on the wheel so that one streaked into another leaving traces of unblended color creating the styrated or marbleized effect.

Hyten made arrangements with a jewelry shop in Benton to show some of his strange new creations on consignment. They aroused interest and very soon the Hyten Pottery became the Niloak Pottery Company.

Distribution was made to the leading market areas of the country, but Niloak never expanded to the point of actually mass producing its wares. The firm's most successful decade was the 1920s. Like other art potteries it was hit hard by the depression and never regained momentum, though it managed to survive into the 1940s.

MARKS: Niloak pottery will either have an impressed mark or a circular paper label, reading simple *NILOAK POTTERY.* The mark is contained in a collar and is printed in plain block letters. Paper labels became standard with Niloak in its later years. As with other pottery bearing paper labels, the labels sometimes came loose, leaving the item without any indication of its origin. A more elaborate form of the mark reads *FROM THE NILOAK POTTERIES AT BENTON, ARKANSAS.* Some pieces carry model numbers and some do not. It is incorrect to refer to these as MOLD numbers, since the Niloak ware was always thrown on the wheel, not pressed from molds.

HYWOOD *(Introduced 1930s)*

This line was less expensive to produce. It was finished with either high gloss or semi-matte glazes.

	Current Price Range		P/Y Average
☐ **Ewer,** *10", brown and green semi-matte glaze, eagle molded on side*	30.00	35.00	32.00
☐ **Pitcher,** *miniature*	12.00	14.00	13.00
☐ **Vase,** *matte white glaze*	130.00	140.00	132.00
☐ **Vase,** *6", applied handles, matte glaze*	32.00	37.00	34.00
☐ **Vase,** *7½ ", matte rose glaze*	38.00	43.00	39.00
☐ **Vase,** *8", two handled, scalloped rim, rose to blue glaze*	48.00	55.00	49.00

MISSION WARE *(Introduced early 1900s)*

This line is the most desirable of Niloak's production. It features hand-thrown clay decoration in various colors.

	Current Price Range		P/Y Average
☐ **Bowl,** *10", earth tone swirls*	65.00	75.00	67.00
☐ **Holder,** *match, swirls*	40.00	45.00	42.00
☐ **Vase,** *3½ ", swirls*	37.00	43.00	38.00
☐ **Vase,** *4", dark blue, cream and blue swirls* ..	40.00	50.00	41.00
☐ **Vase,** *4½ ", tan and blue swirls*	48.00	55.00	49.00
☐ **Vase,** *5", brown, blue and cream swirls*	37.00	42.00	38.00
☐ **Vase,** *5½ ", blue and brown swirls*	40.00	45.00	41.00
☐ **Vase,** *5½ ", blue and white swirls*	45.00	50.00	46.00
☐ **Vase,** *6", bulbous body, flared rim, swirls* ...	55.00	62.00	56.00
☐ **Vase,** *6", swirls*	40.00	45.00	41.00
☐ **Vase,** *6¾ ", brown, tan, ivory and blue swirls* .	60.00	65.00	61.00
☐ **Vase,** *9", swirls*	92.00	100.00	93.00
☐ **Vase,** *10", swirls*	130.00	140.00	131.00

NIPPON

DESCRIPTION: Nippon porcelain ware is the result of an American tarriff act in the late 19th century which required imports to be marked with the country of their origin. Nippon ware is something of an enigma to all but experienced collectors as it also represents Satsuma, Noritake, Imari and other Japanese wares of a certain period. Nippon ware really is quite beautiful combining a relatively contemporary look with old style crafts-manship and exquisite taste.

COMMENTS: Nippon was not a popular collectible until the mid 1950s. It is still possible to find Nippon porcelain in flea markets, thrift shops, yard sales, attics or Grandma's china closet. Really choice pieces are difficult to locate, however, as the owners withhold them from the market to increase their value, or because of sentimental attachment.

MARKS: Nippon marks most frequently depict an M within a green wreath, and the word "Nippon" printed in curved letters underneath. There are many, many variations, however. By the early 20th century, the Nippon emblem was replaced with "Japan," thus ending an era.

ADDITIONAL TIPS: Typical of any lucrative collectible field, Nippon ware has been faked and reproduced on the antique market. Items are arranged according to function, material and colors.

RECOMMENDED READING: For more in-depth information on Nippon you may refer to *The Official Price Guide to Oriental Collectibles,* published by The House of Collectibles.

	Current Price Range		P/Y Average
☐ **Basket,** *1900s, blown out, molded, acorns, brown, handle extends over the top of the basket*	150.00	200.00	175.00
☐ **Bowl,** *6" in diameter, 1900s, bisque finish, small bowl, tiny brown beading on the out-side, scalloped trim, hand painted acorns, leaves, twigs inside the bowl, yellow, brown, maroon and green*	65.00	75.00	70.00
☐ **Bowl,** *9" in diameter, c. 1900s, bisque, walnut motif, green M mark*	50.00	100.00	75.00

	Current Price Range		P/Y Average

☐ **Bowl,** 7" in diameter, c. 1900s, blue, white background, pink, red floral medallions, handles, green M mark . . . . | 100.00 | 20.00 | 15.00

☐ **Bowl,** 9" in diameter, c. 1900s, mustard color, hand painted, M wreath, blue mark, gold, jewels, rose motif . . . . | 35.00 | 75.00 | 55.00

☐ **Bowl,** 9" in diameter, c. 1900s, red, black, figural, scenic, floral motif, green, red border, unmarked . . . . | 40.00 | 80.00 | 60.00

☐ **Bowl,** c. 1900s, strawberries, leaves and flowers, leaf shaped handles . . . . | 270.00 | 290.00 | 280.00

☐ **Box,** 2" high, c. 1900s, blue, gold-raised motif, green M mark . . . . | 80.00 | 120.00 | 100.00

☐ **Candy Bowl,** c. 1900s, hand painted scene of palm trees, lake with sailboat, mountains in pastel colors, beaded gold trim around outer rim, two pierced, upturned handles . . . . | 55.00 | 65.00 | 60.00

☐ **Candy Bowl,** 6" square, c. 1900s, square, beaded, gold rim, blown out sides, two gold handles, floral design, purple, green, yellow and brown, pastel background . . . . | 77.00 | 85.00 | 82.50

☐ **Ewer,** 10" high, c. 1900s, bulbous body, band of violets, greens and violets, cabinet item, unmarked . . . . | 175.00 | 190.00 | 182.50

☐ **Ewer,** 12" high, 1900s, bulbous body, long 5½" neck, handle extends from body to neck, folial center piece, red and violet . . . . | 200.00 | 300.00 | 250.00

☐ **Fruit Bowl,** 9" in diameter, c. 1900s, handles, scalloped gold rim, geometric designs, wide beaded gold ribbons, hand painted red flowers and buds outlined in gold, signed with the blue leaf mark . . . . | 80.00 | 90.00 | 85.00

☐ **Humidore,** c. 1900s, bisque finish, blown out, molded horse heads . . . . | 750.00 | 800.00 | 775.00

☐ **Humidore,** 5" high, c. 1900s, bisque finish, scenic, body is six sided, country scene, cottage, tree, extends onto the lid, tan and brown tones . . . . | 150.00 | 185.00 | 167.50

☐ **Humidore,** 6" high, 5¾" in diameter, c. 1900s, deep rich brown background, lion panels, raised enamel work lid . . . . | 425.00 | 475.00 | 450.00

☐ **Humidore,** 4" high, c. 1900s, bisque finish, gray, trimmed in gold, scene depicts playing cards . . . . | 425.00 | 475.00 | 450.00

☐ **Humidore,** 8" high, c. 1900s, bisque finish, motif of playing cards 10, J, Q, K and Ace of diamonds, background medium brown, top of body and lid lip depicts dice, symbols for diamonds, hearts, clubs and spades, top of lid depicts dice, the queen of hearts . . . . | 375.00 | 425.00 | 400.00

☐ **Humidore,** 5" high, 18" in diameter, c. 1900s, bisque finish, scenic Art Nouveau, desert, tent, palm trees, browns and tans, age line on bottom . . . . | 100.00 | 130.00 | 115.00

	Current Price Range		P/Y Average

Humidore, *11" x 7", c. 1900s, bisque finish, tray, match holder, small tray, open cigar cup, seven pieces in all, scene of Arab astride a camel, beside a desert tent, fire and palm trees, sunset colors, flat lid gold round finial (set)* **750.00 800.00 775.00**

Humidore, *5" high, c. 1900s, bisque finish, winter scene, purple, enamel tracings of leaves* **45.00 55.00 50.00**

Humidore, *c. 1900s, metal top, glass, painted, roses, base flares out* **55.00 65.00 60.00**

Humidore, *9" in diameter, c. 1900s, satin finish, round tray, match, ash tray, five pieces, scene of swamp, tree extends onto the lid* . . . **450.00 500.00 475.00**

Nut Bowl, *5" in diameter, c. 1900s, black, gold background, green floral motif, floral medallion, three blue leaf mask* **40.00 80.00 60.00**

Nut Bowl, *6" wide, c. 1900s, brown raised enamel, bisque finish, walnut motif, three legs, green M mark* **95.00 110.00 100.00**

Stamp Box, *c. 1900s, slanting top, compartment* **25.00 50.00 37.50**

Vase, *9" high, c. 1900s, amphore shaped body, no handles, small neck, scenic panel, sunset colors, thatched farm cottage, trees, pond, two swans in the water, top of the vase covered with heavy brown putty in fancy designs, green* **350.00 400.00 375.00**

Vase, *7" high, c. 1900s, bisque finish, autumn swamp scene, swan on water, orange, yellows, scenic panel on the bottom, one-half of vase, upper portion gold, some jeweling* **90.00 100.00 95.00**

Vase, *6" high, c. 1900s, bisque, Dutch country side, windmill, browns, lavender, black, neck is fluted, two handles, gold, cabinet piece* . . . **65.00 75.00 70.00**

Vase, *8" high, c. 1900s, bisque finish, Dutch river scene, sunset colors, two sailboats in foreground and one plus a windmill in background, handles, olive green and brown, trimmed in raised black enamel tracings, some red* **95.00 110.00 102.50**

Vase, *9" high, c. 1900s, tall bisque finish, scenic, country, trees in foreground, brown and tan, small handles* **90.00 100.00 95.00**

Vase, *9" high, c. 1900s, bisque finish, scenic desert ruins, sunset colors* **60.00 70.00 65.00**

OCCUPIED JAPAN

DESCRIPTION: Collectibles from this category represent Japanese exported items made after World War II, when Japan was "occupied" by a foreign country for the first time in history. The term "occupied" was essential to Japanese economic recovery. Hostile feelings towards the Eastern nation still ran high for many years after the war; people absolutely refused to buy anything with "Made in Japan" as it's trademark, believing that American dollars could not go to a more unworthy cause than to support a country responsible for such economic, personal, and political worldwide upheaval. Since Japanese exports still retained such superior craftsmanship, beauty and aesthetic symmetry despite the scarcity of materials and manpower, the trademark "Occupied Japan," assured consumers, that they were in no way contributing their hard earned dollars to the menancing powers of the pre War era.

COMMENTS: Like Nippon, Occupied Japanese items are steadily growing in value as collectibles, and more and more dealers are scrambling to supply these items to their Orientalia buyers. Identification is fairly simple of course; the trademark is self explanatory. Do not be put off by Westernized motifs and design; the Japanese were, after all, in a state of national transition marking the beginning of their conversion to Westernized ideals and modes of living.

Items are arranged according to category. In large sections, these are further broken down according to type of object. Within the listings, articles are alphabetically arranged by dimension, smallest to largest.

RECOMMENDED READING: For more in-depth information on Occupied Japan, you may refer to *The Official Price Guide to Oriental Collectibles,* published by The House of Collectibles.

	Current Price Range		P/Y Average
☐ **Ashtray,** 3″ x 2½″, cigarette and match holder, pickanny between pants hanging to dry, "Who left this behind?"	20.00	30.00	25.00
☐ **Ashtray,** 3″ octagonal, iris in relief, gold trim .	5.00	10.00	7.50
☐ **Ashtray,** 3½″ high, boot, cigarette rest, brown flowers and trim	8.00	12.00	10.00

Lamps, *pair,* **$70.00-$90.00**

	Current Price Range		P/Y Average
☐ **Ashtray,** 3½" high, white leaf, gold trim	4.00	6.00	5.00
☐ **Ashtray,** 3¾" high, leaf, fancy, green-red and gold	8.00	12.00	10.00
☐ **Ashtray,** 4" high, long green leaf	4.00	6.00	5.00
☐ **Ashtray,** 4" x 4", porcelain, green floral, marked	7.00	9.00	8.00
☐ **Ashtray,** 4" long, Indian in canoe	15.00	20.00	17.50
☐ **Ashtray,** 4½" square, two cherubs in relief, fancy trim	8.00	12.00	10.00
☐ **Ashtray,** 6¼" long, map of North Carolina, Indian with bear and dogwood	10.00	15.00	12.50
☐ **Ashtray,** 5" x 3", bronze, detailed filigree on sides and top, rest area for cigarette pack . . .	20.00	25.00	22.50
☐ **Bookend,** 4" high, lady in green bonnet, yellow bodice, blue shawl, lavender layered skirt carries closed parasol, on two books	8.00	10.00	9.00
☐ **Boot,** 2½" x 1½", silver plate, etched floral design	15.00	18.00	17.50
☐ **Pin Cushion,** tin, red velvet top, mirror inside lid, marked	20.00	22.00	21.00
☐ **Plaque,** 4" x 5", landscape, gold filigree border	13.00	15.00	14.00
☐ **Plaque,** 5" x 4", "It's Later Than You Think" in Japanese and English	9.00	11.00	10.00
☐ **Plaques,** 7¼" high, in orange, yellow and green, Dutch children hold flower, pair	15.00	17.00	16.00
☐ **Powder Bowl,** 10" diameter, pale blue, dome lid	13.00	15.00	14.00

	Current Price Range		P/Y Average
Sweater Clips, 1¼" high, porcelain buttons with pansies joined by pearl chain	18.00	22.00	20.00
Toy Bear, wind-up, string of fish in mouth	31.00	33.00	32.00
Toy Car, rer, remote control	26.00	28.00	27.00
Vase, 4½" high, Hummel boy next to 2¼" vase, holds basket of apples	14.00	16.00	15.00
Vase, 4½" high, lakeside scene, side shoulders	9.50	11.00	10.25
Vase, 4¾" high, bud vase, concertina player in brick hat, green and brown jacket, blue pants in front of vase	10.00	12.00	11.00
Vase, 4¾" high, Hummel girl next to 3¼" vase	14.00	16.00	15.00
Vase, 5" high, bud vase, sax player in red hat, green jacket, yellow pants in front of vase . . .	10.00	12.00	11.00
Vase, 5" high, Oriental girl in green jacket, fancy fan, pin pantaloons next to bamboo vase containing artificial flowers	14.00	16.00	15.00
Vase, 6" high, lady in yellow bonnet, green ruffled blouse, red bodice, blue and gold ruffled flowered, tiered skirt holds green basket vase	18.00	20.00	19.00
Vase, 6½" high, winged cherub next to bud vase, iridized colors, blue smock, red shoes, plays violin	10.00	12.00	11.00
Wall Vase, 4¾" high, blue deep relief ducks dives	15.00	17.00	16.00
Wall Vase, 6" high, relief decoration of cockatoo and flowers	24.00	28.00	26.00

OCEAN LINER COLLECTIBLES

DESCRIPTION: Ocean Liner collectibles are items pertaining to steam powered sea vessels, chiefly commercial ocean liners.

TYPES: Menus, schedules, postcards, brochures, ashtrays or any part of the ship are types of items that can be included in a collection of ocean liner memorabilia.

COMMENTS: Usually collectors are interested in the ships which attracted the most notoriety. These include Britain's Queen Mary and Queen Elizabeth, France's Normandie and the White Star ships which include the Titanic, Olympic, Brittanic and Oceanic.

	Current Price Range		P/Y Average
☐ **Advertising Broadside,** one sheet, Pacific Mail steamships from New York to San Francisco, the ship Colon, 1889, 7″ x 11″	175.00	225.00	200.00
☐ **Advertising Lithograph,** Starnis Excursions, New York, four pictures in one, lithographed by Donaldson Brothers, undated, c. 1875, very large size	1000.00	1400.00	1175.00
☐ **Ashtray,** aluminum, Holland-America lines, c. 1950, 4⅜″	2.00	3.00	2.50
☐ **Ashtray,** from the liner France, cobalt glass, gold picture of steamship, 4½″	7.00	10.00	8.00
☐ **Bath Towels,** set of two, Queen Elizabeth I, 22″ x 40″	35.00	45.00	39.00
☐ **Brochure,** Cruises on Holland-America line, foldout, multicolored, undated	1.50	2.00	1.75
☐ **Cuspidor,** porcelain, Eastern Steamship Lines, marked "Ye Olde Ivory, Buffalo China, Marine, Made Especially for ESS Co. for Thompson Winchester Co., Boston," 7½″	20.00	26.00	23.00
☐ **Faucet Knob,** brass and porcelain, Queen Mary	40.00	55.00	46.00
☐ **Life Preserver,** Queen Elizabeth II, with original white rope attached	70.00	90.00	80.00
☐ **Menu,** Leonardo DaVinci, three sheet foldout on stiff paper, c. 1970	1.50	2.00	1.75
☐ **Newspaper,** Chicago Tribune, 1954 with front page story of the wreck of the Andria Doria . .	2.50	3.50	3.00
☐ **Pamphlet,** Pacific Coast Official Railway and Steamship Guide, timetables and ads from San Francisco businesses, vignette of steam and sail ship on cover, 140 pages, 1891	80.00	100.00	90.00
☐ **Playing Cards,** Cunard Line, Goodall, gold edges, linen finish, full deck, c. 1915	20.00	30.00	23.00
☐ **Playing Cards,** Lamport and Holt Steamship Line, full deck	20.00	30.00	23.00
☐ **Playing Cards,** SS Norway, Norwegian Caribbean Line, full deck	6.00	8.00	6.50
☐ **Toy Model of Lusitania,** lightweight brass, cast unpainted, c. 1920, 4½″ long	60.00	80.00	70.00

OLD COMMONWEALTH

ORIGIN: Old Commonwealth is produced by J.P. Van Winkle and Son. The company, which began operating in 1974, is one of the newest companies producing collector decanters filled with high quality whiskey.

TYPES: Most of the company's decanters are produced in regular and miniature sizes.

COMMENT: The company's decanters are easily identified by the titles placed on front plaques on most pieces.

ADDITIONAL INFORMATION: For more information, consult *The Official Price Guide to Bottles Old & New,* published by The House of Collectibles.

	Current Price Range		P/Y Average
☐ **Alabama Crimson Tide,** (1981), University of Alabama symbol, front of elephant thrusting through a large red A, elephant's foot propped on top of a football, "Crimson Tide" printed on the front	35.00	45.00	40.00
☐ **Bulldogs,** (1982), the mascot of the Georgia Bulldogs, front portion of a bulldog stands in the center of a large G with one front paw propped on a football	45.00	55.00	50.00
☐ **Chief Illini,** (1979), #1, the mascot for the University of Illinois, warrior stands with arms up and spread wide, dressed in beige buckskin and ceremonial warbonnet	72.00	78.00	75.00
☐ **Chief Illini,** (1981), #2, the mascot of the University of Illinois, warrior running with arms flung back to the sides, dressed in beige buckskins and orange feathered headdress, a large letter "I" in orange and blue stands behind him	50.00	60.00	55.00
☐ **Cottontail,** (1981), jumping rabbit lands on front feet with hind feet extended in the air, short stump	35.00	45.00	40.00
☐ **Coal Miner,** (1975), #1, man stands holding shovel in one hand, and other hand on jacket, bucket of coal at his feet	90.00	120.00	105.00
☐ Mini, (1980)	40.00	60.00	50.00

Old Commonwealth Coal Miner, (1982), *#2, mini, man stands with pick in one hand and a lantern in the other, blue mining outfit with red kerchief, plaque reads "Old Time Coal Miner,"* **$15.00-$20.00**

	Current Price Range		P/Y Average
☐ **Coal Miner,** (1976), #2, man stands with pick in one hand and a lantern in the other, wears blue mining outfit with red kerchief, plaque reads "Old Time Coal Miner"	30.00	40.00	35.00
☐ Mini, (1982)	12.00	18.00	15.00
☐ **Coal Miner,** (1977), #3, miner kneels on one leg, holding a shovel in one hand and coal in the other hand, bucket of coal at his feet	30.00	40.00	35.00
☐ Mini, (1981)	12.00	18.00	15.00
☐ **Coal Miner - Lunch Time,** (1980), #4, miner sits eating lunch, red apple in one hand, wears blue overalls and red miner's hat	35.00	45.00	40.00
☐ **Elusive Leprechaun,** (1980), leprechaun sits on top of a pot of gold with arms wrapped around bent knees, wears dark green hat and boots, and red jacket	35.00	45.00	40.00

	Current Price Range		P/Y Average
☐ **Fisherman, "A Keeper,"** (1980), old man sits holding fish in both hands, his pole tucked in one arm, fishing tackle sits on the ground ...	35.00	45.00	40.00
☐ **Golden Retriever,** (1979), dog sits with game laying between front feet	30.00	40.00	35.00
☐ **Kentucky Thoroughbreds,** (1976), red mare and colt with dark manes and tails, prancing on blue grass	30.00	40.00	35.00
☐ **L.S.U. Tiger,** (1979), the mascot for Louisiana State University, ferocious tiger stands with front legs resting on stone structure, a football under one paw, "LSU" in yellow on structure .	45.00	55.00	50.00

OLD SLEEPY EYE POTTERY

DESCRIPTION: Old Sleepy Eye is an interesting pottery produced by Western Stoneware Company of Monmouth, Illinois. Sleepy Eye ware sports an Indian head motif. The name "Old Sleepy Eye" refers to an Indian chief whose tribe lived in Minnesota. The town of Sleepy Eye, Minnesota was named after him.

TYPES: The common color of this line was cobalt blue on white. Other colors such as brown on white, solid green, solid brown and green on white are rare.

ADDITIONAL TIPS: Also scarce are pieces produced by the Weir Pottery Company of Monmouth, Illinois which merged with six other companies in 1906 to form the Western Stoneware Company.

☐ **Mustache Cup,** *cobalt blue on white, rare* ...	2500.00	3000.00	2550.00
☐ **Pitcher,** *4", cobalt blue on white, "monmouth" printed below spout, Indian head on handle, 1920s*	1000.00	1100.00	1050.00
☐ **Pitcher,** *5¼" cobalt blue on gray, Indian head on handle, 1915*	195.00	225.00	198.00

	Current Price Range		P/Y Average
☐ **Pitcher**, 5¼", cobalt blue on yellow, Indian head on handle	750.00	780.00	755.00
☐ **Pitcher**, 7¾", cobalt blue on white, Indian head on handle, early 1900s	200.00	225.00	205.00
☐ **Pitcher**, 7¾", solid green	1300.00	1400.00	1325.00
☐ **Pitcher**, flemish blue on gray, standing Indian	950.00	1050.00	955.00
☐ **Stein**, 7¾", brown on white	750.00	800.00	760.00
☐ **Stein**, any stein made for the Board of Directors Western Stoneware Co. from 1968 to 1973, each	280.00	320.00	285.00

OLD WEST MEMORABILIA

DESCRIPTION: Old West memorabilia generally refers to the cowboy era which existed in the western United States during the 1800s.

TYPES: Old West memorabilia comprises a wide range of items with the most common being cowboy gear. Items dealing with outlaws, Indians and ghost towns are also widely collected.

PERIOD: Many of the collectible Old West items date from the 1800s.

ADDITIONAL TIPS: A good source for identifying Old West collectibles is through catalogs of the 1800s which can be bought through auction houses or dealers specializing in Old West collectibles.

☐ **Arrest Warrant**, state of California, Sacramento, February 7, 1876, warrant from Executive Department signed by Governor William Irwin for arrest of Christian Henke, fugitive from Missouri wanted for grand larceny, 11" x 16"	43.00	57.00	50.00
☐ **Belt Buckle**, tradesman's belt buckle in cast brass, found at California ghost town, c. 1860	70.00	90.00	80.00
☐ **Bill Heads**, San Francisco merchants, price shown is for a typical bill head with vignette illustration dating from 1870 to 1890	2.00	3.00	2.50
☐ **Book**, Reminiscences of a Ranger by Horace Bell, published in Los Angeles in 1881, cloth bound, 457 pages	250.00	300.00	275.00

Spurs, *Thomas Beck, Dallas TX, Steel, 4″ x 3″,*
1879, $120.00-$150.00
(photo courtesy of ©Bret Farnum)

	Current Price Range		P/Y Average
☐ **Book,** *The Log of a Cowboy* by Andy Adams, published in Boston in 1903, 387 pages, bound in pictorial cloth	70.00	90.00	80.00
☐ **Book,** *They Died With Their Boots On* by Thomas Ripley, published in New York in 1935, cloth bound, 285 pages	110.00	140.00	120.00
☐ **Boot Heel Plate,** iron, shaped like horseshoe, late 19th century	6.00	8.00	7.00
☐ **Button,** ranger's button from Ft. Fetterman, Wyoming	1.00	1.50	1.25
☐ **Cartridge Box,** brass, found in Wyoming, some corrosion	8.00	10.00	9.00
☐ **Cattle Skull,** sun bleached skull of steer found on Arizona plains, teeth intact, horns missing, shellacked	40.00	50.00	45.00
☐ **Check,** Idaho Territory, Bank of Idaho, J.T. Morgan and Co., Bankers, Blackfoot, Idaho, unused check with a pair of vignettes, one of them showing a cowboy roping a steer, undated, c. 1885	4.00	6.00	5.00
☐ **Check,** Virginia City, Nevada, Agency of the Bank of California, has two revenue stamps and signature of John Mackay, 1870	50.00	70.00	60.00
☐ **Check,** Wells Fargo, drawn on Wells Fargo and Co.'s bank in San Francisco, undated, signed by J. Hyman	13.00	17.00	15.00
☐ **Contract for Mail Route,** State of California, from North San Juan to North Bloomfield, issued to John Hogan, one half is a printed list of instructions, 1870, 13″ x 16½″	26.00	34.00	30.00

	Current Price Range		P/Y Average

☐ **County Warrant,** Mono County, California, relating to the paying of a bill, 1877 . . . . — 13.00 — 17.00 — 15.00

☐ **Fork,** nickel silver, stamped Fort D.A., Russell, Wyoming . . . . — 9.00 — 12.00 — 10.00

☐ **Knapsack Hook,** brass, found in Wyoming, 19th century . . . . — 1.50 — 2.00 — 1.75

☐ **Magazine,** *The Galaxy,* New York, March, 1873, with article "Life on the Plains" by General George Armstrong Custer . . . . — 25.00 — 35.00 — 30.00

☐ **Map,** hand-drawn survey map of Dakota Territory, executed by Charles W. Irish for the C. & N.W. Railroad, 1880, on a roll measuring 6′ x 19″ . . . . — 600.00 — 800.00 — 700.00

☐ **Nail,** iron, hand forged, square head, 19th century . . . . — 1.00 — 1.50 — 1.25

☐ **Newspaper,** *U.S. Telegraph,* Washington, D.C., for July 10, 1832, with reports of Black Hawk War . . . . — 10.00 — 13.00 — 11.00

☐ **Oil Painting,** Bringing in the Saddle Stock by Gordon Phillips, oil on canvas, 20th century, 22″ x 30″ . . . . — 2200.00 — 3000.00 — 2600.00

☐ **Pamphlet,** *Marshall's Gold Discovery,* a lecture by John S. Hittell, published in San Francisco, 20 pages, 1893, 9″ x 6″ . . . . — 42.00 — 58.00 — 50.00

☐ **Pay Warrant,** Columbia, Texas, certificate entitling Robert Middleton to pay off $48 for six months employment by Paratts Company in 1836, countersigned by paymaster, 3½″ x 7″ . . . . — 40.00 — 50.00 — 45.00

☐ **Pistol Hammer,** from unidentified percussion pistol, iron with subdued engraving . . . . — 3.00 — 4.50 — 3.75

☐ **Proclamation,** appointment of deputy sheriff, state of Colorado, county of El Paso, W.R. Buergelin is appointed a Deputy Sheriff, signed by George G. Birdsall, Sheriff of El Paso County, 1913, 7″ x 8¼″ . . . . — 18.00 — 23.00 — 20.00

☐ **Reward Poster,** the state of California offers $200 for the arrest of Frank Revada for the crime of murder of Thomas Leahey at Williams' ranch in the county of Mono, 1892, 9″ x 14″ . . . . — 130.00 — 180.00 — 150.00

☐ **Spoon,** nickel silver, stamped Fort D.A., Russell, Wyoming . . . . — 9.00 — 12.00 — 10.50

☐ **Spurs,** pair, brass, six-pointed stars, moderately to heavily corroded, place of manufacture unknown, c. 1880 . . . . — 30.00 — 35.00 — 32.00

☐ **Ticket,** Montana Stage and Railroad ticket, three part ticket of the North Western Overland Mail Line and the Northern Pacific Railroad, unused, undated, 19th century, 3″ x 6″ . — 9.00 — 12.00 — 10.50

☐ **Voting List,** Great Register of the County of Mono, California, lists all registered voters, 46 pages, undated, 19th century, 9″ x 12″ . . . — 90.00 — 115.00 — 103.00

☐ **Way Bill,** Ft. Apache Stage Line, list of passengers and freight, vignette of wagon and team of horses, 1901, 7″ x 17″ . . . . — 23.00 — 28.00 — 25.00

OPERA MEMORABILIA

COMMENTS: Items from the well-known artists, Enrico Caruso, Nicolai Gedda; well-known opera houses, The Metropolitan Opera House; and well-known operas are the most sought after and collectible. Opera recordings are fairly readily available, though many collectors seek 78 r.p.m. records.

ADDITIONAL TIPS: The listings are alphabetical according to item.
For more complete listings and information, see *The Official Price Guide to Music Collectibles.*

	Current Price Range		P/Y Average
☐ **Album Cover,** autographed by Kirsten Flagstad, records missing	60.00	75.00	65.00
☐ **Annual,** Metropolitan Opera Annual, signed by Regine Crespin	12.00	15.00	13.00
☐ **Book,** *Bubbles,* autographed by Beverly Sills .	30.00	40.00	33.00
☐ **Book,** *Songs of Stephen Foster,* signed by John Charles Thomas	25.00	35.00	28.00
☐ **Bracelet,** gold colored costume bracelet worn by Leontyne Price	60.00	75.00	63.00
☐ **Brochure,** opera company brochure signed by Regina Resnik, c. 1952	8.00	12.00	10.00
☐ **Calling Card,** signed by Enrico Caruso	60.00	80.00	70.00
☐ **Check,** endorsed by John Brownlee	10.00	13.00	11.00
☐ **Christmas Card,** autographed by Anna Moffo .	21.00	26.00	23.00
☐ **Contract,** opera company contract signed by Patrice Munsel	30.00	40.00	33.00
☐ **Contract,** opera contract signed by Giuseppe Deluca	70.00	90.00	80.00
☐ **Contract,** record company contract signed by Robert Merrill	40.00	50.00	42.00
☐ **Contract,** signed by Richard Tucker	70.00	95.00	80.00
☐ **Earrings,** once belonged to Zinka Milanor	60.00	80.00	70.00
☐ **Envelope,** addressed by Dorothy Kirsten, contents missing	12.00	16.00	13.00
☐ **Fan,** used by Grace Moore	30.00	40.00	33.00

Theatrical Program, *Adelina Patti, farewell tour,* **$25.00-$35.00**

	Current Price Range		P/Y Average
☐ **Gloves,** pair of long silver gloves worn by Patrice Munsel in an opera production, with letter of authentication	42.00	50.00	46.00
☐ **Helmet,** reputedly worn by Birgit Nilsson in a production	77.00	99.00	85.00
☐ **Letter,** handwritten in Russian by Fyodor Chaliapin	430.00	560.00	450.00
☐ **Libretto,** opera libretto signed by Cesare Siepi	13.00	18.00	15.00

	Current Price Range		P/Y Average
Libretto, opera libretto signed by Helen Traubel	13.00	18.00	15.00
Magazine, *Opera News,* signed by Justino Diaz who is on the cover	25.00	35.00	28.00
Magazine Cover, signed by Joan Sutherland	25.00	35.00	28.00
Magazine Cover, signed by Richard Tucker, c. 1962	20.00	26.00	22.00
Menu, signed by Enrico Caruso, c. 1915	160.00	200.00	170.00
Menu, signed by Joan Sutherland	8.00	12.00	10.00
Menu, signed by Lorenzo Alvary	9.00	16.00	11.00
Photograph, autographed photo of Beverly in costume from *Daughter of the Regiment,* 8″ x 10″	25.00	35.00	27.00
Photograph, autographed by Charles Anthony, 8″ x 10″	10.00	15.00	11.50
Photograph, autographed photo of Dorothy Kirsten, 8″ x 10″	55.00	70.00	65.00
Photograph, autographed photo of Enrico Caruso in *Rigoletto* costume, 5″ x 7″	145.00	185.00	150.00
Photograph, autographed portrait of Enrico Caruso, c. 1906, 8″ x 10″	180.00	220.00	200.00
Photograph, autographed portrait of Fyodor Chaliapin, c. 1925, 5″ x 7″	185.00	265.00	200.00
Photograph, autographed photo of James Melton in costume, 8″ x 10″	23.00	35.00	27.00
Photograph, autographed photo of John Brownlee in *Rigoletto* costume, c. 1940, 8″ x 10″	23.00	30.00	26.00
Photograph, autographed photo of Jussi Bjoerling in *Boheme* costume, 8″ x 10″	23.00	33.00	26.00
Photograph, autographed photo of Leontyne Price in costume, 8″ x 10″	30.00	40.00	33.00
Photograph, autographed photo of Lorenzo Alvary, 8″ x 10″	10.00	15.00	11.50
Photograph, autographed photo of Nadine Conner	21.00	26.00	22.00
Photograph, autographed photo of Rosalind Elias, 8″ x 10″	11.00	15.00	12.00
Photograph, autographed photo of Tito Gobbi, c. 1959, 8″ x 10″	30.00	37.00	32.00
Pinback Button, "Beverly Sills Is a Good High," red and white, c. 1975	3.00	4.00	3.50
Poster, advertising appearance of Salvatore Baccaloni, c. 1940	13.00	18.00	14.50
Poster, autographed opera poster of Nicolai Gedda	23.00	32.00	35.00
Poster, Metropolitan Opera poster, *Emperor Jones,* signed by Lawrence Tibbett	250.00	325.00	275.00
Poster, Metropolitan Opera poster featuring Enrico Caruso	230.00	330.00	260.00
Program, concert program, signed by Roberta Peters	10.00	15.00	12.00
Program, Metropolitan Opera, signed by Frances Alda	26.00	38.00	29.00
Program, Metropolitan Opera, signed by Kirsten Flagstad	35.00	45.00	38.00

	Current Price Range		P/Y Average
☐ **Program,** Metropolitan Opera House, pre-1900	10.00	14.00	12.00
☐ **Program,** Metropolitan Opera House, 1901-1910	8.00	12.00	10.00
☐ **Program,** Metropolitan Opera House, 1911-1920	6.00	10.00	8.00
☐ **Program,** Metropolitan Opera House, 1921-1930	5.00	9.00	7.00
☐ **Program,** Metropolitan Opera House, 1931-1940	4.00	6.00	5.00
☐ **Program,** Metropolitan Opera House, 1941-1950	3.00	5.00	4.00
☐ **Program,** Metropolitan Opera House, 1951-1960	2.00	4.00	3.00
☐ **Program,** Metropolitan Opera House, 1961-1970	1.00	2.50	1.50
☐ **Program,** opera program, signed by Jan Peerce	12.00	18.00	14.00
☐ **Score,** from *Traviata,* signed by Lily Pons	30.00	40.00	33.00
☐ **Sheet Music,** *Some Enchanted Evening,* signed by Ezio Pinza	35.00	48.00	38.00
☐ **Sheet Music,** *When Irish Eyes Are Smiling,* signed by John McCormack	85.00	110.00	90.00
☐ **Signature,** on a card of Cesare Siepi	4.00	5.50	4.50
☐ **T-Shirt,** with likeness of Leontyne Price	8.00	11.00	9.25

ORIENTAL FURNITURE

DESCRIPTION: Oriental furniture differed from European furniture in several ways:
  1) it was lower.
  2) it was built to be arranged against walls, never jutting out or dividing a room.
  3) it was built to conceal daily functions; writing tables folded into cabinets, chests were used for clothes, tables as altar frontals.
  4) it was joined by grooves, not nails, and rarely glue.

CONSTRUCTION: Hardwood, particularly rosewood was the preferred furniture material in more northerly climates, and bamboo or lacquer in the warmer southerly regions. Oriental furniture cannot really be typified much more than this. It was ornate, it was simple, some pieces were of superior workmanship, others fell apart easily.

ADDITIONAL TIPS: Up until now, Oriental furniture has represented only a small percentage of the Oriental collectibles market, although that trend seems to be changing. Now would be a good time to purchase some of these interesting relics, before prices are swept upwards and out of the sight of the average collector.

RECOMMENDED READING: For more in-depth information on Oriental furniture you may refer to *The Official Price Guide to Oriental Collectibles*, published by The House of Collectibles.

	Current Price Range		P/Y Average
☐ **Altar Coffer,** *Chinese, rectangular with drawers, carved scrolls and dragons, Huang Huali, 60" x 32" x 19"*	6000.00	8000.00	6250.00
☐ **Altar Table,** *Chinese, carved hardwood, rectangular, apron pierced with fruit carvings, trestle supports, 82" x 35" x 17", 19th century*	1800.00	2200.00	1850.00
☐ **Altar Table,** *Chinese, carved rectangular, top features scrolled ends above apron, slender legs, Hongmu, 57" x 32" x 15", 19th century*	1500.00	2000.00	1550.00
☐ **Altar Table,** *Chinese, low rosewood with marble inset top, maroon finish, pierced apron panels, mask and flame carved knees, scrolled feet, 25" x 8" x 5"*	75.00	150.00	80.00
☐ **Altar Table,** *rosewood, carved pierced apron, phoenix bird motif, 46" x 23" x 15¼"*	800.00	1200.00	850.00
☐ **Armchair,** *Chinese, simple toprail above splat carved with medallion, seat features cane matting, Jigi Mu, 17th century*	4000.00	6000.00	4200.00
☐ **Armchair,** *hardwood, intricately carved in high relief, dragon and serpent motif, cabriole legs, 40" high, 19th century*	1000.00	1100.00	1100.00
☐ **Armchair,** *hardwood, carved back, coiling dragon amidst clouds, panel with a phoenix, lathed arms, cabriole legs, 19th century*	750.00	1050.00	765.00
☐ **Armchair,** *teakwood, horseshoe shape, pierced trelliswork decoration, 20th century*	450.00	500.00	425.00
☐ **Bar,** *mahogany, hinged top, reliefed landscape decor, footed, 40" high, 20th century*	600.00	625.00	625.00
☐ **Bed,** *hardwood, headboard, foot fretted design, high polish, 32" high, 19th century*	1400.00	1600.00	1450.00
☐ **Bed,** *fruitwood, carved canopy, paneled sides, frieze borders, 8' high, 19th century*	3000.00	4000.00	3025.00
☐ **Bed,** *Chinese, carved hardwood, paneled backrest, open arms with carved fretwork, carved fretwork base, silk cushions, 65" x 29" x 43", 19th century*	2500.00	3500.00	2575.00
☐ **Bench,** *rosewood, inlaid cane top, straight legs, 22" high, 20th century*	6500.00	7000.00	6575.00
☐ **Box,** *tiered, Chinese Export, black and gold lacquer, oval shaped with compartments, 11" high, 19th century*	600.00	900.00	625.00
☐ **Breakfront,** *Chinese, teakwood, upper section has double glass doors with two shelves and mirrored back, bottom features carved double doors, 6'3" x 2'10" x 16"*	900.00	1200.00	925.00
☐ **Cabinet,** *bamboo, four legs, 19th century*	350.00	450.00	375.00
☐ **Cabinet,** *burlwood, open shelves, bamboo doors and drawers, 48" high, 19th century*	3500.00	3850.00	3550.00
☐ **Cabinet,** *camphorwood, carved top, Chinese, 18" x 13"*	175.00	200.00	180.00
☐ **Cabinet,** *Chinese design Chippendale, lighted, 74" high*	15000.00	17000.00	15500.00

	Current Price Range		P/Y Average
☐ **Chaise,** *Chinese, hardwood, carved, high back with openwork medallion carving, rectangular arms with openwork carving, long rectangular seat, short legs with scrollwork, 54" x 77" x 27"*	700.00	1000.00	725.00
☐ **Chaise,** *hardwood, long back panel, carved design, low legs, 37" high, 19th century*	3000.00	3500.00	3025.00
☐ **Chest,** *camphor, heavily carved with sailing ships in landscape, hinged cover, 34" x 16" x 19"*	250.00	350.00	275.00
☐ **Chest,** *cedar lined, oak exterior, elaborate all-over carving, decorative scalloped brass lock with floral and leaf chasing, stepped bracket feet, 40" long, 21" deep, 23" high*	400.00	600.00	425.00
☐ **Chest on Chest,** *Chinese, black lacquer, mother-of-pearl inlay fish, trees, bats, kites, birds, animals, two double doors, bracket feet, 31" wide, 16" deep, 50" high, 19th century*	1500.00	2000.00	1550.00
☐ **Clothes Cupboards,** *Chinese, doors, shelves and drawers, some fruit carving, brass lockplates and hinges, Han Mu, pair, 8'7" x 49" x 21"*	20000.00	30000.00	20500.00
☐ **Commode,** *19th century*	1000.00	1500.00	1100.00
☐ **Console Tables,** *Chinese, black lacquer, gilt decoration, half-moon shape with gilt painted landscape, fret and foliate border, shaped apron with four legs with scrolled flanks, 31" x 34" x 17", 19th century*	6500.00	9500.00	6550.00
☐ **Cupboard,** *Chinese, Ming style, hardwood, rectangular, molded edges, hinged doors, square stiles form feet, 62" x 31" x 16"*	1200.00	1500.00	1250.00
☐ **Cupboard,** *Korean, elm, rectangular, paneled front features drawers and doors, 68" x 44"* .	700.00	1000.00	750.00
☐ **Daybed,** *Chinese Export, mahogany with canework, carved roll supports, caned lid that opens, drawers, 7' long, 19th century* ...	5000.00	8000.00	5500.00
☐ **Desk,** *burlwood, carved decoration on top, squared simple legs, three top drawers, brass fittings, 33" high, 19th century*	3500.00	4000.00	3600.00
☐ **Dining Chair,** *hardwood, knobbed ends, sculptured borders, 29" high, 18th century* ..	2900.00	3200.00	2950.00
☐ **Dining Table,** *hardwood, rectangular top, two medallion decorations on surface, 32" high, 19th century*	700.00	900.00	750.00
☐ **Dining Table,** *rectangular, geometric carved border, 36" high, 20th century*	800.00	900.00	850.00
☐ **Dining Room Set,** *Chinese, teakwood and blond Honduran mahogany, table has Chinese dragon carving and plate glass top, six side chairs have straight legs, upholstered seats, table is 72" long, 42" wide, 29" high, 20th century*	500.00	800.00	550.00

	Current Price Range		P/Y Average

☐ **Display Cabinets,** *Chinese, painted lacquer, rectangular with assortment of shelves, a pair of pierced lattice doors and drawers, decorated with gilt phoenix and dragon medallions, 75" x 36" x 15", 19th century, pair* — 5000.00 / 7000.00 / 5500.00

☐ **Dressing Table,** *padouk wood, carved, 3' wide* — 700.00 / 730.00 / 710.00

☐ **Dressing Table,** *rectangular top, three drawers, above two pedestals with three drawers each, drawer fronts lacquered in red and gold, 30" x 4'6"* .... 575.00 / 700.00 / 580.00

☐ **Etagere,** *hardwood, rectangular top, scrolled design, shelves open and with sliding doors, gilded decoration, 40" high, 19th century* ... 400.00 / 500.00 / 420.00

☐ **Etagere,** *huoli, veneer inset, trellis supports, scroll work, 40" high, 19th century* .... 3000.00 / 4000.00 / 3100.00

☐ **Game Table,** *Chinese, hardwood, carved, rounded and shaped top with raised border, apron contains four drawers, supported by an x-form stand and hipped legs, 32" high, 19th century* .... 1100.00 / 1600.00 / 1150.00

☐ **Game Table,** *hardwood, drawers all around, x-shaped brackets, 32" high, 20th century* ... 1000.00 / 1100.00 / 1150.00

☐ **Garden Seat,** *hardwood, round marble inlaid seat, 20" high, 20th century* .... 1000.00 / 1100.00 / 1150.00

☐ **Garden Seat,** *green lacquered wood, landscape decor, 19" high* .... 900.00 / 1100.00 / 925.00

☐ **Garden Seat,** *Chinese, barrel shape, mahogany, five supports and floor stretcher, piercing on apron and legs and beading at the borders, inset handpainted porcelain top depicts storks in floral landscape, artist's seal, 14" diameter, 18" high* .... 200.00 / 400.00 / 210.00

☐ **Headboard,** *hardwood, red lacquer and gilt decoration, elaborately carved with birds and foliage, 60" high, 19th century* .... 2000.00 / 2500.00 / 2100.00

☐ **Lamp,** *patinated, polished bronze, 19th century* .... 900.00 / 1000.00 / 925.00

☐ **Lantern,** *bronze, lidded, pierced grate, 22" high, 19th century* .... 1400.00 / 1800.00 / 1450.00

☐ **Lantern,** *metal, gilded, relief design, set of four, 18" high, 19th century* .... 1500.00 / 1700.00 / 1550.00

☐ **Loveseat,** *Chinese, carved hardwood, rectangular, spindleback sides and apron, round legs joined by stretchers and footrest, 36" x 33" x 19"* .... 3000.00 / 4000.00 / 3100.00

☐ **Pedestal,** *Chinese, teakwood, inset white marble circular top, pierced tendril and floral apron, curved legs, 12" diameter, 36" high* .. 300.00 / 500.00 / 325.00

☐ **Pedestal,** *Chinese, teakwood, pierced and carved apron and curved legs, 16" diameter, 37" high* .... 400.00 / 500.00 / 425.00

☐ **Pedestal,** *Chinese, teakwood, round top with marble inlay, beaded border, carved and pierced floral apron, high cabriole legs, x-form base, 11" diameter, 36" high* .... 400.00 / 600.00 / 425.00

	Current Price Range		P/Y Average
☐ **Screen,** *coromandel, four panels, front of each decorated with various landscape, figural and pagoda scenes, back decorated with birds and flowers, 72" x 72"*	500.00	700.00	525.00
☐ **Screen,** *hardwood, four panels, carved figural domestic scenes, each panel measures 72" high by 17⅞" wide, 20th century*	1500.00	2500.00	1550.00
☐ **Screen,** *Chinese, black lacquered wood, four panels, figures in garden scene, border features dragons, 9' x 88"*	1600.00	2100.00	1650.00
☐ **Settee,** *Chinese, Ming style, rosewood, horseshoe shape with shell and whorl open arm terminations, open back with two curved splats, featuring carved Taoist and Greek key motifs, straight legs, single loose Shou embroidered cushion in two-tone gold, 50" long, 20th century*	1200.00	1600.00	1250.00
☐ **Pair of Matching,** *open armchairs to above settee*	1200.00	1600.00	1250.00
☐ **Settee,** *Southeast Asian, mahogany, finely carved all over floral, leaf and scroll design on sides, back and apron, back panel has carved landscape scene with train of elephants, scrolled arm terminals, plank seat for cushion, stylized paw feet, 70" long, 26" deep, 33" high*	800.00	1200.00	850.00
☐ **Matching Cocktail Table,** *to above settee, 50" long, 24" deep, 16" high*	300.00	500.00	350.00
☐ **Side Chairs,** *Chinese, shaped top rail, paneled splat, openwork apron, legs joined by stretchers, foot rest, Hongmu, pair*	1200.00	1400.00	1250.00
☐ **Side Chairs,** *Chinese, simple design of top rail and plain splat, cane seat joins to shaped brackets and tapered legs, Hongmu, 19th century*	450.00	650.00	475.00
☐ **Side Chairs,** *Chinese, Ming style, hardwood, four chairs, shaped top rails, each splat has a different floral carving, solid seat, square legs, stretchers and foot rest, 19th century* . .	1500.00	2000.00	1550.00
☐ **Side Table,** *Chinese, Ming style, hardwood, shaped rectangular top, plain apron, carved flanks support legs joined by double stretchers, 49" x 30" x 15"*	600.00	1000.00	650.00
☐ **Side Tables,** *Chinese, Ming style, inlaid square top, shaped stretchers on square legs, hoofed feet, 16" x 20", 19th century* . . .	800.00	950.00	850.00
☐ **Stand,** *hardwood with mother-of-pearl inlay, claw feet, carved decor, 36" high, 20th century*	575.00	625.00	580.00
☐ **Stand,** *hardwood, round shape, red lacquer, 24" high, 19th century*	1800.00	2000.00	1850.00
☐ **Stand,** *hardwood, three shelves, key work frieze, 31" high, 19th century*	900.00	1100.00	950.00
☐ **Stool,** *Chinese, painted black lacquer, barrel shaped, with landscape scenes, mock ring handles, 19" high, 19th century*	800.00	1000.00	850.00

	Current Price Range		P/Y Average
☐ **Stool,** *eight sided, scroll feet, frieze decor, 18" high, 19th century*	1000.00	2000.00	1100.00
☐ **Stool,** *Chinese, carved barrel shape, top inlaid above pierced apron, Hongmu, 10" high, 19th century*	600.00	900.00	650.00
☐ **Table,** *burlwood, geometric frieze, scroll toes, 36" high, 19th century*	800.00	1000.00	825.00
☐ **Table,** *burlwood, leather inset top, side table on simple squared legs, 20" high, 19th century*	2000.00	2250.00	2100.00
☐ **Table,** *burlwood, turned legs, squared supports, polished top, 16" high, 19th century* . .	700.00	800.00	725.00
☐ **Table,** *cinnabar, highly ornate, tall, decor overall, lacquered, 30" high, 18th century* . . .	7000.00	8000.00	7050.00

ORIENTAL PAINTINGS

COMMENTS: Early Chinese paintings consisted of mostly landscapes, though later works incorporated people, animals, court scenes, portraits and calligraphy. Paintings was done on a variety of materials including silk and paper.

RECOMMENDED READING: For further information refer to *The Official Price Guide to Oriental Collectibles,* published by The House of Collectibles.

	Current Price Range		P/Y Average
☐ **Album,** *Chinese, ink and color on paper, eight leaves in album, various landscapes, Yuan Bei, 8" x 11", 19th century*	1400.00	1800.00	1450.00
☐ **Album,** *Chinese, ink and color on paper, twelve leaves, Chinese erotica, 7" x 6", 19th century*	600.00	800.00	650.00
☐ **Album,** *Chinese, ink and color on paper, twelve leaves, animals and vegetables, 10" x 6", 20th century*	250.00	400.00	275.00
☐ **Fan Painting,** *Chinese, ink and color on gold paper, scenic view of figure on bridge, by Chen Guan, 7" x 20", 17th century*	1500.00	2500.00	1550.00

	Current Price Range		P/Y Average

☐ **Fan Painting,** *Chinese, ink and color on paper, house scene with scholar and attendant, Hua Yan, 6" x 20", 18th century* . . . . — 1000.00 — 1300.00 — 1050.00

☐ **Fan Painting,** *Chinese, ink and color on paper, scenic view, Pu Ru, 7" x 20", 20th century* . . . . — 650.00 — 850.00 — 675.00

☐ **Fan Painting,** *Chinese, ink and color on paper, vegetables, Wang Xuetao, 7" x 21", 20th century* . . . . — 650.00 — 850.00 — 675.00

☐ **Fan Painting,** *Chinese, ink on gold paper, scenic landscape with two figures, Bian Wenyu, 6" x 19", 17th century* . . . . — 2500.00 — 4000.00 — 2550.00

☐ **Hanging Scroll,** *Chinese, ink on paper, running script calligraphy, Wang Wenzhi, 48" x 15", 18th century* . . . . — 700.00 — 1000.00 — 725.00

☐ **Hanging Scroll,** *Chinese, ink on paper, scene with flower, rock and bamboo, Fang Xun, 55" x 19", 18th century* . . . . — 2000.00 — 2500.00 — 2050.00

☐ **Hanging Scroll,** *Chinese, ink on paper, scenic view, Pu Ru, 36" x 13", 20 century* . . . . — 850.00 — 1050.00 — 875.00

☐ **Hanging Scroll,** *Chinese, ink on paper, scenic view with flowers, rocks and bamboo, Jian Ting Xi, 51" x 19", 18th century* . . . . — 2000.00 — 4000.00 — 2100.00

☐ **Hanging Scroll,** *Chinese, ink on paper, two fish, Li Ku Chan, 27" x 19", 20th century* . . . . — 750.00 — 950.00 — 775.00

☐ **Hanging Scroll,** *Chinese, ink on satin, scenic landscape, Cai Jia, 39" x 26", 18th century* . . — 4000.00 — 6000.00 — 4100.00

☐ **Hanging Scroll,** *Chinese, ink on satin, scenic landscape, Fa Ruozhen, 90" x 19", 17th century* . . . . — 22000.00 — 25000.00 — 22500.00

☐ **Hanging Scroll,** *Chinese, ink on silk, bamboo, 63" x 19", 18th century* . . . . — 1000.00 — 1250.00 — 1100.00

☐ **Hanging Scroll,** *Chinese, ink on silk, landscape, gold color, Qiang Guozhong, 25" x 14", 17th century* . . . . — 15000.00 — 19000.00 — 15500.00

☐ **Hanging Scroll,** *Chinese, ink on silk, Lohan, 52" x 33", 17 century* . . . . — 1800.00 — 2300.00 — 1900.00

☐ **Hanging Scroll,** *Chinese, ink on silk, scenic landscape, Wang Jian, 18" x 10", 17th century* . . . . — 11000.00 — 14000.00 — 11500.00

☐ **Hanging Scroll,** *Chinese, ink on silk, scenic view, by Dong Qichang, 42" x 21", 16th century* . . . . — 9000.00 — 12000.00 — 9500.00

☐ **Hanging Scroll,** *Chinese, ink on silk, scenic view, Mingshan Qingyong, 73" x 40", 17th century* . . . . — 5000.00 — 7000.00 — 5200.00

☐ **Hanging Scroll,** *Chinese, ink on silk, scenic view of trees and water, Pu Ru, 14" x 23", 20th century* . . . . — 1200.00 — 1500.00 — 1250.00

☐ **Hanging Scroll,** *Chinese, rubbing of calligraphy, repainted in gold, Qing Gaozong, 62" x 29", 18th century* . . . . — 700.00 — 1000.00 — 750.00

☐ **Portraits,** *Chinese, ink and color on silk, ancestor portraits, pair, 57" x 36", 18th century* . . . . — 3000.00 — 5000.00 — 3100.00

	Current Price Range		P/Y Average
☐ **Portraits,** *Chinese, ink and color on paper, Deities, pair, 56" x 29", 19th century*	800.00	1000.00	850.00

ORIENTAL PRINTS

COMMENTS: The method of color printing that became popular in Japan, or at least widely adopted by publishers of illustrated books, bore little relationship to Western lithography — the artform of Currier and Ives. Nor could it be directly linked to any of the earlier Western efforts in color printing. Originating c. 1765, it involved the cutting of numerous duplicate blocks to achieve "nishiki-e"; brocade-like pictures. To the Japanese, who had not painted in oils on canvas, colored prints were likened to woven fabrics. It was not unusual for two or three dozen blocks, or even more, to be cut for a single picture. Each was used to print a particular color shade which the printer was responsible for applying. Each color hue, some of them differing so slightly that none but a keen eye could distinguish it, was applied in such a way that subtle blends and tonal effects could be achieved. So delicate was this work that every step had to be carried out flawlessly; cutting the blocks, choosing colors, mixing them, applying them to the blocks, and pulling impressions. The alignment in printing could not be off by even a millimeter, without destroying visual quality. Considering that each was printed by hand, without machinery of any kind, this was surely a proof of dedication and innate skill.

RECOMMENDED READING: For further information refer to *The Official Price Guide to Oriental Collectibles,* published by The House of Collectibles.

☐ **The Basket of Medlar Fruit,** *artist: Paul Jacoulet; carver: Maeda; printers: Fujii, Onodera, pencil signature, published May 23, 1950, 18" x 14"*	150.00	300.00	175.00
☐ **Chinese Mask Seller,** *artist: Paul Jacoulet; carver: Maeda; printers: Honda, Uchikawa, Ogawa, pencil signature, published December 30, 1940, 18" x 14"*	350.00	550.00	375.00

	Current Price Range		P/Y Average
☐ **Chinese Puppets,** *artist: Paul Jacoulet; carver: Yamagishi; printer: Urushibara, pencil signature, published April 29, 1935, 18" x 14"*	450.00	650.00	475.00
☐ **Jade Lady,** *artist: Paul Jacoulet; carver: Maeda; printers: Honda, Uchikawa, pencil signature, published February 2, 1940, 18" x 14"*	600.00	900.00	625.00
☐ **The Love Letter,** *artist: Paul Jacoulet; carver: Maeda; printers: Onodera, Honda, pencil signature, published May 1955, 18" x 14"*	650.00	850.00	675.00
☐ **The Miraculous Catch,** *artist: Paul Jacoulet; carver: Maeda; printers: Honda, Uchikawa, pencil signature, published December 12, 1939, 18" x 14"*	350.00	550.00	375.00
☐ **Sawara Fisherman,** *artist: Paul Jacoulet; carver: Maeda; printers: Honda, Fujii, pencil signature, published January 15, 1936, 18" x 14"*	400.00	600.00	425.00
☐ **Shepherds Of The High Mountains,** *artist: Paul Jacoulet; carver: Maeda; printer: Ogawa, pencil signature, published April 20, 1941, 18" x 14"*	300.00	500.00	325.00
☐ **The Water Pipe,** *artist: Paul Jacoulet; carver: Maeda; printer: Onodera, pencil signature, published December 31, 1952, 18" x 14"*	300.00	500.00	325.00
☐ **Winter Flowers,** *artist: Paul Jacoulet; carver: Maeda; printers: Onodera, Honda, pencil signature, published June1955, 18" x 14"*	400.00	600.00	425.00
☐ **Young Girl of Saipan And Hibiscus Flowers,** *artist: Paul Jacoulet; carver: Yamagishi; printer: Urushibara, pencil signature, published June 30, 1934, 18" x 14"*	200.00	425.00	225.00

ORIENTAL TEXTILES

DESCRIPTION: Collectible Oriental textiles are based primarily upon silk, and silk brocade products, though satin, cotton and gauze are also acceptable. Silk garments were cherished and given special treatment over other materials. They were reserved mainly for special occasions.

MATERIAL: Silk was a carefully kept secret of the Chinese for many centuries, and even today there are only a few places in the world where it can be successful cultivated (the United States is not one of them). For years envious countries — particularly Japan who prized the textile as an esential commodity during warm weather — believed silk was made from some kind of plant, like flax or cotton. The real secret lay with a simple moth, who happened to lay her eggs on the leaves of a mulberry tree. When the eggs hatched and the silkworms appeared, they would steadily eat the leaves of their birthplace, before wrapping themselves in a gorgeous, very strong cocoon comprised of around 1000 yards of silken thread filament. Nevertheless, it takes thousands of silkworms to make one yard of silk, which is one reason it is still such a expensive natural fabric. In the old days the silken filaments were woven on hand looms and distributed to a very profitable foreign trade. Now power looms are used for the same purposes, but silkworms continue to be raised in carefully monitored incubators and are our only source to this valuable commodity.

COMMENTS: Prized Oriental textiles frequently feature some type of embroidery, stitched in satin or silk thread in colorful motifs. Small personal items can often be found in good condition, as can whole garments or swatches of fabric. Othen collectors like to mount their finds within frames as gorgeous wall hangings — care must be taken, however, to avoid direct sunlight. The main problem with old silks is not that they fall apart, but that they fade so easily.

The main clothing articles in Oriental wardrobes included kimono, jackets, chuba (longer than a jacket, shorter than a robe), robes, obi (sash), hakama (loose trousers), fun dashi (loin cloth) and the mo (apron).

RECOMMENDED READING: For more in-depth information on Oriental textiles, you may refer to *The Official Price Guide to Oriental Collectibles,* published by The House of Collectibles.

Japanese Robe, *1820-50,* **$1700.00-$1800.00**
(photo courtesy of ©Marc Bernsau, Sanford, ME, 1984)

	Current Price Range		P/Y Average

CEREMONIAL

☐ **Altar Frontal,** *30" long, c. 1800s, red silk, gold stitched dragon, lotus bat motif*	710.00	920.00	815.00
☐ **Altar Frontal,** *32" long, c. 1800s, blue silk, gold stitched floral motif*	510.00	752.00	631.00
☐ **Altar Robe,** *40" x 70", c. 1900s, silk, rectangular, embroidered figurines, marked*	930.00	960.00	945.00
☐ **Badge,** *10" x 11", c. 1800s, blue satin, blue green, orange, white stitches, duck motif* . . .	350.00	450.00	400.00
☐ **Badge,** *12" x 12", c. 1800s, gold satin, multicolored stitches, pheasant motif*	300.00	400.00	350.00
☐ **Badge,** *12" x 12", c. 1800s, satin, multi-colored stitches, egret shape, floral motif*	200.00	300.00	250.00
☐ **Badge,** *12" x 12", c. 1800s, silk, bird shape, multicolored stitches*	150.00	200.00	175.00
☐ **Banner,** *8" x 26", c. 1700s, yellow damask, dragon, loud motif, Korean*	750.00	950.00	850.00
☐ **Court Robe,** *50" long, c. 1770s, red silk, embroidered cranes, flowers, fruit, butterflies, waves, emblems*	1000.00	1250.00	1150.00
☐ **Court Vest,** *50" long, c. 1800s, black satin, embroidered, bats, clouds, birds, dragons, waves*	1100.00	1600.00	1350.00
☐ **Holy Robe,** *58" x 65", c. 1800s, yellow damask, embroidered dragons, clouds and bird motifs*	2100.00	3200.00	2650.00
☐ **Robe,** *1600s, ceremonial, brilliant floral and dragon motif*	350.00	375.00	362.50
☐ **Throne Back Cover,** *25" x 15", yellow satin, embroidered lotus, foliage, bat, fan, bamboo motif*	450.00	550.00	500.00
☐ **Warrior Outfit,** *60" long, c. 1700s, multicolored brocade, embroidered gold floral motif* .	650.00	850.00	750.00

DECORATIVE

☐ **Embroidery,** *9" x 23", c. 1900s, beige background, multicolored, vase with flowers motif, brocade border*	20.00	30.00	25.00
☐ **Embroidery,** *10" x 24", c. 1900s, beige background, multicolored bird, floral motif, brocade border*	40.00	50.00	45.00
☐ **Embroidery,** *12" x 12", c. 1600s, multicolored satin, oval shape, embroidered floral, foliage motifs*	450.00	650.00	550.00
☐ **Embroidery,** *12" x 13", c. 1900s, multicolored background, floral, bird, butterfly motif, brocade border*	20.00	30.00	25.00
☐ **Embroidery,** *13" x 26", c. 1900s, beige background, hand stitched black border, multicolored vase, incense burner, floral motif*	80.00	100.00	90.00
☐ **Embroidery,** *13" x 26", c. 1900s, beige background, multicolored bird motif, brocade border*	60.00	90.00	75.00
☐ **Embroidery,** *15" x 12", c. 1600s, multicolored satin, oval shape, embroidered bird, tree motifs*	450.00	650.00	550.00

	Current Price Range		P/Y Average
☐ **Embroidery,** 36" x 77", c. 1900s, multicolored, phoenix, peony blossom, magnolia tree	600.00	900.00	750.00
☐ **Embroidery,** 36" x 78", c. 1900s, silk, multicolored, hoo birds, cranes, ducks, lilies, peonies, cherry blossom motif	600.00	700.00	650.00
☐ **Embroidery,** 36" x 78", c. 1900s, silk, multicolored, two cranes, pine tree, peony, cherry blossoms	600.00	700.00	650.00
☐ **Embroidery,** 40" x 80", c. 1900s, silk, multicolored, male and female peacock, magnolia tree, roses	400.00	600.00	500.00
☐ **Embroidery,** 42" x 10", c. 1900s, silk, multicolored, dragon, flaming pearl motif	1000.00	2000.00	1100.00
☐ **Embroidery,** 46" x 84", c. 1900s, silk, red, bat, fungus, boy, butterfly motif	800.00	1000.00	900.00
☐ **Embroidery,** 60" x 25", c. 1700s, multicolored silk, embroidered dragon, clouds, bats and emblems motifs	650.00	850.00	750.00
☐ **Embroidery,** 110" x 60", c. 1800s, multicolored satin, immortals, attendants, deer motifs ...	4100.00	6200.00	5150.00
☐ **Panel,** 18" x 60", c. 1700s, yellow satin, embroidered dragons, bats, fruit, trees, rocks motifs	550.00	850.00	700.00
☐ **Panel,** 20" x 20", c. 1700s, gray satin, embroidered vase, floral, bat motif	450.00	550.00	500.00
☐ **Panel,** 30" x 20", c. 1700s, greenish gold brocade, embroidered dragon, cloud motif	250.00	350.00	300.00
☐ **Panel,** 30" x 20", c. 1700s, light orange satin, embroidered immortals, birds, fruit motifs ..	150.00	200.00	175.00
☐ **Panel,** 36" x 18", c. 1700s, orange satin, figural, immortal motif river scape, garden scene	800.00	1250.00	1025.00
☐ **Panel,** 50" x 30", c. 1800s, blue velvet, embroidered dragons, lotus, lion motifs	250.00	350.00	300.00
☐ **Panel,** 60" x 25", c. 1800s, brown gauze, embroidered dragon, clouds, bats, trees, rocks motifs	350.00	550.00	450.00
☐ **Panel,** 65" x 15", c. 1800s, gold satin, motif of religious haven	800.00	1200.00	1000.00
☐ **Panel,** 65" x 50", c. 1800s, red satin, embroidered trees, bats motif	650.00	850.00	750.00
☐ **Panel,** 70" x 35", c. 1800s, off white satin, embroidered Buddhist heaven motif	3100.00	5200.00	4150.00
☐ **Pillar Hanging,** 90" x 60", c. 1700s, peach silk, embroidered ons, birds, clouds, religious emblems	8100.00	11000.00	9550.00
☐ **Silk Cover,** 9' x 6', c. 1800s, pink embroidered floral, fowl, tree motif	1100.00	1500.00	1300.00
☐ **Table Frontal,** 35" x 34", c. 1800s, red gauze, embroidered floral fruit motif	250.00	350.00	300.00
☐ **Table Frontal,** 40" x 30", c. 1700s, red silk, embroidered gold elephant motif	350.00	550.00	450.00
☐ **Tapestry,** 70" x 92", c. 1900s, sheared velvet, lake, toreii gate, pine tree hills, Japanese ...	500.00	600.00	550.00
☐ **Wall Hanging,** 40" x 60", c. 1900s, silk, multicolored, child, dragon, wave motif	2000.00	2500.00	2250.00
☐ **Wall Hanging,** 90" x 60", c. 1700s, blue brocade, embroidered gold dragon motif	8100.00	10000.00	9050.00

	Current Price Range		P/Y Average

FUNCTIONAL

	Current Price Range		P/Y Average
☐ **Blanket,** *6'8" x 5', c. 1900s, green, maroon, white, embroiderery, vine motif, Turkish*	2100.00	3100.00	2600.00
☐ **Chair Panel,** *70" x 20", c. 1600s, orange satin seascape, dragon, phoenix motif*	1100.00	1600.00	1350.00
☐ **Chair Panel,** *70" x 22", c. 1700s, orange velvet, lotus, phoenix motif*	650.00	850.00	750.00
☐ **Chair Panel,** *70" x 25", c. 1700s, pink brocade, dragon phoenix, bird motif*	1600.00	2600.00	2100.00
☐ **Cushion Covers,** *40" x 40", c. 1800s, yellow brocade, embroidered dragon, cloud motif* . .	612.00	820.00	716.00
☐ **Pillow Cover,** *20" x 20", c. 1800s, yellow satin, embroidered red flowers, green foliage motif*	350.00	550.00	450.00

GARMENTS

	Current Price Range		P/Y Average
☐ **Apron,** *40" long, c. 1800s, green silk, embroidered dragon, phoenix, bat motif*	800.00	1100.00	750.00
☐ **Chuba,** *50" long, c. 1700s, yellow brocade, dragon motif*	3100.00	3600.00	3350.00
☐ **Chuba,** *60" long, c. 1800s, red brocade, floral motif*	650.00	850.00	750.00
☐ **Coat,** *45" long, c. 1800s, black satin, embroidered floral, wave motif*	450.00	650.00	550.00
☐ **Coat,** *45" long, c. 1800s, black satin, embroidered multicolored fruit, floral motif*	350.00	550.00	450.00
☐ **Coat,** *45" long, c. 1800s, black satin, embroidered phoenix, dragon, clouds, bats, floral motif*	350.00	550.00	450.00
☐ **Coat,** *45" long, c. 1800s, yellow satin, embroidered floral, figurals, landscape, cloud motif*	650.00	850.00	750.00
☐ **Coat,** *52" long, c. 1800s, purple silk, embroidered floral, bamboo, bat motif*	810.00	1300.00	1055.00
☐ **Coat,** *55" long, c. 1800s, quilted black satin, embroidered cranes, wave motif*	650.00	850.00	750.00
☐ **Jacket,** *30" long, c. 1800s, red silk, embroidered lion motif*	700.00	900.00	800.00
☐ **Jacket,** *35" long, c. 1800s, white gauze, embroidered floral, pavilion, tree motifs*	550.00	750.00	650.00
☐ **Jacket,** *38" long, c. 1800s, purple silk, embroidered, cloud, garden motifs*	150.00	200.00	175.00
☐ **Jacket,** *40" long, c. 1800s, blue silk, embroidered gold dragon*	350.00	450.00	400.00
☐ **Jacket,** *40" long, c. 1600s, green brocade, embroidered dragon motif*	1100.00	1600.00	1350.00
☐ **Jacket,** *40" long, c. 1800s, red silk, embroidered dragon, cloud motifs*	1100.00	1600.00	1350.00
☐ **Jacket,** *42" long, c. 1800s, red satin, embroidered gold dragons, blue clouds*	650.00	850.00	750.00
☐ **Jacket,** *45" long, c. 1800s, orange silk, embroidered floral motif*	800.00	1300.00	1050.00
☐ **Jacket,** *45" long, c. 1800s, red silk, embroidered floral, butterfly motif*	800.00	1000.00	900.00
☐ **Obi,** *6" x 9", c. 1900s, silk, multicolored, ferns and mums motif*	160.00	200.00	180.00
☐ **Obi,** *6" x 9", c. 1900s, silk, multicolored, phoenix, garden house, trees motif*	160.00	200.00	180.00

	Current Price Range		P/Y Average
□ **Obi,** 6" x 10", c. 1900s, silk, multicolored, bamboo motif	200.00	300.00	250.00
□ **Obi,** 6" x 36", c. 1900s, silk, multicolored, kirin, bamboo, floral motif	200.00	300.00	250.00
□ **Obi,** 9" x 9", c. 1900s, silk, red background overlapping decorated balls, gold geometric motif, leaves and flowers	160.00	200.00	180.00
□ **Obi,** 13" x 13", c. 1900s, silk, multicolored, fans, floral motif	800.00	1600.00	1200.00
□ **Obi,** 12" x 12", c. 1900s, rayon, multicolored, fan, leaves, vine motif	325.00	450.00	387.50
□ **Obi,** 12" x 12", c. 1900s, silk, multicolored, peacocks, fans, cranes, pine, mums motif ..	200.00	300.00	250.00
□ **Obi,** 12" x 12", c. 1900s, silk, multicolored, phoenix, crane motif	600.00	700.00	650.00
□ **Obi,** 13" wide, c. 1900s, silk, multicolored, bird, branch, floral motif	700.00	900.00	750.00
□ **Obi,** 13" x 12", c. 1900s, light brown background, multicolored peacocks, mums, pine trees motif	400.00	500.00	450.00
□ **Obi,** 13" x 12", c. 1900s, silk, multicolored, fans, scrolls, folded papers motif	400.00	500.00	450.00
□ **Obi,** 13" x 13", c. 1900s, rayon, multicolored, floral, fence tree motif	300.00	400.00	350.00
□ **Obi,** 13" x 13", c. 1900s, silk, black and brown pines on tan background, swirls of gold snow	400.00	500.00	450.00
□ **Obi,** 13" x 13", c. 1900s, silk, multicolored, fans, floral motif	800.00	1600.00	1200.00
□ **Obi,** 13" x 13", c. 1900s, silk, multicolored, floral, cart, crane	500.00	600.00	550.00
□ **Overcoat,** 40" long, c. 1800s, black silk, embroidered dragon, rabbit, bird motif	850.00	1100.00	675.00
□ **Robe,** 50" long, c. 1800s, black satin, orange satin, embroidered with trees, flowers, waves, fruit and butterfly motifs	1100.00	1600.00	1350.00
□ **Robe,** 50" long, c. 1800s, blue silk, embroidered dragon, cloud, bat motif	800.00	1200.00	1000.00
□ **Robe,** 50" long, c. 1800s, dragon, aqua silk, gold dragons, red bats, blue clouds	150.00	200.00	175.00
□ **Robe,** 50" long, c. 1800s, dragon, blue satin, dragon, cloud motif	650.00	850.00	750.00
□ **Robe,** 54" long, c. 1800s, blue dragon, satin, gold dragon motif	350.00	550.00	450.00
□ **Robe,** 55" long, c. 1800s, aqua silk, embroidered floral motif	800.00	1200.00	1000.00
□ **Robe,** 55" long, c. 1800s, dragon, black satin, gold and silver dragon motif	1300.00	1600.00	1450.00
□ **Robe,** 55" long, c. 1800s, dragon, blue satin, gold and silver dragon motif	550.00	850.00	700.00
□ **Robe,** 55" long, c. 1800s, dragon, brown gauze, dragon, cloud motif	850.00	1300.00	1075.00
□ **Robe,** 60" long, c. 1800s, dragon, blue satin, dragon cloud motif	1100.00	1600.00	1350.00
□ **Robe,** 60" long, c. 1800s, dragon, blue silk, dragon, cloud, wave, bat motif	1100.00	1600.00	1350.00

	Current Price Range		P/Y Average
☐ **Robe**, *60" long, c. 1800s, dragon, blue silk, embroidered, gold dragons, blue, green clouds, blossoms, waves, shells, sea creatures*	450.00	650.00	550.00
☐ **Robe**, *60" long, c. 1800s, dragon, rust colored silk, gold, dragons, red bats, blue clouds*	1100.00	1500.00	1300.00
☐ **Robe**, *60" long, c. 1800s, dragon, yellow satin, embroidered dragons, clouds, bats, fruit motifs*	6100.00	8200.00	7150.00

OTT & BREWER POTTERY

ORIGIN: The company which was later to be known as Ott & Brewer was founded in May 1863, by Bloor, Ott and Booth. Booth left the business in 1864, and his part of the company was bought by Garret S. Burroughs. Due to illness, Burroughs also lasted only one year. It was at this point that John Hart Brewer entered the firm, and items which are marked "O.B.B." could mean Bloor, Ott & **Booth,** Bloor, Ott & **Burroughs,** or Bloor, Ott & **Brewer.**

Isaac Broome came to Ott & Brewer in 1875 or 1876 and greatly expanded the parian line there. Many of his items were shown at the Philadelphia exposition in 1876.

DECORATION: Ott & Brewer used the full range of decorating methods on their wares, including transfer decoration of various types (primarily on their non-porcelain wares), hand-painting, gold paste, Royal Worcester "cloisonne" style artwork, and Irish Belleek type pearlized glazes. Pate-sur-pate work was done there, primarily by a man named Saunders. (Where is all that pate-sur-pate now?)

PRICES: Ott & Brewer Belleek has never been cheap. The recent rise in prices has eliminated the middle class collector. Most collectors do not distinguish between the ivory porcelain and the true Belleek, although most are aware that items with the crown marks can be a little heavier than those with the crescent marks. There is also little difference in pricing between the two types. (Remember that although the true Belleek is thinner, the ivory porcelain is older.)

Non-porcelain items are still found at popular prices, although this situation may not last. As more O&B Belleek becomes unreachable, the granite wares and cream-colored wares will become more interesting to collectors. This could raise prices.

Parian items and pieces signed by Broome are the most expensive. During the past year, the only known sale of a Broome item was the egg shown in the color section. It sold for $1,200. It is marked with a variation of mark F, and has the date 1877 and the Broome signature. Expect to pay a minimum of $1,500 for a marked parian bust.

RECOMMENDED READING: For further information refer to *The Official Price Guide to Pottery and Porcelain,* published by The House of Collectibles.

Plate, *game bird*

PORCELAIN ITEMS

No attempt will be made to differentiate between ivory porcelain and true Belleek.

	Current Price Range		P/Y Average
☐ **Basket,** 6″, *rustic handle, raised gold paste trim in thistle pattern on beige matte finish, mark I, see photo in color section*	600.00	700.00	620.00
☐ **Chocolate Pot,** 12″, *green bottom section, top section has raised gold paste trim in several shades of gold, on bottom section, top section has raised gold paste trim in several shades of gold, gold trim on dragon handle and spout and on finial and rims, mark I*	700.00	820.00	720.00
☐ **Cup And Saucer,** *after dinner size, gold paste trim, mark K and Tiffany & Co. mark, saucer only marked, gold is not the same color on the cup as on the saucer for some reason, but it is obvious the pieces belong together*	115.00	130.00	120.00

OTT & BREWER / 793

	Current Price Range		P/Y Average

☐ **Cup And Saucer,** *after dinner size, plain shape, spray of raised enamel flowers across front of cup, smaller spray on back, two sprays on saucer, pearlized pink interior, gold trim on rims and handle, mark J with New Orleans inscription, saucer broken in half and glued back together* .... — 135.00 — 155.00 — 140.00

☐ **Cup And Saucer,** *Tridacna pattern, teacup size, pearlized yellow interior, gold trim on handle and rims, mark K* .... — 150.00 — 175.00 — 155.00

☐ **Cup And Saucer,** *Tridacna pattern, bouillon, pearlized pink interior, gold trim on handle and rims, mark K, small fleck on underside of saucer* .... — 140.00 — 170.00 — 145.00

☐ **Cup And Saucer,** *cactus pattern, teacup size, pearlized white finish, gold trim on handle and rim, crack in handle* .... — 120.00 — 140.00 — 125.00

☐ **Cup And Saucer,** *after dinner size, enamel ribbon design, gold trim, mark I* .... — 180.00 — 220.00 — 185.00

☐ **Ewer,** *double spouted, rustic handle, top section covered with gold, bottom section has hand-painted coral colored water lilies, two small chips on top section, mark I* .... — 750.00 — 850.00 — 760.00

☐ **Ewer,** *raised gold paste cattail pattern, two turtle figurines applied to side of piece, turtles and coral handle decorated in green and gold, small fleck on one of the turtles, mark I* .... — 800.00 — 1000.00 — 820.00

☐ **Ewer,** *8", bulbous shape, raised gold paste in thistle pattern on beige matte finish, gold trim on handle and rims, mark I* .... — 650.00 — 750.00 — 670.00

☐ **Ewer,** *similar in size and shape to the one with turtles listed above, hand-painted water lilies outlined in gold, handle is formed like stem to buds and leaves which are applied near the rim, piece has been totally devastated in the back and is held together with glue, damage does not show very much in front, handle badly cracked so piece has to be picked up by the body, mark I* .... — 210.00 — 255.00 — 220.00

☐ **Ewer,** *7", shaped like a vinegar cruet, raised gold paste trim in chrysanthemum design on beige matte finish, mark K* .... — 385.00 — 455.00 — 390.00

☐ **Ewer,** *8", melon-ribbed, white glazed background with gold paste trim in oak leaf pattern, mark I, spider crack in bottom of piece* . — 170.00 — 200.00 — 175.00

☐ **Shell,** *raised on coral and seashell base, pearlized pink interior to shell, gold trim on rim and on base, one of the small shells that form the base has been broken off, mark I* ... — 400.00 — 470.00 — 420.00

☐ **Shell,** *1½" high, 3¼" wide, (handle included), very delicate and thin, forked handle and two small shell feet decorated in gold, gold trim on rim, little shells are misplaced so the item wobbles ever so slightly, mark I* .... — 90.00 — 110.00 — 95.00

	Current Price Range		P/Y Average
☐ **Shell,** *similar to one above but with no handle, pearlized blue interior, mark J*	90.00	110.00	95.00
☐ **Shoe,** *5", hand-painted small flowers in scatter pattern, gold trim, marks I and J*	400.00	470.00	420.00
☐ **Sugar And Creamer,** *cactus pattern, pearlized finish, gold trim on rim, bronze trim on handles, mint condition, mark I*	385.00	455.00	390.00
☐ **Sugar And Creamer,** *Tridacna pattern, pearlized pink inside, gold trim on handles and rims, mark J*	260.00	320.00	270.00
☐ **Sugar And Creamer,** *ruffled top sugar, creamer fits inside of sugar, raised gold paste trim in oak leaf pattern on beige matte finish, mark K*	300.00	400.00	310.00
☐ **Sugar And Creamer,** *same shape as above, transfer print with raised enamel work, gold trim on rims, mark I*	260.00	320.00	270.00
Note: Sugars and creamers are frequently found without their mates, and in this event a creamer is probably worth a hint more than a sugar bowl alone. The little creamer shown by itself in the photo is probably worth $10 to $15 more than a matching sugar bowl alone. The creamer sold recently for $125.			
☐ **Teapot,** *dented sides, covered with grotesque coral trim, raised gold paste work on bottom half, gold trim on coral branches, spout has been repaired and there is a small crack coming down from the rim, mark I*	260.00	320.00	270.00

OWLS

ORIGIN: The owl was first used as a decoration on coins in ancient Greece.

COMMENTS: A popular collectible, owls have been used on emblems, shields and beginning in the 19th century, on decorative items.

ADDITIONAL TIPS: The listings are alphabetical according to item. Following the items is a description, followed by maker, date and other information as available.

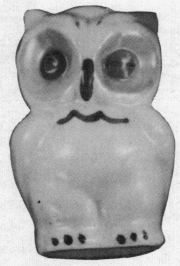

Salt And Pepper Shakers, *white with tan trim, winking eye, shawnee pottery.* **$8.50 - $12.50**

	Current Price Range		P/Y Average
☐ **Bookends,** rookwood, tan glaze, pair	120.00	160.00	130.00
☐ **Book Rack,** expanding, cast brass, two owls	36.00	46.00	40.00
☐ **Chatelaine,** wire plaque, link chains, silver plated	140.00	170.00	150.00
☐ **Cookie Jar,** tan and white, one eye closed, Shawnee Pottery Company	10.00	15.00	12.00
☐ **Doorstop,** carved wood with glass eyes, c. 1920s	21.50	30.00	24.00
☐ **Fairy Lamp,** bisque, owl face, glass eyes, 4½ " high	165.00	240.00	185.00
☐ **Figurine,** carved wooden owl	55.00	75.00	65.00
☐ **Figurine,** character owl in checked shawl with ermine collar, Royal Doulton	775.00	875.00	825.00
☐ **Figurine,** Great Horned Owl, ceramic	40.00	60.00	50.00
☐ **Figurine,** Great Horned Owl, porcelain, Royal Copenhagen	450.00	550.00	500.00
☐ **Figurine,** veined owl, Rouge Flambe, Royal Doulton, No. 2249	310.00	360.00	340.00
☐ **Figurine,** wise old owl in red cloak with ermine collar	425.00	525.00	475.00
☐ **Inkwell,** alabaster, owl on pile of books, 19th century	125.00	175.00	150.00
☐ **Jar,** Atterbury, opal glass, inserted red eyes, 7" high	125.00	165.00	135.00
☐ **Jar,** owl on a pedestal, pastel bisque, head is the jar lid, Royal Doulton-Lambeth	390.00	440.00	400.00
☐ **Painting,** primitive, two owls, late 19th century	107.00	140.00	117.00

	Current Price Range		P/Y Average
☐ **Paperweight,** crystal, round, frosted horned owl, copper engraving	425.00	525.00	475.00
☐ **Pitcher,** owl design, etched, clear green glass	30.00	45.00	35.00
☐ **Plate,** "1981 First Light - Great Horned Owl, The Prowlers of the Clouds Series," by Larry Toschik	60.00	70.00	65.00
☐ **Plate,** "1981 His Golden Throne - Screech Owl, The Prowlers of the Clouds Series," by Larry Toschik	60.00	70.00	65.00
☐ **Print,** Baby Saw-Whet Owls, released 1981, by Guy Coheleach	30.00	60.00	45.00
☐ **Print,** Barn Owl, released, 1980, by Owen J. Gromme	100.00	120.00	105.00
☐ **Print,** Barred Owl, released 1982, by Guy Coheleach	120.00	140.00	130.00
☐ **Print,** Burrowing Owl, released 1975, by Arthur Singer	30.00	60.00	45.00
☐ **Print,** "Eyes of the Night," Great Horned Owl, released 1979 by Owen J. Gromme	100.00	115.00	105.00
☐ **Print,** Great Horned Owl, released 1974, by Roger Tory Peterson	150.00	200.00	175.00
☐ **Print,** Great Horned Owl, released 1979, by Jill Fogelsong	50.00	75.00	60.00
☐ **Print,** Long-Eared Owl, released 1976, by James A. Carson	85.00	100.00	90.00
☐ **Print,** Oval Owl, released 1978, by Stan Brod .	45.00	60.00	50.00
☐ **Print,** Pigmy Owl, released 1972, by Peter Parnall	30.00	180.00	80.00
☐ **Print,** Richardson's Owl, released 1972, by Peter Parnall	30.00	215.00	150.00
☐ **Print,** Screech Owls, by E. Gordon West	30.00	45.00	37.00
☐ **Print,** Screech Owl, released 1972, by Gene Gray	25.00	50.00	35.00
☐ **Print,** Snowy Owls, released 1979, by Charles Frace	65.00	95.00	75.00
☐ **Print,** Snowy Owl, released 1972, by Roger Tory Peterson	175.00	575.00	250.00
☐ **Print,** Spectacled Owl, released 1979, by Jill Fogelsong	100.00	150.00	125.00
☐ **Purse,** mesh, diamonds, rubies, gold, owl motif frame, Art Nouveau, c. 1890	23000.00	25000.00	24000.00
☐ **Salt and Pepper Shakers,** tan and white, one eye closed, Shawnee Pottery Company	8.00	14.00	11.00
☐ **Sculpture,** Snowy Owl, female, by Robert Jefferson, Royal Doulton, 1974	2150.00	2400.00	2250.00
☐ **Sculpture,** Snowy Owl, male, by Robert Jefferson, Royal Doulton, 1974	1750.00	2000.00	1850.00
☐ **Stick Pin,** 14K gold, c. 1895	70.00	80.00	75.00
☐ **Stick Pin,** gold, two diamond chip eyes, 14K gold	140.00	175.00	155.00
☐ **Stick Pin,** gold filled, c. 1895	30.00	40.00	35.00
☐ **Vase,** hand painted owl profile, tan and brown, Weller Hudson	1050.00	1200.00	1100.00
☐ **Vase,** primitive owl design, pottery, Avon Pottery	800.00	950.00	850.00

PAPER COLLECTIBLES

TOPIC: This section covers business correspondence, celebrity items, checks and documents. For listings of other paper items such as autographs or books, please refer directly to those individual sections.

TYPES: There is a huge variety of paper items that people collect. If the item is of historical importance it probably has a value to collectors.

COMMENTS: Collectors of paper goods specialize as to the type of item they collect, since the field is too vast for general collecting.

ADDITIONAL TIPS: For further information and listings, please refer to *The Official Price Guide to Paper Collectibles,* published by The House of Collectibles.

BUSINESS CORRESPONDENCE

	Current Price Range		P/Y Average
☐ **California Aeronautics Firm,** 651 letters covering the period January to June 1938, a few of later date, some stained or damaged, in three plywood flip-top cartons with lettered labels (one carton broken).	150.00	170.00	160.00
☐ **Chicago Ice-House,** 421 letters covering the period December 1890 to July 1896, some invoices, etc. included.	90.00	120.00	105.00
☐ **Connecticut Clock Manufacturer,** 68 letters covering the period September 1851 to January 1852, bound in a half morocco case.	180.00	220.00	200.00
☐ **Massachusetts Leather Goods Manufacturer,** 81 letters covering the period July to October 1870, loose, some letters have a page or more missing.	65.00	85.00	75.00
☐ **New York Cigar Wholesaler,** 223 letters covering the period April 1889 to October 1889.	48.00	68.00	58.00
☐ **New York Optical Goods Company,** 17 letters, 1862.	85.00	105.00	95.00
☐ **Parisian Hat Manufacturer,** 367 letters (plus miscellaneous bills, a few photos and design sketches) covering the period August 1906 to March 1907, enclosed in a buckram folder.	55.00	65.00	60.00

Advertising, *booklet and blotters, c. 1930s,* **$2.00-$5.00**
*Photo courtesy of Lou McCulloch, Highland Heights, OH
44143.*

	Current Price Range		P/Y Average

Tiffany & Co., New York Fancy Goods Retailer, 891 letters (plus promotional items, notes, memos, etc.) of 1911-1915, enclosed in six cardboard felt-lined cases. . . . . — **850.00 | 1050.00 | 950.00**

CELEBRITY ITEMS

Amos and Andy Map of Weber City, Pepsodent radio premium, 1935.	38.00	48.00	43.00
Amos and Andy, 8″ x 10″ photo, n.d., c. 1935.	13.00	17.00	15.00
Amos and Andy, four page brochure about the program, c. 1935.	13.00	17.00	15.00
Astaire, Fred, brochure of Fred Astaire Dance School, c. 1954.	2.00	3.00	2.50
Hopalong Cassidy Western Magazine, Vol. 1, No. 2, colored cover, published by Best Books, 162 pages, Winter, 1951.	60.00	70.00	65.00
Hopalong Cassidy with Cole Bros. Circus, souvenir program, color cover, 32 pages, 1950.	25.00	35.00	30.00
Hopalong Cassidy Coloring Book, Abbott Publishing Co., 10″ x 15″, unused, 1950.	18.00	22.00	20.00
Hopalong Cassidy Returns, by Clarence E. Mulford, colored cover, "Pocket Book", 250 pages, published 1946.	10.00	12.00	11.00
Doomed Caravan Featuring William Boyd, lobby card for motion picture, 1942.	25.00	30.00	27.50
Hopalong Canasta, boxed game, includes deck of Hoppy cards, score sheet, rules and plastic card holder designed as a saddle, 1950.	35.00	45.00	40.00
Judy Garland, "Wizard of Oz" scrapbook belonging to her, containing numerous press cuttings and other memorabilia.	1000.00	1200.00	1100.00
Judy Garland, "Over the Rainbow", musical arrangement prepared for her, for motion picture "Wizard of Oz".	2700.00	3100.00	2900.00
Judy Garland, "A Star is Born," first-draft copy of the Moss Hart script for motion picture in which she starred.	1400.00	1600.00	1500.00
Judy Garland, telegram sent by her to Louis B. Mayer, 1945.	300.00	340.00	320.00
"Shirley Temple — in Warner Bros. Pictures," 5″ x 7″ photo sold originally as a picture frame insert, probably about 1940.	10.00	14.00	12.00
"Love, Shirley Temple," printed card sent in reply to fan request for photo, listing prices of various photos.	10.00	14.00	12.00
"Shirley Temple Grows Up," cover story from Life magazine, 1942.	11.00	15.00	13.00
Shirley Temple Edition of the Littlest Rebel, Random House, 214 pages with photo illustrations taken from movie stills, 1939.	8.00	12.00	10.00
Rudolph Valentino, full color embossed cigar box label, 7″ x 9″.	11.00	16.00	13.50
Jane Withers — Her Life Story, Whitman picture book, 32 pages, 1936.	18.00	22.00	20.00

	Current Price Range		P/Y Average

CHECKS, CELEBRITY

	Current Price Range		P/Y Average
☐ Authors; Maxwell Anderson, n.d.	16.00	24.00	20.00
☐ Susan B. Anthony, 1889.	22.00	28.00	25.00
☐ Henry W. Beecher, 1884.	16.00	26.00	21.00
☐ John Fiske, 1889.	10.00	14.00	12.00
☐ FitzGreen Halleck, 1846.	8.00	12.00	10.00
☐ Military; G. T. Beauregard, three checks dating 1878-1880.	23.00	29.00	26.00
☐ John A. Dix, filled out by a clerk but signed by him, 1836.	8.00	12.00	10.00
☐ Admiral R. P. Hobson, 1911.	4.00	6.00	5.00
☐ General Henry Knox, 1792.	35.00	42.00	38.50
☐ John A. Logan, 1879.	8.00	12.00	10.00
☐ Partly printed (red and black) check on the Treasurer of the Confederate States, made out to an officer, signed by Captain Barksdale, Richmond, 1861.	10.00	14.00	12.00
☐ Winfield Scott, 1827.	20.00	26.00	23.00
☐ Winfield Scott, 1851.	17.00	23.00	20.00
☐ Statesmen; Robert Morris, 1812.	8.00	14.00	10.00
☐ James Oliver, two checks, 1896.	8.00	14.00	10.00
☐ Gerrit Smith, 1871.	5.00	9.00	7.00
☐ Andrew Stevenson, two checks, both 1828. . .	8.00	12.00	10.00
☐ Charles Summer, 1871.	7.00	8.00	7.50
☐ John Cleves Symmes, 1797.	13.00	17.00	15.00
☐ Daniel Webster, on Corcoran and Riggs bank, 1845.	27.00	37.00	32.00
☐ Gideon Wells, on Riggs and Co., 1869.	7.00	9.00	8.00
☐ Theatrical; George Burns, 1955.	25.00	35.00	30.00
☐ Enrico Caruso, Hudson Trust Co., NY, 1920. .	45.00	55.00	50.00
☐ Lotta Crabtree, 1888.	17.00	23.00	20.00
☐ Erroll Flynn, 1941.	35.00	45.00	40.00
☐ Cary Grant, 1966.	25.00	30.00	27.50
☐ Victor Herbert, Corn Exchange Bank, NY, 1924.	20.00	28.00	24.00
☐ Marilyn Monroe, 1951.	300.00	380.00	340.00
☐ Elvis Presley, 1963.	420.00	520.00	470.00

CHECKS, NON-CELEBRITY

	Current Price Range		P/Y Average
☐ Pre-1800.	20.00	26.00	23.00
☐ 1800-1830.	13.00	17.00	15.00
☐ 1831-1859.	9.00	13.00	11.00
☐ 1860-1889.	6.00	10.00	8.00
☐ 1890-1910.	3.00	5.00	4.00

DOCUMENTS

	Current Price Range		P/Y Average
☐ Amherst, Jeffrey, Commander-in-chief in North America (1759), military document signed, one page, 1774.	210.00	260.00	235.00
☐ Audubon, John James, artist, legal document signed, Henderson Circuit Court, Kentucky, five pages, 1820.	850.00	1050.00	950.00
☐ Bacon, Nathaniel, (1593-1660), holograph document signed, on behalf of Oliver Cromwell, 1656.	125.00	155.00	140.00

	Current Price Range		P/Y Average

☐ **Bacon, Sir Francis,** document signed as Baron Verulam, two pages, large folio, repaired, February 11, 1618. . . . . | 1300.00 | 1800.00 | 1550.00

☐ **Burke, Edmund,** document signed as Paymaster General of the Forces, one page, April 10, 1782. . . . . | 90.00 | 120.00 | 105.00

☐ **Carleton, Sir Guy,** Governor of Quebec, document signed, two pages, 1789. . . . . | 150.00 | 210.00 | 180.00

☐ **Cary, Robert,** document signed, one page, 1622. . . . . | 65.00 | 85.00 | 75.00

☐ **Catherine the Great,** Empress of Russia, document signed, with the great seal attached, decorating an officer for outstanding service, 1785. . . . . | 270.00 | 370.00 | 320.00

☐ **Catherine de Medici,** document signed, vellum, 9″ x 19″, one page, 1579. . . . . | 120.00 | 270.00 | 195.00

☐ **Charles IX,** King of France, document signed, a record of gifts and payments by the king, two pages, 1567. . . . . | 200.00 | 260.00 | 230.00

☐ **Chase, Samuel,** Maryland signer of the Declaration of Independence, holograph document signed, about 100 words, silked. . . . . | 220.00 | 260.00 | 240.00

☐ **Choate, Rufus,** lawyer, document signed, Boston, one page, 1845. . . . . | 18.00 | 22.00 | 20.00

☐ **Christian IV,** (1577-1648), King of Norway and Denmark, vellum document, signed, 1647. . . . | 100.00 | 130.00 | 115.00

☐ **Clemenceau, Georges,** Premier of France, document signed, Paris, two pages, 1912. . . . | 130.00 | 150.00 | 140.00

☐ **Coleridge, Samuel Taylor,** poet, document signed, folio, June, two pages, 1805. . . . . | 130.00 | 150.00 | 140.00

☐ **Cromwell, Richard,** Lord Protector of England, document on vellum, one page, December 16, 1658. . . . . | 320.00 | 380.00 | 350.00

☐ **Cutler, Manasseh,** Ohio pioneer, short holograph document signed, Ipswich, 1773. . . . . . | 90.00 | 110.00 | 100.00

☐ **DeLesseps, Ferdinand,** official document, signed by Queen Victoria, August, 1870. . . . . | 125.00 | 145.00 | 135.00

☐ **Dudley, Robert,** Earl of Leicester, 1532-88, Proclamation signed as Governor of the Netherlands, 16″ x 12″, 1586. . . . . | 480.00 | 580.00 | 530.00

☐ **Dummer, Jeremiah,** holograph document signed, Boston, 1701. | 170.00 | 210.00 | 190.00

☐ **Elizabeth I of England,** vellum document signed, June, 1559, one page, quarto, 9″ x 12″. . . . . | 2100.00 | 2600.00 | 2350.00

☐ **Elizabeth I,** vellum document, unsigned but bearing a good impression of her Great Seal, attached to the document with silken twine, fleece-lined case, 7″ x 4½″. . . . . | 1400.00 | 1600.00 | 1500.00

☐ **Ellery, William,** signer of the Declaration of Independence from Rhode Island, document signed, 5″ x 7″, 1768. . . . . | 80.00 | 120.00 | 100.00

☐ **Evelyn, John,** English diarist, vellum document, 1654. . . . . | 160.00 | 200.00 | 180.00

☐ **Francis of Sales,** Saint. document signed, 10½″ x 14″. . . . . | 620.00 | 720.00 | 670.00

PAPER DOLLS

COMMENTS: Paper dolls were first produced in the 1400s and first used as children's toys in the late 1700s. Collectors usually specialize in two ways either by antique examples or by specific types such as celebrity, advertising, works of favorite artists or companies.

A paper doll's collectibility depends upon several factors including artist, subject, age, construction, condition and size. Because paper dolls have been produced for such a long time, examples from the 1800s in excellent condition can be readily found.

MAKERS: Some companies which produced paper dolls include Whitman, Colorforms, Childrens Press, Avalon Industries, American Toy Works, Samuel Gabriel Sons and Co., Dennison Manufacturing Co. and Saalfield Co.

RECOMMENDED READING: For further information you may refer to *The Official Price Guide to Paper Collectibles,* published by The House of Collectibles.

	Current Price Range		P/Y Average
☐ BETSY McCALL, *1965-66 Saalfield book #1370, reprint, uncut.*	12.00	18.00	13.00
☐ BETSY McCALL, *1971 Whitman box #4744, one doll, assorted clothes, boxed, uncut.*	12.00	18.00	13.00
☐ BETSY ROSS, *by Queen Holden, 1963 Platt and Munk book #224B, assorted dresses, uncut.*	25.00	35.00	26.00
☐ BETSY ROSS AND HER FRIENDS, *by Queen Holden, 1969 Platt and Murk #1251, Tom, Betsy, Dolly and John, Colonial costumes, boxed, uncut.*	8.00	12.00	9.00
☐ BETTY AND BOB, *by Queen Holden, 1952, #991, largedolls — boy is brunette, the girl is a blonde, assorted outfits, cut.*	15.00	25.00	14.00
☐ BETTY BLUE AND PATTY PINK, *1958 Merrill, wrap-around clothes.*	12.00	18.00	13.00
☐ BETTY BOBBS BABY BROTHER BUDDY BOBBS, *(Pictorial Review), February 1925, cut.*	4.00	8.00	5.00

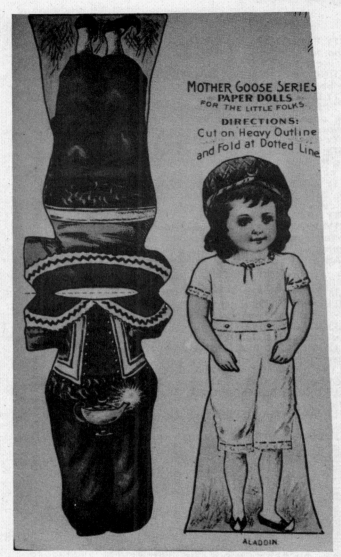

Mother Goose series, c. *1885,* **$5.00-$8.00**
Photo courtesy of Lou McCulloch, Highland Heights, OH
44143.

	Current Price Range		P/Y Average
☐ **BETTY BONNETT PAPER DOLLS**, *by Sheila Young, includes sixteen original Betty Bonnet sheets.*	2.00	6.00	3.00
☐ **BETTINA AND HER PLAYMATE ROSALIE,** *1931 Saalfield, uncut.*	25.00	35.00	26.00
☐ **BETTY DAVIS,** *1942 Merrill, uncut.*	55.00	65.00	57.00
☐ **BETTY FIELD,** *1943 Saalfield book #332, two large dolls, gowns and assorted clothes, jewelry and jewelry box, cut.*	45.00	55.00	46.00
☐ **BETTY GRABLE,** *1953 Merrill, uncut.*	40.00	50.00	41.00
☐ **BETTY GRABLE,** *1941 Whitman #989, two dolls, thirty-six outfits, twenty-eight accessories, cut.*	12.00	18.00	13.00
☐ **BETTY GRABLE,** *1943 Whitman #976, two dolls, twenty-five outfits, fourteen accessories, cut.*	20.00	30.00	21.00
☐ **BETTY GRABLE,** *1951 Merrill.*	75.00	125.00	78.00
☐ **BETTY HUTTON AND DAUGHTERS,** *1958 Saalfield book #4423, three statuette dolls, assorted outfits, cut.*	30.00	40.00	31.00
☐ **DINAH SHORE AND GEORGE MONTGOMERY,** *1959 Whitman book #1970, statuette dolls, assorted clothes, folder, uncut.*	60.00	70.00	62.00
☐ **DOLLY DINGLE'S PAPER DOLLS AND HER LITTLE FRIEND JULIE,** *July 1924, dresses, cut.*	2.00	6.00	62.00
☐ **DOLLY DINGLE'S PARTY,** *March 1930, one doll, clothes, dog Comfy, uncut.*	8.00	12.00	3.00
☐ **DOLLY DINGLE'S PLAYMATES,** *May 1929, matching Raggedy Andy costume, uncut.*	8.00	12.00	9.00
☐ **DOLLY DINGLE'S SAMMY SNOOKS,** *December 1921, one doll, coat and hat, cut.*	2.00	6.00	9.00
☐ **DOLLY DINGLE'S SWEETHEART,** *July 1929, uncut.*	8.00	12.00	3.00
☐ **DOLLY DINGLE'S SWEETHEART,** *July 1929, cut.*	4.00	8.00	9.00
☐ **DOLLY DINGLE'S TRAVELS,** *September 1929, alsace costume, day dress, uncut.*	8.00	12.00	5.00
☐ **DOLLY DINGLE'S TRIP AROUND THE WORLD — SOMEWHERE IN FRANCE,** *August 1917, small doll, cut.*	2.00	8.00	9.00
☐ **DOLLY DINGLE'S VACATION,** *September 1927, story, playsuit, backed, cut.*	5.00	10.00	3.00
☐ **DOLLY DINGLE'S WEEKEND PAPER,** *August 1929, Colonial costume, uncut.*	8.00	12.00	6.00
☐ **DOLLY DINGLE'S WEEKEND,** *August 1929, one doll, assorted outfits, cut.*	6.00	10.00	7.00
☐ **DOLLY DINGLE'S WEEKEND GUEST VIRGINIA,** *November 1926, one doll, gown, hat, purse and flower, cut.*	8.00	12.00	9.00
☐ **DOTTY DOUBLE,** *1933, 13" front and back doll, cut.*	6.00	10.00	7.00
☐ **DOUBLE DATE,** *1957 Saalfield, uncut.*	5.00	10.00	6.00
☐ **DOUBLE DOLLS,** *five dolls — two girls and three boys, dressed in different styles, no outfits.*	18.00	22.00	19.00

	Current Price Range		P/Y Average

☐ **DOUBLE WEDDING,** *1939 Merrill, uncut.*	25.00	35.00	26.00
☐ **DOWN ON THE FARM,** *Samuel Lowe, uncut.*	10.00	18.00	11.00
☐ **DREAM GIRL,** *1947 Merrill, uncut.*	10.00	18.00	11.00
☐ **DRESSES WORN BY THE FIRST LADIES OF THE WHITE HOUSE,** *by Mabelle Mercer, 1939 Saalfield book #2164, three dolls, assorted costumes, cut.*	16.00	24.00	17.00
☐ **DRESS ME,** *by Queen Holden, 1950 Whitman book #972, nude baby, one suit and several other outfits, cut.*	12.00	18.00	13.00
☐ **ELAINE STEWART,** *1955 Whitman book #2048, two dolls, assorted outfits, cut.*	30.00	40.00	29.00
☐ **ELIZABETH,** *1963 Samuel Lowe, uncut.*	2.00	6.00	3.00
☐ **ELIZABETH TAYLOR,** *1949 Whitman book #968, assorted outfits, cut.*	40.00	50.00	41.00
☐ **ELIZABETH TAYLOR,** *1955 Whitman book #1951, two large dolls, cut.*	30.00	40.00	32.00
☐ **ELLY MAY,** *1963 Watkins/Strathmore book #1819S, small book, two dolls, eight pages of clothes, uncut.*	40.00	50.00	41.00
☐ **EMILIE,** *Merrill.*	45.00	55.00	46.00
☐ **EMILY AND MIMI,** *by Queen Holden, 1971 James and Jonathan book #2711, assorted dresses, uncut.*	8.00	12.00	9.00
☐ **ESTHER WILLIAMS,** *1950 Merrill book #1563, three dolls, numerous outfits, uncut.*	55.00	65.00	56.00
☐ **ESTHER WILLIAMS,** *1950 Merrill book #1563, two dolls, several outfits, cut.*	35.00	45.00	36.00
☐ **GISELE MacKENZIE,** *1957 Saalfield book #4421, two dolls, assorted clothes, uncut.*	40.00	50.00	41.00
☐ **GISELE MacKENZIE,** *1957 Saalfield, cut.* . . .	15.00	25.00	16.00
☐ **GISELE MacKENZIE,** *1958 book #4475, uncut.*	30.00	40.00	31.00
☐ **GLAMOUR PARADE,** *c. early 1950s, Stevens.*	2.00	6.00	3.00
☐ **GLAMOROUS MOVIE STARS OF THE THIR-TIES PAPER DOLLS,** *by Tom Tierney, eight famous actresses, thirty-eight authentic costumes from films; includes Garbo, Harlow, Crawford, Lombard and others, thirty-two pages, 9¼″ x 12¼″.*	3.00	9.00	4.00
☐ **GLORIA JEAN,** *1940 Saalfield #1661, two dolls, fifteen outfits, four accessories, cut.* . . .	10.00	18.00	11.00
☐ **GLORIA JEAN,** *1941 Saalfield #223, uncut.* . . .	35.00	45.00	36.00
☐ **GLORIA'S MAKE UP,** *1952 book #2585, later became Rosemary Clooney, one doll, assorted outfits, cut.*	16.00	24.00	17.00
☐ **GOLDEN BOOK OF DOLLS AND TOYS,** *by Milouche and Kane, five dolls — two are babies, assorted clothes, cut.*	18.00	22.00	19.00
☐ **GOLDEN GIRL,** *1953 Merrill book #1543, two dolls, large assortment of clothes, cut.*	25.00	35.00	26.00
☐ **GOLDILOCKS AND THE THREE BEARS,** *1939 Saalfield, uncut.*	35.00	45.00	36.00
☐ **GONE WITH THE WIND,** *1940 Merrill #3405, uncut.*	85.00	95.00	86.00
☐ **GONE WITH THE WIND,** *1940 Merrill, eigh-teen dolls, assorted clothes, cut.*	125.00	175.00	127.00

	Current Price Range		P/Y Average
GONE WITH THE WIND, *1940 Merrill #3404, uncut.*	85.00	95.00	86.00
GONE WITH THE WIND, *by Charlotte Whatley, two dolls — Rhett 13" and Scarlette 11", sixteen authentic movie costumes, black and white, limited edition of 500.*	8.00	12.00	9.00
GONE WITH THE WIND, *characters from the movie: Scarlette, Rhett, Melanine, Carreen, Ellen Suellen, Aunt Pittypat, Mammy and Gerald, assorted outfits.*	35.00	45.00	36.00
GOOD LITTLE DOLLS, *1941 Saalfield, uncut.*	15.00	25.00	16.00
GOOD NEIGHBOR, *1944 Saalfield, uncut.*	10.00	18.00	11.00
GRACE KELLY, *1955 Whitman book #2049, dolls punch out an dput back in, assorted outfits, uncut.*	90.00	100.00	91.00
GRACE KELLY, *1956 Whitman book #2064, assorted outfits, cut.*	30.00	40.00	31.00
JILL'S CHRISTMAS DOLL, *by Tina Lee, December 1941, Jack and Jill set, uncut.*	8.00	12.00	9.00
JILL WITH THE KISSING LIPS, *by Queen Holden, 1963 James and Jonathan, large doll, assorted outfits, uncut.*	40.00	50.00	41.00
JIMMY AND JANE VISIT GENE AUTRY AT MELODY RANCH, *1951 Whitman book #11484115, western outfits, uncut.*	60.00	70.00	61.00
JOAN, *by Miloche, statuette doll, five outfits, cut.*	4.00	10.00	5.00
KIDDIES KOASTING KARNIVAL, *by Durand Chapman, January 1915, assortment of dolls, sleds, uncut.*	12.00	18.00	13.00
KIM NOVAK PAPERDOLLS AND COLOR-BOOK, *1957 Saalfield book #4459, two dolls, four pages of dresses, colorin book, uncut.*	55.00	65.00	56.00
KIM NOVAK, *1958 Saalfield, uncut.*	25.00	35.00	26.00
KISSEY, *1963 Saalfield, Idel doll, has kissing disc on mouth, large doll, uncut.*	15.00	25.00	16.00
KIT, *by Queen Holden, 1952 Whitman book #210625, one doll, large assortment of clothes and toys, cut.*	30.00	40.00	31.00
KITCHEN PLAY, *1938 Saalfield, uncut.*	10.00	18.00	11.00
KITTY GOES TO KINDERGARDEN, *1956 Merrill, uncut.*	2.00	6.00	2.50
LACE AND DRESS PUPPY, *1975 Samuel Lowe, uncut.*	2.00	4.00	2.50
LADY AND GIRL, *World War I, Decalco Lithography Co. set #, costumes, uncut.*	6.00	12.00	7.00
LANA TURNER, *1942 Whitman #988, uncut.*	30.00	40.00	31.00
LANA TURNER, *1945 Whitman #975, uncut.*	30.00	40.00	31.00
LANA TURNER, *1945 Whitman #975, two dolls, twenty-seven outfits, nineteen accessories, cut.*	20.00	30.00	21.00
LARGE BABIES, *c. early 1950s, three dolls, thirty-one pieces of clothing.*	2.00	8.00	3.00
LARGE-SIZED DOLL, *Raphael Tuck, white top, lavender petticoat, three dresses, two coats — one brown and one red.*	45.00	55.00	46.00

	Current Price Range		P/Y Average

☐ **LAUGH-IN,** *1969 Saalfield book #6045, assorted clothes and punchlines, uncut.* **12.00 18.00 13.00**

☐ **LAUGH-IN PARTY,** *1969 Saalfield, cut.* **2.00 4.00 2.50**

☐ **LENNON SISTERS,** *1957 Whitman book #1979, four dolls, assorted outfits, uncut.* . . . **40.00 50.00 41.00**

☐ **LENNON SISTERS,** *1959 Whitman book #1991, four dolls, assorted clothes, tri-folder, uncut.* **45.00 55.00 46.00**

☐ **LENNON SISTERS,** *1961 Whitman book #1983, assorted dresses, tri-folder, uncut.* . . . **45.00 55.00 46.00**

☐ **LENNON SISTERS,** *1963 Whitman book #1991, statuette dolls, assorted clothes, tri-folder, uncut.* **40.00 50.00 41.00**

☐ **LETTIE LANE PAPER DOLLS,** *by Shelia Young, reproduction of twenty-four antique paper dolls published in Ladies Home Journal 1908-1910, assorted outfits — evening dress, summer wear and haute couture, thirty-two pages, 9¼" x 12¼", uncut.* **3.00 9.00 4.00**

☐ **LET'S PLAY HOUSE,** *by Robert Bezucha, 1932 Whitman book #W968B, three rooms, uncut.* . . **45.00 55.00 46.00**

☐ **LET'S PLAY STORE,** *by Fran Bisel Peat, 1933 Saalfield book #971, grocery store, uncut.* . . . **70.00 80.00 71.00**

☐ **LET'S PLAY WITH THE BABY,** *1948 Merrill book #1550, cut.* **4.00 8.00 5.00**

☐ **MY VERY OWN BABY DOLL,** *by Queen Holden, 1974, James and Jonathan book #3719, baby, assorted outfits, uncut.* **12.00 18.00 13.00**

☐ **NANNY AND THE PROFESSOR,** *1970/1971 Artcraft book #5114, window on Prudence, five dolls and a dog, punch-out clothes, uncut.* **30.00 40.00 31.00**

☐ **NATALIE WOOD,** *1958 Whitman book #2086, assorted outfits, cut.* **40.00 50.00 41.00**

☐ **NATIONAL VELVET,** *1961 Whitman book #1958, from the T.V. show, folder, uncut.* **20.00 30.00 21.00**

☐ **NATIONAL VELVET,** *1962 Whitman book #1948, one doll, assorted clothes, uncut.* **30.00 40.00 31.00**

☐ **NURSE AND DOCTOR PAPER DOLLS,** *from T.V. Show, by Betty Campbell, Saalfield book #2777, five doll set, uncut.* **30.00 40.00 31.00**

☐ **NURSE AND DOCTORS,** *by Betty Campbell, 1952 Saalfield.* **5.00 10.00 6.00**

☐ **NURSERY RHYME PARTY DOLLS IN COSTUME,** *McLoughlin Brothers, #574, cut.* **30.00 40.00 31.00**

☐ **NURSES THREE,** *1964 Whitman book #1964, based on T.V. show, three dolls — Penny, Kelly and Tracy, assorted outfits, uncut.* **12.00 18.00 13.00**

☐ **OFFICIAL NEW YORK WORLD'S FAIR PAPER DOLL BOOK,** *1964-1965 Spertus book #700-59, assorted foreign costumes, pictures of fair buildings, uncut.* **8.00 12.00 9.00**

☐ **OKLAHOMA,** *1956 Whitman book #1954, Gordon MacRae, Shirley Jones, assorted costumes, uncut.* **70.00 80.00 71.00**

	Current Price Range		P/Y Average

☐ **ONCE UPON A TIME,** c. 1960s Saalfield, ten dolls, ninety-four costumes from Mother Goose, reprint of The Old Woman Who Lived In A Shoe, uncut. . . . . 12.00 18.00 — 13.00

☐ **ONCE UPON A WEDDING DAY,** Saalfield, cut. 2.00 6.00 — 3.00

☐ **ONE HUNDRED AND ONE DALMATIONS,** Walt Disney, Whitman book #1993:59, twenty-five stand up figures, fifteen costumes, accessories, tri-folder, uncut. . . . . 60.00 70.00 — 61.00

☐ **OUR LITTLE PET,** Raphael Tuck Artistic Series #106, one doll, two dresses. . . . . 18.00 22.00 — 19.00

☐ **OUR NEW BABY,** 1936 Merrill, uncut. . . . . 15.00 25.00 — 16.00

☐ **OUR WAVE JOAN,** by Miloche and Kane, 1943 Whitman book #1012, die cut cover, four pages of clothes, uncut. . . . . 30.00 40.00 — 31.00

☐ **OUTDOOR PAPER DOLLS,** 1941 Saalfield book #1958, fourteen dolls, outdoor outfits, thin covers, uncut. . . . . 8.00 12.00 — 9.00

☐ **OZZIE AND HARRIETT,** 1954 Saalfield, uncut. 15.00 25.00 — 16.00

☐ **PAGEANT,** #4412, reprint of Brenda Starr (faces changed), assorted outfits same as Brenda Starr, uncut. . . . . 8.00 12.00 — 9.00

☐ **PALMER COX BROWNIES,** 1895, jointed, uncut. . . . . 55.00 65.00 — 56.00

☐ **PAM AND HER DOLLY,** Saalfield #1010, blonde doll — Dolly Ellen, assorted outfits, punch outs, uncut. . . . . 10.00 18.00 — 11.00

☐ **PAVLOVA AND NIJINSKY PAPER DOLLS,** by Tom Tierney, two dolls of two famous Russian dancers, thirty authentic costumes, uncut. . . . . 2.00 6.00 — 3.00

☐ **PEASANT COSTUMES OF EUROPE,** 1934 Whitman #900, uncut. 15.00 25.00 — 16.00

☐ **PEEK-A-BOO,** 1955 Whitman, four babies, 6". 5.00 10.00 — 6.00

☐ **ROY ROGERS AND DALE EVANS,** 1950 Whitman book #1186-15, dolls and Trigger, reproduction of Roy's autograph, uncut. . . . . 60.00 70.00 — 61.00

☐ **ROY ROGERS AND DALE EVANS,** 1954 Whitman book #1950, statuette dolls, western outfits, brown leather-like cover, uncut. . . . . 45.00 55.00 — 46.00

☐ **ROY ROGERS AND DALE EVANS,** 1956 Whitman book #1956, assorted western outfits, uncut. . . . . 45.00 55.00 — 46.00

☐ **ROY ROGERS AND DALE EVANS AND DUSTY AT THE DOUBLE R-BAR RANCH,** 1957 Whitman book #1950, three statuette dolls, western outfits, uncut. . . . . 45.00 55.00 — 46.00

☐ **ROYAL FAMILY,** by Charlotte Whatley, three dolls — Prince Charles, Princess Diana and baby; nineteen pages, thirty-five costumes, black and white, limited edition of 500. . . . . . 8.00 12.00 — 9.00

☐ **ROYAL WEDDING, LADY DIANA AND PRINCE CHARLES,** made in England, book 12" x 18". . . . . 14.00 20.00 — 15.00

☐ **RUB A DUB DOLLY,** 1977 Whitman. . . . . 2.00 6.00 — 3.00

PAPERWEIGHTS

TYPES: Millefiori weights contain arrays of small ornamental glass beads or stems arranged in a striking pattern. They are quite colorful. Sulfides are ceramic relief plaques encased in glass. Many other artistic types of paperweights were made, and souvenir paperweights featuring some company or place are also common, though not as desirable.

PERIOD: Paperweights were not seen before the 1700s; they are a recent item. The most important paperweights were made in the 1800s.

MAKERS: Clichy, Baccarat and St. Louis are all important producers of artistic glass paperweights. Prices for famous makers like these are high, although less known craftsmen can also produce exquisite items.

MATERIALS: For the most part, glass is the medium used for artistic paperweights. Functional weights are rarely made of metal.

COMMENTS: The weight of the specimen is not an indication of quality. Rather, the name of the maker and the level of artistry evident determine the value of a paperweight.

ADDITIONAL TIPS: Famous makers like Clichy, Baccarat and St. Louis sometimes put their initials on one of the canes in a millefiori weight. This makes certain specimens easy to identify.

	Current Price Range		P/Y Average
☐ **Baccarat,** millefiori canes, 1847, 2½ ″ diameter	600.00	660.00	630.00
☐ **Baccarat,** Primrose, pink, red and green, 3″ diameter	200.00	250.00	225.00
☐ **Baccarat,** sulfide, Eleanor Roosevelt	50.00	100.00	75.00
☐ **Baccarat,** sulfide, John Kennedy	225.00	275.00	250.00
☐ **Baccarat,** sulfide, Will Rogers	150.00	200.00	175.00
☐ **Banford, Ray,** stylized roses, c. 1974	275.00	325.00	300.00
☐ **Bonnel,** pine key	40.00	60.00	50.00
☐ **Coca-Cola,** blue lettering, dome	13.00	19.00	16.00
☐ **Crider,** most designs, large	40.00	50.00	45.00
☐ **Crider,** most designs, small	25.00	35.00	30.00
☐ **Davis, Jim,** bell shape, swirl design	14.00	18.00	16.00
☐ **Davis, Jim,** bird shape, large	10.00	15.00	12.50

	Current Price Range		P/Y Average
☐ **Davis, Jim,** bird shape, small	5.00	7.00	6.00
☐ **Davis, Jim,** five flowers in vase	20.00	28.00	24.00
☐ **Gentile,** bubble, clear, small	5.00	8.00	6.50
☐ **Gentile,** butterfly, small	13.00	15.00	14.00
☐ **Gentile,** cabbage leaf	16.00	18.00	17.00
☐ **Gentile,** Elks lodge	14.00	16.00	15.00
☐ **Gentile,** five petaled flower, colored, small ...	7.00	8.00	7.50
☐ **Gentile,** millefiori butterfly and flower	40.00	50.00	45.00
☐ **Gentile,** millefiori heart	20.00	39.00	30.00
☐ **Gentile,** millefiori pinwheel	30.00	40.00	35.00
☐ **Gentile,** mushroom, colored, small	12.00	16.00	14.00
☐ **Gentile,** Remember Pearl Harbor	22.00	30.00	26.00
☐ **Gentile,** sign of the zodiac	14.00	18.00	16.00
☐ **Gentile,** spotted pattern	12.00	14.00	13.00
☐ **Gentile,** tear drop bubble, clear	13.00	14.00	13.50
☐ **Gentile,** three lilies	13.00	15.00	14.00
☐ **Gentile,** white goose	15.00	20.00	17.50
☐ **Hamon, Bob,** millefiori cane weight, signed ..	70.00	80.00	75.00
☐ **Kaziun, Charles,** miniature, floral motif, pedestal, 2" high	400.00	430.00	415.00
☐ **New England Glass Co.,** posy bouquet, millefiori canes, 2⅝" diameter	440.00	500.00	470.00
☐ **Oriental,** flower, elongated pedestal, 5½" tall	25.00	31.00	28.00
☐ **Oriental,** open rose, 3½" tall	25.00	30.00	27.50
☐ **Oriental,** stemmed apple, 2⅞" tall	15.00	22.00	18.50
☐ **Oriental,** two frogs, 4" tall	20.00	26.00	23.00
☐ **Perthshire,** sunflower, 1979, 3⅛" diameter	140.00	170.00	155.00
☐ **St. Clair,** apple, crimped	15.00	20.00	17.50
☐ **St. Clair,** bell with five flowers	10.00	14.00	12.00
☐ **St. Clair,** crimped	8.00	12.00	10.00
☐ **St. Clair,** floral design with five flowers	14.00	20.00	17.00
☐ **St. Louis,** dahlia, star cut base, 2⅛" diameter .	1000.00	1100.00	1050.00
☐ **St. Louis,** fruit in a basket, 2⅞" diameter	2000.00	2200.00	2100.00
☐ **St. Louis,** King Tut mask, 1979	270.00	330.00	300.00
☐ **Tiffany,** favrile, red sides with internal yellow blossoms, 1906	4500.00	5500.00	5000.00
☐ **Tiffany,** favrile scarab, 4½" long, c. 1900	440.00	600.00	520.00
☐ **Vandermark,** latticinio design	50.00	60.00	55.00
☐ **Ysart Paul,** clematis in lattininio basket, 2⅞" diameter	500.00	600.00	550.00
☐ **Ysart, Paul,** fish with multicolored sea bed, 3" diameter	450.00	550.00	500.00

PATTERN GLASS

ORIGIN: Glass historians are still undecided as to whether the Americans or the British first invented pressed glass. Small objects and feet for footed bowls were first hand pressed in England in the early 1800's, but this method was crude compared to the mechanical process which later evolved. Pressing glass with machinery to produce a wide range of glass objects appears to have originated in America. Glass companies began producing pressed glass in matching tableware sets during the 1840's.

COMMENTS: Although identification of pieces is mainly by pattern name, the novice collector will have some confusion in this area. This is due to the fact that most of the original names have been discarded by advanced collectors who have renamed the pattern in descriptive terms. For the most part these collectors have found it impossible to attribute most patterns to a particular maker.

ADDITIONAL TIPS: Although pattern glass was originally made to imitate cut glass, you will have no problem differentiating one from the other. Despite the similarities pattern glass lacks the deep faceted appearance of cut — the edges of the patterns look rounded, the earlier pieces contain many imperfections — bubbles, lumps, impurities, and sometimes cloudiness.

MARKS: Manufacturers' marks are exceedingly rare and there are few catalogs available from the period before 1850. By studying the old catalogs that do exist, along with shards found at old factory sites, some sketchy information has been provided. But because patterns were so quickly copied by the competition, absolute verification of the manufacturer is impossible.

REPRODUCTIONS: Reproductions can pose a definite problem to the beginning pattern glass collector. Two very popular patterns, Bellflower and Daisy and Button, have been reproduced extensively. With careful, informed scrutiny, you will be able to detect the dullness and lack of sparkle characteristic of remakes. If the reproduction was made from a new mold (formed from an original object), the details will not possess the clarity and preciseness of the original article.

RECOMMENDED READING: For more in-depth information on pattern glass you may refer to *The Official Price Guide to Glassware* and *The Official Identification Guide to Glassware,* published by The House of Collectibles.

BAKEWELL BLOCK	Current Price Range		P/Y Average
☐ Celery	100.00	107.00	96.00
☐ Champagne	100.00	108.00	95.00
☐ Creamer	165.00	175.00	160.00
☐ Decanter	135.00	145.00	131.00
☐ Spooner	65.00	75.00	60.00
☐ Sugar Bowl, covered	85.00	95.00	80.00
☐ Tumbler, bar	85.00	95.00	81.00
☐ Tumbler, whiskey	85.00	95.00	80.00
☐ Whiskey Tumbler, handle	105.00	115.00	100.00
☐ Wine	70.00	80.00	64.00

CANADIAN			
☐ Butter, with cover	60.00	70.00	62.50
☐ Celery	45.00	55.00	4750
☐ Compote, high, with cover	65.00	75.00	67.50
☐ Compote, low	45.00	65.00	55.00
☐ Cordial	40.00	50.00	42.50
☐ Creamer	40.00	50.00	42.50
☐ Goblet	55.00	65.00	57.50
☐ Jam Jar	50.00	60.00	55.00
☐ Milk Pitcher, large	85.00	95.00	87.50
☐ Milk Pitcher, small	70.00	80.00	72.50
☐ Plate, diameter 6½ "	45.00	55.00	47.50
☐ Plate, diameter 7½ "	60.00	70.00	65.50
☐ Sauce, flat	16.00	18.00	16.50
☐ Sauce, footed	22.00	32.00	22.50
☐ Spooner	40.00	50.00	42.50
☐ Sugar, with cover	65.00	75.00	67.50
☐ Water Pitcher, large	90.00	100.00	95.00
☐ Water Pitcher, small	70.00	80.00	72.50
☐ Wine Glass	50.00	60.00	52.50

DIAMOND THUMBPRINT			
☐ Butter Dish, covered	147.00	157.00	145.00
☐ Cake Stand	220.00	250.00	222.00
☐ Celery	180.00	190.00	175.00
☐ Champagne Glass, rare	230.00	250.00	220.00
☐ Creamer	125.00	140.00	120.00
☐ Compote, footed, scalloped edge	40.00	50.00	42.00
☐ Decanter, no stopper, pint size	75.00	80.00	75.00
☐ Decanter, original stopper, quart size	150.00	165.00	150.00
☐ Goblet, rare	350.00	365.00	345.00
☐ Honey Dish	15.00	20.00	15.00
☐ Sauce Dish	10.00	15.00	11.00
☐ Spooner	80.00	90.00	75.00
☐ Sugar Bowl, covered	150.00	170.00	155.00
☐ Tumbler	100.00	110.00	95.00
☐ Waste Bowl	85.00	95.00	80.00
☐ Water Pitcher, rare	350.00	370.00	352.00

	Current Price Range		P/Y Average
☐ Whiskey Tumbler, handled	275.00	300.00	280.00
☐ Wine Glass, rare	220.00	240.00	205.00
☐ Wine Jug, places for holding glasses	750.00	950.00	600.00

FLUTE

☐ Ale Glass	30.00	40.00	28.00
☐ Bottle, bitters	30.00	37.00	28.00
☐ Bowl, scalloped edge	30.00	38.00	27.00
☐ Candlesticks, pair	40.00	50.00	37.00
☐ Champagne	30.00	35.00	27.00
☐ Compote, open, diameter 8″	32.00	38.00	30.00
☐ Decanter, quart	50.00	56.00	47.00
☐ Egg Cup, single	15.00	19.00	13.00
☐ Egg Cup, double	30.00	35.00	28.00
☐ Goblet	30.00	40.00	25.00
☐ Honey Dish	15.00	19.00	13.00
☐ Lamp	70.00	77.00	67.00
☐ Mug	50.00	60.00	48.00
☐ Pitcher, water	60.00	70.00	55.00
☐ Salt, footed	20.00	25.00	17.00
☐ Sauce, flat	14.00	18.00	12.00
☐ Sugar Bowl, open	27.00	35.00	25.00
☐ Tumbler	28.00	34.00	27.00
☐ Whiskey, handled	25.00	33.00	23.00
☐ Wine	25.00	30.00	23.00

LEE

☐ Celery Dish	110.00	120.00	105.00
☐ Champagne Glass	140.00	148.00	135.00
☐ Creamer	130.00	140.00	125.00
☐ Decanter	75.00	90.00	75.00
☐ Goblet	135.00	145.00	130.00
☐ Sugar Bowl, covered	130.00	140.00	125.00
☐ Tumbler	100.00	110.00	96.00

MINERVA

☐ Butter, with cover	110.00	115.00	112.50
☐ Cake Plate, diameter 12″	115.00	125.00	117.50
☐ Compote, high	85.00	110.00	95.00
☐ Compote, low	75.00	100.00	78.00
☐ Compote, with lid	70.00	75.00	72.50
☐ Creamer	65.00	85.00	67.50
☐ Goblet, small	75.00	85.00	75.50
☐ Goblet, large	90.00	100.00	95.00
☐ Jam Jar, with cover	85.00	95.00	87.50
☐ Plate, tab handled	65.00	75.00	67.50
☐ Platter, oval	50.00	60.00	52.50
☐ Pickle Dish, oval, says "Love's Request is Pickles"	40.00	50.00	42.50
☐ Relish Dish, three compartment	35.00	45.00	37.50
☐ Sauce, flat	25.00	35.00	27.50
☐ Sauce, footed	30.00	35.00	32.50
☐ Spooner	40.00	50.00	42.50
☐ Sugar	75.00	85.00	77.50

	Current Price Range		P/Y Average
☐ Sugar, with cover	90.00	100.00	92.50
☐ Water Pitcher	125.00	135.00	130.00

PICKET

☐ Butter, with cover	70.00	80.00	75.00
☐ Celery	45.00	55.00	47.50
☐ Compote, high, with cover	60.00	70.00	65.00
☐ Compote, low	45.00	55.00	47.50
☐ Creamer	45.00	55.00	47.50
☐ Goblet	55.00	60.00	57.50
☐ Jam Jar	44.00	50.00	46.00
☐ Pickle Dish, with cover	45.00	55.00	47.50
☐ Salt	20.00	30.00	25.00
☐ Spooner	25.00	35.00	27.50
☐ Sugar, with cover	52.00	55.00	53.00
☐ Toothpick	35.00	40.00	37.50
☐ Tumbler	40.00	50.00	42.50
☐ Water Pitcher	65.00	75.00	67.50
☐ Wine Glass	30.00	40.00	32.50

SCROLL

☐ Butter	30.00	40.00	32.50
☐ Celery	30.00	40.00	35.00
☐ Compote, high	25.00	30.00	32.50
☐ Compote, low	20.00	30.00	22.50
☐ Creamer	25.00	30.00	27.50
☐ Egg Cup	30.00	40.00	32.50
☐ Goblet	15.00	20.00	17.50
☐ Relish Bowl	20.00	30.00	22.50
☐ Salt	15.00	20.00	17.50
☐ Sauce, flat	10.00	12.00	11.00
☐ Sauce, footed	20.00	30.00	25.00
☐ Spooner	22.00	30.00	24.00
☐ Sugar, with cover	30.00	40.00	32.50
☐ Water Pitcher	40.00	60.00	45.00
☐ Wine Glass	20.00	30.00	22.50

PENS AND PENCILS

TYPES: Pens can be either dip pens, the earliest type, fountain pens or ball-point pens. Dip pens are the style of modern calligraphy pens: a pointed nib is dipped in ink and used quickly. Fountain pens carry their own ink supply, as do ball-points. Pencils are either traditional or mechanical.

PERIOD: The fountain pen, which is the most collectible type, experienced its heyday in the 1920s and 1930s.

ORIGIN: The fountain pen was invented in the 1880s by Lewis Waterman.

MAKERS: The big names in pen and pencil production are Waterman, Parker, Conklin, Sheaffer and Wahl. All of these companies produced fine pens that are currently in great demand by collectors.

COMMENTS: As mentioned before, few ball-point or dip pens are collected by modern enthusiasts. Additional, collectors focus on post-1880 specimens.

ADDITIONAL TIPS: Rarity and condition are very important; the second more so than the first. Historical importance may also play a part, though only in isolated instances.

	Current Price Range		P/Y Average
☐ **Autopoint,** gold filled, 1930s	12.00	18.00	15.00
☐ **Blaisdell,** green, gold plated trim, pencil, 1920s	10.00	20.00	15.00
☐ **Century,** Durapoint, red woodgrain, marbled, 1928	125.00	175.00	150.00
☐ **Chilton,** cream and gold, marbled, gold plated trim, golf pencil, 1930	20.00	30.00	25.00
☐ **Conklin,** 2P black chased hard rubber, crescent filler, 1918	25.00	40.00	32.50
☐ **Conklin,** Endura, orange, lever filler, gold plated trim, 1920s	30.00	40.00	35.00
☐ **Conklin,** Nozak, gray and red pearl, gold plated trim, 1931	25.00	45.00	35.00
☐ **Cross,** 1888	60.00	70.00	65.00

	Current Price Range		P/Y Average
☐ **Doric,** pearly lined nickle plated trim, pencil, 1935	20.00	40.00	35.00
☐ **Dunn,** sterling silver, fine point, 1922	110.00	150.00	130.00
☐ **Eversharp,** green, chrome gold banded cap, 1951	25.00	35.00	30.00
☐ **Eversharp,** Skyline, black, 1945	15.00	20.00	17.50
☐ **Lincoln,** red, marbled, 1926	25.00	40.00	32.50
☐ **Majestic,** black and cream, 1930s	25.00	35.00	30.00
☐ **Parker,** # 51, Blue Diamond, black, gold plated trim, Lustraloy cap, 1945	32.00	52.00	42.00
☐ **Parker,** Deluxe Challenger, gold plated trim, 1930s	30.00	40.00	35.00
☐ **Parker,** Duofold, gold pearl and black, gold plated trim, 1939	50.00	60.00	55.00
☐ **Parker,** Duofold Sr., Big Red, gold plated trim, 1924	100.00	150.00	125.00
☐ **Parker,** Duofold Jr., black, gold plated trim, 1927	35.00	40.00	37.50
☐ **Parker,** gold filled metal, button filler, 1926	50.00	70.00	60.00
☐ **Parker,** Lady Duofold, red, gold plated trim	30.00	50.00	40.00
☐ **Parker,** Pastel, blue, gold plated trim, 1926	35.00	45.00	40.00
☐ **Parker,** silver plate, pencil, 1921	60.00	70.00	65.00
☐ **Parker,** Vacumatic, black, 1947	25.00	35.00	30.00
☐ **Peerless,** black and cream, gold plated trim, lever filler, 1930	20.00	30.00	25.00
☐ **Peerless,** lever filler, gold plated trim, black veined cream, 1920s	18.00	28.00	23.00
☐ **Pilot,** black lacquer and hand painted design, gold fittings, Japanese	50.00	70.00	60.00
☐ **Rider,** black, eye dropper filler, # 6 nib Mabie Todd	50.00	100.00	75.00
☐ **Royal,** Parker Duofold imitation, yellow, gold plated trim, 1928	35.00	45.00	40.00
☐ **Sanford and Bennett,** black, eye dropper filler, 1904	30.00	50.00	40.00
☐ **Sheaffer,** 5-30, black, lever filler, gold plated trim, ladies', 1930s	15.00	25.00	20.00
☐ **Sheaffer,** Balance, pearl and black marbled, pencil, 1931	40.00	60.00	50.00
☐ **Sheaffer,** black, gold plated trim, pencil, 1925	30.00	45.00	37.50
☐ **Sheaffer,** Lifetime, black and pearl, lever filler, gold plated trim, 1925	50.00	60.00	55.00
☐ **Sheaffer,** Lifetime, black and pearl, lever filler, gold plated trim, 1932	90.00	110.00	100.00
☐ **Sheaffer,** sterling silver, early feed, ladies, lever filler, 1916	40.00	50.00	45.00
☐ **Sheaffer,** Triumph, striped, plunger filled, 1946	30.00	45.00	37.50
☐ **Swann,** solid gold 14K, fine point, 1920s	60.00	80.00	70.00
☐ **Wahl,** # 4, gold filled metal, 1924	80.00	100.00	90.00
☐ **Wahl,** lever filler, gold filled, 1926	35.00	45.00	40.00
☐ **Wahl-Eversharp,** gold filled metal, pen and pencil set, 1924	100.00	130.00	115.00
☐ **Waterman,** # 52, black chased hard rubber, nickle plated trim, 1923	20.00	30.00	25.00

	Current Price Range		P/Y Average
☐ **Waterman,** #412, orange with silver overlay, eye dropper filler, 1905	330.00	370.00	350.00
☐ **Waterman,** #452, gothic sterling silver, 1925 .	120.00	130.00	125.00
☐ **Waterman,** #554, lower end covered, solid 14K gold, gothic, 1928	430.00	470.00	450.00
☐ **Waterman,** #5116, Ink View, gray pearl, gold plated trim, 1939	40.00	50.00	45.00
☐ **Waterman,** black, chased hard rubber, pencil, 1920	15.00	25.00	20.00
☐ **Waterman,** Taperite, gold filled cap, 1946	20.00	30.00	25.00

PHONOGRAPHS

DESCRIPTION: An instrument that reproduces sound by the use of a needle playing on a cylinder record or flat disc.

PERIOD: Thomas Edison invented the phonograph in 1877 and was issued a patent in 1878.

MAKER: There were several major manufacturers of phonographs including Columbia Phonograph Company, North American Phonograph Company and Berliner Gramophone Company which later became RCA Victor. Lesser known companies which produced phonographs included Vitaphone, Euphonic and Echophone.

COMMENTS: Although all types of phonographs are valuable, collectors especially seek those with the visible sound horn. Collectors also search for obscure company's phonographs.

ADDITIONAL TIPS: For more information, consult *The Official Price Guide to Music Collectibles,* published by The House of Collectibles.

☐ **Apollo (Disc),** table model, plain oak case, outside blue fluted metal (painted) horn, crank wind, plays 78rpm records, Apollo, Jr. reproducer (sound box) European maker. . . .	250.00	350.00	300.00
☐ **Apollo Floor Model (Disc),** highly styled fruitwood case, curved legs, storage for records, cover lifts to reveal turntable, nickel plated exposed parts, European maker.	285.00	385.00	325.00

Edison Triumph, *with polyphone attachment*

	Current Price Range		P/Y Average
☐ **Adler (Disc) "Box Camera,"** style portable, tone arm fits into opening in cover, "horn" is drawer in the cover which opens out on one side to form a horn, turntable is three spokes which open out to hold record, hand crank, 7″ x 4″ x 7″	125.00	200.00	162.00
☐ **Boston Talking Machine Co. (Disc),** "Little Wonder Disc Phonograph," cast iron case and horn, tone arm comes out from center of 6 sided horn rests on rear mount bracket, 6½″ turntable, single spring, records must have vertical cut grooves, plays "Little Wonder" discs, c. 1909-12.	125.00	200.00	162.00
☐ **Brunswick,** c. 1921 (Disc), mahogany table model, plain square sided case, rotating reproducer plays both lateral and vertical groove records. 11¾″ turntable.	100.00	200.00	150.00

	Current Price Range		P/Y Average

☐ **Brunswick Model 105 (Disc),** table model, c. 1921, mahogany case, 19½" high, two headed reproducer will play both lateral and vertical cut record, 11¾" turntable, simple rectangular case style with cover, oval fretwork grill, crank wind. 150.00 250.00 **200.00**

☐ **Columbia Type AT,** c. 1898 (Cylinder), oak case, decorative moulding along top edge, corner columns, ribbon decal, nickel plated mechanism (also black with gold decoration), double spring, Eagle Aluminum Reproducer, High Trunion Model c. 1903, oak case, decorative corner mouldings, new style "D" reproducer, 14" bell aluminum horn with bell, reproducer sits in horizontal position over cylinder. 375.00 600.00 **462.00**

☐ **Columbia Type AU,** c. 1903 (Disc). Open works mounted on base, 7" (6¾") turntable, 16" metal horn with bell, horn support and metal "tone arm," reproducer attached at end of horn. 300.00 400.00 **350.00**

☐ **Columbia Graphophone Model B 1 (Disc),** rear mount outside horn table model, 8 petal morning glory horn, decorative corner and base mouldings, crank wind, nickel metal fittings and horn. 850.00 1000.00 **925.00**

☐ **Columbia Graphophone Model Bn (Disc),** oak outside horn table model, 11 petal morning glory, simple case style, rear mount horn bracket and tone arm. 650.00 950.00 **800.00**

☐ **Columbia Grand Type AG (Cylinder),** oak case (similar to Type AT) decorative top, corner and base mouldings, large ribbon decal, 5" diameter mandrel plays Grand cylinders, black painted exposed metal parts, gold decoration, type "D" reproducer (Heavy Eagle Reproducer). 1000.00 2000.00 **1500.00**

☐ **Columbia Type QQ,** c. 1898-1902 (Cylinder), keywind, exposed works, mounted on oak base, single spring, aluminum reproducer Type Q, belled horn with nickel finish, 'bent' wood oak cover with large "The Graphophone" decal. 220.00 260.00 **240.00**

☐ **Columbia "Q" Second Series,** c. 1903 (Cylinder), black and gold base open works simple mechanism, plays 2-minute cylinders, key wind, type "D" reproducer. 185.00 250.00 **217.00**

☐ Also sold as the "Languagephone" with special language cylinders (Rosenthal). 200.00 275.00 **237.00**

	Current Price Range		P/Y Average

☐ **Columbia Regent or Grafonola Regent (Disc)**, floor model, mahogany "desk" style, console case style (walnut, oak) some case decoration, carved claw feet, top drawer pulls out to reveal 78rpm phonograph, two storage compartments for 200-12″ records, small doors on one side near top open to reveal grilled speaker (electric). **750.00   1500.00   1120.00**

☐ **Edison School Phonograph**, c. 1912 (Cylinder), table model, metal case fits into metal floor stand, on wheels with four storage boxes for 96 cylinders (Blue Amberol), self-supporting cygnet type black metal horn, Diamond Model "A" reproducer (Opera mechanism). **1000.00   1500.00   1250.00**

☐ **Edison Standard Model A**, c. 1897 (Cylinder), oak case, "suitcase" style model with metal clips to hold cover, plays 2-minute cylinders, slotted crank, plays 3 cylinders on one winding, squared off corners on base of case, 14″ brass belled horn, shaving device, single spring. **300.00   450.00   375.00**

☐ **Edison Standard Model B**, c. 1905 (Cylinder), oak case and rounded cover, base moulding, mechanism screwed to lid of base, Model "C" reproducer, ribbon decal, speed control, screw on crank, single spring, plays 2-minute cylinder records (no shaving device), 14″ brass belled horn, may be fitted with manual language repeater mechanism operated by pressing on lever attached to front of mechanism. The reproducer is set back several grooves to repeat last phrases, usually accompanied by a small plate on front of machine, e.g. "International Textbook Co." Special language cylinders were made with a whole course of instruction. **275.00   375.00   325.00**

☐ With language repeat (International Correspondence School). **350.00   500.00   425.00**

☐ **Pathe Coquet (Cylinder)**, simple walnut case, Orpheus attachment, bakelite reproducer and recorder, slip on Salon mandrel, aluminum horn, plays both 2″ diameter and 4″diameter Salon cylinders, shallow cover. ... **400.00   450.00   425.00**

☐ **Pathe "Duplex" Grand Concert (Cylinder)**, simple oak case, carrying handles, small aluminum bell horn, plays both regular and Salon size cylinders, slightly smaller than the Concert Cylinder, Orpheus attachment. **225.00   450.00   337.00**

☐ **Pathe "Elf,"** c. 1915 (Disc), table model, "horn" built into the cover of the machine and finished to match the oak case, the tone arm comes down from the center of the "horn," hand crank wind, simple lines. **225.00   325.00   275.00**

	Current Price Range		P/Y Average

☐ **Victor III,** oak case, fluted corner columns, heavy base moulding, Exhibition Reproducer, tapering tone arm, brake, speed regulator, 10″ turntable, double spring, 23″ long ribbed horn (black metal with gold decoration) rear mount. (Also brass belled horn, oak wood horn or flowered horn)..................... **650.00 1200.00 925.00**

☐ **Victor IV,** mahogany case with rounded corner columns, base and top moulding, rear mount 24″ ribbed horn (black metal with gold decoration), tapering tone arm, brake, speed control, 10″ turntable, heavy double spring, Exhibition Reproducer (also black tapered horn with brass bell, flowered horn or mahogany horn)............................. **750.00 1250.00 1000.00**

☐ **Victor V,** oak case with corner columns, heavy base and top moulding, 12″ turntable, triple spring, tapering tone arm, brake, speed control, Exhibition Reproducer, 26″ black ribbed horn (flowered or oak horn).......... **750.00 1500.00 1125.00**

☐ **Victor VI,** c. 1906, mahogany case with fluted Corinthian corner columns, with carved capitals, gold decoration on columns, 14 karat triple gold plated Exhibition or Concert reproducer and tone arm, triple spring, 24″ bell brass Morning Glory horn or mahogany horn, 12″ turntable........................... **1800.00 2400.00 2100.00**

☐ **Victrola XI (Floor model),** mahogany (oak) floor model, inside horn with cover, plain case, 43″ high, slightly curving corner mouldings down to legs, two doors over speaker, storage in base for records, nickel plated metal parts, Exhibition Reproducer, brake, speed regulator and indicator, double spring. **100.00 200.00 150.00**

☐ **Victrola XII,** mahogany, inside horn, table model with cover, two small doors on front open to reveal louvered speaker, gold plated metal parts. **75.00 125.00 100.00**

PHOTOGRAPHS

TYPES: Photographs are usually one of four varieties: dageurreotypes, ambrotypes, tintypes or modern paper prints. Ambrotypes and tintypes are less valuable but are often collected. Three varieties of pictures made from negatives are original prints, later prints or reproductions. Original prints are those made by the photographer, or someone in his employ, shortly after taking the negative. Later prints are made from the original negative at a later date, sometimes fifty or more years later. Reproductions are made by making a new negative from the photo print. In most instances, original prints are most desired by collectors.

PERIOD: Photographs taken during the 1800s are most in demand by collectors. Early 1900s scenes, especially of the outdoor environment, are becoming more popular.

ORIGIN: The dageurroetype was invented in 1839 by Louis Dageurre.

MAKERS: Works by famous photographers such as Edward Curtis, Mathew Brady, Alfred Stieglitz or Carleton Watkins all command high prices in the collector market.

COMMENTS: Value is determined by age and subject matter. Of course the quality of the print in important; it must be in good condition to merit its full value.

TIPS: For further information, please refer to *The Official Price Guide to Paper Collectibles,* published by The House of Collectibles.

	Current Price Range		P/Y Average
☐ **Abbott, Berenice,** "Flatiron Building," silver print, mounted, 19¼ ″ x 14¾ ″, 1930s, printed later, date unknown	1200.00	1300.00	1250.00
☐ **Abbott, Berenice,** "New York Fifth Avenue at Eighth Street," plate from Berenice Abbott's New York, silver print, mounted, signed, 18¼ ″ x 23¼ ″, 1930s, printed c. 1979	950.00	1000.00	975.00
☐ **Adams, Ansel,** "Aspens, Northern New Mexico," silver print, mounted, signed, 15⅜ ″ x 19½ ″, 1958, printed c. 1963	4800.00	4900.00	4850.00

Engagement Picture,
*sepia tones, Fox Studios,
Chicago, January, 1915,*
$5.00-$10.00

	Current Price Range		P/Y Average
☐ **Adams, Ansel,** "Frozen Lake and Cliffs, Sierra Nevada, California," silver print, mounted, signed, 10″ x 13″, c. 1927, printed in 1973	2100.00	2200.00	2150.00
☐ **Adams, Ansel,** "Leaves, Mt. Rainier National Park," silver print, mounted, signed, 15½ ″ x 19½ ″, c. 1942, printed c. 1963	2500.00	2600.00	2550.00
☐ **Adams, Ansel,** portrait of Mrs. Gunn, silver print, mounted, signed, matted, 13¼ ″ x 10″, c. 1944, printed c. 1955	2200.00	2300.00	2250.00
☐ **Adams, Ansel,** "Sonoma County Hills," silver print, mounted, signed, 15½ ″ x 19½ ″, late 1950s, printed c. 1962	1850.00	1950.00	1900.00
☐ **Adams, Ansel,** "Three Eggs in a Bowl," silver print, mounted, signed, 8½ ″ x 6¾ ″, 1931, printed in 1931	1950.00	2150.00	2050.00
☐ **Adams, Ansel,** "White Post and Spandrel," plate 7 from Portfolio VI, silver print, mounted, signed, framed, 19¼ ″ x 14″, 1953, printed c. 1974	325.00	375.00	350.00
☐ **Allen, Frances and Mary,** "Out West" and "Running Water Ranch," two photographic panoramas, platinum prints, matted, each 3¼ ″ x 11¼ ″, early 1900s, the specific printing dates unknown	150.00	170.00	160.00
☐ **American Missionary Association Jubilee Singers,** Fisk University, Nashville, carte-de-visite of group of black gospel singers	30.00	38.00	33.00

	Current Price Range		P/Y Average

☐ **Booth, Edwin,** as Cardinal Richelieu, carte-de-visite by Sarony 17.00 23.00 **19.00**

☐ **Brandt, Bill,** "Race-Goers," silver print, mounted, signed, 13¼ ″ x 11½ ″, printed later, the specific date unknown 325.00 345.00 **335.00**

☐ **Brady (Mathew) Studio,** album containing 1,120 mounted prints on 119 pages, mostly carte-de-visite size, almost all identified, some measuring 8″ x 10″, includes 18 U.S. Presidents, 84 Union officers, 66 Confederate officers, 11 Confederate statesmen, 130 American statesmen and authors, 95 European statesmen and royalty, etc., small folio, full leather, c. 1860s 13000.00 17000.00 **15000.00**

☐ **Brassai,** "Conchita With an Admirer at the Place D'Italie," silver print, signed, 11½ ″ x 9″, 1930s, printed later, the specific date unknown 1550.00 1650.00 **1600.00**

☐ **Brassai,** "Lovers in a Park," silver print, signed, 12″ x 9½ ″, 1930s, printed later, the specific date unknown 950.00 1000.00 **975.00**

☐ **Bravo, Manuel Alvarez,** "La Buena Fama Durmiendo," silver print, signed, matted, 7⅛″ x 9½ ″, 1938, printed later, the specific date unknown 550.00 600.00 **575.00**

☐ **Brazil and Mexico,** album of 60 mounted photographs, folio, half leather, c. 1870 .... 150.00 200.00 **175.00**

☐ **Briquet, A.,** group of 14 mounted photos, ranging from 5″ x 8″ to 8″ x 10″, showing indians, views of Mexico City, etc., c. 1875 ... 300.00 400.00 **350.00**

☐ **British Snapshots,** album with over 100 small amateur shapshots, mostly 3½ ″ x 4½ ″, showing views of Oxford, Chester, Devonshire, etc., boards, back cover lacking 45.00 55.00 **50.00**

☐ **Bunker Hill Monument,** carte-de-visite, historical information printed on reverse 9.00 12.00 **10.00**

☐ **Business and Commerce,** collection of over 40 mounted photos showing shops, factories, work crews, wagons and other aspects of 19th-century American commerce, mostly from Connecticut, sizes 13″ x 16″ and smaller, mixed condition, c. 1880s-1910 .... 85.00 125.00 **105.00**

☐ **Callahan, Harry,** "Eleanor, Chicago," silver print, signed, matted, 7⅜″ x 7″, 1948, printed later, the specific date unknown 480.00 530.00 **505.00**

☐ **Callahan, Harry,** "Ivy Tentacles on Glass," silver print, signed, framed, 8″ x 10″, c. 1952, printed later, the specific date unknown 425.00 475.00 **450.00**

☐ **Canada and Alaska,** group of 32 stereograms, some colored lithoprints, by various photographers, showing Yukon Gold Rush and other subjects, 3¼ ″ x 7″, mostly c. 1890s 45.00 65.00 **55.00**

☐ **Caponigro, Paul,** "Blue Ridge Parkway," silver print, mounted, 14¼ ″ x 18″, 1965, printed later, the specific date unknown 530.00 570.00 **550.00**

	Current Price Range		P/Y Average

☐ **Civil War State Militiaman,** *ambrotype, half length seated portrait holding M1816 musket with bayonet in belt, cased* . . . . — 170.00 — 190.00 — 175.00

☐ **Cody, Buffalo Bill,** carte-de-visite, portrait wearing his theatrical costuming . . . . — 35.00 — 45.00 — 38.00

☐ **Dassonville, William,** "Study in black and white, No. II," silver print, signed, matted, 9½″ x 7″, early 1920s, printed before 1924 . . . — 540.00 — 580.00 — 560.00

☐ **Dassonville, William,** "Study of Iris," platinum print, signed, 7⅜″ x 4⅜″, early 1900s, the specific printing date unknown . . . . — 570.00 — 630.00 — 600.00

☐ **Dassonville, William,** "Yosemite, Cathedral Rocks," platinum print, signed, matted, 6″ x 8″, 1907-8, the specific printing date unknown — 275.00 — 325.00 — 300.00

☐ **Dater, Judy,** "Imogen and Twinka at Yosemite," silver print, mounted, signed, matted and framed, 9½″ x 7⅜″, 1974, printed later, the specific date unknown . . . . — 625.00 — 675.00 — 650.00

☐ **De Meyer, Baron,** photo of an actress in royal medieval dress, 9½″ x 7½″, signed "DeMeyer," c. 1924 . . . . — 220.00 — 280.00 — 250.00

☐ **Doisneau, Robert,** "Le Petit Balcon," silver print, signed, matted, 12⅛″ x 10″, 1953, printed later, the specific date unknown . . . . — 370.00 — 430.00 — 400.00

☐ **Doisneau, Robert,** "Venus Prise a la Gorge," silver print, signed, matted 12¾″ x 9⅝″, 1965, printed in 1977 . . . . — 480.00 — 520.00 — 500.00

☐ **Dwarf,** Mrs. Tom Thumb, carte-de-visite by Fredericks . . . . — 9.00 — 12.00 — 10.00

☐ **Dwarf,** General Grant Jr., carte-de-visite of dwarf said to be sixteen years old, standing 27″ and weighing twenty three pounds, dressed in military attire and posing alongside a normal size adult for contrast, c. 1875 . — 15.00 — 20.00 — 16.75

☐ **Dwarf,** Little Lord Robert, carte-de-visite of dwarf said to be twenty years old, standing 22″, weighing thirteen and a half pounds . . . — 18.00 — 23.00 — 19.75

☐ **Edgarton, Harold,** "Bullet in Apple," dye-transfer print, signed, matted and framed, 9¾″ x 12″, c. 1964, printed later, the specific date unknown . . . . — 400.00 — 460.00 — 430.00

☐ **Fire Brigade Officer,** ambrotype, three quarter length portrait, embossed contemporary case . . . . — 100.00 — 135.00 — 110.00

☐ **Frank, Robert,** "Florer Seller in Paris," silver print, signed, matted 9″ x 13½″, c. 1949-50, the specific printing date unknown . . . . — 700.00 — 750.00 — 725.00

☐ **Freaks,** nine carte-de-visites and two cabinet cards, showing sideshow attractions, c. 1860s-1870s . . . . — 75.00 — 105.00 — 90.00

☐ **Gardner, Alexander,** photographic sketch book of the (Civtl) war, two volumes, oblong folio, with 100 mounted albumen prints, Washington, D.C. 1866 . . . . — 17000.00 — 22000.00 — 19500.00

☐ **Genthe, Arnold,** photo, "Elderly Woman with Baby on Her Back," Japan, 7½″ x 10″ . . . . . . — 250.00 — 350.00 — 300.00

	Current Price Range		P/Y Average

☐ **Genthe, Arnold,** photo, "Woman Standing in Front of Temple," Japan, 10″ x 6½″ . . . . — 250.00 / 350.00 / 300.00

☐ **Genthe, Arnold,** photo, "Mountain in Guatemala," 8″ x 9¾″ . . . . — 170.00 / 230.00 / 200.00

☐ **Grand Canyon,** group of 14 mounted photos by C. Osborn of Flagstaff, AZ, showing the canyon rim and interior, 4½″ x 7½″ on 7″ x 10″ mounts, c. 1870s . . . . — 125.00 / 175.00 / 150.00

☐ **Grand Canyon Of The Arkansas,** cabinet photo . . . . — 55.00 / 70.00 / 61.00

☐ **Greene, Milton,** "Portrait of Marilyn Monroe," silver print, matted, 16″ x 20″, 1953, printed in 1978 . . . . — 440.00 / 460.00 / 450.00

☐ **Green, Milton H.,** "Portrait of Marilyn Monroe," silver print, matted, 16″ x 20″, 1953, printed in 1979 . . . . — 375.00 / 425.00 / 400.00

☐ **Gruen, John,** "Two Coffee Pots," silver print, signed, matted, 13″ x 17″, 1975, printed c. 1980 . . . . — 370.00 / 430.00 / 400.00

☐ **Halsman, Philippe,** "Portrait of Albert Einstein," silver print, signed, matted and framed, 13⅝″ x 10½″, 1947, the specific printing date unknown . . . . — 1200.00 / 1300.00 / 1250.00

☐ **Iron Spring Hotel,** cabinet photo . . . . — 40.00 / 50.00 / 43.00

☐ **Lady In Bonnet,** ⅑ plate daguerreotype of lady with corkscrew curls and frilly bonnet, cased . . . . — 50.00 / 65.00 / 56.75

☐ **Lynes, George Platt,** "Bill Miller," a group of three portraits, silver prints, one matted, each approximately 9¼″ x 7½″, 1942-46, the specific printing dates unknown . . . . — 950.00 / 1050.00 / 1000.00

☐ **Mammy With Baby,** ambrotype, black girl holding sleeping white child, cased, Civil War era . . . . — 200.00 / 250.00 / 215.00

☐ **Mapplethorpe, Robert,** "Cowboy, San Francisco," silver print, 14½″ x 13¾″, c. 1976, the specific printing date unknown . . . . — 775.00 / 825.00 / 800.00

☐ **Meyerowitz, Joel,** "Provincetown," a group of six photographs, five from the Porch Series and one from the Bayl Sky series, C prints, frames, each approximately 7¾″ x 9¾″, 1976-77, printed c. 1979 . . . . — 1750.00 / 1850.00 / 1800.00

☐ **Michals, Duane,** "Magritte," silver print, matted, 4⅞″ x 7¼″, 1965, printed later in an edition of 100, the specific date unknown . . . . . . — 425.00 / 475.00 / 450.00

☐ **Monsen, Frederick I.,** "Children of the Desert, Rio Grande, New Mexico," silver print, mounted; title label on the mount, matted, 18⅝″ x 13⅛″, 1920s, the specific printing date unknown . . . . — 150.00 / 180.00 / 165.00

☐ **Moon, Karl,** "Home from the Hunt," silver print, triple-mounted, 11⅜″ x 14⅜″, 1920s, the specific printing date unknown . . . . — 425.00 / 475.00 / 450.00

	Current Price Range		P/Y Average

☐ **Morse, Samuel F. B.,** lantern slide reproduction of Bogardus' famous portrait of Morse with his Daguerrotype camera by his side, 3¼" x 4¼", c. 1880 . . . . **60.00 70.00 65.00**

☐ **Niagara Falls In Summer,** albumen cabinet photo by G.E. Curtis, 21" x 17" **100.00 130.00 115.00**

☐ **As Above,** in winter **90.00 115.00 97.00**
Note: These must have been originally made to sell to tourists. They would date about 1885.

☐ **Princess of Wales,** carte-de-visite, profile by Downey **15.00 20.00 16.50**

☐ **Revels, Hiram,** cabinet card from Mathew Brady's National Photographic Galleries, Washington, D.C., showing profile of Revels (Senator from Mississippi), 6½" x 4¼", c. 1870 . . . . **125.00 175.00 150.00**

☐ **Reward Poster,** broadside advertising $1,000 reward for capture of James Burns, charged with robbing Post Office in Brooklyn, NY., mounted on poster in a carte-de-visite of Burns, overall size 9" x 5½", Brooklyn, 1883 . **60.00 90.00 75.00**

☐ **Rhodesia,** album with 20 photos of botanical experiments, crops, etc., in Rhodesia, dated 1914 . . . . **45.00 60.00 52.50**

☐ **Robertson, James,** mounted albumen print believed to be by Robertson but not positively identified, showing view of the Parthenon with yobng top-hatted man standing near, 10¼" x 15", on mount 17" x 21", c. 1857 **290.00 390.00 340.00**

☐ **Ross, Charlie,** *$20,000 Reward, carte-de-visite surrounded by imprinted foil, these were distributed in mass quantities in 1874 in hopes someone would recognize the kidnapped boy* **50.00 60.00 56.00**
Note: Charlie Ross, the first child kidnapped for ransom in the U.S., was never found.

☐ **San Francisco,** group of five mounted photos of views in San Francisco: Cliff House, Sutro Heights, Golden Gate and Fort Point, Band Stand, Seal Rocks, 5¼" x 8½", c. 1870s **110.00 150.00 130.00**

☐ **Savage, Charles R.,** three carte-de-visites of Indians, c. 1870s **125.00 175.00 150.00**

☐ **Sheridan, General,** carte-de-visite, three quarter length portrait in full dress uniform by E. Anthony **35.00 45.00 39.00**

☐ **Siamese Twins,** carte-de-visite, infants photographed by Beach **13.00 17.00 14.00**
Note: These are not the famous Barnum Siamese twins, who were already adults by the time they reached the U.S.

☐ **Spirit Photographs,** 10 photos of male medium demonstrating levitation, ectroplasm, "Marjorie the Medium, 10 Lime Street, Boston," 7" x 5", c. 1935 . . . . **55.00 85.00 70.00**

	Current Price Range		P/Y Average
☐ **Stereograms,** 72 cards by Keystone View Co., mostly of scenes in Africa, India and Sweden, 3½" x 7", c. 1900	55.00	75.00	65.00
☐ **Stieglitz, Alfred,** photo, "Sunlight and Shadow," 8" x 10", (negative made 1889, date of print unknown)	150.00	220.00	185.00
☐ **Stieglitz, Alfred,** photo, "The Steerage," 8" x 10", (negative made 1907, date of print unknown)	150.00	220.00	185.00
☐ **Supreme Court Of The U.S.,** albumen cabinet photo by C.M. Bell, group portrait of Supreme Court members of 1882, 20" x 24"	250.00	300.00	267.00
☐ **Uncompahgre Canon/Mears Toll Road,** Colorado Springs, cabinet photo by George Mellen	20.00	25.00	22.00
☐ **Waino And Plutano: Wild Men of Borneo,** cabinet photo by Eisenmann, undated, c. 1900	23.00	29.00	25.00

PIPES

DESCRIPTION: A pipe is an item used for smoking which consists of a tube with a bowl and mouthpiece at opposite ends.

ORIGIN: American Indians are believed to be the first known people to make pipes. Europeans picked up the custom from them during the 1500s.

MATERIAL: Clay, porcelain and wood are different materials used to produce pipes. Meerschaum, a white clay, was discovered during the middle 1600s. This soft clay produced beautiful pipes that are highly prized collector's items today.

COMMENTS: Meerschaum pipes carved in Vienna during the 19th and 20th centuries, pipes made by famous German porcelain factories during the 18th century and briar pipes produced in the early 1900s by famous British pipe makers like Alfred Dunhill of London and Comoy's of London are some of the most sought after pipes by collectors.

ADDITIONAL TIPS: Factors to consider when searching for collectible pipes are design, maker and user. Value is added when a noteable person owns the pipe, a famous company produces the pipe or the pipe is intricately designed.

CLASSIC PIPE SHAPES

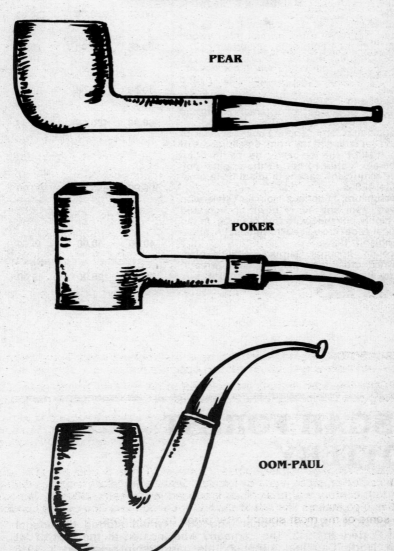

PEAR

POKER

OOM-PAUL

	Current Price Range		P/Y Average
□ **Corn Cob,** American, large tapering bowl with light incised carving, grayish patina, 1890s ..	20.00	25.00	22.00
□ **Ivory,** the bowl in oval form carved with an oriental scene of peasants carrying trays and buckets, with intricate leaf and vinework, 1870s	200.00	250.00	220.00
□ **Meerschaum,** bowl carved in the likeness of a female figure with flowing hair, cherrywood stem, horn mouthpiece, age uncertain	60.00	80.00	70.00
□ **Meerschaum,** British "bull dog" type soldier's pipe from World War I, carved with the date 1915 and word "Dardanelles," plated ferrule	30.00	40.00	35.00
□ **Meerschaum,** large size, fully sculptured bowl in the likeness of a female head and neck, in a leather case, 1870s	80.00	100.00	90.00
□ **Meerschaum,** large tapering bowl carved with a cavalier's face at the front, small figures of elks at sides, the top carved as the rim of an elaborate feathered hat, in the original polished mahogany case with inlaid bone ornaments, 1830s	500.00	650.00	560.00
□ **Meerschaum,** "Sherlock Holmes" style with curved stem and heavy bowl, undecorated but highly polished with fine graining, in the original cedar case lined in white satin, made in England, 1920s	40.00	50.00	45.00
□ **Porcelain,** Imperial German soldier's pipe, crowned cross and painted floral wreath, cherry stem and horn mouthpiece, 1914	75.00	95.00	85.00

PISGAH FOREST POTTERY

DESCRIPTION: Walter Stephen and C.P. Ryman started the Pisgah Forest Pottery in 1913. The company was located at the foot of Mt. Pisgah, North Carolina. Although this partnership dissolved in 1916, Stephen began to produce pottery again in 1920. Currently, the firm is still producing wares.

The company produced many types of pieces including vases, jugs, tea sets and mugs.

MARKS: Early pieces are marked Stephen or W.B. Stephen with either a raised figure of a potter at his wheel or without. After 1926, "Pisgah Forest" was the mark used. Again, the potter figure was sometimes used with this mark.

RECOMMENDED READING: For further information, refer to *The Official Price Guide to Pottery and Porcelain,* published by The House of Collectibles.

Bowl, *5"*, **$30.00-$40.00**

	Current Price Range		P/Y Average
☐ **Bowl,** *3", flat, very bulbous shaped body*	30.00	40.00	32.00
☐ **Vase,** *4¾", green and pink, 1948*	40.00	50.00	42.00
☐ **Vase,** *5", bulbous body, green, three handled*	25.00	35.00	27.00
☐ **Vase,** *6", red and green, collared neck*	40.00	50.00	42.00
☐ **Vase,** *6", white and creme glaze*	150.00	175.00	152.00

PLATES

DESCRIPTION: Collector plates have a painting or design usually by a well-known or studio artist portrayed on its face.

TYPES: There are two types of limited edition collector plates. Either the number of plates or the number of production days is limited.

PERIOD: Collector plates first began with the 1895 blue and white porcelain Christmas plate by Bing and Grondahl. Companies have been producing collector plates since that time.

COMMENTS: Most plate collectors display their plates as artwork and derive the same sense of pleasure and satisfaction from them that they would from original paintings, except at a small fraction of the cost of a painting. Yet, plates usually appreciate at a phenomenal rate.

ADDITIONAL TIPS: For more information, consult *The Official Price Guide to Collector Plates,* published by The House of Collectibles.

	Issue Price	Current Price
☐ **American Express,** Birds of North America Series, 1978, Saw Whet Owls, production quantity 9,800	38.00	40.00
☐ **American Rose Society,** All American Rose Series, 1975, Oregold, production quantity 9,800	39.00	120.00
☐ **Anna-Perenna,** American Silhouettes Collection I, The Children Series, 1981, Fiddlers Two, artist: P. Buckley Moss, production quantity 5,000	75.00	75.00
☐ **Antique Trader,** Bible Series, 1973, David and Goliath, production quantity 2,000	10.75	11.00
☐ **Artists of the World,** The Anthony Sidoni Series, 1982, The Little Yankee, artist: Anthony Sidoni, production quantity 15,000	35.00	40.00
☐ **Bareuther,** Christmas Series, 1967, Stiftskirche, artist: Hans Mueller, porcelain, 8″	12.00	125.00
☐ **Bing & Grondahl,** Christmas Series, 1895, Frozen Window, artist: Frans August Hallin, porcelain, blue underglaze	.50	4050.00
☐ **Boehm Studios,** Boehm Owl Collection, 1980, Boreal Owl, artist: Boehm Studio Artists, production quantity 15,000 . .	62.50	65.00
☐ **Canadian Collector Plates,** Discover Canada Series, 1980, Sawmill-Kings Landing, artist: Keirstead, production quantity 10,000	98.00	240.00

UNCLE TAD'S CATS SERIES
"Walter's Window," 1981,
Thaddeus Krumeich,
Anna-Perenna,

$85.00-$87.00

UNCLE TAD'S CATS SERIES
"Princess Aurora, Queen
Of The Night," 1981
Thaddeus Krumeich
Anna-Perenna

$80.00-$82.00

	Issue Price	Current Price
☐ **Carson Mint,** América Has Heart Series, 1980, My Heart's Desire, artist: Jan Hagara, production; one year	24.50	90.00
☐ **Coalport,** Mother's Day series, 1978, Clematis, production: one year	16.00	18.00
☐ **Danbury Mint,** Bicentennial Silver Series, 1973, Boston Tea Party, production quantity 7,500	125.00	130.00
☐ **D'Arceau Limoges,** Ganeau's Women, 1976, Scarlet en Crinoline, artist: Francois Ganeau, porcelain, overglaze decorated	17.67	35.00

	Issue Price	Current Price
☐ **Daum,** Nymphea Series, 1979, Waterlilies, production quantity 4,000	125.00	140.00
☐ **Dresden,** Mother's Day Series, 1972, Doe and Fawns, artist: Hans Waldheimer, production quantity 8,000	15.00	22.00
☐ **Fairmont China,** America's Most Beloved Series, 1980, John Wayne, artist: Clarence Thorpe, production quantity 5,000 .	13.95	16.00
☐ **Franklin Mint,** Audubon Society Series, 1972, The Goldfinch, artist: James Fenwick Lansdowne, production quantity 10,193	125.00	125.00
☐ **Franklin Mint,** Rockwell American Sweethearts Series, 1977, Youngsters at Play, artist: Norman Rockwell, production quantity 1,004	120.00	140.00
☐ **Frankoma Pottery,** Teenagers of the Bible Series, 1973, Jesus The Carpenter, artist: John Frank, pottery, low relief .	5.00	18.00
☐ **George Washington Mint,** Picasso Series, 1972, Rites of Spring, production quantity 9,800	150.00	185.00
☐ **Ghent Collection,** American Bicentennial Wildlife Series, 1976, American Bald Eagle, artist: Harry J. Moeller, production quantity 2,500	95.00	335.00
☐ **Goebel Collection,** American Heritage Series, 1978, Freedom and Justice Soaring, production: one year	100.00	115.00
☐ **Gorham Collection,** American Artists Series, 1976, Apache Mother and Child, production quantity 9,800	52.00	58.00
☐ **Hacket American Collectors,** Classical American Beauties Series, 1978, Collen, artist: Vincent, production quantity 7,500	60.00	85.00
☐ **Kaiser,** Mother's Day Series, 1976, Swan and Cygnets, artist: Toni Schoener	25.00	21.00
☐ **Lynell,** Betsy Bates Annual Series, 1979, Olde Country Inn, production quantity 7,500	38.50	45.00
☐ **Pemberton and Oakes,** Moments Alone Series, 1980, The Dreamer, artist: Robert Bentley, production: less than one year	28.80	32.00
☐ **Reco International,** Arabelle and Friends Series, 1982, Ice Delight, artist: Carol Greunke, production quantity 15,000 .	35.00	37.00
☐ **Ridgewood,** Vasils Series, 1976, All Hallows Eve, production quantity 5,000	38.50	40.00
☐ **Norman Rockwell Museum,** American Family Series I, 1978, Baby's First Step, artist: Norman Rockwell, bisque porcelain, production quantity 9,900	28.50	85.00
☐ **Royal Copenhagen,** Historical Series, 1975, R.C. Bicentennial, production: one year	30.00	32.00
☐ **Royal Delft,** Christmas Series, 1915, Christmas Bells, production: one year	2.25	6250.00
☐ **Royal Doulton,** All God's Children Series, 1979, A Brighter Day, artist: Lisette DeWinne, production quantity 10,000 ...	60.00	75.00
☐ **Schmid Germany,** Cat Tales Series, 1982, Right Church, Wrong Pew, artist: Lowell Davis, production quantity 12,500	37.50	40.00
☐ **Signature Collection,** Angler's Dream Series, 1983, Brook Trout, artist: John Eggert, production quantity 9,800	55.00	55.00
☐ **Vague Shadows,** The Plainsmen Series, 1978, Buffalo Hunt, artist: Gregory Perillo, production quantity 2,500	300.00	300.00
☐ **Veneto Flair,** Bellini Series, 1971, Madonna, production quantity 500	45.00	420.00
☐ **Viletta China,** The Carefree Days Series, 1982, Autumn Wanderer, artist: Thornton Utz, production: 10 days	24.50	25.00

PLAYER PIANOS

DESCRIPTION: A self-playing instrument which uses suction, that is controlled by a paper roll passing over a bar, to produce sound.

TYPES: The three types of player mechanisms used through the 1930s are Welte-Mignon, Duo-Art and Ampico.

COMMENTS: Note the reputation of the piano manufacturer, the type of player mechanism used in the piano and whether the piano is restored when determining the value of any player piano.

ADDITIONAL TIPS: For more information, consult *The Official Price Guide to Music Collectibles.*

	Unrestored	Restored
☐ **Apollo Piano Co. (IL),** used foot pump player actions made by Melville and Simplex in their pianos.	200.00-275.00	2000.00-2500.00
☐ **Apollophone,** upright player piano, foot pump, with built in disc phonograph inside front left panel next to paper roll assembly.	2500.00	3500.00
☐ **Artemis (KRELL),** Player action used in Thompson, Steger, Reid and Sons, Krell and other pianos.	250.00	1500.00-2000.00
☐ **Godfrey Pianos (New York),** melodic upright, 88-note regular players.	250.00	2500.00-2750.00
☐ **Gordon & Sons (Kohler & Campbell),** used the Standard and Pratt and Read Player mechanisms.	250.00	2500.00 2750.00
☐ **Grinnell Bros. (Detroit, MI),** used the Aeolian and Lester Player mechanisms.	250.00-300.00	2500.00-3000.00
☐ **Guest Piano Co. (Burlington, IA),** made a line of Players. . . .	250.00	2500.00
☐ **Gulbransen (Chicago, IL),** made their own player mechanisms, they made what they called a "Registering Piano" Player mechanism, early model was screwed together, later the stack was glued together and is much more difficult to restore, Gulbransen Player mechanisms found in many pianos.	200.00-250.00	2500.00

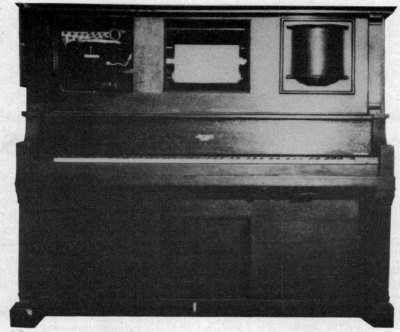

Apollophone Upright Player-Phonograph . $2500.00-$3500.00

	Unrestored	Restored
☐ **Gulbransen-Dickinson (Chicago, IL)**, used their own player mechanism.	250.00	2500.00-2750.00
☐ **Haddorf Piano Co. (Rockford, IL)**, used the Amphion Player mechanism.	250.00	2500.00-3000.00
☐ **Story and Clark Piano Co. (Chicago, IL)**, used their own player mechanism. Also made miniature upright players. Their mechanism also used in Gibbs, Irvington, Iverson and other pianos.	275.00-325.00	2500.00-3000.00
☐ **Straube Piano Co. (Chicago, IL)**, made their own player mechanism and also used the Standard mechanism. Straube mechanism also used in Woodward, Hammond and Gilmore Pianos.	250.00	2500.00-2750.00
☐ **Stroud Pianos (Aeolian)**, used the Aeolian and Duo-Art Reproducing Player mechanism.	350.00	3500.00
☐ **Stultz and Bauer (NY)**, used the Standard Player mechanism.	250.00	2500.00
☐ **Stutz and Co. (NY)**, used the Bjur Bros. Player mechanism.	200.00-250.00	2500.00 2750.00
☐ **Stuyvesant Pianos (NY)**, used the Aeolian Player mechanism.	250.00	2500.00

PLAYING CARDS

TYPES: Standard playing cards feature a king, a queen and a jack as the court subjects on a face card. The subjects will differ on a nonstandard deck. Tarot cards are also very collectible; they are used in fortune-telling.

ORIGIN: Playing cards are believed to have first appeared in the Far East around the 1100s. Printed playing cards probably were developed in Switzerland around 1430.

COMMENTS: Age usually determines value, although the quality of the artwork will have some influence. Very old playing cards do not often appear on the collectible market.

Playing Card, *Kinney Tobacco Co., 1889,* **$16.00-$20.00**

	Current Price Range		P/Y Average
☐ **Advertising,** Lorrilard Splendid Cut Plug Tobacco, 52 cards plus joker, American Playing Card Co., backs in red/white/blue, c. 1880, believed to be the earliest American advertising deck with pictorial backs	150.00	200.00	165.00

	Current Price Range		P/Y Average

□ **Advertising,** souvenir of the 11th Annual Convention of the United Drug Co., 52 cards, each with photographs of Rexall club officers, 1913 — 150.00 · 200.00 · 165.00

□ **American Indian Souvenir Playing Cards,** 52 cards plus joker and title card, Lazarus and Melzer, 1900 — 80.00 · 100.00 · 89.00

□ **Art Nouveaux,** deck depicts turn of the century artists, Grimaud, 1900 — 4.00 · 6.00 · 5.00

□ **At Sea,** 52 cards, Congress, gold borders — 20.00 · 25.00 · 21.75

□ **Barking Dog,** pinochle deck, Standard Playing Card Co., gold edges, c. 1910 — 18.00 · 23.00 · 20.00

□ **Bezique,** Samuel Hart, square corners, one way courts, believed to be pre-Civil War — 110.00 · 150.00 · 125.00

□ **Bicycle Bridge,** 52 cards plus joker, United States Playing Card Co., c. 1945 — 7.00 · 10.00 · 8.35

□ **Brown Derby,** 52 cards plus two jokers, each card has caricature of a show business personality (including Ronald Reagan), 1951 — 26.00 · 34.00 · 29.00

□ **Canary Playing Cards,** 52 cards plus joker, backs have black and white picture of lady with long curls and large hat, c. 1910 — 12.00 · 16.00 · 13.50

□ **Chicago World's Fair,** deck, c. 1934 — 15.00 · 21.00 · 18.00

□ **Chinese Art Treasures,** double deck — 13.00 · 18.00 · 15.50

□ **Circus World Museum Souvenir Deck,** 52 cards, backs picture Buffalo Bill's Wild West Show, c. 1970-1980 — 6.00 · 8.00 · 7.00

□ **Civil War Pack,** Union Playing Cards, American Card Co., NY, 2-color, eagles, stars, flags, shields, suits — 550.00 · 850.00 · 700.00

□ **Coca-Cola,** double deck — 5.00 · 10.00 · 7.50

□ **Culbertson's Own,** 52 cards, Russell, each card has bridge tips printed on it, 1932 — 25.00 · 32.00 · 28.00

□ **Cupid's Secret,** 52 cards, gold edges, 1907 — 20.00 · 25.00 · 22.25

□ **Deck,** 52 cards, Andrew Dougherty, tiny picture of card in two corners, c. 1870 — 120.00 · 200.00 · 160.00

□ **Deck,** Andrew Dougherty, NY, Owen Jones designs, c. 1880 — 50.00 · 130.00 · 90.00

□ **Deck,** 36 cards, two information cards, The Game of Kings, Adams, NY, portraits of British monarchs, 1845 — 220.00 · 320.00 · 270.00

□ **Double Action,** 52 cards, 1935 — 30.00 · 40.00 · 34.00

□ **Fish Up,** 52 cards plus two jokers, Creative Playing Card Co., all have cartoon backs with fishing themes, 1963 — 7.00 · 10.00 · 8.25

□ **Fleet Wing Gasoline,** advertising deck, c. 1910 — 16.00 · 22.00 · 19.00

□ **Flinch Cards,** c. 1910 — 25.00 · 30.00 · 27.50

□ **France Royale,** double deck, by Piatnik — 8.00 · 11.00 · 9.50

□ **French Suited Pack,** L.I. Cohen, large size, gold trim, mint — 220.00 · 320.00 · 270.00

□ **Grover Cleveland,** campaign deck, reprint of 1888 issue — 3.00 · 7.00 · 5.00

□ **Gypsy Witch,** fortune telling deck — 10.00 · 15.00 · 12.50

□ **Hard-A-Port-Cut Plug,** tobacco premium, 52 cards plus joker, c. late 1880s — 170.00 · 350.00 · 260.00

□ **Hollyhocks,** 52 cards, Dougherty, 1921 — 13.00 · 17.00 · 14.50

	Current Price Range		P/Y Average

Huntress, 52 cards, Andrew Dougherty, gold edges, ace of spades is neutral 13.00 17.00 14.75

Illuminated Deck, 52 cards, A. Dougherty, all pips gold outlined in style of medieval cards, Civil War era, considered one of the classic American packs 200.00 250.00 220.00

Indian Wars, 52 cards, Humphrey, with black spades, red hearts, yellow diamonds, blue clubs, rare 1300.00 1600.00 1425.00

Jack Daniels, 1972 edition 4.00 6.00 5.00

Jaws, double deck, Stancraft, motion picture inspired with shark reverses, c. 1978 . . . . 7.00 10.00 8.35

Mardi Gras, deck, reprint of 1925 issue 3.00 6.00 4.50

Nixon, politicards, 1971 edition 8.00 12.00 10.00

Panama Souvenir Cards, 53 plus information cards, USPC, real photos, c. 1908 . . . . 40.00 80.00 60.00

Picturesque Canada, 52 cards plus joker, backs picture Chateau Frontenac 20.00 25.00 22.00

Picturesque Nova Scotia, 52 cards plus joker, Canadian Playing Card Co., Montreal, illustrated on both sides, c. 1920 . . . . 25.00 35.00 29.00

Rita, double deck in double box, total of four jokers 25.00 33.00 28.75

Sebago, pinochle deck, Dougherty, gold edges, World War I era 12.00 17.00 13.25

Serenader, 52 cards, Russell, gold edges 9.00 12.00 10.25

Shooting The Rapids, 52 cards, 1910 . . . . 70.00 100.00 83.00

Souvenir Of The Canary Islands, 52 cards, Fournier, 1973 . . . . 10.00 15.00 11.50

Steamboats, 52 cards plus joker, U.S. Printing Co., pre-1900 . . . . 50.00 65.00 56.00

Texas Souvenir Deck, 52 cards plus joker, gold edges, c. 1900-1910 . . . . 75.00 100.00 83.00

Uncle Sam's Cabinet, 1901 . . . . 30.00 40.00 35.00

Vanity Fair Transformation Deck, United States Playing Card Co., America's first true transformation deck, 1895 . . . . 450.00 650.00 550.00

Verkehrvelt Tarock, reproduction of 1810 edition, "Topsy Turvy Animal Tarot" 50.00 70.00 60.00

Washable Plastic Deck, 52 cards plus joker, Dale, c. 1950 . . . . 7.00 10.00 8.25

W.C. Fields, 52 cards plus two jokers, J.L. Brown, scenes from his movies on courts and aces plus booklet with hints on cheating, 1971 . . . . 13.00 17.00 15.00

POLICE MEMORABILIA

DESCRIPTION: Police memorabilia includes any items pertaining to the policeman or a police station from ephemera to toys and paintings.

PERIOD: The early 1800s saw the first use of paid policemen in America. It wasn't until the middle 1800s, that police uniforms were used. During the early years of police duty, the officers carried items that were later outlawed. These items such as a bully club with nails are sought after by collectors.

TYPES: All types of police memorabilia from different law enforcement agencies including city police, sheriffs, rangers and private guards are collected especially uniforms, badges, night sticks and headgear.

MAKER: Most police badges from the 19th and early 20th centuries were produced by either the Waterbury Button Company of Waterbury, CT or Danbury Button Company of Danbury, Connecticut.

COMMENTS: The type of material, style changes and rarity play important roles in determing value of police collectibles.

	Current Price Range		P/Y Average
☐ **Badge,** Bangor Police 3, Bangor, Maine, silver, star in center with openwork around it, c. 1900	90.00	110.00	97.00
☐ **Badge,** Boston Police, embossed brass, first issue, pictures Justice with scales and date 1630, large size, issued 1853-1854, 4″	300.00	400.00	340.00
☐ **Badge,** Chief of Police, western, made from a Mexican silver coin of the 1800s with engraved wording added and a pin on the back.	225.00	275.00	250.00
☐ **Badge,** Federal Protective Service Police, 1981 Inauguration of the President (Ronald Reagan), gold and blue, special badge worn on that occasion only	175.00	235.00	197.00
☐ **Badge,** Fire Police, place of origin unknown, brass with light silver overlay, shield shape with wording on thin banners at top and bottom, c. 1880	35.00	45.00	40.00

Presentation Police Baton, *rosewood, handcarved ivory sections, gold plate inset inscribed "Presented to Sgt. William McCarthy, Jan. 8, 1901,"* *original silk cord and tassel, 22½",* **$200.00-$250.00** *(photo courtesy of ©Alfred J. Young Collection, NYC)*

	Current Price Range		P/Y Average
☐ **Badge,** Metropolitan Police Conference, New York City, enamel, shield shape, a special occasion badge worn by officers to gain admission to a function, date of origin unknown	20.00	25.00	22.00
☐ **Badge,** Newark, New Jersey, Police #189, brass with applied numerals, shield shape, c. 1890	65.00	85.00	72.00
☐ **Badge,** New Bedford Police, Massachusetts, brass with silver overlay, circular, word "Police" in large letters near bottom	36.00	44.00	39.00
☐ **Badge,** New York City Department of Correction Elevator Operator, gold washed	35.00	45.00	39.00
☐ **Badge,** Office of the Sheriff, Jacksonville Police, The Bold New City of the South, enameled bronze, illustration of skyline of Jacksonville, Florida on large elaborate shield shaped badge, early 1900s	33.00	43.00	35.00
☐ **Badge,** P. Morton, Police Chief, Ashland, New Hampshire, gilt copper, large with ornate eagle at top, c. 1910	45.00	55.00	49.00

	Current Price Range		P/Y Average

☐ **Badge,** Railroad Police, New York, New Haven and Hartford Railroad, brass with black enamel, pointed at top and bottom, late 1800s 75.00 95.00 82.00

☐ **Badge,** Saco Police, Maine, brass with silver overlay, plain incised lettering, shield shape, late 1800s or early 1900s 43.00 57.00 46.00

☐ **Badge,** Safety Patrol, Providence, brass with silver overlay and containing a small celluloid insert, spreadwing eagle at top, cross at center, late 1800s 27.00 34.00 29.00

☐ **Badge,** Sheriff's Officer, Camden County, New Jersey, brass with inlaid enamel, star shape, early 1900s 36.00 44.00 38.00

☐ **Badge,** Waltham Police, Massachusetts, plated silver, beehive center, shellwork at sides, large pin 80.00 100.00 88.00

☐ **Badge,** White House Police, Honorary Badge, gold filled, engraved "with best wishes, Harry S. Truman," c. 1945-1952 .... 200.00 300.00 230.00

☐ **Badge,** White House Police Chief, second issue (1940-1951), 10K golf face 250.00 350.00 285.00

☐ **Brass Knuckles,** iron, stamped Loudons Patent, Oct. 20, 1885, three joined loops for fitting over the first three fingers 40.00 50.00 42.00

☐ **Coat,** frock type worn by Providence (R.I.) police force, 19 buttons, c. 1900 .... 90.00 115.00 102.00

☐ **Flask,** in shape of nightstick or "billy club," glass with screw on tin lid, dark brown to resemble wood, said to have been carried by some police in Victorian era to circumvent orders against drinking on duty, 10½", c. 1850-1860 .... 100.00 130.00 110.00

☐ **Handcuffs,** nickel plated, oval shaped connected by rectangular loop links, working order with key, c. 1925 .... 25.00 32.00 27.00

☐ **Hat,** felt, bonnet type as worn by many metropolitan forces in the 1890s, oil cloth strap, badge in front states "Precinct Three" but no further details 130.00 160.00 142.00

☐ **Hat,** straw, for summer wear by an unidentified metropolitan force, c. 1915 .... 60.00 80.00 68.00

☐ **Helmet,** New York City Police Force, iron, dome shape, painted dark blue, name "Edwards" and number "261" written inside in white paint, c. 1885 .... 150.00 200.00 165.00

☐ **Nightstick,** rosewood, unmarked, rubber grip, leather thong, c. 1935, 21" 15.00 20.00 17.00

☐ **Nightstick,** wood with metal weighted end, leather strap, 17½", c. 1910 .... 30.00 40.00 34.00

☐ **Photograph,** Springfield (Massachusetts) Police Department group photo in uniform with accessories, mounted, 7½" x 10", 1891 . 90.00 115.00 101.75

☐ **Toy,** Patrol wagon with two horses, four police figures, moveable wheels, 1890s, 13" . 300.00 350.00 325.00

POLITICAL BUTTONS

DESCRIPTION: Political buttons usually have a portrait of a politician produced on it with a pin attached to the back.

TYPE: There are several types of buttons produced including celluloids and jugates, which are buttons having both presidential and vice presidential candidates pictured.

MATERIAL: Early pictures used on the pin back buttons from the late 1800s and early 1900s were printed on paper with a metal backing and covered with celluloid. By 1920, pictures were lithographed to the metal with the plastic covering omitted.

ADDITIONAL TIPS: Celluloids and jugates are both sought after collector's items. Rarity plays one of the most important factors in determining the value of political buttons.

	Current Price Range		P/Y Average
☐ **Bryan/Kern Jugate,** picture of eagle, multi-colored	245.00	290.00	265.00
☐ **Coolidge,** lithographed tin, blue and white ..	13.00	17.00	14.00
☐ **Coolidge/Davis Jugate,** celluloid, black and white, ⅞″	35.00	43.00	38.00
☐ **Eugene Chafin for President,** 1908 Prohibition Party candidate, ⅞″	40.00	55.00	45.00
☐ **Eugene Debs,** celluloid, red, white and black	70.00	100.00	80.00
☐ **Franklin Roosevelt,** celluloid, "We Are Going to Win This War," red, white and blue, 1½″ ..	13.00	17.00	14.00
☐ **Franklin Roosevelt,** "New Deal, Cowlitz County, Washington," red, white, blue and black	90.00	115.00	100.00
☐ **Governor Franklin D. Roosevelt,** "The People's Choice for President," 1932, brass 1¼″	18.00	23.00	20.00
☐ **Hoover,** black and white, 1¼″	30.00	40.00	33.00
☐ **Hoover/Curtis Jugate,** lithographed tin, red, white and blue, 2½″	110.00	140.00	120.00
☐ **I Like Ike,** lithographed tin, red lettering on white background, no illustration, used in 1952	2.00	3.00	2.50

	Current Price Range		P/Y Average
☐ **Landon for President Club,** red rim	15.00	20.00	17.00
☐ **Lucky Willkie,** red letters on white background, no illustration, used for the 1940 Republican candidacy of Wendell Willkie . . .	7.00	10.00	8.50
☐ **Lyndon Johnson/Hubert Humphrey Jugate,** "Let us Continue," 1964 campaign, ⅞ "	38.00	46.00	41.00
☐ **McKinley,** celluloid, red, white and black, "An Honest Dollar Earned and Spent at Home" . .	65.00	85.00	72.00
☐ **McKinley/Theodore Roosevelt Jugate,** photos in brass shell with flags in red, white and blue, used in 1900 campaign	23.00	29.00	25.00
☐ **Nixon/Lodge Jugate,** lithographed tin, from campaign of 1960 which Richard Nixon lost to John Kennedy	1.00	1.50	1.20
☐ **Ronald Reagan for Governor,** lithographed tin, white border	2.00	3.00	2.30
☐ **Smith/Robinson Jugate,** lithographed tin, from 1928 campaign	20.00	30.00	23.00
☐ **Stevenson,** celluloid, blue and white, shoulder length portrait, reading 1960 beneath	50.00	65.00	56.00
☐ **Support FDR,** Elect Satini Secretary of State, local button from Massachusetts, blue and white, 1936	13.00	17.00	14.00
☐ **Taft,** oval, celluloid, red, white, blue and green	30.00	35.00	32.00
☐ **Taft/Sherman Jugate,** celluloid, multicolored	35.00	43.00	38.00
☐ **Truman,** lithographed tin, pictures dome of U.S. Capitol, mentions his running mate Barkley	14.00	18.00	15.00
☐ **Willkie,** white and black with shoulder length portrait, wording "For President" at top	16.00	21.00	18.00
☐ **Wilson/Dunne Jugate,** celluloid, blue and white, 1¼ "	55.00	70.00	62.00
☐ **Young Republican Hoover League,** blue and white, not illustrated	27.00	34.00	30.00

POLITICAL MEMORABILIA

COMMENTS: Every political campaign from dog catcher to President produces memorabilia. In addition to the familiar campaign buttons, there is sure to be literature of all types, including posters, pictures, brochures and newspaper ads. Collectors naturally place the highest values on items pertaining to historic statesmen but even the memorabilia from campaigns of recent Presidents is highly favored by hobbyists.

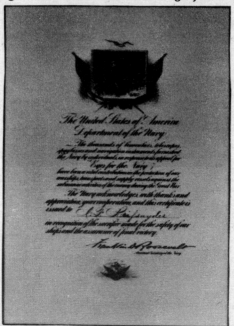

Document, *Donation of Binoculars as "Eyes for the Navy" by FDR, 1918,* **$40.00-$50.00**
Photo courtesy of Lou McCulloch, Highland Heights, OH 44143.

Political, *General Grant carte de visite,* **$20.00-$25.00** *Photo courtesy of Lou McCulloch, Highland Heights, OH 44143.*

	Current Price Range		P/Y Average
☐ **"AMERICA'S PRIDE,"** *colored and embossed cigar box label. Pictures George Washington. 7" x 9". c. 1910.*	6.75	13.50	7.00
☐ **BOTTOM IS OUT OF THE FULL DINNER PAIL, THE.** *Postcard, 1908.*	9.50	16.50	10.00
☐ **BACK TO THE FARM - THREE STRIKES AND OUT.** *Anti-Bryan cartoon postcard.*	13.50	20.00	14.00
☐ **DEE-LIGHTED.** *A postcard picturing Teddy Roosevelt, 1905.*	6.75	13.50	7.00
☐ **"FIRST BANNER,"** *cigar box label picturing Washington, an eagle and a shield. 7" x 10".*	6.75	13.50	7.00
☐ **F. D.R.,** *paper window poster, 8" x 11".*	6.75	11.00	7.00
☐ **F. D.R., "RAIN OR SHINE,"** *paper poster, 8" x 11".*	11.00	16.00	12.00
☐ **"GOLD WATER - THE RIGHT DRINK FOR THE CONSERVATIVE TASTE."** *Cardboard carton that once held six cans of soda; soda cans missing, 1964.*	16.00	24.00	17.00
☐ **"GREAT ISSUES AND NATIONAL LEADERS, THE VOTER'S GUIDE FOR THE CAMPAIGN OF 1908."** *Book, with photos on cover of Taft and Bryan.*	8.00	11.00	9.00
☐ **"HORACE GREELEY."** *Photo printed on heavy cardboard, set into brass frame.*	9.00	13.50	10.00

	Current Price Range		P/Y Average
□ **"I LIKE IKE."** 3" x 3½" sticker. 1952 or 1956.	6.75	9.00	7.00
□ **"INTERVIEW, THE."** Playboy Magazine folder with 2½" button, "Carter Talks in Playboy." 1976 campaign.	6.75	11.00	7.00
□ **"I THINK WE'VE GOT ANOTHER WASHINGTON AND WILSON IS HIS NAME."** Song sheet, 1915.	13.50	20.00	14.00
□ **"LET'S BACK NIXON."** 4" x 6" paper sticker showing Nixon pointing his finger at Khrushchev. 1960 campaign.	13.50	20.00	14.00
□ **"LINCOLN BOUQUET,"** colored and embossed cigar box label. 6" x 10". c. 1910.	6.75	13.50	7.00
□ **"LIEUT.-GENERAL WINFIELD SCOTT, FAITHFUL TO THE LAST."** 19th century ferrotype photo by Abbot, set in brass frame, 1½" x 1¾".	27.00	40.00	28.00
□ **NATION'S CHOICE, THE.** Embossed postcard picturing Taft and Sherman.	6.75	11.00	7.00
□ **"NEVER SWAP HORSES WHEN YOU'RE CROSSING A STREAM."** Song sheet with portrait of Woodrow Wilson, 1916.	13.50	20.00	14.00
□ **NEXT OCCUPANT OF THE WHITE HOUSE.** Campaign postcard for William J. Bryan.	6.75	11.00	7.00
□ **"ONE WORLD"** by Wendell L. Wilkie, autographed copy of book, 1943.	13.50	20.00	14.00
□ **OUR NEXT PRESIDENT WILLIAM H. TAFT: GLORY AND PROSPERITY FOR OUR COUNTRY.** Colored postcard picturing Taft.	6.75	11.00	7.00
□ **OUR NEXT PRESIDENT.** Full color picture of the Capitol with Taft pictured in the corner. Postcard, 1908.	6.75	11.00	7.00
□ **OUR NEXT PRESIDENT AND VICE PRESIDENT.** Postcard picturing Taft and Sherman.	6.75	11.00	7.00
□ **"PUCK" MAGAZINE.** Issue contains two large political cartoons, one of Teddy Roosevelt, 1906.	9.00	13.50	10.00
□ **"U. S. GRANT."** Photo printed on heavy cardboard, set into brass frame.	9.00	13.50	10.00
□ **"VOTE DEMOCRATIC,"** paper window sticker, 4" x 4". c. 1948.	6.75	11.00	7.00
□ **WILLIAM HOWARD TAFT FOR PRESIDENT.** Tinte photo on white background.	6.75	11.00	7.00

POSTCARDS

DESCRIPTION: Postcards are cards with a picture on one side and a place to write a message on the other. Postcards can also be mailed without an envelope.

PERIOD: Postcard collecting began in Europe in 1902 and by 1906 Americans were purchasing them at the rate of 700 million a year. The postcard boom dropped off around 1914 but began again in the 1960s.

TYPES: Hobbyists usually collect postcards by subject with the most popular portraying transportation, political events and advertising.

COMMENTS: The cards from pre-World War I are highly valuable. Artist, signature and category are items that determine value.

	Current Price Range		P/Y Average
☐ **Bosselman,** Eastern States, color, undivided back	7.00	10.00	8.25
☐ **Clinton & Close,** The Iron Ore Docks of Toledo, color, undivided back	7.00	10.00	8.25
☐ **Detroit Photo Co. #9100,** Indias Amatecas/Mexico, color, undivided back	6.00	8.00	6.85
☐ **Erker #221,** Levee Scene, color, undivided back	5.00	7.00	5.85
☐ **Erker #246,** Soulard Market, color, undivided back	5.00	7.00	5.85
☐ **Erker #250,** Wabash Freight Station, color, undivided back	5.00	7.00	5.85
☐ **Holmes & Warren,** Branding Calves, two-tone, undivided back	5.00	7.00	5.85
☐ **Illinois Postcard Co.,** Indian Encampment on River Bank, color, undivided back	5.00	7.00	5.85
☐ **Leighton,** "Indians," Chief Spotted Tail, color, undivided back	5.00	7.00	5.85
☐ **Louis Levy,** Horse Drawn Double Decker Buses in London's Ludgate Circus, color, divided back	6.00	8.00	6.80
☐ **MacFarlane,** "Wild West" Series, Fur Canoe, color, undivided back	10.00	14.00	11.25
☐ **MacFarlane,** "Wild West" Series, Red River Carts, color, divided back	10.00	14.00	11.25

Postcards, *Left: Gruss aus of postman-the pouch attachment contains views of Bremen; Right: A postcard street seller of 1910,* **$5.00-$20.00** *Photo courtesy of Lou McCulloch, Highland Heights, OH 44143.*

	Current Price Range		P/Y Average
☐ **Miller,** Two Crow Papooses, black and white, undivided back	5.00	7.00	5.90
☐ **Morris & Kirby,** A Beef Herd on Water, black and white, undivided back	6.00	8.00	6.85
☐ **Ridley,** "Wild West" Series, A Roper, two-tone, undivided back, artwork by Charles M. Russell	20.00	25.00	22.00
☐ **Ridley,** "Wild West" Series, Antelope Hunting, two-tone, undivided back, artwork by Charles M. Russell	22.00	28.00	24.00
☐ **Samuel Cupples,** "German Tyrolean Alps" Series, Red Roof Tower at Left of Mountains	15.00	20.00	17.00
☐ **Samuel Cupples,** "German Tyrolean Alps" Series, Residence House at Roof Square	15.00	20.00	17.00

	Current Price Range		P/Y Average
☐ **Samuel Cupples,** "German Tyrolean Alps" Series, The Village Square	15.00	20.00	17.00
☐ **Samuel Cupples,** Oklahoma Building, color, undivided back	7.00	10.00	6.75
☐ **Sunday Post Dispatch (St. Louis),** Missouri State Building, color, undivided back, c. 1900 .	7.00	10.00	6.75
☐ **Tammen,** Home Sweet Home, color, undivided back	11.00	15.00	12.50
☐ **Underwood & Underwood,** Austrian Cavalry Patrol Crossing River, color	7.00	10.00	8.20
☐ **Valentine,** The Westmount Club of Montreal, color, divided back	6.00	8.00	6.75

PREMIUMS

DESCRIPTION: Premiums are advertising giveaways used to promote a company's product.

ORIGIN: Premiums proved to be quite successful for radio during the 1930s to 1940s. Giveaways were also used to a smaller extent on television and for some foods like cereal or Cracker Jacks.

COMMENTS: Radio premiums, which comprise a large portion of the premium collector market, are more readily available in the Midwest than on the East or West Coast. There were many successful radio shows originating in cities like Detroit, Chicago, Cincinnati and Kansas City, therefore prices are generally lower in these areas than in New York or Los Angeles.

ADDITIONAL TIPS: Paper items are considered more valuable than metal objects simply because paper does not hold up through the years like metal. Character popularity, type of item and rarity are important factors to consider in the premium market.

For additional information, consult *The Official Price Guide to Radio, TV and Movie Memorabilia,* published by The House of Collectibles.

Left to Right: Little Orphan Annie, *ceramic cup, Ovaltine premium,* **$5.00-$10.00;** *and* **Quaker Oats** *mug, Quaker Oats premium,* **$2.00-$5.00**

	Current Price Range		P/Y Average
☐ **Ali Baba And The 40 Thieves,** cardboard album with story and accompanying record, late 1940s, Post Cereal premium	10.00	15.00	12.50
☐ **Amos 'N Andy,** cardboard figure, 1930 Pepsodent premium, large figure of Andy	17.00	25.00	20.50
☐ **Bob Hope,** *They Got Me Covered,* first edition of Hope's book, 1941 Pepsodent premium, illustrated envelope	15.00	25.00	20.00
☐ **Bobby Benson,** card game, 1934 Hecker-H-O premium, 32 card deck with 32 page instruction booklet	15.00	25.00	20.00
☐ **Buck Rogers Map Of The Solar System,** Cocomalt, c. 1933	200.00	220.00	205.00
☐ **Buck Rogers,** Scout badge, 1935 Cream of Wheat premium	25.00	35.00	20.00
☐ **Captain Gallant Of The Foreign Legion,** Junior Legionnaires Kit, Heinz 57 Varieties, contains Captain Gallant comic book, photos of Buster Crabbe in the role of Captain Gallant, and membership card, all in the original Heinz mailing envelope, 1955	55.00	70.00	61.50
☐ **Captain Hawks,** badge, 1935 newspaper premium, sky patrol member propeller badge	10.00	15.00	12.50
☐ **Captain Marvel Club Key Holder,** plastic over picture, featuring Captain Marvel and lightning bolt	40.00	55.00	46.00
☐ **Captain Midnight's "Air Heroes" Stamp Album,** Skelly Oil, 16 stamps, c. 1940	39.00	49.00	43.00
☐ **Captain Midnight Cold Ovaltine Shake-Up Mug,** orange mug, c. 1942	55.00	70.00	61.00
☐ **Captain Midnight Letter,** Ovaltine, dated 1945, printed form letter sent to listeners who wrote to Captain Midnight, 8½ " x 11"	40.00	50.00	42.75
☐ **Captain Midnight Membership Token,** Skelly Oil, brass with spinner, 1940	30.00	37.00	33.00

	Current Price Range		P/Y Average
☐ **Captain Midnight Whistle Decoder,** Ovaltine, plastic, blue and red, c. 1947	50.00	60.00	53.00
☐ **Donald Duck,** blotter, 1942 Sunoco premium, Donald Duck driving a car	8.00	15.00	12.00
☐ **Ed East,** booklet, *Greetings and Good Morning from Ed East's Breakfast in Bedlan,* 1939, 12 pages	5.00	10.00	7.50
☐ **Eddie Cantor,** *Book of Magic,* 1935 Pebeco toothpaste premium	35.00	45.00	40.00
☐ **Gargantua The Gorilla,** Muffet's Shredded Wheat, colored cardboard (to be assembled) *Note: This was not a fictional character but a real gorilla from the Ringling Brothers circus.*	4.00	6.00	4.80
☐ **Howdy Doody,** Climber, 1951 Welch Grape Juice premium	35.00	45.00	40.00
☐ **Howdy Doody,** History Album, 1950s Wonder Bread premium, 8 page book	15.00	25.00	20.00
☐ **Howie Wing Good Luck Coin,** Kellogg Cereal, aluminum, 1930s	22.00	30.00	25.00
☐ **Jack Armstrong,** bowl, 1939 Wheaties premium	30.00	40.00	35.00
☐ **Jack Armstrong,** flashlight, 1939 Wheaties premium	20.00	30.00	25.00
☐ **Jack Armstrong,** gun, 1933 Wheaties premium, daisy shooting propeller plane gun	25.00	35.00	30.00
☐ **Jack Armstrong Magic Answer Box,** tin	45.00	60.00	51.00
☐ **Jack Armstrong Pre-Flight Trainer Model,** Wheaties, three pages of stiff paper punchouts, 1945	60.00	80.00	67.00
☐ **Jack Armstrong Tailsman,** Wheaties, brass, 1936	65.00	85.00	72.00
☐ **Jim Babcock,** book, 1936 Log Cabin Syrup premium, 36 page illustrated book shows rope tricks, explains tracking and trailing of animals, trail blazing, branding, has dictionary of cowboy words	25.00	40.00	32.00
☐ **Jimmie Allen,** identification bracelet, 1935 Richfield Oil premium	45.00	55.00	50.00
☐ **Kellogg's Magic Color Cards,** Rice Krispies, set of four cards in original mailing envelope with paint brush, 1933	18.00	23.00	20.00
☐ **Klicko The Climbing Monkey Punch-Out,** Post Cereal, colored stiff paper, 6″ x 8″, 1947	9.00	12.00	10.35
☐ **Lone Ranger,** badge, 1949 Cheerios premium	25.00	35.00	30.00
☐ **Lone Ranger,** belt, 1941 Kix premium, rare . .	80.00	100.00	90.00
☐ **Mickey Mouse,** blotter, 1940 Sunoco premium, shows Mickey Mouse driving a car	10.00	15.00	12.50
☐ **Mickey Mouse,** magic kit, 1955 Mars Candy premium, instructions for 20 tricks	35.00	45.00	40.00
☐ **Monko The Chattering Ape Punch-Out,** Muffet's Shredded Wheat, colored cardboard (to be assembled), 1940s	4.00	6.00	4.90
☐ **Radio Orphan Annie,** manual, 1935 Ovaltine premium, 12 page illustrated book shows how to operate 1935 decoder	35.00	50.00	42.00
☐ **Roy Roger,** coin, 1952 Post's Cereal premium	10.00	15.00	12.50

	Current Price Range		P/Y Average
☐ **Roy Roger,** ring, 1949 Quaker Oats premium .	35.00	45.00	40.00
☐ **Scrappy's Animated Puppet Theater Punch-Out,** Pillsbury, four page book of colored punch-outs, 1936	45.00	60.00	52.00
☐ **Secretary Hawkins,** membership card, 1932 Ralston premium, has oath on back, rare . . .	35.00	45.00	40.00
☐ **Shield G-Man,** badge, 1942 Pep Comics premium, full color picture of the shield bending an iron bar	50.00	60.00	55.00
☐ **Shield G-Man,** membership card, 1942 Pep Comics premium	50.00	75.00	62.00
☐ **Sky King,** writer, 1949 Powerhouse candy bar premium, magnifying glass, printing kit, ruler and decoder built into one	100.00	125.00	112.00
☐ **Smitty,** button, 1930s premium, color picture of Smitty with saying, "Smitty Sweater, What A Sweater," rare	30.00	40.00	35.00
☐ **Stretcho The Indian Rubber Man Punch-Out,** Muffet's Shredded Wheat, colored cardboard (to be assembled), 1940s	4.00	6.00	4.80
☐ **Sundial,** Kellogg Cereal, aluminum, can be worn as wristwatch, in original mailing envelope, 1940s	14.00	18.00	15.50
☐ **Superman Pep Model War Plane,** Kellogg Cereal, Russian Stormovik #18, wood, in original paper wrapper	9.00	12.00	10.00
☐ **Superman Pep Model War Plane,** Kellogg Cereal, Grumman Avenger #19, wood, in original paper wrapper	9.00	12.00	10.00
☐ **Tom Mix,** charm, 1940 Ralston premium	20.00	30.00	25.00
☐ **Tom Mix,** compass, 1946 Ralston premium, includes magnifier, glows in the dark	15.00	30.00	22.00
☐ **Tom Mix,** decoder, 1941 Ralston premium, rare	75.00	95.00	85.00

PRINTS

DESCRIPTION: Often referred to as limited edition or collector prints, this type of artwork is completed by a printmaking process.

TYPES: The three common forms of printmaking are original lithography, offset lithography or serigraphy. Original lithographs are made from hand drawn stones or plates. The artist paints directly on the stone or plate. The artist must reverse his drawing so when it is transferred to the paper, it will be viewed in the proper perspective. An offset lithograph is a photomechanical reproduction of the original work. Serigraph or silk screening is a method of printing using a squeegie. The squeegie forces the ink through a screen in which a stencil forms the area where the ink will go.

COMMENTS: Several factors are used to compile prices for collector prints including authenticity, subject, condition, size, artist's workmanship, printing technique, and quality of material.

ADDITIONAL TIPS: This section is organized by artist followed by the name of the print, release date, edition number, size and publisher or distributor. The listing also tells if the print is signed and numbered (sn), numbered only (n/o) or signed only (s/o).

For more information, consult *The Official Price Guide to Collector Prints,* published by The House of Collectibles.

Money To Spend *by Jay Schmidt*

	ISSUE PRICE	CURRENT PRICE
☐ **Adamson, Harry,** Winging In-Pintails, rel. 1971, ed. 450, s/n, 17″ x 25″, pub Wild Wings, Inc.	50.00	675.00
☐ **Allison, Betty,** Cascades In Shade, rel. 1979, ed. 1,000, s/n, 15″ x 30″	40.00	80.00
☐ **Antis, Harry,** Whitetail Buck, rel. 1970, ed. 500, s/n, 24″ x 30″	25.00	60.00
☐ **Baize, Wayne,** Lazy Summer Days, rel. 1974, ed. 2,500, s/o, 27″ x 15″, pub Frame House Gallery, Inc.	30.00	125.00
☐ **Balke, Don,** Barn Owl, rel. 1976, ed. 1,000, s/n, 20″ x 26″, distributor Masterpiece Moulding and Frame	40.00	100.00
☐ **Bama, James,** Ken Hunder, Working Cowboy, rel. 1974, ed. 1,000, s/n, 21″ x 24″, pub Greenwich Workshop	55.00	375.00
☐ **Barber, John,** Atlantic Sentinel, ed. 750, s/n, 18″ x 28″, distributor Commodore Art Publishing	40.00	200.00
☐ **Bateman, Robert,** Cheetah with Cubs, rel. 1978, ed. 950, s/n, 21″ x 27″, pub Mill Pond Press, Inc.	95.00	175.00
☐ **Bergsma, Jody,** First Boat Boy, rel. 1979, ed. 1,000, s/o, 8″ x 10″, pub Bergsma Illustrations	3.00	40.00
☐ **Bierly, Edward,** Winter Woods, rel. 1977, ed. 600, s/n, 24″ x 32″, pub EJB Editions	100.00	350.00
☐ **Bollar, Sean,** Red-Headed Woodpecker, rel. 1975, ed. 800, s/n, 12″ x 16″, pub Pandion Gallery Ltd.	24.00	30.00
☐ **Boren, James,** Rainy Day at Hillsboro, rel. 1977, ed. 950, s/n, 20″ x 27″, pub Mill Pond Press, Inc.	75.00	185.00
☐ **Boutwell, George,** Fence Line, rel. 1970, ed. 1,000, s/n, 5″ x 7″, pub George Boutwell	1.00	15.00
☐ **Burger, Howard,** back home, rel. 1975, ed. 1,000, s/n, 18″ x 20″, pub Paul Sawyier Galleries, Inc.	30.00	250.00
☐ **Chapple, Dave,** Backwater Mallards, rel. 1978, ed. 150, etching, pub Etchings, Etc.	90.00	150.00
☐ **Coheleach, Guy,** Great Blue Heron, rel. 1968, ed. 2,500, s/o, 22½″ x 26″, pub Frame House Gallery	40.00	75.00
☐ **Combes, Simon,** Facing The Wind, rel. 1980, ed. 1,500, s/n, 32″ x 22″, pub Greenwich Workshop	75.00	120.00
☐ **Cowan, John,** Sunken Blind, ed. 600, s/n, 22″ x 28″, pub Meredith Long & Company	85.00	650.00
☐ **Crandall, Jerry,** Smoke Up Ahead, rel. 1977, ed. 450, s/n, 20″ x 30″, pub Guildhall, Inc.	60.00	450.00
☐ **Day, Ray,** Mail Pouch Barn, plate 1, rel. 1973, ed. 500, s/n, 20″ x 24″, distributor Masterpiece Moulding And Frame	15.00	100.00
☐ **Dodson, Larry,** Springtime in Elijay, rel. 1975, ed. 1,000, s/n, 18″ x 19″, pub Swan Graphics, Inc.	20.00	175.00
☐ **Dunnington, Tom,** American Bald Eagle #1, rel. 1971, ed. 4,700, s/o, 32″ x 23″, pub Cottage Hill Wildlife Art	30.00	60.00
☐ **Dye, Burton,** Country Afternoon, rel. 1977, ed. 1,000, s/n, 15″ x 21″, pub Burton Dye Prints	30.00	40.00
☐ **Faner, Ron,** Keeper of the Owls, rel. 1980, ed. 375, s/n, 26″ x 33″, pub Frame House Gallery	100.00	185.00
☐ **Farnsworth, Imogene,** Bengal Tiger, rel. 1973, ed. 1,000, s/n, 20″ x 24″	35.00	750.00
☐ **Ferrandiz, Juan,** He Seems to Sleep, rel. 1981, ed. 450, s/n, 18″ x 11″, pub Schmid Bros.	125.00	400.00
☐ **Forbes, Bart,** Shaker Girl, ed. 150, s/n, 22″ x 30″, pub Salt Creek Graphics	150.00	250.00

	ISSUE PRICE	CURRENT PRICE
☐ **Forrest, Christopher,** Woody's Rest, rel. 1983, ed. 300, s/n, 21″ x 28″, pub Hang Ups, Inc.	250.00	300.00
☐ **Frace, Charles,** African Leopard, rel. 1981, ed. 12,500, s/o, 16″ x 20″, pub American Masters Foundation ...	25.00	35.00
☐ **Frisino, Louis,** single mallard, ed. 500, s/n, 11″ x 14″, pub Russell A. Fink	15.00	30.00
☐ **Getsinger, Joseph,** Antique Show, ed. 175, s/n, 10″ x 15″, etching, pub Joseph Getsinger Enterprises	20.00	30.00
☐ **Gill, Lunda,** Lundy in the Sand, rel. 1972, ed. 1,000, s/n, 31″ x 23″, pub Frame House Gallery...............	35.00	100.00
☐ **Granstaff, Bill,** At East, rel. 1973, ed. 200, s/n, 12″ x 16″, pub Granstaff Prints Ltd.	12.00	100.00
☐ **Gray, Gene,** Eastern Gray Squirrel, rel. 1968, ed. 5,000, s/o, 22″ x 18″	8.00	110.00
☐ **Haney, Enoch,** Spirit of Osceola, ed. 1,500, s/n, pub American Indian Arts Collection	40.00	175.00
☐ **Harm, Ray,** American Butterflies, rel. 1966, ed. 5,000, s/o, 22″ x 17″, pub Frame House Gallery	10.00	75.00
☐ **Harper, Bret,** Consider the Lillies, rel. 1975, ed. 250, s/n, 12″ x 20″, pub Frame House Gallery	20.00	40.00
☐ **Harper, Charles,** Ladybug, rel. 1968, ed. 500, s/n, 15″ x 20″, pub Frame House Gallery	20.00	250.00
☐ **Hibel, Edna,** Bouquet, ed. 101, s/n, 13″ x 19″, pub Jar Publishers	85.00	550.00
☐ **Hughes, Allen,** Returning Woodies, rel. 1975, ed. 750, s/n, 18″ x 23″, pub Swan Graphics, Ltd.	65.00	100.00
☐ **Joyce, Marshall,** Sea Ghost, rel. 1979, ed. 950, s/n, 20″ x 24″, pub Mill Pond Press Inc.	85.00	110.00
☐ **Maass, David,** Wild Wings Logo-Greenwing Teal, rel. 1981, ed. 950, s/n, pub Wild Wings, Inc.	75.00	100.00
☐ **Martin, Bernard,** Eastern Bluebird, rel. 1974, ed. 500, s/n, 16″ x 18″, pub Bernard Martin	20.00	200.00
☐ **McGaughy, Clay,** Bachelor, rel. 1970, ed. 500, s/n, 34″ x 27″, pub Arts Limited, Inc.	50.00	300.00
☐ **Moore, Wayland,** America's Champion, rel. 1977, ed. 500, s/n, 40″ x 30″, pub Felicie, Inc.	200.00	800.00
☐ **Nute, Cherrie,** Governor's Mansion, rel. 1975, ed. 1,000, s/n, 25″ x 22″, pub Foxfire Fine Arts, Inc.	25.00	150.00
☐ **Parker, Ron,** Raccoon Pair, rel. 1982, ed. 950, s/n, 21″ x 17″, pub Mill Pond Press, Inc.	95.00	120.00
☐ **Parnall, Peter,** Fox, rel. 1972, ed. 1,500, s/n, 28″ x 21″, pub Greenwich Workshop	60.00	150.00
☐ **Perillo, Gregory,** Madre, rel. 1977, ed. 500, s/n, 22″ x 28″, pub Vague Shadows Limited	125.00	300.00
☐ **Peterson, Roger Tory,** Baltimore Oriole, rel. 1973, ed. 450, s/n, 18″ x 18″, pub Mill Pond Press, Inc.	150.00	300.00
☐ **Preuss, Roger,** American Widgeon, rel. 1958, ed. 1,140, s/ in plate, 38″ x 48″, pub Wildlife of American .	15.00	130.00
☐ **Reece, Maynard,** Bobwhites, rel. 1964, ed. 950, 14″ x 18″	20.00	650.00
☐ **Ren, Chuck,** The Mountain Men, rel. 1981, ed. 600, s/n, 22″ x 24″, pub Grey Stone Press	75.00	150.00
☐ **Sander, Tom,** From Cover, rel. 1977, ed. 500, s/n, 24″ x 30″, pub Frame House Gallery	40.00	115.00

	ISSUE PRICE	CURRENT PRICE
☐ **Sawyier, Paul,** Elkhorn Creek Scene, rel. 1965, ed. 1,000, n/o, pub Sawyier Galleries, Inc.	15.00	45.00
☐ **Singer, Arthur,** Peregrine Falcon, rel. 1978, ed. 800, s/n, 37″ x 18″, pub Frame House Gallery	60.00	115.00
☐ **Sloan, Richard,** Eastern Bluebird, rel. 1968, ed. 5,000, s/o, 22″ x 28″, pub Nature House, Inc.	30.00	400.00
☐ **Solberg, Morton,** Chippewa Lake, rel. 1978, ed. 1,000, s/n, 29″ x 22″, pub Greenwich Workshop	65.00	115.00
☐ **Spencer, Irene,** Beyond the Sun, ed. 400, s/n, pub Irene Spencer	185.00	400.00
☐ **Timberlake, Bob,** Ella's Cupboard, rel. 1971, ed. 250, s/n, pub The Heritage Company	35.00	500.00
☐ **Vickers, Mary,** Age of Innocence, rel. 1970, ed. 200, s/n, pub Art Spectrum	40.00	325.00
☐ **Ward, Edward,** Caribe, rel. 1981, ed. 175, s/n, 11″ x 13″, pub Ed Ward	18.00	24.00
☐ **Wilson, Charles Banks,** New Rich, rel. 1939, ed. 10, 14″ x 10″, pub Charles Banks Wilson	5.00	250.00
☐ **Wright, David,** A Way of Life, ed. 1,500, s/n, 19″ x 25″, pub Grey Stone Press	40.00	80.00

PUPPETS

TYPES: There are four basic puppet types: hand puppets are controlled by puppeteers who wear puppets on their hands; rod puppets have rods attached to their jointed legs, arms and head; shadow puppets are flat and are used behind a screen or sheet to cast shadows; and marionettes or string puppets have much detail and are usually large.

COMMENTS: Made for the theatre and for children's toys, puppets have been collected since the 1920s. Those made before 1920 are currently the most valuable, but those from the 1930s and 1940s are usually easier to find and just as collectible.

ADDITIONAL TIPS: The listings are alphabetical and placed under puppet-type subheads. Ventriloquist dummies are also included here.

For further information on puppets, contact The Puppeteers of America, Inc., 2311 Connecticut Ave., NW #501, Washington, D.C. 20008.

	Current Price Range		P/Y Average

HAND PUPPETS

☐ **Figure of an old woman,** wearing long dress and apron, carved wood head, painted, French or Swiss, late 18th or early 19th c. . . . 610.00 / 725.00 / 650.00

☐ **Oliver J. Dragon,** of the "Kukla, Fran and Ollie" television program, the original puppet made and used by Burr Tilstrom, c. 1940's . . . . 7000.00 / 9000.00 / 8000.00

☐ **Policeman,** old style uniform and hat, the head carved of balsa wood, painted and gilded, American, first quarter of the 20th c. . . . . 175.00 / 225.00 / 200.00

☐ **Punch,** long crooked nose, red cheeks, brightly colored costume, porcelain head and hands, chipped, probably English, mid-Victorian . . . . 1250.00 / 1550.00 / 1350.00

MARIONETTES

☐ **"Black Sambo,"** composition head and hands, checkered shirt, brown striped pants, brown jacket, in original box with 78 r.p.m. phonograph record, America, 11½" H., c. 1947 . . . . 75.00 / 95.00 / 85.00

☐ **"Buffalo Bill,"** composition head, dressed in western outfit, belt with two guns, one hand missing, signs of wear, 46" H. . . . . 1600.00 / 2000.00 / 1800.00

☐ **Figure in the likeness of a skeleton,** painted wood, may be Mexican, 16½" H., first half of the 20th c. . . . . 450.00 / 550.00 / 500.00

☐ **Figure of a dragon,** entirely of wood, green, purple and other colors, prominent eyes, Chinese, 56" H., 20th c. . . . . 1050.00 / 1350.00 / 1150.00

☐ **Figure of Satan,** papier-mache head, garishly painted, the body made of red plush, wooden shoes, carved wooden pitchfork, 29" H., 20th c. . . . . 850.00 / 1150.00 / 950.00

☐ **Figure of a woman,** possibly a princess, silk attire in multicolors, composition head, Japanese modern . . . . 85.00 / 105.00 / 95.00

☐ **Fish, carved and painted wood,** moveable lower jaw, fins and tail, approx. 2' H. . . . . 512.00 / 575.00 / 543.00

☐ **Howdy Doody,** replica of the TV puppet, reduced size sold in toy stores in the early 1950's, 12" H. . . . . 82.00 / 110.00 / 93.00

☐ **Howdy Doody,** the orginal puppet used when the TV program first appeared on the air in 1948 . . . . 20000.00 / 30000.00 / 25000.00

☐ **Man with round face,** bulging eyes, in tuxedo, American, carved and painted wooden face, 37" H., 20th c. . . . . 1050.00 / 1350.00 / 1200.00

ROD PUPPETS (Operated by sticks)

☐ **Man on a horse,** stuffed bodies, papier-mache heads . . . . 425.00 / 525.00 / 475.00

☐ **Monkey with smiling face,** long arms, rods attached to arms, 21" H. . . . . 350.00 / 450.00 / 400.00

VENTRILOQUIST "DUMMIES"

	Current Price Range		P/Y Average
☐ **Jerry Mahoney,** composition head and hands, a small but exact replica, American, 21″ H., c. 1950 (was not sold with phonograph record)	105.00	135.00	120.00
☐ **Jerry Mahoney,** composition head and hands, wearing suit and white shirt, American, 32″ H., c. 1950	180.00	220.00	200.00
☐ **As above,** in original suitcase-like carrying case with phonograph record	350.00	450.00	400.00
☐ **Original Charlie McCarthy dummy** of radio fame, head of carved wood (for a long while Edgar Bergen worked with just a single model of Charlie, then made another in case something happened to the first)	32500.00	47500.00	40000.00
☐ **Original Jerry Mahoney** used by Paul Winchell, head of carved wood. Jerry was by far the best designed of all the "famous dummies," with many special features	8500.00	11500.00	10000.00

QUILTS

DESCRIPTION: Quilts have been absorbed into the category of Folk Art, though their creators seldom intended them as works of art. Early America, and especially early rural America, thrived on its self-sufficiency: its ability to cultivate foodstuffs and manufacture the necessities of everyday life. Quilts are one example (of many) of our ancestors using their creative skills and their sense of thrift: oddments of fabric were cut and sewn into various patterns, to make clothing, bed coverings, etc. Not only was some money saved, but the owner was sure to possess a very unique "original," which made the shopkeeper's merchandise seem pale by comparison.

COMMENTS: Collecting specimens of old quilts was once a very restricted hobby, which seemed destined never to get beyond rural New England, Pennsylvania and some other areas. It has blossomed to full flower today, aided by museum interest and antique shows. On the whole, *Amish* quilts are the leaders in hobbyist appeal and in value, though they are not invariably the most valuable. The self-contained

Amish community (of western Pennsylvania) was intent on "doing for itself," unconcerned about what was fashionable in the world's eyes; its quilts are ample testimony to its artistic spirit.

Doll Quilt, *patchwork, wool,* **$30.00-$40.00**

	Current Price Range		P/Y Average
☐ **Arkansas Star,** 1930s, cotton, blocks are pieced with various solid colors for star points, prints for center of star, set in blocks of unbleached muslin, lattice strips of yellow, red, white and green print, solid red corner blocks and border, unbleached muslin backing which has been turned up and machine stitched to form binding, leaf and vine quilting design on lattice strips, never washed, excellent condition, 85" x 67"	150.00	155.00	150.00
☐ **Baseball,** cotton, all-over pattern made of gingham and calico, many colors, good light and dark contrast, border on one end, no set-up blocks or strips, good condition, 70" x 73"	130.00	155.00	142.00
☐ **Bowtie,** cotton, pieced 5" red bowties set in white squares alternate diagonally with gold and white blocks, wide inner white border with cable quilting, red outer border with diagonal quilting, white muslin back and binding, good used condition, 65" x 81"	190.00	215.00	197.00

	Current Price Range		P/Y Average

☐ **Bowtie,** cotton, pieced 7″ blocks of various old calicoes, set up with beige print, border on two sides in same beige print, unbleached muslin back, some damage, 70″ x 84″ . . . . . . — 90.00 — 115.00 — 96.00

☐ **Butterfly Applique,** cotton, sixty 5″ x 4½″ butterflies pieced of solid color percale, coordinating print and black percale body with embroidered antennae, appliqued to white block with black button hole stitching, gold percale strips, border and binding, lavender percale backing, fine fancy quilting, good used condition, 70″ x 75″ . . . . — 150.00 — 175.00 — 162.00

☐ **Butterfly Applique,** 1930s, cotton, each butterfly pieced with various coordinating prints and solids, appliqued onto unbleached muslin blocks with running stitch in black embroidery thread, set up lattice strips in yellow and white print, smaller butterflies in blocks form border, unbleached muslin binding and backing, lovely quilting, never washed, excellent condition, 76″ x 80″ . . . . — 180.00 — 200.00 — 190.00

☐ **Cactus Basket,** also called basket of scraps, cotton, blocks are pieced in purple calico and pink gingham with white muslin background, set diagonally with squares of light lime-yellow calico, lime yellow binding, unbleached muslin back, very good condition, 80″ x 68″ . . — 130.00 — 155.00 — 140.00

☐ **Checkerboard,** cotton, 13″ blocks are pieced with various old calicoes, chambrays and ginghams, set diagonally with yellow, red and black calico print blocks, unbleached muslin back, machine stitched binding, fan quilting, very good condition, 82″ x 60″ . . . . — 100.00 — 125.00 — 112.00

☐ **Colonial Tulip Applique,** 1930s, cotton, tulips are of solid lavender and lavender, purple and white print, green leaves and stems, hand appliqued onto sixteen inch square unbleached muslin blocks, lavender binding, diagonal quilting, no set-up strips or border, never washed, excellent condition, 77″ x 85″ . . . . — 170.00 — 195.00 — 180.00

☐ **Double Irish Chain With Shamrocks,** cotton, alternating 2″ squares of solid red and green, larger white blocks with appliqued green shamrocks, green binding, white backing, good used condition, 72″ x 85″ . . . . — 200.00 — 225.00 — 210.00

☐ **Double T,** Ohio Amish, cotton sateen, blue, turquoise, mauve and green pieced TS are set in diamond block arrangement, deep blue background, blue border with cable stiching, bright green, binding . . . . — 675.00 — 725.00 — 700.00

	Current Price Range		P/Y Average

☐ **Double Wedding Ring,** 1930s, cotton, pieced rings of various prints and solids, squares where rings meet are solid blue and solid yellow, white background, blue binding, straight rather than scalloped edges, intricate spider web quilting in medium blue thread, good used condition, 70″ x 84″ **130.00 155.00 140.00**

☐ **Double Wedding Ring,** 1930s, cotton, rings and squares where rings meet are all made of various color prints, white background and backing, green binding, good used condition, 86″ x 75″ **195.00 215.00 200.00**

☐ **Dresden Plate,** 1930s, cotton, each 12″ plate is pieced from calico prints and hand appliqued to solid pink blocks, darker pink background, never washed, excellent condition, 65″ x 82″ **90.00 115.00 100.00**

☐ **Dresden Plate,** 1930s, cotton, prints and solids appliqued by hand to white muslin background, centers of plates are yellow and so are lattice strips, borderless, white backing and binding, diagonal quilting, excellent condition, 69″ x 89″ **150.00 175.00 160.00**

☐ **Embroidered Flowers In A Basket,** cotton, 1938, four blocks with embroidered red, gold, blue and purple flowers, green leaves in large brown handled basket, three large embroidered flowers surround each basket, green squares placed diagonally between white triangular pieces form lattice strips which separate the four large embroidered blocks, inner border matches lattice strips, outside border of larger white and green triangular pieces with green pieces forming scalloped edge, green binding, unbleached muslin back, lovely handwork, never washed, very good condition, 86″ x 79″ **225.00 250.00 235.00**

☐ **Embroidered State Flowers,** cotton, forty eight pink blocks are each embroidered with state flower and abbreviated state name, solid red, pastel pink and pastel blue lattice strips separate the blocks, blue corner blocks, dark pink, backing, very good condition, 85″ x 67″ **150.00 175.00 160.00**

☐ **Flower Applique,** cotton, two shades of pink form four petal flowers with buds, green leaves, large dramatic repetition, very intricate quilting with swag border forming corner teardrops, never washed, excellent condition **450.00 475.00 460.00**

	Current Price Range		P/Y Average

☐ **Flower Applique,** Ohio, 1950, cotton, original design, red and pink calico flowers with yellow centers, green calico leaves and stems, each flower is surrounded by four leaves and curved stems with four buds, white background with tan band in border, signed and dated with quilters name, town and date in ink on back **650.00 675.00 660.00**

☐ **Flower Baskets,** 1930s, cotton, assorted calico prints form pieced baskets on white background, good quilting between baskets, good used condition **200.00 225.00 210.00**

☐ **Flower Wreath Applique,** crib, cotton, pink and blue flowers form wreath in center of white background, cable quilted border, new blue binding **250.00 275.00 260.00**

☐ **Flyfoot,** 1920s, cotton, large 15″ blocks are pieced with various prints having backgrounds, solid pink cotton is used for the foot, solid green lattice set-up strips, pink corner blocks, green binding, green and white polka dot backing with green, red and yellow apples and green leaves, crossing lines quilting, good handwork never washed, excellent condition, 90″ x 73″ **100.00 125.00 110.00**

☐ **Four Patch,** Indiana Amish, 1910, cotton, tan, black, yellow are pieced to form each of the four patches, indigo blue background and border with light blue band **800.00 825.00 810.00**

☐ **Grape Vine Wreath,** applique, cotton, deep red grapes, dark green leaves form large wreath which covers entire off-white background of top, applique done by old machine stitching, hand quilted, cotton seeds throughout batting, never washed, excellent condition **475.00 500.00 485.00**

☐ **Hexagon,** cotton, 1½″ hexagons made of pastel, 1930s, percale prints and solids, 5″ solid pink percale border, white backing, pink binding, crossing lines quilting, very good condition, 74″ x 85″ **150.00 175.00 160.00**

☐ **Hole In The Barn Door,** Amish, cotton, wine pieced pattern mounted on black diamond blocks, medium blue blackground, medium blue border with black band and binding, quilted in white thread **550.00 575.00 560.00**

☐ **Indiana Puzzle,** also called monkey wrench, cotton, solid white and bright red, machine bound, fan quilting, never washed, good condition, 75″ x 85″ **140.00 165.00 150.00**

☐ **Jacob's Ladder,** cotton, made entirely of two old calico prints, one red and the other dark green, set diagonally in rows with no set-up strips or blocks in between, green calico border with cable quilting, very good condition, 78″ x 79″ **350.00 375.00 360.00**

	Current Price Range		P/Y Average

☐ **Jeweled Chain,** 1930s, cotton, pieced with various 1¼" squares of various cotton prints set with larger areas of white fancy quilted muslin, narrow inside border of white muslin, 2¾" outside border composed of 1¼" printed squares arranged diagonally with white triangular pieces, good used condition, 90" x 71" **250.00 275.00 260.00**

☐ **Johnny In The Corner In A Garden Maze,** Indiana, cotton, red pieced geometric pattern, slate blue background, gold back and binding, never washed, mint condition **375.00 400.00 385.00**

☐ **Le Moyne Star,** cotton, each 9" square block contains a star which is pieced of alternating dark and light calicoes, chambrays, and ginghams surrounded by sold light orange background, set up diagonally with indigo blue and white geometric print, unbleached muslin back, never washed, excellent condition, 78" x 85" **170.00 195.00 180.00**

☐ **LeMoyne Star,** 1930s, cotton, 9" star blocks are pieced with various prints on solid green background, green binding, whitebacking, fine quilting, never washed, very good condition, 80" x 71" **150.00 175.00 160.00**

☐ **Log Cabin,** cotton, blocks are pieced with old calico prints, red border, navy, white and red print backing, lovely quilting, good used condition, 66" x 80" **175.00 195.00 182.00**

☐ **Lone Star,** 1930s, cotton, pieced large star is made of various percale prints, background and backing are solid green, machine stitched, binding, crossing lines design quilting, good used condition, 82" x 85" **225.00 250.00 235.00**

☐ **Nine Patch,** Ohio Amish, crib, cotton sateen, pieced wine squares form pattern, black blackground and border, wine binding, new . **75.00 85.00 80.00**

☐ **Nine Patch,** Pennsylvania Amish, wool, pieced with burgundy, plum, brown, navy and teal, loden green background, wine blocks in foot-end corners, wide green border with tulip quilting **600.00 625.00 610.00**

☐ **Nine Patch,** Pennsylvania, crib, various old prints, form blocks, background is pieced from mostly pink prints, used condition with some fading and wear **85.00 90.00 87.00**

☐ **Oak Leaf Applique,** nine repeats, four yellow-green leaves with four gold flowers, gold eight point star in center of each repeat, vine and bud border, good used condition **300.00 325.00 310.00**

☐ **Picture Frame,** Ohio Amish, cotton, solid black with bright blue band in border, bright blue binding, exceptional quilting, very contemporary **250.00 275.00 260.00**

	Current Price Range		P/Y Average

☐ **Plain,** Iowa Amish, cotton sateen, one solid piece of celery green sateen, exceptional quilting ... **350.00 375.00 360.00**

☐ **Rainbow Tile,** also called Diamond Field, bright prints and solids are pieced to form pattern, unbleached muslin backing, machine stitched binding, never washed ... **100.00 125.00 110.00**

☐ **Rising Star,** cotton, large 13″ blocks pieced with old calicoes, ginghams and solid percales, solid turquoise percale lattice strips and narrow border, backing is white, turquoise, gold and black print, diagonal line quilting, good used, 66″ x 79″ ... **80.00 100.00 90.00**

☐ **Rose Applique,** cotton, large oval design of roses, buds, stems and leaves in two shades of green and four shades of pink hand appliqued using whipstitch in matching thread, embroidered veins in leaves, white background and binding, fine quilting in shell, feather, diagonal lines and other designs, white binding, scalloped edges on two sides, excellent condition, 60″ x 85″ ... **130.00 155.00 145.00**

☐ **Shooting Star,** 1920s, cotton, tiny old rose print calico and white muslin is pieced to form blocks which are set diagonally with squares of pieced white, tan and rose prints, rose calico inside border on two sides with narrow outside white border on all sides, white cotton backing, lovely quilting, good used, 76″ x 80″ ... **190.00 215.00 200.00**

☐ **Squares,** Ohio Mennonite, crib, 1″ bands of wine, green, olive and black are pieced to form squares with black centers, black background, fifteen squares with black border .. **300.00 325.00 315.00**

☐ **Star String,** cotton, large four point stars are pieced with various 1930s print and solids, large, solid pink diamond shaped pieces between stars and border, pink binding, unbleached muslin backing, diagonal line quilting, never washed, excellent condition, several years old, 68″ x 69″ ... **150.00 175.00 162.00**

☐ **Streak Of Lightning,** crib, cotton, pieced solid red, white, and blue zig-zag pattern, red binding, good used condition ... **350.00 375.00 362.00**

☐ **T Block,** cotton, old solid red and white blocks recently pieced with additional white cotton to form 10″ blocks, white binding and backing, fine quilting, never washed, very good condition, 94″ x 72″ ... **180.00 200.00 190.00**

☐ **Texas Star,** also called Dolly Madison Star and Star Garden, 1930s, cotton, all over pattern consisting of 6″ pieced yellow stars, green, white and black print binding, solid yellow backing, good used condition, ... **170.00 195.00 185.00**

	Current Price Range		P/Y Average
☐ **Triple Irish Chain,** 1893, pieced with solid red and white, 1¾″ squares, inside red border, outside white border, white binding and backing, quilted in lines only one half inch apart, embroidered date Dec. 25, 1893, very good condition, 73″ x 68″	325.00	350.00	333.00
☐ **Wild Goose Chase,** cotton, blocks are pieced with triangles of old ginghams, calicoes, chambrays and solids, strips between rows of triangular pieces are solid aqua, unbleached muslin back, aqua binding, nice diagonal quilting, never washed, good condition, 82″ x 72″	150.00	175.00	162.00

RADIOS

TYPES: Most collectors seek vintage radio types including: early radio sets that required headphones; battery operated loudspeaker models; and loudspeaker models that ran on house currents. Even some transistor models are collectible today.

PERIOD: Collectible radios date from 1920, the start of commercial radio broadcasting.

COMMENTS: Most valuable are working radios with all of their original parts. Though they are expensive, large console models are sought after.

ADDITIONAL TIPS: The radio listings are in alphabetical order.

☐ **A. C. Dayton Co.,** crystal set, c. 1923	118.00	150.00	128.00
☐ **A. C. Dayton Co.,** Super Six, c. 1924	148.00	190.00	160.00
☐ **Adams-Morgan,** Paragon Regen, c. 1921 . . .	215.00	260.00	230.00
☐ **Adams-Morgan,** R10 Short Wave, c. 1921 . . .	268.00	320.00	280.00
☐ **Atwater Kent,** #10, c. 1923	282.00	325.00	295.00
☐ **Beaver Baby Grand,** c. 1924	125.00	160.00	135.00
☐ **Crosley,** Vlm, c. 1922	305.00	370.00	330.00
☐ **Crosley,** X, c. 1922	212.00	245.00	220.00
☐ **Crosley,** Pup, c. 1925	310.00	370.00	340.00
☐ **Crosley,** 5-38, c. 1926	205.00	255.00	230.00
☐ **DeForest,** D6, c. 1923	315.00	365.00	340.00

	Current Price Range		P/Y Average
☐ DeForest, D10, c. 1923	405.00	465.00	435.00
☐ DeForest, Everyman, crystal, c. 1923	230.00	270.00	250.00
☐ Federal, 58DX, c. 1922	418.00	468.00	440.00
☐ Federal, 57DX, c. 1922	395.00	445.00	420.00
☐ Federal, 61DX, c. 1923	413.00	458.00	435.00
☐ Freshman, Masterpiece, c. 1924	255.00	305.00	280.00
☐ Grebe, CR6, c. 1919	495.00	565.00	530.00
☐ Grebe, CR5, c. 1921	285.00	335.00	310.00
☐ Grebe, Synchrophase, c. 1925	400.00	450.00	425.00
☐ Lafayette, ivory deco, plastic case	25.00	40.00	30.00
☐ Magnavox, TRF-5, c. 1925	250.00	350.00	300.00
☐ Philco, 551, c. 1928	145.00	165.00	155.00
☐ Philco, 525, c. 1929	100.00	120.00	110.00
☐ Philco, Super-heterodyne Cathedral, c. 1931	130.00	150.00	140.00
☐ Philco Transitone, portable, maroon and brown plastic case, leather handle	25.00	40.00	30.00
☐ RCA, Radiola X, c. 1925	420.00	470.00	450.00
☐ RCA, Radiola 26, c. 1925	515.00	575.00	530.00
☐ RCA, Radiola c. 1923	170.00	210.00	185.00
☐ RCA, Radiola special, c. 1923	175.00	225.00	200.00
☐ RCA, Aeriola Jr. (crystal), c. 1922	140.00	170.00	155.00
☐ Zenith, 835, c. 1932	150.00	200.00	175.00

RAILROADIANA

DESCRIPTION: Any items that pertain to the railroad make up railroadiana. This includes items from the steam powered, diesel and electric eras.

TYPES: Paper and hardware are the two basic types of railroadiana. The most collected paper item is timetables while uniforms are an especially sought after hardware item.

ADDITIONAL TIPS: Some collectors obtain any object of railroadiana while others specialize in such areas as dining car items, ashtrays or keys.

☐ Ashtray, Erie, glass, diamond in center	7.00	10.00	8.00
☐ Ashtray, New York Central Railroad, crystal, blue, pictures diesel	15.00	19.00	16.00
☐ Beer Mug, Chessie System, glass, side logo with illustration of cat	7.00	10.00	8.00

Railroad Passes and Timetables, c. 1903, **$12.00-$16.00**
Photo courtesy of Lou McCulloch, Highland Heights, OH 44143.

	Current Price Range		P/Y Average
☐ **Booklet,** New York, New Haven and Hartford, "Arranged Freight Train Service," c. 1920-1930	7.00	10.00	8.20
☐ **Brochure,** Erie Railroad, "The Erie Limited," with timetables and maps, 8½ x 11″, 1929 . .	6.00	8.00	6.90
☐ **Candle Holders,** Pennsylvania Railroad, silver plated, 3½″, pair	200.00	250.00	220.00
☐ **Cordial Glass,** New York Central System, tall, side logo	9.00	12.00	10.00
☐ **Cordial Glass,** Santa Fe, etched glass	14.00	18.00	15.00
☐ **Cordial Glass,** 20th Century Limited, embossed glass	16.00	20.00	17.00
☐ **Dessert Fork,** New York Central Railroad, "New Pattern" by Hall and Elton, silver, 6½″	16.00	20.00	17.00
☐ **Folder,** Union Pacific, "Along the Union Pacific Railroad," c. 1930-1940	3.00	4.00	3.45

	Current Price Range		P/Y Average
☐ **Formal Dinner Fork,** New York Central Railroad, "King's Pattern", silver, 8″	15.00	19.00	16.00
☐ **Horseradish Pot Holder,** Pennsylvania Railroad, glass and silver plated (two pieces), dated 1926	100.00	130.00	110.00
☐ **Juice Glass,** Chesapeake and Ohio, embossed glass, wording "For Progress"	7.50	10.00	8.00
☐ **Juice Glass,** New York Central Railroad, embossed glass, side marked, 6 oz.	6.00	8.00	6.50
☐ **Liquor License,** New York State, issued to New York Central Railroad, 8 x 11″, c. 1960	4.50	6.00	5.10
☐ **Map,** New York Central System, color, 1924	11.00	15.00	12.75
☐ **Menu,** Burlington Northern, Beverage List, 4 sided folder, states "form 2813", undated	2.00	3.00	2.35
☐ **Menu,** Burlington Northern, Breakfast, folder, April, 1970, 5″ x 7″	2.00	3.00	2.35
☐ **Menu,** California Zephyr Lines, Cable Car Room cocktail menu, 4 sided folder, 1968	2.50	3.50	2.90
☐ **Menu,** Silver Meteor (Amtrack), Breakfast, 4-sided folder, October, 1962	4.00	6.00	4.75
☐ **Menu,** Wabash Railroad, undated	2.00	3.00	2.35
☐ **Napkin,** Rock Island Line, linen with logo	3.50	4.50	4.00
☐ **Pass,** Maine Central Railroad, 1898	6.75	8.75	7.50
☐ **Pass,** Memphis and Little Rock Railroad Co., 1883	7.00	9.00	8.00
☐ **Pass,** Milwaukee and Northern, 1888	7.00	9.50	8.00
☐ **Pass,** Lake Shore and Western, 1882	7.00	9.00	8.00
☐ **Pass,** Lake Shore and Western, 1887	7.00	9.00	8.00
☐ **Pass,** Minneapolis and St. Louis, 1896	6.75	8.75	7.50
☐ **Pass,** Minneapolis and St. Louis, 1900	6.50	8.50	7.25
☐ **Pass,** Minneapolis, St. Paul and Sault Ste. Marie, 1895	6.75	8.75	7.50
☐ **Pass,** Missouri, Kansas and Texas Railway, 1889	7.00	9.00	8.00
☐ **Pass,** Missouri Pacific Railway Co., 1894	6.75	8.75	7.50
☐ **Pass,** Missouri Pacific Railway Co., 1898	6.75	8.75	7.50
☐ **Pass,** New York, Chicago and St. Louis Railroad, 1895	6.75	8.75	7.50
☐ **Placard,** Delaware and Western, "Switch Carefully," 3½″ x 7″	.75	1.00	.85
☐ **Placard,** Delaware and Western, "Warning, Poisonous Fumes, Heated Car," 9½″ x 9½″	2.00	3.00	2.40
☐ **Poster,** Brotherhood of Railroad Trainmen, various scenes in the life and death of a rail employee, final scene shows widow receiving death benefit check, c. 1900-1910, 22″ x 28″	75.00	100.00	87.00
☐ **Poster,** New York Central, "Low Fare Excursions to Watkins Glen, July 12, 1931," 6″ x 15″	4.00	5.00	4.35
☐ **Poster,** New York Central, "State Fair, Syracuse, September 7 to 12, 1931, " fare chart plus list of events and attractions, 7″ x 14″	4.50	6.00	5.15
☐ **Poster,** New York Central, "Weekend Excursion, Rochester to Montreal, Quebec, and Return, " schedule plus points of interest, c. 1930	4.00	5.00	4.35

	Current Price Range		P/Y Average
☐ **Serving Spoon,** New York Central Railroad, "King's Pattern", silver, 8″	15.00	19.00	16.00
☐ **Stock Certificate,** Market Street Railway Co., San Francisco, green and black with eagle vignette, c. 1925	9.00	12.00	10.00
☐ **Sugar Bowl,** Pennsylvania Railroad, silver plated with raised keystone emblem, dated 1929, 4″	80.00	100.00	88.00
☐ **Timetable,** Angelina and Neches River System, July, 1938	9.00	12.00	10.00
☐ **Timetable,** Ashley Drew and Northern System, December, 1938	11.00	14.00	12.00
☐ **Timetable,** Atlanta Birmingham and Coast Line System, November, 1936	9.00	12.00	10.00
☐ **Timetable,** Atlanta and West Point, Western Railway of Alabama, September, 1942	7.00	10.00	8.00
☐ **Timetable,** Baltimore and Ohio, Baltimore Division, October, 1965	3.50	5.00	4.15
☐ **Timetable,** Baltimore and Ohio, Buffalo Division, October, 1965	3.50	5.00	4.15
☐ **Timetable,** Baltimore and Ohio, Chicago Terminal, April, 1969	2.50	3.50	2.90
☐ **Timetable,** Baltimore and Ohio, Cumberland Division, October, 1970	3.50	5.00	4.15
☐ **Timetable,** Baltimore and Ohio, Maryland Division, January, 1974	3.50	5.00	4.15
☐ **Timetable,** Baltimore and Ohio, Monogah Division, October, 1965	3.50	5.00	4.15
☐ **Timetable,** Baltimore and Ohio, St. Louis Division, April, 1967	3.50	5.00	4.15
☐ **Timetable,** Barre and Chelsea Railroad System, September, 1949	7.00	10.00	8.00
☐ **Timetable,** Beaver/Meade/Englewood, October, 1956	7.00	10.00	8.00
☐ **Timetable,** Belfast and Moosehead Lake System, April, 1953	4.50	6.00	5.10
☐ **Timetable,** Bennetsville and Cheraw Railroad System, May, 1939	11.00	14.00	12.00
☐ **Timetable,** Blue Ridge Railway System, May, 1942	8.00	11.00	9.00
☐ **Timetable,** Bonhomie and Hattiesburg System, November, 1928	13.00	17.00	14.00
☐ **Timetable,** Bonhomie and Hattiesburg System, April, 1954	7.00	10.00	8.00
☐ **Timetable,** Boston and Albany Railroad, poster style with large woodcut, c. 1870-1880, 18½″ x 24″	50.00	65.00	56.00
☐ **Timetable,** Boston Terminal Co., South Station, April, 1954	4.50	6.00	5.10
☐ **Timetable,** Central New Jersey Railroad, Central Division, September, 1953	5.00	7.00	5.75
☐ **Timetable,** Central New Jersey Railroad, Central Division, October, 1955	5.00	7.00	5.75
☐ **Timetable,** Central New Jersey Railroad, Central Division, October, 1961	4.50	6.00	5.20

	Current Price Range		P/Y Average
☐ **Timetable,** Central New Jersey Railroad, Pennsylvania Division, April, 1959	5.00	7.50	6.10
☐ **Timetable,** Central Vermont System, April, 1964	4.50	6.00	5.00
☐ **Timetable,** Central Terminal of Toledo System, February, 1958	4.50	6.00	5.00
☐ **Timetable,** Charleston and Western Carolina System, April, 1946	8.00	11.00	9.20
☐ **Timetable,** Chicago and Alton, Northern Division, September, 1929	14.00	19.00	15.50
☐ **Timetable,** Chessie System, Covington and Cincinnati Elevated Railroad, April, 1941 . . .	8.00	11.00	9.00
☐ **Timetable,** Chessie System, Covington and Cincinnati Elevated Railroad, April, 1961 . . .	4.50	6.00	5.00
☐ **Timetable,** Chessie System, Ashland and Russell-Hocking Division, April, 1961	3.50	5.00	4.00
☐ **Timetable,** Chessie System, Cincinnati and Chicago Division, April, 1966	3.50	5.00	4.00
☐ **Timetable,** Chessie System, Grand Rapids-Saginaw Division, October, 1965	3.50	5.00	4.00
☐ **Timetable,** Chessie System, Hinton Division, April, 1961	4.50	6.00	5.10
☐ **Timetable,** Chessie System, Hinton and Huntington Division, April, 1966	3.50	5.00	4.00
☐ **Timetable,** Erie Railroad, Wyoming and Jefferson Division, April, 1939	7.00	10.00	8.00
☐ **Timetable,** Erie Railroad, New York Division, April, 1660	4.50	6.00	5.00
☐ **Timetable,** Ft. Worth and Denver, Wichita Falls and Amarillo Division, October, 1936 . .	9.00	12.00	10.00
☐ **Timetable,** Ft. Worth and Denver, Wichita Falls and Amarillo Division, December, 1942	7.00	10.00	8.00
☐ **Timetable,** Ft. Worth and Denver, Wichita Falls and Amarillo Division, October, 1945 . .	6.00	8.00	6.75
☐ **Timetable,** Ft. Worth and Denver, Wichita Falls and Amarillo Division, June, 1949	6.00	8.00	6.75
☐ **Timetable,** Ft. Worth and Denver, Wichita Falls and Amarillo Division, June, 1954	5.00	7.00	5.45
☐ **Timetable,** Galveston Houston and Henderson, April, 1928	11.00	14.00	12.00
☐ **Timetable,** Galveston Houston and Henderson, December, 1932	9.00	12.00	10.00
☐ **Timetable,** Gulf Mobile and Ohio, Southern Division, October, 1940	7.00	10.00	8.00
☐ **Timetable,** Gulf Mobile and Ohio, Southern Division, January, 1952	5.00	7.00	5.70
☐ **Timetable,** Gulf Mobile and Ohio, Western Division, September, 1948	7.00	10.00	8.00
☐ **Timetable,** Gulf Mobile and Ohio, Western Division, April, 1960	4.50	6.00	5.00
☐ **Timetable,** Gulf and Ship Island Railroad System, June, 1930	11.00	14.00	12.00

	Current Price Range		P/Y Average

☐ **Timetable,** Harlem Line, operating between Grand Central Depot and Mott Haven (Manhattan to Bronx, New York), broadside poster with rules on reverse side, c. 1881 . . . . — 8.00 / 11.00 — 9.25

Note: The Harlem Line with its short borough-to-borough runs was the direct ancester of the subway train in New York City

☐ **Timetable,** Houston and Texas Central System, March, 1960 . . . . — 18.00 / 23.00 — 19.00

☐ **Timetable,** Houston Belt and Terminal System, August, 1926 . . . . — 9.00 / 12.00 — 10.00

☐ **Timetable,** Houston Belt and Terminal System, October, 1933 . . . . — 8.00 / 11.00 — 9.00

☐ **Timetable,** Houston Belt and Terminal System, April, 1943 . . . . — 6.00 / 8.00 — 6.75

☐ **Timetable,** Houston Belt and Terminal System, January, 1948 . . . . — 5.00 / 7.00 — 5.50

☐ **Timetable,** Houston Belt and Terminal System, January, 1965 . . . . — 4.50 / 6.00 — 5.00

☐ **Timetable,** Houston Belt and Terminal System, December, 1972 . . . . — 3.50 / 5.00 — 4.10

☐ **Timetable,** Illinois Central, Louisville Division, August, 1900 . . . . — 23.00 / 28.00 — 25.00

☐ **Timetable,** Illinois Central, Louisville Division, September, 1950 . . . . — 5.00 / 7.00 — 5.60

☐ **Timetable,** Illinois Central, Louisville Division, September, 1953 . . . . — 4.50 / 6.00 — 5.00

☐ **Timetable,** Illinois Central, Louisville Division, October, 1958 . . . . — 4.50 / 6.00 — 5.00

☐ **Timetable,** Illinois Central, Paducah Division, April, 1972 . . . . — 3.50 / 5.00 — 4.10

☐ **Timetable,** Illinois Central, St. Louis Division, July, 1919 . . . . — 18.00 / 23.00 — 19.00

☐ **Timetable,** Illinois Central, St. Louis Division, June, 1923 . . . . — 14.00 / 19.00 — 15.50

☐ **Timetable,** Illinois Central, St. Louis Division, Januray, 1931 . . . . — 9.00 / 12.00 — 10.00

☐ **Timetable,** Illinois Central, St. Louis Division, October, 1965 . . . . — 3.50 / 5.00 — 4.15

☐ **Timetable,** Illinois Central, St. Louis Division, April, 1967 . . . . — 3.50 / 5.00 — 4.15

☐ **Timetable,** Illinois Central Gulf, Kentucky Division, January, 1978 . . . . — 3.50 / 5.00 — 4.15

☐ **Timetable,** Illinois Central Gulf, Mississippi Division, April, 1976 . . . . — 3.50 / 5.00 — 4.15

☐ **Timetable,** Illinois Central Gulf, Missouri Division, April, 1976 . . . . — 3.50 / 5.00 — 4.15

☐ **Timetable,** Illinois Central Gulf, Midwest Division, October, 1978 . . . . — 2.50 / 3.50 — 2.85

☐ **Waiter's Clipboard,** Pennsylvania Railroad, silver plated with raised keystone emblem at top, 8¾ ″ . . . . — 170.00 / 200.00 — 180.00

☐ **Water Glass,** Baltimore and Ohio, embossed glass, side logo with diesel and steam locomotives, 6 oz. . . . . — 14.00 / 18.00 — 15.00

	Current Price Range		P/Y Average
☐ **Water Glass,** Baltimore and Ohio, embossed glass, pictures Capitol Dome, undated	9.00	12.00	10.00
☐ **Water Glass,** New York Central Railroad, embossed glass, side marked, 10 oz.	9.00	12.00	10.00
☐ **Water Glass,** Santa Fe, embossed glass, 8 oz.	6.00	8.00	6.60
☐ **Water Glass,** 20th Century Limited, embossed glass, 8 oz.	18.00	23.00	19.25
☐ **Water Glass,** Union Pacific, crest at side, 8 oz.	3.50	5.00	3.80
☐ **Wine Glass,** New York Central Railroad, embossed glass, side marked, 4 oz.	7.00	10.00	8.15
☐ **Wine List,** Burlington Northern, with insert, undated	2.00	3.00	2.35

RAZORS

MATERIALS: Most commonly, razor handles are made of wood, hard rubber and imitation bone. Finer razors had handles of ivory, bone or sterling silver.

COMMENTS: As with most collectibles, old and rare razors are the most valuable. Along with flea markets and antiques shops, knife shows often feature razors.

ADDITIONAL TIPS: The listings in this section are alphabetical according to manufacturer. When the manufacturer isn't known, the razor is listed by type.

☐ **Amber,** straight razor, high carbon steel blade with gold plated end, extra full hollow grinding, transparent celluloid handle, ½″ wide blade (narrower than standard)	9.00	12.00	10.50
☐ **Antonio Tadros,** straight edge	8.50	12.00	10.00
☐ **Army/Navy,** straight razor, Wardlow English steel blade, three-quarter hollow grinding, oval handle of black hard rubber, ¾″ wide blade (wider than standard), commercially sold razor of World War I era said to be duplicate of military issue	10.00	13.00	11.50
☐ **Barber,** straight edge in original box	51.50	60.00	53.00

Straight Razor, *Red Injun, ivory celluloid handle, made in Germany, original box,* **$35.00 - $40.00**

	Current Price Range		P/Y Average
☐ **Cattaraugus Cutlery Co.** with "The Sovereign's Own" imprint	22.50	30.00	26.50
☐ **Chip-A-Way Cutlery Co., England** with "Chip-A-Way" imprint	10.50	13.50	12.00
☐ **Colquhoun and Cadman, Sheffield** with "Little Favorite" imprint	6.50	9.50	8.00
☐ **Curvit,** for women, in flannel pouch	4.00	10.00	6.00
☐ **Electric Cutlery, New York** with "Arlington" imprint	6.50	9.50	8.00
☐ **Elsener, Switzerland** with "Ideal" imprint . .	7.50	10.50	9.00
☐ **Euchler,** straight, with bakelite handle	6.00	10.00	8.00
☐ **Ever-Ready,** safety razor, c. 1920-1930	5.00	7.00	6.00
☐ **Favorite,** straight razor, Wardlow English steel blade, extra full hollow grinding, plain handle of hard black rubber, ⅝" wide blade .	8.00	11.00	9.50
☐ **Genco Barber,** straight razor, extra full hollow grinding, celluloid handle in imitation of golden oak, ⅝" wide blade	16.00	21.00	18.25
☐ **Genco Heavy,** Geneva Cutlery Co., straight razor, full hollow grinding, plain hard black rubber handle with nickel silver ends, ⅝" wide blade	12.00	17.00	14.50
☐ **Gillette New Standard,** safety razor, triple silver plating	7.00	10.00	8.35

RECORDS

TYPES: There are two primary types of records: 45s and LPs. A 45 is a small record that usually features one song on each side. It turns on the turntable at a rate of 45 revolutions per minute; thus, the name. An LP is a long playing album that has several songs on each side. It turns at a rate of 33 revolutions per minute.

PERIOD: Records from the 1950s and 1960s are most popular among collectors.

MATERIALS: Records are almost exclusively made of vinyl. Rare platinum and gold specimens are produced occasionally for superstars, but these almost never make it into the collectible market.

COMMENTS: Rare releases by famous groups and singers are in great demand. Bands like The Beatles and The Rolling Stones command top prices for scarce recordings.

ADDITIONAL TIPS: for further information and listings, please refer to *The Official Price Guide to Records,* published by the House of Collectibles.

	Current Price Range		P/Y Average
☐ **Johnny Ace,** Flair, #1015, Midnight Hours/-Journey/Trouble And Me	20.00	50.00	35.00
☐ **Aladdins,** Frankie, #6, My Charlene/Dot, My Love	50.00	90.00	68.00
☐ **Paul Anka,** RPM, #472, I Confess/Blau-Wile Deveest Fontaine	23.00	32.00	28.00
☐ **Marty Balin,** Challenge, #9146, Nobody But You/You Made Me Fall	8.50	14.00	12.00
☐ **Baritones,** Dore, #501, After School Rock/Sentimental Baby	14.00	24.00	18.00
☐ **Beach Boys,** X, #301, Surfin'/Luau	80.00	130.00	100.00
☐ **Beach Boys,** Candix, #301, Surfin'/Luau	33.00	55.00	40.00
☐ **Beatles,** Decca, #9-31382, My Bonnie/The Saints	375.00	860.00	500.00
☐ **Beatles,** Vee Jay, #581, From Me To You/Please Please Me (promo)	35.00	75.00	50.00

	Current Price Range		P/Y Average
☐ **Beatles,** Swan, #4152, She Loves You/I'll Get You	30.00	65.00	40.00
☐ **Dell Vikings,** Luniverse, #106, Over The Rainbow/Hey Senorita	17.00	30.00	24.00
☐ **Dell Vikings,** Fee Bee, #205, Come Go With Me/How Can I Find True Love	40.00	65.00	50.00
☐ **Dominoes,** Federal, #12010, Harbor Lights/No Says My Heart	160.00	275.00	220.00
☐ **Five Satins,** Standard, #105, All Mine/ Rosemarie	55.00	100.00	75.00
☐ **Ronnie Gill,** Rio, #129, Geraldine/Standing On The Mountain	12.00	46.00	28.00

RED WING POTTERY

DESCRIPTION: Red Wing Stoneware Company was founded in 1878 in Red Wing, Minnesota. It was one of the earliest midwestern potteries outside of Ohio. Pottery factories straying from the eastern Ohio region were usually doomed to an early failure, but Red Wing showed remarkable staying power. As the population of the area increased, its production increased, and the business thrived. The concept of expanding its line beyond stoneware was first explored in the early 1920's when the market for pottery in general broadened out as never before. The first new item put into production at that time was a line of flowerpots, followed in later years by artware cookie jars, jugs, trays, candleholders and vases. Also, a general line of dinnerware was added to the factory's schedule in the depression years to take up slack from the loss of artware sales. The best years for Red Wing art pottery were from the middle 1920's to the early 1930's.

MARKS: Red Wing manufactured under its own name and also as Rumrill sometimes spelled RumRill. When the Rumrill mark is used, it will generally be with the second R capitalized, The Red Wing housemarks changed through the years. If one includes the early stoneware markings a long list would be necessary to record them all. In the era of its art pottery, there were at least three distinctive marks. One consisted of the wording RED WING ART POTTERY arranged in a circle with ART at the center and other symbols or decoration. An impressed mark from the

1930's states simply RED WING followed by the mold or model number. The most elaborate mark is a badge, with the company name in bold script lettering in Art Deco style.

Pitcher, *green mottled glaze,* **$35.00-$40.00**

	Current Price Range		P/Y Average
☐ **Ashtray,** red, semi gloss, of bird's-wing form with textured molding, special anniversary product, marked 1879-1953	22.00	25.00	23.50
☐ **Ashtray,** #738, salmon, matte glaze, oval, flattened, no lip marked RED WING U.S.A.	6.00	8.00	7.00
☐ **Bowl,** black, matte glaze, oval with rising lip, marked RED WING U.S.A.	8.00	10.00	9.00
☐ **Bowl,** item #1493, black, matte glaze, oval with square handles, marked RED WING U.S.A.	8.00	10.00	9.00
☐ **Candleholder,** item #847, blue, matte glaze, in the form of a classical urn with fluted sides and vaulted scrolling terminals at the rim, resting on a flat base, marked RED WING U.S.A.	8.00	10.00	9.00
☐ **Candleholder,** bright blue, matte glaze, of spherical shape with molded leaves at the base, marked RED WING U.S.A.	4.00	5.00	4.50

	Current Price Range		P/Y Average
□ **Cookie Jar,** rooster, item #249, pale sea green with various tonal effects, semi gloss, in the form of a realistically modeled rooster, seated, upper portion serves as the jar lid, the dividing line occurring just above the wings, tail is the lid handle, marked RED WING U.S.A.	24.00	28.00	26.00
□ **Dish, Candy,** item #801, mud brown, semi gloss, of shaped triangular form, consisting of three bowls in one, each formed by a hexagon of diagonal wedges, marked RED WING U.S.A.	11.00	13.00	12.00
□ **Ewer,** item #1219, ivory white, matte glaze, of cruet form with bulbous bowl and tall narrow cylindrical neck, with vertical handle rising from the bowl and connecting with the lip. Decorated at the bowl with molded leafwork, highlighted with pale burgundy coloring, marked RED WING U.S.A.	28.00	32.00	30.00
□ **Figurine,** Chinaman, item #1309, ivory white, matte glaze, a priest dressed in long flowing robes, hands clasped, wearing a cermonial headpiece, marked RED WING U.S.A.	16.00	19.00	17.50

ROBOTS

COMMENTS: There is a tremendous amount of activity in this area of toy collecting. The best place to see toy robots is at an antique toy show. Condition is very important in this field.

RECOMMENDED READING: For further information refer to *The Official Price Guide to Toys and The Official Price Guide to Science Fiction and Fantasy Collectibles,* published by The House of Collectibles.

□ **Acrobat Robot,** *made by S. H. of Japan, all plastic, battery powered, chrome-like finish with very modernistic design, box reads (in English), "Mystery Action, Lited Eyes, Turn Over Action," 5½".*	20.00	30.00	14.00

Attacking Martian, *hips swivel, moves forward and back,* $100.00-$180.00

	Current Price Range		P/Y Average
☐ **Action Packed Robot,** *made in Japan, battery operated, lithographed tin with plastic arms and feet, doors on chest open to reveal machine guns, turns as he walks, 11½"*	75.00	95.00	75.00
☐ **Action Robot,** *made in Hong Kong, all plastic, guns mounted on either side of head, 10".* ..	15.00	20.00	12.50
☐ **Amazing Magic Robot,** *4th Edition, Merritt Toys Ltd. (Great Britain), actually a game which includes a 3" lithographed tin robot, price is for complete game, enclosed in 10" x 15" box, 1953*	60.00	80.00	62.00
☐ **Apollo Astroid Robot,** *made by Durham of Japan, plastic with silver-colored radar screen that rotates as he walks, 6".*	25.00	35.00	30.00
☐ **Artoo-Detoo,** *Kenner Corp., stuffed toy of the little robot in Star Wars, 100% polyester with painted features and moveable legs.*	5.00	7.00	6.00
☐ **Atomic Robot,** *maker unidentified, clockwork, tin, primitive styling with "tin can" appearance, lithographed dials, walks, 7"* ...	275.00	325.00	260.00

Note: *One of the early mechanical robots, perhaps from the late 1940s.*

	Current Price Range		P/Y Average

☐ **Big Max Robot,** *made by Remco, all plastic, battery powered, robot hoists loads by electromagnet, places them on belt which deposits them into truck, was featured in 1958 Sears Roebuck catalogue.* **180.00 220.00 177.50**

☐ **Buck Rogers Walking Twiki,** *made by Mego under license from Robert C. Dille, clockwork, hard molded plastic, his head turns while he walks, has grip-lock hands, 1979, 6½".* **15.00 20.00 17.00**

☐ **Busy Robot,** *made by S. H. of Japan, battery powered, wears "hard hat" of construction worker and wheels wheelbarrow, 11½".* **375.00 450.00 387.00**

☐ **Crank-Powered Robot,** *made in Japan, lithographed tin, plastic space helmet on head, small claw-like hands, crank is turned to make robot walk (has no motor), 7"* **300.00 350.00 280.00**

☐ **Dalek Robot,** *Palitoy, battery powered, gray plastic body, 6½".* **9.00 12.00 10.00**

☐ **Dia Attacker,** *made by S. T. of Japan, Japanese lettering on box, in the likeness of a shogun (outlaw of old Japan) which changes into a robot, box has large colored illustration of him in giant size menacing city.* **40.00 50.00 38.50**

☐ **Doug Davis, Major Matt Mason's Space Buddy,** *Mattel, plastic, 1968, 6½". Price is for specimen in original unopened blister-pack.* . . **11.00 14.00 12.10**

☐ **Electric Remote Control Battery Operated Robot** *(so named by maker), lithographed tin, wire leading from control box to robot, box reads, "Eyes Light Up, Arms Swing, Walks Forward, Backward," has illustration of him walking right with powerful beams shining from eyes, 7½".* **190.00 230.00 180.00**

☐ **Electric Robot,** *Marx, plastic, battery powered, black and red, antenna attached to head, 15".* **140.00 170.00 137.50**

☐ **Family Robots,** *made by T.N. of Hong Kong, plastic, a set of three robots representing Poppa (blue), Momma (red), and Baby (green), Momma Robot has knobs on chest for female appearance, 3½".* **9.00 12.00 10.00**

☐ **Jupiter Robot,** *made by K.O. of Japan, plastic, clockwork, walks, sparks and makes noise, modeled after Robbie in the Anne Francis movie "Forbidden Planet," 7".* **180.00 225.00 167.50**

☐ **Mr. Robot,** *made in Japan, battery operated, tin body with plastic head, bump-and-go action, names across chest, 11"* **430.00 530.00 445.00**

☐ **Piston Robot,** *lithographed tin, battery powered, has eight pistons that can be viewed through clear plastic shield, makes sound, motor lights up, arms move, 11".* **80.00 100.00 65.00**

	Current Price Range		P/Y Average

☐ **R2-D2 Model,** *Fundimensions, General Mills Fun Group, retractable third leg, moves on rollers, pivoting support leg, dome spins, front panel opens and computer extends, height 6", 1977* 4.00 6.00 5.00

☐ **Radar Robot,** *made by KY of Japan, clockwork, plastic, walks and moves arms, holds sparking gum, makes engine noise, multicolored, 10",* 60.00 80.00 63.00

☐ **Radio Controlled R2-D2,** *Kenner Corp., replica of popular robot, beeping speech, fully automated, height 8", 1978.* 30.00 60.00 45.00

☐ **Remote Control Robot,** *Modern Toys of Japan, lithographed and silvered tin, remote control action with wire leading to control box, robot has primitive "nailed together" appearance with cylindrical head and protruding eyes, control box features large lithographed picture, 7½ "* 600.00 750.00 575.00

☐ **Robot Bubble Bath,** *no indication of maker or place of origin, plastic, stationery figure of robot which is actually a bottle holding bubble bath liquid, 7½ ". Price is for empty specimen.* 9.00 12.00 10.25

☐ **Robot Bus,** *made by Woodhaven Metal Stamping Co., lithographed tin, clockwork, bump-'n-go action, 14"* 75.00 95.00 83.00

☐ **Robot 2500,** *no indication of maker, battery operated, steel and chrom-plated plastic, blinking eye, arms and legs move, 10"* 90.00 115.00 95.00

☐ **Robot Carrying Case,** *no indication of maker or place of origin, probably Oriental, all plastic, blue with yellow wheels, a coffin-like case in the form of a large robot, carrying handle at top, 24"* 9.00 12.00 10.25

☐ **Robot-7,** *made in Taiwan, lithographed tin, clockwork, miniature robot with melancholy expression on its face, 4"* 18.00 23.00 20.00

☐ **Robot Commando,** *Ideal, plastic, remote control (with cord), blue body, red head and arms, "bullseye" eyes, movable arms, a very large robot, 18½ "* 150.00 200.00 140.00

ROOKWOOD

DESCRIPTION: Rookwood pottery features large, bold underglaze painting which gives the wares the appearance of oil painting on porcelain.

PERIOD: Rookwood manufactured pottery from 1879 to 1967. Its heyday was from 1890-1930.

ORIGIN: Rookwood was founded in 1879 in Cincinnati, Ohio. While other manufacturers of the day made stoneware, Rookwood strove to design artistic ware and maintain high quality. Rookwood proved that the buying public would buy American art pottery instead of European pottery.

MARKS: Products bore a factory artist mark, and they sometimes bore a clay mark, size mark and process mark as well. Those with a process mark are always worth a premium.

COMMENTS: In terms of length of operation, pieces manufactured and collector interest, Rookwood is the leader of art pottery makers. Rookwood vases are the most famous and popular. While prices for Rookwood pottery are fairly high, the market has stabilized in recent years.

ADDITIONAL TIPS: The listings are alphabetical by item. For more complete information on Rookwood, refer to *The Official Price Guide to Pottery and Porcelain.*

	Current Price Range		P/Y Average
☐ **Advertising Sign,** 4½", cream, highly glazed, says "Rookwood, Cincinnati," dated 1947 ..	575.00	600.00	587.50
☐ **Apple,** 3", with cover, dark brown slip with a redstone glaze, dated 1933	110.00	140.00	125.00
☐ **Ashtray,** 5", shell shape, red goldstone glaze, dated 1932	90.00	110.00	100.00
☐ **Ashtray,** 5½", fish, light blue, high glaze, dated 1951	35.00	45.00	40.00
☐ **Basket,** 5", item #1641, dark turquoise, high glazed, dated 1920	110.00	140.00	130.00
☐ **Box,** 3¼", dark green and blue, red reliefed flowers on top, by K. Van Horn, dated 1910 ...	650.00	750.00	700.00

Vase, c. *1949*

	Current Price Range		P/Y Average
☐ **Bookends,** 5½ ″, item #2695, turquoise, in the form of a yacht, by William P. McDonald, dated 1925	95.00	120.00	110.00
☐ **Bookends,** 6″, blue, highly glazed, models of owls, by Margaret Helen McDonald, dated 1940	110.00	125.00	115.00
☐ **Bowl,** 4¼ ″, item #1222, frog design, dated 1921	65.00	70.00	67.50
☐ **Bowl,** 4½ ″, brown shades to dark brown, incised leaf decoration, dated 1927	60.00	70.00	67.50
☐ **Box,** 5¼ ″, item #6286, brown aventurine glaze, lidded, of dome form, decorated by Louise Abel (signed with full signature), bearing an impressed factory mark and the date 1930 . . .	1800.00	2300.00	2100.00
☐ **Candlesticks,** 6″, item #2199, embossed columns, dated 1922	50.00	60.00	55.00
☐ **Candlesticks,** 10″, item #1630, rose, matte finish, embossed tulips, dated 1922	125.00	150.00	135.00
☐ **Cigarette Box,** item #6856, green, glazed, Dogwood design, dated 1944	55.00	65.00	60.00
☐ **Creamer,** item #547, turquoise, matte finish, dated 1940	20.00	25.00	22.50
☐ **Dish,** 5″, cameo glaze, peach shades to green, white flowers, log shape, dated 1890	115.00	125.00	120.00
☐ **Figurine,** goat 6¼ ″, item #6170, white, matte finish, impressed Louis Abel, dated 1945	65.00	75.00	70.00
☐ **Figurine,** 4½ ″, woman reclining on high glaze green tray	75.00	85.00	80.00
☐ **Ginger Jar,** 3½ ″, item #1321E, pink, with lid . .	70.00	80.00	75.00

	Current Price Range		P/Y Average
☐ **Honey Jug,** 4¾″, bisque, light brown, intaglio clover design, by H. Wendroth, dated 1883 . . .	140.00	160.00	150.00
☐ **Honey Jug,** 4¾″, brown high glaze, black birds and reeds with gold inlay, by M. Rettig, dated 1883	375.00	450.00	420.00
☐ **Humidor,** item #1019, mustard, matte finish, molded design, dated 1921	75.00	85.00	80.00
☐ **Inkwell,** 2½″, brown and green glaze, lily pads and floral decoration, by C. Steinle, dated 1897	90.00	120.00	97.50
☐ **Jar,** 9″, yellow-brown, lidded pot form with shaped shoulder, hat-type lid, decorated with a painting of red flowers by Laura Fry (signed with initials), marked ROOKWOOD 1885	950.00	1125.00	1000.00
☐ **Jardiniere,** 5¼″, brown, three handles, slip-painted blue berries and leaf yellow leaves, by F. Rothenbush, dated 1900	425.00	450.00	437.50

ROSEVILLE POTTERY

HISTORY: The Roseville factory opened up in 1885 in Roseville, Ohio. It was operated by George Young, C.F. Allison and other partners, and got off to a modest beginning as a maker of general stoneware lines. Cuspidors were among its early products. In 1902, the factory bought out an old stoneware plant in Zanesville, and soon began making art pottery at Zanesville. This phase of its operations overshadowed the stoneware business at Roseville. In 1910, the Roseville arm of the company was closed down. After this, all manufacturing was at Zanesville, but the name Roseville Pottery Co. was retained. Because it had already built up a number of lines of moderately-priced ware, Roseville was not hurt as much by the 1930s financial depression as Rookwood. It nevertheless did, feel the pinch; sales declined and never again reached their peaks of the 1920s and earlier years. In 1954, Roseville went out of business.

DESCRIPTION: Roseville called its artware Rozane, a name coined from ROseville and ZANEsville. At first all the products were in deep brown, similar to those being produced by Rookwood. Soon the shades were lightened and variety was worked into the pottery. Various lines were introduced, including "Egypto," "Mongol," "Woodland," "Mara," and "Royal." Although, water pitchers, jugs, lamp bases, ashtrays, and a full array of other decorative products were made, the main line was vases.

222222222222222222

MARKS: Most of the art pottery is marked Rozane or Rozane Ware, in conjunction with an artist's mark. There might be another mark indicating the line from which the piece has come. Apparently one of the earliest marks used at Zanesville was a three-line block-letter arrangement reading *ROSEVILLE POTTERY CO., ZANESVILLE, O.* On much of the earlier ware, the name *ROZANE WARE* is enclosed in a circular border, with a banner beneath giving the line name (*MONGOL, ROYAL,* etc.). A figure of a rose appears within the circle. This mark was heavily outlined and always impressed into the ware. Sometimes the marking was done by circular paper labels, which had decorative borders. These labels carried printing in red ink, which is often blurry and poorly centered.

RECOMMENDED READING: For more in-depth information on Roseville, you may refer to *The Official Price Guide to Pottery and Porcelain,* published by The House of Collectibles.

Vase, *Roseville, Sunflower pattern,*
$90.00-$100.00

	Current Price Range		P/Y Average
☐ **Antique Green Matt,** jardiniere, shape #550, 4″	40.00	50.00	45.00
☐ **Apple Blossom,** planter, shape #368, 8″, green	28.00	30.00	29.00
☐ **Azurine,** vase, 6″ x 8½″, turquoise, flared wide rim stamped RV	60.00	65.00	62.50
☐ **Baneda,** jardiniere, 4″ x 5½″, green with two handles	65.00	75.00	70.00
☐ **Bittersweet,** basket, shape #811, 10″, green	75.00	85.00	80.00
☐ **Blackberry,** console bowl, oval, 13″ x 13½″	185.00	200.00	192.50
☐ **Bleeding Heart,** hanging basket, 8½″ x 4″, pink	85.00	95.00	90.00
☐ **Bushberry,** cornucopia, shape #154, 8″, blue	33.00	35.00	34.00
☐ **Carnelian I,** wall pocket, 7½″, green and tan	50.00	60.00	55.00

	Current Price Range		P/Y Average
□ **Carnelian II,** bowl, 3″ x 8¼″, blue and green mottled, marked RV	40.00	50.00	45.00
□ **Ceramic Design,** wall pocket, 10″, two small cut-outs, V shape, no mark	145.00	170.00	155.00
□ **Cherry Blossom,** bookends, green with pink blossoms, pair	110.00	120.00	115.00
□ **Chloron,** vase, 6½″, textured design, cone shape, no trim, no mark	210.00	230.00	220.00
□ **Clematis,** jardiniere and pedestal, 25″, brown, pair	300.00	350.00	325.00
□ **Columbine,** vase, shape #19, 8″, pink and green	55.00	65.00	60.00
□ **Corinthian,** bowl, 8″ x 3″	42.00	45.00	43.00
□ **Cosmos,** basket, shape #358, 12″, blue	155.00	175.00	165.00
□ **Cremona,** vase, pillow-shaped, 6″ x 6″, pink . .	45.00	55.00	50.00
□ **Dahlrose,** rose bowl, 4½″ x 4¾″, with two handles	35.00	40.00	37.50
□ **Dogwood,** bowl, 7″ x 2½″	48.00	55.00	51.00
□ **Dogwood II,** tub, 5″ x 8½″	85.00	95.00	90.00
□ **Donatello,** flower frog, green, ivory and tan . . .	15.00	18.00	16.50
□ **Dutch,** humidor and lid, creamware with Dutch decals	125.00	150.00	137.50
□ **Earlem,** candlesticks, 3″ x 5″, blue-green with two handles, pair	95.00	110.00	102.50
□ **Egypto,** pitcher, wine, 12″	225.00	250.00	237.50
□ **Falline,** vase, 7″ x 6¼″, red and turquoise with two handles	200.00	250.00	225.00

ROYAL DOULTON

DESCRIPTION: Royal Doulton figures are ceramic works of art. Although the English company produces other items, its HN series is the best known.

ORIGIN: The Royal Doulton Company began in the early 1800s by John Doulton. The HN series was introduced in 1913 and named after Harry Nixon, head colorist at the time.

TYPES: Besides their figurines, there are many different Royal Doulton collectibles including toby jugs, plates, limited editions and bird and animal figures.

MARKS: Royal Doulton figures are identified by the HN prefix followed by numbers in a chronological sequence.

COMMENTS: Subjects in the HN series are highly diverse representing the works of many different artists at different time periods. This series is good for topical collecting.

ADDITIONAL TIPS: HN figures one through twenty-six are listed. These are among the earliest Royal Doulton figures and usually the most desirable to collectors.

For more information, consult *The Official Price Guide to Royal Doulton,* published by The House of Collectibles.

Odds And Ends,
HN1844,
$800.00-$900.00

		Current Price Range		P/Y Average
☐HN	1, Darling (1st version), 1913-28	1000.00	1150.00	1050.00
☐HN	2, Elizabeth Fry, 1913-38	4000.00	4500.00	4200.00
☐HN	3, Milking Time, 1913-38	3000.00	3500.00	3200.00
☐HN	4, Picardy Peasant (female), 1913-38	1500.00	2000.00	1750.00
☐HN	5, Picardy Peasant (female), 1913-38	1500.00	2000.00	1750.00
☐HN	6, Dunce, 1913-38	2750.00	3000.00	2850.00
☐HN	7, Pedlar Wolf, 1913-38	2000.00	2500.00	2200.00
☐HN	8, The Crinoline, 1913-38	1300.00	1450.00	1350.00
☐HN	9, The Crinoline, 1913-38	1300.00	1450.00	1350.00
☐HN	9A, The Crinoline, 1913-38	1300.00	1450.00	1350.00
☐HN	10, Madonna of the Square, 1913-38	1450.00	1600.00	1550.00
☐HN	10A, Madonna of the Square, 1913-38 . . .	1350.00	1500.00	1050.00

	Current Price Range		P/Y Average
☐ HN 11, Madonna of the Square, 1913-38	1450.00	1700.00	1750.00
☐ HN 12, Baby, 1913-38	2050.00	2200.00	2125.00
☐ HN 13, Picardy Peasant (male), 1913-38	1950.00	2000.00	1975.00
☐ HN 14, Madonna of the Square, 1913-38	1450.00	1850.00	1800.00
☐ HN 15, The Sleepy Scholar, 1913-38	1650.00	1800.00	1250.00
☐ HN 16, The Sleepy Scholar, 1913-38	1550.00	1700.00	1250.00
☐ HN 17, Picardy Peasant (male), 1913-38	1850.00	2000.00	1925.00
☐ HN 17A, Picardy Peasant (female), 1913-38 . .	1850.00	2000.00	1925.00
☐ HN 18, Pussy, 1913-38	2400.00	2600.00	2600.00
☐ HN 19, Picardy Peasant (male), 1913-38	1600.00	1850.00	1050.00
☐ HN 20, The Coquette, 1913-38	2500.00	3000.00	2750.00
☐ HN 21, The Crinoline, 1913-38	1300.00	1450.00	1325.00
☐ HN 21A, The Crinoline, 1913-38	1250.00	1400.00	1325.00
☐ HN 22, The Lavender Woman, 1913-38	1750.00	2000.00	1850.00
☐ HN 23, The Lavender Woman, 1913-38	1750.00	2000.00	1850.00
☐ HN 23A, The Lavender Woman, 1913-38	1750.00	2000.00	1850.00
☐ HN 24, Sleep, 1913-38	2200.00	2250.00	2300.00
☐ HN 24A, Sleep, 1913-38	2200.00	2400.00	2300.00
☐ HN 25, Sleep, 1913-38	2500.00	2800.00	2650.00
☐ HN 25A, Sleep, 1913-38	2500.00	2800.00	2650.00
☐ HN 26, The Diligent Scholar, 1913-38	1750.00	2000.00	1125.00

SAMPLERS

DESCRIPTION: Samplers are needlework pieces using a variety of stitches.

TYPES: Most common are samplers that feature the alphabet along with the name of the girl who did the work, the date and some decoration. Specialized samplers, which are more rare, feature such designs as maps, genealogy and mourning scenes.

PERIOD: The oldest samplers date back to 16th century England, while the oldest American samplers date to the 18th century.

ORIGIN: Samplers were first made by schoolgirls as part of their schoolwork.

COMMENTS: Most samplers found today date from the 18th to the mid-19th centuries. European samplers tend to be less valuable than American ones, though value is determined by color choice, design, needlework ability and condition.

A sampler on a colored background is usually more valuable than one on a natural linen colored background. Samplers with personal inscriptions and bright scenes are also sought after. A sampler in its original frame adds to its value.

ADDITIONAL TIPS: The listings are in alphabetical order according to sampler design.

Sampler, *wool and linen, Nova Scotia, c. 1840s, 17", $1000.00-$2000.00*

	Current Price Range		P/Y Average
☐ **Adam and Eve,** in good condition, c. 1740	35000.00	37000.00	35000.00
☐ **Alphabet,** 19th century	700.00	1200.00	900.00
☐ **Alphabet,** script and block letters, c. 1800	900.00	1200.00	1050.00
☐ **Alphabet and Flowers,** c. 1855	350.00	500.00	425.00
☐ **Alphabet and Numbers,** c. 1842	350.00	500.00	400.00
☐ **Alphabet,** bands of alphabets, floral panels, red, green, blue and brown stitches on linen, c. 1840	1200.00	1400.00	1250.00
☐ **Alphabet,** bands of alphabets, inscription, c. 1800	1300.00	1500.00	1350.00
☐ **Alphabet,** bands of alphabets and numbers, vine borders and flowering urns, c. 1820	400.00	550.00	475.00
☐ **Alphabet,** geometric designs, long horizontal shape, c. 1680	1600.00	2400.00	1800.00
☐ **Alphabet,** three bands of alphabets, dog, cat, house, c. 1840	500.00	700.00	575.00
☐ **Alphabet,** wool stitches on linen, 19th century	450.00	600.00	525.00

	Current Price Range		P/Y Average
☐ **Cain and Abel,** c. 1800	850.00	1050.00	925.00
☐ **Farmhouse,** with "God Bless This House," c. 1840	600.00	800.00	700.00
☐ **Patriotic,** "The Union Forever," nineteenth century	1000.00	1400.00	1180.00
☐ **Landscape,** house and paths, probably from New England	1100.00	1450.00	1250.00
☐ **Landscape,** house, birds, cow, c. 1830	700.00	900.00	800.00
☐ **Landscape,** trees, flowers and animals, inscription, c. 1840	500.00	800.00	650.00
☐ **Scene,** farmyard with animals, c. 1820	800.00	1000.00	875.00
☐ **Scene,** snowy landscape, probably New England, c. 1820-1840	1300.00	1700.00	1475.00
☐ **Scene,** "View of Walton's Inn," large building, walled garden, figures, animals, c. 1810	2000.00	2900.00	2400.00
☐ **Traditional,** c. 1830	375.00	475.00	400.00
☐ **Tree,** with various flowers, bright colors, 18th century	750.00	950.00	850.00

SATURDAY EVENING GIRLS

COMMENTS: Teenage girls belonging to the Saturday Evening Girls Club of Boston, Massachusetts produced this pottery. Although the company was called Paul Revere Pottery, many collectors refer to the pottery as Saturday Evening Girls or S.E.G. since this is usually the mark found on the ware.

Under the direction of Edith Brown, the girls made a wide variety of ware including vases, bowls, pitchers, jars, mugs, candlesticks, tiles and children's dishes.

The pottery closed in 1942, ten years after Edith Brown's death.

MARKS: S.E.G. placed in a bowl design is often used. Also used was a paper label of a man on a horse and Revere Pottery printed underneath.

☐ **Bowl,** 5½", silver and blue flecks, marked S.E.G.	65.00	75.00	62.00
☐ **Bowl,** speckled motif, footed, marked S.E.G. . .	70.00	80.00	72.00

	Current Price Range		P/Y Average
☐ **Egg Cup,** *blue, chicken motif*	40.00	50.00	42.00
☐ **Pitcher,** *3½ ", cream background, tree, mountain and sky scene, marked S.E.G.*	340.00	360.00	345.00
☐ **Plate,** *8", yellow, marked S.E.G.*	20.00	30.00	22.00
☐ **Plate,** *rabbit motif in center, marked S.E.G.* . .	280.00	310.00	285.00
☐ **Vase,** *15", green glaze, marked S.E.G., 1915* .	240.00	260.00	245.00

SCHOENHUT DOLLS AND TOYS

COMMENTS: When Albert Schoenhut arrived in America from Wurttenberg Germany at the age of 17, he was already an accomplished wood carver. The Schoenhut family had been wood carvers in Germany for generations. Albert continued this family tradition, teaching the trade to his six sons and, in the 1870s, the Schoenhut family opened a toy factory in Philadelphia, Pennsylvania. However, it was not until 1911 that he began to market his unique all wood dolls. These first Schoenhut dolls had swivel necks and spring jointed bodies with a hole in the bottom of each foot which permitted the use of a stand for display purposes.

When Albert Schoenhut died in 1912, his sons carried on the Schoenhut doll and toy business. In 1913, Albert's oldest son designed a bent-limb baby and toddler doll, and in the 1920s a less expensive elastic jointed doll was introduced into production. Before it ceased operation in the 1930s, Schoenhut also marketed a fully jointed, all composition doll.

RECOMMENDED READING: For further information consult *The Official Price Guide to Collectible Toys* and *The Official Price Guide to Antique and Modern Dolls* published by The House of Collectibles.

☐ **Acrobat,** *wooden toy man, hinged at hips, tall molded red fez and tassel, goatee and moustache, two-piece brown patterned cotton suit, 7"*	60.00	70.00	63.00
☐ **Baby,** *all wood, molded wooden head, doweled bent limb wooden body, painted blue eyes, open/closed moth, 12"*	350.00	450.00	350.00

Clown, Roly-Poly,
Schoenhut, musical, 14",
$35.00-$45.00

	Current Price Range		P/Y Average
☐ **Baby,** *bent limb, blonde skin wig, closed mouth, 11"*	350.00	400.00	365.00
☐ **Baby,** wooden head, bent limb body, painted eyes, no eyebrows, closed mouth, individually modeled fingers, dark skin tone, wearing a vertically striped infant's suit with rounded collar and tam o'shanter cap, marked H.E. Schoenhut/1913, 14½"	200.00	250.00	215.00
☐ **Baby Character,** *wooden head, jointed wooden body, brown intaglio eyes, original wig, pouty mouth, original clothes and shoes, 21"*	1200.00	1300.00	1200.00
☐ **Baby,** wooden construction carved features, ball-joint body, painted eyes, open mouth, layette suit with bonnet, c. 1911, 12"	300.00	400.00	325.00
☐ **Boy,** carved wooden head and spring jointed wood body, painted brown eyes, with blonde wig, two-piece black velvet suit and white shirt, paint peeling across fahe, marks: Schoenhut Doll Pat. Jan. 17'11, USA, 14"	95.00	100.00	200.00
☐ **Boy,** sombre face, blonde wig, sailor suit, 16"	350.00	400.00	365.00

	Current Price Range		P/Y Average

☐ **Boy,** *spring jointed, bald, painted blue eyes, partially open mouth* .... 400.00 450.00 — 410.00

☐ **Boy,** *wooden, blue painted eyes, closed pouty mouth, striped woolen suit, marked head and marked incised body* .... 550.00 650.00 — 550.00

☐ **Circus Clown,** *wooden, striped cotton suit in green, pink, and white, large red feet, 8"* .... 90.00 100.00 — 92.00

☐ **Dolly Face,** *brown mohair wig, 22"* .... 275.00 325.00 — 295.00

☐ **Dolly Face,** *red pigtail mohair wig, sticker, 17"* .... 225.00 275.00 — 240.00

☐ **Dolly Face,** *15½"* .... 400.00 450.00 — 420.00

☐ **Female Acrobat,** *wood, painted eyes, molded and painted hair, jointed at neck, arms and legs, wearing a fabric outfit of pink and green, 8"* .... 250.00 300.00 — 265.00
Note: sold as an accessory in the company's Humpty Dumpty Circus set.

☐ **Girl,** *all-wood, jointed wooden body, blue intaglio eyes, brown wig, dressed in sailor suit, 16"* .... 625.00 725.00 — 600.00

☐ **Girl,** *character, wooden head, jointed wooden body, pouty, brown wig, painted features, original clothes, 16"* .... 900.00 1000.00 — 950.00

☐ **Girl,** *molded brown pulled over ears and tied in back with molded blue ribbon, fully jointed wooden body, painted blue eyes, pink gingham dress, 16"* .... 975.00 1175.00 — 900.00

☐ **Girl,** *sombre face, blonde wig, 15"* .... 350.00 400.00 — 360.00

☐ **Lady Bareback Rider,** *bisque head, painted blue eyes, brown hair, pink and green outfit, 7½"* .... 425.00 475.00 — 440.00

☐ **Pouty,** *wooden head on spring jointed wooden body, painted blue intaglio eyes, new blonde human hair wig, wearing pink checked pinafore over white lace trimmed blouse, nose rub, discreet retouching of face, marks: oval label reads "Schoenhut Doll, Pat. Jan. 17th, 1911 U.S.A., 14"* .... 275.00 300.00 — 270.00

☐ **Ringmaster,** *wood, painted eyes, molded and painted hair with mustache and whiskers, jointed at neck, arms and legs, representing a circus ringmaster in traditional costume with tall hat, vest, tailed jacket and black polished riding boots, 8"* .... 250.00 300.00 — 245.00
Note: sold as an accessory in the Humpty Dumpty Circus set.

☐ **Rolly Dollys,** *clown, 9"* .... 100.00 150.00 — 120.00

☐ **Rolly Dollys,** *policeman, 7"* .... 90.00 110.00 — 98.00

☐ **Toddler,** *brown, mohair wig, painted eyes, partially open mouth, 11"* .... 350.00 450.00 — 365.00

☐ **Walker,** *wooden head, jointed wooden five piece body, painted blue eyes, blonde mohair wig, open/closed mouth, sailor suit, paper label* .... 400.00 575.00 — 425.00

	Current Price Range		P/Y Average
□ **Walker**, wooden, original mohair wig, blue painted eyes, closed pouty mouth, walker body, cute sailor suite, marked head and body, 16½"	695.00	850.00	650.00
□ **Walker**, wood, spring jointed, carved head, blue ribbon headband with bow in back, brown intaglio eyes, Schoenhut stick in back, original sailor suit, underwear and shoes, 14"	1500.00	1700.00	1450.00

SCOUTING

DESCRIPTION: Scouting memorabilia includes items for scouting groups including Boy Scouts, Cub Scouts, Camp Fire Girls, Brownies and Girl Scouts.

TYPES: All types of scouting treasures are considered collectible, from cloth badges to metal neckerchief rings and tools, backpacks, uniforms and manuals.

ORIGIN: Englishman Sir Robert S.S. Baden-Powell is the original founder of Boy Scouts and Girls Scouts in England.

The development of scouting in America is due to Daniel Carter Beard, William Boyce and James E. West for Boy Scouts of America, and Juliette Gordon Low for Girl Scouts of America. Both groups are separate and distinct.

COMMENTS: There are more collectors of Boy Scout treasures than of Girl Scout memorabilia. Prices are reasonable and fairly stable.

For more complete information, refer to *The Official Price Guide to Scouting Collectibles,* published by The House of Collectibles.

□ **Ash Tray**, Kit Carson House, Philmont, 1950 ..	7.00	8.50	7.25
□ **Bank**, Conn., has another scout behind kettle, 1915	250.00	325.00	275.00
□ **Bank**, tin lithographed scout, 1912	22.00	28.00	23.50
□ **Binoculars**, tan leather, 1920's	77.00	88.00	79.00
□ **Blotter**, BSA/Coca-cola, "Be Prepared, Be Refreshed"	6.00	8.00	7.00
□ **Belt**, belt and buckle, gun medal, 1930's	7.50	9.50	8.00

Badge Sash, $3.00-$7.50

	Current Price Range		P/Y Average
☐ **Bookends,** bronze metal, Girl Scout feeding rabbit	20.50	26.00	21.00
☐ **Bookends,** metal, first class Emblem 6″ x 6″	24.00	32.00	26.00
☐ **Bookmark,** green and gold, first class emblem, BSA National Council	4.25	5.50	4.75
☐ **Books,** Holy Bible, early BSA seal on cover	45.00	57.00	47.00
☐ **Cachet Cover,** Boy Scout stamp club, 1932	9.00	11.00	9.50
☐ **Calendar Holder,** cast metal, BSA perpetual, first class emblem	18.50	22.00	19.25
☐ **Camera,** Official 7-Piece flash camera kit	12.00	17.00	13.00
☐ **Canteen,** Wearever seamless, felt cover, 1930's	17.00	22.00	18.00
☐ **Cards,** 65 BSA job description cards, 1949-1962	5.00	7.00	5.50
☐ **Collar Monogram,** BSA, brass collar monograms, 1920's	40.00	60.00	46.00
☐ **Comb,** Official BSA comb and clippers in a case	4.00	7.00	5.00
☐ **Compass,** Sylva pathfinder, BSA	2.00	4.00	2.50
☐ **Cut Outs,** Camping with the Scouts, gummed paper in book form, 1930's	22.00	27.00	23.00
☐ **Drum,** "Boy Scout Drum" tin, 6″ round 3½″ high, 1908	40.00	60.00	44.00

	Current Price Range		P/Y Average
☐ **Figurine,** Head Scout, signaller, arms move, 2″	18.00	24.00	20.00
☐ **Figurine,** Kenner doll, Craig Cub Scout	15.00	21.00	17.00
☐ **Figurine,** Scout with pack and rifle, cardboard, 6″ high	4.50	5.50	4.75
☐ **Figurine,** Lead Scout kneeling, frying eggs ...	11.00	14.00	12.00
☐ **Figurine,** Scout plastic figure, tree and flag-pole, 3″	8.50	11.00	9.25
☐ **First Aid Kit,** Bauer and Black, gray, oval belt loop kit, rare, 1932	20.00	27.00	22.00
☐ **First Aid Kit,** Johnson and Johnson, swing clasp, 1942	16.00	22.00	17.50

SCRIMSHAW

TOPIC: Scrimshaw is artwork done on bone.

TYPES: Scrimshaw can be carved or painted. Carved scrimshaw, which seldom has any painted decoration, is mostly in the nature of little trinkets — boxes, pins or forks, for example. Painted scrimshaw is done directly on the tooth or bone. It is accomplished by scratching the design into the surface with needles, then working India ink into the scratches.

MATERIALS: Whalebone is the most commonly found material, followed by walrus tusk. Occasionally a low-grade ivory such as whale tooth is used.

COMMENTS: The age, size, artistic quality, subject matter and state of preservation all go into determining the value of scrimshaw.

☐ **Box,** whalebone and wood, 10″ L.	525.00	775.00	650.00
☐ **Bust of Man,** 4″ H.	150.00	250.00	200.00
☐ **Cane,** dove on knob, brass tip, 38″ H.	380.00	480.00	430.00
☐ **Carpenter's Molding Plane,** 9½″ L.	540.00	640.00	590.00
☐ **Carpenter's Square,** teakwood handle	160.00	200.00	180.00
☐ **Corset Stays,** whalebone, home scenes, 14″ L.	200.00	250.00	225.00
☐ **Hammer,** dolphin on handle, 7″ L.	270.00	330.00	300.00
☐ **Horn,** 10″ L., c. 19th c.	210.00	250.00	230.00
☐ **Napkin Holder,** with cats	50.00	70.00	60.00
☐ **Pie Crimper,** fancy with rosewood handle	180.00	220.00	200.00
☐ **Walrus' Tusk,** cribbage board	900.00	1200.00	1050.00
☐ **Walrus' Tusk,** dagger, 10″ L.	130.00	170.00	150.00

Powderhorn, *scrimshaw, 1700s,* **$4500.00-$4700.00**
(photo courtesy of ©Marc Bernsau, Sanford, ME, 1984)

	Current Price Range		P/Y Average
☐ **Walrus' Tusk,** Indians, 6″ L.	680.00	880.00	780.00
☐ **Walrus' Tusk,** mother and child on swing, 11″ L.	470.00	630.00	550.00
☐ **Whale's Tooth,** crucifix, 6″ L.	290.00	390.00	340.00
☐ **Whale's Tooth,** eagle and flag, 5″ L.	580.00	780.00	680.00
☐ **Whale's Tooth,** children playing	590.00	810.00	700.00
☐ **Whale's Tooth,** whaling scene, 5″ L.	680.00	880.00	780.00

SEARS-ROEBUCK CATALOGS

COMMENTS: Sears Roebuck catalogs were first collected in the 1960s. They are still popular and prices, especially for rare or mint copies, tend to be high.

CONDITION: Condition standards for such catalogs are fairly liberal, because they were large, soft bound and received much use.

ADDITIONAL TIPS: The listings are in chronological order with a price range.

Sears Catalog,
general catalog no. 111,
50¢ cover price,
1902, **$100.00-$125.00**

	Current Price Range		P/Y Average
☐ **1897,** general catalogue, Chicago, IL	200.00	250.00	220.00
☐ **1899,** general catalogue	175.00	225.00	200.00
☐ **1900-1910,** most editions, food, groceries, tobacco	50.00	65.00	55.00
☐ **1902,** general catalogue #111, 50¢ cover price .	120.00	140.00	130.00
☐ **1902,** general catalogue, 1969 reprint (Crown Pub., NY)	10.00	15.00	12.00
☐ **1905,** general catalogue	130.00	155.00	140.00
☐ **1906,** general catalogue	145.00	175.00	155.00
☐ **1907,** general catalogue, 1,240 pages	150.00	185.00	160.00
☐ **1908,** general catalogue, 1,232 pages	175.00	200.00	185.00
☐ **1910,** general catalogue, spring and summer, 1,182 pages	175.00	200.00	185.00
☐ **1911-1920,** most editions, food, groceries, tobacco	40.00	55.00	47.00
☐ **1916,** furniture	60.00	85.00	73.00
☐ **1922,** general catalogue, spring and summer .	125.00	145.00	135.00
☐ **1926,** general catalogue, autumn and winter ..	110.00	130.00	120.00
☐ **1931,** general catalogue, spring and summer .	110.00	140.00	125.00
☐ **1944,** general catalogue, autumn and winter ..	80.00	110.00	95.00
☐ **1947,** Christmas catalogue	45.00	60.00	53.00
☐ **1949,** general catalogue, autumn and winter ..	40.00	55.00	47.00
☐ **1951,** business equipment	8.00	12.00	10.00
☐ **1951,** Christmas catalogue	35.00	45.00	40.00
☐ **1955,** general catalogue, spring and summer .	27.00	40.00	32.00
☐ **1960,** Christmas catalogue	20.00	30.00	25.00
☐ **1963,** general catalogue, autumn and winter ..	18.00	28.00	23.00
☐ **1965-1975,** general catalogues, most editions	12.00	18.00	14.00

SHAKER

DESCRIPTION: The Shakers were a socio-religious organization formed in the 18th century. A very disciplined group with purity as the basis of their beliefs, Shaker doctrines were precise and leadership was strict.

PERIOD: Shaker items were made from the early 19th century to the 20th century. Most pieces date to the mid 19th century when Shaker communities were at their largest.

ORIGIN: A combination of the English Quaker Church and the French Prophets, the first Shaker society was formed in England in 1747. Formally called "The United Society of Believers in Christ's Second Appearing," they were nicknamed "Shakers" because of the devotional dancing they did in religious services.

English woman Ann Lee became the first spiritual leader and led a group to America in 1776 where they attracted many American converts.

COMMENTS: All Shaker products were made for practical use and they symbolized Shaker beliefs of purity, unity, simplicity and utility. Shakers used fine building techniques and did not hide carpentry details. Such details add charm and grace to Shaker pieces.

While much Shaker furniture was made for their own use, some was made for commercial sale.

ADDITIONAL TIPS: The listings are alphabetical according to item. Descriptions, dates and price ranges follow.

	Current Price Range		P/Y Average
☐ **Almanac,** 1885	65.00	85.00	75.00
☐ **Basket,** double handle, 7″	125.00	165.00	130.00
☐ **Basket,** cover, red-painted handle	232.00	280.00	250.00
☐ **Basket,** draining	85.00	110.00	95.00
☐ **Bed,** plain headboard with rounded edges, square legs with wooden casters, usually made of pine, c. 1850	450.00	550.00	400.00
☐ **Bed,** plain headboard and footboard, springs, carved wooden legs with casters, c. 1850	650.00	750.00	700.00
☐ **Bonnet,** woven with straw	150.00	190.00	170.00

Shaker Pantry Boxes, *set of five, ea.,* **$110.00-$175.00**

	Current Price Range		P/Y Average
☐ **Bookcase,** combination secretary and bookcase in two parts, simple molding, shelves, drawers, late 19th century	850.00	1000.00	925.00
☐ **Box,** oval or round, made of wood with overlapping, tapered fingers	140.00	175.00	150.00
☐ **Box,** 8½″ oval	117.50	150.00	130.00
☐ **Box,** 10½″ oval	137.50	175.00	150.00
☐ **Box,** pincushion	210.00	270.00	230.00
☐ **Box,** sewing	232.00	280.00	250.00
☐ **Bucket,** wood with handle and lid, 12″ high	127.50	160.00	140.00
☐ **Bucket,** 1 gallon, dove-tailed, fair condition	12.50	20.00	15.00
☐ **Candlestand,** round top, tapering pedestal, cabriole legs and snake feet, 19th century	300.00	450.00	325.00
☐ **Chair,** ladderback side chair, seat is either rush, wood splint or woven tape, 19th century	400.00	650.00	500.00
☐ **Chair,** ladderback armchair, mushroom post arms, tapering legs, seat usually of woven tape, 19th century	500.00	750.00	625.00
☐ **Chair,** rocking side chair, 19th century	550.00	750.00	650.00
☐ **Chair,** rocking armchair, 19th century	700.00	900.00	800.00
☐ **Chair,** rocking armchair with shawl rail, late 19th century	850.00	1000.00	925.00

	Current Price Range		P/Y Average

- ☐ **Chair,** dining, modified ladderback, built low so it could be placed under the dining table when not in use, 19th century .... 750.00 850.00 — 800.00
- ☐ **Chest,** blanket, storage, lifting top, drawers, c. 1830 .... 600.00 800.00 — 700.00
- ☐ **Chest,** storage, work, case has two drawers and one door, plain top with hinged drop leaves .... 600.00 750.00 — 675.00
- ☐ **Chest,** tall, several drawers with top drawers in pairs, early 19th century .... 975.00 1250.00 — 1100.00
- ☐ **Chest,** drawers with side cabinet .... 800.00 950.00 — 875.00
- ☐ **Clothes Hanger** .... 70.00 90.00 — 80.00
- ☐ **Clothes Hanger,** six-peg .... 55.00 75.00 — 65.00
- ☐ **Comb,** wood .... 26.00 34.00 — 30.00
- ☐ **Cradle,** simple carving, shaped hood, carved handholds and rockers, c. 1800 .... 550.00 700.00 — 625.00
- ☐ **Cupboard,** two sets of doors on top of each other, simple molding and slight cornice, c. 1850 .... 950.00 1250.00 — 1100.00
- ☐ **Desk,** slanted work area with opening lid, pedestal, cabriole legs, snake feet, c. 1850 ...... 600.00 850.00 — 775.00
- ☐ **Desk,** high, made for Shaker deacons, identical sets of everything so it could be shared, 19th century .... 975.00 1200.00 — 1100.00
- ☐ **Dry Sink,** rectangular drawer, doors, round sink, splashboard, corner shelf, c. 1850 ...... 500.00 750.00 — 625.00
- ☐ **Dust Pan** .... 60.00 80.00 — 70.00
- ☐ **Foot Stool,** decorated .... 232.00 285.00 — 260.00
- ☐ **Hay Winder With Rope** .... 50.00 70.00 — 60.00
- ☐ **Jelly Cupboard,** red stained wood, c. 1890 .... 525.00 625.00 — 575.00
- ☐ **Pegboard,** wood .... 210.00 270.00 — 230.00
- ☐ **Plantation Desk** .... 900.00 1200.00 — 1100.00
- ☐ **Rack,** spice dryer .... 190.00 230.00 — 210.00
- ☐ **Rocker,** ladderback, mushroom arms, splint seat .... 750.00 1000.00 — 850.00
- ☐ **Sap Bucket,** Enfield, New Hampshire .... 47.50 60.00 — 53.00
- ☐ **Sewing Stand,** sliding drawers so two people can use it at the same time, pedestal, cabriole legs, 19th century .... 550.00 750.00 — 650.00
- ☐ **Sewing Stand,** similar to desk with many small drawers, large work area, c. 1850 .... 750.00 900.00 — 825.00
- ☐ **Sideboard,** doors, work area, top board, 19th century .... 775.00 975.00 — 875.00
- ☐ **Soap Shaver** .... 102.50 130.00 — 115.00
- ☐ **Spinning Wheel** .... 325.00 400.00 — 370.00
- ☐ **Steps,** utility, also called one-stepper, two-stepper, etc. .... 250.00 350.00 — 300.00
- ☐ **Table,** dining, trestle table with plank top, 19th century .... 950.00 1200.00 — 1100.00
- ☐ **Table,** drop leaf, plain skirt, 19th century ..... 450.00 550.00 — 500.00
- ☐ **Table,** oval, top overlaps frame, often used in Shaker shops, 19th century .... 450.00 550.00 — 500.00
- ☐ **Table,** square, drawer, dove tailed skirting, c. 1850 .... 500.00 650.00 — 575.00
- ☐ **Washstand,** rectangular, dovetailed, boards shaped wash area, one drawer, 19th century .. 450.00 550.00 — 500.00

▭▭▭▭▭▭▭▭▭▭▭▭▭▭▭▭▭▭▭▭▭▭▭▭▭▭▭▭▭

SHAWNEE POTTERY

DESCRIPTION: The Shawnee Pottery Company was founded in 1937 in Zanesville, Ohio. Its first president was Addis Hull Jr. of the Hull pottery family which had been one of the leading factories in neighboring Crooksville. Discovering an Indian arrow on the grounds when the factory was being readied for opening led to the company being called Shawnee. Shawnee played up the Indian theme at various times in its history, notably with its line of corn-pattern dinnerware. This famous set in yellow and green was textured on every piece to resemble an ear of corn. It was officially known as Corn King, then as Corn Queen beginning in the mid 1950s. The final year of the Shawnee operations was 1961.

MARKS: The trademarks used by Shawnee usually carry the letters *U.S.A.*, together with the factory name and a mold number. A low mold number is not necessarily an indication of early production. Most pieces of Shawnee figureware and such novelties as toy banks, ashtrays, etc., can be easily dated (approximately) on the basis of style. The vases are a little more difficult to accurately date, but a collector who makes educated guesses will probably score more hits than misses.

RECOMMENDED READING: For more in-depth information on Shawnee pottery, you may refer to *The Offical Price Guide to Pottery and Porcelain* and *The Official Identification Guide to Pottery and Porcelain,* published by The House of Collectibles.

CORN LINE *(Introduced early 1940s)*

Perhaps the company's most popular line, this pattern was called Corn King before 1954. After the company installed John Bonistall as the new president, he changed the glaze to a darker green and renamed the line Corn Queen. The mark and number remained the same.

	Current Price Range		P/Y Average
☐ **Butter Dish,** *covered, marked Shawnee U.S.A. #72*	25.00	30.00	26.00
☐ **Bowl,** *large, marked Shawnee U.S.A. #6*	12.00	16.00	13.00
☐ **Bowl,** *mixing, marked Shawnee U.S.A. #5* . . .	10.00	14.00	11.00

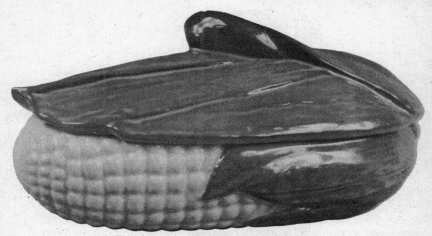

Dish, *Corn King Pattern,* **$30.00-$40.00**

	Current Price Range		P/Y Average
☐ **Bowl,** *small, marked Shawnee U.S.A. #94* ...	8.00	12.00	9.00
☐ **Casserole,** *11", covered, marked Shawnee U.S.A. oven proof #74*	25.00	35.00	26.00
☐ **Casserole,** *covered, marked Shawnee U.S.A. oven proof #73*	30.00	40.00	31.00
☐ **Cookie Jar,** *lidded, marked Shawnee U.S.A. #66*	45.00	55.00	46.00
☐ **Mug,** *marked Shawnee U.S.A. #69*	10.00	15.00	11.00
☐ **Pitcher,** *8½", marked Shawnee U.S.A. #71* ..	24.00	34.00	25.00
☐ **Pitcher,** *small, marked Shawnee U.S.A. #70* ..	8.00	11.00	9.00
☐ **Plate,** *dinner, marked Shawnee U.S.A. #68* ..	9.00	14.00	10.00
☐ **Platter,** *marked Shawnee U.S.A. oven proof #96*	14.00	18.00	15.00
☐ **Relish,** *oblong, marked Shawnee U.S.A. #79* .	14.00	18.00	5.00
☐ **Saucer,** *marked Shawnee U.S.A. #91*	4.00	7.00	5.00
☐ **Shakers,** *3½", salt and pepper, pair, no mark*	10.00	14.00	11.00
☐ **Shakers,** *5½", salt and pepper, no mark*	13.00	16.00	14.00
☐ **Sugar Bowl,** *covered, marked Shawnee U.S.A. #78*	7.00	12.00	8.00
☐ **Teacup,** *marked Shawnee U.S.A. #90*	4.00	6.00	5.00
☐ **Teapot,** *covered, marked Shawnee U.S.A. #75*	25.00	32.00	26.00

MISCELLANEOUS

☐ **Ashtray,** *oak leaf shape, blue, yellow and red blend, detailed vein lines, marked U.S.A. #350*	8.00	10.00	8.50
☐ **Ashtray,** *orange interior, brown exterior, marked U.S.A. #1014*	11.00	13.00	11.50
☐ **Basket,** *blue, swirled handled, marked Rum RILL#358*	30.00	35.00	31.00
☐ **Bookends,** *pair, two dark green and red flying geese on each bookend, bottom decorated with flowers, marked Shawnee U.S.A. #4000* .	16.00	20.00	17.00

Cookie Jar, *pig,*
$35.00-$40.00

	Current Price Range		P/Y Average
☐ **Bowl,** *blue, ruffled edge, marked Shawnee U.S.A. #2500*	11.00	14.00	12.00
☐ **Bowl,** *green and white, ruffled edge, marked Shawnee U.S.A. #2507*	11.00	13.00	12.00

SHEET MUSIC

DESCRIPTION: Sheet music is a musical composition.

COMMENTS: Condition and rarity determine the value of sheet music. Specimens are not always in top condition due to music store stamps, tape marks, staples, binder holes and ownership signatures. Worn copies sell for considerably less than those in good or mint condition.

ADDITIONAL TIPS: Often prices in major hobby marketplaces such as New York and California are higher than prices in more remote areas. Collectors should also beware of high prices placed on sheet music at flea markets.

For more information, consult *The Official Price Guide to Radio, TV and Movie Memorabilia,* or *The Official Price Guide to Music,* both published by The House of Collectibles.

	Current Price Range		P/Y Average
☐ **After I've Called You Sweetheart (How Can I Call You Friend),** words by Bernie Grossman, music by Little Jack Little, pub. Milton Weil, inset Little Jack Little, c. 1927	3.00	5.00	4.00
☐ **Alexander's Ragtime Band,** by Irving Berlin, pub. Standard Music (reprint)	2.00	3.00	2.50
☐ **All I Want Is You,** lyric and music by Benny Davis, Harry Akst and Sidney Clare, Starmer cover, inset Corinne Arbuckle, c. 1927	3.00	5.00	4.00
☐ **Along The Santa Fe Trail,** words by Al Dubin and Edwina Coolidge, music by Will Grosz, pub. Harms, 1940	3.50	4.50	4.00
☐ **Around The World In 80 Days,** words by Harold Adamson, music by Victor Young, pub. Victor Young, 1956	2.50	3.50	3.00
☐ **Bebe,** lyric by Sam Coslow, music by Abner Silver, pub. W, inset Bebe Daniels, c. 1923 . .	2.00	4.00	3.00
☐ **Breeze (Blow My Baby Back to Me),** by Ballard MacDonald, Joe Goodwin and James F. Hanley, small inset Owsley and O'Day, black face, c. 1919	3.00	5.00	4.00
☐ **Champagne Waltz, The,** by Con Conrad, Ben Oakland and Milton Drake, inset Fred MacMurray and Gladys Swarthout, pub. Famous Music	2.50	5.00	3.75
☐ **Climb Every Mountain,** words by Oscar Hammerstein, II, music by Richard Rodgers, pub. Williamson Music, 1959	2.00	4.00	3.00
☐ **Cryin' For The Carolines,** words by Sam Lewis and Joe Young, music by Harry Warren, 1930	2.50	5.00	3.75
☐ **Desert Song, The,** words by Otto Harbach, Oscar Hammerstein, II and Frank Mandel, music by Sigmund Romberg, 1926	3.00	7.00	5.00
☐ **As above,** different cover issued when picture was released, inset Dennis Morgan and Irene Manning	2.00	4.00	3.00
☐ **Did You Ever See A Dream Walking,** words by Mack Gordon, music by Harry Revel, insets Jack Oakie, Jack Haley and Ginger Rogers, 1933	3.50	7.00	4.20
☐ **Ending With A Kiss,** words by Harlan Thompson, music by Lewis E. Gensler, inset Lanny Ross and Mary Boland, pub. Famous, 1934 .	3.50	7.50	5.50
☐ **Faithful Forever,** words and music by Ralph Grainger	2.50	5.00	3.50

	Current Price Range		P/Y Average
☐ **From The Top Of Your Head To The Tip Of Your Toes,** words and music by Mack Gordon and Harry Revel, photo Bing Crosby and Joan Bennett, pub. Crawford, 1935	2.50	5.00	3.50
☐ **Good Night Angel,** words by Herb Magidson, music by Allie Wrubel, insets Bob Burns, Jack Oakie, Kenny Baker, Milton Berle, Ann Miller, Helen Broderick, Hal Kemp, Jane Fromna, Victor Moore, Eric Blore	3.00	7.00	5.00
☐ **Happy Days Are Here Again,** words by Jack Yellen, music by Milton Ager, 1929	3.00	7.00	5.00

SHENANDOAH VALLEY POTTERY

DESCRIPTION: The Shenandoah Valley in Maryland and Virginia became known for its varied, brightly colored pottery. The most notable of the many potters was Peter Bell, Jr., who operated in Hagerstown, Maryland and then Winchester, Virginia from 1800-1845. Bell's sons John, Solomon and Samuel also started potteries. John established his pottery at Waynesboro, Pennsylvania in 1833, while Solomon and Samuel began a pottery in Strasburg, Virginia. Their descendants continued to run the potteries in the early 20th century. Shenandoah Valley redware pottery is eagerly sought by collectors because of the colorful glazes found in each piece.

MARKS: Although the Shenandoah Valley Pottery includes several companies, the concentration here is on the Bell family. Since both father and sons owned their own companies, the marks are made up of several names. They include: S. Bell & Son, Strasburg; S. Bell, Strasburg; John Bell, Waynesboro, Pennsylvania; Solomon Bell, Strasburg; or Upton Bell, Waynesboro, Pa.

	Current Price Range		P/Y Average
Bowl, 15", white, handled, marked S. Bell & Son, Strasburg	420.00	435.00	425.00
Cuspidor, 6¾" redware with cream, green and brown	190.00	200.00	192.00
Flowerpot, 8", brown and green, flared body, marked S. Bell & Sons, Strasburg	140.00	160.00	142.00
Flowerpot, 8", bulbous body, scroll design, cream, green and brown, handled, marked S. Bell & Son	320.00	340.00	322.00
Dish, 9", marked Upton Bell, Waynesboro, Pa.	140.00	160.00	142.00
Dish, 10", circular shape, green, orange and cream, marked S. Bell & Son, Strasburg	540.00	560.00	545.00
Figurine, 3½", lamb, sleeping position, cream, green and brown	1700.00	1750.00	1720.00
Figurine, 4", dog, yellow, orange and brown, oval base	1350.00	1375.00	1355.00
Figurine, 8", dog, seated, basket and bottle in mouth, black and brown	2300.00	2350.00	2310.00
Figurine, 9", dog, cream and black, marked John Bell, Waynesboro, Pennsylvania	1100.00	1400.00	1150.00
Jar, 4¾", cylinder body, straight sides, narrow neck, white, green and brown with redware	345.00	355.00	345.00
Jar, 9½", gray with three blue floral designs on shoulder, marked S. Bell & Son, Strasburg, c. 1882	130.00	140.00	132.00
Jar, 9½", blue flower design, marked Solomon Bell, Strasburg	180.00	190.00	182.00
Pitcher, 6½", brown and green, marked S. Bell, Strasburg	345.00	355.00	347.00
Pitcher, 9", handled, gray and green, angels and grapevine motif, marked John Bell, Waynesboro, Pennsylvania	840.00	860.00	842.00
Pitcher, 10¼", bulbous green body, tall brown neck, marked John Bell, Waynesboro, Pennsylvania	540.00	560.00	545.00
Pitcher, 10½", cylinder shape, one handle, green, brown and cream	670.00	685.00	672.00
Pitcher, 16", bulbous body, small handles, flower design, marked Solomon Bell, Strasburg	370.00	385.00	372.00

◨▬◨▬◨▬◨▬◨▬◨▬◨▬◨▬◨▬◨

SHIP MODELS

TOPIC: Ship models are small replicas of ships that may or may not have actually been full-size sailing vessels.

TYPES: There are four main types of ship models: the wright's model, the sailor's model, the collector's model and the kit model. The wright's model is made by a shipwright (a ship builder) as a working model for an actual ship. The sailor's model is one made while the sailor served on that actual ship, for the purpose of selling when the ship called at port or for presentation to a relative. A collector's model is one made long after the ship itself was constructed, and often after it ceased to exist, by using photographs or drawings in books. Finally, a kit model is built from components and directions furnished in a commercially sold kit.

COMMENTS: Wright's models are the most desirable and expensive. Sailor's models may be crude, but they are highly regarded by collectors. The value of a collector's model is determined by age, size, intricacy of detail and state of preservation.

ADDITIONAL TIPS: Models of steamships, no matter how big or how nicely done, are not as valuable in the collector market as sailing vessels.

	Current Price Range		P/Y Average
☐ **American cargo ship "Explorer,"** masts and sails, mounted on a metal base, well-preserved except for portions of the rigging, 27″ L., c. 1880	700.00	900.00	800.00
☐ **American gunner "Victory,"** meticulous workmanship, some detail work damaged, overall well-preserved, mounted on a new stand made of polished walnut, 41″ L., c. 1900	1400.00	1900.00	1650.00
☐ **American battleship "Kentucky,"** the hull carved from a solid block of wood, painted, traces of original paint, one mast restored, the sails not original, mounted on a wooden platform painted deep blue, 19″ L., c. 1870 . .	1100.00	1500.00	1300.00

	Current Price Range		P/Y Average

☐ **American battleship "Maine,"** the guns made of real brass, figures of seamen in carved wood, tins and crates on board, the work of a master modeler, 24″ L., c. 1890 ... **2500.00 3000.00 2750.00**

☐ **American cargo ship "Explorer,"** masts and sails, mounted on a metal base, well-preserved except for portions of the rigging, 27″ L., c. 1880 .... **900.00 1200.00 1050.00**

☐ **American gunner "Victory,"** meticulous workmanship, some detail work damaged, overall well-preserved, mounted on a new stand made of polished walnut, 41″ L., c. 1900 .... **1700.00 2200.00 1950.00**

☐ **English battleship "Great Harry,"** brass guns, made largely of oak, some components of other wood, gilded work with most of the original gilding intact, rare model, probably English or Scottish, of a ship dating to the 16th c., 57″ L., c. 1810 .... **6100.00 9100.00 7600.00**

☐ **English liner "Titanic,"** wood and metal painted in various shades of gray, mounted on wooden stand, American or English, 32″ L., recent **850.00 1100.00 975.00**

☐ **English liner "Queen Mary,"** wood and metal, scale built by a modeler down to the smallest detail, rubber life preservers, scale-built lifeboats, etc., mounted on a copper and wood stand with engraved nameplate, 55″ L., c. 1940 .... **3900.00 5300.00 4600.00**

☐ **English schooner "Admiral V,"** 26″ L., c. 1900 .... **450.00 590.00 520.00**

☐ **German-built model of an unnamed sailing ship,** 15th c. design, well detailed, weathered wood, wormholes, some parts restored, unmounted, c. 1750-1800 .... **2200.00 3200.00 2700.00**

☐ **Model of an early Viking sailing ship,** 10th or 11th c. A.D., wood and canvas, probably German (not entirely accurate in design), 31″ L., c. 1860 .... **1900.00 2300.00 2100.00**

SHIRLEY TEMPLE DOLLS

COMMENTS: Child star Shirley Temple captured the heart of America during the 1930s and 40s. There is a tremendous interest in Shirley Temple collectibles today and a huge variety of items to choose from. Dolls are listed here.

RECOMMENDED READING: For in-depth information on all kinds of Shirley Temple collectibles refer to *The Official Price Guide to Radio, TV and Movie Memorabilia, The Official Price Guide to Collectible Toys* and *The Official Price Guide to Antique and Modern Dolls,* published by The House of Collectibles.

IDEAL

	Current Price Range		P/Y Average
☐ Shirley Temple, *Captain January, c.1982, 8"* .	22.00	27.00	22.50
☐ Shirley Temple, *Heidi, c.1982, 8"*	22.00	27.00	22.50
☐ Shirley Temple, *Heidi, c.1982, 12"*	33.00	43.00	35.00
☐ Shirley Temple, *Little Colonel, c.1982, 8"*	22.00	27.00	22.50
☐ Shirley Temple, *Little Colonel, c.1982, 12"* ...	33.00	43.00	35.00
☐ Shirley Temple, *Little Miss Marker, c.1983, 8"*	12.00	16.00	12.50
☐ Shirley Temple, *Little Miss Marker, c.1983, 12"*	17.00	22.00	17.50
☐ Shirley Temple, *Littlest Rebel, c.1982, 8"*	22.00	27.00	22.50
☐ Shirley Temple, *Poor Little Rich Girl, c.1983, 8"*	12.00	17.00	12.50
☐ Shirley Temple, *Poor Little Rich Girl, c.1983, 12"*	17.00	22.00	17.50
☐ Shirley Temple, *Rebecca of Sunnybrook Farm, c.1983, 8"*	12.00	17.00	12.50
☐ Shirley Temple, *Rebecca of Sunnybrook Farm, c.1983, 12"*	17.00	22.00	17.50
☐ Shirley Temple, *Stand Up and Cheer, c.1982, 8"*	22.00	27.00	22.50
☐ Shirley Temple, *Stowaway, c.1982, 8"*	22.00	27.00	22.50
☐ Shirley Temple, *Stowaway, c.1982, 12"*	33.00	43.00	35.00
☐ Shirley Temple, *Susannah of the Mounties, c.1983, 8"*	12.00	17.00	12.50

Shirley Temple, *Ideal,*
composition, c. 1930,
$560.00-$660.00

	Current Price Range		P/Y Average
☐ **Shirley Temple,** *Susannah of the Mounties,* *c.1983, 12"*	17.00	24.00	17.50
☐ **Shirley Temple,** *Wee Willie Winkle, c.1983, 8"*	12.00	17.00	12.50
☐ **Shirley Temple,** *Wee Willie Winkle, c.1983, 12"*	17.00	22.00	17.50
☐ **Shirley Temple,** *all composition, 27"*	300.00	360.00	330.00
☐ **Shirley Temple,** *all composition, 25"*	175.00	200.00	187.00
☐ **Shirley Temple,** *all composition, 23"*	155.00	200.00	165.00
☐ **Shirley Temple,** *all composition, 18"*	125.00	150.00	135.00
☐ **Shirley Temple,** *all composition, 17"*	120.00	140.00	133.00
☐ **Shirley Temple,** *all composition, 16"*	120.00	140.00	133.00
☐ **Shirley Temple,** *all composition, 15"*	105.00	135.00	120.00
☐ **Shirley Temple,** *all composition, 13"*	70.00	85.00	72.00
☐ **Shirley Temple,** *all composition, 11"*	170.00	190.00	175.00
☐ **Shirley Temple,** *all composition, jointed, blonde curly mohair wig, brown sleep eyes, open mouth, six teeth, Heidi style dress and pinafore not original, c. 1938, marked on head and body: 13 SHIRLEY TEMPLE, 22"*	530.00	580.00	550.00

	Current Price Range		P/Y Average

☐ **Shirley Temple,** *all composition jointed neck, shoulders and hips, green sleep eyes, open smiling mouth, original full blonde mohair wig styled in ringlets, original red and white polka dot dress, marked: Original Shirley Temple dress tag, head and body signed Shirley Temple, 25"* 740.00   780.00   750.00

☐ **Shirley Temple,** *character, vinyl head, plastic body, jointed shoulders and hips, rooted hair painted eyes, smiling mouth, red-polka dot dress, original, mint, 16"* 72.00   82.00   75.00

☐ **Shirley Temple,** *composition, curly top, Shirley pin, polka dotted red and white dress, c. 1935, 22"* 560.00   660.00   600.00

☐ **Shirley Temple,** *composition, jointed body, glazed eyes, blonde wig, open smiling mouth, original clothes, marked on head and body: 13 SHIRLEY TEMPLE, 13"* 460.00   560.00   500.00

☐ **Shirley Temple,** *composition, jointed body, glazed eyes, blonde wig, open smiling mouth, original clothes, marked on head and body: 13 SHIRLEY TEMPLE, 25"* 725.00   825.00   750.00

☐ **Shirley Temple,** *composition, pink organdy dress, snap dress, 15"* 300.00   350.00   300.00

☐ **Shirley Temple,** *original, ruffled lace dress, 22"* 500.00   600.00   540.00

☐ **Shirley Temple,** *vinyl and hard plastic jointed neck, shoulders and hips, rooted blonde hair, green sleep eyes, smiling mouth with four porcelain teeth, dimples, original mint condition, petite 1957 model with complete wardrobe, all clothing tagged Shirley Temple, flannel nightgown with cap, pink ballet dress, two piece plaid dress with cap, Swiss dirndl, sunglasses and Shirley Temple pin and purse, wearing a pale yellow organdy dress, marked: Ideal Doll ST-12, 12"*   220.00   230.00   222.00

☐ **Shirley Temple,** *vinyl head, jointed vinyl body, vinyl wig, sleep eyes, sheer blue gown, c. 1950, 17"* 125.00   140.00   130.00

☐ **Shirley Temple,** *vinyl, print dress, marked: Ideal, 12"* 90.00   100.00   90.00

SHOTGUNS

TOPIC: A shotgun is a firearm that has a long, smooth barrel and fires "shot" (small pellets held together in a cartridge).

TYPES: A shotgun can be of many types, such as double barrel, semi-automatic, singleshot, slide action, bolt action or percussion. A double barrel shotgun has two barrels, which can be side-by-side or over-under. A semi-automatic ejects the spent case and cycles the new round into the chamber using energy from the fired round. A singleshot has no magazine and can only fire one shot. Slide action is a repeating action which uses a reciprocating forestock connected to the breechbolt. Bolt action is done manually by moving a reciprocating breechbolt. Percussion refers to the use of a percussion cap to ignite the powder charge.

ORIGIN: Firearms were developed in Europe.

MAKERS: Prominent manufacturers include Browning, Marlin, Remington and Winchester.

COMMENTS: Documented evidence of historical significance increases a gun's value to a marked degree. Any collectible firearm, even if in poor condition, should fetch at least twenty to thirty percent of the Very Good price. Refinished guns are worth signficantly less than their unrefinished counterparts which are still in good condition.

ADDITIONAL TIPS: For more information, please refer to *The Official Price Guide to Antique and Modern Firearms* by David Byron, published by The House of Collectibles.

Savage Model 110-C, $165.00-$230.00

	Current Price Range		P/Y Average

BROWNING

SHOTGUN, DOUBLE BARREL, OVER — UNDER

	Current Price Range		P/Y Average
☐ **Citori,** 12 gauge, trap grade, vent rib, checkered stock, modern	435.00	575.00	550.00
☐ **Citori,** 12 and 20 gauges, standard grade, vent rib, checkered stock, modern	425.00	550.00	535.00
☐ **Citori,** 12 and 20 gauges, skeet grade, vent rib, checkered stock, modern	435.00	575.00	550.00
☐ **Citori International,** 12 gauge, trap grade, vent rib, checkered stock, modern	485.00	625.00	600.00
☐ **Citori International,** 12 gauge, skeet grade, vent rib, checkered stock, modern	485.00	625.00	600.00
☐ **Citori Grade II,** various gauges, hunting model, engraved, checkered stock, single selective trigger, modern	670.00	885.00	850.00
☐ **Citori Grade II,** trap and skeet models, add 10%.			
☐ Citori Grade V, various gauges, fancy engraving, checkered stock, single selective trigger, modern	900.00	1400.00	1350.00

WINCHESTER REPEATING ARMS COMPANY

SHOTGUN, DOUBLE BARREL, OVER-UNDER

	Current Price Range		P/Y Average
☐ **Model 101,** 12 gauges, trap grade, Monte Carlo stock, single trigger, automatic ejector, engraved, modern	575.00	750.00	675.00
☐ **Model 101,** 12 gauges, trap grade, single trigger, automatic ejector, checkered stock, engraved, modern	575.00	750.00	675.00
☐ **Model 101,** 12 gauges, Mag. 3″, vent rib, single trigger, automatic ejector, checkered stock, engraved, modern	550.00	725.00	650.00
☐ **Model 101,** various gauges, skeet grade, single trigger, automatic ejector, checkered stock, engraved, modern	575.00	750.00	675.00
☐ **Model 101,** various gauges, featherweight, single trigger, automatic ejector, checkered stock, engraved, modern	575.00	750.00	675.00
☐ **Model 101,** 3 gauges set, skeet grade, single trigger, automatic ejector, checkered stock, engraved, modern	1100.00	1650.00	1325.00
☐ **Model 101 Field,** various gauges, vent rib, single trigger, automatic ejector, checkered stock, engraved, modern	500.00	725.00	612.00

SILHOUETTES

TOPIC: Silhouettes are profiles cut out of one color paper and attached to a background of contrasting color. They can have detail added in chalk, pen or watercolors.

PERIOD: Silhouettes became popular in the 1700s and did not fall from popular favor until the middle of the 1800s.

MAKERS: Famous silhouette artists include Martha Anne Honeywell, William Henry Brown, Sanders Nellis and Auguste Edouart. Any silhouette bearing the name of Jean Millette is a fake; this was a name created by forgers.

COMMENTS: The value of a silhouette depends on the age, quality and size of the specimen; the notoriety of the subject is also very important. Any information marked on the silhouette increases its value.

ADDITIONAL TIPS: Modern and semi-modern silhouettes are not valued in the collector market.

	Current Price Range		P/Y Average
☐ **Aaron Burr,** bust portrait, black watercolor. Signed Jos. Wood, dated 1812, 3″ x 2¾″	390.00	450.00	420.00
☐ **Admiral,** unidentified, English wax, bowled glass, gilt rim, 3½″ diameter	180.00	210.00	195.00
☐ **Charles Carroll Of Carrollton** (last surviving signer of the Declaration of Independence), holding trowel and cane, dated 1828, 13″ x 10″	260.00	390.00	325.00
☐ **Civil War Officer,** unidentified, violet paper against light pink background, matted and framed, believed to be of Virginia origin, 5½″ x 4″, c. 1865	195.00	260.00	220.00
☐ **Hon. Henry Clay,** bust portrait, inscribed J. W. Jarvis, dated 1810, 8″ x 6¼″	95.00	160.00	140.00
☐ **Couple,** in double frame, 19th-century	285.00	315.00	300.00

Portrait Silhouettes of Governor and Mrs. S.W. Kearney, *1840s,*
$400.00-$500.00

	Current Price Range		P/Y Average
☐ **Double Portrait,** of gentleman and lady, full length figures. Signed Aug. Edouart, dated 1844, 9″ x 7⅛″, Edouart was the Stradivari of silhouettists	225.00	325.00	275.00
☐ **Elderly Man,** unidentified, half-length profile. c. 1880	95.00	130.00	115.00
☐ **Miss Elizabeth Frobiser,** clad in bonnet, dress and white pantalettes. Signed Frith, dated 1821	325.00	390.00	360.00
☐ **Gentleman,** wearing top hat, landscape setting. Signed Aug. Edouart, dated 1829, 8⅞″ x 6⅝″	285.00	360.00	320.00
☐ **Alexander Hamilton,** bust portrait wearing frilled smock. Signed J. W. Jarvis, dated 1804, 4½″ x 3½″	520.00	650.00	575.00
☐ **Gentleman,** unidentified, English wax, 18th century style, 1¼″ high	290.00	320.00	305.00

SILVER

DESCRIPTION: Silver collectibles include all objects made of silver.

TYPES: All types of items are made from silver including tableware, household ornaments, artwork and jewelry.

MAKERS: American silverware includes both factory merchandise and items made by individual craftsmen. Some chief manufacturers include Gorham, Reed and Barton, Towle, Wallace, Rogers, Oneida, Reliance, Kirk and International.

MATERIALS: Silver is always alloyed with base metal, usually copper, in manufacturing. This is done to provide durability, as silver in its pure state is soft and vulnerable. The grade of silver is determined by the amount or percentage of alloy material contained. Sterling silver, the traditional American grade for silverware, is .925 fine.

ADDITIONAL TIPS: For more information, consult *The Official Price Guide to American Silver and Silver Plate,* published by The House of Collectibles.

VERSAILLES — STERLING	Current Price Range		P/Y Average
GORHAM — 1898 · Inactive			
☐ Bouillon Spoon.	25.00	30.00	25.00
☐ Citrus Spoon.	37.00	42.00	37.00
☐ Cocktail Fork.	25.00	30.00	25.00
☐ Cream Soup Spoon.	45.00	50.00	45.00
☐ Cream Soup Spoon, *small*.	35.00	40.00	35.00
☐ Demitasse Spoon.	20.00	25.00	20.00
☐ Dessert Spoon.	40.00	45.00	40.00
☐ Dinner Fork.	45.00	50.00	45.00
☐ Dinner Knife.	55.00	60.00	55.00
☐ Five O'Clock Teaspoon.	14.00	19.00	14.00
☐ Fruit Knife.	35.00	40.00	35.00
☐ Ice Cream Spoon.	40.00	45.00	40.00
☐ Iced Tea Spoon.	50.00	55.00	50.00
☐ Luncheon Fork.	35.00	40.00	35.00

Punch Bowl, *Tiffany "Chrysanthemum," c. 1895, diameter 17", 114 ounces,* **$7250.00**

	Current Price Range		P/Y Average
☐ Luncheon Knife.	43.00	48.00	43.00
☐ Salad Fork.	45.00	50.00	45.00
☐ Steak Knife.	35.00	40.00	35.00
☐ Teaspoon.	19.00	24.00	19.00
☐ Berry Spoon, *large.*	125.00	135.00	125.00
☐ Carving Fork.	65.00	70.00	65.00
☐ Cheese Scoop, *large.*	145.00	155.00	145.00
☐ Cold Meat Fork, *buffet fork.*	110.00	120.00	110.00
☐ Fish Fork.	40.00	45.00	40.00
☐ Fish Knife.	35.00	40.00	35.00
☐ Flat Server.	30.00	35.00	30.00
☐ Gravy Ladle.	95.00	100.00	95.00
☐ Ice Cream Fork.	40.00	45.00	40.00
☐ Jelly Server, *large.*	135.00	145.00	135.00
☐ Lettuce Fork.	95.00	100.00	95.00
☐ Nut Picks.	25.00	30.00	25.00
☐ Olive or Pickle Fork.	45.00	50.00	45.00
☐ Pie Server.	40.00	45.00	40.00
☐ Soup Ladle.	250.00	260.00	250.00
☐ Sugar Shell.	35.00	40.00	35.00
☐ Sugar Tongs.	45.00	50.00	45.00
☐ Tablespoon/Serving Spoon.	50.00	55.00	50.00

STAMPS

DESCRIPTION: Stamps are small pieces of printed paper, issued by post offices for the prepayment of postage. In most cases they have a gummed back which, when moistened, adheres to a letter or parcel. All U.S. stamps have had gummed backs, but certain early foreign stamps needed to be glued. In modern times, all stamps have had "perforations" by which they can easily be separated from each other. The first stamps of many nations including the U.S. did not have perforations, and had to be cut apart with scissors. These are called "imperforates". Due to the scissor cutting, which was rarely methodical, some "imperforates" have much larger or straighter margins than others.

ORIGIN: Postage stamps were introduced by Great Britain in 1840, and soon thereafter by other nations, the U.S. following in 1847. Prior to the first federally issued U.S. stamps, several city postmasters issued their own stamps. This was done in New York and St. Louis, as well as elsewhere. These are called "postmasters' provisionals" and are very rare in most cases.

MAKER: Today, all U.S. stamps are printed by the U.S. Department of Printing and Engraving in Washington, D.C. Our early stamps were printed under contract by private firms.

COMMENTS: Frequently called "the hobby of kings" (largely because of Britain's George V, an avid collector), stamp collecting is now enjoyed by more than 20 million persons in this country and a much larger total worldwide.

CONDITION AND CARE: It is vital to consider the condition of a stamp before purchasing it. Points such as a bent corner, a missing perforation, or a heavy cancel can greatly reduce the value of a stamp.

ADDITIONAL TIPS: Learn about the hobby before venturing after rarities or unusual pieces. Get a good magnifying glass and handle your stamps with tongs rather than fingers. Subscribe to one of the stamp periodicals and visit stamp shows as you have the opportunity.

More detailed information on stamps and their current values is available in *The Official Blackbook Price Guide to U.S. Stamps,* published by The House of Collectibles.

Scott No.			Fine Unused Each	Ave. Unused Each	Fine Used Each	Ave. Used Each
GENERAL ISSUES						
1847. FIRST ISSUE						
☐ 1	5¢	Red Brown	—	4250.00	1300.00	900.00
☐ 2	10¢	Black	—	16500.00	3275.00	2500.00
1875. REPRODUCTIONS OF 1847 ISSUE						
☐ 3	5¢	Red Brown	2425.00	2000.00	—	—
☐ 4	10¢	Black	3100.00	2475.00	—	—
1851-56. REGULAR ISSUE — IMPERFORATE						
☐ 5A	1¢	Blue (Ib)	—	—	3325.00	2600.00
☐ 6	1¢	Blue (Ia)	—	—	4100.00	3175.00
☐ 7	1¢	Blue (II)	675.00	500.00	175.00	125.00
☐ 8	1¢	Blue (III)	—	—	1575.00	1150.00
☐ 8A	1¢	Blue (IIa)	—	1325.00	800.00	590.00
☐ 9	1¢	Blue (IV)	435.00	350.00	135.50	90.00
☐ 10	3¢	Orange Brown (I)	—	1200.00	95.00	75.00
☐ 11	3¢	Dull Red (I)	275.00	195.00	14.00	9.75
☐ 12	5¢	Red Brown (I)	—	—	1480.00	1025.00
☐ 13	10¢	Green (I)	—	—	940.00	675.00
☐ 14	10¢	Green (II)	—	1150.00	435.00	330.00
☐ 15	10¢	Green (III)	—	1120.00	390.00	280.00
☐ 16	10¢	Green (IV)	—	—	1575.00	1250.00
☐ 17	12¢	Black	—	1500.00	340.00	245.00
1857-61. SAME DESIGNS AS 1851-56 ISSUE — PERF. 15						
☐ 18	1¢	Blue (I)	925.00	650.00	550.00	350.00
☐ 19	1¢	Blue (Ia)	—	—	2425.00	1825.00
☐ 20	1¢	Blue (II)	635.00	430.00	260.00	200.00
☐ 21	1¢	Blue (III)	—	2475.00	1175.00	850.00
☐ 22	1¢	Blue (IIIa)	700.00	525.00	300.00	210.00
☐ 23	1¢	Blue (IV)	—	1400.00	395.00	270.00
☐ 24	1¢	Blue (V)	190.00	135.00	50.00	37.00
☐ 25	3¢	Rose (I)	—	600.00	39.00	29.00
☐ 26	3¢	Dull Red (II)	130.00	75.00	10.00	7.00
☐ 26A	3¢	Dull Red (IIa)	180.00	130.00	28.00	21.00
☐ 27	5¢	Brick Red (I)	—	5750.00	1100.00	780.00
☐ 28	5¢	Red Brown (I)	—	1350.00	460.00	315.00
☐ 28A	5¢	Indian Red (I)	—	—	1435.00	1000.00
☐ 29	5¢	Brown (I)	875.00	600.00	340.00	215.00
☐ 30	5¢	Orange Brown (II)	1025.00	675.00	1150.00	780.00
☐ 30A	5¢	Brown (II)	500.00	360.00	275.00	190.00
☐ 31	10¢	Green (I)	—	3700.00	610.00	400.00
☐ 32	10¢	Green (II)...................	1520.00	1125.00	240.00	180.00
☐ 33	10¢	Green (III)	1475.00	1085.00	235.00	175.00
☐ 34	10¢	Green (IV)	—	—	1425.00	1065.00
☐ 35	10¢	Green (V)	295.00	185.00	140.00	100.00
☐ 36	12¢	Black (I)	435.00	295.00	135.00	90.00
☐ 36b	12¢	Black (II)..................	410.00	310.00	165.00	110.00
☐ 37	24¢	Gray Lilac.................	825.00	625.00	350.00	230.00
1893. COLUMBIAN ISSUE (N-H ADD 95%)						
☐ 230	1¢	Blue	300.00	220.00	60.00	42.00	.70	.48
☐ 231	2¢	Violet	280.00	200.00	55.00	38.00	.13	.09
☐ 231c	2¢	"Broken Hat" .	510.00	350.00	112.00	80.00	1.05	.65
☐ 232	3¢	Green	485.00	320.00	110.00	85.00	35.00	23.00
☐ 233	4¢	Ultramarine ...	875.00	700.00	165.00	120.00	13.73	11.00

Scott No.			Fine Unused Each		Ave. Unused Each	Fine Used Each	Ave. Used Each
☐ 234	5¢	Chocolate	1000.00	825.00	180.00	127.00	17.00	13.00
☐ 235	6¢	Purple........	950.00	775.00	175.00	125.00	62.00	47.00
☐ 236	8¢	Magenta......	915.00	650.00	170.00	115.00	21.00	15.00
☐ 237	10¢	Black Brown ..	1600.00	1275.00	320.00	215.00	15.00	11.00
☐ 238	15¢	Dark Green ...	2800.00	2300.00	445.00	320.00	145.00	115.00
☐ 239	30¢	Orange Brown .	3750.00	3000.00	625.00	450.00	215.00	170.00
☐ 240	50¢	Slate Blue	4500.00	3800.00	775.00	570.00	300.00	210.00
☐ 241	$1	Salmon.......	—	—	2580.00	2000.00	1075.00	700.00
☐ 242	$2	Brown Red	—	—	2715.00	1875.00	900.00	610.00
☐ 243	$3	Yellow Green ..	—	—	4600.00	3545.00	1625.00	1175.00
☐ 244	$4	Crimson Lake .	—	—	6000.00	4380.00	2100.00	1450.00
☐ 245	$5	Black	—	—	6775.00	4965.00	2465.00	1250.00

Scott No.			Mint Sheet	Plate Block	Fine Unused Each	Fine Used Each
1969. W. C. HANDY — MUSICIAN						
☐ 1372	6¢	Multicolored	10.50	1.25	.19	.06
1969. SETTLEMENT OF CALIFORNIA						
☐ 1373	6¢	Multicolored	10.50	1.25	.19	.06
1969. MAJOR JOHN WESLEY POWELL — GEOLOGIST						
☐ 1374	6¢	Multicolored	10.50	1.25	.19	.06
1969. ALABAMA STATEHOOD						
☐ 1375	6¢	Red, Yellow, Brown	10.50	1.25	.19	.06
1969. XI INTL. BOTANICAL CONGRESS						
☐ 1376	6¢	Multicolored	—	—	2.00	.10
☐ 1377	6¢	Multicolored	—	—	2.00	.10
☐ 1378	6¢	Multicolored	—	—	2.00	.10
☐ 1379	6¢	Multicolored	—	—	2.00	.10
1969. DARTMOUTH COLLEGE CASE						
☐ 1380	6¢	Green	13.00	1.50	.20	.06
1969. PROFESSIONAL BASEBALL CENTENARY						
☐ 1381	6¢	Multicolored	14.00	1.50	.30	.07
1969. INTERCOLLEGIATE FOOTBALL CENTENARY						
☐ 1382	6¢	Red & Green	13.00	1.50	.27	.06
1969. DWIGHT D. EISENHOWER MEMORIAL						
☐ 1383	6¢	Blue, Black & Red	8.00	1.50	.29	.06
1969. CHRISTMAS ISSUE						
☐ 1384	6¢	Multicolored	10.50	4.50	.27	.05
1969. HOPE FOR THE CRIPPLED						
☐ 1385	6¢	Multicolored	12.00	1.50	.27	.06
1969. WILLIAM M. HARNETT PAINTING						
☐ 1386	6¢	Multicolored	8.00	1.50	.27	.06

1970. COMMEMORATIVES

Scott No.		Mint Sheet	Plate Block	Fine Unused Each	Fine Used Each
1970. NATURAL HISTORY					
□ 1387	6¢ Multicolored	—	—	.22	.10
□ 1388	6¢ Multicolored	—	—	.22	.10
□ 1389	6¢ Multicolored	—	—	.22	.10
□ 1390	6¢ Multicolored	—	—	.22	.10
1970. MAINE STATEHOOD SESQUICENTENNIAL					
□ 1391	6¢ Multicolored	14.00	1.50	.32	.06
1970. WILDLIFE CONSERVATION — BUFFALO					
□ 1392	6¢ Black on Tan	14.00	1.50	.32	.06
1970-74. REGULAR ISSUE					
□ 1393	6¢ Blue Gray	18.00	1.25	.14	.06
□ 1393D	7¢ Light Blue	21.00	1.50	.16	.07
□ 1394	8¢ Black, Blue, Red	21.00	1.25	.16	.06

Scott No.		Fine Unused Plate Blk	Ave. Unused Plate Blk	Fine Unused Each	Ave. Unused Each	Fine Used Each	Ave. Used Each
1939. GOLDEN GATE INTERNATIONAL EXPOSITION (N-H ADD 25%)							
□ 852	3¢ Bright Purple	3.75	3.25	.25	.20	.10	.07
1939. NEW YORK WORLD'S FAIR (N-H ADD 20%)							
□ 853	3¢ Deep Purple	3.75	2.80	.25	.20	.10	.07
1939. WASHINGTON INAUGURATION SESQUICENTENNIAL (N-H ADD 20%)							
□ 854	3¢ Bright Red Violet	8.25	6.75	.32	.23	.15	.10
1939. BASEBALL CENTENNIAL (N-H ADD 20%)							
□ 855	3¢ Violet	9.00	7.00	.70	.55	.12	.09
1939. 25TH ANNIVERSARY PANAMA CANAL (N-H ADD 20%)							
□ 856	3¢ Deep Red Violet	10.00	8.00	.40	.32	.14	.09
1939. COLONIAL PRINTING TERCENTENARY (N-H ADD 20%)							
□ 857	3¢ Rose Violet	4.50	3.75	.30	.25	.12	.09
1939. 50TH ANNIVERSARY OF STATEHOOD (N-H ADD 20%)							
□ 858	3¢ Rose Violet	4.50	3.75	.35	.29	.12	.09
1940. FAMOUS AMERICANS SERIES							
AMERICAN AUTHORS (N-H ADD 20%)							
□ 859	1¢ Bright Blue Green	3.25	2.50	.13	.09	.12	.08
□ 860	2¢ Rose Carmine........	3.50	2.75	.20	.16	.14	.10
□ 861	3¢ Bright Red Violet	6.00	4.85	.22	.17	.10	.07
□ 862	5¢ Ultramarine..........	40.00	30.00	.80	.65	.42	.32
□ 863	10¢ Dark Brown	140.00	120.00	5.00	3.90	4.00	3.15
AMERICAN POETS (N-H ADD 20%)							
□ 864	1¢ Bright Blue Green	6.00	4.50	.18	.14	.19	.15
□ 865	2¢ Rose Carmine........	6.35	4.75	.18	.14	.12	.08
□ 866	3¢ Bright Red Violet	10.00	8.00	.25	.20	.10	.07
□ 867	5¢ Ultramarine..........	50.00	40.00	1.25	.95	.43	.32
□ 868	10¢ Dark Brown	145.00	125.00	7.00	5.50	5.00	3.85
AMERICAN EDUCATORS (N-H ADD 20%)							
□ 869	1¢ Bright Blue Green	6.00	4.85	.27	.22	.12	.08
□ 870	2¢ Rose Carmine........	6.00	4.85	.23	.18	.11	.08

STANGL POTTERY

HISTORY: Stangl was an outgrowth of the Fulper Pottery Company of Flemington, New Jersey. In 1910, J.M. Stangl assumed the post of ceramic engineer at Fulper and was directly responsible for much of its creative work during the next two decades. During the 1920s, Fulper with its business rapidly expanding bought out the old Anchor Pottery Company factory in Trenton. When the main Fulper plant was destroyed in a fire in 1929, the firm was reorganized as Stangl Pottery and Trenton became its headquarters. The Stangl Pottery Company was taken over by Pfaltzgraff, a division of Susquehanna Broadcasting Company of York, Pennsylvania in July 1878.

DESCRIPTION: The Stangl Pottery Company was one of the later producers of fine artware and dinnerware. Among its best-known works are the famous "Stangl birds" a series of statuettes released during the early part of World War I. These charming pieces were produced in limited numbers, probably because of the war, and are now valuable "finds". Stangl was also well known for its fine vases with rich colors and satiny glazes, similar to the wares turned out by Grueby (and then by Tiffany, which acquired Grueby) some 30 or 40 years earlier.

MARKS: It appears as though the first mark used by the Stangl Pottery Company was *STANGL USA*, without periods between the initial letters. This was followed by a series of others, including an oval mark in which the trade name of the line appears at the center, with *MADE IN TRENTON, U.S.A.* beneath. A more elaborate version has the name *STANGL, TRENTON, N.J.* within an oval, accompanied by such wording as *HAND-PAINTED, OVEN PROOF, COUNTRY GARDEN* or *HAND-PAINTED, GRANADA GOLD*, denoting different lines of ware.

RECOMMENDED READING: For more in-depth information on Stangl Pottery you may refer to *The Official Price Guide to Pottery and Porcelain*, published by The House of Collectibles.

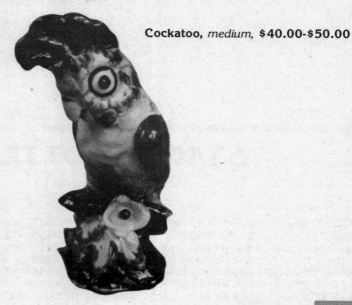

Cockatoo, *medium,* $40.00-$50.00

BIRDS

	Current Price Range		P/Y Average
☐ **Audubon Warbler,** item #3755, 4″	90.00	100.00	92.00
☐ **Bird Of Paradise,** item #2040	85.00	95.00	87.00
☐ **Bird Of Paradise,** item #3408	60.00	70.00	62.00
☐ **Blackpoll Warbler,** item #3810	40.00	50.00	42.00
☐ **Black Throated Warbler,** item #3814	55.00	70.00	57.00
☐ **Bluebird,** item #3276, 5″	80.00	90.00	82.00
☐ **Bluebirds,** item #32760, 5″, pair (resting on a single base)	135.00	150.00	140.00
☐ **Blueheaded Vireo,** item #3448, 4″	45.00	55.00	47.00
☐ **Bobalink,** item #3595, 4½ ″	80.00	90.00	82.00
☐ **Brewer's Blackbird,** item #3591	35.00	45.00	37.00
☐ **Cardinal,** item #3444, matt finish	60.00	70.00	62.00
☐ **Carolina Wren,** item #33590	55.00	65.00	57.00
☐ **Cerulean Warbler,** item #3456, 4¼ ″	40.00	50.00	42.00
☐ **Chat,** item #3590, 4″	50.00	60.00	52.00
☐ **Chestnut-backed Chickadee,** item #3811	80.00	90.00	82.00
☐ **Chestnut-sided Warbler,** item #3812, 5″	50.00	60.00	52.00
☐ **Chickadee Grouping,** item #3581	95.00	105.00	97.00
☐ **Cockatoo,** item #3405, 6″	40.00	50.00	42.00
☐ **Cockatoo, pair,** item #3405D, (resting on a single base)	75.00	85.00	77.00
☐ **Cockatoo,** item #3492, 9″	65.00	75.00	67.00
☐ **Cock Pheasant,** item #3492, 6″	120.00	135.00	122.00
☐ **Duck,** item #3250B	210.00	235.00	215.00
☐ **Duck,** item #3281, 4″	45.00	55.00	47.00
☐ **Duck In Flight,** item #3443, 8¾ ″	225.00	245.00	230.00
☐ **Duck, Preening,** item #3250, 2¾ ″	40.00	45.00	42.00
☐ **Evening Grosbeak,** 5″	75.00	88.00	77.00
☐ **Gold Crowned Kinglet,** 5¼ ″ x 5″, grouping ..	50.00	60.00	52.00

	Current Price Range		P/Y Average
☐ Golden Crowned Kinglet, item #3848, 4¼ " ..	50.00	60.00	52.00
☐ Goldfinch, item #3635, grouping (four birds resting on a single base)	155.00	165.00	160.00
☐ Goldfinch, item #3849	70.00	80.00	72.00
☐ Gray Cardinal, item #3596, 4½ "	55.00	70.00	57.00
☐ Gray Cardinal, item #3596, 5½ ", (larger version of the above)	65.00	75.00	67.00
☐ Hen, item #3446, 7"	75.00	85.00	72.00
☐ Hen Pheasant, item #3491, 6"	130.00	140.00	132.00
☐ Hummingbird, item #3585	35.00	40.00	37.00
☐ Hummingbird, item #3634, 3½ "	45.00	55.00	47.00
☐ Indigo Bunting, item #3589, 3¼ "	50.00	60.00	52.00
☐ Kentucky Warbler, item #3598, 3"	35.00	45.00	37.00
☐ Key West Quail Dove, item #3454, 9"	150.00	160.00	152.00
☐ Kingfisher, item #3406, 3½ "	40.00	50.00	42.00
☐ Lovebird, item #3400, 4"	35.00	45.00	37.00
☐ Lovebird, pair, (resting on a single base)	105.00	115.00	107.00
☐ Nuthatch, item #3593, 2½ "	40.00	45.00	42.00
☐ Oriole, item #3402, 3½ "	50.00	60.00	52.00
☐ Oriole, pair, item #3402D, (resting on a single base)	80.00	90.00	82.00
☐ Painted Bunting, item #3452, 5"	65.00	75.00	67.00

STAR TREK COLLECTIBLES

DESCRIPTION: Star Trek Collectibles include all items dealing with or made for the Television series, cartoon series or its movies.

ORIGIN: Star Trek, a science fiction space thriller, began as a television series which ran from 1966 to 1969. After its cancellation, the series was syndicated and by 1978 was shown 300 times per day worldwide. A cartoon series was produced which ran from 1972 to 1974. *Star Trek: The Motion Picture* and *The Wrath of Khan* were two Star Trek movies.

TYPES: There are all kinds of Star Trek memorabilia including animated cels, toys, costumes, books and household ware.

COMMENTS: After the television series, Star Trek Fan Clubs, magazines and conventions sprang up worldwide. With more fans interested in these collectibles, the prices are rising into the double digits.

ADDITIONAL TIPS: For more information, consult *The Official Price Guide to Star Trek and Star Wars Collectibles,* published by The House of Collectibles.

Star Trek Adventure Set, *made by Colorforms under license from Paramount Pictures Corp., punch-out cardboard figures of characters, 1975,* **$5.00-$7.00**

	Current Price Range		P/Y Average
☐ **Animated Cel Of McCoy,** reproduction of drawings by studio animators, clear acetate, 4″ x 8″	3.00	5.00	4.00
☐ **Badge,** card stock with plastic pinback holder, says "Boarding pass, U.S.S. Enterprise" with the picture of the starship	.75	1.00	.87
☐ **Billfold, TV show, vinyl with zipper, shows Enterprise, 1977**	5.00	8.00	6.50
☐ **Blueprints Enterprise,** Franz Joseph, rolled edition, few produced prior to professional production by Ballantine Books, desirable collectible	150.00	175.00	162.00
☐ **Blueprints Star Trek The Motion Picture,** by David Kimble, shows exterior detail only of the Enterprise bridge, Klingon ship and bridge, Valcan shuttle, travel pod and more, blue pack, out of print	10.00	30.00	20.00
☐ **Blueprints,** Shuttlecraft plans of the Galileo, set of two, 18″ x 24″ Starcraft Productions	4.00	6.00	5.00

	Current Price Range		P/Y Average
☐ **Book Best Of Trek, The,** W. Irwin and G. Love, volume #1, interviews, convention close ups, close up on special effects, compiled from Trek, the magazine for Star Trek fans, 1974 ..	2.00	3.00	2.50
☐ **Book Making Of Star Trek, The,** G. Roddenberry, a complete and authorized history of television series, how it was conceived, written, produced and sold, paperback, Ballantine Books, 1968.			
☐ First edition	15.00	30.00	22.50
☐ Later edition	6.00	12.00	9.00
☐ **Book Official Star Trek Cooking Manual,** Ann Riccard, Bantam, 1978	15.00	25.00	20.00
☐ **Book Official Star Trek Trivia Book,** hardcover, 205 pp	10.00	15.00	12.50
☐ **Bumper Sticker,** says "Dr. McCoy Doesn't Make House Calls," Aviva Enterprises, blue and white printed on orange	1.00	2.00	1.50
☐ **Bumper Sticker,** says "Spock For President .	1.00	2.00	1.50
☐ **Button With Captain Kirk,** Langley Associates, close-up of head, diameter 2¼"	1.00	2.00	1.50
☐ **Button With Dr. McCoy,** Langley Associates, looking puzzled, diameter 2¼"	1.00	2.00	1.50
☐ **Button With Spock,** Star Trek Galore, with harp	1.00	2.00	1.50
☐ **Calendar,** Pocket Books, photos from the first movie, star dates, 1982	10.00	12.00	11.00
☐ **Patch Enterprise,** black background with white silhouette captioned "Star Trek," 2" x 3"	3.00	4.00	3.50
☐ **Figure,** Mego Corporation, Mr. Spock, dressed in science officer uniform with phaser, 1980, 12½"	25.00	35.00	30.00
☐ **Helmet,** Enco Industries, a similar version of the same thing by Remco, flashing light and sound, 1976	25.00	27.00	26.00
☐ **Memo Pads,** Lincoln Enterprises, miniatue versions of the official stationary used in the Star Trek offices	.50	.75	.62
☐ **Postcard Of Sulu,** Lincoln Enterprises, full color, played by George Takei, 5" x 7"	.20	.60	.40
☐ **Puzzle,** H.G. Toys Inc., 150 pieces, series II, cartoons, "The Alien," 14" x10"	4.00	8.00	6.00
☐ **Ship Recognition Manual,** The Federation F. A.S.A. all ships of The Federation in color, magazine format, 1983	7.00	8.00	7.50
☐ **Spock Ears,** Don Post Studios, custom handmade, soft plastic	5.00	7.00	6.00
☐ **Still Khan,** sitting at table turning to side talking	1.00	3.00	2.00
☐ **Still Kirk,** looking to side with bridge in background looking determined	1.00	3.00	2.00
☐ **Still Spock,** in brown coveralls talking in corridor, wall in background	1.00	3.00	2.00

	Current Price Range		P/Y Average
☐ **Still Sulu,** at post listening to Kirk speaking by control panel	1.00	3.00	2.00
☐ **View Master,** series of three reels from "The Omega Glory," in three dimension, 1968	5.00	10.00	8.00

STAR WARS COLLECTIBLES

DESCRIPTION: Star Wars collectibles include all items made for or about the three Star Wars movies.

ORIGIN: *Star Wars,* a space fantasy, is the name of a movie released in the 1980s. Because of its popularity, two other movies were produced including *The Empire Strikes Back* and *Return of the Jedi.*

TYPES: All types of movie articles and promotional items were produced including posters, toys, patches, household ware and action figures.

COMMENTS: The three Star Wars movies were big hits with movie audiences worldwide. Thousands of Star Wars fans keep the collectible market booming.

ADDITIONAL TIPS: For more information, consult *The Official Price Guide to Star Trek and Star Wars Collectibles,* published by The House of Collectibles.

	Current Price Range		P/Y Average
☐ **Alarm Clock,** Star Wars Talking Alarm, three dimensional R2-D2 and C-3PO, the Robot's voices are alarm, clock is 30 hour manual wind, 4″ x 6¾″ x 7¾″	10.00	15.00	12.50
☐ **Belt,** Lee, stretch, metal buckle says "Return Of The Jedi," belt is red and black with "Star Wars/Return Of The Jedi" repeated around it, 1982	2.50	3.50	3.00

Press Book,
The World of Star Wars,
Lucasfilm Ltd., 1981,
10½" x 16", **$35.00-$45.00**

	Current Price Range		P/Y Average
☐ **Book, Empire Strikes Back, The,** Archie Goodwin and Al Williamson, illustrators, from screenplay by L. Brackett and L. Kasdan, Marvel Comics Group, 1980, paperback, 224 pages	5.00	7.00	6.00
☐ **Book, Han Solo At Star's End,** B. Daley, Chewbacca is kidnapped and Han can only save himself or his friends, hardcover, Del Rey, 1979	6.00	10.00	8.00
☐ **Candy Heads,** Topps, the Empire Strikes Back, Yoda series, plastic figurine heads of Yoda, Tauntaun, Bounty Hunter Bossk, 2-1B, heads, filled with candy, each	1.00	2.00	1.50
☐ **Costume,** Darth Vader, Halloween type, with mask	5.00	7.00	6.00
☐ **Imperial Cruiser,** Kenner, sliding cargo door, captured royal command ship inside, die cast metal and high impact plastic	25.00	35.00	30.00
☐ **Key Chain,** "Darth Vader Lives"	2.00	4.00	3.00
☐ **Lobby Card,** Empire Strikes Back, 11" x 14" .	4.00	6.00	5.00
☐ **Mask,** Chewbacca, by Don Post, soft latex, hand applied hair	50.00	70.00	60.00
☐ **Puppet, Yoda,** Kenner, from the planet Dagobah, finely sculpted, head and hands can be manipulated, height 8½ "	8.00	10.00	9.00
☐ **Puzzle,** jigsaw, Kenner, 1000 pieces, same as promotional poster for first movie, Star Wars Adventure, 19⅜" x 26¾", 1977	9.00	12.00	10.50

	Current Price Range		P/Y Average
Sheet Music, "Princess Leia's Theme" by John Williams, from Star Wars, Fox Fanfare Music, Inc., 1977	2.00	3.00	2.50
Shoelaces, Stride-Rite, repeat of Star Wars, light blue, 1983	1.50	2.00	1.75
Tumblers, Pepperidge Farm, free with purchase of Star Wars cookies, plastic, four different pictures	6.00	10.00	8.00
Wrapping Paper, Empire Strikes Back, pictures Yoda and Obi-Wan Kenobi	2.00	3.00	2.50

STEINS

DESCRIPTION: Steins are ornately decorated large mugs which have a lid.

ORIGIN: Although steins were produced in the thirteenth century, they are extremely rare. In fact, steins from the thirteenth through the seventeenth centuries are usually found in museums. Collectors seek steins from the 1800s and 1900s.

MANUFACTURERS: Steins produced by the Villeroy & Bock Company of Mettlach, Germany are especially valuable. Collectors also seek steins manufactured by Merkelbach & Wick and Simon Peter Gerz.

COMMENTS: Since few steins were produced in America, they are rare and sought after by collectors. Quality, condition and maker are all items which determine value.

Art Nouveau, copper and brass, 14"	110.00	130.00	110.00
Bacchus, silver, Sheffield, 11½"	580.00	675.00	605.00
Character, drunken monkey, Musterschutz, one litre	400.00	465.00	415.00
Crying Radish, Musterschutz, ³⁄₁₀ litre	450.00	550.00	475.00
David And Goliath, handle with four finger holes, ½ litre	590.00	670.00	605.00
Firefighting Scene, pewter top, ½ litre	340.00	390.00	330.00
Happy Turnip, Musterschutz, 3 litre	490.00	565.00	500.00
Ivory, battle scene, carved, 13¾"	2375.00	2950.00	2500.00
Lithophanes, clown, ½ litre	400.00	485.00	415.00
Lithophanes, German scene, 6½"	110.00	130.00	110.00
Mettlach, No. 1527, ½ litre	575.00	675.00	580.00

Beer Stein, *Germany,*
porcelain with pewter lid,
decorated with trio of
merry makers in relief,
1900s, **$175.00-$250.00**

	Current Price Range		P/Y Average
☐ **Mettlach,** No. 1675, Heidelberg, ½ litre	500.00	585.00	515.00
☐ **Mettlach,** No. 1934, soldiers, inlaid lid	650.00	825.00	720.00
☐ **Mettlach,** No. 2002, Munich, ½ litre	400.00	460.00	415.00
☐ **Mettlach,** No. 2038, Black Forest, ½ litre	3900.00	4400.00	4000.00
☐ **Mettlach,** No. 2082, inlaid top, featuring Robin Hood character firing crossbow	1250.00	1450.00	1325.00
☐ **Mettlach,** No. 2136, Brewmaster, ½ litre	350.00	425.00	365.00
☐ **Mettlach,** No. 2181, Pug, ½ litre	350.00	425.00	365.00
☐ **Mettlach,** No. 2277, inlaid top, castle and clock tower	425.00	525.00	460.00
☐ **Mettlach,** No. 2333, dancing gnomes, pewter top	135.00	160.00	145.00
☐ **Mettlach,** No. 2388, pretzel, ½ litre	490.00	575.00	500.00
☐ **Mettlach,** No. 2833F, inlaid top, tavern scene of men toasting, brick wall motif around base	370.00	450.00	385.00
☐ **Mettlach,** No. 2958, bowling, 16″	775.00	925.00	780.00
☐ **Monk,** Gesetzlicht, ½ litre	200.00	230.00	200.00
☐ **Pewter,** Kayserzinn, 10″	190.00	220.00	190.00

	Current Price Range		P/Y Average
☐ **Porcelain,** pewter top, blacksmith crest	180.00	220.00	185.00
☐ **Pottery,** figural top, Roman soldier on sides . .	150.00	180.00	155.00
☐ **Pottery,** Marzi Remi, tavern scene	35.00	49.00	39.00
☐ **Pottery,** pewter top, border of grapes on top edge, seated men and women talking	55.00	70.00	62.00
☐ **Pottery,** pewter top, eagle crest in oval medallion	85.00	120.00	97.00
☐ **Pottery,** pewter top, monks drinking, keg taps border bottom	80.00	120.00	93.00
☐ **Pottery,** soldier figural top, relief, featuring Diana, Mars and Minerva	100.00	140.00	114.00
☐ **Puss In Boots,** 6½ "	55.00	70.00	61.00
☐ **Regimental,** 18th Infantry, 1 litre	340.00	400.00	360.00
☐ **Regimental,** Franco-Prussian War, 1 litre	340.00	400.00	360.00
☐ **Schlitz Beer,** ceramic, 7½ "	33.00	39.00	34.00
☐ **Singing Pig,** Musterschutz, ¼ litre	340.00	410.00	360.00
☐ **Stoneware,** pewter top, blue saltglaze	100.00	140.00	109.00
☐ **Stoneware,** pewter top, blue saltglaze, band of musicians outdoors	110.00	140.00	117.00
☐ **Stoneware,** pewter top, blue saltglaze, hunters	100.00	120.00	105.00

STEREOGRAPHS

BACKGROUND: Stereographs were first introduced in the U.S. on glass. Those stereographs (or stereo cards, views) made before 1858 are easiest to place. They are unusually thin, and in most French and English examples, they have no identifying signatures or titles.

Those stereographs with a revenue stamp on the back can be easily dated between 1864-1866, when the U.S. taxed many minute luxuries. In 1868, many publishers listed the views in a particular stereographic series by underlining or outlining a card number or title.

After 1880, stereographs that were curved came on the market since it was believed that it carried a more three dimensional quality.

COMMENTS: A stereograph's value is determined by condition, subject, rarity, photographer and age. Of course, a series or set is usually more valuable than an individual card.

ADDITIONAL TIPS: Listed below is a sampling of stereographs recently purchased, or found, on today's market. They are listed alphabetically by category. For further information, please contact National Stereoscopic Association, Box 14801, Columbus, OH 43214.

The Great Stone Face.

Photographica, stereograph, c. 1880, **$3.00-$15.00.**
Photo Credit: Lou McCulloch, Highland Heights, OH 44143.

CELEBRITIES	Current Price Range		P/Y Average
☐ **William Jennings Bryan,** In New York City, Keystone Davis #15539	15.00	25.00	20.00
☐ **Calvin Coolidge,** with cabinet, Keystone Davis #26303, rare	45.00	55.00	49.50
☐ **Major Doolittle,** Keystone Davis #28031	30.00	40.00	34.50
☐ **Thomas Alva Edison,** Keystone Davis #V28007	45.00	55.00	49.50
☐ **Henry Ford,** Keystone Davis #28023	45.00	55.00	49.50
☐ **Herbert Hoover,** Keystone Davis #28012	15.00	35.00	25.00
☐ **Charles Lindberg,** next to plane, Keystone Davis #32062T	25.00	35.00	29.50
☐ **John D. Rockefeller,** Keystone Davis #V11961	10.00	30.00	19.50
☐ **Evangelist Billy Sunday**	7.00	12.00	9.50

EVENTS			
☐ **Boxer Rebellion**	3.50	7.00	4.50
☐ **Chicago Fire of 1871**	3.00	9.00	7.00
☐ **Civil War,** set of 75	385.00	430.00	400.00
☐ **Mill Creek Flood of 1874**	3.00	5.00	3.75
☐ **San Francisco Earthquake**	10.00	20.00	15.00
☐ **Spanish American War**	3.00	12.00	9.00
☐ **Wedding,** of Tom Thumb, by Anthony Brady, c. 1860s	75.00	125.00	102.00
☐ **World War I,** set of 100	125.00	175.00	145.00

PLACES

	Current Price Range		P/Y Average
China, set of 100	325.00	375.00	345.00
Death Valley, Keystone Davis #32666	4.00	8.00	5.50
France, set of 30	40.00	50.00	46.00
New York City, views of various landmarks, set of eight	30.00	50.00	41.50
Philadelphia, by James Cremer, 19th century, set of five	20.00	30.00	24.75
United States, set of five	20.00	30.00	24.50
Virginia City, Nevada, by C.E. Watkins	60.00	80.00	69.50
World Tour, set of 200	275.00	325.00	305.00
Yosemite Falls, by C.E. Watkins	19.00	30.00	22.50

MISCELLANEOUS

Household Scene, hand tinted, features children, 19th century, set of nine	20.00	30.00	28.00
Nineteenth Century, time capsule, by Anthony, Gardner and Bierstadt, set of 50	75.00	125.00	95.00
Nude, woman, black and white, rare	9.50	15.00	12.50
Six Men Who Circled The Earth, Keystone Davis #26408T, set of six	15.00	25.00	19.50

STOCK CERTIFICATES

DESCRIPTION: Stock certificates are printed paper documents designating ownership of shares in a company.

TYPES: Some hobbyists collect stock certificates according to the nature of the business like railroad or mining, while others collect all types including canceled, elaborately illustrated and unissued certificates.

PERIOD: Stocks from the 1800s are the most common collected by hobbyists.

Acme Uranium Mines, Inc., Delaware, allegorical vignette of a woman and two men, c. 1955	2.00	3.00	2.50
Aircraft Acceptance Corp., Columbus, Ohio, eagle in black with green border, 1960s	1.75	2.50	2.00

Photographica, *stereograph, c. 1880,* **$3.00-$15.00**
Photo courtesy of Lou McCulloch, Highland Heights, OH 44143.

	Current Price Range		P/Y Average
☐ **Allied Chemical Corporation,** New York, vignette representing chemistry with classical figures, blue border	2.00	3.00	2.50
☐ **Boston Elevated Railway Co.,** Boston, vignette of elevated train	4.00	6.00	5.00
☐ **Calpetro Producers Syndicate,** San Francisco, vignette of oil field	3.00	4.00	3.50
☐ **Cavanagh-Dobbs, Inc.,** Connecticut, male and female figures flanking emblem, 1930s	1.50	2.00	1.75
☐ **Chicago and North Western Railway Co.,** Wisconsin, company name in medallion flanked by cherubs	3.50	4.50	4.00
☐ **Citizens' National Bank,** Gastonia, North Carolina, eagle with outstretched wings	1.75	2.50	2.10
☐ **Fairchild Engine and Airplane Corp.,** Maryland, male and female figures, flying horse	2.00	3.00	2.50
☐ **Milk Row Bleachery Co.,** Somerville, Massachusetts, printed on blue paper, 1850	2.00	3.00	2.50
☐ **New Toledo Apartments,** $500 face value gold bond, Illinois, dated 1910	3.50	4.50	4.00
☐ **People's Shoe Store,** Perryville, Missouri, eagle with wings outspread	2.00	3.00	2.50
☐ **Sovereign Hotel Corp.,** Illinois, unillustrated, printed in brown, early 1920s	2.00	2.50	3.00
☐ **United States Plywood Corp.,** New York, man turning wheel, orange border, 1950s	2.00	3.00	2.50
☐ **Van Buren Hotel Corp.,** Maine, vignette of eagle against gold background	2.00	3.00	2.50

STOVES

PERIOD: Collectible stoves are those made in the 19th and early 20th centuries.

ORIGIN: Kitchen ranges with ovens were first made in the early 19th century. Before that time most cooking was done over an open fire.

COMMENTS: Stoves are usually sought after by kitchen enthusiasts. In 1850 the first gas cookers appeared on the market. Electric cookers were introduced in 1894 and stoves didn't come with thermostats until 1923.

ADDITIONAL TIPS: The listings include a description of each stove and the price range. For more complete information, refer to *The Official Price Guide to Kitchen Collectibles.*

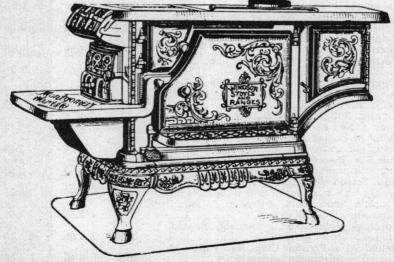

Cook Stove, *cast iron, 1890s,* **$300.00-$600.00**

	Current Price Range		P/Y Average
☐ **Stove,** Acme Champion, wood burner, early 20th century, 25″ high	405.00	430.00	415.00
☐ **Stove,** Adam type, iron, stoked via surface cover, early 19th century, 38″ high	525.00	720.00	540.00
☐ **Stove,** Art Grand, circular shape uses coal, northern origin	326.00	360.00	330.00
☐ **Stove,** blue iron range, complete with reservoir and warming closet, six-hole, fully nickeled, 14″ oven, late 19th century	298.00	315.00	205.00
☐ **Stove,** Blue Poppy, blue enameling, done by hand, open-worked cover, stoked via surface cover, early 20th century, 27″ x 18″	795.00	965.00	810.00
☐ **Stove,** Charm, Acme, four legs, six hole range, reservoir, warming closet, and oven door thermometer	1800.00	2000.00	1850.00
☐ **Stove,** Globe, Acme, porcelain lined reservoir, burns coal, coke, wood, side embellishments, four legs, nickeled, late 19th century	1450.00	1700.00	1500.00
☐ **Stove,** Royal Redwood, Acme, six hole, combination coal and wood burning, duplex grate, oven thermometer, reservoir, scroll carved base, four legs, deep skirt strips on all four sides, early 20th century	1250.00	1550.00	1300.00
☐ **Stove,** step, two burners on top and one double burner on step, surface area 14″ x 22″, 24″ high, Sears, early 20th century	1450.00	1900.00	1550.00
☐ **Stove,** small, cast iron, hot plate underneath cover that comes off, three footed, European make, early 20th century, 15″ x 38″ surface area	472.00	560.00	480.00
☐ **Stove,** stands on hearth that comes out, enameled in green, hot plate, openworked cover, European make, early 20th century, 17″ x 45″	472.00	565.00	480.00
☐ **Stove,** Scandanavian make, mid 19th century, 55″ x 35″	1450.00	1850.00	1600.00
☐ **Stove,** stands on three legs, European make, enameled in dark red, handle in the shape of a winged creature, early 20th century, 27″ x 11″	525.00	700.00	540.00
☐ **Stove,** Scandanavian make, cast iron, a trio of ovens above hearth, wooden base, late 18th century, 88″ x 30″	5750.00	7500.00	6000.00
☐ **Stove,** Victorian	148.00	190.00	152.00
☐ **Stove,** lid lifters, factory made, coil handle ..	8.50	17.00	9.00
☐ **Stove,** stove lid lifters, hand wrought	8.50	24.00	12.00
☐ **Stove,** wood heating, salesman's sample, large, early 20th century	236.00	280.00	240.00
☐ **Stove,** wood burner, Acme Empress, four hole top, burns knots, hard or soft wood, rococo design, adjustable tea shelves, large fire box, tin lined oven door, nickel plated medallions, early 20th century	685.00	870.00	690.00
☐ **Stove,** wood burning, 2' long	225.00	310.00	230.00
☐ **Stove,** wood burning, round	310.00	360.00	315.00

	Current Price Range		P/Y Average
☐ **Stove,** wire handled, stove poker, straight sided	8.50	17.00	9.00
☐ **Stove,** woodburning, pot belly, late 19th century	262.00	295.00	240.00
☐ **Stove,** woodburning, pot belly, late 19th century, ornate lion's paw foot	120.00	210.00	125.00
☐ **Stove,** Wehrle, combination stove, four hole coal and wood, pig iron, rococo design, four slightly splayed legs, early 20th century	840.00	1250.00	860.00
☐ **Stove,** wood or coal, for heating or cooking . .	335.00	370.00	340.00
☐ **Stove,** wood burning, round, chrome trimmings	550.00	630.00	560.00
☐ **Stove,** wood burning, restored, 20″ high	1050.00	1150.00	1100.00
☐ **Stove,** with burning box at the base, three sections above, each holding a hot-plate, Norwegian, late 19th century, 26″ x 78″	840.00	1250.00	900.00
☐ **Stove,** Wildwood, Acme, diving return flue, ornamental urn, swing top, nickel trimmings, fire door, cast iron stove plate, early 20th century	525.00	625.00	550.00

SUPERMAN

DESCRIPTION: Items pertaining to the comic book character Superman are collectible.

TYPES: Toys, games, comic books, newpaper strips, original comic art, and premiums are some examples of Superman memorabilia.

PERIOD: The comic book Superman first appeared in 1938. It was created by Jerry Siegel and Joe Shuster.

COMMENTS: Besides comic books, Superman was portrayed in a television series, radio series and motion pictures.

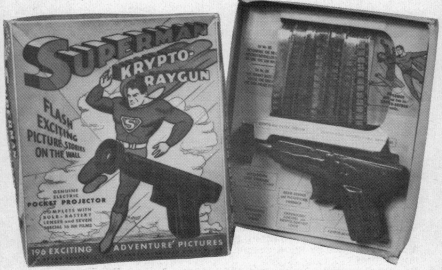

Superman Krypto-Ray Gun, *Daisy Manufacturing Company,*
$80.00-$90.00

	Current Price Range		P/Y Average
☐ **Badge,** movie promotional, emblem shaped (for Superman I)	3.00	4.00	3.25
☐ **Bank,** dime register bank, lithographed tin, square, picture of Superman facing left, breaking chain by expanding his chest	90.00	115.00	100.00
☐ **Belt Buckle,** tin, blue and red on silvered brass, half-length portrait, name at bottom, 1940	90.00	115.00	102.00
☐ **Birthday Card,** You're Ten Today, Birthday Greetings From Superman, copyright by Superman, Inc., 1940s	13.00	17.00	15.00
☐ **Button,** Kelloggs Pep Cereal premium, lithographed tin, multicolored, 1940s	7.00	10.00	8.50
☐ **Button,** Muscle Building Club, lithographed tin, head and chest portrait, c. 1940.	75.00	100.00	86.00
☐ **Button,** Superman of America, club button given to members of the Supermen of America, shows him breaking chains across his chest, 1939	35.00	45.00	40.00
☐ **Clothing,** Superman the Movie T-shirt, with iron-on, made in four different colors, has full standing portrait	6.00	8.00	7.00
☐ **Clothing,** T-shirt with iron-on, made in four different colors, pictures American flag	6.00	8.00	7.00
☐ **Clothing,** T-shirt with iron-on, made in four different colors, has wording "Run, Jump, Fly."	6.00	8.00	7.00
☐ **Clothing,** T-shirt with iron-on, has "S" symbol	6.00	8.00	7.00

	Current Price Range		P/Y Average

☐ **Cookie Jar,** California Originals, ceramic, figural, painted, shows him leaving phone booth after switching from Clark Kent identity, 1970s **22.00 29.00 24.00**

☐ **Decoder,** Superman's Secret Code, premium from Action Comics sent to members of the Supermen of America club, 1938-1942 ...... **45.00 57.00 50.00**

☐ **Doll,** made by The Toy Works, stuffed fabric, full length with cape, 25½ " **22.00 28.00 24.00**

☐ **Figure,** Ideal, composition and wood, painted, with cape, one of the earliest Superman figures, 13 " **300.00 400.00 350.00**

☐ **Figure,** Syrocco, 1940s, 5¾ " **165.00 200.00 175.00**

☐ **Figure,** Brass Hanging Ornament, shows him standing on top of world, 4 " **2.50 3.50 3.00**

☐ **Food Carton,** Superman Candy Coated Peanuts, box only, illustrated lid, multicolors, 1966, 5½ " **20.00 27.00 23.00**

☐ **Mug,** tankard type, made by California Originals, ceramic, high relief, painted, 1978 ..... **20.00 25.00 22.00**

☐ **Music Box,** made by Price, ceramic, figural, late 1970s, 7 " **22.00 29.00 24.85**

☐ **Novelty,** Glow-in-the-Dark picture, shows him riding on a bomb with airplanes in background, 9 " x 11 " **22.00 28.00 25.00**

☐ **Pencil Case,** stiff paper, maroon and silver, illustration at top, 8¼ " **35.00 45.00 39.00**

☐ **Pendant,** lithographed tin, movable arms, 1970s, 2½ " **4.00 6.00 5.00**

☐ **Pen,** fountain pen, small colored decal of Superman standing with hands on hips, c. 1942 .... **32.00 40.00 35.00**

☐ **Phongraph Record,** Superman and the Magic Ring, set of two seven-inch 78 r.p.m. records, Musette label, contains story that was broadcast on the radio with original radio cast, accompanied by a booklet, c. 1947 .... **40.00 50.00 42.00**

☐ **Purse,** yellow, 1966 .... **27.00 35.00 30.00**

☐ **Vehicle,** Supermobile, made by Corgi of Great Britain, diecast metal, bearing the number 265 .... **9.00 12.00 10.25**

TELEPHONES

DESCRIPTION: A telephone is a device which converts sounds into electrical impulses which are then transmitted by wire.

ORIGIN: Telephones were first installed for public use in the U.S. in 1877. This form of communication was developed by Alexander Graham Bell.

ADDITIONAL TIPS: Many small independent companies produced telephones which are highly collectible today. These companies include Stromberg-Carlson Telephone Manufacturing Company, Manhattan Electrical Supply Company and Strowger Automatic Telephone Exchange.

Pay Telephone, *3 slot, 1930,* **$75.00-$95.00**

	Current Price Range		P/Y Average
Adapter Plug, modular receiver for four prongs, World War I era	3.00	4.00	3.50
Back Cup For Transmitter, brass, patented November 1910, 3″	4.00	6.00	5.00
Bell, from wall phone, single, solid brass with hole in center, dome shape, c. 1895	7.00	10.00	8.25
Candlestick Phone, Western Electric, brass with black paint, cord missing, all internal parts intact, some scuffing to paint, c. 1928 .	2.00	2.50	2.20
Clapper Cover, brass, c. 1915	3.00	4.50	3.65
Directory, 1881 Boston Telephone Directory, 56 pages with paper cover, gives list of subscribers plus ads for various phone equipment	250.00	325.00	285.00
Magneto Wall Phone, box style, cabinet of golden oak, quarter sawn, early 1900s, 21″ high by 9″ wide	200.00	250.00	220.00
Magneto Wall Phone, box style, cabinet of walnut, quarter sawn, 1900s, 21″ high by 9″ wide	170.00	215.00	185.00
Mouthpiece From Candlestick Phone, black, c. 1925	2.50	3.50	3.00
Mouthpiece From Candlestick Phone, brass, c. 1930	18.00	23.00	20.00
Mouthpiece From Wood Magneto Phone, black, early 1900s	2.50	3.50	3.00
Pay Phone, wall model, wood and brass, bells and crank at top, receiver hangs at left side, mouthpiece stationary at center, slots for deposit of coins of various denominations, c. 1900	500.00	700.00	600.00
Receiver, outside terminal, 1882, 7½ ″	50.00	65.00	57.00
Receiver Cap, Stromberg Carlson, 1¾ ″	10.00	14.00	12.00
Shelf For Wall Mounted Phone, oak, late 1800s	18.00	23.00	20.00
Shelf For Wall Mounted Phone, oak, late 1800s	18.00	23.00	20.00
Swivel Bracket, Kellog, early 1900s, 4½ ″	5.00	7.00	6.00
Swivel Transmitter, small, all brass except for mouthpiece, front casting, c. 1901, five ounces	12.00	16.00	14.00
Transmitter, Kellog type, brass, 1910 patent date, 7″	15.00	20.00	17.00
Transmitter, Western Electric, brass back cup, brass front plate with brass cap nuts, 1910 patent date, 8½ ″	15.00	20.00	17.00

TELEVISION MEMORABILIA

COMMENTS: Since the television industry itself is still rather young, collecting TV memorabilia is a relatively new hobby. It probably first emerged as part of the nostalgia craze in the 1970s. But its current popularity may be attributed to the recent market explosion of video tape recorders. With these, viewers can record and watch popular old TV programs that may no longer run. This often sparks an interest in collecting memorabilia from these shows.

RECOMMENDED READING: For further information refer to *The Official Price Guide to Radio, TV and Movie Memorabilia*, published by The House of Collectibles.

Howdy Doody Television Crayons and Pictures, *shadow box coloring set, 5" x 6½", $4.00-$9.00 Photo courtesy of Hake's Americana, York, PA.*

	Current Price Range		P/Y Average
Addams Family, The, card game, Milton Bradley, 1965	12.50	15.00	13.00
Addams Family, The, ½ hour, 16mm original print, "Morticia the Writer"	35.00	45.00	36.00
All In The Family, original TV soundtrack, first album	5.00	8.00	6.00
Archies, The, paper doll, Sabrina	12.00	15.00	13.00
Archies, The, paper doll, other Archies character	12.00	15.00	13.00
Batman, Batman flashlight, 1976	3.50	5.00	3.75
Batman, fork, metal 6½", Imperial, 1966	18.00	23.00	20.00
Batman, hair brush, plastic figural handle, white bristles, 8½", Avon, 1976	20.00	25.00	22.00
Batman, plastic assembly kit, Robin the Teen Wonder, Aurora, 1974	22.00	25.00	23.00
Batman, Robin flashlight, 1976	3.50	5.00	3.25
Beverly Hillbillies, The, card game, "Set back," Milton Bradley, 1963	15.00	20.00	16.00
Beverly Hillbillies, The, Magic Eyes story set	4.00	6.00	4.50
Bonanza, album, "Party Time"	15.00	18.00	15.50
Bonanza, Big Little Book, The Bubble Gum Kid, Whitman, 1967	3.50	4.00	3.75
Bonanza, color postcard, cast, 6" x 4"	1.50	4.00	1.75
Bonanza, comic book	1.75	2.00	1.25
Bonanza, hardcover book, Bonanza Heroes of the Wild West, Whitman, 210 pages, 1970	5.00	7.00	5.50
Bonanza, hardcover book, Bonanza Killer Lion, Whitman, 212 pages, 1956	6.50	8.50	6.75
Bonanza, Hoss Cartwright doll	25.00	30.00	26.00
Bonanza, jigsaw puzzle, Ponderosa Ranch	5.00	7.00	5.50
Bonanza, lunch pail with thermos, Alladin, 1963	7.50	9.00	7.75
Bonanza, movie viewer, National Broadcasting Co., Inc.	13.00	16.00	13.50
Bonanza, paperback, The Living Legend of Bonanza, 7" x 10"	8.00	10.00	8.50
Bonanza, paperback, One Man with Courage, Media Books, 1966	7.00	9.00	7.50
Bonanza, View-Master with 12-page story booklet and three reels, 1964	10.00	13.00	10.50
Brady Bunch, The, original TV soundtrack, Paramount	10.00	15.00	10.50
Buck Rogers 25th Century A.D., pencil box, 6" x 10½", 1935	35.00	45.00	36.00
Bugs Bunny, watch with carrot hands	45.00	50.00	46.00
Bullwinkle, plastic coin, Old London, 1960's	2.50	3.00	2.75
Burke's Law, one hour, 16mm original print, "Who Killed the 13th Clown"	55.00	70.00	56.00
Captain Kangaroo, Sears' Captain Kangaroo doll, 1967	15.00	20.00	16.00
Charlie's Angels, Farrah Fawcett Wella Balsam poster	10.00	15.00	11.00
Cheyenne, comic book, #6, 1958	5.00	8.00	6.00
Dallas, glossy color TV still, Patrick Duffy and Victoria Principal, 8" x 10"	4.00	7.00	5.00
Daniel Boone, plate	3.00	5.00	3.50

	Current Price Range		P/Y Average
☐ Dark Shadows, *comic book, #4*	1.25	1.75	1.50
☐ Dark Shadows, *glossy color TV still, Jonathan Frid, 8" x 10"*	4.00	7.00	4.25
☐ Dark Shadows, *gum card*	2.00	3.00	2.25
☐ Dark Shadows, *original TV soundtrack, Philips*	20.00	25.00	21.00
☐ Davy Crockett, *ceramic wall vase*	15.00	20.00	16.00
☐ Davy Crockett, *character pocket knife*	6.50	8.50	7.00
☐ Davy Crockett, *comic book, "Indian Fighter," 1955*	6.50	8.50	7.00
☐ Davy Crockett, *comic book, "Walt Disney's Davy Crockett and The River Pirates," 1955* . .	6.50	8.50	7.00
☐ Davy Crockett, *pinback button*	3.50	4.00	3.75
☐ Davy Crockett, *wall light, 6", c. 1955*	30.00	40.00	31.00
☐ Dennis The Menace, *graphic, Jay North, Sunday supplement from the Pittsburgh Press, color cover, October 4, 1959*	2.50	3.50	2.75
☐ Dick Van Dyke Show, The, *½ hour, 16mm original print, "Farewell to Writing"*	35.00	45.00	36.00
☐ Dragnet, *official Jack Webb whistle, 1968* . . .	3.00	5.00	3.25
☐ Ed Sullivan Show, The, *glossy color TV still, The Beatles, 8" x 10"*	4.00	7.00	4.25
☐ Flintstones, The, *cookie jar, glazed ceramic, 12", Hanna-Barbera*	60.00	80.00	65.00
☐ Flintstones, The, *Fred Flintstone figural radio*	22.00	27.00	22.50
☐ Flintstones, The, *original TV soundtrack, "Christmas with Pebbles," Hanna-Barbera* . .	8.00	12.00	8.50
☐ Flipper, *jigsaw puzzle, 99 pieces, Whitman, Big Little Book, 10" x 13" 1967*	10.00	15.00	10.50
☐ Fugitive, The, *paperback "Fear in a Desert Town"*	1.00	3.50	1.25
☐ Gene Autry, *coloring book, "Chuck Wagon Chatter," 1953*	15.00	18.00	16.00
☐ Gene Autry, *viewmaster reel # 950, "Gene Autry and his Wonder Horse, 'Champion,'"* . .	7.00	14.00	7.50
☐ Get Smart, *card game, Ideal, 1966*	15.00	20.00	16.00
☐ Girl From U.N.C.L.E., The, *original TV soundtrack, MGM*	20.00	25.00	21.00
☐ Good Times, *gum cards, set of 55, 1976*	5.00	8.00	5.50
☐ Green Hornet, The, *spoon, metal, 6", Imperial, 1966*	9.00	12.00	10.00
☐ Gunsmoke, *Big Little Book, Whitman 1958* . .	8.50	10.00	8.75
☐ Gunsmoke, *cardboard pencil box*	15.00	20.00	15.50
☐ Gunsmoke, *comic book, #2, 1960*	3.50	4.00	3.75
☐ Happy Days, *play set, 1976*	15.00	18.00	15.50
☐ Hardy Boys Mysteries, The, *glossy color TV still, Shaun Cassidy and Parker Stevenson 8" x 10"*	4.00	7.00	4.25
☐ Have Gun Will Travel, *comic book, #10*	5.00	7.00	5.25
☐ Have Gun Will Travel, *hardcover book, Have Gun, Will Travel, Whitman, 282 pages, 1959* .	8.00	10.00	8.25
☐ Hawaii Five-O, *Police badge*	25.00	30.00	26.00
☐ Hawaiian Eye, *original TV soundtrack, Warner Brothers*	8.00	12.00	8.50

	Current Price Range		P/Y Average
□ Hogan's Heroes, *Peri-peeper periscope, ID card, badge*	10.00	13.00	11.00
□ Hopalong Cassidy, *dental kit, Dr. West's, 8" x 9"*	25.00	35.00	26.00
□ Hopalong Cassidy, *Ingraham alarm clock* ...	148.00	160.00	149.00
□ Hopalong Cassidy, *leather belt*	12.00	16.00	13.00
□ Hopalong Cassidy, *milk container, c. 1955, half gallon*	8.00	10.00	9.00
□ Hopalong Cassidy, *milk container, c. 1955, quart*	6.00	9.00	7.00
□ Hopalong Cassidy, *milk container, c. 1955, pint*	2.00	4.00	3.00
□ Hopalong Cassidy, *pinback button, Hopalong and Topper*	7.50	10.00	7.75
□ Hopalong Cassidy, *record album*	30.00	35.00	31.00
□ Hopalong Cassidy, *Viewmaster reel #956, "The Cattle Rustler"*	4.00	12.00	4.50
□ Hopalong Cassidy, *wallet, 3½" x 4½"*	8.00	12.00	8.50
□ Howdy Doody, *figural ear muffs*	18.00	25.00	18.50
□ Howdy Doody, *plastic Jack-in-the-box, 5" high*	20.00	25.00	21.50
□ Howdy Doody, *paper bag, fudge bar*	6.00	10.00	6.50
□ Howdy Doody, *plate*	16.00	20.00	16.50
□ Howdy Doody, *shadow box, for coloring, 5½" x 6"*	4.00	9.00	4.25
□ Immortal, The, *1 hour, 16mm original print, "My Brother"*	72.00	80.00	73.00
□ Invaders, The, *UFO model kit, Aurora, 1968* ..	15.00	20.00	15.50
□ Ironsides, *graphic, Raymond Burr, Sunday supplement from the Pittsburgh Press, color cover, January 26, 1958*	1.50	2.50	1.75
□ It Takes A Thief, *paperback, #1*	1.00	3.50	1.25
□ Johnny Quest, *½ hour, 16mm original print, "Antarctica"*	25.00	30.00	26.00
□ Kojak, *playing cards, set of 56, color, original cast, Monty Gum*	15.00	18.00	16.00
□ Lassie, *hardcover book,* The Secret Of The Smelter's Cave, *Whitman, 1968*	5.00	7.00	5.50
□ Laugh-In, *original TV soundtrack, Epic*	4.00	7.00	4.25
□ Leave It To Beaver, *graphic, Sunday supplement from the Pittsburgh Press, color cover, September 6, 1959*	2.00	4.00	2.25
□ Lone Ranger, The, *holsters, fiberboard, set of 2, 11", c. 1945*	15.00	25.00	15.50
□ Lone Ranger, The, *ink blotter, 3½" x 8"*	5.00	10.00	5.25
□ Lone Ranger, The, *paperweight, snowy*	35.00	40.00	36.00
□ Lost In Space, *color 16mm print, "The Questing Beast"*	125.00	140.00	126.00
□ Lost In Space, *glossy color TV still, Jonathan Harris, 8" x 10"*	4.00	10.00	4.25
□ I Love Lucy, *paper doll, Lucille Ball, Whitman, 1953*	30.00	35.00	31.00
□ I Love Lucy, *paper doll, Desi Arnaz, Whitman, 1953*	30.00	35.00	31.00
□ Man From U.N.C.L.E., The, *action doll*	15.00	25.00	16.00
□ Man From U.N.C.L.E., The, *board game*	15.00	18.00	16.00

	Current Price Range		P/Y Average
☐ Munsters, The, *figure, Herman*	15.00	20.00	16.00
☐ Munsters, The, *figure, Lily*	15.00	20.00	16.00
☐ Partridge Family, The, *paper doll, cast*	12.00	15.00	13.00
☐ Peter Gunn, *original TV soundtrack, Henry Mancini, Vol. 1, RCA*	10.00	15.00	11.00
☐ Peter Gunn, *original TV soundtrack, Henry Mancini, Vol. 2, RCA*	10.00	15.00	11.00
☐ Planet Of The Apes, *gum cards, set of 66*	10.00	15.00	11.00
☐ Popeye, *bifbat, 11½", 1929*	20.00	30.00	21.00
☐ Prisoner, The, *glossy color TV still, Patrick McGoohan, 8" x 10"*	4.00	7.00	5.00
☐ Rango, *comic book, #1*	2.00	4.00	3.00
☐ Rich Man, Poor Man, *original TV soundtrack, MCA*	10.00	15.00	11.00
☐ Richard II, *glossy color TV still, Derek Jacoby, 8" x 10"*	4.00	7.00	5.00
☐ Rifleman, The, *hardcover book, Whitman* ...	7.50	9.00	8.00
☐ Route 66, *original TV soundtrack, Nelson Riddle Orchestra, Capitol*	8.00	12.00	9.00
☐ Roy Rogers, *color cards, set of 25, Kane Products*	20.00	25.00	21.00
☐ Roy Rogers, *color photo, Roy and Trigger, 8" x 10", c. 1950s-60s*	10.00	20.00	11.00
☐ Roy Rogers, *coloring book, "Roy Rogers and Dale Evans," Whitman, 1951*	16.50	20.00	17.00
☐ Roy Rogers, *flashlight lantern, 7½"*	4.00	8.00	5.00
☐ Roy Rogers, *horseshoe*	5.00	7.00	6.00
☐ Roy Rogers, *jeep with figures*	50.00	60.00	51.00
☐ Roy Rogers, *Lincoln Logs cabin construction set, early 1905s*	38.00	45.00	39.00
☐ Roy Rogers, *modeling clay set, 8" x 12", c. 1948*	12.00	18.00	13.00
☐ Sanford & Son, *original TV soundtrack, RCA* .	6.00	8.00	7.00
☐ Secret Agent, *paperback, "Departure Deferred"*	1.00	3.50	2.00
☐ Shogun, *glossy color TV still, Richard Chamberlain, 8" x 10"*	4.00	7.00	5.00
☐ Shotgun Slade, *original TV soundtrack, Mercury*	40.00	50.00	41.00
☐ Six Million Dollar Man, *model kit, FunDimension, 1975*	10.00	13.00	11.00
☐ Six Million Dollar Man, *fan club kit, with certificate, membership card, color sticker and 8" x 10" color photo of Steve Austin, 1973* ...	12.50	14.00	13.00
☐ Sky King, *½ hour, 16mm original print, "Designing Woman"*	29.00	35.00	30.00
☐ Space: 1999, *gum card set, 1976, stun saucer gun*	6.50	8.00	7.00
☐ Star Trek, *card, black and white, Leaf, 1967* ..	9.00	12.00	10.00
☐ Star Trek, *model kit, U.S.S. Enterprise*	30.00	35.00	31.00
☐ Star Trek, *Spock action figure, Mego, 8", 1974*	12.50	15.00	13.00
☐ Starsky and Hutch, *glossy color TV still, Paul Michael Glaser and David Soul, 8" x 10"* ...	4.00	7.00	5.00
☐ Streets Of San Francisco, The, *glossy color TV still, Michael Douglas, 8" x 10"*	4.00	7.00	5.00
☐ 77 Sunset Strip, *game*	15.00	18.00	16.00

◻━━◻━━◻━━◻━━◻━━◻━━◻━━◻━━◻━━◻━━◻━━◻

THEATRICAL MEMORABILIA

COMMENTS: Items from every phase of the theater are highly collectible and are beginning to command high prices among hobbyists.

RECOMMENDED READING: For further information refer to *The Official Price Guide to Paper Collectibles,* published by The House of Collectibles.

	Current Price Range		P/Y Average
◻ **BOOK.** *Songs of Stephen Foster, signed by John Charles Thomas.*	25.00	35.00	26.00
◻ **BROADWAY PLAYBILL.** *Advise and Consent, 1961.*	1.50	3.00	1.75
◻ **BROADWAY PLAYBILL.** *Amadeus, 1981.*	1.50	3.00	1.75
◻ **BROADWAY PLAYBILL.** *American Buffalo, 1977.*	1.50	3.00	1.75
◻ **BROADWAY PLAYBILL.** *Annie Get Your Gun, 1966.*	1.50	3.00	1.75
◻ **BROADWAY PLAYBILL.** *Any Wednesday, 1964.*	1.50	3.00	1.75
◻ **BROADWAY PLAYBILL.** *Bell, Book and Candle, 1951.*	1.50	3.00	1.75
◻ **BROADWAY PLAYBILL.** *Bells are Ringing, 1957.*	1.50	3.00	1.75
◻ **BROADWAY PLAYBILL.** *Brigadoon, 1948.*	1.50	3.00	1.75
◻ **BROADWAY PLAYBILL.** *Chicago, 1976.*	1.50	3.00	1.75
◻ **BROADWAY PLAYBILL.** *Coco, 1970.*	1.50	3.00	1.75
◻ **BROADWAY PLAYBILL.** *Dear Liar, 1960.*	1.50	3.00	1.75
◻ **BROADWAY PLAYBILL.** *Diary of Anne Frank, 1955.*	1.50	3.00	1.75
◻ **BROADWAY PLAYBILL.** *Eddie Fisher at the Winter Garden, 1962.*	1.50	3.00	1.75
◻ **BROADWAY PLAYBILL.** *Fiddler on the Roof, 1977.*	1.50	3.00	1.75
◻ **BROADWAY PLAYBILL.** *Forty Carats, 1969.*	1.50	3.00	1.75
◻ **BROADWAY PLAYBILL.** *Golden Boy, 1964.*	1.50	3.00	1.75
◻ **BROADWAY PLAYBILL.** *Grease, 1976.*	1.50	3.00	1.75

	Current Price Range		P/Y Average

☐ **BROADWAY PLAYBILL.** *Guys and Dolls, 1953.* . . . . | 1.50 | 3.00 | 1.75

☐ **BROADWAY PLAYBILL.** *Hamlet, 1964.* . . . . . . | 1.50 | 3.00 | 1.75

☐ **BROADWAY PLAYBILL.** *I Remember Mama, 1944.* . . . . | 3.50 | 4.00 | 1.75

☐ **BROADWAY PLAYBILL.** *Irene, 1974.* . . . . | 1.50 | 3.00 | 1.75

☐ **BROADWAY PLAYBILL.** *Life with Father, 1940.* . . . . | 1.50 | 3.00 | 1.75

☐ **BROADWAY PLAYBILL.** *Look Back in Anger, 1958.* . . . . | 1.50 | 3.00 | 1.75

☐ **BROADWAY PLAYBILL.** *Master Harold and the Boys, 1982.* . . . . | 1.50 | 3.00 | 1.75

☐ **BROADWAY PLAYBILL.** *Much Ado About Nothing, 1959.* . . . . | 1.50 | 3.00 | 1.75

☐ **BROADWAY PLAYBILL.** *No Strings, 1963.* . . . | 1.50 | 3.00 | 1.75

☐ **BROADWAY PLAYBILL.** *No Time for Sergeants, 1956.* . . . . | 1.50 | 3.00 | 1.75

☐ **BROADWAY PLAYBILL.** *One Touch of Venus, 1944.* . . . . | 3.50 | 5.00 | 1.75

☐ **BROADWAY PLAYBILL.** *On the Town, 1971.* . | 1.50 | 3.00 | 1.75

☐ **BROADWAY PLAYBILL.** *Over Here, 1974.* . . . | 1.50 | 3.00 | 1.75

☐ **BROADWAY PLAYBILL.** *Pippin, 1972.* . . . . . . | 1.50 | 3.00 | 1.75

☐ **BROADWAY PLAYBILL.** *Play it Again, Sam, 1969.* . . . . | 1.50 | 3.00 | 1.75

☐ **BROADWAY PLAYBILL.** *Plaza Suite, 1970.* . . | 1.50 | 3.00 | 1.75

☐ **BROADWAY PLAYBILL.** *Private Lives, 1975.* . | 1.50 | 3.00 | 1.75

☐ **BROADWAY PLAYBILL.** *Same Time Next Year, 1975.* . . . . | 1.50 | 3.00 | 1.75

☐ **BROADWAY PLAYBILL.** *Sugar Babies, 1979.* | 1.50 | 3.00 | 1.75

☐ **BROADWAY PLAYBILL.** *Sunday in New York, 1963.* . . . . | 1.50 | 3.00 | 1.75

☐ **BROADWAY PLAYBILL.** *Sweeney Todd, 1979.* | 1.50 | 3.00 | 1.75

☐ **BROADWAY PLAYBILL.** *There's a Girl in My Soup, 1968.* . . . . | 1.50 | 3.00 | 1.75

☐ **BROADWAY PLAYBILL.** *They're Playing Our Song, 1979.* . . . . | 1.50 | 3.00 | 1.75

☐ **BROADWAY PLAYBILL.** *Tribute, 1978.* . . . . . . | 1.50 | 3.00 | 1.75

☐ **BROADWAY PLAYBILL.** *Under the Yum Yum Tree, 1960.* . . . . | 1.50 | 3.00 | 1.75

☐ **BROADWAY PLAYBILL.** *Witness for the Prosecution, 1956.* . . . . | 1.50 | 3.00 | 1.75

☐ **BROADWAY PLAYBILL.** *Woman of the Year, 1982.* . . . . | 1.50 | 3.00 | 1.75

☐ **BROCHURE.** *Opera company brochure signed by Regina Resnik, c. 1952.* | 8.00 | 12.00 | 8.50

☐ **CALLING CARD.** *Signed by Enrico Caruso.* . . | 60.00 | 80.00 | 61.00

☐ **CONTRACT.** *Opera company contract signed by Patrice Munsel.* . . . . | 30.00 | 40.00 | 31.00

☐ **CONTRACT.** *Opera contract signed by Giuseppe Deluca.* . . . . | 70.00 | 90.00 | 71.00

☐ **CONTRACT.** *Record company contract signed by Robert Merrill.* . . . . | 40.00 | 50.00 | 41.00

☐ **LETTER.** *Handwritten in Russian by Fyodor Chaliapin.* . . . . | 430.00 | 560.00 | 435.00

☐ **LIBRETTO.** *Opera libretto signed by Cesare Siepi.* . . . . | 13.00 | 18.00 | 14.00

	Current Price Range		P/Y Average
☐ **LIBRETTO.** Opera libretto signed by Helen Traubel.	13.00	18.00	14.00
☐ **MAGAZINE COVER.** Signed by Joan Sutherland.	25.00	35.00	26.00
☐ **MENU.** Signed by Enrico Caruso, c. 1915.	160.00	200.00	162.00
☐ **MENU.** Signed by Joan Sutherland.	8.00	12.00	9.00
☐ **MENU.** Signed by Lorenzo Alvary.	9.00	16.00	10.00
☐ **PHOTOGRAPH.** Autographed photo of Beverly in costume from Daughter of the Regiment, 8" x 10".	25.00	35.00	26.00
☐ **PHOTOGRAPH.** Autographed by Charles Anthony, 8" x 10".	10.00	15.00	11.00
☐ **PHOTOGRAPH.** Autographed photo of Dorothy Kirsten, 8" x 10".	55.00	70.00	56.00
☐ **PHOTOGRAPH.** Autographed photo of Enrico Caruso in Rigoletto costume, 5" x 7".	145.00	185.00	150.00
☐ **PHOTOGRAPH.** Autographed portrait of Enrico Caruso, c. 1906, 8" x 10".	180.00	220.00	185.00
☐ **PHOTOGRAPH.** Autographed portrait of Fyodor Chaliapin, c. 1925, 5" x 7".	185.00	265.00	190.00
☐ **PHOTOGRAPH.** Autographed photo of James Melton in costume, 8" x 10".	23.00	35.00	25.00
☐ **PHOTOGRAPH.** Autographed photo of John Brownlee in Rigoletto costume, c. 1940, 8" x 10".	23.00	30.00	25.00
☐ **PHOTOGRAPH.** Autographed photo of Jussi Bjoerling in Boheme costume, 8" x 10".	23.00	33.00	25.00
☐ **PHOTOGRAPH.** Autographed photo of Leontype Price in costume, 8" x 10".	30.00	40.00	31.00
☐ **PHOTOGRAPH.** Autographed photo of Lorenzo Alvary, 8" x 10".	10.00	15.00	12.00
☐ **PHOTOGRAPH.** Autographed photo of Nadine Conner.	21.00	26.00	22.00
☐ **PHOTOGRAPH.** Autographed photo of Rosalind Elias, 8" x 10".	11.00	15.00	12.00
☐ **PHOTOGRAPH.** Autographed photo of Tito Gobbi, c. 1959, 8" x 10".	30.00	37.00	32.00
☐ **POSTER.** Advertising appearance of Salvatore Baccaloni, c. 1940.	13.00	18.00	14.00
☐ **POSTER.** Autographed opera poster of Nicolai Gedda.	23.00	32.00	24.00
☐ **POSTER.** Darkest Russia, 20" x 30", 1895.	135.00	165.00	140.00
☐ **POSTER.** "A Happy Little Home," 40" x 80", 1895.	225.00	300.00	230.00
☐ **POSTER.** East Lynne, 30" x 40", early 1900s.	165.00	210.00	170.00
☐ **POSTER.** Girl of the Golden West, 20" x 30".	60.00	75.00	65.00
☐ **POSTER.** In Gay Atlantic City, 30" x 40", 1890.	300.00	375.00	320.00
☐ **POSTER.** In Old Kentucky, 30" x 40", 1897.	275.00	330.00	280.00
☐ **POSTER.** Metropolitan Opera poster, Emperor Jones, signed by Lawrence Tibbett.	250.00	325.00	255.00
☐ **POSTER.** Metropolitan Opera poster featuring Enrico Caruso.	230.00	330.00	235.00
☐ **POSTER.** Saved from the Sea, 40" x 80", 1895.	145.00	195.00	150.00
☐ **POSTER.** William Gillette's Private Secretary, 20" x 30", 1900.	90.00	120.00	95.00

	Current Price Range		P/Y Average
☐ **PROGRAM.** *Concert program, signed by Roberta Peters.*	10.00	15.00	15.00
☐ **PROGRAM.** *Metropolitan Opera, signed by Frances Alda.*	26.00	38.00	30.00
☐ **PROGRAM.** *Metropolitan Opera, signed by Kirsten Flagstad.*	35.00	45.00	40.00
☐ **PROGRAM.** *Metropolitan Opera House, pre-1900.*	10.00	14.00	11.00
☐ **PROGRAM.** *Metropolitan Opera House, 1901-1910.*	8.00	12.00	9.00
☐ **PROGRAM.** *Metropolitan Opera House, 1911-1920.*	6.00	10.00	7.00

THIMBLES

TOPIC: Thimbles are small fingertip protectors used during sewing.

MATERIALS: Porcelain and silver are the most popular materials for making thimbles.

COMMENTS: Designs of thimbles are very diverse; the decorations on many thimbles are so exquisite that collectors may devote themselves soley to the porcelain painted or other varieties.

ADDITIONAL TIPS: Since thimbles are very difficult to accurately date, their decoration and design remain paramount to most collectors. Some individuals focus on advertising thimbles, while others prefer the artistic type.

☐ **Beer Company Advertising,** porcelain, set of three	2.50	3.00	2.75
☐ **Currier & Ives,** porcelain, blue and white, set of four	1.00	1.50	1.25
☐ **Damron,** Butterfly, cystal	10.00	18.00	14.00
☐ **Delft,** blue, Holland	5.00	10.00	7.50
☐ **Friia,** goldplate, presidents	5.00	10.00	7.50
☐ **General Store Advertising,** porcelain, set of four	3.25	3.75	3.50
☐ **Goldplate Cloisonne,** Disney character	5.00	10.00	7.50

	Current Price Range		P/Y Average
□ **Hummel,** Apple Girl, porcelain	16.00	26.00	21.00
□ **Hurley,** Calico Cuties, porcelain	12.00	20.00	16.00
□ **Lefton,** porcelain, floral motif, set of three ..	.75	1.25	1.00
□ **Limoges,** bird motif, porcelain	10.00	18.00	14.00
□ **Partrige,** bisque, gold raised lettering, signed Joel	15.00	20.00	17.50
□ **Silver,** engraved scenic design	21.00	26.00	24.00
□ **Silver,** engraved scenic design on border ...	15.00	18.00	16.50
□ **Silver,** hallmarked	25.00	35.00	30.00
□ **Silver,** size 9	7.00	13.00	10.00
□ **Silver,** size 6, star trade mark	20.00	26.00	23.00
□ **Spode,** Heavenly cherubs, china	25.00	35.00	30.00
□ **Tobacco Company Advertising,** porcelain, set of three	2.50	3.00	2.75
□ **Whiskey Company Advertising,** porcelain, set of three	2.50	3.00	2.75

THIRD REICH COLLECTIBLES

DESCRIPTION: Items relating to the German Nazi government headed by Adolph Hilter from 1933 to 1945.

COMMENTS: Far from being sympathizers of the Third Reich and its policies, collectors of this memorabilia are usually concerned only with its historical significance.

ADDITIONAL TIPS: For more information, consult *The Official Price Guide to Collectibles of the Third Reich,* published by The House of Collectibles.

Nazi Sun Helmet, *with tan (khaki) cover, early model,* **$80.00-$90.00**

	Current Price Range		P/Y Average
Belt Buckle Pistol, four short .22 caliber barrels are concealed behind a large heavy brass buckle attached to a heavy black belt. When a release is tripped the hinged buckle swings down and the barrels swing out. Each barrel is fired by slight pressure on a small trigger. On the front of the buckle appears the Nazi Party insignia of an eagle grasping a wreath encircling a swastika	17500.00	19400.00	18200.00
Goblet of Honor For Distinguished Achievements in the Air War, silver, cup section is attached to a wide collar and base. The obverse of the cup part has raised figures of eagles in combat. The reverse has a large Iron Cross in raised relief.			
Goblet of Honor, Uncased	1200.00	1400.00	1290.00
Goblet of Honor, Cased. Very rarely offered .	3000.00	4500.00	3700.00
Goering's Wedding Sword, large, heavy sword with genuine damascus blade. On one side in raised gold letters appears "10 APRIL 1935 DIE REICHSLUFTWAFFE IHREM OBERFEFEHL-SHABER" (The National Air Force to its Commander-in-Chief). On the other side of the blade appears "GETREU DEM FUHRER FUR VOLK UND REICH" (Loyal to the Fuhrer for the People and Nation)			**VERY RARE**

	Current Price Range		P/Y Average

☐ **Goering Leaded and Stained Glass Plaque,** this beautiful piece intended for hanging is reputed to have been a wedding gift from Adolph Hitler to Herman Goering and his new bride. Of circular form the principal motif consists of two shields one bearing Goering's coat of arms and the other the arms of his bride, A banner between the helmet crest of each coat of arms bears the legend "10 APRIL 1935," the date of the wedding, in Gothic letters. The background is composed of an intricate floral design. A wreath encircles the plaque. . . . . **VERY RARE**

☐ **Goering Yacht,** this yacht was a wedding present to Herman Goering from the German automobile industry. Tastefully decorated and appointed throughout. The white hull on the bow of each side bears in color the Goering arms . . . . **VERY RARE**

☐ **Hitler's Pocket Watch,** silver cased pocket watch with the authentication that it belonged to Adolph Hitler. Plain white face with black Arabic numerals and gold hour and second hands 3500.00   4000.00   3700.00

☐ **German Order,** the cross patee is of black enamel with raised gold edges within which are gold oak leaves. The cross design itself resembles the shape of the well known Iron Cross. A gold party eagle, swastika and wreath appears between the arms of the cross. The obverse center of the cross is occupied by a gold wreath encircling a white enamel disk upon which appears a circular red enameled band bearing in gold the legend "National Sozialistische D.A.P." (National Socialist German Workers Party) all in capital Roman letters. In the center of the band is a black enameled swastika. The reverse of the cross is generally the same except that there is a second edging of gold in lieu of the oak leaf border and the central disk is of black enamel upon which appears the signature of Adolph Hitler engraved in gold . . . . **VERY RARE**

☐ **Salver of Honor for Distinguished Achievements in Action Badge,** broad rim about a rather shallow dish, the rim had raised edging on both outer and inner sides. A design of widely spaced oak leaves and laurel sprigs in raised relief decorated the surface of the rim. In the center of the dish in raised design is a Luftwaffe eagle grasping a large swastika. Behind the swastika are crossed field marshall batons. On two scrolls above the eagle appear the name and rank of the receiver of

	Current Price Range		P/Y Average

the award. Under the baton design appears a long curved scroll bearing the legend "IN ANERIKENNUNG HERVORRAGENDER KAMPFLEISTUNGEN" (In recognition of distinguished achievements in action) in raised Roman Letters **3500.00 4000.00 3700.00**

☐ **SS First Type Field Cap,** black cloth trimmed with white piping about the tip of the cap and about the upper and lower band. On the front appears the Party eagle, wreath and swastika over a skull and cross bones, all in silver color. Has waterproof lining and leather sweatband. Has paper RZM label **1350.00 1500.00 1410.00**

☐ **Luftwaffe Chaplain's DAK Tropical Cap.** Tan cloth cap with cloth covered vospr and silver piping, At top front of cap is Bevo Eagle, swastika and wreath and cockade. Enclosing the cockage is an inverted purple "V." Between the apex of the "V" and the eagle is a silver embroidered Gothic cross **500.00 600.00 540.00**

TIFFANY GLASS

MAKER: Louis Comfort Tiffany produced decorative accessories in glass, pottery and metal from the 1880s through the 1920s. He grew up in affluence, the son of the famous jeweler, Charles Louis Tiffany, founder of Tiffany and Company of New York. Louis studied art abroad as a young man and spent ten years pursuing a career as a fine artist, achieving some success as a painter, but not the worldwide recognition he sought. He decided to enter the new field of interior decoration where he quickly gained enormous fame. While the foremost exponent of the Art Nouveau movement in America, Tiffany did not strictly adhere to its precepts. Fascinated with the exotic and ornate, Tiffany's unique sense of design and great love of beauty produced a style unlike any other. It was his goal to bring beauty and artistic appreciation into every home in America. In his older years Tiffany's popularity declined as America moved into the streamlined world of the Art Deco period. There was a tremendous resurgence of interest in his work in the 1960s and now his decorative pieces are avidly sought by collectors.

PERIOD: Louis Comfort Tiffany was a well known decorator by the 1880s and a devotee of the infant Art Nouveau movement in America. The Art Nouveau style was a rebellion against the imitativeness of the Victorian period and the mass production of the Industrial Revolution. It came out of the Arts and Crafts movement in England and the belief of its founder, William Morris, that all decorative arts should be handmade. The Art Nouveau style is characterized by a return to nature in motifs executed by sensual, flowing lines with a heavy oriental influence.

CHARACTERISTICS: Tiffany had been collecting ancient glass for years and was particularly captivated by the iridescence found on ancient glass as a result of chemical changes. In 1880 he obtained a patent for his "favrile" glass, favrile meaning handmade. Gold chloride was used either in the glass or as a spray to achieve the iridized gold sheen which characterized favrile. Indeed, Tiffany's colored glass was incredibly deep and true in its color due to the use of expensive metal oxides which produced the most intense colors. His blown glass was reheated as many as twenty times to achieve the desired effect. He absolutely believed that the decoration in glass must be a part of the glass itself, not applied externally.

TYPES: Tiffany Studios produced a wide range of decorative accessories in glass, enamel pottery and bronze. However, Tiffany is most remembered for his exquisite art glass which was fashioned into leaded glass lamp shades and windows, vases, bowls, screens, tableware, desk sets and jewelry boxes to name just a few.

COMMENTS: Tiffany lamps are commanding astronomical prices these days and as a result, many forged marks are appearing. Therefore deal only with an established dealer if you are considering an expensive purchase. Furthermore, be suspicious if you should run across bargain prices for Tiffany items. They probably aren't genuine.

RECOMMENDED READING: For more in-depth information on Tiffany glass, you may refer to *The Offical Price Guide to Glassware* and *The Official Indentification Guide to Glassware,* published by The House of Collectibles.

	Current Price Range		P/Y Average
☐ **Bottle,** scent, bulbous body, teardrop-shaped neck, short circular foot, flattened knopped stopper, silvery-blue iridescent, c. 1899-1928	300.00	400.00	325.00
☐ **Bowl,** circular with paneled sides, scalloped rim, dark blue iridescent, 7" diameter, c. 1928	5000.00	6000.00	4200.00
☐ **Bowl,** Favrile, circular expanding towards rim, incurvate rim, clear, white paperweight flowers with orange and yellow, green leaves, signed, 4¾" diameter, c. 1925	2000.00	3000.00	2100.00
☐ **Bread plates,** Favrile, circular, wide flat rim with ruffling, green shading to opalescent ribbing in the center, 8" diameter, c. 1920, set of six	600.00	700.00	625.00
☐ **Candlestick,** elongated candle socket, openwork, green background, thin cylinder stem, flattened circular foot, 22½" high, c. 1892-1920	600.00	700.00	625.00

Tiffany Lamp, *1930s,*
$6000.00-$6200.00
*(photo courtesy of
©Marc Bernsau,
Sanford, ME, 1984)*

	Current Price Range		P/Y Average
☐ **Candlestick,** free form, indented swirls and flared sides, iridescent amber, signed, 9½″ high c. 1906	600.00	800.00	700.00
☐ **Clock,** carriage, Favrile, rectangular shape, green sides overlaid with bronze filigree in grapevine pattern, angular handle at top, stepped rectangular base, 8″ high, c. 1900 ..	1400.00	1600.00	1500.00
☐ **Compote,** circular shape, spiraling bands, scalloped rim, amber iridescent, 4⅛″ high, c. 1892-1928	175.00	225.00	200.00
☐ **Decanter And Stopper,** double-gourd shape body, circular foot, slender tapering neck, flared rim, amber-colored body, lily pad with tendrils continuing into base, flattened knopped stopper, signed, 11″ high, c. 1904 ..	800.00	900.00	700.00
☐ **Desk Set,** includes a pair of bookends, a pen-tray, a letter rack, a rocker blotter, four-corner blotter ends, a pen knife, an inkwell, a calendar holder, and a paper clip, abalone pattern, c. 1899-1920	800.00	1200.00	850.00

	Current Price Range		P/Y Average

☐ **Lamp,** cone-shaped shade, bronze cylinder standard with fluted sections, flaring circular foot, bands running vertically and horizontally of striated ochre, band of opalescent turtle-back tiles in amber iridescent, 24⅜" high, c. 1899-1920 . . . . — **7000.00 8000.00 — 7500.00**

☐ **Lamp,** desk, domed shade, irregular border, slightly domed finial with bud tip, baluster standard expanding, molded with leaves separating at base, rolled foot with openwork, five feet, shade with pattern of laburnum blossoms and leaves in yellow, ochre, green, blue, lavender and brown, 29" high, c. 1899-1920 . . . . — **35000.00 45000.00 — 40000.00**

☐ **Lamp,** desk, domed shade, pivots on a harp-shaped support, flaring base, foot molded in petals, blue-green iridescent background, loops and trails in silvery-blue iridescence, signed, 18" high, c. 1899-1920 . . . . — **1400.00 1600.00 — 1500.00**

☐ **Lamp,** desk, Favrile, cone-shaped shade, flattened dome finial, gilt-bronze Romanesque standard with scrolling foliage and two bands of glass bosses in green, shade with mottled yellow background and borders, graduated bands of medallions in green, blue, and red, 19¾" high, c. 1899-1920 . . . . . . — **14000.00 16000.00 — 13000.00**

☐ **Lamp,** desk, Favrile, domed shade, wide bell-shaped finial, cylinder flaring base in openwork honeycomb pattern of bronze, mottled blue shading to mottled green background, band of spread winged dragonflies, ochre bodies, yellow, green, and blue wings, green cabochons set above, 31" high, c. 1899-1920 — **35000.00 45000.00 — 36000.00**

☐ **Lamp,** dome shade, emerald green background, with pattern of cherry blossoms and leaves in pink and olive green, mounted on three serpentine supports, ribbed stand in cylinder shape, circular gadroon base, five ball feet, 22" high, c. 1899-1920 . . . . — **5000.00 7000.00 — 5200.00**

☐ **Vase,** compressed spherical body, long, slender cylinder neck expanding to slightly bulbous above body, opalescent, brown and amber lappets, pale yellow background, 11¾" high, c. 1905 . . . . — **1200.00 1600.00 — 1250.00**

☐ **Vase,** cylindrical body, sloping shoulder, waisted neck, circular foot, amber body with amber and tan swirls and loop design, signed, 12" high . . . . — **900.00 1100.00 — 950.00**

☐ **Vase,** cylindrical body, sloping shoulder, waisted neck, circular foot, amber body with amber and tan swirls and loop design, signed, 12" high . . . . — **3500.00 4500.00 — 3600.00**

	Current Price Range		P/Y Average
☐ **Vase,** elongated ovoid shape, paneled sides, short circular foot, casing around neck in blue and amber and yellow iridescent design, overlapping lappets, signed, 8″ high, c. 1921	3500.00	4500.00	3600.00
☐ **Vase,** elongated tulip-shaped body, triangular section, tapering to cylinder stem, slightly domed foot, opalescent, striated amber iridescent and green feathering, 6″ high, c. 1905 . . .	900.00	1100.00	915.00

TIFFANY POTTERY

COMMENTS: Louis Comfort Tiffany, one of America's most illustrious artists known primarily for his work with glass, also produced pottery, jewelry and paintings.

Tiffany first showed his pottery at the St. Louis Exposition in 1904. Both Tiffany and Company and Tiffany Studios produced pottery with production ceasing by 1920.

MARKS: LCT is a mark often found on Tiffany Pottery. Other backstamps include variations of the inscription "L.C. Tiffany Favrile Pottery." Some pieces are also marked with code numbers or letters.

☐ **Bowl,** 7″, collared foot and neck with bulbous body, blue, marked LCT	500.00	550.00	510.00
☐ **Vase,** 6″, narrow base, bulbous shoulders, very narrow neck, green and maroon, marked LCT	500.00	600.00	510.00
☐ **Vase,** 6½″, yellow exterior, green interior, marked LCT	350.00	450.00	360.00
☐ **Vase,** 9¾″, long cylindrical shape, berry and leaf motif, green	600.00	700.00	610.00
☐ **Vase,** 11″, waisted cylindrical shape, artichoke leaf motif molded on bottom half of piece, cream and green exterior, blue and green interior, marked LCT	900.00	1100.00	920.00
☐ **Vase,** 20½″, narrow foot and neck with bulbous shoulders, leaf motif, green	1000.00	2000.00	1100.00

TIN

TYPES: All types of tin items are sought after collectibles. This section concerns tin kitchen utensils.

COMMENTS: A light, fusible metal, tin was often used to coat other metals. Early pieces were usually soldered together. Prices are fairly reasonable.

ADDITIONAL TIPS: The listings are alphabetical according to item. For further information, refer to *The Official Price Guide to Kitchen Collectibles.*

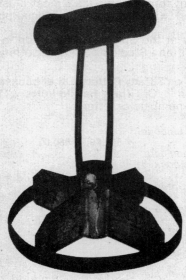

Apple Quarterer, *tin, wood,*
c. 1870s, **$15.00-$25.00**

	Current Price Range		P/Y Average
☐ **Apple Corer**, *19th century*	6.00	9.00	7.00
☐ **Apple Corer**, *handled, T shape*	7.00	13.00	8.50
☐ **Apple Corer**, *with wooden knob handle, 19th century*	6.00	9.00	7.00
☐ **Apple Corer**, *says "The Boye Needle Company," c. 1910*	6.00	9.00	7.00
☐ **Basket**, *wire, for deep frying, with hook to hang for draining*	18.00	22.00	19.00
☐ **Bathtub**, *with high back, round*	90.00	100.00	93.00
☐ **Batter Beater**, *wire coated, c. 1930*	3.50	7.00	4.50
☐ **Bee Smoker**, *leather bellows*	40.00	50.00	43.00
☐ **Betty Lamp**, *on stand, late, 9" long*	95.00	120.00	105.00
☐ **Bird Nest Fryer**, *with wire mesh, c. 1920*	8.00	14.00	9.50
☐ **Biscuit Cutter**, *Victorian, pig shaped*	10.00	20.00	13.00
☐ **Biscuit or Cookie Cutter**, *c. 1910*	10.00	14.00	11.50
☐ **Body Flask**, *concave shape, 11" high*	17.00	23.00	19.00
☐ **Boiler**, *fish, pierced, c. 1890, two parts*	10.00	17.00	12.00
☐ **Border Mold**, *fruit design*	9.00	14.50	11.00
☐ **Bowl**, *beating, c. 1890*	8.00	14.00	9.50
☐ **Bowl**, *handmade, tooled relief of ornate flowers, scrolls and medallions, with lid, 8" x 4¾"*	30.00	50.00	39.50
☐ **Box**, *cake, brown, japanned, c. 1890*	14.00	23.00	16.00
☐ **Box**, *tobacco accessories, wooden with hinged lid, 5" long*	80.00	100.00	87.00
☐ **Box**, *lunch, oval, hinged door, child picture, c. 1910*	90.00	105.00	96.00
☐ **Bread Box**, *brown, rectangular, 13" long*	30.00	45.00	33.00
☐ **Bread Box**, *bubble design, round, 10" diameter*	33.00	47.00	36.00
☐ **Bread Box**, *oak, round, 13" diameter*	35.00	45.00	36.00
☐ **Bread Mixer**, *tin bowl, lidded and crank, dual blades knead dough, clamp, c. 1900*	39.00	50.00	42.00
☐ **Bread Mixer**, *Universal*	35.00	45.00	38.00
☐ **Bread Pan**, *round, two halves fastened together with wire hoop at one end*	12.00	23.00	15.00
☐ **Bread Pan**, *two loaf, round, tin and sheet iron*	36.00	50.00	40.00
☐ **Bread Tin**, *double loaf size, clamps together*	15.00	28.00	18.00
☐ **Bread Raiser**, *tin bowl, handles, lidded with air holes, knob top, 14" diameter*	30.00	52.00	33.00
☐ **Bread Raiser**, *metal finger grip lid handle, 12" diameter*	25.00	37.00	28.00
☐ **Broiler**, *wire, c. 1880s*	10.00	20.00	13.00
☐ **Broom Holder**, *decorated with reliefed blue jays, c. 1900*	80.00	105.00	90.00
☐ **Bucket**, *squared handle, wood grip, factory made*	35.00	50.00	39.00
☐ **Butter Press**, *assorted patterns, c. 1870s* ...	13.00	25.00	16.00
☐ **Cake Cutters**, *c. 1870s*	5.00	10.00	6.50
☐ **Cake Maker**, *crank with gears, handle grip, c. 1900, 8" high*	58.00	70.00	62.00
☐ **Cake Mold**	20.00	30.00	22.00
☐ **Cake Mold**, *9" long*	25.00	35.00	28.00
☐ **Cake Pan**, *bundt style*	10.50	13.50	11.00
☐ **Cake Pan**, *set of three*	25.00	35.00	27.00
☐ **Cake Pan**, *Calumet Baking Powder Company*	10.00	17.00	12.00
☐ **Cake Pan**, *F.A. Walker, c. 1880s*	25.00	35.00	28.00

	Current Price Range		P/Y Average
☐ **Cake Pan,** *star shape tube*	14.00	22.00	16.00
☐ **Cake Pan,** *scalloped, tart, 9" diameter*	6.00	13.00	7.50
☐ **Cake Pan,** *scalloped, tart, 11" diameter*	7.00	15.00	8.50
☐ **Cake Pan,** *scalloped, tart, 13" diameter*	8.00	17.00	10.00
☐ **Cake Pan,** *says "Swans Down Cake Flour Makes Better Cakes," 9" diameter*	18.00	35.00	22.00
☐ **Cake or Pie Tin,** *two pieces, c. 1895*	12.00	20.00	14.00
☐ **Cake Pan,** *tube, fluted, 8" long*	14.00	22.00	16.00
☐ **Cake Spoons,** *c. 1908*	12.00	18.00	14.00
☐ **Candle Box,** *hanging hole*	230.00	270.00	240.00
☐ **Candle Box,** *black, c. 1800*	240.00	290.00	260.00
☐ **Candle Box,** *hinged cover, with hanging hole, c. 1820*	230.00	270.00	240.00
☐ **Candle Holder,** *sheet tin, loop handle*	30.00	55.00	37.00
☐ **Candle Holder,** *flat plate, push up, loop handle, c. 1810, 6" diameter*	110.00	135.00	120.00
☐ **Candle Holder,** *5" high*	15.00	30.00	18.00
☐ **Candle Holder,** *sheet tin, flat drip pan, with snuffer, 8" diameter*	135.00	155.00	142.00
☐ **Candle Lantern,** *sheet tin and mica, hinged door, 5" high*	82.00	115.00	95.00
☐ **Candle Lantern,** *perforated tin and wood, 12" high*	250.00	280.00	262.00
☐ **Candle Light,** *shaped like a Christmas tree, stained glass panels, 3" high*	100.00	150.00	120.00
☐ **Candle Maker,** *c. 1840, 7" diameter*	400.00	450.00	415.00
☐ **Candle Mold,** *one hole, 6"*	14.00	28.00	17.00
☐ **Candle Mold,** *two hole, 6"*	40.00	70.00	55.00
☐ **Candle Mold,** *three hole, 6"*	45.00	70.00	55.00
☐ **Candle Mold,** *four hole*	50.00	65.00	57.00
☐ **Candle Mold,** *footed*	165.00	195.00	175.00
☐ **Candle Mold,** *footed, c. 1860, 13"*	380.00	400.00	385.00
☐ **Carrot Curler,** *tin sheeting, says "Dandy," c. 1900*	4.50	10.00	6.00
☐ **Chamberstick,** *darkened tin, push up candleholder with ring handle, mid 19th century, 5⅜" bottom, 3½" high*	60.00	75.00	63.00
☐ **Chamberstick,** *tin, saucer base with handle, 2¾" tall*	45.00	60.00	48.00
☐ **Cheese Strainer,** *perforated*	184.00	215.00	195.00
☐ **Cheese Strainer,** *legged, perforated, heart shape*	26.00	55.00	35.00
☐ **Churn,** *sheet tin and wood*	242.00	300.00	260.00
☐ **Coal Hod,** *japanned, half covered, c. 1879* . . .	21.00	35.00	26.00
☐ **Coddler,** *egg, lift out rack holds 16 eggs, oval, 7" x 9"*	103.00	118.00	107.00
☐ **Coffee Boiler,** *pierced, c. 1890*	33.00	55.00	38.00
☐ **Coffee Canister,** *japanned and stenciled tin, c. 1890s*	25.00	40.00	28.00
☐ **Coffee Grinder,** *with bottom drawer*	53.00	65.00	56.00
☐ **Coffee Grinder,** *wall type, crank, George Washington pictured*	205.00	235.00	210.00
☐ **Coffee Grinder,** *blue paint, old*	47.00	62.00	50.00
☐ **Coffee Grinder,** *red label, Universal Company, crank*	68.00	85.00	73.00

	Current Price Range		P/Y Average
☐ **Coffee Pot,** *multicolored, green decoration, 10" high*	250.00	285.00	265.00
☐ **Coffee Pot,** *blue and yellow, 5" high*	250.00	270.00	258.00
☐ **Coffee Pot,** *spouted, eight cup*	84.00	105.00	90.00
☐ **Coffee Pot**	89.00	105.00	93.00
☐ **Coffee Roaster,** *for fireplace, tube shape, hinged door*	32.00	43.00	35.00
☐ **Coffee Roaster,** *for fireplace, box shape, iron handle*	37.00	48.00	39.00
☐ **Coffee Roaster,** *for coal stove, round, with crank*	26.00	40.00	28.00
☐ **Colander,** *pierced tin, handles, c. 1890s*	15.00	25.00	18.00
☐ **Cookie Cutter,** *handled, c. 1890*	8.50	16.00	10.00
☐ **Cookie Cutter,** *animals*	8.50	18.00	12.00
☐ **Cookie Cutter,** *bear, 4" high*	16.00	30.00	21.00
☐ **Cookie Cutter,** *bird, 3" long*	26.00	40.00	30.00
☐ **Cookie Cutter,** *bird*	19.00	33.00	25.00
☐ **Cookie Cutter,** *butterfly*	19.00	33.00	25.00
☐ **Cookie Cutter,** *chick*	10.50	24.00	14.00
☐ **Cookie Cutter,** *donkey, laying*	19.00	30.00	22.00
☐ **Cookie Cutter,** *Santa Claus*	13.00	22.00	15.00
☐ **Cookie Cutter,** *hearts*	5.50	13.00	7.00
☐ **Dipper,** *large size, 25" long*	10.50	18.00	12.00
☐ **Dipper,** *enameled*	42.00	60.00	53.00
☐ **Dinner Horn,** *c. 1890*	4.50	15.00	8.00
☐ **Dish Cover,** *blue japanned, c. 1890*	5.50	16.00	9.00
☐ **Dish Pan,** *wooden handles*	16.00	25.00	18.00
☐ **Dish Pan,** *strap handles*	37.00	50.00	41.00
☐ **Dish Dryer,** *hinged utensil rack, tin and wire, c. 1930*	14.00	22.00	16.00
☐ **Dispenser,** *sheet tin, reinforced, c. 1870, 5" diameter*	15.00	33.00	20.00
☐ **Dustpan**	63.00	80.00	69.00
☐ **Dustpan,** *hammered tin, star design in center, wood handle*	33.00	50.00	38.00
☐ **Eclair Pan,** *makes 12 eclairs*	13.00	22.00	15.00
☐ **Egg Basket,** *wire, 9" wide, 3" high*	18.00	22.00	19.00
☐ **Eggbeater-Cream Whipper,** *combination, tank churn, crank, two pieces, c. 1860*	37.00	52.00	42.00
☐ **Eggbeater-Cream Whipper,** *tank churn, crank, says "Lightning Cream and Whip and Egg Beater"*	35.00	50.00	40.00
☐ **Eggbeater-Cream Whipper,** *box churn, crank, clamp and legs, lidded, 7" high*	21.00	35.00	26.00
☐ **Eggbeaters,** *grip handle, crank, two blades, c. 1900*	8.50	18.00	11.00
☐ **Eggbeater,** *grip and crank, rotating action, c. 1900*	8.50	18.00	11.00
☐ **Eggbeater,** *grip and crank, says "A & J," c. 1920*	6.00	13.00	8.50
☐ **Flour Bin and Sifter,** *15 pound*	37.00	50.00	41.00
☐ **Flour Bin and Sifter,** *20 pound*	47.00	60.00	52.00
☐ **Flour Bin and Sifter,** *30 pound*	68.00	81.00	73.00
☐ **Flour Dredger,** *tin, 5½"*	40.00	52.00	42.00
☐ **Flour Sifter,** *says "Acme," c. 1900*	10.00	22.00	13.00

	Current Price Range		P/Y Average
☐ Flour Sifter, *mesh basket, wood handle, c. 1850*	84.00	105.00	93.00
☐ Flour Sifter, *mesh bucket*	8.00	14.00	10.00
☐ Flour Sifter, *combination, crank action*	37.00	50.00	41.00
☐ Funnel, *loop for hanging, 2" diameter*	5.00	8.00	6.00
☐ Funnel, *with handle*	10.00	16.00	12.00
☐ Funnel, *says "C.D. Kenny Co's Teas-Coffees-Sugars"*	23.00	40.00	30.00
☐ Funnel, *says "canning containers," c. 1900*	23.00	40.00	30.00
☐ Funnel, *loop for hanging*	10.00	18.00	13.00
☐ Grater, *tin, nutmeg, place to store nutmeg, ring for hanging*	16.00	20.00	17.00
☐ Grater, *perforated tin, wooden handle*	13.00	22.00	16.00
☐ Grater, *perforated tin with an intricate design*	20.00	30.00	22.00
☐ Grater, *long oval shape, perforated tin, wood handle, 13" length*	10.00	16.00	12.00
☐ Grater, *tin, rectangular, 7" x 11"*	28.00	32.00	29.00
☐ Grater, *two sided for grating, slaw cutter also, with handle and feet, 9" long*	12.00	20.00	14.00
☐ Grater, *says "Gilmore Co.," c. 1890, 11" long*	20.00	30.00	23.00
☐ Ladle, *gravy, 13" long*	16.00	26.00	20.00
☐ Ladyfingers Pan, *c. 1890*	43.00	58.00	46.00
☐ Lamp, *tin and iron, flat base, acorn design on shaft*	224.00	270.00	244.00
☐ Lamp, *shaped like coal stove, red glass door, 6" high*	58.00	75.00	67.00
☐ Lantern, *c. 1890, 11" high*	89.00	125.00	100.00
☐ Lard Lamp Front, *3" high*	155.00	175.00	162.00
☐ Loaf Pan, *lidded, 20" long*	30.00	55.00	40.00
☐ Lunch Box, *with cup and dish*	40.00	70.00	53.00
☐ Lunch Box, *with dishes, hinged lid, wooden handle*	53.00	70.00	63.00
☐ Masher, *potato, tin and wood, zig zag pattern, c. 1936*	5.00	11.00	7.00
☐ Match Holder, *match box case and safe*	8.00	12.00	9.00
☐ Match Holder, *match box holder and safe with advertising*	13.00	20.00	15.00
☐ Match Holder, *match box holder and safe*	13.00	22.00	16.00
☐ Match Holder, *small, hinged lid*	9.00	16.00	11.00
☐ Match Holder, *open holder, intricate embossed design, 3½" high*	12.00	18.00	14.00
☐ Match Holder, *two compartment with striker, wall type, 5" high*	20.00	35.00	26.00
☐ Match Safe, *c. 1900*	18.00	30.00	22.00
☐ Match Safe, *enamelled "matches"*	12.00	18.00	14.00

TINTYPES

DESCRIPTION: Early photographs, usually but not exclusively portraits, made by a special process distinctive from other photographs of their era.

TYPES: The most familiar tintype is a portrait measuring approximately 2½ by 3½ inches, though tintypes of larger and smaller sizes exist. This size became standard as it permitted the photographer to make four different exposures on one plate. These are known as "Quarter-Plate" tintypes.

PERIOD: The tintype process was short lived. It was invented in 1856 and declined by the 1870s.

MATERIALS: Tintypes were exposed from metal plates whose surfaces had been coated with varnish. This was the point of departure from earlier processes, which had used silver coating.

COMMENTS: Tintypes are the earliest photographs widely available on the collector market at moderate prices. Anonymous portraits of anonymous persons are collected simply as specimens of pioneer photography, and are of interest even if no identification can ever be made of the photograher, subject, or locale. Of great appeal are topical specimens such as photos of Civil War soldiers and officers and circus performers.

ADDITIONAL TIPS: Today there are specialist dealers who regularly stock early photographs, including tintypes, but fine selections may also be found at auction sales of photographica and Americana.

	Current Price Range		P/Y Average
☐ **Actress,** ¼ plate of Ella Rathbun in a dancing pose, enclosed in a pink and red cardboard mat, c. 1885	42.00	53.00	46.00
☐ **Anonymous Domestic Portrait,** husband and wife, wife seated in ornate chair, husband standing with hand on her shoulder, 1865 ...	11.00	15.00	13.00
☐ **Anonymous Portrait,** middle aged man with frock coat, eyeglasses, sideburns, head and shoulders view, mounted in a wood frame with oval opening, 1860s	11.00	15.00	13.00

	Current Price Range		P/Y Average

☐ **Bishop Baker,** Abbot & Co., commercially issued tintype picturing abolishionists and ministers, 1863, 1½″ x 1½″ . . . . **15.00 20.00** — **17.00**

☐ **Boy With Dog,** ⅙ plate, black dog on fringed chair, uncased . . . . **13.00 17.00** — **14.75**

☐ **Civil War Infantryman Loading Musket,** ⅙ plate, standing three quarter portrait holding M1861 musket and ramrod, cased . . . . **190.00 230.00** — **205.00**

☐ **Civil War Officer,** whole plate, three quarter length portrait holding bayoneted rifle over right shoulder . . . . **90.00 115.00** — **102.00**

☐ **Commodore DuPont,** Abbot & Co., commercially issued tintype, printed reverse, 1864 . . **40.00 55.00** — **46.00**

☐ **Coney Island (New York),** ⅙ plate, roller skaters from "Coney Rink" . . . . **27.00 35.00** — **30.00**

☐ **Croquet Players,** ⅙ plate, distant view of players against wooded background, housed in a pink paper mat . . . . **20.00 25.00** — **22.00**

☐ **Cyclist,** ⅙ plate, man wearing bowtie stands next to his cycle, uncased, c. 1890 . . . . **15.00 20.00** — **17.00**

☐ **Farm House,** whole plate, family gathered outside frame farm house, uncased, unmounted, c. 1870s . . . . **60.00 80.00** — **67.00**

☐ **Female Pilot,** woman in aviator outfit standing alongside early aircraft, housed in a decorated cardboard mat with shield and the word "Greetings," World War I era . . . . **32.00 39.00** — **34.00**

☐ **Foreign Costume,** large tintype portrait of man wearing Eastern European or Turkish national costume, full length . . . . **22.00 28.00** — **24.50**

☐ **Gamblers,** ⅙ plate, half length portraits of two men playing cards at a small table, uncased . . . . **30.00 38.00** — **33.50**

☐ **General Burnside,** Abbot & Co., commercially issued tintype, printed reverse, 1864 . . . . **45.00 60.00** — **51.00**

☐ **General Halleck,** Abbot & Co., commercially issued tintype, printed reverse, 1864 . . . . **40.00 55.00** — **46.00**

☐ **General Walbridge,** Abbot & Co., commercially issued tintype picturing abolishionists and ministers, 1863, 1½″ x 1¼″ . . . . **15.00 20.00** — **17.00**

☐ **Grocer In Wagon,** ⅙ plate, man driving wagon which reads "City Grocery," pulled by horse, half case . . . . **50.00 65.00** — **56.00**

☐ **Hunter,** ¼ plate, full length portrait of man in dress suit with rifle over his left shoulder . . . **23.00 30.00** — **26.00**

☐ **Louis Blenker,** Abbot & Co., Union commercially issued tintype, printed reverse, 1864 . . **40.00 55.00** — **44.00**

☐ **Pair of Union Cavalry Soldiers,** wearing jackets and trousers, one has broadbrim hat with cavalry boots, a quarter-plate tintype . . . . **68.00 85.00** — **74.00**

☐ **Patriot,** ¼ plate of man standing next to large American flag, probably made during Civil War to show patriotism . . . . **36.00 44.00** — **39.00**

☐ **Post-Civil War,** officer in dress uniform, 1870s **35.00 45.00** — **39.00**

	Current Price Range		P/Y Average
☐ **Rev. Theodore Parker,** Abbot & Co., commercially issued tintype picturing abolishionists and ministers, c. 1863, 1½ ″ x 1¼ ″	15.00	20.00	17.00
☐ **Soldier and Wife Seated on Ornate Victorian Sofa,** quarter plate tintype	45.00	60.00	49.00
☐ **Tennis Players,** ⅙ plate, group shot of six persons with racquets and balls, half case, c. 1880	35.00	45.00	39.00
☐ **Union Chaplain William Bryan,** ⅙ plate, half length portrait with shoulder bars and clerical collar, housed in a gutta percha case, dated March 26, 1863	200.00	250.00	215.00
☐ **Union Corporal,** ⅙ plate, half length seated portrait with right arm resting on table, cased	70.00	100.00	82.00
☐ **Union Soldier,** young, seated in front of photography backdrop	30.00	40.00	34.00
☐ **Violin Player,** ⅙ plate, young man holding violin and bow, gutta percha case	50.00	60.00	53.50
☐ **Watermelon Feast,** ⅙ plate, group shot of seven people (white) eating watermelon, c. 1880	15.00	20.00	17.00
☐ **Zouave,** ⅙ plate tinted, half length portrait, housed in an embossed contemporary case .	110.00	140.00	115.00
☐ **Bust Portrait,** Union soldier, in uniform, mounted in frame with oval opening	32.00	40.00	35.00

TOBACCO JARS

DESCRIPTION: The tobacco jar is generally a combination of a humidor and pipe holder.

MATERIALS: Tobacco jars are made from a variety of items including wood, china, pottery, iron and other metals.

COMMENTS: Many tobacco jars were not only functional but quite ornately decorated. Sculptured heads, figures or animals are commonly found on tabacco jars.

ADDITIONAL TIPS: Price ranges listed are for original jars in good condition.

	Current Price Range		P/Y Average
☐ **Arab,** wearing headdress, 7″ H.	60.00	75.00	67.50
☐ **Boy,** bisque, 6¾″ H.	60.00	75.00	67.50
☐ **Buffalo,** pottery, Dedare ware	220.00	265.00	240.00
☐ **Bulldog,** Bristolware tan colored ceramic . . .	60.00	75.00	65.00
☐ **Devil's Head,** red, bee on side of head	50.00	65.00	57.00
☐ **Elephant,** Majolica	90.00	115.00	102.50
☐ **Egyptian Queen,** exotic face, very colorful, 4″ H.	80.00	100.00	90.00
☐ **Frog With Pipe**	85.00	110.00	97.00
☐ **Girl's Face,** with light hair, hat functions as cover	85.00	110.00	97.00
☐ **Human Skull**	95.00	120.00	107.00
☐ **Indian Chief,** Majolica, feathered headdress, 10″ H.	95.00	120.00	107.00
☐ **Indian Head,** mahogany, top of head is lid, 1900s, 7″	130.00	160.00	145.00
☐ **Jester With Dog,** Staffordshire, 9½″ H.	250.00	300.00	275.00
☐ **Lion's Head,** Austrian hallmarks	50.00	70.00	60.00
☐ **Man,** with derby hat, pipe in mouth, Austrian	50.00	70.00	60.00
☐ **Man,** with skull cap, English pottery	95.00	120.00	97.00
☐ **Monk,** fat with laughing face, bisque china- ware	65.00	85.00	75.00
☐ **Monkeys,** face on lid and around base	140.00	175.00	157.00
☐ **Old Salt Sea Captain,** with cap and pipe	90.00	115.00	102.50
☐ **Owl,** Majolica, 7″ H.	55.00	75.00	65.00
☐ **Pipes On Cover,** pink and green pottery	70.00	95.00	82.50
☐ **Pirate,** shirt and hat, Majolica	95.00	120.00	107.00
☐ **Ram's Head,** Majolica	90.00	115.00	102.50
☐ **Royal Bayreuth,** tapestry ware, cows in field .	275.00	340.00	302.00
☐ **Sea Captain,** pipe in mouth, Majolica	100.00	135.00	117.50

TOOLS

DESCRIPTION: A tool is a device used by hand. Those who use tools include carpenters, farmers, plumbers, cabinetmakers and wheelwrights.

TYPES: There are several different types of tools but woodworking tools which include planes, saws, measuring implements, augers, bits and bladed instruments are the items most sought after by collectors.

COMMENTS: Handmade tools of the 1800s and factory produced tools of the early 1900s are the most desirable among collectors.

ADDITIONAL TIPS: Some hobbyists collect tools by type while others collect by craft. An entire collection could be comprised of tools used only by a shipwright or it could contain every type of bladed instrument from various occupations.

	Current Price Range		P/Y Average
☐ **Adze,** *bowl, curved blade, 7", signed "Ream"*	111.00	118.00	113.00
☐ **Adze,** *carpenter's, blade, 4½"*	8.50	12.00	9.00
☐ **Adze,** *shipbuilder's, blade, 5"*	18.00	22.00	19.00
☐ **Anvil,** *cooper's, wrought iron, 8"*	42.00	48.00	43.00
☐ **Auger,** *hand-forged stem is Y-shaped at hickory handle, 24" x 1¼", 1850s*	22.00	32.00	27.00
☐ **Auger,** *hand-forged crude hickory handles, unreadable mark, 15" x 1¼", 1850s*	20.00	29.00	23.50
☐ **Auger,** *pod, wooden cross handle, 20"*	13.00	17.00	14.00
☐ **Auger,** *reamer, cooper's, 14" with 17" wooden cross handle*	10.00	13.00	11.00
☐ **Auger,** *stamped #5, no manufacturer's mark, well shaped hickory handle, 15" x 1½", c. 1880*	14.00	20.00	17.00
☐ **Axe,** *camp, Marble's #10, "Gladstone, Mich."*	107.00	113.00	108.00
☐ **Axe,** *ceremonial, red and black paint, curved blade, 13" x 38"*	61.00	69.00	62.00
☐ **Axe,** *felling type, marked "Stohler"*	32.00	40.00	35.00
☐ **Axe,** *felling, wrought iron, blade, 5"*	8.50	12.00	9.00
☐ **Axe,** *felling, wrought iron, blade, 5" x 30"*	10.00	13.00	11.00
☐ **Axe,** *fireman's, "Warren Axe and Tool Co., Warren, Pa."*	33.00	37.00	34.00
☐ **Axe,** *goose wing, wrought iron, blade, 12"*	155.00	165.00	158.00
☐ **Axe,** *hand, head, 5"*	20.00	24.00	21.00
☐ **Axe,** *post hole, center bit of wrought iron*	42.00	49.00	43.00
☐ **Axe,** *post hole type, made by Hagen of Lancaster, Pennsylvania, wrought single center bit*	42.00	55.00	45.00
☐ **Bale Hook,** *wooden handle, 5"*	2.00	4.00	2.50
☐ **Beader,** *Stanley #66, with cutter and straight fence*	41.00	49.00	43.00
☐ **Beader,** *Windsor style, brass, wooden handles, 10½"*	90.00	100.00	93.00
☐ **Bench Stop,** *wrought iron*	12.00	17.00	13.00
☐ **Bitstock,** *beechwood, 13½"*	240.00	256.00	245.00
☐ **Bitstock,** *cooper's, beechwood, fixed spoon bit, head 3½"*	230.00	250.00	235.00
☐ **Bitstock,** *wooden with iron ferrules, 14"*	267.00	283.00	270.00
☐ **Blades,** *for planes, set of three*	3.00	7.00	5.00
☐ **Bolt Header,** *wrought iron, 22" long*	8.50	12.00	9.00
☐ **Brace,** *Beech Sheffield, unplated*	90.00	100.00	93.00
☐ **Brace,** *chairmaker's, beechwood, 13"*	157.00	173.00	160.00
☐ **Brace,** *chairmaker's, spoon bit, beechwood, 13"*	145.00	190.00	160.00
☐ **Brace,** *crank, geared, "Millers Falls #182"*	28.00	34.00	30.00
☐ **Brace,** *four-post cage head, 13"*	295.00	320.00	302.00
☐ **Brace,** *gentleman's, beechwood head, 11"*	32.00	38.00	33.00
☐ **Brace,** *gentleman's, "H & R Boker"*	10.50	14.00	11.00

	Current Price Range		P/Y Average

☐ **Cutter,** *brush, blade 12" with laid on steel edge, 38"*	51.00	59.00	52.50
☐ **Cutter,** *circle, brass with wooden head, engraved decoration on one side, 2½" x 9½"*	243.00	258.00	246.00
☐ **Cutter,** *for corn or sugar cane*	17.00	22.00	18.00
☐ **Darning Tool,** *made of wood with round knob, turned handle, c. 1915*	7.50	11.00	9.50
☐ **Drill,** *bow, beechwood drill, hickory bow*	282.00	307.00	288.00
☐ **Drill,** *breast, brass, 15"*	240.00	260.00	245.00
☐ **Drill,** *hand, marked Goodel Bros., bit dispenser made of brass*	17.00	25.00	20.00
☐ **Drill,** *hand, marked Metro Tool Works, Ger., 14"*	10.00	15.00	12.00
☐ **Drill,** *hand, marked Millers' Falls 2-A, red, ornamental wheel, hollow handle, glossy wood, 14½"*	20.00	30.00	24.50
☐ **Drill,** *striped gilt decoration, in decorated tin case with nine original bits, "Johnson & Tainter's. Pat. Oct. 5, '69"*	60.00	70.00	62.00
☐ **Filletster,** *moving, fence and brass depth stop, #54 "Child, Pratt & Co., St. Louis, MO".*	46.00	53.00	47.00
☐ **Filletster,** *sash, beechwood with brass tips and depth adjustment, "John Mosely & Son"*	90.00	100.00	92.00
☐ **Float,** *cabinetmaker's, rosewood handle, "W. Drummond & Sons," 14" long*	61.00	69.00	62.00
☐ **Floor Scraper,** *for wood floors, flat, 5" blade.*	5.00	10.00	7.00
☐ **Framing Square,** *wrought iron with hand lettering*	22.00	28.00	23.00
☐ **Froe,** *gratting, 8"*	6.00	8.00	6.50
☐ **Froe,** *splitting, basket maker's, 5" long*	36.00	43.00	37.50
☐ **Froe,** *splitting, blade 10"*	17.00	21.00	18.00
☐ **Froe,** *splitting, blade 12"*	17.00	23.00	18.00
☐ **Gaff,** *iceman's or lumberman's, 6" length*	8.50	12.00	9.00
☐ **Garden Sprayer,** *turned wood handle, three attached nozzles, cast brass, 20"*	40.00	50.00	44.50
☐ **Gauge,** *clapboard, mahogany, 3" x 7"*	36.00	42.00	37.50
☐ **Gauge,** *clapboard setting, maple and mahogany, 8" wide*	75.00	85.00	78.00
☐ **Gauge,** *marking, boxwood with brass fence, "D. M. Lyon & Co., Newark, NJ"*	37.00	43.00	38.50
☐ **Gauge,** *pattern maker's, rosewood and walnut*	26.00	30.00	27.00
☐ **Gauge,** *rope and cable, "J. Rabone & Sons, Makers, #1207," 2" x 6½"*	70.00	80.00	73.00
☐ **Gauge,** *rope and cable, "Rabone #1208," 2" x 4½"*	51.00	59.00	53.00
☐ **Gauge,** *veneer splitting, beechwood*	13.00	17.00	14.00
☐ **Gauge,** *vertical height, brass, three-footed, 3½" high*	39.00	45.00	40.00
☐ **Gig,** *eel, wooden handle with five prongs, handle 62" long*	14.00	18.00	15.00
☐ **Gimlet,** *bell hanger's, ebony handle, 41" long*	18.00	22.00	19.00
☐ **Glass Cutter,** *marked France, made of brass, 4"*	2.00	6.00	4.50
☐ **Glue Pot,** *cast iron, "Marietta" #1 size, 6" diameter*	13.00	17.00	14.00

	Current Price Range		P/Y Average

☐ **Glue Pot,** *copper, miniature*	51.00	59.00	53.00
☐ **Hack Saw,** *Old Miller Falls, brass ferrule, straight handle with adjustable top notch* . . .	10.00	15.00	12.00
☐ **Hammer,** *broom maker's*	22.00	28.00	23.50
☐ **Hammer,** *broom maker's, brass ferrule, 9"* . .	26.00	34.00	28.00
☐ **Hammer,** *caulking, slotted head, iron wings, 1880s*	12.00	15.00	13.50
☐ **Hammer,** *claw, hand wrought, head 4½"* . . .	10.00	14.00	11.00
☐ **Hammer,** *cobbler's, marked "Steel drop forged champion," handle replaced, 1920s* . .	5.00	8.00	6.50
☐ **Hammer,** *cobbler's or upholstery, "Made in Germany," hand-forged tool, steel, unusually angled head, 1920s*	7.00	10.00	8.50
☐ **Hammer,** *double clawed*	142.00	158.00	146.00
☐ **Hammer,** *Sawyer, head 5½"*	47.00	53.00	48.50
☐ **Hammer Head,** *embossed Des Moines Ice and Fuel Co., Ph. 3-4221 on both sides, used to break up coal lumps, no handle, rare*	17.00	22.00	19.00
☐ **Hand Beader,** *Stanley #66, straight fence with cutter*	28.00	32.00	29.00
☐ **Hat Brimmer,** *tool used to cut felt for hats, has adjustable blade holder that slides away from curved base so that brim can be cut to 2"-5" W. as desired, maple with brass-locking nuts, 1800s*	27.00	36.00	30.00
☐ **Hatchet,** *LL beam, 9" straight handle, blade 2½" W., 1920s*	12.00	17.00	14.50
☐ **Hatchet,** *plumb, boy scout holster, 10½" curved handle, blade 3" W., 1920s*	7.00	10.00	8.50
☐ **Hatchet,** *steel, 6½"*	3.00	7.00	5.00
☐ **Hinge Butt Mortiser,** *made by Waller Tool Co. of Chicago*	60.00	80.00	67.00
☐ **Holder,** *horse rein, wrought iron*	19.00	25.00	20.50
☐ **Hook,** *hay, hand-wrought, hickory handle, 1800s*	5.00	7.50	6.75
☐ **Hoop Driver,** *cooper's, wrought iron, 24"*	22.00	28.00	23.00
☐ **Howelling Tool,** *cooper's*	58.00	67.00	60.50
☐ **Inshave,** *cooper's, beechwood with brass bottom, 9"*	46.00	52.00	47.00
☐ **Jack,** *mitre, mahogany, 30"*	55.00	61.00	57.00
☐ **Jack,** *steel, Stanley, model #S5, rosewood handle and knob, 14"*	145.00	170.00	155.00
☐ **Knife,** *chamfer, cooper's, wooden handle, 16"*	37.00	43.00	38.00
☐ **Knife,** *chamfer, cooper's, wooden handle, blade 7", 18"*	46.00	52.00	47.00
☐ **Knife,** *clogger's hollowing, wrought iron, curved cutter, 1½"*	120.00	131.00	123.00
☐ **Knife,** *clogger's hollowing, cutter 1½", 30" long*	90.00	100.00	92.50
☐ **Knife,** *clogger's hollowing, wrought iron, curved cutter, 2"*	120.00	132.00	123.00
☐ **Knife,** *draw, cooper's tangs bent through handles, brass ferrule, 1840s*	12.00	17.00	14.50
☐ **Knife,** *draw, folding handle, cherrywood handle, "A.J. Wilkinson, Boston," Pat. July 16, 1895, blade 7"*	29.00	35.00	30.50

	Current Price Range		P/Y Average

☐ **Knife**, *draw, leather working "Snell & Atherton," #5, all metal scraper, c. 1870* . . . . — 14.00 — 19.00 — 16.50

☐ **Knife**, *draw, open scorp, brass ferrule, 1800s* — 14.00 — 19.00 — 16.50

☐ **Knife**, *draw, wagon maker's, "Ohio Tool Co." #9, 9" blade, eggshaped handles, maple, c. 1870* . . . . — 15.00 — 20.00 — 17.50

☐ **Knife**, *for trimming hooves, 1890s* . . . . — 2.50 — 4.00 — 3.25

☐ **Knife**, *hay, brass ferrules on both handles, 1870s* . . . . — 17.00 — 24.00 — 20.00

☐ **Knife**, *hay, Connecticut style, 36"* . . . . — 20.00 — 24.00 — 21.00

☐ **Knife**, *hay, "Pat. Jan. 20, '68," blade 8", 34" long* . . . . — 46.00 — 52.00 — 48.00

☐ **Knife**, *hay, wood handle, 17" blade* . . . . — 17.00 — 21.00 — 18.00

☐ **Knife**, *race, bone handle, 7"* . . . . — 22.00 — 28.00 — 23.00

☐ **Knife**, *race, folding, rosewood handle* . . . . . . — 31.00 — 39.00 — 33.00

☐ **Knife**, *splint, basket maker's, 12"* . . . . — 70.00 — 80.00 — 72.50

☐ **Level**, *cherrywood with two adjustable vials, "J.M. Davidson, New York"* . . . . — 80.00 — 90.00 — 82.00

☐ **Level**, *inclinometer, brass, patented "Adams, Dubuque"* . . . . — 18.00 — 22.00 — 19.00

☐ **Level**, *iron, marked "Stanley Rule & Level Co." and "Wm. T. Nicholson," Patentee, Prov. R.I., May 1, 1860," 14"* . . . . — 132.00 — 148.00 — 136.00

☐ **Level**, *mahogany, top level adjustment with two adjustable vials* . . . . — 80.00 — 90.00 — 83.00

☐ **Level**, *rosewood and brass, Stratton Bros. #10, "Pat. July 16, 1872" and "Oct. 4, 1887"* . . — 215.00 — 233.00 — 220.00

☐ **Log Dog**, *jointed, 22" long* . . . . — 14.00 — 18.00 — 15.00

☐ **Log Dog**, *one piece, 14"* . . . . — 4.00 — 6.00 — 4.50

☐ **Log Dog**, *pivot-type, 21" long* . . . . — 13.00 — 17.00 — 14.00

☐ **Lumber Rule**, *brass end, handmade, 29"* . . . . — 25.50 — 31.00 — 27.00

☐ **Lumber Rule**, *brass end, "Lufkin Rule Co.," 42"* . . . . — 16.00 — 20.00 — 17.00

☐ **Lumber Stick**, *brass end, 1" x 1" x 36"* . . . . . . — 15.00 — 19.00 — 16.00

☐ **Mallet**, *wood, head has two 1½" wide iron bands* . . . . — 10.00 — 20.00 — 15.00

☐ **Map Plotting Scale**, *boxwood, beveled edges, 1¾" x 6"* . . . . — 22.00 — 27.00 — 23.50

☐ **Map Scale**, *ivory, 2" x 6"* . . . . — 61.00 — 69.00 — 62.00

☐ **Mortise Gauge**, *ebony fence with solid brass stem* . . . . — 41.00 — 49.00 — 43.00

☐ **Mortise Gauge**, *rosewood, Stanley #77* . . . . . — 20.00 — 24.00 — 21.00

☐ **Mortise Tool**, *hinge butt, "Waller Tool Co., Chicago"* . . . . — 61.00 — 69.00 — 62.00

☐ **Mortise Tool**, *wrought iron with strapped handle attached to head, head 18"* . . . . — 70.00 — 80.00 — 71.00

☐ **Mouse Trap**, *wood, five holes, round, rare* . . . — 10.00 — 18.00 — 14.50

☐ **Mouse Trap**, *wood, four holes, round, rare* . . . — 8.00 — 16.00 — 12.00

☐ **Nail Header**, *wrought iron, round, 10" long* . . — 8.50 — 11.00 — 9.00

☐ **Parallel Rule**, *rosewood with brass, 15"* . . . . . — 41.00 — 49.00 — 43.00

☐ **Plane**, *nosing, beechwood, #466 "Greenfield Tool Co."* . . . . — 18.00 — 22.00 — 19.00

☐ **Plane**, *panel raising, nickel blade and two adjustable fences, Greenfield Tool Co., #688* — 215.00 — 235.00 — 220.00

☐ **Plane**, *pencil sharpener, mahogany* . . . . — 46.00 — 53.00 — 47.00

	Current Price Range		P/Y Average
☐ **Router,** *maple, metal clad bottom, 4" x 7"* ...	32.00	38.00	33.50
☐ **Rule,** *boxwood, one foot, four fold, "Stephens & Co., #70, Riverton, CT"*	15.00	19.00	16.00
☐ **Rule,** *caliper, hatter's ebony and silver with ivory caliper slide*	118.00	132.00	121.00
☐ **Rule,** *brass trim all around, Chapin Stephens Co., stamped "JRP," 1880s*	22.00	29.00	25.00
☐ **Rule,** *ivory, four fold, brass fittings, 18" long*	215.00	235.00	220.00
☐ **Rule,** *ivory, 24" L., 1800s*	55.00	70.00	62.50
☐ **Rule,** *Lufkin #651, brass trim, marked "Boxwood — Made in England"*	14.00	19.00	16.50
☐ **Rule,** *Lufkin, pat'd. 12/3/18, brass trim, marked "Boxwood," stamped "Maguire," 1920s*	13.00	18.00	15.00
☐ **Rule,** *Stanley, #66½, brass at hinges and end, "Warrented Boxwood," 36" L., 1800s* ...	22.00	29.00	23.00
☐ **Rule,** *Stanley, #68, brass trim on hinges and ends, "Boxwood," 1900s*	14.00	19.00	16.50
☐ **Sash Filleter,** *made by John Moseley and Son, beechwood, brass tips with depth adjustment*	90.00	110.00	97.00
☐ **Saw,** *backsaw, Wright & Co. on blade, extra heavy back, beech handle, 11" L., 1890s*	14.00	19.00	16.50
☐ **Saw,** *bow, beechwood with boxwood handles, 9" x 15"*	86.00	92.00	88.00
☐ **Saw,** *fret, beechwood handle, "Hobbie's Patent," 18" high*	60.00	70.00	63.00
☐ **Saw,** *jeweler's piercing, beechwood handle, 12" long*	36.00	43.00	38.00

TOY CARS

TOPIC: Toy cars are scaled-down models of automobiles. The detail on them can be extremely intricate, with working windshield wipers and rubber tires, or it can be minimal. Toy cars as a rule do not run under their own power.

PERIOD: Collectible toy cars date back to around 1910.

MAKERS: Corgi, Dinky, Matchbox and Tootsietoy are major names in the production of toy cars. Other less well known companies are F & F Corporation, Gamda Koor, Hubley and Play Art.

COMMENTS: Large toy cars are generally more valuable than smaller ones. Whether the car does what it was designed to do is immaterial, since it is mainly for display and not play.

ADDITIONAL TIPS: Most collectors do not play with their miniature toy cars, because the value of the item depends greatly on condition. Restored specimens have little value on the collector market. For additional information, please refer to *The Official Price Guide to Collectible Toys,* published by The House of Collectibles.

James Bond Aston Martin #271, $5.00-$7.00
Photo courtesy of Dick Starr.

Iso Grifo #301, $15.00-$18.00
Photo courtesy of Dick Starr.

MATCHBOX 1 - 75 SERIES

	Current Price Range		P/Y Average
No. 1C Dodge Challenger, *c. 1976, red body, silver interior, white roof*	2.00	3.00	2.75
No. 2C Mercedes Benz—Binz Ambulance, *c. 1968, white with red cross decal*	4.00	6.00	4.00
No. 2D Monteverdi Hai, *c. 1974, red body, white interior, silver trim, opening doors*	2.00	3.00	2.75
No. 2F Porsche Turbo, *c. 1979, brown body, yellow interior, opening doors*	2.00	3.00	2.75
No. 5E Gruesome Twosome, *c. 1972, gold body, white interior, exposed engine at front and rear*	3.00	4.00	3.25
No. 5F Pontiac Firebird, *c. 1976, blue body, silver interior, tinted windows*	2.00	3.00	2.75
No. 5G '57 Chevy, *c. 1981, pink body, silver interior, opening hood*	2.00	3.00	2.75
No. 6E Lotus Europa, *c. 1969, blue body, white interior, opening doors*	3.00	5.00	4.00
No. 6H 4 x 4 Jeep Off Road, *c. 1982, bronze body, black crash bars and grill*	3.00	4.00	3.75
No. 6E Mercedes Tourer 3505L, *c. 1974, yellow interior, silver trim, white hood*	3.00	4.00	3.75
No. 6F Mercedes 350 Convertible, *c. 1982, silver body, white interior, silver trim*	2.00	3.00	3.75
No. 7B Ford Anglia, *c. 1961, light blue body, grey plastic wheels*	5.25	8.00	5.00
No. 7E Volkswagen Golf, *c. 1977, green body, yellow interior, two surf boards*	4.00	5.00	4.25
No. 8E Ford Mustang Fastback, *c. 1967, orange body, white interior*	5.25	8.00	5.00
No. 8F Ford Mustang Wildcat Dragster, *c. 1971, orange body, yellow interior*	2.00	3.00	3.75
No. 8G De Tomaso Pantera, *c. 1975, white body, red interior, No. 8 decal*	2.00	3.00	3.75
No. 8H Rover 3500, *c. 1981, bronze body cream interior, sliding roof*	4.00	5.00	4.75
No. 9E AMX Javelin, *c. 1972, green body, orange interior, silver trim*	4.00	5.00	4.25
No. 9F Ford Escort RS 2000, *c. 1978, white body, black trim, "Shell" decal*	3.00	4.00	3.25
No. 10F Plymouth "Granfury" Police Car, *c. 1979, white body, white interior, silver base* ..	3.50	4.50	3.75
No. 11E Flying Bug, *c. 1973, red body, yellow jets on roof*	3.00	4.00	3.75
No. 12A Land Rover, *c. 1955, green body, silver trim*	8.80	12.50	8.00
No. 12B Land Rover (Series II), *c. 1959, olive green body, tow hook*	7.00	10.00	7.50
No. 12C Safari Land Rover, *c. 1966, green body, white interior*	6.00	8.00	6.50
No. 12F Citroen CX, *c. 1980, light blue body, yellow interior, silver base*	4.00	5.00	4.75
No. 13E Baja Buggy, *c. 1972, green body, black trim*	2.50	3.50	3.00
No. 14A Daimler Ambulance, *c. 1956, cream body, silver trim, Red Cross decal*	12.00	14.00	11.50

	Current Price Range		P/Y Average
☐ No. 14B Daimler Ambulance, c. 1958, cream and silver, Red Cross decal	10.50	12.00	9.50
☐ No. 14C Bedford Lomas Ambulance, c. 1962, white body, white interior, silver trim	6.00	8.00	6.50
☐ No. 14D Iso Grifo, c. 1968, blue body, light blue interior, silver grille	2.50	4.00	2.75
☐ No. 30A Ford Prefect, c. 1957, blue body	12.50	14.50	13.00
☐ No. 30D Beach Buggy, c. 1971, metallic mauve body, yellow interior	5.50	6.50	5.25
☐ No. 31A American Ford Customline Station Wagon, c. 1957, yellow body, silver trim	11.00	14.00	13.50
☐ No. 31B American Ford Fairlane Station Wagon, c. 1960, metallic green body, silver wheels	5.60	6.25	5.75
☐ No. 31C Lincoln Continental, c. 1964, metallic blue body, white interior	5.00	7.00	5.65
☐ No. 31D Volks Dragon, c. 1972, red body, yellow interior	4.00	5.00	4.75
☐ No. 31E Caravan, c. 1978, white body, yellow interior	4.00	5.00	4.75
☐ No. 32A Jaguar XK140, c. 1957, red body	10.00	13.50	12.00
☐ No. 32B E Type Jaguar, c. 1962, red body, white interior, white spoked wheels	6.00	8.00	7.25
☐ No. 32E Masserati Bora, c. 1973, pink body, yellow interior	4.00	5.00	4.25
☐ No. 33A Ford Zodiac Sedan, c. 1957, sea green body	10.50	13.50	11.20
☐ No. 33B Ford Zephyr 6, c. 1963, sea green body, white interior	4.50	6.00	4.75
☐ No. 33C Lamborghini Miura, c. 1969, yellow body, red interior	2.75	3.25	3.00
☐ No. 33D Datsun 126X, c. 1973, red body with black motifs, silver interior	3.50	5.50	3.75
☐ No. 34D Formula 1 Racing Car, c. 1971, yellow body, "16" decal	1.75	2.75	2.50
☐ No. 36A Austin A50, c. 1957, turquoise body, silver trim	12.00	14.00	12.50
☐ No. 36B Lambretta TV175 Motor Scooter And Sidecar, c. 1960, pale green body	12.00	14.00	12.50
☐ No. 36C Opel Diplomat, c. 1966, gold body, white interior	4.50	6.50	4.75
☐ No. 36D Hot Rod Draguar, c. 1971, red purple body, white interior	3.00	4.00	3.25
☐ No. 36E Formula 5000, c. 1976, orange body, "Formula 5000" decal	3.00	4.00	3.25
☐ No. 38B Vauxhall Victor Estate, c. 1963, yellow body, green interior	6.50	8.50	6.75
☐ No. 39A Ford Zodiac Convertible, c. 1957, pink body, fawn interior	11.00	14.00	11.50
☐ No. 39B Pontiac Convertible, c. 1962, violet body, white interior	12.00	16.00	12.75
☐ No. 39D Clipper, c. 1973, metallic cerise body, yellow interior	3.00	4.00	3.25
☐ No. 39E Rolls Royce, Silver Shadow MK.11, c. 1979, silver body, red interior, silver trim	3.00	4.00	3.25

TOY SOLDIERS

TOPIC: Toy soldiers are miniature figures of military personnel.

TYPES: Soldiers, officers, medical personnel and related figures are all collected avidly.

PERIOD: Figures from the World Wars are most popular, and the majority of the pieces were manufactured in the mid-20th century. Toy soldiers can date back to the late 1800s.

MAKERS: Major producers of toy soldiers are Barclay and Manoil. Many other manufacturers are also prominent.

MATERIALS: Lead, plastic and metals are usually used.

COMMENTS: Collectors have recently become more interesting in this field. Many collect a certain set of figures, while others focus on soldiers from a certain era.

ADDITIONAL TIPS: For further information, please refer to *The Official Price Guide to Collectible Toys,* published by The House of Collectibles.

AMERICAN MADE TOY SOLDIERS

	Current Price Range		P/Y Average
BARCLAY - EARLY 20th CENTURY			
☐ **Cadet,** *New Jersey, lead, painted, advancing, with rifle*	10.00	15.00	11.00
☐ **Officer,** *Italian, New Jersey, lead, painted, standing, hands at sides*	25.00	50.00	26.00
☐ **Officer,** *New Jersey, lead, painted, standing, with sword*	8.00	16.00	9.00
☐ **Officer,** *New Jersey, #743, lead, painted, advancing, with sword*	5.00	10.00	6.00
☐ **Officer,** *New Jersey, #773, lead, painted, standing, with paperwork*	10.00	15.00	11.00
☐ **Officer,** *New Jersey, #778, lead, painted, with gas mask*	15.00	20.00	17.00
☐ **Pilot,** *New Jersey, #741, lead, painted, standing, in uniform*	10.00	15.00	11.00
☐ **Sailor,** *New Jersey, lead, painted, holding flag*	6.00	12.00	7.00

Machine Gunner with Helper, *Manoil,* **$5.00-$15.00**
Photo courtesy of Hake's Americana, York, PA.

	Current Price Range		P/Y Average
☐ **Sailor,** *New Jersey, #719, lead, painted, in uniform, armed*	10.00	15.00	11.00
☐ **Sentry,** *New Jersey, #736, lead, painted, standing, wearing overcoat*	5.00	10.00	5.50
☐ **Soldier,** *New Jersey, lead, painted, crouched, on motorcycle*	10.00	20.00	11.00
☐ **Soldier,** *New Jersey, lead, painted, kneeling, aiming anti-tank gun*	10.00	15.00	11.00
☐ **Soldier,** *New Jersey, lead, painted, lying flat, gazing through binoculars*	5.00	10.00	11.00
☐ **Solider,** *New Jersey, lead, painted, mounted* .	10.00	15.00	11.00
☐ **Soldier,** *New Jersey, lead, painted, sitting, on K.P.*	15.00	20.00	17.00

BARCLAY - MID 20th CENTURY

☐ **Aviator,** *New Jersey, #941, lead, painted, pod foot, standing*	2.00	5.00	2.50
☐ **Marine,** *New Jersey, #922, lead, unpainted, pod foot, standing, with rifle*	2.00	5.00	2.50
☐ **Officer,** *New Jersey, plastic, marching with sword*	5.00	8.00	5.50
☐ **Officer,** *New Jersey, #208, lead, unpainted, pod foot, standing*	2.00	5.00	2.50
☐ **Radioman,** *New Jersey, plastic, antenna*	4.00	8.00	4.50
☐ **Soldiers,** *three, New Jersey, #82, lead, painted, pod foot, at range finder*	6.00	18.00	6.50
☐ **Soldier,** *New Jersey, plastic, advancing, with rifle*	5.00	8.00	5.50

GREY IRON

☐ **Sailor,** *Pennsylvania, #14, cast iron, painted, in uniform, armed*	7.00	14.00	7.50

	Current Price Range		P/Y Average
☐ **Officer,** *Naval, Pennsylvania, #14AW, cast iron, painted, in uniform*	9.00	18.00	10.00
☐ **Officer,** *U.S., Pennsylvania, #3, cast iron, painted, one of three pieces*	8.00	16.00	9.00
☐ **Soldier,** *Colonial, Pennsylvania, #1, cast iron, painted, standing, rifle held diagonally*	6.00	15.00	6.50
☐ **Soldier,** *U.S., Pennsylvania, #3, cast iron, painted, armed*	10.00	15.00	11.00
☐ **Soldier,** *U.S., Pennsylvania, #5, cast iron, painted, charging, armed*	8.00	11.00	9.00
☐ **Soldier,** *Pennsylvania, #6, cast iron, painted, armed*	5.00	10.00	5.00
☐ **Soldier,** *Pennsylvania, #7, cast iron, painted, charging, with rifle*	6.00	12.00	7.00
☐ **Soldier,** *Pennsylvania, #13, cast iron, painted, kneeling, manning machine gun*	16.00	22.00	19.00

MANOIL

☐ **Sailor,** *New York, #14, lead, painted, standing*	30.00	60.00	35.00
☐ **Soldier,** *New York, #25, lead, painted, kneeling, sniper with rifle*	10.00	15.00	11.00
☐ **Soldier,** *New York, #45, lead, painted, lying flat, with periscope*	10.00	15.00	11.00
☐ **Soldier,** *New York, #47, lead, painted, sitting with antiaircraft searchlight*	9.00	12.00	10.00
☐ **Soldier,** *New York, #52, lead, painted, on motorcycle*	15.00	20.00	16.00
☐ **Soldier,** *New York, #63, lead, painted, with gas mask, holding flare pistol*	10.00	15.00	11.00
☐ **Soldier,** *New York, #64, lead, painted, sitting, playing banjo*	10.00	15.00	11.00

MANOIL - MID 20th CENTURY

☐ **General,** *New York, #45/15, lead, painted, on base, at attention, saluting, in uniform*	35.00	55.00	38.00
☐ **Soldier,** *New York, #45/7, lead, painted, marching, holding flag*	6.00	12.00	6.50
☐ **Soldier,** *New York, #45/8, lead, painted, marching, parade*	10.00	15.00	11.00
☐ **Soldier,** *New York, #45/9, lead, painted, standing, at ease, with rifle*	15.00	25.00	17.00
☐ **Soldier,** *New York, #45/10, lead, painted, at attention, rifle upright*	10.00	20.00	11.00
☐ **Soldier,** *New York, #45/11, lead, painted, kneeling, aiming rifle upwards*	20.00	30.00	22.00
☐ **Soldier,** *New York, #45/12, lead, painted, standing, aiming tommy gun*	15.00	20.00	16.00

MARX

☐ **Army Combat Training Center,** *U.S. #2654, plastic*	85.00	95.00	89.00
☐ **Army Training Center,** *U.S., #4122, plastic* ...	90.00	110.00	99.00
☐ **General Grant,** *plastic*	3.00	6.00	3.25
☐ **Soldier,** *Union, plastic, advancing, with bayonet*	2.00	3.00	2.50
☐ **Soldier,** *Union, plastic, crawling, with rifle* ...	2.00	3.00	2.50
☐ **Soldier,** *Union, plastic, wounded*	2.00	3.00	2.50

MULTIPLE PLASTICS CORPORATION	Current Price Range		P/Y Average
☐ **Officer,** *American Revolution, plastic*	4.00	8.00	5.00
☐ **Soldier,** *American Revolution, plastic, advancing, bearing flag*	2.00	5.00	2.50
☐ **Soldier,** *American Revolution, plastic, kneeling, firing*	2.00	5.00	2.50
☐ **Soldier,** *American Revolution, plastic, kneeling, loading rifle*	2.00	5.00	2.50
☐ **Soldier,** *American Revolution, plastic, mounted, sans horse*	2.00	3.00	2.50
☐ **Soldier,** *American Resolution, plastic, running, holding rifle*	2.00	5.00	2.50
☐ **Soldier,** *American Resolution, plastic, standing, firing*	2.00	5.00	2.50
☐ **Soldier,** *American Revolution, plastic, standing, rifle held diagonally*	2.00	5.00	2.50
MULTIPLE PLASTICS CORPORATION - MID 20th CENTURY			
☐ **Soldier,** *Japanese, plastic, kneeling, firing* ..	2.00	3.00	2.50
☐ **Soldier,** *Japanese, plastic, lying flat, firing machine gun*	2.00	3.00	2.50
☐ **Soldier,** *Japanese, plastic, running*	2.00	5.00	2.50
☐ **Soldier,** *Japanese, plastic, standing, firing* ..	2.00	3.00	2.50
☐ **Soldier,** *Japanese, plastic, standing guard, with bayonet*	2.00	3.00	2.50
☐ **Soldier,** *Japanese, plastic, standing, throwing bomb*	2.00	3.00	2.50
☐ **Soldier,** *Russian, plastic, charging, with bayonet*	2.00	3.00	2.50
☐ **Soldier,** *Russian, plastic, lunging with saber* .	3.00	5.00	3.00

TOY TRAINS

TOPIC: Toy trains are scaled-down models of locomotives and stock cars. They are designed to be operational on miniature tracks in miniature landscapes.

TYPES: The two major types of trains are distinguished by track size. The space between the outermost rails of the tracks will measure 2⅛″ if the set is standard gauge. This measurement will be 1¼" if the set is O gauge. Other sizes are common, but these are the most popular.

PERIOD: Toy trains were first made in the late 1800s. They reached a peak of popularity in the 1940s and 1950s.

MAKERS: The primary manufacturers of toy trains in the United States were Lionel Corporation, American Flyer Manufacturing Company, Ives Corporation and Louis Marx and Company.

MATERIALS: Trains are commonly made of tinplate, cast iron, aluminum or plastic.

COMMENTS: Toy train collecting is an expensive hobby. Collectors may focus on a particular manufacturer, size or period of trains. The most valuable specimens were made prior to the second World War.

ADDITIONAL TIPS: The serious collector does not play with his trains; they are for display only. Use will result in wear and tear that lowers the value of the set. For more information and extensive listings, please refer to *The Official Price Guide to Collectible Toys,* published by The House of Collectibles.

AMERICAN FLYER

	Current Price Range		P/Y Average
NARROW GAUGE TRAIN SETS			
☐ No. 1312, The Vanguard, *locomotive #3100, pullman car #3141, observation car #3142, train length 21", circular track, 88" circumference*	65.00	95.00	85.00
☐ No. 1314, The Dixie Queen, *locomotive #3105, baggage car #3150, pullman car #3151, observation car #3152, train length 31", oval track 51" x 31"*	85.00	140.00	145.00
☐ No, 1316, The Clipper, *locomotive #3103, sand car #3013, automobile car #3012, caboose #3014, train length 31", oval track 41½" x 31"*	75.00	125.00	100.00
NARROW GAUGE LOCOMOTIVES			
☐ No. 1093 Locomotive, *runs forward only, headlight and brass trim, two-tone green, 7"*	75.00	95.00	77.00
☐ No. 3100 Locomotive, *runs forward only, red, 7½"*	100.00	125.00	115.00
☐ No. 3103 Locomotive, *runs forward only, brass trim, red, 8"*	80.00	100.00	90.00
☐ No. 3105 Locomotive, *runs forward only, blue, 8½"*	85.00	95.00	90.00
☐ No. 3109 Locomotive, *manual control reverse, 9"*	150.00	200.00	175.00
☐ No. 3115 Locomotive, *track switch reverse, two headlights, 10¼"*	150.00	200.00	175.00
STANDARD GAUGE TRAIN SETS			
☐ Freight Set, *diesel locomotive #4680 engine with tender, tank car #4010, mechanics car #4022, caboose #4017*	1100.00	1400.00	1200.00
☐ Freight Set, *electric locomotive #4692 with golden state tender, cattle car #4020, gondola #4017, boxcar #4018, caboose #4021*	1600.00	2000.00	1750.00

	Current Price Range		P/Y Average

☐ **Freight Set,** *Hiawatha locomotive with tender, lumber, crane, gondola, tank and caboose* — 700.00 / 750.00 / 725.00

☐ **Passenger Set,** *electric locomotive #4000, with baggage #4040, America coach, Pleasantview observation car, green, yellow, black and white* . . . . 700.00 / 750.00 / 725.00

☐ **Passenger Set,** *electric locomotive #4643 0-4-0, American coach, Pleasantview observation, green* . . . . 300.00 / 400.00 / 325.00

STANDARD GAUGE LOCOMOTIVES

☐ **No. 88 Franklin Locomotive,** *with tender* . . . . — 80.00 / 100.00 / 90.00

☐ **No. 290 Electric Locomotive,** *4-6-2* . . . . — 65.00 / 75.00 / 65.00

☐ **No. 300 Reading Lines Locomotive,** *with tender* . . . . — 40.00 / 60.00 / 45.00

☐ **No. 301 Reading Lines Locomotive,** *with tender* . . . . — 30.00 / 35.00 / 32.50

☐ **No. 302 Reading Lines Locomotive,** *plastic body* . . . . — 30.00 / 35.00 / 32.50

☐ **No. 303 Electric Locomotive,** *4-4-0, plastic body* . . . . — 45.00 / 55.00 / 48.50

☐ **No. 307 Reading Lines Locomotive,** *with tender, plastic body* . . . . — 40.00 / 60.00 / 50.00

IVES

O GAUGE ELECTRICAL TRAIN SETS

☐ **No. 500 Locomotive #3250,** *baggage car #550, chair car #51, round setup, track length 96"* . . — 450.00 / 550.00 / 470.00

☐ **No. 501 Steel Locomotive #3251,** *with headlight, baggage car #550, chair car #551, parlor car #552, oval setup, track length 126"* . . . . . . — 375.00 / 475.00 / 400.00

☐ **No. 502 Steel Locomotive #3252,** *with headlight and reverse, baggage car #70, two parlor cars #72, oval setup, track length 145"* . . . . . . — 350.00 / 450.00 / 375.00

☐ **No. 503 Steel Locomotive #3253,** *with headlight and reverse, buffet car #130, parlor car #129, oval setup, track length 130"* . . . . — 900.00 / 1000.00 / 1150.00

LIONEL

LOCOMOTIVES

☐ **No. 10E Electric,** *with steam wheels, black, chrome and brass trim* . . . . — 165.00 / 200.00 / 175.00

☐ **No. 21D Texas Special AA,** *without motor* . . . — 25.00 / 30.00 / 27.50

☐ **No. 201 Union Pacific AA,** *orange* . . . . — 22.50 / 25.00 / 23.00

☐ **No. 204 Santa Fe AA,** *blue and yellow* . . . . . . — 55.00 / 60.00 / 57.50

☐ **No. 205 Missouri Pacific Steam Type,** *large apron* . . . . — 20.00 / 25.00 / 22.50

☐ **No. 208 Sante Fe AA,** *with horn* . . . . — 75.00 / 80.00 / 72.50

☐ **No. 212 Sante Fe AA,** *two way reverse, no magnetraction, horn, red and silver* . . . . — 40.00 / 45.00 / 42.50

☐ **No. 215 Sante Fe AA,** *with double axle magnetraction, orange* . . . . — 90.00 / 95.00 / 92.50

MARX

LOCOMOTIVES

	Current Price Range		P/Y Average
☐ **Clockwork Type,** *plastic, gears, key, steam-chest*	8.00	12.00	8.75
☐ **Commodore Vanderbilt,** *copper nameplate, no tender*	12.00	15.00	12.50
☐ **Power Car,** *#M10005, blue and red*	9.00	12.00	9.50
☐ **Power Car,** *#M10005, snub nose, green and white*	12.50	17.00	15.50
☐ **REA Car,** *#M10005, snub nose, cream colored and white*	10.00	15.00	12.50
☐ **"Sparkling Friction RR,"** *#242, with tender, rubberized friction action, black*	10.25	15.00	11.50
☐ **Steam Type,** *#400, plastic, electric*	7.00	11.00	7.50

TRADE CARDS

DESCRIPTION: Trade cards are usually made of very stiff paper advertising a business, product or service.

ORIGIN: Trade cards are an outgrowth of advertising handbills.

ADDITIONAL TIPS: Be wary of specimens that are heavily stained, torn or wrinkled. Light soiling is to be expected as are small pinholes in the upper corners. It was a frequent practice to post trade cards with thumbtacks.

☐ **Ayers' Cherry Pectoral,** J.C. Ayers Co., Lowell, Massachusetts, girl on front, list of ailments on back	1.50	2.00	1.70
☐ **Ayers' Sasaparilla,** J.C. Ayers Co., Lowell, Massachusetts, picture of two women with children and dog on front	1.50	2.50	1.95
☐ **C.I. Hood & Co.,** Lowell, Massachusetts, telephone series, testimonials on reverses, price for group	5.00	7.00	6.00
☐ **Columbia Bicycles,** pictures cyclists on high-wheelers riding at night, with lanterns	13.00	17.00	14.50

	Current Price Range		P/Y Average
□ **Dobbins' Soap,** six cards illustrating Shakespeare's "Six Ages of Man"	13.00	17.00	14.50
□ **Freese's Clementine Glue,** has two illustrations, one vertical at left, the other in a circular medallion at right, wording above, 1885	4.00	6.00	5.00
□ **Hall's Vegetable Sicilian Hair Renewer,** Nashua, New Hampshire, testimonials on reverse side, portrait of girl on front	1.25	1.75	1.50
□ **Horseford's Self-Raising Bread Preparation,** Rumford Chemical Works, Providence, R.I. ..	1.00	1.50	1.20
□ **Hoyt's Cologne,** perfumed card picturing large frog, 1883	2.00	2.50	2.20
□ **Jumbo,** P.T. Barnum's famous circus elephant	5.00	6.00	5.45
□ **Latest Novelty, Secret Motto Ring,** unillustrated but for engravings of ring in each of the four corners, decorative border like early paper money, ornamental lettering, 1870s ...	6.50	8.50	7.50
□ **Minard's Liniment, King of Pain,** pictures black man riding mule cart, reverse side lists various complaints for which product is supposedly effective	2.50	3.50	2.90
□ **Nature's Remedy — Vegetine — The Blood Purifier,** girl	1.25	1.75	1.50
□ **Page's Glue,** humorous card showing men stuck to bench with maker's product, printed by Bufford, 1890	6.50	8.50	7.25
□ **Ponds Extract Co.,** New York, gives cures on reverse side	1.25	1.75	1.50
□ **Rising Sun Stove Polish,** pictures delivery boy stealing a kiss from housewife who has just finished polishing stove, 1890	6.50	8.50	7.25
□ **Rough On Rats,** E.R. Wells, Jersey City, New Jersey, reads "A 15¢ Box Will Keep Your House Free."	1.00	1.25	1.10
□ **Tarrant's Seltzer Aperient,** little girl and sewing basket, cures on reverse side	1.50	2.00	1.60
□ **Waterbury Watch Co.,** shows multi-panel illustrated story in cartoon format, picture of watch at upper right, vertical format, 1884 ..	15.00	20.00	17.00
□ **Willimantic Thread,** pictures Brooklyn Bridge, printed by Forbes Lithography Co. ..	9.00	12.00	10.25
□ **Worcester Salt,** card in the form of a pair of eyeglasses with eye holes at the center, 1885	11.00	14.00	12.00
□ **World's Largest Fruithouse,** pictures tall building that looks like a hotel, 1885	7.00	9.00	8.00

TRADE CATALOGS

DESCRIPTION: Catalogs issued by manufacturers, wholesalers and retail merchants are called trade catalogs.

CARE AND CONDITION: Since many of the early specimens are rare, allowances are made for their condition. Usually trade catalogs received a great deal of use making it difficult for collectors to find them in excellent condition.

ADDITIONAL TIPS: Watch for specialized catalogs which pertain to one subject rather than general merchandise catalogs.

	Current Price Range		P/Y Average
☐ **Automobile Supplies,** Sears, Roebuck and Co., Chicago, 112 pp, 1913	22.00	28.00	25.00
☐ **Bicycles, Tires, Motorcycle and Bicycle Accessories,** Edwards and Crist Co., Chicago and Philadelphia, 122 pp, 1923	22.00	30.00	26.00
☐ **Blymyer Bells for Churches, Schools, Colleges, Court Houses, Fire Alarms, Factories, Farms, Plantations, Etc.,** Cincinnati Bell Foundry Co., Cincinnati, 31 pp, 1916	20.00	25.00	22.50
☐ **Bottling Supplies and Household Utensils,** Consumers Products Company, Brooklyn, N.Y., 20 pp, 1927	9.00	12.00	10.00
☐ **Brooms,** The Most Modern Broom Manufacturing Plant in the World, Hamburg Broom Works, Hamburg, Pennsylvania, 28 pp, 1911 .	8.00	11.00	10.00
☐ **Busiest House in America,** illustrated catalogue of general merchandise, 640 pp, 1908 .	60.00	80.00	70.00
☐ **Civil Engineers' and Surveyors' Instruments,** W. and L.E. Gurley, Troy, New York, 34 pp, 1878	45.00	60.00	55.00
☐ **Columbia Bicycles,** Pope Manufacturing Co., Hartford, Connecticut, 31 pp, 1897	33.00	41.00	37.00
☐ **Counting Machines,** W.N. Durant, Milwaukee, 20 pp, c. 1905	22.00	30.00	26.00

	Current Price Range		P/Y Average

☐ **Descriptive and Illustrated Catalogue,** Iron Cutting Shears, Bolt Forging Machinery, Pawtucket Manufacturing Co., Central Falls, Rhode Island, 74 pp, 1892 . . . .   32.00 40.00 36.00

☐ **Florence Home Needle-Work,** Nonotuck Silk Co., Florence, Massachusetts, 96 pp, 1891 . .   13.00 17.00 15.00

☐ **Galvanized Patent Stock Trough,** Foltz Manufacturing and Supply Co., Hagerstown, Maryland, 8 pp, c. 1902, price list of pig and other livestock troughs 6.50 8.50 7.00

☐ **Great Western Gun Works,** Catalogue #40, J.H. Johnston Co., Pittsburgh, 64 pp, 1888 . .   45.00 60.00 55.00

☐ **Hand-Book and Illustrated Catalogue of the Engineers' and Surveyor's Instruments of Precision,** C.L. Berger and Sons, Boston, 212 pp, 1902 . . . .   40.00 50.00 45.00

☐ **Hersey Water Meters,** price list, Hersey Manufacturing Co., South Boston, Massachusetts, 7 pp, 1908 . . . .   4.00 5.00 4.50

☐ **Hibbard Baskets,** price list, Hibbard Basket Works, Lyons, New York, 12 pp, 1900 . . . .   14.00 18.00 16.00

☐ **High Grade Bicycles,** Special Catalogue, Cash Buyers' Union, Chicago, 40 pp, 1895 . . .   35.00 45.00 40.00

☐ **Illustrated Catalogue of Metal Broom Locks and Braces,** M. Gould's Son and Co., Newark, New Jersey, 16 pp, 1906 . . . .   16.00 20.00 18.00

☐ **Jaros Hygienic Wear,** I. Jaros, New York, 79 pp, 1890 . . . .   23.00 28.00 25.00

☐ **Keating Bicycles,** 1896 Catalogue, Keating Wheel Co., Holyoke, Massachusetts, 32 pp . .   25.00 30.00 27.50

☐ **Masonic Lodge Supplies,** Catalogue #2, Henderson Ames Co., Kalamazoo, Michigan, 110 pp, 1905 . . . .   25.00 32.00 28.00

☐ **Photographic Card Stock,** A.M. Collins Manufacturing Co. price list, Philadelphia, 47 pp, 1898 . . . .   25.00 32.00 28.00

☐ **Powell Brothers Shoe Co.,** Spring Catalogue, New York, 49 pp, 1902 . . . .   11.00 15.00 13.00

☐ **Prices Current,** Soda Fountain Supplies, Fuller and Fuller Co., Chicago, 189 pp, c. 1906   25.00 32.00 28.00

☐ **Prices Current,** Patent Medicines, Propritary Articles, Plasters, Antiseptic Dressings, Etc., Fuller and Fuller Co., Chicago, 189 pp, c. 1906   17.00 21.00 19.00

☐ **Saddlery and Horse Furnishings,** Carriage and Sleigh Trimmings, James Bailey Co., Portland, Maine, 1913, 7″ x 10″ 30.00 40.00 35.00

☐ **Schoenhut's Marvelous Toys,** A. Schoenhut Company, Philadelphia, 36 pp, 1904 . . . .   90.00 115.00 102.00

☐ **Vertical Gas,** Gasoline, Kerosene and Distillate Engines for All Power Purposes, Fairbanks, Morse and Co., Chicago, 32 pp, 1904 .   10.00 14.00 12.00

☐ **Washington Stoves and Ranges,** Grey and Dudley Hardware Co., Nashville, Tennessee, 110 pp, c. 1918 . . . .   20.00 25.00 22.00

TRUCKS

ORIGIN: The U.S. trucking industry dates to the early twentieth century when trucks were tested in New York for their capacity, speed and economy.

MAKERS: The best-known truck makers include Dodge, Ford, General Motors Corporation and International Harvester.

COMMENTS: Pick-up trucks are currently among the most collectible trucks. Rare trucks are always sought after and the collectible truck industry is rising in popularity.

ADDITIONAL TIPS: These listings are alphabetical according to the truck maker. Following the maker is the date of manufacture, model, type of engine, type of body and price range. Prices do vary according to the condition of the truck. For further information, see *The Official Price Guide to Cars, Trucks and Motorcycles*

GMC — *1948 "Pickup, FC-100",* **$2750.00-$3500.00**
Photo courtesy of General Motors Corporations, Pontiac, MI.

YEAR	MODEL	ENGINE	BODY	F	G	E
DODGE						
1930	Stake Truck (V)	8 cyl. Flathead	1½ Ton	2100	2450	2700
1936	Dump		Garwood	2000	2300	2500
1936	Humpback (V)	8 cyl. 318	Deluxe Package	3500	4000	4500
1937	Pickup	Slant 6	¾ Ton	1950	2200	2600
1938	Humpback (V)	8 cyl. 350	½ Ton	3000	3200	3500
1947	WC Pickup	Slant 6	½ Ton	2000	2400	2700
1948	Tow	6 cyl., 5-Speed		1700	2000	2300
1950	Pickup (V)	8 cyl.	Long Bed	2500	2750	3000
1950	Pickup	6 cyl.	½ Ton, Slant Bed	2250	2500	2800
1953	Pickup	3-Speed	½ Ton, Short Bed	2200	2500	2800
1953	Pickup	4-Speed	½ Ton	2300	2500	2800
FORD						
1920	Model A	4 cyl.	C. Cab	4500	4900	5300
1923	Model T	4 cyl.	Short Back	4200	4500	4900
1925	Model TT	2-Speed	1 Ton	3500	3800	4200
1925	Stake	4 cyl.	1 Ton	3200	3500	3900
1928	Tow	2-Speed	Shortbed	1950	2450	2800
1930	Flatbed	4 cyl.	1½ Ton	1200	1500	1800
1931	Model A		½ Ton	4000	4300	4600
1931	Model AA	4-Speed		3800	4100	4400
1931	Model AA (V)	8 cyl.	Short Box	4000	4200	4500
1932	Flatbed	4 cyl.	1½ Ton	2000	2200	2400
1933	Stake Truck	AB Motor	Grainbed	2000	2450	2700
1934	Pickup (V)	8 cyl.	Sidemount	2800	3000	3300
1935	Panel (V)	8 cyl., automatic		3000	3400	3900

TV GUIDES

DESCRIPTION: *TV Guide* is a weekly magazine which includes local television listings and articles about Hollywood stars.

PERIOD: The nationally distributed editions of *TV Guide* began in 1953. Before 1953, there were local forerunners.

COMMENTS: Issues which have popular Hollywood stars on the cover are usually more valuable than other editions. Editions with Lucille Ball, Ronald Reagan and Elvis Presley on the cover are highly valued by collectors.

ADDITIONAL TIPS: For more information, consult *The Official Price Guide to Radio, TV and Movie Memorabilia,* published by The House of Collectibles.

	Current Price Range		P/Y Average
☐ April 3-9, 1953, issue #1, photo of Lucille Ball's baby on cover, with small photo of Lucy in upper right corner, headline "Lucy's $50,000,000 Baby." This referred to the fact that many episodes of "I Love Lucy" in late 1952 and early 1953 were built around Lucy's pregnancy, and the fact that the baby ("Little Ricky") became an instant TV star. Though the issue is labeled #1, it was actually not the first issue of TV Guide, as regional issues had been published previously; it was the first coast-to-coast issue, and the first with a glossy cover	140.00	160.00	145.00
☐ April 10-16, 1953, issue #2, Jack Webb on cover	50.00	65.00	55.00
☐ April 17-23, 1953, issue #3, caricatures of Lucille Ball, Arthur Godfrey, Milton Berle, Sid Caesar and Imogene Coca on cover	20.00	27.50	23.00
☐ April 24-30, 1953, issue #4, Ralph Edwards on cover	22.50	30.00	25.00
☐ May 1-7, 1953, issue #5, Eve Arden on cover	36.00	45.00	39.00
☐ May 8-14, 1953, issue #6, Arthur Godfrey on cover	25.00	35.00	28.00
☐ May 22-28, 1953, issue #8, Red Buttons on cover	20.00	30.00	24.00
☐ June 12-18, 1953, issue #11, Eddie Fisher on cover	15.00	25.00	19.00
☐ June 19-25, 1953, issue #12, Ed Sullivan on cover	10.00	20.00	14.00
☐ July 3-9, 1953, issue #14, Perry Como on cover	8.00	15.00	11.00
☐ July 17-23, 1953, issue #16, Lucille Ball and Desi Arnez on cover	25.00	35.00	29.00
☐ July 24-30, 1953, issue #17, caricature of Groucho Marx on cover	25.00	37.00	30.00
☐ August 14-20, 1953, issue #20, Patti Page on cover	15.00	25.00	19.00
☐ August 21-27, 1953, issue #21, Mary Hartline and Claude Kirchner of Super Circus on cover	25.00	35.00	29.00
☐ August 28-September 3, 1953, issue #22, Jane and Audrey Meadows on cover	12.50	20.00	14.00
☐ October 2-8, 1953, issue #27, Red Skelton on cover	17.00	23.00	19.00
☐ October 16-22, 1953, issue #29, TV beauty contestants on cover	10.00	20.00	14.00
☐ October 23-29, 1953, issue #30, Arthur Godfrey on cover	14.00	17.00	15.00
☐ October 30-November 5, 1953, issue #31, Beulah Witch, Kukla and Ollie on cover	15.00	25.00	19.00

	Current Price Range		P/Y Average
☐ *November 6-12, 1953, issue #32, Warren Hull on cover*	15.00	25.00	19.00
☐ *November 20-26, 1953, issue #34, Dorothy McGuire and Julius LaRosa on cover*	25.00	35.00	29.00
☐ *November 27-December 3, 1953, issue #35, Lugene Sanders on cover*	10.00	18.00	13.00
☐ *December 4-10, 1953, issue #36, Loretta Young on cover*	10.00	18.00	13.00
☐ *December 25-31, 1953, issue #39, Perry Como, Patti Page and Eddie Fisher on cover*	10.00	20.00	14.00
☐ *March 19-25, 1954, issue #51, Groucho Marx on cover*	36.00	45.00	40.00
☐ *December 24-31, 1954, issue #91, Nelson family on cover (before Ricky Nelson launched pop music career)*	45.00	55.00	49.00
☐ *January 15-21, 1955, issue #94, Gary Moore on cover, and an article on Johnny Carson*	16.00	20.00	17.00
☐ *March 5-11, 1955, issue #101, Liberace on cover (he was doing a daily late-afternoon show)*	15.00	20.00	16.00
☐ *October 22-28, 1955, issue #134, George Gobel on cover*	9.00	12.00	10.00
☐ *December 17-23, 1955, issue #142, Robert Montgomery on cover*	14.00	17.00	15.00
☐ *January 21-27, 1956, issue #147, Lawrence Welk on cover*	7.00	10.00	8.00
☐ *April 14-20, 1956, issue #159, Grace Kelly wedding issue*	22.00	29.00	24.00
☐ *April 28-May 4, 1956, issue #161, Red Skelton on cover*	5.00	10.00	7.00
☐ *September 8-14, 1956, issue #180, Elvis Presley on cover, first TV Guide cover of Elvis; he had just hit the big time via appearances on the Jackie Gleason show*	75.00	110.00	85.00
☐ *December 1-7, 1956, issue #192, caricature of George Burns on cover*	22.00	29.00	24.00
☐ *January 19-25, 1957, issue #199, Jerry Lewis on cover*	9.00	12.00	10.00
☐ *February 23-March 1, 1957, issue #204, Charles van Doren on cover (he was a national sensation after winning a fortune on Jack Barry's quiz program)*	9.00	12.00	10.00
☐ *August 31-September 6, 1957, issue #231, Clint Walker on cover*	32.00	40.00	32.00
☐ *November 23-29, 1957, issue #243, Mary Martin on cover (Larry Hagman's mother)*	7.00	10.00	8.00

UNCLE SAM AND STATUE OF LIBERTY COLLECTIBLES

TOPIC: Uncle Sam and Statue of Liberty items are highly collectible, and rare, on the Americana market. Most items range from toys to posters, souvenirs to postcards.

ORIGIN: Uncle Sam originated in the 19th century, and became solidly established as a national symbol during the Civil War. Uncle Sam, as we know him today, was created by Thomas Nast in his *Harper's Weekly* drawings, and James Montgomery Flagg's World War I recruiting poster.

The Statue of Liberty was brought to America in 1876 as a gift from France. Next year, she will celebrate her 100th year of providing safe harbor to millions of Americans. For this gala event, she is currently receiving a much needed refurbishing.

COMMENTS: Authentic Statue of Liberty and Uncle Sam items are extremely rare on today's market. Be careful of careless reproductions and fakes. The next two years should provide a wealth of Statue of Liberty collectibles that will be cherished for years to come.

ADDITIONAL TIPS: For further information, please contact THE STATUE OF LIBERTY COMMEMORATIVE CORP.; their address is listed in the directory section of this book.

	Current Price Range		P/Y Average
☐ **Astray,** Uncle Sam, glazed china	50.00	70.00	62.00
☐ **Bookmark,** Statue of Liberty, silk, Paris, 1878	65.00	70.00	67.00
☐ **Commemorative Plate,** Statue of Liberty, Pickard China	150.00	—	—
☐ **Costume,** Uncle Sam, traditional cloth coat and pants, applied stars, painted straw hat, three pieces	50.00	100.00	76.00
☐ **Doll,** Uncle Sam, bisque, c. 1890s	850.00	950.00	880.00

	Current Price Range		P/Y Average
□ **Doll,** Uncle Sam, papier mache and cloth, 20″, c. 1910	100.00	150.00	125.00
□ **Fan,** Uncle Sam, with flag, paper	5.00	10.00	7.00
□ **Mail Box Holder,** Uncle Sam, cut out wood, 75½″, c. 1920-1940	40.00	60.00	52.00
□ **Model,** Statue of Liberty, bronze casting of original model, limited edition, 1985	2500.00	—	—
□ **Sign,** Uncle Sam, carved and painted wood, flat, on a black base made of steel, 77½″	720.00	975.00	835.00
□ **Whirligig,** United States, painted red, white, black and blue, wood, 10″	350.00	450.00	400.00

VALENTINES

ORIGIN: Valentines have been given for centuries. The first Valentines were handwritten and homemade statements of love and affection. Commercial Valentines were produced by the end of the 18th century.

MAKERS: Popular Valentine makers and companies include, Whitney, Taft, Strong, Tuck, Mansell, and others.

COMMENTS: Handmade Valentines are quite desirable and quite rare. Period Valentines are also sought after, such as those from the Civil War, Victorian era, or the World Wars.

ADDITIONAL TIPS: The listings are in alphabetical order according to country of origin, type of Valentine or company, depending on available information.

□ **American,** heart shaped, lace, c. 1905	9.00	16.00	12.00
□ **American,** honeycomb, "Cupid's Temple of Love," c. 1928	8.00	16.00	12.00
□ **American,** Maggie and Jiggs, c. 1940	4.00	12.00	8.00
□ **American,** Popeye, c. 1940	4.00	10.00	6.50
□ **Art Nouveau,** heart shaped folder	4.50	6.50	5.50
□ **Carrington,** folder, lace, c. 1937	1.50	4.50	3.00
□ **Comic Valentine,** the "Hat Trimmer," Elton and Co., New York, illustration of glum-looking woman sewing hat, with verse, c. 1860	22.00	30.00	25.00

Valentine Postcard,
1911, **$2.00-$3.00**

	Current Price Range		P/Y Average
☐ **"Dainty Dimples" series,** per card	3.00	8.00	4.00
☐ **Easel Valentine,** fold back, free standing, c. early 1900s	34.00	44.00	38.00
☐ **German,** 5 layer, pulldown, religious sentiment, flowers	45.00	65.00	55.00
☐ **German,** large ship, mechanical pulldown ...	55.00	85.00	70.00
☐ **German,** pulldown, children, c. 1915	4.50	10.00	6.50
☐ **German,** pulldown, gold	10.00	20.00	15.00
☐ **German,** pullout and stand up cottage, c. 1910	7.00	15.00	12.00
☐ **German,** pullout and stand up steam boiler, c. 1910	12.00	18.00	14.00
☐ **German,** stand up, little girl holding opening parasol	15.00	25.00	20.00
☐ **German,** three layers, pulldown, lavendar, pink, gold, green, c. 1920	6.50	15.00	8.50
☐ **Gibson Art,** paper doll mechanical stand up, little girl holding doll, German	20.00	35.00	27.00
☐ **"Hearts Are Ripe,"** children picking heart shaped apples from tree	3.00	7.00	5.00
☐ **H. Dobbs and Co.,** "Pillar Post," illustration of mailbox, c. 1800	22.00	27.00	23.50
☐ **"It Must Be Fine, To Have a Valentine,"** from "Valentine Wishes" series	7.00	12.00	9.00
☐ **"Lady Killer,"** comic valentine by A.J. Fisher, N.Y., c. 1850	29.00	39.00	33.00
☐ **McLoughlin,** folder, no lace, c. 1905	5.00	12.00	7.00

	Current Price Range		P/Y Average
☐ **McLoughlin,** three layer, silver, white, lace, c. 1880	5.00	12.00	7.50
☐ **McLoughlin,** three layer, white, gold, lace, c. 1880	5.00	12.00	7.50
☐ **Mansell,** lace, handwritten verse, c. 1846	75.00	100.00	85.00
☐ **Mansell,** lace paper, lovers in a park, heavily ornamented, white with silver, c. 1855	44.00	54.00	48.00
☐ **Mansell,** cameo embossing, two lovers walking along woodland path, c. 1845	39.00	49.00	43.00
☐ **Mechanical,** set of fifteen, c. 1920	34.00	44.00	38.00
☐ **Mechanical,** "Such is Married Life," c. 1850 .	39.00	49.00	43.00
☐ **Mechanical,** various animals, c. 1930	10.00	15.00	12.00
☐ **Mechanical,** Walt Disney character, c. 1930 .	17.00	24.00	20.00
☐ **Meek & Son.,** Gibson Girl (from photo), surrounded by lace in various ornamental patterns, cherub heads, c. 1890	54.00	65.00	58.00
☐ **Meek,** layered folder, lace, c. 1870	8.00	15.00	12.00
☐ **"Temple of Love,"** from Raphael Tuck's "Betsy Beauties" series, young girl chasing butterfly	5.00	9.00	7.00
☐ **"To My Valentine,"** from Raphael Tuck's "Innocence Abroad" series, two young children, brief verse	5.00	8.00	6.00
☐ **"To My Wife,"** embossed woman, hearts and flowers, cutout flowers tied with satin ribbon, real lace surrounds cutout heart, c. 1936	11.00	16.00	12.00
☐ **Tuck,** folder, heart shaped, little girl on front	4.00	10.00	6.50
☐ **Victorian Valentine,** fold out, paper lace	20.00	25.00	22.00
☐ **Whitney,** embossed paper in pattern, a child delivering a note to a lady, with original embossed envelope, c. 1870	39.00	49.00	43.00
☐ **Whitney,** folder, lace, c. 1920	3.50	8.00	6.00
☐ **Whitney,** heart shape, World War I soldier valentine	5.00	13.00	8.00
☐ **Whitney,** three layer, Art Nouveau design, lace, gold, pink, rose, hearts, c. 1912	15.00	30.00	23.00
☐ **Whitney,** three layer, lace, Art Deco, children .	4.50	6.50	5.50
☐ **Whitney,** three layer, lace, Art Nouveau	10.00	18.00	14.00
☐ **Whitney,** three piece, heart shaped, little girls	1.75	3.50	2.10

VAN BRIGGLE

DESCRIPTION: Van Briggle was one of the earliest and most sucessful art potteries in the west. Founded in 1901 and located in Colorado Springs, it acquired a grasp on the western market from Denver to San Francisco which nearly equaled the hold that Rookwood had on the east. Van Briggle's wares perfectly reflected the western taste. They weren't frilly or delicated like the Old World porcelains. Instead, they had a rugged charm. Their creative shapes suggested the gnarled limbs of old trees, driftwood, cactus, and other products of nature. They proved to be quite an influence on the potters of the east who adapted some of Van Briggle's innovative ideas into their own wares. Color used by Van Briggle also suggested the west. They included Mountain Craig (green to brown), Midnight (black), Moonglo (off-white), Persian Rose, Turquoise Ming, and Russet. In terms of its importance to the art pottery movement, Van Briggle stands very high. It continues in operation to the present day.

MARKS: The first and most famous mark used by this firm consisted of the letters AA, the initials of the first names of Van Briggle and his wife, Anne. It was used in conjunction with an incised mark reading *VAN BRIGGLE,* scratched by hand into the ware itself. The date of production usually accompanied these markings, and often (especially at a later period) a stock number. Sometimes, the word *ORIGINAL* appears along with the mark. *HAND CARVED* is likewise found, occasionally, along with the factory mark on pieces with raised decoration.

RECOMMENDED READING: For more in-depth information on Van Briggle pottery you may refer to *The Official Price Guide to Pottery and Porcelain* and the *The Official Identification Guide to Pottery and Porcelain,* published by The House of Collectibles.

	Current Price Range		P/Y Average
☐ Ashtray, 5⅜″, rose, spiral interior	20.00	30.00	25.00
☐ Ashtray, 6¾″, trapezoid shape, turquoise ming	20.00	28.00	24.00
☐ Bookends, pair, rams, red and blue glaze	130.00	140.00	135.00
☐ Bowl, 3″, acorn form, brown, c. 1915	140.00	160.00	150.00
☐ Bowl, 3″, rose, butterfly decor	60.00	70.00	65.00

Vase, Van Briggle,
Loreli Pattern,
$75.00-$85.00

	Current Price Range		P/Y Average
☐ **Bowl,** 3½", rose glaze, cherry, leaf and vine motif	80.00	90.00	85.00
☐ **Bowl,** 4", flat, small base, brown, leaf motif across top, c. 1917	80.00	90.00	85.00
☐ **Bowl,** 4", red, leaf motif across top, c. 1914	30.00	40.00	35.00
☐ **Bowl,** 5", rose, scalloped rim, flared ends	20.00	28.00	24.00
☐ **Bowl,** 5½", green, floral and leaf motif	110.00	120.00	115.00
☐ **Bowl,** 6", acorn and leaf motif across top, marked III	30.00	40.00	35.00
☐ **Bowl,** 6", flat, yellow, leaf motif, c. 1903	450.00	480.00	465.00
☐ **Bowl,** 6", rose, swirled ivy motif	32.00	38.00	35.00
☐ **Bowl,** 12½", rose glaze, leaf motif	200.00	220.00	210.00
☐ **Bowl,** pattern #283, 10½", small base flaring out to shoulder, shoulder slopes inward to rim, moonglo background, blue flower and stem motif, c. 1906	150.00	170.00	160.00
☐ **Bowl,** pattern #678, 2", bulbous shape, band of berries and leaves across top, pink and green, c. 1908	140.00	160.00	150.00
☐ **Bowl,** pattern #903D, 8½", frog and dragonfly motif, turquoise ming	65.00	75.00	70.00
☐ **Candlesticks,** 6", pair, rose, double tulip motif	30.00	40.00	35.00
☐ **Conch,** 9", turquoise ming, marked 42	30.00	40.00	35.00
☐ **Creamer,** 2", hexagon, turquoise ming	12.00	18.00	15.00
☐ **Cup,** 3½", six incised panel lines, turquoise ming, c. 1917	30.00	38.00	34.00
☐ **Figurine,** 3". elephant, on base, yellow and brown	30.00	40.00	35.00
☐ **Figurine,** 4", donkey, turquoise ming	30.00	40.00	35.00

	Current Price Range		P/Y Average
Figurine, 4″, elephant, rose, triangular ears ..	70.00	80.00	75.00
Figurine, 4¼″, elephant, turquoise ming, trunk raised	30.00	40.00	35.00
Figurine, 6″, detailed girl grinding corn, on base, turquoise ming	30.00	40.00	35.00
Figurine, 8″, cat, sits on base, tail curled around body, long neck	50.00	60.00	55.00
Figurine, 8½″, rearing horse, on stand, brown .	45.00	55.00	50.00
Figurine, 9¾″, owl on stump, brown	275.00	300.00	287.50
Lamp, 18″, flat base, narrow neck, running horse motif, red	65.00	75.00	70.00
Lamp, 20″, bulbous base, narrow middle, bulbous top, moonglo	45.00	55.00	50.00
Mug, 4¾″, unglazed, c. 1908	180.00	190.00	185.00
Ornament, 1978, 4″, has word "noel" on front, limited to 1,000, natural glaze	27.00	32.00	29.00
Ornament, 1980, 3″, oval, angel blowing trumpet, words "The Herald" on front, natural glaze, limited to 1,000	20.00	25.00	22.50
Paperweight, 3½″, rabbit, green and brown .	60.00	70.00	65.00
Pitcher, 3″, moonglo	18.00	25.00	22.00
Pitcher, 3½″, bulbous body, handled, collared neck, turquois ming, c. 1908	140.00	160.00	150.00
Pitcher, 11″, bulbous base, slender body and neck, slender handle, turquoise ming	50.00	60.00	55.00
Planter, 9″, blue, floral motif	32.00	42.00	37.00
Planter, 12½″, rose shell form	47.00	52.00	50.00
Plaque, 4½″, oval, rise glaze, Indian head design	50.00	60.00	55.00
Vase, 2″, bulbous body, red, leaf and stem motif, c. 1919	50.00	60.00	55.00
Vase, 2″, rose, c. 1918	80.00	90.00	85.00
Vase, 3″, bulbous body, narrow neck, small opening, red background, blue butterfly motif, c. 1921	65.00	75.00	70.00
Vase, 3″, flared rim, feather motif, turquoise ming	20.00	25.00	22.50
Vase, 4″, rose, ivy and floral motif	30.00	40.00	35.00
Vase, 4″, rose, tulip shaped, scalloped rim ..	15.00	25.00	20.00
Vase, 4″, rose, c. 1917	135.00	145.00	140.00
Vase, 4½″, rose, butterfly motif	80.00	90.00	85.00
Vase, 4¾″, ivy and floral motif, turquoise ming	20.00	30.00	25.00
Vase, 5″, bulbous body, collared neck, green, leaf motif, c. 1908	75.00	85.00	80.00
Vase, 5″, rose, floral motif	28.00	35.00	32.00
Vase, 5″, rose and green, floral motif, c. 1905	390.00	410.00	400.00
Vase, 5¼″, rose, heart shaped, ivy motif	30.00	38.00	34.00
Vase, 7″, cylinder shape, collared neck, turquoise ming, c. 1916	240.00	260.00	250.00
Vase, 8″, bulbous body, narrow neck, two handled, red and blue, leaf motif, c. 1920	45.00	55.00	50.00
Vase, 8¾″, moonglow, bird of paradise motif	20.00	30.00	25.00
Vase, 9″, rose, flower and leaf motif	65.00	75.00	70.00

VANITY FAIR LITHOGRAPHS

DESCRIPTION: Vanity Fair was a weekly periodical published in London from 1860 to 1914. Each issue featured a lithograph depicting an influential man or woman usually in a satirical fashion.

TYPES: The Vanity Fair Lithographs covered every topic imaginable from ambassadors and boxers to ministers and criminals.

PROCESS: Lithography is a printing process from which the image to be printed accepts ink while the blank area repels it.

COMMENTS: Two of the most famous Vanity Fair artists were SPY (Leslie Ward) and APE (Carlo Pilligrini).

ADDITIONAL TIPS: This section is arranged by topic followed by the name of the work, year produced, artist and price. For more information, consult *The Official Price Guide to Collector Prints,* published by The House of Collectibles.

	Current Price
☐ **Ambassadors From England,** Diplomacy, 1873, unsigned	18.00
☐ **Ambassadors From England,** Siam, 1879, artist SPY	18.00
☐ **Americans,** An Arbitrator, 1872, unsigned	20.00
☐ **Americans,** Captain, Tanner, Farmer, 1872, unsigned	26.00
☐ **Americans,** President of the New York, 1889, artist SPY	20.00
☐ **Americans,** The New President, 1913, artist HESTER	24.00
☐ **Automobile Devotees,** Steam, 1907, artist SPY	24.00
☐ **Aviators,** The Deutsch Prize, 1901, artist GEO HUM	80.00
☐ **Boxers,** A Good Lightweight, 1877, artist SPY	24.00
☐ **Businessmen and Empire Builders,** Manchester, 1875, artist APE	18.00
☐ **Businessmen and Empire Builders,** Long John, 1910, artist QUIP	24.00
☐ **Businessmen and Empire Builders,** Sir Horace, J.P., 1909, artist SPY	18.00
☐ **Clergy,** The Chief Rabbi, 1904, artist SPY	36.00
☐ **Clergy,** A Fashion Canon, 1898, artist FTD	16.00
☐ **Freemasons,** The Lord Mayor, 1902, artist SPY	14.00
☐ **Game Hunters,** Pointers, 1885, artist SPY	30.00
☐ **Horse Trainers,** Sollie, 1910, artist HCO	16.00
☐ **Jockeys,** Top of the List, 1906, artist SPY	40.00

	Current Price
☐ **Legal,** Dick, 1900, artist SPY	40.00
☐ **Legal,** The Majesty of the Law, 1870, artist APE	40.00
☐ **Literary,** Waterloo, 1883, artist T	20.00
☐ **Music,** English Tenor, 1892, artist LIB	24.00
☐ **Music,** Wagnerian Opera, 1899, artist, WAG	24.00
☐ **Newspapermen,** New York Herald, 1884, artist NEMO	20.00
☐ **Orientals,** Li, 1896, artist GUTH	20.00
☐ **Photographers,** East Birmingham, 1902, artist SPY	36.00
☐ **Policemen,** Criminal Investigation, 1883, artist SPY	18.00
☐ **Politicians,** The Kent Gang, 1885, artist APE	14.00
☐ **Politicians,** A Sticker, 1908, artist SPY	20.00
☐ **Prime Ministers,** The Greatest Liberal, 1869, artist APE	20.00
☐ **Red Robe Judges,** The Recorder, 1903, artist SPY	60.00
☐ **Rowing,** Pembroke, 1888, artist, HAY	30.00
☐ **Royalty,** Oh Child, Mayst Thou, 1905, artist GUTH	20.00
☐ **Shipping Officials,** Plymouth, 1888, artist SPY	14.00
☐ **Theater,** The St. James's, 1909, artist MAX	20.00
☐ **Turf Devotees,** Bunny, 1876, artist SPY	20.00
☐ **Turf Devotees,** Sundown Park, 1891, artist SPY	20.00
☐ **Yachting Devotees,** Alisa, 1896, artist MILLER	20.00

WATCHES

DECRIPTION: Collectible watches include both the pocket and wrist style. Fobs which attached to pocket watches are another item that is valuable.

TYPES: All types of watches are collectible including 1930s Walt Disney character children's wristwatches, 1920s men and women's wristwatches and European pocket watches.

COMMENTS: Watches are available from antique dealers, pawnshops and flea markets. Even inoperative watches can be quite valuable after repair.

ADDITIONAL TIPS: Age, manufacturer, movement's complexity and accuracy, design and material are all factors which determine the value of a watch.

Purse Watch, *black enamel, opening and closing the sliding case winds the watch, face marked "Chronometer, Movado," silver, Swiss, c. 1930,* **$325.00-$425.00**

	Current Price Range		P/Y Average
☐ **Pocket Watch,** size 12 Hamilton, 19 jewels, model 900, 14K yellow gold in mahogany box, arabic dial, floral seal on back	400.00	500.00	450.00
☐ **Pocket Watch,** size 16 Hamilton, 17 jewels, model 974, arabic dial with red 5's, case made of Illinois nickel, 1918	50.00	70.00	60.00
☐ **Pocket Watch,** size 18 Hampden, bridge model, gold train, 1904	35.00	45.00	40.00
☐ **Pocket Watch,** size 16 Ingersoll Buck, 1922 ..	13.00	17.00	15.00
☐ **Pocket Watch,** size 16 Ingersoll Yankee, 1933	16.00	20.00	18.00
☐ **Pocket Watch,** size 16 New England Scout, gun metal case with duplex movement	45.00	60.00	52.00
☐ **Pocket Watch,** size 18 Seth Thomas, Philadelphia silverode arabic dial, case, 1912	40.00	55.00	46.00
☐ **Pocket Watch,** size 10 Waltham, 7 jewels, gold filled floral train model, 1894	65.00	80.00	72.00
☐ **Pocket Watch,** size 12 Waltham Ensign, 7 jewels, roman dial, 1897	65.00	80.00	72.00
☐ **Pocket Watch,** size 6 Waltham Seaside, gold train model with roman dial and case, "warranted 20 years," 1902	75.00	95.00	85.00
☐ **Pocket Watch,** size 18 Waltham, leaver set, stem wind, 17 jewels, demascenced, roman dial, case, 1903	70.00	85.00	76.00
☐ **Pocket Watch,** size 11 Lignes Girard Perregaux, 15 jewels automatic, model 300 case, stainless	35.00	45.00	40.00
☐ **Wristwatch,** Bugs Bunny, made by Lafayette under license from Warner Brothers, colored dial, in display box	25.00	33.00	28.00
☐ **Wristwatch,** Mary Marvel, has copyright of Fawcett Publications and is made in Switzerland, picture of Mary Marvel on dial, 1948 ...	125.00	150.00	135.00
☐ **Wristwatch,** Mighty Mouse, made in Switzerland, pictorial dial, red vinyl band, dates from 1960s	11.00	15.00	12.50
☐ **Wristwatch,** Superman, made by Dabs under license from National Periodical Publications, child size, with wrist strip, boxed, mid to late 1970s	20.00	25.00	21.00

WATERFORD CRYSTAL

ORIGIN: Waterford, the most famous Irish glass, was made from 1783 until 1850. Produced at the Waterford Glass House, an establishment formed by brothers George and William Penrose, Waterford is known for its fine cutting, lovely clarity and design.

DESCRIPTION: Blank items were cut by a revolving iron wheel combined with sand and a water trickle. Cuts were then polished with a soft powder. After 1800 glass cutters used a wider variety of cutting strokes to make an even more brilliant product. Manufacturers most often marked their glass with raised words under the base; Waterford items are marked "Penrose Waterford." The color of Waterford is much whiter than other Irish glass, though it is often mistakenly thought to have a blue tinge.

PERIOD: Much Waterford was imported from 1790 to 1850 and popular import items were decanters, glasses, lamps, chandeliers, candlesticks and candelabra. However, the characteristic Waterford items, most often associated with Ireland and Irish glass, include covered vases and jars for food, large serving bowls, oil and vinegar bottles, glasses, jugs and salts.

A new company was started at Waterford in the late 1940s. Along with a variety of fine cut glass items, they also make some copies of the original Waterford pieces. The Waterford crystal listed here was produced during this period.

RECOMMENDED READING: For further information refer to *The Official Price Guide to Glassware,* published by The House of Collectibles.

	Current Price Range		P/Y Average
☐ **Ashtray,** *vesicas on sides, starcut base, 1¼" high, 7" diameter*	20.00	60.00	35.00
☐ **Bowl,** *fruit, spiked diamond panels flank cut fans in reserves, notched rim, cut crescents, signed, 3½" high, 8" diameter*	110.00	150.00	130.00
☐ **Bowl,** *fruit, spiked diamonds with panels and thumbprints, tapered sides, signed, 4½" high, 12" diameter*	70.00	130.00	100.00

	Current Price Range		P/Y Average

□ **Bowl,** *fruit, tapered sides, cut vesieas on sides and base, round shape, 3½" high, 8" long* **80.00 110.00 90.00**

□ **Bowl,** *fruit, tapered sides, cut stars within a square design, notched rim, round shape, signed, 4" high, 7¾" diameter* **45.00 85.00 65.00**

□ **Bowl,** *notched diamonds, notched and paneled edge, starcut design on base, oblong shape, signed, 4¼" high, 13½" long* **80.00 130.00 100.00**

□ **Bowl,** *salad, cut diamond design, notched edge, starcut base on tapered base, signed, 4¼" high, 10" diameter* **80.00 130.00 100.00**

□ **Bowl,** *salad, marquise shape with daisy and button motif, flared rim, cylindrical shape, signed, 3¾" high, 9" diameter* **80.00 110.00 90.00**

□ **Bowl,** *salad, slanted sides, cut zigzag vesicas, starcut design on base, round, signed, 4" high, 8½" diameter* **80.00 110.00 90.00**

□ **Bowl,** *wide diamond cut band, pinwheel cut in pedestal base, signed, 3" high, 10¼" diameter* **80.00 120.00 90.00**

□ **Candlesticks,** *starcut design on bases, 6" high,* **55.00 80.00 65.00**

□ **Compote,** *spiked diamond band, cut fans around scalloped rim, starcut design on base, signed, 5½" high, 5½" diameter* **80.00 110.00 90.00**

□ **Compote,** *spiked diamond band with thumbprint band, round, notched rim, notched base, signed, 6" high, 7½" diameter* **130.00 160.00 140.00**

□ **Compotes,** *pair, notched thumbprint, lid has spiral finials, base is six-sided, 14½" high* .. **150.00 250.00 200.00**

□ **Decanter,** *cut diamonds with sunburst design, thumbprints, notched neck, starcut design stopper, signed* **65.00 90.00 75.00**

□ **Decanter,** *paneled neck, base has cut sawtooth band, signed, 11½" high* **80.00 110.00 95.00**

□ **Dish,** *round shape spiked diamond bands, ball finial, starcut design on base, signed, 6" high, 6" diameter* **55.00 80.00 65.00**

□ **Dishes,** *pair, star design in center, 3½" diameter* **35.00 50.00 40.00**

□ **Jar,** *marmalade, pedestal base, 6" high* **55.00 75.00 60.00**

□ **Jar,** *starcut design on lid, cut crosses and panels, signed, 3¾" high* **90.00 165.00 125.00**

□ **Mug,** *notched sides, 4½" high* **55.00 70.00 60.00**

□ **Mugs,** *marquise shapes alternate with cane design in reserves, starcut design on base, signed, set of four, 4½" high* **90.00 160.00 120.00**

□ **Napkin Ring,** *cut diamond pattern* **20.00 30.00 25.00**

□ **Vase,** *cut diamond design, cylindrical shape, 6" high* **35.00 55.00 40.00**

□ **Vase,** *cut diamond panels with tapered sides, cylindrical shape, 10" high* **80.00 130.00 100.00**

	Current Price Range		P/Y Average
☐ **Vase,** *fine panels of double shield form notching, cylindrical shape, signed, 8" high* .	40.00	80.00	55.00
☐ **Vase,** *trumpet shape, grid design formed from cut vesicas, starburst design on base, signed, 10" high*	110.00	150.00	130.00

WEATHER VANES

MAKERS: The two best known makers of weather vanes were Cushing and White of Waltham, MA, and the J. Howard Company of East Bridgewater, MA.

MATERIALS: Weather vanes are usually made of copper, sheet iron or wood.

COMMENTS: The most valued weather vanes are those handmade of sheet copper before 1850. These are mostly museum pieces. Most collectors seek factory made weather vanes of copper hammered in iron molds. These date to the 19th and early 20th centuries. Three dimensional weather vanes are rare. More common among collectors are silhouettes cut from sheet iron. Condition, beauty and rarity decide prices of weather vanes. Many reproductions have been made from original molds.

ADDITIONAL TIPS: The listings are alphabetical according to weather vane figure. A description, date and price range follow.

☐ **American Eagle,** with spread wings mounted on wooden block	700.00	900.00	775.00
☐ **Automobile,** open roadster, intricate detail, heavy copper, gilded gold leaf, full bodies, 26" L.	475.00	650.00	525.00
☐ **Automobile,** open top, complete with goggled old green patina navigator and driver, heavy copper, full bodied, 24" L.	1050.00	1400.00	1150.00
☐ **Banneret,** banner pierced with a letter, applied decorations, sheet metal and copper, 19th century	700.00	900.00	750.00

	Current Price Range		P/Y Average
☐ **Banneret and Scroll,** ornately gilded copper, 3' L.	110.00	150.00	125.00
☐ **Beaver,** Quebec, made of tin, c. 1860	1250.00	1700.00	1400.00
☐ **Cannon,** mounted on spoked gun carriage, reinforced barrel and stand, copper	200.00	275.00	215.00
☐ **Chicken,** old decorations made of tin with iron rods	850.00	1200.00	950.00
☐ **Cow,** mounted on 20½ " arrow, 9½ " L.	175.00	275.00	225.00
☐ **Cow,** molded copper, weathered, 19th century	1900.00	2300.00	2000.00
☐ **Cricket,** copper with red glass eyes	250.00	350.00	275.00
☐ **Crowing Cock,** made of copper, 28½ " L.	1200.00	1600.00	1400.00
☐ **Deer,** running buck with curved antlers, full-bodied, copper, old green patina with traces of old gilt, 50" L.	335.00	500.00	400.00
☐ **Dog,** full figure of a retriever, molded copper, c. 1870	3500.00	5000.00	4000.00
☐ **Donkey Cart,** three men riding donkey cart, painted metal, 19th century	800.00	1000.00	875.00
☐ **Dragon,** winged beast with snake-like tail, crouching on stand above scrolled direction indicators, 54 " L.	250.00	350.00	300.00
☐ **Eagle,** American eagle in flight, molded and gilded copper mounted on cast iron, 19th century	700.00	900.00	800.00
☐ **Eagle,** hollow copper, speadwing, 24" W., c. 19th century	1400.00	2000.00	1600.00
☐ **Eagle,** clawed feet resting on ball, old green patina, 5' wing span	205.00	250.00	220.00
☐ **Eagle,** perched on sphere, cast iron with directional lettering	1250.00	1750.00	1450.00
☐ **Eagle,** spread in flight, wings and head tilted up, molded copper, 19th century	250.00	350.00	275.00
☐ **Fish,** contemporary folk art, painted galvanized tin, 18" L.	60.00	80.00	70.00
☐ **Fish,** copper, 26" L.	1050.00	1400.00	1150.00
☐ **Fiske Running Horse,** black hawk #201, 33" L.	4200.00	6000.00	5200.00
☐ **Flag,** unfurled 48-star banner with pointed standard	140.00	180.00	160.00
☐ **Fox,** running, scrolled pointers, copper, full-bodied, 30" L.	210.00	280.00	235.00
☐ **Fox and Hound,** hound chasing fox, full-bodied figures, molded copper, c. 1880	8000.00	10000.00	8500.00
☐ **Goose,** cast iron, 23" wing span	750.00	1050.00	900.00
☐ **Grasshopper,** molded copper and cast iron, 19th century	1200.00	2300.00	1600.00
☐ **Greyhound,** long-legged animal standing on reinforced pedestal, ¾ full-bodied, green patina, 30" L.	197.00	250.00	220.00
☐ **Hackney Horse,** full-bodied horse, in a prance, molded copper, 19th century	3000.00	4000.00	3500.00
☐ **Heraldic Arrowwith Loins,** wrought iron with scrolling base	325.00	475.00	400.00
☐ **Horse,** elegant standing horse, molded copper, 19th century	1900.00	2300.00	2000.00

	Current Price Range		P/Y Average
☐ **Horse,** full-bodied in a trot, molded and gilded copper with some paint, 19 century	700.00	900.00	775.00
☐ **Horse,** full-bodied, running, 19th century	650.00	850.00	750.00
☐ **Horse and Arrow,** gold globe	375.00	500.00	425.00
☐ **Horse and Rider,** hollow copper, directional roof finial	2600.00	3400.00	3000.00
☐ **Horse and Rider,** silhouettes, rider has top hat and one arm raised, painted sheet metal	700.00	900.00	750.00
☐ **Horse and Sulky,** running horse pulling cart, molded copper	700.00	900.00	775.00
☐ **Indian,** full-bodied, detailed Indian chief with bow and arrow, molded copper, 19th century	700.00	900.00	750.00
☐ **Indian,** profile of Indian with bow and arrow, painted sheet iron, 19th century	400.00	600.00	500.00
☐ **Locomotive with Tender,** large model of late 19th c. railroad machine, full-bodied copper, 5' L.	350.00	450.00	300.00
☐ **Lion,** large head with carved mane, copper, ¾ full-bodied, 4' L.	237.00	325.00	275.00
☐ **Peacock,** full-bodied, copper, 19th century . .	2600.00	2900.00	2700.00
☐ **Pig,** molded and gilded copper pig, c. 1880 . .	8500.00	10500.00	9000.00
☐ **Race Horse with Jockey,** Kentucky thoroughbred, full-bodied copper, 32" L.	350.00	450.00	300.00
☐ **Railroad,** engine car, painted sheet metal . . .	675.00	875.00	750.00
☐ **Rooster,** full-bodied copper, c. 1880	2250.00	2400.00	2300.00
☐ **Rooster,** full-bodied game rooster, molded copper, c. 1880	1200.00	1700.00	1400.00
☐ **Ram,** full-bodied, molded copper, 19th century	2700.00	3700.00	3000.00
☐ **Rooster,** molded and painted copper, c. 1880	2700.00	3700.00	3000.00
☐ **Rooster,** painted metal	450.00	600.00	500.00
☐ **Rooster,** strutting, molded copper, 19th century	1200.00	1700.00	1400.00
☐ **Sailing Vessel,** painted green	315.00	400.00	350.00
☐ **Standing Indian,** original zinc finish, single direction indicator	480.00	600.00	515.00
☐ **Winged Horse,** with arrow, carved wood	650.00	850.00	750.00

○▭▭○▭▭○▭▭○▭▭○▭▭○▭▭○▭▭○▭▭○▭

WICKER

DESCRIPTION: Wicker is the general term for pieces made of woven rattan, cane, dried grasses, willow, reed or other pliable material.

PERIOD: The wicker heyday in the U.S. was from about 1860 to 1930.

ORIGIN: Wicker can be dated to about 4000 B.C. when the Egyptians used it. The interest in wicker in the U.S. began in the 1850s.

MAKERS: Cyrus Wakefield and the Heywood Brothers were the best known wicker manufacturers. They later joined to become the Heywood-Wakefield Company. Other companies include American Rattan Company and Paine's Manufacturing Company.

COMMENTS: While 19th century wicker is more valuable, pieces from the 1920s and 1930s are also very collectible and easier to find. Natural finish wicker is most desirable and less common pieces are the most sought after.

ADDITIONAL TIPS: For more information on wicker, see *The Official Price Guide to Wicker.*

	Current Price Range		P/Y Average
☐ **Basket,** sewing, natural finish, c. 1880	165.00	225.00	180.00
☐ **Basket,** sewing, natural finish, loop design on bottom shelf, crisscross weave on basket, c. 1880	250.00	325.00	275.00
☐ **Basket,** sewing, natural finish, rare curlicue and spool design on basket, large birdcage design at middle of brace, c. 1880	300.00	425.00	330.00
☐ **Chair,** fancy, white, often used as a photo rapher's chair, four rows of wooden beadwork in backrest and scrollwork at bottom right, c. 1890	675.00	850.00	700.00
☐ **Chair,** high, natural finish, c. 1880	250.00	325.00	275.00
☐ **Chair,** high, white, wooden tray and footrest, c. 1880	275.00	375.00	300.00
☐ **Chair,** Morris, rare, serpentine arms and back, cushions, c. 1890	900.00	1200.00	1000.00

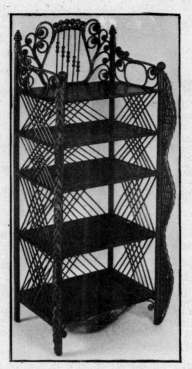

Music Stand, *natural finish, rare, lyre motif at top embellished with curlicues, reed latticework, thick braiding, turned wood frame, c. 1890s,* **$675.00-$900.00**
Photo courtesy of The Wicker Garden.

	Current Price Range		P/Y Average
☐ **Chair,** piano, natural finish, rare, adjustable seat, birdcage design on back braces, turned wooden legs, c. 1880	500.00	700.00	550.00
☐ **Chair,** side chair, natural finish, intricate weaving and unique use of wooden beadwork set into the back, c. 1880	385.00	485.00	400.00
☐ **Chair,** side chair, natural finish, elaborate fancywork set into back panel, c. 1890	235.00	325.00	250.00
☐ **Chair,** side chair, natural finish, tall back employs canewrapped squares, birdcage design on back and legs, horizontally woven seat, c. 1880	200.00	285.00	230.00
☐ **Chair,** side chair, white, full circle shell-back design, woven reed seat, c. 1880	350.00	400.00	365.00
☐ **Chair,** turkish, natural finish, closely woven arms and seat, wooden beadwork under arms and seat, c. 1890	325.00	400.00	340.00

	Current Price Range		P/Y Average

☐ **Crib,** standing, natural finish, drop-side panel, flower motif set into headboard, c. 1870	1200.00	1500.00	1300.00
☐ **Crib,** swinging, natural finish, elaborate fancywork, canopy, c. 1890	1000.00	1400.00	1200.00
☐ **Doll Buggy,** natural finish, wickerwork emphasizes flowing design, silk parasol, wooden wheel has metal rims, c. 1880	350.00	450.00	375.00
☐ **Hanging Music Rack,** natural finish, elaborate scrollwork, c. 1880	225.00	350.00	250.00
☐ **Lounge,** natural finish, rare upholstered design, c. 1890	900.00	1500.00	1100.00
☐ **Rocker,** child's, natural finish, serpentine back and arms, wooden beadwork, c. 1890 . .	200.00	300.00	225.00
☐ **Rocker,** platform, natural finish, curved backrest, serpentine back and arms, c. 1890	525.00	650.00	550.00
☐ **Rocker,** platform, white, serpentine, arms and arched platform, c. 1890	600.00	750.00	625.00
☐ **Rocker,** natural finish, chevron-shaped back panel, serpentine back and arms, turned wooden legs, c. 1890	275.00	375.00	300.00
☐ **Rocker,** natural finish, crisscross beadwork, serpentine back and arms, c. 1890	450.00	625.00	500.00
☐ **Rocker,** natural finish, leaf motif set into back panel, hand-caned seat, c. 1880	475.00	575.00	500.00
☐ **Rocker,** natural finish, spider-web caned back panel, c. 1880	275.00	350.00	300.00
☐ **Rocker,** white, banjo motif set into back panel, loop design on back and arms, c. 1880 .	400.00	575.00	450.00
☐ **Rocker,** white, circular braidwork, spider-web cane back panel, c. 1880	400.00	550.00	475.00
☐ **Sofa,** divan, natural finish, rolled backs and arms employ wooden beadwork, rosette arm tips, set-in cane seat, c. 1890	800.00	1000.00	875.00
☐ **Sofa,** settee, natural finish, serpentine back and arms, closely woven back panel, turned-wood legs, c. 1890	750.00	900.00	800.00
☐ **Sofa,** settee, white, peacock design dominates back panel, birdcage legs, c. 1880	950.00	1300.00	1000.00
☐ **Stand,** music stand, natural finish, oak shelves, beveled mirror, c. 1890	1500.00	2000.00	1700.00
☐ **Stand,** music, white, angled sides, two reed shelves, ball feet, c. 1890	250.00	350.00	280.00
☐ **Stand,** washstand, white, side towel racks, rustic design, tightly woven back, crisscross legs, c. 1880	350.00	500.00	400.00
☐ **Stool,** piano, white, circular woven reed seat, c. 1890	200.00	285.00	225.00
☐ **Stool,** ottoman, white, closely woven top, round rosette design on both ends, c. 1890 . .	175.00	245.00	180.00
☐ **Table,** end table, white, large center birdcage design, c. 1890	225.00	325.00	260.00
☐ **Table,** oblong table, white, wooden beadwork, c. 1890	285.00	350.00	300.00

	Current Price Range		P/Y Average
□ **Table,** round, white, cabriole legs, wooden beadwork frames top and bottom shelf, c. 1890	500.00	750.00	575.00
□ **Table,** square, white, closely woven top, beadwork set into skirting, c. 1880	300.00	385.00	330.00

WOOD

TYPES: While many types of wood items are highly sought after collectibles, this section lists wooden kitchen utensils.

COMMENTS: Wooden utensils are most commonly made of maple. Other woods used include cedar, pine, hickory, ash and oak. Prices vary depending on item and type of wood.

ADDITIONAL TIPS: The listings are alphabetized according to item. For further information, refer to *The Official Price Guide to Kitchen Collectibles.*

□ **Apple Butter Bucket,** *bail handle, c. 1850, 10" long*	110.00	140.00	120.00
□ **Apple Butter Paddle,** *paddle stirrer, perforated spatula, 60" long*	50.00	75.00	63.00
□ **Apple Butter Paddle,** *drilled holes, 30" long* .	65.00	85.00	72.00
□ **Apple Butter Scoop,** *maple, c. 1850s*	260.00	300.00	265.00
□ **Apple Drying Rack,** *open slats, three sided, legged, c. 1870*	125.00	150.00	135.00
□ **Apple Parers,** *clamp, clank, two gears, drip board*	200.00	225.00	210.00
□ **Apple Peelers,** *hardwood gears, c. 1700s*	225.00	250.00	230.00
□ **Apple Peelers,** *crank handle, two size, belt driven gears*	175.00	188.00	177.00
□ **Apple Peelers,** *wooden with iron gears, 7" x 14"*	170.00	200.00	178.00
□ **Barrel,** *nutmeg storage, enameled yellow, 4" diameter*	35.00	50.00	41.00
□ **Barrel,** *for pickles, staved, three concentric wooden bands, 12" x 20"*	35.00	60.00	40.00

Coffee Grinder, *wood and cast iron,* **$50.00-$100.00**

	Current Price Range		P/Y Average
☐ **Bandbox,** *egg shaped, plain, 5" long*	70.00	95.00	83.00
☐ **Bread Peel,** *poplar, long handle, mid 1800s, 54" long*	82.00	100.00	88.00
☐ **Bread Raiser,** *with lid, tin, 12" long*	50.00	70.00	58.00
☐ **Broom,** *flat, birch splint, bound with iron, spindled, maple handle*	163.00	185.00	171.00
☐ **Broom,** *oak splint*	78.00	99.00	85.00
☐ **Bucket,** *oak, for well*	48.00	60.00	52.00
☐ **Bucket,** *sap, 9¼" diameter*	150.00	175.00	160.00
☐ **Bucket,** *mincemeat, lid, concave, 11" diameter*	88.00	105.00	93.00
☐ **Bucket,** *sugar, floor standing, red*	270.00	300.00	280.00
☐ **Bucket,** *sugar, stave constructed, enameled, 13" diameter*	128.00	140.00	133.00
☐ **Bucket,** *sugar, loop handles, lid, flat handle, c. 1890, 5" diameter*	175.00	200.00	179.00
☐ **Bucket,** *water, one piece wood, side handles, rope bail*	110.00	130.00	117.00
☐ **Bucket,** *tin top, walnut, "S" shaped legs, 17" diameter*	160.00	185.00	170.00
☐ **Bung Pusher,** *barrel, all wood, with lid and stem*	15.00	24.00	19.00
☐ **Butcher's Block,** *sycamore, decoratively carved*	720.00	750.00	730.00
☐ **Butter Churn,** *cylinder type, white cedar, one gallon capacity*	62.00	80.00	68.00

	Current Price Range		P/Y Average

☐ **Candlestick,** *adjustable stem, English, c. 1790, 8" high*	1450.00	1560.00	1470.00
☐ **Candlestick,** *walnut, c. 1760, 6" diameter* ...	300.00	340.00	314.00
☐ **Clothes Wringer,** *crank, handle and roller* ...	18.00	30.00	22.00
☐ **Coaster,** *oak, English, c. 1810, 12" diameter* .	1100.00	1250.00	1150.00
☐ **Coaster,** *18th century, treen, octagonal*	225.00	260.00	235.00
☐ **Coffee Grinder,** *box type*	90.00	110.00	97.00
☐ **Coffee Grinder,** *lap, oak*	80.00	95.00	86.00
☐ **Coffee Grinder,** *lap, cherry box, brass fittings, crank*	95.00	115.00	103.00
☐ **Coffee Grinder,** *lap type, handled, cherry* ...	100.00	120.00	106.00
☐ **Coffee Grinder,** *wood, carved handle*	70.00	89.00	76.00
☐ **Coffee Grinder,** *drawer, wooden base*	85.00	100.00	92.00
☐ **Coffee Grinder,** *19th century, wooden, French maker*	82.00	110.00	95.00
☐ **Coffee and Spice Mill,** *c, 1760, 9" high*	1300.00	1450.00	1355.00
☐ **Coffee Mill,** *hand crank, iron blade, storage box*	60.00	80.00	67.00
☐ **Colander,** *wooden, circular, c. 1700s*	280.00	310.00	291.00
☐ **Cookie Board,** *carved pattern, walnut, 8" long*	70.00	90.00	78.00
☐ **Cookie Board,** *walnut construction, grape relief design, 9" long*	20.00	30.00	22.00
☐ **Cookie Board,** *divided into squares, different molded design, 6" long*	24.00	36.00	27.00
☐ **Lemon Squeezer,** *11"*	25.00	35.00	30.00
☐ **Lemon Squeezer,** *all wood construction, short handle, ridged press*	22.00	31.00	25.00
☐ **Lemon Squeezer,** *on frame, indentation and drain holes, three turned legs, mid 18th century*	150.00	250.00	120.00
☐ **Lemon Squeezer,** *hinged, all wood*	30.00	45.00	35.00
☐ **Lemon Squeezer,** *hinged, wood frame, wood and ceramic, hinged, press is perforated*	30.00	45.00	33.00
☐ **Lemon Squeezer,** *wood and tin, hinged, perforated*	30.00	43.00	33.00
☐ **Lemon Squeezer,** *wood and nickel alloy, juicer is perforated*	35.00	50.00	41.00
☐ **Lemon Squeezer,** *wooden, on stand, 14" x 9"*	113.00	138.00	118.00
☐ **Lemon Squeezer,** *8" long*	52.00	68.00	56.00
☐ **Lemon Squeezer,** *9" long*	62.00	78.00	67.00
☐ **Mortar And Pestle,** *bird's eye maple, early* ...	80.00	100.00	88.00
☐ **Muffineer,** *Tunbridge ware, c. 1790*	180.00	210.00	195.00
☐ **Noggin,** *wood, carved decor, 8" high*	175.00	210.00	195.00
☐ **Noodle Board,** *wooden circle with paddle handle, 24" long*	82.00	96.00	85.00
☐ **Noodle Roller,** *maple, perforated crank, c. 1840, 21" long*	67.00	99.00	70.00
☐ **Noodle Rolling Pin**	15.00	25.00	18.00
☐ **Notion Cabinet,** *oak counter, pegged construction, framed compartments*	495.00	525.00	512.00
☐ **Nutcracker,** *bear's head, 9" long*	70.00	85.00	73.00
☐ **Nutcracker,** *wood with iron presses, c. 1650, 5½" long*	350.00	380.00	363.00
☐ **Nutcracker,** *large size, c. 1750, 10" long*	190.00	215.00	200.00
☐ **Nutcracker,** *18th century*	225.00	250.00	231.00

	Current Price Range		P/Y Average
☐ **Toddy Stick,** *pestle style, hand carved, turned wood*	12.00	20.00	14.00
☐ **Toddy Sticks,** *early 19th century*	20.00	42.00	32.00
☐ **Washtub,** *oak slats, natural varnish, 23" long*	75.00	100.00	82.00
☐ **Whisk Broom,** *Fuller Brush Company, 8" long*	45.00	60.00	50.00
☐ **Wooden Box,** *Shaker*	200.00	230.00	210.00
☐ **Wood Frame Churn,** *windmill paddles, side turn handle, 15" high*	220.00	250.00	230.00
☐ **Wooden Shovel,** *grain*	285.00	310.00	295.00
☐ **Wood Churn,** *staved, dasher, four gallon capacity*	225.00	260.00	238.00
☐ **Wooden Wash Bowl,** *chestnut, c. 1790*	145.00	170.00	155.00
☐ **Wool Comb,** *carved handle, 13"*	15.00	30.00	20.00
☐ **Yarn Winder,** *box-type, spindle suspended on spike over box, turns in circular motion, 18"* .	30.00	50.00	40.00
☐ **Yarn Winder,** *duck feet*	110.00	135.00	120.00
☐ **Yarn Winder,** *floor model, spindled legs, yard counter, knobbed end*	90.00	120.00	103.00
☐ **Yarn Winder,** *maple*	115.00	140.00	120.00

THE OFFICIAL PRICE GUIDES TO:

☐ 465-8	**American Silver & Silver Plate** 4th Ed.	10.95
☐ 482-8	**Antique Clocks** 3rd Ed.	10.95
☐ 455-0	**Antique & Modern Dolls** 2nd Ed.	9.95
☐ 483-6	**Antique & Modern Firearms** 5th Ed.	10.95
☐ 271-X	**Antiques & Other Collectibles** 6th Ed.	9.95
☐ 466-6	**Antique Jewelry** 4th Ed.	10.95
☐ 270-1	**Beer Cans & Collectibles**, 3rd Ed.	7.95
☐ 262-0	**Bottles Old & New** 9th Ed.	10.95
☐ 255-8	**Carnival Glass** 1st Ed.	10.95
☐ 453-4	**Collectible Cameras** 2nd Ed.	10.95
☐ 277-9	**Collectibles of the Third Reich** 2nd Ed.	10.95
☐ 454-2	**Collectible Toys** 2nd Ed.	9.95
☐ 490-9	**Collector Cars** 6th Ed.	11.95
☐ 267-1	**Collector Handguns** 3rd Ed.	11.95
☐ 459-3	**Collector Knives** 7th Ed.	10.95
☐ 266-3	**Collector Plates** 4th Ed.	11.95
☐ 476-3	**Collector Prints** 6th Ed.	11.95
☐ 489-5	**Comic Books & Collectibles** 8th Ed.	9.95
☐ 433-X	**Depression Glass** 1st Ed.	9.95
☐ 472-0	**Glassware** 2nd Ed.	10.95
☐ 492-5	**Hummel Figurines & Plates** 5th Ed.	9.95
☐ 451-8	**Kitchen Collectibles** 2nd Ed.	10.95
☐ 460-7	**Military Collectibles** 4th Ed.	10.95
☐ 268-X	**Music Collectibles** 5th Ed.	11.95
☐ 491-7	**Old Books & Autographs** 6th Ed.	10.95
☐ 452-6	**Oriental Collectibles** 2nd Ed.	11.95
☐ 461-5	**Paper Collectibles** 4th Ed.	10.95
☐ 276-0	**Pottery & Porcelain** 5th Ed.	10.95
☐ 263-9	**Radio, T.V. & Movie Memorabilia** 2nd Ed.	11.95
☐ 484-4	**Records** 6th Ed.	9.95
☐ 485-2	**Royal Doulton** 4th Ed.	10.95
☐ 418-6	**Science Fiction & Fantasy Collectibles** 1st Ed.	9.95
☐ 477-1	**Wicker** 3rd Ed.	10.95

THE OFFICIAL:

☐ 369-4	**Guide to Buying & Selling Antiques** 1st Ed.	9.95
☐ 448-8	**Identification Guide to Gunmarks** 2nd Ed.	9.95
☐ 412-7	**Identification Guide to Pottery & Porcelain** 1st Ed.	9.95
☐ 415-1	**Identification Guide to Victorian Furniture** 1st Ed.	9.95

THE OFFICIAL (POCKET SIZE) PRICE GUIDES TO:

☐ 473-9	**Antiques & Flea Markets** 3rd Ed.	3.95
☐ 442-9	**Antique Jewelry** 2nd Ed.	3.95
☐ 264-7	**Baseball Cards** 5th Ed.	4.95
☐ 488-7	**Bottles** 2nd Ed.	4.95
☐ 468-2	**Cars & Trucks** 2nd Ed.	4.95
☐ 260-4	**Collectible Americana** 1st Ed.	4.95
☐ 463-1	**Collectible Records** 2nd Ed.	3.95
☐ 469-0	**Collector Guns** 2nd Ed.	4.95
☐ 474-7	**Comic Books** 3rd Ed.	3.95
☐ 486-0	**Dolls** 3rd Ed.	4.95
☐ 462-3	**Football Cards** 4th Ed.	3.95
☐ 258-2	**Glassware** 2nd Ed.	4.95
☐ 487-9	**Hummels** 3rd Ed.	4.95
☐ 441-0	**Military Collectibles** 2nd Ed.	3.95
☐ 480-1	**Paperbacks & Magazines** 3rd Ed.	4.95
☐ 278-7	**Pocket Knives** 3rd Ed.	4.95
☐ 479-8	**Scouting Collectibles** 3rd Ed.	4.95
☐ 439-9	**Sports Collectibles** 2nd Ed.	3.95
☐ 494-1	**Star Trek/Star Wars Collectibles** 3rd Ed.	3.95
☐ 493-3	**Toys** 3rd Ed.	4.95

THE OFFICIAL BLACKBOOK PRICE GUIDES TO:

☐ 284-1	**U.S. Coins** 24th Ed.	3.95
☐ 286-8	**U.S. Paper Money** 18th Ed.	3.95
☐ 285-X	**U.S. Postage Stamps** 8th Ed.	3.95

THE OFFICIAL INVESTORS GUIDE TO BUYING & SELLING:

☐ 496-8	**Gold, Silver and Diamonds** 2nd Ed.	9.95
☐ 497-6	**Gold Coins** 2nd Ed.	9.95
☐ 498-4	**Silver Coins** 2nd Ed.	9.95
☐ 499-2	**Silver Dollars** 2nd Ed.	9.95

TOTAL	

SEE REVERSE SIDE FOR ORDERING INSTRUCTIONS

FOR IMMEDIATE DELIVERY

VISA & MASTER CARD CUSTOMERS

ORDER TOLL FREE!
1-800-327-1384

This number is for orders only, it is not tied into the customer service or business office. Customers not using charge cards must use mail for ordering since payment is required with the order — sorry no C.O.D.'s. Florida residents call (305) 857-9095 — ask for order department.

OR SEND ORDERS TO

THE HOUSE OF COLLECTIBLES, *ORLANDO CENTRAL PARK*
1904 PREMIER ROW, ORLANDO, FL 32809   (305) 857-9095

— POSTAGE & HANDLING RATE CHART —

TOTAL ORDER/POSTAGE	TOTAL ORDER/POSTAGE	
0 to $10.00 - **$1.25**	$20.01 to $30.00 - **$2.00**	$50.01 & Over -
$10.01 to $20.00 - **$1.60**	$30.01 to $40.00 - **$2.75**	**Add 10% of your total order**
	$40.01 to $50.00 - **$3.50**	(Ex. $75.00 x .10 = $7.50)

Total from columns on reverse side. Quantity_____ $ _____

| | Check or money order enclosed $_____ (include postage and handling)

| | Please charge $_____ to my: | | MASTERCARD | | VISA

Charge Card Customers Not Using Our Toll Free Number Please Fill Out The Information Below.

Account No. (All Digits) _____ Expiration Date _____

Signature_____

NAME (please print) _____ PHONE _____

ADDRESS _____ APT. # _____ (10)

CITY _____ STATE _____ ZIP _____